DATA AND COMPUTER COMMUNICATIONS

Tenth Edition

William Stallings

International Edition contributions by

Moumita Mitra Manna

Bangabasi College, Kolkata

PEARSON

Boston   Columbus   Indianapolis   New York   San Francisco   Upper Saddle River
Amsterdam   Cape Town   Dubai   London   Madrid   Milan   Munich   Paris   Montréal   Toronto
Delhi   Mexico City   São Paulo   Sydney   Hong Kong   Seoul   Singapore   Taipei   Tokyo

Editorial Director, ECS: Marcia Horton
Executive Editor: Tracy Johnson (Dunkelberger)
Editorial Assistant: Jenah Blitz-Stoehr
Director of Marketing: Christy Lesko
Marketing Manager: Yez Alayan
Marketing Assistant: Jon Bryant
Director of Program Management: Erin Gregg
Program Management–Team Lead: Scott Disanno
Program Manager: Carole Snyder
Project Management–Team Lead: Laura Burgess
Project Manager: Robert Engelhardt
Publishing Operations Director, International Edition:
 Angshuman Chakraborty
Manager, Publishing Operations, International Edition:
 Shokhi Shah Khandelwal

Associate Print and Media Editor, International Edition:
 Anuprova Dey Chowdhuri
Acquisitions Editor, International Edition:
 Sandhya Ghoshal
Publishing Administrator, International Edition:
 Hema Mehta
Project Editor, International Edition: Daniel Luiz
Editorial Assistant, International Edition: Sinjita Basu
Procurement Specialist: Linda Sager
**Senior Manufacturing Controller, Production, International
 Edition:** Trudy Kimber
Art Director: Jayne Conte
Cover Designer: Karen Noferi
Cover Photo Credit: Fotolia/Female photographer
Cover Printer: Courier Westford

Pearson Education Limited
Edinburgh Gate
Harlow
Essex CM20 2JE
England

and Associated Companies throughout the world

Visit us on the World Wide Web at: www.pearsoninternationaleditions.com

© Pearson Education Limited 2014

ISBN 10: 1-29-201438-5
ISBN 13: 978-1-29-201438-8

British Library Cataloguing-in-Publication Data
A catalogue record for this book is available from the British Library

10 9 8 7 6 5 4 3 2 1
14 13 12 11 10

Typeset in Times LT Std-Roman by Integra Software Services Pvt. Ltd.

Printed and bound by Courier Westford in The United States of America

PEARSON

For Tricia

CONTENTS

8 CONTENTS

---

[1]Online chapters and appendices are Premium Content, available via the access card at the front of this book.

PREFACE

Since the ninth edition of this book went to press, the pace of change in this field continues unabated. In this new edition, I try to capture these changes while maintaining a broad and comprehensive coverage of the entire field. To begin the process of revision, the ninth edition of this book was extensively reviewed by a number of professors who teach the subject and by professionals working in the field. The result is that, in many places, the narrative has been clarified and tightened, and illustrations have been improved.

Beyond these refinements to improve pedagogy and user friendliness, there have been major substantive changes throughout the book. The chapter organization has been changed somewhat so that now the material is organized into two Units, with Unit Two containing more advanced material and an expansion of the material related to the Internet. Beyond this organizational revision, the most noteworthy changes include the following:

- **Sockets programming:** A new section introduces sockets programming. Plus a number of sockets programming assignments, with sample solutions, are available for instructors.

- **Software-defined networks:** A new section covers this widely used technology.

- **Wireless transmission technology:** The book provides a unified treatment of important transmission technologies for wireless networks, including FDD, TDD, FDMA, TDMA, CDMA, OFDM, OFDMA, SC-FDMA, and MIMO.

- **4G cellular networks:** A new section covers 4G networks and the LTE-Advanced specification.

- **Gigabit Wi-Fi:** A new section covers the two new Wi-Fi standards, IEEE 802.11ac and 802.11ad, which provide Wi-Fi in the Gbps range.

- **Fixed broadband wireless access:** New sections cover fixed broadband wireless access to the Internet and the related WiMAX standard.

- **Forward error correction:** Forward error correction techniques are essential in wireless networks. This new edition contains substantially expanded coverage of this important topic.

- **Personal area networks:** New sections cover personal area networks and the Bluetooth standard.

- **Dynamic Host Configuration Protocol (DHCP):** DHCP is a widely used protocol that enables dynamic IP address assignment. A new section covers this protocol.

- **Datagram Congestion Control Protocol:** DCCP is a new protocol that meets the needs of multimedia applications for a congestion control transport protocol without the overhead of TCP. A new section covers DCCP.

- **Protocol Independent Multicast (PIM):** PIM, the most important Internet multicast routing algorithm, is covered in a new section.
- **Quality of service (QoS) architectural framework:** A new section covers ITU-T Recommendation Y.1291, which provides an overall framework for provision of Internet QoS facilities.
- **Electronic mail:** The section on e-mail in Chapter 24 has been expanded to include a discussion of the standard Internet mail architecture.
- **Animations:** As a powerful aid to understanding the material, over 150 online animations are provided covering a wide range of topics from the book. An icon at the beginning of many chapters indicates that supporting animations are available to enhance the student's understanding.
- **Learning objectives:** Each chapter now begins with a list of learning objectives.
- **Sample syllabus:** The text contains more material than can be conveniently covered in one semester. Accordingly, instructors are provided with several sample syllabi that guide the use of the text within limited time (e.g., 16 weeks or 12 weeks). These samples are based on real-world experience by professors with the ninth edition.

In addition, the material that carries over from the ninth edition has been revised, with new figures and revised and updated content.

OBJECTIVES

This book attempts to provide a unified overview of the broad field of data and computer communications. The organization of the book reflects an attempt to break this massive subject into comprehensible parts and to build, piece by piece, a survey of the state of the art. The book emphasizes basic principles and topics of fundamental importance concerning the technology and architecture of this field and provides a detailed discussion of leading-edge topics.

The following basic themes serve to unify the discussion:

- **Principles:** Although the scope of this book is broad, there are a number of basic principles that appear repeatedly as themes and that unify this field. Examples are multiplexing, flow control, and error control. The book highlights these principles and contrasts their application in specific areas of technology.
- **Design approaches:** The book examines alternative approaches to meeting specific communication requirements.
- **Standards:** Standards have come to assume an increasingly important, indeed dominant, role in this field. An understanding of the current status and future direction of technology requires a comprehensive discussion of the related standards.

SUPPORT OF ACM/IEEE COMPUTER SCIENCE CURRICULA 2013

The book is intended for both an academic and a professional audience. For the professional interested in this field, the book serves as a basic reference volume and is suitable for self-study. As a textbook, it can be used for a one-semester or two-semester course. This edition is designed to support the recommendations of the current (February 2013) draft version of the ACM/IEEE Computer Science Curricula 2013 (CS2013). The CS2013 curriculum recommendation includes Networking and Communication (NC) as one of the Knowledge Areas in the Computer Science Body of Knowledge. CS2013 divides all course work into three categories: Core-Tier 1 (all topics should be included in the curriculum), Core-Tier-2 (all or almost all topics should be included), and elective (desirable to provide breadth and depth). In the NC area, CS2013 includes two Tier 1 topics and five Tier 2 topics, each of which has a number of subtopics. This text covers all of the topics and subtopics listed by CS2013 in these two tiers.

Table P.1 shows the support for the NC Knowledge Area provided in this textbook.

Table P.1 Coverage of CS2013 Networking and Communication (NC) Knowledge Area

Topic	Chapter Coverage
Introduction (Tier 1) —Organization of the Internet (Internet Service Providers, Content Providers, etc.) —Switching techniques (Circuit, packet, etc.) —Physical pieces of a network (hosts, routers, switches, ISPs, wireless, LAN, access point, firewalls, etc.) —Layering principles (encapsulation, multiplexing) —Roles of the different layers (application, transport, network, datalink, physical)	1-Data Communications 2-Protocol Architecture 9-WAN Technology
Networked Applications (Tier 1) —Naming and address schemes (DNS, IP addresses, Uniform Resource Identifiers, etc.) —Distributed applications (client/server, peer-to-peer, cloud, etc.) —HTTP as an application layer protocol —Multiplexing with TCP and UDP —Socket APIs	24-Electronic mail, DNS, HTTP 2-Protocol Architecture
Reliable Data Delivery (Tier 2) —Error control (retransmission techniques, timers) —Flow control (acknowledgments, sliding window) —Performance issues (pipelining) —TCP	6-Error Detection and Correction 7-Data Link Control 15-Transport Protocols

Table P.1 Continued

Topic	Chapter Coverage
Routing And Forwarding (Tier 2) —Routing versus forwarding —Static routing —Internet Protocol (IP) —Scalability issues (hierarchical addressing)	19-Routing 14-The Internet Protocol
Local Area Networks (Tier 2) —Multiple Access Problem —Common approaches to multiple access (exponential-backoff, time division multiplexing, etc.) —Local Area Networks —Ethernet —Switching	11-Local Area Network Overview 12-Ethernet
Resource Allocation (Tier 2) —Need for resource allocation —Fixed allocation (TDM, FDM, WDM) versus dynamic allocation —End-to-end versus network-assisted approaches —Fairness —Principles of congestion control —Approaches to Congestion (Content Distribution Networks, etc.)	8-Multiplexing 20-Congestion Control 21-Internetwork QoS
Mobility (Tier 2) —Principles of cellular networks —802.11 networks —Issues in supporting mobile nodes (home agents)	10-Cellular Wireless Networks 13-Wireless LANs

PLAN OF THE TEXT

The book is divided into two units, comprising nine parts, which are described in Chapter 0:

- Unit One: Fundamentals of Data Communications and Networking
  - Overview
  - Data Communications
  - Wide Area Networks
  - Local Area Networks
  - Internet and Transport Layers
- Unit Two: Advanced Topics in Data Communications and Networking
  - Data Communications and Wireless Networks
  - Internetworking
  - Internet Applications
  - Network Security

The book includes a number of pedagogic features, including the use of animations and numerous figures and tables to clarify the discussions. Each chapter includes a list of key words, review questions, homework problems, and suggestions for further reading. The book also includes an extensive online glossary, a list of frequently used acronyms, and a reference list. In addition, a test bank is available to instructors.

The chapters and parts of the book are sufficiently modular to provide a great deal of flexibility in the design of courses. See Chapter 0 for a number of detailed suggestions for both top-down and bottom-up course strategies.

INSTRUCTOR SUPPORT MATERIALS

The major goal of this text is to make it as effective a teaching tool for this exciting and fast-moving subject as possible. This goal is reflected both in the structure of the book and in the supporting material. The text is accompanied by the following supplementary material to aid the instructor:

- **Solutions manual:** Solutions to all end-of-chapter Review Questions and Problems.
- **Projects manual:** Suggested project assignments for all of the project categories in the next section.
- **PowerPoint slides:** A set of slides covering all chapters, suitable for use in lecturing.
- **PDF files:** Reproductions of all figures and tables from the book.
- **Test bank:** A chapter-by-chapter set of questions with a separate file of answers.
- **Sample syllabuses:** The text contains more material than can be conveniently covered in one semester. Accordingly, instructors are provided with several sample syllabuscs that guide the use of the text within limited time. These samples are based on real-world experience by professors with the ninth edition.

All of these support materials are available at the **Instructor Resource Center (IRC)** for this textbook, which can be reached through the publisher's Web site www. pearsoninternationaleditions.com/stallings or by clicking on the link labeled *Pearson Resources for Instructors* at this book's Companion Web site at WilliamStallings.com/ DataComm. To gain access to the IRC, please contact your local Pearson sales representative.

The **Companion Web site**, at WilliamStallings.com/DataComm (click on *Instructor Resources* link), includes the following:

- Links to Web sites for other courses being taught using this book.
- Sign-up information for an Internet mailing list for instructors using this book to exchange information, suggestions, and questions with each other and with the author.

PROJECTS AND OTHER STUDENT EXERCISES

For many instructors, an important component of a data communications or networking course is a project or set of projects by which the student gets hands-on experience to reinforce concepts from the text. This book provides an unparalleled degree of support for including a projects component in the course. The IRC not only provides guidance on how to assign and structure the projects but also includes a set of User's Manuals for various project types plus specific assignments, all written especially for this book. Instructors can assign work in the following areas:

- **Animation assignments:** Described in the following section.
- **Practical exercises:** Using network commands, the student gains experience in network connectivity.
- **Sockets programming projects:** Described subsequently in this Preface.
- **Wireshark projects:** Wireshark is a protocol analyzer that enables students to study the behavior of protocols. A video tutorial is provided to get students started, in addition to a set of Wireshark assignments.
- **Simulation projects:** The student can use the simulation package *cnet* to analyze network behavior. The IRC includes a number of student assignments.
- **Performance modeling projects:** Two performance modeling techniques are introduced: a *tools* package and OPNET. The IRC includes a number of student assignments.
- **Research projects:** The IRC includes a list of suggested research projects that would involve Web and literature searches.
- **Reading/report assignments:** The IRC includes a list of papers that can be assigned for reading and writing a report, plus suggested assignment wording.
- **Writing assignments:** The IRC includes a list of writing assignments to facilitate learning the material.
- **Discussion topics:** These topics can be used in a classroom, chat room, or message board environment to explore certain areas in greater depth and to foster student collaboration.

This diverse set of projects and other student exercises enables the instructor to use the book as one component in a rich and varied learning experience and to tailor a course plan to meet the specific needs of the instructor and students. See Appendix B for details.

ANIMATIONS

Animations provide a powerful tool for understanding the complex mechanisms discussed in this book, including forward error correction, signal encoding, and protocols. Over 150 Web-based animations are used to illustrate many of the data communications and protocol concepts in this book. These animations are available online at the Premium Web site. For those chapters for which animations are available, this icon appears at the beginning of the chapter: .

Twelve of the animations have been designed to allow for two types of assignments. First, the student can be given a specific set of steps to invoke and watch the animation, and then be asked to analyze and comment on the results. Second, the student can be given a specific end point and is required to devise a sequence of steps that achieve the desired result. The IRC includes a set of assignments for each of these animations, plus suggested solutions so that instructors can assess the student's work.

SOCKETS PROGRAMMING

Sockets are the fundamental element behind any kind of network communication using the TCP/IP protocol suite. Sockets programming is a relatively straightforward topic that can result in very satisfying and effective hands-on projects for students. This book provides considerable support to enable students to learn and use Sockets programming to enhance their understanding of networking, including:

1. Chapter 2 provides a basic introduction to Sockets programming and includes a detailed analysis of a TCP server and a TCP client program.

2. Chapter 2 also includes some end-of-chapter programming assignments using Sockets. Sample solutions are available at the IRC for this book.

3. Additional Sockets programming assignments, plus sample solutions, are available for instructors at the IRC. These include a number of moderate-size assignments and a more substantial project that, step by step, implements a simplified instant messaging client and server.

4. A different, additional set of Sockets assignments, plus sample solutions, are included in the supplemental homework problems available to students at the Premium Web site.

Taken together, these resources provide students with a solid understanding of Sockets programming and experience in developing networking applications.

ONLINE DOCUMENTS FOR STUDENTS

For this new edition, a substantial amount of original supporting material for students has been made available online, at two Web locations. The **Companion Web site**, at WilliamStallings.com/DataComm (click on *Student Resources* link), includes a list of relevant links organized by chapter and an errata sheet for the book.

Purchasing this textbook new also grants the reader six months of access to the **Premium Content site**, which includes the following materials:

- **Online chapters:** To limit the size and cost of the book, two chapters of the book, covering security, are provided in PDF format. The chapters are listed in this book's table of contents.

- **Online appendices:** There are numerous interesting topics that support material found in the text but whose inclusion is not warranted in the printed text.

A total of 18 online appendices cover these topics for the interested student. The appendices are listed in this book's table of contents.

- **Homework problems and solutions:** To aid the student in understanding the material, a separate set of homework problems with solutions is available.

To access the Premium Content site, click on the *Premium Content* link at the Companion Web site or at www.pearsoninternationaleditions.com/stallings and enter the student access code found on the card in the front of the book.

ACKNOWLEDGMENTS

Through its multiple editions this book has benefited from review by hundreds of instructors and professionals, who gave generously of their time and expertise. Here I acknowledge those whose help contributed to this latest edition.

The following instructors reviewed all or a large part of the manuscript: Tibor Gyires (Illinois State University), Hossein Hosseini (University of Wisconsin-Milwaukee), Naeem Shareef (Ohio State University), Adrian Lauf (University of Louisville), and Michael Fang (University of Florida).

Thanks also to the many people who provided detailed technical reviews of a single chapter: Naji A. Albakay, Prof. (Dr). C. Annamalai, Rakesh Kumar Bachchan, Alan Cantrell, Colin Conrad, Vineet Chadha, George Chetcuti, Rajiv Dasmohapatra, Ajinkya Deshpande, Michel Garcia, Thomas Johnson, Adri Jovin, Joseph Kellegher, Robert Knox, Bo Lin, Yadi Ma, Luis Arturo Frigolet Mayo, Sushil Menon, Hien Nguyen, Kevin Sanchez-Cherry, Mahesh S. Sankpal, Gaurav Santhalia, Stephanie Sullivan, Doug Tiedt, Thriveni Venkatesh, and Pete Zeno.

Thanks also to the following contributors. Yadi Ma contributed homework problems on Sockets programming. Yunzhao Li developed some of the animation applets. Larry Tan of the University of Stirling in Scotland developed the animation assignments. Michael Harris of Indiana University initially developed the Wireshark exercises and user's guide. Dave Bremer, a principal lecturer at Otago Polytechnic in New Zealand, updated the material for the most recent Wireshark release; he also developed an online video tutorial for using Wireshark. Kim McLaughlin produced the PPT lecture slides.

Finally, I thank the many people responsible for the publication of this book, all of whom did their usual excellent job. This includes the staff at Pearson, particularly my editor Tracy Johnson, her assistant Jenah Blitz-Stoehr, program manager Carole Snyder, and permissions supervisor Bob Engelhardt. I also thank Shiny Rajesh and the production staff at Integra for another excellent and rapid job. Thanks also to the marketing and sales staffs at Pearson, without whose efforts this book would not be in front of you.

The publishers wish to thank Somitra Kumar Sanadhya, of the Indraprastha Institute of Information Technology, Delhi, for reviewing the content of the International Edition.

About the Author

Dr. William Stallings has authored 17 titles, and counting revised editions, over 40 books on computer security, computer networking, and computer architecture. His writings have appeared in numerous publications, including the *Proceedings of the IEEE, ACM Computing Reviews* and *Cryptologia.*

He has 12 times received the award for the best Computer Science textbook of the year from the Text and Academic Authors Association.

In over 30 years in the field, he has been a technical contributor, technical manager, and an executive with several high-technology firms. He has designed and implemented both TCP/IP-based and OSI-based protocol suites on a variety of computers and operating systems, ranging from microcomputers to mainframes. As a consultant, he has advised government agencies, computer and software vendors, and major users on the design, selection, and use of networking software and products.

He created and maintains the *Computer Science Student Resource Site* at ComputerScienceStudent.com. This site provides documents and links on a variety of subjects of general interest to computer science students (and professionals). He is a member of the editorial board of *Cryptologia,* a scholarly journal devoted to all aspects of cryptology.

Dr. Stallings holds a PhD from MIT in Computer Science and a BS from Notre Dame in electrical engineering.

CHAPTER 0

GUIDE FOR READERS AND INSTRUCTORS

This book, with its accompanying Web support, covers a lot of material. Here, we give the reader some basic background information.

0.1   OUTLINE OF THE BOOK

The book is organized into two units. Unit One provides a survey of the fundamentals of data communications, networks, and Internet protocols. Unit Two covers more advanced or difficult topics in data communications and networks, and provides a more comprehensive discussion of Internet protocols and operation.
Unit One is organized into five parts:

> **Part One. Overview:** Provides an introduction to the range of topics covered in the book. This part includes a general overview of data communications and networking, and a discussion of protocols and the TCP/IP protocol suite.
>
> **Part Two. Data Communications:** Presents material concerned primarily with the exchange of data between two directly connected devices. Within this restricted scope, the key aspects of transmission, transmission media, error detection, link control, and multiplexing are examined.
>
> **Part Three. Wide Area Networks:** Examines the technologies and protocols that have been developed to support voice, data, and multimedia communications over long-distance networks. The traditional technologies of packet switching and circuit switching, as well as the more contemporary ATM and cellular networks, are examined.
>
> **Part Four. Local Area Networks:** Explores the technologies and architectures that have been developed for networking over shorter distances. The transmission media, topologies, and medium access control protocols that are the key ingredients of a LAN design are explored. This is followed by a detailed discussion of Ethernet and Wi-Fi networks.
>
> **Part Five. Internet and Transport Protocols:** Discusses protocols at the Internet and Transport layers.

Unit Two consists of three parts:

> **Part Six. Data Communications and Wireless Networks:** Treats important topics in these areas not covered in Unit One.
>
> **Part Seven. Internetworking:** Examines a range of protocols and standards related to the operation of the Internet, including routing, congestion control, and quality of service.
>
> **Part Eight. Internet Applications:** Looks at a range of applications that operate over the Internet.

In addition, there is an online **Part Nine. Security:** It covers security threats and techniques for countering these threats. A number of online appendices cover additional topics relevant to the book.

0.2 A ROADMAP FOR READERS AND INSTRUCTORS

The text contains more material than can be conveniently covered in one semester. Accordingly, the Instructor Resource Center (IRC) for this book includes several sample syllabi that guide the use of the text within limited time (e.g., 16 weeks or 12 weeks). Each alternative syllabus suggests a selection of chapters and a weekly schedule. These samples are based on real-world experience by professors with the previous edition.

The organization of the book into two units is intended to divide the material, roughly, into introductory and fundamental topics (Unit One) and advanced topics (Unit Two). Thus, a one-semester course could be limited to all or most of the material in Unit One.

In this section, we provide some other suggestions for organizing the material for a course.

Course Emphasis

The material in this book is organized into four broad categories: data transmission and communication, communications networks, network protocols, and applications and security. The chapters and parts of the book are sufficiently modular to provide a great deal of flexibility in the design of courses. The following are suggestions for three different course designs:

- **Fundamentals of Data Communications:** Parts One (overview), Two (data communications), and Three (wired WANs and cellular networks).
- **Communications Networks:** If the student has a basic background in data communications, then this course could cover Parts One (overview), Three (WAN), and Four (LAN).
- **Computer Networks:** If the student has a basic background in data communications, then this course could cover Part One (overview), Chapters 6 and 7 (error detection and correction, and data link control), Part Five (internet and transport protocols), and part or all of Parts Seven (internetworking) and Eight (applications).

In addition, a more streamlined course that covers the entire book is possible by eliminating certain chapters that are not essential on a first reading. The sample syllabi document at the IRC provides guidance on chapter selection.

Bottom–Up versus Top–Down

The book is organized in a modular fashion. After reading Part One, the other parts can be read in a number of possible sequences. Table 0.1a shows the bottom–up approach provided by reading the book from front to back. With this approach, each part builds on the material in the previous part, so that it is always clear how

Table 0.1   Suggested Reading Orders

(a) A bottom–up approach	(b) A shorter bottom–up approach
Part One: Overview	Part One: Overview
Part Two: Data Communications	Part Two: Data Communications (Chapters 3, 6, 7, 8)
Part Three: Wide Area Networks	Part Three: Wide Area Networks
Part Four: Local Area Networks	Part Four: Local Area Networks
Part Five: Internet and Transport Layers	Part Five: Internet and Transport Layers
Part Seven: Internetworking	
Part Eight: Internet Applications	
(c) A top–down approach	**(d) A shorter top–down approach**
Part One: Overview	Part One: Overview
Chapter 14: The Internet Protocol	Chapter 14: The Internet Protocol
Part Eight: Internet Applications	Part Eight: Internet Applications
Chapter 15: Transport Protocols	Chapter 15: Transport Protocols
Part Seven: Internetworking	Part Seven: Internetworking (Chapters 19, 20, 21)
Part Three: Wide Area Networks	Part Three: Wide Area Networks
Part Four: Local Area Networks	Part Four: Local Area Networks (Chapter 11)
Part Two: Data Communications	

a given layer of functionality is supported from below. There is more material than can be comfortably covered in a single semester, but the book's organization makes it easy to eliminate some chapters and maintain the bottom–up sequence. Table 0.1b suggests one approach to a survey course.

Some readers, and some instructors, are more comfortable with a top–down approach. After the background material (Part One), the reader continues at the application level and works down through the protocol layers. This has the advantage of immediately focusing on the most visible part of the material, the applications, and then seeing, progressively, how each layer is supported by the next layer down. Table 0.1c is an example of a comprehensive treatment, and Table 0.1d is an example of a survey treatment.

0.3   INTERNET AND WEB RESOURCES

There are a number of resources available on the Internet and the Web that support this book and help readers keep up with developments in this field.

Web Sites for This Book

Three Web sites provide additional resources for students and instructors.

There is a **Companion Website** for this book at http://williamstallings.com/ DataComm. For students, this Web site includes a list of relevant links, organized by chapter, and an errata list for the book. For instructors, this Web site provides links to course pages by professors teaching from this book and provides a number of other useful documents and links.

There is also an access-controlled **Premium Content Website**, which provides a wealth of supporting material, including additional online chapters, additional online appendices, and a set of homework problems with solutions. See the card at the front of this book for access information.

Finally, additional material for instructors, including a solutions manual and a projects manual, is available at the **Instructor Resource Center (IRC)** for this book. See Preface for details and access information.

Computer Science Student Resource Site

I also maintain the **Computer Science Student Resource Site**, at ComputerScience Student.com. The purpose of this site is to provide documents, information, and links for computer science students and professionals. Links and documents are organized into seven categories:

- **Math:** Includes a basic math refresher, a queuing analysis primer, a number system primer, and links to numerous math sites.
- **How-to:** Advice and guidance for solving homework problems, writing technical reports, and preparing technical presentations.
- **Research resources:** Links to important collections of papers, technical reports, and bibliographies.
- **Other useful:** A variety of other useful documents and links.
- **Computer science careers:** Useful links and documents for those considering a career in computer science.
- **Writing help:** Help in becoming a clearer, more effective writer.
- **Miscellaneous topics and humor:** You have to take your mind off your work once in a while.

Other Web Sites

Numerous Web sites provide information related to the topics of this book. The Companion Website provides links to these sites, organized by chapter.

0.4 STANDARDS

Standards have come to play a dominant role in the information communications marketplace. Virtually all vendors of products and services are committed to supporting international standards. Throughout this book, we describe the most important standards in use or being developed for various aspects of data communications and networking. Various organizations have been involved in the development or promotion of these standards. The most important (in the current context) of these organizations are as follows:

- **Internet Society:** The Internet SOCiety (ISOC) is a professional membership society with worldwide organizational and individual membership. It provides leadership in addressing issues that confront the future of the Internet and is the organization home for the groups responsible for Internet infrastructure standards, including the Internet Engineering Task Force (IETF) and the Internet Architecture Board (IAB). These organizations develop Internet standards and related specifications, all of which are published as Requests for Comments (RFCs).

- **IEEE 802:** The IEEE (Institute of Electrical and Electronics Engineers) 802 LAN/MAN Standards Committee develops local area network standards and metropolitan area network standards. The most widely used standards are for the Ethernet family, wireless LAN, bridging, and virtual bridged LANs. An individual working group provides the focus for each area.

- **ITU-T:** The International Telecommunication Union (ITU) is a United Nations agency in which governments and the private sector coordinate global telecom networks and services. The ITU Telecommunication Standardization Sector (ITU-T) is one of the three sectors of the ITU. ITU-T's mission is the production of standards covering all fields of telecommunications. ITU-T standards are referred to as Recommendations.

- **ISO:** The International Organization for Standardization (ISO)[1] is a worldwide federation of national standards bodies from more than 140 countries, one from each country. ISO is a nongovernmental organization that promotes the development of standardization and related activities with a view to facilitating the international exchange of goods and services, and to developing cooperation in the spheres of intellectual, scientific, technological, and economic activity. ISO's work results in international agreements that are published as International Standards.

A more detailed discussion of these organizations is contained in Appendix C.

---

[1]ISO is not an acronym (in which case it would be IOS), but a word, derived from the Greek, meaning *equal.*

UNIT ONE
FUNDAMENTALS

CHAPTER 1

DATA COMMUNICATIONS, DATA NETWORKS, AND THE INTERNET

LEARNING OBJECTIVES

After studying this chapter, you should be able to:

◆ Present an overview of data communications traffic volume trends.

◆ Understand the key elements of a data communications system.

◆ Summarize the types of data communications networks.

◆ Present an overview of the overall architecture of the Internet.

This book aims to provide a unified view of the broad field of data and computer communications. The organization of the book reflects an attempt to break this massive subject into comprehensible parts and to build, piece by piece, a survey of the state of the art. This introductory chapter begins with a general model of communications. Then a brief discussion introduces each of the Parts Two through Four and Six of this book. Chapter 2 provides an overview to Parts Five, Eight, and Nine.

1.1 DATA COMMUNICATIONS AND NETWORKING FOR TODAY'S ENTERPRISE

Effective and efficient data communication and networking facilities are vital to any enterprise. In this section, we first look at trends that are increasing the challenge for the business manager in planning and managing such facilities. Then we look specifically at the requirement for ever-greater transmission speeds and network capacity.

Trends

Three different forces have consistently driven the architecture and evolution of data communications and networking facilities: traffic growth, development of new services, and advances in technology.

Communication **traffic**, both local (within a building or business campus) and long distance, has been growing at a high and steady rate for decades. Network traffic is no longer limited to voice and data and increasingly includes image and video. Increasing business emphasis on web services, remote access, online transactions, and social networking means that this trend is likely to continue. Thus, business managers are constantly pressured to increase communication capacity in cost-effective ways.

As businesses rely more and more on information technology, the range of **services** that business users desire to consume is expanding. For example, mobile broadband traffic growth is exploding as is the amount of data being pushed over mobile networks by business users' smart phones and tablets. In addition, over time, mobile users are increasingly demanding high-quality services to support their high-resolution camera phones, favorite video streams, and high-end audio. Similar demand growth is seen in landline access to the Internet and private networks. To keep up with mushrooming traffic generated by both consumers and business users, mobile service providers have to keep investing in high-capacity networking and transmission facilities. In turn, the growth in high-speed network offerings at competitive price points encourages the expansion of mobile applications and services. Thus, growth in services and in traffic capacity go hand in hand. As an example, Figure 1.1 [IEEE12] shows the mix of traffic and the growth trend for cable Internet subscribers.

Finally, trends in **technology** enable the provision of increasing traffic capacity and the support of a wide range of services. Four technology trends are particularly notable:

1. The trend toward faster and cheaper, in both computing and communications, continues. In terms of computing, this means more powerful computers and clusters of computers capable of supporting more demanding applications, such as multimedia applications. In terms of communications, the increasing use of optical fiber and high-speed wireless has brought transmission prices down and greatly increased capacity. For example, for long-distance telecommunication and data network links, dense wavelength division multiplexing (DWDM)

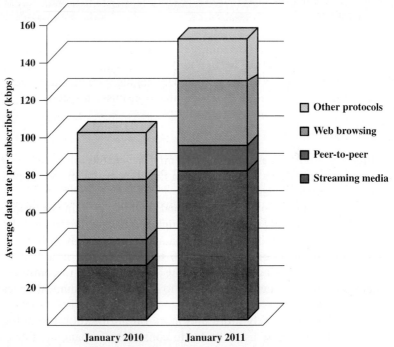

Figure 1.1   Average Downstream Traffic per Internet Subscriber

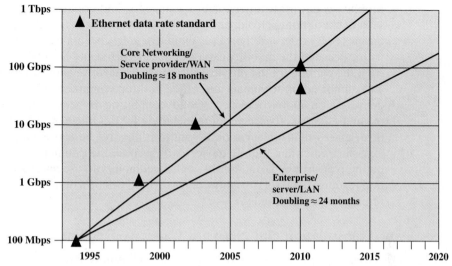

Figure 1.2 Past and Projected Growth in Ethernet Data Rate Demand Compared to Existing Ethernet Data Rates

enables communication traffic to be carried by fiber optic cables at rates of multiple terabits per second. For local area networks (LANs), many enterprises now have 40-Gbps Ethernet or 100-Gbps Ethernet backbone networks.[1] Figure 1.2 [IEEE12] indicates the Ethernet demand trend. As shown, usage statistics indicate that Internet backbone data rate demand in the network core doubles approximately every 18 months, while demand in enterprise/LAN applications doubles approximately every 24 months.

2. Today's networks are more "intelligent" than ever. Two areas of intelligence are noteworthy. First, today's networks can offer differing levels of quality of service (QoS), which include specifications for maximum delay, minimum throughput, and so on to ensure high-quality support for applications and services. Second, today's networks provide a variety of customizable services in the areas of network management and security.

3. The Internet, the Web, and associated applications have emerged as dominant features for both business and personal network landscapes. The migration to "everything over IP" continues and has created many opportunities and challenges for information and communications technology (ICT) managers. In addition to exploiting the Internet and the Web to reach customers, suppliers, and partners enterprises have formed intranets and extranets[2] to isolate proprietary information to keep it free from unwanted access.

---

[1]An explanation of numerical prefixes, such as *tera* and *giga*, is provided in the document *Prefix.pdf*, available at box.com/dcc10e.

[2]Briefly, an intranet uses Internet and Web technology in an isolated facility internal to an enterprise; an extranet extends a company's intranet out onto the Internet to allow selected customers, suppliers, and mobile workers to access the company's private data and applications.

4. Mobility is newest frontier for ICT managers, and popular consumer devices such as the iPhone, Droid, and iPad have become drivers of the evolution of business networks and their use. While there has been a trend toward mobility for decades, the mobility explosion has occurred and has liberated workers from the confines of the physical enterprise. Enterprise applications traditionally supported on terminals and office desktop computers are now routinely delivered on mobile devices. Cloud computing is being embraced by all major business software vendors including SAP, Oracle, and Microsoft, and this ensures that further mobility innovations will be forthcoming. Industry experts predict that mobile devices will become the dominant business computing platform by 2015 and that enhanced ability to use enterprise information resources and services anywhere-anytime will be a dominant trend for the remainder of the decade.

Data Transmission and Network Capacity Requirements

Momentous changes in the way organizations do business and process information have been driven by changes in networking technology and at the same time have driven those changes. It is hard to separate chicken and egg in this field. Similarly, the use of the Internet by both businesses and individuals reflects this cyclic dependency: The availability of new image-based services on the Internet (i.e., the Web) has resulted in an increase in the total number of users and the traffic volume generated by each user. This, in turn, has resulted in a need to increase the speed and efficiency of the Internet. On the other hand, it is only such increased speed that makes the use of Web-based applications palatable to the end user.

In this section, we survey some of the end-user factors that fit into this equation. We begin with the need for high-speed LANs in the business environment, because this need has appeared first and has forced the pace of networking development. Then we look at business WAN requirements. Finally, we offer a few words about the effect of changes in commercial electronics on network requirements.

THE EMERGENCE OF HIGH-SPEED LANS   Personal computers and microcomputer workstations began to achieve widespread acceptance in business computing in the early 1980s and have now achieved virtually the status of the telephone: an essential tool for office workers. Until relatively recently, office LANs provided basic connectivity services—connecting personal computers and terminals to mainframes and midrange systems that ran corporate applications, and providing workgroup connectivity at the departmental or divisional level. In both cases, traffic patterns were relatively light, with an emphasis on file transfer and electronic mail. The LANs that were available for this type of workload, primarily Ethernet and token ring, are well suited to this environment.

In the last 20 years, two significant trends altered the role of the personal computer and therefore the requirements on the LAN:

1. The speed and computing power of personal computers continued to enjoy explosive growth. These more powerful platforms support graphics-intensive applications and ever more elaborate graphical user interfaces to the operating system.

2. MIS (management information systems) organizations have recognized the LAN as a viable and essential computing platform, resulting in the focus on network computing. This trend began with client/server computing, which has become a dominant architecture in the business environment and the more recent Web-focused intranet trend. Both of these approaches involve the frequent transfer of potentially large volumes of data in a transaction-oriented environment.

The effect of these trends has been to increase the volume of data to be handled over LANs and, because applications are more interactive, to reduce the acceptable delay on data transfers. The earlier generation of 10-Mbps Ethernets and 16-Mbps token rings was simply not up to the job of supporting these requirements.

The following are examples of requirements that call for higher-speed LANs:

- **Centralized server farms:** In many applications, there is a need for user, or client, systems to be able to draw huge amounts of data from multiple centralized servers, called server farms. An example is a color publishing operation, in which servers typically contain tens of gigabytes of image data that must be downloaded to imaging workstations. As the performance of the servers themselves has increased, the bottleneck has shifted to the network.

- **Power workgroups:** These groups typically consist of a small number of cooperating users who need to draw massive data files across the network. Examples are a software development group that runs tests on a new software version, or a computer-aided design (CAD) company that regularly runs simulations of new designs. In such cases, large amounts of data are distributed to several workstations, processed, and updated at very high speed for multiple iterations.

- **High-speed local backbone:** As processing demand grows, LANs proliferate at a site, and high-speed interconnection is necessary.

CORPORATE WIDE AREA NETWORKING NEEDS   As recently as the early 1990s, there was an emphasis in many organizations on a centralized data processing model. In a typical environment, there might be significant computing facilities at a few regional offices, consisting of mainframes or well-equipped midrange systems. These centralized facilities could handle most corporate applications, including basic finance, accounting, and personnel programs, as well as many of the business-specific applications. Smaller, outlying offices (e.g., a bank branch) could be equipped with terminals or basic personal computers linked to one of the regional centers in a transaction-oriented environment.

This model began to change in the early 1990s, and the change accelerated since then. Many organizations have dispersed their employees into multiple smaller offices. There is a growing use of telecommuting. Most significant, the nature of the application structure has changed. First client/server computing and, more recently, intranet computing have fundamentally restructured the organizational data processing environment. There is now much more reliance on personal computers, workstations, and servers and much less use of centralized mainframe and midrange systems. Furthermore, the virtually universal deployment of graphical user interfaces to the desktop enables the end user to exploit graphic applications, multimedia, and other data-intensive applications. In addition, most organizations require access to the Internet. When a few clicks of the mouse can trigger huge volumes of data, traffic patterns have become more unpredictable while the average load has risen.

All of these trends mean that more data must be transported off premises and into the wide area. It has long been accepted that in the typical business environment, about 80% of the traffic remains local and about 20% traverses wide area links. But this rule no longer applies to most companies, with a greater percentage of the traffic going into the WAN environment. This traffic flow shift places a greater burden on LAN backbones and, of course, on the WAN facilities used by a corporation. Thus, just as in the local area, changes in corporate data traffic patterns are driving the creation of high-speed WANs.

DIGITAL ELECTRONICS   The rapid conversion of consumer electronics to digital technology is having an impact on both the Internet and corporate intranets. As these new gadgets come into view and proliferate, they dramatically increase the amount of image and video traffic carried by networks.

Two noteworthy examples of this trend are digital versatile disks (DVDs) and digital still cameras. With the capacious DVD, the electronics industry at last found an acceptable replacement for the analog video home system (VHS) tapes. The DVD has replaced the videotape used in videocassette recorders (VCRs) and the CD-ROM in personal computers and servers. The DVD takes video into the digital age. It delivers movies with picture quality that outshines laser disks, and it can be randomly accessed like audio CDs, which DVD machines can also play. Vast volumes of data can be crammed onto the disk. With DVD's huge storage capacity and vivid quality, PC games have become more realistic and educational software incorporates more video. Following in the wake of these developments is a new crest of traffic over the Internet and corporate intranets, as this material is incorporated into Web sites.

A related product development is the digital camcorder. This product has made it easier for individuals and companies to make digital video files to be placed on corporate and Internet Web sites, again adding to the traffic burden.

Convergence

Convergence refers to the merger of previously distinct telephony and information technologies and markets. We can think of this convergence in terms of a three-layer model of enterprise communications:

- **Applications:** These are seen by the end users of a business. Convergence integrates communications applications, such as voice calling (telephone), voice mail, e-mail, and instant messaging, with business applications, such as workgroup collaboration, customer relationship management, and other back-office functions. With convergence, applications provide features that incorporate voice, data, and video in a seamless, organized, and value-added manner. One example is multimedia messaging, which enables a user to employ a single interface to access messages from a variety of sources (e.g., office voice mail, office e-mail, beeper, and fax).

- **Enterprise services:** At this level, the manager deals with the information network in terms of the services it provides to support applications. The network manager needs design, maintenance, and support services related to the deployment of convergence-based facilities. Also at this level, network managers deal with the enterprise network as a function-providing system. Such management services may include setting up authentication schemes; capacity management for various users, groups, and applications; and QoS provision.

- **Infrastructure:** The network and communications infrastructure consists of the communication links, LANs, WANs, and Internet connections available to the enterprise. Increasingly, enterprise network infrastructure also includes private and/or public cloud connections to data centers which host high-volume data storage and Web services. A key aspect of convergence at this level is the ability to carry voice, image, and video over networks that were originally designed to carry data traffic. Infrastructure convergence has also occurred for networks that were designed for voice traffic. For example, video, image, text, and data are routinely delivered to smart phone users over cell phone networks.

In simple terms, convergence involves moving voice into a data infrastructure, integrating all the voice and data networks inside a user organization into a single data network infrastructure, and then extending that into the wireless arena. The foundation of this convergence is packet-based transmission using the Internet Protocol (IP). Convergence increases the function and scope of both the infrastructure and the application base.

1.2 A COMMUNICATIONS MODEL

This section introduces a simple model of communications, illustrated by the block diagram in Figure 1.3a.

The fundamental purpose of a communications system is the exchange of data between two parties. Figure 1.3b presents one particular example, which is communication between a workstation and a server over a public telephone network. Another example is the exchange of voice signals between two telephones over the same network. The following are key elements of the model:

- **Source:** This device generates the data to be transmitted; examples are telephones and personal computers.

- **Transmitter:** Usually, the data generated by a source system are not transmitted directly in the form in which they were generated. Rather, a transmitter transforms and encodes the information in such a way as to produce electromagnetic signals that can be transmitted across some sort of transmission system. For example, a modem takes a digital bit stream from an attached device such as a personal computer and transforms that bit stream into an analog signal that can be handled by the telephone network.

- **Transmission system:** This can be a single transmission line or a complex network connecting source and destination.

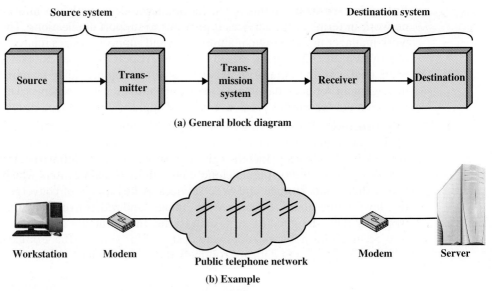

Figure 1.3   Simplified Communications Model

- **Receiver:** The receiver accepts the signal from the transmission system and converts it into a form that can be handled by the destination device. For example, a modem will accept an analog signal coming from a network or transmission line and convert it into a digital bit stream.

- **Destination:** Takes the incoming data from the receiver.

This simple narrative conceals a wealth of technical complexity. To get some idea of the scope of this complexity, Table 1.1 lists some of the key tasks that must be performed in a data communications system. The list is somewhat arbitrary: Elements could be added; items on the list could be merged; and some items represent several tasks that are performed at different "levels" of the system. However, the list as it stands is suggestive of the scope of this book.

The first item, **transmission system utilization**, refers to the need to make efficient use of transmission facilities that are typically shared among a number of communicating devices. Various techniques (referred to as multiplexing) are used to allocate the total capacity of a transmission medium among a number of users.

Table 1.1   Communications Tasks

Transmission system utilization	Addressing
Interfacing	Routing
Signal generation	Recovery
Synchronization	Message formatting
Exchange management	Security
Error detection and correction	Network management
Flow control	

Congestion control techniques may be required to assure that the system is not overwhelmed by excessive demand for transmission services.

To communicate, a device must **interface** with the transmission system. All forms of communication discussed in this book depend on the use of electromagnetic signals propagated over a transmission medium. Thus, once an interface is established, **signal generation** is required for communication. The properties of the signal, such as form and intensity, must be such that the signal is (1) capable of being propagated through the transmission system, and (2) interpretable as data at the receiver.

Not only must the signals be generated to conform to the requirements of the transmission system and receiver, but also there must be some form of **synchronization** between transmitter and receiver. The receiver must be able to determine when a signal begins to arrive and when it ends. It must also know the duration of each signal element.

Beyond the basic matter of deciding on the nature and timing of signals, there is a variety of requirements for communication between two parties that might be collected under the term **exchange management**. If data are to be exchanged in both directions over a period of time, the two parties must cooperate. For example, for two parties to engage in a telephone conversation, one party must dial the number of the other, causing signals to be generated that result in the ringing of the called phone. The called party completes a connection by lifting the receiver. For data processing devices, more will be needed than simply establishing a connection; certain conventions must be decided on. These conventions might include whether both devices may transmit simultaneously or must take turns, the amount of data to be sent at one time, the format of the data, and what to do if certain contingencies such as an error arise.

The next two items might have been included under exchange management, but they seem important enough to list separately. In all communications systems, there is a potential for error; transmitted signals are distorted to some extent before reaching their destination. **Error detection and correction** are required in circumstances where errors cannot be tolerated. This is usually the case with data processing systems. For example, in transferring a file from one computer to another, it is simply not acceptable for the contents of the file to be accidentally altered. **Flow control** is required to assure that the source does not overwhelm the destination by sending data faster than they can be processed and absorbed.

Next are the related but distinct concepts of **addressing** and **routing**. When more than two devices share a transmission facility, a source system must indicate the identity of the intended destination. The transmission system must assure that the destination system, and only that system, receives the data. Further, the transmission system may itself be a network through which various paths may be taken. A specific route through this network must be chosen.

Recovery is a concept distinct from that of error correction. Recovery techniques are needed in situations in which an information exchange, such as a database transaction or file transfer, is interrupted due to a fault somewhere in the system. The objective is either to be able to resume activity at the point of interruption or at least to restore the state of the systems involved to the condition prior to the beginning of the exchange.

Message formatting has to do with an agreement between two parties as to the form of the data to be exchanged or transmitted, such as the binary code for characters.

Frequently, it is important to provide some measure of **security** in a data communications system. The sender of data may wish to be assured that only the intended receiver actually receives the data. And the receiver of data may wish to be assured that the received data have not been altered in transit and that the data actually come from the purported sender.

Finally, a data communications facility is a complex system that cannot create or run itself. **Network management** capabilities are needed to configure the system, monitor its status, react to failures and overloads, and plan intelligently for future growth.

Thus, we have gone from the simple idea of data communication between source and destination to a rather formidable list of data communications tasks. In this book, we elaborate this list of tasks to describe and encompass the entire set of activities that can be classified under data and computer communications.

1.3 DATA COMMUNICATIONS

A Data Communications Model

To get some flavor for the focus of Part Two, Figure 1.4 provides a new perspective on the communications model of Figure 1.3a. We trace the details of this figure using electronic mail as an example.

Suppose that the input device and transmitter are components of a personal computer. The user of the PC wishes to send a message m to another user. The user activates the electronic mail package on the PC and enters the message via the keyboard (input device). The character string is briefly buffered in main memory. We can view it as a sequence of bits (g) in memory. The personal computer is connected to some transmission medium, such as a local area network, a digital subscriber line, or a wireless connection, by an I/O device (transmitter), such as a local network transceiver or a DSL modem. The input data are transferred to the transmitter as a

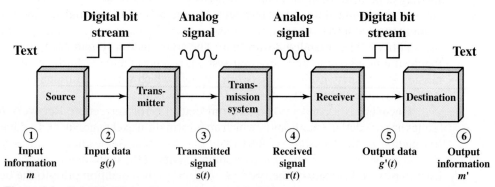

Figure 1.4   Simplified Data Communications Model

sequence of voltage shifts [$g(t)$] representing bits on some communications bus or cable. The transmitter is connected directly to the medium and converts the incoming stream [$g(t)$] into a signal [$s(t)$] suitable for transmission; specific alternatives will be described in Chapter 5.

The transmitted signal $s(t)$ presented to the medium is subject to a number of impairments, discussed in Chapter 3, before it reaches the receiver. Thus, the received signal $r(t)$ may differ from $s(t)$. The receiver will attempt to estimate the original $s(t)$, based on $r(t)$ and its knowledge of the medium, producing a sequence of bits $g'(t)$. These bits are sent to the output personal computer, where they are briefly buffered in memory as a block of bits (g'). In many cases, the destination system will attempt to determine if an error has occurred and, if so, cooperate with the source system to eventually obtain a complete, error-free block of data. These data are then presented to the user via an output device, such as a printer or screen. The message (m') as viewed by the user will usually be an exact copy of the original message (m).

Now consider a telephone conversation. In this case the input to the telephone is a message (m) in the form of sound waves. The sound waves are converted by the telephone into electrical signals of the same frequency. These signals are transmitted without modification over the telephone line. Hence the input signal $g(t)$ and the transmitted signal $s(t)$ are identical. The signal $s(t)$ will suffer some distortion over the medium, so that $r(t)$ will not be identical to $s(t)$. Nevertheless, the signal $r(t)$ is converted back into a sound wave with no attempt at correction or improvement of signal quality. Thus, m' is not an exact replica of m. However, the received sound message is generally comprehensible to the listener.

The discussion so far does not touch on other key aspects of data communications, including data link control techniques for controlling the flow of data and detecting and correcting errors, and multiplexing techniques for transmission efficiency.

The Transmission of Information

The basic building block of any enterprise network infrastructure is the transmission line. Much of the technical detail of how information is encoded and transmitted across a line is of no real interest to the business manager. The manager is concerned with whether the particular facility provides the required capacity, with acceptable reliability, at minimum cost. However, there are certain aspects of transmission technology that a manager must understand to ask the right questions and make informed decisions.

One of the basic choices facing a business user is the transmission medium. For use within the business premises, this choice is generally completely up to the business. For long-distance communications, the choice is generally but not always made by the long-distance carrier. In either case, changes in technology are rapidly changing the mix of media used. Of particular note are *fiber optic* transmission and *wireless* transmission (e.g., satellite and cellular communications). These two media are now driving the evolution of data communications transmission.

The ever-increasing availability of fiber optic communication circuits is making channel capacity a virtually free resource. Since the early 1980s, the growth of the market for optical fiber transmission systems is without precedent. During the past 10 years, the cost of fiber optic transmission has dropped by more than an order of magnitude, and the capacity of such systems has grown at almost as rapid a rate. Almost all of the long-distance telephone communications trunks within the United States and the highest speed links on the Internet consist of fiber optic cable. Because of its high capacity and its security characteristics (fiber is difficult to tap), it is becoming increasingly used within office buildings and local area networks to carry the growing load of business information. The spreading use of fiber optic cable is also spurring advancements in communication switching technologies and network management architectures.

The increasing use of the second medium, wireless transmission, is a result of the trend toward universal personal telecommunications and universal access to communications. The first concept refers to the ability of a person to a single account to use any communication system anytime-anywhere, ideally globally. The second refers to the ability to use one's preferred computing device in a wide variety of environments to connect to information services (e.g., to have a laptop, smartphone, or tablet that will work equally well in the office, on the street, and on an airplane, bus, or train). Today, both concepts are subsumed under the business push to support mobility. Wireless LANs have become common components of enterprise networks as well as small office/home office networks, and smartphones and tablets with wireless capabilities are rapidly becoming mainstream business user communications devices. Mobility has the potential to unleash higher performance at all business levels: personal, workgroup, and enterprise-wide. This provides compelling rationale for further business investment in wireless technologies.

Despite the growth in the capacity and the drop in cost of transmission facilities, transmission services remain the most costly component of a communications budget for most businesses. Thus, the manager needs to be aware of techniques that increase the efficiency of the use of these facilities. The two major approaches to greater efficiency are multiplexing and compression. *Multiplexing* refers to the ability of a number of devices to share a transmission facility. If each device needs the facility only a fraction of the time, then a sharing arrangement allows the cost of the facility to be spread over many users. *Compression*, as the name indicates, involves squeezing the data down so that a lower-capacity, cheaper transmission facility can be used to meet a given demand. These two techniques show up separately and in combination in a number of types of communications equipment. The manager needs to understand these technologies to assess the appropriateness and cost-effectiveness of the various products on the market.

TRANSMISSION AND TRANSMISSION MEDIA   Information can be communicated by converting it into an electromagnetic signal and transmitting that signal over some medium, such as a twisted-pair telephone line. The most commonly used transmission media are twisted-pair lines, coaxial cable, optical fiber cable, and terrestrial and satellite microwave. The data rates that can be achieved and the rate at which errors can occur depend on the nature of the signal and the type of medium. Chapters 3 and 4 examine the significant properties of electromagnetic signals and compare the various transmission media in terms of cost, performance, and applications.

COMMUNICATION TECHNIQUES   The transmission of information across a transmission medium involves more than simply inserting a signal on the medium. The technique used to encode the information into an electromagnetic signal must be determined. There are various ways in which the encoding can be done, and the choice affects performance and reliability. Furthermore, the successful transmission of information involves a high degree of cooperation between the various components. The interface between a device and the transmission medium must be agreed on. Some means of controlling the flow of information and recovering from its loss or corruption must be used. These latter functions are performed by a data link control protocol. All these issues are examined in Chapters 5 through 7.

TRANSMISSION EFFICIENCY   A major cost in any computer/communications facility is transmission cost. Because of this, it is important to maximize the amount of information that can be carried over a given resource or, alternatively, to minimize the transmission capacity needed to satisfy a given information communications requirement. Two ways of achieving this objective are multiplexing and compression. The two techniques can be used separately or in combination. Chapter 8 examines the three most common multiplexing techniques: frequency division, synchronous time division, and statistical time division, as well as the important compression techniques.

1.4 NETWORKS

Globally, the number of Internet users is forecast to increase from approximately 2 billion in 2011 to 3 billion users in 2016. This figure is in fact misleading, as a single end user may have multiple types of devices. The estimate for 2016 is that there will be over 20 billion fixed and mobile networked devices and machine-to-machine connections, up from about 7 billion devices in 2011. The increase in the number of user devices, especially broadband devices, affects traffic volume in a number of ways. It enables a user to be continuously consuming network capacity, as well as to be consuming capacity on multiple devices simultaneously. Also, different broadband devices enable different applications, which may have greater traffic generation capability. The result is that the total annual traffic generated over the Internet and other IP-based networks is forecast to rise from 372 exabytes (372×2^{60} bytes) to 1.3 zettabytes (1.3×2^{70} bytes) in 2016 [CISC12a]. This traffic demand imposes stiff performance requirements on communications protocols, which is previewed in Chapter 2, and on communications and computer networks.

One type of network that has become commonplace is the local area network. Indeed, LANs are to be found in virtually all medium- and large-size office buildings. LANs, especially Wi-Fi LANs, are also increasingly used for small office and home networks. As the number and power of computing devices have grown, so have the number and capacity of LANs found in business networks. The development of internationally recognized standards for LANs has contributed to their proliferation in enterprises. Although Ethernet has emerged as the dominant LAN architecture, business managers still have choices to make about transmission rates (ranging from 100 Mbps to 100 Gbps) and the degree to which both wired and wireless LANs will be combined within an enterprise network. Interconnecting and managing a diverse collection of local area networks and computing devices within today's business networks presents ongoing challenges for networking professionals.

A business need for a robust network to support voice, data, image, and video traffic is not confined to a single office building or LAN; today, it is an enterprise-wide communication requirement. Advances in LAN switches and other data communication technologies have led to greatly increased local area network transmission capacities and the concept of integration. *Integration* means that the communication equipment and networks can deal simultaneously with voice, data, image, and even video. Thus, a memo or report can be accompanied by voice commentary, presentation graphics, and perhaps even a short video introduction, demonstration, or summary. Image and video services that perform adequately within LANs often impose large demands on wide area network transmission and can be costly. Moreover, as LANs become ubiquitous and as their transmission rates increase, the need for enterprise networks to support interconnections among geographically dispersed areas has increased. This, in turn, has forced businesses increase wide area network transmission and switching capacity. Fortunately, the enormous and ever-increasing capacity of fiber optic and wireless transmission services provides ample resources to meet these business data communication needs. However, the development of switching systems that are capable of responding to the increasing capacities of transmission links and business communication traffic requirements is an ongoing challenge not yet conquered.

The opportunities for a business to use its enterprise network as an aggressive competitive tool and as a means of enhancing productivity and slashing costs are great. When business managers understand these technologies, they can deal effectively with data communication equipment vendors and service providers to enhance the company's competitive position.

In the remainder of this section, we provide a brief overview of various networks. Parts Three and Four cover these topics in depth.

Wide Area Networks

Wide area networks generally cover a large geographical area. They often require the crossing of public right-of-ways, and typically rely at least in part on circuits provided by one or more *common carriers*—companies that offer communication services to the general public. Typically, a WAN consists of a number of interconnected switching nodes. A trans-mission from any one device is routed through these internal nodes to the specified destination device. These nodes (including the boundary nodes) are not concerned with the content of the data; rather, their purpose is to provide a switching facility that will move the data from node to node until they reach their destination.

Traditionally, WANs have been implemented using one of two technologies: circuit switching and packet switching. Subsequently, frame relay and ATM networks assumed major roles. While ATM and, to some extent frame relay, are still widely used, their use is gradually being supplanted by services based on gigabit Ethernet and Internet Protocol technologies.

Circuit Switching In a circuit-switching network, a dedicated communications path is established between two stations through the nodes of the network. That path is a connected sequence of physical links between nodes. On each link, a logical channel is dedicated to the connection. Data generated by the source station are transmitted along the dedicated path as rapidly as possible. At each node, incoming data are routed or switched to the appropriate outgoing channel without delay. The most common example of circuit switching is the telephone network.

PACKET SWITCHING   In a packet-switching network, it is not necessary to dedicate transmission capacity along a path through the network. Rather, data are sent out in a sequence of small chunks, called packets. Each packet is passed through the network from node to node along some path leading from source to destination. At each node, the entire packet is received, stored briefly, and then transmitted to the next node. Packet-switching networks are commonly used for terminal-to-computer and computer-to-computer communications.

FRAME RELAY   Packet switching was developed at a time when digital long-distance transmission facilities exhibited a relatively high error rate compared to today's facilities. As a result, there is a considerable amount of overhead built into packet-switching schemes to compensate for errors. The overhead includes additional bits added to each packet to introduce redundancy and additional processing at the end stations and the intermediate switching nodes to detect and recover from errors.

With modern high-speed telecommunications systems, this overhead is unnecessary and counterproductive. It is unnecessary because the rate of errors has been dramatically lowered and any remaining errors can easily be caught in the end systems by logic that operates above the level of the packet-switching logic. It is counterproductive because the overhead involved soaks up a significant fraction of the high capacity provided by the network.

Frame relay was developed to take advantage of these high data rates and low error rates. Whereas the original packet-switching networks were designed with a data rate to the end user of about 64 kbps, frame relay networks are designed to operate efficiently at user data rates of up to 2 Mbps. The key to achieving these high data rates is to strip out most of the overhead involved with error control.

ATM   Asynchronous transfer mode, sometimes referred to as cell relay, is a culmination of developments in circuit switching and packet switching. ATM can be viewed as an evolution from frame relay. The most obvious difference between frame relay and ATM is that frame relay uses variable-length packets, called frames, and ATM uses fixed-length packets, called cells. As with frame relay, ATM provides little overhead for error control, depending on the inherent reliability of the transmission system and on higher layers of logic in the end systems to catch and correct errors. By using a fixed packet length, the processing overhead is reduced even further for ATM compared to frame relay. The result is that ATM is designed to work in the range of 10s and 100s of Mbps, and in the Gbps range.

ATM can also be viewed as an evolution from circuit switching. With circuit switching, only fixed-data-rate circuits are available to the end system. ATM allows the definition of multiple virtual channels with data rates that are dynamically defined at the time the virtual channel is created. By using small, fixed-size cells, ATM is so efficient that it can offer a constant-data-rate channel even though it is using a packet-switching technique. Thus, ATM extends circuit switching to allow multiple channels with the data rate on each channel dynamically set on demand.

Local Area Networks

As with WANs, a LAN is a communications network that interconnects a variety of devices and provides a means for information exchange among those devices. There are several key distinctions between LANs and WANs:

1. The scope of the LAN is small, typically a single building or a cluster of buildings. This difference in geographic scope leads to different technical solutions, as we shall see.

2. It is usually the case that the LAN is owned by the same organization that owns the attached devices. For WANs, this is less often the case, or at least a significant fraction of the network assets is not owned. This has two implications. First, care must be taken in the choice of LAN, because there may be a substantial capital investment (compared to dial-up or leased charges for WANs) for both purchase and maintenance. Second, the network management responsibility for a LAN falls solely on the user.

3. The internal data rates of LANs are typically much greater than those of WANs.

LANs come in a number of different configurations. The most common are switched LANs and wireless LANs. The most common switched LAN is a switched Ethernet LAN, which may consist of a single switch with a number of attached devices, or a number of interconnected switches. The most common type of wireless LANs are Wi-Fi LANs.

Wireless Networks

As was just mentioned, wireless LANs are widely used in business environments. Wireless technology is also common for both wide area voice and data networks. Wireless networks provide advantages in the areas of mobility and ease of installation and configuration.

1.5 THE INTERNET

Origins of the Internet

The Internet evolved from the ARPANET, which was developed in 1969 by the Advanced Research Projects Agency (ARPA) of the U.S. Department of Defense. It was the first operational packet-switching network. ARPANET began operations in four locations. Today the number of hosts is in the hundreds of millions, the number of users in the billions, and the number of countries participating nearing 200. The number of connections to the Internet continues to grow exponentially.

The network was so successful that ARPA applied the same packet-switching technology to tactical radio communication (packet radio) and to satellite communication (SATNET). Because the three networks operated in very different communication environments, the appropriate values for certain parameters, such as maximum packet size, were different in each case. Faced with the dilemma of integrating these networks, Vint Cerf and Bob Kahn of ARPA developed methods and protocols for *internetworking*—that is, communicating across arbitrary, multiple, packet-switched networks. They published a very influential paper in May 1974 [CERF74] outlining their approach to a Transmission Control Protocol. The proposal was refined and details filled in by the ARPANET community, with major contributions from participants from European networks eventually leading to the TCP (Transmission Control Protocol) and IP (Internet Protocol) protocols, which, in turn, formed the basis for what eventually became the TCP/IP protocol suite. This provided the foundation for the Internet.

Key Elements

Figure 1.5 illustrates the key elements that comprise the Internet. The purpose of the Internet, of course, is to interconnect end systems, called **hosts**; these include PCs, workstations, servers, mainframes, and so on. Most hosts that use the Internet are connected to a **network**, such as a local area network or a wide area network (WAN). These networks are in turn connected by **routers**. Each router attaches to two or more networks. Some hosts, such as mainframes or servers, connect directly to a router rather than through a network.

In essence, the Internet operates as follows. A host may send data to another host anywhere on the Internet. The source host breaks the data to be sent into a

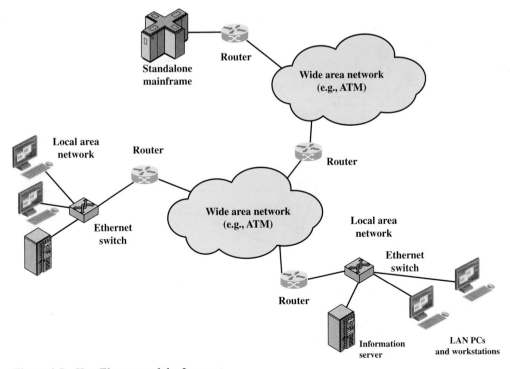

Figure 1.5 Key Elements of the Internet

sequence of packets, called **IP datagrams** or **IP packets**. Each packet includes a unique numeric address of the destination host. This address is referred to as an **IP address**, because the address is carried in an IP packet. Based on this destination address, each packet travels through a series of routers and networks from source to destination. Each router, as it receives a packet, makes a routing decision and forwards the packet along its way to the destination.

Internet Architecture

The Internet today is made up of thousands of overlapping hierarchical networks. Because of this, it is not practical to attempt a detailed description of the exact architecture or topology of the Internet. However, an overview of the common, general characteristics can be made. Figure 1.6 illustrates the discussion and Table 1.2 summarizes the terminology.

A key element of the Internet is the set of hosts attached to it. Simply put, a host is a computer. Today, computers come in many forms, including mobile phones and even cars. All of these forms can be hosts on the Internet. Hosts are sometimes grouped together in a LAN. This is the typical configuration in a corporate environment. Individual hosts and LANs are connected to an **Internet service provider (ISP)** through a **point of presence (POP)**. The connection is made in a series of steps starting with the **customer premises equipment (CPE)**. The CPE is the communications equipment located onsite with the host.

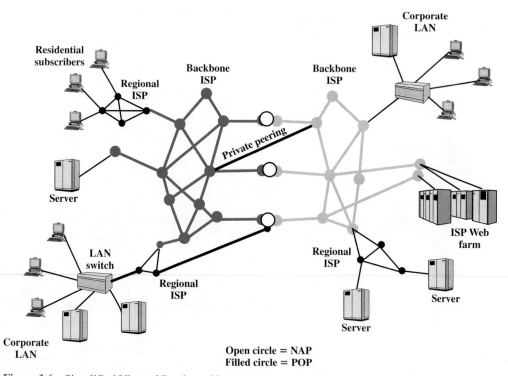

Figure 1.6 Simplified View of Portion of Internet

Table 1.2   Internet Terminology

Central Office (CO)

The place where telephone companies terminate customer lines and locate switching equipment to interconnect those lines with other networks.

Customer Premises Equipment (CPE)

Telecommunications equipment that is located on the customer's premises (physical location) rather than on the provider's premises or in between. Telephone handsets, modems, cable TV set-top boxes, and digital subscriber line routers are examples. Historically, this term referred to equipment placed at the customer's end of the telephone line and usually owned by the telephone company. Today, almost any end-user equipment can be called customer premises equipment and it can be owned by the customer or by the provider.

Internet Service Provider (ISP)

A company that provides other companies or individuals with access to, or presence on, the Internet. An ISP has the equipment and the telecommunication line access required to have a POP on the Internet for the geographic area served. The larger ISPs have their own high-speed leased lines so that they are less dependent on the telecommunication providers and can provide better service to their customers.

Network Access Point (NAP)

In the United States, a network access point (NAP) is one of several major Internet interconnection points that serve to tie all the ISPs together. Originally, four NAPs—in New York, Washington, D.C., Chicago, and San Francisco—were created and supported by the National Science Foundation as part of the transition from the original U.S. government–financed Internet to a commercially operated Internet. Since that time, several new NAPs have arrived, including WorldCom's "MAE West" site in San Jose, California, and ICS Network Systems' "Big East."

The NAPs provide major switching facilities that serve the public in general. Companies apply to use the NAP facilities. Much Internet traffic is handled without involving NAPs, using peering arrangements and interconnections within geographic regions.

Network Service Provider (NSP)

A company that provides backbone services to an Internet service provider. Typically, an ISP connects at a point called an Internet exchange (IX) to a regional ISP that in turn connects to an NSP backbone.

Point of Presence (POP)

A site that has a collection of telecommunications equipment, usually refers to ISP or telephone company sites. An ISP POP is the edge of the ISP's network; connections from users are accepted and authenticated here. An Internet access provider may operate several POPs distributed throughout its area of operation to increase the chance that their subscribers will be able to reach one with a local telephone call. The largest national ISPs have POPs all over the country.

For a number of home users, the CPE was traditionally a 56-kbps modem. This was adequate for e-mail and related services but marginal for graphics-intensive Web surfing. Today's CPE offerings provide greater capacity and guaranteed service in some cases. A sample of these access technologies includes DSL, cable modem, terrestrial wireless, and satellite. Users who connect to the Internet through their work often use workstations or PCs connected to their employer-owned LANs, which in turn connect through shared organizational trunks to an ISP. In these cases the shared circuit is often a T-1 connection (1.544 Mbps), while for very large organizations T-3 connections (44.736 Mbps) are sometimes found. Alternatively, an organization's LAN may be hooked to a WAN, such as a frame relay network, which in turn connects to an ISP.

The CPE is physically attached to the "local loop" or "last mile." This is the infrastructure between a provider's installation and the site where the host is located. For example, a residential user with a DSL modem attaches the modem to the telephone line. The telephone line is typically a pair of copper wires that runs from the house to a **central office (CO)** owned and operated by the telephone company, with perhaps the use of optical fiber for a large portion of that link. If the home user has a cable modem, the local loop is the coaxial cable that runs from the home to the cable company facilities. The preceding examples are a bit of an oversimplification, but they suffice for this discussion. In many cases the wires that leave a home are aggregated with wires from other homes and then converted to a different media such as fiber. In these cases the term *local loop* still refers to the path from the home to the CO or cable facility. The local loop provider is not necessarily the ISP. In many cases the local loop provider is the telephone company and the ISP is a large, national service organization. Often, however, the local loop provider is also the ISP.

Other forms of CPE-ISP connection do not go through a telephone company CO. For example, a cable link would connect the local user to the cable company site, which would include or link to an ISP. Mobile users can take advantage of a wireless link to a Wi-Fi access point that provides access to the Internet. And corporate access to an ISP may be by dedicated high-speed links or through a wide area network, such as an asynchronous transfer mode or frame relay network.

The ISP provides access to its larger network through a POP. A POP is simply a facility where customers can connect to the ISP network. The facility is sometimes owned by the ISP, but often the ISP leases space from the local loop carrier. A POP can be as simple as a bank of modems and an access server installed in a rack at the CO. The POPs are usually spread out over the geographic area where the provider offers service. The ISP acts as a gateway to the Internet, providing many important services. For most home users, the ISP provides the unique numeric IP address needed to communicate with other Internet hosts. Most ISPs also provide name resolution and other essential network services. The most important service an ISP provides, though, is access to other ISP networks. Access is facilitated by formal peering agreements between providers. Physical access can be implemented by connecting POPs from different ISPs. This can be done directly with a local connection if the POPs are collocated or with leased lines when the POPs are not collocated. A more commonly used mechanism is the **network access point (NAP)**.

A NAP is a physical facility that provides the infrastructure to move data between connected networks. In the United States, the National Science Foundation (NSF) privatization plan called for the creation of four NAPs. The NAPs were built and operated by the private sector. The number of NAPs has grown significantly over the years, and the technology employed has shifted from Fiber Distributed Data Interface (FDDI) and Ethernet to ATM and Gigabit Ethernet. Most NAPs today have an ATM core. The networks connected at a NAP are owned and operated by **network service providers (NSPs)**. A NSP can also be an ISP but this is not always the case. Peering agreements are between NSPs and do not include the NAP operator. The NSPs install routers at the NAP and connect them to the NAP infrastructure. The NSP equipment is responsible for routing, and the NAP infrastructure provides the physical access paths between routers.

1.6   AN EXAMPLE CONFIGURATION

To give some feel for the scope of concerns of this book, Figure 1.7 illustrates some of the typical communications and network elements in use today. At the center of the figure is an IP backbone network, which could represent a portion of the Internet or an enterprise IP network. Typically, the backbone consists of high-performance routers, called *core routers*, interconnected with high-volume optical links. The optical links make use of what is known as wavelength division multiplexing (WDM), such that each link has multiple logical channels occupying different portions of the optical bandwidth.

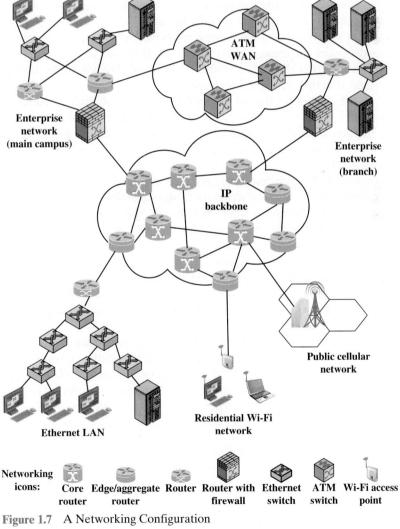

Figure 1.7   A Networking Configuration

At the periphery of an IP backbone are routers that provide connectivity to external networks and users. These routers are sometimes referred to as *edge routers,* or *aggregate routers.* Aggregate routers are also used within an enterprise network to connect a number of routers and switches to external resources, such as an IP backbone or a high-speed WAN. As an indication of the capacity requirements for core and aggregate routers, [XI11] reports on an analysis that projects these requirements for Internet backbone providers and large enterprise networks in China. The analysis concludes the aggregation router requirements to be in the range of 200 Gbps to 400 Gbps per optical link by 2020, and 400 Gbps to 1 Tbps per optical link for core routers by 2020.

The upper part of the figure depicts a portion of what might be a large enterprise network. The figure shows two sections of the network connected via a private high-speed asynchronous transfer mode (ATM) WAN, with switches interconnected with optical links. Enterprise assets are connected to, and protected from, an IP backbone or the Internet via routers with firewall capability, a not uncommon arrangement for implementing the firewall.

The lower left of the figure depicts what might be a configuration for a small or medium-size business, which relies on an Ethernet LAN configuration. Connection to the Internet through a router could be through a cable digital subscriber line connection or a dedicated high-speed link.

The lower portion of the figure also shows an individual residential user connected to an Internet service provider through some sort of subscriber connection. Common examples of such a connection are a digital subscriber line, which provides a high-speed link over telephone lines and requires a special DSL modem; and a cable TV facility, which requires a cable modem, or some type of wireless connection. In each case, there are separate issues concerning signal encoding, error control, and the internal structure of the subscriber network.

Finally, mobile devices, such as smartphones and tablets, can connect to the Internet through the public cellular network, which has a high-speed connection, typically optical, to the Internet.

The ISPs are not explicitly shown in the figure. Typically, an ISP network will consist of a number of interconnected routers connected to the Internet through a high-speed link. The Internet consists of a number of interconnected routers that span the globe. The routers forward packets of data from source to destination through the Internet.

A variety of design issues, such as signal encoding and error control, relate to the links between adjacent elements, such as between routers on the Internet or between switches in the ATM network, or between a subscriber and an ISP. The internal structure of the various networks (telephone, ATM, Ethernet) raises additional issues. We will be occupied throughout much of this book with the design features suggested by Figure 1.7.

CHAPTER 2

PROTOCOL ARCHITECTURE, TCP/IP, AND INTERNET-BASED APPLICATIONS

55

LEARNING OBJECTIVES

After reading this chapter, you should be able to:

♦ Define the term *protocol architecture* and explain the need for and benefits of a communications architecture.

♦ Describe the TCP/IP architecture and explain the functioning of each layer.

♦ Explain the motivation for the development of a standardized architecture and the reasons why a customer should use products based on a protocol architecture standard in preference to products based on a proprietary architecture.

♦ Explain the need for internetworking.

♦ Describe the operation of a router within the context of TCP/IP to provide internetworking.

This chapter provides a context for the detailed material that follows. It shows how the concepts of Parts Two through Five fit into the broader area of computer networks and computer communications. This chapter may be read in its proper sequence or it may be deferred until the beginning of Part Three, Four, or Five.[1]

We begin this chapter by introducing the concept of a layered **protocol architecture**. We then examine the most important such architecture, the TCP/IP protocol suite. TCP/IP is an Internet-based protocol suite and is the framework for developing a complete range of computer communications standards. Another well-known architecture is the **Open Systems Interconnection (OSI)** reference model. OSI is a standardized architecture that is often used to describe communications functions but that is now rarely implemented. OSI is examined in Appendix E.

2.1 THE NEED FOR A PROTOCOL ARCHITECTURE

When computers, terminals, and/or other data processing devices exchange data, the procedures involved can be quite complex. Consider, for example, the transfer of a file between two computers. There must be a data path between the two

---

[1]The reader may find it helpful just to skim this chapter on a first reading and then reread it more carefully just before embarking on Part Five.

computers, either directly or via a communication network. But more is needed. Typical tasks to be performed:

1. The source system must either activate the direct data communication path or inform the communication network of the identity of the desired destination system.
2. The source system must ascertain that the destination system is prepared to receive data.
3. The file transfer application on the source system must ascertain that the file management program on the destination system is prepared to accept and store the file for this particular user.
4. If the file formats used on the two systems are different, one or the other system must perform a format translation function.

It is clear that there must be a high degree of cooperation between the two computer systems. Instead of implementing the logic for this as a single module, the task is broken up into subtasks, each of which is implemented separately. In a protocol architecture, the modules are arranged in a vertical stack. Each layer in the stack performs a related subset of the functions required to communicate with another system. It relies on the next lower layer to perform more primitive functions and to conceal the details of those functions. It provides services to the next higher layer. Ideally, layers should be defined so that changes in one layer do not require changes in other layers.

Of course, it takes two to communicate, so the same set of layered functions must exist in two systems. Communication is achieved by having the corresponding, or **peer**, layers in two systems communicate. The **peer layers** communicate by means of formatted blocks of data that obey a set of rules or conventions known as a **protocol**. The key features of a protocol are as follows:

- **Syntax**: Concerns the format of the data blocks
- **Semantics**: Includes control information for coordination and error handling
- **Timing**: Includes speed matching and sequencing

Appendix 2A provides a specific example of a protocol, the **Internet** standard Trivial File Transfer Protocol (TFTP).

2.2   A SIMPLE PROTOCOL ARCHITECTURE

In very general terms, distributed data communications can be said to involve three agents: applications, computers, and networks. Examples of applications include file transfer and electronic mail. These applications execute on computers that typically support multiple simultaneous applications. Computers are connected to networks, and the data to be exchanged are transferred by the network from one computer to another. Thus, the transfer of data from one application to another involves first getting the data to the computer in which the application resides and then getting it to the intended application within the computer.

With these concepts in mind, it appears natural to organize the communication task into three relatively independent layers: network access layer, transport layer, and application layer.

The **network access layer** is concerned with the exchange of data between a computer and the network to which it is attached. The sending computer must provide the network with the address of the destination computer, so that the network may route the data to the appropriate destination. The sending computer may wish to invoke certain services, such as priority, that might be provided by the network. The specific software used at this layer depends on the type of network to be used; different standards have been developed for circuit switching, packet switching, local area networks (LANs), and others. For example, IEEE 802 is a standard that specifies the access to a LAN; this standard is described in Part Three. It makes sense to put those functions having to do with network access into a separate layer. By doing this, the remainder of the communications software, above the network access layer, need not be concerned about the specifics of the network to be used. The same higher-layer software should function properly regardless of the particular network to which the computer is attached.

Regardless of the nature of the applications that are exchanging data, there is usually a requirement that data be exchanged reliably. That is, we would like to be assured that all of the data arrive at the destination application and that the data arrive in the same order in which they were sent. As we shall see, the mechanisms for providing reliability are essentially independent of the nature of the applications. Thus, it makes sense to collect those mechanisms in a common layer shared by all applications; this is referred to as the **transport layer**.

Finally, the **application layer** contains the logic needed to support the various user applications. For each different type of application, such as file transfer, a separate module is needed that is peculiar to that application.

Figures 2.1 and 2.2 illustrate this simple architecture. Figure 2.1 shows three computers connected to a network. Each computer contains software at the network access and transport layers and at the application layer for one or more applications. For successful communication, every entity in the overall system must have a unique address. In the three-layer model, two levels of addressing are needed. Each computer on the network has a unique network address; this allows the network to deliver data to the proper computer. Each application on a computer has an address that is unique within that computer; this allows the transport layer to support multiple applications at each computer. These latter addresses are known as **service access points** (SAPs), or **ports**, connoting the fact that each application is individually accessing the services of the transport layer.

Figure 2.1 indicates that modules at the same level (peers) on different computers communicate with each other by means of a protocol. An application entity (e.g., a file transfer application) in one computer communicates with an application in another computer via an application-level protocol (e.g., the File Transfer Protocol). The interchange is not direct (indicated by the dashed line) but is mediated by a transport protocol that handles many of the details of transferring data between two computers. The transport protocol is also not direct, but relies on a network-level protocol to achieve network access and to route data through the network to the destination system. At each level, the cooperating peer entities focus on what they need to communicate to each other.

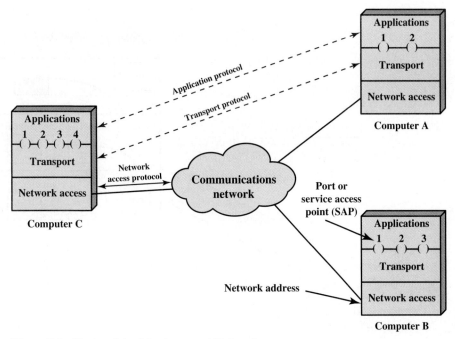

Figure 2.1 Protocol Architectures and Networks

Let us trace a simple operation. Suppose that an application, associated with port 1 at computer A, wishes to send a message to another application, associated with port 2 at computer B. The application at A hands the message over to its transport layer with instructions to send it to port 2 on computer B. The transport layer hands the message over to the network access layer, which instructs the network to send the message to computer B. Note that the network need not be told the identity of the destination port. All that it needs to know is that the data are intended for computer B.

To control this operation, control information, as well as user data, must be transmitted, as suggested in Figure 2.2. Let us say that the sending application generates a block of data and passes this to the transport layer. The transport layer may break this block into two smaller pieces for convenience, as discussed subsequently. To each of these pieces the transport layer appends a transport **header**, containing protocol control information. The addition of control information to data is referred to as **encapsulation**. The combination of data from the next higher layer and control information is known as a **protocol data unit (PDU)**; in this case, it is referred to as a transport PDU. Transport PDUs are typically called **segments**. The header in each segment contains control information to be used by the peer transport protocol at computer B. Examples of items that may be stored in this header include the following:

- **Source port:** This indicates the application that sent the data.
- **Destination port:** When the destination transport layer receives the segment, it must know to which application the data are to be delivered.

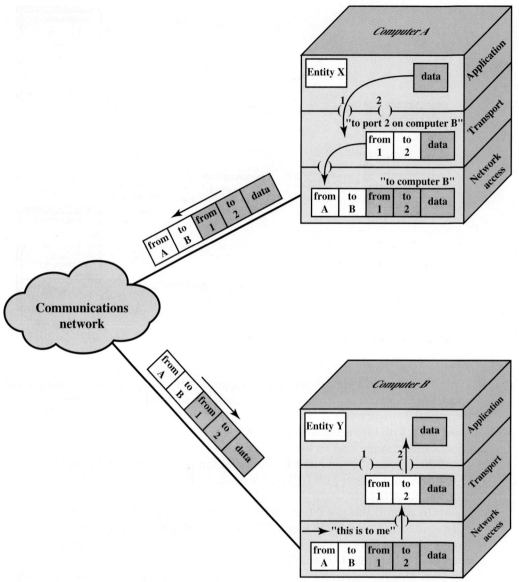

Figure 2.2 Protocols in a Simplified Architecture

- **Sequence number:** Because the transport protocol is sending a sequence of segments, it numbers them sequentially so that if they arrive out of order, the destination transport entity may reorder them.

- **Error-detection code:** The sending transport entity may include a code that is a function of the contents of the segment. The receiving transport protocol performs the same calculation and compares the result with the incoming code. A discrepancy results if there has been some error in transmission. In that case, the receiver can discard the segment and take corrective action. This code is also referred to as a **checksum** or **frame check sequence**.

The next step is for the transport layer to hand each segment over to the network layer, with instructions to transmit it to the destination computer. To satisfy this request, the network access protocol must present the data to the network with a request for transmission. As before, this operation requires the use of control information. In this case, the **network access protocol (NAP)** appends a network access header to the data it receives from the transport layer, creating a network access PDU, typically called a **packet**. Examples of the items that may be stored in the header include the following:

- **Source computer address:** Indicates the source of this packet.
- **Destination computer address:** The network must know to which computer on the network the data are to be delivered.
- **Facilities requests:** The network access protocol might want the network to make use of certain facilities, such as priority.

Note that the transport header is not "visible" at the network access layer; the network access layer is not concerned with the contents of the transport segment.

The network accepts the network packet from A and delivers it to B. The network access module in B receives the packet, strips off the packet header, and transfers the enclosed transport segment to B's transport layer module. The transport layer examines the segment header and, on the basis of the port field in the header, delivers the enclosed record to the appropriate application, in this case the file transfer module in B.

2.3 THE TCP/IP PROTOCOL ARCHITECTURE

TCP/IP is a result of protocol research and development conducted on the experimental packet-switched network, ARPANET, funded by the Defense Advanced Research Projects Agency (DARPA), and is generally referred to as the TCP/IP protocol suite. This protocol suite consists of a large collection of protocols that have been issued as Internet standards by the Internet Activities Board (IAB). Appendix C provides a discussion of Internet standards.

The TCP/IP Layers

In general terms, computer communications can be said to involve three agents: applications, computers, and networks. Examples of applications include file transfer and electronic mail. The applications that we are concerned with here are distributed applications that involve the exchange of data between two computer systems. These applications, and others, execute on computers that can often support multiple simultaneous applications. Computers are connected to networks, and the data to be exchanged are transferred by the network from one computer to another. Thus, the transfer of data from one application to another involves first getting the data to the computer in which the application resides and then getting the data to the intended application within the computer. With these concepts in mind, we can organize the communication task into five relatively independent layers (Figure 2.3):

- Physical layer
- Network access/data link layer
- Internet layer
- Host-to-host, or transport layer
- Application layer

The **physical layer** covers the physical interface between a data transmission device (e.g., workstation, computer) and a transmission medium or network. This layer is concerned with specifying the characteristics of the transmission medium, the nature of the signals, the data rate, and related matters.

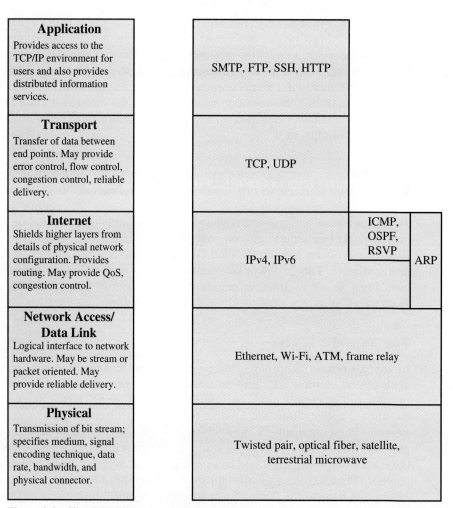

Figure 2.3 The TCP/IP Layers and Example Protocols

The **network access/data link layer** is discussed in Section 2.2. This layer is concerned with access to and routing data across a network for two end systems attached to the same network. In those cases where two devices are attached to different networks, procedures are needed to allow data to traverse multiple interconnected networks. This is the function of the **internet layer**. The **Internet Protocol (IP)** is used at this layer to provide the routing function across multiple networks. This protocol is implemented not only in the end systems but also in **routers**. A router is a processor that connects two networks and whose primary function is to relay data from one network to the other on its route from the source to the destination end system.

The **host-to-host layer**, or **transport layer**, may provide reliable end-to-end service, as discussed in Section 2.2, or merely an end-to-end delivery service without reliability mechanisms. The **Transmission Control Protocol (TCP)** is the most commonly used protocol to provide this functionality.

Finally, the *application layer* contains the logic needed to support the various user applications. For each different type of application, such as file transfer, a separate module is needed that is peculiar to that application.

Operation of TCP and IP

Figure 2.4 indicates how these protocols are configured for communications. To make clear that the total communications facility may consist of multiple networks, the constituent networks are usually referred to as **subnetworks**. Some sort of

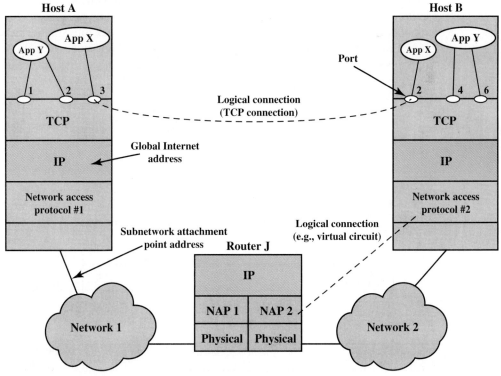

Figure 2.4   TCP/IP Concepts

network access protocol, such as the Ethernet or Wi-Fi logic, is used to connect a computer to a subnetwork. This protocol enables the host to send data across the subnetwork to another host or, if the target host is on another subnetwork, to a router that will forward the data. IP is implemented in all of the end systems and the routers. It acts as a relay to move a block of data from one host, through one or more routers, to another host. TCP is implemented only in the end systems; it keeps track of the blocks of data to assure that all are delivered reliably to the appropriate application.

As is mentioned in Section 2.2, every entity in the overall system must have a unique address. Each host on a subnetwork must have a unique global internet address; this allows the data to be delivered to the proper host. Each process with a host must have an address that is unique within the host; this allows the host-to-host protocol (TCP) to deliver data to the proper process. These latter addresses are known as *ports*.

Let us trace a simple operation. Suppose that a process, associated with port 3 at host A, wishes to send a message to another process, associated with port 2 at host B. The process at A hands the message down to TCP with instructions to send it to host B, port 2. TCP hands the message down to IP with instructions to send it to host B. Note that IP need not be told the identity of the destination port. All it needs to know is that the data are intended for host B. Next, IP hands the message down to the network access layer (e.g., Ethernet logic) with instructions to send it to router J (the first hop on the way to B).

To control this operation, control information, as well as user data, must be transmitted, as suggested in Figure 2.5. Let us say that the sending process generates a block of data and passes this to TCP. TCP may break this block into smaller pieces to make it more manageable. To each of these pieces, TCP appends control information known as the TCP header, forming a **TCP segment**. The control information

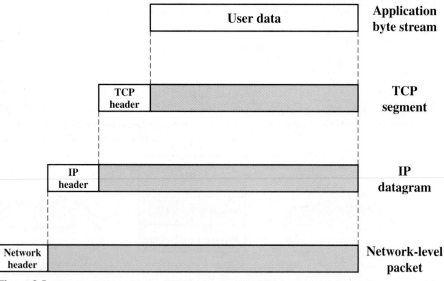

Figure 2.5   Protocol Data Units (PDUs) in the TCP/IP Architecture

is to be used by the peer TCP entity at host B. Examples of items in this header include:

- **Destination port:** When the TCP entity at B receives the segment, it must know to whom the data are to be delivered.

- **Sequence number:** TCP numbers the segments that it sends to a particular destination port sequentially, so that if they arrive out of order, the TCP entity at B can reorder them.

- **Checksum:** The sending TCP includes a code that is a function of the contents of the remainder of the segment. The receiving TCP performs the same calculation and compares the result with the incoming code. A discrepancy results if there has been some error in transmission.

Next, TCP hands each segment over to IP, with instructions to transmit it to B. These segments must be transmitted across one or more subnetworks and relayed through one or more intermediate routers. This operation, too, requires the use of control information. Thus IP appends a header of control information to each segment to form an **IP datagram**. An example of an item stored in the IP header is the destination host address (in this example, B).

Finally, each IP datagram is presented to the network access layer for transmission across the first subnetwork in its journey to the destination. The network access layer appends its own header, creating a packet, or frame. The packet is transmitted across the subnetwork to router J. The packet header contains the information that the subnetwork needs to transfer the data across the subnetwork.

At router J, the packet header is stripped off and the IP header is examined. On the basis of the destination address information in the IP header, the IP module in the router directs the datagram out across subnetwork 2 to B. To do this, the datagram is again augmented with a network access header.

When the data are received at B, the reverse process occurs. At each layer, the corresponding header is removed, and the remainder is passed on to the next higher layer, until the original user data are delivered to the destination process.

TCP and UDP

For most applications running as part of the TCP/IP architecture, the transport layer protocol is TCP. TCP provides a reliable connection for the transfer of data between applications. A connection is simply a temporary logical association between two entities in different systems. A logical connection refers to a given pair of port values. For the duration of the connection, each entity keeps track of TCP segments coming and going to the other entity, in order to regulate the flow of segments and to recover from lost or damaged segments.

Figure 2.6a shows the header format for TCP, which is a minimum of 20 octets, or 160 bits. The Source Port and Destination Port fields identify the applications at the source and destination systems that are using this connection. The Sequence Number, Acknowledgment Number, and Window fields provide flow control and error control. The checksum is a 16-bit frame check sequence used to detect errors in the TCP segment. Chapter 15 provides more details.

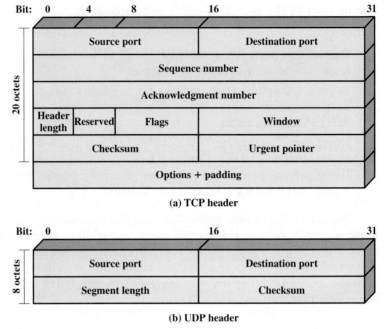

Figure 2.6   TCP and UDP Headers

In addition to TCP, there is one other transport-level protocol that is in common use as part of the TCP/IP protocol suite: the **User Datagram Protocol (UDP)**. UDP does not guarantee delivery, preservation of sequence, or protection against duplication. UDP enables a procedure to send messages to other procedures with a minimum of protocol mechanism. Some transaction-oriented applications make use of UDP; one example is SNMP (Simple Network Management Protocol), the standard network management protocol for TCP/IP networks. Because it is connectionless, UDP has very little to do. Essentially, it adds a port addressing capability to IP. This is best seen by examining the UDP header, shown in Figure 2.6b. UDP also includes a checksum to verify that no error occurs in the data; the use of the checksum is optional.

IP and IPv6

For decades, the keystone of the TCP/IP architecture has been IPv4, generally referred to as IP. Figure 2.7a shows the IP header format, which is a minimum of 20 octets, or 160 bits. The header, together with the segment from the transport layer, forms an IP-level PDU referred to as an IP datagram or an IP packet. The header includes 32-bit source and destination addresses. The Header Checksum field is used to detect errors in the header to avoid misdelivery. The Protocol field indicates which higher-layer protocol is using IP. The ID, Flags, and Fragment Offset fields are used in the fragmentation and reassembly process. Chapter 14 provides more details.

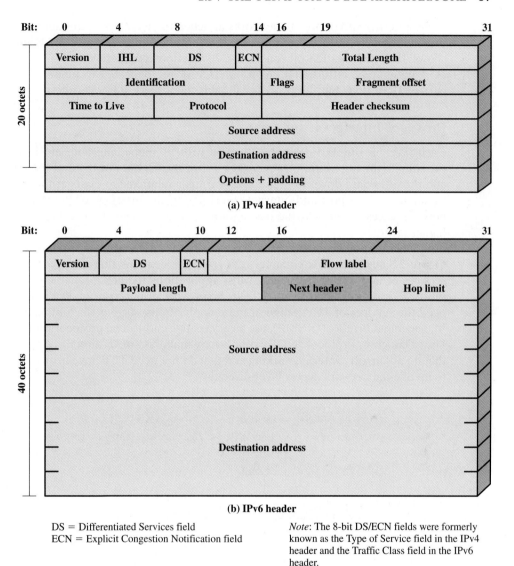

Figure 2.7 IP Headers

DS = Differentiated Services field
ECN = Explicit Congestion Notification field

Note: The 8-bit DS/ECN fields were formerly known as the Type of Service field in the IPv4 header and the Traffic Class field in the IPv6 header.

In 1995, the Internet Engineering Task Force (IETF), which develops protocol standards for the Internet, issued a specification for a next-generation IP, known then as IPng. This specification was turned into a standard in 1996 known as IPv6. IPv6 provides a number of functional enhancements over the existing IP, designed to accommodate the higher speeds of today's networks and the mix of data streams, including graphic and video, that are becoming more prevalent. But the driving force behind the development of the new protocol was the need for more addresses. IPv4 uses a 32-bit address to specify a source or destination. With the explosive growth of the Internet and of private networks attached to the Internet, this address length became insufficient to accommodate all systems needing addresses. As Figure 2.7b shows, IPv6 includes 128-bit source and destination address fields.

Ultimately, all installations using TCP/IP are expected to migrate from the current IP to IPv6, but this process will take many years, if not decades.

Protocol Interfaces

Each layer in the TCP/IP suite interacts with its immediate adjacent layers. At the source, the application layer makes use of the services of the end-to-end layer and provides data down to that layer. A similar relationship exists at the interface between the transport and internet layers and at the interface of the internet and network access layers. At the destination, each layer delivers data up to the next higher layer.

This use of each individual layer is not required by the architecture. As Figure 2.8 suggests, it is possible to develop applications that directly invoke the services of any one of the layers. Most applications require a reliable end-to-end protocol and thus make use of TCP. Some special-purpose applications do not need the services of TCP. Some of these applications, such as the Simple Network Management Protocol (SNMP), use an alternative end-to-end protocol known as the User Datagram Protocol (UDP); others may make use of IP directly. Applications that do not involve **internetworking** and that do not need TCP have been developed to invoke the network access layer directly.

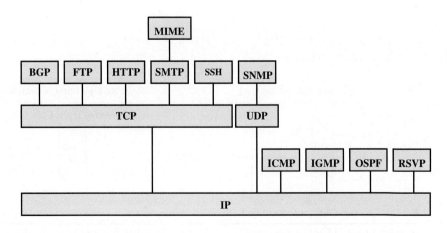

BGP	=	Border Gateway Protocol	OSPF	=	Open Shortest Path First
FTP	=	File Transfer Protocol	RSVP	=	Resource ReSerVation Protocol
HTTP	=	Hypertext Transfer Protocol	SMTP	=	Simple Mail Transfer Protocol
ICMP	=	Internet Control Message Protocol	SNMP	=	Simple Network Management Protocol
IGMP	=	Internet Group Management Protocol	SSH	=	Secure Shell
IP	=	Internet Protocol	TCP	=	Transmission Control Protocol
MIME	=	Multipurpose Internet Mail Extension	UDP	=	User Datagram Protocol

Figure 2.8 Some Protocols in the TCP/IP Protocol Suite

2.4 STANDARDIZATION WITHIN A PROTOCOL ARCHITECTURE

Standards and Protocol Layers

A protocol architecture, such as the TCP/IP architecture or OSI, provides a framework for standardization. Within the model, one or more protocol standards can be developed at each layer. The model defines in general terms the functions to be performed at that layer and facilitates the standards-making process in two ways:

- Because the functions of each layer are well defined, standards can be developed independently and simultaneously for each layer. This speeds up the standards-making process.

- Because the boundaries between layers are well defined, changes in standards in one layer need not affect already existing software in another layer. This makes it easier to introduce new standards.

Figure 2.9 illustrates the use of a protocol architecture as such a framework. The overall communications function is decomposed into a number of distinct layers. That is, the overall function is broken up into a number of modules, making the interfaces between modules as simple as possible. In addition, the design

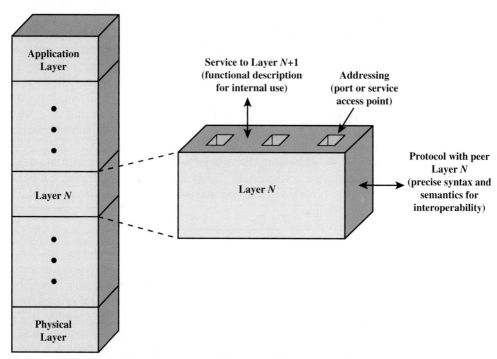

Figure 2.9   A Protocol Architecture as a Framework for Standardization

principle of information hiding is used: Lower layers are concerned with greater levels of detail; upper layers are independent of these details. Each layer provides services to the next higher layer and implements a protocol to the peer layer in other systems.

Figure 2.9 also shows more specifically the nature of the standardization required at each layer. Three elements are key:

- **Protocol specification:** Two entities at the same layer in different systems cooperate and interact by means of a protocol. Because two different open systems are involved, the protocol must be specified precisely. This includes the format of the protocol data units exchanged, the semantics of all fields, and the allowable sequence of PDUs.
- **Service definition:** In addition to the protocol or protocols that operate at a given layer, standards are needed for the services that each layer provides to the next higher layer. Typically, the definition of services is equivalent to a functional description that defines what services are provided, but not how the services are to be provided.
- **Addressing:** Each layer provides services to entities at the next higher layer. These entities are referenced by means of a port, or **service access point (SAP)**. Thus, a network service access point (NSAP) indicates a transport entity that is a user of the network service.

The need to provide a precise protocol specification for open systems is self-evident. The other two items listed warrant further comment. With respect to service definitions, the motivation for providing only a functional definition is as follows. First, the interaction between two adjacent layers takes place within the confines of a single open system and is not the concern of any other open system. Thus, as long as peer layers in different systems provide the same services to their next higher layers, the details of how the services are provided may differ from one system to another without loss of interoperability. Second, it will usually be the case that adjacent layers are implemented on the same processor. In that case, we would like to leave the system programmer free to exploit the hardware and operating system to provide an interface that is as efficient as possible.

With respect to addressing, the use of an address mechanism at each layer, implemented as a service access point, allows each layer to multiplex multiple users from the next higher layer. Multiplexing may not occur at each layer, but the model allows for that possibility.

Service Primitives and Parameters

The services between adjacent layers in a protocol architecture are expressed in terms of primitives and parameters. A primitive specifies the function to be performed, and the parameters are used to pass data and control information. The actual form of a primitive is implementation dependent. An example is a procedure call.

Four types of primitives are used in standards to define the interaction between adjacent layers in the architecture. These are defined in Table 2.1. The

Table 2.1 Service Primitive Types

Request	A primitive issued by a service user to invoke some service and to pass the parameters needed to specify fully the requested service.

Indication	A primitive issued by a service provider either to
	  1. indicate that a procedure has been invoked by thwe peer service user on the connection and to provide the associated parameters, or
	  2. notify the service user of a provider-initiated action.

Response	A primitive issued by a service user to acknowledge or complete some procedure previously invoked by an indication to that user.
Confirm	A primitive issued by a service provider to acknowledge or complete some procedure previously invoked by a request by the service user.

layout of Figure 2.10a suggests the time ordering of these events. For example, consider the transfer of data from an (N) entity to a peer (N) entity in another system. The following steps occur:

1. The source (N) entity invokes its $(N-1)$ entity with a *request* primitive. Associated with the primitive are the parameters needed, such as the data to be transmitted and the destination address.
2. The source $(N-1)$ entity prepares an $(N-1)$ PDU to be sent to its peer $(N-1)$ entity.
3. The destination $(N-1)$ entity delivers the data to the appropriate destination (N) entity via an *indication* primitive, which includes the data and source address as parameters.
4. If an acknowledgment is called for, the destination (N) entity issues a *response* primitive to its $(N-1)$ entity.
5. The $(N-1)$ entity conveys the acknowledgment in an $(N-1)$ PDU.
6. The acknowledgment is delivered to the (N) entity as a *confirm* primitive.

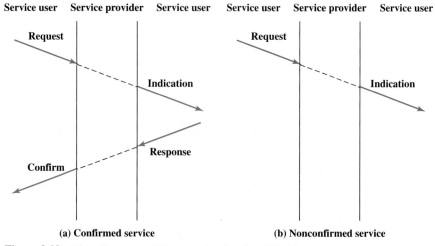

Figure 2.10 Time Sequence Diagrams for Service Primitives

This sequence of events is referred to as a *confirmed service*, as the initiator receives confirmation that the requested service has had the desired effect at the other end. If only request and indication primitives are involved (corresponding to steps 1 through 3), then the service dialog is a *nonconfirmed service*; the initiator receives no confirmation that the requested action has taken place (Figure 2.10b).

2.5 TRADITIONAL INTERNET-BASED APPLICATIONS

A number of applications have been standardized to operate on top of TCP. We mention three of the most common here.

The **Simple Mail Transfer Protocol (SMTP)** provides a basic electronic mail transport facility. It provides a mechanism for transferring messages among separate hosts. Features of SMTP include mailing lists, return receipts, and forwarding. SMTP does not specify the way in which messages are to be created; some local editing or native electronic mail facility is required. Once a message is created, SMTP accepts the message and makes use of TCP to send it to an SMTP module on another host. The target SMTP module will make use of a local electronic mail package to store the incoming message in a user's mailbox.

The **File Transfer Protocol (FTP)** is used to send files from one system to another under user command. Both text and binary files are accommodated, and the protocol provides features for controlling user access. When a user wishes to engage in file transfer, FTP sets up a TCP connection to the target system for the exchange of control messages. This connection allows user ID and password to be transmitted and allows the user to specify the file and file actions desired. Once a file transfer is approved, a second TCP connection is set up for the data transfer. The file is transferred over the data connection, without the overhead of any headers or control information at the application level. When the transfer is complete, the control connection is used to signal the completion and to accept new file transfer commands.

SSH (Secure Shell) provides a secure remote logon capability, which enables a user at a terminal or personal computer to log on to a remote computer and function as if directly connected to that computer. SSH also supports file transfer between the local host and a remote server. SSH enables the user and the remote server to authenticate each other; it also encrypts all traffic in both directions. SSH traffic is carried on a TCP connection.

2.6 MULTIMEDIA

With the increasing availability of broadband access to the Internet has come an increased interest in Web-based and Internet-based **multimedia** applications. The terms *multimedia* and *multimedia applications* are used rather loosely in the literature and in commercial publications, and no single definition of the term *multimedia* has been agreed. For our purposes, the definitions in Table 2.2 provide a starting point.

Table 2.2 Multimedia Terminology

Media
Refers to the form of information and includes text, still images, audio, and video.
Multimedia
Human–computer interaction involving text, graphics, voice, and video. Multimedia also refers to storage devices that are used to store multimedia content.
Streaming media
Refers to multimedia files, such as video clips and audio, that begin playing immediately or within seconds after it is received by a computer from the Internet or Web. Thus, the media content is consumed as it is delivered from the server rather than waiting until an entire file is downloaded.

One way to organize the concepts associated with multimedia is to look at a taxonomy that captures a number of dimensions of this field. Figure 2.11 looks at multimedia from the perspective of three different dimensions: type of media, applications, and the technology required to support the applications.

Media Types

Typically, the term *multimedia* refers to four distinct types of media: text, audio, graphics, and video.

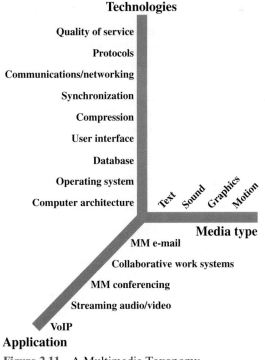

Figure 2.11 A Multimedia Taxonomy

From a communications perspective, the term **text** is self-explanatory, referring to information that can be entered via a keyboard and is directly readable and printable. Text messaging, instant messaging, and text (non-html) e-mail are common examples, as are chat rooms and message boards. However, the term often is used in the broader sense of data that can be stored in files and databases and that does not fit into the other three categories. For example, an organization's database may contain files of numerical data, in which the data are stored in a more compact form than printable characters.

The term **audio** generally encompasses two different ranges of sound. Voice, or speech, refers to sounds that are produced by the human speech mechanism. Generally, a modest bandwidth (under 4 kHz) is required to transmit voice. Telephony and related applications (e.g., voice mail, audio teleconferencing, and telemarketing) are the most common traditional applications of voice communications technology. A broader frequency spectrum is needed to support music applications, including the download of music files.

The **image** service supports the communication of individual pictures, charts, or drawings. Image-based applications include facsimile, computer-aided design (CAD), publishing, and medical imaging. Images can be represented in a vector graphics format, such as is used in drawing programs and PDF files. In a raster graphics format, an image is represented as a two-dimensional array of spots, called pixels.[2] The compressed JPG format is derived from a raster graphics format.

The **video** service carries sequences of pictures in time. In essence, video makes use of a sequence of raster-scan images.

Multimedia Applications

The Internet, until recently, has been dominated by information retrieval applications, e-mail, and file transfer, plus Web interfaces that emphasized text and images. Increasingly, the Internet is being used for multimedia applications that involve massive amounts of data for visualization and support of real-time interactivity. Streaming audio and video are perhaps the best known of such applications. An example of an interactive application is a virtual training environment involving distributed simulations and real-time user interaction [VIN98]. Some other examples are shown in Table 2.3.

Table 2.3   Domains of Multimedia Systems and Example Applications

Domain	Example Application
Information management	Hypermedia, multimedia-capable databases, content-based retrieval
Entertainment	Computer games, digital video, audio (MP3)
Telecommunication	Videoconferencing, shared workspaces, virtual communities
Information publishing/delivery	Online training, electronic books, streaming media

---

[2]A pixel, or picture element, is the smallest element of a digital image that can be assigned a gray level. Equivalently, a pixel is an individual dot in a dot-matrix representation of a picture.

[GONZ00] lists the following multimedia application domains:

- **Information systems:** These applications present information using multimedia. Examples include information kiosks, electronic books that include audio and video, and multimedia expert systems.

- **Communication systems:** These applications support collaborative work, such as videoconferencing.

- **Entertainment systems:** These applications include computer and network games and other forms of audiovisual entertainment.

- **Business systems:** These applications include business-oriented multimedia presentation, video brochures, and online shopping.

- **Educational systems:** These applications include electronic books with a multimedia component, simulation and modeling applets, and other teaching support systems.

One point worth noting is highlighted in Figure 2.11. Although traditionally the term *multimedia* has connoted the simultaneous use of multiple media types (e.g., video annotation of a text document), it has also come to refer to applications that require real-time processing or communication of video or audio alone. Thus, voice over IP (VoIP), streaming audio, and streaming video are considered multimedia applications even though each involves a single media type.

Multimedia Technologies

Figure 2.11 lists some of the technologies that are relevant to the support of multimedia applications. As can be seen, a wide range of technologies is involved. The lowest four items on the list are beyond the scope of this book. The other items represent only a partial list of communications and networking technologies for multimedia. These technologies and others are explored throughout the book. Here, we give a brief comment on each area.

- **Compression:** Digitized video, and to a much lesser extent audio, can generate an enormous amount of traffic on a network. A streaming application, which is delivered to many users, magnifies the traffic. Accordingly, standards have been developed for producing significant savings through compression. The most notable standards are JPG for still images and MPG for video.

- **Communications/networking:** This broad category refers to the transmission and networking technologies (e.g., SONET, ATM) that can support high-volume multimedia traffic.

- **Protocols:** A number of protocols are instrumental in supporting multimedia traffic. One example is the Real-time Transport Protocol (RTP), which is designed to support **inelastic traffic** (traffic that does not easily adapt, if at all, to changes in delay and throughput across an internet). RTP uses buffering and discarding strategies to assure that real-time traffic is received by the end user in a smooth continuous stream. Another example is the Session Initiation Protocol (SIP), an application-level control protocol for setting up, modifying, and terminating real-time sessions between participants over an IP data network.

- **Quality of service (QoS)**: The Internet and its underlying local area and wide area networks must include a QoS capability to provide differing levels of service to different types of application traffic. A QoS capability can deal with priority, delay constraints, delay variability constraints, and other similar requirements.

All of these matters are explored subsequently in this text.

2.7 SOCKETS PROGRAMMING

The concept of sockets and sockets programming was developed in the 1980s in the UNIX environment as the Berkeley Sockets Interface. In essence, a socket enables communication between a client and server process and may be either connection oriented or connectionless. A socket can be considered an end point in a communication. A client socket in one computer uses an address to call a server socket on another computer. Once the appropriate sockets are engaged, the two computers can exchange data.

Typically, computers with server sockets keep a TCP or UDP port open, ready for unscheduled incoming calls. The client typically determines the socket identification of the desired server by finding it in a Domain Name System (DNS) database. Once a connection is made, the server switches the dialogue to a different port number to free up the main port number for additional incoming calls.

Internet applications, such as TELNET and remote login (rlogin), make use of sockets, with the details hidden from the user. However, sockets can be constructed from within a program (in a language such as C, Java, or Python), enabling the programmer to easily support networking functions and applications. The sockets programming mechanism includes sufficient semantics to permit unrelated processes on different hosts to communicate.

The Berkeley Sockets Interface is the de facto standard **application programming interface (API)** for developing networking applications, spanning a wide range of operating systems. Windows Sockets (WinSock) is based on the Berkeley specification. The Sockets API provides generic access to interprocess communications services. Thus, the sockets capability is ideally suited for students to learn the principles of protocols and distributed applications by hands-on program development.

The Socket

Recall that each TCP and UDP header includes Source Port and Destination Port fields (Figure 2.6). These port values identify the respective users (applications) of the two TCP or UDP entities. Also, each IPv4 and IPv6 header includes Source Address and Destination Address fields (Figure 2.7); these **IP addresses** identify the respective host systems. The concatenation of a port value and an IP address forms a **socket**, which is unique throughout the Internet. Thus, in Figure 2.4, the combination of the IP address for host B and the port number for application X uniquely identifies the socket location of application X in host B. As the figure indicates, an application may have multiple socket addresses, one for each port into the application.

The socket is used to define an API, which is a generic communication interface for writing programs that use TCP or UDP. In practice, when used as an API, a socket is identified by the triple (protocol, local address, local process). The local address is an IP address and the local process is a port number. Because port numbers are unique within a system, the port number implies the protocol (TCP or UDP). However, for clarity and ease of implementation, sockets used for an API include the protocol as well as the IP address and port number in defining a unique socket.

Corresponding to the two protocols, the Sockets API recognizes two types of sockets: stream sockets and datagram sockets. **Stream sockets** make use of TCP, which provides a connection-oriented reliable data transfer. Therefore, with stream sockets, all blocks of data sent between a pair of sockets are guaranteed for delivery and arrive in the order that they were sent. **Datagram sockets** make use of UDP, which does not provide the connection-oriented features of TCP. Therefore, with datagram sockets, delivery is not guaranteed, nor is order necessarily preserved.

There is a third type of socket provided by the Sockets API: raw sockets. **Raw sockets** allow direct access to lower-layer protocols, such as IP.

Sockets Interface Calls

This subsection summarizes the key system calls. Table 2.4 lists the core Socket functions.

SOCKETS SETUP   The first step in using Sockets is to create a new socket using the socket() command. This command includes three parameters. The domain parameter refers to the area where the communicating processes exist. Commonly used domains include:

- AF_UNIX for communication between processes on one system;
- AF_INET for communication between processes using the IPv4 Internet Protocol;
- AF_INET6 for communication between processes using the IPv6 Internet Protocol.

Type specifies whether this is a stream or datagram socket, and protocol specifies either TCP or UDP. The reason that both type and protocol need to be specified is to allow additional transport-level protocols to be included in a future implementation. Thus, there might be more than one datagram-style transport protocol or more than one connection-oriented transport protocol. The socket() command returns an integer result that identifies this socket; it is similar to a UNIX file descriptor. The exact socket data structure depends on the implementation. It includes the source port and IP address and, if a connection is open or pending, the destination port and IP address and various options and parameters associated with the connection.

Table 2.4 Core Socket Functions

Format	Function	Parameters
socket( )	Initialize a socket	**domain** Protocol family of the socket to be created (AF_UNIX, AF_INET, AF_INET6) **type** Type of socket to be opened (stream, datagram, raw) **protocol** Protocol to be used on socket (UDP, TCP, ICMP)
bind( )	Bind a socket to a port address	**sockfd** Socket to be bound to the port address **localaddress** Socket address to which the socket is bound **addresslength** Length of the socket address structure
listen( )	Listen on a socket for inbound connections	**sockfd** Socket on which the application is to listen **queuesize** Number of inbound requests that can be queued at any time
accept( )	Accept an inbound connection	**sockfd** Socket on which the connection is to be accepted **remoteaddress** Remote socket address from which the connection was initiated **addresslength** Length of the socket address structure
connect( )	Connect outbound to a server	**sockfd** Socket on which the connection is to be opened **remoteaddress** Remote socket address to which the connection is to be opened **addresslength** Length of the socket address structure
send( ) recv( ) read( ) write( )	Send and receive data on a stream socket (either send/recv or read/write can be used)	**sockfd** Socket across which the data will be sent or read **data** Data to be sent, or buffer into which the read data will be placed **datalength** Length of the data to be written, or amount of data to be read
sendto( ) recvfrom( )	Send and receive data on a datagram socket	**sockfd** Socket across which the data will be sent or read **data** Data to be sent, or buffer into which the read data will be placed **datalength** Length of the data to be written, or amount of data to be read
close( )	Close a socket	**sockfd** Socket which is to be closed

After a socket is created, it must have an address to listen to. The bind() function binds a socket to a socket address. The address has the structure:

```
struct sockaddr_in {
    short int sin_family;         //Address family (TCP/IP)
    unsigned short int sin_port;  //Port number
    struct in_addr sin_addr;      //Internet address
    unsigned char sin_zero[8];    //Padding to make structure same
                                  //size as struct sockaddr
};
```

SOCKETS CONNECTION   For a stream socket, once the socket is created, a connection must be set up to a remote socket. One side functions as a client and requests a connection to the other side, which acts as a server.

The server side of a connection setup requires two steps. First, a server application issues a `listen()`, indicating that the given socket is ready to accept incoming connections. The parameter *backlog* is the number of connections allowed on the incoming queue. Each incoming connection is placed in this queue until a matching `accept()` is issued by the server side. Next, the `accept()` call is used to remove one request from the queue. If the queue is empty, the `accept()` blocks the process until a connection request arrives. If there is a waiting call, then `accept()` returns a new file descriptor for the connection. This creates a new socket, which has the IP address and port number of the remote party, the IP address of this system, and a new port number. The reason that a new socket with a new port number is assigned is that this enables the local application to continue to listen for more requests. As a result, an application may have multiple connections active at any time, each with a different local port number. This new port number is returned across the TCP connection to the requesting system.

A client application issues a `connect()` that specifies both a local socket and the address of a remote socket. If the connection attempt is unsuccessful `connect()` returns the value −1. If the attempt is successful, `connect()` returns a 0 and fills in the file descriptor parameter to include the IP address and port number of the local and foreign sockets. Recall that the remote port number may differ from that specified in the `foreignAddress` parameter because the port number is changed on the remote host.

Once a connection is set up, `getpeername()` can be used to find out who is on the other end of the connected stream socket. The function returns a value in the `sockfd` parameter.

SOCKETS COMMUNICATION   For **stream communication**, the functions `send()` and `recv()` are used to send or receive data over the connection identified by the `sockfd` parameter. In the `send()` call, the `*msg` parameter points to the block of data to be sent and the `len` parameter specifies the number of bytes to be sent. The `flags` parameter contains control flags, typically set to 0. The `send()` call returns the number of bytes sent, which may be less than the number specified in the `len` parameter. In the `recv()` call, the `*buf` parameter points to the buffer for storing incoming data, with an upper limit on the number of bytes set by the `len` parameter.

At any time, either side can close the connection with the `close()` call, which prevents further sends and receives. The `shutdown()` call allows the caller to terminate sending or receiving or both.

Figure 2.12 shows the interaction of the clients and server sides in setting up, using, and terminating a connection.

For **datagram communication**, the functions `sendto()` and `recvfrom()` are used. The `sendto()` call includes all the parameters of the `send()` call plus a specification of the destination address (IP address and port). Similarly, the `recvfrom()` call includes an address parameter, which is filled in when data are received.

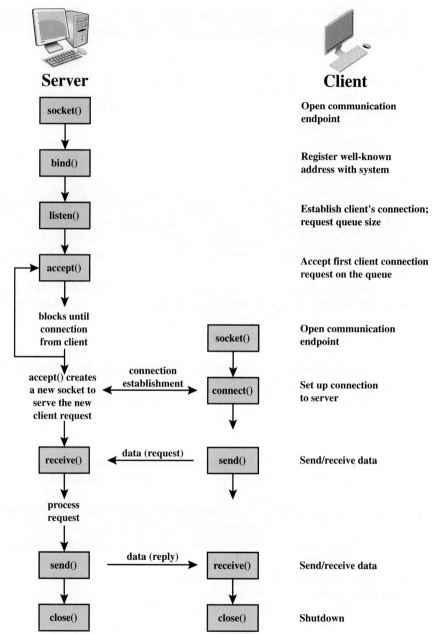

Figure 2.12 Socket System Calls for Connection-Oriented Protocol

Example

In this section, we give an example of a simple client and server implemented in C, and communicating using stream sockets over the Internet. The two programs are shown in Figures 2.13 and 2.14. Before reading the following discussion, the reader is advised to compile and execute the two programs to understand their operation.[3]

```
1   #include <stdio.h>
2   #include <sys/types.h>
3   #include <sys/socket.h>
4   #include <netinet/in.h>

5   void error(char *msg)
6   {
7       perror(msg);
8       exit(1);
9   }

10  int main(int argc, char *argv[])
11  {
12      int sockfd, newsockfd, portno, clilen;
13      char buffer[256];
14      struct sockaddr_in serv_addr, cli_addr;
15      int n;
16      if (argc < 2) {
17          fprintf(stderr,"ERROR, no port provided\n");
18          exit(1);
19      }
20      sockfd = socket(AF_INET, SOCK_STREAM, 0);
21      if (sockfd < 0)
22          error("ERROR opening socket");
23      bzero((char *) &serv_addr, sizeof(serv_addr));
24      portno = atoi(argv[1]);
25      serv_addr.sin_family = AF_INET;
26      serv_addr.sin_port = htons(portno);
27      serv_addr.sin_addr.s_addr = INADDR_ANY;
28      if (bind(sockfd, (struct sockaddr *) &serv_addr,
29              sizeof(serv_addr)) < 0)
30              error("ERROR on binding");
31      listen(sockfd,5);
32      clilen = sizeof(cli_addr);
33      newsockfd = accept(sockfd, (struct sockaddr *) &cli_addr, &clilen);
34      if (newsockfd < 0)
35          error("ERROR on accept");
36      bzero(buffer,256);
37      n = read(newsockfd,buffer,255);
38      if (n < 0) error("ERROR reading from socket");
39      printf("Here is the message: %s\n",buffer);
40      n = write(newsockfd,"I got your message",18);
41      if (n < 0) error("ERROR writing to socket");
42      return 0;
43  }
```

Figure 2.13 Sockets Server

---

[3]The two programs, without the line numbers, are available at box.com/dcc10e.

```
1    #include <stdio.h>
2    #include <sys/types.h>
3    #include <sys/socket.h>
4    #include <netinet/in.h>
5    #include <netdb.h>

6    void error(char *msg)
7    {
8        perror(msg);
9        exit(0);
10   }

11   int main(int argc, char *argv[])
12   {
13     int sockfd, portno, n;
14     struct sockaddr_in serv_addr;
15     struct hostent *server;
16     char buffer[256];
17     if (argc < 3) {
18         fprintf(stderr,"usage %s hostname port\n", argv[0]);
19         exit(0);
20     }
21     portno = atoi(argv[2]);
22     sockfd = socket(AF_INET, SOCK_STREAM, 0);
23     if (sockfd < 0)
24         error("ERROR opening socket");
25     server = gethostbyname(argv[1]);
26     if (server == NULL) {
27         fprintf(stderr,"ERROR, no such host\n");
28         exit(0);
29     }
30     bzero((char *) &serv_addr, sizeof(serv_addr));
31     serv_addr.sin_family = AF_INET;
32     bcopy((char *)server->h_addr,
33         (char *)&serv_addr.sin_addr.s_addr,
34         server->h_length);
35     serv_addr.sin_port = htons(portno);
36     if (connect(sockfd,(struct sockaddr *)&serv_addr,sizeof(serv_addr)) < 0)
37         error("ERROR connecting");
38     printf("Please enter the message: ");
39     bzero(buffer,256);
40     fgets(buffer,255,stdin);
41     n = write(sockfd,buffer,strlen(buffer));
42     if (n < 0)
43          error("ERROR writing to socket");
44     bzero(buffer,256);
45     n = read(sockfd,buffer,255);
46     if (n < 0)
47          error("ERROR reading from socket");
48     printf("%s\n",buffer);
49     return 0;
50   }
```

Figure 2.14   Sockets Client

1. Download the client and server programs into files called server.c and
   client.c and compile them into two executables called server and
   client. The commands would look something like this:

   ```
   gcc server.c -o server
   gcc client.c -o client
   ```

Ideally, you should run the client and server on separate hosts on the Internet. You can, if necessary, run the server in one window and the client in another on the same machine.

2. Start the server first by issuing a command to the server with a port number as the argument. This is the port on which the server will listen. Choose a number between 2000 and 65535. If the port is in use, the server will return a message. In that case, pick another number and try again. A typical command line is the following:

```
server 62828
```

3. Issue a command to start the client, with two arguments: the name of the host on which the server is running and the port number on which the server is listening. So, if the server is on host X, the command line would be:

```
client X 62828
```

If client and server are on the same machine, then the first argument is *localhost*.

4. The client will prompt you to enter a message. Subsequently, if there are no errors, the server will display the message on *stdout*, send an acknowledgment message to the client and terminate. The client then prints the acknowledgment message and terminates.

SERVER PROGRAM   Now that you see what the two programs do, we can examine the code, starting with the server (Figure 2.13). Lines 1–4 define header files: stdio.h contains declarations used in most input and output operations; types.h defines a number of data types used in system calls; socket.h defines a number of structures needed for sockets; and netinet/in.h contains constants and structures needed for Internet domain addresses.

When a system call fails, the error program void, which contains the function perror, displays an error message on stderr and then aborts the program (lines 5–9).

Line 10 begins the definition of the main program. The first two integer variables, sockfd and newsockfd, are array subscripts into the file descriptor table. They store the values returned by the socket system call and the accept system call. portno stores the port number on which the server accepts connections. clilen stores the size of the address of the client, which is needed for the accept system call. The server reads characters from the socket connection into the buffer char.

Line 14 defines the client and server address structures, using the sockaddr_ in Internet address structure. This structure is defined in netinet/in.h. The variable n designates the number of characters read or written by the read() and write() calls.

Lines 16–19 check that the user has provided a port number argument and displays an error message if the argument is not present.

Lines 20–22 deal with creating a new socket. The first parameter of the socket() call specifies the IPv4 domain. The second parameter specifies that a stream socket is requested. The third parameter, which defines the protocol to be used, is set to zero. The zero value indicates that the default protocol should be used, which is TCP for a stream socket. The socket() call returns an entry into the file descriptor table, which defines the socket. If the call fails, it returns the value −1. The if statement in the code then displays the error message.

The function bzero() sets all values in a buffer to zero (line 23). It takes two arguments, the first is a pointer to the buffer and the second is the size of the buffer. Thus, this line initializes serv_addr to zeros.

Line 24 retrieves the port number that was supplied as an argument to the server program. This statement uses the atoi() function to convert the parameter from a string of digits to an integer stored in portno.

Lines 25–27 assign values to the variable serv_addr, which is a structure of type struct sockaddr_in. As shown earlier in this section, sockaddr_in has four fields, of which the first three must be assigned values. serv_addr.sin_family is set to AF_INET, for IPv4 communication. serv_addr.sin_port is derived from the port number argument. However, instead of simply copying the port number to this field, it is necessary to convert this to network byte order using the function htons(), which converts a port number in host byte order to a port number in network byte order. The field serv_addr.sin_addr.s_addr is assigned the Internet IPv4 address of the server, which is obtained from the symbolic constant INADDR_ANY.

Lines 28–30 include the bind() function, which, as mentioned earlier, binds a socket to a socket address. Its three arguments are the socket file descriptor, the address to which the socket is bound, and the size of the address. The second argument is a pointer to a structure of type sockaddr, but what is passed in is a structure of type sockaddr_in, and so this must be cast to the correct type. This can fail for a number of reasons, the most obvious being that this socket is already in use on this machine.

If the bind() operation succeeds, the server is now ready to listen on this socket. The listen() on line 31 takes as arguments the file descriptor for the socket and the size of the backlog queue, which is the number of connections that can be waiting while the process is handling a particular connection. Typically, the queue size is set to 5.

Lines 32–35 deal with the accept() system call, which causes the process to block until a client connects to the server. Thus, it wakes up the process when a connection from a client has been successfully established. It returns a new file descriptor, and all communication on this connection should be done using the new file descriptor. The second argument is a reference pointer to the address of the client on the other end of the connection, and the third argument is the size of this structure.

After a client has successfully connected to the server, lines 36–39 are executed. The variable buffer is set to all zeroes. Then, the read() function is invoked to read up to 255 bytes into buffer. The read call uses the new file descriptor, which was returned by accept(), not the original file descriptor returned by socket(). In addition to filling the buffer, read() returns the number of character read. Note also that the read() will block until there is something for it to read in the socket, that is, after the client has executed a write(). The read operation concludes when the server displays the message received over the connection.

After a successful read, the server writes a message that will be delivered over the socket connection to the client (lines 40–41). The parameters for the `write()` function are the socket file descriptor, the message, and a character count of the message.

Lines 42–43 terminate `main` and thus the program. Since `main` was declared to be of type `int`, many compilers complain if it does not return anything.

CLIENT PROGRAM   The client program is shown in Figure 2.14. Lines 1–4 are the same header files as for the server. Line 5 adds the header file `netdb.h`, which defines the structure `hostent`, which is used in the client program.

In lines 6–14, the `error()` function is the same as for the server, as are the variables `sockfd`, `portno`, and `n`. The variable `serv_addr` will be assigned the address of the server to which the client wants to connect.

Line 15 defines the variable server as a pointer to a structure of type `hostent`, defined in `netdb.h`. The structure includes the following fields: `*h_name`, the name of the host; `**h_aliases`, a list of alternate names for the host; `h_addrtype`, currently always `AF_INET`; `h_length`, the length in bytes of the address; and `**h_addr_list`, a pointer to a list of network addresses for the named host.

Lines 16–24 are almost the same as that in the server.

In lines 25–29, the client attempts to get the `hostent` structure for the server. `argv[1]` is the first argument in the call to the client program and contains the name of the desired server host. The function `*gethostbyname(char, *name)` is defined in `netdb.h` as `struct hostent`. It takes a name as an argument and returns a pointer to a `hostent` structure for the named host. If the name is not known locally, the client machine uses the Domain Name System, described in a subsequent chapter.

Lines 30–35 set the fields in `serv_addr`, similar to what is done in the server program. However, because the field `server->h_addr` is a character string, we use the function `void bcopy(char *s1, char *s2, int length)`, which copies length bytes from `s1` to `s2`.

The client is now ready to make a request for a connection to the server, on lines 36–37. The function `connect()` takes three arguments: the client's socket file descriptor, the address of the requested host, and the size of this address. The function returns 0 on success and –1 on failure.

The remaining code, lines 38–50, should be fairly clear. It prompts the user to enter a message, uses `fgets` to read the message from `stdin`, writes the message to the socket, reads the reply from the socket, and displays this reply.

2.8 RECOMMENDED READING AND ANIMATION

For the reader interested in greater detail on TCP/IP, there are two three-volume works that are more than adequate. The works by Comer and Stevens have become classics and are considered definitive [COME14, COME99, COME01]. The works by Stevens, Wright, and Fall are equally worthwhile and more detailed with respect to protocol operation [FALL12, STEV96, WRIG95]. A more compact and very useful reference work is [PARZ06], which covers the spectrum of TCP/IP-related protocols in a technically concise but thorough fashion, including coverage of some protocols not found in the other two works.

[GREE80] is a good tutorial overview of the concept of a layered protocol architecture. Two early papers that provide good discussions of the design philosophy of the TCP/IP protocol suite are [LEIN85] and [CLAR88].

Although somewhat dated, [FURH94] remains a good overview of multimedia topics. [VOGE95] is a good introduction to QoS considerations for multimedia. [HELL01] is a lengthy and worthwhile theoretical treatment of multimedia. An excellent concise introduction to using sockets is [DONA01]; another good overview is [HALL01].

CLAR88 Clark, D. "The Design Philosophy of the DARPA Internet Protocols." *ACM SIGCOMM Computer Communications Review*, August 1988.

COME99 Comer, D., and Stevens, D. *Internetworking with TCP/IP, Volume II: Design Implementation, and Internals.* Upper Saddle River, NJ: Prentice Hall, 1999.

COME01 Comer, D., and Stevens, D. *Internetworking with TCP/IP, Volume III: Client-Server Programming and Applications.* Upper Saddle River, NJ: Prentice Hall, 2001.

COME14 Comer, D. *Internetworking with TCP/IP, Volume I: Principles, Protocols, and Architecture.* Upper Saddle River, NJ: Prentice Hall, 2014.

DONA01 Donahoo, M., and Clavert, K. *The Pocket Guide to TCP/IP Sockets.* San Francisco, CA: Morgan Kaufmann, 2001.

FALL12 Fall, K., and Stevens, W. *TCP/IP Illustrated, Volume 1: The Protocols.* Reading, MA: Addison-Wesley, 2012.

FURH94 Furht, B. "Multimedia Systems: An Overview." *IEEE Multimedia*, Spring 1994.

GREE80 Green, P. "An Introduction to Network Architecture and Protocols." *IEEE Transactions on Communications*, April 1980.

HALL01 Hall, B. *Beej's Guide to Network Programming Using Internet Sockets.* 2001. http://beej.us/guide/bgnet.

HELL01 Heller, R., et al. "Using a Theoretical Multimedia Taxonomy Framework." *ACM Journal of Educational Resources in Computing*, Spring 2001.

LEIN85 Leiner, B.; Cole, R.; Postel, J.; and Mills, D. "The DARPA Internet Protocol Suite." *IEEE Communications Magazine*, March 1985.

PARZ06 Parziale, L., et al. *TCP/IP Tutorial and Technical Overview.* IBM Redbook GG24-3376-07, 2006, http://www.redbooks.ibm.com/abstracts/gg243376.html

STEV96 Stevens, W. *TCP/IP Illustrated, Volume 3: TCP for Transactions, HTTP, NNTP, and the UNIX(R) Domain Protocol.* Reading, MA: Addison-Wesley, 1996.

VIN98 Vin, H. "Supporting Next-Generation Distributed Applications." *IEEE Multimedia*, July–September 1998,

VOGE95 Vogel, A., et al. "Distributed Multimedia and QoS: A Survey." *IEEE Multimedia*, Summer 1995.

WRIG95 Wright, G., and Stevens, W. *TCP/IP Illustrated, Volume 2: The Implementation.* Reading, MA: Addison-Wesley, 1995.

Animations

Animations that illustrate protocol encapsulation, data flow through a protocol stack, and TFTP are available at the Premium Web site. The reader is encouraged to view these animations to reinforce concepts from this chapter.

2.9 KEY TERMS, REVIEW QUESTIONS, AND PROBLEMS

Key Terms

application programming interface (API)	IP datagram	service access point (SAP)
application layer	multimedia	Simple Mail Transfer Protocol (SMTP)
audio	network access protocol (NAP)	socket
checksum	network access layer	socket programming
datagram communication	Open Systems Interconnection (OSI)	SSH (Secure Shell)
datagram sockets		stream communication
encapsulation	packet	stream sockets
File Transfer Protocol (FTP)	peer layer	subnetwork
frame check sequence	physical layer	syntax
header	port	TCP segment
image	protocol	text
host-to-host layer	protocol architecture	timing
inelastic traffic	protocol data unit (PDU)	Transmission Control Protocol (TCP)
Internet	quality of service (QoS)	transport layer
Internet layer	raw sockets	User Datagram Protocol (UDP)
Internet Protocol (IP)	router	
Internetworking	segments	video
	semantics	

Review Questions

2.1. What is the major function of the network access layer?

2.2. What tasks are performed by the transport layer?

2.3. What is a protocol?

2.4. What is a protocol data unit (PDU)?

2.5. What is a protocol architecture?

2.6. What is TCP/IP?

2.7. What are some advantages to layering as seen in the TCP/IP architecture?

2.8. What is a router?

2.9.   Which version of IP is the most prevalent today?

2.10.   Does all traffic running on the Internet use TCP?

2.11.   Compare the address space between IPv4 and IPv6. How many bits are used in each?

Problems

2.1.   Using the layer models in Figure 2.15, describe the ordering and delivery of a pizza, indicating the interactions at each level.

2.2.   **a.** The French and Chinese prime ministers need to come to an agreement by telephone, but neither speaks the other's language. Further, neither has on hand a translator that can translate to the language of the other. However, both prime ministers have English translators on their staffs. Draw a diagram similar to Figure 2.15 to depict the situation, and describe the interaction at each level.

   b. Now suppose that the Chinese prime minister's translator can translate only into Japanese and that the French prime minister has a German translator available. A translator between German and Japanese is available in Germany. Draw a new diagram that reflects this arrangement and describe the hypothetical phone conversation.

2.3.   List the major disadvantages with the layered approach to protocols.

2.4.   Two blue armies are each poised on opposite hills preparing to attack a single red army in the valley. The red army can defeat either of the blue armies separately but will fail to defeat both blue armies if they attack simultaneously. The blue armies communicate via an unreliable communications system (a foot soldier). The commander with one of the blue armies would like to attack at noon. His problem is this: If he

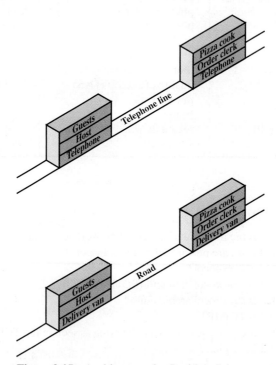

Figure 2.15   Architecture for Problem 2.1

sends a message to the other blue army, ordering the attack, he cannot be sure it will get through. He could ask for acknowledgment, but that might not get through. Is there a protocol that the two blue armies can use to avoid defeat?

2.5. A broadcast network is one in which a transmission from any one attached station is received by all other attached stations over a shared medium. Examples are a bus-topology local area network, such as Ethernet, and a wireless radio network. Discuss the need or lack of need for a network layer (OSI layer 3) in a broadcast network.

2.6. In Figure 2.5, exactly one protocol data unit (PDU) in layer N is encapsulated in a PDU at layer $(N - 1)$. It is also possible to break one N-level PDU into multiple $(N - 1)$-level PDUs (segmentation) or to group multiple N-level PDUs into one $(N - 1)$-level PDU (blocking).

    a. In the case of segmentation, is it necessary that each $(N - 1)$-level segment contain a copy of the N-level header?

    b. In the case of blocking, is it necessary that each N-level PDU retain its own header, or can the data be consolidated into a single N-level PDU with a single N-level header?

2.7. Suppose a protocol architecture has defined four layers for communication, say, base layer, net layer, transport layer, and max layer. The header length of the base layer and of the net layer is 2 bytes; the transport layer, 3 bytes; and max layer, 4 bytes. Besides this, each layer has a 4-bit end marker. If a 50-byte packet is received, what is the size of the actual message?

2.8. Can you identify some areas where UDP may be preferable to TCP?

2.9. IP, TCP, and UDP all discard a packet that arrives with a checksum error and do not attempt to notify the source. Why?

2.10. Why does the TCP header have a header length field while the UDP header does not?

2.11. The previous version of the TFTP specification, RFC 783, included the following statement:

> All packets other than those used for termination are acknowledged individually unless a timeout occurs.

The RFC 1350 specification revises this to say:

> All packets other than duplicate ACK's and those used for termination are acknowledged unless a timeout occurs.

The change was made to fix a problem referred to as the "Sorcerer's Apprentice." Deduce and explain the problem.

2.12. What is the limiting factor in the time required to transfer a file using TFTP?

2.13. Data comprising 5000 bytes needs to be transmitted. How many TFTP packets would be required? For transmission, each TFTP packet is handed to UDP, which adds an 8-byte header to form a UDP segment, which is in turn handed to IP, which adds a 20-byte header file to form an IP datagram. What is the size of this IP datagram? What is the total size of all the packets actually being transmitted? Find the overhead as a ratio of the size of headers to the size of the data file.

2.14. The TFTP specification (RFC 1350) states that the transfer identifiers (TIDs) for a connection should be randomly chosen, so that the probability that the same number is chosen twice in immediate succession is very low. What would be the problem of using the same TIDs twice in immediate succession?

2.15. In order to be able to retransmit lost packets, TFTP must keep a copy of the data it sends. How many packets of data must TFTP keep at a time to implement this retransmission mechanism?

2.16. TFTP, like most protocols, will never send an error packet in response to an error packet it receives. Why?

2.17. We have seen that in order to deal with lost packets, TFTP implements a timeout-and-retransmit scheme, by setting a retransmission timer when it transmits a packet to the remote host. Most TFTP implementations set this timer to a fixed value of about 5 seconds. Discuss the advantages and the disadvantages of using a fixed value for the retransmission timer.

2.18. TFTP's timeout-and-retransmission scheme implies that all data packets will eventually be received by the destination host. Will these data also be received uncorrupted? Why or why not?

2.19. This problem concerns material in Appendix E. Based on the principles enunciated in Table E.1.

    a. Design an architecture with eight layers and make a case for it.
    b. Design one with six layers and make a case for that.

2.10 SOCKETS PROGRAMMING ASSIGNMENTS

2.1. Determining a local machine's IP address is useful when you are handling network communication tasks. Write code to find the IP address of a local machine. Hint: You may use some public DNS, for example, Google public DNS is 8.8.8.8.

2.2. Write a sockets program to get a host name for a given IP address.

2.3. How to broadcast a message on the Internet? Two questions need to be answered: What address should be used as the broadcast address. How to send data to the broadcast address? A broadcast address is the subnet's network number with all one-bits set for the host portion of the address. For instance, if a network IP address is 192.168.1.0, and the netmask is 255.255.255.0, the last byte of the address is the host number (because the first three bytes, according to the netmask, correspond to the network number). So the broadcast address is 192.168.1.255. Under Unix, the ifconfig command will actually give you all this information.

    a. Determine the broadcast address of your local machine;
    b. Send a broadcast packet to your broadcast address. Write a code to implement this task.

2.4. Write a stream-based echo server and a client sending messages to it, and receiving back each message in turn. Hint: Modify the stream-based TCP client and server programs in this chapter or similar programs to transfer multiple messages back and forth (until the client terminates the connection).

2.5. Modify the server program from Exercise 2.4 to set the TCP window size for the server socket. Hint: Set the SO_RCVBUF size through a call to setsockopt(). Be aware that setting the TCP window size in this way would not guarantee the size for the entire life of the socket because of the inherent TCP window flow control. This exercise solely intends to demonstrate the use of setsockopt() and getsockopt() calls.

2.6. Use poll() function and socket programming to receive out-of-band data. Out-of-band data is also called urgent data in TCP, and is often received with first priority via a separate data stream. Hint: Check events and select POLLPRI.

APPENDIX 2A THE TRIVIAL FILE TRANSFER PROTOCOL

This appendix provides an overview of the Internet standard Trivial File Transfer Protocol (TFTP), defined in RFC 1350. Our purpose is to give the reader some flavor for the elements of a protocol. TFTP is simple enough to provide a concise example, but includes most of the significant elements found in other, more complex, protocols.

Introduction to TFTP

TFTP is far simpler than the Internet standard FTP (RFC 959). There are no provisions for access control or user identification, so TFTP is only suitable for public access file directories. Because of its simplicity, TFTP is easily and compactly implemented. For example, some diskless devices use TFTP to download their firmware at boot time.

TFTP runs on top of UDP. The TFTP entity that initiates the transfer does so by sending a read or write request in a UDP segment with a destination port of 69 to the target system. This port is recognized by the target UDP module as the identifier of the TFTP module. For the duration of the transfer, each side uses a transfer identifier (TID) as its port number.

TFTP Packets

TFTP entities exchange commands, responses, and file data in the form of packets, each of which is carried in the body of a UDP segment. TFTP supports five types of packets (Figure 2.16); the first two bytes contain an opcode that identifies the packet type:

- **RRQ:** The read request packet requests permission to transfer a file from the other system. The packet includes a file name, which is a sequence of ASCII[4] bytes terminated by a zero byte. The zero byte is the means by which the receiving TFTP entity knows when the file name is terminated. The packet also includes a mode field, which indicates whether the data file is to be interpreted as a string of ASCII bytes (netascii mode) or as raw 8-bit bytes (octet mode) of data. In netascii mode, the file is transferred as lines of characters, each terminated by a carriage return, line feed. Each system must translate between its own format for character files and the TFTP format.

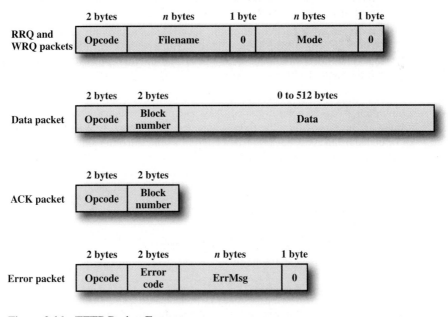

Figure 2.16 TFTP Packet Formats

---

[4]ASCII is the American Standard Code for Information Interchange, a standard of the American National Standards Institute. It designates a unique 7-bit pattern for each letter, with an eighth bit used for parity. ASCII is equivalent to the International Reference Alphabet (IRA), defined in ITU-T Recommendation T.50. See Appendix F for a discussion.

Table 2.5 TFTP Error Codes

Value	Meaning
0	Not defined, see error message (if any)
1	File not found
2	Access violation
3	Disk full or allocation exceeded
4	Illegal TFTP operation
5	Unknown transfer ID
6	File already exists
7	No such user

- **WRQ:** The write request packet requests permission to transfer a file to the other system.
- **Data:** The block numbers on data packets begin with one and increase by one for each new block of data. This convention enables the program to use a single number to discriminate between new packets and duplicates. The data field is from zero to 512 bytes long. If it is 512 bytes long, the block is not the last block of data; if it is from zero to 511 bytes long, it signals the end of the transfer.
- **ACK:** This packet is used to acknowledge receipt of a data packet or a WRQ packet. An ACK of a data packet contains the block number of the data packet being acknowledged. An ACK of a WRQ contains a block number of zero.
- **Error:** An error packet can be the acknowledgment of any other type of packet. The error code is an integer indicating the nature of the error (Table 2.5). The error message is intended for human consumption and should be in ASCII. Like all other strings, it is terminated with a zero byte.

All packets other than duplicate ACKs (explained subsequently) and those used for termination are to be acknowledged. Any packet can be acknowledged by an error packet. If there are no errors, then the following conventions apply. A WRQ or a data packet is acknowledged by an ACK packet. When a RRQ is sent, the other side responds (in the absence of error) by beginning to transfer the file; thus, the first data block serves as an acknowledgment of the RRQ packet. Unless a file transfer is complete, each ACK packet from one side is followed by a data packet from the other, so that the data packet functions as an acknowledgment. An error packet can be acknowledged by any other kind of packet, depending on the circumstance.

Figure 2.17 shows a TFTP data packet in context. When such a packet is handed down to UDP, UDP adds a header to form a UDP segment. This is then passed to IP, which adds an IP header to form an IP datagram.

Overview of a Transfer

The example illustrated in Figure 2.18 is of a simple file transfer operation from A to B. No errors occur and the details of the option specification are not explored.

The operation begins when the TFTP module in system A sends a write request (WRQ) to the TFTP module in system B. The WRQ packet is carried as the body of a UDP segment. The write request includes the name of the file (in this case, XXX) and a mode of octet, or raw data. In the UDP header, the destination port number is 69, which alerts the

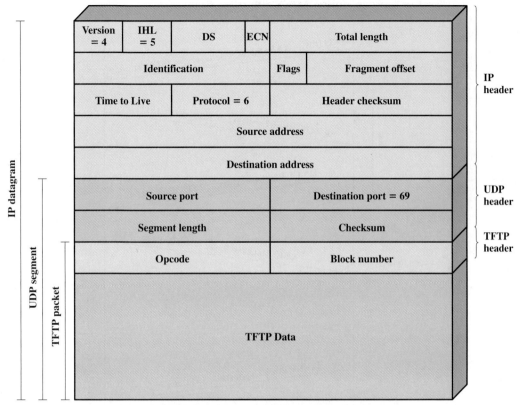

Figure 2.17 A TFTP Packet in Context

receiving UDP entity that this message is intended for the TFTP application. The source port number is a TID selected by A, in this case 1511. System B is prepared to accept the file and so responds with an ACK with a block number of 0. In the UDP header, the destination port is 1511, which enables the UDP entity at A to route the incoming packet to the TFTP module, which can match this TID with the TID in the WRQ. The source port is a TID selected by B for this file transfer, in this case 1660.

Following this initial exchange, the file transfer proceeds. The transfer consists of one or more data packets from A, each of which is acknowledged by B. The final data packet contains less than 512 bytes of data, which signals the end of the transfer.

Errors and Delays

If TFTP operates over a network or internet (as opposed to a direct data link), it is possible for packets to be lost. Because TFTP operates over UDP, which does not provide a reliable delivery service, there needs to be some mechanism in TFTP to deal with lost packets. TFTP uses the common technique of a timeout mechanism. Suppose that A sends a packet to B that requires an acknowledgment (i.e., any packet other than duplicate ACKs and those used for termination). When A has transmitted the packet, it starts a timer. If the timer expires before the acknowledgment is received from B, A retransmits the same packet. If in fact the original packet was lost, then the retransmission will be the first copy of this packet received by B. If the original packet was not lost but the acknowledgment from B was lost, then B will receive

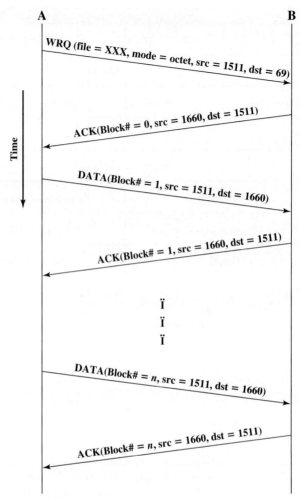

Figure 2.18 Example TFTP Operation

two copies of the same packet from A and simply acknowledges both copies. Because of the use of block numbers, this causes no confusion. The only exception to this rule is for duplicate ACK packets. The second ACK is ignored.

Syntax, Semantics, and Timing

In Section 2.1, it was mentioned that the key features of a protocol can be classified as syntax, semantics, and timing. These categories are easily seen in TFTP. The formats of the various TFTP packets form the **syntax** of the protocol. The **semantics** of the protocol are shown in the definitions of each of the packet types and the error codes. Finally, the sequence in which packets are exchanged, the use of block numbers, and the use of timers are all aspects of the **timing** of TFTP.

DATA TRANSMISSION

LEARNING OBJECTIVES

After studying this chapter, you should be able to:

♦ Distinguish between digital and analog information sources.

♦ Explain the various ways in which audio, data, image, and video can be represented by electromagnetic signals.

♦ Discuss the characteristics of analog and digital waveforms.

♦ Discuss the various transmission impairments that affect signal quality and information transfer over communication media.

♦ Identify the factors that affect channel capacity.

The successful transmission of **data** depends principally on two factors: the quality of the signal being transmitted and the characteristics of the transmission medium. The objective of this chapter and the next is to provide the reader with an intuitive feeling for the nature of these two factors.

The first section presents some concepts and terms from the field of electrical engineering. This should provide sufficient background to deal with the remainder of the chapter. Section 3.2 clarifies the use of the terms *analog* and *digital*. Either analog or **digital data** may be transmitted using either analog or digital signals. Furthermore, it is common for intermediate processing to be performed between source and destination, and this processing has either an analog or digital character.

Section 3.3 looks at the various impairments that may introduce errors into the data during transmission. The chief impairments are **attenuation**, **attenuation distortion**, **delay distortion**, and the various forms of noise. Finally, we look at the important concept of channel capacity.

3.1 CONCEPTS AND TERMINOLOGY

In this section, we introduce some concepts and terms that will be referred to throughout the rest of the chapter and, indeed, throughout Part Two.

Transmission Terminology

Data transmission occurs between transmitter and receiver over some transmission medium. Transmission media may be classified as guided or unguided. In both cases, communication is in the form of electromagnetic waves. With **guided media**, the waves are guided along a physical path; examples of guided media are twisted pair, coaxial cable, and optical fiber. **Unguided media**, also called **wireless**, provide a means for transmitting electromagnetic waves but do not guide them; examples are propagation through air, vacuum, and seawater.

The term **direct link** is used to refer to the transmission path between two devices in which signals propagate directly from transmitter to receiver with no intermediate devices, other than amplifiers or repeaters used to increase signal strength. Note that this term can apply to both guided and unguided media.

A guided transmission medium is **point to point** if it provides a direct link between two devices and those are the only two devices sharing the medium. In a **multipoint** guided configuration, more than two devices share the same medium.

A transmission may be simplex, **half duplex**, or **full duplex**. In **simplex** transmission, signals are transmitted in only one direction; one station is transmitter and the other is receiver. In **half-duplex** operation, both stations may transmit, but only one at a time. In **full-duplex** operation, both stations may transmit simultaneously. In the latter case, the medium is carrying signals in both directions at the same time. We should note that the definitions just given are the ones in common use in the United States (ANSI definitions). Elsewhere (ITU-T definitions), the term *simplex* is used to correspond to *half duplex*, and *duplex* is used to correspond to *full duplex* as just defined.

Frequency, Spectrum, and Bandwidth

In this book, we are concerned with electromagnetic signals used as a means to transmit data. At point 3 in Figure 1.5, a signal is generated by the transmitter and transmitted over a medium. The signal is a function of time, but it can also be expressed as a function of frequency; that is, the signal consists of components of different frequencies. It turns out that the **frequency domain** view of a signal is more important to an understanding of data transmission than a **time domain** view. Both views are introduced here.

TIME DOMAIN CONCEPTS   Viewed as a function of time, an electromagnetic signal can be either analog or digital. An **analog signal** is one in which the signal intensity varies in a smooth, or **continuous**, fashion over time. In other words, there are no breaks or discontinuities in the signal.[1] A **digital signal** is one in which the signal intensity maintains a constant level for some period of time and then abruptly changes to another constant level, in a **discrete** fashion.[2] Figure 3.1 shows an example of each kind of signal. The analog signal might represent speech, and the digital signal might represent binary 1s and 0s.

---

[1]A mathematical definition: a signal $s(t)$ is continuous if $\lim_{t \to a} s(t) = s(a)$ for all a.

[2]This is an idealized definition. In fact, the transition from one voltage level to another will not be instantaneous, but there will be a small transition period. Nevertheless, an actual digital signal approximates closely the ideal model of constant voltage levels with instantaneous transitions.

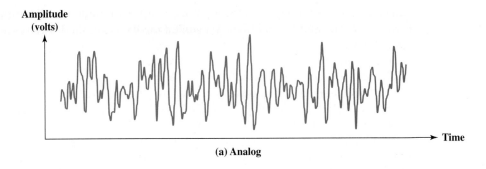

(a) Analog

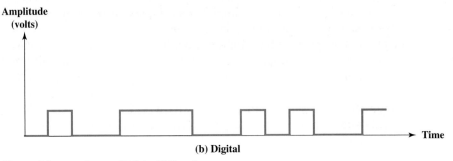

(b) Digital

Figure 3.1   Analog and Digital Waveforms

The simplest sort of signal is a **periodic signal**, in which the same signal pattern repeats over time. Figure 3.2 shows an example of a periodic continuous signal (sine wave) and a periodic discrete signal (square wave). Mathematically, a signal $s(t)$ is defined to be periodic if and only if

$$s(t + T) = s(t) \qquad -\infty < t < +\infty$$

where the constant T is the period of the signal (T is the smallest value that satisfies the equation). Otherwise, a signal is **aperiodic**.

The sine wave is the fundamental periodic signal. A general sine wave can be represented by three parameters: peak amplitude (A), frequency (f), and phase (ϕ). The **peak amplitude** is the maximum value or strength of the signal over time; typically, this value is measured in volts. The **frequency** is the rate [in cycles per second, or hertz (Hz)] at which the signal repeats. An equivalent parameter is the **period** (T) of a signal, which is the amount of time it takes for one repetition; therefore, $T = 1/f$. **Phase** is a measure of the relative position in time within a single period of a signal, as is illustrated subsequently. More formally, for a periodic signal $f(t)$, phase is the fractional part t/T of the period T through which t has advanced relative to an arbitrary origin. The origin is usually taken as the last previous passage through zero from the negative to the positive direction.

The general sine wave can be written

$$s(t) = A \sin(2\pi ft + \phi)$$

A function with the form of the preceding equation is known as a **sinusoid**. Figure 3.3 shows the effect of varying each of the three parameters. In part (a) of

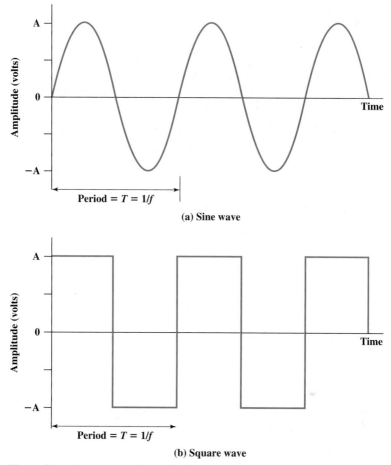

Figure 3.2   Examples of Periodic Signals

the figure, the frequency is 1 Hz; thus the period is $T = 1$ second. Part (b) has the same frequency and phase but a peak amplitude of 0.5. In part (c) we have $f = 2$, which is equivalent to $T = 0.5$. Finally, part (d) shows the effect of a phase shift of $\pi/4$ radians, which is 45 degrees (2π radians $= 360° = 1$ period).

In Figure 3.3, the horizontal axis is time; the graphs display the value of a signal at a given point in space as a function of time. These same graphs, with a change of scale, can apply with horizontal axes in space. In this case, the graphs display the value of a signal at a given point in time as a function of distance. For example, for a sinusoidal transmission (e.g., an electromagnetic radio wave some distance from a radio antenna, or sound some distance from a loudspeaker), at a particular instant of time, the intensity of the signal varies in a sinusoidal way as a function of distance from the source.[3]

There is a simple relationship between the two sine waves, one in time and one in space. The **wavelength** (λ) of a signal is the distance occupied by a single

---

[3] An electromagnetic signal attenuates as it propagates, as a function of distance from the source of the signal. This effect is ignored in Figure 3.3.

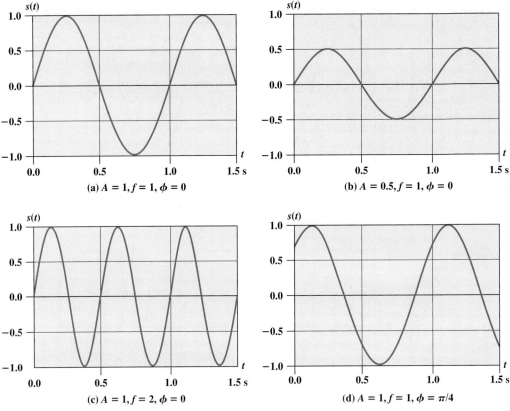

Figure 3.3 $s(t) = A \sin(2\pi f t + \phi)$

cycle, or, put another way, the distance between two points of corresponding phase of two consecutive cycles. Assume that the signal is traveling with a velocity v. Then the wavelength is related to the period as follows: $\lambda = vT$. Equivalently, $\lambda f = v$. Of particular relevance to this discussion is the case where $v = c$, the speed of light in free space, which is approximately 3×10^8 m/s.

EXAMPLE 3.1 In the United States, ordinary household current is typically supplied at a frequency of 60 Hz with a peak voltage of about 170 V. Thus the power line voltage can be expressed as

$$170 \sin(2\pi \times 60 \times t)$$

The period of this current is $1/60 = 0.0167$ s $= 16.7$ ms. A typical velocity of propagation is about 0.9 c, so the wavelength of the current is $\lambda = vT = 0.9 \times 3 \times 10^8 \times 0.0167 = 4.5 \times 10^6$ m $= 4500$ km.

Household voltage is normally stated as being 120 V. This is what is known as the root mean square (square the voltage to make everything positive, find the average, take the square root) value. For a sine wave, the value is calculated as $\sqrt{(A^2 - 0)/2} = 0.707A$. In this case, $0.707 \times 170 = 120$.

FREQUENCY DOMAIN CONCEPTS   In practice, an electromagnetic signal will be made up of many frequencies. For example, the signal

$$s(t) = (4/\pi) \times [\sin(2\pi ft) + (1/3)\sin(2\pi(3f)t)]$$

is shown in Figure 3.4c. The components of this signal are just sine waves of frequencies f and $3f$; parts (a) and (b) of the figure show these individual components.[4] There are two interesting points that can be made about this figure:

- The second frequency is an integer multiple of the first frequency. When all of the frequency components of a signal are integer multiples of one frequency, the latter frequency is referred to as the **fundamental frequency**. Each multiple of the fundamental frequency is referred to as a **harmonic frequency** of the signal.

- The period of the total signal is equal to the period of the fundamental frequency. The period of the component $\sin(2\pi ft)$ is $T = 1/f$, and the period of $s(t)$ is also T, as can be seen from Figure 3.4c.

It can be shown, using a discipline known as Fourier analysis, that any signal is made up of components at various frequencies, in which each component is a sinusoid. By adding together enough sinusoidal signals, each with the appropriate amplitude, frequency, and phase, any electromagnetic signal can be constructed. Put another way, any electromagnetic signal can be shown to consist of a collection of periodic analog signals (sine waves) at different amplitudes, frequencies, and phases. The importance of being able to look at a signal from the frequency perspective (frequency domain) rather than a time perspective (time domain) should become clear as the discussion proceeds. For the interested reader, the subject of Fourier analysis is introduced in Appendix A.

So we can say that for each signal, there is a time domain function $s(t)$ that specifies the amplitude of the signal at each instant in time. Similarly, there is a frequency domain function $S(f)$ that specifies the peak amplitude of the constituent frequencies of the signal. Figure 3.5a shows the frequency domain function for the signal of Figure 3.4c. Note that, in this case, $S(f)$ is discrete. Figure 3.5b shows the frequency domain function for a single square pulse that has the value 1 between $-X/2$ and $X/2$, and is 0 elsewhere.[5] Note that in this case $S(f)$ is continuous and that it has nonzero values indefinitely, although the magnitude of the frequency components rapidly shrinks for larger f. These characteristics are common for real signals.

The **spectrum** of a signal is the range of frequencies that it contains. For the signal of Figure 3.4c, the spectrum extends from f to $3f$. The **absolute bandwidth** of a signal is the width of the spectrum. In the case of Figure 3.4c, the bandwidth is $3f - f = 2f$ Many signals, such as that of Figure 3.5b, have an infinite bandwidth. However, most of the energy in the signal is contained in a relatively narrow band of frequencies. This band is referred to as the **effective bandwidth**, or just **bandwidth**.

---

[4]The scaling factor of $4/\pi$ is used to produce a wave whose peak amplitude is close to 1.

[5]In fact, the function $S(f)$ for this case is symmetric around $f = 0$ and so has values for negative frequencies. The presence of negative frequencies is a mathematical artifact whose explanation is beyond the scope of this book.

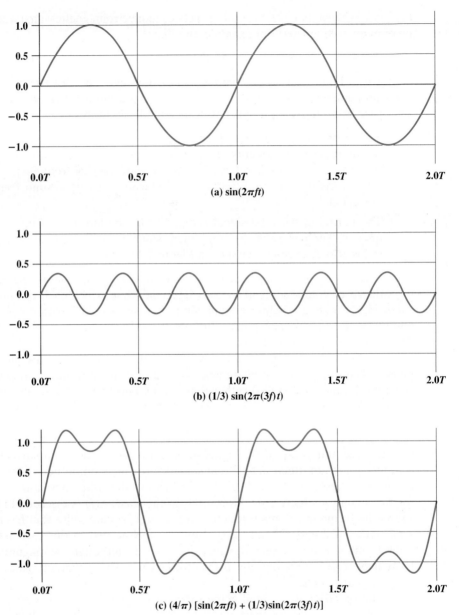

Figure 3.4   Addition of Frequency Components ($T = 1/f$)

One final term to define is **dc component**. If a signal includes a component of zero frequency, that component is a direct current (dc) or constant component. For example, Figure 3.6 shows the result of adding a dc component to the signal of Figure 3.4c. With no dc component, a signal has an average amplitude of zero, as seen in the time domain. With a dc component, it has a frequency term at $f = 0$ and a nonzero average amplitude.

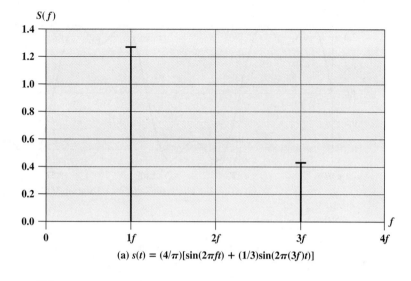

(a) $s(t) = (4/\pi)[\sin(2\pi ft) + (1/3)\sin(2\pi(3f)t)]$

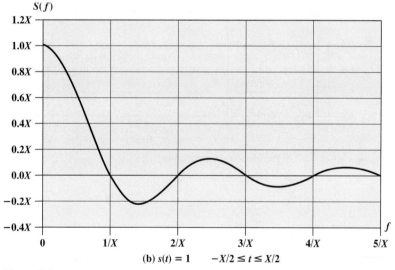

(b) $s(t) = 1 \qquad -X/2 \leq t \leq X/2$

Figure 3.5 Frequency Domain Representations

RELATIONSHIP BETWEEN DATA RATE AND BANDWIDTH   We have said that effective bandwidth is the band within which most of the signal energy is concentrated. The meaning of the term *most* in this context is somewhat arbitrary. The important issue here is that, although a given waveform may contain frequencies over a very broad range, as a practical matter any transmission system (transmitter plus medium plus receiver) will be able to accommodate only a limited band of frequencies. This, in turn, limits the data rate that can be carried on the transmission medium.

To try to explain these relationships, consider the square wave of Figure 3.2b. Suppose that we let a positive pulse represent binary 0 and a negative pulse

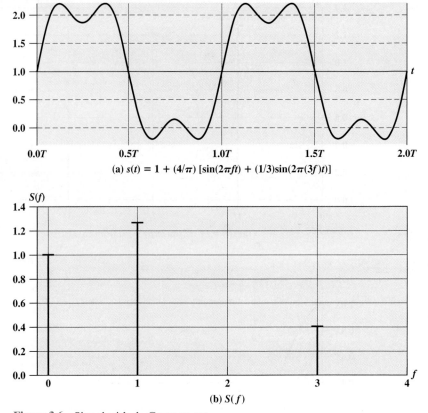

(a) $s(t) = 1 + (4/\pi) \, [\sin(2\pi ft) + (1/3)\sin(2\pi(3f)t)]$

(b) $S(f)$

Figure 3.6   Signal with dc Component

represent binary 1. Then the waveform represents the repetitive binary stream 0101.…The duration of each pulse is $1/(2f)$; thus the data rate is $2f$ bits per second (bps). What are the frequency components of this signal? To answer this question, consider again Figure 3.4. By adding together sine waves at frequencies f and $3f$, we get a waveform that begins to resemble the original square wave. Let us continue this process by adding a sine wave of frequency $5f$, as shown in Figure 3.7a, and then adding a sine wave of frequency $7f$, as shown in Figure 3.7b. As we add additional odd multiples of f, suitably scaled, the resulting waveform approaches that of a square wave more and more closely.

Indeed, it can be shown that the frequency components of the square wave with amplitudes A and $-A$ can be expressed as follows:

$$s(t) = A \times \frac{4}{\pi} \times \sum_{k\,\text{odd},k=1}^{\infty} \frac{\sin\left(2\pi kft\right)}{k}$$

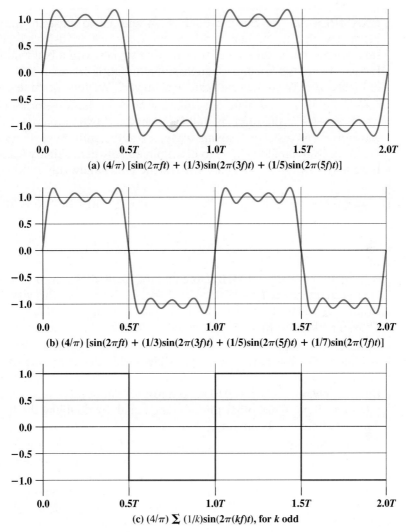

Figure 3.7   Frequency Components of Square Wave ($T = 1/f$)

Thus, this waveform has an infinite number of frequency components and hence an infinite bandwidth. However, the peak amplitude of the kth frequency component, kf, is only $1/k$, so most of the energy in this waveform is in the first few frequency components. What happens if we limit the bandwidth to just the first three frequency components? We have already seen the answer in Figure 3.7a. As we can see, the shape of the resulting waveform is reasonably close to that of the original square wave.

EXAMPLE 3.2 We can use Figures 3.4 and 3.7 to illustrate the relationship between data rate and bandwidth. Suppose that we are using a digital transmission system that is capable of transmitting signals with a bandwidth of 4 MHz. Let us attempt to transmit a sequence of alternating 1s and 0s as the square wave of Figure 3.7c. What data rate can be achieved? We look at three cases.

Case I. Let us approximate our square wave with the waveform of Figure 3.7a, which consists of the fundamental frequency and two harmonics. Although this waveform is a "distorted" square wave, it is sufficiently close to the square wave that a receiver should be able to discriminate between a binary 0 and a binary 1. If we let $f = 10^6$ cycles/second $= 1$ MHz, then the bandwidth of the signal

$$s(t) = \frac{4}{\pi} \times \left[\sin\left((2\pi \times 10^6)t \right) + \frac{1}{3} \sin\left((2\pi \times 3 \times 10^6)t \right) \right.$$
$$\left. + \frac{1}{5} \sin\left((2\pi \times 5 \times 10^6)t \right) \right]$$

is $(5 \times 10^6) - 10^6 = 4$ MHz. Note that for $f = 1$ MHz, the period of the fundamental frequency is $T = 1/10^6 = 10^{-6} = 1 \mu$s. If we treat this waveform as a bit string of 1s and 0s, 1 bit occurs every 0.5μs, for a data rate of $2 \times 10^6 = 2$ Mbps. Thus, for a bandwidth of 4 MHz, a data rate of 2 Mbps is achieved.

Case II. Now suppose that we have a bandwidth of 8 MHz. Let us look again at Figure 3.7a, but now with $f = 2$ MHz. Using the same line of reasoning as before, the bandwidth of the signal is $(5 \times 2 \times 10^6) - (2 \times 10^6) = 8$ MHz. But in this case $T = 1/f = 0.5 \mu$s. As a result, 1 bit occurs every 0.25μs for a data rate of 4 Mbps. Thus, other things being equal, by doubling the bandwidth, we double the potential data rate.

Case III. Now suppose that the waveform of Figure 3.4c is considered adequate for approximating a square wave. That is, the difference between a positive and negative pulse in Figure 3.4c is sufficiently distinct that the waveform can be successfully used to represent a sequence of 1s and 0s. Assume as in Case II that $f = 2$ MHz and $T = 1/f = 0.5 \mu$s, so that 1 bit occurs every 0.25μs for a data rate of 4 Mbps. Using the waveform of Figure 3.4c, the bandwidth of the signal is $(3 \times 2 \times 10^6) - (2 \times 10^6) = 4$MHz. Thus, a given bandwidth can support various data rates depending on the ability of the receiver to discern the difference between 0 and 1 in the presence of noise and other impairments.

To summarize,

Case I: Bandwidth = 4 MHz; data rate = 2 Mbps
Case II: Bandwidth = 8 MHz; data rate = 4 Mbps
Case III: Bandwidth = 4 MHz; data rate = 4 Mbps

We can draw the following conclusions from the preceding example. In general, any digital waveform will have infinite bandwidth. If we attempt to transmit this waveform as a signal over any medium, the transmission system will limit the bandwidth that can be transmitted. Furthermore, for any given medium, the greater the bandwidth transmitted, the greater the cost. Thus, on the one hand, economic

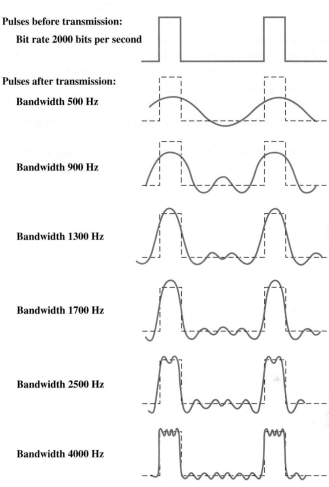

Figure 3.8   Effect of Bandwidth on a Digital Signal

and practical reasons dictate that digital information be approximated by a signal of limited bandwidth. On the other hand, limiting the bandwidth creates distortions, which makes the task of interpreting the received signal more difficult. The more limited the bandwidth, the greater the distortion, and the greater the potential for error by the receiver.

One more illustration should serve to reinforce these concepts. Figure 3.8 shows a digital bit stream with a data rate of 2000 bits per second. With a bandwidth of 2500 Hz, or even 1700 Hz, the representation is quite good. Furthermore, we can generalize these results. If the data rate of the digital signal is W bps, then a very good representation can be achieved with a bandwidth of $2W$ Hz. However, unless noise is very severe, the bit pattern can be recovered with less bandwidth than this (see the discussion of channel capacity in Section 3.4).

Thus, there is a direct relationship between data rate and bandwidth: The higher the data rate of a signal, the greater is the bandwidth required for transmission.

Another way of stating this is that the greater the bandwidth of a transmission system, the higher the data rate that can be transmitted over that system.

Another observation worth making is this: If we think of the bandwidth of a signal as being centered about some frequency, referred to as the **center frequency**, then the higher the center frequency, the higher the potential bandwidth and therefore the higher the potential data rate. For example, if a signal is centered at 2 MHz, its maximum potential bandwidth is 4 MHz.

We return to a discussion of the relationship between bandwidth and data rate in Section 3.4, after a consideration of transmission impairments.

3.2 ANALOG AND DIGITAL DATA TRANSMISSION

The terms *analog* and *digital* correspond, roughly, to *continuous* and *discrete*, respectively. These two terms are used frequently in data communications in at least three contexts: data, signaling, and transmission.

Briefly, we define **data** as entities that convey meaning, or information. **Signals** are electric or electromagnetic representations of data. **Signaling** is the physical propagation of the signal along a suitable medium. **Transmission** is the communication of data by the propagation and processing of signals. In what follows, we try to make these abstract concepts clear by discussing the terms *analog* and *digital* as applied to data, signals, and transmission.

Analog and Digital Data

The concepts of analog and digital data are simple enough. **Analog data** take on continuous values in some interval. For example, voice and video are continuously varying patterns of intensity. Most data collected by sensors, such as temperature and pressure, are continuous valued. Digital data take on discrete values; examples are **text** and integers.

The most familiar example of analog data is audio, which, in the form of acoustic sound waves, can be perceived directly by human beings. Figure 3.9 shows the acoustic spectrum for human speech and for music.[6] Frequency components of typical speech may be found between approximately 100 Hz and 7 kHz. Although much of the energy in speech is concentrated at the lower frequencies, tests have shown that frequencies below 600 or 700 Hz add very little to the intelligibility of speech to the human ear. Typical speech has a dynamic range of about 25 dB;[7] that is, the power produced by the loudest shout may be as much as 300 times greater than the least whisper.

A familiar example of digital data is text or character strings. While textual data are most convenient for human beings, they cannot, in character form, be easily stored or transmitted by data processing and communications systems. Such

---

[6]Note the use of a log scale for the *x*-axis. Because the *y*-axis is in units of **decibels**, it is effectively a log scale also. A basic review of log scales is in the math refresher document at the Computer Science Student Resource Site at http://www.computersciencestudent.com

[7]The concept of decibels is explained in Appendix 3A.

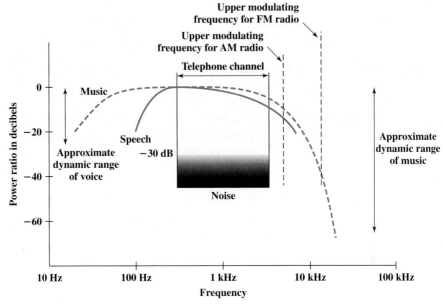

Figure 3.9   Acoustic Spectrum of Speech and Music [CARN99]

systems are designed for binary data. Thus a number of codes have been devised by which characters are represented by a sequence of bits. Perhaps the earliest common example of this is the Morse code. Today, the most commonly used text code is the International Reference Alphabet (IRA).[8] Each character in this code is represented by a unique 7-bit pattern; thus 128 different characters can be represented. This is a larger number than is necessary, and some of the patterns represent invisible *control characters*. IRA-encoded characters are almost always stored and transmitted using 8 bits per character. The eighth bit is a parity bit used for error detection. This bit is set such that the total number of binary 1s in each octet is always odd (odd parity) or always even (even parity). Thus a transmission error that changes a single bit, or any odd number of bits, can be detected.

Video transmission carries sequences of pictures in time. In essence, video makes use of a sequence of raster-scan images. Here it is easier to characterize the data in terms of the viewer's (destination's) television or computer display monitor rather than the original scene (source) that is recorded by the video camera.

Video can be captured by either analog or digital video recorders. The video that is captured can be transmitted using continuous (analog) or discrete (digital) signals, can be received by either analog or digital display devices, and can be stored in either analog or digital file formats.

The first televisions and computer monitors used cathode-ray-tube (CRT) technology. CRT monitors are inherently analog devices that use an electron gun to

---

[8]IRA is defined in ITU-T Recommendation T.50 and was formerly known as International Alphabet Number 5 (IA5). The U.S. national version of IRA is referred to as the American Standard Code for Information Interchange (ASCII). Appendix F provides a description and table of the IRA code.

"paint" pictures on the screen. The gun emits an electron beam that scans across the surface of the screen from left to right and top to bottom. For black-and-white television, the amount of illumination produced (on a scale from black to white) at any point is proportional to the intensity of the beam as it passes that point. Thus at any instant in time the beam takes on an analog value of intensity to produce the desired brightness at that point on the screen. Further, as the beam scans, the analog value changes. Thus the video image can be thought of as a time-varying analog signal.

The term *digital video* refers to the capture, manipulation, and storage of video in digital formats. Digital video cameras capture moving images digitally. In essence, this is done by taking a series of digital photographs, at a rate of at least 30 frames per second.

Analog and Digital Signals

In a communications system, data are propagated from one point to another by means of electromagnetic signals. An **analog signal** is a continuously varying electromagnetic wave that may be propagated over a variety of media, depending on spectrum; examples are wire media, such as twisted pair and coaxial cable; fiber optic cable; and unguided media, such as atmosphere or space propagation. A **digital signal** is a sequence of voltage pulses that may be transmitted over a wire medium; for example, a constant positive voltage level may represent binary 0 and a constant negative voltage level may represent binary 1.

The principal advantages of digital signaling are that it is generally cheaper than analog signaling and is less susceptible to noise interference. The principal disadvantage is that digital signals suffer more from attenuation than do analog signals. Figure 3.10 shows a sequence of voltage pulses, generated by a source using two voltage levels, and the received voltage some distance down a conducting medium. Because of the attenuation, or reduction, of signal strength at higher frequencies, the pulses become rounded and smaller. It should be clear that this attenuation can lead rather quickly to the loss of the information contained in the propagated signal.

In what follows, we first look at some specific examples of signal types and then discuss the relationship between data and signals.

EXAMPLES Let us return to the three examples in the preceding subsection. For each example, we will describe the signal and estimate its bandwidth.

First, we consider **audio**, or acoustic, information. One form of acoustic information, of course, is human speech. This form of information is easily converted to an electromagnetic signal for transmission (Figure 3.11). In essence, all of the sound frequencies, whose amplitude is measured in terms of loudness, are converted into electromagnetic frequencies, whose amplitude is measured in volts. The telephone handset contains a simple mechanism for making such a conversion.

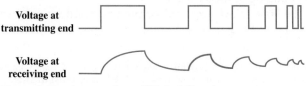

Figure 3.10 Attenuation of Digital Signals

In this graph of a typical analog voice signal, the variations in amplitude and frequency convey the gradations of loudness and pitch in speech or music. Similar signals are used to transmit television pictures, but at much higher frequencies.

Figure 3.11 Conversion of Voice Input to Analog Signal

In the case of acoustic data (voice), the data can be represented directly by an electromagnetic signal occupying the same spectrum. However, there is a need to compromise between the fidelity of the sound as transmitted electrically and the cost of transmission, which increases with increasing bandwidth. As mentioned, the spectrum of speech is approximately 100 Hz to 7 kHz, although a much narrower bandwidth will produce acceptable voice reproduction. The standard spectrum for a voice channel is 300 to 3400 Hz. This is adequate for speech transmission, minimizes required transmission capacity, and allows the use of rather inexpensive telephone sets. The telephone transmitter converts the incoming acoustic voice signal into an electromagnetic signal over the range 300 to 3400 Hz. This signal is then transmitted through the telephone system to a receiver, which reproduces it as acoustic sound.

Now let us look at the **video** signal. To produce a video signal, a TV camera, which performs similar functions to the TV receiver, is used. One component of the camera is a photosensitive plate, upon which a scene is optically focused. An electron beam sweeps across the plate from left to right and top to bottom. As the beam sweeps, an analog electric signal is developed proportional to the brightness of the scene at a particular spot. We mentioned that a total of 483 lines are scanned at a rate of 30 complete scans per second. This is an approximate number taking into account the time lost during the vertical retrace interval. The actual U.S. standard is 525 lines, but of these about 42 are lost during vertical retrace. Thus the horizontal scanning frequency is (525 lines) × (30 scan/s) = 15,750 lines per second, or 63.5 μs/line. Of the 63.5 μs, about 11 μs are allowed for horizontal retrace, leaving a total of 52.5 μs per video line.

Now we are in a position to estimate the bandwidth required for the video signal. To do this we must estimate the upper (maximum) and lower (minimum) frequency of the band. We use the following reasoning to arrive at the maximum frequency: The maximum frequency would occur during the horizontal scan if the scene were alternating between black and white as rapidly as possible. We can estimate this maximum value by considering the resolution of the video image. In the vertical dimension, there are 483 lines, so the maximum vertical resolution would be 483. Experiments have shown that the actual subjective resolution is about 70% of that number, or about 338 lines. In the interest of a balanced picture, the horizontal and vertical resolutions should be about the same. Because the ratio of width to height of a TV screen is 4 : 3, the horizontal resolution should be about 4/3 × 338 = 450 lines. As a worst case, a scanning line would be made up of 450 elements alternating black and white. The scan would result in a wave, with each cycle of the wave consisting of one higher (black) and one lower (white) voltage level. Thus, there would be 450/2 = 225 cycles of the wave in 52.5 μs, for a maximum frequency of about 4.2 MHz. This rough reasoning, in fact, is fairly accurate. The lower limit is a dc or zero frequency, where the dc component corresponds to the average illumination of the scene (the average value by which the brightness exceeds the reference black level). Thus the bandwidth of the video signal is approximately 4 MHz − 0 = 4 MHz.

The foregoing discussion did not consider color or audio components of the signal. It turns out that, with these included, the bandwidth remains about 4 MHz.

Finally, the third example described is the general case of **binary data**. Binary data is generated by terminals, computers, and other data processing equipment and then converted into digital voltage pulses for transmission, as illustrated in Figure 3.12. A commonly used signal for such data uses two constant (dc) voltage levels: one level for binary 1 and one level for binary 0. (In Chapter 5, we shall see that this is but one alternative, referred to as nonreturn to zero (NRZ).) Again, we are interested in the bandwidth of such a signal. This will depend, in any specific case, on the exact shape of the waveform and the sequence of 1s and 0s. We can obtain some understanding by considering Figure 3.8 (compare with Figure 3.7). As can be seen, the greater the bandwidth of the signal, the more faithfully it approximates a digital pulse stream.

DATA AND SIGNALS   In the foregoing discussion, we have looked at analog signals, used to represent analog data, and digital signals, used to represent digital data. Generally, analog data are a function of time and occupy a limited frequency

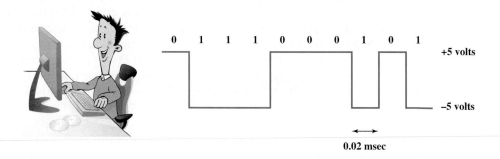

User input at a PC is converted into a stream of binary
digits (1s and 0s). In this graph of a typical digital signal,
binary one is represented by –5 volts and binary zero is
represented by +5 volts. The signal for each bit has a duration
of 0.02 msec, giving a data rate of 50,000 bits per second (50 kbps).

Figure 3.12   Conversion of PC Input to Digital Signal

spectrum; such data can be represented by an electromagnetic signal occupying the same spectrum. Digital data can be represented by digital signals, with a different voltage level for each of the two binary digits.

As Figure 3.13 illustrates, these are not the only possibilities. Digital data can also be represented by analog signals by use of a modem (modulator/demodulator). The modem converts a series of binary (two-valued) voltage pulses into an analog signal by encoding the digital data onto a carrier frequency. The resulting signal occupies a certain spectrum of frequency centered about the carrier and may be propagated across a medium suitable for that carrier. The most common modems represent digital data in the voice spectrum and hence allow those data to be propagated over ordinary voice-grade telephone lines. At the other end of the line, another modem demodulates the signal to recover the original data.

In an operation very similar to that performed by a modem, analog data can be represented by digital signals. The device that performs this function for voice data is a codec (coder-decoder). In essence, the codec takes an analog signal that directly represents the voice data and approximates that signal by a bit stream. At the receiving end, the bit stream is used to reconstruct the analog data.

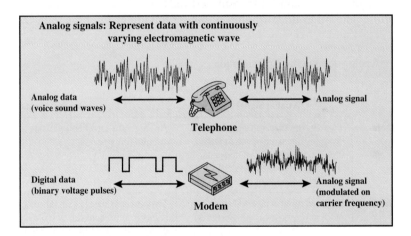

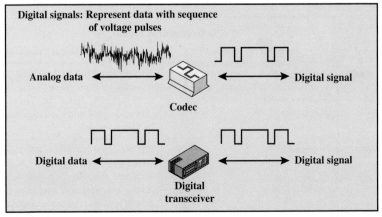

Figure 3.13   Analog and Digital Signaling of Analog and Digital Data

Thus, Figure 3.13 suggests that data may be encoded into signals in a variety of ways. We return to this topic in Chapter 5.

Analog and Digital Transmission

Both analog and digital signals may be transmitted on suitable transmission media. The way these signals are treated is a function of the transmission system. Table 3.1 summarizes the methods of data transmission. **Analog transmission** is a means of transmitting analog signals without regard to their content; the signals may represent analog data (e.g., voice) or digital data (e.g., binary data that pass through a modem). In either case, the analog signal will become weaker (attenuate) after a certain distance. To achieve longer distances, the analog transmission system includes amplifiers that boost the energy in the signal. Unfortunately, the amplifier also boosts the noise components. With amplifiers cascaded to achieve long distances, the signal becomes more and more distorted. For analog data, such as voice, quite a bit of distortion can be tolerated and the data remain intelligible. However, for digital data, cascaded amplifiers will introduce errors.

Digital transmission, by contrast, assumes a binary content to the signal. A digital signal can be transmitted only to a limited distance before attenuation, noise, and other impairments endanger the integrity of the data. To achieve greater

Table 3.1 Analog and Digital Transmission

(a) Data and Signals

	Analog Signal	Digital Signal
Analog Data	Two alternatives: (1) signal occupies the same spectrum as the analog data; (2) analog data are encoded to occupy a different portion of spectrum.	Analog data are encoded using a codec to produce a digital bit stream.
Digital Data	Digital data are encoded using a modem to produce analog signal.	Two alternatives: (1) signal consists of two voltage levels to represent the two binary values; (2) digital data are encoded to produce a digital signal with desired properties.

(b) Treatment of Signals

	Analog Transmission	Digital Transmission
Analog Signal	Is propagated through amplifiers; same treatment whether signal is used to represent analog data or digital data.	Assumes that the analog signal represents digital data. Signal is propagated through repeaters; at each repeater, digital data are recovered from inbound signal and used to generate a new analog outbound signal.
Digital Signal	Not used	Digital signal represents a stream of 1s and 0s, which may represent digital data or may be an encoding of analog data. Signal is propagated through repeaters; at each repeater, stream of 1s and 0s is recovered from inbound signal and used to generate a new digital outbound signal.

distances, repeaters are used. A repeater receives the digital signal, recovers the pattern of 1s and 0s, and retransmits a new signal. Thus the attenuation is overcome.

The same technique may be used with an analog signal if it is assumed that the signal carries digital data. At appropriately spaced points, the transmission system has repeaters rather than amplifiers. The repeater recovers the digital data from the analog signal and generates a new, clean analog signal. Thus noise is not cumulative.

The question naturally arises as to which is the preferred method of transmission. The answer being supplied by the telecommunications industry and its customers is digital. Both long-haul telecommunications facilities and intrabuilding services have moved to digital transmission and, where possible, digital signaling techniques. The most important reasons are the following:

- **Digital technology:** The advent of large-scale integration (LSI) and very-large-scale integration (VLSI) technology has caused a continuing drop in the cost and size of digital circuitry. Analog equipment has not shown a similar drop.
- **Data integrity:** With the use of repeaters rather than amplifiers, the effects of noise and other signal impairments are not cumulative. Thus, it is possible to transmit data longer distances and over lower quality lines by digital means while maintaining the integrity of the data.
- **Capacity utilization:** It has become economical to build transmission links of very high bandwidth, including satellite channels and optical fiber. A high degree of multiplexing is needed to utilize such capacity effectively, and this is more easily and cheaply achieved with digital (time division) rather than analog (frequency division) techniques. This is explored in Chapter 8.
- **Security and privacy:** Encryption techniques can be readily applied to digital data and to analog data that have been digitized.
- **Integration:** By treating both analog and digital data digitally, all signals have the same form and can be treated similarly. Thus economies of scale and convenience can be achieved by integrating voice, video, and digital data.

Asynchronous and Synchronous Transmission

The reception of digital data involves sampling the incoming signal once per bit time to determine the binary value. One of the difficulties encountered in such a process is that various transmission impairments will corrupt the signal so that occasional errors will occur. This problem is compounded by a timing difficulty: In order for the receiver to sample the incoming bits properly, it must know the arrival time and duration of each bit that it receives.

Suppose that the sender simply transmits a stream of data bits. The sender has a clock that governs the timing of the transmitted bits. For example, if data are to be transmitted at 1 million bits per second (1 Mbps), then one bit will be transmitted every $1/10^6 = 1$ microsecond (μs), as measured by the sender's clock. Typically, the receiver will attempt to sample the medium at the center of each bit time. The receiver will time its samples at intervals of one bit time. In our example, the sampling would occur once every 1 μs. If the receiver times its samples based on its own clock, then there will be a problem if the transmitter's and receiver's clocks are not precisely aligned. If there is a drift of 1% (the receiver's clock is 1% faster or slower than the transmitter's clock), then the first sampling will be 0.01 of a bit time (0.01 μs) away from the center of the bit (center of bit is 0.5 μs from beginning and end of bit). After 50 or more samples, the receiver may be in error because it is sampling in the wrong bit time ($50'.01 = 0.5\,\mu s$). For smaller timing differences, the error would occur later, but eventually the receiver will be out of step with the transmitter if the transmitter sends a sufficiently long stream of bits and if no steps are taken to synchronize the transmitter and receiver.

Two approaches are common for achieving the desired synchronization. The first is called, oddly enough, **asynchronous transmission**. The strategy with this scheme is to avoid the timing problem by not sending long, uninterrupted streams of bits. Instead, data are transmitted one character at a time, where each character is 5 to 8 bits in length. Timing or synchronization must only be maintained within each character; the receiver has the opportunity to resynchronize at the beginning of each new character.

With **synchronous transmission**, a block of bits is transmitted in a steady stream without start and stop codes. The block may be many bits in length. To prevent timing drift between transmitter and receiver, their clocks must somehow be synchronized. One possibility is to provide a separate clock line between transmitter and receiver. One side (transmitter or receiver) pulses the line regularly with one short pulse per bit time. The other side uses these regular pulses as a clock. This technique works well over short distances, but over longer distances the clock pulses are subject to the same impairments as the data signal, and timing errors can occur. The other alternative is to embed the clocking information in the data signal. For digital signals, this can be accomplished with Manchester or differential Manchester encoding. For analog signals, a number of techniques can be used; for example, the carrier frequency itself can be used to synchronize the receiver based on the phase of the carrier.

With synchronous transmission, there is another level of synchronization required to allow the receiver to determine the beginning and end of a block of data. To achieve this, each block begins with a *preamble* bit pattern and generally ends with a *postamble* bit pattern. In addition, other bits are added to the block that conveys control information used in the data link control procedures. The data plus preamble, postamble, and control information are called a **frame**. The exact format of the frame depends on which data link control procedure is being used.

Appendix D contains more detail on this topic.

3.3 TRANSMISSION IMPAIRMENTS

With any communications system, the signal that is received may differ from the signal that is transmitted, due to various transmission impairments. For analog signals, these impairments introduce various random modifications that degrade the signal quality. For digital signals, bit errors may be introduced, such that a binary 1 is transformed into a binary 0 or vice versa. In this section, we examine the various impairments and how they may affect the information-carrying capacity of a communication link; Chapter 5 looks at measures that can be taken to compensate for these impairments.

The most significant impairments are

- Attenuation and attenuation distortion
- Delay distortion
- Noise

Attenuation

The strength of a signal falls off with distance over any transmission medium. For guided media (e.g., twisted-pair wire, optical fiber), this reduction in strength, or attenuation, is generally exponential and thus is typically expressed as a constant number of decibels per unit distance.[9] For unguided media (wireless transmission), attenuation is a more complex function of distance and the makeup of the atmosphere. Attenuation introduces three considerations for the transmission engineer.

1. A received signal must have sufficient strength so that the electronic circuitry in the receiver can detect and interpret the signal.
2. The signal must maintain a level sufficiently higher than noise to be received without error.
3. Attenuation is greater at higher frequencies, and this causes distortion.

The first and second considerations are dealt with by attention to signal strength and the use of amplifiers or repeaters. For a point-to-point link, the signal strength of the transmitter must be strong enough to be received intelligibly, but not so strong as to overload the circuitry of the transmitter or receiver, which would cause distortion. Beyond a certain distance, the attenuation becomes so great that repeaters or amplifiers must be installed at regular intervals to boost the signal. These problems are more complex for multipoint lines where the distance from transmitter to receiver is variable.

The third consideration, known as attenuation distortion, is particularly noticeable for analog signals. Because attenuation is different for different frequencies, and the signal is made up of a number of components at different frequencies, the received signal is not only reduced in strength but is also distorted. To overcome this problem, techniques are available for equalizing attenuation across a band of frequencies. This is commonly done for voice-grade telephone lines by using loading coils that change the electrical properties of the line; the result is to smooth out attenuation effects. Another approach is to use amplifiers that amplify high frequencies more than lower frequencies.

An example is provided in Figure 3.14a, which shows attenuation as a function of frequency for a typical leased line. In the figure, attenuation is measured relative to the attenuation at 1000 Hz. Positive values on the y-axis represent attenuation greater than that at 1000 Hz. A 1000-Hz tone of a given power level is applied to the

---

[9]Standards documents generally use the term *insertion loss* when referring to losses associated with cabling, because it is more descriptive of a loss caused by the insertion of a link between transmitter and receiver. Because it remains a more familiar term, we generally use *attenuation* in this book.

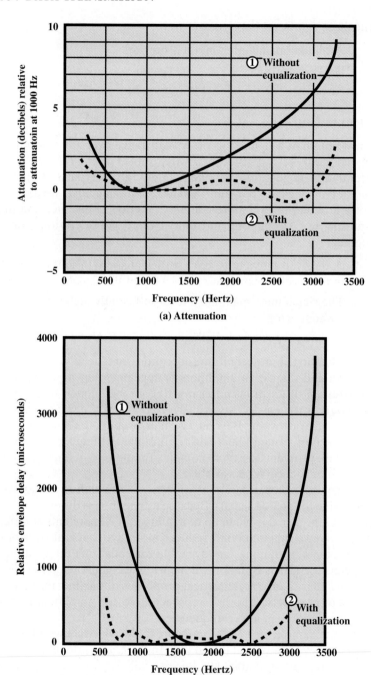

Figure 3.14 Attenuation and Delay Distortion Curves for a Voice Channel

input, and the power, P_{1000}, is measured at the output. For any other frequency f, the procedure is repeated and the relative attenuation in decibels is[10]

$$N_f = -10\log_{10}\frac{P_f}{P_{1000}}$$

The solid line in Figure 3.14a shows attenuation without equalization. As can be seen, frequency components at the upper end of the voice band are attenuated much more than those at lower frequencies. It should be clear that this will result in a distortion of the received speech signal. The dashed line shows the effect of equalization. The flattened response curve improves the quality of voice signals. It also allows higher data rates to be used for digital data that are passed through a modem.

Attenuation distortion can present less of a problem with digital signals. As we have seen, the strength of a digital signal falls off rapidly with frequency (Figure 3.5b); most of the content is concentrated near the fundamental frequency or bit rate of the signal.

Delay Distortion

Delay distortion is a phenomenon that occurs in transmission cables (such as twisted pair, coaxial cable, and optical fiber); it does not occur when signals are transmitted through the air by means of antennas. Delay distortion is caused by the fact that the velocity of propagation of a signal through a cable is different for different frequencies. For a signal with a given bandwidth, the velocity tends to be highest near the center frequency of the signal and to fall off toward the two edges of the band. Thus, various components of a signal will arrive at the receiver at different times.

This effect is referred to as delay distortion because the received signal is distorted due to varying delays experienced at its constituent frequencies. Delay distortion is particularly critical for digital data. Consider that a sequence of bits is being transmitted, using either analog or digital signals. Because of delay distortion, some of the signal components of 1 bit position will spill over into other bit positions, causing **intersymbol interference**, which is a major limitation to maximum bit rate over a transmission channel.

Equalizing techniques can also be used for delay distortion. Again using a leased telephone line as an example, Figure 3.14b shows the effect of equalization on delay as a function of frequency.

Noise

For any data transmission event, the received signal will consist of the transmitted signal, modified by the various distortions imposed by the transmission system, plus additional unwanted signals that are inserted somewhere between transmission and reception. The latter, undesired signals are referred to as **noise**. Noise is the major limiting factor in communications system performance.

---

[10]In the remainder of this book, unless otherwise indicated, we use $\log(x)$ to mean $\log_{10}(x)$.

Noise may be divided into four categories:

- Thermal noise
- Intermodulation noise
- Crosstalk
- Impulse noise

Thermal noise is due to thermal agitation of electrons. It is present in all electronic devices and transmission media and is a function of temperature. Thermal noise is uniformly distributed across the bandwidths typically used in communications systems and hence is often referred to as **white noise**. Thermal noise cannot be eliminated and therefore places an upper bound on communications system performance. Because of the weakness of the signal received by satellite earth stations, thermal noise is particularly significant for satellite communication.

The amount of thermal noise to be found in a bandwidth of 1 Hz in any device or conductor is

$$N_0 = kT \, (\text{W/Hz})$$

where[11]

N_0 = noise power density in watts per 1 Hz of bandwidth
k = Boltzmann's constant = 1.38×10^{-23} J/K
T = temperature, in kelvins (absolute temperature) where the symbol K is used to represent 1 kelvin

---

EXAMPLE 3.3 Room temperature is usually specified as $T = 17°C$, or 290 K. At this temperature, the thermal noise power density is

$$N_0 = (1.38 \times 10^{-23}) \times 290 = 4 \times 10^{-21} \, \text{W/H}_Z = -204 \, \text{dBW/H}_Z$$

where dBW is the decibel-watt, defined in Appendix 3A.

The noise is assumed to be independent of frequency. Thus the thermal noise in watts present in a bandwidth of B hertz can be expressed as

$$N = kTB$$

or, in decibel-watts,

$$N = 10 \log k + 10 \log T + 10 \log B$$
$$= -228.6 \, \text{dBW} + 10 \log T + 10 \log B$$

---

[11]A joule (J) is the International System (SI) unit of electrical, mechanical, and thermal energy. A watt is the SI unit of power, equal to one joule per second. The kelvin (K) is the SI unit of thermodynamic temperature. For a temperature in kelvins of T, the corresponding temperature in degrees Celsius is equal to $T - 273.15$.

EXAMPLE 3.4 Given a receiver with an effective noise temperature of 294 K and a 10-MHz bandwidth, the thermal noise level at the receiver's output is

$$N = -228.6\,\text{dBW} + 10\log(294) + 10\log 10^7$$
$$= -228.6 + 24.7 + 70$$
$$= -133.9\,\text{dBW}$$

When signals at different frequencies share the same transmission medium, the result may be **intermodulation noise**. The effect of intermodulation noise is to produce signals at a frequency that is the sum or difference of the two original frequencies or multiples of those frequencies. For example, if two signals, one at 4000 Hz and one at 8000 Hz, share the same transmission facility, they might produce energy at 12,000 Hz. This noise could interfere with an intended signal at 12,000 Hz.

Intermodulation noise is produced by nonlinearities in the transmitter, receiver, and/or intervening transmission medium. Ideally, these components behave as linear systems; that is, the output is equal to the input times a constant. However, in any real system, the output is a more complex function of the input. Excessive nonlinearity can be caused by component malfunction or overload from excessive signal strength. It is under these circumstances that the sum and difference frequency terms occur.

Crosstalk has been experienced by anyone who, while using the telephone, has been able to hear another conversation; it is an unwanted coupling between signal paths. It can occur by electrical coupling between nearby twisted pairs or, rarely, coax cable lines carrying multiple signals. Crosstalk can also occur when microwave antennas pick up unwanted signals; although highly directional antennas are used, microwave energy does spread during propagation. Typically, crosstalk is of the same order of magnitude as, or less than, thermal noise.

All of the types of noise discussed so far have reasonably predictable and relatively constant magnitudes. Thus it is possible to engineer a transmission system to cope with them. **Impulse noise**, however, is noncontinuous, consisting of irregular pulses or noise spikes of short duration and of relatively high amplitude. It is generated from a variety of causes, including external electromagnetic disturbances, such as lightning, and faults and flaws in the communications system.

Impulse noise is generally only a minor annoyance for analog data. For example, voice transmission may be corrupted by short clicks and crackles with no loss of intelligibility. However, impulse noise is the primary source of error in digital data communication. For example, a sharp spike of energy of 0.01s duration would not destroy any voice data but would wash out about 560 bits of digital data being transmitted at 56 kbps. Figure 3.15 is an example of the effect of noise on a digital signal. Here the noise consists of a relatively modest level of thermal noise plus occasional spikes of impulse noise. The digital data can be recovered from the signal by sampling the received waveform once per bit time. As can be seen, the noise is occasionally sufficient to change a 1 to a 0 or a 0 to a 1.

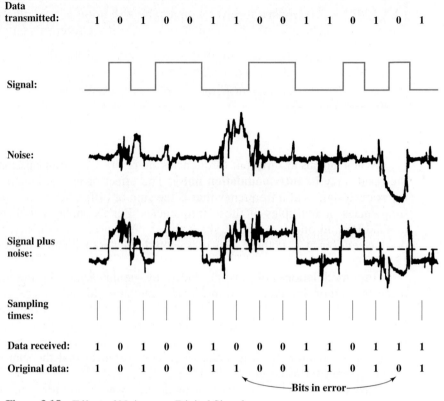

Figure 3.15 Effect of Noise on a Digital Signal

3.4 CHANNEL CAPACITY

We have seen that there are a variety of impairments that distort or corrupt a signal. For digital data, the question that then arises is to what extent these impairments limit the data rate that can be achieved. The maximum rate at which data can be transmitted over a given communication path, or channel, under given conditions, is referred to as the **channel capacity**.

There are four concepts here that we are trying to relate to one another.

- **Data rate:** The rate, in bits per second (bps), at which data can be communicated
- **Bandwidth:** The bandwidth of the transmitted signal as constrained by the transmitter and the nature of the transmission medium, expressed in cycles per second, or hertz
- **Noise:** The average level of noise over the communications path
- **Error rate:** The rate at which errors occur, where an error is the reception of a 1 when a 0 was transmitted or the reception of a 0 when a 1 was transmitted

The problem we are addressing is this: Communications facilities are expensive, and, in general, the greater the bandwidth of a facility, the greater the cost.

Furthermore, all transmission channels of any practical interest are of limited bandwidth. The limitations arise from the physical properties of the transmission medium or from deliberate limitations at the transmitter on the bandwidth to prevent interference from other sources. Accordingly, we would like to make as efficient use as possible of a given bandwidth. For digital data, this means that we would like to get as high a data rate as possible at a particular limit of error rate for a given bandwidth. The main constraint on achieving this efficiency is noise.

Nyquist Bandwidth

To begin, let us consider the case of a channel that is noise free. In this environment, the limitation on data rate is simply the bandwidth of the signal. A formulation of this limitation, due to **Nyquist**, states that if the rate of signal transmission is $2B$, then a signal with frequencies no greater than B is sufficient to carry the signal rate. The converse is also true: Given a bandwidth of B, the highest signal rate that can be carried is $2B$. This limitation is due to the effect of intersymbol interference, such as is produced by delay distortion. The result is useful in the development of digital-to-analog encoding schemes and is, in essence, based on the same derivation as that of the sampling theorem, described in Appendix G.

Note that in the preceding paragraph, we referred to signal rate. If the signals to be transmitted are binary (two voltage levels), then the data rate that can be supported by B Hz is $2B$ bps. However, as we shall see in Chapter 5, signals with more than two levels can be used; that is, each signal element can represent more than 1 bit. For example, if four possible voltage levels are used as signals, then each signal element can represent 2 bits. With multilevel signaling, the Nyquist formulation becomes

$$C = 2B \log_2 M$$

where M is the number of discrete signal or voltage levels.

So, for a given bandwidth, the data rate can be increased by increasing the number of different signal elements. However, this places an increased burden on the receiver: Instead of distinguishing one of two possible signal elements during each signal time, it must distinguish one of M possible signal elements. Noise and other impairments on the transmission line will limit the practical value of M.

EXAMPLE 3.5 Consider a voice channel being used, via modem, to transmit digital data. Assume a bandwidth of 3100 Hz. Then the Nyquist capacity, C, of the channel is $2B = 6200$ bps. For $M = 8$, a value used with some modems, C becomes 18,600 bps for a bandwidth of 3100 Hz.

Shannon Capacity Formula

Nyquist's formula indicates that, all other things being equal, doubling the bandwidth doubles the data rate. Now consider the relationship among data rate, noise, and error rate. The presence of noise can corrupt 1 or more bits. If the data rate is increased, then the bits become "shorter" so that more bits are affected by a given pattern of noise.

Figure 3.15 illustrates this relationship. If the data rate is increased, then more bits will occur during the interval of a noise spike, and hence more errors will occur.

All of these concepts can be tied together neatly in a formula developed by the mathematician Claude Shannon [SHAN48]. As we have just illustrated, the higher the data rate, the more damage that unwanted noise can do. For a given level of noise, we would expect that a greater signal strength would improve the ability to receive data correctly in the presence of noise. The key parameter involved in this reasoning is the **signal-to-noise ratio** (SNR, or S/N),[12] which is the ratio of the power in a signal to the power contained in the noise that is present at a particular point in the transmission. Typically, this ratio is measured at a receiver, because it is at this point that an attempt is made to process the signal and recover the data. For convenience, this ratio is often reported in decibels:

$$\text{SNR}_{\text{dB}} = 10\log_{10}\frac{\text{signal power}}{\text{noise power}}$$

This expresses the amount, in decibels, that the intended signal exceeds the noise level. A high SNR will mean a high-quality signal and a low number of required intermediate repeaters.

The signal-to-noise ratio is important in the transmission of digital data because it sets the upper bound on the achievable data rate. Shannon's result is that the maximum channel capacity, in bits per second, obeys the equation

$$C = B\log_2\left(1 + \text{SNR}\right) \tag{3.1}$$

where C is the capacity of the channel in bits per second and B is the bandwidth of the channel in hertz.[13] The Shannon formula represents the theoretical maximum that can be achieved. In practice, however, only much lower rates are achieved. One reason for this is that the formula assumes white noise (thermal noise). Impulse noise is not accounted for, nor are attenuation distortion and delay distortion. Even in an ideal white noise environment, present technology still cannot achieve Shannon capacity due to encoding issues, such as coding length and complexity.

The capacity indicated in the preceding equation is referred to as the **error-free capacity**. Shannon proved that if the actual information rate on a channel is less than the error-free capacity, then it is theoretically possible to use a suitable signal code to achieve error-free transmission through the channel. Shannon's theorem unfortunately does not suggest a means for finding such codes, but it does provide a yardstick by which the performance of practical communication schemes may be measured.

---

[12]Some of the literature uses SNR; others use S/N. Also, in some cases the dimensionless quantity is referred to as SNR or S/N and the quantity in decibels is referred to as SNR_{dB} or $(\text{S/N})_{\text{dB}}$. Others use just SNR or S/N to mean the dB quantity. This text uses SNR and SNR_{dB}.

[13]An intuitive proof of Shannon's equation is contained in a document at box.com/dcc10e.

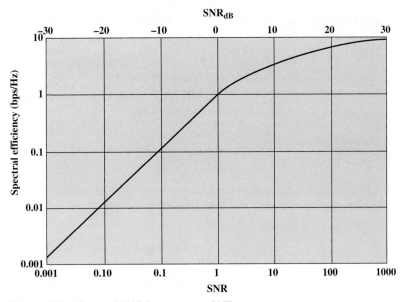

Figure 3.16   Spectral Efficiency versus SNR

We define the **spectral efficiency**, also called **bandwidth efficiency**, of a digital transmission as the number of bits per second of data that can be supported by each hertz of bandwidth. The theoretical maximum spectral efficiency can be expressed using Equation (3.1) by moving the bandwidth B to the left-hand side, resulting in $C/B = \log_2(1 + \text{SNR})$. C/B has the dimensions bps/Hz. Figure 3.16 shows the results on a log/log scale. At SNR = 1, we have $C/B = 1$. For SNR < 1 (signal power is less than noise power), the plot is linear; above SNR = 1, the plot flattens but continues to increase with increasing SNR.

We can make several observations about Figure 3.16. Below 0 dB SNR, noise is the dominant factor in the capacity of a channel. Shannon's theorem shows that communications is possible in this region, but at a relatively low data rate, a rate that is reduced in proportion to the SNR (on a log/log scale). In the region of at least 6 dB above 0 dB SNR, noise is no longer the limiting factor in communications speed. In this region, there is little ambiguity in a signal's relative amplitude and phase, and achieving a high-channel capacity depends on the design of the signal, including such factors as modulation type and coding.

Several other observations concerning the preceding equation may be instructive. For a given level of noise, it would appear that the data rate could be increased by increasing either signal strength or bandwidth. However, as the signal strength increases, the effects of nonlinearities in the system also increase, leading to an increase in intermodulation noise. Note also that, because noise is assumed to be white, the wider the bandwidth, the more noise is admitted to the system. Thus, as B increases, SNR decreases.

EXAMPLE 3.6 Let us consider an example that relates the Nyquist and Shannon formulations. Suppose that the spectrum of a channel is between 3 MHz and 4 MHz and $SNR_{dB} = 24$ dB. Then

$$B = 4\ \text{MH}_Z - 3\ \text{MH}_Z = 1\ \text{MH}_Z$$
$$SNR_{dB} = 24\,dB = 10\log_{10}(SNR)$$
$$SNR = 251$$

Using Shannon's formula,

$$C = 10^6 \times \log_2(1 + 251) \approx 10^6 \times 8 = 8\ \text{Mbps}$$

This is a theoretical limit and, as we have said, is unlikely to be reached. But assume we can achieve the limit. Based on Nyquist's formula, how many signaling levels are required? We have

$$C = 2B\log_2 M$$
$$8 \times 10^6 = 2 \times (10^6) \times \log_2 M$$
$$4 = \log_2 M$$
$$M = 16$$

The Expression E_b/N_0

Finally, we mention a parameter related to SNR that is more convenient for determining digital data rates and error rates and that is the standard quality measure for digital communication system performance. The parameter is the ratio of signal energy per bit to noise power density per hertz, E_b/N_0. Consider a signal, digital or analog, that contains binary digital data transmitted at a certain bit rate R. Recalling that 1 watt = 1 J/s, the energy per bit in a signal is given by $E_b = ST_b$, where S is the signal power and T_b is the time required to send 1 bit. The data rate R is just $R = 1/T_b$. Thus

$$\frac{E_b}{N_0} = \frac{S/R}{N_0} = \frac{S}{kTR}$$

or, in decibel notation,

$$\left(\frac{E_b}{N_0}\right)_{dB} = S_{dBW} - 10\log R - 10\log k - 10\log T$$
$$= S_{dBW} - 10\log R + 228.6\ dBW - 10\log T$$

The ratio E_b/N_0 is important because the bit error rate for digital data is a (decreasing) function of this ratio. Given a value of E_b/N_0 needed to achieve a desired error rate, the parameters in the preceding formula may be selected. Note that as the bit rate R increases, the transmitted signal power, relative to noise, must increase to maintain the required E_b/N_0.

Let us try to grasp this result intuitively by considering again Figure 3.15. The signal here is digital, but the reasoning would be the same for an analog signal. In several instances, the noise is sufficient to alter the value of a bit. If the data rate were doubled, the bits would be more tightly packed together, and the same passage of noise might destroy 2 bits. Thus, for constant signal-to-noise ratio, an increase in data rate increases the error rate.

The advantage of E_b/N_0 over SNR is that the latter quantity depends on the bandwidth.

EXAMPLE 3.7 For binary phase-shift keying (defined in Chapter 5), $E_b/N_0 = 8.4\,\text{dB}$ is required for a bit error rate of 10^{-4} (1 bit error out of every 10,000). If the effective noise temperature is 290 K (room temperature) and the data rate is 2400 bps, what received signal level is required?

We have

$$8.4 = S(\text{dBW}) - 10 \log 2400 + 228.6\,\text{dBW} - 10 \log 290$$
$$= S(\text{dBW}) - (10)(3.38) + 228.6 - (10)(2.46)$$
$$S = -161.8\ \text{dBW}$$

We can relate E_b/N_0 to SNR as follows. We have

$$\frac{E_b}{N_0} = \frac{S}{N_0 R}$$

The parameter N_0 is the noise power density in watts/hertz. Hence, the noise in a signal with bandwidth B is $N = N_0 B$. Substituting, we have

$$\frac{E_b}{N_0} = \frac{S}{N}\frac{B}{R} \tag{3.2}$$

Another equation of interest relates Eb/N_0 to spectral efficiency. Shannon's result (Equation 3.1) can be rewritten as:

$$\frac{S}{N} = 2^{C/B} - 1$$

Using Equation (3.2), and equating R with C, we have

$$\frac{E_b}{N_0} = \frac{B}{C}\left(2^{C/B} - 1\right)$$

This is a useful formula that relates the achievable spectral efficiency C/B to E_b/N_0.

EXAMPLE 3.8 Suppose we want to find the minimum Eb/N_0 required to achieve a spectral efficiency of 6 bps/Hz. Then $E_b/N_0 = (1/6)(2^6 - 1) = 10.5 = 10.21\,\text{dB}$.

3.5 RECOMMENDED READING

There are many books that cover the fundamentals of analog and digital transmission. [COUC13] is quite thorough. Other good reference works are [FREE05], which includes some of the examples used in this chapter, and [HAYK09].

COUC13 Couch, L. *Digital and Analog Communication Systems.* Upper Saddle River, NJ: Pearson, 2013.

FREE05 Freeman, R. *Fundamentals of Telecommunications.* New York: Wiley, 2005.

HAYK09 Haykin, S. *Communication Systems.* New York: Wiley, 2009.

3.6 KEY TERMS, REVIEW QUESTIONS, AND PROBLEMS

Key Terms

absolute bandwidth	digital transmission	period
analog data	direct link	periodic signal
analog signal	discrete	point-to-point link
analog transmission	effective bandwidth	phase
aperiodic	error-free capacity	signal
asynchronous transmission	frame	signal-to-noise ratio (SNR)
attenuation	frequency	signaling
attenuation distortion	frequency domain	simplex
audio	full duplex	sinusoid
bandwidth	fundamental frequency	spectral efficiency
bandwidth efficiency	gain	spectrum
binary data	guided media	synchronous transmission
center frequency	half duplex	text
channel capacity	harmonic frequency	thermal noise
continuous	impulse noise	time domain
crosstalk	intermodulation noise	transmission
data	intersymbol interference	unguided media
dc component	loss	video
decibel (dB)	multipoint link	wavelength
delay distortion	noise	white noise
digital data	Nyquist bandwidth	wireless
digital signal	peak amplitude	

Review Questions

3.1. Differentiate between guided media and unguided media.

3.2. Differentiate between an analog and a digital electromagnetic signal.

3.3. What are three important characteristics of a periodic signal?

3.4. How many radians are there in a complete circle of 360 degrees?
3.5. What is the relationship between the wavelength and frequency of a sine wave?
3.6. Define *fundamental frequency*.
3.7. What is the relationship between a signal's spectrum and its bandwidth?
3.8. What is attenuation?
3.9. Define *channel capacity*.
3.10. What key factors affect channel capacity?

Problems

3.1. **a.** For multipoint configuration, only one device at a time can transmit. Why?
  b. There are two methods of enforcing the rule that only one device can transmit. In the centralized method, one station is in control and can either transmit or allow a specified other station to transmit. In the decentralized method, the stations jointly cooperate in taking turns. What do you see as the advantages and disadvantages of the two methods?

3.2. The period of a signal is 10^6 ms. What is its frequency in megahertz?

3.3. A sine wave is shifted left by a 1/8 cycle at time 0.
  a. Express its phase shift in degrees.
  b. Express its phase shift in radians.

3.4. Sound may be modeled as sinusoidal functions. Compare the relative frequency and wavelength of musical notes. Use 330 m/s as the speed of sound and the following frequencies for the musical scale.

Note	C	D	E	F	G	A	B	C
Frequency	264	297	330	352	396	440	495	528

3.5. If the solid curve in Figure 3.17 represents $\sin(2\pi t)$, what does the dotted curve represent? That is, the dotted curve can be written in the form $A \sin(2\pi ft + \phi)$; what are A, f, and ϕ?

3.6. Decompose the signal $(1 + 0.1 \cos 5t) \cos 100t$ into a linear combination of sinusoidal functions, and find the amplitude, frequency, and phase of each component. *Hint:* Use the identity for $\cos a \cos b$.

3.7. Find the wavelength of a 600-THz green light ray in air.

3.8. Consider two periodic functions $f_1(t)$ and $f_2(t)$, with periods T_1 and T_2, respectively. Is it always the case that the function $f(t) = f_1(t) + f_2(t)$ is periodic? If so, demonstrate this fact. If not, under what conditions is $f(t)$ periodic?

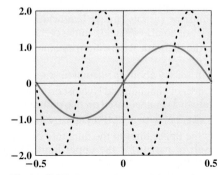

Figure 3.17 Figure for Problem 3.5

3.9. Figure 3.4 shows the effect of eliminating higher-harmonic components of a square wave and retaining only a few lower harmonic components. What would the signal look like in the opposite case—that is, retaining all higher harmonics and eliminating a few lower harmonics?

3.10. Figure 3.5b shows the frequency domain function for a single square pulse. The single pulse could represent a digital 1 in a communication system. Note that an infinite number of higher frequencies of decreasing magnitudes is needed to represent the single pulse. What implication does that have for a real digital transmission system?

3.11. IRA is a 7-bit code that allows 128 characters to be defined. In the 1970s, many newspapers received stories from the wire services in a 6-bit code called TTS. This code carried upper- and lower case characters as well as many special characters and formatting commands. The typical TTS character set allowed over 100 characters to be defined. How do you think this could be accomplished?

3.12. Commonly, medical digital radiology ultrasound studies consist of about 25 images extracted from a full-motion ultrasound examination. Each image consists of 512 by 512 pixels, each with 8 b of intensity information.
   a. How many bits are there in the 25 images?
   b. Ideally, however, doctors would like to use 512×512 8-bit frames at 30 fps (frames per second). Ignoring possible compression and overhead factors, what is the minimum channel capacity required to sustain this full-motion ultrasound?
   c. Suppose each full-motion study consists of 25 s of frames. How many bytes of storage would be needed to store a single study in uncompressed form?

3.13. a. Suppose that a digitized TV picture is to be transmitted from a source that uses a matrix of 480×500 picture elements (pixels), where each pixel can take on one of 32 intensity values. Assume that 30 pictures are sent per second. (This digital source is roughly equivalent to broadcast TV standards that have been adopted.) Find the source rate R (bps).
   b. Assume that the TV picture is to be transmitted over a channel with 4.5-MHz bandwidth and a 35-dB signal-to-noise ratio. Find the capacity of the channel (bps).
   c. Discuss how the parameters given in part (a) could be modified to allow transmission of color TV signals without increasing the required value for R.

3.14. Compare the white noise density levels in closed rooms in London and Sydney in January, with average temperatures of 5°C and 24°C respectively.

3.15. A telephone line has a bandwidth of 2800 Hz and its signal-to-noise ratio has been computed as 3000. Compute the highest bit rate of this line.

3.16. Data needs to be sent over a noiseless channel of 30-kHz bandwidth.
   a. Find the number of signal levels M needed if the bit rate desired is approximately 400 kbps.
   b. What maximum bit rate will you get with M signal levels found in part (a)?

3.17. In a communication channel, the power of a signal is 75 mW and the power of noise is 50 µW. What are the values of SNR and SNR_{dB}?

3.18. Given the narrow (usable) audio bandwidth of a telephone transmission facility, a nominal SNR of 56 dB (400,000), and a certain level of distortion
   a. What is the theoretical maximum channel capacity (kbps) of traditional telephone lines?
   b. What can we say about the actual maximum channel capacity?

3.19. Study the works of Shannon and Nyquist on channel capacity. Each places an upper limit on the bit rate of a channel based on two different approaches. How are the two related?

3.20. Consider a channel with a 1 MHz capacity and an SNR of 63.
   a. What is the upper limit to the data rate that the channel can carry?
   b. The result of part (a) is the upper limit. However, as a practical matter, better error performance will be achieved at a lower data rate. Assume we choose a data rate of 2/3 as the maximum theoretical limit. How many signal levels are needed to achieve this data rate?

BEER & CIDER FESTIVAL

28th Feb & 1st March

Live Rugby 6 Nations

Ireland v England Sunday 3pm

Open 12 Noon

Wolverhampton Rugby Club WV3 8NA

FREE ENTRY

www.pitchero.com/wolverhampton

3.21. A channel can transmit signals in the frequency range of 2500 kHz to 4000 kHz. Compute its bandwidth. Assuming $SNR_{dB} = 40$, what will be the theoretical maximum capacity of this channel?

3.22. The square wave of Figure 3.7c, with $T = 1$ ms, is passed through a lowpass filter that passes frequencies up to 8 kHz with no attenuation.
   a. Find the power in the output waveform.
   b. Assuming that at the filter input there is a thermal noise voltage with $N_0 = 0.1 \, \mu W/Hz$, find the output signal-to-noise ratio in dB.

3.23. A 6-km-long cable has an attenuation of –0.25 dB/km. A signal with a power of 2.84 mW has been received at the end of the cable. Find out the power at which the signal was transmitted from the source.

3.24. In a 1939 letter to Vannevar Bush, Claude Shannon said he was working on a theorem, which states that for any transmitter and receiver the length of an arbitrary message multiplied by its essential spectrum and divided by the distortion of the system is less than a certain constant times the time of transmission of the message multiplied by its essential spectrum width or, roughly speaking, it is impossible to reduce bandwidth times transmission time for a given distortion. Relate the theorem to Equation (3.1).

3.25. Fill in the missing elements in the following table of approximate power ratios for various dB levels.

Decibels	1	2	3	4	5	6	7	8	9	10
Losses			0.5							0.1
Gains			2							10

3.26. Find the minimum E_b/N_0 required to achieve a spectral efficiency of 10 bps/Hz.

3.27. An amplifier has an input of 5 W and a voltage gain of 20 dBW. Find its output in dBW.

APPENDIX 3A   DECIBELS AND SIGNAL STRENGTH

An important parameter in any transmission system is the signal strength. As a signal propagates along a transmission medium, there will be a loss, or *attenuation*, of signal strength. To compensate, amplifiers may be inserted at various points to impart a gain in signal strength.

It is customary to express gains, losses, and relative levels in decibels because

- Signal strength often falls off exponentially, so loss is easily expressed in terms of the decibel, which is a logarithmic unit.

- The net gain or loss in a cascaded transmission path can be calculated with simple addition and subtraction.

The decibel is a measure of the ratio between two signal levels. The decibel gain is given by:

$$G_{dB} = 10 \log_{10} \frac{P_{out}}{P_{in}}$$

where

$$G_{dB} = \text{gain, in decibels}$$
$$P_{in} = \text{input power level}$$
$$P_{out} = \text{output power level}$$
$$\log_{10} = \text{logarithm to the base 10}$$

Table 3.2 Decibel Values

Power Ratio	dB	Power Ratio	dB
1	0	0.5	−3.01
2	3.01	10^{-1}	−10
10^1	10	10^{-2}	−20
10^2	20	10^{-3}	−30
10^3	30	10^{-4}	−40
10^4	40	10^{-5}	−50
10^5	50	10^{-6}	−60

Table 3.2 shows the relationship between decibel values and powers of 10. The table also includes the decibel values for 2 and 1/2.

There is some inconsistency in the literature over the use of the terms **gain** and **loss.** If the value of G_{dB} is positive, this represents an actual gain in power. For example, a gain of 3 dB means that the power has approximately doubled. If the value of G_{dB} is negative, this represents an actual loss in power. For example, a gain of −3 dB means that the power has approximately halved, and this is a loss of power. Normally, this is expressed by saying there is a loss of 3 dB. However, some of the literature would say that this is a loss of −3 dB. It makes more sense to say that a negative gain corresponds to a positive loss. Therefore, we define a decibel loss as:

$$L_{dB} = -10\log_{10}\frac{P_{out}}{P_{in}} = 10\log_{10}\frac{P_{in}}{P_{out}} \quad (3.3)$$

EXAMPLE 3.9 If a signal with a power level of 10 mW is inserted onto a transmission line and the measured power some distance away is 5 mW, the loss can be expressed as

$$L_{dB} = 10\log(10/5) = 10(0.301) = 3.01\,dB.$$

Note that the decibel is a measure of relative, not absolute, difference. A loss from 1000 mW to 500 mW is also a loss of approximately 3 dB.

The decibel is also used to measure the difference in voltage, taking into account that power is proportional to the square of the voltage:

$$P = \frac{V^2}{R}$$

where

$$P = \text{power dissipated across resistance } R$$
$$V = \text{voltage across resistance } R$$

Thus,

$$L_{dB} = 10\log\frac{P_{in}}{P_{out}} = 10\log\frac{V_{in}^2/R}{V_{out}^2/R} = 20\log\frac{V_{in}}{V_{out}}$$

EXAMPLE 3.10 Decibels are useful in determining the gain or loss over a series of transmission elements. Consider a series in which the input is at a power level of 4 mW, the first element is a transmission line with a 12-dB loss (−12-dB gain), the second element is an amplifier with a 35-dB gain, and the third element is a transmission line with a 10-dB loss. The net gain is (−12 + 35 − 10) = 13 dB. To calculate the output power P_{out}:

$$G_{dB} = 13 = 10 \log (P_{out}/4 \text{ mW})$$
$$P_{out} = 4 \times 10^{1.3} \text{ mW} = 79.8 \text{ mW}$$

Decibel values refer to relative magnitudes or changes in magnitude, not to an absolute level. It is convenient to be able to refer to an absolute level of power or voltage in decibels so that gains and losses with reference to an initial signal level may be calculated easily. The **dBW (decibel-watt)** is used extensively in microwave applications. The value of 1 W is selected as a reference and defined to be 0 dBW. The absolute decibel level of power in dBW is defined as:

$$\text{Power}_{dBW} = 10 \log \frac{\text{Power}_W}{1 \text{ W}}$$

EXAMPLE 3.11 A power of 1000 W is 30 dBW, and a power of 1 mW is −30 dBW.

Another common unit is the **dBm (decibel-milliwatt)**, which uses 1 mW as the reference. Thus 0 dBm = 1 mW. The formula is:

$$\text{Power}_{dBm} = 10 \log \frac{\text{Power}_{mW}}{1 \text{ mW}}$$

Note the following relationships:

$$+30 \text{ dBm} = 0 \text{ dBW}$$
$$0 \text{ dBm} = -30 \text{ dBW}$$

A unit in common use in cable television and broadband LAN applications is the **dBmV (decibel-millivolt)**. This is an absolute unit with 0 dBmV equivalent to 1 mV. Thus,

$$\text{Voltage}_{dBmV} = 20 \log \frac{\text{Voltage}_{mV}}{1 \text{ mV}}$$

In this case, the voltage levels are assumed to be across a 75-Ω resistance.

CHAPTER 4

TRANSMISSION MEDIA

In a data transmission system, the **transmission medium** is the physical path between transmitter and receiver. Recall from Chapter 3 that for **guided media**, electromagnetic waves are guided along a solid medium, such as copper twisted pair, copper coaxial cable, and optical fiber. For **unguided media**, wireless transmission occurs through the atmosphere, outer space, or water.

The characteristics and quality of a data transmission are determined both by the characteristics of the medium and by the characteristics of the signal. In the case of guided media, the medium itself is more important in determining the limitations of transmission.

For unguided media, the bandwidth of the signal produced by the transmitting antenna is more important than the medium in determining transmission characteristics. One key property of signals transmitted by antenna is directionality. In general, signals at lower frequencies are omnidirectional; that is, the signal propagates in all directions from the antenna. At higher frequencies, it is possible to focus the signal into a directional beam.

Data rate and distance are the key considerations in data transmission system design, with emphasis placed on achieving the highest data rates over the longest distances. A number of design factors relating to the transmission medium and the signal determine the data rate and distance:

- **Bandwidth:** All other factors remaining constant, the greater the bandwidth of a signal, the higher the data rate that can be achieved.
- **Transmission impairments:** Impairments, such as attenuation, limit the distance. For guided media, twisted pair generally suffers more impairment than coaxial cable, which in turn suffers more than optical fiber.

- **Interference:** Interference from competing signals in overlapping frequency bands can distort or cancel out a signal. Interference is of particular concern for unguided media, but is also a problem with guided media. For guided media, interference can be caused by emanations from nearby cables (alien crosstalk) or adjacent conductors under the same cable sheath (internal crosstalk). For example, twisted pairs are often bundled together and conduits often carry multiple cables. Interference can also be caused by electromagnetic coupling from unguided transmissions. Proper shielding of a guided medium can minimize this problem.

- **Number of receivers:** A guided medium can be used to construct a point-to-point link or a shared link with multiple attachments. In the latter case, each attachment introduces some attenuation and distortion on the line, limiting distance and/or data rate.

Figure 4.1 depicts the electromagnetic spectrum and indicates the frequencies at which various guided media and unguided transmission techniques operate. In this chapter, we examine these guided and unguided alternatives. In all cases, we describe the systems physically, briefly discuss applications, and summarize key transmission characteristics.

4.1 GUIDED TRANSMISSION MEDIA

For guided transmission media, the transmission capacity, in terms of either data rate or bandwidth, depends critically on the distance and on whether the medium is point-to-point or multipoint. Table 4.1 indicates the characteristics typical for the common guided media for long-distance point-to-point applications; we defer a discussion of the use of these media for local area networks (LANs) to Part Four.

The three guided media commonly used for data transmission are twisted pair, coaxial cable, and optical fiber (Figure 4.2). We examine each of these in turn.

Twisted Pair

The least expensive and most widely used guided transmission medium is twisted pair.

PHYSICAL DESCRIPTION   A twisted pair consists of two insulated copper wires arranged in a regular spiral pattern. A wire pair acts as a single communication link. Typically, a number of these pairs are bundled together into a cable by wrapping them in a tough protective sheath, or jacket. Over longer distances, cables may contain hundreds of pairs. The twisting tends to decrease the crosstalk interference between adjacent pairs in a cable. Neighboring pairs in a bundle typically have somewhat different twist lengths to reduce the crosstalk interference. On long-distance links, the twist length typically varies from 5 to 15 cm. The wires in a pair have thicknesses of from 0.4 to 0.9 mm.

APPLICATIONS   By far the most common guided transmission medium for both analog and digital signals is twisted pair. It is the most commonly used medium in the telephone network and is the workhorse for communications within buildings.

Frequency
(Hertz)

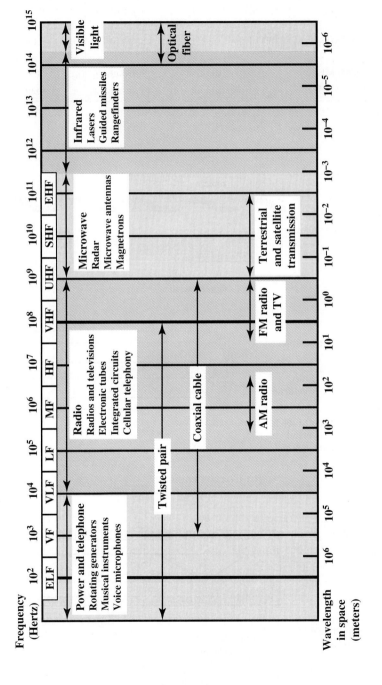

ELF = Extremely low frequency   MF = Medium frequency   UHF = Ultrahigh frequency
VF = Voice frequency   HF = High frequency   SHF = Superhigh frequency
VLF = Very low frequency   VHF = Very high frequency   EHF = Extremely high frequency
LF = Low frequency

Figure 4.1 Electromagnetic Spectrum for Telecommunications

137

Table 4.1   Point-to-Point Transmission Characteristics of Guided Media

	Frequency Range	**Typical Attenuation**	**Typical Delay**	**Repeater Spacing**
Twisted pair (with loading)	0 to 3.5 kHz	0.2 dB/km @ 1 kHz	50 μs/km	2 km
Twisted pairs (multipair cables)	0 to 1 MHz	0.7 dB/km @ 1 kHz	5 μs/km	2 km
Coaxial cable	0 to 500 MHz	7 dB/km @ 10 MHz	4 μs/km	1 to 9 km
Optical fiber	186 to 370 THz	0.2 to 0.5 dB/km	5 μs/km	40 km

THz = terahertz = 10^{12} Hz

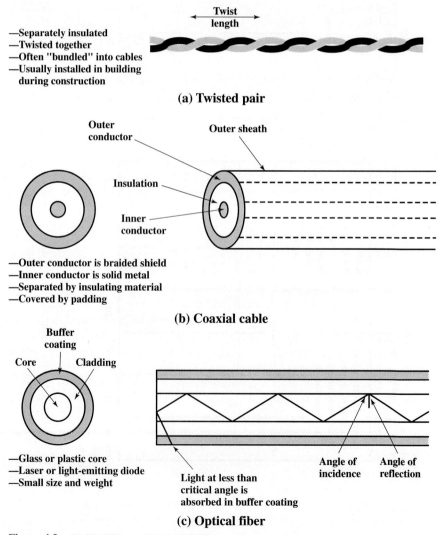

—Separately insulated
—Twisted together
—Often "bundled" into cables
—Usually installed in building
  during construction

(a) Twisted pair

—Outer conductor is braided shield
—Inner conductor is solid metal
—Separated by insulating material
—Covered by padding

(b) Coaxial cable

—Glass or plastic core
—Laser or light-emitting diode
—Small size and weight

(c) Optical fiber

Figure 4.2   Guided Transmission Media

In the telephone system, individual residential telephone sets are connected to the local telephone exchange, or "end office," by twisted-pair wire. These are referred to as **subscriber loops**. Within an office building, each telephone is also connected to a twisted pair, which goes to the in-house private branch exchange (PBX) system or to a Centrex facility at the end office. These twisted-pair installations were designed to support voice traffic using analog signaling. However, by means of a modem, these facilities can handle digital data traffic at modest data rates.

Twisted pair is also the most common medium used for digital signaling. For connections to a digital data switch or digital PBX within a building, a data rate of 64 kbps is common. Ethernet operating over twisted-pair cabling is commonly used within a building for LANs supporting personal computers. Data rates for Ethernet products are typically in the neighborhood of 100 Mbps to 1 Gbps. Emerging twisted-pair cabling Ethernet technology can support data rates of 10 Gbps. For long-distance applications, twisted pair can be used at data rates of 4 Mbps or more.

Twisted pair is much less expensive than the other commonly used guided transmission media (coaxial cable, optical fiber) and is easier to work with.

TRANSMISSION CHARACTERISTICS   Twisted pair may be used to transmit both analog and digital transmission. For analog signals, amplifiers are required for about every 5 to 6 km. For digital transmission (using either analog or digital signals), repeaters are required every 2 or 3 km.

Compared to other commonly used guided transmission media, twisted pair is limited in distance, bandwidth, and data rate. As Figure 4.3a shows, the attenuation for twisted pair is a very strong function of frequency. Twisted-pair cabling is also susceptible to signal reflections, or return loss, caused by impedance mismatches along the length of the transmission line and crosstalk from adjacent twisted-pairs or twisted-pair cables. Due to the well-controlled geometry of the twisted pair itself (pairs are manufactured with a unique and precise twist rate that varies from pair to pair within a cable) and the media's differential mode transmission scheme (discussed in Chapter 5), twisted-pair cabling used for data transmission is highly immune to interference from low frequency (i.e., 60 Hz) disturbers. Note that twisted-pair cabling is usually run separately from cables transmitting ac power in order to comply with local safety codes, which protect low-voltage telecommunications installers from high-voltage applications. The possibility of electromagnetic interference from high frequency (i.e., greater than 30 MHz) disturbers such as walkie-talkies and other wireless transmitters can be alleviated by using shielded twisted-pair cabling.

For point-to-point analog signaling, a bandwidth of up to about 1 MHz is possible. This accommodates a number of voice channels. For long-distance digital point-to-point signaling, data rates of up to a few Mbps are possible. Ethernet data rates of up to 10 Gbps can be achieved over 100 m of twisted-pair cabling.

UNSHIELDED AND SHIELDED TWISTED PAIR   Twisted pair comes in two varieties: unshielded and shielded. As the name implies, **unshielded twisted pair (UTP)** consists of one or more twisted-pair cables, typically enclosed within an overall thermoplastic jacket, which provides no electromagnetic shielding. The most common form of UTP is ordinary voice-grade telephone wire, which is pre-wired in residential and office buildings. For data transmission purposes, UTP may vary

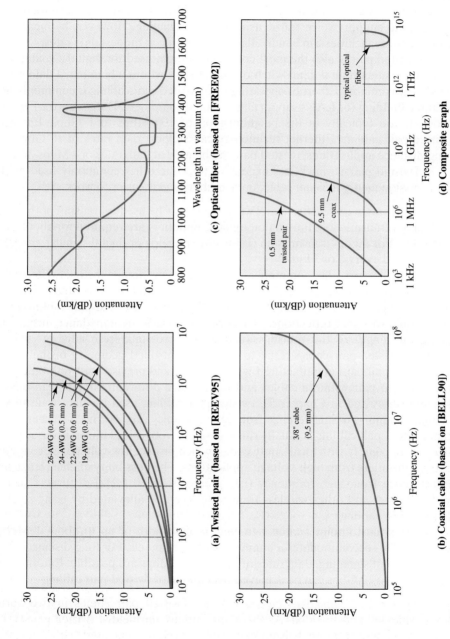

Figure 4.3 Attenuation of Typical Guided Media

from voice-grade to very high-speed cable for LANs. For high-speed LANs, UTP typically has four pairs of wires inside the jacket, with each pair twisted with a different number of twists per centimeter to help eliminate interference between adjacent pairs. The tighter the twisting, the higher the supported transmission rate, and the greater the cost per meter.

Unshielded twisted pair is subject to external electromagnetic interference, including interference from nearby twisted pair and from noise generated in the environment. In an environment with a number of sources of potential interference (e.g., electric motors, wireless devices, and RF transmitters), **shielded twisted pair (STP)** may be a preferred solution. Shielded twisted pair cable is manufactured in three different configurations:

1. Each pair of wires is individually shielded with metallic foil, generally referred to as foil twisted pair (FTP).

2. There is a foil or braid shield inside the jacket covering all wires (as a group). This configuration is sometimes designated as screened twisted pair (F/UTP).

3. There is a shield around each individual pair, as well as around the entire group of wires. This is referred to as fully shielded twisted pair or shielded/foil twisted pair (S/FTP).

The shielding reduces interference and provides better performance at higher data rates. However, it may be more expensive and installers familiar with UTP technology may be reluctant to work with a new media type.

Categories of Twisted Pair for Data Transmission In 1991, the Electronic Industries Association published standard ANSI/EIA/TIA-568, *Commercial Building Telecommunications Cabling Standard*, which specifies the use of voice- and data-grade UTP and F/UTP cabling for in-building data applications. At that time, the specification was felt to be adequate for the range of frequencies and data rates found in office environments. With continuing advances in cable and connector design and test methods, this standard has undergone a number of iterations to provide support for higher data rates using higher-quality cable and connectors. The current version is the responsibility of the Telecommunications Industry Association, and was issued in 2009 as four American National Standards Institute (ANSI) standards:

- **ANSI/TIA-568-C.0 Generic Telecommunications Cabling for Customer Premises:** Enables the planning and installation of a structured cabling system for all types of customer premises.

- **ANSI/TIA-568-C.1 Commercial Building Telecommunications Cabling Standard:** Enables the planning and installation of a structured cabling system for commercial buildings.

- **ANSI/TIA-568-C.2 Balanced Twisted-Pair Telecommunications Cabling and Components Standards:** Specifies minimum requirements for balanced twisted-pair telecommunications cabling (e.g., channels and permanent links) and components (e.g., cable, connectors, connecting hardware, patch cords, equipment cords, work area cords, and jumpers) that are used up to and including the telecommunications outlet/connector and between buildings in a campus environment. This standard also specifies field test procedures and applicable laboratory reference measurement procedures for all transmission parameters.

- **ANSI/TIA-568-C.3 Optical Fiber Cabling Components Standard:** Specifies cable and component transmission performance requirements for premises optical fiber cabling.

The 568-C standards identify a number of categories of cabling and associated components that can be used for premises and campus-wide data distribution. An overlapping standard, jointly issued by the International Standards Organization and the International Electrotechnical Commission (IEC), known as ISO/IEC 11801, second edition, identifies a number of classes of cabling and associated components, which correspond to the 568-C categories.

Table 4.2 summarizes key characteristics of the various categories and classes recognized in the current standards. The categories listed in the table are the following:

- **Category 5e/Class D:** This specification was first published in 2000 in order to address the transmission performance characterization required by applications such as 1-Gbps Ethernet that utilize bidirectional and full four-pair transmission schemes (described in Chapter 12).

- **Category 6/Class E:** In recent years, the majority of structured cabling specified for new buildings has been category 6/class E. This category provides a greater performance margin (also called performance headroom) than category 5e to ensure that the cabling plant could withstand the rigors of the cabling environment and still support 1-Gbps Ethernet when it was time for an application upgrade from 100-Mbps Ethernet. This category was published in 2002, with a targeted lifetime of 10 years, so its use is likely to decline rapidly in new installations.

- **Category 6A/Class E_A:** This specification is targeted at 10-Gbps Ethernet applications.

Table 4.2   Twisted Pair Categories and Classes

	Category 5e Class D	Category 6 Class E	Category 6A Class E_A	Category 7 Class F	Category 7_A Class F_A
Bandwidth	100 MHz	250 MHz	500 MHz	600 MHz	1,000 MHz
Cable type	UTP	UTP/FTP	UTP/FTP	S/FTP	S/FTP
Insertion loss (dB)	24	21.3	20.9	20.8	20.3
NEXT loss (dB)	30.1	39.9	39.9	62.9	65
ACR (dB)	6.1	18.6	19	42.1	44.1

UTP = Unshielded twisted pair

FTP = Foil twisted pair

S/FTP = Shielded/foil twisted pair

- **Category 7/Class F:** This specification uses fully shielded twisted pair (i.e., cabling with an overall shield and individually shielded pairs). The advantage of this category over lower grades of cabling is that the use of both an overall shield and a foil shield around individual pairs dramatically decreases internal pair-to-pair crosstalk and external alien crosstalk. This class is targeted for support of next-generation applications beyond 10-Gbps Ethernet.

- **Category 7A/Class F_A:** The requirements for this class are based on class F cabling requirements. The main enhancement is to extend the frequency bandwidth to 1 GHz. This enhancement enables support of all channels of broadband video (e.g., CATV) that operate up to 862 MHz. It is likely that all fully shielded cabling solutions specified in the near future will be class F_A.

Table 4.2 includes three key performance parameters. **Insertion loss** in this context refers to the amount of **attenuation** across the link from the transmitting system to the receiving system. Thus, lower dB values are better. The table shows the amount of attenuation at a frequency of 100 MHz. This is the standard frequency used in tables comparing various classes of twisted pair. However, attenuation is an increasing function of frequency, and the 568 standards specify the attenuation at various frequencies. In accordance with ANSI/TIA-568-C.2 and ISO/IEC 11801 second edition, all transmission characteristics are specified as a worst-case value for a 100 m length. While cabling lengths may be less than 100 m, no provisions are provided in the standards for the scaling of the specified limits. Attenuation in decibels is a linear function of distance, so attenuation for shorter or longer distances is easily calculated. In practice, as is shown in Chapter 12, distances much less than 100 m are typical for Ethernet at data rates of 1 GB and above.

Near-end crosstalk (NEXT) loss as it applies to twisted-pair wiring systems is the coupling of the signal from one pair of conductors to another pair. These conductors may be the metal pins in a connector or wire pairs in a cable. The near end refers to coupling that takes place when the transmit signal entering the link couples back to the receive conductor pair at that same end of the link (i.e., the near-end transmitted signal is picked up by the near-receive pair). We can think of this as noise introduced into the system, so higher dB loss values are better; that is, greater NEXT loss magnitudes are associated with less crosstalk noise. Figure 4.4 illustrates the relationship between NEXT loss and insertion loss at system A. A transmitted signal from system B, with a transmitted signal power of P_t is received at A with a reduced signal power of P_r. At the same time, system A is transmitting to B, and we assume that the transmission is at the same transmit signal power of P_t. Due to crosstalk, a certain level of signal from A's transmitter is induced on the receive wire pair at A with a power level of P_c; this is the crosstalk signal. Clearly, we need to have $P_r > P_c$ to be able to intelligibly receive the intended signal, and the greater the difference between P_r and P_c, the better. Unlike insertion loss, NEXT loss does not vary as a function of the length of the link, because, as Figure 4.4 indicates, NEXT loss is an end phenomenon. NEXT loss varies as a function of frequency, with losses increasing as a function of frequency. That is, the amount of signal power from the near-end transmitter that couples over to an adjacent transmission line increases as a function of frequency.

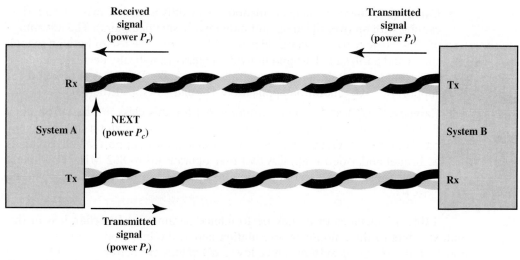

Figure 4.4   Signal Power Relationships (from System A Viewpoint)

For Table 4.2, insertion loss and NEXT loss are defined using the same form as Equation (3.3):

$$A_{dB} = 10 \log_{10} \frac{P_t}{P_r} \quad NEXT_{dB} = 10 \log_{10} \frac{P_t}{P_c}$$

Note that NEXT loss is defined in terms of the amount of signal loss between the local transmitter and the local receiver. Thus, smaller values of NEXT loss correspond to increasing amount of crosstalk.

Another important parameter used in the ISO/IEC 11801, second edition specification, is the **attenuation-to-crosstalk ratio (ACR)**, which is defined as $ACR_{dB} = NEXT_{dB} - A_{dB}$. ACR is a measure of how much larger the received signal strength is compared to the crosstalk on the same pair. A positive value is required for successful operation. To see that this is so, consider the following derivation. We want $NEXT_{dB} > A_{dB}$. This implies

$$10 \log_{10} \frac{P_t}{P_c} > 10 \log_{10} \frac{P_t}{P_r}$$

$$\log_{10} P_t - \log_{10} P_c > \log_{10} P_t - \log_{10} P_r$$

$$\log_{10} P_r > \log_{10} P_c$$

$$P_r > P_c$$

which is the desired condition.

EXAMPLE 4.1 Figure 4.5 shows attenuation (insertion loss) and NEXT loss as a function of frequency for category 6A twisted pair. As usual, a link of 100 m is assumed. The figure suggests that above a frequency of about 250 MHz, communication is impractical. Yet Table 4.2 indicates that category 6A is specified to operate up to 500 MHz. The explanation is that the 10-Gbps application employs crosstalk cancellation, which effectively provides a positive ACR margin out to 500 MHz. The standard indicates a worst-case situation, and engineering practices, such as crosstalk cancellation, are used to overcome the worst-case limitations.

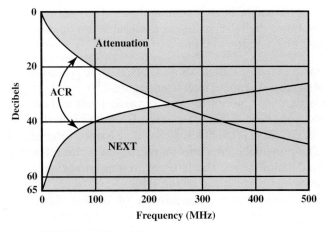

NEXT = near-end crosstalk
ACR = attenuation-to-crosstalk ratio

Figure 4.5   Category 6A Channel Requirements

Coaxial Cable

PHYSICAL DESCRIPTION   Coaxial cable, like twisted pair, consists of two conductors, but is constructed differently to permit it to operate over a wider range of frequencies. It consists of a hollow outer cylindrical conductor that surrounds a single inner wire conductor (Figure 4.2b). The inner conductor is held in place by either regularly spaced insulating rings or a solid dielectric material. The outer conductor is covered with a jacket or shield. A single coaxial cable has a diameter of from 1 to 2.5 cm. Coaxial cable can be used over longer distances and support more stations on a shared line than twisted pair.

APPLICATIONS   Coaxial cable is a versatile transmission medium, used in a wide variety of applications. The most important of these are:

- Television distribution
- Long-distance telephone transmission
- Short-run computer system links
- Local area networks

Coaxial cable is widely used as a means of distributing TV signals to individual homes—cable TV. From its modest beginnings as Community Antenna Television (CATV), designed to provide service to remote areas, cable TV reaches almost as many homes and offices as the telephone. A cable TV system can carry dozens or even hundreds of TV channels at ranges up to a few tens of kilometers.

Coaxial cable has traditionally been an important part of the long-distance telephone network. Today, it faces increasing competition from optical fiber, terrestrial microwave, and satellite. Using frequency division multiplexing (FDM, see Chapter 8), a coaxial cable can carry over 10,000 voice channels simultaneously.

Coaxial cable is also commonly used for short-range connections between devices. Using digital signaling, coaxial cable can be used to provide high-speed I/O channels on computer systems.

TRANSMISSION CHARACTERISTICS   Coaxial cable is used to transmit both analog and digital signals. As can be seen from Figure 4.3b, coaxial cable has frequency characteristics that are superior to those of twisted pair and can hence be used effectively at higher frequencies and data rates. Because of its shielded, concentric construction, coaxial cable is much less susceptible to interference and crosstalk than twisted pair. The principal constraints on performance are attenuation, thermal noise, and intermodulation noise. The latter is present only when several channels (FDM) or frequency bands are in use on the cable.

For long-distance transmission of analog signals, amplifiers are needed every few kilometers, with closer spacing required if higher frequencies are used. The usable spectrum for analog signaling extends to about 500 MHz. For digital signaling, repeaters are needed every kilometer or so, with closer spacing needed for higher data rates.

Optical Fiber

PHYSICAL DESCRIPTION   An optical fiber is a thin, flexible medium capable of guiding an optical ray. Various glasses and plastics can be used to make optical fibers. The lowest losses have been obtained using fibers of ultrapure fused silica. Ultrapure fiber is difficult to manufacture; higher-loss multicomponent glass fibers are more economical and still provide good performance. Plastic fiber is even less costly and can be used for short-haul links, for which moderately high losses are acceptable.

An **optical fiber strand** (also called an *optical waveguide*) has a cylindrical shape and consists of three concentric sections: the core, the cladding, and the buffer coating (Figure 4.2c). The core is the innermost section and consists of thin strands made of glass or plastic; the core has a diameter in the range of 8 to 62.5 μm. The core is surrounded by a **cladding**, which is a glass or plastic coating that has optical properties different from those of the core and a diameter of 125 μm. The interface between the core and cladding acts as a reflector to confine light that would otherwise escape the core. The outermost layer is the **buffer coating**, which is a hard plastic coating that protects the glass from moisture and physical damage.

Fiber optic cable provides protection to the fiber from stress during installation and from the environment once it is installed. Cables may contain from only one to hundreds of fibers inside. The outermost layer of the cable, surrounding one or a bundle of fibers, is the **jacket**. The jacket is composed of plastic and other materials, layered to protect against moisture, abrasion, crushing, and other environmental dangers.

APPLICATIONS   Optical fiber already enjoys considerable use in long-distance telecommunications, and its use in military applications is growing. The continuing improvements in performance and decline in prices, together with the inherent advantages of optical fiber, have made it increasingly attractive for local area networking. The following characteristics distinguish optical fiber from twisted pair or coaxial cable:

- **Greater capacity:** The potential bandwidth, and hence data rate, of optical fiber is immense; data rates of hundreds of Gbps over tens of kilometers have been demonstrated. Compare this to the practical maximum of hundreds of Mbps over about 1 km for coaxial cable and just a few Mbps over 1 km or up to 100 Mbps to 10 Gbps over a few tens of meters for twisted pair.

- **Smaller size and lighter weight:** Optical fibers are considerably thinner than coaxial cable or bundled twisted-pair cable—at least an order of magnitude thinner for comparable information transmission capacity. For cramped conduits in buildings and underground along public rights-of-way, the advantage of small size is considerable. The corresponding reduction in weight reduces structural support requirements.

- **Lower attenuation:** Attenuation is significantly lower for optical fiber than for coaxial cable or twisted pair (Figure 4.3c) and is constant over a wide range.

- **Electromagnetic isolation:** Optical fiber systems are not affected by external electromagnetic fields. Thus the system is not vulnerable to interference, impulse noise, or crosstalk. By the same token, fibers do not radiate energy, so there is little interference with other equipment and there is a high degree of security from eavesdropping. In addition, fiber is inherently difficult to tap.

- **Greater repeater spacing:** Fewer repeaters mean lower cost and fewer sources of error. The performance of optical fiber systems from this point of view has been steadily improving. Repeater spacing in the tens of kilometers for optical fiber is common, and repeater spacings of hundreds of kilometers have been demonstrated. Coaxial and twisted-pair systems generally have repeaters every few kilometers.

Five basic categories of application have become important for optical fiber:

- Long-haul trunks
- Metropolitan trunks
- Rural exchange trunks
- Subscriber loops
- Local area networks

Telephone networks were the first major users of fiber optics. Fiber optic links were used to replace copper or digital radio links between telephone switches, beginning with long-distance links, called long lines or long haul, where fiber's distance and bandwidth capabilities made fiber significantly more cost-effective. Optical fiber is used to connect all central offices and long-distance switches because it has thousands of times the bandwidth of copper wire and can carry signals hundreds of times further before needing a repeater, making the cost of a phone connection over fiber only a few percent of the cost of the same connection on copper. Long-haul routes average about 1500 km in length and offer high capacity (typically 20,000 to 60,000 voice channels). Undersea optical fiber cables have also enjoyed increasing use.

Metropolitan trunking circuits have an average length of 12 km and may have as many as 100,000 voice channels in a trunk group. Most facilities are installed in underground conduits and are repeaterless, joining telephone exchanges in a metropolitan or city area. Included in this category are routes that link long-haul microwave facilities that terminate at a city perimeter to the main telephone exchange building downtown.

Rural exchange trunks have circuit lengths ranging from 40 to 160 km that link towns and villages. In the United States, they often connect the exchanges of different telephone companies. Most of these systems have fewer than 5000 voice channels. With the exception of some rugged or remote locations, the entire telephone backbone is now optical fiber. Cables on the land are run underground or aerially, depending on the geography and local regulations. Connections around the world are run primarily on undersea cables, which now link every continent and most island nations with the exception of Antarctica.

Subscriber loop circuits are fibers that run directly from the central exchange to a subscriber. These facilities are beginning to displace twisted pair and coaxial cable links as the telephone networks evolve into full-service networks capable of handling not only voice and data, but also image and video. The initial penetration of optical fiber in this application has been for the business subscriber, but fiber transmission into the home is now a significant presence in many areas.

A final important application of optical fiber is for local area networks. Standards have been developed and products introduced for optical fiber networks that have a total capacity of up to 100 Gbps and can support thousands of stations in a large office building or a complex of buildings.

TRANSMISSION CHARACTERISTICS   Figure 4.6 shows the general structure of a fiber optic link, which consists of a transmitter on one end of a fiber and a receiver on the other end. Most systems operate by transmitting in one direction on one fiber and in the reverse direction on another fiber for full duplex operation. The transmitter takes as input a digital electrical signal. This signal feeds into a LED or laser light source through an electronic interface. The light source produces a series of lightwave pulses that encode the digital data from the electrical input. The receiver includes a light sensor that detects the incoming light signal and converts it back to a digital electrical signal.

Optical fiber transmits a signal-encoded beam of light by means of total internal reflection. Total internal reflection can occur in any transparent medium that has a higher index of refraction than the surrounding medium. In effect, the optical

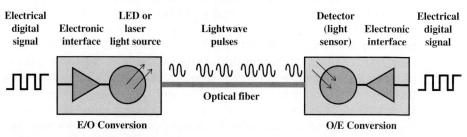

Figure 4.6   Optical Communication

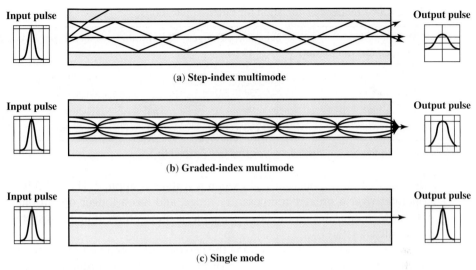

Figure 4.7   Optical Fiber Transmission Modes

fiber acts as a waveguide for frequencies in the range of about 10^{14} to 10^{15} Hz; this covers portions of the infrared and visible spectra.

Figure 4.7 shows the principle of optical fiber transmission. Light from a source enters the cylindrical glass or plastic core. Rays at shallow angles are reflected and propagated along the fiber; other rays are absorbed by the surrounding material. This form of propagation is called **step-index multimode**, referring to the variety of angles that reflect. With multimode transmission, multiple propagation paths exist, each with a different path length and hence time to traverse the fiber. This causes signal elements (light pulses) to spread out in time, which limits the rate at which data can be accurately received. Put another way, the need to leave spacing between the pulses limits data rate. This type of fiber is best suited for transmission over very short distances. When the fiber core radius is reduced, fewer angles will reflect. By reducing the radius of the core to the order of a **wavelength**, only a single angle or mode can pass: the axial ray. This **single-mode propagation** provides superior performance for the following reason. Because there is a single transmission path with single-mode transmission, the distortion found in multimode cannot occur. Single mode is typically used for long-distance applications, including telephone and cable television. Finally, by varying the index of refraction of the core, a third type of transmission, known as **graded-index multimode**, is possible. This type is intermediate between the other two in characteristics. The higher refractive index (discussed subsequently) at the center makes the light rays moving down the axis advance more slowly than those near the cladding. Rather than zig-zagging off the cladding, light in the core curves helically because of the graded index, reducing its travel distance. The shortened path and higher speed allows light at the periphery to arrive at a receiver at about the same time as the straight rays in the core axis. Graded-index fibers are often used in LANs.

Two different types of light source are used in fiber optic systems: the light-emitting diode (LED) and the injection laser diode (ILD). Both are semiconductor

Table 4.3 Frequency Utilization for Fiber Applications

Wavelength (in vacuum) range (nm)	Frequency Range (THz)	Band Label	Fiber Type	Application
820 to 900	366 to 333		Multimode	LAN
1280 to 1350	234 to 222	S	Single mode	Various
1528 to 1561	196 to 192	C	Single mode	WDM
1561 to 1620	192 to 185	L	Single mode	WDM

WDM = wavelength division multiplexing (see Chapter 8)

devices that emit a beam of light when a voltage is applied. The LED is less costly, operates over a greater temperature range, and has a longer operational life. The ILD, which operates on the laser principle, is more efficient and can sustain greater data rates.

There is a relationship among the wavelength employed, the type of transmission, and the achievable data rate. Both single mode and multimode can support several different wavelengths of light and can employ laser or LED light sources. In optical fiber, based on the attenuation characteristics of the medium and on properties of light sources and receivers, four transmission windows are appropriate, as shown in Table 4.3.

Note the tremendous bandwidths available. For the four windows, the respective bandwidths are 33, 12, and 7 THz.[1] This is several orders of magnitude greater than the bandwidth available in the radio-frequency spectrum.

One confusing aspect of reported attenuation figures for fiber optic transmission is that, invariably, fiber optic performance is specified in terms of wavelength rather than frequency. The wavelengths that appear in graphs and tables are the wavelengths corresponding to transmission in a vacuum. However, on the fiber, the velocity of propagation is less than c, the speed of light in a vacuum; the result is that although the frequency of the signal is unchanged, the wavelength is changed.

EXAMPLE 4.2 For a wavelength in vacuum of 1550 nm, the corresponding frequency is $f = c/\lambda = (3 \times 10^8)/(1550 \times 10^{-9}) = 193.4 \times 10^{12} = 193.4\,\text{THz}$. For a typical single-mode fiber, the velocity of propagation is approximately $v = 2.04 \times 10^8$. In this case, a frequency of 193.4 THz corresponds to a wavelength of $\lambda = v/f = (2.04 \times 10^8)/(193.4 \times 10^{12}) = 1055\,\text{nm}$. Therefore, on this fiber, when a wavelength of 1550 nm is cited, the actual wavelength on the fiber is 1055 nm.

The four transmission windows are in the infrared portion of the frequency spectrum, below the visible-light portion, which is 400 to 700 nm. The loss is lower at higher wavelengths, allowing greater data rates over longer distances. Many local applications today use 850-nm LED light sources. Although this combination

[1] 1 THz = 10^{12} Hz. For a definition of numerical prefixes in common use, see the supporting document at box.com/dcc10e.

is relatively inexpensive, it is generally limited to data rates under 100 Mbps and distances of a few kilometers. To achieve higher data rates and longer distances, a 1300-nm LED or laser source is needed. The highest data rates and longest distances require 1500-nm laser sources.

Figure 4.3c shows attenuation versus wavelength for a typical optical fiber. The unusual shape of the curve is due to the combination of a variety of factors that contribute to attenuation. The two most important of these are absorption and scattering. In this context, the term *scattering* refers to the change in direction of light rays after they strike small particles or impurities in the medium.

4.2 WIRELESS TRANSMISSION

Three general ranges of frequencies are of interest in our discussion of wireless transmission. Frequencies in the range of about 1 GHz (gigahertz = 10^9 hertz) to 40 GHz are referred to as **microwave frequencies**. At these frequencies, highly directional beams are possible, and microwave is quite suitable for point-to-point transmission. Microwave is also used for satellite communications. Frequencies in the range of 30 MHz to 1 GHz are suitable for omnidirectional applications. We refer to this range as the **radio** range.

Another important frequency range, for local applications, is the infrared portion of the spectrum. This covers, roughly, from 3×10^{11} to 2×10^{14} Hz. Infrared is useful to local point-to-point and multipoint applications within confined areas, such as a single room.

For unguided media, transmission and reception are achieved by means of an antenna. Before looking at specific categories of wireless transmission, we provide a brief introduction to antennas.

Antennas

An antenna can be defined as an electrical conductor or system of conductors used either for radiating electromagnetic energy or for collecting electromagnetic energy. For transmission of a signal, radio-frequency electrical energy from the transmitter is converted into electromagnetic energy by the antenna and radiated into the surrounding environment (atmosphere, space, water). Reception occurs when the electromagnetic signal intersects the antenna, where the electromagnetic energy is converted into radio-frequency electrical energy and fed into the receiver.

In two-way communication, the same antenna can be and often is used for both transmission and reception. This is possible because any antenna transfers energy from the surrounding environment to its input receiver terminals with the same efficiency that it transfers energy from the output transmitter terminals into the surrounding environment, assuming that the same frequency is used in both directions. Put another way, antenna characteristics are essentially the same whether an antenna is sending or receiving electromagnetic energy.

An antenna radiates power in all directions but, typically, does not perform equally well in all directions. A common way to characterize the performance of an antenna is the radiation pattern, which is a graphical representation of the radiation properties of an antenna as a function of space coordinates. The simplest pattern is produced by an idealized antenna known as the isotropic antenna. An **isotropic antenna**, also called an **omnidirectional antenna**, is a point in space that radiates power in all directions equally. The actual radiation pattern for the isotropic antenna is a sphere with the antenna at the center.

PARABOLIC REFLECTIVE ANTENNA   An important type of antenna is the **parabolic reflective antenna**, which is used in terrestrial microwave and satellite applications. A parabola is the locus of all points equidistant from a fixed line and a fixed point not on the line. The fixed point is called the *focus* and the fixed line is called the *directrix* (Figure 4.8a). If a parabola is revolved about its axis, the surface generated is called a *paraboloid*. A cross section through the paraboloid parallel to its axis forms a parabola and a cross section perpendicular to the axis forms a circle. Such surfaces are used in automobile headlights, optical and radio telescopes, and microwave antennas because of the following property: If a source of electromagnetic energy (or sound) is placed at the focus of the paraboloid, and if the paraboloid is a reflecting surface, then the wave bounces back in lines parallel to the axis of the paraboloid; Figure 4.8b shows this effect in cross section. In theory, this effect creates a parallel beam without dispersion. In practice, there is some dispersion, because the source of energy must occupy more than one point. The larger the diameter of the antenna, the more tightly directional is the beam. On reception, if incoming waves are parallel to the axis of the reflecting paraboloid, the resulting signal is concentrated at the focus.

ANTENNA GAIN   **Antenna gain** is a measure of the directionality of an antenna. Antenna gain is defined as the power output, in a particular direction, compared to that produced in any direction by a perfect omnidirectional antenna (isotropic antenna). Specifically, $G_{dB} = 10 \log (P_2/P_1)$, where G is the antenna gain, P_1 is the

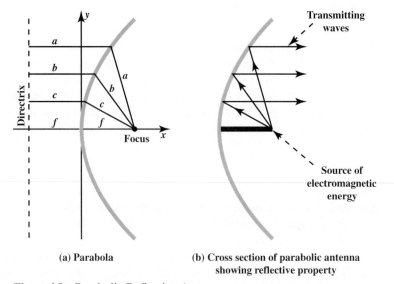

(a) Parabola

(b) Cross section of parabolic antenna showing reflective property

Figure 4.8   Parabolic Reflective Antenna

radiated power of the directional antenna, and P_2 is the radiated power from the reference antenna. For example, if an antenna has a gain of 3 dB, that antenna improves upon the isotropic antenna in that direction by 3 dB, or a factor of 2. The increased power radiated in a given direction is at the expense of other directions. In effect, increased power is radiated in one direction by reducing the power radiated in other directions. It is important to note that antenna gain does not refer to obtaining more output power than input power but rather to directionality.

EXAMPLE 4.3 Consider a directional antenna that has a gain of 6 dB over a reference antenna and that radiates 700 W. How much power must the reference antenna radiate to provide the same signal power in the preferred direction? To solve, we have

$$6 = 10 \ \log(P_2/700)$$
$$P_2/700 = 10^{0.6} = 3.98$$
$$P_2 = 2786 \, \text{W}$$

A concept related to that of antenna gain is the **effective area** of an antenna. The effective area of an antenna is related to the physical size of the antenna and to its shape. The relationship between antenna gain and effective area is:

$$G = \frac{4\pi A_e}{\lambda^2} = \frac{4\pi f^2 A_e}{c^2} \qquad\qquad \textbf{(4.1)}$$

where

$\qquad G =$ antenna gain (dimensionless number or ratio)

$\qquad A_e =$ effective area (m^2)

$\qquad f =$ carrier frequency (Hz)

$\qquad c =$ speed of light ($\approx 3 \times 10^8$ m/s)

$\qquad \lambda =$ carrier wavelength (m)

Expressed in decibels, we have $G_{dB} = 10 \log G$

For example, the effective area of an ideal isotropic antenna is $\lambda^2/4\pi$, with a power gain of 1; the effective area of a parabolic antenna with a face area of A is $0.56A$, with a power gain of $7A/\lambda^2$.

EXAMPLE 4.4 For a parabolic reflective antenna with a diameter of 2 m, operating at 12 GHz, what are the effective area and the antenna gain? We have an area of $A \times \pi r^2 = \pi$ and an effective area of $A_e = 0.56\pi$. The wavelength is $\lambda = c/f = (3 \times 10^8)/(12 \times 10^9) = 0.025$ m. Then

$$G = (7A)/\lambda^2 = (7 \times \pi)/(0.025)^2 = 35{,}186$$
$$G_{dB} = 10 \log 35{,}186 = 45.46 \, \text{dB}$$

Terrestrial Microwave

PHYSICAL DESCRIPTION The most common type of microwave antenna is the parabolic "dish." A typical size is about 3 m in diameter. The antenna is fixed rigidly and focuses a narrow beam to achieve line-of-sight transmission to the receiving antenna. Microwave antennas are usually located at substantial heights above ground level to extend the range between antennas and to be able to transmit over intervening obstacles. To achieve long-distance transmission, a series of microwave relay towers is used, with point-to-point microwave links strung together over the desired distance.

APPLICATIONS The primary use for terrestrial microwave systems is in long-haul telecommunications service, as an alternative to coaxial cable or optical fiber. The microwave facility requires far fewer amplifiers or repeaters than coaxial cable over the same distance, but requires line-of-sight transmission. Microwave is commonly used for both voice and television transmission.

Another increasingly common use of microwave is for short point-to-point links between buildings. This can be used for closed-circuit TV or as a data link between LANs. Short-haul microwave can also be used for the so-called bypass application. A business can establish a microwave link to a long-distance telecommunications facility in the same city, bypassing the local telephone company.

Another important use of microwave is in cellular systems, examined in Chapter 10.

TRANSMISSION CHARACTERISTICS Microwave transmission covers a substantial portion of the electromagnetic spectrum. Common frequencies used for transmission are in the range 1 to 40 GHz. The higher the frequency used, the higher the potential bandwidth, and therefore the higher the potential data rate. Table 4.4 indicates bandwidth and data rate for some typical systems.

As with any transmission system, a main source of loss is attenuation. For microwave (and radio frequencies), the loss can be expressed as

$$L = 10 \log \left(\frac{4\pi d}{\lambda} \right)^2 \text{ dB} \qquad (4.2)$$

where d is the distance and λ is the wavelength, in the same units. Thus, loss varies as the square of the distance. By contrast, for twisted pair and coaxial cable, loss varies exponentially with distance (linear in decibels). Thus repeaters or amplifiers may be placed farther apart for microwave systems—10 to 100 km is typical. Attenuation

Table 4.4 Typical Digital Microwave Performance

Band (GHz)	Bandwidth (MHz)	Data Rate (Mbps)
2	7	12
6	30	90
11	40	135
18	220	274

is increased with rainfall. The effects of rainfall become especially noticeable above 10 GHz. Another source of impairment is interference. With the growing popularity of microwave, transmission areas overlap and interference is always a danger. Thus the assignment of frequency bands is strictly regulated.

The most common bands for long-haul telecommunications are the 4-GHz to 6-GHz bands. With increasing congestion at these frequencies, the 11-GHz band is now coming into use. The 12-GHz band is used as a component of cable TV systems. Microwave links are used to provide TV signals to local CATV installations; the signals are then distributed to individual subscribers via coaxial cable. Higher-frequency microwave is being used for short point-to-point links between buildings; typically, the 22-GHz band is used. The higher microwave frequencies are less useful for longer distances because of increased attenuation but are quite adequate for shorter distances. In addition, at the higher frequencies, the antennas are smaller and cheaper.

Satellite Microwave

PHYSICAL DESCRIPTION   A communication satellite is, in effect, a microwave relay station. It is used to link two or more ground-based microwave transmitter/receivers, known as **earth stations**, or ground stations. The satellite receives transmissions on one frequency band (**uplink**), amplifies or repeats the signal, and transmits it on another frequency (**downlink**). A single orbiting satellite will operate on a number of frequency bands, called **transponder channels**, or simply **transponders**.

Figure 4.9 depicts in a general way two common configurations for satellite communication. In the first, the satellite is being used to provide a point-to-point link between two distant ground-based antennas. In the second, the satellite provides communications between one ground-based transmitter and a number of ground-based receivers.

For a communication satellite to function effectively, it is generally required that it remain stationary with respect to its position over the Earth. Otherwise, it would not be within the line of sight of its earth stations at all times. To remain stationary, the satellite must have a period of rotation equal to the Earth's period of rotation. This match occurs at a height of 35,863 km at the equator.

Two satellites using the same frequency band, if close enough together, interfere with each other. To avoid this, current standards require a 4° spacing (angular displacement as measured from the Earth) in the 4/6-GHz band and a 3° spacing at 12/14 GHz. Thus the number of possible satellites is quite limited.

APPLICATIONS   The following are the most important applications for satellites:

- Television distribution
- Long-distance telephone transmission
- Private business networks
- Global positioning

Because of their broadcast nature, satellites are well suited to television distribution and are being used extensively in the United States and throughout the world for this purpose. In its traditional use, a network provides programming from

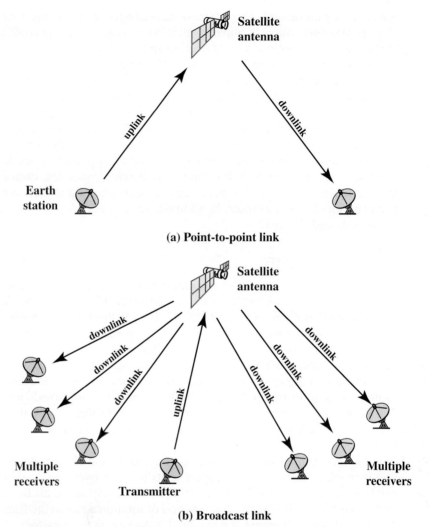

Figure 4.9   Satellite Communication Configurations

a central location. Programs are transmitted to the satellite and then broadcast down to a number of stations, which then distribute the programs to individual viewers. One network, the Public Broadcasting Service (PBS), distributes its television programming almost exclusively by the use of satellite channels. Other commercial networks also make substantial use of satellite, with cable television systems receiving an ever-increasing proportion of their programming from satellites. The most recent application of satellite technology to television distribution is direct broadcast satellite (DBS), in which satellite video signals are transmitted directly to the home user. The decreasing cost and size of receiving antennas have made DBS economically feasible.

Satellite transmission is also used for point-to-point trunks between telephone exchange offices in public telephone networks. It is the optimum medium for high-usage international trunks and is competitive with terrestrial systems for many long-distance intranational links.

There are a number of business data applications for satellite. The satellite provider can divide the total capacity into a number of channels and lease these channels to individual business users. A user equipped with the antennas at a number of sites can use a satellite channel for a private network. Traditionally, such applications have been quite expensive and limited to larger organizations with high-volume requirements. A recent development is the very small aperture terminal (VSAT) system, which provides a low-cost alternative. Figure 4.10 depicts a typical VSAT configuration. A number of subscriber stations are equipped with low-cost VSAT antennas. Using some discipline, these stations share a satellite transmission capacity for transmission to a hub station. The hub station can exchange messages with each of the subscribers and can relay messages between subscribers.

A final application of satellites, which has become pervasive, is worthy of note. The Navstar **Global Positioning System**, or GPS for short, consists of three segments or components:

- A constellation of satellites (currently 27) orbiting about 20,000 km above the Earth's surface, which transmits ranging signals on two frequencies in the microwave part of the radio spectrum
- A control segment which maintains GPS through a system of ground monitor stations and satellite upload facilities
- The user receivers—both civil and military

Each satellite transmits a unique digital code sequence of 1s and 0s, precisely timed by an atomic clock, which is picked up by a GPS receiver's antenna and

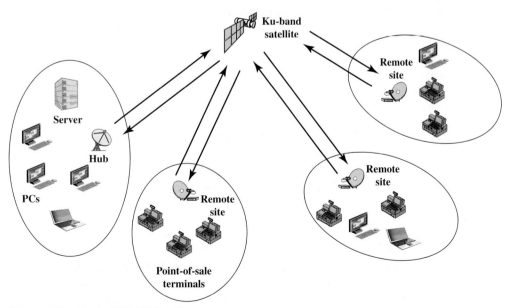

Figure 4.10   Typical VSAT Configuration

matched with the same code sequence generated inside the receiver. By lining up or matching the signals, the receiver determines how long it takes the signals to travel from the satellite to the receiver. These timing measurements are converted to distances using the speed of light. Measuring distances to four or more satellites simultaneously and knowing the exact locations of the satellites (included in the signals transmitted by the satellites), the receiver can determine its latitude, longitude, and height while also synchronizing its clock with the GPS time standard which also makes the receiver a precise time piece.

TRANSMISSION CHARACTERISTICS   The optimum frequency range for satellite transmission is in the range 1 to 10 GHz. Below 1 GHz, there is significant noise from natural sources, including galactic, solar, and atmospheric noise, and human-made interference from various electronic devices. Above 10 GHz, the signal is severely attenuated by atmospheric absorption and precipitation.

Most satellites providing point-to-point service today use a frequency bandwidth in the range 5.925 to 6.425 GHz for transmission from Earth to satellite (uplink) and a bandwidth in the range 3.7 to 4.2 GHz for transmission from satellite to Earth (downlink). This combination is referred to as the 4/6-GHz band. Note that the uplink and downlink frequencies differ. For continuous operation without interference, a satellite cannot transmit and receive on the same frequency. Thus signals received from a ground station on one frequency must be transmitted back on another.

The 4/6 GHz band is within the optimum zone of 1 to 10 GHz but has become saturated. Other frequencies in that range are unavailable because of sources of interference operating at those frequencies, usually terrestrial microwave. Therefore, the 12/14-GHz band has been developed (uplink: 14 to 14.5 GHz; downlink: 11.7 to 12.2 GHz). At this frequency band, attenuation problems must be overcome. However, smaller and cheaper earth-station receivers can be used. It is anticipated that this band will also saturate, and use is projected for the 20/30-GHz band (uplink: 27.5 to 30.0 GHz; downlink: 17.7 to 20.2 GHz). This band experiences even greater attenuation problems but will allow greater bandwidth (2500 MHz versus 500 MHz) and even smaller and cheaper receivers.

Several properties of satellite communication should be noted. First, because of the long distances involved, there is a propagation delay of about a quarter second from transmission from one earth station to reception by another earth station. This delay is noticeable in ordinary telephone conversations. It also introduces problems in the areas of error control and flow control, which we discuss in later chapters. Second, satellite microwave is inherently a broadcast facility. Many stations can transmit to the satellite, and a transmission from a satellite can be received by many stations.

Broadcast Radio

PHYSICAL DESCRIPTION   The principal difference between broadcast radio and microwave is that the former is omnidirectional and the latter is directional. Thus broadcast radio does not require dish-shaped antennas, and the antennas need not be rigidly mounted to a precise alignment.

APPLICATIONS   Radio is a general term used to encompass frequencies in the range of 3 kHz to 300 GHz. We are using the informal term **broadcast radio** to cover the VHF and part of the UHF band: 30 MHz to 1 GHz. This range covers FM radio and UHF and VHF television. This range is also used for a number of data networking applications.

TRANSMISSION CHARACTERISTICS   The range 30 MHz to 1 GHz is an effective one for broadcast communications. Unlike the case for lower-frequency electromagnetic waves, the ionosphere is transparent to radio waves above 30 MHz. Thus transmission is limited to the line of sight, and distant transmitters will not interfere with each other due to reflection from the atmosphere. Unlike the higher frequencies of the microwave region, broadcast radio waves are less sensitive to attenuation from rainfall.

As with microwave, the amount of attenuation due to distance obeys Equation (4.2), namely $10 \log\left(\frac{4\pi d}{\lambda}\right)^2$ dB. Because of the longer wavelength, radio waves suffer relatively less attenuation.

A prime source of impairment for broadcast radio waves is multipath interference. Reflection from land, water, and natural or human-made objects can create multiple paths between antennas.

Infrared

Infrared communications is achieved using transmitters/receivers (transceivers) that modulate noncoherent infrared light. Transceivers must be within the line of sight of each other either directly or via reflection from a light-colored surface such as the ceiling of a room.

One important difference between infrared and microwave transmission is that the former does not penetrate walls. Thus the security and interference problems encountered in microwave systems are not present. Furthermore, there is no frequency allocation issue with infrared, because no licensing is required.

4.3 WIRELESS PROPAGATION

A signal radiated from an antenna travels along one of three routes: ground wave, sky wave, or line of sight (LOS). Table 4.5 shows in which frequency range each predominates. In this book, we are almost exclusively concerned with LOS communication, but a short overview of each mode is given in this section.

Ground Wave Propagation

Ground wave propagation (Figure 4.11a) more or less follows the contour of the Earth and can propagate considerable distances, well over the visual horizon. This effect is found in frequencies up to about 2 MHz. Several factors account for the tendency of electromagnetic wave in this frequency band to follow the Earth's curvature. One factor is that the electromagnetic wave induces a current in the Earth's surface, the result of which is to slow the wavefront near the Earth, causing the wavefront to tilt downward and hence follow the Earth's curvature. Another factor

Table 4.5 Frequency Bands

Band	Frequency Range	Free-Space Wavelength Range	Propagation Characteristics	Typical Use
ELF (extremely low frequency)	30 to 300 Hz	10,000 to 1000 km	GW	Power line frequencies; used by some home control systems
VF (voice frequency)	300 to 3000 Hz	1000 to 100 km	GW	Used by the telephone system for analog subscriber lines
VLF (very low frequency)	3 to 30 kHz	100 to 10 km	GW; low attenuation day and night; high atmospheric noise level	Long-range navigation; submarine communication
LF (low frequency)	30 to 300 kHz	10 to 1 km	GW; slightly less reliable than VLF; absorption in daytime	Long-range navigation; marine communication radio beacons
MF (medium frequency)	300 to 3000 kHz	1,000 to 100 m	GW and night SW; attenuation low at night, high in day; atmospheric noise	Maritime radio; direction finding; AM broadcasting
HF (high frequency)	3 to 30 MHz	100 to 10 m	SW; quality varies with time of day, season, and frequency	Amateur radio; military communication
VHF (very high frequency)	30 to 300 MHz	10 to 1 m	LOS; scattering because of temperature inversion; cosmic noise	VHF television; FM broadcast and two-way radio, AM aircraft communication; aircraft navigational aids
UHF (ultra high frequency)	300 to 3000 MHz	100 to 10 cm	LOS; cosmic noise	UHF television; cellular telephone; radar; microwave links; personal communications systems
SHF (super high frequency)	3 to 30 GHz	10 to 1 cm	LOS; rainfall attenuation above 10 GHz; atmospheric attenuation due to oxygen and water vapor	Satellite communication; radar; terrestrial microwave links; wireless local loop
EHF (extremely high frequency)	30 to 300 GHz	10 to 1 mm	LOS; atmospheric attenuation due to oxygen and water vapor	Experimental; wireless local loop; radio astronomy
Infrared	300 GHz to 400 THz	1 mm to 770 nm	LOS	Infrared LANs; consumer electronic applications
Visible light	400 to 900 THz	770 to 330 nm	LOS	Optical communication

160

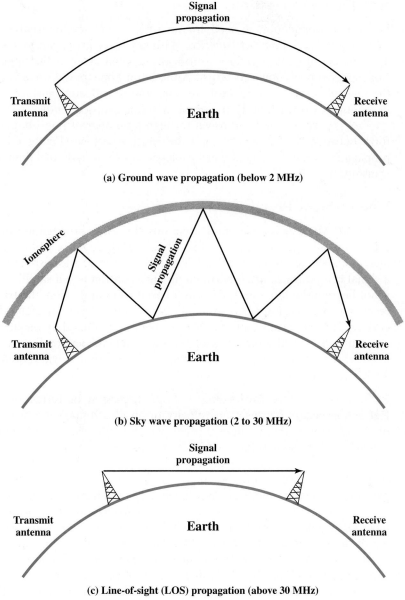

Figure 4.11   Wireless Propagation Modes

is diffraction, which is a phenomenon having to do with the behavior of electromagnetic waves in the presence of obstacles. Electromagnetic waves in this frequency range are scattered by the atmosphere in such a way that they do not penetrate the upper atmosphere.

The best-known example of ground wave communication is AM radio.

Sky Wave Propagation

Sky wave propagation is used for amateur radio and international broadcasts such as *BBC* and *Voice of America*. With sky wave propagation, a signal from an earth-based antenna is reflected from the ionized layer of the upper atmosphere (ionosphere) back down to Earth. Although it appears the wave is reflected from the ionosphere as if the ionosphere were a hard reflecting surface, the effect is in fact caused by refraction. Refraction is described subsequently.

A sky wave signal can travel through a number of hops, bouncing back and forth between the ionosphere and the Earth's surface (Figure 4.11b). With this propagation mode, a signal can be picked up thousands of kilometers from the transmitter.

Line-of-Sight Propagation

Above 30 MHz, neither ground wave nor sky wave propagation modes operate, and communication must be by line of sight (Figure 4.11c). For satellite communication, a signal above 30 MHz is not reflected by the ionosphere and therefore a signal can be transmitted between an earth station and a satellite overhead that is not beyond the horizon. For ground-based communication, the transmitting and receiving antennas must be within an *effective* line of sight of each other. The term *effective* is used because microwaves are bent or refracted by the atmosphere. The amount and even the direction of the bend depend on conditions, but generally microwaves are bent with the curvature of the Earth and will therefore propagate farther than the optical line of sight.

REFRACTION Before proceeding, a brief discussion of refraction is warranted. Refraction occurs because the velocity of an electromagnetic wave is a function of the density of the medium through which it travels. In a vacuum, an electromagnetic wave (such as light or a radio wave) travels at approximately 3×10^8 m/s. This is the constant, c, commonly referred to as the speed of light, but actually referring to the speed of light in a vacuum.[2] In air, water, glass, and other transparent or partially transparent media, electromagnetic waves travel at speeds less than c.

When an electromagnetic wave moves from a medium of one density to a medium of another density, its speed changes. The effect is to cause a one-time bending of the direction of the wave at the boundary between the two media. Moving from a less dense to a more dense medium, the wave bends toward the more dense medium. This phenomenon is easily observed by partially immersing a stick in water.

The **index of refraction**, or **refractive index**, of one medium relative to another is the sine of the angle of incidence divided by the sine of the angle of refraction. The index of refraction is also equal to the ratio of the respective velocities in the two media. The absolute index of refraction of a medium is calculated in comparison with that of a vacuum. Refractive index varies with wavelength, so that refractive effects differ for signals with different wavelengths.

Although an abrupt, one-time change in direction occurs as a signal moves from one medium to another, a continuous, gradual bending of a signal occurs if it is

---

[2]The exact value is 299,792,458 m/s.

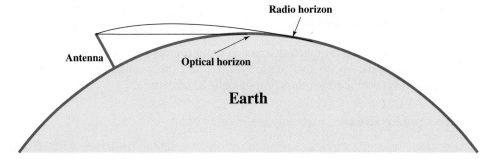

Figure 4.12 Optical and Radio Horizons

moving through a medium in which the index of refraction gradually changes. Under normal propagation conditions, the refractive index of the atmosphere decreases with height so that radio waves travel more slowly near the ground than at higher altitudes. The result is a slight bending of the radio waves toward the Earth.

OPTICAL AND RADIO LINE OF SIGHT The term **optical line of sight** refers to the straight-line propagation of light waves; the term **radio line of sight**, or effective line of sight, refers to the propagation of radio waves bent by the curvature of the earth. With no intervening obstacles, the optical LOS can be expressed as

$$d = 3.57\sqrt{h}$$

where d is the distance between an antenna and the horizon in kilometers and h is the antenna height in meters. The radio LOS to the horizon is expressed as (Figure 4.12)

$$d = 3.57\sqrt{Kh}$$

where K is an adjustment factor to account for the refraction. A good rule of thumb is $K = 4/3$. Thus, the maximum distance between two antennas for LOS propagation is $3.57\sqrt{Kh_1} + \sqrt{Kh_2}$, where h_1 and h_2 are the heights of the two antennas.

EXAMPLE 4.5 The maximum distance between two antennas for LOS transmission if one antenna is 100 m high and the other is at ground level is:

$$d = 3.57\sqrt{Kh} = 3.57\sqrt{133} = 41\,\text{km}$$

Now suppose that the receiving antenna is 10 m high. To achieve the same distance, how high must the transmitting antenna be? The result is:

$$41 = 3.57\left(\sqrt{Kh_1} + \sqrt{13.3}\right)$$

$$\sqrt{Kh_1} = \frac{41}{3.57} - \sqrt{13.3} = 7.84$$

$$h_1 = 7.84^2/1.33 = 46.2\,\text{m}$$

This is a savings of over 50 m in the height of the transmitting antenna. This example illustrates the benefit of raising receiving antennas above ground level to reduce the necessary height of the transmitter.

4.4 LINE-OF-SIGHT TRANSMISSION

Section 3.3 discusses various transmission impairments common to both guided and wireless transmission. In this section, we extend the discussion to examine some impairments specific to wireless line-of-sight transmission.

Free Space Loss

For any type of wireless communication the signal disperses with distance. Therefore, an antenna with a fixed area receives less signal power the farther it is from the transmitting antenna. For satellite communication this is the primary mode of signal loss. Even if no other sources of attenuation or impairment are assumed, a transmitted signal attenuates over distance because the signal is being spread over a larger and larger area. This form of attenuation is known as **free space loss**, which can be expressed in terms of the ratio of the radiated power P_t to the power P_r received by the antenna or, in decibels, by taking 10 times the log of that ratio. For the ideal isotropic antenna, free space loss is

$$\frac{P_t}{P_r} = \frac{(4\pi d)^2}{\lambda^2} = \frac{(4\pi f d)^2}{c^2} \tag{4.3}$$

where

$$P_t = \text{signal power at the transmitting antenna}$$
$$P_r = \text{signal power at the receiving antenna}$$
$$\lambda = \text{carrier wavelength}$$
$$d = \text{propagation distance between antennas}$$
$$c = \text{speed of light } (3 \times 10^8 \, \text{m/s})$$

where d and λ are in the same units (e.g., meters).

This can be recast as:[3]

$$L_{dB} = 10 \log \frac{P_t}{P_r} = 10 \log\left(\frac{4\pi d}{\lambda^2}\right)^2 = 20 \log\left(\frac{4\pi d}{\lambda}\right) \text{substituting from Equation (4.3)}$$

$$L_{dB} = -20 \log(\lambda) + 20 \log(d) + 21.98 \, \text{dB}$$

And using $\lambda f = c$.

$$L_{dB} = 20 \log\left(\frac{4\pi f d}{c}\right) = 20 \log(f) + 20 \log(d) - 147.56 \, \text{dB} \tag{4.4}$$

Figure 4.13 illustrates the free space loss equation.

---

[3]As was mentioned in Appendix 3A, there is some inconsistency in the literature over the use of the terms *gain* and *loss*. Equation (4.4) follows the convention of Equation (3.3).

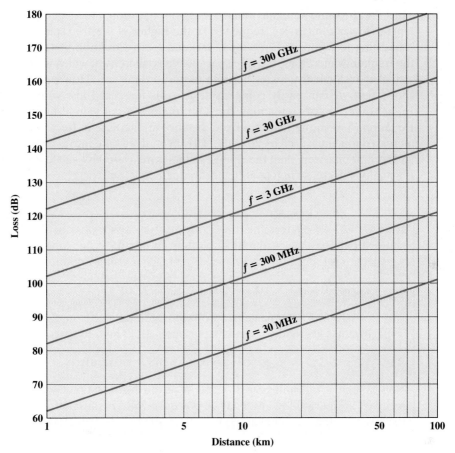

Figure 4.13   Free Space Loss

For other antennas, we must take into account the gain of the antenna, which yields the following free space loss equation:

$$\frac{P_t}{P_r} = \frac{(4\pi)^2(d)^2}{G_r G_t \lambda^2} = \frac{(\lambda d)^2}{A_r A_t} = \frac{(cd)^2}{f^2 A_r A_t}$$

where

G_t = gain of the transmitting antenna

G_r = gain of the receiving antenna

A_t = effective area of the transmitting antenna

A_r = effective area of the receiving antenna

The third fraction is derived from the second fraction using the relationship between antenna gain and effective area defined in Equation (4.1). We can recast the loss equation as:

$$L_{dB} = 20 \log(\lambda) + 20 \log(d) - 10 \log(A_t A_r)$$
$$= -20 \log(f) + 20 \log(d) - 10 \log(A_t A_r) + 169.54 \text{ dB} \qquad \textbf{(4.5)}$$

Thus, for the same antenna dimensions and separation, the longer the carrier wavelength (lower the carrier frequency f), the higher is the free space path loss. It is interesting to compare Equations (4.4) and (4.5). Equation (4.4) indicates that as the frequency increases, the free space loss also increases, which would suggest that at higher frequencies, losses become more burdensome. However, Equation (4.5) shows that we can easily compensate for this increased loss with antenna gains. In fact other factors remaining constant, there is a net gain at higher frequencies. Equation (4.4) shows that at a fixed distance an increase in frequency results in an increased loss measured by $20 \log(f)$. However, if we take into account antenna gain and fix antenna area, then the change in loss is measured by $-20 \log(f)$; that is, there is actually a decrease in loss at higher frequencies.

EXAMPLE 4.6 Determine the isotropic free space loss at 4 GHz for the shortest path to a synchronous satellite from Earth (35,863 km). At 4 GHz, the wavelength is $(3 \times 10^8)/(4 \times 10^9) = 0.075$ m. Then, using Equation (4.4)

$$L_{dB} = 20 \log(4 \times 10^9) + 20 \log(35.853 \times 10^6) - 147.56 = 195.6 \, dB$$

Now consider the antenna gain of both the satellite- and ground-based antennas. Typical values are 44 dB and 48 dB, respectively. The free space loss is

$$L_{dB} = 195.6 - 44 - 48 = 103.6 \, dB$$

Now assume a transmit power of 250 W at the earth station. What is the power received at the satellite antenna? A power of 250 W translates into 24 dBW, so the power at the receiving antenna is $24 - 103.6 = -79.6 \, dBW$.

Atmospheric Absorption

An additional loss between the transmitting and receiving antennas is atmospheric absorption. Water vapor and oxygen contribute most to attenuation. A peak attenuation occurs in the vicinity of 22 GHz due to water vapor. At frequencies below 15 GHz, the attenuation is less. The presence of oxygen results in an absorption peak in the vicinity of 60 GHz but contributes less at frequencies below 30 GHz. Rain and fog (suspended water droplets) cause scattering of radio waves that results in attenuation. In this context, the term *scattering* refers to the production of waves of changed direction or frequency when radio waves encounter matter. This can be a major cause of signal loss. Thus, in areas of significant precipitation, either path lengths have to be kept short or lower-frequency bands should be used.

Multipath

For wireless facilities where there is a relatively free choice of where antennas are to be located, they can be placed so that if there are no nearby interfering obstacles, there is a direct line-of-sight path from transmitter to receiver. This is generally the case for many satellite facilities and for point-to-point microwave. In other cases, such as mobile telephony, there are obstacles in abundance. The signal can be reflected by such obstacles so that multiple copies of the signal with varying delays can be received. In fact, in extreme cases, there may be no direct signal. Depending on the differences in the path lengths of the direct and reflected waves, the composite signal can be either larger or smaller than the direct signal. Reinforcement and cancellation of the signal resulting from the signal following multiple paths can be controlled for communication between fixed, well-sited antennas, and between satellites and fixed ground stations. One exception is when the path goes across water, where the wind keeps the reflective surface of the water in motion. For mobile telephony and communication to antennas that are not well sited, multipath considerations can be paramount.

Figure 4.14 illustrates in general terms the types of multipath interference typical in terrestrial, fixed microwave and in mobile communications. For fixed microwave, in addition to the direct line of sight, the signal may follow a curved path through the atmosphere due to refraction and the signal may also reflect from the ground. For mobile communications, structures and topographic features provide reflection surfaces.

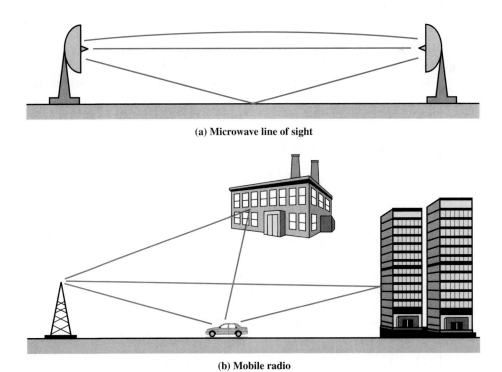

(a) Microwave line of sight

(b) Mobile radio

Figure 4.14   Examples of Multipath Interference

Refraction

Radio waves are refracted (or bent) when they propagate through the atmosphere. The refraction is caused by changes in the speed of the signal with altitude or by other spatial changes in the atmospheric conditions. Normally, the speed of the signal increases with altitude, causing radio waves to bend downward. However, on occasion, weather conditions may lead to variations in speed with height that differ significantly from the typical variations. This may result in a situation in which only a fraction or no part of the line-of-sight wave reaches the receiving antenna.

4.5 RECOMMENDED READING

Detailed descriptions of the transmission characteristics of the transmission media discussed in this chapter can be found in [FREE98b]. A less technical but excellent resource is [OLIV09]. [BORE97] is a thorough treatment of optical fiber transmission components. Another good paper on the subject is [WILL97]. [RAMA06] surveys optical network technologies. [FREE02] is a detailed technical reference on optical fiber. [STAL00] discusses the characteristics of transmission media for LANs in greater detail.

For a more thorough treatment on wireless transmission and propagation, see [STAL05] and [RAPP02]. [FREE07] is an excellent detailed technical reference on wireless topics.

BORE97 Borella, M., et al. "Optical Components for WDM Lightwave Networks." *Proceedings of the IEEE*, August 1997.

FREE98b Freeman, R. *Telecommunication Transmission Handbook.* New York: Wiley, 1998.

FREE02 Freeman, R. *Fiber-Optic Systems for Telecommunications.* New York: Wiley, 2002.

FREE07 Freeman, R. *Radio System Design for Telecommunications.* New York: Wiley, 2007.

OLIV09 Oliviero, A., and Woodward, B. *Cabling: The Complete Guide to Copper and Fiber-Optic Networking.* Indianapolis: Sybex, 2009.

RAMA06 Ramaswami, R. "Optical Network Technologies: What Worked and What Didn't." *IEEE Communications Magazine*, September 2006.

RAPP02 Rappaport, T. *Wireless Communications.* Upper Saddle River, NJ: Prentice Hall, 2002.

STAL00 Stallings, W. *Local and Metropolitan Area Networks,* Sixth Edition. Upper Saddle River, NJ: Prentice Hall, 2000.

STAL05 Stallings, W. *Wireless Communications and Networks*, Second Edition. Upper Saddle River, NJ: Prentice Hall, 2005.

WILL97 Willner, A. "Mining the Optical Bandwidth for a Terabit per Second." *IEEE Spectrum*, April 1997.

4.6 KEY TERMS, REVIEW QUESTIONS, AND PROBLEMS

Key Terms

antenna	guided media	satellite
antenna gain	index of refraction	shielded twisted pair
atmospheric absorption	infrared	(STP)
attenuation	insertion loss	single-mode propagation
attenuation-to-crosstalk	isotropic antenna	sky wave propagation
ratio (ACR)	jacket	step-index multimode
broadcast radio	line of sight (LOS)	subscriber loops
buffer coating	microwave frequencies	terrestrial microwave
cladding	multipath	total internal reflection
coaxial cable	near-end crosstalk (NEXT)	transmission medium
core	loss	transponder channels
directional antenna	omnidirectional antenna	transponders
downlink	optical fiber strand	twisted pair
earth stations	optical LOS	unguided media
effective area	parabolic reflective antenna	unshielded twisted pair
fiber optic cable	radio	(UTP)
free space loss	radio LOS	uplink
global positioning system	reflection	wavelength division
(GPS)	refraction	multiplexing (WDM)
graded-index multimode	refractive index	wireless transmission
ground wave propagation	scattering	

Review Questions

4.1. Why are the wires twisted in twisted-pair copper wire?

4.2. What are some major limitations of twisted-pair wire?

4.3. What is the difference between unshielded twisted pair and shielded twisted pair?

4.4. Describe the components of optical fiber cable.

4.5. What are some major advantages and disadvantages of microwave transmission?

4.6. What is direct broadcast satellite (DBS)?

4.7. Why must a satellite have distinct uplink and downlink frequencies?

4.8. Indicate some significant differences between broadcast radio and microwave.

4.9. What two functions are performed by an antenna?

4.10. What is an isotropic antenna?

4.11. What is the advantage of a parabolic reflective antenna?

4.12. What factors determine antenna gain?

4.13. What is the primary cause of signal loss in satellite communications?

4.14. What is refraction?

4.15. What is the difference between diffraction and scattering?

Problems

4.1. A UTP cable has a bit rate of 10 Mbps and a propagation delay of 4 μs/km. A sender intends to transmit a file of size 500 KB to a receiver who is connected with a cable length of 10,000 km. What are the propagation time and transmission time for transmitting this file? What is the latency of this communication?

4.2. A light signal is traveling through a single-mode fiber where the velocity of propagation is approximately 2.04 $\times$ 10^8 m/s. What will be the delay in the signal if the length of the cable is 8 km?

4.3. Given a 100-watt power source, what is the maximum allowable length for the following transmission media if a signal of 1 watt is to be received?
   a. 24-gauge (0.5 mm) twisted pair operating at 300 kHz
   b. 24-gauge (0.5 mm) twisted pair operating at 1 MHz
   c. 0.375-inch (9.5 mm) coaxial cable operating at 1 MHz
   d. 0.375-inch (9.5 mm) coaxial cable operating at 25 MHz
   e. optical fiber operating at its optimal frequency

4.4. Coaxial cable is a two-wire transmission system. What is the advantage of connecting the outer conductor to ground?

4.5. A microwave has a wavelength of 10 cm. What is the attenuation at a distance of 50 m?

4.6. It turns out that the depth in the ocean to which airborne electromagnetic signals can be detected grows with the wavelength. Therefore, the military got the idea of using very long wavelengths corresponding to about 30 Hz to communicate with submarines throughout the world. It is desirable to have an antenna that is about one-half wavelength long. How long would that be?

4.7. The audio power of the human voice is concentrated at about 300 Hz. Antennas of the appropriate size for this frequency are impracticably large, so that to send voice by radio the voice signal must be used to modulate a higher (carrier) frequency for which the natural antenna size is smaller.
   a. What is the length of an antenna one-half wavelength long for sending radio at 300 Hz?
   b. An alternative is to use a modulation scheme, as described in Chapter 5, for transmitting the voice signal by modulating a carrier frequency, so that the bandwidth of the signal is a narrow band centered on the carrier frequency. Suppose we would like a half-wave antenna to have a length of 1 m. What carrier frequency would we use?

4.8. Stories abound of people who receive radio signals in fillings in their teeth. Suppose you have one filling that is 2.5 mm (0.0025 m) long that acts as a radio antenna. That is, it is equal in length to one-half the wavelength. What frequency do you receive?

4.9. You are communicating between two satellites. The transmission obeys the free space law. The signal is too weak. Your vendor offers you two options. The vendor can use a higher frequency that is twice the current frequency or can double the effective area of both of the antennas. Which will offer you more received power or will both offer the same improvement, all other factors remaining equal? How much improvement in the received power do you obtain from the best option?

4.10. In satellite communications, different frequency bands are used for the uplink and the downlink. Discuss why this pattern occurs.

4.11. For radio transmission in free space, signal power is reduced in proportion to the square of the distance from the source, whereas in wire transmission, the attenuation is a fixed number of dB per kilometer. The following table is used to show the dB reduction relative to some reference for free space radio and uniform wire. Fill in the missing numbers to complete the table.

Distance (km)	Radio (dB)	Wire (dB)
1	−6	−3
2		
4		
8		
16		

4.12. Section 4.2 states that if a source of electromagnetic energy is placed at the focus of the paraboloid, and if the paraboloid is a reflecting surface, then the wave will bounce back in lines parallel to the axis of the paraboloid. To demonstrate this, consider the parabola $y^2 = 2px$ shown in Figure 4.15. Let $P(x_1, y_1)$ be a point on the parabola, and PF be the line from P to the focus. Construct the line L through P parallel to the x-axis and the line M tangent to the parabola at P. The angle between L and M is β, and the angle between PF and M is α. The angle α is the angle at which a ray from F strikes the parabola at P. Because the angle of incidence equals the angle of reflection, the ray reflected from P must be at an angle α to M. Thus, if we can show that $\alpha = \beta$, we have demonstrated that rays reflected from the parabola starting at F will be parallel to the x-axis.

    a. First show that $\tan \beta = (p/y_1)$. *Hint:* Recall from trigonometry that the slope of a line is equal to the tangent of the angle the line makes with the positive x-direction. Also recall that the slope of the line tangent to a curve at a given point is equal to the derivative of the curve at that point.

    b. Now show that $\tan \alpha = (p/y_1)$, which demonstrates that $\alpha = \beta$. *Hint:* Recall from trigonometry that the formula for the tangent of the difference between two angles α_1 and α_2 is $\tan(\alpha_2 - \alpha_1) = (\tan \alpha_2 - \tan \alpha_1)/(1 + \tan \alpha_2 \times \tan \alpha_1)$.

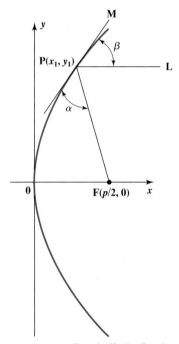

Figure 4.15 Parabolic Reflection

4.13. What is the maximum distance at which two antennas at heights of 100 m and 80 m may be placed for optical line-of-sight transmission?

4.14. Suppose a transmitter produces 50 W of power.

   a. Express the transmit power in units of dBm and dBW.
   b. If the transmitter's power is applied to a unity gain antenna with a 900 MHz carrier frequency, what is the received power in dBm at a free space distance of 100 m?
   c. Repeat (b) for a distance of 10 km.
   d. Repeat (c) but assume a receiver antenna gain of 2.

4.15. A microwave transmitter has an output of 0.1 W at 2 GHz. Assume that this transmitter is used in a microwave communication system where the transmitting and receiving antennas are parabolas, each 1.2 m in diameter.

   a. What is the gain of each antenna in decibels?
   b. Taking into account antenna gain, what is the effective radiated power of the transmitted signal?
   c. If the receiving antenna is located 24 km from the transmitting antenna over a free space path, find the available signal power out of the receiving antenna in dBm units.

4.16. Section 4.3 states that with no intervening obstacles, the optical line of sight can be expressed as $d = 3.57\sqrt{h}$, where d is the distance between an antenna and the horizon in kilometers and h is the antenna height in meters. Using a value for the Earth's radius of 6370 km, derive this equation. *Hint:* Assume that the antenna is perpendicular to the Earth's surface, and note that the line from the top of the antenna to the horizon forms a tangent to the Earth's surface at the horizon. Draw a picture showing the antenna, the line of sight, and the Earth's radius to help visualize the problem.

4.17. An isotropic antenna is transmitting signals at a frequency of 600 MHz. What will be the free space loss at a distance of 10 km?

4.18. A beam of light is moving from a fiber glass of high optical density to a fiber glass of low optical density. The critical angle is 45°. State what happens if the light ray is incident at angles 40°, 45°, and 50°, and compute the relative refractive indexes of the fiber glass.

CHAPTER 5

SIGNAL ENCODING TECHNIQUES

LEARNING OBJECTIVES

After studying this chapter, you should be able to:

◆ Understand how both analog and digital information can be encoded as either analog or digital signals.

◆ Present an overview of the basic methods of encoding digital data into a digital signal.

◆ Present an overview of the basic methods of encoding digital data into an analog signal.

◆ Present an overview of the basic methods of encoding analog data into a digital signal.

In Chapter 3 a distinction was made between analog and digital data, and analog and digital signals. Figure 3.14 suggested that either form of data could be encoded into either form of signal.

Figure 5.1 is another depiction that emphasizes the process involved. For **digital signaling**, a data source $g(t)$, which may be either digital or analog, is encoded into a digital signal $x(t)$. The actual form of $x(t)$ depends on the encoding technique and is chosen to optimize use of the transmission medium. For example, the encoding may be chosen to conserve bandwidth or to minimize errors.

The basis for **analog signaling** is a continuous constant-frequency signal known as the **carrier signal**. The frequency of the carrier signal is chosen to be compatible with the transmission medium being used. Data may be transmitted using a carrier signal by modulation. **Modulation** is the process of encoding source data onto a carrier signal with frequency f_c. All modulation techniques involve operation on one or more of the three fundamental carrier signal parameters: amplitude, frequency, and phase.

The input signal $m(t)$ may be analog or digital and is called the modulating signal or **baseband signal**. The result of modulating the carrier signal is called the modulated signal $s(t)$. As Figure 5.1b indicates, $s(t)$ is a bandlimited (bandpass) signal. The location of the bandwidth on the spectrum is related to f_c and is often centered on f_c. Again, the actual form of the encoding is chosen to optimize some characteristics of the transmission.

Each of the four possible combinations depicted in Figure 5.1 is in widespread use. The reasons for choosing a particular combination for any given communication task vary. We list here some representative reasons:

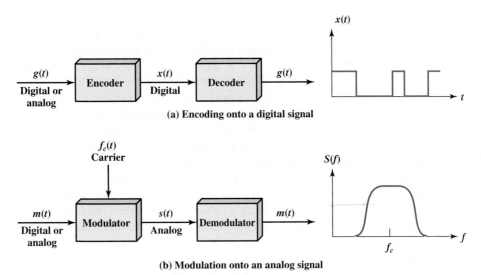

Figure 5.1   Encoding and Modulation Techniques

- **Digital data, digital signal:** In general, the equipment for encoding digital data into a digital signal is less complex and less expensive than digital-to-analog modulation equipment.
- **Analog data, digital signal:** Conversion of analog data to digital form permits the use of modern digital transmission and switching equipment. The advantages of the digital approach were outlined in Section 3.2.
- **Digital data, analog signal:** Some transmission media, such as optical fiber and unguided media, will only propagate analog signals.
- **Analog data, analog signal:** Analog data in electrical form can be transmitted as baseband signals easily and cheaply. This is done with voice transmission over voice-grade lines. One common use of modulation is to shift the bandwidth of a baseband signal to another portion of the spectrum. In this way multiple signals, each at a different position on the spectrum, can share the same transmission medium. This is known as frequency division multiplexing.

This chapter discusses the encoding for the first three of these combinations. The case of encoding analog data as analog signals is somewhat more complex mathematically.

5.1   DIGITAL DATA, DIGITAL SIGNALS

A digital signal is a sequence of discrete, discontinuous voltage pulses. Each pulse is a signal element. Binary data are transmitted by encoding each data bit into signal elements. In the simplest case, there is a one-to-one correspondence between bits and signal elements. An example is shown in Figure 3.16, in which binary 1 is represented by a lower voltage level and binary 0 by a higher voltage level. We show in this section that a variety of other encoding schemes are also used.

First, we define some terms. If the signal elements all have the same algebraic sign, that is, all positive or negative, then the signal is **unipolar**. In **polar** signaling, one logic state is represented by a positive voltage level and the other by a negative voltage level. The **data signaling rate**, or just **data rate**, of a signal is the rate, in bits per second, that data are transmitted. The duration or length of a bit is the amount of time it takes for the transmitter to emit the bit; for a data rate R, the bit duration is $1/R$. The **modulation rate**, by contrast, is the rate at which the signal level is changed. This will depend on the nature of the digital encoding, as explained later. The modulation rate is expressed in baud, which means signal elements per second. Finally, the terms *mark* and *space*, for historical reasons, refer to the binary digits 1 and 0, respectively. Table 5.1 summarizes key terms; these should be clearer when we see an example later in this section.

The tasks involved in interpreting digital signals at the receiver can be summarized by again referring to Figure 3.16. First, the receiver must know the timing of each bit; that is, the receiver must know with some accuracy when a bit begins and ends. Second, the receiver must determine whether the signal level for each bit position is high (0) or low (1). In Figure 3.16, these tasks are performed by sampling each bit position in the middle of the interval and comparing the value to a threshold. Because of noise and other impairments, there will be errors, as shown.

What factors determine how successful the receiver will be in interpreting the incoming signal? We saw in Chapter 3 that three factors are important: the signal-to-noise ratio (SNR), the data rate, and the bandwidth. With other factors held constant, the following statements are true:

- An increase in data rate increases **bit error rate** (BER).[1]
- An increase in SNR decreases bit error rate.
- An increase in bandwidth allows an increase in data rate.

Table 5.1   Key Data Transmission Terms

Term	Units	Definition
Data element	Bits	A single binary one or zero
Data rate	Bits per second (bps)	The rate at which data elements are transmitted
Signal element	Digital: a voltage pulse of constant amplitude	That part of a signal that occupies the shortest interval of a signaling code
	Analog: a pulse of constant frequency, phase, and amplitude	
Signaling rate or modulation rate	Signal elements per second (baud)	The rate at which signal elements are transmitted

[1]The BER is the most common measure of error performance on a data circuit and is defined as the probability that a bit is received in error. It is also called the bit error ratio. This latter term is clearer, because the term *rate* typically refers to some quantity that varies with time. Unfortunately, most books and standards documents refer to the R in BER as *rate*.

Table 5.2   Definition of Digital Signal Encoding Formats

Nonreturn to Zero-Level (NRZ-L)
0 = high level
1 = low level
Nonreturn to Zero Inverted (NRZI)
0 = no transition at beginning of interval (one bit time)
1 = transition at beginning of interval
Bipolar-AMI
0 = no line signal
1 = positive or negative level, alternating for successive ones
Pseudoternary
0 = positive or negative level, alternating for successive zeros
1 = no line signal
Manchester
0 = transition from high to low in middle of interval
1 = transition from low to high in middle of interval
Differential Manchester
Always a transition in middle of interval
0 = transition at beginning of interval
1 = no transition at beginning of interval
B8ZS
Same as bipolar AMI, except that any string of eight zeros is replaced by a string with two code violations
HDB3
Same as bipolar AMI, except that any string of four zeros is replaced by a string with one code violation

There is another factor that can be used to improve performance, and that is the encoding scheme. The encoding scheme is simply the mapping from data bits to signal elements. A variety of approaches have been tried. In what follows, we describe some of the more common ones; they are defined in Table 5.2.

> **EXAMPLE 5.1** Figure 5.2 shows the signal encoding for the binary sequence 01001100011 using six different signal encoding schemes.

Before describing these techniques, let us consider the following ways of evaluating or comparing the various techniques.

- **Signal spectrum:** Several aspects of the signal spectrum are important. A lack of high-frequency components means that less bandwidth is required for transmission. In addition, lack of a direct-current (dc) component is also desirable. With a dc component to the signal, there must be direct physical attachment of transmission components. With no dc component, ac coupling via transformer is possible; this provides excellent electrical isolation, reducing interference.

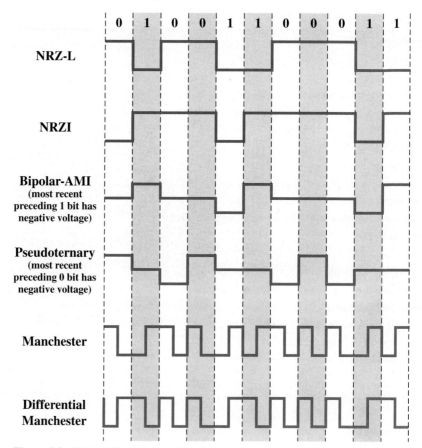

Figure 5.2 Digital Signal Encoding Formats

Finally, the magnitude of the effects of signal distortion and interference depends on the spectral properties of the transmitted signal. In practice, it usually happens that the transmission characteristics of a channel are worse near the band edges. Therefore, a good signal design should concentrate the transmitted power in the middle of the transmission bandwidth. In such a case, a smaller distortion should be present in the received signal. To meet this objective, codes can be designed with the aim of shaping the spectrum of the transmitted signal.

• **Clocking:** We mentioned the need to determine the beginning and end of each bit position. This is no easy task. One rather expensive approach is to provide a separate clock lead to synchronize the transmitter and receiver. The alternative is to provide some synchronization mechanism that is based on the transmitted signal. This can be achieved with suitable encoding, as explained subsequently.

• **Error detection:** We will discuss various error-detection techniques in Chapter 6 and show that these are the responsibility of a layer of logic above the signaling level that is known as data link control. However, it is useful to have some error-detection capability built into the physical signaling encoding scheme. This permits errors to be detected more quickly.

- **Signal interference and noise immunity:** Certain codes exhibit superior performance in the presence of noise. Performance is usually expressed in terms of a BER.

- **Cost and complexity:** Although digital logic continues to drop in price, this factor should not be ignored. In particular, the higher the signaling rate to achieve a given data rate, the greater the cost. We shall see that some codes require a signaling rate that is greater than the actual data rate.

We now turn to a discussion of various techniques.

Nonreturn to Zero (NRZ)

The most common, and easiest, way to transmit digital signals is to use two different voltage levels for the two binary digits. Codes that follow this strategy share the property that the voltage level is constant during a bit interval; there is no transition (no return to a zero voltage level). For example, the absence of voltage can be used to represent binary 0, with a constant positive voltage used to represent binary 1. More commonly, a negative voltage represents one binary value and a positive voltage represents the other. This latter code, known as **Nonreturn to Zero-Level (NRZ-L)**, is illustrated[2] in Figure 5.2. NRZ-L is typically the code used to generate or interpret digital data by terminals and other devices. If a different code is to be used for transmission, it is generated from an NRZ-L signal by the transmission system [in terms of Figure 5.1, NRZ-L is $g(t)$ and the encoded signal is $x(t)$].

A variation of **NRZ** is known as **NRZI** (Nonreturn to Zero, invert on ones). As with NRZ-L, NRZI maintains a constant voltage pulse for the duration of a bit time. The data themselves are encoded as the presence or absence of a signal transition at the beginning of the bit time. A transition (low to high or high to low) at the beginning of a bit time denotes a binary 1 for that bit time; no transition indicates a binary 0.

NRZI is an example of **differential encoding**. In differential encoding, the information to be transmitted is represented in terms of the changes between successive signal elements rather than the signal elements themselves. The encoding of the current bit is determined as follows: If the current bit is a binary 0, then the current bit is encoded with the same signal as the preceding bit; if the current bit is a binary 1, then the current bit is encoded with a different signal than the preceding bit. One benefit of differential encoding is that it may be more reliable to detect a transition in the presence of noise than to compare a value to a threshold. Another benefit is that with a complex transmission layout, it is easy to lose the sense of the polarity of the signal. For example, on a multidrop twisted-pair line, if the leads from an attached device to the twisted pair are accidentally inverted, all 1s and 0s for NRZ-L will be inverted. This does not happen with differential encoding.

The NRZ codes are the easiest to engineer and, in addition, make efficient use of bandwidth. This latter property is illustrated in Figure 5.3, which compares the

---

[2]In this figure, a negative voltage is equated with binary 1 and a positive voltage with binary 0. This is the opposite of the definition used in virtually all other textbooks. The definition here conforms to the use of NRZ-L in data communications interfaces and the standards that govern those interfaces.

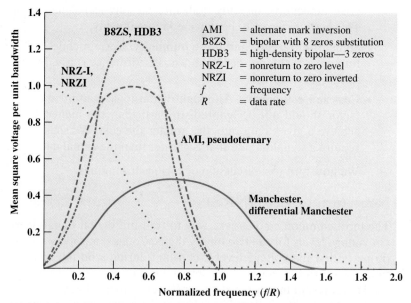

Figure 5.3   Spectral Density of Various Signal Encoding Schemes

spectral density of various encoding schemes. In the figure, frequency is normalized to the data rate. Most of the energy in NRZ and NRZI signals is between dc and half the bit rate. For example, if an NRZ code is used to generate a signal with data rate of 9600 bps, most of the energy in the signal is concentrated between dc and 4800 Hz.

The main limitations of NRZ signals are the presence of a dc component and the lack of synchronization capability. To picture the latter problem, consider that with a long string of 1s or 0s for NRZ-L or a long string of 0s for NRZI, the output is a constant voltage over a long period of time. Under these circumstances, any drift between the clocks of transmitter and receiver will result in loss of synchronization between the two.

Because of their simplicity and relatively low-frequency response characteristics, NRZ codes are commonly used for digital magnetic recording. However, their limitations make these codes unattractive for signal transmission applications.

Multilevel Binary

Multilevel binary encoding techniques address some of the deficiencies of the NRZ codes. These codes use more than two signal levels. Two examples of this scheme are illustrated in Figure 5.2, bipolar-AMI (alternate mark inversion) and pseudoternary.[3]

In the case of the **bipolar-AMI** scheme, a binary 0 is represented by no line signal, and a binary 1 is represented by a positive or negative pulse. The binary

---

[3]These terms are not used consistently in the literature. In some books, these two terms are used for different encoding schemes than those defined here, and a variety of terms have been used for the two schemes illustrated in Figure 5.2. The nomenclature used here corresponds to the usage in various ITU-T standards documents.

1 pulses must alternate in polarity. There are several advantages to this approach. First, there will be no loss of synchronization if a long string of 1s occurs. Each 1 introduces a transition, and the receiver can resynchronize on that transition. A long string of 0s would still be a problem. Second, because the 1 signals alternate in voltage from positive to negative, there is no net dc component. Also, the bandwidth of the resulting signal is considerably less than the bandwidth for NRZ (Figure 5.3). Finally, the pulse alternation property provides a simple means of error detection. Any isolated error, whether it deletes a pulse or adds a pulse, causes a violation of this property.

The comments of the previous paragraph also apply to **pseudoternary**. In this case, it is the binary 1 that is represented by the absence of a line signal, and the binary 0 by alternating positive and negative pulses. There is no particular advantage of one technique versus the other, and each is the basis of some applications.

Although a degree of synchronization is provided with these codes, a long string of 0s in the case of AMI or 1s in the case of pseudoternary still presents a problem. Several techniques have been used to address this deficiency. One approach is to insert additional bits that force transitions. This technique is used in ISDN (integrated services digital network) for relatively low data rate transmission. Of course, at a high data rate, this scheme is expensive, because it results in an increase in an already high signal transmission rate. To deal with this problem at high data rates, a technique that involves **scrambling** the data is used. We examine two examples of this technique later in this section.

Thus, with suitable modification, multilevel binary schemes overcome the problems of NRZ codes. Of course, as with any engineering design decision, there is a trade-off. With multilevel binary coding, the line signal may take on one of three levels, but each signal element, which could represent $\log_2 3 = 1.58$ bits of information, bears only one bit of information. Thus multilevel binary is not as efficient as NRZ coding. Another way to state this is that the receiver of multilevel binary signals has to distinguish between three levels $(+A, -A, 0)$ instead of just two levels in the signaling formats previously discussed. Because of this, the multilevel binary signal requires approximately 3 dB more signal power than a two-valued signal for the same probability of bit error. This is illustrated in Figure 5.4. Put another way, the bit error rate for NRZ codes, at a given signal-to-noise ratio, is significantly less than that for multilevel binary.

Biphase

There is another set of coding techniques, grouped under the term **biphase**, that overcomes the limitations of NRZ codes. Two of these techniques, Manchester and differential Manchester, are in common use.

In the **Manchester** code, there is a transition at the middle of each bit period. The midbit transition serves as a clocking mechanism and also as data: A low-to-high transition represents a 1, and a high-to-low transition represents a 0.[4] In **differential**

---

[4]The definition of Manchester presented here is the opposite of that used in a number of respectable textbooks, in which a low-to-high transition represents a binary 0 and a high-to-low transition represents a binary 1. Here, we conform to industry practice and to the definition used in the various LAN standards, such as IEEE 802.3.

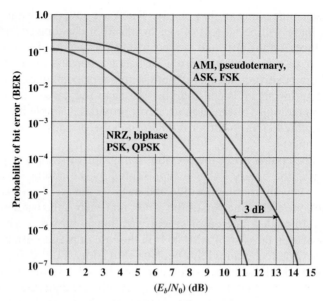

Figure 5.4 Theoretical Bit Error Rate for Various Encoding Schemes

Manchester, the midbit transition is used only to provide clocking. The encoding of a 0 is represented by the presence of a transition at the beginning of a bit period, and a 1 is represented by the absence of a transition at the beginning of a bit period. Differential Manchester has the added advantage of employing differential encoding.

All of the biphase techniques require at least one transition per bit time and may have as many as two transitions. Thus, the maximum modulation rate is twice that for NRZ; this means that the bandwidth required is correspondingly greater. On the other hand, the biphase schemes have several advantages:

- **Synchronization:** Because there is a predictable transition during each bit time, the receiver can synchronize on that transition. For this reason, the biphase codes are known as self-clocking codes.

- **No dc component:** Biphase codes have no dc component, yielding the benefits described earlier.

- **Error detection:** The absence of an expected transition can be used to detect errors. Noise on the line would have to invert both the signal before and after the expected transition to cause an undetected error.

As can be seen from Figure 5.3, the bandwidth for biphase codes is reasonably narrow and contains no dc component. However, it is wider than the bandwidth for the multilevel binary codes.

Biphase codes are popular techniques for data transmission. The more common Manchester code has been specified for the IEEE 802.3 (Ethernet) standard for baseband coaxial cable and twisted-pair bus LANs. Differential Manchester has been specified for the IEEE 802.5 token ring LAN, using shielded twisted pair.

Modulation Rate

When signal encoding techniques are used, a distinction needs to be made between data rate (expressed in bits per second) and modulation rate (expressed in baud). The data rate, or bit rate, is $1/T_b$, where T_b = bit duration. The modulation rate is the rate at which signal elements are generated. Consider, for example, Manchester encoding. The minimum size signal element is a pulse of one-half the duration of a bit interval. For a string of all binary 0s or all binary 1s, a continuous stream of such pulses is generated. Hence, the maximum modulation rate for Manchester is $2/T_b$. This situation is illustrated in Figure 5.5, which shows the transmission of a stream of binary 1s at a data rate of 1 Mbps using NRZI and Manchester. In general,

$$D = \frac{R}{L} = \frac{R}{\log_2 M} \qquad \text{(5.1)}$$

where

D = modulation rate, baud

R = data rate, bps

M = number of different signal elements = 2^L

L = number of bits per signal element

One way of characterizing the modulation rate is to determine the average number of transitions that occur per bit time. In general, this will depend on the exact sequence of bits being transmitted. Table 5.3 compares transition rates for various techniques. It indicates the signal transition rate in the case of a data stream of alternating 1s and 0s, and for the data stream that produces the minimum and maximum modulation rate.

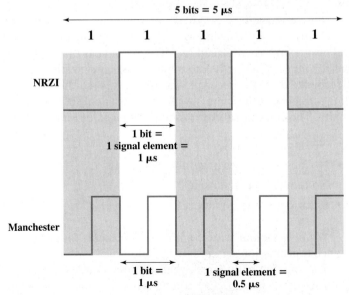

Figure 5.5   A Stream of Binary 1s at 1 Mbps

Table 5.3 Normalized Signal Transition Rate of Various Digital Signal Encoding Schemes

	Minimum	**101010...**	**Maximum**
NRZ-L	0 (all 0s or 1s)	1.0	1.0
NRZI	0 (all 0s)	0.5	1.0 (all 1s)
Bipolar-AMI	0 (all 0s)	1.0	1.0
Pseudoternary	0 (all 1s)	1.0	1.0
Manchester	1.0 (1010...)	1.0	2.0 (all 0s or 1s)
Differential Manchester	1.0 (all 1s)	1.5	2.0 (all 0s)

EXAMPLE 5.2 For the 11-bit binary string 01001100011 (Figure 5.2) the number of transitions for the encoding schemes discussed in this section is:

NRZ-L	5	Pseudoternary	8
NRZI	5	Manchester	16
Bipolar-AMI	7	Differential Manchester	16

Scrambling Techniques

Although the biphase techniques have achieved widespread use in local area network applications at relatively high data rates (up to 10 Mbps), they have not been widely used in long-distance applications. The principal reason for this is that they require a high signaling rate relative to the data rate. This sort of inefficiency is more costly in a long-distance application.

Another approach is to make use of some sort of scrambling scheme. The idea behind this approach is simple: Sequences that would result in a constant voltage level on the line are replaced by filling sequences that will provide sufficient transitions for the receiver's clock to maintain synchronization. The filling sequence must be recognized by the receiver and replaced with the original data sequence. The filling sequence is the same length as the original sequence, so there is no data rate penalty. The design goals for this approach can be summarized as follows:

- No dc component
- No long sequences of zero-level line signals
- No reduction in data rate
- Error-detection capability

We now look at two scrambling techniques that are commonly used in long-distance transmission services: B8ZS and HDB3.

The **bipolar with 8-zeros substitution (B8ZS)** coding scheme is commonly used in North America. The coding scheme is based on a bipolar-AMI. We have seen that the drawback of the AMI code is that a long string of zeros may result in loss of synchronization. To overcome this problem, the encoding is amended with the following rules:

- If an octet of all zeros occurs and the last voltage pulse preceding this octet was positive, then the eight zeros of the octet are encoded as 000+−0−+.
- If an octet of all zeros occurs and the last voltage pulse preceding this octet was negative, then the eight zeros of the octet are encoded as 000−+0+−.

This technique forces two code violations (signal patterns not allowed in AMI) of the AMI code, an event unlikely to be caused by noise or other transmission impairment. The receiver recognizes the pattern and interprets the octet as consisting of all zeros.

A coding scheme that is commonly used in Europe and Japan is known as the **high-density bipolar-3 zeros (HDB3)** code (Table 5.4). As before, it is based on the use of AMI encoding. In this case, the scheme replaces strings of four zeros with sequences containing one or two pulses. In each case, the fourth zero is replaced with a code violation. In addition, a rule is needed to ensure that successive violations are of alternate polarity so that no dc component is introduced. Thus, if the last violation was positive, this violation must be negative and vice versa. Table 5.4 shows that this condition is tested for by determining (1) whether the number of pulses since the last violation is even or odd and (2) the polarity of the last pulse before the occurrence of the four zeros.

EXAMPLE 5.3 Figure 5.6 shows the signal encoding for the binary sequence 1100000000110000010 using AMI, and then scrambled using B8ZS and HDB3. The original sequence includes a continuous strings of eight zeros and five zeros. B8ZS eliminates the string of eight zeros. HDB3 eliminates both strings. The total number of transitions for this sequence is 7 for Bipolar-AMI, 12 for B8ZS, and 14 for HDB3.

Figure 5.3 shows the spectral properties of these two codes. As can be seen, neither has a dc component. Most of the energy is concentrated in a relatively sharp spectrum around a frequency equal to one-half the data rate. Thus, these codes are well suited to high data rate transmission.

Table 5.4 HDB3 Substitution Rules

Polarity of Preceding Pulse	Number of Bipolar Pulses (ones) since Last Substitution	
	Odd	Even
−	000−	+00+
+	000+	−00−

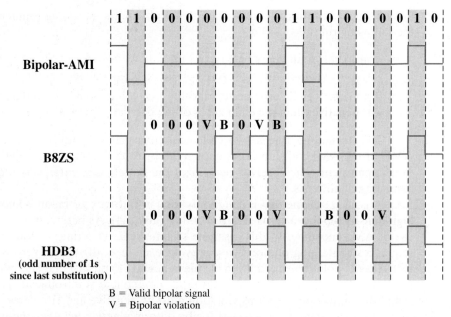

B = Valid bipolar signal
V = Bipolar violation

Figure 5.6   Encoding Rules for B8ZS and HDB3

5.2 DIGITAL DATA, ANALOG SIGNALS

We turn now to the case of transmitting digital data using analog signals. The most familiar use of this transformation is for transmitting digital data through the public telephone network. The telephone network was designed to receive, switch, and transmit analog signals in the voice-frequency range of about 300 to 3400 Hz. It is not at present suitable for handling digital signals from the subscriber locations (although this is beginning to change). Thus digital devices are attached to the network via a modem (modulator-demodulator), which converts digital data to analog signals, and vice versa.

For the telephone network, modems are used that produce signals in the voice-frequency range. The same basic techniques are used for modems that produce signals at higher frequencies (e.g., microwave). This section introduces these techniques and provides a brief discussion of the performance characteristics of the alternative approaches.

We mentioned that modulation involves operation on one or more of the three characteristics of a carrier signal: amplitude, frequency, and phase. Accordingly, there are three basic encoding or modulation techniques for transforming digital data into analog signals, as illustrated in Figure 5.7: amplitude shift keying (ASK), frequency shift keying (FSK), and phase shift keying (PSK). In all these cases, the resulting signal occupies a bandwidth centered on the carrier frequency. The term **carrier frequency** refers to a continuous frequency capable of being modulated or impressed with a second (information-carrying) signal.

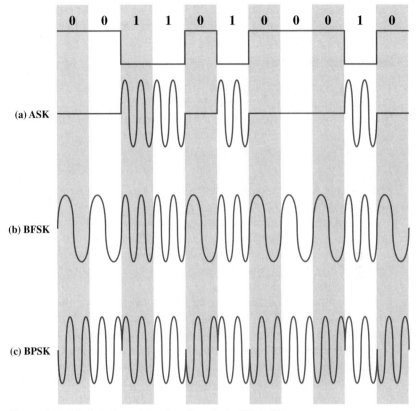

Figure 5.7 Modulation of Analog Signals for Digital Data

Amplitude Shift Keying

In ASK, the two binary values are represented by two different amplitudes of the carrier frequency. Commonly, one of the amplitudes is zero; that is, one binary digit is represented by the presence, at constant amplitude, of the carrier, the other by the absence of the carrier (Figure 5.7a). The resulting transmitted signal for one bit time is

$$\textbf{ASK} \quad s(t) = \begin{cases} A\cos(2\pi f_c t) & \text{binary 1} \\ 0 & \text{binary 0} \end{cases} \tag{5.2}$$

where the carrier signal is $A\cos(2\pi f_c t)$. ASK is susceptible to sudden gain changes and is a rather inefficient modulation technique. On voice-grade lines, it is typically used only up to 1200 bps.

The ASK technique is used to transmit digital data over optical fiber. For LED (light-emitting diode) transmitters, Equation (5.2) is valid. That is, one signal element is represented by a light pulse while the other signal element is represented by the absence of light. Laser transmitters normally have a fixed "bias" current that causes the device to emit a low light level. This low level represents one signal element, while a higher-amplitude lightwave represents another signal element.

Frequency Shift Keying

The most common form of FSK is binary FSK (BFSK), in which the two binary values are represented by two different frequencies near the carrier frequency (Figure 5.7b). The resulting transmitted signal for one bit time is

$$\textbf{BFSK} \quad s(t) = \begin{cases} A \cos(2\pi f_1 t) & \text{binary 1} \\ A \cos(2\pi f_2 t) & \text{binary 0} \end{cases} \qquad \textbf{(5.3)}$$

where f_1 and f_2 are typically offset from the carrier frequency f_c by equal but opposite amounts.

Figure 5.8 shows an example of the use of BFSK for full-duplex operation over a voice-grade line. The figure is a specification for the Bell System 108 series modems. Recall that a voice-grade line will pass frequencies in the approximate range 300 to 3400 Hz, and that *full duplex* means that signals are transmitted in both directions at the same time. To achieve full-duplex transmission, this bandwidth is split. In one direction (transmit or receive), the frequencies used to represent 1 and 0 are centered on 1170 Hz, with a shift of 100 Hz on either side. The effect of alternating between those two frequencies is to produce a signal whose spectrum is indicated as the shaded area on the left in Figure 5.8. Similarly, for the other direction (receive or transmit) the modem uses frequencies shifted 100 Hz to each side of a center frequency of 2125 Hz. This signal is indicated by the shaded area on the right in Figure 5.8. Note that there is little overlap and thus little interference.

BFSK is less susceptible to error than ASK. On voice-grade lines, it is typically used up to 1200 bps. It is also commonly used for high-frequency (3 to 30 MHz) radio transmission. It can also be used at even higher frequencies on local area networks that use coaxial cable.

A signal that is more bandwidth efficient, but also more susceptible to error, is multiple FSK (MFSK), in which more than two frequencies are used. In this case

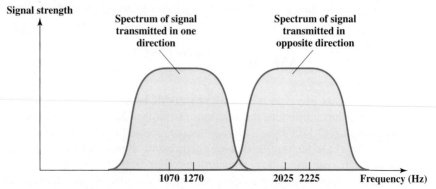

Figure 5.8   Full-Duplex FSK Transmission on a Voice-Grade Line

each signaling element represents more than one bit. The transmitted MFSK signal for one signal element time can be defined as follows:

$$\textbf{MFSK} \qquad s_i(t) = A \cos 2\pi f_i t, \qquad 1 \le i \le M \qquad \textbf{(5.4)}$$

where

$$f_i = f_c + (2i - 1 - M)f_d$$

f_c = the carrier frequency

f_d = the difference frequency

M = number of different signal elements = 2^L

L = number of bits per signal element

To match the data rate of the input bit stream, each output signal element is held for a period of $T_s = LT$ seconds, where T is the bit period (data rate = $1/T$). Thus, one signal element, which is a constant-frequency tone, encodes L bits. The total bandwidth required is $2Mf_d$. It can be shown that the minimum frequency separation required is $2f_d = 1/T_s$. Therefore, the modulator requires a bandwidth of $W_d = 2Mf_d = M/T_s$.

EXAMPLE 5.4 With $f_c = 250$ kHz, $f_d = 25$ kHz, and $M = 8$ ($L = 3$ bits), we have the following frequency assignments for each of the eight possible 3-bit data combinations:

$f_1 = 75$ kHz 000 $\quad f_2 = 125$ kHz 001 $\quad f_3 = 175$ kHz 010 $\quad f_4 = 225$ kHz 011
$f_5 = 275$ kHz 100 $\quad f_6 = 325$ kHz 101 $\quad f_7 = 375$ kHz 110 $\quad f_8 = 425$ kHz 111

This scheme can support a data rate of $1/T = 2Lf_d = 150$ kbps.

EXAMPLE 5.5 Figure 5.9 shows an example of MFSK with $M = 4$. An input bit stream of 20 bits is encoded 2 bits at a time, with each of the four possible 2-bit combinations transmitted as a different frequency. The display in the figure shows the frequency transmitted (y-axis) as a function of time (x-axis). Each column represents a time unit T_s in which a single 2-bit signal element is transmitted. The shaded rectangle in the column indicates the frequency transmitted during that time unit.

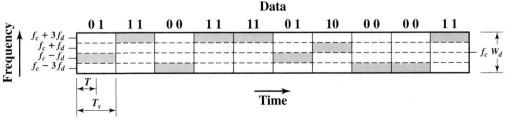

Figure 5.9   MFSK Frequency Use ($M = 4$)

Phase Shift Keying

In PSK, the phase of the carrier signal is shifted to represent data.

TWO-LEVEL PSK The simplest scheme uses two phases to represent the two binary digits (Figure 5.7c) and is known as binary phase shift keying. The resulting transmitted signal for one bit time is

$$\textbf{BPSK} \quad s(t) = \begin{cases} A\cos(2\pi f_c t) \\ A\cos(2\pi f_c t + \pi) \end{cases} = \begin{cases} A\cos(2\pi f_c t) & \text{binary 1} \\ -A\cos(2\pi f_c t) & \text{binary 0} \end{cases} \quad \textbf{(5.5)}$$

Because a phase shift of 180° (π) is equivalent to flipping the sine wave or multiplying it by −1, the rightmost expressions in Equation (5.5) can be used. This leads to a convenient formulation. If we have a bit stream, and we define $d(t)$ as the discrete function that takes on the value of +1 for one bit time if the corresponding bit in the bit stream is 1 and the value of −1 for one bit time if the corresponding bit in the bit stream is 0, then we can define the transmitted signal as

$$\textbf{BPSK} \quad s_d(t) = A\,d(t)\cos(2\pi f_c t) \quad \textbf{(5.6)}$$

An alternative form of two-level PSK is **differential PSK (DPSK)**. Figure 5.10 shows an example. In this scheme, a binary 0 is represented by sending a signal burst of the same phase as the previous signal burst sent. A binary 1 is represented by sending a signal burst of opposite phase to the preceding one. This term *differential* refers to the fact that the phase shift is with reference to the previous bit transmitted rather than to some constant reference signal. In differential encoding, the information to be transmitted is represented in terms of the changes between successive data symbols rather than the signal elements themselves. DPSK avoids the requirement for an accurate local oscillator phase at the receiver that is matched with the transmitter. As long as the preceding phase is received correctly, the phase reference is accurate.

FOUR-LEVEL PSK More efficient use of bandwidth can be achieved if each signaling element represents more than one bit. For example, instead of a phase shift

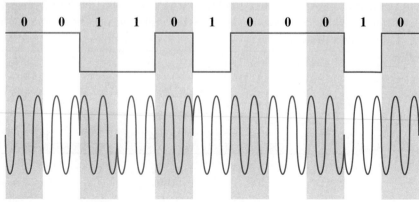

Figure 5.10 Differential Phase−Shift Keying (DPSK)

of 180°, as allowed in BPSK, a common encoding technique known as quadrature phase shift keying (QPSK) uses phase shifts separated by multiples of $\pi/2$ (90°).

$$\textbf{QPSK}\quad s(t) = \begin{cases} A\cos\left(2\pi f_c t + \dfrac{\pi}{4}\right) & 11 \\[2ex] A\cos\left(2\pi f_c t + \dfrac{3\pi}{4}\right) & 01 \\[2ex] A\cos\left(2\pi f_c t - \dfrac{3\pi}{4}\right) & 00 \\[2ex] A\cos\left(2\pi f_c t - \dfrac{\pi}{4}\right) & 10 \end{cases} \tag{5.7}$$

Thus each signal element represents two bits rather than one.

Figure 5.11 shows the QPSK modulation scheme in general terms. The input is a stream of binary digits with a data rate of $R = 1/T_b$, where T_b is the width of each bit. This stream is converted into two separate bit streams of $R/2$ bps each, by taking alternate bits for the two streams. The two data streams are referred to as the I (in-phase) and Q (quadrature phase) streams. In the diagram, the upper stream is modulated on a carrier of frequency f_c by multiplying the bit stream by the carrier. For convenience of modulator structure we map binary 1 to $\sqrt{1/2}$ and binary 0 to $-\sqrt{1/2}$. Thus, a binary 1 is represented by a scaled version of the carrier wave and a binary 0 is represented by a scaled version of the negative of the carrier wave, both at a constant amplitude. This same carrier wave is shifted by 90° and used for modulation of the lower binary stream. The two modulated signals are then added together and transmitted. The transmitted signal can be expressed as follows:

$$\textbf{QPSK}\quad s(t) = \frac{1}{\sqrt{2}} I(t)\cos 2\pi f_c t - \frac{1}{\sqrt{2}} Q(t)\sin 2\pi f_c t$$

Figure 5.12 shows an example of QPSK coding. Each of the two modulated streams is a BPSK signal at half the data rate of the original bit stream. Thus, the

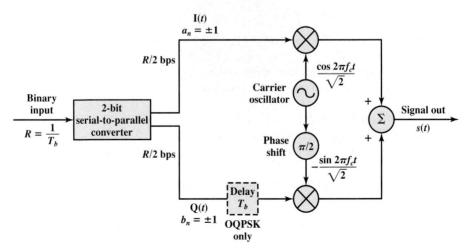

Figure 5.11 QPSK and OQPSK Modulators

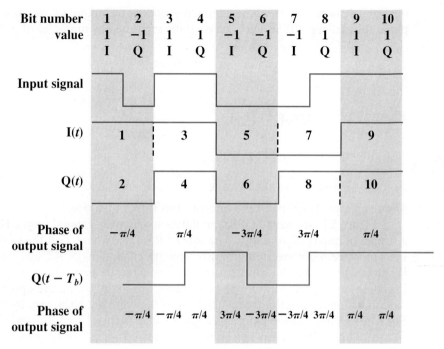

Figure 5.12 Example of QPSK and OQPSK Waveforms

combined signals have a symbol rate that is half the input bit rate. Note that from one symbol time to the next, a phase change of as much as 180° (π) is possible.

Figure 5.11 also shows a variation of QPSK known as offset QPSK (OQPSK), or orthogonal QPSK. The difference is that a delay of one bit time is introduced in the Q stream, resulting in the following signal:

$$s(t) = \frac{1}{\sqrt{2}} I(t) \cos 2\pi f_c t \; - \; \frac{1}{\sqrt{2}} Q(t \; - \; T_b) \sin 2\pi f_c t$$

Because OQPSK differs from QPSK only by the delay in the Q stream, its spectral characteristics and bit-error performance are the same as that of QPSK. From Figure 5.12, we can observe that only one of two bits in the pair can change sign at any time and thus the phase change in the combined signal never exceeds 90° ($\pi/2$). This can be an advantage because physical limitations on phase modulators make large phase shifts at high transition rates difficult to perform. OQPSK also provides superior performance when the transmission channel (including transmitter and receiver) has significant nonlinear components. The effect of nonlinearities is a spreading of the signal bandwidth, which may result in adjacent channel interference. It is easier to control this spreading if the phase changes are smaller, hence the advantage of OQPSK over QPSK.

MULTILEVEL PSK The use of multiple levels can be extended beyond taking bits two at a time. It is possible to transmit bits three at a time using eight different phase angles. Further, each angle can have more than one amplitude. For example, a standard 9600 bps modem uses 12 phase angles, four of which have two amplitude values, for a total of 16 different signal elements.

This latter example points out very well the difference between the data rate R (in bps) and the modulation rate D (in baud) of a signal. Let us assume that this scheme is being employed with digital input in which each bit is represented by a constant voltage pulse, one level for binary 1 and one level for binary 0. The data rate is $R = 1/T_b$. However, the encoded signal contains $L = 4$ bits in each signal element using $M = 16$ different combinations of amplitude and phase. The modulation rate can be seen to be $R/4$, because each change of signal element communicates four bits. Thus the line signaling speed is 2400 baud, but the data rate is 9600 bps. This is the reason that higher bit rates can be achieved over voice-grade lines by employing more complex modulation schemes.

Performance

In looking at the performance of various digital-to-analog modulation schemes, the first parameter of interest is the bandwidth of the modulated signal. This depends on a variety of factors, including the definition of bandwidth used and the filtering technique used to create the bandpass signal. We will use some straightforward results from [COUC13].

The transmission bandwidth B_T for ASK is of the form

$$\textbf{ASK} \qquad B_T = (1 + r)R \qquad \textbf{(5.8)}$$

where R is the bit rate and r is related to the technique by which the signal is filtered to establish a bandwidth for transmission, typically $0 < r < 1$. Thus the bandwidth is directly related to the bit rate. The preceding formula is also valid for PSK and, under certain assumptions, FSK.

With multilevel PSK (MPSK), significant improvements in bandwidth can be achieved. In general

$$\textbf{MPSK} \qquad B_T = \left(\frac{1 + r}{L}\right)R = \left(\frac{1 + r}{\log_2 M}\right)R \qquad \textbf{(5.9)}$$

where L is the number of bits encoded per signal element and M is the number of different signal elements.

For multilevel FSK (MFSK), we have

$$\textbf{MFSK} \qquad B_T = \left(\frac{(1 + r)M}{\log_2 M}\right)R \qquad \textbf{(5.10)}$$

Table 5.5 shows the ratio of data rate, R, to transmission bandwidth for various schemes. This ratio is also referred to as the **bandwidth efficiency**. As the name suggests, this parameter measures the efficiency with which bandwidth can be used to transmit data. The advantage of multilevel signaling methods now becomes clear.

Of course, the preceding discussion refers to the spectrum of the input signal to a communications line. Nothing has yet been said of performance in the presence of noise. Figure 5.4 summarizes some results based on reasonable assumptions concerning the transmission system [COUC13]. Here bit error rate is plotted as a function of the ratio E_b/N_0 defined in Chapter 3. Of course, as that ratio increases,

Table 5.5 Bandwidth Efficiency (R/B_T) for Various Digital-to-Analog Encoding Schemes

	$r = 0$	$r = 0.5$	$r = 1$
ASK	1.0	0.67	0.5
Multilevel FSK			
$M = 4, L = 2$	0.5	0.33	0.25
$M = 8, L = 3$	0.375	0.25	0.1875
$M = 16, L = 4$	0.25	0.167	0.125
$M = 32, L = 5$	0.156	0.104	0.078
PSK	1.0	0.67	0.5
Multilevel PSK			
$M = 4, L = 2$	2.00	1.33	1.00
$M = 8, L = 3$	3.00	2.00	1.50
$M = 16, L = 4$	4.00	2.67	2.00
$M = 32, L = 5$	5.00	3.33	2.50

the bit error rate drops. Further, DPSK and BPSK are about 3 dB superior to ASK and BFSK.

Figure 5.13 shows the same information for various levels of M for MFSK and MPSK. There is an important difference. For MFSK, the error probability for a given value of E_b/N_0 decreases as M increases, while the opposite is true for MPSK. On the other hand, comparing Equations (5.9) and (5.10), the bandwidth efficiency of MFSK decreases as M increases, while the opposite is true of MPSK. Thus, in both cases, there is a trade-off between bandwidth efficiency and error performance: An increase in bandwidth efficiency results in an increase in error probability. The fact that these trade-offs move in opposite directions with respect

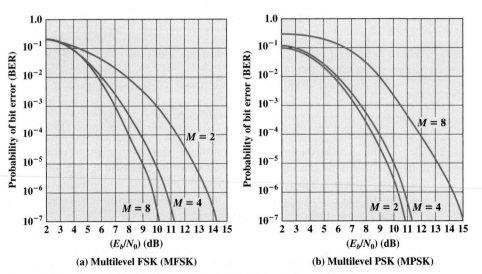

(a) Multilevel FSK (MFSK) (b) Multilevel PSK (MPSK)

Figure 5.13 Theoretical Bit Error Rate for Multilevel FSK and PSK

to the number of levels M for MFSK and MPSK can be derived from the underlying equations. A discussion of the reasons for this difference is beyond the scope of this book. See [SKLA01] for a full treatment.

EXAMPLE 5.6 What is the bandwidth efficiency for FSK, ASK, PSK, and QPSK for a bit error rate of 10^{-7} on a channel with an SNR of 12 dB?

Using Equation (3.2), we have

$$\left(\frac{E_b}{N_0}\right)_{dB} = 12\,dB - \left(\frac{R}{B_T}\right)_{dB}$$

For FSK and ASK, from Figure 5.4,

$$\left(\frac{E_b}{N_0}\right)_{dB} = 14.2\,dB$$

$$\left(\frac{R}{B_T}\right)_{dB} = -2.2\,dB$$

$$\frac{R}{B_T} = 0.6$$

For PSK, from Figure 5.4

$$\left(\frac{E_b}{N_0}\right)_{dB} = 11.2\,dB$$

$$\left(\frac{R}{B_T}\right)_{dB} = 0.8\,dB$$

$$\frac{R}{B_T} = 1.2$$

The result for QPSK must take into account that the baud rate $D = R/2$. Thus

$$\frac{R}{B_T} = 2.4$$

As the preceding example shows, ASK and FSK exhibit the same bandwidth efficiency; PSK is better, and even greater improvement can be achieved with multilevel signaling.

It is worthwhile to compare these bandwidth requirements with those for digital signaling. A good approximation is

$$B_T = 0.5(1 + r)D$$

where D is the modulation rate. For NRZ, $D = R$, and we have

$$\frac{R}{B_T} = \frac{2}{1 + r}$$

Thus digital signaling is in the same ballpark, in terms of bandwidth efficiency, as ASK, FSK, and PSK. A significant advantage for analog signaling is seen with multilevel techniques.

Quadrature Amplitude Modulation

Quadrature amplitude modulation (QAM) is a popular analog signaling technique that is used in the asymmetric digital subscriber line (ADSL) and in cable modems, described in Chapter 8, and in some wireless standards. This modulation technique is a combination of ASK and PSK. QAM can also be considered a logical extension of QPSK. QAM takes advantage of the fact that it is possible to send two different signals simultaneously on the same carrier frequency, by using two copies of the carrier frequency, one shifted by 90° with respect to the other. For QAM, each carrier is ASK modulated. The two independent signals are simultaneously transmitted over the same medium. At the receiver, the two signals are demodulated and the results are combined to produce the original binary input.

Figure 5.14 shows the QAM modulation scheme in general terms. The input is a stream of binary digits arriving at a rate of R bps. The binary digits are represented by 1 and –1 for binary 1 and binary 0, respectively. This stream is converted into two separate bit streams of $R/2$ bps each, by taking alternate bits for the two streams. In the diagram, the upper stream is ASK modulated on a carrier of frequency f_c by multiplying the bit stream by the carrier. Thus, a binary 0 is represented by $-\cos 2\pi f_c t$ and a binary 1 is represented by $+\cos 2\pi f_c t$, where f_c is the carrier frequency. This same carrier wave is shifted by 90 and used for ASK modulation of the lower binary stream. The two modulated signals are then added together and transmitted. The transmitted signal can be expressed as follows:

$$\textbf{QAM} \qquad s(t) = d_1(t)\cos 2\pi f_c t + d_2(t)\sin 2\pi f_c t$$

If two-level ASK is used, then each of the two streams can be in one of two states and the combined stream can be in one of $4 = 2 \times 2$ states. This is essentially QPSK. If four-level ASK is used (i.e., four different amplitude levels), then

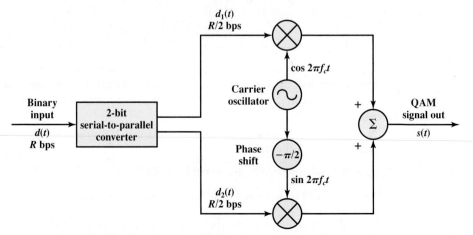

Figure 5.14 QAM Modulator

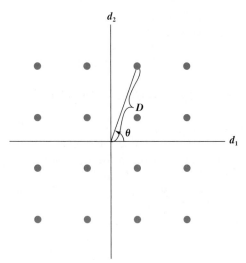

Figure 5.15   16-QAM Constellation

the combined stream can be in one of $16 = 4 \times 4$ states. This is known as 16-QAM. Figure 5.15 shows the possible combinations of instantaneous values of the digital signals $d_1(t)$ and $d_2(t)$. For 16-QAM, each digital signals encodes two bits and takes on one of four values, two positive and two negative.

QAM can also be viewed as a combination of digital-amplitude and digital-phase modulation. Using trigonometric identities, we can rewrite the QAM equation in the form $s(t) = D(t) \cos(2\pi f_c t + \theta(t))$, where

$$D(t) = \sqrt{d_1(t)^2 + d_2(t)^2}, \quad \theta(t) = tan^{-1}\left(\frac{d_2(t)}{d_1(t)}\right)$$

Systems using 64 and even 256 states have been implemented. The greater the number of states, the higher the data rate that is possible within a given bandwidth. Of course, as discussed previously, the greater the number of states, the higher the potential error rate due to noise and attenuation.

5.3   ANALOG DATA, DIGITAL SIGNALS

In this section, we examine the process of transforming analog data into digital signals. Strictly speaking, it might be more correct to refer to this as a process of converting analog data into digital data; this process is known as digitization. Once analog data have been converted into digital data, a number of things can happen. The three most common outcomes are the following:

1. The digital data can be transmitted using NRZ-L. In this case, we have in fact gone directly from analog data to a digital signal.
2. The digital data can be encoded as a digital signal using a code other than NRZ-L. Thus an extra step is required.
3. The digital data can be converted into an analog signal, using one of the modulation techniques discussed in Section 5.2.

Figure 5.16   Digitizing Analog Data

   This last, seemingly curious, procedure is illustrated in Figure 5.16, which shows voice data that are digitized and then converted to an analog ASK signal. This allows digital transmission in the sense defined in Chapter 3. The voice data, because they have been digitized, can be treated as digital data, even though transmission requirements (e.g., use of microwave) dictate that an analog signal be used.

   The device used for converting analog data into digital form for transmission, and subsequently recovering the original analog data from the digital, is known as a **codec** (coder-decoder). In this section, we examine the two principal techniques used in codecs: pulse code modulation and delta modulation. The section closes with a discussion of comparative performance.

Pulse Code Modulation

Pulse code modulation (PCM) is based on the sampling theorem:

> **SAMPLING THEOREM:** If a signal $f(t)$ is sampled at regular intervals of time and at a rate higher than twice the highest signal frequency, then the samples contain all the information of the original signal. The function $f(t)$ may be reconstructed from these samples by the use of a lowpass filter.

   For the interested reader, a proof is provided in Appendix G. If voice data are limited to frequencies below 4000 Hz, a conservative procedure for intelligibility, 8000 samples per second would be sufficient to characterize the voice signal completely. Note, however, that these are analog samples, called **pulse amplitude modulation (PAM)** samples. To convert to digital, each of these analog samples must be assigned a binary code.

> **EXAMPLE 5.7** Figure 5.17 shows an example in which the original signal is assumed to be bandlimited with a bandwidth of B. PAM samples are taken at a rate of $2B$, or once every $T_s = 1/2B$ seconds. Each PAM sample is approximated by being *quantized* into one of 16 different levels. Each sample can then be represented by 4 bits. The resulting digital code for this analog signal is 0001100111111010010100100010.
>   Because the quantized values are only approximations, it is impossible to recover the original signal exactly. By using an 8-bit sample, which allows 256 quantizing levels, the quality of the recovered voice signal is comparable with that achieved via analog transmission. Note that this implies that a data rate of 8000 samples per second $\times$ 8 bits per sample $= 64$ kbps is needed for a single voice signal.

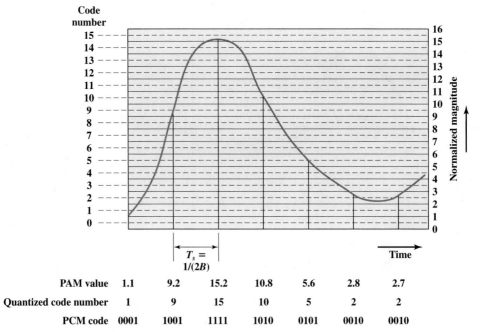

PAM value	1.1	9.2	15.2	10.8	5.6	2.8	2.7
Quantized code number	1	9	15	10	5	2	2
PCM code	0001	1001	1111	1010	0101	0010	0010

Figure 5.17   Pulse Code Modulation Example

Thus, PCM starts with a continuous-time, continuous-amplitude (analog) signal, from which a digital signal is produced (Figure 5.18). The digital signal consists of blocks of n bits, where each n-bit number is the amplitude of a PCM pulse. On reception, the process is reversed to reproduce the analog signal. Notice, however, that this process violates the terms of the sampling theorem. By quantizing the PAM pulse, the original signal is now only approximated and cannot be recovered exactly. This effect is known as **quantizing error** or **quantizing noise**. The signal-to-noise ratio for quantizing noise can be expressed as [BENN48]

$$\text{SNR}_{dB} = 20 \log 2^n + 1.76 \text{ dB} = 6.02n + 1.76 \text{ dB}$$

Thus each additional bit used for quantizing increases SNR by about 6 dB, which is a factor of 4.

Typically, the PCM scheme is refined using a technique known as nonlinear encoding, which means, in effect, that the quantization levels are not equally spaced. The problem with equal spacing is that the mean absolute error for each

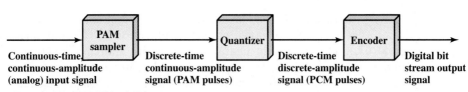

Figure 5.18   PCM Block Diagram

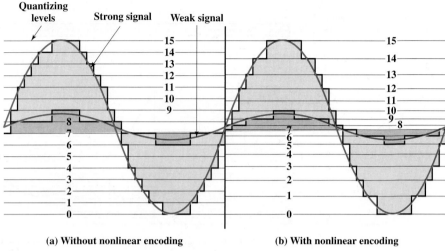

(a) Without nonlinear encoding   (b) With nonlinear encoding

Figure 5.19   Effect of Nonlinear Coding

sample is the same, regardless of signal level. Consequently, lower amplitude values are relatively more distorted. By using a greater number of quantizing steps for signals of low amplitude, and a smaller number of quantizing steps for signals of large amplitude, a marked reduction in overall signal distortion is achieved (e.g., see Figure 5.19).

The same effect can be achieved by using uniform quantizing but companding (compressing-expanding) the input analog signal. Companding is a process that compresses the intensity range of a signal by imparting more gain to weak signals than to strong signals on input. At output, the reverse operation is performed. Figure 5.20 shows typical companding functions. Note that the effect on the input side is to compress the sample so that the higher values are reduced with respect to the lower values. Thus, with a fixed number of quantizing levels, more levels are available for lower-level signals. On the output side, the compander expands the samples so the compressed values are restored to their original values.

Nonlinear encoding can significantly improve the PCM SNR. For voice signals, improvements of 24 to 30 dB have been achieved.

Delta Modulation (DM)

A variety of techniques have been used to improve the performance of PCM or to reduce its complexity. One of the most popular alternatives to PCM is delta modulation (DM).

With delta modulation, an analog input is approximated by a staircase function that moves up or down by one quantization level (δ) at each sampling interval (T_s). The important characteristic of this staircase function is that its behavior is binary: At each sampling time, the function moves up or down a constant amount δ. Thus, the output of the delta modulation process can be represented as a single binary digit for each sample. In essence, a bit stream is produced

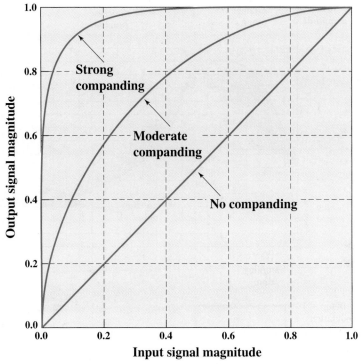

Figure 5.20   Typical Companding Functions

by approximating the derivative of an analog signal rather than its amplitude: A 1 is generated if the staircase function is to go up during the next interval; a 0 is generated otherwise.

EXAMPLE 5.8   Figure 5.21 shows an example, with the staircase function overlaid on the original analog waveform. The resulting digital code for this analog signal is 0111111100000000001010101110.

The transition (up or down) that occurs at each sampling interval is chosen so that the staircase function tracks the original analog waveform as closely as possible. Figure 5.22 illustrates the logic of the process, which is essentially a feedback mechanism. For transmission, the following occurs: At each sampling time, the analog input is compared to the most recent value of the approximating staircase function. If the value of the sampled waveform exceeds that of the staircase function, a 1 is generated; otherwise, a 0 is generated. Thus, the staircase is always changed in the direction of the input signal. The output of the DM process is therefore a binary sequence that can be used at the receiver to reconstruct the staircase function. The staircase function can then be smoothed by some type of integration process or by passing it through a lowpass filter to produce an analog approximation of the analog input signal.

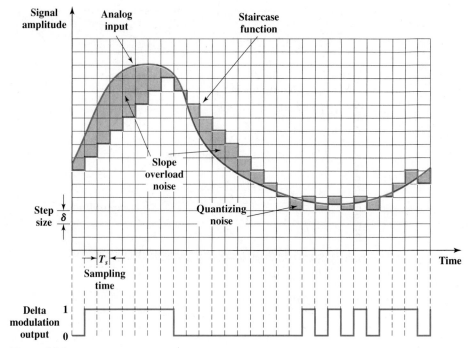

Figure 5.21   Example of Delta Modulation

There are two important parameters in a DM scheme: the size of the step assigned to each binary digit, δ, and the sampling rate. As Figure 5.21 illustrates, δ must be chosen to produce a balance between two types of errors or noise. When the analog waveform is changing very slowly, there will be quantizing noise. This noise increases as δ is increased. On the other hand, when the analog waveform is changing more rapidly than the staircase can follow, there is slope overload noise. This noise increases as δ is decreased.

It should be clear that the accuracy of the scheme can be improved by increasing the sampling rate. However, this increases the data rate of the output signal.

The principal advantage of DM over PCM is the simplicity of its implementation. In general, PCM exhibits better SNR characteristics at the same data rate.

Performance

Good voice reproduction via PCM can be achieved with 128 quantization levels, or 7-bit coding ($2^7 = 128$). A voice signal, conservatively, occupies a bandwidth of 4 kHz. Thus, according to the sampling theorem, samples should be taken at a rate of 8000 samples per second. This implies a data rate of $8000 \times 7 = 56$ kbps for the PCM-encoded digital data.

Consider what this means from the point of view of bandwidth requirement. An analog voice signal occupies 4 kHz. Using PCM this 4-kHz analog signal can be converted into a 56-kbps digital signal. But using the Nyquist criterion from Chapter 3, this digital signal could require on the order of 28 kHz of bandwidth.

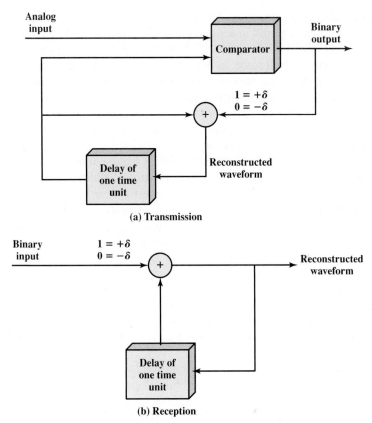

Figure 5.22 Delta Modulation

Even more severe differences are seen with higher bandwidth signals. For example, a common PCM scheme for color television uses 10-bit codes, which works out to 92 Mbps for a 4.6-MHz bandwidth signal. In spite of these numbers, digital techniques continue to grow in popularity for transmitting analog data. The principal reasons for this are the following:

- Repeaters are used instead of amplifiers, so there is no cumulative noise.
- As we shall see, time division multiplexing (TDM) is used for digital signals instead of the frequency division multiplexing (FDM) used for analog signals. With TDM, there is no intermodulation noise, whereas we have seen that this is a concern for FDM.
- The conversion to digital signaling allows the use of the more efficient digital switching techniques.

Furthermore, techniques have been developed to provide more efficient codes. In the case of voice, a reasonable goal appears to be in the neighborhood of 4 kbps. With video, advantage can be taken of the fact that from frame to frame, most picture elements will not change. Interframe coding techniques should allow the video requirement to be reduced to about 15 Mbps, and for slowly changing scenes, such as found in a video teleconference, down to 64 kbps or less.

As a final point, we mention that in many instances, the use of a telecommunications system will result in both digital-to-analog and analog-to-digital processing. The overwhelming majority of local terminations into the telecommunications network is analog, and the network itself uses a mixture of analog and digital techniques. Thus digital data at a user's terminal may be converted to analog by a modem, subsequently digitized by a codec, and perhaps suffer repeated conversions before reaching its destination.

Thus, telecommunications facilities handle analog signals that represent both voice and digital data. The characteristics of the waveforms are quite different. Whereas voice signals tend to be skewed to the lower portion of the bandwidth (Figure 3.9), analog encoding of digital signals has a more uniform spectral content over the bandwidth and therefore contains more high-frequency components. Studies have shown that, because of the presence of these higher frequencies, PCM-related techniques are preferable to DM-related techniques for digitizing analog signals that represent digital data.

5.4 RECOMMENDED READING AND ANIMATIONS

It is difficult, for some reason, to find solid treatments of digital-to-digital encoding schemes. [SKLA01] provides a useful account.

There are many good references on analog modulation schemes for digital data. Good choices are [COUC013], [XION00], and [PROA05]; these three also provide comprehensive treatment of digital and analog modulation schemes for analog data.

An instructive treatment of the concepts of bit rate, baud, and bandwidth is [FREE98a]. A recommended tutorial that expands on the concepts treated in the past few chapters relating to bandwidth efficiency and encoding schemes is [SKLA93].

COUC13   Couch, L. *Digital and Analog Communication Systems.* Upper Saddle River, NJ: Pearson, 2013.

FREE98a   Freeman, R. "Bits, Symbols, Baud, and Bandwidth." *IEEE Communications Magazine,* April 1998.

PROA05   Proakis, J. *Fundamentals of Communication Systems.* Upper Saddle River, NJ: Prentice Hall, 2005.

SKLA93   Sklar, B. "Defining, Designing, and Evaluating Digital Communication Systems." *IEEE Communications Magazine,* November 1993.

SKLA01   Sklar, B. *Digital Communications: Fundamentals and Applications.* Englewood Cliffs, NJ: Prentice Hall, 2001.

XION00   Xiong, F. *Digital Modulation Techniques.* Boston: Artech House, 2000.

Animations

Animations that illustrate various signal encoding schemes are available at the Premium Web site. The reader is encouraged to view these animations to reinforce concepts from this chapter.

5.5 KEY TERMS, REVIEW QUESTIONS, AND PROBLEMS

Key Terms

alternate mark inversion (AMI)	delta modulation (DM)	phase shift keying (PSK)
amplitude shift keying (ASK)	differential encoding	polar
	differential Manchester	pseudoternary
analog signaling	differential PSK (DPSK)	pulse amplitude modulation (PAM)
bandwidth efficiency	digital signaling	
baseband signal	frequency shift keying (FSK)	pulse code modulation (PCM)
biphase	high-density bipolar-3 zeros (HDB3)	
bipolar-AMI		pulse position modulation (PPM)
bipolar with 8-zeros substitution (B8ZS)	Manchester	
	modulation	quadrature amplitude modulation (QAM)
bit error rate (BER)	modulation rate	
carrier frequency	multilevel binary	quadrature PSK (QPSK)
carrier signal	nonreturn to zero (NRZ)	quantizing error
codec	nonreturn to zero, inverted (NRZI)	quantizing noise
data rate		scrambling
data signaling rate	nonreturn to zero-level (NRZ-L)	unipolar

Review Questions

5.1. List and briefly define important factors that can be used in evaluating or comparing the various digital-to-digital encoding techniques.

5.2. What is differential encoding?

5.3. Explain the difference between NRZ-L and NRZI.

5.4. Describe two multilevel binary digital-to-digital encoding techniques.

5.5. Define biphase encoding and describe two biphase encoding techniques.

5.6. Explain the function of scrambling in the context of digital-to-digital encoding techniques.

5.7. What function does a modem perform?

5.8. How are binary values represented in amplitude shift keying, and what is the limitation of this approach?

5.9.   What is the difference between QPSK and offset QPSK?

5.10. What is QAM?

5.11. What does the sampling theorem tell us concerning the rate of sampling required for an analog signal?

Problems

5.1.   Which of the signals in Table 5.2 has a dc component problem?

5.2.   Develop algorithms for generating each of the codes of Table 5.2 from NRZ-L.

5.3.   A certain system needs to transfer data at the rate of 100 Mbps. What will be the average signal rate if the NRZ-L and NRZ-I coding schemes are used? What will be the minimum bandwidth that is required? If a biphase scheme like Manchester encoding or differential Manchester encoding is used, determine the minimum bandwidth that will be required.

5.4.   Develop a state diagram (finite state machine) representation of NRZI coding.

5.5.   Consider the following signal encoding technique. Binary data are presented as input, a_m, for $m = 1, 2, 3, \ldots$. Two levels of processing occur. First, a new set of binary numbers are produced:

$$b_0 = 0$$
$$b_m = (a_m + b_{m-1}) \bmod 2$$

These are then encoded as

$$c_m = b_m - b_{m-1}$$

On reception, the original data are recovered by

$$a_m = c_m \bmod 2$$

a.   Verify that the received values of a_m equal the transmitted values of a_m.
b.   What sort of encoding is this?

5.6.   For the bit stream 01001110, sketch the waveforms for each of the codes of Table 5.2. Assume that: the signal level for the preceding bit for NRZI was high; the most recent preceding 1 bit (AMI) has a negative voltage; and the most recent preceding 0 bit (pseudoternary) has a negative voltage.

5.7.   The waveform of Figure 5.23 belongs to a Manchester-encoded binary data stream. Determine the beginning and end of bit periods (i.e., extract clock information) and give the data sequence.

5.8.   Consider the bit string 1100 0000 0110. Sketch its waveform using
a.   NRZ-L.
b.   Bipolar AMI, assuming that the most recent preceding bit has negative voltage.
What major problem do you observe in the sequence of these waveforms? Can this problem be eliminated by using the bipolar with 8 zeros substitution (B8ZS) coding scheme? Support your answer by sketching the waveform using B8ZS.

5.9.   The bipolar-AMI waveform representing the binary sequence 0100101011 is transmitted over a noisy channel. The received waveform is shown in Figure 5.24; it contains a single error. Locate the position of this error and explain your answer.

5.10. One positive side-effect of bipolar encoding is that a bipolar violation (two consecutive + pulses or two consecutive − pulses separated by any number of zeros)

Figure 5.23   A Manchester Stream

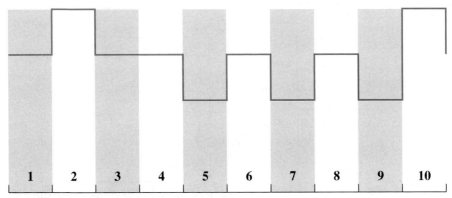

Figure 5.24 A Received Bipolar-AMI Waveform

indicates to the receiver that an error has occurred in transmission. Unfortunately, upon the receipt of such a violation, the receiver does not know which bit is in error (only that an error has occurred). The received bipolar sequence

$$+ - 0 + - 0 - +$$

has one bipolar violation. Construct two scenarios (each of which involves a different transmitted bit stream with one transmitted bit being converted via an error) that will produce this same received bit pattern.

5.11. Given the bit pattern 01100, encode this data using ASK, BFSK, and BPSK.

5.12. A sine wave is to be used for two different signaling schemes: (a) PSK; (b) QPSK. The duration of a signal element is 10^{-5} s. If the received signal is of the following form:

$$s(t) = 0.005 \sin(2\pi 10^6 t + \theta)\,\text{V}$$

and if the measured noise power at the receiver is 2.5×10^{-8} watts, determine the E_b/N_0 (in dB) for each case.

5.13. How many bits are needed for a QPSK signal? If the baud rate is 500 Mbaud, what will be the bit rate?

5.14. What is the carrier frequency if available frequencies range from 300 kHz to 500 kHz? If data is modulated by using ASK with $r = 1$, then what is its bit rate?

5.15. Given that $r = 0.5$, what is the required bandwidth for each of the following cases if the data rate is 8000 bps?

  a. ASK
  b. QPSK
  c. 64-QAM

5.16. A certain system has a bandpass of 400 kHz–600 kHz. If the data is modulated using BFSK, what should be the carrier frequencies? What will be the bit rate if $r = 0.8$? If a data rate of 100 kbps is desired, what is the minimum bandwidth needed? Assume that the difference between carrier frequencies is half of a bandwidth.

5.17. Figure 5.25 shows the QAM demodulator corresponding to the QAM modulator of Figure 5.14. Show that this arrangement does recover the two signals $d_1(t)$ and $d_2(t)$, which can be combined to recover the original input.

5.18. A signal needs to be sent 3 bits at a time at a bit rate of 18 Mbps. Find the number of signal levels and the baud rate of this transmission.

5.19. Are the modem and the codec functional inverses (i.e., could an inverted modem function as a codec, or vice versa)?

5.20. How many bits are needed for a signal to achieve a minimum PCM SNR of 55 dB?

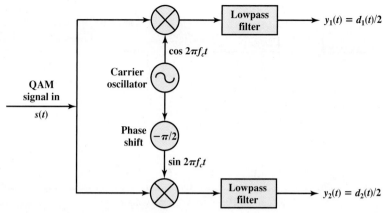

Figure 5.25   QAM Demodulator

5.21. A telephone subscriber line has a frequency range of 300 Hz to 3300 Hz and a minimum SNR_{dB} of 48.

 a. Find the minimum sampling rate for a signal in this line.
 b. What is the minimum number of bits per sample?
 c. What is the bit rate?

5.22. Find the step size δ required to prevent slope overload noise as a function of the frequency of the highest-frequency component of the signal. Assume that all components have amplitude A.

5.23. A PCM encoder accepts a signal with a full-scale voltage of 10 V and generates 8-bit codes using uniform quantization. The maximum normalized quantized voltage is $1 - 2^{-8}$. Determine: (a) normalized step size, (b) actual step size in volts, (c) actual maximum quantized level in volts, (d) normalized resolution, (e) actual resolution, and (f) percentage resolution.

5.24. The analog waveform shown in Figure 5.26 is to be delta modulated. The sampling period and the step size are indicated by the grid on the figure. The first DM output

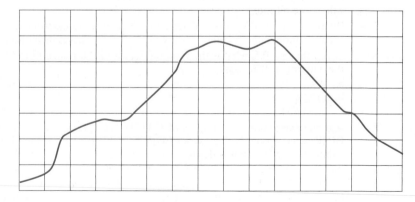

Figure 5.26   Delta Modulation Example

and the staircase function for this period are also shown. Show the rest of the staircase function and give the DM output. Indicate regions where slope overload distortion exists.

5.25. **Pulse position modulation (PPM)** is an encoding scheme in which the digital input value determines the position of a narrow pulse relative to the clocking time. This method is used in optical communication systems such as optical fiber, IR local area networks, and IR remote controls, where efficiency is required and little or no external interference occurs. Transmission uses an intensity modulation scheme, in which the presence of a signal corresponds to a binary 1 and the absence of a signal corresponds to binary 0.

 a. A 16-PPM scheme is used for the 1-Mbps IEEE 802.11 infrared standard. Each group of 4 data bits is mapped into one of the 16-PPM symbols; each symbol is a string of 16 bits. Each 16-bit string consists of fifteen 0s and one binary 1, such that the position of the binary 1 in the string encodes a value from 0 through 15.

   a1. What is the period of transmission (time between bits)?
       For the corresponding infrared pulse transmission:
   a2. What is the average time between pulses (1 values) and the corresponding average rate of pulse transmission?
   a3. What is the minimum time between adjacent pulses?
   a4. What is the maximum time between pulses?

 b. Repeat (a) for the 4-PPM scheme used for the 2-Mbps infrared standard. In this scheme, each group of 2 data bits is mapped into one of four 4-bit sequences.

CHAPTER 6

ERROR DETECTION AND CORRECTION

After studying this chapter, you should be able to:

◆ Explain the basic mechanism for the use of error-detecting codes.

◆ Present an overview of the Internet checksum.

◆ Understand the operation of the cyclic redundancy check.

◆ Define Hamming distance.

◆ Explain the basic principles for forward error correction using a block code.

In earlier chapters, we talked about transmission impairments and the effect of data rate and signal-to-noise ratio on bit error rate. Regardless of the design of the transmission system, there will be errors, resulting in the change of one or more bits in a transmitted block of data.

Three approaches are in common use for coping with data transmission errors:

• Error-detection codes

• Error-correction codes, also called forward error correction (FEC) codes

• Automatic repeat request (ARQ) protocols

All three approaches are applied to individual blocks of data, called frames, packets, or cells, depending on the protocol used for data exchange. The first two approaches, which are the subject of this chapter, use **redundancy**. In essence, for error detection and error correction, additional bits, which are a function of the data bits, are appended to the data bits by the sender. These redundant bits are used by the receiver for the purpose of error detection or correction.

An error-detection code simply detects the presence of an error. Typically, such codes are used in conjunction with a protocol at the data link or transport level (see Figure 2.3) that uses an ARQ scheme. With an ARQ scheme, a receiver discards a block of data in which an error is detected and the transmitter retransmits that block of data. FEC codes are designed not just to detect but correct errors, avoiding the need for retransmission. FEC schemes are frequently used in wireless transmission, where retransmission schemes are highly inefficient and error rates may be high.

This chapter examines error-detecting and error-correcting codes. ARQ protocols are discussed in Chapter 7. After a brief discussion of the distinction between single-bit errors and burst errors, this chapter describes three approaches to error detection: the use of parity bits, the Internet checksum technique, and the cyclic redundancy check (CRC). The CRC error-detecting code is used in a wide variety of applications. Because of its complexity, we present three different approaches to describing the CRC algorithm.

For error correction, this chapter provides an overview of the general principles of error-correcting codes. Specific examples are provided in Chapter 16.

6.1 TYPES OF ERRORS

In digital transmission systems, an error occurs when a bit is altered between transmission and reception; that is, a binary 1 is transmitted and a binary 0 is received, or a binary 0 is transmitted and a binary 1 is received. Two general types of errors can occur: single-bit errors and burst errors. A single-bit error is an isolated error condition that alters one bit but does not affect nearby bits. A burst error of length B is a contiguous sequence of B bits in which the first and last bits and any number of intermediate bits are received in error. More precisely, IEEE Std 100 and ITU-T Recommendation Q.9 both define an error burst as follows:

> **Error burst:** A group of bits in which two successive erroneous bits are always separated by less than a given number x of correct bits. The last erroneous bit in the burst and the first erroneous bit in the following burst are accordingly separated by x correct bits or more.

Thus, in an error burst, there is a cluster of bits in which a number of errors occur, although not necessarily all of the bits in the cluster suffer an error. Figure 6.1 provides an example of both types of errors.

A single-bit error can occur in the presence of white noise, when a slight random deterioration of the signal-to-noise ratio is sufficient to confuse the receiver's decision of a single bit. Burst errors are more common and more difficult to deal with. Burst errors can be caused by impulse noise, which was described in Chapter 3. Another cause is fading in a mobile wireless environment; fading is described in Chapter 10.

Note that the effects of burst errors are greater at higher data rates.

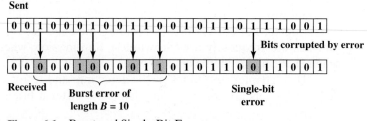

Figure 6.1 Burst and Single-Bit Errors

EXAMPLE 6.1 An impulse noise event or a fading event of 1 μs occurs. At a data rate of 10 Mbps, there is a resulting error burst of 10 bits. At a data rate of 100 Mbps, there is an error burst of 100 bits.

6.2 ERROR DETECTION

Regardless of the design of the transmission system, there will be errors, resulting in the change of one or more bits in a transmitted frame. In what follows, we assume that data are transmitted as one or more contiguous sequences of bits, called frames. We define these probabilities with respect to errors in transmitted frames:

P_b: Probability that a bit is received in error; also known as the bit error rate (BER)

P_1: Probability that a frame arrives with no bit errors

P_2: Probability that, with an error-detecting algorithm in use, a frame arrives with one or more undetected errors

P_3: Probability that, with an error-detecting algorithm in use, a frame arrives with one or more detected bit errors but no undetected bit errors

First consider the case in which no means are taken to detect errors. Then the probability of detected errors (P_3) is zero. To express the remaining probabilities, assume the probability that any bit is in error (P_b) is constant and independent for each bit. Then we have

$$P_1 = (1 - P_b)^F$$
$$P_2 = 1 - P_1$$

where F is the number of bits per frame. In words, the probability that a frame arrives with no bit errors decreases when the probability of a single bit error increases, as you would expect. Also, the probability that a frame arrives with no bit errors decreases with increasing frame length; the longer the frame, the more bits it has and the higher the probability that one of these is in error.

EXAMPLE 6.2 A defined objective for ISDN (integrated services digital network) connections is that the BER on a 64-kbps channel should be less than 10^{-6} on at least 90% of observed 1-minute intervals. Suppose now that we have the rather modest user requirement that on average one frame with an undetected bit error should occur per day on a continuously used 64-kbps channel, and let us assume a frame length of 1000 bits. The number of frames that can be transmitted in a day comes out to 5.529×10^6, which yields a desired frame error rate of $P_2 = 1/(5.529 \times 10^6) = 0.18 \times 10^{-6}$. But if we assume a value of P_b of 10^{-6}, then $P_1 = (0.999999)^{1000} = 0.999$ and therefore $P_2 = 10^{-3}$, which is about three orders of magnitude too large to meet our requirement.

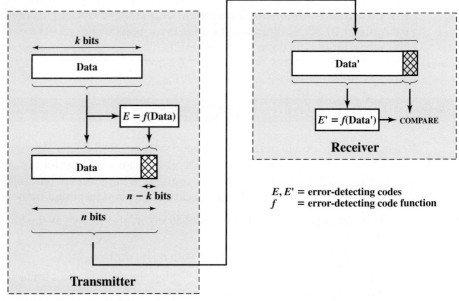

Figure 6.2 Error-Detection Process

This is the kind of result that motivates the use of error-detecting techniques to achieve a desired frame error rate on a connection with a given BER. All of these techniques operate on the following principle (Figure 6.2). For a given frame of bits, additional bits that constitute an **error-detecting code** are added by the transmitter. This code is calculated as a function of the other transmitted bits. Typically, for a data block of k bits, the error-detecting algorithm yields an error-detecting code of $n - k$ bits, where $(n - k) < k$. The error-detecting code, also referred to as the **check bits**, is appended to the data block to produce a frame of n bits, which is then transmitted. The receiver separates the incoming frame into the k bits of data and $(n - k)$ bits of the error-detecting code. The receiver performs the same error-detecting calculation on the data bits and compares this value with the value of the incoming error-detecting code. A detected error occurs if and only if there is a mismatch. Thus P_3 is the probability that a frame contains errors and that the error-detecting scheme will detect that fact. P_2 is known as the residual error rate and is the probability that an error will be undetected despite the use of an error-detecting scheme.

6.3 PARITY CHECK

Parity Bit

The simplest error-detecting scheme is to append a parity bit to the end of a block of data. A typical example is character transmission, in which a parity bit is attached to each 7-bit IRA character. The value of this bit is selected so that the character has an even number of 1s (even parity) or an odd number of 1s (odd parity).

EXAMPLE 6.3 If the transmitter is transmitting an IRA character G (1110001) and using odd parity, it will append a 1 and transmit 11110001.[1] The receiver examines the received character and, if the total number of 1s is odd, assumes that no error has occurred. If one bit (or any odd number of bits) is erroneously inverted during transmission (e.g., 11100001), then the receiver will detect an error.

Note, however, that if two (or any even number) of bits are inverted due to error, an undetected error occurs. Typically, even parity is used for synchronous transmission and odd parity for asynchronous transmission.

The use of the parity bit is not foolproof, as noise impulses are often long enough to destroy more than one bit, particularly at high data rates.

Two-Dimensional Parity Check

The two-dimensional parity scheme, illustrated in Figure 6.3, is more robust than the single parity bit. The string of data bits to be checked is arranged in a two-dimensional array. Appended to each row i is an even parity bit r_i for that row, and appended to each column j is an even parity bit c_j for that column. An overall parity bit p completes the matrix. Thus the error-detecting code consists of $i + j + 1$ parity bits.

In this scheme, every bit participates in two parity checks. As with a simple parity bit, any odd number of bit errors is detected.

EXAMPLE 6.4 Figure 6.3b shows a string of 20 data bits arranged in a 4×5 array, with the parity bits calculated, to form a 5×6 array. When a single-bit error occurs in Figure 6.3c, both the corresponding row and column parity bits now indicate an error. Furthermore, the error can be determined to be at the intersection of that row and column. Thus it is possible to not only detect but also correct the bit error.

If an even number of errors occur in a row, the errors are detected by the column parity bits. Similarly, if an even number of errors occur in a column, the errors are detected by the row parity bits. However, any pattern of four errors forming a rectangle, as shown in Figure 6.3d, is undetectable. If the four circled bits change value, the corresponding row and column parity bits do not change value.

---

[1]Recall from our discussion in Section 5.1 that the least significant bit of a character is transmitted first and that the parity bit is the most significant bit.

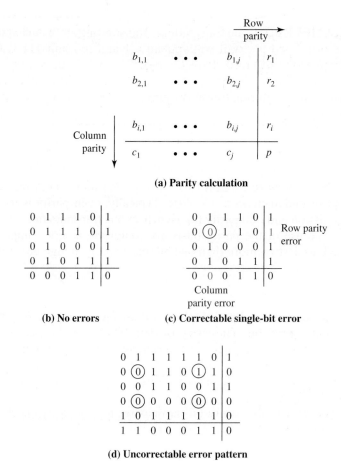

(a) Parity calculation

```
0  1  1  1  0 | 1              0  1  1  1  0 | 1
0  1  1  1  0 | 1              0 (0) 1  1  0 | 1   Row parity
0  1  0  0  0 | 1              0  1  0  0  0 | 1   error
0  1  0  1  1 | 1              0  1  0  1  1 | 1
0  0  0  1  1 | 0              0  0  0  1  1 | 0
                                    Column
                                  parity error
   (b) No errors              (c) Correctable single-bit error
```

```
0  1  1  1  1  1  0 | 1
0 (0) 1  1  0 (1) 1 | 0
0  0  1  1  0  0  1 | 1
0 (0) 0  0  0 (0) 0 | 0
1  0  1  1  1  1  1 | 0
1  1  0  0  0  1  1 | 0
```

(d) Uncorrectable error pattern

Figure 6.3 A Two-Dimensional Even Parity Scheme

6.4 THE INTERNET CHECKSUM

The Internet checksum is an error-detecting code used in many Internet standard protocols, including IP, TCP, and UDP. The calculation makes use of the ones-complement operation and ones-complement addition.[2] To perform the **ones-complement operation** on a set of binary digits, replace 0 digits with 1 digits and 1 digits with 0 digits. The **ones-complement addition** of two binary integers of equal bit length is performed as follows:

1. The two numbers are treated as unsigned binary integers and added.
2. If there is a carry out of the leftmost bit, add 1 to the sum. This is called an *end-around carry*.

---

[2]See Appendix H for a further discussion of ones-complement arithmetic.

Here are two examples:

$$
\begin{array}{r}
0011 \\
+1100 \\
\hline
1111
\end{array}
\qquad
\begin{array}{r}
1101 \\
+1011 \\
\hline
11000 \\
+\ \ \ \ \ 1 \\
\hline
1001
\end{array}
$$

Typically, the checksum is included as a field in the header of a protocol data unit, such as in IP datagram. To compute the checksum, the checksum field is first set to all zeros. The checksum is then calculated by performing the ones-complement addition of all the words in the header, and then taking the ones-complement operation of the result. This result is placed in the checksum field.

To verify a checksum, the ones-complement sum is computed over the same set of octets, including the checksum field. If the result is all 1 bits (−0 in ones-complement arithmetic), the check succeeds.

EXAMPLE 6.5 Consider a header that consists of 10 octets, with the checksum in the last two octets (this does not correspond to any actual header format) with the following content (in hexadecimal):

00 01 F2 03 F4 F5 F6 F7 00 00

Note that the checksum field is set to zero.

Figure 6.4a shows the results of the calculation. Thus, the transmitted packet is 00 01 F2 03 F4 F5 F6 F7 0D. Figure 6.4b shows the calculation carried out by the receiver on the entire data block, including the checksum. The result is a value of all ones, which verifies that no errors have been detected.

(a) Checksum calculation by sender		(b) Checksum verification by receiver	
Partial sum	0001 F203 F204	**Partial sum**	0001 F203 F204
Partial sum	F204 F4F5 1E6F9	**Partial sum**	F204 F4F5 1E6F9
Carry	E6F9 1 E6FA	**Carry**	E6F9 1 E6FA
Partial sum	E6FA F6F7 1DDF1	**Partial sum**	E6FA F6F7 1DDF1
Carry	DDF1 1 DDF2	**Carry**	DDF1 1 DDF2
Ones complement of the result	220D	**Partial sum**	DDF2 220D FFFF

(a) Checksum calculation by sender   (b) Checksum verification by receiver

Figure 6.4 Example of Internet Checksum

The Internet checksum provides greater error-detection capability than a parity bit or two-dimensional parity scheme but is considerably less effective than the cyclic redundancy check (CRC), discussed next. The primary reason for its adoption in Internet protocols is efficiency. Most of these protocols are implemented in software and the Internet checksum, involving simple addition and comparison operations, causes very little overhead. It is assumed that at the lower link level, a strong error-detection code such as CRC is used, and so the Internet checksum is simply an additional end-to-end check for errors.

6.5   CYCLIC REDUNDANCY CHECK (CRC)

One of the most common, and one of the most powerful, error-detecting codes is the cyclic redundancy check, which can be described as follows. Given a k-bit block of bits, or message, the transmitter generates an $(n - k)$-bit sequence, known as a **frame check sequence (FCS)**, such that the resulting frame, consisting of n bits, is exactly divisible by some predetermined number. The receiver then divides the incoming frame by that number and, if there is no remainder, assumes there was no error.[3]

To clarify this, we present the procedure in three equivalent ways: modulo 2 arithmetic, polynomials, and digital logic.

Modulo 2 Arithmetic

Modulo 2 arithmetic uses binary addition with no carries, which is just the exclusive-OR (XOR) operation. Binary subtraction with no carries is also interpreted as the XOR operation: For example

$$
\begin{array}{rrr}
1111 & 1111 & 11001 \\
+1010 & -0101 & \times\,11 \\
\hline
0101 & 1010 & 11001 \\
& & 11001 \\
\hline
& & 101011 \\
\end{array}
$$

Now define

$T = n$-bit frame to be transmitted

$D = k$-bit block of data, or message, the first k bits of T

$F = (n - k)$-bit FCS, the last $(n - k)$ bits of T

$P = $ pattern of $n - k + 1$ bits; this is the predetermined divisor

We would like T/P to have no remainder. It should be clear that

$$
T = 2^{n-k}D + F
$$

---

[3]This procedure is slightly different from that of Figure 6.2. As shall be seen, the CRC process could be implemented as follows. The receiver could perform a division operation on the incoming k data bits and compare the result to the incoming $(n - k)$ check bits.

That is, by multiplying D by 2^{n-k}, we have in effect shifted it to the left by $n-k$ bits and padded out the result with zeroes. Adding F yields the concatenation of D and F, which is T. We want T to be exactly divisible by P. Suppose that we divide 2^{n-k} D by P:

$$\frac{2^{n-k}D}{P} = Q + \frac{R}{P} \tag{6.1}$$

There is a quotient and a remainder. Because division is modulo 2, the remainder is always at least one bit shorter than the divisor. We will use this remainder as our FCS. Then

$$T = 2^{n-k}D + R \tag{6.2}$$

Does this R satisfy our condition that T/P has no remainder? To see that it does, consider:

$$\frac{T}{P} = \frac{2^{n-k}D + R}{P} = \frac{2^{n-k}D}{P} + \frac{R}{P}$$

Substituting Equation (6.1), we have

$$\frac{T}{P} = Q + \frac{R}{P} + \frac{R}{P}$$

However, any binary number added to itself modulo 2 yields zero. Thus

$$\frac{T}{P} = Q + \frac{R+R}{P} = Q$$

There is no remainder, and therefore T is exactly divisible by P. Thus, the FCS is easily generated: Simply divide $2^{n-k} D$ by P and use the $(n-k)$-bit remainder as the FCS. On reception, the receiver will divide T by P and will get no remainder if there have been no errors.

EXAMPLE 6.6

1. Given

$$\text{Message } D = 1010001101 \,(10 \text{ bits})$$
$$\text{Pattern } P = 110101 \,(6 \text{ bits})$$
$$\text{FCS } R = \text{ to be calculated } (5 \text{ bits})$$

Thus, $n = 15$, $k = 10$, and $(n-k) = 5$.

2. The message is multiplied by 2^5, yielding 101000110100000.

3. This product is divided by P:

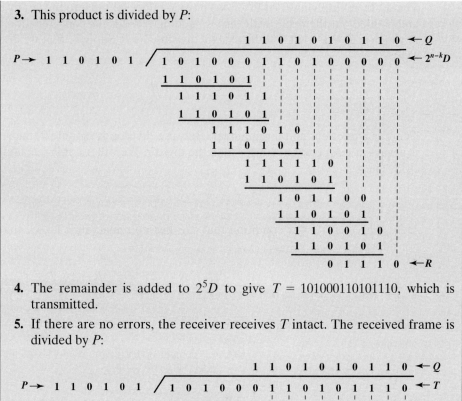

4. The remainder is added to $2^5 D$ to give $T = 101000110101110$, which is transmitted.

5. If there are no errors, the receiver receives T intact. The received frame is divided by P:

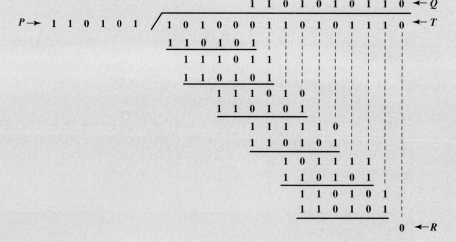

Because there is no remainder, it is assumed that there have been no errors.

The pattern P is chosen to be one bit longer than the desired FCS, and the exact bit pattern chosen depends on the type of errors expected. At minimum, both the high- and low-order bits of P must be 1.

There is a concise method for specifying the occurrence of one or more errors. An error results in the reversal of a bit. This is equivalent to taking the XOR of the bit and 1 (modulo 2 addition of 1 to the bit): $0 + 1 = 1$; $1 + 1 = 0$. Thus, the errors in an n-bit frame can be represented by an n-bit field with 1s in each error position. The resulting frame T_r can be expressed as

$$T_r = T \oplus E$$

where

T = transmitted frame

E = error pattern with 1s in positions where errors occur

T_r = received frame

$\oplus$ = bitwise exclusive-OR (XOR)

If there is an error ($E \neq 0$), the receiver will fail to detect the error if and only if T_r is divisible by P, which is equivalent to E divisible by P. Intuitively, this seems an unlikely occurrence.

Polynomials

A second way of viewing the CRC process is to express all values as polynomials in a dummy variable X, with binary coefficients. The coefficients correspond to the bits in the binary number. Thus, for $D = 110011$, we have $D(X) = X^5 + X^4 + X + 1$, and for $P = 11001$, we have $P(X) = X^4 + X^3 + 1$. Arithmetic operations are again modulo 2. The CRC process can now be described as

$$\frac{X^{n-k}D(X)}{P(X)} = Q(X) + \frac{R(X)}{P(X)}$$

$$T(X) = X^{n-k}D(X) + R(X)$$

Compare these equations with Equations (6.1) and (6.2).

EXAMPLE 6.7 Using the preceding example, for $D = 1010001101$, we have $D(X) = X^9 + X^7 + X^3 + X^2 + 1$, and for $P = 110101$, we have $P(X) = X^5 + X^4 + X^2 + 1$. We should end up with $R = 01110$, which corresponds to $R(X) = X^3 + X^2 + X$. Figure 6.5 shows the polynomial division that corresponds to the binary division in the preceding example.

An m-bit CRC is typically generated by a polynomial of the form

$$P(X) = q(X) \text{ or}$$
$$P(X) = (X + 1)q(X)$$

Where $q(X)$ is a special type of polynomial called a primitive polynomial.[4]

---

[4]A document at box.com/dcc10e provides an explanation of primitive polynomials.

$$
\begin{array}{c}
\phantom{P(X)\rightarrow X^5+X^4+X^2+1\sqrt{}}\underset{\leftarrow\,Q(X)}{X^9 + X^8 + X^6 + X^4 + X^2 + X}\\[2pt]
P(X)\rightarrow X^5 + X^4 + X^2 + 1\,\big/\,\overline{X^{14}\qquad X^{12}\qquad\qquad X^8 + X^7 +\quad X^5}\quad\leftarrow X^5 D(X)\\[2pt]
\underline{X^{14} + X^{13} +\qquad X^{11} +\qquad X^9}\\[2pt]
\underline{X^{13} + X^{12} + X^{11} +\qquad X^9 + X^8}\\[2pt]
\underline{X^{13} + X^{12} +\qquad X^{10} +\qquad X^8}\\[2pt]
\underline{X^{11} + X^{10} + X^9 +\qquad X^7}\\[2pt]
\underline{X^{11} + X^{10} +\qquad X^8 +\qquad X^6}\\[2pt]
\underline{X^9 + X^8 + X^7 + X^6 + X^5}\\[2pt]
\underline{X^9 + X^8 +\qquad X^6 +\qquad X^4}\\[2pt]
\underline{X^7 +\qquad X^5 + X^4}\\[2pt]
\underline{X^7 + X^6 +\qquad X^4 +\quad X^2}\\[2pt]
\underline{X^6 + X^5 +\qquad\qquad X^2}\\[2pt]
\underline{X^6 + X^5 +\qquad X^3 +\qquad X}\\[2pt]
\underset{\leftarrow R(X)}{X^3 + X^2 + X}
\end{array}
$$

Figure 6.5 Example of Polynomial Division

An error $E(X)$ will only be undetectable if it is divisible by $P(X)$. It can be shown [PETE61, RAMA88] that all of the following errors are not divisible by a suitably chosen $P(X)$ and hence are detectable:

- All single-bit errors, if $P(X)$ has more than one nonzero term
- All double-bit errors, as long as $P(X)$ is of one of the two forms shown above
- Any odd number of errors, as long as $P(X)$ contains a factor $(X + 1)$
- Any burst error for which the length of the burst is less than or equal to $n - k$; that is, less than or equal to the length of the FCS
- A fraction of error bursts of length $n - k + 1$; the fraction equals $1 - 2^{-(n-k-1)}$
- A fraction of error bursts of length greater than $n - k + 1$; the fraction equals $1 - 2^{-(n-k)}$

In addition, it can be shown that if all error patterns are considered equally likely, then for a burst error of length $r + 1$, the probability of an undetected error ($E(X)$ is divisible by $P(X)$) is $1/2^{r-1}$, and for a longer burst, the probability is $1/2^r$, where r is the length of the FCS.

Four versions of $P(X)$ are widely used:

$$\text{CRC-12} = X^{12} + X^{11} + X^3 + X^2 + X + 1 = (X + 1)(X^{11} + X^2 + 1)$$
$$\text{CRC-ANSI} = X^{16} + X^{15} + X^2 + 1 = (X + 1)(X^{15} + X + 1)$$
$$\text{CRC-CCITT} = X^{16} + X^{12} + X^5 + 1 = (X + 1)(X^{15} + X^{14} + X^{13} + X^{12}$$
$$+ X^4 + X^3 + X^2 + X + 1)$$
$$\text{IEEE-802} = X^{32} + X^{26} + X^{23} + X^{22} + X^{16} + X^{12} + X^{11} + X^{10} + X^8$$
$$+ X^7 + X^5 + X^4 + X^2 + X + 1$$

The CRC-12 system is used for transmission of streams of 6-bit characters and generates a 12-bit FCS. Both CRC-16 and CRC-CCITT are popular for 8-bit characters in the United States and Europe, respectively, and both result in a 16-bit FCS. This would seem adequate for most applications, although CRC-32 is specified as an option in some point-to-point synchronous transmission standards and is used in IEEE 802 LAN standards.

Digital Logic

The CRC process can be represented by, and indeed implemented as, a dividing circuit consisting of XOR gates and a shift register. The shift register is a string of 1-bit storage devices. Each device has an output line, which indicates the value currently stored, and an input line. At discrete time instants, known as clock times, the value in the storage device is replaced by the value indicated by its input line. The entire register is clocked simultaneously, causing a 1-bit shift along the entire register.

The circuit is implemented as follows:

1. The register contains $n - k$ bits, equal to the length of the FCS.
2. There are up to $n - k$ XOR gates.
3. The presence or absence of a gate corresponds to the presence or absence of a term in the divisor polynomial, $P(X)$, excluding the terms 1 and X^{n-k}.

EXAMPLE 6.8 The architecture of a CRC circuit is best explained by first considering an example, which is illustrated in Figure 6.6. In this example, we use:

$$\text{Data } D = 1010001101; \quad D(X) = X^9 + X^7 + X^3 + X^2 + 1$$
$$\textit{Divisor } P = 110101; \qquad P(X) = X^5 + X^4 + X^2 + 1$$

which were used earlier in the discussion.

Figure 6.6a shows the shift-register implementation. The process begins with the shift register cleared (all zeros). The message, or dividend, is then entered one bit at a time, starting with the most significant bit. Figure 6.6b is a table that shows the step-by-step operation as the input is applied one bit at a time. Each row of the table shows the values currently stored in the five shift-register elements. In addition, the row shows the values that appear at the outputs of the three XOR circuits. Finally, the row shows the value of the next input bit, which is available for the operation of the next step.

Note that the XOR operation affects C_4, C_2, and C_0 on the next shift. This is identical to the binary long division process illustrated earlier. The process continues through all the bits of the message. To produce the proper output, two switches are used. The input data bits are fed in with both switches in the A position. As a result, for the first 10 steps, the input bits are fed into the shift register and also used as output bits. After the last data bit is processed, the shift register contains the remainder (FCS) (shown shaded). As soon as the last data bit is provided to the shift register, both switches are set to the B position.

> This has two effects: (1) all of the XOR gates become simple pass-throughs; no bits are changed, and (2) as the shifting process continues, the 5 CRC bits are output.
>
> At the receiver, the same logic is used. As each bit of M arrives, it is inserted into the shift register. If there have been no errors, the shift register should contain the bit pattern for R at the conclusion of M. The transmitted bits of R now begin to arrive, and the effect is to zero out the register so that, at the conclusion of reception, the register contains all 0s.

Figure 6.7 indicates the general architecture of the shift-register implementation of a CRC for the polynomial $P(X) = \sum_{i=0}^{n-k} A_i X^i$, where $A_0 = A_{n-k} = 1$ and all other A_i equal either 0 or 1.[5]

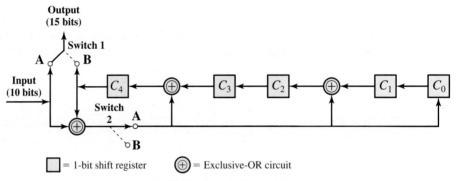

(a) **Shift-register implementation**

	C_4	C_3	C_2	C_1	C_0	$C_4 \oplus C_3 \oplus I$	$C_4 \oplus C_1 \oplus I$	$C_4 \oplus I$	I = input	
Initial	0	0	0	0	0	1	1	1	1	
Step 1	1	0	1	0	1	1	1	1	0	
Step 2	1	1	1	1	1	1	1	0	1	
Step 3	1	1	1	1	0	0	0	1	0	
Step 4	0	1	0	0	1	1	0	0	0	Message to
Step 5	1	0	0	1	0	1	0	1	0	be sent
Step 6	1	0	0	0	1	0	0	0	1	
Step 7	0	0	0	1	0	1	0	1	1	
Step 8	1	0	0	0	1	1	1	1	0	
Step 9	1	0	1	1	1	0	1	0	1	
Step 10	0	1	1	1	0					

(b) **Example with input of 1010001101**

Figure 6.6 Circuit with Shift Registers for Dividing by the Polynomial $X^5 + X^4 + X^2 + 1$

---

[5]It is common for the CRC register to be shown shifting to the right, which is the reverse of the analogy to binary division. Because binary numbers are usually shown with the most significant bit on the left, a left-shifting register, as is used here, is more appropriate.

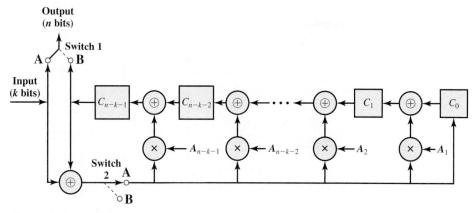

Figure 6.7   General CRC Architecture to Implement Divisor $(1 + A_1 X + A_2 X + \cdots + A_{n-k-1}X^{n-k-1} + X^{n-k})$

6.6   FORWARD ERROR CORRECTION

Error detection is a useful technique, found in data link control protocols, such as HDLC, and in transport protocols, such as TCP. As explained in Chapter 7, an error-detecting code can be used as part of a protocol that corrects errors in transmitted data by requiring the blocks of data be retransmitted. For wireless applications this approach is inadequate for two reasons:

1. The BER on a wireless link can be quite high, which would result in a large number of retransmissions.

2. In some cases, especially satellite links, the propagation delay is very long compared to the transmission time of a single frame. The result is a very inefficient system. As is discussed in Chapter 7, the common approach to retransmission is to retransmit the frame in error plus all subsequent frames. With a long data link, an error in a single frame necessitates retransmitting many frames.

Instead, it would be desirable to enable the receiver to correct errors in an incoming transmission on the basis of the bits in that transmission. Figure 6.8 shows in general how this is done. On the transmission end, each k-bit block of data is mapped into an n-bit block $(n > k)$ called a **codeword**, using an FEC (forward error correction) encoder. The codeword is then transmitted. During transmission, the signal is subject to impairments, which may produce bit errors in the signal. At the receiver, the incoming signal is demodulated to produce a bit string that is similar to the original codeword but may contain errors. This block is passed through an FEC decoder, with one of four possible outcomes:

- **No errors:** If there are no bit errors, the input to the FEC decoder is identical to the original codeword, and the decoder produces the original data block as output.

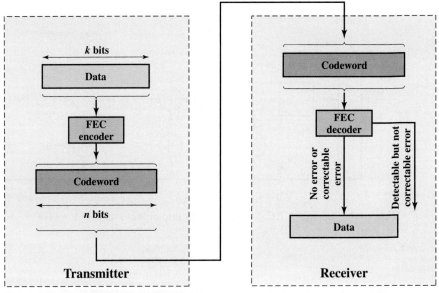

Figure 6.8   Error-Correction Process

- **Detectable, correctable errors:** For certain error patterns, it is possible for the decoder to detect and correct those errors. Thus, even though the incoming data block differs from the transmitted codeword, the FEC decoder is able to map this block into the original data block.

- **Detectable, not correctable errors:** For certain error patterns, the decoder can detect but not correct the errors. In this case, the decoder simply reports an uncorrectable error.

- **Undetectable errors:** For certain, typically rare, error patterns, the decoder does not detect the error and maps the incoming n-bit data block into a k-bit block that differs from the original k-bit block.

How is it possible for the decoder to correct bit errors? In essence, error correction works by adding sufficient redundancy to the transmitted message. The redundancy makes it possible for the receiver to deduce what the original message was, even in the face of a certain level of error rate. In this section, we look at a widely used form of error-correcting code known as a block error-correcting code. Our discussion here only deals with basic principles; a discussion of specific error-correcting codes is provided in Chapter 16.

Before proceeding, we note that in many cases, the error-correcting code follows the same general layout as shown for error-detecting codes in Figure 6.2. That is, the FEC algorithm takes as input a k-bit block and adds $(n - k)$ check bits to that block to produce an n-bit block; all of the bits in the original k-bit block show up in the n-bit block. For some FEC algorithms, the FEC algorithm maps the k-bit input into an n-bit codeword in such a way that the original k bits do not appear in the codeword.

Block Code Principles

To begin, we define a term that shall be of use to us. The **Hamming distance** $d(v_1, v_2)$ between two n-bit binary sequences v_1 and v_2 is the number of bits in which v_1 and v_2 disagree. For example, if

$$v_1 = 011011, \quad v_2 = 110001$$

then

$$d(v_1, v_2) = 3$$

Now let us consider the block code technique for error correction. Suppose we wish to transmit blocks of data of length k bits. Instead of transmitting each block as k bits, we map each k-bit sequence into a unique n-bit codeword.

EXAMPLE 6.9

For $k = 2$ and $n = 5$, we can make the following assignment:

Data Block	Codeword
00	00000
01	00111
10	11001
11	11110

Now, suppose that a codeword block is received with the bit pattern 00100. This is not a valid codeword, and so the receiver has detected an error. Can the error be corrected? We cannot be sure which data block was sent because 1, 2, 3, 4, or even all 5 of the bits that were transmitted may have been corrupted by noise. However, notice that it would require only a single-bit change to transform the valid codeword 00000 into 00100. It would take two bit changes to transform 00111 to 00100, three bit changes to transform 11110 to 00100, and it would take four bit changes to transform 11001 into 00100. Thus, we can deduce that the most likely codeword that was sent was 00000 and that therefore the desired data block is 00. This is error correction. In terms of Hamming distances, we have

$$d(00000, 00100) = 1; \quad (00111, 00100) = 2;$$
$$d(11001, 00100) = 4; \quad d(11110, 00100) = 3$$

So the rule we would like to impose is that if an invalid codeword is received, then the valid codeword that is closest to it (minimum distance) is selected. This will only work if there is a unique valid codeword at a minimum distance from each invalid codeword.

For our example, it is not true that for every invalid codeword there is one and only one valid codeword at a minimum distance. There are $2^5 = 32$ possible codewords of which 4 are valid, leaving 28 invalid codewords. For the invalid codewords, we have the following:

Invalid Codeword	Minimum Distance	Valid Codeword	Invalid Codeword	Minimum Distance	Valid Codeword
00001	1	00000	10000	1	00000
00010	1	00000	10001	1	11001
00011	1	00111	10010	2	00000 or 11110
00100	1	00000	10011	2	00111 or 11001
00101	1	00111	10100	2	00000 or 11110
00110	1	00111	10101	2	00111 or 11001
01000	1	00000	10110	1	11110
01001	1	11001	10111	1	00111
01010	2	00000 or 11110	11000	1	11001
01011	2	00111 or 11001	11010	1	11110
01100	2	00000 or 11110	11011	1	11001
01101	2	00111 or 11001	11100	1	11110
01110	1	11110	11101	1	11001
01111	1	00111	11111	1	11110

There are eight cases in which an invalid codeword is at a distance 2 from two different valid codewords. Thus, if one such invalid codeword is received, an error in 2 bits could have caused it and the receiver has no way to choose between the two alternatives. An error is detected but cannot be corrected. However, in every case in which a single-bit error occurs, the resulting codeword is of distance 1 from only one valid codeword and the decision can be made. This code is therefore capable of correcting all single-bit errors but cannot correct double-bit errors. Another way to see this is to look at the pairwise distances between valid codewords:

$$d(00000, 00111) = 3; \quad d(00000, 11001) = 3; \quad d(00000, 11110) = 4;$$
$$d(00111, 11001) = 4; \quad d(00111, 11110) = 3; \quad d(11001, 11110) = 3$$

The minimum distance between valid codewords is 3. Therefore, a single-bit error will result in an invalid codeword that is a distance 1 from the original valid codeword but a distance at least 2 from all other valid codewords. As a result, the code can always correct a single-bit error. Note that the code also will always detect a double-bit error.

The preceding example illustrates the essential properties of a block error-correcting code. An (n, k) block code encodes k data bits into n-bit codewords. Typically, each valid codeword reproduces the original k data bits and adds to them $(n - k)$ check bits to form the n-bit codeword. Thus the design of a block code is equivalent to the design of a function of the form $\mathbf{v_c} = f(\mathbf{v_d})$, where $\mathbf{v_d}$ is a vector of k data bits and $\mathbf{v_c}$ is a vector of n codeword bits.

With an (n, k) block code, there are 2^k valid codewords out of a total of 2^n possible codewords. The ratio of redundant bits to data bits, $(n - k)/k$, is called the **redundancy** of the code, and the ratio of data bits to total bits, k/n, is called the **code rate**. The code rate is a measure of how much additional bandwidth is required to carry data at the same data rate as without the code. For example, a code rate of 1/2 requires double the transmission capacity of an uncoded system to maintain the same data rate. Our example has a code rate of 2/5 and so requires 2.5 times the capacity of an uncoded system. For example, if the data rate input to the encoder is 1 Mbps, then the output from the encoder must be at a rate of 2.5 Mbps to keep up.

For a code consisting of the codewords $\mathbf{w}_1, \mathbf{w}_2, \cdots, \mathbf{w}_s$, where $s = 2^n$, the minimum distance $d_{\min}$ of the code is defined as

$$d_{\min} = \min_{i \neq j} [d(\mathbf{w}_i, \mathbf{w}_j)]$$

It can be shown that the following conditions hold. For a given positive integer t, if a code satisfies $d_{\min} \geq (2t + 1)$, then the code can correct all bit errors up to and including errors of t bits. If $d_{\min} \geq 2t$, then all errors $\leq (t - 1)$ bits can be corrected and errors of t bits can be detected but not, in general, corrected. Conversely, any code for which all errors of magnitude $\leq t$ are corrected must satisfy $d_{\min} \geq (2t + 1)$, and any code for which all errors of magnitude $\leq (t - 1)$ are corrected and all errors of magnitude t are detected must satisfy $d_{\min} \geq 2t$.

Another way of putting the relationship between $d_{\min}$ and t is to say that the maximum number of guaranteed correctable errors per codeword satisfies

$$t = \left\lfloor \frac{d_{\min} - 1}{2} \right\rfloor$$

where $\lfloor x \rfloor$ means the largest integer not to exceed x (e.g., $\lfloor 6.3 \rfloor = 6$). Furthermore, if we are concerned only with error detection and not error correction, then the number of errors, t, that can be detected satisfies

$$t = d_{\min} - 1$$

To see this, consider that if $d_{\min}$ errors occur, this could change one valid codeword into another. Any number of errors less than $d_{\min}$ cannot result in another valid codeword.

The design of a block code involves a number of considerations.

1. For given values of n and k, we would like the largest possible value of $d_{\min}$.
2. The code should be relatively easy to encode and decode, requiring minimal memory and processing time.
3. We would like the number of extra bits $(n - k)$ to be small, to reduce bandwidth.
4. We would like the number of extra bits $(n - k)$ to be large, to reduce error rate.

Clearly, the last two objectives are in conflict, and trade-offs must be made.

It is instructive to examine Figure 6.9. The literature on error-correcting codes frequently includes graphs of this sort to demonstrate the effectiveness of various

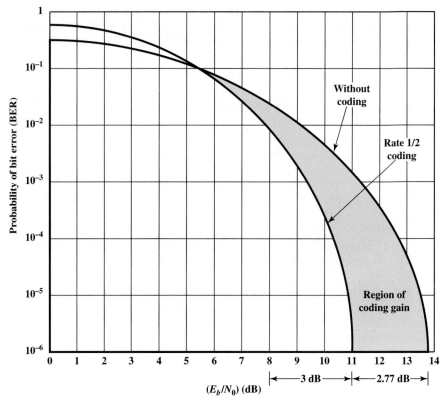

Figure 6.9 How Coding Improves System Performance

encoding schemes. Recall from Chapter 5 that coding can be used to reduce the required E_b/N_0 value to achieve a given bit error rate.[6] The coding discussed in Chapter 5 has to do with the definition of signal elements to represent bits. The coding discussed in this chapter also has an effect on E_b/N_0. In Figure 6.9, the curve on the right is for an uncoded modulation system. To the left of that curve is the area in which improvement can be achieved. In this region, a smaller BER (bit error rate) is achieved for a given E_b/N_0, and conversely, for a given BER, a smaller E_b/N_0 is required. The other curve is a typical result of a code rate of one-half (equal number of data and check bits). Note that at an error rate of 10^{-6}, the use of coding allows a reduction in E_b/N_0 of 2.77 dB. This reduction is referred to as the **coding gain**, which is defined as the reduction, in decibels, in the required E_b/N_0 to achieve a specified BER of an error-correcting coded system compared to an uncoded system using the same modulation.

It is important to realize that the BER for the second rate 1/2 curve refers to the rate of uncorrected errors and that the E_b value refers to the energy per data bit.

---

[6]E_b/N_0 is the ratio of signal energy per bit to noise power density per Hz; it is defined and discussed in Chapter 3.

Because the rate is 1/2, there are two bits on the channel for each data bit, and the energy per coded bit is half that of the energy per data bit, or a reduction of 3 dB to a value of 8 dB. If we look at the energy per coded bit for this system, then we see that the channel bit error rate is about 2.4×10^{-2}, or 0.024.

Finally, note that below a certain threshold of E_b/N_0, the coding scheme actually degrades performance. In our example of Figure 6.9, the threshold occurs at about 5.4 dB. Below the threshold, the extra check bits add overhead to the system that reduces the energy per data bit causing increased errors. Above the threshold, the error-correcting power of the code more than compensates for the reduced E_b, resulting in a coding gain.

6.7 RECOMMENDED READING AND ANIMATIONS

The classic treatment of error-detecting codes and CRC is [PETE61]. [RAMA88] is an excellent tutorial on CRC.

[ADAM91] provides comprehensive treatment of error-correcting codes. [SKLA01] contains a clear, well-written section on the subject. Two useful survey articles are [BERL87] and [BHAR83]. A quite readable theoretical and mathematical treatment of error-correcting codes is [ASH90]. [LIN04] is a thorough treatment of both error-detecting and error-correction codes.

ADAM91 Adamek, J. *Foundations of Coding.* New York: Wiley, 1991.

ASH90 Ash, R. *Information Theory.* New York: Dover, 1990.

BERL87 Berlekamp, E.; Peile, R.; and Pope, S. "The Application of Error Control to Communications." *IEEE Communications Magazine,* April 1987.

BHAR83 Bhargava, V. "Forward Error Correction Schemes for Digital Communications." *IEEE Communications Magazine,* January 1983.

LIN04 Lin, S., and Costello, D. *Error Control Coding.* Upper Saddle River, NJ: Prentice Hall, 2004.

PETE61 Peterson, W., and Brown, D. "Cyclic Codes for Error Detection." *Proceedings of the IEEE,* January 1961.

RAMA88 Ramabadran, T., and Gaitonde, S. "A Tutorial on CRC Computations." *IEEE Micro,* August 1988.

SKLA01 Sklar, B. *Digital Communications: Fundamentals and Applications.* Upper Saddle River, NJ: Prentice Hall, 2001.

Animations

Animations that illustrate CRC and parity are available at the Premium Web site. The reader is encouraged to view these animations to reinforce concepts from this chapter.

6.8 KEY TERMS, REVIEW QUESTIONS, AND PROBLEMS

Key Terms

check bits	error-correcting code (ECC)	Hamming distance
checksum	error detection	ones-complement addition
codeword	error-detecting code	ones-complement operation
code rate	forward error correction	parity bit
coding gain	(FEC)	parity check
cyclic redundancy check	frame	redundancy
(CRC)	frame check sequence	two-dimensional parity
error correction	(FCS)	check

Review Questions

6.1 What is a parity bit?

6.2 What is the CRC?

6.3 Why would you expect a CRC to detect more errors than a parity bit?

6.4 List three different ways in which the CRC algorithm can be described.

6.5 Is it possible to design an ECC that will correct some double-bit errors but not all double-bit errors? Why or why not?

6.6 In an (n, k) block ECC, what do n and k represent?

Problems

6.1 For the example of Figure 6.1, what is the minimum and maximum value of x that satisfies the formal definition of error burst in Section 6.1?

6.2 Would you expect that the inclusion of a parity bit with each character would change the probability of receiving a correct message?

6.3 Two communicating devices are using single-bit odd parity check for error detection. What will the transmitter send if the data word is 1010110? State the cases in which the receiver will be able to detect errors on receiving the message.

6.4 Consider a frame consisting of two characters of four bits each. Assume that the probability of bit error is 10^{-3} and that it is independent for each bit.
a. What is the probability that the received frame contains at least one error?
b. Now add a parity bit to each character. What is the probability?

6.5 Show that the value of p in Figure 6.3a is the same whether it is calculated as the parity of all the data bits, the parity of all the row parity bits, or the parity of all the column parity bits.

6.6 If the Internet checksum method is adopted, what message will be sent if data is 5AD3 EE35? If the message received is 59D3 EF35 B6F6, will the message be accepted?

6.7 One nice property of the Internet checksum is that it is endian-independent. Little Endian computers store hex numbers with the least significant byte last (Intel processors, for example). Big Endian computers put the least significant byte first (IBM mainframes, for example). Explain why the checksum does not need to take into account endianness.

6.8 The high-speed transport protocol XTP (Xpress Transfer Protocol) uses a 32-bit checksum function defined as the concatenation of two 16-bit functions: XOR and

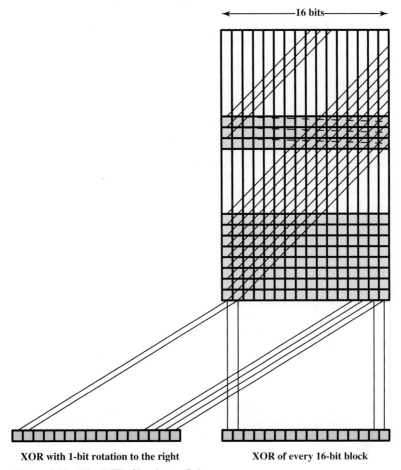

XOR with 1-bit rotation to the right **XOR of every 16-bit block**

Figure 6.10 The XTP Checksum Scheme

RXOR are illustrated in Figure 6.10. The XOR function calculates the column parity. RXOR is a diagonal parity check, achieved by rotating each successive 16-bit word in the data block one bit and then performing a bitwise XOR.

   a. Will this checksum detect all errors caused by an odd number of error bits? Explain.

   b. Will this checksum detect all errors caused by an even number of error bits? If not, characterize the error patterns that will cause the checksum to fail.

6.9 What is the purpose of using modulo 2 arithmetic rather than binary arithmetic in computing an FCS?

6.10 A CRC-4-ITU uses the polynomial $X^4 + X + 1$ as the divisor. There is a message in the form of a polynomial $D = X^8 + X^5 + X$.

   a. What will be appended to this message using CRC-4-ITU?

   b. What message will be sent in binary?

6.11 In CRC code with C(11, 7), the bit string 110011 has been chosen as the divisor. Is this divisor suitable?

6.12 If the divisor is 1011 in a CRC code with C(7,4), how will 1101 be encoded?

6.13 A CRC is constructed to generate a 4-bit FCS for an 11-bit message. The generator polynomial is $X^4 + X^3 + 1$.

a. Draw the shift-register circuit that would perform this task (see Figure 6.4).

b. Encode the data bit sequence 10011011100 (leftmost bit is the least significant) using the generator polynomial and give the codeword.

c. Now assume that bit 7 (counting from the LSB) in the codeword is in error and show that the detection algorithm detects the error.

6.14 a. In a CRC coding scheme, is the generator $(X+1)$ suitable for guaranteeing detection of all single-bit errors?

b. If a CRC coding scheme has the generator (X^4+1), in what situations does it fail to detect two isolated single-bit errors?

c. Is the generator $X^5 + X^3 + X + 1$ in a CRC coding scheme suitable for detecting all odd-numbered errors?

6.15 A modified CRC procedure is commonly used in communications standards. It is defined as follows:

$$\frac{X^{16}D(X) + X^k L(X)}{P(X)} = Q + \frac{R(X)}{P(X)}$$

$$\text{FCS} = L(X) + R(X)$$

where

$$L(X) = X^{15} + X^{14} + X^{13} + \cdots + X + 1$$

and k is the number of bits being checked (address, control, and information fields).

a. Describe in words the effect of this procedure.

b. Explain the potential benefits.

c. Show a shift-register implementation for $P(X) = X^{16} + X^{12} + X^5 + 1$.

6.16 A code scheme has a Hamming distance $d_{\min} = 6$.

a. What is its error detection capability?

b. What is its error correction capability?

6.17 Section 6.6 discusses block error-correcting codes that make a decision on the basis of minimum distance. That is, given a code consisting of s equally likely codewords of length n, for each received sequence $\mathbf{v}$, the receiver selects the codeword $\mathbf{w}$ for which the distance $d(\mathbf{w}, \mathbf{v})$ is a minimum. We would like to prove that this scheme is "ideal" in the sense that the receiver always selects the codeword for which the probability of $\mathbf{w}$ given $\mathbf{v}$, $p(\mathbf{w}|\mathbf{v})$, is a maximum. Because all codewords are assumed equally likely, the codeword that maximizes $p(\mathbf{w}|\mathbf{v})$ is the same as the codeword that maximizes $p(\mathbf{v}|\mathbf{w})$.

a. In order that $\mathbf{w}$ be received as $\mathbf{v}$, there must be exactly $d(\mathbf{w}, \mathbf{v})$ errors in transmission, and these errors must occur in those bits where $\mathbf{w}$ and $\mathbf{v}$ disagree. Let β be the probability that a given bit is transmitted incorrectly and n be the length of a codeword. Write an expression for $p(\mathbf{v}|\mathbf{w})$ as a function of β, $d(\mathbf{w}, \mathbf{v})$, and n. *Hint:* The number of bits in error is $d(\mathbf{w}, \mathbf{v})$ and the number of bits not in error is $n - d(\mathbf{w}, \mathbf{v})$.

b. Now compare $p(\mathbf{v}|\mathbf{w}_1)$ and $p(\mathbf{v}|\mathbf{w}_2)$ for two different codewords $\mathbf{w}_1$ and $\mathbf{w}_2$ by calculating $p(\mathbf{v}|\mathbf{w}_1)/p(\mathbf{v}|\mathbf{w}_2)$.

c. Assume that $0 < \beta < 0.5$ and show that $p(\mathbf{v}|\mathbf{w}_1) > p(\mathbf{v}|\mathbf{w}_2)$ if and only if $d(\mathbf{v},\mathbf{w}_1) < d(\mathbf{v},\mathbf{w}_2)$. This proves that the codeword $\mathbf{w}$ that gives the largest value of $p(\mathbf{v}|\mathbf{w})$ is that word whose distance from $\mathbf{v}$ is a minimum.

6.18 A 16-bit block of data needs to be encoded by a block error-correcting code (n,k).

a. Find the values of n and k.

b. Find the redundancy of the code.

c. Find the code rate.

6.19 A common technique for implementing CRC is to use a table lookup algorithm. The document site at box.com/dcc10e contains several papers describing this approach. Write a short paper that summarizes the general approach to implementing CRC using table lookup.

DATA LINK CONTROL PROTOCOLS

LEARNING OBJECTIVES

After reading this chapter, you should be able to:

♦ Explain the need for a flow control and error control.

♦ Present an overview of the basic mechanisms of stop-and-wait flow control and sliding-window flow control.

♦ Present an overview of the basic mechanisms of stop-and-wait ARQ, go-back-N ARQ, and selective reject flow control.

♦ Present an overview of HDLC.

Our discussion so far has concerned *sending signals over a transmission link*. For effective digital data communications, much more is needed to control and manage the exchange. In this chapter, we shift our emphasis to that of *sending data over a data communications link*. To achieve the necessary control, a layer of logic is added above the physical layer discussed in Chapter 6; this logic is referred to as **data link control** or a **data link control protocol**. When a data link control protocol is used, the transmission medium between systems is referred to as a **data link**.

To see the need for data link control, we list some of the requirements and objectives for effective data communication between two directly connected transmitting-receiving stations:

• **Frame synchronization:** Data are sent in blocks called frames. The beginning and end of each frame must be recognizable. We briefly introduced this topic with the discussion of synchronous frames (Figure 6.2).

• **Flow control:** The sending station must not send frames at a rate faster than the receiving station can absorb them.

• **Error control:** Bit errors introduced by the transmission system should be corrected.

• **Addressing:** On a shared link, such as a local area network (LAN), the identity of the two stations involved in a transmission must be specified.

• **Control and data on same link:** It is usually not desirable to have a physically separate communications path for control information. Accordingly, the receiver must be able to distinguish control information from the data being transmitted.

• **Link management:** The initiation, maintenance, and termination of a sustained data exchange require a fair amount of coordination and cooperation among stations. Procedures for the management of this exchange are required.

None of these requirements is satisfied by the techniques described in Chapter 6. We shall see in this chapter that a data link protocol that satisfies these requirements is a rather complex affair. We begin by looking at two key mechanisms that are part of data link control: flow control and error control. Following this background we look at the most important example of a data link control protocol: HDLC (high-level data link control). This protocol is important for two reasons: First, it is a widely used standardized data link control protocol. Second, HDLC serves as a baseline from which virtually all other important data link control protocols are derived.

7.1 FLOW CONTROL

Flow control is a technique for assuring that a transmitting entity does not overwhelm a receiving entity with data. The receiving entity typically allocates a data buffer of some maximum length for a transfer. When data are received, the receiver must do a certain amount of processing before passing the data to the higher-level software. In the absence of flow control, the receiver's buffer may fill up and overflow while it is processing old data.

To begin, we examine mechanisms for flow control in the absence of errors. The model we will use is depicted in Figure 7.1a, which is a vertical time sequence diagram. It has the advantages of showing time dependencies and illustrating the correct send–receive relationship. Each arrow represents a single frame transiting a data link between two stations. The data are sent in a sequence of frames, with each frame containing a portion of the data and some control information. The time it takes for a station to emit all of the bits of a frame onto the medium is the **transmission time**; this is proportional to the length of the frame. The **propagation time** is the time it takes for a bit to traverse the link between source and destination. For this section, we assume that all frames that are transmitted are successfully received; no frames are lost and none arrive with errors. Furthermore, frames arrive in the same order in which they are sent. However, each transmitted frame suffers an arbitrary and variable amount of delay before reception.[1]

Stop-and-Wait Flow Control

The simplest form of flow control, known as stop-and-wait flow control, works as follows. A source entity transmits a frame. After the destination entity receives the frame, it indicates its willingness to accept another frame by sending back an acknowledgment to the frame just received. The source must wait until it receives the acknowledgment before sending the next frame. The destination can thus stop

---

[1]On a direct point-to-point link, the amount of delay is fixed rather than variable. However, a data link control protocol can be used over a network connection, such as a circuit-switched or ATM network, in which case the delay may be variable.

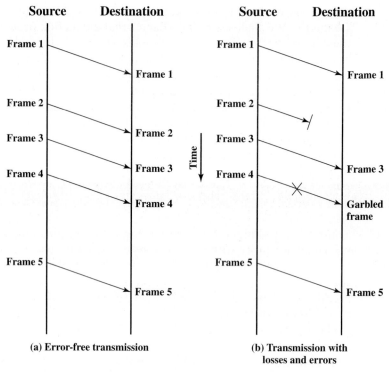

Figure 7.1 Model of Frame Transmission

the flow of data simply by withholding acknowledgment. This procedure works fine and, indeed, can hardly be improved upon when a message is sent in a few large frames. However, it is often the case that a source will break up a large block of data into smaller blocks and transmit the data in many frames. This is done for the following reasons:

- The buffer size of the receiver may be limited.
- The longer the transmission, the more likely that there will be an error, necessitating retransmission of the entire frame. With smaller frames, errors are detected sooner, and a smaller amount of data needs to be retransmitted.
- On a shared medium, such as a LAN, it is usually desirable not to permit one station to occupy the medium for an extended period, thus causing long delays at the other sending stations.

With the use of multiple frames for a single message, the stop-and-wait procedure may be inadequate. The essence of the problem is that only one frame at a time can be in transit. To explain we first define the **bit length of a link** as follows:

$$B = R \times \frac{d}{V} \tag{7.1}$$

where

    B = length of the link in bits; this is the number of bits present on the link at an instance in time when a stream of bits fully occupies the link

    R = data rate of the link, in bps

    d = length, or distance, of the link in meters

    V = velocity of propagation, in m/s

In situations where the bit length of the link is greater than the frame length, serious inefficiencies result. This is illustrated in Figure 7.2. In the figure, the transmission time is normalized to one, and the propagation delay is expressed as the variable a. Thus, we can express a as

$$a = \frac{B}{L} \tag{7.2}$$

where L is the number of bits in the frame (length of the frame in bits).

When a is less than 1, the propagation time is less than the transmission time. In this case, the frame is sufficiently long that the first bits of the frame have arrived

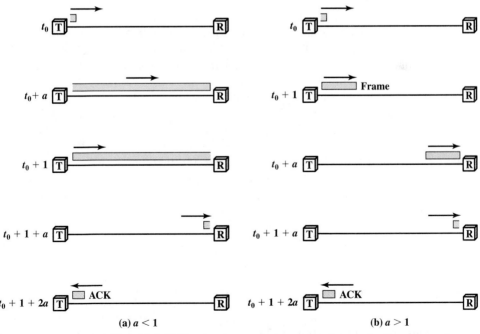

(a) $a < 1$ (b) $a > 1$

Figure 7.2 Stop-and-Wait Link Utilization (transmission time = 1; propagation time = a)

at the destination before the source has completed the transmission of the frame. When *a* is greater than 1, the propagation time is greater than the transmission time. In this case, the sender completes transmission of the entire frame before the leading bits of that frame arrive at the receiver. Put another way, larger values of *a* are consistent with higher data rates and/or longer distances between stations. Chapter 16 discusses *a* and data link performance.

Both parts of Figure 7.2 (a and b) consist of a sequence of snapshots of the transmission process over time. In both cases, the first four snapshots show the process of transmitting a frame containing data, and the last snapshot shows the return of a small acknowledgment frame. Note that for *a* > 1, the line is always underutilized and even for *a* < 1, the line is inefficiently utilized. In essence, for very high data rates, for very long distances between sender and receiver, stop-and-wait flow control provides inefficient line utilization.

EXAMPLE 7.1 Consider a 200-m optical fiber link operating at 1 Gbps. The velocity of propagation of optical fiber is typically about 2×10^8 m/s. Using Equation (7.1), $B = (10^9 \times 200)/(2 \times 10^8) = 1000$ bits. Assume a frame of 1000 octets, or 8000 bits, is transmitted. Using Equation (7.2), $a = (1000/8000) = 0.125$. Using Figure 7.2a as a guide, assume transmission starts at time $t = 0$. After 1 μs (a normalized time of 0.125 frame times), the leading edge (first bit) of the frame has reached R, and the first 1000 bits of the frame are spread out across the link. At time $t = 8$ μs, the trailing edge (final bit) of the frame has just been emitted by T, and the final 1000 bits of the frame are spread out across the link. At $t = 9$ μs, the final bit of the frame arrives at R. R now sends back an ACK frame. If we assume the frame transmission time is negligible (very small ACK frame) and that the ACK is sent immediately, the ACK arrives at T at $t = 10$ μs. At this point, T can begin transmitting a new frame. The actual transmission time for the frame was 8 μs, but the total time to transmit the first frame and receive an ACK is 10 μs.

Now consider a 1-Mbps link between two ground stations that communicate via a satellite relay. A geosynchronous satellite has an altitude of roughly 36,000 km. Then $B = (10^6 \times 2 \times 36,000,000)/(3 \times 10^8) = 240,000$ bits. For a frame length of 8000 bits, $a = (240,000/8000) = 30$. Using Figure 7.2b as a guide, we can work through the same steps as before. In this case, it takes 240 ms for the leading edge of the frame to arrive and an additional 8 ms for the entire frame to arrive. The ACK arrives back at T at $t = 488$ ms. The actual transmission time for the first frame was 8 ms, but the total time to transmit the first frame and receive an ACK is 488 ms.

Sliding-Window Flow Control

The essence of the problem described so far is that only one frame at a time can be in transit. In situations where the bit length of the link is greater than the frame length ($a > 1$), serious inefficiencies result. Efficiency can be greatly improved by allowing multiple frames to be in transit at the same time.

Let us examine how this might work for two stations, A and B, connected via a full-duplex link. Station B allocates buffer space for W frames. Thus, B can accept W frames, and A is allowed to send W frames without waiting for any acknowledgments. To keep track of which frames have been acknowledged, each is labeled with a sequence number. B acknowledges a frame by sending an acknowledgment that includes the sequence number of the next frame expected. This acknowledgment also implicitly announces that B is prepared to receive the next W frames, beginning with the number specified. This scheme can also be used to acknowledge multiple frames. For example, B could receive frames 2, 3, and 4 but withhold acknowledgment until frame 4 has arrived. By then returning an acknowledgment with sequence number 5, B acknowledges frames 2, 3, and 4 at one time. A maintains a list of sequence numbers that it is allowed to send, and B maintains a list of sequence numbers that it is prepared to receive. Each of these lists can be thought of as a *window* of frames. The operation is referred to as **sliding-window flow control**.

Several additional comments need to be made. Because the sequence number to be used occupies a field in the frame, it is limited to a range of values. For example, for a 3-bit field, the sequence number can range from 0 to 7. Accordingly, frames are numbered modulo 8; that is, after sequence number 7, the next number is 0. In general, for a k-bit field the range of sequence numbers is 0 through $2^k - 1$, and frames are numbered modulo 2^k. As will be shown subsequently, the maximum window size is $2^k - 1$.

Figure 7.3 is a useful way of depicting the sliding-window process. It assumes the use of a 3-bit sequence number, so that frames are numbered sequentially from

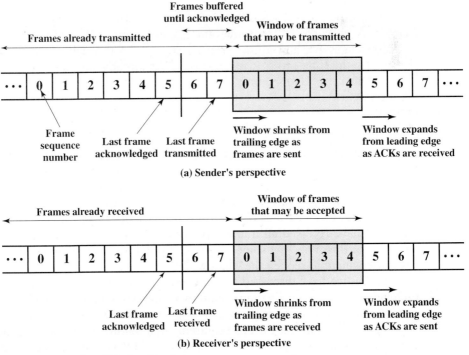

Figure 7.3 Sliding-Window Depiction

0 through 7, and then the same numbers are reused for subsequent frames. The shaded rectangle indicates the frames that may be sent; in this figure, the sender may transmit five frames, beginning with frame 0. Each time a frame is sent, the shaded window shrinks; each time an acknowledgment is received, the shaded window grows. Frames between the vertical bar and the shaded window have been sent but not yet acknowledged. As we shall see, the sender must buffer these frames in case they need to be retransmitted.

The window size need not be the maximum possible size for a given sequence number length. For example, using a 3-bit sequence number, a window size of 5 could be configured for the stations using the sliding-window flow control protocol.

> **EXAMPLE 7.2** An example is shown in Figure 7.4. The example assumes a 3-bit sequence number field and a maximum window size of seven frames. Initially, A and B have windows indicating that A may transmit seven frames, beginning with frame 0 (F0). After transmitting three frames (F0, F1, F2) without acknowledgment, A has shrunk its window to four frames and maintains a copy of the three transmitted frames. The window indicates that A may transmit four frames, beginning with frame number 3. B then transmits an RR (receive ready) 3, which means "I have received all frames up through frame number 2 and am ready to receive frame number 3; in fact, I am prepared to receive seven frames, beginning with frame number 3." With this acknowledgment, A is back up to permission to transmit seven frames, still beginning with frame 3; also A may discard the buffered frames that have now been acknowledged. A proceeds to transmit frames 3, 4, 5, and 6. B returns RR 4, which acknowledges F3, and allows transmission of F4 through the next instance of F2. By the time this RR reaches A, it has already transmitted F4, F5, and F6, and therefore A may only open its window to permit sending four frames beginning with F7.

The mechanism so far described provides a form of flow control: The receiver must only be able to accommodate seven frames beyond the one it has last acknowledged. Most data link control protocols also allow a station to cut off the flow of frames from the other side by sending a Receive Not Ready (RNR) message, which acknowledges former frames but forbids transfer of future frames. Thus, RNR 5 means, "I have received all frames up through number 4 but am unable to accept any more at this time." At some subsequent point, the station must send a normal acknowledgment to reopen the window.

So far, we have discussed transmission in one direction only. If two stations exchange data, each needs to maintain two windows, one for transmit and one for receive, and each side needs to send the data and acknowledgments to the other. To provide efficient support for this requirement, a feature known as **piggybacking** is typically provided. Each **data frame** includes a field that holds the sequence number of that frame plus a field that holds the sequence number used for acknowledgment.

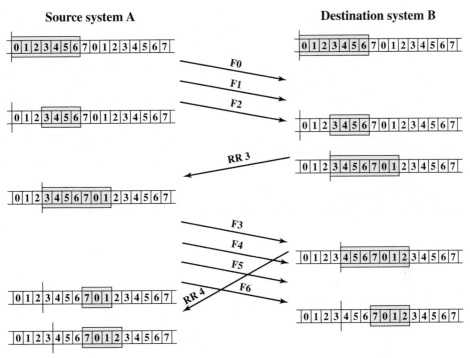

Figure 7.4   Example of a Sliding-Window Protocol

Thus, if a station has data to send and an acknowledgment to send, it sends both together in one frame, saving communication capacity. Of course, if a station has an acknowledgment but no data to send, it sends a separate **acknowledgment frame,** such as RR or RNR. If a station has data to send but no new acknowledgment to send, it must repeat the last acknowledgment sequence number that it sent. This is because the data frame includes a field for the acknowledgment number, and some value must be put into that field. When a station receives a duplicate acknowledgment, it simply ignores it.

Sliding-window flow control is potentially much more efficient than stop-and-wait flow control. The reason is that, with sliding-window flow control, the transmission link is treated as a pipeline that may be filled with frames in transit. By contrast, with stop-and-wait flow control, only one frame may be in the pipe at a time. Chapter 16 quantifies the improvement in efficiency.

EXAMPLE 7.3 Let us consider the use of sliding-window flow control for the two configurations of Example 7.1. As was calculated in Example 7.1, it takes 10 μs for an ACK to the first frame to be received. It takes 8 μs to transmit one frame, so the sender can transmit one frame and part of a second frame by the time the ACK to the first frame is received. Thus, a window size of 2 is adequate to enable the sender to transmit frames continuously, or at a rate of one frame every 8 μs. With stop-and-wait, a rate of only one frame per 10 μs is possible.

> For the satellite configuration, it takes 488 ms for an ACK to the first frame to be received. It takes 8 ms to transmit one frame, so the sender can transmit 61 frames by the time the ACK to the first frame is received. With a window field of 6 bits or more, the sender can transmit continuously, or at a rate of one frame every 8 ms. If the window size is 7, using a 3-bit window field, then the sender can only send 7 frames and then must wait for an ACK before sending more. In this case, the sender can transmit at a rate of 7 frames per 488 ms, or about one frame every 70 ms. With stop-and-wait, a rate of only one frame per 488 ms is possible.

7.2   ERROR CONTROL

Error control refers to mechanisms to detect and correct errors that occur in the transmission of frames. The model that we will use, which covers the typical case, is illustrated in Figure 7.1b. As before, data are sent as a sequence of frames; frames arrive in the same order in which they are sent; and each transmitted frame suffers an arbitrary and potentially variable amount of delay before reception. In addition, we admit the possibility of two types of errors:

- **Lost frame:** A frame fails to arrive at the other side. In the case of a network, the network may simply fail to deliver a frame. In the case of a direct point-to-point data link, a noise burst may damage a frame to the extent that the receiver is not aware that a frame has been transmitted.

- **Damaged frame:** A recognizable frame does arrive, but some of the bits are in error (have been altered during transmission).

The most common techniques for error control are based on some or all of the following ingredients:

- **Error detection:** The destination detects frames that are in error, using the techniques described in the preceding chapter, and discards those frames.

- **Positive acknowledgment:** The destination returns a positive acknowledgment to successfully received, error-free frames.

- **Retransmission after timeout:** The source retransmits a frame that has not been acknowledged after a predetermined amount of time.

- **Negative acknowledgment and retransmission:** The destination returns a negative acknowledgment to frames in which an error is detected. The source retransmits such frames.

Collectively, these mechanisms are all referred to as **automatic repeat request (ARQ)**. The effect of ARQ is to turn a potentially unreliable data link into a reliable one. Three versions of ARQ have been standardized:

- Stop-and-wait ARQ
- Go-back-N ARQ
- Selective-reject ARQ

All of these forms are based on the use of the flow control techniques discussed in Section 7.1. We examine each in turn.

Stop-and-Wait ARQ

Stop-and-wait ARQ is based on the stop-and-wait flow control technique outlined previously. The source station transmits a single frame and then must await an acknowledgment (ACK). No other data frames can be sent until the destination station's reply arrives at the source station.

Two sorts of errors could occur. First, the frame that arrives at the destination could be damaged. The receiver detects this by using the error-detection technique referred to earlier and simply discards the frame. To account for this possibility, the source station is equipped with a timer. After a frame is transmitted, the source station waits for an acknowledgment. If no acknowledgment is received by the time that the timer expires, then the same frame is sent again. Note that this method requires that the transmitter maintain a copy of a transmitted frame until an acknowledgment is received for that frame.

The second sort of error is a damaged acknowledgment. Consider the following situation. Station A sends a frame. The frame is received correctly by station B, which responds with an acknowledgment. The ACK is damaged in transit and is not recognizable by A, which will therefore time out and resend the same frame. This duplicate frame arrives and is accepted by B. B has therefore accepted two copies of the same frame as if they were separate. To avoid this problem, frames are alternately labeled with 0 or 1, and positive acknowledgments are of the form ACK0 and ACK1. In keeping with the sliding-window convention, an ACK0 acknowledges receipt of a frame numbered 1 and indicates that the receiver is ready for a frame numbered 0.

Figure 7.5 gives an example of the use of stop-and-wait ARQ, showing the transmission of a sequence of frames from source A to destination B.[2] The figure shows the two types of errors just described. The third frame transmitted by A is lost or damaged and therefore B does not return an ACK. A times out and retransmits the frame. Later, A transmits a frame labeled 1 but the ACK0 for that frame is lost. A times out and retransmits the same frame. When B receives two frames in a row with the same label, it discards the second frame but sends back an ACK0 to each.

The principal advantage of stop-and-wait ARQ is its simplicity. Its principal disadvantage, as discussed in Section 7.1, is that stop-and-wait is an inefficient mechanism. The sliding-window flow control technique can be adapted to provide more efficient line use; in this context, it is sometimes referred to as *continuous ARQ*.

Go-Back-N ARQ

The form of error control based on sliding-window flow control that is most commonly used is called go-back-N ARQ. In this method, a station may send a series of frames sequentially numbered modulo some maximum value. The number of unacknowledged frames outstanding is determined by window size, using the

---

[2]This figure indicates the time required to transmit a frame. For simplicity, other figures in this chapter do not show this time.

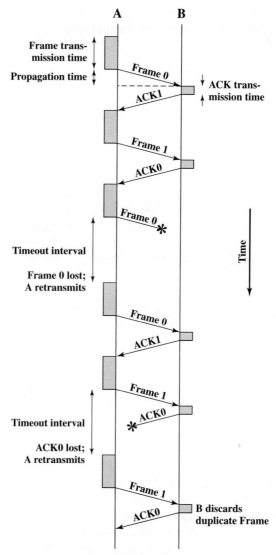

Figure 7.5 Stop-and-Wait ARQ

sliding-window flow control technique. While no errors occur, the destination will acknowledge incoming frames as usual (RR = receive ready, or piggybacked acknowledgment). If the destination station detects an error in a frame, it may send a negative acknowledgment (REJ = reject) for that frame, as explained in the following rules. The destination station will discard that frame and all future incoming frames until the frame in error is correctly received. Thus, the source station, when it receives a REJ, must retransmit the frame in error plus all succeeding frames that were transmitted in the interim.

Suppose that station A is sending frames to station B. After each transmission, A sets an acknowledgment timer for the frame just transmitted. Suppose that B has previously successfully received frame $(i - 1)$ and A has just transmitted frame i. The go-back-N technique takes into account the following contingencies:

1. **Damaged frame.** If the received frame is invalid (i.e., B detects an error, or the frame is so damaged that B does not even perceive that it has received a frame), B discards the frame and takes no further action as the result of that frame. There are two subcases:

    a. Within a reasonable period of time, A subsequently sends frame $(i + 1)$. B receives frame $(i + 1)$ out of order and sends a REJ i. A must retransmit frame i and all subsequent frames.

    b. A does not soon send additional frames. B receives nothing and returns neither an RR nor a REJ. When A's timer expires, it transmits an RR frame that includes a bit known as the P bit, which is set to 1. B interprets the RR frame with a P bit of 1 as a command that must be acknowledged by sending an RR indicating the next frame that it expects, which is frame i. When A receives the RR, it retransmits frame i. Alternatively, A could just retransmit frame i when its timer expires.

2. **Damaged RR.** There are two subcases:

    a. B receives frame i and sends RR $(i + 1)$, which suffers an error in transit. Because acknowledgments are cumulative (e.g., RR 6 means that all frames through 5 are acknowledged), it may be that A will receive a subsequent RR to a subsequent frame and that it will arrive before the timer associated with frame i expires.

    b. If A's timer expires, it transmits an RR command as in Case 1b. It sets another timer, called the P-bit timer. If B fails to respond to the RR command, or if its response suffers an error in transit, then A's P-bit timer will expire. At this point, A will try again by issuing a new RR command and restarting the P-bit timer. This procedure is tried for a number of iterations. If A fails to obtain an acknowledgment after some maximum number of attempts, it initiates a reset procedure.

3. **Damaged REJ.** If a REJ is lost, this is equivalent to Case 1b.

EXAMPLE 7.4 Figure 7.6a is an example of the frame flow for go-back-N ARQ. Because of the propagation delay on the line, by the time that an acknowledgment (positive or negative) arrives back at the sending station, it has already sent at least one additional frame beyond the one being acknowledged. In this example, frame 4 is damaged. Frames 5 and 6 are received out of order and are discarded by B. When frame 5 arrives, B immediately sends a REJ 4. When the REJ to frame 4 is received, not only frame 4 but frames 5 and 6 must be retransmitted. Note that the transmitter must keep a copy of all unacknowledged frames. Figure 7.6a also shows an example of retransmission after timeout. No acknowledgment is received for frame 5 within the timeout period, so A issues an RR to determine the status of B.

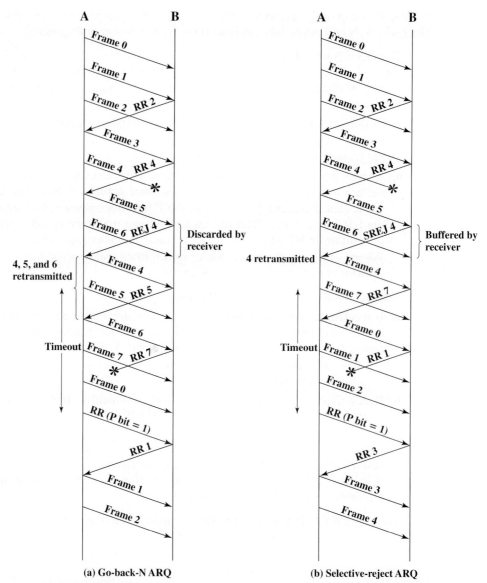

Figure 7.6   Sliding-Window ARQ Protocols

In Section 7.1, we mentioned that for a k-bit sequence number field, which provides a sequence number range of 2^k, the maximum window size is limited to $2^k - 1$. This has to do with the interaction between error control and acknowledgment. Consider that if data are being exchanged in both directions, station B must send piggybacked acknowledgments to station A's frames in the data frames being transmitted by B, even if the acknowledgment has already been sent. As we have mentioned, this is because B must put some number in the acknowledgment field of its data frame. As an example, assume a 3-bit sequence number (sequence number space = 8). Suppose a station sends frame 0 and gets back an RR 1 and then sends frames 1, 2, 3, 4, 5, 6, 7, 0 and gets another RR 1. This could mean that all eight frames were received correctly and the RR 1 is a cumulative acknowledgment. It could also mean that all eight frames were damaged or lost in transit, and the receiving station is repeating its previous RR 1. The problem is avoided if the maximum window size is limited to 7 $(2^3 - 1)$.

Selective-Reject ARQ

With **selective-reject ARQ**, the only frames retransmitted are those that receive a negative acknowledgment, in this case called SREJ, or those that time out.

> **EXAMPLE 7.5** Figure 7.6b illustrates this scheme. When frame 5 is received out of order, B sends a SREJ 4, indicating that frame 4 has not been received. However, B continues to accept incoming frames and buffers them until a valid frame 4 is received. At that point, B can place the frames in the proper order for delivery to higher-layer software.

Selective reject would appear to be more efficient than go-back-N, because it minimizes the amount of retransmission. On the other hand, the receiver must maintain a buffer large enough to save post-SREJ frames until the frame in error is retransmitted and must contain logic for reinserting that frame in the proper sequence. The transmitter, too, requires more complex logic to be able to send a frame out of sequence. Because of such complications, selective-reject ARQ is much less widely used than go-back-N ARQ. Selective reject is a useful choice for a satellite link because of the long propagation delay involved.

The window size limitation is more restrictive for selective-reject than for go-back-N. Consider the case of a 3-bit sequence number size for selective-reject. Allow a window size of seven, and consider the following scenario:

1. Station A sends frames 0 through 6 to station B.
2. Station B receives all seven frames and cumulatively acknowledges with RR 7.
3. Because of a noise burst, the RR 7 is lost.
4. A times out and retransmits frame 0.
5. B has already advanced its receive window to accept frames 7,0,1,2,3,4, and 5. Thus it assumes that frame 7 has been lost and that this is a new frame 0, which it accepts.

The problem with the preceding scenario is that there is an overlap between the sending and receiving windows. To overcome the problem, the maximum window size should be no more than half the range of sequence numbers. In the preceding scenario, if only four unacknowledged frames may be outstanding, no confusion can result. In general, for a k-bit sequence number field, which provides a sequence number range of 2^k, the maximum window size is limited to 2^{k-1}.

7.3 HIGH-LEVEL DATA LINK CONTROL (HDLC)

The most important data link control protocol is HDLC (ISO 3009, ISO 4335). Not only is HDLC widely used, but it is the basis for many other important data link control protocols, which use the same or similar formats and the same mechanisms as employed in HDLC.

Basic Characteristics

To satisfy a variety of applications, HDLC defines three types of stations, two link configurations, and three data transfer modes of operation. The three station types are:

- **Primary station:** Responsible for controlling the operation of the link. Frames issued by the primary are called commands.
- **Secondary station:** Operates under the control of the primary station. Frames issued by a secondary are called responses. The primary maintains a separate logical link with each secondary station on the line.
- **Combined station:** Combines the features of primary and secondary. A combined station may issue both commands and responses.

The two link configurations are

- **Unbalanced configuration:** Consists of one primary and one or more secondary stations and supports both full-duplex and half-duplex transmission.
- **Balanced configuration:** Consists of two combined stations and supports both full-duplex and half-duplex transmission.

The three data transfer modes are

- **Normal response mode (NRM):** Used with an unbalanced configuration. The primary may initiate data transfer to a secondary, but a secondary may only transmit data in response to a command from the primary.
- **Asynchronous balanced mode (ABM):** Used with a balanced configuration. Either combined station may initiate transmission without receiving permission from the other combined station.
- **Asynchronous response mode (ARM):** Used with an unbalanced configuration. The secondary may initiate transmission without explicit permission of the primary. The primary still retains responsibility for the line, including initialization, error recovery, and logical disconnection.

NRM is used on multidrop lines, in which a number of terminals are connected to a host computer. The computer polls each terminal for input. NRM is also sometimes used on point-to-point links, particularly if the link connects a terminal or other peripheral to a computer. ABM is the most widely used of the three modes; it makes more efficient use of a full-duplex point-to-point link because there is no polling overhead. ARM is rarely used; it is applicable to some special situations in which a secondary may need to initiate transmission.

Frame Structure

HDLC uses synchronous transmission. All transmissions are in the form of frames, and a single frame format suffices for all types of data and control exchanges.

Figure 7.7 depicts the structure of the HDLC frame. The flag, address, and control fields that precede the information field are known as a **header**. The frame check sequence and flag fields following the data field are referred to as a **trailer**.

FLAG FIELDS   **Flag fields** delimit the frame at both ends with the unique pattern 01111110. A single flag may be used as the closing flag for one frame and the opening flag for the next. On both sides of the user-network interface, receivers are continuously hunting for the flag sequence to synchronize on the start of a frame. While receiving a frame, a station continues to hunt for that sequence to determine the end of the frame. Because the protocol allows the presence of arbitrary bit patterns (i.e., there are no restrictions on the content of the various fields imposed by the link protocol), there is no assurance that the pattern 01111110 will not appear somewhere inside the frame, thus destroying synchronization. To avoid this problem, a procedure known as **bit stuffing** is used. For all bits between the starting and ending

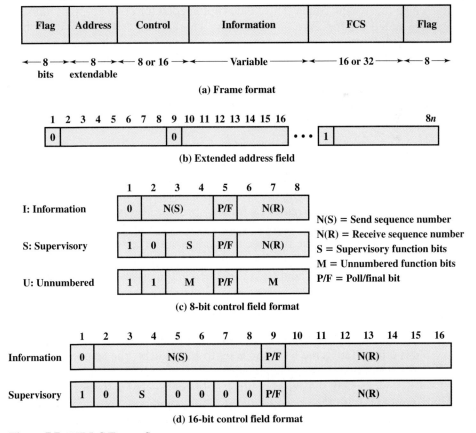

Figure 7.7   HDLC Frame Structure

Original pattern:

111111111111011111101111110

After bit-stuffing:

111110011111011101111101011111010

Figure 7.8   Bit Stuffing

flags, the transmitter inserts an extra 0 bit after each occurrence of five 1s in the frame. After detecting a starting flag, the receiver monitors the bit stream. When a pattern of five 1s appears, the sixth bit is examined. If this bit is 0, it is deleted. If the sixth bit is a 1 and the seventh bit is a 0, the combination is accepted as a flag. If the sixth and seventh bits are both 1, the sender is indicating an abort condition.

With the use of bit stuffing, arbitrary bit patterns can be inserted into the data field of the frame. This property is known as **data transparency**.

Figure 7.8 shows an example of bit stuffing. Note that in the first two cases, the extra 0 is not strictly necessary for avoiding a flag pattern but is necessary for the operation of the algorithm.

ADDRESS FIELD   The address field identifies the secondary station that transmitted or is to receive the frame. This field is not needed for point-to-point links but is always included for the sake of uniformity. The address field is usually 8 bits long but, by prior agreement, an extended format may be used in which the actual address length is a multiple of 7 bits. The leftmost bit of each octet is 1 or 0 according as it is or is not the last octet of the address field. The remaining 7 bits of each octet form part of the address. The single-octet address of 11111111 is interpreted as the all-stations address in both basic and extended formats. It is used to allow the primary to broadcast a frame for reception by all secondaries.

CONTROL FIELD   HDLC defines three types of frames, each with a different control field format. **Information frames** (I-frames) carry the data to be transmitted for the user (the logic above HDLC that is using HDLC). Additionally, flow and error control data, using the ARQ mechanism, are piggybacked on an information frame. **Supervisory frames** (S-frames) provide the ARQ mechanism when piggy-backing is not used. **Unnumbered frames** (U-frames) provide supplemental link control functions. The first one or two bits of the control field serves to identify the frame type. The remaining bit positions are organized into subfields as indicated in Figures 7.7c and d. Their use is explained in the discussion of HDLC operation later in this chapter.

All of the control field formats contain the poll/final (P/F) bit. Its use depends on context. Typically, in command frames, it is referred to as the P bit and is set to 1 to solicit (poll) a response frame from the peer HDLC entity. In response frames, it is referred to as the F bit and is set to 1 to indicate the response frame transmitted as a result of a soliciting command.

Note that the basic control field for S- and I-frames uses 3-bit sequence numbers. With the appropriate set-mode command, an extended control field can be used for S- and I-frames that employs 7-bit sequence numbers. U-frames always contain an 8-bit control field.

INFORMATION FIELD   The information field is present only in I-frames and some U-frames. The field can contain any sequence of bits but must consist of an integral number of octets. The length of the information field is variable up to some system-defined maximum.

FRAME CHECK SEQUENCE FIELD   The frame check sequence (FCS) is an error-detecting code calculated from the remaining bits of the frame, exclusive of flags. The normal code is the 16-bit CRC-CCITT defined in Section 6.3. An optional 32-bit FCS, using CRC-32, may be employed if the frame length or the line reliability dictates this choice.

Operation

HDLC operation consists of the exchange of I-frames, S-frames, and U-frames between two stations. The various commands and responses defined for these frame types are listed in Table 7.1. In describing HDLC operation, we will discuss these three types of frames.

The operation of HDLC involves three phases. First, one side or another initializes the data link so that frames may be exchanged in an orderly fashion. During this phase, the options that are to be used are agreed upon. After initialization, the two sides exchange user data and the control information to exercise flow and error control. Finally, one of the two sides signals the termination of the operation.

INITIALIZATION   Either side may request initialization by issuing one of the six set-mode commands. This command serves three purposes:

1. It signals the other side that initialization is requested.
2. It specifies which of the three modes (NRM, ABM, ARM) is requested.
3. It specifies whether 3- or 7-bit sequence numbers are to be used.

If the other side accepts this request, then the HDLC module on that end transmits an unnumbered acknowledged (UA) frame back to the initiating side. If the request is rejected, then a disconnected mode (DM) frame is sent.

DATA TRANSFER   When the initialization has been requested and accepted, then a logical connection is established. Both sides may begin to send user data in I-frames, starting with sequence number 0. The N(S) and N(R) fields of the I-frame are sequence numbers that support flow control and error control. An HDLC module sending a sequence of I-frames will number them sequentially, modulo 8 or 128, depending on whether 3- or 7-bit sequence numbers are used, and place the sequence number in N(S). N(R) is the acknowledgment for I-frames received; it enables the HDLC module to indicate which number I-frame it expects to receive next.

S-frames are also used for flow control and error control. The receive ready (RR) frame acknowledges the last I-frame received by indicating the next I-frame expected. The RR is used when there is no reverse user data traffic (I-frames) to carry an acknowledgment. Receive not ready (RNR) acknowledges an I-frame, as with RR, but also asks the peer entity to suspend transmission of I-frames. When the

Table 7.1 HDLC Commands and Responses

Name	Command/ Response	Description
Information (I)	C/R	Exchange user data
Supervisory (S)		
Receive ready (RR)	C/R	Positive acknowledgment; ready to receive I-frame
Receive not ready (RNR)	C/R	Positive acknowledgment; not ready to receive
Reject (REJ)	C/R	Negative acknowledgment; go back N
Selective reject (SREJ)	C/R	Negative acknowledgment; selective reject
Unnumbered (U)		
Set normal response/extended mode (SNRM/SNRME)	C	Set mode; extended = 7-bit sequence numbers
Set asynchronous response/ extended mode (SARM/SARME)	C	Set mode; extended = 7-bit sequence numbers
Set asynchronous balanced/ extended mode (SABM, SABME)	C	Set mode; extended = 7-bit sequence numbers
Set initialization mode (SIM)	C	Initialize link control functions in addressed station
Disconnect (DISC)	C	Terminate logical link connection
Unnumbered Acknowledgment (UA)	R	Acknowledge acceptance of one of the set-mode commands
Disconnected mode (DM)	R	Responder is in disconnected mode
Request disconnect (RD)	R	Request for DISC command
Request initialization mode (RIM)	R	Initialization needed; request for SIM command
Unnumbered information (UI)	C/R	Used to exchange control information
Unnumbered poll (UP)	C	Used to solicit control information
Reset (RSET)	C	Used for recovery; resets N(R), N(S)
Exchange identification (XID)	C/R	Used to request/report status
Test (TEST)	C/R	Exchange identical information fields for testing
Frame reject (FRMR)	R	Report receipt of unacceptable frame

entity that issued RNR is again ready, it sends an RR. REJ initiates the go-back-N ARQ. It indicates that the last I-frame received has been rejected and that retransmission of all I-frames beginning with number N(R) is required. Selective reject (SREJ) is used to request retransmission of just a single frame.

DISCONNECT   Either HDLC module can initiate a disconnect, either on its own initiative if there is some sort of fault, or at the request of its higher-layer user. HDLC issues a disconnect by sending a disconnect (DISC) frame. The remote entity must accept the disconnect by replying with a UA and informing its layer 3 user that the connection has been terminated. Any outstanding unacknowledged I-frames may be lost, and their recovery is the responsibility of higher layers.

EXAMPLES OF OPERATION   To better understand HDLC operation, several examples are presented in Figure 7.9. In the example diagrams, each arrow includes a legend that specifies the frame name, the setting of the P/F bit, and, where appropriate, the values of N(R) and N(S). The setting of the P or F bit is 1 if the designation is present and 0 if absent.

Figure 7.9a shows the frames involved in link setup and disconnect. The HDLC protocol entity for one side issues an SABM command to the other side and starts

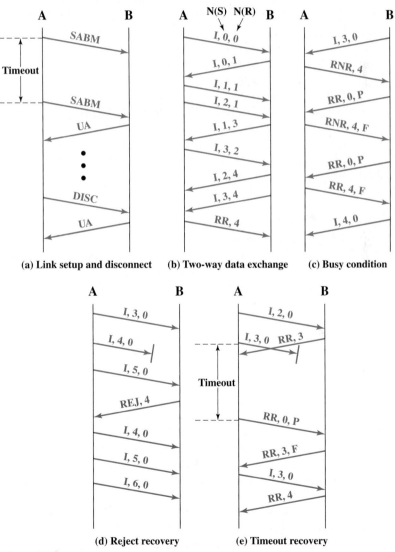

(a) Link setup and disconnect   (b) Two-way data exchange   (c) Busy condition

(d) Reject recovery   (e) Timeout recovery

Figure 7.9   Examples of HDLC Operation

a timer. The other side, upon receiving the SABM, returns a UA response and sets local variables and counters to their initial values. The initiating entity receives the UA response, sets its variables and counters, and stops the timer. The logical connection is now active, and both sides may begin transmitting frames. Should the timer expire without a response to an SABM, the originator will repeat the SABM, as illustrated. This would be repeated until a UA or DM is received or until, after a given number of tries, the entity attempting initiation gives up and reports failure to a management entity. In such a case, higher-layer intervention is necessary. The same figure (Figure 7.9a) shows the disconnect procedure. One side issues a DISC command, and the other responds with a UA response.

Figure 7.9b illustrates the full-duplex exchange of I-frames. When an entity sends a number of I-frames in a row with no incoming data, then the receive sequence number is simply repeated (e.g., I,1,1; I,2,1 in the A-to-B direction). When an entity receives a number of I-frames in a row with no outgoing frames, then the receive sequence number in the next outgoing frame must reflect the cumulative activity (e.g., I,1,3 in the B-to-A direction). Note that, in addition to I-frames, data exchange may involve supervisory frames.

Figure 7.9c shows an operation involving a busy condition. Such a condition may arise because an HDLC entity is not able to process I-frames as fast as they are arriving, or the intended user is not able to accept data as fast as they arrive in I-frames. In either case, the entity's receive buffer fills up and it must halt the incoming flow of I-frames, using an RNR command. In this example, A issues an RNR, which requires B to halt transmission of I-frames. The station receiving the RNR will usually poll the busy station at some periodic interval by sending an RR with the P bit set. This requires the other side to respond with either an RR or an RNR. When the busy condition has cleared, A returns an RR, and I-frame transmission from B can resume.

An example of error recovery using the REJ command is shown in Figure 7.9d. In this example, A transmits I-frames numbered 3, 4, and 5. Number 4 suffers an error and is lost. When B receives I-frame number 5, it discards this frame because it is out of order and sends an REJ with an N(R) of 4. This causes A to initiate retransmission of I-frames previously sent, beginning with frame 4. A may continue to send additional frames after the retransmitted frames.

An example of error recovery using a timeout is shown in Figure 7.9e. In this example, A transmits I-frame number 3 as the last in a sequence of I-frames. The frame suffers an error. B detects the error and discards it. However, B cannot send an REJ, because there is no way to know if this was an I-frame. If an error is detected in a frame, all of the bits of that frame are suspect, and the receiver has no way to act upon it. A, however, would have started a timer as the frame was transmitted. This timer has a duration long enough to span the expected response time. When the timer expires, A initiates recovery action. This is usually done by polling the other side with an RR command with the P bit set to determine the status of the other side. Because the poll demands a response, the entity will receive a frame containing an N(R) field and be able to proceed. In this case, the response indicates that frame 3 was lost, which A retransmits.

These examples are not exhaustive. However, they should give the reader a good feel for the behavior of HDLC.

7.4 RECOMMENDED READING AND ANIMATIONS

An excellent and very detailed treatment of flow control and error control is to be found in [BERT92]. [FIOR95] points out some of the real-world reliability problems with HDLC.

BERT92 Bertsekas, D., and Gallager, R. *Data Networks*. Englewood Cliffs, NJ: Prentice Hall, 1992.

FIOR95 Fiorini, D.; Chiani, M.; Tralli, V.; and Salati, C. "Can We Trust HDLC?" *ACM Computer Communications Review*, October 1995.

Animations

An animation that illustrates data link control protocol operation is available at the Premium Web site. The reader is encouraged to view the animation to reinforce concepts from this chapter.

7.5 KEY TERMS, REVIEW QUESTIONS, AND PROBLEMS

Key Terms

automatic repeat request (ARQ)	flag field	piggybacking
acknowledgment frame	flow control	propagation time
data frame	frame	selective-reject ARQ
data link	frame synchronization	sliding-window flow control
data link control protocol	go-back-N ARQ	stop-and-wait ARQ
data transparency	header	stop-and-wait flow control
error control	high-level data link control (HDLC)	trailer
		transmission time

Review Questions

7.1 List and briefly define some of the requirements for effective communications over a data link.

7.2 Define *flow control*.

7.3 Describe stop-and-wait flow control.

7.4 What are reasons for breaking up a long data transmission into a number of frames?

7.5 Describe sliding-window flow control.

7.6 What is the advantage of sliding-window flow control compared to stop-and-wait flow control?

7.7   What is piggybacking?

7.8   Define *error control*.

7.9   List common ingredients for error control for a link control protocol.

7.10   Describe automatic repeat request (ARQ).

7.11   List and briefly define three versions of ARQ.

7.12   What are the station types supported by HDLC? Describe each.

7.13   What are the transfer modes supported by HDLC? Describe each.

7.14   What is the purpose of the flag field?

7.15   Define *data transparency*.

7.16   What are the three frame types supported by HDLC? Describe each.

Problems

7.1   Consider a half-duplex point-to-point link using a stop-and-wait scheme, in which a series of messages is sent, with each message segmented into a number of frames. Ignore errors and frame overhead.

   a.   What is the effect on line utilization of increasing the message size so that fewer messages will be required? Other factors remain constant.

   b.   What is the effect on line utilization of increasing the number of frames for a constant message size?

   c.   What is the effect on line utilization of increasing frame size?

7.2   A 300-m optical fiber has a data rate of 900 Mbps. The length of the data frame is 2000 bits. Assume a propagation speed of 2×10^8 m/s.

   a.   What is the bit length of the link?

   b.   What is the propagation delay a of a bit?

   c.   What inference can you draw from this value of a?

7.3   In Figure 7.10 frames are generated at node A and sent to node C through node B. Determine the minimum data rate required between nodes B and C so that the buffers of node B are not flooded, based on the following:

- The data rate between A and B is 100 kbps.
- The propagation delay is 5 μs/km for both lines.
- There are full-duplex lines between the nodes.
- All data frames are 1000 bits long; ACK frames are separate frames of negligible length.
- Between A and B, a sliding-window protocol with a window size of 3 is used.
- Between B and C, stop-and-wait is used.
- There are no errors.

  Hint: In order not to flood the buffers of B, the average number of frames entering and leaving B must be the same over a long interval.

7.4   A channel has a data rate of R bps and a propagation delay of t s/km. The distance between the sending and receiving nodes is L kilometers. Nodes exchange fixed-size frames of B bits. Find a formula that gives the minimum sequence field size of the frame as a function of R, t, B, and L (considering maximum utilization). Assume that ACK frames are negligible in size and the processing at the nodes is instantaneous.

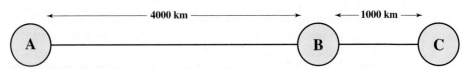

Figure 7.10   Configuration for Problem 7.3

7.5 Frames from a sending station are using a 4-bit sequence number starting from 0. What will be the sequence numbers of the 17th and 64th frames that are sent?

7.6 Suppose that a selective-reject ARQ is used where $W = 4$. Show, by example, that a 3-bit sequence number is needed.

7.7 In a stop-and-wait ARQ system, the bandwidth of the line is 10 Mbps. A bit takes 3 ms to travel from source to destination. The length of the data frame is 5000 bits.
  a. For a round trip, what is the bandwidth delay in bits?
  b. What percentage of this link will be utilized?
  c. If a protocol is designed so that up to 10 frames can be sent before receiving acknowledgements, what will be the utilization percentage? Assume that no frames are re-sent due to damage or otherwise.

7.8 Out-of-sequence acknowledgment cannot be used for selective-reject ARQ. That is, if frame i is rejected by station X, all subsequent I-frames and RR frames sent by X must have $N(R) = i$ until frame i is successfully received, even if other frames with $N(S) > i$ are successfully received in the meantime. One possible refinement is the following: $N(R) = j$ in an I-frame or an RR frame is interpreted to mean that frame $j - 1$ and all preceding frames are accepted except for those that have been explicitly rejected using an SREJ frame. Comment on any possible drawback to this scheme.

7.9 The ISO standard for HDLC procedures (ISO 4335) includes the following definitions: (1) an REJ condition is considered cleared upon the receipt of an incoming I-frame with an N(S) equal to the N(R) of the outgoing REJ frame; and (2) a SREJ condition is considered cleared upon the receipt of an I-frame with an N(S) equal to the N(R) of the SREJ frame. The standard includes rules concerning the relationship between REJ and SREJ frames. These rules indicate what is allowable (in terms of transmitting REJ and SREJ frames) if an REJ condition has not yet been cleared and what is allowable if an SREJ condition has not yet been cleared. Deduce the rules and justify your answer.

7.10 Two neighbouring nodes are sending frames using 5-bit sequence numbers. What will be the maximum size of the send-and-receive windows for each of the following protocols?
  a. Stop-and-wait ARQ
  b. Go-back-N ARQ
  c. Selective-reject ARQ

7.11 It is clear that bit stuffing is needed for the address, data, and FCS fields of an HDLC frame. Is it needed for the control field?

7.12 Because of the provision that a single flag can be used as both an ending and a starting flag, a single-bit error can cause problems.
  a. Explain how a single-bit error can merge two frames into one.
  b. Explain how a single-bit error can split a single frame into two frames.

7.13 Suggest improvements to the bit stuffing-algorithm to overcome the problems of single-bit errors described in the preceding problem.

7.14 Using the example bit string of Figure 7.8, show the signal pattern on the line using NRZ-L coding. Does this suggest a side benefit of bit stuffing?

7.15 Assume that the primary HDLC station in NRM has sent six I-frames to a secondary. The primary's N(S) count was three (011 binary) prior to sending the six frames. If the poll bit is on in the sixth frame, what will be the N(R) count back from the secondary after the last frame? Assume error-free operation.

7.16 Consider that several physical links connect two stations. We would like to use a "multilink HDLC" that makes efficient use of these links by sending frames on a FIFO basis on the next available link. What enhancements to HDLC are needed?

7.17 A World Wide Web server is usually set up to receive relatively small messages from its clients but to transmit potentially very large messages to them. Explain, then, which type of ARQ protocol (selective reject, go-back-N) would provide less of a burden to a particularly popular WWW server.

CHAPTER **8**

MULTIPLEXING

After reading this chapter, you should be able to:

◆ Explain the need for transmission efficiency and list the two major approaches used to achieve efficiency.

◆ Discuss the use of frequency-division multiplexing in voice networks.

◆ Describe the use of multiplexing in digital carrier systems.

◆ Discuss the T-1 service and describe its importance and the applications that are using it.

◆ Discuss the SONET standard and its significance for wide area networking.

In Chapter 7, we described efficient techniques for utilizing a data link under heavy load. Specifically, with two devices connected by a point-to-point link, it is generally desirable to have multiple frames outstanding so that the data link does not become a bottleneck between the stations. Now consider the opposite problem. Typically, two communicating stations will not utilize the full capacity of a data link. For efficiency, it should be possible to share that capacity. A generic term for such sharing is **multiplexing**.

A common application of multiplexing is in long-haul communications. Trunks on long-haul networks are high-capacity fiber, coaxial, or microwave links. These links can carry large numbers of voice and data transmissions simultaneously using multiplexing.

Figure 8.1 depicts the multiplexing function in its simplest form. There are n inputs to a multiplexer. The multiplexer is connected by a single data link to a **demultiplexer**. The link is able to carry n separate channels of data. The multiplexer combines (multiplexes) data from the n input lines and transmits over a higher-capacity data link. The demultiplexer accepts the multiplexed

Figure 8.1 Multiplexing

data stream, separates (demultiplexes) the data according to channel, and delivers data to the appropriate output lines.

The widespread use of multiplexing in data communications can be explained by the following:

- The higher the data rate, the more cost-effective the transmission facility. That is, for a given application and over a given distance, the cost per kbps declines with an increase in the data rate of the transmission facility. Similarly, the cost of transmission and receiving equipment, per kbps, declines with increasing data rate.
- Most individual data communicating devices require relatively modest data rate support. For example, for many terminal and personal computer applications that do not involve Web access or intensive graphics, a data rate of between 9600 bps and 64 kbps is generally adequate.

The preceding statements were phrased in terms of data communicating devices. Similar statements apply to voice communications. That is, the greater the capacity of a transmission facility, in terms of voice channels, the less the cost per individual voice channel, and the capacity required for a single voice channel is modest.

This chapter presents two types of multiplexing techniques. The first, frequency-division multiplexing (FDM), is the most heavily used and is familiar to anyone who has ever used a radio or television set. The second is a particular case of time-division multiplexing (TDM) known as synchronous TDM. This is commonly used for multiplexing digitized voice streams and data streams. We then look at two schemes that combine both types of multiplexing, cable modems and digital subscriber lines.

8.1   FREQUENCY-DIVISION MULTIPLEXING

Characteristics

FDM is possible when the useful bandwidth of the transmission medium exceeds the required bandwidth of signals to be transmitted. A number of signals can be carried simultaneously if each signal is modulated onto a different carrier frequency and the carrier frequencies are sufficiently separated that the bandwidths of the signals do not significantly overlap. A general case of FDM is shown in Figure 8.2a. Six signal sources are fed into a multiplexer, which modulates each signal onto a different frequency $(f_1, \ldots, f_6)$. Each modulated signal requires a certain bandwidth centered on its carrier frequency, referred to as a **channel**. To prevent interference, the channels are separated by guard bands, which are unused portions of the spectrum.

The composite signal transmitted across the medium is analog. Note, however, that the input signals may be either digital or analog. In the case of digital input, the input signals must be passed through modems to be converted to analog. In either case, each input analog signal must then be modulated to move it to the appropriate frequency band.

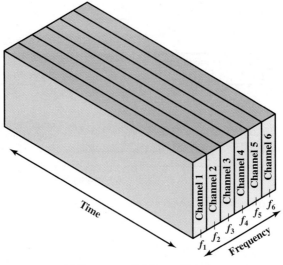

(a) Frequency-division multiplexing

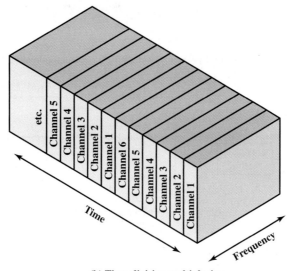

(b) Time-division multiplexing

Figure 8.2   FDM and TDM

A generic depiction of an FDM system is shown in Figure 8.3. A number of analog or digital signals [$m_i(t)$, $i = 1, n$] are to be multiplexed onto the same transmission medium. Each signal $m_i(t)$ is modulated onto a carrier f_i; because multiple carriers are to be used, each is referred to as a **subcarrier**. Any type of modulation may be used. The resulting analog, modulated signals are then summed to produce a composite **baseband**[1] signal $m_b(t)$. Figure 8.3b shows the result. The spectrum of

---

[1]The term *baseband* is used to designate the band of frequencies of the signal delivered by the source and potentially used as a modulating signal. Typically, the spectrum of a baseband signal is significant in a band that includes or is in the vicinity of $f = 0$.

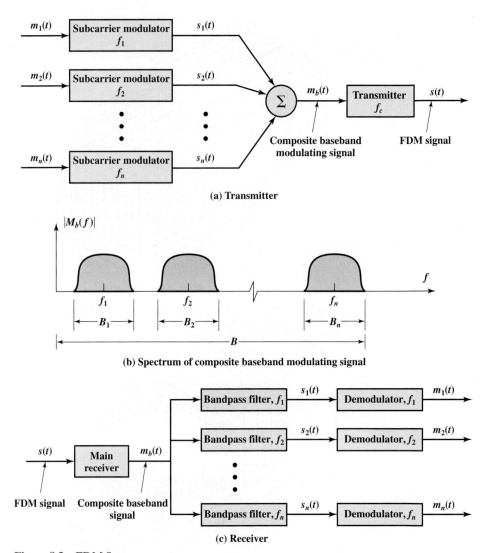

(a) Transmitter

(b) Spectrum of composite baseband modulating signal

(c) Receiver

Figure 8.3 FDM System

signal $m_i(t)$ is shifted to be centered on f_i. For this scheme to work, f_i must be chosen so that the bandwidths of the various signals do not significantly overlap. Otherwise, it will be impossible to recover the original signals.

The composite signal may then be shifted as a whole to another carrier frequency by an additional modulation step. We will see examples of this later. This second modulation step need not use the same modulation technique as the first.

The FDM signal $s(t)$ has a total bandwidth B, where $B > \sum_{i=1}^{n} B_i$. This analog signal may be transmitted over a suitable medium. At the receiving end, the FDM signal is demodulated to retrieve $m_b(t)$, which is then passed through n bandpass filters, each filter centered on f_i and having a bandwidth B_i, for $1 \le i \le n$. In this way, the signal is again split into its component parts. Each component is then demodulated to recover the original signal.

EXAMPLE 8.1 Let us consider a simple example of transmitting three voice signals simultaneously over a medium. As was mentioned, the bandwidth of a voice signal is generally taken to be 4 kHz, with an effective spectrum of 300 to 3400 Hz (Figure 8.4a). If such a signal is used to amplitude-modulate a 64-kHz carrier, the spectrum of Figure 8.4b results. The modulated signal has a bandwidth of 8 kHz, extending from 60 to 68 kHz. To make efficient use of bandwidth, we elect to transmit only the lower sideband. If three voice signals are used to modulate carriers at 64 kHz, 68 kHz, and 72 kHz, and only the lower sideband of each is taken, the spectrum of Figure 8.4c results.

Figure 8.4 points out two problems that an FDM system must cope with. The first is crosstalk, which may occur if the spectra of adjacent component signals overlap significantly. In the case of voice signals, with an effective bandwidth of

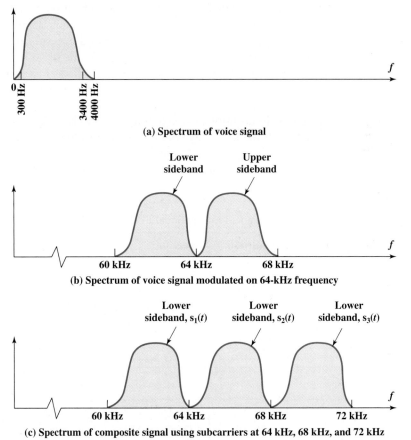

(a) Spectrum of voice signal

(b) Spectrum of voice signal modulated on 64-kHz frequency

(c) Spectrum of composite signal using subcarriers at 64 kHz, 68 kHz, and 72 kHz

Figure 8.4 FDM of Three Voiceband Signals

only 3100 Hz (300 to 3400), a 4-kHz bandwidth is adequate. The spectra of signals produced by modems for voiceband transmission also fit well in this bandwidth. Another potential problem is intermodulation noise, which was discussed in Chapter 3. On a long link, the nonlinear effects of amplifiers on a signal in one channel could produce frequency components in other channels.

Analog Carrier Systems

The long-distance carrier system provided in the United States and throughout the world is designed to transmit voiceband signals over high-capacity transmission links, such as coaxial cable and microwave systems. The earliest, and still a very common, technique for utilizing high-capacity links is FDM. In the United States, AT&T has designated a hierarchy of FDM schemes to accommodate transmission systems of various capacities. A similar, but unfortunately not identical, system has been adopted internationally under the auspices of ITU-T (Table 8.1).

At the first level of the AT&T hierarchy, 12 voice channels are combined to produce a group signal with a bandwidth of $12 \times 4 \text{ kHz} = 48 \text{ kHz}$, in the range 60 to 108 kHz. The signals are produced in a fashion similar to that described previously, using subcarrier frequencies of from 64 to 108 kHz in increments of 4 kHz. The next basic building block is the 60-channel supergroup, which is formed by frequency-division multiplexing five group signals. At this step, each group is treated as a single signal with a 48-kHz bandwidth and is modulated by a subcarrier. The subcarriers have frequencies from 420 to 612 kHz in increments of 48 kHz. The resulting signal occupies 312 to 552 kHz.

There are several variations to supergroup formation. Each of the five inputs to the supergroup multiplexer may be a group channel containing 12 multiplexed voice signals. In addition, any signal up to 48 kHz wide whose bandwidth is contained within 60 to 108 kHz may be used as input to the supergroup multiplexer. As another variation, it is possible to combine 60 voiceband channels into a supergroup. This may reduce multiplexing costs where an interface with existing group multiplexer is not required.

Table 8.1 North American and International FDM Carrier Standards

Number of Voice Channels	Bandwidth	Spectrum	AT&T	ITU-T
12	48 kHz	60–108 kHz	Group	Group
60	240 kHz	312–552 kHz	Supergroup	Supergroup
300	1.232 MHz	812–2044 kHz		Mastergroup
600	2.52 MHz	564–3084 kHz	Mastergroup	
900	3.872 MHz	8.516–12.388 MHz		Supermaster group
$N \times 600$			Mastergroup multiplex	
3,600	16.984 MHz	0.564–17.548 MHz	Jumbogroup	
10,800	57.442 MHz	3.124–60.566 MHz	Jumbogroup multiplex	

The next level of the hierarchy is the mastergroup, which combines 10 super-group inputs. Again, any signal with a bandwidth of 240 kHz in the range 312 to 552 kHz can serve as input to the mastergroup multiplexer. The mastergroup has a bandwidth of 2.52 MHz and can support 600 voice frequency (VF) channels. Higher-level multiplexing is defined above the mastergroup, as shown in Table 8.1.

Note that the original voice or data signal may be modulated many times. For example, a data signal may be encoded using QPSK (quadrature phase shift keying) to form an analog voice signal. This signal could then be used to modulate a 76-kHz carrier to form a component of a group signal. This group signal could then be used to modulate a 516-kHz carrier to form a component of a supergroup signal. Each stage can distort the original data; this is so, for example, if the modulator/multi-plexer contains nonlinearities or introduces noise.

Wavelength Division Multiplexing

The true potential of optical fiber is fully exploited when multiple beams of light at different frequencies are transmitted on the same fiber. This is a form of frequency-division multiplexing but is commonly called **wavelength division multiplexing (WDM)**. With WDM, the light streaming through the fiber consists of many colors, or wavelengths, each carrying a separate channel of data. In 1997, a landmark was reached when Bell Laboratories was able to demonstrate a WDM system with 100 beams each operating at 10 Gbps, for a total data rate of 1 trillion bits per second (also referred to as 1 terabit per second or 1 Tbps). Commercial systems with 160 channels of 10 Gbps are now available. In a lab environment, Alcatel has carried 256 channels at 39.8 Gbps each, a total of 10.1 Tbps, over a 100-km span.

A typical WDM system has the same general architecture as other FDM systems. A number of sources generate a laser beam at different wavelengths. These are sent to a multiplexer, which consolidates the sources for transmission over a single fiber line. Optical amplifiers, typically spaced tens of kilometers apart, amplify all of the wavelengths simultaneously. Finally, the composite signal arrives at a demultiplexer, where the component channels are separated and sent to receivers at the destination point (Figure 8.5).

Most WDM systems operate in the 1550-nm range. In early systems, 200 GHz was allocated to each channel, but today most WDM systems use 50-GHz spacing.

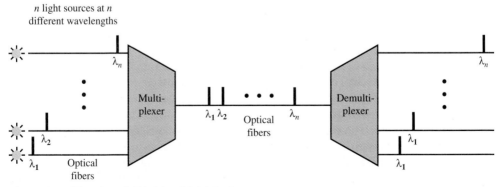

Figure 8.5 Wavelength Division Multiplexing

Table 8.2 ITU WDM Channel Spacing (G.692)

Frequency (THz)	Wavelength in Vacuum (nm)	50 GHz	100 GHz	200 GHz
196.10	1528.77	X	X	X
196.05	1529.16	X		
196.00	1529.55	X	X	
195.95	1529.94	X		
195.90	1530.33	X	X	X
195.85	1530.72	X		
195.80	1531,12	X	X	
195.75	1531.51	X		
195.70	1531.90	X	X	X
195.65	1532.29	X		
195.60	1532.68	X	X	
...	...			
192.10	1560.61	X	X	X

The channel spacing defined in ITU-T G.692, which accommodates 80 50-GHz channels, is summarized in Table 8.2.

The term **dense wavelength division multiplexing (DWDM)** is often seen in the literature. There is no official or standard definition of this term. The term connotes the use of more channels, more closely spaced, than ordinary WDM. In general, a channel spacing of 200 GHz or less could be considered dense.

8.2 SYNCHRONOUS TIME-DIVISION MULTIPLEXING

Characteristics

Synchronous time-division multiplexing is possible when the achievable data rate (sometimes, unfortunately, called bandwidth) of the medium exceeds the data rate of digital signals to be transmitted. Multiple digital signals (or analog signals carrying digital data) can be carried on a single transmission path by interleaving portions of each signal in time. The interleaving can be at the bit level or in blocks of bytes or larger quantities. For example, the multiplexer in Figure 8.2b has six inputs that might each be, say, 1 Mbps. A single line with a capacity of at least 6 Mbps (plus overhead capacity) could accommodate all six sources.

A generic depiction of a synchronous TDM system is provided in Figure 8.6. A number of signals $[m_i(t), i = 1, n]$ are to be multiplexed onto the same transmission medium. The signals carry digital data and are generally digital signals. The incoming data from each source are briefly buffered. Each buffer is typically one bit or one character in length. The buffers are scanned sequentially to form a composite digital data stream $m_c(t)$. The scan operation is sufficiently rapid so that each buffer is emptied before more data can arrive. Thus, the data rate of $m_c(t)$ must at

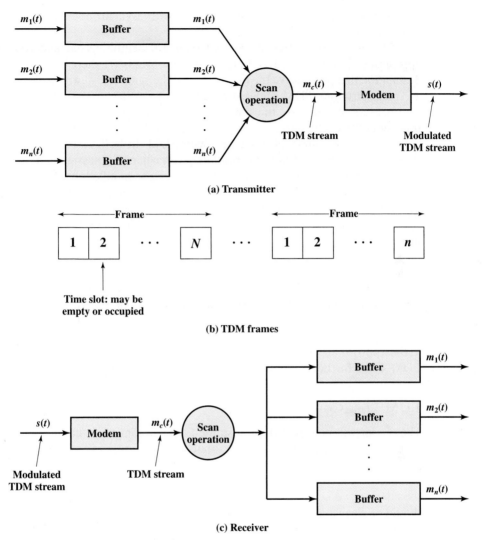

(a) Transmitter

(b) TDM frames

(c) Receiver

Figure 8.6   Synchronous TDM System

least equal the sum of the data rates of the $m_i(t)$. The digital signal $m_c(t)$ may be transmitted directly, or passed through a modem so that an analog signal is transmitted. In either case, transmission is typically synchronous.

The transmitted data may have a format something like Figure 8.6b. The data are organized into **frames**. Each frame contains a cycle of time slots. In each frame, one or more slots are dedicated to each data source. The sequence of slots dedicated to one source, from frame to frame, is called a **channel**. The slot length equals the transmitter buffer length, typically a bit or a byte (character).

The byte-interleaving technique is used with asynchronous and synchronous sources. Each time slot contains one character of data. Typically, the start and stop bits of each character are eliminated before transmission and reinserted by the receiver, thus improving efficiency. The bit-interleaving technique is used with synchronous sources and may also be used with asynchronous sources. Each time slot contains just one bit.

At the receiver, the interleaved data are demultiplexed and routed to the appropriate destination buffer. For each input source $m_i(t)$, there is an identical output destination that will receive the output data at the same rate at which it was generated.

Synchronous TDM is called synchronous not because synchronous transmission is used, but because the time slots are preassigned to sources and fixed. The time slots for each source are transmitted whether or not the source has data to send. This is, of course, also the case with FDM. In both cases, capacity is wasted to achieve simplicity of implementation. Even when fixed assignment is used, however, it is possible for a synchronous TDM device to handle sources of different data rates. For example, the slowest input device could be assigned one slot per cycle, while faster devices are assigned multiple slots per cycle.

An alternative to synchronous TDM is **statistical TDM**. The statistical multiplexer dynamically allocates time slots on demand. As with a synchronous TDM, the statistical multiplexer has a number of I/O lines on one side and a higher speed multiplexed line on the other. Each I/O line has a buffer associated with it. In the case of the statistical multiplexer, there are n I/O lines, but only k, where $k < n$, time slots available on the TDM frame. For input, the function of the multiplexer is to scan the input buffers, collecting data until a frame is filled, and then send the frame. On output, the multiplexer receives a frame and distributes the slots of data to the appropriate output buffers. Packet switching is, in effect, a form of statistical TDM. For a further discussion of statistical TDM, see Appendix I.

TDM Link Control

The reader will note that the transmitted data stream depicted in Figure 8.6b does not contain the headers and trailers that we have come to associate with synchronous transmission. The reason is that the control mechanisms provided by a data link protocol are not needed. It is instructive to ponder this point, and we do so by considering two key data link control mechanisms: flow control and error control. It should be clear that, as far as the multiplexer and demultiplexer (Figure 8.1) are concerned, flow control is not needed. The data rate on the multiplexed line is fixed, and the multiplexer and demultiplexer are designed to operate at that rate. But suppose that one of the individual output lines attaches to a device that is temporarily unable to accept data. Should the transmission of TDM frames cease? Clearly not, because the remaining output lines are expecting to receive data at predetermined times. The solution is for the saturated output device to cause the flow of data from the corresponding input device to cease. Thus, for a while, the channel in question will carry empty slots, but the frames as a whole will maintain the same transmission rate.

The reasoning for error control is the same. It would not do to request retransmission of an entire TDM frame because an error occurs on one channel. The devices using the other channels do not want a retransmission nor would they know that a retransmission has been requested by some other device on another channel. Again, the solution is to apply error control on a per-channel basis.

Flow control and error control can be provided on a per-channel basis by using a data link control protocol such as HDLC on a per-channel basis.

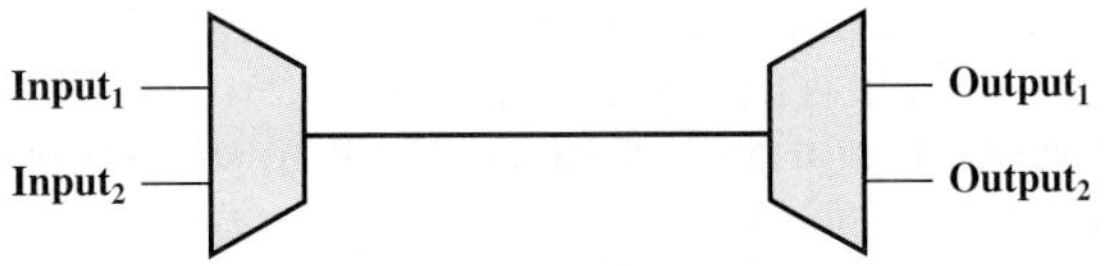

(a) Configuration

Input$_1$⋯⋯⋯   F$_1$ f$_1$ f$_1$ d$_1$ d$_1$ d$_1$ C$_1$ A$_1$ F$_1$ f$_1$ f$_1$ d$_1$ d$_1$ d$_1$ C$_1$ A$_1$ F$_1$

Input$_2$⋯F$_2$ f$_2$ f$_2$ d$_2$ d$_2$ d$_2$ d$_2$ C$_2$ A$_2$ F$_2$ f$_2$ f$_2$ d$_2$ d$_2$ d$_2$ d$_2$ C$_2$ A$_2$ F$_2$

(b) Input data streams

⋯ f$_2$ F$_1$ d$_2$ f$_1$ d$_2$ f$_1$ d$_2$ d$_1$ d$_2$ d$_1$ C$_2$ d$_1$ A$_2$ C$_1$ F$_2$ A$_1$ f$_2$ F$_1$ f$_2$ f$_1$ d$_2$ f$_1$ d$_2$ d$_1$ d$_2$ d$_1$ d$_2$ d$_1$ C$_2$ C$_1$ A$_2$ A$_1$ F$_2$ F$_1$

(c) Multiplexed data stream

Legend: F = flag field   d = one octet of data field
         A = address field   f = one octet of FCS field
         C = control field

Figure 8.7 Use of Data Link Control on TDM Channels

EXAMPLE 8.2 Figure 8.7 provides a simplified example. We assume two data sources, each using HDLC. One is transmitting a stream of HDLC frames containing three octets of data each, and the other is transmitting HDLC frames containing four octets of data. For clarity, we assume that character-interleaved multiplexing is used, although bit interleaving is more typical. Notice what is happening. The octets of the HDLC frames from the two sources are shuffled together for transmission over the multiplexed line. The reader may initially be uncomfortable with this diagram, because the HDLC frames have lost their integrity in some sense. For example, each frame check sequence (FCS) on the line applies to a disjointed set of bits. Even the FCS is not in one piece. However, the pieces are reassembled correctly before they are seen by the device on the other end of the HDLC protocol. In this sense, the multiplexing/demultiplexing operation is transparent to the attached stations; to each communicating pair of stations, it appears that they have a dedicated link.

One refinement is needed in Figure 8.7. Both ends of the line need to be a combination multiplexer/demultiplexer with a full-duplex line in between. Then each channel consists of two sets of slots, one traveling in each direction. The individual devices attached at each end can, in pairs, use HDLC to control their own channel. The multiplexer/demultiplexers need not be concerned with these matters.

FRAMING We have seen that a link control protocol is not needed to manage the overall TDM link. There is, however, a basic requirement for framing. Because we are not providing flag or SYNC characters to bracket TDM frames, some means is needed to assure frame synchronization. It is clearly important to maintain framing synchronization because, if the source and destination are out of step, data on all channels are lost.

Perhaps the most common mechanism for framing is known as added-digit framing. In this scheme, typically, one control bit is added to each TDM frame. An identifiable pattern of bits, from frame to frame, is used as a "control channel." A typical example is the alternating bit pattern, 101010.... This is a pattern unlikely to be sustained on a data channel. Thus, to synchronize, a receiver compares the incoming bits of one frame position to the expected pattern. If the pattern does not match, successive bit positions are searched until the pattern persists over multiple frames. Once framing synchronization is established, the receiver continues to monitor the framing bit channel. If the pattern breaks down, the receiver must again enter a framing search mode.

Pulse Stuffing   Perhaps the most difficult problem in the design of a synchronous time-division multiplexer is that of synchronizing the various data sources. If each source has a separate clock, any variation among clocks could cause loss of synchronization. Also, in some cases, the data rates of the input data streams are not related by a simple rational number. For both these problems, a technique known as **pulse stuffing** is an effective remedy. With pulse stuffing, the outgoing data rate of the multiplexer, excluding framing bits, is higher than the sum of the maximum instantaneous incoming rates. The extra capacity is used by stuffing extra dummy bits or pulses into each incoming signal until its rate is raised to that of a locally generated clock signal. The stuffed pulses are inserted at fixed locations in the multiplexer frame format so that they may be identified and removed at the demultiplexer.

EXAMPLE 8.3 An example, from [COUC13], illustrates the use of synchronous TDM to multiplex digital and analog sources (Figure 8.8). Consider that there are 11 sources to be multiplexed on a single link:

Source 1:   Analog, 2-kHz bandwidth

Source 2:   Analog, 4-kHz bandwidth

Source 3:   Analog, 2-kHz bandwidth

Sources 4–11:   Digital, 7200 bps synchronous

As a first step, the analog sources are converted to digital using pulse code modulation (PCM). Recall from Chapter 5 that PCM is based on the sampling theorem, which dictates that a signal be sampled at a rate equal to twice its bandwidth. Thus, the required sampling rate is 4000 samples per second for sources 1 and 3, and 8000 samples per second for source 2. These samples, which are analog (PAM), must then be quantized or digitized. Let us assume that 4 bits are used for each analog sample. For convenience, these three sources will be multiplexed first, as a unit. At a scan rate of 4 kHz, one PAM sample each is taken from sources 1 and 3, and two PAM samples are taken from source 2 per scan. These four samples are interleaved and converted to 4-bit PCM samples. Thus, a total of 16 bits is generated at a rate of 4000 times per second, for a composite bit rate of 64 kbps.

For the digital sources, pulse stuffing is used to raise each source to a rate of 8 kbps, for an aggregate data rate of 64 kbps. A frame can consist of multiple cycles of 32 bits, each containing 16 PCM bits and two bits from each of the eight digital sources.

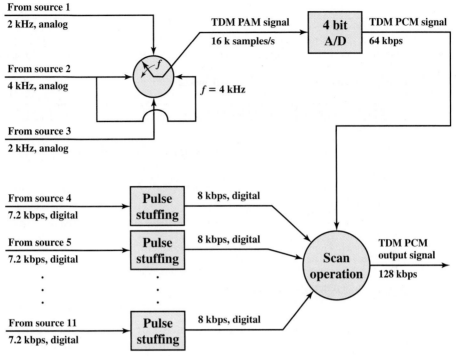

Figure 8.8   TDM of Analog and Digital Sources

Digital Carrier Systems

The long-distance carrier system provided in the United States and throughout the world was designed to transmit voice signals over high-capacity transmission links, such as optical fiber, coaxial cable, and microwave. Part of the evolution of these telecommunications networks to digital technology has been the adoption of synchronous TDM transmission structures. In the United States, AT&T developed a hierarchy of TDM structures of various capacities; this structure is used in Canada and Japan as well as the United States. A similar, but unfortunately not identical, hierarchy has been adopted internationally under the auspices of ITU-T (Table 8.3).

Table 8.3   North American and International TDM Carrier Standards

North American			International (ITU-T)		
Designation	Number of Voice Channels	Data Rate (Mbps)	Level	Number of Voice Channels	Data Rate (Mbps)
DS-1	24	1.544	1	30	2.048
DS-1C	48	3.152	2	120	8.448
DS-2	96	6.312	3	480	34.368
DS-3	672	44.736	4	1920	139.264
DS-4	4032	274.176	5	7680	565.148

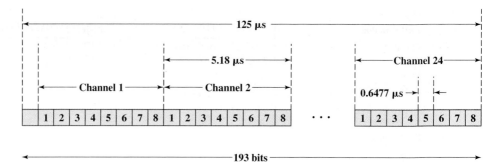

Notes:
1. The first bit is a framing bit, used for synchronization.
2. Voice channels:
   ·8-bit PCM used on five of six frames.
   ·7-bit PCM used on every sixth frame; bit 8 of each channel is a signaling bit.
3. Data channels:
   ·Channel 24 is used for signaling only in some schemes.
   ·Bits 1–7 used for 56-kbps service.
   ·Bits 2–7 used for 9.6-kbps, 4.8-kbps, and 2.4-kbps service.

Figure 8.9 DS-1 Transmission Format

The basis of the TDM hierarchy (in North America and Japan) is the DS-1 transmission format (Figure 8.9), which multiplexes 24 channels. Each frame contains 8 bits per channel plus a framing bit for $24 \times 8 + 1 = 193$ bits. For voice transmission, the following rules apply. Each channel contains one word of digitized voice data. The original analog voice signal is digitized using pulse code modulation at a rate of 8000 samples per second. Therefore, each channel slot and hence each frame must repeat 8000 times per second. With a frame length of 193 bits, we have a data rate of $8000 \times 193 = 1.544$ Mbps. For five of every six frames, 8-bit PCM samples are used. For every sixth frame, each channel contains a 7-bit PCM word plus a *signaling bit*. The signaling bits form a stream for each voice channel that contains network control and routing information. For example, control signals are used to establish a connection or terminate a call.

The same DS-1 format is used to provide digital data service. For compatibility with voice, the same 1.544-Mbps data rate is used. In this case, 23 channels of data are provided. The twenty-fourth channel position is reserved for a special sync byte, which allows faster and more reliable reframing following a framing error. Within each channel, 7 bits per frame are used for data, with the eighth bit used to indicate whether the channel, for that frame, contains user data or system control data. With 7 bits per channel, and because each frame is repeated 8000 times per second, a data rate of 56 kbps can be provided per channel. Lower data rates are provided using a technique known as subrate multiplexing. For this technique, an additional bit is robbed from each channel to indicate which subrate multiplexing rate is being provided. This leaves a total capacity per channel of $6 \times 8000 = 48$ kbps. This capacity is used to multiplex five 9.6-kbps channels, ten 4.8-kbps channels, or twenty 2.4-kbps channels. For example, if channel 2 is used to provide 9.6-kbps service, then up to five data subchannels share this channel. The data for each subchannel appear as six bits in channel 2 every fifth frame.

Finally, the DS-1 format can be used to carry a mixture of voice and data channels. In this case, all 24 channels are utilized; no sync byte is provided.

Above the DS-1 data rate of 1.544 Mbps, higher-level multiplexing is achieved by interleaving bits from DS-1 inputs. For example, the DS-2 transmission system combines four DS-1 inputs into a 6.312-Mbps stream. Data from the four sources are interleaved 12 bits at a time. Note that $1.544 \times 4 = 6.176$ Mbps. The remaining capacity is used for framing and control bits.

SONET/SDH

SONET (Synchronous Optical Network) is an optical transmission interface originally proposed by BellCore and standardized by ANSI. A compatible version, referred to as Synchronous Digital Hierarchy (SDH), has been published by ITU-T in Recommendation G.707.[2] SONET is intended to provide a specification for taking advantage of the high-speed digital transmission capability of optical fiber.

SIGNAL HIERARCHY   The SONET specification defines a hierarchy of standardized digital data rates (Table 8.4). The lowest level, referred to as STS-1 (Synchronous Transport Signal level 1) or OC-1 (Optical Carrier level 1),[3] is 51.84 Mbps. This rate can be used to carry a single DS-3 signal or a group of lower-rate signals, such as DS1, DS1C, DS2, plus ITU-T rates (e.g., 2.048 Mbps).

Multiple STS-1 signals can be combined to form an STS-N signal. The signal is created by interleaving bytes from N STS-1 signals that are mutually synchronized.

For the ITU-T Synchronous Digital Hierarchy, the lowest rate is 155.52 Mbps, which is designated STM-1. This corresponds to SONET STS-3.

FRAME FORMAT   The basic SONET building block is the STS-1 frame, which consists of 810 octets and is transmitted once every 125 μs, for an overall data rate of 51.84 Mbps (Figure 8.10a). The frame can logically be viewed as a matrix of 9 rows of 90 octets each, with transmission being one row at a time, from left to right and top to bottom.

Table 8.4   SONET/SDH Signal Hierarchy

SONET Designation	ITU-T Designation	Data Rate	Payload Rate (Mbps)
STS-1/OC-1		51.84 Mbps	50.112 Mbps
STS-3/OC-3	STM-1	155.52 Mbps	150.336 Mbps
STS-12/OC-12	STM-4	622.08 Mbps	601.344 Mbps
STS-48/OC-48	STM-16	2.48832 Gbps	2.405376 Gbps
STS-192/OC-192	STM-64	9.95328 Gbps	9.621504 Gbps
STS-768	STM-256	39.81312 Gbps	38.486016 Gbps
STS-3072		159.25248 Gbps	153.944064 Gbps

---

[2]In what follows, we will use the term *SONET* to refer to both specifications. Where differences exist, these will be addressed.

[3]An OC-*N* rate is the optical equivalent of an STS-*N* electrical signal. End-user devices transmit and receive electrical signals; these must be converted to and from optical signals for transmission over optical fiber.

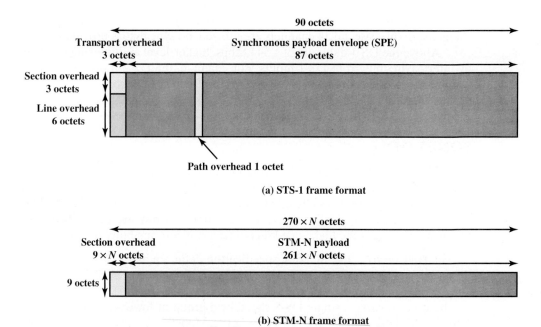

(a) STS-1 frame format

(b) STM-N frame format

Figure 8.10 SONET/SDH Frame Formats

The first three columns (3 octets × 9 rows = 27 octets) of the frame are devoted to overhead octets. Nine octets are devoted to section-related overhead and 18 octets are devoted to line overhead. Figure 8.11a shows the arrangement of overhead octets, and Table 8.5 defines the various fields.

	Framing A1	Framing A2	trc/growth J0/Z0
Section overhead	BIP-8 B1	Orderwire E1	User F1
	DataCom D1	DataCom D2	DataCom D3
	Pointer H1	Pointer H2	Pointer Action H3
	BIP-8 B2	APS K1	APS K2
Line overhead	DataCom D4	DataCom D5	DataCom D6
	DataCom D7	DataCom D8	DataCom D9
	DataCom D10	DataCom D11	DataCom D12
	Status S1/Z1	Error M0/M1	Orderwire E2

Trace J1
BIP-8 B3
Signal Label C2
Path Status G1
User F2
Multiframe H4
Growth Z3
Growth Z4
Growth Z5

(a) Transport overhead

(b) Path overhead

Figure 8.11 SONET STS-1 Overhead Octets

Table 8.5 STS-1 Overhead Bits

	Section Overhead
A1, A2:	Framing bytes = F6,28 hex; used to indicate the beginning of the frame.
J0/Z0:	Allows two connected sections to verify the connections between them by transmitting a 16-byte message. This message is transmitted in 16 consecutive frames with first byte (J0) carried in first frame, second byte in second frame, and so on (Z0).
B1:	Bit-interleaved parity byte providing even parity over previous STS-N frame after scrambling; the ith bit of this octet contains the even parity value calculated from the ith bit position of all octets in the previous frame.
E1:	Section level 64-kbps PCM orderwire; optional 64-kbps voice channel to be used between section terminating equipment, hubs, and remote terminals.
F1:	64-kbps channel set aside for user purposes.
D1-D3:	192-kbps data communications channel for alarms, maintenance, control, and administration between sections.

	Line Overhead
H1-H3:	Pointer bytes used in frame alignment and frequency adjustment of payload data.
B2:	Bit-interleaved parity for line level error monitoring.
K1, K2:	Two bytes allocated for signaling between line level automatic protection switching equipment; uses a bit-oriented protocol that provides for error protection and management of the SONET optical link.
D4-D12:	576-kbps data communications channel for alarms, maintenance, control, monitoring, and administration at the line level.
S1/Z1:	In the first STS-1 of an STS-N signal, used for transporting synchronization message (S1). Undefined in the second through Nth STS-1 (Z1).
M0/M1:	Remote error indication in first STS-1 (M0) and third frames.
E2:	64-kbps PCM voice channel for line level orderwire.

	Path Overhead
J1:	64-kbps channel used to send repetitively a 64-octet fixed-length string so a receiving terminal can continuously verify the integrity of a path; the contents of the message are user programmable.
B3:	Bit-interleaved parity at the path level, calculated over all bits of the previous SPE.
C2:	STS path signal label to designate equipped versus unequipped STS signals. *Unequipped* means the line connection is complete but there is no path data to send. For equipped signals, the label can indicate the specific STS payload mapping that might be needed in receiving terminals to interpret the payloads.
G1:	Status byte sent from path terminating equipment back to path originating equipment to convey status of terminating equipment and path error performance.
F2:	64-kbps channel for path user.
H4:	Multiframe indicator for payloads needing frames that are longer than a single STS frame; multiframe indicators are used when packing lower rate channels (virtual tributaries) into the SPE.
Z3-Z5:	Reserved for future use.

The remainder of the frame is payload. The payload includes a column of path overhead, which is not necessarily in the first available column position; the line overhead contains a pointer that indicates where the path overhead starts. Figure 8.11b shows the arrangement of path overhead octets, and Table 8.5 defines these.

Figure 8.10b shows the general format for higher-rate frames, using the ITU-T designation.

8.3 CABLE MODEM

A **cable modem** is a device that allows a user to access the Internet and other online services through a cable TV network. To support data transfer to and from a cable modem, a cable TV provider dedicates two 6-MHz channels, one for transmission in each direction. Each channel is shared by a number of subscribers, and so some scheme is needed for allocating capacity on each channel for transmission. Typically, a form of statistical TDM is used, as illustrated in Figure 8.12. In the downstream direction, cable **headend** to subscriber, a cable scheduler delivers data in the form of small packets. Because the channel is shared by a number of subscribers, if more than one subscriber is active, each subscriber gets only a fraction of the downstream capacity. An individual cable modem subscriber may experience access speeds from 500 kbps to 1.5 Mbps or more, depending on the network architecture and traffic load. The downstream direction is also used to grant time slots to subscribers. When a subscriber has data to transmit, it must first request time slots on the shared upstream channel. Each subscriber is given dedicated time slots for this request purpose. The headend scheduler responds to a request packet by sending back an assignment of future time slots to be used by this subscriber. Thus, a number of subscribers can share the same upstream channel without conflict.

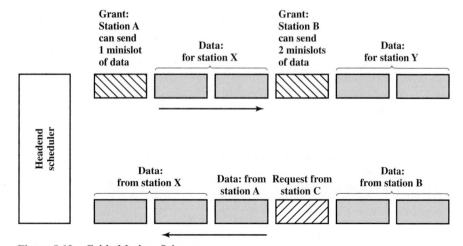

Figure 8.12   Cable Modem Scheme

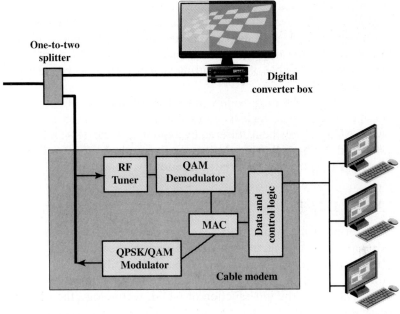

Figure 8.13 Cable Modem Configuration

To support both cable television programming and data channels, the cable spectrum is divided in to three ranges, each of which is further divided into 6-MHz channels. In North America, the spectrum division is as follows:

- User-to-network data (upstream): 5–40 MHz
- Television delivery (downstream): 50–550 MHz
- Network to user data (downstream): 550–750 MHz

Figure 8.13 shows a typical cable modem configuration at a residential or office location. At the interface to the external cable, a one-to-two splitter enables the subscriber to continue to receive cable television service through numerous FDM 6-MHz channels, while simultaneously supporting data channels to one or more computers in a local area network. The inbound channel first goes through a radio frequency (RF) tuner that selects and demodulates the data channel down to a spectrum of 0 to 6 MHz. This channel provides a data stream encoded using 64-QAM (quadrature amplitude modulation) or 256-QAM. The QAM demodulator extracts the encoded data stream and converts it to a digital signal that it passes to the media access control (MAC) module. In the outbound direction, a data stream is modulated using either QPSK or 16-QAM.

8.4 ASYMMETRIC DIGITAL SUBSCRIBER LINE

In the implementation and deployment of a high-speed wide area public digital network, the most challenging part is the link between subscriber and network: the digital subscriber line. With billions of potential endpoints worldwide, the prospect of installing new cable for each new customer is daunting. Instead, network designers have sought ways of exploiting the installed base of twisted-pair wire that links virtually all residential and business customers to telephone networks. These links were installed to carry voice-grade signals in a bandwidth from 0 to 4 kHz. However, the wires are capable of transmitting signals over a far broader spectrum—1 MHz or more.

ADSL is the most widely publicized of a family of new modem technologies designed to provide high-speed digital data transmission over ordinary telephone wire. ADSL is now being offered by a number of carriers and is defined in an ANSI standard. In this following section, we first look at the overall design of ADSL and then examine the key underlying technology, known as DMT.

ADSL Design

The term *asymmetric* refers to the fact that ADSL provides more capacity downstream (from the carrier's central office to the customer's site) than upstream (from customer to carrier). ADSL was originally targeted at the expected need for video on demand and related services. This application has not materialized. However, since the introduction of ADSL technology, the demand for high-speed access to the Internet has grown. Typically, the user requires far higher capacity for downstream than for upstream transmission. Most user transmissions are in the form of keyboard strokes or transmission of short e-mail messages, whereas incoming traffic, especially Web traffic, can involve large amounts of data and include images or even video. Thus, ADSL provides a perfect fit for the Internet requirement.

ADSL uses frequency-division multiplexing in a novel way to exploit the 1-MHz capacity of twisted pair. There are three elements of the ADSL strategy (Figure 8.14):

- Reserve lowest 25 kHz for voice, known as POTS (plain old telephone service). The voice is carried only in the 0 to 4 kHz band; the additional bandwidth is to prevent crosstalk between the voice and data channels.
- Use either echo cancellation[4] or FDM to allocate two bands, a smaller upstream band and a larger downstream band.
- Use FDM within the upstream and downstream bands. In this case, a single bit stream is split into multiple parallel bit streams and each portion is carried in a separate frequency band.

When echo cancellation is used, the entire frequency band for the upstream channel overlaps the lower portion of the downstream channel. This has two advantages compared to the use of distinct frequency bands for upstream and downstream.

---

[4]Echo cancellation is a signal-processing technique that allows transmission of digital signals in both directions on a single transmission line simultaneously. In essence, a transmitter must subtract the echo of its own transmission from the incoming signal to recover the signal sent by the other side.

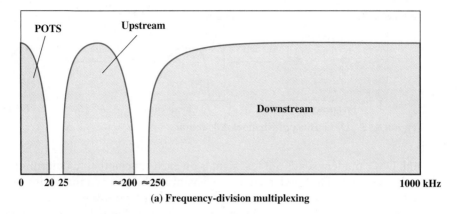

(a) Frequency-division multiplexing

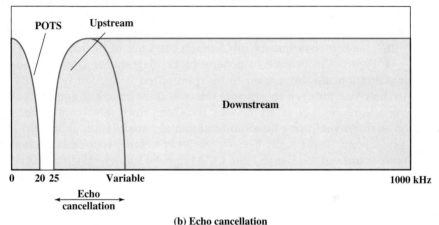

(b) Echo cancellation

Figure 8.14 ADSL Channel Configuration

- The higher the frequency, the greater the attenuation. With the use of echo cancellation, more of the downstream bandwidth is in the "good" part of the spectrum.
- The echo cancellation design is more flexible for changing upstream capacity. The upstream channel can be extended upward without running into the downstream; instead, the area of overlap is extended.

The disadvantage of the use of echo cancellation is the need for echo cancellation logic on both ends of the line.

The ADSL scheme provides a range of up to 5.5 km, depending on the diameter of the cable and its quality. This is sufficient to cover about 95% of all U.S. subscriber lines and should provide comparable coverage in other nations.

Discrete Multitone

Discrete multitone (DMT) uses multiple carrier signals at different frequencies, sending some of the bits on each channel. The available transmission band (upstream or downstream) is divided into a number of 4-kHz subchannels. On initialization,

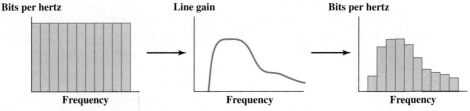

Figure 8.15 DMT Bits per Channel Allocation

the DMT modem sends out test signals on each subchannel to determine the signal-to-noise ratio. The modem then assigns more bits to channels with better signal transmission qualities and less bits to channels with poorer signal transmission qualities. Figure 8.15 illustrates this process. Each subchannel can carry a data rate of from 0 to 60 kbps. The figure shows a typical situation in which there is increasing attenuation and hence decreasing signal-to-noise ratio at higher frequencies. As a result, the higher-frequency subchannels carry less of the load.

Figure 8.16 provides a general block diagram for DMT transmission. After initialization, the bit stream to be transmitted is divided into a number of substreams, one for each subchannel that will carry data. The sum of the data rates of the substreams is equal to the total data rate. Each substream is then converted to an analog signal using quadrature amplitude modulation, described in Chapter 5. This scheme works easily because of QAM's ability to assign different numbers of bits per transmitted signal. Each QAM signal occupies a distinct frequency band, so these signals can be combined by simple addition to produce the composite signal for transmission.

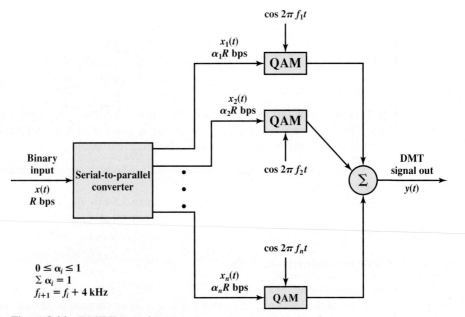

Figure 8.16 DMT Transmitter

Present ADSL/DMT designs employ 256 downstream subchannels. In theory, with each 4-kHz subchannel carrying 60 kbps, it would be possible to transmit at a rate of 15.36 Mbps. In practice, transmission impairments prevent attainment of this data rate. Current implementations operate at from 1.5 to 9 Mbps, depending on line distance and quality.

Broadband Access Configuration

Figure 8.17 shows a typical configuration for broadband service using DSL. The DSL link is between the provider central office and the residential or business premises. On the customer side, a splitter allows simultaneous telephone and data service. The data service makes use of a DSL modem, sometimes referred to as a G.DMT modem, because the modem conforms to the ITU-T G.992.1 recommendation for DMT over DSL. The DSL data signal can be further divided into a video stream and a data stream. The latter connects the modem to either a single local computer or to a wireless modem/router, which enables the customer to support a wireless local area network.

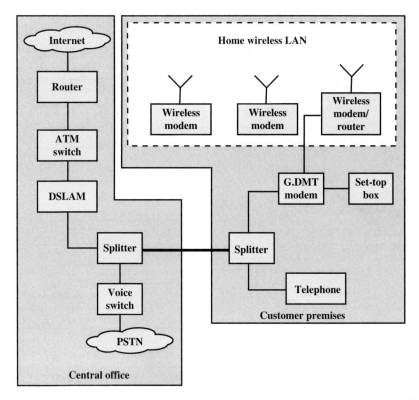

ATM = asynchronous transfer mode
DSLAM = digital subscriber line access multiplexer
PSTN = public switched telephone network
G.DMT = G.992.1 discrete multitone

Figure 8.17 DSL Broadband Access

On the provider side, a splitter is also used to separate the telephone service from the Internet service. The voice traffic is connected to the public switched telephone network (PSTN), thus providing the same service as an ordinary telephone line to the subscriber. The data traffic connects to a DSL access multiplexer (DSLAM), which multiplexes multiple customer DSL connections on to a single high-speed asynchronous transfer mode line. The ATM line connects via one or more ATM switches to a router that provides an entry point to the Internet.

8.5 xDSL

ADSL is one of a number of recent schemes for providing high-speed digital transmission of the subscriber line. Table 8.6 summarizes and compares some of the most important of these new schemes, which collectively are referred to as xDSL.

High Data Rate Digital Subscriber Line

HDSL was developed in the late 1980s by BellCore to provide a more cost-effective means of delivering a T1 data rate (1.544 Mbps). The standard T1 line uses alternate mark inversion (AMI) coding, which occupies a bandwidth of about 1.5 MHz. Because such high frequencies are involved, the attenuation characteristics limit the use of T1 to a distance of about 1 km between repeaters. Thus, for many subscriber lines one or more repeaters are required, which adds to the installation and maintenance expense.

HDSL uses the 2B1Q coding scheme to provide a data rate of up to 2 Mbps over two twisted-pair lines within a bandwidth that extends only up to about 196 kHz. This enables a range of about 3.7 km to be achieved.

Table 8.6   Comparison of xDSL Alternatives

	ADSL	HDSL	SDSL	VDSL
Data Rate	1.5–9 Mbps downstream 16–640 kbps upstream	1.544 or 2.048 Mbps	1.544 or 2.048 Mbps	13–52 Mbps downstream 1.5–2.3 Mbps upstream
Mode	Asymmetric	Symmetric	Symmetric	Asymmetric
Copper Pairs	1	2	1	1
Range (24-Gauge UTP)	3.7–5.5 km	3.7 km	3.0 km	1.4 km
Signaling	Analog	Digital	Digital	Analog
Line Code	CAP/DMT	2B1Q	2B1Q	DMT
Frequency	1–5 MHz	196 kHz	196 kHz	≥10 MHz
Bits/Cycle	Varies	4	4	Varies

UTP = unshielded twisted pair

Single-Line Digital Subscriber Line

Although HDSL is attractive for replacing existing T1 lines, it is not suitable for residential subscribers because it requires two twisted pair, whereas the typical residential subscriber has a single twisted pair. SDSL was developed to provide the same type of service as HDSL but over a single twisted-pair line. As with HDSL, 2B1Q coding is used. Echo cancellation is used to achieve full-duplex transmission over a single pair.

Very High Data Rate Digital Subscriber Line

One of the newest xDSL schemes is VDSL. As of this writing, many of the details of this signaling specification remain to be worked out. The objective is to provide a scheme similar to ADSL at a much higher data rate by sacrificing distance. The likely signaling technique is DMT/QAM.

VDSL does not use echo cancellation but provides separate bands for different services, with the following tentative allocation:

- POTS: 0–4 kHz
- ISDN: 4–80 kHz
- Upstream: 300–700 kHz
- Downstream: $\geq$ 1 MHz

8.6 MULTIPLE CHANNEL ACCESS

In this section, we look at four multiplexing techniques used for sharing channel capacity among multiple transmitter/receiver stations. These techniques differ from the FDM and TDM techniques so far discussed, because no physical multiplexer is involved. Rather, individual stations are assigned a frequency band or a sequence of time slots and transmit directly on the channel and not through a multiplexer.

The techniques discussed in this section are used as building blocks in a number of wireless schemes, including wireless LANs such as Wi-Fi, cellular networks, satellite networks, and wireless broadband Internet access, such as WiMAX.

Frequency-Division Duplex (FDD)

FDD, by itself, is not a particularly interesting case. FDD simply means that two stations have a full-duplex connection in which each station transmits on a separate frequency band. The two frequency bands are separated from each other and from other bands on the network by guard bands, to prevent interference (Figure 8.18a). The combination of the two frequency bands is often referred to as a **subchannel**, with the combination of the two subchannels viewed as a full-duplex channel between the stations.

Time-Division Duplex (TDD)

In TDD, also known as **time-compression multiplexing (TCM)**, data are transmitted in one direction at a time, with transmission alternating between the two directions.

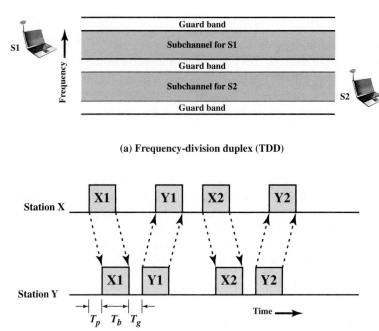

(a) Frequency-division duplex (TDD)

T_p = Propagation delay

T_b = Burst transmission time

T_g = Guard time

(b) Time-division duplex (TDD)

Figure 8.18 Duplex Access Techniques

To achieve the desired subscriber data rate with simple TDD, the transmitter's bit stream is divided into equal segments, compressed in time to a higher transmission rate, and transmitted in bursts, which are expanded at the other end to the original rate. A short quiescent period is used between bursts going in opposite directions to allow the channel to settle down. Thus, the actual data rate on the channel must be greater than twice the data rate required by the two end systems.

The timing implications are shown in Figure 8.19b. The two sides alternate in the transmission of data. Each side sends blocks of some fixed length, which take a time T_b to transmit; this time is a linear function of the number of bits in a block. In addition, a time T_p is required for the propagation of a signal from transmitter to receiver; this time is a linear function of the distance between transmitter and receiver. Finally, a guard time T_g is introduced to turn the channel around. Thus, the time to send one block is $(T_p + T_b + T_g)$. However, because the two sides must alternate transmissions, the rate at which blocks can be transmitted by either side is only $1/[2(T_p + T_b + T_g)]$. We can relate this to the effective data rate, R, as seen by the two endpoints. Let B be the size of a block in bits. Then the effective number of bits transmitted per second, or effective data rate, is

$$R = \frac{B}{2(T_p + T_b + T_g)}$$

The actual data rate, A, on the medium can easily be seen to be

$$A = B/T_b$$

Combining the two, we have

$$A = 2R\left(1 + \frac{T_p + T_g}{T_b}\right)$$

The choice of block size, B, is a compromise between competing requirements. For a larger block size, the value of T_b becomes larger compared to the values of T_p and T_g. Now consider that we have a fixed value of R, which is the data rate required for the link, and we need to determine the value of A. If B is increased, there is a decrease in the actual data rate, A. This makes the task of implementation easier. On the other hand, this is accompanied by an increase in the signal delay due to buffering, which is undesirable for voice traffic.

EXAMPLE 8.4 One of the standard interfaces defined for ISDN (Integrated Services Digital Network) is the basic interface, which provides a data rate of 192 kbps and uses a frame size of 48 bits. Suppose we use TDD with a block size equal to the frame size. Assume the distance between the subscriber and the network switch is 1 km and a guard time 10 μs is used. What is the actual data rate?

First, we need to determine the burst transmission time T_b. The propagation delay is $(1 \text{ km})/(3 \times 10^8 \text{ m/s}) = 3.33 \ \mu$s. We have $\dfrac{B}{2R} = (T_p + T_b + T_g)$, so that

$$T_b = \frac{B}{2R} - T_p - T_g = \frac{48}{0.384 \times 10^6} - (10 \times 10^{-6}) - (3.33 \times 10^{-6}) = 111.67 \ \mu s.$$

Thus,

$$A = 2 \times 192 \times [1 + (3.33 + 10)/111.67] \approx 430 \,\text{kbps}$$

TDD is used in cordless telephones and is a building block for a number of wireless network systems.

Frequency-Division Multiple Access (FDMA)

FDMA is a technique used to share the spectrum among multiple stations. In a typical configuration, there is a base station that communicates with a number of subscriber stations. Such a configuration is found in satellite networks, cellular networks, Wi-Fi, and WiMAX. Typically, the base station assigns bandwidths to stations within the overall bandwidth available. Figure 8.19a is an example. Three stations are assigned separate frequency bands (subchannels) for transmission to the base station (uplink direction), with guard bands between the assigned transmission bands. Another frequency band, typically wider, is reserved for transmission from the base station to the other stations (downlink direction).

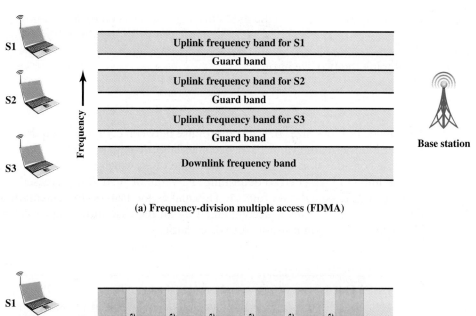

(a) Frequency-division multiple access (FDMA)

(b) Time-division multiple access (TDMA)

Figure 8.19 Multiple Channel Access Techniques

Key features of FDMA include the following:

- Each subchannel is dedicated to a single station; it is not shared.
- If a subchannel is not in use, it is idle; the capacity is wasted.
- FDMA is relatively less complex than TDMA and requires fewer overhead bits because each subchannel is dedicated.
- Individual subchannels must be separated by guard bands to minimize interference.

Time-Division Multiple Access (TDMA)

As with FDMA, TDMA is typically used in a configuration that consists of a base station and a number of subscriber stations. With TDMA there is a single, relatively large, uplink frequency band that is used to transmit a sequence of time slots. Repetitive time slots are assigned to an individual subscriber station to form a logical subchannel. Figure 8.19b is an example. In this example, each station gets an equal amount of the overall capacity of the uplink channel. Thus, each channel is assigned every third slot. Similarly, each subscriber station listens on designated time slots on the downlink channel, which may have the same slot assignment as the uplink channel, or a different one. In this example, the downlink channel is also equally distributed among the three stations.

Key features of TDMA include the following:

- Each subchannel is dedicated to a single station; it is not shared.
- For an individual station, data transmission occurs in bursts rather than continuously.
- Guard times are needed between time slots, to account for lack of perfect synchronization among the subscriber station.
- The downlink channel may be on a separate frequency band, as in our example. This is referred to as TDMA/FDD. With TDMA/FDD, the time slots assigned for subscriber station reception are typically nonoverlapping with that station's transmit time slots.
- The uplink and downlink transmission may be on the same frequency band, which is referred to as TDMA/TDD.

8.7 RECOMMENDED READING AND ANIMATIONS

A discussion of FDM and TDM carrier systems can be found in [FREE98b]. SONET is treated in greater depth in [STAL99] and in [TEKT01]. Useful articles on SONET are [BALL89] and [BOEH90]. A good overview of WDM is [MUKH00].

Two good articles on cable modems are [FELL01] and [CICI01].

[MAXW96] provides a useful a discussion of ADSL. Recommended treatments of xDSL are [HAWL97] and [HUMP97].

BALL89 Ballart, R., and Ching, Y. "SONET: Now It's the Standard Optical Network." *IEEE Communications Magazine*, March 1989.

BOEH90 Boehm, R. "Progress in Standardization of SONET." *IEEE LCS*, May 1990.

CICI01 Ciciora, W. "The Cable Modem Traffic Jam." *IEEE Spectrum*, June 2001.

FELL01 Fellows, D., and Jones, D. "DOCSIS Cable Modem Technology." *IEEE Communications Magazine*, March 2001.

FREE98b Freeman, R. *Telecommunications Transmission Handbook*. New York: Wiley, 1998.

HAWL97   Hawley, G. "Systems Considerations for the Use of xDSL Technology for Data Access." *IEEE Communications Magazine*, March 1997.

HUMP97   Humphrey, M., and Freeman, J. "How xDSL Supports Broadband Services to the Home." *IEEE Network*, January/March 1997.

MAXW96   Maxwell, K. "Asymmetric Digital Subscriber Line: Interim Technology for the Next Forty Years." *IEEE Communications Magazine*, October 1996.

MUKH00   Mukherjee, B. "WDM Optical Communication Networks: Progress and Challenges." *IEEE Journal on Selected Areas in Communications*, October 2000.

STAL99   Stallings, W. *ISDN and Broadband ISDN, with Frame Relay and ATM*. Upper Saddle River, NJ: Prentice Hall, 1999.

TEKT01   Tektronix. *SONET Telecommunications Standard Primer*. Tektronix White Paper, 2001, www.tek.com/document/primer/sonet-telecommunications-standard-primer.

Animations

An animation that illustrates multiplexing is available at the Premium Web site. The reader is encouraged to view the animation to reinforce concepts from this chapter.

8.8   KEY TERMS, REVIEW QUESTIONS, AND PROBLEMS

Key Terms

ADSL	downstream	SONET
baseband	echo cancellation	statistical TDM
cable modem	frame	subcarrier
channel	frequency-division	synchronous TDM
demultiplexer	multiplexing (FDM)	time-division multiplexing
dense wavelength division	headend	(TDM)
multiplexing (DWDM)	multiplexer	upstream
dense WDM	multiplexing	wavelength division
digital carrier system	pulse stuffing	multiplexing (WDM)
discrete multitone	SDH	

Review Questions

8.1   Why is multiplexing so cost-effective?

8.2   How is interference avoided by using frequency-division multiplexing?

8.3   What is echo cancellation?

8.4   Define *upstream* and *downstream* with respect to subscriber lines.

8.5   Explain how synchronous time-division multiplexing (TDM) works.

8.6   Why is a statistical time-division multiplexer more efficient than a synchronous time-division multiplexer?

8.7   Using Table 8.3 as a guide, indicate the major difference between North American and international TDM carrier standards.

Problems

8.1   The information in four analog signals is to be multiplexed and transmitted over a telephone channel that has a 400- to 3100-Hz bandpass. Each of the analog baseband signals is bandlimited to 500 Hz. Design a communication system (block diagram) that will allow the transmission of these four sources over the telephone channel using

    a. Frequency-division multiplexing with SSB (single sideband) subcarriers
    b. Time-division multiplexing using PCM; assume 4-bit samples

    Show the block diagrams of the complete system, including the transmission, channel, and reception portions. Include the bandwidths of the signals at the various points in the systems.

8.2   To paraphrase Lincoln: "…all of the channel some of the time, some of the channel all of the time…." Refer to Figure 8.2 and relate the preceding to the figure.

8.3   How can you combine four voice channels, each of 5 kHz bandwidth, in a link having a minimum frequency of 20 kHz?

8.4   Three channels, each sending 128 bytes/second, are multiplexed using TDM. Multiplexing is done 1 byte per channel.

    a. What will be the size of the frame?
    b. What will be the frame rate and the bit rate of the output channel?

8.5   Why is it that the start and stop bits can be eliminated when character interleaving is used in synchronous TDM?

8.6   Five 4-kbps connections are multiplexed together, 1 bit at a time, in synchronous TDM. What will be the data rate of the output connection and the duration of the output slot?

8.7   One of the 193 bits in the DS-1 transmission format is used for frame synchronization. Explain its use.

8.8   In the DS-1 format, what is the control signal data rate for each voice channel?

8.9   Six channels, each with a bandwidth of 150 kHz, have to be multiplexed together using FDM. A guard band of 10 kHz is needed between any two adjacent channels to prevent interference. What should be the minimum bandwidth of the link in order to enable the communication?

8.10 Four channels are multiplexed using TDM. If the input bit rate is 600 kbps and the multiplexer uses a time slot of 4 bits, what will be the frame duration and the bit duration in the output channel?

8.11 A character-interleaved time-division multiplexer is used to combine the data streams of a number of 110-bps asynchronous terminals for data transmission over a 2400-bps digital line. Each terminal sends asynchronous characters consisting of 7 data bits, 1 parity bit, 1 start bit, and 2 stop bits. Assume that one synchronization character is sent every 19 data characters and, in addition, at least 3% of the line capacity is reserved for pulse stuffing to accommodate speed variations from the various terminals.

    a. Determine the number of bits per character.
    b. Determine the number of terminals that can be accommodated by the multiplexer.
    c. Sketch a possible framing pattern for the multiplexer.

8.12 Find the number of the following devices that could be accommodated by a T1-type TDM line if 1% of the T1 line capacity is reserved for synchronization purposes.

    a. 110-bps teleprinter terminals
    b. 300-bps computer terminals

    c. 1200-bps computer terminals

    d. 9600-bps computer output ports

    e. 64-kbps PCM voice-frequency lines

    How would these numbers change if each of the sources were transmitting an average of 10% of the time and a statistical multiplexer was used?

8.13 Three channels need to be multiplexed using TDM. Their bit rates are 150 kbps, 50 kbps, and 100 kbps.

    a. How can this be achieved?

    b. What will be the minimum frame size and the corresponding frame duration?

8.14 A synchronous nonstatistical TDM is to be used to combine four 4.8-kbps and one 9.6-kbps signals for transmission over a single leased line. For framing, a block of 7 bits (pattern 1011101) is inserted for each 48 data bits. The reframing algorithm (at the receiving demultiplex) is as follows:

    1. Arbitrarily select a bit position.

    2. Consider the block of 7 contiguous bits starting with that position.

    3. Observe that block of 7 bits each frame for 12 consecutive frames.

    4. If 10 of the 12 blocks match the framing pattern the system is "in-frame"; if not advance one bit position and return to step 2.

        a. Draw the multiplexed bit stream (note that the 9.6 kbps input may be treated as two 4.8-kbps inputs).

        b. What is the percentage overhead in the multiplexed bit stream?

        c. What is the multiplexed output bit rate?

        d. What is the minimum reframe time? What is the maximum reframe time? What is the average reframe time?

8.15 A company has two locations: a headquarters and a factory about 25 km away. The factory has four 300-bps terminals that communicate with the central computer facilities over leased voice-grade lines. The company is considering installing TDM equipment so that only one line will be needed. What cost factors should be considered in the decision?

8.16 In synchronous TDM, the I/O lines serviced by the two multiplexers may be either synchronous or asynchronous although the channel between the two multiplexers must be synchronous. Is there any inconsistency in this? Why or why not?

8.17 A channel with a propagation rate of 2.4×10^8 m/s and a data rate of 480 kbps is using time-division duplex. It has a block size of 32 bits and a guard time of 10 μs. If a message needs to be sent at a distance of 1.2 km, what is the effective data rate?

8.18 For a statistical time-division multiplexer, define the following parameters:

$$F = \text{frame length, bits}$$
$$OH = \text{overhead in a frame, bits}$$
$$L = \text{load of data in the frame, bps}$$
$$C = \text{capacity of link, bps}$$

    a. Express F as a function of the other parameters. Explain why F can be viewed as a variable rather than a constant.

    b. Plot F versus L for $C = 9.6$ kbps and values of $OH = 40, 80, 120$. Comment on the results and compare to Figure I.1 in Appendix I.

    c. Plot F versus L for $OH = 40$ and values of $C = 9.6$ kbps and 8.2 kbps. Comment on the results and compare to Figure I.1 in Appendix I.

8.19 In statistical TDM, there may be a length field. What alternative could there be to the inclusion of a length field? What problem might this solution cause and how could it be solved?

WAN TECHNOLOGY AND PROTOCOLS

LEARNING OBJECTIVES

After reading this chapter, you should be able to:

◆ Define circuit switching and describe the key elements of circuit-switching networks.

◆ Define packet switching and describe the key elements of packet-switching technology.

◆ Discuss the relative merits of circuit switching and packet switching and analyze the circumstances for which each is most appropriate.

◆ Describe the features and characteristics of ATM networks.

Part Two describes how information can be encoded and transmitted over a communications link. We now turn to the broader discussion of networks, which can be used to interconnect many devices. The chapter begins with a general discussion of switched communications networks. The remainder of the chapter focuses on wide area networks and, in particular, on traditional approaches to wide area network design: circuit switching and packet switching.

Since the invention of the telephone, circuit switching has been the dominant technology for voice communications, and it has remained so well into the digital era. This chapter looks at the key characteristics of a circuit-switching network.

Around 1970, research began on a new form of architecture for long-distance digital data communications: packet switching. Although the technology of packet switching has evolved substantially since that time, it is remarkable that (1) the basic technology of packet switching is fundamentally the same today as it was in the early 1970s networks, and (2) packet switching remains one of the few effective technologies for long-distance data communications.

This chapter provides an overview of packet-switching technology. We will see, in this chapter and later in this part, that many of the advantages of packet switching (flexibility, resource sharing, robustness, responsiveness) come with a cost. The packet-switching network is a distributed collection of packet-switching nodes. Ideally, all packet-switching nodes would always know the state of the entire network. Unfortunately, because the nodes are distributed, there is a time delay between a change in status in one portion of the network and knowledge of that change elsewhere. Furthermore, there is overhead involved in communicating status information. As a result, a packet-switching network can never perform "perfectly," and elaborate algorithms are used to cope with the time delay and overhead penalties of network operation. These same issues will appear again when we discuss internetworking in Part Five.

9.1 SWITCHED COMMUNICATIONS NETWORKS

For transmission of data[1] beyond a local area, communication is typically achieved by transmitting data from source to destination through a network of intermediate switching nodes; this switched network design is typically used to implement LANs as well. The switching nodes are not concerned with the content of the data; rather, their purpose is to provide a switching facility that will move the data from node to node until they reach their destination. Figure 9.1 illustrates a simple network. The devices attached to the network may be referred to as *stations*. The stations may be computers, terminals, telephones, or other communicating devices. We refer to

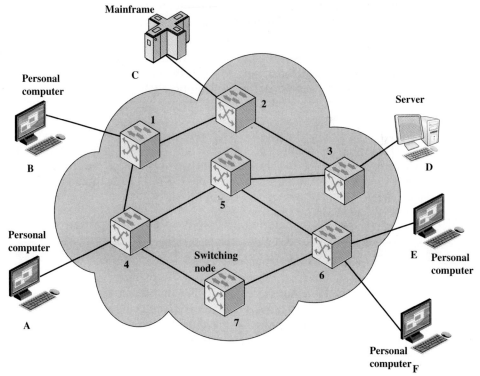

Figure 9.1   Simple Switching Network

---

[1]We use this term here in a very general sense, to include voice, image, and video, as well as ordinary data (e.g., numbers, text).

the switching devices whose purpose is to provide communication as *nodes*. Nodes are connected to one another in some topology by transmission links. Each station attaches to a node, and the collection of nodes is referred to as a *communications network*.

In a *switched communication network*, data entering the network from a station are routed to the destination by being switched from node to node.

EXAMPLE 9.1 In Figure 9.1, data from station A intended for station F are sent to node 4. They may then be routed via nodes 5 and 6 or nodes 7 and 6 to the destination. Several observations are in order:

1. Some nodes connect only to other nodes (e.g., 5 and 7). Their sole task is the internal (to the network) switching of data. Other nodes have one or more stations attached as well; in addition to their switching functions, such nodes accept data from and deliver data to the attached stations.

2. Node–station links are generally dedicated point-to-point links. Node–node links are usually multiplexed, using either frequency-division multiplexing (FDM) or time-division multiplexing (TDM).

3. Usually, the network is not fully connected; that is, there is not a direct link between every possible pair of nodes. However, it is always desirable to have more than one possible path through the network for each pair of stations. This enhances the reliability of the network.

Two different technologies are used in wide area switched networks: circuit switching and packet switching. These two technologies differ in the way the nodes switch information from one link to another on the way from source to destination.

9.2 CIRCUIT-SWITCHING NETWORKS

Communication via circuit switching implies that there is a dedicated communication path between two stations. That path is a connected sequence of links between network nodes. On each physical link, a logical channel is dedicated to the connection. Communication via circuit switching involves three phases, which can be explained with reference to Figure 9.1.

1. **Circuit establishment**. Before any signals can be transmitted, an end-to-end (station-to-station) circuit must be established. For example, station A sends a request to node 4 requesting a connection to station E. Typically, the link from A to 4 is a dedicated line, so that part of the connection already exists. Node 4 must find the next leg in a route leading to E. Based on routing information and measures of availability and perhaps cost, node 4 selects the link to node

5, allocates a free channel (using FDM or TDM) on that link, and sends a message requesting connection to E. So far, a dedicated path has been established from A through 4 to 5. Because a number of stations may attach to 4, it must be able to establish internal paths from multiple stations to multiple nodes. How this is done is discussed later in this section. The remainder of the process proceeds similarly. Node 5 allocates a channel to node 6 and internally ties that channel to the channel from node 4. Node 6 completes the connection to E. In completing the connection, a test is made to determine if E is busy or is prepared to accept the connection.

2. **Data transfer**. Data can now be transmitted from A through the network to E. The transmission may be analog or digital, depending on the nature of the network. As the carriers evolve to fully integrated digital networks, the use of digital (binary) transmission for both voice and data is becoming the dominant method. The path is A-4 link, internal switching through 4, 4-5 channel, internal switching through 5, 5-6 channel, internal switching through 6, 6-E link. Generally, the connection is full duplex.

3. **Circuit disconnect**. After some period of data transfer, the connection is terminated, usually by the action of one of the two stations. Signals must be propagated to nodes 4, 5, and 6 to deallocate the dedicated resources.

Note that the connection path is established before data transmission begins. Thus, channel capacity must be reserved between each pair of nodes in the path, and each node must have available internal switching capacity to handle the requested connection. The switches must have the intelligence to make these allocations and to devise a route through the network.

Circuit switching can be rather inefficient. Channel capacity is dedicated for the duration of a connection, even if no data are being transferred. For a voice connection, utilization may be rather high, but it still does not approach 100%. For a client/server or terminal-to-computer connection, the capacity may be idle during most of the time of the connection. In terms of performance, there is a delay prior to signal transfer for call establishment. However, once the circuit is established, the network is effectively transparent to the users. Information is transmitted at a fixed data rate with no delay other than the propagation delay through the transmission links. The delay at each node is negligible.

Circuit switching was developed to handle voice traffic but is now also used for data traffic. The best-known example of a circuit-switching network is the public telephone network (Figure 9.2). This is actually a collection of national networks interconnected to form the international service. Although originally designed and implemented to service analog telephone subscribers, it handles substantial data traffic via modem and is gradually being converted to a digital network. Another well-known application of circuit switching is the private branch exchange (PBX), used to interconnect telephones within a building or office. Circuit switching is also used in private networks. Typically, such a network is set up by a corporation or other large organization to interconnect its various sites. Such a network usually consists of PBX systems at each site interconnected by dedicated, leased lines obtained from one of the carriers, such as AT&T. A final common example of the application of circuit switching is the data switch. The data switch is similar to the

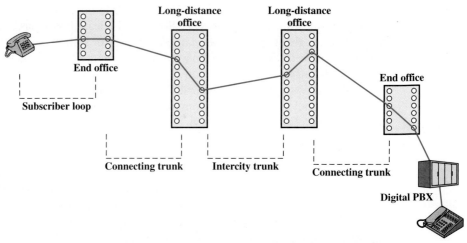

Figure 9.2   Example Connection Over a Public Circuit-Switching Network

PBX but is designed to interconnect digital data processing devices, such as terminals and computers.

A public telecommunications network can be described using four generic architectural components:

- **Subscribers**: The devices that attach to the network. It is still the case that most subscriber devices to public telecommunications networks are telephones, but the percentage of data traffic increases year by year.

- **Subscriber line**: The link between the subscriber and the network, also referred to as the **subscriber loop** or **local loop**. Almost all local loop connections use twisted-pair wire. The length of a local loop is typically in a range from a few kilometers to a few tens of kilometers.

- **Exchanges**: The switching centers in the network. A switching center that directly supports subscribers is known as an end office. Typically, an end office will support many thousands of subscribers in a localized area. There are over 19,000 end offices in the United States, so it is clearly impractical for each end office to have a direct link to each of the other end offices; this would require on the order of 2×10^8 links. Rather, intermediate switching nodes are used.

- **Trunks**: The branches between exchanges. Trunks carry multiple voice-frequency circuits using either FDM or synchronous TDM. We referred to these as carrier systems in Chapter 8.

Subscribers connect directly to an end office, which switches traffic between subscribers and between a subscriber and other exchanges. The other exchanges are responsible for routing and switching traffic between end offices. This distinction is shown in Figure 9.3. To connect two subscribers attached to the same end office, a circuit is set up between them in the same fashion as described before. If two subscribers connect to different end offices, a circuit between them consists of a chain of circuits through one or more intermediate offices. In the figure, a connection is established between lines a and b by simply setting up the connection through the end office. The

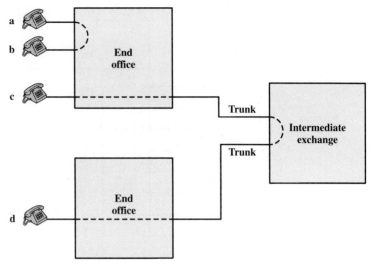

Figure 9.3   Circuit Establishment

connection between c and d is more complex. In c's end office, a connection is established between line c and one channel on a TDM trunk to the intermediate switch. In the intermediate switch, that channel is connected to a channel on a TDM trunk to d's end office. In that end office, the channel is connected to line d.

Circuit-switching technology has been driven by those applications that handle voice traffic. One of the key requirements for voice traffic is that there must be virtually no transmission delay and certainly no variation in delay. A constant signal transmission rate must be maintained, because transmission and reception occur at the same signal rate. These requirements are necessary to allow normal human conversation. Further, the quality of the received signal must be sufficiently high to provide, at a minimum, intelligibility.

Circuit switching achieved its widespread, dominant position because it is well suited to the analog transmission of voice signals. In today's digital world, its inefficiencies are more apparent. However, despite its inefficiencies, circuit switching will remain an attractive choice for both local area and wide area networking. One of its key strengths is that it is transparent. Once a circuit is established, it appears as a direct connection to the two attached stations; no special networking logic is needed at the station.

9.3   CIRCUIT-SWITCHING CONCEPTS

The technology of circuit switching is best approached by examining the operation of a single circuit-switching node. A network built around a single circuit-switching node consists of a collection of stations attached to a central switching unit. The central switch establishes a dedicated path between any two devices that wish to communicate. Figure 9.4 depicts the major elements of such a one-node network. The dotted lines inside the switch symbolize the connections that are currently active.

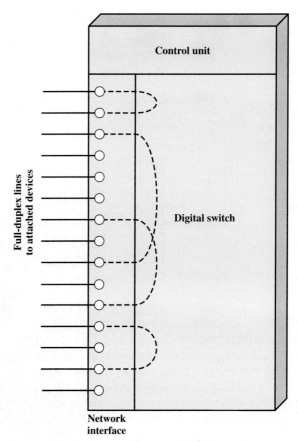

Figure 9.4 Elements of a Circuit-Switch Node

The heart of a modern system is a **digital switch**. The function of the digital switch is to provide a transparent signal path between any pair of attached devices. The path is transparent in that it appears to the attached pair of devices that there is a direct connection between them. Typically, the connection must allow full-duplex transmission.

The **network interface** element represents the functions and hardware needed to connect digital devices, such as data processing devices and digital telephones, to the network. Analog telephones can also be attached if the network interface contains the logic for converting to digital signals. Trunks to other digital switches carry TDM signals and provide the links for constructing multiple-node networks.

The **control unit** performs three general tasks. First, it establishes connections. This is generally done on demand, that is, at the request of an attached device. To establish the connection, the control unit must handle and acknowledge the request, determine if the intended destination is free, and construct a path through the switch. Second, the control unit must maintain the connection. Because the digital switch uses time-division principles, this may require ongoing manipulation of the switching elements. However, the bits of the communication are transferred transparently (from the point of view of the attached devices). Third, the control unit must tear down the connection, either in response to a request from one of the parties or for its own reasons.

An important characteristic of a circuit-switching device is whether it is blocking or nonblocking. Blocking occurs when the network is unable to connect two stations because all possible paths between them are already in use. A blocking network is one in which such blocking is possible. Hence a nonblocking network permits all stations to be connected (in pairs) at once and grants all possible connection requests as long as the called party is free. When a network is supporting only voice traffic, a blocking configuration is generally acceptable, because it is expected that most phone calls are of short duration and that therefore only a fraction of the telephones will be engaged at any time. However, when data processing devices are involved, these assumptions may be invalid. For example, for a data entry application, a terminal may be continuously connected to a computer for hours at a time. Hence, for data applications, there is a requirement for a nonblocking or "nearly nonblocking" (very low probability of blocking) configuration.

We turn now to an examination of the switching techniques internal to a single circuit-switching node.

Space Division Switching

Space division switching was originally developed for the analog environment and has been carried over into the digital realm. The fundamental principles are the same, whether the switch is used to carry analog or digital signals. As its name implies, a space division switch is one in which the signal paths are physically separate from one another (divided in space). Each connection requires the establishment of a physical path through the switch that is dedicated solely to the transfer of signals between the two endpoints. The basic building block of the switch is a metallic crosspoint or semiconductor gate that can be enabled and disabled by a control unit.

EXAMPLE 9.2 Figure 9.5 shows a simple **crossbar matrix** with 10 full-duplex I/O lines. The matrix has 10 inputs and 10 outputs; each station attaches to the matrix via one input and one output line. Interconnection is possible between any two lines by enabling the appropriate crosspoint. Note that a total of 100 crosspoints is required.

The crossbar switch has a number of limitations:

* The number of crosspoints grows with the square of the number of attached stations. This is costly for a large switch.
* The loss of a crosspoint prevents connection between the two devices whose lines intersect at that crosspoint.
* The crosspoints are inefficiently utilized; even when all of the attached devices are active, only a small fraction of the crosspoints are engaged.

To overcome these limitations, multiple-stage switches are employed.

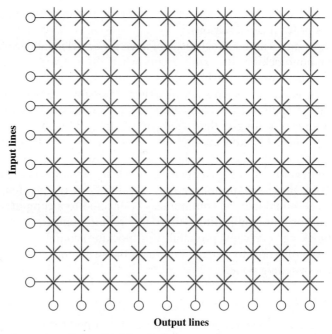

Figure 9.5   Space Division Switch

> **EXAMPLE 9.3** Figure 9.6 is an example of a three-stage switch.

A multiple-stage switch has two advantages over a single-stage crossbar matrix:

- The number of crosspoints is reduced, increasing crossbar utilization. In Examples 9.2 and 9.3, the total number of crosspoints for 10 stations is reduced from 100 to 48.
- There is more than one path through the network to connect two endpoints, increasing reliability.

Of course, a multistage network requires a more complex control scheme. To establish a path in a single-stage network, it is only necessary to enable a single gate. In a multistage network, a free path through the stages must be determined and the appropriate gates enabled.

A consideration with a multistage space division switch is that it may be blocking. It should be clear from Figure 9.5 that a single-stage crossbar matrix is nonblocking; that is, a path is always available to connect an input to an output. That this may not be the case with a multiple-stage switch can be seen in Figure 9.6. The heavier lines indicate the lines that are already in use. In this state, input line 10, for example, cannot be connected to output line 3, 4, or 5, even though all of these output lines are available. A multiple-stage switch can be made nonblocking

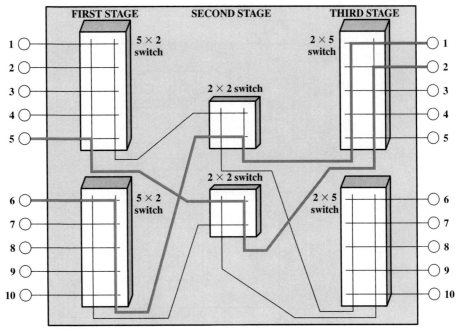

Figure 9.6   Three-Stage Space Division Switch

by increasing the number or size of the intermediate switches, but of course this increases the cost.

Time–Division Switching

The technology of switching has a long history, most of it covering an era when analog signal switching predominated. With the advent of digitized voice and synchronous TDM techniques, both voice and data can be transmitted via digital signals. This has led to a fundamental change in the design and technology of switching systems. Instead of the relatively dumb space division approach, modern digital systems rely on intelligent control of space and time-division elements.

Virtually all modern circuit switches use digital time-division techniques for establishing and maintaining "circuits." Time-division switching involves the partitioning of a lower-speed bit stream into pieces that share a higher-speed stream with other bit streams. The individual pieces, or slots, are manipulated by control logic to route data from input to output.

Time–Slot Interchange

The basic building block of many time-division switches is the time-slot interchange (TSI) mechanism. A TSI unit operates on a synchronous TDM stream of time slots, or channels, by interchanging pairs of slots to achieve a full-duplex operation. Figure 9.7a shows how the input line of device I is connected to the output line of device J, and vice versa.

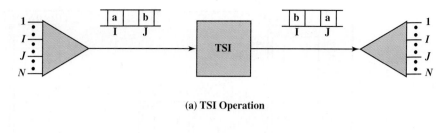

(a) TSI Operation

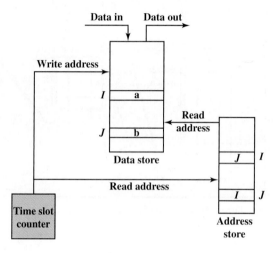

(b) TSI Mechanism

Figure 9.7   Time-Slot Interchange

The input lines of *N* devices are passed through a synchronous time-division multiplexer to produce a TDM stream with *N* slots. To allow the interchange of any two slots, to create a full-duplex connection, the incoming data in a slot must be stored until the data can be sent out on the correct channel in the next TDM frame cycle. Hence, the TSI introduces a delay and produces output slots in the desired order. The output stream of slots is then demultiplexed and routed to the appropriate output line. Because each channel is provided a time slot in each TDM frame, whether or not it transmits data, the size of the TSI unit must be chosen for the capacity of the line, not for the actual data rate.

Figure 9.7b shows a mechanism for implementing TSI. A random access data store whose width equals one time slot of data and whose length equals the number of slots in a frame is used. An incoming TDM frame is written sequentially, slot by slot, into the data store. An outgoing data frame is created by reading slots from the memory in an order dictated by an address store that reflects the existing connections. In the figure, the data in channels *I* and *J* are interchanged, creating a full-duplex connection between the corresponding stations.

TSI is a simple, effective way to switch TDM data. However, the size of such a switch, in terms of the number of connections, is limited by the amount of latency that can be tolerated. The greater the number of channels, the greater the average delay that each channel experiences.

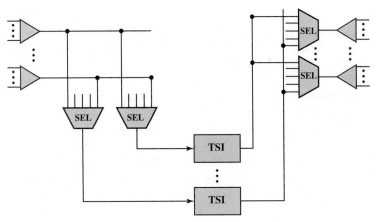

Figure 9.8 A Time-Multiplexed Switch

Time–Multiplexed Switching

To overcome the latency problems of TSI, contemporary time-division switches use multiple TSI units, each of which carries a portion of the total traffic. To connect two channels entering a single TSI unit, their time slots can be interchanged, as just described. However, to connect a channel on one TDM stream (going into one TSI) to a channel on another TDM stream (going into another TSI), some form of space division switching is needed. Naturally, we do not wish to switch all of the time slots from one TDM stream to another; we would like to do it one slot at a time. This technique is known as **time-multiplexed switching (TMS)**.

One means of implementing a TMS switch is the crossbar switch discussed earlier. This requires the crosspoints to be manipulated at each time slot. More commonly, the TMS switch is implemented using digital selectors. The selector (SEL) device selects an input line based on a channel assignment provided from a store controlled by a time-slot counter.

To reduce or eliminate blocking, multiple stage networks can be built by concatenating TMS (S) and TSI (T) stages. Systems are generally described by an enumeration of their stages from input to output using the symbols T and S. Figure 9.8 shows an example of a three-stage switch implemented with SEL units.

9.4 SOFTSWITCH ARCHITECTURE

The latest trend in the development of circuit-switching technology is generally referred to as the softswitch. In essence, a softswitch is a general-purpose computer running specialized software that turns it into a smart phone switch. Softswitches cost significantly less than traditional circuit switches and can provide more functionality. In particular, in addition to handling the traditional circuit-switching functions, a softswitch can convert a stream of digitized voice bits into packets. This opens up a number of options for transmission, including the increasingly popular voice over IP (Internet Protocol) approach.

In any telephone network switch, the most complex element is the software that controls call processing. This software performs call routing and implements call-processing logic for hundreds of custom-calling features. Typically, this software runs on a proprietary processor that is integrated with the physical circuit-switching hardware. A more flexible approach is to physically separate the call-processing function from the hardware-switching function. In softswitch terminology, the physical-switching function is performed by a **media gateway (MG)** and the call-processing logic resides in a **media gateway controller (MGC)**.

Figure 9.9 contrasts the architecture of a traditional telephone network circuit switch with the softswitch architecture. In the latter case, the MG and MGC are distinct entities and may be provided by different vendors. To facilitate interoperability, ITU-T has issued a standard for a media gateway control protocol between the MG and MGC: H.248.1 (*Gateway Control Protocol, Version 3*, 2005). RFC 2805 (*Media Gateway Control Protocol Architecture and Requirements*, 2000) provides an overview of media gateway concepts.

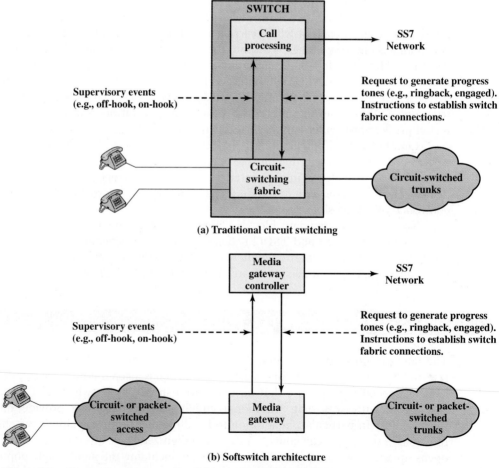

Figure 9.9   Comparison between Traditional Circuit Switching and Softswitch

9.5 PACKET-SWITCHING PRINCIPLES

The long-haul circuit-switching telecommunications network was originally designed to handle voice traffic, and the majority of traffic on these networks continues to be voice. A key characteristic of circuit-switching networks is that resources within the network are dedicated to a particular call. For voice connections, the resulting circuit will enjoy a high percentage of utilization because, most of the time, one party or the other is talking. However, as the circuit-switching network began to be used increasingly for data connections, two shortcomings became apparent:

- In a typical user/host data connection (e.g., personal computer user logged on to a database server), much of the time the line is idle. Thus, with data connections, a circuit-switching approach is inefficient.
- In a circuit-switching network, the connection provides for transmission at a constant data rate. Thus, each of the two devices that are connected must transmit and receive at the same data rate as the other. This limits the utility of the network in interconnecting a variety of host computers and workstations.

To understand how packet switching addresses these problems, let us briefly summarize packet-switching operation. Data are transmitted in short packets. A typical upper bound on packet length is 1000 octets (bytes). If a source has a longer message to send, the message is broken up into a series of packets (Figure 9.10). Each packet contains a portion (or all for a short message) of the user's data plus some control information. The control information, at a minimum, includes the information that the network requires to be able to route the packet through the network and deliver it to the intended destination. At each node en route, the packet is received, stored briefly, and passed on to the next node.

Let us return to Figure 9.1, but now assume that it depicts a simple packet-switching network. Consider a packet to be sent from station A to station E. The packet includes control information that indicates that the intended destination is E. The packet is sent from A to node 4. Node 4 stores the packet, determines the

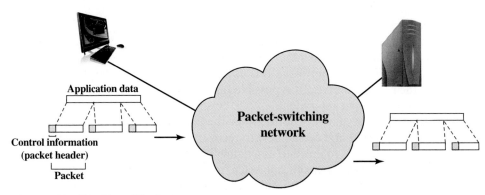

Figure 9.10   The Use of Packets

next leg of the route (say 5), and queues the packet to go out on that link (the 4-5 link). When the link is available, the packet is transmitted to node 5, which forwards the packet to node 6, and finally to E. This approach has a number of advantages over circuit switching:

- Line efficiency is greater, because a single node-to-node link can be dynamically shared by many packets over time. The packets are queued up and transmitted as rapidly as possible over the link. By contrast, with circuit switching, time on a node-to-node link is preallocated using synchronous time-division multiplexing. Much of the time, such a link may be idle because a portion of its time is dedicated to a connection that is idle.

- A packet-switching network can perform data-rate conversion. Two stations of different data rates can exchange packets because each connects to its node at its proper data rate.

- When traffic becomes heavy on a circuit-switching network, some calls are blocked; that is, the network refuses to accept additional connection requests until the load on the network decreases. On a packet-switching network, packets are still accepted, but delivery delay increases.

- Priorities can be used. If a node has a number of packets queued for transmission, it can transmit the higher-priority packets first. These packets will therefore experience less delay than lower-priority packets.

Switching Technique

If a station has a message to send through a packet-switching network that is of length greater than the maximum packet size, it breaks the message up into packets and sends these packets, one at a time, to the network. A question arises as to how the network will handle this stream of packets as it attempts to route them through the network and deliver them to the intended destination. Two approaches are used in contemporary networks: datagram and virtual circuit.

In the **datagram** approach, each packet is treated independently, with no reference to packets that have gone before. This approach is illustrated in Figure 9.11, which shows a time sequence of snapshots of the progress of three packets through the network. Each node chooses the next node on a packet's path, taking into account information received from neighboring nodes on traffic, line failures, and so on. So the packets, each with the same destination address, do not all follow the same route, and they may arrive out of sequence at the exit point. In this example, the exit node restores the packets to their original order before delivering them to the destination. In some datagram networks, it is up to the destination rather than the exit node to do the reordering. Also, it is possible for a packet to be destroyed in the network. For example, if a packet-switching node crashes momentarily, all of its queued packets may be lost. Again, it is up to either the exit node or the destination to detect the loss of a packet and decide how to recover it. In this technique, each packet, treated independently, is referred to as a datagram.

In the **virtual circuit** approach, a preplanned route is established before any packets are sent. Once the route is established, all the packets between a pair of communicating parties follow this same route through the network. This is illustrated in

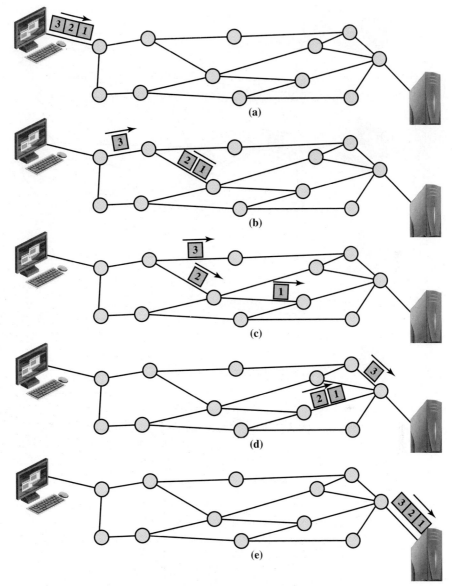

Figure 9.11   Packet Switching: Datagram Approach

Figure 9.12. Because the route is fixed for the duration of the logical connection, it is somewhat similar to a circuit in a circuit-switching network and is referred to as a virtual circuit. Each packet contains a virtual circuit identifier as well as data. Each node on the preestablished route knows where to direct such packets; no routing decisions are required. At any time, each station can have more than one virtual circuit to any other station and can have virtual circuits to more than one station.

So the main characteristic of the virtual circuit technique is that a route between stations is set up prior to data transfer. Note that this does not mean that this is a dedicated path, as in circuit switching. A transmitted packet is buffered at

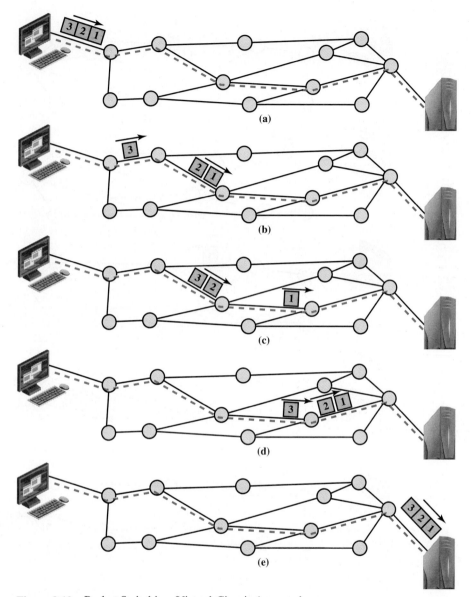

Figure 9.12 Packet Switching: Virtual-Circuit Approach

each node, and queued for output over a line, while other packets on other virtual circuits may share the use of the line. The difference from the datagram approach is that, with virtual circuits, the node need not make a routing decision for each packet. It is made only once for all packets using that virtual circuit.

If two stations wish to exchange data over an extended period of time, there are certain advantages to virtual circuits. First, the network may provide services related to the virtual circuit, including sequencing and error control. Sequencing refers to the fact that, because all packets follow the same route, they arrive in the original order. Error control is a service that assures not only that packets arrive in proper sequence, but also that all packets arrive correctly. For example, if a packet in a sequence from node 4 to node 6 fails to arrive at node 6, or arrives with an error, node 6 can request a retransmission of that packet from node 4. Another advantage is that packets should transit the network more rapidly with a virtual circuit; it is not necessary to make a routing decision for each packet at each node.

One advantage of the datagram approach is that the call setup phase is avoided. Thus, if a station wishes to send only one or a few packets, datagram delivery will be quicker. Another advantage of the datagram service is that, because it is more primitive, it is more flexible. For example, if congestion develops in one part of the network, incoming datagrams can be routed away from the congestion. With the use of virtual circuits, packets follow a predefined route, and thus it is more difficult for the network to adapt to congestion. A third advantage is that datagram delivery is inherently more reliable. With the use of virtual circuits, if a node fails, all virtual circuits that pass through that node are lost. With datagram delivery, if a node fails, subsequent packets may find an alternate route that bypasses that node. A datagram-style of operation is common in internetworks, discussed in Part Five.

Packet Size

There is a significant relationship between packet size and transmission time, as shown in Figure 9.13. In this example, it is assumed that there is a virtual circuit from station X through nodes a and b to station Y. The message to be sent comprises 40 octets, and each packet contains 3 octets of control information, which is placed at the beginning of each packet and is referred to as a header. If the entire message is sent as a single packet of 43 octets (3 octets of header plus 40 octets of data), then the packet is first transmitted from station X to node a (Figure 9.13a). When the entire packet is received, it can then be transmitted from a to b. When the entire packet is received at node b, it is then transferred to station Y. Ignoring switching time, total transmission time is 129 octet-times (43 octets × 3 packet transmissions).

Suppose now that we break up the message into two packets, each containing 20 octets of the message and, of course, 3 octets each of header, or control information. In this case, node a can begin transmitting the first packet as soon as it has arrived from X, without waiting for the second packet. Because of this overlap in transmission, the total transmission time drops to 92 octet-times. By breaking the message up into five packets, each intermediate node can begin transmission even sooner and the savings in time is greater, with a total of 77 octet-times for transmission. However, this process of using more and smaller packets eventually results in increased, rather than reduced, delay as illustrated in Figure 9.13d. This is because each packet contains a fixed amount of header, and more packets mean more of these headers. Furthermore, the example does not show the processing and queuing delays at each node. These delays are also greater when more packets are handled for a single message. However, we shall see in the next chapter that an extremely small packet size (53 octets) can result in an efficient network design.

External Network Interface

One technical aspect of packet-switching networks remains to be examined: the interface between attached devices and the network. We have seen that a circuit-switching

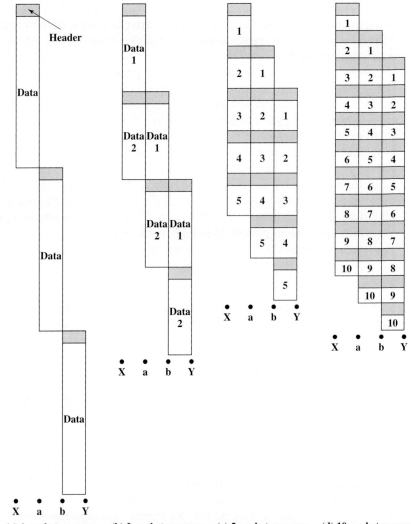

(a) 1-packet message   (b) 2-packet message   (c) 5-packet message   (d) 10-packet message

Figure 9.13 Effect of Packet Size on Transmission Time

network provides a transparent communications path for attached devices that makes it appear that the two communicating stations have a direct link. However, in the case of packet-switching networks, the attached stations must organize their data into packets for transmission. This requires a certain level of cooperation between the network and the attached stations. This cooperation is embodied in an interface standard. The standard used for traditional packet-switching networks is X.25, which is described in Appendix U. Another interface standard is frame relay, also discussed in Appendix U.

Typically, standards for packet-switching network interfaces define a virtual circuit service. This service enables any subscriber to the network to set up logical connections, called virtual circuits, to other subscribers. An example is shown in Figure 9.14 (compare Figure 9.1). In this example, station A has a virtual circuit

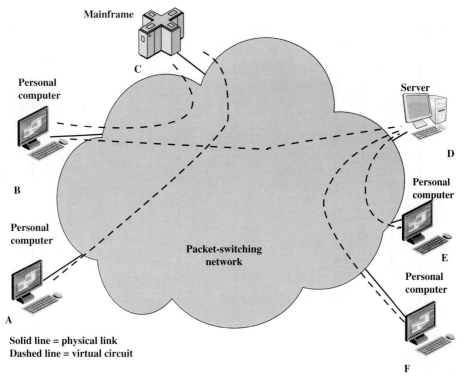

Figure 9.14   The Use of Virtual Circuits

connection to C; station B has two virtual circuits established, one to C and one to D; and stations E and F each have a virtual circuit connection to D.

   In this context, the term *virtual circuit* refers to the logical connection between two stations through the network; this is perhaps best termed an **external virtual circuit**. Earlier, we used the term *virtual circuit* to refer to a specific preplanned route through the network between two stations; this could be called an **internal virtual circuit**. Typically, there is a one-to-one relationship between external and internal virtual circuits. However, it is also possible to employ an external virtual circuit service with a datagram-style network. What is important for an external virtual circuit is that there is a logical relationship, or logical channel, established between two stations, and all of the data associated with that logical channel are considered as part of a single stream of data between the two stations. For example, in Figure 9.14, station D keeps track of data packets arriving from three different workstations (B, E, F) on the basis of the virtual circuit number associated with each incoming packet.

Comparison of Circuit Switching and Packet Switching

Having looked at the internal operation of packet switching, we can now return to a comparison of this technique with circuit switching. We first look at the important issue of performance and then examine other characteristics.

PERFORMANCE   A simple comparison of circuit switching and the two forms of packet switching is provided in Figure 9.15. The figure depicts the transmission of a

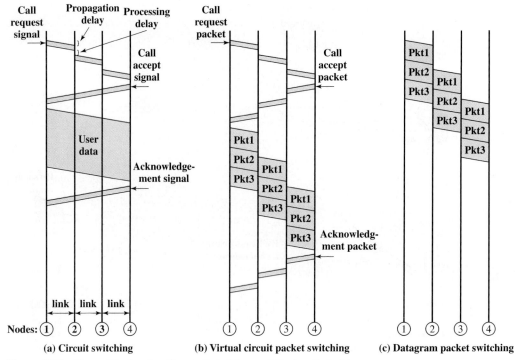

Figure 9.15 Event Timing for Circuit Switching and Packet Switching

message across four nodes, from a source station attached to node 1 to a destination station attached to node 4. In this figure, we are concerned with three types of delay:

- **Propagation delay:** The time it takes a signal to propagate from one node to the next. This time is generally negligible. The speed of electromagnetic signals through a wire medium, for example, is typically 2×10^8 m/s.

- **Transmission time:** The time it takes for a transmitter to send out a block of data. For example, it takes 1 s to transmit a 10,000-bit block of data onto a 10-kbps line.

- **Node delay:** The time it takes for a node to perform the necessary processing as it switches data.

For circuit switching, there is a certain amount of delay before the message can be sent. First, a Call Request signal is sent through the network, to set up a connection to the destination. If the destination station is not busy, a Call Accepted signal returns. Note that a processing delay is incurred at each node during the call request; this time is spent at each node setting up the route of the connection. On the return, this processing is not needed because the connection is already set up. After the connection is set up, the message is sent as a single block, with no noticeable delay at the switching nodes.

Virtual circuit packet switching appears quite similar to circuit switching. A virtual circuit is requested using a Call Request packet, which incurs a delay at each node. The virtual circuit is accepted with a Call Accept packet. In contrast to the circuit-switching case, the call acceptance also experiences node delays, even though the virtual circuit route is now established. The reason is that this packet is queued at each node and must wait its turn for transmission. Once the virtual circuit is established, the message is transmitted in packets. It should be clear that this phase of the operation can be no faster than circuit switching for comparable networks. This is because circuit switching is an essentially transparent process, providing a constant data rate across the network. Packet switching involves some delay at each node in the path. Worse, this delay is variable and will increase with increased load.

Datagram packet switching does not require a call setup. Thus, for short messages, it will be faster than virtual circuit packet switching and perhaps circuit switching. However, because each individual datagram is routed independently, the processing for each datagram at each node may be longer than for virtual circuit packets. Thus, for long messages, the virtual circuit technique may be superior.

Figure 9.15 is intended only to suggest what the relative performance of the techniques might be; actual performance depends on a host of factors, including the size of the network, its topology, the pattern of load, and the characteristics of typical exchanges.

OTHER CHARACTERISTICS   Besides performance, there are a number of other characteristics that may be considered in comparing the techniques we have been discussing. Table 9.1 summarizes the most important of these. Most of these characteristics have already been discussed. A few additional comments follow.

Table 9.1   Comparison of Communication Switching Techniques

Circuit Switching	Datagram Packet Switching	Virtual Circuit Packet Switching
Dedicated transmission path	No dedicated path	No dedicated path
Continuous transmission of data	Transmission of packets	Transmission of packets
Fast enough for interactive	Fast enough for interactive	Fast enough for interactive
Messages are not stored	Packets may be stored until delivered	Packets stored until delivered
The path is established for entire conversation	Route established for each packet	Route established for entire conversation
Call setup delay; negligible transmission delay	Packet transmission delay	Call setup delay; packet transmission delay
Busy signal if called party busy	Sender may be notified if packet not delivered	Sender notified of connection denial
Overload may block call setup; no delay for established calls	Overload increases packet delay	Overload may block call setup; increases packet delay
Electromechanical or computerized switching nodes	Small switching nodes	Small switching nodes
User responsible for message loss protection	Network may be responsible for individual packets	Network may be responsible for packet sequences
Usually no speed or code conversion	Speed and code conversion	Speed and code conversion
Fixed bandwidth	Dynamic use of bandwidth	Dynamic use of bandwidth
No overhead bits after call setup	Overhead bits in each packet	Overhead bits in each packet

As was mentioned, circuit switching is essentially a transparent service. Once a connection is established, a constant data rate is provided to the connected stations. This is not the case with packet switching, which typically introduces variable delay, so that data arrive in a choppy manner. Indeed, with datagram packet switching, data may arrive in a different order than they were transmitted.

An additional consequence of transparency is that there is no overhead required to accommodate circuit switching. Once a connection is established, the analog or digital data are passed through, as is, from source to destination. For packet switching, analog data must be converted to digital before transmission; in addition, each packet includes overhead bits, such as the destination address.

9.6   ASYNCHRONOUS TRANSFER MODE

Asynchronous transfer mode is a switching and multiplexing technology that employs small, fixed-length packets called **cells**. A fixed-size packet was chosen to ensure that the switching and multiplexing function could be carried out efficiently, with little delay variation. A small cell size was chosen primarily to support delay-intolerant interactive voice service with a small packetization delay. ATM is a connection-oriented packet-switching technology that was designed to provide the performance of a circuit-switching network and the flexibility and efficiency of a packet-switching network. A major thrust of the ATM standardization effort was to provide a powerful set of tools for supporting a rich QoS capability and a powerful traffic management capability. ATM was intended to provide a unified networking standard for both circuit-switched and packet-switched traffic, and to support data, voice, and video with appropriate QoS mechanisms. With ATM, the user can select the desired level of service and obtain guaranteed service quality. Internally, the ATM network makes reservations and preplans routes so that transmission allocation is based on priority and QoS characteristics.

ATM was intended to be a universal networking technology, with much of the switching and routing capability implemented in hardware, and with the ability to support IP-based networks and circuit-switched networks. It was also anticipated that ATM would be used to implement local area networks. ATM never achieved this comprehensive deployment. However, ATM remains an important technology. ATM is commonly used by telecommunications providers to implement wide area networks. Many DSL implementations use ATM over the basic DSL hardware for multiplexing and switching, and ATM is used as a backbone network technology in numerous IP networks and portions of the Internet.

A number of factors have led to this lesser role for ATM. IP, with its many associated protocols, provides an integrative technology that is more scalable and less complex than ATM. In addition, the need to use small fixed-sized cells to reduce jitter has disappeared as transport speeds have increased. The development of voice and video over IP protocols has provided an integration capability at the IP level.

Perhaps the most significant development related to the reduced role for ATM is the widespread acceptance of Multiprotocol Label Switching (MPLS). MPLS is a layer-2 connection-oriented packet-switching protocol that, as the name suggests, can provide a switching service for a variety of protocols and applications, including IP, voice, and video. We introduce MPLS in Chapter 23.

ATM Logical Connections

ATM is a packet-oriented transfer mode. It allows multiple logical connections to be multiplexed over a single physical interface. The information flow on each logical connection is organized into fixed-size packets called cells. Logical connections in ATM are referred to as **virtual channel connections (VCCs)**. A VCC is analogous to a virtual circuit; it is the basic unit of switching in an ATM network. A VCC is set up between two end users through the network, and a variable-rate, full-duplex flow of fixed-size cells is exchanged over the connection. VCCs are also used for user–network exchange (control signaling) and network–network exchange (network management and routing).

For ATM, a second sublayer of processing has been introduced that deals with the concept of virtual path (Figure 9.16). A **virtual path connection (VPC)** is a bundle of VCCs that have the same endpoints. Thus, all of the cells flowing over all of the VCCs in a single VPC are switched together.

The virtual path concept was developed in response to a trend in high-speed networking in which the control cost of the network is becoming an increasingly higher proportion of the overall network cost. The virtual path technique helps contain the control cost by grouping connections sharing common paths through the network into a single unit. Network management actions can then be applied to a small number of groups of connections instead of a large number of individual connections.

Several advantages can be listed for the use of virtual paths:

- **Simplified network architecture:** Network transport functions can be separated into those related to an individual logical connection (virtual channel) and those related to a group of logical connections (virtual path).

- **Increased network performance and reliability:** The network deals with fewer, aggregated entities.

- **Reduced processing and short connection setup time:** Much of the work is done when the virtual path is set up. By reserving capacity on a virtual path connection in anticipation of later call arrivals, new virtual channel connections can be established by executing simple control functions at the endpoints

Figure 9.16   ATM Connection Relationships

of the virtual path connection; no call processing is required at transit nodes. Thus, the addition of new virtual channels to an existing virtual path involves minimal processing.

- **Enhanced network services:** The virtual path is used internal to the network but is also visible to the end user. Thus, the user may define closed user groups or closed networks of virtual channel bundles.

VIRTUAL PATH/VIRTUAL CHANNEL CHARACTERISTICS ITU-T Recommendation I.150 lists the following as characteristics of virtual channel connections:

- **Quality of service (QoS):** A user of a VCC is provided with a QoS specified by parameters such as cell loss ratio (ratio of cells lost to cells transmitted) and cell delay variation.
- **Switched and semipermanent virtual channel connections:** A switched VCC is an on-demand connection, which requires a call control signaling for setup and tearing down. A semipermanent VCC is one that is of long duration and is set up by configuration or network management action.
- **Cell sequence integrity:** The sequence of transmitted cells within a VCC is preserved.
- **Traffic parameter negotiation and usage monitoring:** Traffic parameters can be negotiated between a user and the network for each VCC. The network monitors the input of cells to the VCC to ensure that the negotiated parameters are not violated.

The types of traffic parameters that can be negotiated include average rate, peak rate, burstiness, and peak duration. The network may need a number of strategies to deal with congestion and to manage existing and requested VCCs. At the crudest level, the network may simply deny new requests for VCCs to prevent congestion. Additionally, cells may be discarded if negotiated parameters are violated or if congestion becomes severe. In an extreme situation, existing connections might be terminated.

I.150 also lists characteristics of VPCs. The first four characteristics listed are identical to those for VCCs. That is, QoS; switched and semipermanent VPCs; cell sequence integrity; and traffic parameter negotiation and usage monitoring are all also characteristics of a VPC. There are a number of reasons for this duplication. First, this provides some flexibility in how the network service manages the requirements placed upon it. Second, the network must be concerned with the overall requirements for a VPC, and within a VPC may negotiate the establishment of virtual channels with given characteristics. Finally, once a VPC is set up, it is possible for the end users to negotiate the creation of new VCCs. The VPC characteristics impose a discipline on the choices that the end users may make.

In addition, a fifth characteristic is listed for VPCs:

- **Virtual channel identifier restriction within a VPC:** One or more virtual channel identifiers, or numbers, may not be available to the user of the VPC but may be reserved for network use. Examples include VCCs used for network management.

CONTROL SIGNALING   In ATM, a mechanism is needed for the establishment and release of VPCs and VCCs. The exchange of information involved in this process is referred to as control signaling and takes place on separate connections from those that are being managed.

For VCCs, I.150 specifies four methods for providing an establishment/release facility. One or a combination of these methods will be used in any particular network:

1. **Semipermanent VCCs** may be used for user-to-user exchange. In this case, no control signaling is required.

2. If there is no preestablished call control signaling channel, then one must be set up. For that purpose, a control signaling exchange must take place between the user and the network on some channel. Hence we need a permanent channel, probably of low data rate, that can be used to set up VCCs that can be used for call control. Such a channel is called a **meta-signaling channel**, as the channel is used to set up signaling channels.

3. The meta-signaling channel can be used to set up a VCC between the user and the network for call control signaling. This **user-to-network signaling virtual channel** can then be used to set up VCCs to carry user data.

4. The meta-signaling channel can also be used to set up a **user-to-user signaling virtual channel**. Such a channel must be set up within a preestablished VPC. It can then be used to allow the two end users, without network intervention, to establish and release user-to-user VCCs to carry user data.

For VPCs, three methods are defined in I.150:

1. A VPC can be established on a **semipermanent** basis by prior agreement. In this case, no control signaling is required.

2. VPC establishment/release may be **customer controlled**. In this case, the customer uses a signaling VCC to request the VPC from the network.

3. VPC establishment/release may be **network controlled**. In this case, the network establishes a VPC for its own convenience. The path may be network-to-network, user-to-network, or user-to-user.

ATM Cells

ATM makes use of fixed-size cells, consisting of a 5-octet header and a 48-octet information field. There are several advantages to the use of small, fixed-size cells. First, the use of small cells may reduce queuing delay for a high-priority cell, because it waits less if it arrives slightly behind a lower-priority cell that has gained access to a resource (e.g., the transmitter). Second, fixed-size cells can be switched more efficiently, which is important for the very high data rates of ATM. With fixed-size cells, it is easier to implement the switching mechanism in hardware.

Figure 9.17a shows the cell header format at the user–network interface. Figure 9.17b shows the cell header format internal to the network.

The **Generic Flow Control (GFC)** field does not appear in the cell header internal to the network, but only at the user–network interface. Hence, it can be used for control of cell flow only at the local user–network interface. The field could

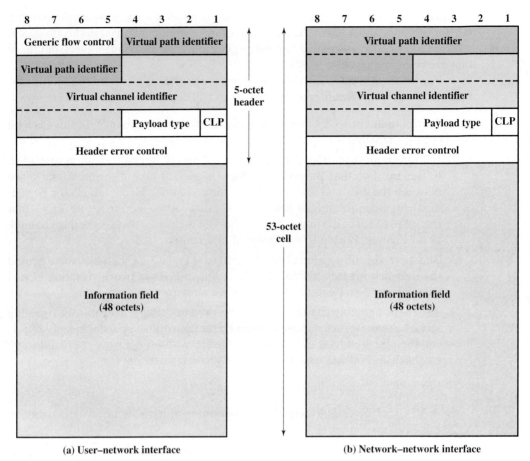

Figure 9.17 ATM Cell Format

be used to assist the customer in controlling the flow of traffic for different qualities of service. In any case, the GFC mechanism is used to alleviate short-term overload conditions in the network.

The **virtual path identifier (VPI)** constitutes a routing field for the network. It is 8 bits at the user–network interface and 12 bits at the network–network interface. The latter allows support for an expanded number of VPCs internal to the network, to include those supporting subscribers and those required for network management. The **virtual channel identifier (VCI)** is used for routing to and from the end user.

The **Payload Type (PT)** field indicates the type of information in the information field. Table 9.2 shows the interpretation of the PT bits. A value of 0 in the first bit indicates user information (i.e., information from the next higher layer). In this case, the second bit indicates whether congestion has been experienced; the third bit, known as the Service Data Unit (SDU) type bit, is a one-bit field that can be used to discriminate two types of ATM SDUs associated with a connection. The term *SDU* refers to the 48-octet payload of the cell. A value of 1 in the first bit of

Table 9.2 Payload Type (PT) Field Coding

PT Coding	Interpretation		
0 0 0	User data cell,	congestion not experienced,	SDU-type = 0
0 0 1	User data cell,	congestion not experienced,	SDU-type = 1
0 1 0	User data cell,	congestion experienced,	SDU-type = 0
0 1 1	User data cell,	congestion experienced,	SDU-type = 1
1 0 0	OAM segment associated cell		
1 0 1	OAM end-to-end associated cell		
1 1 0	Resource management cell		
1 1 1	Reserved for future function		

SDU = Service Data Unit

OAM = Operations, Administration, and Maintenance

the Payload Type field indicates that this cell carries network management or maintenance information. This indication allows the insertion of network-management cells onto a user's VCC without impacting the user's data. Thus, the PT field can provide inband control information.

The **Cell Loss Priority (CLP)** bit is used to provide guidance to the network in the event of congestion. A value of 0 indicates a cell of relatively higher priority, which should not be discarded unless no other alternative is available. A value of 1 indicates that this cell is subject to discard within the network. The user might employ this field so that extra cells (beyond the negotiated rate) may be inserted into the network, with a CLP of 1, and delivered to the destination if the network is not congested. The network may set this field to 1 for any data cell that is in violation of an agreement concerning traffic parameters between the user and the network. In this case, the switch that does the setting realizes that the cell exceeds the agreed traffic parameters but that the switch is capable of handling the cell. At a later point in the network, if congestion is encountered, this cell has been marked for discard in preference to cells that fall within agreed traffic limits.

The **Header Error Control (HEC)** field is an 8-bit error code that can be used to correct single-bit errors in the header and to detect double-bit errors. In the case of most existing data link layer protocols, such as LAPD and HDLC, the data field that serves as input to the error code calculation is in general much longer than the size of the resulting error code. This allows for error detection. In the case of ATM, there is also sufficient redundancy in the code to recover from certain error patterns.

9.7 RECOMMENDED READING

As befits its age, circuit switching has inspired a voluminous literature. Two good books on the subject are [BELL00] and [FREE04].

The literature on packet switching is enormous. [BERT92] is a good treatment of this subject. [ROBE78] is a classic paper on how packet-switching technology evolved. [BARA02] and [HEGG84] are also interesting. [IBM95] provides a detailed treatment of ATM technology.

BARA02   Baran, P. "The Beginnings of Packet Switching: Some Underlying Concepts." *IEEE Communications Magazine*, July 2002.

BELL00   Bellamy, J. *Digital Telephony*. New York: Wiley, 2000.

BERT92   Bertsekas, D., and Gallager, R. *Data Networks*. Englewood Cliffs, NJ: Prentice Hall, 1992.

FREE04   Freeman, R. *Telecommunication System Engineering*. New York: Wiley, 2004.

HEGG84   Heggestad, H. "An Overview of Packet Switching Communications." *IEEE Communications Magazine*, April 1984.

IBM95   IBM International Technical Support Organization. *Asynchronous Transfer Mode (ATM) Technical Overview*. IBM Redbook SG24-4625-00, 1995. www.redbooks.ibm.com

ROBE78   Roberts, L. "The Evolution of Packet Switching." *Proceedings of the IEEE*, November 1978.

[BERT92]   is a good treatment of this subject.

9.8   KEY TERMS, REVIEW QUESTIONS, AND PROBLEMS

Key Terms

asynchronous transfer mode (ATM)	header error control (HEC)	time-division switching
cell	internal virtual circuit	time-multiplexed switching (TMS)
circuit switching	local loop	time-slot interchange (TSI)
circuit-switching network	media gateway controller (MGC)	trunk
crossbar matrix	packet switching	virtual channel connection (VCC)
datagram	softswitch	virtual circuit
digital switch	space division switching	virtual path connection (VPC)
exchange	subscriber	
external virtual circuit	subscriber line	
generic flow control (GFC)	subscriber loop	

Review Questions

9.1   Why is it useful to have more than one possible path through a network for each pair of stations?

9.2   What are the four generic architectural components of a public communications network? Define each term.

9.3   What is the principal application that has driven the design of circuit-switching networks?

9.4   What are the advantages of packet switching compared to circuit switching?

9.5   Explain the difference between datagram and virtual circuit operation.

9.6   What is the significance of packet size in a packet-switching network?

9.7   What types of delay are significant in assessing the performance of a packet-switching network?

9.8 What are the characteristics of a virtual channel connection?
9.9 What are the characteristics of a virtual path connection?
9.10 List and briefly explain the fields in an ATM cell.

Problems

9.1 Consider a simple telephone network consisting of two end offices and one intermediate switch with a 1-MHz full-duplex trunk between each end office and the
intermediate switch. Assume a 4-kHz channel for each voice call. The average telephone is used to make four calls per 8-hour workday, with a mean call duration of six
minutes. Ten percent of the calls are long distance. What is the maximum number of
telephones an end office can support?

9.2 We need to design a switch with 100 input lines and 100 output lines.
  a. If a crossbar switch has 100 input lines and 100 output lines, how many crosspoints
     will it have?
  b. How many crosspoints will there be if the above crossbar switch is replaced with a
     three-stage switch? You may consider the following specifications:
     • Each switch in the first stage and last stage has $10 \times$ crosspoints.
     • The middle stage has 4 crossbars each with 10×10 crosspoints.

9.3 Consider a three-stage switch such as in Figure 9.6. Assume that there are a total of N
input lines and N output lines for the overall three-stage switch. If n is the number of
input lines to a stage 1 crossbar and the number of output lines to a stage 3 crossbar,
then there are N/n stage 1 crossbars and N/n stage 3 crossbars. Assume each stage 1
crossbar has one output line going to each stage 2 crossbar, and each stage 2 crossbar
has one output line going to each stage 3 crossbar. For such a configuration it can be
shown that, for the switch to be nonblocking, the number of stage 2 crossbar matrices
must equal $2n - 1$.
  a. What is the total number of crosspoints among all the crossbar switches?
  b. For a given value of N, the total number of crosspoints depends on the value of
     n. That is, the value depends on how many crossbars are used in the first stage to
     handle the total number of input lines. Assuming a large number of input lines to
     each crossbar (large value of n), what is the minimum number of crosspoints for a
     nonblocking configuration as a function of n?
  c. For a range of N from 10^2 to 10^6, plot the number of crosspoints for a single-stage
     $N \times N$ switch and an optimum three-stage crossbar switch.

9.4 Consider a TSI system with a TDM input of 8000 frames per second. The TSI requires
one memory read and one memory write operation per slot. What is the maximum
number of slots per frame that can be handled, as a function of the memory cycle time?

9.5 Consider a TDM system with 8 I/O lines, and connections 1-2, 3-7, and 5-8. Draw
several frames of the input to the TSI unit and output from the TSI unit, indicating
the movement of data from input time slots to output time slots.

9.6 Design a three-stage 450×450 crossbar switch, given that the number of input lines
in each switch of the first stage, n, is 18; the number of output lines in each switch of
the last stage is also 18; and the number of crossbars, k, in the middle stage is 8. How
can you redesign the above three-stage switch according to the Clos criteria? The
Clos criteria states that if $n = (N/2)^{1/2}$ and $k \geq 2n - 1$, the switch would prevent blocking during periods of heavy loads.

9.7 Define the following parameters for a switching network:

  N = number of hops between two given end systems
  L = message length in bits
  B = data rate, in bits per second (bps), on all links
  P = fixed packet size, in bits

H = overhead (header) bits per packet

S = call setup time (circuit switching or virtual circuit) in seconds

D = propagation delay per hop in seconds

  a. For $N = 4$, $L = 3200$, $B = 9600$, $P = 1024$, $H = 16$, $S = 0.2$, $D = 0.001$, compute the end-to-end delay for circuit switching, virtual circuit packet switching, and datagram packet switching. Assume that there are no acknowledgments. Ignore processing delay at the nodes.

  b. Derive general expressions for the three techniques of part (a), taken two at a time (three expressions in all), showing the conditions under which the delays are equal.

9.8 Compute the total number of crosspoints in an N $\times$ N three-stage switch that has n input lines per switch in first stage and k crossbars in the middle stage.

9.9 Assuming no malfunction in any of the stations or nodes of a network, is it possible for a packet to be delivered to the wrong destination?

9.10 Although ATM does not include any end-to-end error detection and control functions on the user data, it is provided with a HEC field to detect and correct header errors. Let us consider the value of this feature. Suppose that the bit error rate of the transmission system is B. If errors are uniformly distributed, then the probability of an error in the header is

$$\frac{h}{h+i} \times B$$

and the probability of error in the data field is

$$\frac{i}{h+i} \times B$$

where h is the number of bits in the header and i is the number of bits in the data field.

  a. Suppose that errors in the header are not detected and not corrected. In that case, a header error may result in a misrouting of the cell to the wrong destination; therefore, i bits will arrive at an incorrect destination, and i bits will not arrive at the correct destination. What is the overall bit error rate $B1$? Find an expression for the multiplication effect on the bit error rate: $M1 = B1/B$.

  b. Now suppose that header errors are detected but not corrected. In that case, i bits will not arrive at the correct destination. What is the overall bit error rate $B2$? Find an expression for the multiplication effect on the bit error rate: $M2 = B2/B$.

  c. Now suppose that header errors are detected and corrected. What is the overall bit error rate $B3$? Find an expression for the multiplication effect on the bit error rate: $M3 = B3/B$.

  d. Plot $M1$, $M2$, and $M3$ as a function of header length, for $i = 48 \times 8 = 384$ bits. Comment on the results.

9.11 One key design decision for ATM was whether to use fixed- or variable-length cells. Let us consider this decision from the point of view of efficiency. We can define transmission efficiency as

$$N = \frac{\text{Number of information octets}}{\text{Number of information octets} + \text{Number of overhead octets}}$$

  a. Consider the use of fixed-length packets. In this case the overhead consists of the header octets. Define

    L = Data field size of the cell in octets

    H = Header size of the cell in octets

    X = Number of information octets to be transmitted as a single message

Derive an expression for N. *Hint:* The expression will need to use the operator $\lceil \cdot \rceil$, where $\lceil Y \rceil$ = the smallest integer greater than or equal to Y.

b. If cells have variable length, then overhead is determined by the header, plus the flags to delimit the cells or an additional length field in the header. Let Hv = additional overhead octets required to enable the use of variable-length cells. Derive an expression for N in terms of X, H, and Hv.

c. Let $L = 48$, $H = 5$, and $Hv = 2$. Plot N versus message size for fixed- and variable-length cells. Comment on the results.

9.12 A packet-switching network is using a virtual circuit to transmit data from the source to the destination node. In a given instance of data transmission, a message of size 56 octets is to be transmitted from node X to node Y. The virtual circuit designed has 3 intermediate nodes, a, b, and c. Each packet in the network has a 4-octet header that contains the control information. Determine the time of transmission of the message sent from X to Y in each of the following cases:

a. The entire message is sent as a single packet.
b. The message is sent by dividing it into two packets.
c. The message is sent using 7 packets.
d. The message is sent using 14 packets.

What conclusion can you draw from the above observation? Assume that the transmission time in each hop is the same.

9.13 Consider compressed video transmission in an ATM network. Suppose standard ATM cells must be transmitted through 5 switches. The data rate is 43 Mbps.

a. What is the transmission time for one cell through one switch?
b. Each switch may be transmitting a cell from other traffic all of which we assume to have lower (non-preemptive for the cell) priority. If the switch is busy transmitting a cell, our cell has to wait until the other cell completes transmission. If the switch is free our cell is transmitted immediately. What is the maximum time when a typical video cell arrives at the first switch (and possibly waits) until it is finished being transmitted by the fifth and last one? Assume that you can ignore propagation time, switching time, and everything else but the transmission time and the time spent waiting for another cell to clear a switch.
c. Now suppose we know that each switch is utilized 60% of the time with the other low-priority traffic. By this we mean that with probability 0.6 when we look at a switch it is busy. Suppose that if there is a cell being transmitted by a switch, the average delay spent waiting for a cell to finish transmission is one-half a cell transmission time. What is the average time from the input of the first switch to clearing the fifth?
d. However, the measure of most interest is not delay but jitter, which is the variability in the delay. Use parts (b) and (c) to calculate the maximum and average variability, respectively, in the delay.

In all cases assume that the various random events are independent of one another; for example, we ignore the burstiness typical of such traffic.

9.14 An ATM cell uses fixed-size packets of 53 bytes. Each cell carries a 5-byte header for control information and 48 bytes for user data.
A message of size 1 KB needs to be transmitted using ATM.
a. How many ATM cells will be required for this purpose?
b. If transmission efficiency is computed as the ratio of the size of the message and the total size of cells required, compute the transmission efficiency in this case.

CHAPTER 10

CELLULAR WIRELESS NETWORKS

LEARNING OBJECTIVES

After reading this chapter, you should be able to:

◆ Provide an overview of cellular network organization.

◆ Distinguish among four generations of mobile telephony.

◆ Understand the relative merits of time-division multiple access (TDMA) and code division multiple access (CDMA) approaches to mobile telephony.

◆ Present an overview of LTE-Advanced.

Of all the tremendous advances in data communications and telecommunications, perhaps the most revolutionary is the development of **cellular networks**. Cellular technology is the foundation of mobile wireless communications and supports users in locations that are not easily served by wired networks. Cellular technology is the underlying technology for mobile telephones, personal communications systems, wireless Internet and wireless Web applications, and much more.

We begin this chapter with a look at the basic principles used in all cellular networks. Then we look at specific cellular technologies and standards, which are conveniently grouped into four generations. Finally, we examine LTE-Advanced, which is the standard for the fourth generation, in more detail.

10.1 PRINCIPLES OF CELLULAR NETWORKS

Cellular radio is a technique that was developed to increase the capacity available for mobile radio telephone service. Prior to the introduction of cellular radio, mobile radio telephone service was only provided by a high-power transmitter/ receiver. A typical system would support about 25 channels with an effective radius of about 80 km. The way to increase the capacity of the system is to use lower-power systems with shorter radius and to use numerous transmitters/ receivers.

Cellular Network Organization

The essence of a cellular network is the use of multiple low-power transmitters, on the order of 100 W or less. Because the range of such a transmitter is small, an area can be divided into cells, each one served by its own antenna. Each cell is allocated a band of frequencies and is served by a **base station**, consisting of transmitter, receiver, and control unit. Adjacent cells are assigned different frequencies to avoid interference or crosstalk. However, cells sufficiently distant from each other can use the same frequency band.

The first design decision to make is the shape of cells to cover an area. A matrix of square cells would be the simplest layout to define (Figure 10.1a). However, this geometry is not ideal. If the width of a square cell is d, then a cell has four neighbors at a distance d and four neighbors at a distance $\sqrt{2}d$. As a mobile user within a cell moves toward the cell's boundaries, it is best if all of the adjacent antennas are equidistant. This simplifies the task of determining when to switch the user to an adjacent antenna and which antenna to choose. A hexagonal pattern provides for equidistant antennas (Figure 10.1b). The radius of a hexagon is defined to be the radius of the circle that circumscribes it (equivalently, the distance from the center to each vertex; also equal to the length of a side of a hexagon). For a cell radius R, the distance between the cell center and each adjacent cell center is $d = \sqrt{3}R$.

In practice, a precise hexagonal pattern is not used. Variations from the ideal are due to topographical limitations, local signal propagation conditions, and practical limitation on siting antennas.

A wireless cellular system limits the opportunity to use the same frequency for different communications because the signals, not being constrained, can interfere with one another even if geographically separated. Systems supporting a large number of communications simultaneously need mechanisms to conserve spectrum.

FREQUENCY REUSE   In a cellular system, each cell has a base transceiver. The transmission power is carefully controlled (to the extent that it is possible in the highly variable mobile communication environment) to allow communication within the cell using a given frequency, while limiting the power at that frequency that escapes the cell into adjacent ones. The objective is to use the same frequency in other nearby (but not adjacent) cells, thus allowing the frequency to be used for multiple simultaneous conversations. Generally, 10 to 50 frequencies are assigned to each cell, depending on the traffic expected.

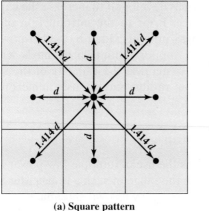
(a) Square pattern

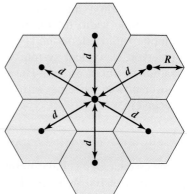
(b) Hexagonal pattern

Figure 10.1   Cellular Geometries

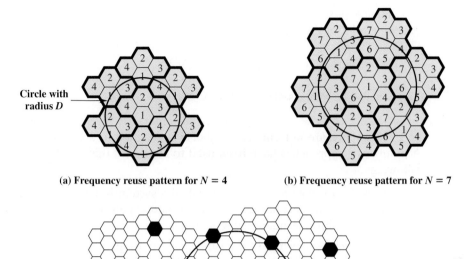

(a) Frequency reuse pattern for $N = 4$ (b) Frequency reuse pattern for $N = 7$

Circle with radius D

(c) Black cells indicate a frequency reuse for $N = 19$

Figure 10.2   Frequency Reuse Patterns

The essential issue is to determine how many cells must intervene between two cells using the same frequency so that the two cells do not interfere with each other. Various patterns of frequency reuse are possible. Figure 10.2 shows some examples. If the pattern consists of N cells and each cell is assigned the same number of frequencies, each cell can have K/N frequencies, where K is the total number of frequencies allotted to the system.

In characterizing frequency reuse, the following parameters are commonly used:

D = minimum distance between centers of cells that use the same band of frequencies (called cochannels)

R = radius of a cell

d = distance between centers of adjacent cells ($d = \sqrt{3}R$)

N = number of cells in a repetitious pattern (each cell in the pattern uses a unique band of frequencies), termed the **reuse factor**

In a hexagonal cell pattern, only the following values of N are possible:

$$N = I^2 + J^2 + (I \times J) \quad I, J = 0, 1, 2, 3, \ldots$$

Hence, possible values of N are 1, 3, 4, 7, 9, 12, 13, 16, 19, 21, and so on. The following relationship holds:

$$\frac{D}{R} = \sqrt{3N}$$

This can also be expressed as $D/d = \sqrt{N}$.

INCREASING CAPACITY   In time, as more customers use the system, traffic may build up so that there are not enough frequencies assigned to a cell to handle its calls. A number of approaches have been used to cope with this situation, including the following:

- **Adding new channels:** Typically, when a system is set up in a region, not all of the channels are used, and growth and expansion can be managed in an orderly fashion by adding new channels.

- **Frequency borrowing:** In the simplest case, frequencies are taken from adjacent cells by congested cells. The frequencies can also be assigned to cells dynamically.

- **Cell splitting:** In practice, the distribution of traffic and topographic features is not uniform, and this presents opportunities for capacity increase. Cells in areas of high usage can be split into smaller cells. Generally, the original cells are about 6.5 to 13 km in size. The smaller cells can themselves be split; however, 1.5-km cells are close to the practical minimum size as a general solution (but see the subsequent discussion of microcells). To use a smaller cell, the power level used must be reduced to keep the signal within the cell. Also, as the mobile units move, they pass from cell to cell, which requires transferring of the call from one base transceiver to another. This process is called a handoff. As the cells get smaller, these handoffs become much more frequent. Figure 10.3 indicates schematically how cells can be divided to provide more

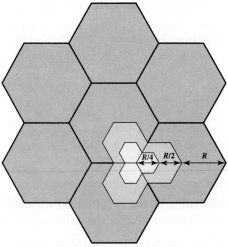

Figure 10.3   Cell Splitting with Cell Reduction Factor of $F = 2$

capacity. A radius reduction by a factor of F reduces the coverage area and increases the required number of base stations by a factor of F^2.

- **Cell sectoring:** With cell sectoring, a cell is divided into a number of wedge-shaped sectors, each with its own set of channels, typically three or six sectors per cell. Each sector is assigned a separate subset of the cell's channels, and directional antennas at the base station are used to focus on each sector.

- **Microcells:** As cells become smaller, antennas move from the tops of tall buildings or hills to the tops of small buildings or the sides of large buildings, and finally to lamp posts, where they form microcells. Each decrease in cell size is accompanied by a reduction in the radiated power levels from the base stations and the mobile units. Microcells are useful in city streets in congested areas, along highways, and inside large public buildings.

EXAMPLE 10.1 Assume a system of 32 cells with a cell radius of 1.6 km, a total frequency bandwidth that supports 336 traffic channels, and a reuse factor of $N = 7$. If there are 32 total cells, what geographic area is covered, how many channels are there per cell, and what is the total number of concurrent calls that can be handled? Repeat for a cell radius of 0.8 km and 128 cells.

Figure 10.4a shows an approximately square pattern. The area of a hexagon of radius R is $1.5R^2\sqrt{3}$. A hexagon of radius 1.6 km has an area of 6.65 km^2, and the total area covered is $6.65 \times 32 = 213$ km^2. For $N = 7$, the number of channels per cell is $336/7 = 48$, for a total channel capacity of $48 \times 32 = 1536$ channels. For the layout of Figure 10.4b, the area covered is $1.66 \times 128 = 213$ km^2. The number of channels per cell is $336/7 = 48$, for a total channel capacity of $48 \times 128 = 6144$ channels.

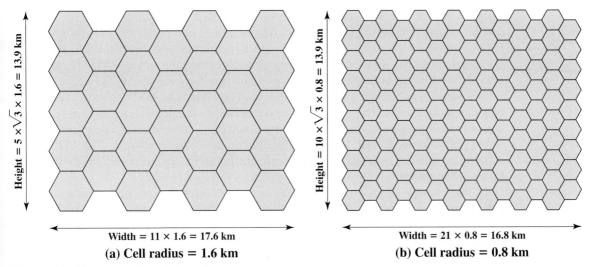

(a) Cell radius = 1.6 km   (b) Cell radius = 0.8 km

Figure 10.4   Frequency Reuse Example

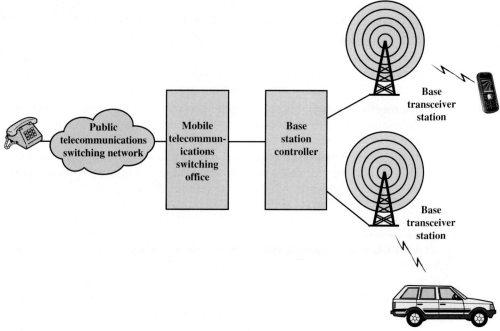

Figure 10.5 Overview of Cellular System

Operation of Cellular Systems

Figure 10.5 shows the principal elements of a cellular system. In the approximate center of each cell is a base station (BS). The BS includes one or more antennas, a controller, and a number of transceivers for communicating on the channels assigned to that cell. The controller is used to handle the call process between the mobile unit and the rest of the network. At any time, a number of mobile user units may be active and moving about within a cell, communicating with the BS. Each BS is connected to a mobile telecommunications switching office (MTSO), with one MTSO serving multiple BSs. Typically, the link between an MTSO and a BS is by a wire line, although a wireless link is also possible. The MTSO connects calls between mobile units. The MTSO is also connected to the public telephone or telecommunications network and can make a connection between a fixed subscriber to the public network and a mobile subscriber to the cellular network. The MTSO assigns the voice channel to each call, performs handoffs, and monitors the call for billing information.

The use of a cellular system is fully automated and requires no action on the part of the user other than placing or answering a call. Two types of channels are available between the mobile unit and the base station: control channels and traffic channels. **Control channels** are used to exchange information having to do with setting up and maintaining calls and with establishing a relationship between a mobile unit and the nearest BS. **Traffic channels** carry a voice or data connection between users. Figure 10.6 illustrates the steps in a typical call between two mobile users within an area controlled by a single MTSO:

- **Mobile unit initialization:** When the mobile unit is turned on, it scans and selects the strongest setup control channel used for this system (Figure 10.6a). Cells with different frequency bands repetitively broadcast on different setup channels. The receiver selects the strongest setup channel and monitors that channel. The effect of this procedure is that the mobile unit has automatically selected the BS antenna of the cell within which it will operate.[1] Then

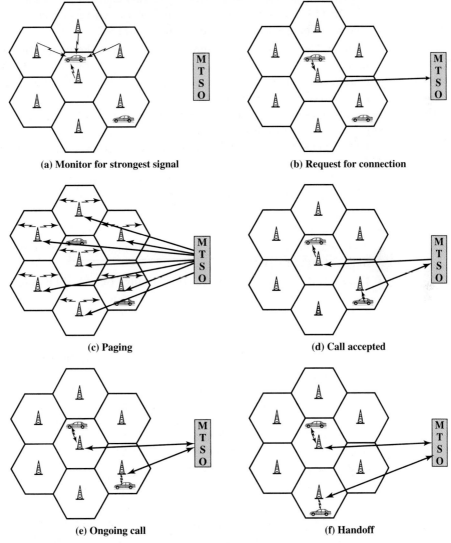

(a) Monitor for strongest signal (b) Request for connection

(c) Paging (d) Call accepted

(e) Ongoing call (f) Handoff

Figure 10.6 Example of Mobile Cellular Cell

---

[1]Usually, but not always, the antenna and therefore the base station selected is the closest one to the mobile unit. However, because of propagation anomalies, this is not always the case.

a handshake takes place between the mobile unit and the MTSO controlling this cell, through the BS in this cell. The handshake is used to identify the user and register its location. As long as the mobile unit is on, this scanning procedure is repeated periodically to account for the motion of the unit. If the unit enters a new cell, then a new BS is selected. In addition, the mobile unit is monitoring for pages, discussed subsequently.

- **Mobile-originated call:** A mobile unit originates a call by sending the number of the called unit on the preselected setup channel (Figure 10.6b). The receiver at the mobile unit first checks that the setup channel is idle by examining information in the forward (from the BS) channel. When an idle condition is detected, the mobile may transmit on the corresponding reverse (to BS) channel. The BS sends the request to the MTSO.

- **Paging:** The MTSO then attempts to complete the connection to the called unit. The MTSO sends a paging message to certain BSs depending on the called mobile number (Figure 10.6c). Each BS transmits the paging signal on its own assigned setup channel.

- **Call accepted:** The called mobile unit recognizes its number on the setup channel being monitored and responds to that BS, which sends the response to the MTSO. The MTSO sets up a circuit between the calling and called BSs. At the same time, the MTSO selects an available traffic channel within each BS's cell and notifies each BS, which in turn notifies its mobile unit (Figure 10.6d). The two mobile units tune to their respective assigned channels.

- **Ongoing call:** While the connection is maintained, the two mobile units exchange voice or data signals, going through their respective BSs and the MTSO (Figure 10.6e).

- **Handoff:** If a mobile unit moves out of range of one cell and into the range of another during a connection, the traffic channel has to change to one assigned to the BS in the new cell (Figure 10.6f). The system makes this change without either interrupting the call or alerting the user.

Other functions performed by the system but not illustrated in Figure 10.6 include the following:

- **Call blocking:** During the mobile-initiated call stage, if all the traffic channels assigned to the nearest BS are busy, then the mobile unit makes a preconfigured number of repeated attempts. After a certain number of failed tries, a busy tone is returned to the user.

- **Call termination:** When one of the two users hangs up, the MTSO is informed and the traffic channels at the two BSs are released.

- **Call drop:** During a connection, because of interference or weak signal spots in certain areas, if the BS cannot maintain the minimum required signal strength for a certain period of time, the traffic channel to the user is dropped and the MTSO is informed.

- **Calls to/from fixed and remote mobile subscriber:** The MTSO connects to the public switched telephone network. Thus, the MTSO can set up a connection between a mobile user in its area and a fixed subscriber via the telephone network. Further, the MTSO can connect to a remote MTSO via the telephone network or via dedicated lines and set up a connection between a mobile user in its area and a remote mobile user.

Mobile Radio Propagation Effects

Mobile radio communication introduces complexities not found in wire communication or in fixed wireless communication. Two general areas of concern are signal strength and signal propagation effects.

- **Signal strength:** The strength of the signal between the base station and the mobile unit must be strong enough to maintain signal quality at the receiver but not so strong as to create too much cochannel interference with channels in another cell using the same frequency band. Several complicating factors exist. Human-made noise varies considerably, resulting in a variable noise level. For example, automobile ignition noise in the cellular frequency range is greater in the city than in a suburban area. Other signal sources vary from place to place. The signal strength varies as a function of distance from the BS to a point within its cell. Moreover, the signal strength varies dynamically as the mobile unit moves.

- **Fading**: Even if signal strength is within an effective range, signal propagation effects may disrupt the signal and cause errors. Fading is discussed subsequently in this section.

In designing a cellular layout, the communications engineer must take account of these various propagation effects, the desired maximum transmit power level at the base station and the mobile units, the typical height of the mobile unit antenna, and the available height of the BS antenna. These factors will determine the size of the individual cell. Unfortunately, as just described, the propagation effects are dynamic and difficult to predict. The best that can be done is to come up with a model based on empirical data and to apply that model to a given environment to develop guidelines for cell size. One of the most widely used models was developed by Okumura et al. [OKUM68] and subsequently refined by Hata [HATA80]. The original was a detailed analysis of the Tokyo area and produced path loss information for an urban environment. Hata's model is an empirical formulation that takes into account a variety of environments and conditions. For an urban environment, predicted path loss is

$$L_{dB} = 69.55 + 26.16 \log f_c - 13.82 \log h_t - A(h_r) + (44.9 - 6.55 \log h_t) \log d \quad \textbf{(10.1)}$$

where

f_c = carrier frequency in MHz from 150 to 1500 MHz

h_t = height of transmitting antenna (base station) in m, from 30 to 300 m

h_r = height of receiving antenna (mobile station) in m, from 1 to 10 m

d = propagation distance between antennas in km, from 1 to 20 km

$A(h_r)$ = correction factor for mobile antenna height

For a small- or medium-sized city, the correction factor is given by

$$A(h_r) = (1.1 \log f_c - 0.7) h_r - (1.56 \log f_c - 0.8) \text{ dB}$$

And for a large city it is given by

$$A(h_r) = 8.29 [\log(1.54 h_r)]^2 - 1.1 \text{ dB} \qquad \text{for } f_c \leq 300 \text{ MHz}$$
$$A(h_r) = 3.2 [\log(11.75 h_r)]^2 - 4.97 \text{ dB} \qquad \text{for } f_c \geq 300 \text{ MHz}$$

To estimate the path loss in a suburban area, the formula for urban path loss in Equation (10.1) is modified as:

$$L_{dB}(\text{suburban}) = L_{dB}(\text{urban}) - 2[\log (f_c/28)]^2 - 5.4$$

And for the path loss in open areas, the formula is modified as

$$L_{dB}(\text{open}) = L_{dB}(\text{urban}) - 4.78(\log f_c)^2 - 18.733 (\log f_c) - 40.98$$

The Okumura/Hata model is considered to be among the best in terms of accuracy in path loss prediction and provides a practical means of estimating path loss in a wide variety of situations [FREE07].

EXAMPLE 10.2 Let $f_c = 900$ MHz, $h_t = 40$ m, $h_r = 5$ m, and $d = 10$ km. Estimate the path loss for a medium-size city.

$$A(h_r) = (1.1 \log 900 - 0.7) 5 - (1.56 \log 900 - 0.8) \text{ dB}$$
$$= 12.75 - 3.8 = 8.95 \text{ dB}$$

$$L_{dB} = 69.55 + 26.16 \log 900 - 13.82 \log 40 - 8.95 + (44.9 - 6.55 \log 40) \log 10$$
$$= 69.55 + 77.28 - 22.14 - 8.95 + 34.4 = 150.14 \text{ dB}$$

Fading in the Mobile Environment

Perhaps the most challenging technical problem facing communications systems engineers is fading in a mobile environment. The term *fading* refers to the time variation of received signal power caused by changes in the transmission medium or path(s). In a fixed environment, fading is affected by changes in atmospheric conditions, such as rainfall. But in a mobile environment, where one of the two antennas is moving relative to the other, the relative location of various obstacles changes over time, creating complex transmission effects.

MULTIPATH PROPAGATION Three propagation mechanisms, illustrated in Figure 10.7, play a role. **Reflection** occurs when an electromagnetic signal encounters a surface that is large relative to the wavelength of the signal. For example, suppose a ground-reflected wave near the mobile unit is received. Because the ground-reflected wave has a 180° phase shift after reflection, the ground wave and the line-of-sight (LOS) wave may tend to cancel, resulting in high signal loss.[2] Further, because the mobile antenna is lower than most human-made structures in the area, multipath

---

[2]On the other hand, the reflected signal has a longer path, which creates a phase shift due to delay relative to the unreflected signal. When this delay is equivalent to half a wavelength, the two signals are back in phase.

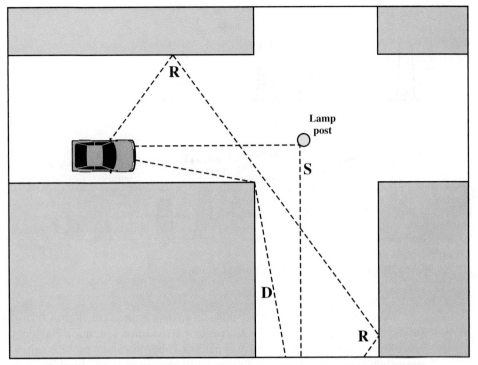

Figure 10.7 Sketch of Three Important Propagation Mechanisms: Reflection (R), Scattering (S), Diffraction (D) [ANDE95]

interference occurs. These reflected waves may interfere constructively or destructively at the receiver.

Diffraction occurs at the edge of an impenetrable body that is large compared to the wavelength of the radio wave. When a radio wave encounters such an edge, waves propagate in different directions with the edge as the source. Thus, signals can be received even when there is no unobstructed LOS from the transmitter.

If the size of an obstacle is on the order of the wavelength of the signal or less, **scattering** occurs. An incoming signal is scattered into several weaker outgoing signals. At typical cellular microwave frequencies, there are numerous objects, such as lamp posts and traffic signs, that can cause scattering. Thus, scattering effects are difficult to predict.

These three propagation effects influence system performance in various ways depending on local conditions and as the mobile unit moves within a cell. If a mobile unit has a clear LOS to the transmitter, then diffraction and scattering are generally minor effects, although reflection may have a significant impact. If there is no clear LOS, such as in an urban area at street level, then diffraction and scattering are the primary means of signal reception.

THE EFFECTS OF MULTIPATH PROPAGATION   As just noted, one unwanted effect of multipath propagation is that multiple copies of a signal may arrive at different phases. If these phases add destructively, the signal level relative to noise declines, making signal detection at the receiver more difficult.

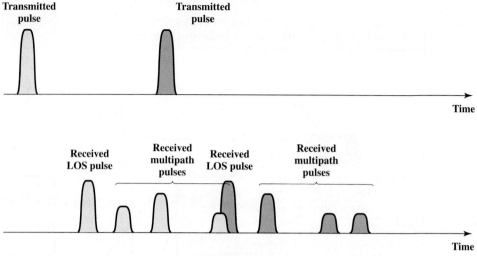

Figure 10.8 Two Pulses in Time-Variant Multipath

A second phenomenon, of particular importance for digital transmission, is intersymbol interference (ISI). Consider that we are sending a narrow pulse at a given frequency across a link between a fixed antenna and a mobile unit. Figure 10.8 shows what the channel may deliver to the receiver if the impulse is sent at two different times. The upper line shows two pulses at the time of transmission. The lower line shows the resulting pulses at the receiver. In each case the first received pulse is the desired LOS signal. The magnitude of that pulse may change because of changes in atmospheric attenuation. Further, as the mobile unit moves farther away from the fixed antenna, the amount of LOS attenuation increases. But in addition to this primary pulse, there may be multiple secondary pulses due to reflection, diffraction, and scattering. Now suppose that this pulse encodes one or more bits of data. In that case, one or more delayed copies of a pulse may arrive at the same time as the primary pulse for a subsequent bit. These delayed pulses act as a form of noise to the subsequent primary pulse, making recovery of the bit information more difficult.

As the mobile antenna moves, the location of various obstacles changes; hence the number, magnitude, and timing of the secondary pulses change. This makes it difficult to design signal-processing techniques that will filter out multipath effects so that the intended signal is recovered with fidelity.

TYPES OF FADING Fading effects in a mobile environment can be classified as either fast or slow. Referring to Figure 10.7, as the mobile unit moves down a street in an urban environment, rapid variations in signal strength occur over distances of about one-half a wavelength. At a frequency of 900 MHz, which is typical for mobile cellular applications, the wavelength is 0.33 m. Changes of amplitude can be as much as 20 or 30 dB over a short distance. This type of rapidly changing fading phenomenon, known as **fast fading**, affects not only mobile phones in automobiles, but even a mobile phone user walking down an urban street.

As the mobile user covers distances well in excess of a wavelength, the urban environment changes, as the user passes buildings of different heights, vacant lots, intersections, and so forth. Over these longer distances, there is a change in the average received power level about which the rapid fluctuations occur. This is referred to as **slow fading**.

Fading effects can also be classified as flat or selective. **Flat fading**, or non-selective fading, is that type of fading in which all frequency components of the received signal fluctuate in the same proportions simultaneously. **Selective fading** affects unequally the different spectral components of a radio signal. The term *selective fading* is usually significant only relative to the bandwidth of the overall communications channel. If attenuation occurs over a portion of the bandwidth of the signal, the fading is considered to be selective; nonselective fading implies that the signal bandwidth of interest is narrower than, and completely covered by, the spectrum affected by the fading.

ERROR COMPENSATION MECHANISMS The efforts to compensate for the errors and distortions introduced by multipath fading fall into three general categories: forward error correction, adaptive equalization, and diversity techniques. In the typical mobile wireless environment, techniques from all three categories are combined to combat the error rates encountered.

Forward error correction is applicable in digital transmission applications: those in which the transmitted signal carries digital data or digitized voice or video data. Typically in mobile wireless applications, the ratio of total bits sent to data bits sent is between 2 and 3. This may seem an extravagant amount of overhead, in that the capacity of the system is cut to one-half or one-third of its potential, but the mobile wireless environment is so difficult that such levels of redundancy are necessary. Chapter 6 discusses forward error correction.

Adaptive equalization can be applied to transmissions that carry analog information (e.g., analog voice or video) or digital information (e.g., digital data, digitized voice or video) and is used to combat intersymbol interference. The process of equalization involves some method of gathering the dispersed symbol energy back together into its original time interval. Equalization is a broad topic; techniques include the use of so-called lumped analog circuits as well as sophisticated digital signal processing algorithms.

Diversity is based on the fact that individual channels experience independent fading events. We can therefore compensate for error effects by providing multiple logical channels in some sense between transmitter and receiver and sending part of the signal over each channel. This technique does not eliminate errors but it does reduce the error rate, since we have spread the transmission out to avoid being subjected to the highest error rate that might occur. The other techniques (equalization, forward error correction) can then cope with the reduced error rate.

Some diversity techniques involve the physical transmission path and are referred to as **space diversity**. For example, multiple nearby antennas may be used to receive the message, with the signals combined in some fashion to reconstruct the most likely transmitted signal. Another example is the use of collocated multiple directional antennas, each oriented to a different reception angle with the incoming signals again combined to reconstitute the transmitted signal.

More commonly, the term *diversity* refers to frequency diversity or time diversity techniques. With **frequency diversity**, the signal is spread out over a larger-frequency bandwidth or carried on multiple frequency carriers. The most important example of this approach is spread spectrum, which is examined in Chapter 17.

10.2 CELLULAR NETWORK GENERATIONS

Since their introduction in the mid-1980s, cellular networks have evolved rapidly. For convenience, industry and standards bodies group the technical advances into "generations." We are now up to the fourth generation (4G) of cellular network technology. In this section, we give a brief overview of the four generations. The following section is devoted to 4G.

Table 10.1 lists some of the key characteristics of the cellular network generations.

First Generation

The original cellular networks, now dubbed 1G, provided analog traffic channels and were designed to be an extension of the public switched telephone networks. Users with brick-sized cell phones placed and received calls in the same fashion as landline subscribers.

The most widely deployed 1G system was the **Advanced Mobile Phone Service (AMPS)**, developed by AT&T. This approach was also common in South America, Australia, and China.

In North America, two 25-MHz bands were allocated to AMPS, one for transmission from the base station to the mobile unit (869–894 MHz) and the other for transmission from the mobile to the base station (824–849 MHz). Each of these bands is split in two to encourage competition (i.e., in each market two operators can be accommodated). An operator is allocated only 12.5 MHz in each direction for its system. The channels are spaced 30 kHz apart, which allows a total of 416 channels per operator. Twenty-one channels are allocated for control, leaving 395 to carry calls. The control channels are data channels operating at 10 kbps. The conversation

Table 10.1 Wireless Network Generations

Technology	1G	2G	2.5G	4G
Design began	1970	1980	1985	2000
Implementation	1984	1991	1999	2012
Services	Analog voice	Digital voice	Higher capacity packetized data	Completely IP based
Data rate	1.9. kbps	14.4 kbps	384 kbps	200 Mbps
Multiplexing	FDMA	TDMA, CDMA	TDMA, CDMA	OFDMA, SC-FDMA
Core network	PSTN	PSTN	PSTN, packet network	IP backbone

channels carry the conversations in analog using frequency modulation (FM). Simple FDMA is used to provide multiple access. Control information is also sent on the conversation channels in bursts as data. This number of channels is inadequate for most major markets, so some way must be found either to use less bandwidth per conversation or to reuse frequencies. Both approaches have been taken in the various approaches to 1G telephony. For AMPS, frequency reuse is exploited.

Second Generation

First-generation cellular networks, such as AMPS, quickly became highly popular, threatening to swamp available capacity. Second-generation systems (2G) were developed to provide higher-quality signals, higher data rates for support of digital services, and greater capacity. Key differences between 1G and 2G networks include:

- **Digital traffic channels:** The most notable difference between the two generations is that 1G systems are almost purely analog, whereas 2G systems are digital. In particular, 1G systems are designed to support voice channels using FM; digital traffic is supported only by the use of a modem that converts the digital data into analog form. 2G systems provide digital traffic channels. These systems readily support digital data; voice traffic is first encoded in digital form before transmitting.

- **Encryption:** Because all of the user traffic, as well as control traffic, is digitized in 2G systems, it is a relatively simple matter to encrypt all of the traffic to prevent eavesdropping. All 2G systems provide this capability, whereas 1G systems send user traffic in the clear, providing no security.

- **Error detection and correction:** The digital traffic stream of 2G systems also lends itself to the use of error detection and correction techniques, such as those discussed in Chapters 6 and 16. The result can be very clear voice reception.

- **Channel access:** In 1G systems, each cell supports a number of channels. At any given time a channel is allocated to only one user. 2G systems also provide multiple channels per cell, but each channel is dynamically shared by a number of users using TDMA (time-division multiple access) or CDMA (**code division multiple access**).

Third Generation

The objective of the third generation (3G) of wireless communication is to provide fairly high-speed wireless communications to support multimedia, data, and video in addition to voice. The ITU's International Mobile Telecommunications for the year 2000 (IMT-2000) initiative has defined the third-generation capabilities as follows:

- Voice quality comparable to the public switched telephone network
- 144 kbps data rate available to users in high-speed motor vehicles over large areas
- 384 kbps available to pedestrians standing or moving slowly over small areas
- Support (to be phased in) for 2.048 Mbps for office use

- Symmetrical and asymmetrical data transmission rates
- Support for both packet-switched and circuit-switched data services
- An adaptive interface to the Internet to reflect efficiently the common asymmetry between inbound and outbound traffic
- More efficient use of the available spectrum in general
- Support for a wide variety of mobile equipment
- Flexibility to allow the introduction of new services and technologies

The dominant technology for 3G systems is CDMA. Although three different CDMA schemes have been adopted, they share the following design features:

- **Bandwidth:** An important design goal for all 3G systems is to limit channel usage to 5 MHz. There are several reasons for this goal. On the one hand, a bandwidth of 5 MHz or more improves the receiver's ability to resolve multipath when compared to narrower bandwidths. On the other hand, available spectrum is limited by competing needs, and 5 MHz is a reasonable upper limit on what can be allocated for 3G. Finally, 5 MHz is adequate for supporting data rates of 144 and 384 kHz, the main targets for 3G services.
- **Chip rate:** Given the bandwidth, the chip rate depends on desired data rate, the need for error control, and bandwidth limitations. A chip rate of 3 Mcps or more is reasonable given these design parameters.
- **Multirate:** The term *multirate* refers to the provision of multiple fixed-data-rate logical channels to a given user, in which different data rates are provided on different logical channels. Further, the traffic on each logical channel can be switched independently through the wireless and fixed networks to different destinations. The advantage of multirate is that the system can flexibly support multiple simultaneous applications from a given user and can efficiently use available capacity by only providing the capacity required for each service.

Fourth Generation

The evolution of smartphones and cellular networks has ushered in a new generation of capabilities and standards, which is collectively called 4G. 4G systems provide ultra-broadband Internet access for a variety of mobile devices including laptops, smartphones, and tablets. 4G networks support Mobile Web access and high-bandwidth applications such as high-definition mobile TV, mobile video conferencing, and gaming services.

These requirements have led to the development of a fourth generation (4G) of mobile wireless technology that is designed to maximize bandwidth and throughput while also maximizing spectral efficiency. The ITU has issued directives for 4G networks. According to the ITU, an IMT-Advanced (or 4G) cellular system must fulfill a number of minimum requirements, including the following:

- Be based on an all-IP packet switched network.
- Support peak data rates of up to approximately 100 Mbps for high-mobility mobile access and up to approximately 1 Gbps for low-mobility access such as local wireless access.

- Dynamically share and use the network resources to support more simultaneous users per cell.
- Support smooth handovers across heterogeneous networks.
- Support high quality of service for next-generation multimedia applications.

In contrast to earlier generations, 4G systems do not support traditional circuit-switched telephony service, providing only IP telephony services. And, as may be observed in Table 10.1, the spread spectrum radio technologies that characterized 3G systems are replaced in 4G systems by OFDMA (orthogonal frequency-division multiple access) multicarrier transmission and frequency-domain equalization schemes.

Figure 10.9 illustrates several major differences between 3G and 4G cellular networks. As shown in Figure 10.9a, the connections between base stations and switching offices in 3G networks are typically cable-based, either copper or fiber wires. Circuit switching is supported to enable voice connections between mobile users and phones connected to the PSTN. Internet access in 3G networks may also be routed through switching offices. By contrast, in 4G networks, IP telephony is the norm as are IP packet-switched connections for Internet access. These are enabled by wireless connections, such as fixed broadband wireless access (BWA)

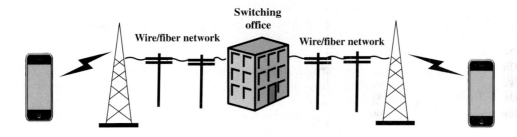

(a) Third-generation (3G) cellular network

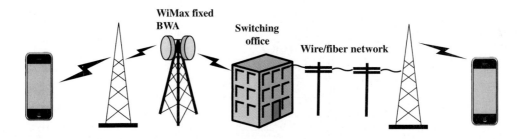

(b) Fourth-generation (4G) cellular network

Figure 10.9 Third vs. Fourth Generation Cellular Networks

WiMAX, between base stations and switching offices (Figure 10.9b). Connections among mobile users with 4G-capable smartphones may never be routed over cable-based, circuit-switched connections—all communications between them can be IP-based and handled by wireless links. This setup facilitates deployment of mobile-to-mobile video call/video conferencing services and the simultaneous delivery of voice and data services (such as Web browsing while engaged in a phone call). 4G mobile users can still connect with 3G network users and PSTN subscribers over cable/fiber circuit-switched connections between the switching offices.

10.3 LTE-ADVANCED

Two candidates emerged for 4G standardization. One is known as **Long Term Evolution (LTE)**, which has been developed by the Third Generation Partnership Project (3GPP), a consortium of Asian, European, and North American telecommunications standards organizations. The other effort is from the IEEE 802.16 committee, which has developed standards for high-speed fixed wireless operations known as WiMAX (described in Chapter 18). The committee has specified an enhancement of WiMAX to meet 4G needs. The two efforts are similar in terms of both performance and technology. Both are based on the use of orthogonal frequency-division multiple access (OFDMA) to support multiple access to network resources. WiMAX uses a pure OFDMA approach for both uplink (UL) and downlink (DL). LTE uses pure OFDMA on the downlink and a technique that is based on OFDMA but offers enhanced power efficiency for the uplink. While WiMAX retains a role as the technology for fixed broadband wireless access, LTE has become the universal standard for 4G wireless. For example, all of the major carriers in the United States, including AT&T and Verizon, have adopted a version of LTE based on **frequency-division duplex (FDD)**, whereas China Mobile, the world's largest telecommunication carrier, has adopted a version of LTE based on time-division duplex (TDD).

LTE development began in the 3G era and its initial releases provided 3G or enhanced 3G services. Beginning with release 10, LTE provides a 4G service, known as **LTE-Advanced**. Table 10.2 compares the performance goals of LTE and LTE-Advanced.

Table 10.2   Comparison of Performance Requirements for LTE and LTE-Advanced

System Performance		LTE	LTE-Advanced
Peak rate	Downlink	100 Mbps @20 MHz	1 Gbps @100 MHz
	Uplink	50 Mbps @20 MHz	500 Mbps @100 MHz
Control plane delay	Idle to connected	<100 ms	<50 ms
	Dormant to active	<50 ms	<10 ms
User plane delay		<5ms	Lower than LTE
Spectral efficiency (peak)	Downlink	5 bps/Hz @2×2	30 bps/Hz @8×8
	Uplink	2.5 bps/Hz @1×2	15 bps/Hz @4×4
Mobility		Up to 350 km/h	Up to 350–500 km/h

The specification for LTE-Advanced is immense. This section provides a brief overview.

LTE-Advanced Architecture

Figure 10.10 illustrates the principal elements in an LTE-Advanced network. The heart of the system is the base station, designated **evolved NodeB (eNodeB)**. In LTE, the base station is referred to as NodeB. The key differences between the two base station technologies are:

- The NodeB station interface with subscriber stations (referred to as user equipment (UE)) is based on CDMA, whereas the eNodeB air interface is based on OFDMA.
- eNodeB embeds its own control functionality, rather than using an RNC (Radio Network Controller) as does a NodeB.

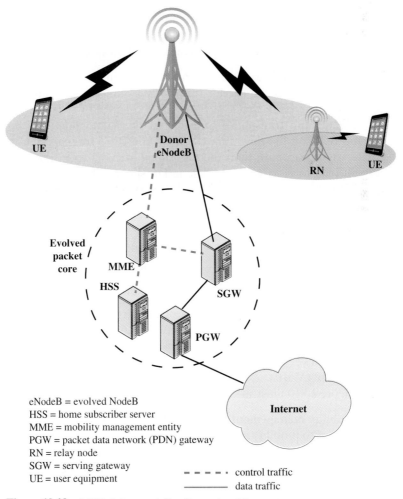

eNodeB = evolved NodeB
HSS = home subscriber server
MME = mobility management entity
PGW = packet data network (PDN) gateway
RN = relay node
SGW = serving gateway
UE = user equipment

- - - - control traffic
———— data traffic

Figure 10.10   LTE-Advanced Configuration Elements

RELAYING   Another key element of an LTE-Advanced cellular network is the use of **relay nodes (RNs)**. As with any cellular system, an LTE-Advanced base station experiences reduced data rates near the edge of its cell, due to lower signal levels and higher interference levels. Rather than use smaller cells, it is more efficient to use small relay nodes, which have a reduced radius of operation compared to an eNodeB, distributed around the periphery of the cell. A UE near an RN communicates with the RN, which in turn communicates with the eNodeB.

An RN is not simply a signal repeater. Instead the RN receives, demodulates, and decodes the data and applies error correction as needed, and then transmits a new signal to the base station, referred to in this context as a **donor eNodeB**. The RN functions as a base station with respect to its communication with the UE and as a UE with respect to its communication with the eNodeB.

- The eNodeB $\rightarrow$ RN transmissions and RN $\rightarrow$ eNodeB transmissions are carried out in the DL frequency band and UL frequency band, respectively, for FDD systems.
- The eNodeB $\rightarrow$ RN transmissions and RN $\rightarrow$ eNodeB transmissions are carried out in the DL subframes of the eNodeB and RN and UL subframes of the eNodeB and RN, respectively, for TDD systems.

Currently, RNs use inband communication, meaning that the RN–eNodeB interface uses the same carrier frequency as the RN–UE interface. This creates an interference issue that can be described as follows. If the RN receives from the eNodeB and transmits to the UE at the same time, it is both transmitting and receiving on the downlink channel. The RN's transmission will have a much greater signal strength than the DL signal arriving from the eNodeB, making it very difficult to recover the incoming DL signal. The same problem occurs in the uplink direction. To overcome this difficulty, frequency resources are partitioned as follows:

- eNodeB $\rightarrow$ RN and RN $\rightarrow$ UE links are time-division multiplexed in a single frequency band and only one is active at any one time.
- RN $\rightarrow$ eNodeB and UE $\rightarrow$ RN links are time-division multiplexed in a single frequency band and only one is active at any one time.

EVOLVED PACKET CORE   The operator, or carrier, network that interconnects all of the base stations of the carrier is referred to as the **evolved packet core (EPC)**. Traditionally, the core cellular network was circuit switched, but for 4G the core is entirely packet switched. It is based on IP and supports voice connections using voice over IP (VoIP).

Figure 10.10 illustrates the essential components of the EPC:

- **Mobility management entity (MME):** The MME deals with control signaling related to mobility and security. The MME is responsible for the tracking and the paging of UEs in idle-mode.
- **Serving gateway (SGW):** The SGW deals with user data transmitted and received by UEs in packet form, using IP. The SGW is the point of interconnect

between the radio side and the EPC. As its name indicates, this gateway serves the UE by routing the incoming and outgoing IP packets. It is the anchor point for the intra-LTE mobility (i.e., in case of handover between eNodeBs). Thus, packets can be routed from an eNodeB to an eNodeB in another area via the SGW, and can also be routed to external networks such as the Internet (via the PGW).

- **Packet data network gateway (PGW):** The PGW is the point of interconnect between the EPC and external IP networks such as the Internet. The PGW routes packets to and from the external networks. It also performs various functions such as IP address/IP prefix allocation and policy control and charging.

- **Home subscriber server (HSS):** The HSS maintains a database that contains user-related and subscriber-related information. It also provides support functions in mobility management, call and session setup, user authentication, and access authorization.

Figure 10.10 shows only a single instance of each configuration element. There are, of course, multiple eNodeBs, and multiple instances of each of the EPC elements. And there are many-to-many links between eNodeBs and MMEs, between MMEs and SGWs, and between SGWs and PGWs.

FEMTOCELLS Industry has responded to the increasing data transmission demands from smartphones, tablets, and similar devices by the introduction of 3G and now 4G cellular networks. As demand continues to increase, it becomes increasingly difficult to satisfy this requirement, particularly in densely populated areas and remote rural areas. An essential component of the 4G strategy for satisfying demand is the use of femtocells.

A **femtocell** is a low-power, short range, self-contained base station. Initially used to describe consumer units intended for residential homes, the term has expanded to encompass higher capacity units for enterprise, rural and metropolitan areas. Key attributes include IP backhaul, self-optimization, low power consumption, and ease of deployment. Femtocells are by far the most numerous type of small cells. The term *small cell* is an umbrella term for low-powered radio access nodes that operate in licensed and unlicensed spectrum that have a range of 10 m to several hundred meters. These contrast with a typical mobile macrocell, which might have a range of up to several tens of kilometers. Femtocells now outnumber macrocells, and the proportion of femtocells in 4G networks is expected to rise.

Figure 10.11 shows the typical elements in a network that uses femtocells. The femtocell access point is a small base station, much like a Wi-Fi hot spot base station, placed in a residential, business, or public setting. It operates in the same frequency band and with the same protocols as an ordinary cellular network base station. Thus, a 4G smartphone or tablet can connect wirelessly with a 4G femtocell with no change. The femtocell connects to the Internet, typically over a DSL, fiber, or cable landline. Packetized traffic to and from the femtocell connects to the cellular operator's core packet network via a femtocell gateway.

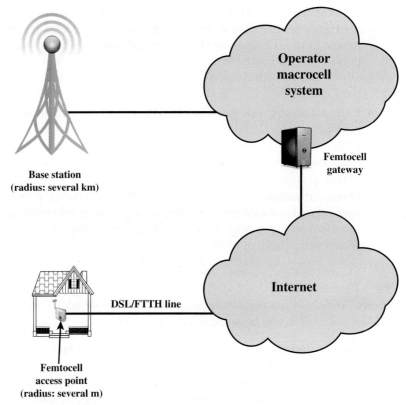

Figure 10.11   The Role of Femtocells

LTE-Advanced Transmission Characteristics

LTE-Advanced relies on two key technologies to achieve high data rates and spectral efficiency: orthogonal frequency-division multiplexing (OFDM) and multiple-input multiple-output (MIMO) antennas. Both of these technologies are explored in Chapter 17.

For the downlink, LTE-Advanced uses OFDMA and for the uplink SC-OFDM (single-carrier OFDM).

OFDM signals have a high peak-to-average power ratio (PAPR), requiring a linear power amplifier with overall low efficiency. This is a poor quality for battery-operated handsets. While complex, SC-FDMA has a lower PAPR and is better suited to portable implementation.

FDD AND TDD   LTE-Advanced has been defined to accommodate both paired spectrum for frequency-division duplex and unpaired spectrum for time-division duplex operation. Both LTE TDD and LTE FDD are being widely deployed as each form of the LTE standard has its own advantages and disadvantages. Table 10.3 compares key characteristics of the two approaches.

FDD systems allocate different frequency bands for uplink and downlink transmissions. The UL and DL channels are usually grouped into two blocks of contiguous

Table 10.3   Characteristics of TDD and FDD for LTE-Advanced

Parameter	LTE-TDD	LTE-FDD
Paired spectrum	Does not require paired spectrum as both transmit and receive occur on the same channel.	Requires paired spectrum with sufficient frequency separation to allow simultaneous transmission and reception.
Hardware cost	Lower cost as no diplexer is needed to isolate the transmitter and receiver. As cost of the UEs is of major importance because of the vast numbers that are produced, this is a key aspect.	Diplexer is needed and cost is higher.
Channel reciprocity	Channel propagation is the same in both directions which enables transmit and receive to use one set of parameters.	Channel characteristics are different in the two directions as a result of the use of different frequencies.
UL/DL asymmetry	It is possible to dynamically change the UL and DL capacity ratio to match demand.	UL/DL capacity is determined by frequency allocation set out by the regulatory authorities. It is therefore not possible to make dynamic changes to match capacity. Regulatory changes would normally be required and capacity is normally allocated so that it is the same in either direction.
Guard period/ guard band	Guard period required to ensure uplink and downlink transmissions do not clash. Large guard period will limit capacity. Larger guard period normally required if distances are increased to accommodate larger propagation times.	Guard band required to provide sufficient isolation between uplink and downlink. Large guard band does not impact capacity.
Discontinuous transmission	Discontinuous transmission is required to allow both uplink and downlink transmissions. This can degrade the performance of the RF power amplifier in the transmitter.	Continuous transmission is required.
Cross slot interference	Base stations need to be synchronized with respect to the uplink and downlink transmission times. If neighboring base stations use different uplink and downlink assignments and share the same channel, then interference may occur between cells.	Not applicable

channels (paired spectrum) that are separated by a guard band of a number of vacant radio frequency (RF) channels for interference avoidance. Figure 10.12a illustrates a typical spectrum allocation in which user i is allocated a pair of channels Ui and Di with bandwidths WU and WD. The frequency offset, WO, used to separate the pair of channels should be large enough for the user terminal to avoid self-interference among the links because both links are simultaneously active.

For TDD, the UL and DL transmissions operate in the same band but alternate in the time domain. Capacity can be allocated more flexibly than with FDD. It

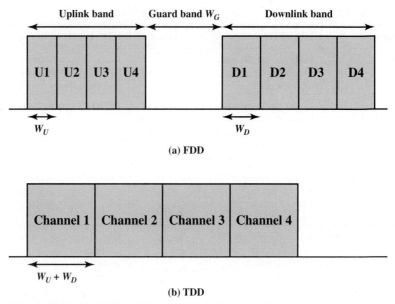

Figure 10.12 Spectrum Allocation for FDD and TDD

is a simple matter of changing the proportion of time devoted to UL and DL within a given channel.

CARRIER AGGREGATION **Carrier aggregation** is used in LTE-Advanced in order to increase the bandwidth, and thereby increase the bit rates. Since it is important to keep backward compatibility with LTE the aggregation is of LTE carriers. Carrier aggregation can be used for both FDD and TDD. Each aggregated carrier is referred to as a component carrier, CC. The component carrier can have a bandwidth of 1.4, 3, 5, 10, 15, or 20 MHz and a maximum of five component carriers can be aggregated, hence the maximum aggregated bandwidth is 100 MHz. In FDD, the number of aggregated carriers can be different in DL and UL. However, the number of UL component carriers is always equal to or lower than the number of DL component carriers. The individual component carriers can also be of different bandwidths. When TDD is used the number of CCs and the bandwidth of each CC are the same for DL and UL.

Figure 10.13a illustrates how three carriers, each of which is suitable for a 3G station, are aggregated to form a wider bandwidth suitable for a 4G station. As Figure 10.13b suggests, there are three approaches used in LTE-Advanced for aggregation:

- **Intra-band contiguous:** This is the easiest form of LTE carrier aggregation to implement. Here, the carriers are adjacent to each other. The aggregated channel can be considered by the terminal as a single enlarged channel from the RF viewpoint. In this instance, only one transceiver is required within the subscriber station. The drawback of this method is the need to have a contiguous spectrum band allocation.

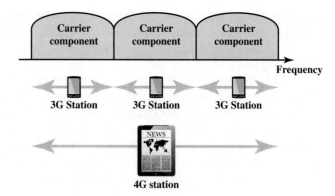

(a) Logical view of carrier aggregation

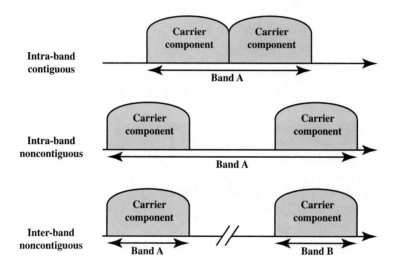

(b) Types of carrier aggregation

Figure 10.13   Carrier Aggregation

- **Intra-band noncontiguous:** Multiple CCs belonging to the same band are used in a noncontiguous manner. In this approach, the multicarrier signal cannot be treated as a single signal and therefore multiple transceivers are required. This adds significant complexity, particularly to the UE where space, power, and cost are prime considerations. This approach is likely to be used in countries where spectrum allocation is noncontiguous within a single band or when the middle carriers are in use by other subscribers.

- **Inter-band noncontiguous:** This form of carrier aggregation uses different bands. It will be of particular use because of the fragmentation of bands—some of which are only 10 MHz wide. For the UE it requires the use of multiple transceivers within the single item, with the usual impact on cost, performance, and power.

10.4 RECOMMENDED READING

[BERT94] and [ANDE95] are instructive surveys of cellular wireless propagation effects. [TANT98] contains reprints of numerous important papers dealing with CDMA in cellular networks. [OJAN98] provides an overview of key technical design considerations for 3G systems. Another useful survey is [ZENG00].

Worthwhile introductions to LTE-Advanced include [FREN13], [BAKE12], [PARK11], and [GHOS10]. [CHAN06] explores the use of FDD and TDD in 4G networks. [IWAM10] provides an overview of LTE-Advanced carrier aggregation. [BAI12] discusses LTE-Advanced modem design issues.

ANDE95 Anderson, J.; Rappaport, T.; and Yoshida, S. "Propagation Measurements and Models for Wireless Communications Channels." *IEEE Communications Magazine*, January 1995.

BAI12 Bai, D., et al. "LTE-Advanced Modem Design: Challenges and Perspectives." *IEEE Communications Magazine*, February 2012.

BAKE12 Baker, M. "From LTE-Advanced to the Future." *IEEE Communications Magazine*, February 2012.

BERT94 Bertoni, H.; Honcharenko, W.; Maciel, L.; and Xia, H. "UHF Propagation Prediction for Wireless Personal Communications." *Proceedings of the IEEE*, September 1994.

CHAN06 Chan, P., et al. "The Evolution Path of 4G Networks: FDD or TDD?" *IEEE Communications Magazine*, December 2006.

FREN13 Frenzel, L. "An Introduction to LTE-Advanced: The Real 4G." *Electronic Design*, February 2013.

GHOS10 Ghosh, A., et al. "LTE-Advanced: Next-Generation Wireless Broadband Technology." *IEEE Wireless Communications*, June 2010.

IWAM10 Iwamura, M., et al. "Carrier Aggregation Framework in 3GPP LTE-Advanced." *IEEE Communications Magazine*, August 2010.

OJAN98 Ojanpera, T., and Prasad, G. "An Overview of Air Interface Multiple Access for IMT-2000/UMTS." *IEEE Communications Magazine*, September 1998.

PARK11 Parkvall, S.; Furuskar, A.; and Dahlman, E. "Evolution of LTE toward IMT-Advanced." *IEEE Communications Magazine*, February 2011.

TANT98 Tantaratana, S., and Ahmed, K., eds. *Wireless Applications of Spread Spectrum Systems: Selected Readings*. Piscataway, NJ: IEEE Press, 1998.

ZENG00 Zeng, M.; Annamalai, A.; and Bhargava, V. "Harmonization of Global Third-generation Mobile Systems." *IEEE Communications Magazine*, December 2000.

10.5 KEY TERMS, REVIEW QUESTIONS, AND PROBLEMS

Key Terms

adaptive equalization	first-generation (1G)	packet data network
Advanced Mobile Phone	network	gateway (PGW)
Service (AMPS)	forward error correction	reflection
base station	fourth-generation (4G)	relay node (RN)
carrier aggregation	network	relaying
cellular network	frequency diversity	reuse factor
code division multiple	frequency-division duplex	scattering
access (CDMA)	(FDD)	second-generation (2G)
diffraction	frequency reuse	network
diversity	handoff	selective fading
donor eNodeB	home subscriber server	serving gateway (SGW)
evolved NodeB (eNodeB)	(HSS)	slow fading
evolved packet core (EPC)	long-term evolution (LTE)	space diversity
fading	LTE-Advanced	third-generation (3G)
fast fading	mobile radio	network
femtocells	mobility management entity	time-division duplex (TDD)
flat fading	(MME)	

Review Questions

10.1 What geometric shape is used in cellular system design?

10.2 What is the principle of frequency reuse in the context of a cellular network?

10.3 List five ways of increasing the capacity of a cellular system.

10.4 Explain the paging function of a cellular system.

10.5 What is fading?

10.6 What is the difference between diffraction and scattering?

10.7 What is the difference between fast and slow fading?

10.8 What is the difference between flat and selective fading?

10.9 What are the key differences between first- and second-generation cellular systems?

10.10 What are some key characteristics that distinguish third-generation cellular systems from second-generation cellular systems?

Problems

10.1 A cellular network has a system of 64 cells, each with a cell radius of 1.2km. It supports 396 traffic channels and has a reuse factor of 9. Find the geometrical area it can cover, the number of channels per cell, and the total channel capacity.

10.2 Consider four different cellular systems that share the following characteristics. The frequency bands are 825 to 845 MHz for mobile unit transmission and 870 to 890 MHz for base station transmission. A duplex circuit consists of one 30-kHz channel in each direction. The systems are distinguished by the reuse factor, which is 4, 7, 12, and 19, respectively.

    a. Suppose that in each of the systems, the cluster of cells (4, 7, 12, 19) is duplicated 16 times. Find the number of simultaneous communications that can be supported by each system.

    b. Find the number of simultaneous communications that can be supported by a single cell in each system.

    c. What is the area covered, in cells, by each system?

    d. Suppose the cell size is the same in all four systems and a fixed area of 100 cells is covered by each system. Find the number of simultaneous communications that can be supported by each system.

10.3 In a small-sized city, mobile radio transmission has the following parameters: 600 MHz carrier frequency, an 80 m high transmitting antenna, an 8 m high receiving antenna, and a distance of 10 km between the antennas. Estimate the path loss.

10.4 A certain mobile communication network has laid down uniform criteria for designing a cellular layout in all places. Their specifications are a carrier frequency of 1000 MHz, transmitting antennas with heights of 100 m, receiving antennas with heights of 10 m, and a distance of 15 km between the antennas. Determine the path loss in

    a. a large city.

    b. a medium-sized city.

    c. a small city.

    d. a suburban area.

    e. open fields.

10.5 A 1G cellular system using FDMA allocates a total of 25 MHz bandwidth to each operator for transmission in both directions. If an operator has a total of 400 channels and guard bands of 8 kHz between adjacent channels, what is the bandwidth of each channel?

10.6 An enhanced 2G cellular system uses a multiframe TDMA system for better performance. All voice input is digitized and compressed into a 5 kbps digital signal. Eight users are multiplexed in time slots of 4 bits in a frame, and then 4 frames are combined to form a multiframe. What will be the bit rate of the output channel?

PART FOUR: LOCAL AREA NETWORKS

CHAPTER 11

LOCAL AREA NETWORK OVERVIEW

 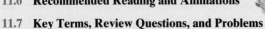

LEARNING OBJECTIVES

After studying this chapter, you should be able to:

♦ Distinguish between bus and star topologies.

♦ Explain the IEEE 802 reference model.

♦ Present an overview of logical link control.

♦ Understand the functionality of bridges.

♦ Distinguish between hubs and switches.

♦ Present an overview of virtual LANs.

This chapter begins our discussion of **local area networks (LANs)**. Whereas wide area networks may be public or private, LANs usually are owned by the organization that is using the network to interconnect equipment. LANs have much greater capacity than wide area networks to carry what is generally a greater internal communications load.

In this chapter, we look at the underlying technology and protocol architecture of LANs. Chapters 12 and 13 are devoted to a discussion of specific LAN systems.

11.1 BUS AND STAR TOPOLOGIES

In the context of a communication network, the term *topology* refers to the way in which the endpoints, or stations, attached to the network are interconnected. Historically, common topologies for LANs are bus, tree, ring, and star. In contemporary LANs, the star topology, based around the use of switches, dominates. However, it is useful to briefly look at the operation of the bus topology because it shares some characteristics with wireless LANs, and key elements of wireless LAN access protocols evolved from bus LAN access protocols. In this section, we first describe the bus topology, and then introduce the star topology.

Bus Topology

In the **bus topology**, all stations attach, through appropriate hardware interfacing known as a tap, directly to a linear transmission medium, or bus. Full-duplex operation between the station and the tap allows data to be transmitted onto the bus and received from the bus. A transmission from any station propagates the length of the medium in both directions and can be received by all other stations. At each end of the bus is a terminator, which absorbs any signal, removing it from the bus.

Two problems present themselves in this arrangement. First, because a transmission from any one station can be received by all other stations, there needs to be some way of indicating for whom the transmission is intended. Second, a mechanism is needed to regulate transmission. To see the reason for this, consider that if two stations on the bus attempt to transmit at the same time, their signals will overlap and become garbled. Or consider that if one station decides to transmit continuously for a long period of time, other stations will be blocked from transmitting.

To solve these problems, stations transmit data in small blocks, known as frames. Each frame consists of a portion of the data that a station wishes to transmit, plus a frame header that contains control information. Each station on the bus is assigned a unique address, or identifier, and the destination address for a frame is included in its header.

EXAMPLE 11.1 Figure 11.1 illustrates the bus scheme. In this example, station C wishes to transmit a frame of data to A. The frame header includes A's address. As the frame propagates along the bus, it passes B. B observes the address and ignores the frame. A, on the other hand, sees that the frame is addressed to itself and therefore copies the data from the frame as it goes by.

So the frame structure solves the first problem mentioned previously: It provides a mechanism for indicating the intended recipient of data. It also provides the basic tool for solving the second problem, the regulation of access. In particular, the stations take turns sending frames in some cooperative fashion. This involves putting additional control information into the frame header, as discussed later.

No special action needs to be taken to remove frames from the bus. When a signal reaches the end of the bus, it is absorbed by the terminator.

Star Topology

In the **star** LAN topology, each station is directly connected to a common central node (Figure 11.2). Typically, each station attaches to a central node via two point-to-point links, one for transmission and one for reception.

In general, there are two alternatives for the operation of the central node. One approach is for the central node to operate in a broadcast fashion. A transmission of a frame from one station to the node is retransmitted on all of the outgoing links. In this case, although the arrangement is physically a star, it is logically a bus: A transmission from any station is received by all other stations, and only one station at a time may successfully transmit. In this case, the central element is referred to as a **hub**. Another approach is for the central node to act as a frame-switching device. An incoming frame is buffered in the node and then retransmitted on an outgoing link to the destination station. These approaches are explored in Section 11.4.

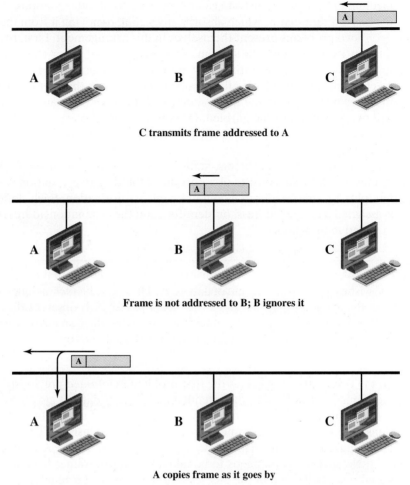

C transmits frame addressed to A

Frame is not addressed to B; B ignores it

A copies frame as it goes by

Figure 11.1 Frame Transmission on a Bus LAN

11.2 LAN PROTOCOL ARCHITECTURE

The architecture of a LAN is best described in terms of a layering of protocols that organize the basic functions of a LAN. This section opens with a description of the standardized protocol architecture for LANs, which encompasses physical, medium access control (MAC), and logical link control (LLC) layers. This section then provides an overview of the MAC and LLC layers.

IEEE 802 Reference Model

Protocols defined specifically for LAN and metropolitan area networks (MAN) transmission address issues relating to the transmission of blocks of data over the network. In OSI (open systems interconnection) terms, higher layer protocols (layer 3 or 4 and above) are independent of network architecture and are applicable

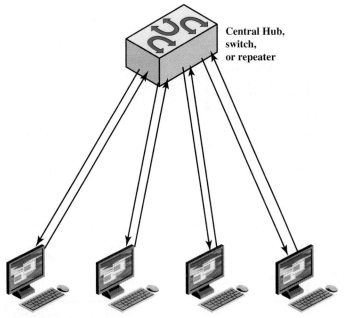

Figure 11.2   Star Topology

to LANs, MANs, and WANs. Thus, a discussion of LAN protocols is concerned principally with lower layers of the OSI model.

Figure 11.3 relates the LAN protocols to the OSI architecture. This architecture was developed by the IEEE 802 LAN standards committee[1] and has been adopted by all organizations working on the specification of LAN standards. It is generally referred to as the IEEE 802 reference model.

Working from the bottom-up, the lowest layer of the IEEE 802 reference model corresponds to the **physical layer** of the OSI model and includes such functions as

- Encoding/decoding of signals
- Preamble generation/removal (for synchronization)
- Bit transmission/reception

In addition, the physical layer of the 802 model includes a specification of the transmission medium and the topology. Generally, this is considered "below" the lowest layer of the OSI model. However, the choice of transmission medium and topology is critical in LAN design, and so a specification of the medium is included.

Above the physical layer are the functions associated with providing service to LAN users. These include the following:

- On transmission, assemble data into a frame with address and error-detection fields.
- On reception, disassemble frame and perform address recognition and error detection.

---

[1]This committee has developed standards for a wide range of LANs. See Appendix C for details.

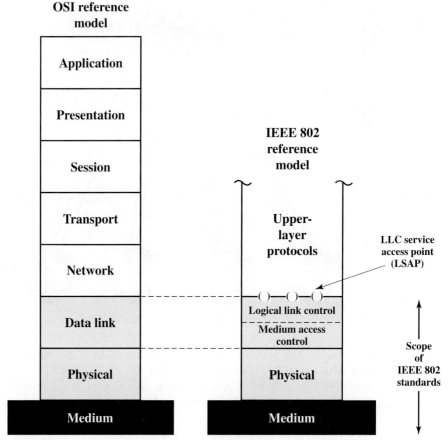

Figure 11.3 IEEE 802 Protocol Layers Compared to OSI Model

- Govern access to the LAN transmission medium.
- Provide an interface to higher layers and perform flow and error control.

These are functions typically associated with OSI layer 2. The set of functions in the last bullet item are grouped into a **logical link control (LLC)** layer. The functions in the first three bullet items are treated as a separate layer, called **medium access control (MAC)**. The separation is done for the following reasons:

- The logic required to manage access to a shared-access medium is not found in traditional layer 2 data link control.
- For the same LLC, several MAC options may be provided.

Figure 11.4 illustrates the relationship between the levels of the architecture (compare Figure 2.5). Higher-level data are passed down to LLC, which appends control information as a header, creating an *LLC protocol data unit (PDU)*. This control information is used in the operation of the LLC protocol. The entire LLC PDU is then passed down to the MAC layer, which appends control information at the front and back of the packet, forming a *MAC frame*. Again, the control information in the frame is needed for the operation of the MAC protocol. For context,

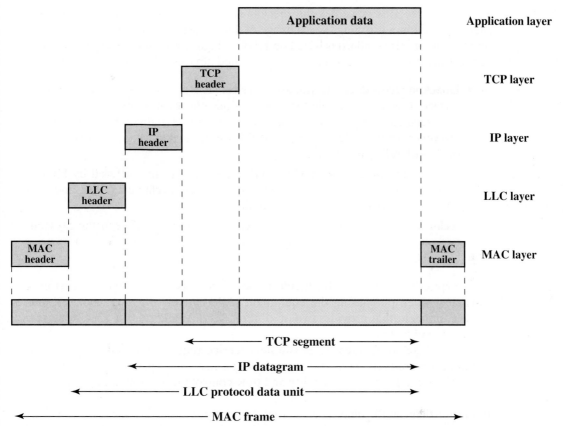

Figure 11.4   LAN Protocols in Context

the figure also shows the use of TCP/IP and an application layer above the LAN protocols.

Logical Link Control

The LLC layer for LANs is similar in many respects to other link layers in common use. Like all link layers, LLC is concerned with the transmission of a link-level PDU between two stations, without the necessity of an intermediate switching node. LLC has two characteristics not shared by most other link control protocols:

1. It must support the multiaccess, shared-medium nature of the link (this differs from a multidrop line in that there is no primary node).
2. It is relieved of some details of link access by the MAC layer.

Addressing in LLC involves specifying the source and destination LLC users. Typically, a user is a higher-layer protocol or a network management function in the station. These LLC user addresses are referred to as service access points (SAPs), in keeping with OSI terminology for the user of a protocol layer.

We look first at the services that LLC provides to a higher-level user, and then at the LLC protocol.

LLC SERVICES   LLC specifies the mechanisms for addressing stations across the medium and for controlling the exchange of data between two users. The operation and format of this standard is based on HDLC (high-level data link control). Three services are provided as alternatives for attached devices using LLC:

- **Unacknowledged connectionless service:** This service is a datagram-style service. It is a very simple service that does not involve any of the flow- and error-control mechanisms. Thus, the delivery of data is not guaranteed. However, in most devices, there will be some higher layer of software that deals with reliability issues.
- **Connection-mode service:** This service is similar to that offered by HDLC. A logical connection is set up between two users exchanging data, and flow control and error control are provided.
- **Acknowledged connectionless service:** This is a cross between the previous two services. It provides that datagrams are to be acknowledged, but no prior logical connection is set up.

Typically, a vendor will provide these services as options that the customer can select when purchasing the equipment. Alternatively, the customer can purchase equipment that provides two or all three services and select a specific service based on application.

The **unacknowledged connectionless service** requires minimum logic and is useful in two contexts. First, it will often be the case that higher layers of software will provide the necessary reliability and flow-control mechanism, and it is efficient to avoid duplicating them. For example, TCP could provide the mechanisms needed to ensure that data is delivered reliably. Second, there are instances in which the overhead of connection establishment and maintenance is unjustified or even counterproductive (e.g., data collection activities that involve the periodic sampling of data sources, such as sensors and automatic self-test reports from security equipment or network components). In a monitoring application, the loss of an occasional data unit would not cause distress, as the next report should arrive shortly. Thus, in most cases, the unacknowledged **connectionless service** is the preferred option.

The **connection-mode service** could be used in very simple devices, such as terminal controllers, that have little software operating above this level. In these cases, it would provide the flow control and reliability mechanisms normally implemented at higher layers of the communications software.

The **acknowledged connectionless service** is useful in several contexts. With the connection-mode service, the logical link control software must maintain some sort of table for each active connection, to keep track of the status of that connection. If the user needs guaranteed delivery but there are a large number of destinations for data, then the connection-mode service may be impractical because of the large number of tables required. An example is a process control or automated factory environment where a central site may need to communicate with a large number of processors and programmable controllers. Another use of this is the handling of important and time-critical alarm or emergency control signals in a factory. Because of their importance, an acknowledgment is needed so that the sender can be assured that the signal got through. Because of the urgency of the signal, the user might not want to take the time first to establish a logical connection and then send the data.

LLC PROTOCOL   The basic LLC protocol is modeled after HDLC and has similar functions and formats. The differences between the two protocols can be summarized as follows:

- LLC makes use of the asynchronous balanced mode of operation of HDLC, to support connection-mode LLC service; this is referred to as type 2 operation. The other HDLC modes are not employed.
- LLC supports an unacknowledged connectionless service using the unnumbered information PDU; this is known as type 1 operation.
- LLC supports an acknowledged connectionless service by using two new unnumbered PDUs; this is known as type 3 operation.
- LLC permits multiplexing by the use of LLC service access points (LSAPs).

All three LLC protocols employ the same PDU format (Figure 11.5), which consists of four fields. The DSAP (Destination Service Access Point) and SSAP (Source Service Access Point) fields each contain a 7-bit address, which specifies the destination and source users of LLC. One bit of the DSAP indicates whether the DSAP is an individual or group address. One bit of the SSAP indicates whether the PDU is a command or response PDU. The format of the LLC control field is identical to that of HDLC (Figure 7.7), using extended (7-bit) sequence numbers.

For **type 1 operation**, which supports the unacknowledged connectionless service, the unnumbered information (UI) PDU is used to transfer user data. There is no acknowledgment, flow control, or error control. However, there is error detection and discard at the MAC level.

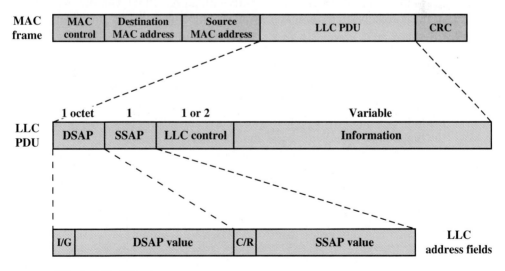

Figure 11.5   LLC PDU in a Generic MAC Frame Format

Two other PDUs are used to support management functions associated with all three types of operation. Both PDUs are used in the following fashion. An LLC entity may issue a command (C/R bit = 0) XID or TEST. The receiving LLC entity issues a corresponding XID or TEST in response. The XID PDU is used to exchange two types of information: types of operation supported and window size. The TEST PDU is used to conduct a loopback test of the transmission path between two LLC entities. Upon receipt of a TEST command PDU, the addressed LLC entity issues a TEST response PDU as soon as possible.

With **type 2 operation**, a data link connection is established between two LLC SAPs prior to data exchange. Connection establishment is attempted by the type 2 protocol in response to a request from a user. The LLC entity issues a SABME PDU[2] to request a logical connection with the other LLC entity. If the connection is accepted by the LLC user designated by the DSAP, then the destination LLC entity returns an unnumbered acknowledgment (UA) PDU. The connection is henceforth uniquely identified by the pair of user SAPs. If the destination LLC user rejects the connection request, its LLC entity returns a disconnected mode (DM) PDU.

Once the connection is established, data are exchanged using information PDUs, as in HDLC. The information PDUs include send and receive sequence numbers, for sequencing and flow control. The supervisory PDUs are used, as in HDLC, for flow control and error control. Either LLC entity can terminate a logical LLC connection by issuing a disconnect (DISC) PDU.

With **type 3 operation**, each transmitted PDU is acknowledged. A new (not found in HDLC) unnumbered PDU, the Acknowledged Connectionless (AC) Information PDU, is defined. User data are sent in AC command PDUs and must be acknowledged using an AC response PDU. To guard against lost PDUs, a 1-bit sequence number is used. The sender alternates the use of 0 and 1 in its AC command PDU, and the receiver responds with an AC PDU with the opposite number of the corresponding command. Only one PDU in each direction may be outstanding at any time.

Medium Access Control

All LANs and MANs consist of collections of devices that must share the network's transmission capacity. Some means of controlling access to the transmission medium is needed to provide for an orderly and efficient use of that capacity. This is the function of a medium access control (MAC) protocol.

The key parameters in any medium access control technique are where and how. *Where* refers to whether control is exercised in a centralized or distributed fashion. In a centralized scheme, a controller is designated that has the authority to grant access to the network. A station wishing to transmit must wait until it receives permission from the controller. In a decentralized network, the stations collectively perform a medium access control function to determine dynamically the order in

---

[2]This stands for Set Asynchronous Balanced Mode Extended. It is used in HDLC to choose ABM and to select extended sequence numbers of seven bits. Both ABM and 7-bit sequence numbers are mandatory in type 2 operation.

which stations transmit. A centralized scheme has certain advantages, including the following:

- It may afford greater control over access for providing such things as priorities, overrides, and guaranteed capacity.
- It enables the use of relatively simple access logic at each station.
- It avoids problems of distributed coordination among peer entities.

The principal disadvantages of centralized schemes are as follows:

- It creates a single point of failure; that is, there is a point in the network that, if it fails, causes the entire network to fail.
- It may act as a bottleneck, reducing performance.

The pros and cons of distributed schemes are mirror images of the points just made.

The second parameter, *how*, is constrained by the topology and is a trade-off among competing factors, including cost, performance, and complexity. In general, we can categorize access control techniques as being either synchronous or asynchronous. With synchronous techniques, a specific capacity is dedicated to a connection. This is the same approach used in circuit switching, frequency-division multiplexing (FDM), and synchronous time-division multiplexing (TDM). Such techniques are generally not optimal in LANs and MANs because the needs of the stations are unpredictable. It is preferable to be able to allocate capacity in an asynchronous (dynamic) fashion, more or less in response to immediate demand. The asynchronous approach can be further subdivided into three categories: round robin, reservation, and contention.

ROUND ROBIN With round robin, each station in turn is given the opportunity to transmit. During that opportunity, the station may decline to transmit or may transmit subject to a specified upper bound, usually expressed as a maximum amount of data transmitted or time for this opportunity. In any case, the station, when it is finished, relinquishes its turn, and the right to transmit passes to the next station in logical sequence. Control of sequence may be centralized or distributed. Polling is an example of a centralized technique.

When many stations have data to transmit over an extended period of time, round-robin techniques can be very efficient. If only a few stations have data to transmit over an extended period of time, then there is a considerable overhead in passing the turn from station to station, because most of the stations will not transmit but simply pass their turns. Under such circumstances other techniques may be preferable, largely depending on whether the data traffic has a stream or bursty characteristic. Stream traffic is characterized by lengthy and fairly continuous transmissions; examples are voice communication, telemetry, and bulk file transfer. Bursty traffic is characterized by short, sporadic transmissions; interactive terminal-host traffic fits this description.

RESERVATION For stream traffic, reservation techniques are well suited. In general, for these techniques, time on the medium is divided into slots, much as with synchronous TDM. A station wishing to transmit reserves future slots for an extended or even an indefinite period. Again, reservations may be made in a centralized or distributed fashion.

CONTENTION   For bursty traffic, contention techniques are usually appropriate. With these techniques, no control is exercised to determine whose turn it is; all stations contend for time in a way that can be, as we shall see, rather rough and tumble. These techniques are of necessity distributed in nature. Their principal advantage is that they are simple to implement and, under light-to-moderate load, efficient. For some of these techniques, however, performance tends to collapse under heavy load.

Although both centralized and distributed reservation techniques have been implemented in some LAN products, round-robin and contention techniques are the most common.

MAC FRAME FORMAT   The MAC layer receives a block of data from the LLC layer and is responsible for performing functions related to medium access and for transmitting the data. As with other protocol layers, MAC implements these functions making use of a protocol data unit at its layer. In this case, the PDU is referred to as a MAC frame.

The exact format of the MAC frame differs somewhat for the various MAC protocols in use. In general, all of the MAC frames have a format similar to that of Figure 11.5. The fields of this frame are as follows:

- **MAC Control:** This field contains any protocol control information needed for the functioning of the MAC protocol. For example, a priority level could be indicated here.
- **Destination MAC Address:** The destination physical attachment point on the LAN for this frame.
- **Source MAC Address:** The source physical attachment point on the LAN for this frame.
- **LLC:** The LLC data from the next higher layer.
- **CRC:** The Cyclic Redundancy Check field (also known as the Frame Check Sequence, FCS, field). This is an error-detecting code, as we have seen in HDLC and other data link control protocols (Chapter 7).

In most data link control protocols, the data link protocol entity is responsible not only for detecting errors using the CRC, but for recovering from those errors by retransmitting damaged frames. In the LAN protocol architecture, these two functions are split between the MAC and LLC layers. The MAC layer is responsible for detecting errors and discarding any frames that are in error. The LLC layer optionally keeps track of which frames have been successfully received and retransmits unsuccessful frames.

11.3 BRIDGES

In virtually all cases, there is a need to expand beyond the confines of a single LAN, to provide interconnection to other LANs and to wide area networks. Two general approaches are used for this purpose: bridges and routers. The **bridge** is the simpler of the two devices and provides a means of interconnecting similar LANs. The router is a more general-purpose device, capable of interconnecting a variety of LANs and WANs. We explore bridges in this section and look at routers in Part Five.

The bridge is designed for use between local area networks that use identical protocols for the physical and link layers (e.g., all conforming to IEEE 802.3). Because the devices all use the same protocols, the amount of processing required at the bridge is minimal. More sophisticated bridges are capable of mapping from one MAC format to another (e.g., to interconnect an Ethernet and a token ring LAN).

Because the bridge is used in a situation in which all the LANs have the same characteristics, the reader may ask, why not simply have one large LAN? Depending on circumstance, there are several reasons for the use of multiple LANs connected by bridges:

- **Reliability:** The danger in connecting all data processing devices in an organization to one network is that a fault on the network may disable communication for all devices. By using bridges, the network can be partitioned into self-contained units.

- **Performance:** In general, performance on a LAN declines with an increase in the number of devices or the length of the wire. A number of smaller LANs will often give improved performance if devices can be clustered so that intranetwork traffic significantly exceeds internetwork traffic.

- **Security:** The establishment of multiple LANs may improve security of communications. It is desirable to keep different types of traffic (e.g., accounting, personnel, strategic planning) that have different security needs on physically separate media. At the same time, the different types of users with different levels of security need to communicate through controlled and monitored mechanisms.

- **Geography:** Clearly, two separate LANs are needed to support devices clustered in two geographically distant locations. Even in the case of two buildings separated by a highway, it may be far easier to use a microwave bridge link than to attempt to string coaxial cable between the two buildings.

Functions of a Bridge

EXAMPLE 11.2 Figure 11.6 illustrates the action of a bridge connecting two LANs, A and B, using the same MAC protocol. In this example, a single bridge attaches to both LANs; frequently, the bridge function is performed by two "half-bridges," one on each LAN. The functions of the bridge are few and simple:

- Read all frames transmitted on A and accept those addressed to any station on B.

- Using the medium access control protocol for B, retransmit each frame on B.

- Do the same for B-to-A traffic.

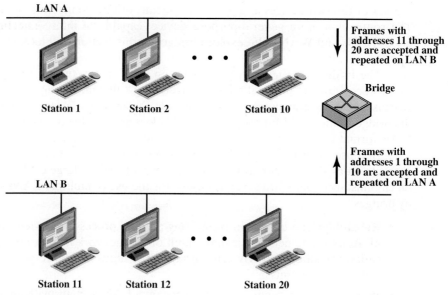

Figure 11.6   Bridge Operation

Several design aspects of a bridge are worth highlighting:

- The bridge makes no modification to the content or format of the frames it receives, nor does it encapsulate them with an additional header. Each frame to be transferred is simply copied from one LAN and repeated with exactly the same bit pattern on the other LAN. Because the two LANs use the same LAN protocols, it is permissible to do this.

- The bridge should contain enough buffer space to meet peak demands. Over a short period of time, frames may arrive faster than they can be retransmitted.

- The bridge must contain addressing and routing intelligence. At a minimum, the bridge must know which addresses are on each network to know which frames to pass. Further, there may be more than two LANs interconnected by a number of bridges. In that case, a frame may have to be routed through several bridges in its journey from source to destination.

- A bridge may connect more than two LANs.

In summary, the bridge provides an extension to the LAN that requires no modification to the communications software in the stations attached to the LANs. It appears to all stations on the two (or more) LANs that there is a single LAN on which each station has a unique address. The station uses that unique address and need not explicitly discriminate between stations on the same LAN and stations on other LANs; the bridge takes care of that.

Bridge Protocol Architecture

The IEEE 802.1D specification defines the protocol architecture for MAC bridges. Within the 802 architecture, the endpoint or station address is designated at the

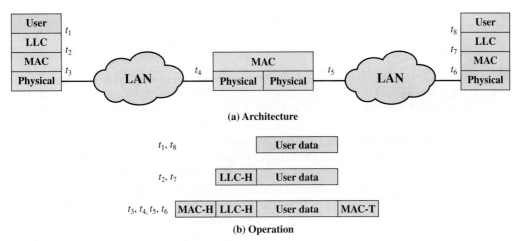

Figure 11.7 Connection of Two LANs by a Bridge

MAC level. Thus, it is at the MAC level that a bridge can function. Figure 11.7 shows the simplest case, which consists of two LANs connected by a single bridge. The LANs employ the same MAC and LLC protocols. The bridge operates as previously described. A MAC frame whose destination is not on the immediate LAN is captured by the bridge, buffered briefly, and then transmitted on the other LAN. As far as the LLC layer is concerned, there is a dialogue between peer LLC entities in the two endpoint stations. The bridge need not contain an LLC layer because it is merely serving to relay the MAC frames.

Figure 11.7b indicates the way in which data are encapsulated using a bridge. Data are provided by some user to LLC. The LLC entity appends a header and passes the resulting data unit to the MAC entity, which appends a header and a trailer to form a MAC frame. On the basis of the destination MAC address in the frame, it is captured by the bridge. The bridge does not strip off the MAC fields; its function is to relay the MAC frame intact to the destination LAN. Thus, the frame is deposited on the destination LAN and captured by the destination station.

The concept of a MAC relay bridge is not limited to the use of a single bridge to connect two nearby LANs. If the LANs are some distance apart, then they can be connected by two bridges that are in turn connected by a communications facility. The intervening communications facility can be a network, such as a wide area packet-switching network, or a point-to-point link. In such cases, when a bridge captures a MAC frame, it must encapsulate the frame in the appropriate packaging and transmit it over the communications facility to a target bridge. The target bridge strips off these extra fields and transmits the original, unmodified MAC frame to the destination station.

Fixed Routing

There is a trend within many organizations to an increasing number of LANs interconnected by bridges. As the number of LANs grows, it becomes important to provide alternate paths between LANs via bridges for load balancing and reconfiguration in response to failure. Thus, many organizations will find that static, preconfigured routing tables are inadequate and that some sort of dynamic routing is needed.

EXAMPLE 11.3 Consider the configuration of Figure 11.8. Suppose that station 1 transmits a frame on LAN A intended for station 6. The frame will be read by bridges 101, 102, and 107. For each bridge, the addressed station is not on a LAN to which the bridge is attached. Therefore, each bridge must make a decision whether or not to retransmit the frame on its other LAN, in order to move it closer to its intended destination. In this case, bridge 102 should repeat the frame on LAN C, whereas bridges 101 and 107 should refrain from retransmitting the frame. Once the frame has been transmitted on LAN C, it will be picked up by both bridges 105 and 106. Again, each must decide whether or not to forward the frame. In this case, bridge 105 should retransmit the frame on LAN F, where it will be received by the destination, station 6.

Thus we see that, in the general case, the bridge must be equipped with a routing capability. When a bridge receives a frame, it must decide whether or not to forward it. If the bridge is attached to two or more networks, then it must decide whether or not to forward the frame and, if so, on which LAN the frame should be transmitted.

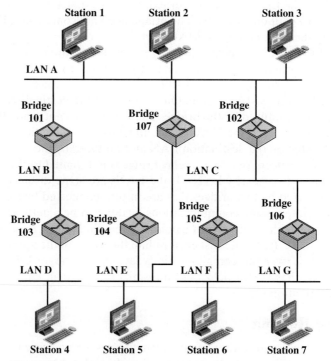

Figure 11.8   Configuration of Bridges and LANs, with Alternate Routes

The routing decision may not always be a simple one. Figure 11.8 also shows that there are two routes between LAN A and LAN E. Such redundancy provides for higher overall Internet availability and creates the possibility for load balancing. In this case, if station 1 transmits a frame on LAN A intended for station 5 on LAN E, then either bridge 101 or bridge 107 could forward the frame. It would appear preferable for bridge 107 to forward the frame, since it will involve only one hop, whereas if the frame travels through bridge 101, it must suffer two hops. Another consideration is that there may be changes in the configuration. For example, bridge 107 may fail, in which case subsequent frames from station 1 to station 5 should go through bridge 101. So we can say that the routing capability must take into account the topology of the internet configuration and may need to be dynamically altered.

A variety of routing strategies have been proposed and implemented in recent years. The simplest and most common strategy is **fixed routing**. This strategy is suitable for small internets and for internets that are relatively stable. In addition, two groups within the IEEE 802 committee have developed specifications for routing strategies. The IEEE 802.1 group has issued a standard for routing based on the use of a **spanning tree** algorithm. The token ring committee, IEEE 802.5, has issued its own specification, referred to as **source routing**. In the remainder of this section, we look at fixed routing and the spanning tree algorithm, which is the most commonly used bridge routing algorithm.

For fixed routing, a route is selected for each source–destination pair of LANs in the configuration. If alternate routes are available between two LANs, then typically the route with the least number of hops is selected. The routes are fixed, or at least only change when there is a change in the topology of the internet.

The strategy for developing a fixed routing configuration for bridges is similar to that employed in a packet-switching network. A central routing matrix is created, to be stored perhaps at a network control center. The matrix shows, for each source–destination pair of LANs, the identity of the first bridge on the route.

EXAMPLE 11.4 The route from LAN E to LAN F begins by going through bridge 107 to LAN A. Again consulting the matrix, the route from LAN A to LAN F goes through bridge 102 to LAN C. Finally, the route from LAN C to LAN F is directly through bridge 105. Thus, the complete route from LAN E to LAN F is bridge 107, LAN A, bridge 102, and LAN C, bridge 105.

From this overall matrix, routing tables can be developed and stored at each bridge. Each bridge needs one table for each LAN to which it attaches. The information for each table is derived from a single row of the matrix. Thus, bridge 105 has two tables, one for frames arriving from LAN C and one for frames arriving from LAN F. The table shows, for each possible destination MAC address, the identity of the LAN to which the bridge should forward the frame.

Once the directories have been established, routing is a simple matter. A bridge copies each incoming frame on each of its LANs. If the destination MAC address corresponds to an entry in its routing table, the frame is retransmitted on the appropriate LAN.

The fixed routing strategy is widely used in commercially available products. It requires that a network manager manually load the data into the routing tables. It has the advantage of simplicity and minimal processing requirements. However, in a complex internet, in which bridges may be dynamically added and in which failures must be allowed for, this strategy is too limited.

The Spanning Tree Approach

The spanning tree approach is a mechanism in which bridges automatically develop a routing table and update that table in response to changing topology. The algorithm consists of three mechanisms: frame forwarding, address learning, and loop resolution.

FRAME FORWARDING   In this scheme, a bridge maintains a **forwarding database** for each port attached to a LAN. The database indicates the station addresses for which frames should be forwarded through that port. We can interpret this in the following fashion. For each port, a list of stations is maintained. A station is on the list if it is on the "same side" of the bridge as the port. For example, for bridge 102 of Figure 11.8, stations on LANs C, F, and G are on the same side of the bridge as the LAN C port, and stations on LANs A, B, D, and E are on the same side of the bridge as the LAN A port. When a frame is received on any port, the bridge must decide whether that frame is to be forwarded through the bridge and out through one of the bridge's other ports. Suppose that a bridge receives a MAC frame on port x. The following rules are applied:

1. Search the forwarding database to determine if the MAC address is listed for any port except port x.

2. If the destination MAC address is not found, forward frame out all ports except the one from which it was received. This is part of the learning process described subsequently.

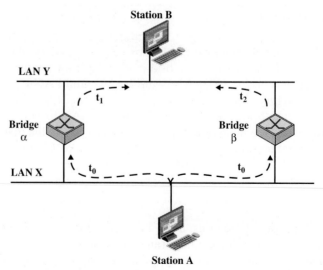

Figure 11.9   Loop of Bridges

3. If the destination address is in the forwarding database for some port y, then determine whether port y is in a blocking or forwarding state. For reasons explained later, a port may sometimes be blocked, which prevents it from receiving or transmitting frames.

4. If port y is not blocked, transmit the frame through port y onto the LAN to which that port attaches.

ADDRESS LEARNING   The preceding scheme assumes that the bridge is already equipped with a forwarding database that indicates the direction, from the bridge, of each destination station. This information can be preloaded into the bridge, as in fixed routing. However, an effective automatic mechanism for learning the direction of each station is desirable. A simple scheme for acquiring this information is based on the use of the Source Address field in each MAC frame.

The strategy is this. When a frame arrives on a particular port, it clearly has come from the direction of the incoming LAN. The Source Address field of the frame indicates the source station. Thus, a bridge can update its forwarding database for that port on the basis of the Source Address field of each incoming frame. To allow for changes in topology, each element in the database is equipped with a timer. When a new element is added to the database, its timer is set. If the timer expires, then the element is eliminated from the database, since the corresponding direction information may no longer be valid. Each time a frame is received, its source address is checked against the database. If the element is already in the database, the entry is updated (the direction may have changed) and the timer is reset. If the element is not in the database, a new entry is created, with its own timer.

SPANNING TREE ALGORITHM   The address learning mechanism described previously is effective if the topology of the internet is a tree, that is, if there are no alternate routes in the network. The existence of alternate routes means that there is a closed loop. For example in Figure 11.8, the following is a closed loop: LAN A, bridge 101, LAN B, bridge 104, LAN E, bridge 107, LAN A.

To see the problem created by a closed loop, consider Figure 11.9. At time t_0, station A transmits a frame addressed to station B. The frame is captured by both bridges. Each bridge updates its database to indicate that station A is in the direction of LAN X, and retransmits the frame on LAN Y. Say that bridge α retransmits at time t_1 and bridge β a short time later t_2. Thus B will receive two copies of the frame. Furthermore, each bridge will receive the other's transmission on LAN Y. Note that each transmission is a frame with a source address of A and a destination address of B. Thus each bridge will update its database to indicate that station A is in the direction of LAN Y. Neither bridge is now capable of forwarding a frame addressed to station A.

To overcome this problem, a simple result from graph theory is used: For any connected graph, consisting of nodes and edges connecting pairs of nodes, there is a spanning tree of edges that maintains the connectivity of the graph but contains no closed loops. In terms of internets, each LAN corresponds to a graph node, and each bridge corresponds to a graph edge. Thus, in Figure 11.8, the removal of one (and only one) of bridges 107, 101, and 104 results in a spanning tree. What is desired is to develop a simple algorithm by which the bridges of the internet can exchange sufficient information to automatically (without user intervention) derive a spanning tree. The algorithm must be dynamic. That is, when a topology change occurs, the bridges must be able to discover this fact and automatically derive a new spanning tree.

The spanning tree algorithm developed by IEEE 802.1, as the name suggests, is able to develop such a spanning tree. All that is required is that each bridge be assigned a unique identifier and that costs be assigned to each bridge port. In the absence of any special considerations, all costs could be set equal; this produces a minimum-hop tree. The algorithm involves a brief exchange of messages among all of the bridges to discover the minimum-cost spanning tree. Whenever there is a change in topology, the bridges automatically recalculate the spanning tree.

For more information on the spanning tree algorithm, see Appendix J.

11.4 HUBS AND SWITCHES

In recent years, there has been a proliferation of types of devices for interconnecting LANs that goes beyond the bridges discussed in Section 11.3 and the routers discussed in Part Five. These devices can conveniently be grouped into the categories of hubs and switches.

Hubs

Earlier, we used the term *hub* in reference to a star-topology LAN. The hub is the active central element of the star layout. Each station is connected to the hub by two lines (transmit and receive). The hub acts as a repeater: When a single station transmits, the hub repeats the signal on the outgoing line to each station. Ordinarily, the line consists of two unshielded twisted pairs. Because of the high data rate and the poor transmission qualities of unshielded twisted pair, the length of a line is limited to about 100 m. As an alternative, an optical fiber link may be used. In this case, the maximum length is about 500 m.

Note that although this scheme is physically a star, it is logically a bus: A transmission from any one station is received by all other stations, and if two stations transmit at the same time there will be a collision.

Multiple levels of hubs can be cascaded in a hierarchical configuration. Figure 11.10 illustrates a two-level configuration. There is one **header hub (HHUB)** and one or more **intermediate hubs (IHUB)**. Each hub may have a mixture of stations and other hubs attached to it from below. This layout fits well with building wiring practices. Typically, there is a wiring closet on each floor of an office building, and a hub can be placed in each one. Each hub could service the stations on its floor.

Layer 2 Switches

In recent years, a new device, the **layer 2 switch**, has replaced the hub in popularity, particularly for high-speed LANs. The layer 2 **switch** is also sometimes referred to as a switching hub.

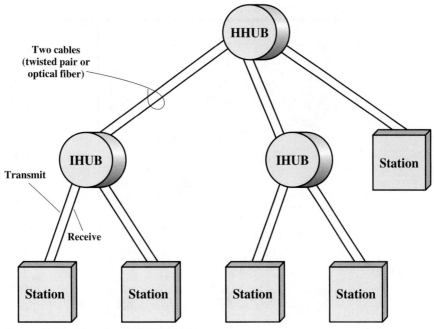

**Two cables
(twisted pair or
optical fiber)**

Transmit

Receive

Figure 11.10   Two-Level Star Topology

To clarify the distinction between hubs and switches, Figure 11.11a shows a typical bus layout of a traditional 10-Mbps LAN. A bus is installed that is laid out so that all the devices to be attached are in reasonable proximity to a point on the bus. In the figure, station B is transmitting. This transmission goes from B, across the lead from B to the bus, along the bus in both directions, and along the access lines of each of the other attached stations. In this configuration, all the stations must share the total capacity of the bus, which is 10 Mbps.

A hub, often in a building wiring closet, uses a star wiring arrangement to attach stations to the hub. In this arrangement, a transmission from any one station is received by the hub and retransmitted on all of the outgoing lines. Therefore, to avoid collision, only one station can transmit at a time. Again, the total capacity of the LAN is 10 Mbps. The hub has several advantages over the simple bus arrangement. It exploits standard building wiring practices in the layout of cable. In addition, the hub can be configured to recognize a malfunctioning station that is jamming the network and to cut that station out of the network. Figure 11.11b illustrates the operation of a hub. Here again, station B is transmitting. This transmission goes from B, across the transmit line from B to the hub, and from the hub along the receive lines of each of the other attached stations.

We can achieve greater performance with a layer 2 switch. In this case, the central hub acts as a switch, much as a packet switch or circuit switch. With a layer 2 switch, an incoming frame from a particular station is switched to the appropriate output line to be delivered to the intended destination. At the same time, other unused lines can be used for switching other traffic. Figure 11.11c shows an example in which B is transmitting a frame to A and at the same time C is transmitting

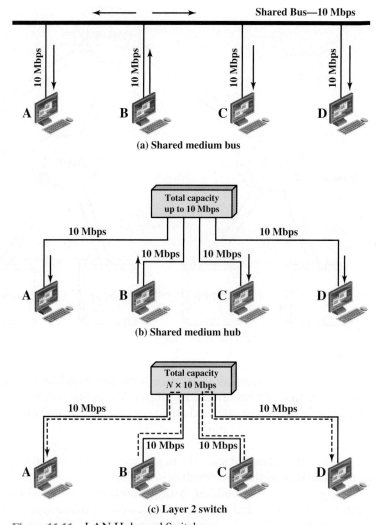

Figure 11.11   LAN Hubs and Switches

a frame to D. So, in this example, the current throughput on the LAN is 20 Mbps, although each individual device is limited to 10 Mbps. The layer 2 switch has several attractive features:

1. No change is required to the software or hardware of the attached devices to convert a bus LAN or a hub LAN to a switched LAN. In the case of an Ethernet LAN, each attached device continues to use the Ethernet medium access control protocol to access the LAN. From the point of view of the attached devices, nothing has changed in the access logic.

2. Each attached device has a dedicated capacity equal to that of the entire original LAN, assuming that the layer 2 switch has sufficient capacity to keep up with all attached devices. For example, in Figure 11.11c, if the layer 2 switch

can sustain a throughput of 20 Mbps, each attached device appears to have a dedicated capacity for either input or output of 10 Mbps.

3. The layer 2 switch scales easily. Additional devices can be attached to the layer 2 switch by increasing the capacity of the layer 2 switch correspondingly.

Two types of layer 2 switches are available as commercial products:

- **Store-and-forward switch:** The layer 2 switch accepts a frame on an input line, buffers it briefly, and then routes it to the appropriate output line.
- **Cut-through switch:** The layer 2 switch takes advantage of the fact that the destination address appears at the beginning of the MAC frame. The layer 2 switch begins repeating the incoming frame onto the appropriate output line as soon as the layer 2 switch recognizes the destination address.

The cut-through switch yields the highest possible throughput but at some risk of propagating bad frames, because the switch is not able to check the CRC prior to retransmission. The store-and-forward switch involves a delay between sender and receiver but boosts the overall integrity of the network.

A layer 2 switch can be viewed as a full-duplex version of the hub. It can also incorporate logic that allows it to function as a multiport bridge. The following are differences between layer 2 switches and bridges:

- Bridge frame handling is done in software. A layer 2 switch performs the address recognition and frame forwarding functions in hardware.
- A bridge can typically only analyze and forward one frame at a time, whereas a layer 2 switch has multiple parallel data paths and can handle multiple frames at a time.
- A bridge uses store-and-forward operation. With a layer 2 switch, it is possible to have cut-through instead of store-and-forward operation.

Because a layer 2 switch has higher performance and can incorporate the functions of a bridge, the bridge has suffered commercially. New installations typically include layer 2 switches with bridge functionality rather than bridges.

11.5 VIRTUAL LANS

Figure 11.12 shows a relatively common type of hierarchical LAN configuration. In this example, the devices on the LAN are organized into four groups, each served by a LAN switch. The three lower groups might correspond to different departments, which are physically separated, and the upper group could correspond to a centralized server farm that is used by all the departments.

Let us consider the transmission of a single MAC frame from workstation X. Suppose the destination MAC address in the frame (see Figure 11.5) is workstation Y. This frame is transmitted from X to the local switch, which then directs the frame along the link to Y. If X transmits a frame addressed to Z or W, then its local switch routes the MAC frame through the appropriate switches to the intended

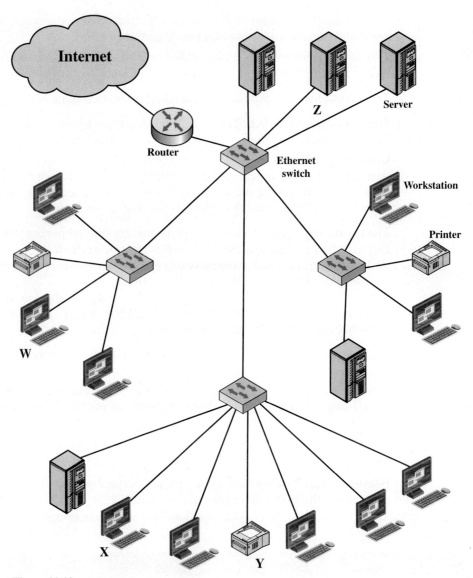

Figure 11.12 A LAN Configuration

destination. All these are examples of **unicast addressing**, in which the destination address in the MAC frame designates a unique destination. A MAC frame may also contain a **broadcast address**, in which case the destination MAC address indicates that all devices on the LAN should receive a copy of the frame. Thus, if X transmits a frame with a broadcast destination address, all of the devices on all of the switches in Figure 11.12 receive a copy of the frame. The total collection of devices that receive broadcast frames from each other is referred to as a **broadcast domain**.

In many situations, a broadcast frame is used for a purpose, such as network management or the transmission of some type of alert, that has a relatively local significance. Thus, in Figure 11.12, if a broadcast frame has information that is only useful to a particular department, then transmission capacity is wasted on the other portions of the LAN and on the other switches.

One simple approach to improving efficiency is to physically partition the LAN into separate broadcast domains, as shown in Figure 11.13. We now have four separate LANs connected by a router. In this case, an IP packet from X intended for Z is handled as follows. The IP layer at X determines that the next hop to the destination is via router V. This information is handed down to X's MAC layer, which prepares a MAC frame with a destination MAC address of router V. When V receives the frame, it strips off the MAC header, determines the destination, and

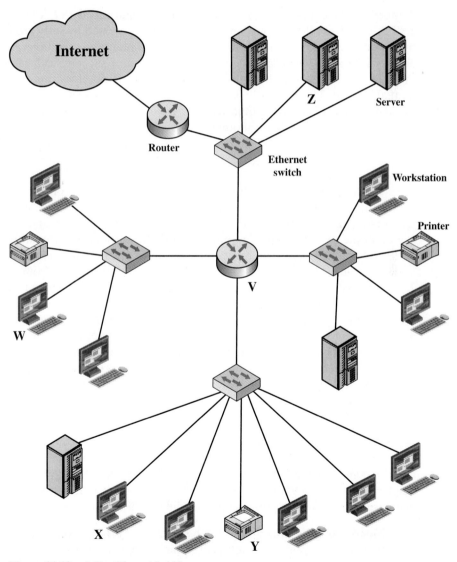

Figure 11.13 A Partitioned LAN

encapsulates the IP packet in a MAC frame with a destination MAC address of Z. This frame is then sent to the appropriate Ethernet switch for delivery.

The drawback to this approach is that the traffic pattern may not correspond to the physical distribution of devices. For example, some departmental workstations may generate a lot of traffic with one of the central servers. Further, as the networks expand, more routers are needed to separate users into broadcast domains and provide connectivity among broadcast domains. Routers introduce more latency than switches because the router must process more of the packet to determine destinations and route the data to the appropriate end node.

The Use of Virtual LANs

A more effective alternative is the creation of **virtual LANs (VLANs)**. In essence, a VLAN is a logical subgroup within a LAN that is created by software rather than by physically moving and separating devices. It combines user stations and network devices into a single broadcast domain regardless of the physical LAN segment they are attached to and allows traffic to flow more efficiently within populations of mutual interest. The VLAN logic is implemented in LAN switches and functions at the MAC layer. Because the objective is to isolate traffic within the VLAN, in order to link from one VLAN to another, a router is required. Routers can be implemented as separate devices, so that traffic from one VLAN to another is directed to a router, or the router logic can be implemented as part of the LAN switch, as shown in Figure 11.14.

VLANs provide the ability for any organization to be physically dispersed throughout the company while maintaining its group identity. For example, accounting personnel can be located on the shop floor, in the research and development center, in the cash disbursement office, and in the corporate offices while all members reside on the same virtual network, sharing traffic only with each other.

In Figure 11.14, five VLANs are defined. A transmission from workstation X to server Z is within the same VLAN, so it is efficiently switched at the MAC level. A broadcast MAC frame from X is transmitted to all devices in all portions of the same VLAN. But a transmission from X to printer Y goes from one VLAN to another. Accordingly, router logic at the IP level is required to move the IP packet from X to Y. In Figure 11.14, that logic is integrated into the switch, so that the switch determines whether or not the incoming MAC frame is destined for another device on the same VLAN. If not, the switch routes the enclosed IP packet at the IP level.

Defining VLANs

A VLAN is a broadcast domain consisting of a group of end stations, perhaps on multiple physical LAN segments, that are not constrained by their physical location and can communicate as if they were on a common LAN. Some means is therefore needed for defining VLAN membership. A number of different approaches have been used for defining membership, including the following:

- **Membership by port group:** Each switch in the LAN configuration contains two types of ports: a trunk port, which connects two switches, and an end port, which connects the switch to an end system. A VLAN can be defined by

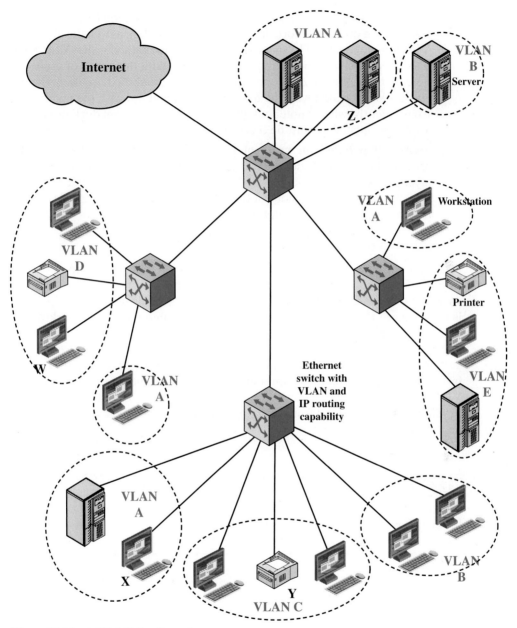

Figure 11.14 A VLAN Configuration

assigning each end port to a specific VLAN. This approach has the advantage that it is relatively easy to configure. The principle disadvantage is that the network manager must reconfigure VLAN membership when an end system moves from one port to another.

- **Membership by MAC address:** Since MAC-layer addresses are hardwired into the workstation's network interface card (NIC), VLANs based on MAC addresses enable network managers to move a workstation to a different physical location on the network and have that workstation automatically retain its VLAN membership. The main problem with this method is that VLAN membership must be assigned initially. In networks with thousands of users, this is no easy task. Also, in environments where notebook PCs are used, the MAC address is associated with the docking station and not with the notebook PC. Consequently, when a notebook PC is moved to a different docking station, its VLAN membership must be reconfigured.

- **Membership based on protocol information:** VLAN membership can be assigned based on IP address, transport protocol information, or even higher-layer protocol information. This is a quite flexible approach, but it does require switches to examine portions of the MAC frame above the MAC layer, which may have a performance impact.

Communicating VLAN Membership

Switches must have a way of understanding VLAN membership (i.e., which stations belong to which VLAN) when network traffic arrives from other switches; otherwise, VLANs would be limited to a single switch. One possibility is to configure the information manually or with some type of network management signaling protocol, so that switches can associate incoming frames with the appropriate VLAN.

A more common approach is frame tagging, in which a header is typically inserted into each frame on interswitch trunks to uniquely identify to which VLAN a particular MAC-layer frame belongs. The IEEE 802 committee has developed a standard for frame tagging, IEEE 802.1Q, which we examine in the next chapter.

11.6 RECOMMENDED READING AND ANIMATIONS

[RAJA97] is a good summary of VLAN principles.

RAJA97 Rajaravivarma, V. "Virtual Local Area Network Technology and Applications." *Proceedings, 29th Southeastern Symposium on System Theory*, 1997.

Animations

Animations that illustrate LAN concepts are available at the Premium Web site. The reader is encouraged to view these animations to reinforce concepts from this chapter.

11.7 KEY TERMS, REVIEW QUESTIONS, AND PROBLEMS

Key Terms

bridge	hub	spanning tree
broadcast address	intermediate hubs (IHUB)	star topology
broadcast domain	layer 2 switch	switch
bus topology	local area network (LAN)	type 1 operation
connectionless service	logical link control (LLC)	type 2 operation
connection-mode service	medium access control	type 3 operation
fixed routing	(MAC)	unicast addressing
forwarding database	physical layer	virtual LAN (VLAN)
header hub (HHUB)	source routing	

Review Questions

11.1 What is network topology?

11.2 List four common LAN topologies and briefly describe their methods of operation.

11.3 What is the purpose of the IEEE 802 committee?

11.4 Why are there multiple LAN standards?

11.5 List and briefly define the services provided by LLC.

11.6 List and briefly define the types of operation provided by the LLC protocol.

11.7 List some basic functions performed at the MAC layer.

11.8 What functions are performed by a bridge?

11.9 What is a spanning tree?

11.10 What is the difference between a hub and a layer 2 switch?

11.11 What is the difference between a store-and-forward switch and a cut-through switch?

Problems

11.1 Instead of LLC, could HDLC be used as a data link control protocol for a LAN? If not, what is lacking?

11.2 An asynchronous device, such as a teletype, transmits characters one at a time with unpredictable delays between characters. What problems, if any, do you foresee if such a device is connected to a LAN and allowed to transmit at will (subject to gaining access to the medium)? How might such problems be resolved?

11.3 Consider the transfer of a file containing one million 8-bit characters from one station to another. What is the total elapsed time and effective throughput for the following cases:

    a. A circuit-switched, star-topology local network. Call setup time is negligible and the data rate on the medium is 64 kbps.

    b. A bus topology local network with two stations a distance D apart, a data rate of B bps, and a frame size of P with 80 bits of overhead per frame. Each frame is acknowledged with an 88-bit frame before the next is sent. The propagation speed on the bus is 200 m/μs. Solve for:

1. $D = 1$ km, $B = 1$ Mbps, $P = 256$ bits
2. $D = 1$ km, $B = 10$ Mbps, $P = 256$ bits
3. $D = 10$ km, $B = 1$ Mbps, $P = 256$ bits
4. $D = 1$ km, $B = 50$ Mbps, $P = 10,000$ bits

11.4 A baseband bus has 5 stations equally spaced at 500 m from one another. The data rate of the bus is 50 Mbps and the propagation speed is 10^5 km/s.

    a. What will be the total time taken to send a packet of 2 KB from any station to its adjacent station, measured from the beginning of transmission to the end of reception?

    b. What will be the total time taken to send the packet from a station at one end to the station at the other end, measured from the beginning of transmission to the end of reception, if the delay at each intermediate node is 10^{-5} seconds?

    c. If two adjacent stations begin to transmit at exactly the same time, when will their packets interfere with each other?

11.5 Repeat Problem 15.4 for a data rate of 100 Mbps.

11.6 Create a LAN system with 4 stations, each connected to one of 4 LANs that are connected by 3 bridges in the following manner:
- Bridge 51 connects LAN1 and LAN2
- Bridge 52 connects LAN2, LAN3, and LAN4
- Bridge 53 connects LAN1 and LAN3

11.7 Six 50-Mbps lines are connected by a star topology with a hub. What is its maximum throughput? What will be its maximum throughput if a switch replaces the hub?

11.8 Develop a spanning tree for the configuration of Figure 11.15.

11.9 A station on a LAN that includes an attached bridge sends out a frame to a device that is not present on any of the segments of the total network. What does the bridge do with this frame?

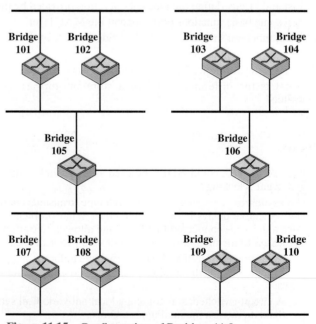

Figure 11.15 Configuration of Problem 11.8

CHAPTER 12

ETHERNET

LEARNING OBJECTIVES

After studying this chapter, you should be able to:

♦ Present an overview of the IEEE 802.3 MAC standard.

♦ Understand the key differences among 1-Gbps, 10-Gbps, and 100-Gbps Ethernet.

♦ Present an overview of the IEEE 802.1Q VLAN standard.

♦ Understand the Ethernet digital signal encoding schemes.

♦ Explain scrambling.

The overwhelmingly dominant scheme for wired local area networks is based on the IEEE 802.3 standard, and is commonly referred to as Ethernet. Ethernet began as an experimental bus-based 3-Mbps system. The first commercially available Ethernet and the first version of IEEE 802.3 were bus-based systems operating at 10 Mbps. As technology has advanced, Ethernet has moved from bus-based to switch-based, and the data rate has periodically increased by an order of magnitude. Currently, Ethernet systems are available at speeds up to 100 Gbps. Figure 12.1, based on data from [IEEE12], shows that systems running at 1 Gbps and above dominate in data centers, and that demand is rapidly evolving toward 100-Gbps systems.

We begin this chapter with an overview of the 10-Mbps system and the basic medium access control (MAC) layer defined for 10-Mbps Ethernet. We

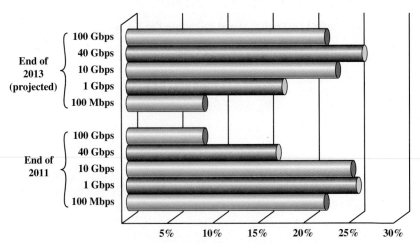

Figure 12.1   Data Center Study—Percentage of Ethernet Links by Speed

then look at subsequent generations of Ethernet, up to the 100-Gbps version, examining the physical layer definitions and the enhancements to the MAC layer. Finally, the chapter looks at the IEEE 802.1Q VLAN standard.

12.1 TRADITIONAL ETHERNET

The most widely used high-speed LANs today are based on Ethernet and were developed by the IEEE 802.3 standards committee. As with other LAN standards, there is both a medium access control layer and a physical layer, which are discussed in turn in what follows.

IEEE 802.3 Medium Access Control

It is easier to understand the operation of CSMA/CD if we look first at some earlier schemes from which CSMA/CD evolved.

PRECURSORS CSMA/CD and its precursors can be termed *random access*, or *contention*, techniques. They are random access in the sense that there is no predictable or scheduled time for any station to transmit; station transmissions are ordered randomly. They exhibit contention in the sense that stations contend for time on the shared medium.

The earliest of these techniques, known as ALOHA, was developed for packet radio networks. However, it is applicable to any shared transmission medium. ALOHA, or pure ALOHA as it is sometimes called, specifies that a station may transmit a frame at any time. The station then listens for an amount of time equal to the maximum possible round-trip propagation delay on the network (twice the time it takes to send a frame between the two most widely separated stations) plus a small fixed time increment. If the station hears an acknowledgment during that time, fine; otherwise, it resends the frame. If the station fails to receive an acknowledgment after repeated transmissions, it gives up. A receiving station determines the correctness of an incoming frame by examining a frame check sequence field, as in HDLC. If the frame is valid and if the destination address in the frame header matches the receiver's address, the station immediately sends an acknowledgment. The frame may be invalid due to noise on the channel or because another station transmitted a frame at about the same time. In the latter case, the two frames may interfere with each other at the receiver so that neither gets through; this is known as a **collision**. If a received frame is determined to be invalid, the receiving station simply ignores the frame.

ALOHA is as simple as can be, and pays a penalty for it. Because the number of collisions rises rapidly with increased load, the maximum utilization of the channel is only about 18%.

To improve efficiency, a modification of ALOHA, known as **slotted ALOHA**, was developed. In this scheme, time on the channel is organized into uniform slots whose size equals the frame transmission time. Some central clock or other technique is needed to synchronize all stations. Transmission is permitted to begin only at a slot boundary. Thus, frames that do overlap will do so totally. This increases the maximum utilization of the system to about 37%.

Both ALOHA and slotted ALOHA exhibit poor utilization. Both fail to take advantage of one of the key properties of both packet radio networks and LANs, which is that propagation delay between stations may be very small compared to frame transmission time. Consider the following observations. If the station-to-station propagation time is large compared to the frame transmission time, then, after a station launches a frame, it will be a long time before other stations know about it. During that time, one of the other stations may transmit a frame; the two frames may interfere with each other and neither gets through. Indeed, if the distances are great enough, many stations may begin transmitting, one after the other, and none of their frames get through unscathed. Suppose, however, that the propagation time is small compared to frame transmission time. In that case, when a station launches a frame, all the other stations know it almost immediately. So, if they had any sense, they would not try transmitting until the first station was done. Collisions would be rare because they would occur only when two stations began to transmit almost simultaneously. Another way to look at it is that a short propagation delay provides the stations with better feedback about the state of the network; this information can be used to improve efficiency.

The foregoing observations led to the development of **carrier sense multiple access (CSMA)**. With CSMA, a station wishing to transmit first listens to the medium to determine if another transmission is in progress (carrier sense). If the medium is in use, the station must wait. If the medium is idle, the station may transmit. It may happen that two or more stations attempt to transmit at about the same time. If this happens, there will be a collision; the data from both transmissions will be garbled and not received successfully. To account for this, a station waits a reasonable amount of time after transmitting for an acknowledgment, taking into account the maximum round-trip propagation delay and the fact that the acknowledging station must also contend for the channel to respond. If there is no acknowledgment, the station assumes that a collision has occurred and retransmits.

One can see how this strategy would be effective for networks in which the average frame transmission time is much longer than the propagation time. Collisions can occur only when more than one user begins transmitting within a short time interval (the period of the propagation delay). If a station begins to transmit a frame, and there are no collisions during the time it takes for the leading edge of the packet to propagate to the farthest station, then there will be no collision for this frame because all other stations are now aware of the transmission.

The maximum utilization achievable using CSMA can far exceed that of ALOHA or slotted ALOHA. The maximum utilization depends on the length of the frame and on the propagation time; the longer the frames or the shorter the propagation time, the higher the utilization.

With CSMA, an algorithm is needed to specify what a station should do if the medium is found busy. Three approaches are depicted in Figure 12.2. One algorithm is **nonpersistent CSMA**. A station wishing to transmit listens to the medium and obeys the following rules:

1. If the medium is idle, transmit; otherwise, go to step 2.
2. If the medium is busy, wait an amount of time drawn from a probability distribution (the retransmission delay) and repeat step 1.

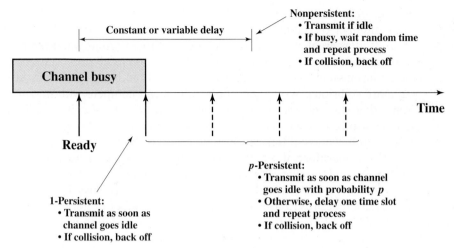

Figure 12.2 CSMA Persistence and Backoff

The use of random delays reduces the probability of collisions. To see this, consider that two stations become ready to transmit at about the same time while another transmission is in progress; if both stations delay the same amount of time before trying again, they will both attempt to transmit at about the same time. A problem with nonpersistent CSMA is that capacity is wasted because the medium will generally remain idle following the end of a transmission even if there are one or more stations waiting to transmit.

To avoid idle channel time, the **1-persistent protocol** can be used. A station wishing to transmit listens to the medium and obeys the following rules:

1. If the medium is idle, transmit; otherwise, go to step 2.

2. If the medium is busy, continue to listen until the channel is sensed idle; then transmit immediately.

Whereas nonpersistent stations are deferential, 1-persistent stations are self-ish. If two or more stations are waiting to transmit, a collision is guaranteed. Things get sorted out only after the collision.

A compromise that attempts to reduce collisions, like nonpersistent, and reduce idle time, like 1-persistent, is **p-persistent**. The rules are given:

1. If the medium is idle, transmit with probability p, and delay one time unit with probability $(1 - p)$. The time unit is typically equal to the maximum propagation delay.

2. If the medium is busy, continue to listen until the channel is idle and repeat step 1.

3. If transmission is delayed one time unit, repeat step 1.

The question arises as to what is an effective value of p. The main problem to avoid is one of instability under heavy load. Consider the case in which n stations have frames to send while a transmission is taking place. At the end of the transmission, the expected number of stations that will attempt to transmit is equal to the number of stations ready to transmit times the probability of transmitting, or np. If np is greater than 1, on average, multiple stations will attempt to transmit and there will be a collision. What is more, as soon as all these stations realize that their transmission suffered a collision, they will be back again, almost guaranteeing more collisions. Worse yet, these retries will compete with new transmissions from other stations, further increasing the probability of collision. Eventually, all stations will be trying to send, causing continuous collisions, with throughput dropping to zero. To avoid this catastrophe, np must be less than one for the expected peaks of n; therefore, if a heavy load is expected to occur with some regularity, p must be small. However, as p is made smaller, stations must wait longer to attempt transmission. At low loads, this can result in very long delays. For example, if only a single station desires to transmit, the expected number of iterations of step 1 is $1/p$ (see Problem 12.2). Thus, if $p = 0.1$, at low load, a station will wait an average of 9 time units before transmitting on an idle line.

DESCRIPTION OF CSMA/CD   CSMA, although more efficient than ALOHA or slotted ALOHA, still has one glaring inefficiency. When two frames collide, the medium remains unusable for the duration of transmission of both damaged frames. For long frames, compared to propagation time, the amount of wasted capacity can be considerable. This waste can be reduced if a station continues to listen to the medium while transmitting. This leads to the following rules for CSMA/CD:

1. If the medium is idle, transmit; otherwise, go to step 2.
2. If the medium is busy, continue to listen until the channel is idle, then transmit immediately.
3. If a collision is detected during transmission, transmit a brief jamming signal to assure that all stations know that there has been a collision and then cease transmission.
4. After transmitting the jamming signal, wait a random amount of time, referred to as the **backoff**, then attempt to transmit again (repeat from step 1).

Figure 12.3 illustrates the technique for a baseband bus. The upper part of the figure shows a bus LAN layout. At time t_0, station A begins transmitting a packet addressed to D. At t_1, both B and C are ready to transmit. B senses a transmission and so defers. C, however, is still unaware of A's transmission (because the leading edge of A's transmission has not yet arrived at C) and begins its own transmission. When A's transmission reaches C, at t_2, C detects the collision and ceases transmission. The effect of the collision propagates back to A, where it is detected by A some time later, t_3, at which time A ceases transmission.

With CSMA/CD, the amount of wasted capacity is reduced to the time it takes to detect a collision. Question: How long does that take? Let us consider the case of a baseband bus and consider two stations as far apart as possible. For example, in Figure 12.3, suppose that station A begins a transmission and that just before that transmission reaches D, D is ready to transmit. Because D is not yet aware of A's transmission, it begins to transmit. A collision occurs almost immediately and is recognized by D. However, the collision must propagate all the way back to A before

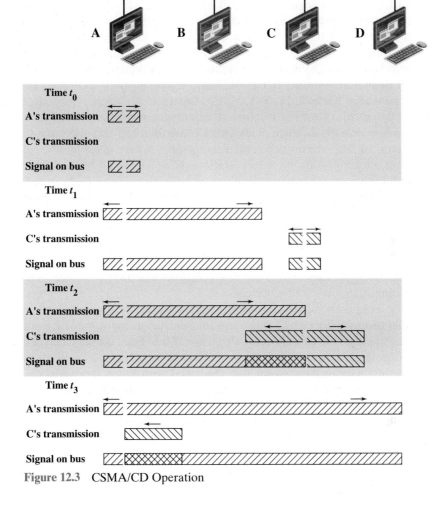

Figure 12.3   CSMA/CD Operation

A is aware of the collision. By this line of reasoning, we conclude that the amount of time that it takes to detect a collision is no greater than twice the end-to-end propagation delay.

An important rule followed in most CSMA/CD systems, including the IEEE standard, is that frames should be long enough to allow collision detection prior to the end of transmission. If shorter frames are used, then collision detection does not occur, and CSMA/CD exhibits the same performance as the less efficient CSMA protocol.

For a CSMA/CD LAN, the question arises as to which persistence algorithm to use. You may be surprised to learn that the algorithm used in the IEEE 802.3 standard is 1-persistent. Recall that both nonpersistent and p-persistent have performance problems. In the nonpersistent case, capacity is wasted because the medium will generally remain idle following the end of a transmission even if there are stations waiting to send. In the p-persistent case, p must be set low enough to avoid instability, with the result of sometimes atrocious delays under light load. The 1-persistent algorithm, which means, after all, that $p = 1$, would seem to be even more unstable than p-persistent due to the greed of the stations. What saves the day is that the wasted time due to collisions is mercifully short (if the frames are long relative to propagation delay), and with random backoff, the two stations involved in a collision are unlikely to collide on their next tries. To ensure that back-off maintains stability, IEEE 802.3 and Ethernet use a technique known as **binary exponential backoff**. A station will attempt to transmit repeatedly in the face of repeated collisions. For the first 10 retransmission attempts, the mean value of the random delay is doubled. This mean value then remains the same for 6 additional attempts. After 16 unsuccessful attempts, the station gives up and reports an error. Thus, as congestion increases, stations back off by larger and larger amounts to reduce the probability of collision.

The beauty of the 1-persistent algorithm with binary exponential backoff is that it is efficient over a wide range of loads. At low loads, 1-persistence guarantees that a station can seize the channel as soon as it goes idle, in contrast to the non- and p-persistent schemes. At high loads, it is at least as stable as the other techniques. However, one unfortunate effect of the backoff algorithm is that it has a last-in first-out effect; stations with no or few collisions will have a chance to transmit before stations that have waited longer.

For baseband bus, a collision should produce substantially higher voltage swings than those produced by a single transmitter. Accordingly, the IEEE standard dictates that the transmitter will detect a collision if the signal on the cable at the transmitter tap point exceeds the maximum that could be produced by the transmitter alone. Because a transmitted signal attenuates as it propagates, there is a potential problem: If two stations far apart are transmitting, each station will receive a greatly attenuated signal from the other. The signal strength could be so small that when it is added to the transmitted signal at the transmitter tap point, the combined signal does not exceed the CD threshold. For this reason, among others, the IEEE standard restricts the maximum length of coaxial cable to 500 m for 10BASE5 and 200 m for 10BASE2.

A much simpler collision detection scheme is possible with the twisted-pair star-topology approach (Figure 11.2). In this case, collision detection is based on logic rather than sensing voltage magnitudes. For any hub, if there is activity (signal) on more than one input, a collision is assumed. A special signal called the collision presence signal is generated. This signal is generated and sent out as long as activity is sensed on any of the input lines. This signal is interpreted by every node as an occurrence of a collision.

For a discussion of LAN performance, see Appendix K.

MAC FRAME   IEEE 802.3 defines three types of MAC frames. The **basic frame** is the original frame format. In addition, to support data link layer protocol encapsulation within the data portion of the frame, two additional frame types have been added. A **Q-tagged frame** supports 802.1Q VLAN capability, as described in Section 12.3. An **envelope frame** is intended to allow inclusion of additional prefixes and suffixes to the data field required by higher-layer encapsulation protocols such as those defined by the IEEE 802.1 working group (such as Provider Bridges and MAC Security), ITU-T, or IETF (such as MPLS).

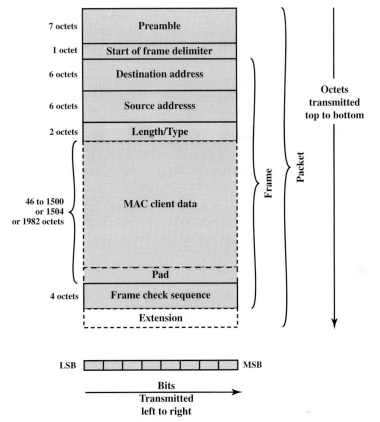

Figure 12.4   IEEE 802.3 MAC Frame Format

Figure 12.4 depicts the frame format for all three types of frames; the differences are contained in the MAC Client Data field. Several additional fields encapsulate the frame to form an 802.3 packet. The fields are as follows:

- **Preamble:** A 7-octet pattern of alternating 0s and 1s used by the receiver to establish bit synchronization.
- **Start Frame Delimiter (SFD):** The sequence 10101011, which that delimits the actual start of the frame and enables the receiver to locate the first bit of the frame.
- **Destination Address (DA):** Specifies the station(s) for which the frame is intended. It may be a unique physical address, a multicast address, or a broadcast address.
- **Source Address (SA):** Specifies the station that sent the frame.
- **Length/Type:** Takes on one of two meanings, depending on its numeric value. If the value of this field is less than or equal to 1500 decimal, then the Length/Type field indicates the number of MAC Client Data octets contained in the subsequent MAC Client Data field of the basic frame (length interpretation).

If the value of this field is greater than or equal to 1536 decimal then the Length/Type field indicates the nature of the MAC client protocol (Type interpretation). The Length and Type interpretations of this field are mutually exclusive.

- **MAC Client Data:** Data unit supplied by LLC. The maximum size of this field is 1500 octets for a basic frame, 1504 octets for a Q-tagged frame, and 1982 octets for an envelope frame.
- **Pad:** Octets added to ensure that the frame is long enough for proper CD operation.
- **Frame Check Sequence (FCS):** A 32-bit cyclic redundancy check, based on all fields except preamble, SFD, and FCS.
- **Extension:** This field is added, if required for 1-Gbps half-duplex operation. The extension field is necessary to enforce the minimum carrier event duration on the medium in half-duplex mode at an operating speed of 1 Gbps.

IEEE 802.3 10–Mbps Specifications (Ethernet)

The IEEE 802.3 committee has defined a number of alternative physical configurations. This is both good and bad. On the good side, the standard has been responsive to evolving technology. On the bad side, the customer, not to mention the potential vendor, is faced with a bewildering array of options. However, the committee has been at pains to ensure that the various options can be easily integrated into a configuration that satisfies a variety of needs. Thus, the user that has a complex set of requirements may find the flexibility and variety of the 802.3 standard to be an asset.

To distinguish the various implementations that are available, the committee has developed a concise notation:

<data rate in Mbps> <signaling method><maximum segment length in hundreds of meters>

The defined alternatives for 10-Mbps are[1]:

- **10BASE5:** Specifies the use of 50-Ω coaxial cable and Manchester digital signaling.[2] The maximum length of a cable segment is set at 500 m. The length of the network can be extended by the use of repeaters. A repeater is transparent to the MAC level; as it does no buffering, it does not isolate one segment from another. So, for example, if two stations on different segments attempt to transmit at the same time, their transmissions will collide. To avoid looping, only one path of segments and repeaters is allowed between any two stations. The standard allows a maximum of four repeaters in the path between any two stations, extending the effective length of the medium to 2.5 km.
- **10BASE2:** Similar to 10BASE5 but uses a thinner cable, which supports fewer taps over a shorter distance than the 10BASE5 cable. This is a lower-cost alternative to 10BASE5.

---

[1]There is also a 10BROAD36 option, specifying a 10-Mbps broadband bus; this option is rarely used.
[2]See Section 5.1.

Table 12.1   IEEE 802.3 10-Mbps Physical Layer Medium Alternatives

	10BASE5	10BASE2	10BASE-T	10BASE-FP
Transmission Medium	Coaxial cable (50 Ω)	Coaxial cable (50 Ω)	Unshielded twisted pair	850-nm optical fiber pair
Signaling Technique	Baseband (Manchester)	Baseband (Manchester)	Baseband (Manchester)	Manchester/on-off
Topology	Bus	Bus	Star	Star
Maximum Segment Length (m)	500	185	100	500
Nodes per Segment	100	30	—	33
Cable Diameter (mm)	10	5	0.4–0.6	62.5/125 μm

- **10BASE-T:** Uses unshielded twisted pair in a star-shaped topology. Because of the high data rate and the poor transmission qualities of unshielded twisted pair, the length of a link is limited to 100 m. As an alternative, an optical fiber link may be used. In this case, the maximum length is 500 m.

- **10BASE-F:** Contains three specifications: a passive-star topology for interconnecting stations and repeaters with up to 1 km per segment, a point-to-point link that can be used to connect stations and repeaters at up to 2 km, and a point-to-point link that can be used to connect repeaters at up to 2 km.

Note that 10BASE-T and 10BASE-F do not quite follow the notation: "T" stands for twisted pair and "F" stands for optical fiber. Table 12.1 summarizes the remaining options. All of the alternatives listed in the table specify a data rate of 10 Mbps.

12.2 HIGH-SPEED ETHERNET

IEEE 802.3 100–Mbps Specifications (Fast Ethernet)

Fast Ethernet refers to a set of specifications developed by the IEEE 802.3 committee to provide a low-cost, Ethernet-compatible LAN operating at 100 Mbps. The blanket designation for these standards is 100BASE-T. The committee defined a number of alternatives to be used with different transmission media.

Table 12.2 summarizes key characteristics of the 100BASE-T options. All of the 100BASE-T options use the IEEE 802.3 MAC protocol and frame format. 100BASE-X refers to a set of options that use two physical links between nodes: one for transmission and one for reception. 100BASE-TX makes use of shielded twisted pair (STP) or high-quality (Category 5) unshielded twisted pair (UTP). 100BASE-FX uses optical fiber.

In many buildings, any of the 100BASE-X options requires the installation of new cable. For such cases, 100BASE-T4 defines a lower-cost alternative that can use Category 3, voice-grade UTP in addition to the higher-quality Category 5 UTP.[3]

---

[3]See Chapter 4 for a discussion of Category 3 and Category 5 cable.

Table 12.2   IEEE 802.3 100BASE-T Physical Layer Medium Alternatives

	100BASE-TX		**100BASE-FX**	**100BASE-T4**
Transmission Medium	2 pair, STP	2 pair, Category 5 UTP	2 optical fibers	4 pair, Category 3, 4, or 5 UTP
Signaling Technique	MLT-3	MLT-3	4B5B, NRZI	8B6T, NRZ
Data Rate	100 Mbps	100 Mbps	100 Mbps	100 Mbps
Maximum Segment Length	100 m	100 m	100 m	100 m
Network Span	200 m	200 m	400 m	200 m

To achieve the 100-Mbps data rate over lower-quality cable, 100BASE-T4 dictates the use of four twisted-pair lines between nodes, with the data transmission making use of three pairs in one direction at a time.

For all of the 100BASE-T options, the topology is similar to that of 10BASE-T, namely a star-wire topology.

100BASE-X   For all of the transmission media specified under 100BASE-X, a unidirectional data rate of 100 Mbps is achieved transmitting over a single link (single twisted pair, single optical fiber). For all of these media, an efficient and effective signal encoding scheme is required. The one chosen is referred to as 4B/5B-NRZI. This scheme is further modified for each option. See Appendix 12A for a description.

The 100BASE-X designation includes two physical medium specifications: one for twisted pair, known as 100BASE-TX, and one for optical fiber, known as 100-BASE-FX.

100BASE-TX makes use of two pairs of twisted-pair cable, one pair used for transmission and one for reception. Both STP and Category 5 UTP are allowed. The MTL-3 signaling scheme is used (described in Appendix 12A).

100BASE-FX makes use of two optical fiber cables: one for transmission and one for reception. With 100BASE-FX, a means is needed to convert the 4B/5B-NRZI code group stream into optical signals. The technique used is known as intensity modulation. A binary 1 is represented by a burst or pulse of light; a binary 0 is represented by either the absence of a light pulse or a light pulse at very low intensity.

100BASE-T4   100BASE-T4 is designed to produce a 100-Mbps data rate over lower-quality Category 3 cable, thus taking advantage of the large installed base of Category 3 cable in office buildings. The specification also indicates that the use of Category 5 cable is optional. 100BASE-T4 does not transmit a continuous signal between packets, which makes it useful in battery-powered applications.

For 100BASE-T4 using voice-grade Category 3 cable, it is not reasonable to expect to achieve 100 Mbps on a single twisted pair. Instead, 100BASE-T4 specifies that the data stream to be transmitted is split up into three separate data streams, each with an effective data rate of $33\frac{1}{3}$ Mbps. Four twisted pairs are used. Data are transmitted using three pairs and received using three pairs. Thus, two of the pairs must be configured for bidirectional transmission.

As with 100BASE-X, a simple NRZ encoding scheme is not used for 100BASE-T4. This would require a signaling rate of 33 Mbps on each twisted pair and does not provide synchronization. Instead, a ternary signaling scheme known as 8B6T is used (described in Appendix 12A).

FULL-DUPLEX OPERATION   A traditional Ethernet is half duplex: A station can either transmit or receive a frame, but it cannot do both simultaneously. With full-duplex operation, a station can transmit and receive simultaneously. If a 100-Mbps Ethernet ran in full-duplex mode, the theoretical transfer rate becomes 200 Mbps.

Several changes are needed to operate in full-duplex mode. The attached stations must have full-duplex rather than half-duplex adapter cards. The central point in the star wire cannot be a simple multiport repeater but rather must be a switching hub. In this case each station constitutes a separate collision domain. In fact, there are no collisions and the CSMA/CD algorithm is no longer needed. However, the same 802.3 MAC frame format is used and the attached stations can continue to execute the CSMA/CD algorithm, even though no collisions can ever be detected.

MIXED CONFIGURATION   One of the strengths of the Fast Ethernet approach is that it readily supports a mixture of existing 10-Mbps LANs and newer 100-Mbps LANs. For example, the 100-Mbps technology can be used as a backbone LAN to support a number of 10-Mbps hubs. Many of the stations attach to 10-Mbps hubs using the 10BASE-T standard. These hubs are in turn connected to switching hubs that conform to 100BASE-T and that can support both 10-Mbps and 100-Mbps links. Additional high-capacity workstations and servers attach directly to these 10/100 switches. These mixed-capacity switches are in turn connected to 100-Mbps hubs using 100-Mbps links. The 100-Mbps hubs provide a building backbone and are also connected to a router that provides connection to an outside WAN.

Gigabit Ethernet

In late 1995, the IEEE 802.3 committee formed a High-Speed Study Group to investigate means for conveying packets in Ethernet format at speeds in the gigabits per second range. The strategy for Gigabit Ethernet is the same as that for Fast Ethernet. While defining a new medium and transmission specification, Gigabit Ethernet retains the CSMA/CD protocol and Ethernet format of its 10-Mbps and 100-Mbps predecessors. It is compatible with 100BASE-T and 10BASE-T, preserving a smooth migration path. As more organizations moved to 100BASE-T, putting huge traffic loads on backbone networks, demand for Gigabit Ethernet intensified.

MEDIA ACCESS LAYER   The 1000-Mbps specification calls for the same CSMA/CD frame format and MAC protocol as used in the 10-Mbps and 100-Mbps version of IEEE 802.3. For shared-medium hub operation (Figure 11.11b), there are two enhancements to the basic CSMA/CD scheme:

- **Carrier extension:** Carrier extension appends a set of special symbols to the end of short MAC frames so that the resulting block is at least 4096 bit-times in duration, up from the minimum 512 bit-times imposed at 10 and 100 Mbps. This is so that the frame length of a transmission is longer than the propagation time at 1 Gbps.

- **Frame bursting:** This feature allows for multiple short frames to be transmitted consecutively, up to a limit, without relinquishing control for CSMA/CD between frames. Frame bursting avoids the overhead of carrier extension when a single station has a number of small frames ready to send.

With a switching hub (Figure 11.11c), which provides dedicated access to the medium, the carrier extension and frame bursting features are not needed. This is because data transmission and reception at a station can occur simultaneously without interference and with no contention for a shared medium.

PHYSICAL LAYER   The 1-Gbps specification for IEEE 802.3 includes the following physical layer alternatives (Figure 12.5):

- **1000BASE-SX:** This short-wavelength option supports duplex links of up to 275 m using 62.5-μm multimode or up to 550 m using 50-μm multimode fiber. Wavelengths are in the range of 770 to 860 nm.

- **1000BASE-LX:** This long-wavelength option supports duplex links of up to 550 m of 62.5-μm or 50-μm multimode fiber or 5 km of 10-μm single-mode fiber. Wavelengths are in the range of 1270 to 1355 nm.

- **1000BASE-CX:** This option supports 1-Gbps links among devices located within a single room or equipment rack, using copper jumpers (specialized shielded twisted-pair cable that spans no more than 25 m). Each link is composed of a separate shielded twisted pair running in each direction.

- **1000BASE-T:** This option makes use of four pairs of Category 5 unshielded twisted pair to support devices over a range of up to 100 m, transmitting and receiving on all four pairs at the same time, with echo cancellation circuitry.

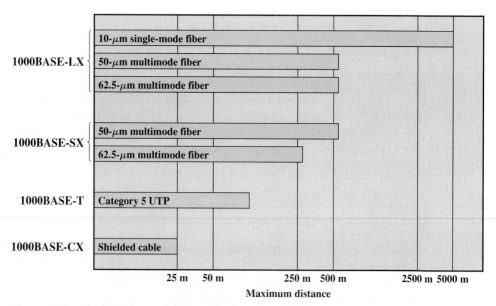

Figure 12.5   Gigabit Ethernet Medium Options (log scale)

The signal encoding scheme used for the first three Gigabit Ethernet options just listed is 8B/10B, which is described in Appendix 12A. The signal encoding scheme used for 1000BASE-T is 4D-PAM5, a complex scheme whose description is beyond our scope.

10-Gbps Ethernet

While gigabit products were still fairly new, attention turned to a 10-Gbps Ethernet capability. The principle driving requirement for 10-Gigabit Ethernet was the increase in Internet and intranet traffic. A number of factors contributed to the explosive growth in both Internet and intranet traffic:

- An increase in the number of network connections
- An increase in the connection speed of each end-station (e.g., 10 Mbps users moving to 100 Mbps, analog 56-kbps users moving to DSL and cable modems)
- An increase in the deployment of bandwidth-intensive applications such as high-quality video
- An increase in Web hosting and application hosting traffic

Initially network managers used 10-Gbps Ethernet to provide high-speed, local backbone interconnection between large-capacity switches. As the demand for bandwidth increased, 10-Gbps Ethernet was deployed throughout the entire network, to include server farm, backbone, and campuswide connectivity. This technology enables Internet service providers (ISPs) and network service providers (NSPs) to create very high-speed links at a low cost, between co-located, carrier-class switches and routers.

The technology also allows the construction of metropolitan area networks (MANs) and WANs that connect geographically dispersed LANs between campuses or points of presence (PoPs). Thus, Ethernet begins to compete with ATM and other wide area transmission and networking technologies. In most cases where the customer requirement is data and TCP/IP transport, 10-Gbps Ethernet provides substantial value over ATM transport for both network end users and service providers:

- No expensive, bandwidth-consuming conversion between Ethernet packets and ATM cells is required; the network is Ethernet, end to end.
- The combination of IP and Ethernet offers quality of service and traffic-policing capabilities that approach those provided by ATM, so that advanced traffic-engineering technologies are available to users and providers.
- A wide variety of standard optical interfaces (wavelengths and link distances) have been specified for 10-Gbps Ethernet, optimizing its operation and cost for LAN, MAN, or WAN applications.

Figure 12.6 illustrates potential uses of 10-Gbps Ethernet. Higher-capacity backbone pipes help relieve congestion for workgroup switches, where Gigabit Ethernet uplinks can easily become overloaded, and for server farms, where 1-Gbps network interface cards are in widespread use.

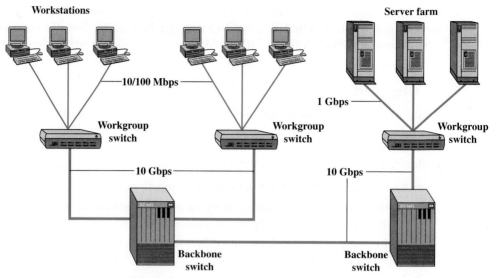

Figure 12.6   Example 10-Gigabit Ethernet Configuration

The goal for maximum link distances covers a range of applications: from 300 m to 40 km. The links operate in full-duplex mode only, using a variety of optical fiber physical media.

Four physical layer options are defined for 10-Gbps Ethernet (Figure 12.7). The first three of these have two suboptions: an "R" suboption and a "W" suboption. The R designation refers to a family of physical layer implementations that use a signal encoding technique known as 64B/66B, described in Appendix 12A. The R implementations are designed for use over *dark fiber*, meaning a fiber optic cable that is not in use and that is not connected to any other equipment. The

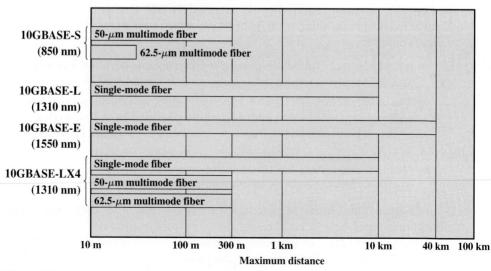

Figure 12.7   10-Gbps Ethernet Distance Options (log scale)

W designation refers to a family of physical layer implementations that also use 64B/66B signaling but that are then encapsulated to connect to SONET equipment.

The four physical layer options are as follows:

- **10GBASE-S (short):** Designed for 850-nm transmission on multimode fiber. This medium can achieve distances up to 300 m. There are 10GBASE-SR and 10GBASE-SW versions.

- **10GBASE-L (long):** Designed for 1310-nm transmission on single-mode fiber. This medium can achieve distances up to 10 km. There are 10GBASE-LR and 10GBASE-LW versions.

- **10GBASE-E (extended):** Designed for 1550-nm transmission on single-mode fiber. This medium can achieve distances up to 40 km. There are 10GBASE-ER and 10GBASE-EW versions.

- **10GBASE-LX4:** Designed for 1310-nm transmission on single-mode or multimode fiber. This medium can achieve distances up to 10 km. This medium uses wavelength division multiplexing (WDM) to multiplex the bit stream across four light waves.

100-Gbps Ethernet

Ethernet is widely deployed and is the preferred technology for wired local area networking. Ethernet dominates enterprise LANs, broadband access, data center networking, and has also become popular for communication across metropolitan and even wide area networks. Further, it is now the preferred carrier wire line vehicle for bridging wireless technologies, such as Wi-Fi and WiMAX, into local Ethernet networks.

This popularity of Ethernet technology is due to the availability of cost-effective, reliable, and interoperable networking products from a variety of vendors. The development of converged and unified communications, the evolution of massive server farms, and the continuing expansion of VoIP, TVoIP, and Web 2.0 applications have driven the need for ever faster Ethernet switches. The following are market drivers for 100-Gbps Ethernet:

- **Data center/Internet media providers:** To support the growth of Internet multimedia content and Web applications, content providers have been expanding data centers, pushing 10-Gbps Ethernet to its limits. Likely to be high-volume early adopters of 100-Gbps Ethernet.

- **Metro-video/service providers:** Video on demand has been driving a new generation of 10-Gbps Ethernet metropolitan/core network buildouts. Likely to be high-volume adopters in the medium term.

- **Enterprise LANs:** Continuing growth in convergence of voice/video/data and in unified communications is driving up network switch demands. However, most enterprises still rely on 1-Gbps or a mix of 1-Gbps and 10-Gbps Ethernet, and adoption of 100-Gbps Ethernet is likely to be slow.

- **Internet exchanges/ISP core routing:** With the massive amount of traffic flowing through these nodes, these installations are likely to be early adopters of 100-Gbps Ethernet.

In 2007, the IEEE 802.3 working group authorized the *IEEE P802.3ba 40Gb/s and 100Gb/s Ethernet Task Force*. The 802.3ba project authorization request cited a number of examples of applications the require greater data rate capacity than 10-Gbps Ethernet offers, including internet exchanges, high performance computing and video-on-demand delivery. The authorization request justified the need for two different data rates in the new standard (40 Gbps and 100 Gbps) by recognizing that aggregate network requirements and end-station requirements are increasing at different rates.

The first products in this category appeared in 2009, and the IEEE 802.3ba standard was finalized in 2010.

An example of the application of 100-Gbps Ethernet is shown in Figure 12.8, taken from [NOWE07]. The trend at large data centers, with substantial banks of blade servers,[4] is the deployment of 10-Gbps ports on individual servers to handle the massive multimedia traffic provided by these servers. Such arrangements are stressing the on-site switches needed to interconnect large numbers of servers. A 100GbE rate was proposed to provide the bandwidth required to handle the

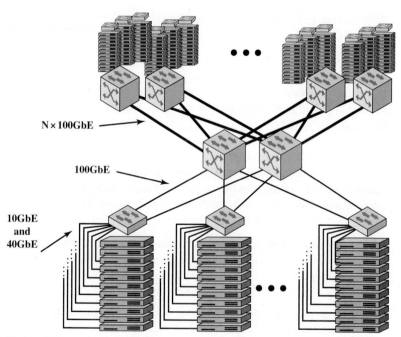

Figure 12.8 Example 100-Gbps Ethernet Configuration for Massive Blade Server Site

---

[4]A blade server is a server architecture that houses multiple server modules ("blades") in a single chassis. It is widely used in data centers to save space and improve system management. Either self-standing or rack mounted, the chassis provides the power supply, and each blade has its own CPU, memory, and hard disk (definition from pcmag.com encyclopedia).

increased traffic load. It is expected that 100GbE will be deployed in switch uplinks inside the data center as well as providing interbuilding, intercampus, MAN, and WAN connections for enterprise networks.

The success of Fast Ethernet, Gigabit Ethernet, and 10-Gbps Ethernet highlights the importance of network management concerns in choosing a network technology. The 40-Gbps and 100-Gbps Ethernet specifications offer compatibility with existing installed LANs, network management software, and applications. This compatibility has accounted for the survival of 30-year-old technology in today's fast-evolving network environment.

MULTILANE DISTRIBUTION The 802.3ba standard uses a technique known as multilane distribution to achieve the required data rates. There are two separate concepts we need to address: multilane distribution and virtual lanes.

The general idea of **multilane distribution** is that, in order to accommodate the very high data rates of 40 and 100 Gbps, the physical link between an end station and an Ethernet switch or the physical link between two switches may be implemented as multiple parallel channels. These parallel channels could be separate physical wires, such as the use of four parallel twisted-pair links between nodes. Alternatively, the parallel channels could be separate frequency channels, such as provided by wavelength division multiplexing over a single optical fiber link.

For simplicity and manufacturing ease, we would like to specify a specific multiple-lane structure in the electrical physical sublayer of the device, known as the physical medium attachment (PMA) sublayer. The lanes produced are referred to as **virtual lanes**. If a different number of lanes are actually in use in the electrical or optical link, then the virtual lanes are distributed into the appropriate number of physical lanes in the physical medium dependent (PMD) sublayer. This is a form of inverse multiplexing.

Figure 12.9a shows the virtual lane scheme at the transmitter. The user data stream is encoded using the 64B/66B, which is also used in 10-Gbps Ethernet. Data is distributed to the virtual lanes one 66-bit word at a time using a simple round robin scheme (first word to first lane, second word to second lane, etc.). A unique 66-bit alignment block is added to each virtual lane periodically. The alignment blocks are used to identify and reorder the virtual lanes and thus reconstruct the aggregate data stream.

The virtual lanes are then transmitted over physical lanes. If the number of physical lanes is smaller than the number of virtual lanes, then bit-level multiplexing is used to transmit the virtual lane traffic. The number of virtual lanes must be an integer multiple (1 or more) of the number of physical lanes.

Figure 12.9b shows the format of the alignment block. The block consists of 8 single-byte fields preceded by the two-bit synchronization field, which has the value 10. The Frm fields contain a fixed framing pattern common to all virtual lanes and used by the receiver to locate the alignment blocks. The VL# fields contain a pattern unique to the virtual lane: one of the fields is the binary inverse of the other.

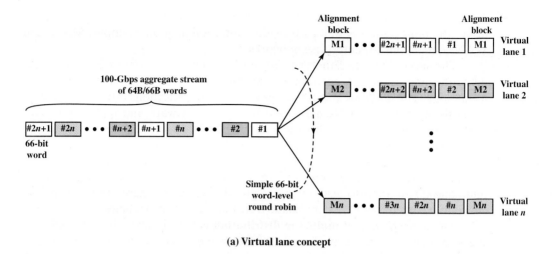

(a) Virtual lane concept

| 1 0 | Frm1 | Frm2 | reserved | reserved | reserved | reserved | ~VL# | VL# |

(b) Alignment block

Figure 12.9 Multilane Distribution for 100-Gbps Ethernet

MEDIA OPTIONS IEEE 802.3ba specifies three types of transmission media (Table 12.3): copper backplane, twin axial (a type of cable similar to coaxial cable), and optical fiber. For copper media, four separate physical lanes are specified. For optical fiber, either 4 or 10 wavelength lanes are specified, depending on data rate and distance.

Table 12.3 Media Options for 40-Gbps and 100-Gbps Ethernet

	40 Gbps	100 Gbps
1m backplane	40GBASE-KR4	
10 m copper	40GBASE-CR4	1000GBASE-CR10
100 m multimode fiber	40GBASE-SR4	1000GBASE-SR10
10 km single-mode fiber	40GBASE-LR4	1000GBASE-LR4
40 km single-mode fiber		1000GBASE-ER4

Naming nomenclature:

    Copper: K = backplane; C = cable assembly

    Optical: S = short reach (100 m); L = long reach (10 km); E = extended long
      reach (40 km)

    Coding scheme: R = 64B/66B block coding

    Final number: number of lanes (copper wires or fiber wavelengths)

12.3 IEEE 802.1Q VLAN STANDARD

The IEEE 802.1Q standard, last updated in 2005, defines the operation of VLAN bridges and switches that permits the definition, operation, and administration of VLAN topologies within a bridged/switched LAN infrastructure. In this section, we will concentrate on the application of this standard to 802.3 LANs.

Recall from Chapter 11 that a A VLAN is an administratively config-ured broadcast domain, consisting of a subset of end stations attached to a LAN. A VLAN is not limited to one switch but can span multiple interconnected switches. In that case, traffic between switches must indicate VLAN membership. This is accomplished in 802.1Q by inserting a tag with a VLAN identifier (VID) with a value in the range from 1 to 4094. Each VLAN in a LAN configuration is assigned a globally unique VID. By assigning the same VID to end systems on many switches, one or more VLAN broadcast domains can be extended across a large network.

Figure 12.10 shows the position and content of the 802.1 tag, referred to as Tag Control Information (TCI). The presence of the 2-octet TCI field is indicated by setting the Length/Type field in the 802.3 MAC frame to a value of 8100 hex. The TCI consists of three subfields:

- **User priority (3 bits):** The priority level for this frame.

- **Canonical format indicator (1 bit):** Is always set to zero for Ethernet switches. CFI is used for compatibility between Ethernet-type networks and token-ring-type networks. If a frame received at an Ethernet port has a CFI set to 1, then that frame should not be forwarded as it is to an untagged port.

- **VLAN identifier (12 bits):** The identification of the VLAN. Of the 4096 pos-sible VIDs, a VID of 0 is used to identify that the TCI contains only a priority value, and 4095 (FFF) is reserved, so the maximum possible number of VLAN configurations is 4094.

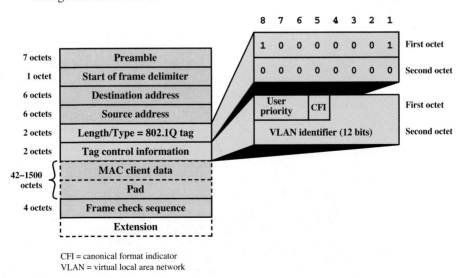

CFI = canonical format indicator
VLAN = virtual local area network

Figure 12.10 Tagged IEEE 802.3 MAC Frame Format

Figure 12.11 illustrates a LAN configuration that includes three switches that implement 802.1Q and one "legacy" switch or bridge that does not. In this case, all of the end systems of the legacy device must belong to the same VLAN. The MAC frames that traverse trunks between VLAN-aware switches include the 802.1Q TCI tag. This tag is stripped off before a frame is routed to a legacy switch. For end systems connected to a VLAN-aware switch, the MAC frame may or may not

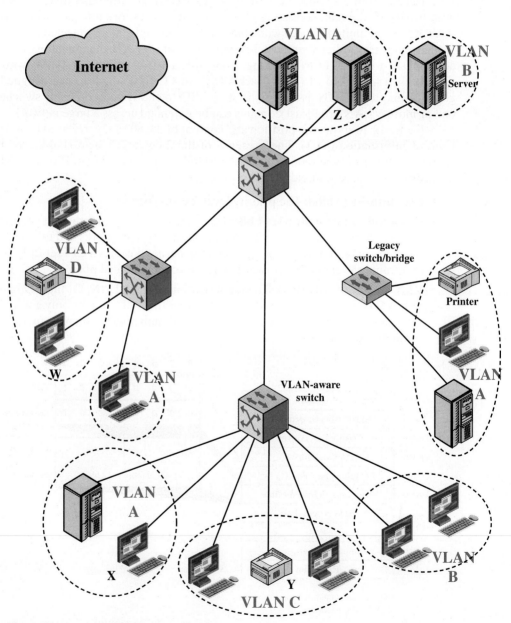

Figure 12.11 A VLAN Configuration

include the TCI tag, depending on the implementation. The important point is that the TCI tag is used between VLAN-aware switches so that appropriate routing and frame handling can be performed.

12.4 RECOMMENDED READING AND ANIMATIONS

The classic paper on Ethernet is [METC76]. A good survey article on Gigabit Ethernet is [FRAZ99]. [TOYO10] provides an overview of 100-Gbps Ethernet and looks at implementation issues.

FRAZ99 Frazier, H., and Johnson, H. "Gigabit Ethernet: From 100 to 1,000 Mbps." *IEEE Internet Computing*, January/February 1999.

METC76 Metcalfe, R., and Boggs, D. "Ethernet: Distributed Packet Switching for Local Computer Networks." *Communications of the ACM,* July 1976.

TOYO10 Toyoda, H.; Ono, G.; and Nishimura, S. "100 GbE PHY and MAC Layer Implementation." *IEEE Communications Magazine*, March 2010.

Animations

Animations that illustrate CSMA/CD and VLAN concepts are available at the Premium Web site. The reader is encouraged to view these animations to reinforce concepts from this chapter.

12.5 KEY TERMS, REVIEW QUESTIONS, AND PROBLEMS

Key Terms

1-persistent CSMA
ALOHA
binary exponential
   backoff
carrier sense multiple access
   (CSMA)
	carrier sense multiple access
	   with collision detection
	   (CSMA/CD)
	collision
	Ethernet
	full-duplex operation
		nonpersistent CSMA
		p-persistent CSMA
		repeater
		scrambling
		slotted ALOHA

Review Questions

12.1 What is a server farm?

12.2 Explain the three persistence protocols that can be used with CSMA.

12.3 What is CSMA/CD?

12.4   Explain binary exponential backoff.

12.5   What are the transmission medium options for Fast Ethernet?

12.6   How does Fast Ethernet differ from 10BASE-T, other than the data rate?

12.7   In the context of Ethernet, what is full-duplex operation?

Problems

12.1   For a pure ALOHA, it can be proved that if the number of frames generated during one frame transmission time is G, then the average number of successful transmissions is $S = G \times e^{-2G}$. Consider a network using pure ALOHA that transmits 150-bit frames on a shared channel of 300 kbps. What will be the throughput if the number of frames produced in a second is 6000?

12.2   For a CSMA/CD, the frame transmission time must be at least twice the maximum propagation time. Suppose that a network using CSMA/CD has a bandwidth of 20 Mbps. The maximum propagation time of this network has been found to be 20 μs.

    a.   What is the frame transmission time?

    b.   What is the minimum size of the frame?

12.3   The backoff time T_B is commonly given by the binary exponential backoff technique using the following method: If K is the number of unsuccessful transmissions, a random integer r is chosen in the range of $0 \leq r < 2^K - 1$, and multiplied by the maximum propagation time, T_p, to give the value of T_B.

    Consider a network in which the stations are located at a maximum of 10 km. The signals in the network propagate at a speed of 2×10^8 m/s. Find the maximum backoff time for $K = 1$, $K = 2$, and $K = 5$.

12.4   Describe the signal pattern produced on the medium by the Manchester-encoded preamble of the IEEE 802.3 MAC frame.

12.5   In a traditional Ethernet, the slot time is 51.2 μs. If the signal propagates at 1.8×10^8 m/s, theoretically, what will be the maximum length of the network?

12.6   With 8B6T coding, the effective data rate on a single channel is 33 Mbps with a signaling rate of 25 Mbaud. If a pure ternary scheme were used, what is the effective data rate for a signaling rate of 25 Mbaud?

12.7   An IEEE 802.3 MAC Frame has 8 octet addresses. A message may be unicast, multicast, or broadcast. If the LSB of the first octet of the destination address is 0, the address is unicast; otherwise it is multicast. A broadcast message has all 1s in its address. If destination addresses of three messages are 4B:6A:03:49:5C:F0, 44:A6:05:E5:32:0B, and FF:FF:FF:FF:FF:FF, state their types.

12.8   Draw the MLT decoder state diagram that corresponds to the encoder state diagram of Figure 12.12.

12.9   For the bit stream 10101101, sketch the waveforms for the NRZ-L, NRZI, Manchester, differential Manchester, and MLT-3 encoding techniques.

12.10 **a.**   Verify that the division illustrated in Figure 12.18a corresponds to the implementation of Figure 12.17a by calculating the result step by step using Equation (12.1).

    b.   Verify that the multiplication illustrated in Figure 12.18b corresponds to the implementation of Figure 12.17b by calculating the result step by step using Equation (12.2).

12.11 Draw a figure similar to Figure 12.16 for the MLT-3 scrambler and descrambler.

APPENDIX 12A   DIGITAL SIGNAL ENCODING FOR LANs

In Chapter 5, we looked at some of the common techniques for encoding digital data for transmission, including Manchester and differential Manchester, which are used in some of the LAN standards. In this appendix, we examine some additional encoding schemes referred to in this chapter.

4B/5B–NRZI

This scheme, which is actually a combination of two encoding algorithms, is used for 100BASE-X. To understand the significance of this choice, first consider the simple alternative of a NRZ (nonreturn to zero) coding scheme. With NRZ, one signal state represents binary 1 and one signal state represents binary 0. The disadvantage of this approach is its lack of synchronization. Because transitions on the medium are unpredictable, there is no way for the receiver to synchronize its clock to the transmitter. A solution to this problem is to encode the binary data to guarantee the presence of transitions. For example, the data could first be encoded using Manchester encoding. The disadvantage of this approach is that the efficiency is only 50%. That is, because there can be as many as two transitions per bit time, a signaling rate of 200 million signal elements per second (200 Mbaud) is needed to achieve a data rate of 100 Mbps. This represents an unnecessary cost and technical burden.

Greater efficiency can be achieved using the 4B/5B code. In this scheme, encoding is done 4 bits at a time; each 4 bits of data are encoded into a symbol with five *code bits*, such that each code bit contains a single signal element; the block of five code bits is called a *code group*. In effect, each set of 4 bits is encoded as 5 bits. The efficiency is thus raised to 80%: 100 Mbps is achieved with 125 Mbaud.

To ensure synchronization, there is a second stage of encoding: Each code bit of the 4B/5B stream is treated as a binary value and encoded using nonreturn to zero inverted (NRZI) (see Figure 5.2). In this code, a binary 1 is represented with a transition at the beginning of the bit interval and a binary 0 is represented with no transition at the beginning of the bit interval; there are no other transitions. The advantage of NRZI is that it employs differential encoding. Recall from Chapter 5 that in differential encoding, the signal is decoded by comparing the polarity of adjacent signal elements rather than the absolute value of a signal element. A benefit of this scheme is that it is generally more reliable to detect a transition in the presence of noise and distortion than to compare a value to a threshold.

Now we are in a position to describe the 4B/5B code and to understand the selections that were made. Table 12.4 shows the symbol encoding. Each 5-bit code group pattern is shown, together with its NRZI realization. Because we are encoding 4 bits with a 5-bit pattern, only 16 of the 32 possible patterns are needed for data encoding. The codes selected to represent the 16 4-bit data blocks are such that a transition is present at least twice for each 5-code group code. No more than three zeros in a row are allowed across one or more code groups.

The encoding scheme can be summarized as follows:

1. A simple NRZ encoding is rejected because it does not provide synchronization; a string of 1s or 0s will have no transitions.
2. The data to be transmitted must first be encoded to assure transitions. The 4B/5B code is chosen over Manchester because it is more efficient.

Table 12.4 4B/5B Code Groups

Data Input (4 bits)	Code Group (5 bits)	NRZI Pattern	Interpretation
0000	11110		Data 0
0001	01001		Data 1
0010	10100		Data 2
0011	10101		Data 3
0100	01010		Data 4
0101	01011		Data 5
0110	01110		Data 6
0111	01111		Data 7
1000	10010		Data 8
1001	10011		Data 9
1010	10110		Data A
1011	10111		Data B
1100	11010		Data C
1101	11011		Data D
1110	11100		Data E
1111	11101		Data F
	11111		Idle
	11000		Start of stream delimiter, part 1
	10001		Start of stream delimiter, part 2
	01101		End of stream delimiter, part 1
	00111		End of stream delimiter, part 2
	00100		Transmit error
	other		Invalid codes

3. The 4B/5B code is further encoded using NRZI so that the resulting differential signal will improve reception reliability.

4. The specific 5-bit patterns for the encoding of the 16 4-bit data patterns are chosen to guarantee no more than three zeros in a row to provide for adequate synchronization.

Those code groups not used to represent data are either declared invalid or assigned special meaning as control symbols. These assignments are listed in Table 12.4. The nondata symbols fall into the following categories:

- **Idle:** The idle code group is transmitted between data transmission sequences. It consists of a constant flow of binary 1s, which in NRZI comes out as a continuous alternation between the two signal levels. This continuous fill pattern establishes and maintains synchronization and is used in the CSMA/CD protocol to indicate that the shared medium is idle.

- **Start of stream delimiter:** Used to delineate the starting boundary of a data transmission sequence; consists of two different code groups.

- **End of stream delimiter:** Used to terminate normal data transmission sequences; consists of two different code groups.

- **Transmit error:** This code group is interpreted as a signaling error. The normal use of this indicator is for repeaters to propagate received errors.

MLT-3

Although 4B/5B-NRZI is effective over optical fiber, it is not suitable as is for use over twisted pair. The reason is that the signal energy is concentrated in such a way as to produce undesirable radiated emissions from the wire. MLT-3, which is used on 100BASE-TX, is designed to overcome this problem.

The following steps are involved:

1. **NRZI to NRZ conversion**. The 4B/5B NRZI signal of the basic 100BASE-X is converted back to NRZ.

2. **Scrambling.** The bit stream is scrambled to produce a more uniform spectrum distribution for the next stage.

3. **Encoder**. The scrambled bit stream is encoded using a scheme known as MLT-3.

4. **Driver**. The resulting encoding is transmitted.

The effect of the MLT-3 scheme is to concentrate most of the energy in the transmitted signal below 30 MHz, which reduces radiated emissions. This in turn reduces problems due to interference.

The MLT-3 encoding produces an output that has a transition for every binary 1 and that uses three levels: a positive voltage (+V), a negative voltage (−V), and no voltage (0). The encoding rules are best explained with reference to the encoder state diagram shown in Figure 12.12:

1. If the next input bit is zero, then the next output value is the same as the preceding value.

2. If the next input bit is one, then the next output value involves a transition:
   a. If the preceding output value was either +V or −V, then the next output value is 0.
   b. If the preceding output value was 0, then the next output value is nonzero, and that output is of the opposite sign to the last nonzero output.

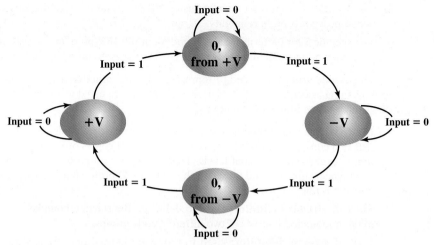

Figure 12.12   MLT-3 Encoder State Diagram

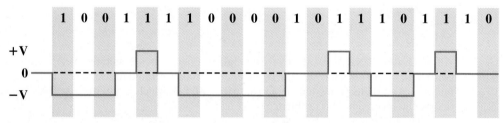

Figure 12.13   Example of MLT-3 Encoding

Figure 12.13 provides an example. Every time there is an input of 1, there is a transition. The occurrences of +V and −V alternate.

8B6T

The 8B6T encoding algorithm uses ternary signaling. With ternary signaling, each signal element can take on one of three values (positive voltage, negative voltage, zero voltage). A pure ternary code is one in which the full information-carrying capacity of the ternary signal is exploited. However, pure ternary is not attractive for the same reasons that a pure binary (NRZ) code is rejected: the lack of synchronization. However, there are schemes referred to as *block-coding methods* that approach the efficiency of ternary and overcome this disadvantage. A new block-coding scheme known as 8B6T is used for 100BASE-T4.

With 8B6T the data to be transmitted are handled in 8-bit blocks. Each block of 8 bits is mapped into a code group of 6 ternary symbols. The stream of code groups is then transmitted in round-robin fashion across the three output channels (Figure 12.14). Thus the ternary transmission rate on each output channel is

$$\frac{6}{8} \times 33\frac{1}{3} = 25 \text{ Mbaud}$$

Table 12.5 shows a portion of the 8B6T code table; the full table maps all possible 8-bit patterns into a unique code group of 6 ternary symbols. The mapping was chosen with two

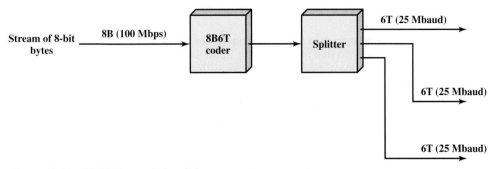

Figure 12.14 8B6T Transmission Scheme

requirements in mind: synchronization and DC balance. For synchronization, the codes were chosen to maximize the average number of transitions per code group. The second requirement is to maintain DC balance, so that the average voltage on the line is zero. For this purpose all of the selected code groups either have an equal number of positive and negative symbols or an excess of one positive symbol. To maintain balance, a DC balancing algorithm is used. In essence, this algorithm monitors the cumulative weight of all code groups transmitted on a single twisted pair. Each code group has a weight of 0 or 1. To maintain balance, the algorithm may negate a transmitted code group (change all + symbols to − symbols and all − symbols to + symbols), so that the cumulative weight at the conclusion of each code group is always either 0 or 1.

Table 12.5 Portion of 8B6T Code Table

Data Octet	6T Code Group	Data Octet	6T Code Group	Data Octet	6T Code Group	Data Octet	6T Code Group
00	+ − 0 0 + −	10	+ 0 + − − 0	20	0 0 − + + −	30	+ − 0 0 − +
01	0 + − + − 0	11	+ + 0 − 0 −	21	− − + 0 0 +	31	0 + − − + 0
02	+ − 0 + − 0	12	+ 0 + − 0 −	22	+ + − 0 + −	32	+ − 0 − + 0
03	− 0 + + − 0	13	0 + + − 0 −	23	+ + − 0 − +	33	− 0 + − + 0
04	− 0 + 0 + −	14	0 + + − − 0	24	0 0 + 0 − +	34	− 0 + 0 − +
05	0 + − − 0 +	15	+ + 0 0 − −	25	0 0 + 0 + −	35	0 + − + 0 −
06	+ − 0 − 0 +	16	+ 0 + 0 − −	26	0 0 − 0 0 +	36	+ − 0 + 0 −
07	− 0 + − 0 +	17	0 + + 0 − −	27	− − + + + −	37	− 0 + + 0 −
08	− + 0 0 + −	18	0 + − 0 + −	28	− 0 − + + 0	38	− + 0 0 − +
09	0 − + + − 0	19	0 + − 0 − +	29	− − 0 + 0 +	39	0 − + − + 0
0A	− + 0 + − 0	1A	0 + − + + −	2A	− 0 − + 0 +	3A	− + 0 − + 0
0B	+ 0 − + − 0	1B	0 + − 0 0 +	2B	0 − − + 0 +	3B	+ 0 − − + 0
0C	+ 0 − 0 + −	1C	0 − + 0 0 +	2C	0 − − + + 0	3C	+ 0 − 0 − +
0D	0 − + − 0 +	1D	0 − + + + −	2D	− − 0 0 + +	3D	0 − + + 0 −
0E	− + 0 − 0 +	1E	0 − + 0 − +	2E	− 0 − 0 + +	3E	− + 0 + 0 −
0F	+ 0 − − 0 +	1F	0 − + 0 + −	2F	0 − − 0 + +	3F	+ 0 − + 0 −

8B/10B

The encoding scheme used for Fibre Channel and Gigabit Ethernet is 8B/10B, in which each 8 bits of data is converted into 10 bits for transmission. This scheme has a similar philosophy to the 4B/5B scheme discussed earlier. The 8B/10B scheme, developed and patented by IBM for use in its 200-megabaud ESCON interconnect system [WIDM83], is more powerful than 4B/5B in terms of transmission characteristics and error-detection capability.

The developers of this code list the following advantages:

- It can be implemented with relatively simple and reliable transceivers at low cost.
- It is well balanced, with minimal deviation from the occurrence of an equal number of 1 and 0 bits across any sequence.
- It provides good transition density for easier clock recovery.
- It provides useful error-detection capability.

The 8B/10B code is an example of the more general mBn B code, in which m binary source bits are mapped into n binary bits for transmission. Redundancy is built into the code to provide the desired transmission features by making $n > m$.

The 8B/10B code actually combines two other codes, a 5B/6B code and a 3B/4B code. The use of these two codes is simply an artifact that simplifies the definition of the mapping and the implementation; the mapping could have been defined directly as an 8B/10B code. In any case, a mapping is defined that maps each of the possible 8-bit source blocks into a 10-bit code block. There is also a function called *disparity control*. In essence, this function keeps track of the excess of zeros over ones or ones over zeros. An excess in either direction is referred to as a disparity. If there is a disparity, and if the current code block would add to that disparity, then the disparity control block complements the 10-bit code block. This has the effect of either eliminating the disparity or at least moving it in the opposite direction of the current disparity.

64B/66B

The 8B/10B code results in an overhead of 25%. To achieve greater efficiency at a higher data rate, the 64B/66B code maps a block of 64 bits into an output block of 66 bits, for an overhead of just 3%. This code is used in 10-Gbps and 100-Gbps Ethernet. The entire Ethernet frame, including control fields, is considered "data" for this process. In addition, there are nondata symbols, called "control," and which include those defined for the 4B/5B code discussed previously plus a few other symbols.

The first step in the process is to encode an input block into a 64-bit block, to which is preopended a 2-bit synchronization field, as show in Figure 12.15. If the input block consists entirely of data octets, then the encoded block consists of the sync field value 10 followed by the 8 data octets unchanged. Otherwise, the input block consists of 8 control octets or a mixture of control octets and data octets. In this case the sync value is 01. This is followed by an 8-bit control type field, which defines the format of the remaining 56 bits of the block. To understand how the 56-bit block is formed, we need to indicate the types of control octets that might be included in the input block, which include the following:

- **Start of packet (S):** Indicates the start of a stream that includes an entire 802.3 MAC packet plus some 64B/66B control characters. This octet is encoded as either 4 bits or 0 bits.
- **End of packet (T):** Marks the termination of the packet. It is encoded using from 0 through 7 bits.

- **Ordered set (0):** Used to adapt clock rates. It is encoded in 4 bits.
- **Other control octets:** Includes idle and error control characters. These octets are encoded in 7 bits.

It is necessary to reduce the number of bits in the input control characters so that the 64-bit input block can be accommodated in 56 bits. Figure 12.15 indicates how this is done. In the input block, the start of packet character is always aligned to be the first or fifth octet. If it occurs as the first octet in the input block, then the remaining seven octets are always data octets. To accommodate all seven data octets, the S field is implied by the block type field but takes up no bits in the encoded block. If the S character is the fifth input octet, then it occupies 4 bits of the encoded block. Similarly, the position and size of the T field is specified

Input data	sync	Data-only field bits							
DDDD DDDD	01	D0	D1	D2	D3	D4	D5	D6	D7

Input data		Type	Data/control field bits							
CCCC CCCC	10	0x1E	C0	C1	C2	C3	C4	C5	C6	C7
CCCC ODDD	10	0x2D	C0	C1	C2	C3	O	D5	D6	D7
CCCC SDDD	10	0x33	C0	C1	C2	C3		D5	D6	D7
ODDD SDDD	10	0x66	D1	D2	D3	O		D5	D6	D7
ODDD ODDD	10	0x55	D1	D2	D3	O	O	D5	D6	D7
SDDD DDDD	10	0x78	D1	D2	D3	D4		D5	D6	D7
ODDD CCCC	10	0x4B	D1	D2	D3	O	C4	C5	C6	C7
TCCC CCCC	10	0x87		C1	C2	C3	C4	C5	C6	C7
DTCC CCCC	10	0x99	D0		C2	C3	C4	C5	C6	C7
DDTC CCCC	10	0xAA	D0	D1		C3	C4	C5	C6	C7
DDDT DDDT	10	0xB4	D0	D1	D2		C4	C5	C6	C7
DDDD TCCC	10	0xCC	D0	D1	D2	D3		C5	C6	C7
DDDD DTCC	10	0xD2	D0	D1	D2	D3	D4		C6	C7
DDDD DDTC	10	0xE1	D0	D1	D2	D3	D4	D5		C7
DDDD DDDT	10	0xFF	D0	D1	D2	D3	D4	D5	D6	

D = data octet
C = input control octet
Ci = 7-bit output control field
S = start of packet field
T = terminate = end of packet field
O = ordered set control character

Figure 12.15 64B/66B Block Formats

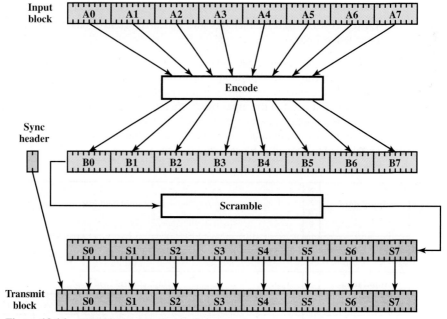

Figure 12.16 64B/66B Transmission Scheme

by the block type field and varies from 0 bits to 7 bits depending on the mixture of control and data octets in the input block.

Figure 12.16 shows the overall scheme for 64B/66B transmission. First, the input block is encoded and the 2-bit sync field is added. Then, scrambling is performed on the encoded 64-bit block using the polynomial $1 + X^{39} + X^{58}$. See Appendix 12B for a discussion of scrambling. The unscrambled 2-bit synchronization field is then prepended to the scrambled block. The sync field provides block alignment and a means of synchronizing when long streams of bits are sent.

Note that for this scheme, no specific coding technique is used to achieve the desired synchronization and frequency of transitions. Rather the scrambling algorithm provides the required characteristics.

APPENDIX 12B SCRAMBLING

For some digital data encoding techniques, a long string of binary 0s or 1s in a transmission can degrade system performance. Also, other transmission properties, such as spectral properties, are enhanced if the data are more nearly of a random nature rather than constant or repetitive. A technique commonly used to improve signal quality is scrambling and descrambling. The scrambling process tends to make the data appear more random.

The scrambling process consists of a feedback shift register, and the matching descrambler consists of a feedforward shift register. An example is shown in Figure 12.17. In this example, the scrambled data sequence may be expressed as follows:

$$B_m = A_m \oplus B_{m-3} \oplus B_{m-5} \tag{12.1}$$

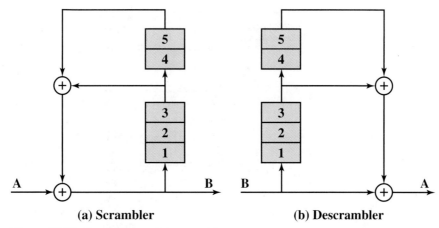

(a) Scrambler   **(b) Descrambler**

Figure 12.17   Scrambler and Descrambler

where $\oplus$ indicates the exclusive-or operation. The shift register is initialized to contain all zeros. The descrambled sequence is

$$
\begin{aligned}
C_m &= B_m \oplus B_{m-3} \oplus B_{m-5} \\
&= (A_m \oplus B_{m-3} \oplus B_{m-5}) \oplus B_{m-3} \oplus B_{m-5} \\
&= A_m (\oplus B_{m-3} \oplus B_{m-3} \oplus) B_{m-5} \oplus B_{m-5} \\
&= A_m
\end{aligned}
\tag{12.2}
$$

As can be seen, the descrambled output is the original sequence.

We can represent this process with the use of polynomials. Thus, for this example, the polynomial is $P(X) = 1 + X^3 + X^5$. The input is divided by this polynomial to produce the scrambled sequence. At the receiver the received scrambled signal is multiplied by the same polynomial to reproduce the original input. Figure 12.18 is an example using the polynomial $P(X)$ and an input of 101010100000111.[5] The scrambled transmission, produced by dividing by $P(X)$ (100101), is 101110001101001. When this number is multiplied by $P(X)$, we get the original input. Note that the input sequence contains the periodic sequence 10101010 as well as a long string of zeros. The scrambler effectively removes both patterns.

For the MLT-3 scheme, which is used for 100BASE-TX, the scrambling equation is:

$$
B_m = A_m \oplus X_9 \oplus X_{11}
$$

In this case the shift register consists of nine elements, used in the same manner as the 5-element register in Figure 12.17. However, in the case of MLT-3, the shift register is not fed by the output . Instead, after each bit transmission, the register is shifted one unit up, and the result of the previous XOR is fed into the first unit. This can be expressed as:

$$
\begin{aligned}
X_i(t) &= X_{i-1}(t-1); \quad 2 \leq i \leq 9 \\
X_i(t) &= X_9(t-1) \oplus X_{11}(t-1)
\end{aligned}
$$

---

[5]We use the convention that the leftmost bit is the first bit presented to the scrambler; thus the bits can be labeled $A_0 A_1 A_2 \dots$. Similarly, the polynomial is converted to a bit string from left to right. The polynomial $B_0 + B_1 X + B_2 X^2 + \dots$ is represented as $B_0 B_1 B_2 \dots$

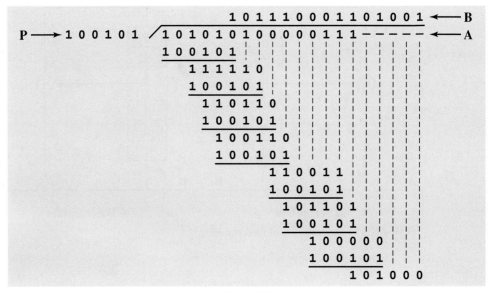

(a) Scrambling

(b) Descrambling

Figure 12.18 Example of Scrambling with $P(X) = 1 + X^{-3} + X^{-5}$

If the shift register contains all zeros, no scrambling occurs (we just have $B_m = A_m$) and the above equations produce no change in the shift register. Accordingly, the standard calls for initializing the shift register with all ones and reinitializing the register to all ones when it takes on a value of all zeros.

For the 4D-PAM5 scheme, two scrambling equations are used, one in each direction:

$$B_m = A_m \oplus B_{m-13} \oplus B_{m-33}$$
$$B_m = A_m \oplus B_{m-20} \oplus B_{m-33}$$

CHAPTER 13

WIRELESS LANS

LEARNING OBJECTIVES

After studying this chapter, you should be able to:

◆ Present an overview of wireless LAN (WLAN) configurations and requirements.

◆ Understand the elements of the 802.11 architecture.

◆ Describe the 802.11 MAC protocol.

◆ Provide an explanation of the individual fields in the 802.11 MAC frame.

◆ Present an overview of the alternative 802.11 physical layer specifications.

In recent years, wireless LANs (WLANs) have come to occupy a significant niche in the local area network market. Increasingly, organizations are finding that WLANs are an indispensable adjunct to traditional wired LANs, to satisfy requirements for mobility, relocation, ad hoc networking, and coverage of locations difficult to wire.

This chapter provides a survey of WLANs. We begin with an overview that looks at the motivations for using WLANs and summarize the various approaches in current use. The next section examines the three principal types of wireless WLANs, classified according to transmission technology: infrared, spread spectrum, and narrowband microwave.

The most prominent specification for WLANs was developed by the IEEE 802.11 working group. This chapter focuses on this standard, and is based on the 2012 version.

13.1 OVERVIEW

Wireless LAN Configurations

Figure 13.1 indicates a simple WLAN configuration that is typical of many environments. There is a backbone wired LAN, such as Ethernet, that supports servers, workstations, and one or more bridges or routers to link with other networks. In addition, there is a control module (CM) that acts as an interface to a WLAN. The control module includes either bridge or router functionality to link the WLAN to the backbone. It includes some sort of access control logic, such as a polling or token-passing scheme, to regulate the access from the end systems. Note that some of the end systems are stand-alone devices, such as a workstation or a server. Hubs

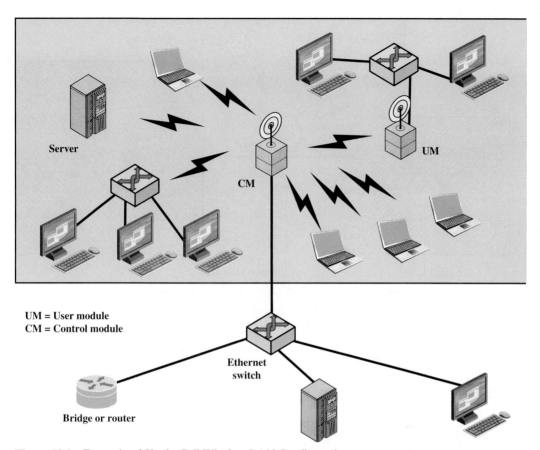

UM = User module
CM = Control module

Figure 13.1   Example of Single-Cell Wireless LAN Configuration

or other user modules (UMs) that control a number of stations off a wired LAN may also be part of the WLAN configuration.

The configuration of Figure 13.1 can be referred to as a single-cell WLAN; all of the wireless end systems are within range of a single control module. Another common configuration, suggested by Figure 13.2, is a multiple-cell WLAN. In this case, there are multiple control modules interconnected by a wired LAN. Each control module supports a number of wireless end systems within its transmission range. For example, with an infrared LAN, transmission is limited to a single room; therefore, one cell is needed for each room in an office building that requires wireless support.

Figure 13.3 illustrates a different type of configuration, referred to as an **ad hoc network**, from that shown in Figures 13.1 and 13.2. Typically, the WLAN forms a stationary infrastructure consisting of one or more cells with a control

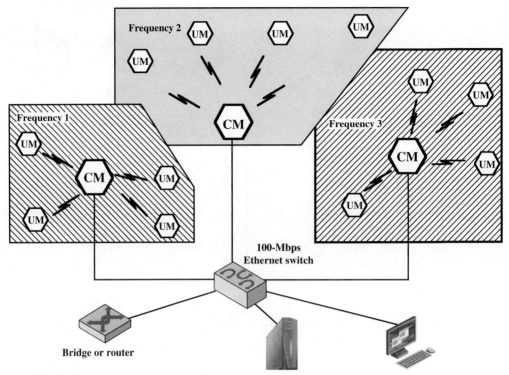

Figure 13.2   Example of Multiple-Cell Wireless LAN Configuration

module for each cell. Within a cell, there may be a number of stationary end systems. Nomadic stations can move from one cell to another. By contrast, there is no infrastructure for an ad hoc network. Rather, a peer collection of stations within a range of each other may dynamically configure themselves into a temporary network.

Figure 13.3   Ad Hoc Wireless LAN Configuration

Wireless LAN Requirements

A WLAN must meet the same sort of requirements typical of any LAN, including high capacity, ability to cover short distances, full connectivity among attached stations, and broadcast capability. In addition, there are a number of requirements specific to the WLAN environment. The following are among the most important requirements for WLANs:

- **Throughput:** The medium access control (MAC) protocol should make as efficient use as possible of the wireless medium to maximize capacity.

- **Number of nodes:** WLANs may need to support hundreds of nodes across multiple cells.

- **Connection to backbone LAN:** In most cases, interconnection with stations on a wired backbone LAN is required. For infrastructure WLANs, this is easily accomplished through the use of control modules that connect to both types of LANs. There may also need to be accommodation for mobile users and ad hoc wireless networks.

- **Service area:** A typical coverage area for a WLAN has a diameter of 100 to 300 m.

- **Battery power consumption:** Mobile workers use battery-powered workstations that need to have a long battery life when used with wireless adapters. This suggests that a MAC protocol that requires mobile nodes to monitor access points constantly or engage in frequent handshakes with a base station is inappropriate. Typical WLAN implementations have features to reduce power consumption while not using the network, such as a sleep mode.

- **Transmission robustness and security:** Unless properly designed, a WLAN may be especially vulnerable to interference and network eavesdropping. The design of a WLAN must permit reliable transmission even in a noisy environment and should provide some level of security from eavesdropping.

- **Collocated network operation:** As WLANs become more popular, it is quite likely for two or more WLANs to operate in the same area or in some area where interference between the LANs is possible. Such interference may thwart the normal operation of a MAC algorithm and may allow unauthorized access to a particular LAN.

- **License-free operation:** Users would prefer to buy and operate WLAN products without having to secure a license for the frequency band used by the LAN.

- **Handoff/roaming:** The MAC protocol used in the WLAN should enable mobile stations to move from one cell to another.

- **Dynamic configuration:** The MAC addressing and network management aspects of the WLAN should permit dynamic and automated addition, deletion, and relocation of end systems without disruption to other users.

13.2 IEEE 802.11 ARCHITECTURE AND SERVICES

In 1990, the IEEE 802 committee formed a new working group, IEEE 802.11, specifically devoted to WLANs, with a charter to develop a MAC protocol and physical medium specification. Since that time, the demand for WLANs, at different frequencies and data rates, has exploded. Keeping pace with this demand, the IEEE 802.11 working group has issued an ever-expanding list of standards (Table 13.1). Table 13.2 briefly defines key terms used in the IEEE 802.11 standard.

Table 13.1 Key IEEE 802.11 Standards

Standard	Scope
IEEE 802.11a	Physical layer: 5-GHz OFDM at rates from 6 to 54 Mbps
IEEE 802.11b	Physical layer: 2.4-GHz DSSS at 5.5 and 11 Mbps
IEEE 802.11c	Bridge operation at 802.11 MAC layer
IEEE 802.11d	Physical layer: Extend operation of 802.11 WLANs to new regulatory domains (countries)
IEEE 802.11e	MAC: Enhance to improve quality of service and security mechanisms
IEEE 802.11g	Physical layer: Extend 802.11b to data rates >20 Mbps
IEEE 802.11i	MAC: Enhance security and authentication mechanisms
IEEE 802.11n	Physical/MAC: Enhancements to enable higher throughput
IEEE 802.11T	Recommended practice for the evaluation of 802.11 wireless performance
IEEE 802.11ac	Physical/MAC: Enhancements to support 0.5–1 Gbps in 5-GHz band
IEEE 802.11ad	Physical/MAC: Enhancements to support ≥ 1 Gbps in the 60-GHz band

Table 13.2 IEEE 802.11 Terminology

Access point (AP)	Any entity that has station functionality and provides access to the distribution system via the wireless medium for associated stations
Basic service set (BSS)	A set of stations controlled by a single coordination function
Coordination function	The logical function that determines when a station operating within a BSS is permitted to transmit and may be able to receive PDUs
Distribution system (DS)	A system used to interconnect a set of BSSs and integrated LANs to create an ESS
Extended service set (ESS)	A set of one or more interconnected BSSs and integrated LANs that appear as a single BSS to the LLC layer at any station associated with one of these BSSs
Frame	Synonym for MAC protocol data unit
MAC protocol data unit (MPDU)	The unit of data exchanged between two peer MAC entities using the services of the physical layer
MAC service data unit (MSDU)	Information that is delivered as a unit between MAC users
Station	Any device that contains an IEEE 802.11 conformant MAC and physical layers

The Wi-Fi Alliance

Although 802.11 products are all based on the same standards, there is always a concern whether products from different vendors will successfully interoperate. To meet this concern, the Wireless Ethernet Compatibility Alliance (WECA), an industry consortium, was formed in 1999. This organization, subsequently renamed the Wi-Fi (Wireless Fidelity) Alliance, created a test suite to certify interoperability for 802.11 products.

IEEE 802.11 Architecture

Figure 13.4 illustrates the model developed by the 802.11 working group. The smallest building block of a WLAN is a **basic service set (BSS)**, which consists of some number of stations executing the same MAC protocol and competing for access to the same shared wireless medium. A BSS may be isolated or it may connect to a backbone **distribution system (DS)** through an **access point (AP)**. The AP functions as a bridge and a relay point. In a BSS, client stations do not communicate directly with one another. Rather, if one station in the BSS wants to communicate with another station in the same BSS, the MAC frame is first sent from the originating station to the AP, and then from the AP to the destination station. Similarly, a MAC frame from a station in the BSS to a remote station is sent from the local station to the AP and then relayed by the AP over the DS on its way to the destination station. The BSS generally corresponds to what is referred to as a cell in the literature. The DS can be a switch, a wired network, or a wireless network.

When all the stations in the BSS are mobile stations, with no connection to other BSSs, the BSS is called an **independent BSS (IBSS)**. An IBSS is typically an

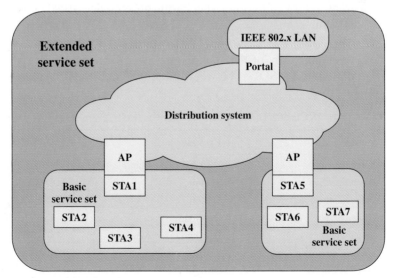

STA = station
AP = access point

Figure 13.4 IEEE 802.11 Architecture

ad hoc network. In an IBSS, the stations all communicate directly, and no AP is involved.

A simple configuration is shown in Figure 13.4, in which each station belongs to a single BSS; that is, each station is within wireless range only of other stations within the same BSS. It is also possible for two BSSs to overlap geographically, so that a single station could participate in more than one BSS. Further, the association between a station and a BSS is dynamic. Stations may turn off, come within range, and go out of range.

An **extended service set (ESS)** consists of two or more BSSs interconnected by a distribution system. Typically, the distribution system is a wired backbone LAN but can be any communications network. The ESS appears as a single logical LAN to the logical link control (LLC) level.

Figure 13.4 indicates that an AP is implemented as part of a station; the AP is the logic within a station that provides access to the DS by providing DS services in addition to acting as a station. To integrate the IEEE 802.11 architecture with a traditional wired LAN, a **portal** is used. The portal logic is implemented in a device, such as a bridge or router, that is part of the wired LAN and that is attached to the DS.

IEEE 802.11 Services

IEEE 802.11 defines a number of services that need to be provided by the WLAN to provide functionality equivalent to that which is inherent to wired LANs. Table 13.3 lists key services and indicates two ways of categorizing them.

1. The service provider can be either the station or the DS. Station services are implemented in every 802.11 station, including AP stations. Distribution services are provided between BSSs; these services may be implemented in an AP or in another special-purpose device attached to the distribution system.

2. Three of the services are used to control IEEE 802.11 LAN access and confidentiality. Six of the services are used to support delivery of MAC service data units (MSDUs) between stations. The MSDU is a block of data passed

Table 13.3 IEEE 802.11 Services

Service	Provider	Used to Support
Association	Distribution system	MSDU delivery
Authentication	Station	LAN access and security
Deauthentication	Station	LAN access and security
Disassociation	Distribution system	MSDU delivery
Distribution	Distribution system	MSDU delivery
Integration	Distribution system	MSDU delivery
MSDU delivery	Station	MSDU delivery
Privacy	Station	LAN access and security
Reassociation	Distribution system	MSDU delivery

down from the MAC user to the MAC layer; typically this is a LLC PDU. If the MSDU is too large to be transmitted in a single MAC frame, it may be fragmented and transmitted in a series of MAC frames.

Following the IEEE 802.11 document, we next discuss the services in an order designed to clarify the operation of an IEEE 802.11 ESS network. **MSDU delivery**, which is the basic service, has already been mentioned. Services related to security are discussed in Section 13.6.

DISTRIBUTION OF MESSAGES WITHIN A DS The two services involved with the distribution of messages within a DS are distribution and integration. **Distribution** is the primary service used by stations to exchange MAC frames when the frame must traverse the DS to get from a station in one BSS to a station in another BSS. For example, suppose a frame is to be sent from station 2 (STA2) to STA7 in Figure 13.4. The frame is sent from STA2 to STA1, which is the AP for this BSS. The AP gives the frame to the DS, which has the job of directing the frame to the AP associated with STA5 in the target BSS. STA5 receives the frame and forwards it to STA7. How the message is transported through the DS is beyond the scope of the IEEE 802.11 standard.

If the two stations that are communicating are within the same BSS, then the distribution service logically goes through the single AP of that BSS.

The **integration** service enables transfer of data between a station on an IEEE 802.11 LAN and a station on an integrated IEEE 802.x LAN. The term *integrated* refers to a wired LAN that is physically connected to the DS and whose stations may be logically connected to an IEEE 802.11 LAN via the integration service. The integration service takes care of any address translation and media conversion logic required for the exchange of data.

ASSOCIATION-RELATED SERVICES The primary purpose of the MAC layer is to transfer MSDUs between MAC entities; this purpose is fulfilled by the distribution service. For that service to function, it requires information about stations within the ESS that is provided by the association-related services. Before the distribution service can deliver data to or accept data from a station, that station must be *associated*. Before looking at the concept of association, we need to describe the concept of mobility. The standard defines three transition types, based on mobility:

- **No transition:** A station of this type is either stationary or moves only within the direct communication range of the communicating stations of a single BSS.
- **BSS transition:** This is defined as a station movement from one BSS to another BSS within the same ESS. In this case, delivery of data to the station requires that the addressing capability be able to recognize the new location of the station.
- **ESS transition:** This is defined as a station movement from a BSS in one ESS to a BSS within another ESS. This case is supported only in the sense that the station can move. Maintenance of upper-layer connections supported by 802.11 cannot be guaranteed. In fact, disruption of service is likely to occur.

To deliver a message within a DS, the distribution service needs to know where the destination station is located. Specifically, the DS needs to know the identity of the AP to which the message should be delivered in order for that message to reach the destination station. To meet this requirement, a station must maintain an association with the AP within its current BSS. Three services relate to this requirement:

- **Association:** Establishes an initial association between a station and an AP. Before a station can transmit or receive frames on a WLAN, its identity and address must be known. For this purpose, a station must establish an association with an AP within a particular BSS. The AP can then communicate this information to other APs within the ESS to facilitate routing and delivery of addressed frames.

- **Reassociation:** Enables an established association to be transferred from one AP to another, allowing a mobile station to move from one BSS to another.

- **Disassociation:** A notification from either a station or an AP that an existing association is terminated. A station should give this notification before leaving an ESS or shutting down. However, the MAC management facility protects itself against stations that disappear without notification.

13.3 IEEE 802.11 MEDIUM ACCESS CONTROL

The IEEE 802.11 MAC layer covers three functional areas: reliable data delivery, access control, and security. This section covers the first two topics.

Reliable Data Delivery

As with any wireless network, a WLAN using the IEEE 802.11 physical and MAC layers is subject to considerable unreliability. Noise, interference, and other propagation effects result in the loss of a significant number of frames. Even with error-correction codes, a number of MAC frames may not successfully be received. This situation can be dealt with by reliability mechanisms at a higher layer, such as TCP. However, timers used for retransmission at higher layers are typically on the order of seconds. It is therefore more efficient to deal with errors at the MAC level. For this purpose, IEEE 802.11 includes a frame exchange protocol. When a station receives a data frame from another station, it returns an acknowledgment (ACK) frame to the source station. This exchange is treated as an atomic unit, not to be interrupted by a transmission from any other station. If the source does not receive an ACK within a short period of time, either because its data frame was damaged or because the returning ACK was damaged, the source retransmits the frame.

Thus, the basic data transfer mechanism in IEEE 802.11 involves an exchange of two frames. To further enhance reliability, a four-frame exchange may be used. In this scheme, a source first issues a Request to Send (RTS) frame to the destination. The destination then responds with a Clear to Send (CTS). After receiving the CTS, the source transmits the data frame, and the destination responds with an ACK. The RTS alerts all stations that are within reception range of the source that an exchange is under way; these stations refrain from transmission in order to avoid a collision between two frames transmitted at the same time. Similarly, the CTS alerts all stations that are within reception range of the destination that an exchange is under way. The RTS/CTS portion of the exchange is a required function of the MAC but may be disabled.

Medium Access Control

The 802.11 working group considered two types of proposals for a MAC algorithm: distributed access protocols, which, like Ethernet, distribute the decision to transmit over all the nodes using a carrier sense mechanism; and centralized access protocols, which involve regulation of transmission by a centralized decision maker. A distributed access protocol makes sense for an ad hoc network of peer workstations (typically an IBSS) and may also be attractive in other WLAN configurations that consist primarily of bursty traffic. A centralized access protocol is natural for configurations in which a number of wireless stations are interconnected with each other and some sort of base station that attaches to a backbone wired LAN; it is especially useful if some of the data is time sensitive or high priority.

The end result for 802.11 is a MAC algorithm called DFWMAC (distributed foundation wireless MAC) that provides a distributed access control mechanism with an optional centralized control built on top of that. Figure 13.5 illustrates the architecture. The lower sublayer of the MAC layer is the distributed coordination function (DCF). DCF uses a contention algorithm to provide access to all traffic. Ordinary asynchronous traffic directly uses DCF. The point coordination function (PCF) is a centralized MAC algorithm used to provide contention-free service. PCF is built on top of DCF and exploits features of DCF to assure access for its users. Let us consider these two sublayers in turn.

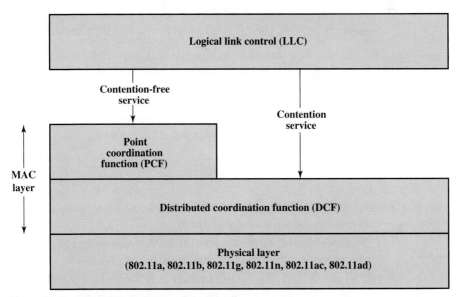

Figure 13.5 IEEE 802.11 Protocol Architecture

DISTRIBUTED COORDINATION FUNCTION The DCF sublayer makes use of a simple CSMA (carrier sense multiple access) algorithm. If a station has a MAC frame to transmit, it listens to the medium. If the medium is idle, the station may transmit; otherwise the station must wait until the current transmission is complete before transmitting. The DCF does not include a collision detection function (i.e., CSMA/CD) because collision detection is not practical on a wireless network. The dynamic range of the signals on the medium is very large, so that a transmitting station cannot effectively distinguish incoming weak signals from noise and the effects of its own transmission.

To ensure the smooth and fair functioning of this algorithm, DCF includes a set of delays that amounts to a priority scheme. Let us start by considering a single delay known as an interframe space (IFS). In fact, there are three different IFS values, but the algorithm is best explained by initially ignoring this detail. Using an IFS, the rules for CSMA access are as follows (Figure 13.6):

1. A station with a frame to transmit senses the medium. If the medium is idle, it waits to see if the medium remains idle for a time equal to IFS. If so, the station may transmit immediately.

2. If the medium is busy (either because the station initially finds the medium busy or because the medium becomes busy during the IFS idle time), the station defers transmission and continues to monitor the medium until the current transmission is over.

3. Once the current transmission is over, the station delays another IFS. If the medium remains idle for this period, then the station backs off a random amount of time and again senses the medium. If the medium is still idle, the station may transmit. During the backoff time, if the medium becomes busy, the backoff timer is halted and resumes when the medium becomes idle.

4. If the transmission is unsuccessful, which is determined by the absence of an acknowledgement, then it is assumed that a collision has occurred.

To ensure that backoff maintains stability, binary exponential backoff, described in Chapter 12, is used. Binary exponential backoff provides a means of handling a heavy load. Repeated failed attempts to transmit result in longer and longer backoff times, which help to smooth out the load. Without such a backoff, the following situation could occur: Two or more stations attempt to transmit at the same time, causing a collision. These stations then immediately attempt to retransmit, causing a new collision.

The preceding scheme is refined for DCF to provide priority-based access by the simple expedient of using three values for IFS:

- **SIFS (short IFS):** The shortest IFS, used for all immediate response actions, as explained in the following discussion

- **PIFS (point coordination function IFS):** A midlength IFS, used by the centralized controller in the PCF scheme when issuing polls

- **DIFS (distributed coordination function IFS):** The longest IFS, used as a minimum delay for asynchronous frames contending for access

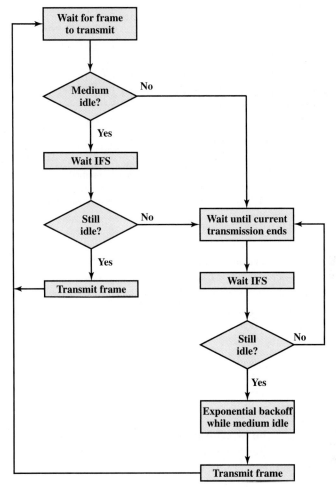

Figure 13.6   IEEE 802.11 Medium Access Control Logic

Figure 13.7a illustrates the use of these time values. Consider first the SIFS. Any station using SIFS to determine transmission opportunity has, in effect, the highest priority, because it will always gain access in preference to a station waiting an amount of time equal to PIFS or DIFS. The SIFS is used in the following circumstances:

- **Acknowledgment (ACK):** When a station receives a frame addressed only to itself (not multicast or broadcast), it responds with an ACK frame after waiting only for an SIFS gap. This has two desirable effects. First, because collision detection is not used, the likelihood of collisions is greater than with CSMA/CD, and the MAC-level ACK provides for efficient collision recovery. Second, the SIFS can be used to provide efficient delivery of an LLC protocol data unit (PDU) that requires multiple MAC frames. In this case, the following scenario occurs. A station with a multiframe LLC PDU to transmit

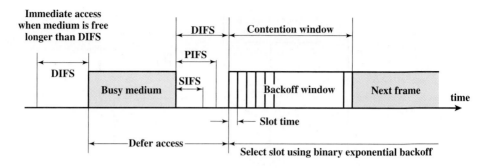

(a) Basic access method

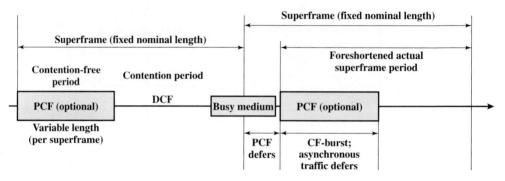

(b) PCF superframe construction

Figure 13.7 IEEE 802.11 MAC Timing

sends out the MAC frames one at a time. Each frame is acknowledged by the recipient after SIFS. When the source receives an ACK, it immediately (after SIFS) sends the next frame in the sequence. The result is that once a station has contended for the channel, it will maintain control of the channel until it has sent all of the fragments of an LLC PDU.

- **Clear to Send (CTS):** A station can ensure that its data frame will get through by first issuing a small RTS frame. The station to which this frame is addressed should immediately respond with a CTS frame if it is ready to receive. All other stations receive the RTS and defer using the medium.

- **Poll response:** This is explained in the following discussion of PCF.

The next longest IFS interval is the PIFS. This is used by the centralized controller in issuing polls and takes precedence over normal contention traffic. However, those frames transmitted using SIFS have precedence over a PCF poll.

Finally, the DIFS interval is used for all ordinary asynchronous traffic.

POINT COORDINATION FUNCTION   PCF is an alternative access method implemented on top of the DCF. The operation consists of polling by the centralized polling master (point coordinator). The point coordinator makes use of PIFS when issuing polls. Because PIFS is smaller than DIFS, the point coordinator can seize the medium and lock out all asynchronous traffic while it issues polls and receives responses.

As an extreme, consider the following possible scenario. A wireless network is configured so that a number of stations with time-sensitive traffic are controlled by the point coordinator while remaining traffic contends for access using CSMA. The point coordinator could issue polls in a round-robin fashion to all stations configured for polling. When a poll is issued, the polled station may respond using SIFS. If the point coordinator receives a response, it issues another poll using PIFS. If no response is received during the expected turnaround time, the coordinator issues a poll.

If the discipline of the preceding paragraph were implemented, the point coordinator would lock out all asynchronous traffic by repeatedly issuing polls. To prevent this, an interval known as the superframe is defined. During the first part of this interval, the point coordinator issues polls in a round-robin fashion to all stations configured for polling. The point coordinator then idles for the remainder of the superframe, allowing a contention period for asynchronous access.

Figure 13.7b illustrates the use of the superframe. At the beginning of a superframe, the point coordinator may optionally seize control and issue polls for a given period of time. This interval varies because of the variable frame size issued by responding stations. The remainder of the superframe is available for contention-based access. At the end of the superframe interval, the point coordinator contends for access to the medium using PIFS. If the medium is idle, the point coordinator gains immediate access and a full superframe period follows. However, the medium may be busy at the end of a superframe. In this case, the point coordinator must wait until the medium is idle to gain access; this results in a foreshortened superframe period for the next cycle.

MAC Frame

Figure 13.8 shows the format of IEEE 802.11 frame, also known as the MAC protocol data unit (MPDU). This general format is used for all data and control frames, but not all fields are used in all contexts. The fields are as follows:

- **Frame Control:** Indicates the type of frame (control, management, or data) and provides control information. Control information includes whether the frame is to or from a DS, fragmentation information, and privacy information.

- **Duration/Connection ID:** If used as a duration field, indicates the time (in microseconds) the channel will be allocated for successful transmission of a MAC frame. In some control frames, this field contains an association, or connection, identifier.

- **Addresses:** The number and meaning of the 48-bit address fields depend on context. The **transmitter address** and **receiver address** are the MAC addresses of stations joined to the BSS that are transmitting and receiving frames over the WLAN. The **service set ID (SSID)** identifies the WLAN over which a frame is transmitted. For an IBSS, the SSID is a random number generated at the time the network is formed. For a WLAN that is part of a larger configuration, the SSID identifies the BSS over which the frame is transmitted; specifically, the SSID is the MAC-level address of the AP for this BSS (Figure 13.4). Finally the **source address** and **destination address** are the MAC addresses of

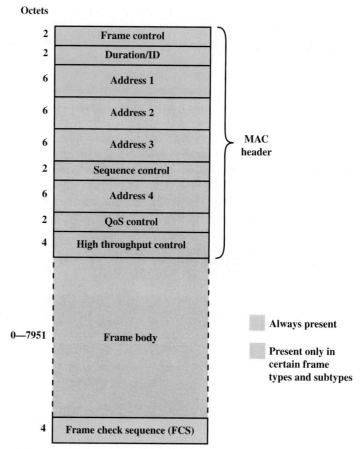

Octets

2	Frame control
2	Duration/ID
6	Address 1
6	Address 2
6	Address 3
2	Sequence control
6	Address 4
2	QoS control
4	High throughput control
0—7951	Frame body
4	Frame check sequence (FCS)

MAC header

Always present

Present only in certain frame types and subtypes

Figure 13.8   IEEE 802.11 MAC Frame Format

stations, wireless or otherwise, that are the ultimate source and destination of this frame. The source address may be identical to the transmitter address and the destination address may be identical to the receiver address.

- **Sequence Control:** Contains a 4-bit fragment number subfield, used for fragmentation and reassembly, and a 12-bit sequence number used to number frames sent between a given transmitter and receiver.

- **QoS Control:** Contains information relating to the IEEE 802.11 quality of service (QoS) facility. A discussion of this facility is beyond our scope.

- **High Throughput Control:** This field contains control bits related to the operation of 802.11n, 802.11ac, and 802.11ad. A discussion of this field is beyond our scope.

- **Frame Body:** Contains an MSDU or a fragment of an MSDU. The MSDU is a LLC PDU or MAC control information.

- **Frame Check Sequence:** A 32-bit cyclic redundancy check.

We now look at the three MAC frame types.

CONTROL FRAMES Control frames assist in the reliable delivery of data frames. There are six control frame subtypes:

- **Power Save-Poll (PS-Poll):** This frame is sent by any station to the station that includes the AP (access point). Its purpose is to request that the AP transmit a frame that has been buffered for this station while the station was in power-saving mode.

- **Request to Send (RTS):** This is the first frame in the four-way frame exchange discussed under the subsection on reliable data delivery at the beginning of this section. The station sending this message is alerting a potential destination, and all other stations within reception range, that it intends to send a data frame to that destination.

- **Clear to Send (CTS):** This is the second frame in the four-way exchange. It is sent by the destination station to the source station to grant permission to send a data frame.

- **Acknowledgment:** Provides an acknowledgment from the destination to the source that the immediately preceding data, management, or PS-Poll frame was received correctly.

- **Contention-Free (CF)-end:** Announces the end of a contention-free period that is part of the point coordination function.

- **CF-End + CF-Ack:** Acknowledges the CF-end. This frame ends the contention-free period and releases stations from the restrictions associated with that period.

DATA FRAMES There are eight data frame subtypes, organized into two groups. The first four subtypes define frames that carry upper-level data from the source station to the destination station. The four data-carrying frames are as follows:

- **Data:** This is the simplest data frame. It may be used in both a contention period and a contention-free period.

- **Data + CF-Ack:** May only be sent during a contention-free period. In addition to carrying data, this frame acknowledges previously received data.

- **Data + CF-Poll:** Used by a point coordinator to deliver data to a mobile station and also to request that the mobile station send a data frame that it may have buffered.

- **Data + CF-Ack + CF-Poll:** Combines the functions of the Data + CF-Ack and Data + CF-Poll into a single frame.

The remaining four subtypes of data frames do not in fact carry any user data. The Null Function data frame carries no data, polls, or acknowledgments. It is used only to carry the power management bit in the frame control field to the AP, to indicate that the station is changing to a low-power operating state. The remaining three frames (CF-Ack, CF-Poll, CF-Ack + CF-Poll) have the same functionality as the corresponding data frame subtypes in the preceding list (Data + CF-Ack, Data + CF-Poll, Data + CF-Ack + CF-Poll) but without the data.

MANAGEMENT FRAMES Management frames are used to manage communications between stations and APs. Functions covered include management of associations (request, response, reassociation, dissociation, and authentication).

13.4 IEEE 802.11 PHYSICAL LAYER

Since its introduction, the IEEE 802.11 standard has been expanded and revised a number of times. The first version of the standard, simply called IEEE 802.11, includes the MAC layer and three physical layer specifications, two in the 2.4-GHz band (ISM) and one in the infrared, all operating at 1 and 2 Mbps. This version is now obsolete and no longer in use. Table 13.4 summarizes key characteristics of the subsequent revisions. In this section, we survey 802.11b, 802.11a, 802.11g, and 802.11n. The following section deals with 802.11ac and 802.11ad, both of which provide for data rates greater than 1 Gbps.

IEEE 802.11b

One of the original 802.11 standards, now obsolete, used direct sequence spread spectrum (DSSS). It operates in the 2.4-GHz ISM band, at data rates of 1 Mbps and 2 Mbps. In the United States, the FCC (Federal Communications Commission) requires no licensing for the use of this band. The number of channels available depends on the bandwidth allocated by the various national regulatory agencies.

IEEE 802.11b is an extension of the IEEE 802.11 DSSS scheme, providing data rates of 5.5 and 11 Mbps in the ISM band. The chipping rate is 11 MHz, which is the same as the original DSSS scheme, thus providing the same occupied bandwidth.

Table 13.4   IEEE 802.11 Physical Layer Standards

Standard	802.11a	802.11b	802.11g	802.11n	802.11ac	802.11ad
Year introduced	1999	1999	2003	2000	2012	2014
Maximum data transfer speed	54 Mbps	11 Mbps	54 Mbps	65 to 600 Mbps	78 Mbps to 3.2 Gbps	6.76 Gbps
Frequency band	5 GHz	2.4 GHz	2.4 GHz	2.4 or 5 GHz	5 GHz	60 GHz
Channel bandwidth	20 MHz	20 MHz	20 MHz	20, 40 MHz	40, 80, 160 MHz	2160 MHz
Highest order modulation	64 QAM	11 CCK	64 QAM	64 QAM	256 QAM	64 QAM
Spectrum usage	DSSS	OFDM	DSSS, OFDM	OFDM	SC-OFDM	SC, OFDM
Antenna configuration	1×1 SISO	1×1 SISO	1×1 SISO	Up to 4×4 MIMO	Up to 8×8 MIMO, MU-MIMO	1×1 SISO

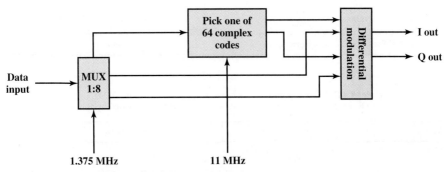

Figure 13.9 11-Mbps CCK Modulation Scheme

To achieve a higher data rate in the same bandwidth at the same chipping rate, a modulation scheme known as **complementary code keying (CCK)** is used.

The CCK modulation scheme is quite complex and is not examined in detail here. Figure 13.9 provides an overview of the scheme for the 11-Mbps rate. Input data are treated in blocks of 8 bits at a rate of 1.375 MHz (8bits/symbol × 1.375MHz = 11Mbps). Six of these bits are mapped into one of 64 code sequences derived from a 64 × 64 matrix known as the Walsh matrix (discussed in Chapter 17). The output of the mapping, plus the two additional bits, forms the input to a QPSK (quadrature phase shift keying) modulator.

An optional alternative to CCK is known as packet binary convolutional coding (PBCC). PBCC provides for potentially more efficient transmission at the cost of increased computation at the receiver. PBCC was incorporated into 802.11b in anticipation of its need for higher data rates for future enhancements to the standard.

Physical-Layer Frame Structure   IEEE 802.11b defines two physical-layer frame formats, which differ only in the length of the preamble. The long preamble of 144 bits is the same as used in the original 802.11 DSSS scheme and allows interoperability with other legacy systems. The short preamble of 72 bits provides improved throughput efficiency. Figure 13.10b illustrates the physical-layer frame format with the short preamble. The **PLCP (physical layer conversion protocol) Preamble** field enables the receiver to acquire an incoming signal and synchronize the demodulator. It consists of two subfields: a 56-bit **Sync** field for synchronization and a 16-bit start-of-frame delimiter (**SFD**). The preamble is transmitted at 1 Mbps using differential BPSK and Barker code spreading.

Following the preamble is the **PLCP Header**, which is transmitted at 2 Mbps using DQPSK. It consists of the following subfields:

- **Signal:** Specifies the data rate at which the MPDU (MAC protocol data unit) portion of the frame is transmitted.
- **Service:** Only 3 bits of this 8-bit field are used in 802.11b. One bit indicates whether the transmit frequency and symbol clocks use the same local oscillator. Another bit indicates whether CCK or PBCC encoding is used. A third bit acts as an extension to the Length subfield.

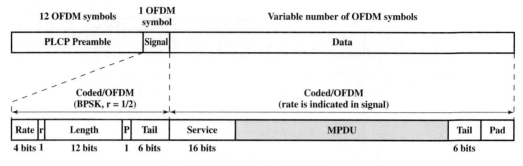

(a) IEEE 802.11a physical PDU

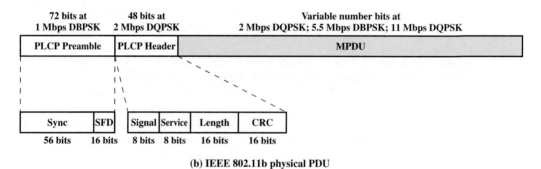

(b) IEEE 802.11b physical PDU

Figure 13.10   IEEE 802.11 Physical-Level Protocol Data Units

- **Length:** Indicates the length of the MPDU field by specifying the number of microseconds necessary to transmit the MPDU. Given the data rate, the length of the MPDU in octets can be calculated. For any data rate over 8 Mbps, the length extension bit from the Service field is needed to resolve a rounding ambiguity.

- **CRC:** A 16-bit error-detection code used to protect the Signal, Service, and Length fields.

The **MPDU** field consists of a variable number of bits transmitted at the data rate specified in the Signal subfield. Prior to transmission, all of the bits of the physical-layer PDU are scrambled (see Appendix 12B for a discussion of scrambling).

IEEE 802.11a

Although 802.11b achieved a certain level of success, its limited data rate results in limited appeal. To meet the needs for a truly high-speed WLAN, **IEEE 802.11a** was developed.

CHANNEL STRUCTURE   IEEE 802.11a makes use of the frequency band called the Universal Networking Information Infrastructure (UNNI), which is divided into three parts. The UNNI-1 band (5.15–5.25 GHz) is intended for indoor use; the UNNI-2 band (5.25–5.35 GHz) can be used either indoor or outdoor; and the UNNI-3 band (5.725–5.825 GHz) is for outdoor use.

IEEE 802.11a has several advantages over IEEE 802.11b/g:

- IEEE 802.11a utilizes more available bandwidth than 802.11b/g. Each UNNI band provides four nonoverlapping channels for a total of 12 across the allocated spectrum.

- IEEE 802.11a provides much higher data rates than 802.11b and the same maximum data rate as 802.11g.

- IEEE 802.11a uses a different, relatively uncluttered frequency spectrum (5 GHz).

CODING AND MODULATION   Unlike the 2.4-GHz specifications, IEEE 802.11a does not use a spread spectrum scheme but rather uses OFDM (orthogonal frequency-division multiplexing). OFDM, also called multicarrier modulation, uses multiple carrier signals at different frequencies, sending some of the bits on each channel. This is similar to FDM. However, in the case of OFDM, all of the subchannels are dedicated to a single data source.

To complement OFDM, the specification supports the use of a variety of modulation and coding alternatives. The system uses up to 48 subcarriers that are modulated using BPSK, QPSK, 16-QAM, or 64-QAM. Subcarrier frequency spacing is 0.3125 MHz, and each subcarrier transmits at a rate of 250 kbaud. A convolutional code at a rate of 1/2, 2/3, or 3/4 provides forward error correction. The combination of modulation technique and coding rate determines the data rate.

PHYSICAL-LAYER FRAME STRUCTURE   The primary purpose of the physical layer is to transmit MAC protocol data units as directed by the 802.11 MAC layer. The PLCP sublayer provides the framing and signaling bits needed for the OFDM transmission and the PMD sublayer performs the actual encoding and transmission operation.

Figure 13.10a illustrates the physical-layer frame format. The **PLCP Preamble** field enables the receiver to acquire an incoming OFDM signal and synchronize the demodulator. Next is the **Signal** field, which consists of 24 bits encoded as a single OFDM symbol. The Preamble and Signal fields are transmitted at 6 Mbps using BPSK. The signal field consists of the following subfields:

- **Rate:** Specifies the data rate at which the data field portion of the frame is transmitted

- **r:** Reserved for future use

- **Length:** Number of octets in the MAC PDU

- **P:** An even parity bit for the 17 bits in the Rate, r, and Length subfields

- **Tail:** Consists of 6 zero bits appended to the symbol to bring the convolutional encoder to zero state

The **Data** field consists of a variable number of OFDM symbols transmitted at the data rate specified in the Rate subfield. Prior to transmission, all of the bits of the Data field are scrambled (see Appendix 12B for a discussion of scrambling). The Data field consists of four subfields:

- **Service:** Consists of 16 bits, with the first 7 bits set to zeros to synchronize the descrambler in the receiver and the remaining 9 bits (all zeros) reserved for future use.

- **MAC PDU:** Handed down from the MAC layer. The format is shown in Figure 13.8.

- **Tail:** Produced by replacing the six scrambled bits following the MPDU end with 6 bits of all zeros; used to reinitialize the convolutional encoder.

- **Pad:** The number of bits required to make the Data field a multiple of the number of bits in an OFDM symbol (48, 96, 192, or 288).

IEEE 802.11g

IEEE 802.11g extends 802.11b to data rates above 20 Mbps, up to 54 Mbps. Like 802.11b, 802.11g operates in the 2.4-GHz range and thus the two are compatible. The standard is designed so that 802.11b devices will work when connected to an 802.11g AP, and 802.11g devices will work when connected to an 802.11b AP, in both cases using the lower 802.11b data rate.

IEEE 802.11g offers a wide array of data rate and modulation scheme options. IEEE 802.11g provides compatibility with 802.11 and 802.11b by specifying the same modulation and framing schemes as these standards for 1, 2, 5.5, and 11 Mbps. At data rates of 6, 9, 12, 18, 24, 36, 48, and 54 Mbps, 802.11g adopts the 802.11a OFDM scheme, adapted for the 2.4-GHz rate; this is referred to as ERP-OFDM, with ERP standing for extended rate physical layer. In addition, an ERP-PBCC scheme is used to provide data rates of 22 and 33 Mbps.

The IEEE 802.11 standards do not include a specification of speed versus distance objectives. Different vendors will give different values, depending on environment. Table 13.5, based on [LAYL04], gives estimated values for a typical office environment.

IEEE 802.11n

With increasing demands being placed on WLANs, the 802.11 committee looked for ways to increase the data throughput and overall capacity of 802.11 networks. The goal of this effort is to not just increase the bit rate of the transmitting antennas but

Table 13.5 Estimated Distance (m) Versus Data Rate

Data Rate (Mbps)	802.11b	802.11a	802.11g
1	90+	—	90+
2	75	—	75
5.5(b)/6(a/g)	60	60+	65
9	—	50	55
11(b)/12(a/g)	50	45	50
18	—	40	50
24	—	30	45
36	—	25	35
48	—	15	25
54	—	10	20

to increase the effective throughput of the network. Increasing effective throughput involves looking not only at the signal encoding scheme, but also at the antenna architecture and the MAC frame structure. The result of these efforts is a package of improvements and enhancements embodied in IEEE 802.11n. This standard is defined to operate in both the 2.4-GHz and the 5-GHz bands and can therefore be made upwardly compatible with either 802.11a or 802.11b/g.

IEEE 802.11n embodies changes in three general areas: use of MIMO, enhancements in radio transmission, and MAC enhancements. We briefly examine each of these.

Multiple-input-multiple-output (MIMO) antenna architecture is the most important of the enhancements provided by 802.11n. A discussion of MIMO is provided in Chapter 17, so we content ourselves with a brief overview. In a MIMO scheme, the transmitter employs multiple antennas. The source data stream is divided into n substreams, one for each of the n transmitting antennas. The individual substreams are the input to the transmitting antennas (multiple input). At the receiving end, m antennas receive the transmissions from the n source antennas via a combination of line-of-sight transmission and multipath. The outputs from the m receiving antennas (multiple output) are combined. With a lot of complex math, the result is a much better receive signal than can be achieved with either a single antenna or multiple frequency channels. 802.11n defines a number of different combinations for the number of transmitters and the number of receivers, from 2×1 to 4×4. Each additional transmitter or receiver in the system increases the SNR (signal-to-noise ratio).

In addition to MIMO, 802.11n makes a number of changes in the **radio transmission scheme** to increase capacity. The most significant of these techniques, known as channel bonding, combines two 20-MHz channels to create a 40-MHz channel. Using OFDM, this allows for twice as many subchannels, doubling the transmission rate.

Finally, 802.11n provides some **MAC enhancements**. The most significant change is to aggregate multiple MAC frames into a single block for transmission. Once a station acquires the medium for transmission, it can transmit long packets without significant delays between transmissions. The receiver sends a single block acknowledgement. The physical header associated with transmission is sent only at the beginning of the aggregated frame, rather than one physical header per individual frame. Frame aggregation can result in significantly improved efficiency in the use of the transmission capacity.

The 802.11n specification includes three forms of aggregation, illustrated in Figure 13.11 [CISC12b]. For simplicity, the 4-octet MAC trailer field is not shown. A-MSDU aggregation combines multiple MSDUs into a single MPDU. Thus there is a single MAC header and single FCS for all of the MSDUs rather than for each of the MSDUs. This provides a certain amount of efficiency because the 802.11 MAC header is potentially quite lengthy. However, if a bit error occurs in one of the MSDU, all of the aggregated MSDUs must be retransmitted. A-MPDU aggregation combines multiple MPDUs in a single physical transmission. Thus, as with A-MSDU, only a single physical-layer header is needed. This approach is less efficient because each MPDU includes the MAC header and FCS. However, if a bit error occurs in one of the MPDUs, only that MPDU

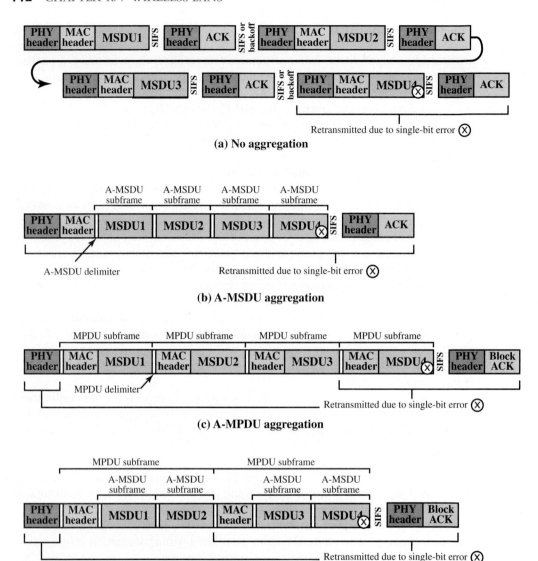

Figure 13.11 Forms of Aggregation

needs to be retransmitted. Finally, the two forms of aggregation can be combined (A-MPDU of A-MSDU).

Figure 13.12 gives an indication of the effectiveness of 802.11n compared to 802.11g [DEBE07]. The chart shows the average throughput per user on a shared system. As expected, the more active users competing for the wireless capacity, the smaller the average throughput per user. IEEE 802.11n provides a significant improvement, especially for networks in which a small number of users are actively competing for transmission time.

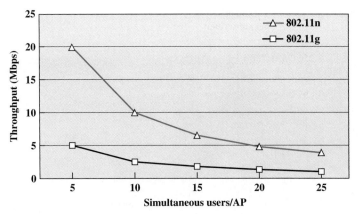

Figure 13.12 Average Throughput per User

13.5 GIGABIT WI-FI

Just as there has been a need to extend the Ethernet standard to speeds in the giga-bit per second range, the same requirement exists for Wi-Fi. Accordingly, IEEE 802.11 has recently introduced two new standards, 802.11ac and 802.11ad, which provide for Wi-Fi networks that operate at well in excess of 1 Gbps. We look at these two standards in turn.

IEEE 802.11ac

IEEE 802.11ac operates in the 5-GHz band, as does 802.11a and 802.11n. It is designed to provide a smooth evolution from 802.11n. The new standard achieves much higher data rates than 802.11n by means of enhancements in three areas (Figure 13.13):

- **Bandwidth:** The maximum bandwidth of 802.11n is 40 MHz; the maximum bandwidth of 802.11ac is 160 MHz.
- **Signal encoding:** 802.11n uses 64 QAM with OFDM, and 802.11ac uses 256 QAM with OFDM. Thus, more bits are encoded per symbol. Both schemes use forward error correction with a code rate of 5/6 (ratio of data bits to total bits).
- **MIMO:** With 802.11n, there can be a maximum of 4 channel input and 4 channel output antennas. 802.11ac increases this to 8×8.

We can quantify these enhancements using the following formula, which yields the physical layer data rate in bps:

$$\text{Data rate} = \frac{(\text{number of data subcarriers}) \times (\text{number of spatial streams}) \times (\text{data bits per subcarrier})}{(\text{time per OFDM symbol, in seconds})}$$

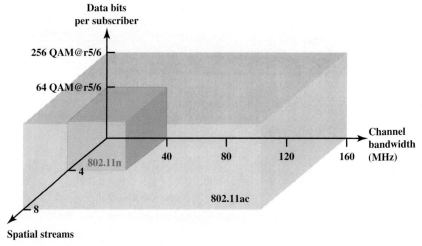

Figure 13.13 IEEE 802.11 Performance Factors

Using this equation, we have the following maximum data rates:

$$802.11\text{n}: \frac{108 \times 4 \times (5/6 \times \log_2 64)}{3.6 \times 10^{-6}} = 600 \times 10^6 \text{ bps} = 600 \text{ Mbps}$$

$$802.11\text{ac}: \frac{468 \times 8 \times (5/6 \times \log_2 256)}{3.6 \times 10^{-6}} = 6937 \times 10^6 \text{ bps} = 6.937 \text{ Gbps}$$

Increasing the channel bandwidth by a factor of 4 approximately quadruples the data rate. The transmit power must now be spread over 4 times as many subcarriers, resulting in a slight reduction in range. Going from 64 QAM to 256 QAM increases the data rate by a factor of 1.33. However, 256 QAM is more sensitive to noise and thus is most effective at shorter ranges. Finally, the speed is directly proportional to the number of spatial streams. Of course, more spatial streams require more antennas, increasing the cost of the subscriber device.

Two other changes going from 802.11n to 802.11ac are noteworthy. 802.11ac includes the option of multiuser MIMO (MU-MIMO). This means that on the downlink, the transmitter is able to use its antenna resources to transmit multiple frames to different stations, all at the same time and over the same frequency spectrum. Thus, each antenna of a MU-MIMO AP can simultaneously communicate with a different single-antenna device, such as a smartphone or tablet. This enables the AP to deliver significantly more data in many environments.

Another difference is that 802.11ac requires that every 802.11ac transmission to be sent as an A-MPDU aggregate. Briefly, this requirement is imposed to guarantee efficient use of the channel. For a more extended explanation, see [CISC12b].

IEEE 802.11ad

IEEE 802.11ad is a version of 802.11 operating in the 60-GHz frequency band. This band offers the potential for much wider channel bandwidth than the 5-GHz band, enabling high data rates with relatively simple signal encoding and antenna characteristics. Few devices operate in the 60-GHz band, which means communications would experience less interference than in the other bands used by 802.11.

However, at 60 GHz, 802.11ad is operating in the millimeter range, which has some undesirable propagation characteristics:

1. Free space loss increases with the square of the frequency [Equation (4.3)]; thus losses are much higher in this range than in the ranges used for traditional microwave systems.

2. Multipath losses can be quite high. Reflection occurs when an electromagnetic signal encounters a surface that is large relative to the wavelength of the signal; scattering occurs if the size of an obstacle is on the order of the wavelength of the signal or less; diffraction occurs when the wavefront encounters the edge of an obstacle that is large compared to the wavelength.

3. Millimeter-wave signals generally don't penetrate solid objects.

For these reasons, 802.11ad is likely to be useful only within a single room. Because it can support high data rates and, for example, could easily transmit uncompressed high-definition video, it is suitable for applications such as replacing wires in a home entertainment system, or streaming high-definition movies from your cell phone to your television.

There are two striking differences between 802.11ac and 802.11ad. Whereas 802.11ac supports a MIMO antenna configuration, 802.11ad is designed for single-antenna operation. And 802.11ad has a huge channel bandwidth of 2160 MHz.

IEEE 802.11ad defines four physical layer modulation and coding schemes (Table 13.6). Each type has a distinct purpose and supports a different range of data rates.

Control PHY (CPHY) is by far the most robustly coded (and consequently, lowest throughput) mode, with a code rate of only 1/2. Its purpose is exclusively to transmit control channel messages. The CPHY robustness is evident from its use of differential encoding, code spreading, and BPSK modulation. Differential encoding eliminates the need for carrier tracking, 32× spreading contributes a theoretical 15 dB gain to the link budget, and BPSK is very noise tolerant.

As with CPHY, **single-carrier PHY (SCPHY)** uses the powerful low-density parity-check (LDPC) code for robust forward error correction and provides three options for modulation. The set of options for code rate and modulation density allow for a trade-off between throughput and robustness to be determined operationally.

OFDM PHY (OFDMPHY) employs multicarrier modulation, which can provide higher modulation densities and hence higher data throughput than the single-carrier options. As with SCPHY, OFDMPHY provides a choice of error protection ratio and the depth of modulation applied to the OFDM data carriers, again to provide operational control over the robustness/throughput trade-off. The choice between SCPHY and OFDMPHY depends on several factors. OFDM modulation will generally impose greater power requirements than SCPHY, but is more robust in the presence of multipath distortion.

Table 13.6   IEEE 802.11ad Modulation and Coding Schemes

Physical Layer	Coding	Modulation	Raw Bit Rate
Control (CPHY)	1/2 LDPC, 32 × spreading	π/2-DBPSK	27.5 Mbps
Single carrier (SCPHY)	1/2 LDPC 1/2 LDPC, 5/8 LDPC 3/4 LDPC 13/16 LDPC	π/2-BPSK π/2-QPSK π/2-16 QAM	385 Mbps to 4.62 Gbps
OFDM (OFDMPHY)	1/2 LDPC 5/8 LDPC 3/4 LDPC 13/16 LDPC	OFDM-OQPSK OFDM-QPSK OFDM-16 QAM OFDM-64 QAM	693 Mbps to 6.76 Gbps
Low-power single carrier (LPSCPHY)	RS(224,208) + Block Code(16/12/9/8,8)	π/2-BPSK π/2-QPSK	636 Mbps to 2.5 Gbps

BPSK = binary phase shift keying

DBPSK = differential binary phase shift keying

LDPC = low-density parity-check code

OFDM = orthogonal frequency-division multiplexing

OQPSK = offset quadrature phase shift keying

QAM = quadrature amplitude modulation

QPSK = quadrature phase shift keying

RS = Reed–Solomon

The LDPC error-correcting coding technique that is common to the CPHY, SCPHY, and OFDMPHY is based on a common codeword length of 672 bits carrying 336, 504, 420, or 546 payload bits to achieve a code rate of 1/2, 3/4, 5/8, or 13/16 as required.

Low-power single carrier (LPSCPHY) employs single-carrier modulation to minimize power consumption. It also uses either Reed–Solomon or Hamming block codes, which require less IC area and hence less power than LDPC, at the expense of less robust error correction. Small battery-powered devices could benefit from the extra power savings.

13.6 IEEE 802.11 SECURITY CONSIDERATIONS

There are two characteristics of a wired LAN that are not inherent in a WLAN.

1. In order to transmit over a wired LAN, a station must be physically connected to the LAN. On the other hand, with a WLAN, any station within radio range of the other devices on the LAN can transmit. In a sense, there is a form of authentication with a wired LAN, in that it requires some positive and presumably observable action to connect a station to a wired LAN.

2. Similarly, in order to receive a transmission from a station that is part of a wired LAN, the receiving station must also be attached to the wired LAN. On the other hand, with a WLAN, any station within radio range can receive. Thus, a wired LAN provides a degree of privacy, limiting reception of data to stations connected to the LAN.

Access and Privacy Services

IEEE 802.11 defines three services that provide a WLAN with these two features:

- **Authentication:** Used to establish the identity of stations to each other. In a wired LAN, it is generally assumed that access to a physical connection conveys authority to connect to the LAN. This is not a valid assumption for a WLAN, in which connectivity is achieved simply by having an attached antenna that is properly tuned. The authentication service is used by stations to establish their identity with stations they wish to communicate with. IEEE 802.11 supports several authentication schemes and allows for expansion of the functionality of these schemes. The standard does not mandate any particular authentication scheme, which could range from relatively unsecure handshaking to public-key encryption schemes. However, IEEE 802.11 requires mutually acceptable, successful authentication before a station can establish an association with an AP.

- **Deauthentication:** This service is invoked whenever an existing authentication is to be terminated.

- **Privacy:** Used to prevent the contents of messages from being read by other than the intended recipient. The standard provides for the optional use of encryption to assure privacy.

Wireless LAN Security Standards

The original 802.11 specification included a set of security features for privacy and authentication that, unfortunately, were quite weak. For **privacy**, 802.11 defined the Wired Equivalent Privacy (WEP) algorithm. The privacy portion of the 802.11 standard contained major weaknesses. Subsequent to the development of WEP, the 802.11i task group has developed a set of capabilities to address the WLAN security issues. In order to accelerate the introduction of strong security into WLANs, the Wi-Fi Alliance promulgated **Wi-Fi Protected Access (WPA)** as a Wi-Fi standard. WPA is a set of security mechanisms that eliminates most 802.11 security issues and was based on the current state of the 802.11i standard. As 802.11i evolves, WPA will evolve to maintain compatibility.

WPA is examined in Chapter 27.

13.7 RECOMMENDED READING

A brief but useful survey of 802.11 is [MCFA03]. [GEIE01] has a good discussion of IEEE 802.11a. [PETR00] summarizes IEEE 802.11b. [SHOE02] provides an overview of IEEE 802.11g. [XIAO04] discusses 802.11e. [CISC07] is a detailed treatment of IEEE 802.11n. [SKOR08] is a thorough examination of the 802.11n MAC frame aggregation scheme. [HALP10] examines the 802.11n MIMO scheme. [ALSA13] is a good technical introduction to 802.11ac. [CORD10] and [PERA10] provide good technical overviews of 802.11ad.

ALSA13 Alsabbagh, E.; Yu, H.; and Gallagher, K. "802.11ac Design Consideration for Mobile Devices." *Microwave Journal,* February 2013.

CISC07 Cisco Systems, Inc. "802.11n: The Next Generation of Wireless Performance." Cisco White Paper, 2007, cisco.com

CORD10 Cordeiro, C.; Akhmetov, D.; and Park, M. "IEEE 802.11ad: Introduction and Performance Evaluation of the First Multi-Gbps WiFi Technology." Proceedings of the 2010 ACM international workshop on mmWave communications: From circuits to networks, 2010.

GEIE01 Geier, J. "Enabling Fast Wireless Networks with OFDM." *Communications System Design*, www.csdmag.com, February 2001.

HALP10 Halperin, D., et al. "802.11 with Multiple Antennas for Dummies." *Computer Communication Review*, January 2010.

MCFA03 McFarland, B., and Wong, M. "The Family Dynamics of 802.11." *ACM Queue*, May 2003.

PERA10 Perahia, E., et al. "IEEE 802.11ad: Defining the Next Generation Multi-Gbps Wi-Fi." Proceedings, 7th IEEE Consumer Communications and Networking Conference, 2010.

PETR00 Petrick, A. "IEEE 802.11b—Wireless Ethernet." *Communications System Design*, June 2000, www.commsdesign.com

SHOE02 Shoemake, M. "IEEE 802.11g Jells as Applications Mount." *Communications System Design*, April 2002, www.commsdesign.com

SKOR08 Skordoulis, D., et al. "IEEE 802.11n MAC Frame Aggregation Mechanisms for Next-Generation High-Throughput WLANs." *IEEE Wireless Communications*, February 2008.

XIAO04 Xiao, Y. "IEEE 802.11e: QoS Provisioning at the MAC Layer." *IEEE Communications Magazine*, June 2004.

13.8 KEY TERMS, REVIEW QUESTIONS, AND PROBLEMS

Key Terms

access point (AP) ad hoc networking basic service set (BSS) complementary code keying (CCK)	coordination function distributed coordination function (DCF) distribution system (DS) extended service set (ESS)	narrowband microwave LAN point coordination function (PCF) wireless LAN (WLAN)

Review Questions

13.1 List and briefly define key requirements for WLANs.

13.2 What is the difference between a single-cell and a multiple-cell WLAN?

13.3 What is the difference between an access point and a portal?

13.4 Is a distribution system a wireless network?

13.5 List and briefly define IEEE 802.11 services.

13.6 How is the concept of an association related to that of mobility?

Problems

13.1 Consider the sequence of actions within a BSS depicted in Figure 13.14. Draw a time-line, beginning with a period during which the medium is busy and ending with a period in which the CF-End is broadcast from the AP. Show the transmission periods and the gaps.

13.2 IEEE 802.11 incorporates collision avoidance. If a collision occurs during the transition of control frames, how can it be handled?

13.3 The 802.11a and 802.11b physical layers make use of data scrambling (see Appendix 12B). For 802.11, the scrambling equation is

$$P(X) = 1 + X^4 + X^7$$

In this case the shift register consists of seven elements, used in the same manner as the five-element register in Figure 12.17. For the 802.11 scrambler and descrambler,

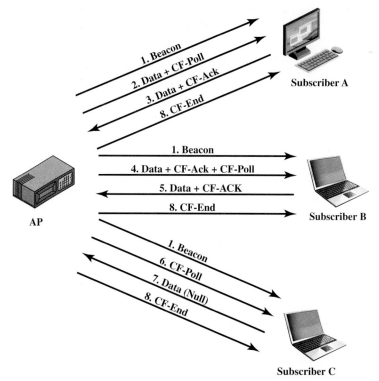

Figure 13.14 Configuration for Problem 13.1

    a. Show the expression with exclusive-or operators that corresponds to the polynomial definition.

    b. Draw a figure similar to Figure 12.17.

13.4 Find the size of an IEEE 802.11 MAC frame with a frame body of 400 bytes.

13.5 Answer the following questions about your wireless network:

    a. What is the SSID?

    b. Who is the equipment vendor?

    c. What standard are you using?

    d. What is the size of the network?

13.6 Network topology generally refers to the physical layout of devices in a network. What is WLAN topology? Briefly describe the most widely used WLAN topologies.

13.7 There are many free tools and applications available for helping decipher wireless networks. One of the most popular is Netstumbler. Obtain the software at www.netstumbler.com and follow the links for downloads. The site has a list of supported wireless cards. Using the Netstumbler software, determine the following:

    a. How many access points in your network have the same SSID?

    b. What is your signal strength to your access point?

    c. How many other wireless networks and access points can you find?

13.8 Most wireless cards come with a small set of applications that can perform tasks similar to Netstumbler. Using your own client software, determine the same items you did with Netstumbler. Do they agree?

13.9 Try this experiment: How far can you go and still be connected to your network? This will depend to a large extent on your physical environment.

13.10 How is IEEE 802.11ad different from IEEE 802.11ac? How have the differences impacted their application areas?

13.11 Two documents related to safety concerns associated with wireless media are the FCC OET-65 Bulletin and the ANSI/IEEE C95.1-1999. Briefly describe the purpose of these documents and briefly outline the safety concerns associated with WLAN technology.

THE INTERNET PROTOCOL

LEARNING OBJECTIVES

After studying this chapter, you should be able to:

◆ Understand the principles of operation of internetworking.

◆ Present an overview of the operation of IP.

◆ Compare and contrast IPv4 and IPv6.

◆ Understand IPv4 and IPv6 address formats.

◆ Explain how IPsec is used to create virtual private networks.

The purpose of this chapter is to examine the Internet Protocol, which is the foundation on which all of the internet-based protocols and internetworking are based. First, it will be useful to provide a general discussion of internetworking. Next, the chapter focuses on the two standard internet protocols: IPv4 and IPv6. Finally, the topic of IP security is introduced.

Refer to Figure 2.8 to see the position within the TCP/IP suite of the protocols discussed in this chapter.

14.1 PRINCIPLES OF INTERNETWORKING

Packet-switching and packet-broadcasting networks grew out of a need to allow the computer user to have access to resources beyond that available in a single system. In a similar fashion, the resources of a single network are often inadequate to meet users' needs. Because the networks that might be of interest exhibit so many differences, it is impractical to consider merging them into a single network. Rather, what is needed is the ability to interconnect various networks so that any two stations on any of the constituent networks can communicate.

Table 14.1 lists some commonly used terms relating to the interconnection of networks, or internetworking. An interconnected set of networks, from a user's point of view, may appear simply as a larger network. However, if each of the constituent networks retains its identity and special mechanisms are needed for communicating across multiple networks, then the entire configuration is often referred to as an **internet.**

Each constituent network in an internet supports communication among the devices attached to that network; these devices are referred to as **end systems (ESs)**. In addition, networks are connected by devices referred to in the

Table 14.1 Internetworking Terms

Communication Network
A facility that provides a data transfer service among devices attached to the network.

Internet
A collection of communication networks interconnected by bridges and/or routers.

Intranet
An internet used by a single organization that provides the key Internet applications, especially the World Wide Web. An intranet operates within the organization for internal purposes and can exist as an isolated, self-contained internet, or may have links to the Internet.

Subnetwork
Refers to a constituent network of an internet. This avoids ambiguity because the entire internet, from a user's point of view, is a single network.

End System (ES)
A device attached to one of the networks of an internet that is used to support end-user applications or services.

Intermediate System (IS)
A device used to connect two networks and permit communication between end systems attached to different networks.

Bridge
An IS used to connect two LANs that use similar LAN protocols. The bridge acts as an address filter, picking up packets from one LAN that are intended for a destination on another LAN and passing those packets on. The bridge does not modify the contents of the packets and does not add anything to the packet. The bridge operates at layer 2 of the OSI model.

Router
An IS used to connect two networks that may or may not be similar. The router employs an internet protocol present in each router and each end system of the network. The router operates at layer 3 of the OSI model.

ISO documents as **intermediate systems (ISs)**. Intermediate systems provide a communications path and perform the necessary relaying and routing functions so that data can be exchanged between devices attached to different networks in the internet.

Two types of ISs of particular interest are bridges and routers. The differences between them have to do with the types of protocols used for the internetworking logic. In essence, a **bridge** operates at layer 2 of the open systems interconnection (OSI) seven-layer architecture and acts as a relay of frames between similar networks; bridges are discussed in Chapter 11. A **router** operates at layer 3 of the OSI architecture and routes packets between potentially different networks.

We begin our examination of internetworking with a discussion of basic principles. We then examine the most important architectural approach to internetworking: the connectionless router.

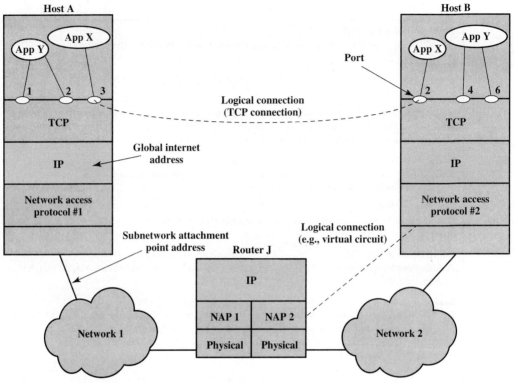

Figure 14.1   TCP/IP Concepts

Requirements

The overall requirements for an internetworking facility are as follows (we refer to Figure 14.1, which repeats Figure 2.4, as an example throughout):

1. Provide a link between networks. At minimum, a physical and link control connection is needed. (Router J has physical links to N1 and N2, and on each link there is a data link protocol.)

2. Provide for the routing and delivery of data between processes on different networks. (Application X on host A exchanges data with application X on host B.)

3. Provide an accounting service that keeps track of the use of the various networks and routers and maintains status information.

4. Provide the services just listed in such a way as not to require modifications to the networking architecture of any of the constituent networks. This means that the internetworking facility must accommodate a number of differences among networks. These include:

   - **Different addressing schemes:** The networks may use different endpoint names and addresses and directory maintenance schemes. Some form of global network addressing must be provided, as well as a directory service. (Hosts A and B and router J have globally unique IP addresses.)

- **Different maximum packet size:** Packets from one network may have to be broken up into smaller pieces for another. This process is referred to as fragmentation. (N1 and N2 may set different upper limits on packet sizes.)
- **Different network access mechanisms:** The network access mechanism between station and network may be different for stations on different networks. (e.g., N1 may be a frame relay network and N2 an Ethernet network.)
- **Different timeouts:** Typically, a connection-oriented transport service will await an acknowledgment until a timeout expires, at which time it will retransmit its block of data. In general, longer times are required for successful delivery across multiple networks. Internetwork timing procedures must allow successful transmission that avoids unnecessary retransmissions.
- **Error recovery:** Network procedures may provide anything from no error recovery up to reliable end-to-end (within the network) service. The internetwork service should not depend on nor be interfered with by the nature of the individual network's error recovery capability.
- **Status reporting:** Different networks report status and performance differently. Yet it must be possible for the internetworking facility to provide such information on internetworking activity to interested and authorized processes.
- **Routing techniques:** Intranetwork routing may depend on fault detection and congestion control techniques peculiar to each network. The internetworking facility must be able to coordinate these to route data adaptively between stations on different networks.
- **User access control:** Each network will have its own user access control technique (authorization for use of the network). These must be invoked by the internetwork facility as needed. Further, a separate internetwork access control technique may be required.
- **Connection, connectionless:** Individual networks may provide connection-oriented (e.g., virtual circuit) or connectionless (datagram) service. It may be desirable for the internetwork service not to depend on the nature of the connection service of the individual networks.

The Internet Protocol meets some of these requirements. Others require additional control and application software, as we shall see in this chapter and the next.

Connectionless Operation

In virtually all implementations, internetworking involves connectionless operation at the level of the Internet Protocol. Whereas connection-oriented operation corresponds to the virtual circuit mechanism of a packet-switching network (Figure 9.12), connectionless-mode operation corresponds to the datagram mechanism of a packet-switching network (Figure 9.11). Each network protocol data unit is treated independently and routed from source ES to destination ES through a series of routers and networks. For each data unit transmitted by A, A makes a decision as to which router should receive the data unit. The data unit hops across the internet from one router to the next until it reaches the destination network. At each router, a routing decision is made (independently for each data unit) concerning the next hop. Thus, different data units may travel different routes between source and destination ES.

All ESs and routers share a common network-layer protocol known generically as the Internet Protocol. An Internet Protocol was initially developed for the DARPA internet project and published as RFC 791 and has become an Internet Standard. Below this Internet Protocol, a protocol is needed to access a particular network. Thus, there are typically two protocols operating in each ES and router at the network layer: an upper sublayer that provides the internetworking function and a lower sublayer that provides network access. Figure 14.2 shows an example. We discuss this example in detail in the next section.

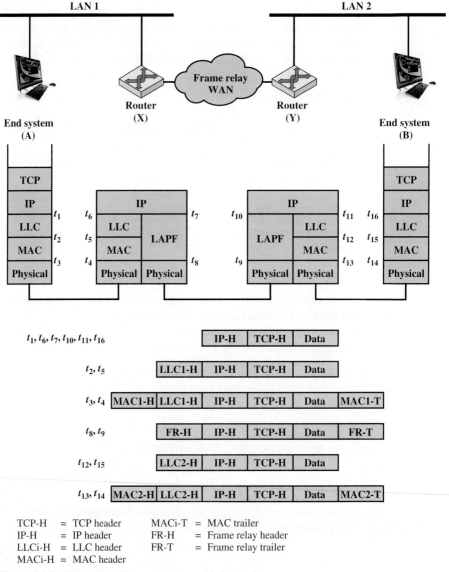

Figure 14.2   Example of Internet Protocol Operation

In this section, we examine the essential functions of an internetwork protocol. For convenience, we refer specifically to the Internet Standard IPv4, but the narrative in this section applies to any connectionless Internet Protocol, such as IPv6.

Operation of a Connectionless Internetworking Scheme

IP provides a connectionless, or datagram, service between end systems. There are a number of advantages to this approach:

- A connectionless internet facility is flexible. It can deal with a variety of networks, some of which are themselves connectionless. In essence, IP requires very little from the constituent networks.
- A connectionless internet service can be made highly robust. This is basically the same argument made for a datagram network service versus a virtual circuit service. For a further discussion, see Section 9.5.
- A connectionless internet service is best for connectionless transport protocols, because it does not impose unnecessary overhead.

Figure 14.2 depicts a typical example using IP, in which two LANs are interconnected by a frame relay WAN. The figure depicts the operation of the Internet Protocol for data exchange between host A on one LAN (network 1) and host B on another LAN (network 2) through the WAN. The figure shows the protocol architecture and format of the data unit at each stage. The end systems and routers must all share a common Internet Protocol. In addition, the end systems must share the same protocols above IP. The intermediate routers need only implement up through IP.

The IP at A receives blocks of data to be sent to B from a higher layer of software in A (e.g., TCP or UDP). IP attaches a header (at time t_1) specifying, among other things, the global internet address of B. That address is logically in two parts: network identifier and end system identifier. The combination of IP header and upper-level data is called an Internet Protocol data unit (PDU), or simply a datagram. The datagram is then encapsulated with the LAN protocol (LLC header at t_2; MAC header and trailer at t_3) and sent to the router, which strips off the LAN fields to read the IP header (t_6). The router modifies the IP header if necessary (t_7) and then encapsulates the datagram with the frame relay protocol fields (t_8) and transmits it across the WAN to another router. This router strips off the frame relay fields and recovers the datagram, which it then wraps in LAN fields appropriate to LAN 2 and sends it to B.

Let us now look at this example in more detail. End system A has a datagram to transmit to end system B; the datagram includes the internet address of B. The IP module in A recognizes that the destination (B) is on another network. So the first step is to send the data to a router, in this case router X. To do this, IP passes the datagram down to the next lower layer (in this case LLC) with instructions to send it to router X. LLC in turn passes this information down to the MAC layer, which inserts the MAC-level address of router X into the MAC header. Thus, the block of data transmitted onto LAN 1 includes data from a layer or layers above TCP, plus a TCP header, an IP header, an LLC header, and a MAC header and trailer (time t_3 in Figure 14.2).

Next, the packet travels through network 1 to router X. The router removes MAC and LLC fields and analyzes the IP header to determine the ultimate destination of the data, in this case B. The router must now make a routing decision. There are three possibilities:

1. The destination B is connected directly to one of the networks to which the router is attached. If so, the router sends the datagram directly to the destination.
2. To reach the destination, one or more additional routers must be traversed. If so, a routing decision must be made: To which router should the datagram be sent?
3. The router does not know the destination address. In this case, the router returns an error message to the source of the datagram.

In both cases 1 and 2, the IP module in the router sends the datagram down to the next lower layer with the destination network address. Please note that we are speaking here of a lower-layer address that refers to this network.

In this example, the data must pass through router Y before reaching the destination. So router X constructs a new frame by appending a frame relay (LAPF) header and trailer to the IP datagram. The frame relay header indicates a logical connection to router Y. When this frame arrives at router Y, the frame header and trailer are stripped off. The router determines that this IP data unit is destined for B, which is connected directly to a network to which this router is attached. The router therefore creates a frame with a layer-2 destination address of B and sends it out onto LAN 2. The data finally arrive at B, where the LAN and IP headers can be stripped off.

At each router, before the data can be forwarded, the router may need to fragment the datagram to accommodate a smaller maximum packet size limitation on the outgoing network. If so, the data unit is split into two or more fragments, each of which becomes an independent IP datagram. Each new data unit is wrapped in a lower-layer packet and queued for transmission. The router may also limit the length of its queue for each network to which it attaches so as to avoid having a slow network penalize a faster one. Once the queue limit is reached, additional data units are simply dropped.

The process just described continues through as many routers as it takes for the data unit to reach its destination. As with a router, the destination end system recovers the IP datagram from its network wrapping. If fragmentation has occurred, the IP module in the destination end system buffers the incoming data until the entire original data field can be reassembled. This block of data is then passed to a higher layer in the end system.[1]

This service offered by IP is an unreliable one. That is, IP does not guarantee that all data will be delivered or that the data that are delivered will arrive in the proper order. It is the responsibility of the next higher layer (e.g., TCP) to recover from any errors that occur. This approach provides for a great deal of flexibility.

---

[1]Appendix O provides a more detailed example, showing the involvement of all protocol layers.

With the Internet Protocol approach, each unit of data is passed from router to router in an attempt to get from source to destination. Because delivery is not guaranteed, there is no particular reliability requirement on any of the networks. Thus, the protocol will work with any combination of network types. Because the sequence of delivery is not guaranteed, successive data units can follow different paths through the internet. This allows the protocol to react to both congestion and failure in the internet by changing routes.

Design Issues

With that brief sketch of the operation of an IP-controlled internet, we now examine some design issues in greater detail:

- Routing
- Datagram lifetime
- Fragmentation and reassembly
- Error control
- Flow control

As we proceed with this discussion, note the many similarities with design issues and techniques relevant to packet-switching networks. To see the reason for this, consider Figure 14.3, which compares an internet architecture with a packet-switching network architecture. The routers (R1, R2, R3) in the internet correspond to the packet-switching nodes (P1, P2, P3) in the network, and the networks (N1, N2, N3) in the internet correspond to the transmission links (T1, T2, T3) in the networks. The routers perform essentially the same functions as packet-switching nodes and use the intervening networks in a manner analogous to transmission links.

ROUTING   For the purpose of routing, each end system and router maintains a routing table that lists, for each possible destination network, the next router to which the internet datagram should be sent.

The routing table may be static or dynamic. A static table, however, could contain alternate routes if a particular router is unavailable. A dynamic table is more flexible in responding to both error and congestion conditions. In the Internet, for example, when a router goes down, all of its neighbors will send out a status report, allowing other routers and stations to update their routing tables. A similar scheme can be used to control congestion. Congestion control is particularly important because of the mismatch in capacity between local and wide area networks. Chapter 19 discusses routing protocols.

Routing tables may also be used to support other internetworking services, such as security and priority. For example, individual networks might be classified to handle data up to a given security classification. The routing mechanism must assure that data of a given security level are not allowed to pass through networks not cleared to handle such data.

Another routing technique is source routing. The source station specifies the route by including a sequential list of routers in the datagram. This, again, could be useful for security or priority requirements.

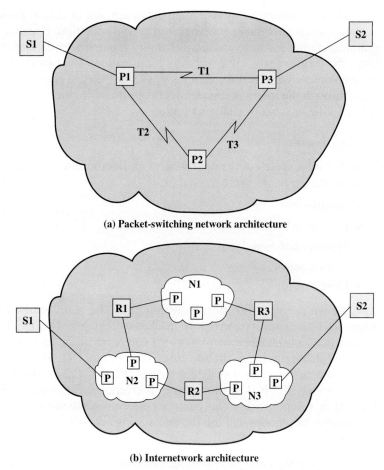

(a) Packet-switching network architecture

(b) Internetwork architecture

Figure 14.3   The Internet as a Network (based on [HIND83])

Finally, we mention a service related to routing: route recording. To record a route, each router appends its internet address to a list of addresses in the datagram. This feature is useful for testing and debugging purposes.

DATAGRAM LIFETIME   If dynamic or alternate routing is used, the potential exists for a datagram to loop indefinitely through the internet. This is undesirable for two reasons. First, an endlessly circulating datagram consumes resources. Second, we will see in Chapter 15 that a transport protocol may depend on the existence of an upper bound on **datagram lifetime**. To avoid these problems, each datagram can be marked with a lifetime. Once the lifetime expires, the datagram is discarded.

A simple way to implement lifetime is to use a hop count. Each time that a datagram passes through a router, the count is decremented. Alternatively, the lifetime could be a true measure of time. This requires that the routers must somehow know how long it has been since the datagram or fragment last crossed a router, to know by how much to decrement the lifetime field. This would seem to require some global clocking mechanism. The advantage of using a true time measure is that it can be used in the reassembly algorithm, described next.

FRAGMENTATION AND REASSEMBLY   The Internet Protocol accepts a block of data from a higher-layer protocol, such as TCP or UDP, and may divide this block into multiple blocks of some smaller bounded size to form multiple IP packets. This process is called **fragmentation**.[2]

There are a number of motivations for fragmentation, depending on the context. Among the typical reasons for fragmentation are the following:

- The communications network may only accept blocks of data up to a certain size. For example, an ATM network is limited to blocks of 53 octets; Ethernet imposes a maximum size of 2008 octets.

- Error control may be more efficient with a smaller PDU size. With smaller PDUs, fewer bits need to be retransmitted when a PDU suffers an error.

- More equitable access to shared transmission facilities, with shorter delay, can be provided. For example, without a maximum block size, one station could monopolize a multipoint medium.

- A smaller PDU size may mean that receiving entities can allocate smaller buffers.

- An entity may require that data transfer comes to some sort of "closure" from time to time, for checkpoint and restart/recovery operations.

There are several disadvantages to fragmentation that argue for making PDUs as large as possible:

- Because each PDU contains a certain amount of control information, smaller blocks have a greater percentage of overhead.

- PDU arrival may generate an interrupt that must be serviced. Smaller blocks result in more interrupts.

- More time is spent processing smaller, more numerous PDUs.

If datagrams can be fragmented (perhaps more than once) in the course of their travel, the question arises as to where they should be reassembled. The easiest solution is to have reassembly performed at the destination only. The principal disadvantage of this approach is that fragments can only get smaller as data move through the internet. This may impair the efficiency of some networks. However, if intermediate router reassembly is allowed, the following disadvantages result:

1. Large buffers are required at routers, and there is the risk that all of the buffer space will be used up storing partial datagrams.

2. All fragments of a datagram must pass through the same router. This inhibits the use of dynamic routing.

---

[2]The term *segmentation* is used in OSI-related documents, but in protocol specifications related to the TCP/IP suite, the term *fragmentation* is used. The meaning is the same.

In IP, datagram fragments are reassembled at the destination end system. The IP fragmentation technique uses the following information in the IP header:

- Data Unit Identifier (ID)
- Data Length[3]
- Offset
- More Flag

The *ID* is a means of uniquely identifying an end-system-originated datagram. In IP, it consists of the source and destination addresses, a number that corresponds to the protocol layer that generated the data (e.g., TCP), and an identification supplied by that protocol layer. The *Data Length* is the length of the user data field in octets, and the *Offset* is the position of a fragment of user data in the data field of the original datagram, in multiples of 64 bits.

The source end system creates a datagram with a *Data Length* equal to the entire length of the data field, with *Offset* = 0 and a *More Flag* set to 0 (false). To fragment a long datagram into two pieces, an IP module in a router performs the following tasks:

1. Create two new datagrams and copy the header fields of the incoming datagram into both.
2. Divide the incoming user data field into two portions along a 64-bit boundary (counting from the beginning), placing one portion in each new datagram. The first portion must be a multiple of 64 bits (8 octets).
3. Set the *Data Length* of the first new datagram to the length of the inserted data, and set *More Flag* to 1 (true). The *Offset* field is unchanged.
4. Set the *Data Length* of the second new datagram to the length of the inserted data, and add the length of the first data portion divided by 8 to the *Offset* field. The *More Flag* remains the same.

EXAMPLE 14.1 Figure 14.4 gives an example in which two fragments are created from an original IP datagram. The procedure is easily generalized to an *n*-way split. In this example, the payload of the original IP datagram is a TCP segment, consisting of a TCP header and application data. The IP header from the original datagram is used in both fragments, with the appropriate changes to the fragmentation-related fields. Note that the first fragment contains the TCP header; this header is not replicated in the second fragment, because all of the IP payload, including the TCP header is transparent to IP. That is, IP is not concerned with the contents of the payload of the datagram.

[3]In the IPv6 header, there is a Payload Length field that corresponds to Data Length in this discussion. In the IPv4 header, there is Total Length field whose value is the length of the header plus data; the data length must be calculated by subtracting the header length.

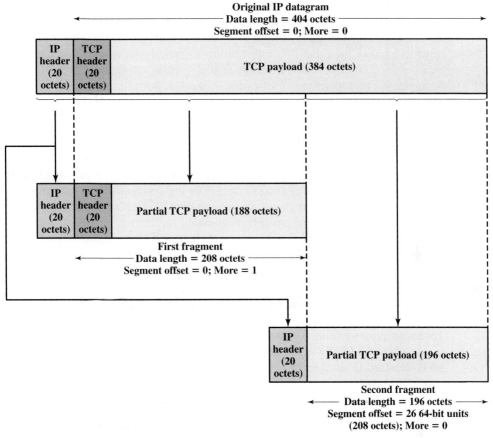

Figure 14.4 Fragmentation Example

To reassemble a datagram, there must be sufficient buffer space at the reassembly point. As fragments with the same ID arrive, their data fields are inserted in the proper position in the buffer until the entire data field is reassembled, which is achieved when a contiguous set of data exists starting with an *Offset* of zero and ending with data from a fragment with a false *More Flag*.

One eventuality that must be dealt with is that one or more of the fragments may not get through; the IP service does not guarantee delivery. Some method is needed to decide when to abandon a reassembly effort to free up buffer space. Two approaches are commonly used. First, assign a reassembly lifetime to the first fragment to arrive. This is a local, real-time clock assigned by the reassembly function and decremented while the fragments of the original datagram are being buffered. If the time expires prior to complete reassembly, the received fragments are discarded. A second approach is to make use of the datagram lifetime, which is part of the header of each incoming fragment. The lifetime field continues to be decremented by the reassembly function; as with the first approach, if the lifetime expires prior to complete reassembly, the received fragments are discarded.

ERROR CONTROL The internetwork facility does not guarantee successful delivery of every datagram. When a datagram is discarded by a router, the router should attempt to return some information to the source, if possible. The source Internet Protocol entity may use this information to modify its transmission strategy and may notify higher layers. To report that a specific datagram has been discarded, some means of datagram identification is needed. Such identification is discussed in the next section.

Datagrams may be discarded for a number of reasons, including lifetime expiration, congestion, and FCS error. In the latter case, notification is not possible because the Source Address field may have been damaged.

FLOW CONTROL Internet flow control allows routers and/or receiving stations to limit the rate at which they receive data. For the connectionless type of service we are describing, flow control mechanisms are limited. The best approach would seem to be to send flow control packets, requesting reduced data flow, to other routers and source stations. We will see one example of this with Internet Control Message Protocol (ICMP), discussed in the next section.

14.3 INTERNET PROTOCOL

In this section, we look at version 4 of IP, officially defined in RFC 791. Although it is intended that IPv4 will ultimately be replaced by IPv6, IPv4 is currently the dominant standard IP used in TCP/IP networks.

IP is part of the TCP/IP suite and is the most widely used internetworking protocol. As with any protocol standard, IP is specified in two parts (see Figure 2.9):

- The interface with a higher layer (e.g., TCP), specifying the services that IP provides
- The actual protocol format and mechanisms

In this section, we examine first IP services and then the protocol. This is followed by a discussion of IP address formats. Finally, the ICMP, which is an integral part of IP, is described.

IP Services

The services to be provided across adjacent protocol layers (e.g., between IP and TCP) are expressed in terms of primitives and parameters. A primitive specifies the function to be performed, and the parameters are used to pass data and control information. The actual form of a primitive is implementation dependent. An example is a procedure call.

IP provides two service primitives at the interface to the next higher layer. The Send primitive is used to request transmission of a data unit. The Deliver primitive is used by IP to notify a user of the arrival of a data unit. The parameters associated with the two primitives are as follows:

- **Source address:** Internetwork address of sending IP entity.
- **Destination address:** Internetwork address of destination IP entity.

- **Protocol:** Recipient protocol entity (an IP user, such as TCP).
- **Type-of-service indicators:** Used to specify the treatment of the data unit in its transmission through component networks.
- **Identification:** Used in combination with the source and destination addresses and user protocol to identify the data unit uniquely. This parameter is needed for reassembly and error reporting.
- **Don't fragment identifier:** Indicates whether IP can fragment data to accomplish delivery.
- **Time to live (TTL):** Measured in seconds.
- **Data length:** Length of data being transmitted.
- **Option data:** Options requested by the IP user.
- **Data:** User data to be transmitted.

The *identification, don't fragment identifier,* and *time to live* parameters are present in the Send primitive but not in the Deliver primitive. These three parameters provide instructions to IP that are not of concern to the recipient IP user.

The options parameter allows for future extensibility and for inclusion of parameters that are usually not invoked. The currently defined options are the following:

- **Security:** Allows a security label to be attached to a datagram.
- **Source routing:** A sequenced list of router addresses that specifies the route to be followed. Routing may be strict (only identified routers may be visited) or loose (other intermediate routers may be visited).
- **Route recording:** A field is allocated to record the sequence of routers visited by the datagram.
- **Stream identification:** Names reserved resources used for stream service. This service provides special handling for volatile periodic traffic (e.g., voice).
- **Timestamping:** The source IP entity and some or all intermediate routers add a timestamp (precision to milliseconds) to the data unit as it goes by.

Internet Protocol

The protocol between IP entities is best described with reference to the IP datagram format, shown in Figure 14.5a. The fields are as follows:

- **Version (4 bits):** Indicates version number, to allow evolution of the protocol; the value is 4.
- **Internet Header Length (IHL) (4 bits):** Length of header in 32-bit words. The minimum value is 5, for a minimum header length of 20 octets.
- **DS (6 bits):** This field supports the Differentiated Service function, described in Chapter 22.
- **ECN (2 bits):** The Explicit Congestion Notification field, defined in RFC 3168, enables routers to indicate to end nodes packets that are experiencing congestion, without the necessity of immediately dropping such packets. A value of 00 indicates a packet that is not using ECN. A value of 01 or 10 is set by

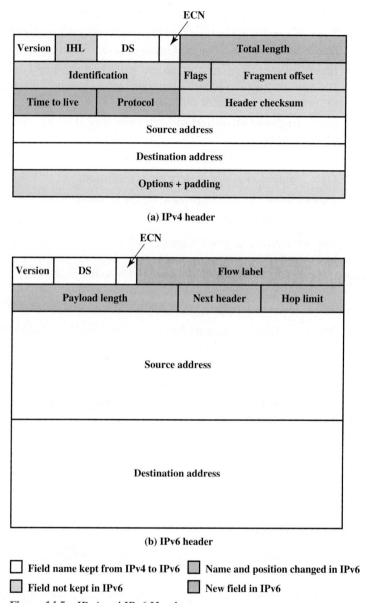

ECN

Version	IHL	DS		Total length	
Identification			Flags	Fragment offset	
Time to live		Protocol	Header checksum		
Source address					
Destination address					
Options + padding					

(a) IPv4 header

ECN

Version	DS		Flow label		
Payload length			Next header	Hop limit	
Source address					
Destination address					

(b) IPv6 header

☐ Field name kept from IPv4 to IPv6   ▨ Name and position changed in IPv6
☐ Field not kept in IPv6   ▨ New field in IPv6

Figure 14.5 IPv4 and IPv6 Headers

the data sender to indicate that the end-points of the transport protocol are ECN-capable. A value of 11 is set by a router to indicate congestion has been encountered. The combination of DS and ECN was originally defined as an 8-bit field called Type of Service, but the DS and ECN interpretation is now used.

- **Total Length (16 bits):** Total datagram length, including header plus data, in octets.

- **Identification (16 bits):** A sequence number that, together with the source address, destination address, and user protocol, is intended to identify a datagram uniquely. Thus, this number should be unique for the datagram's source address, destination address, and user protocol for the time during which the datagram will remain in the internet.

- **Flags (3 bits):** Only two of the bits are currently defined. The More bit is used for fragmentation and reassembly, as previously explained. The Don't Fragment bit prohibits fragmentation when set. This bit may be useful if it is known that the destination does not have the capability to reassemble fragments. However, if this bit is set, the datagram will be discarded if it exceeds the maximum size of an en route network. Therefore, if the bit is set, it may be advisable to use source routing to avoid networks with small maximum packet size.

- **Fragment Offset (13 bits):** Indicates where in the original datagram this fragment belongs, measured in 64-bit units. This implies that fragments other than the last fragment must contain a data field that is a multiple of 64 bits in length.

- **Time to Live (8 bits):** Specifies how long, in seconds, a datagram is allowed to remain in the internet. Every router that processes a datagram must decrease the TTL by at least one, so the TTL is similar to a hop count.

- **Protocol (8 bits):** Indicates the next higher level protocol that is to receive the data field at the destination; thus, this field identifies the type of the next header in the packet after the IP header. Example values are TCP = 6; UDP = 17. A complete list is maintained at http://www.iana.org/assignments/protocol-numbers.

- **Header Checksum (16 bits):** An error-detecting code applied to the header only. Because some header fields may change during transit (e.g., Time to Live, fragmentation-related fields), this is reverified and recomputed at each router. The checksum is formed by taking the ones-complement of the 16-bit ones complement addition of all 16-bit words in the header. For purposes of computation, the checksum field is itself initialized to a value of zero.[4]

- **Source Address (32 bits):** Coded to allow a variable allocation of bits to specify the network and the end system attached to the specified network, as discussed subsequently.

- **Destination Address (32 bits):** Same characteristics as source address.

- **Options (variable):** Encodes the options requested by the sending user.

- **Padding (variable):** Used to ensure that the datagram header is a multiple of 32 bits in length.

- **Data (variable):** The data field must be an integer multiple of 8 bits in length. The maximum length of the datagram (data field plus header) is 65,535 octets.

It should be clear how the IP services specified in the Send and Deliver primitives map into the fields of the IP datagram.

IP Addresses

The Source and Destination Address fields in the IP header each contain a 32-bit global internet address, generally consisting of a network identifier and a host identifier.

---

[4]A discussion of this checksum is contained in Chapter 6.

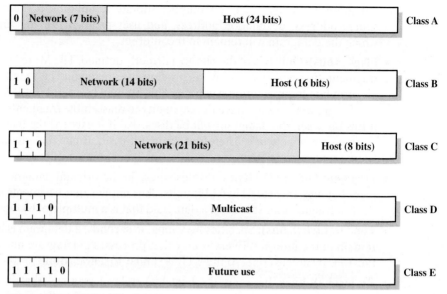

Figure 14.6 IPv4 Address Formats

NETWORK CLASSES   The address is coded to allow a variable allocation of bits to specify network and host, as depicted in Figure 14.6. This encoding provides flexibility in assigning addresses to hosts and allows a mix of network sizes on an internet. The three principal network classes are best suited to the following conditions:

- **Class A:** Few networks, each with many hosts
- **Class B:** Medium number of networks, each with a medium number of hosts
- **Class C:** Many networks, each with a few hosts

In a particular environment, it may be best to use addresses all from one class. For example, a corporate internetwork that consist of a large number of departmental local area networks may need to use Class C addresses exclusively. However, the format of the addresses is such that it is possible to mix all three classes of addresses on the same internetwork; this is what is done in the case of the Internet itself. A mixture of classes is appropriate for an internetwork consisting of a few large networks, many small networks, plus some medium-sized networks.

IP addresses are usually written in **dotted decimal notation,** with a decimal number representing each of the octets of the 32-bit address. For example, the IP address 11000000 11100100 00010001 00111001 is written as 192.228.17.57.

Note that all Class A network addresses begin with a binary 0. Network addresses with a first octet of 0 (binary 00000000) and 127 (binary 01111111) are reserved, so there are 126 potential Class A network numbers, which have a first dotted decimal number in the range 1 to 126. Class B network addresses begin with a binary 10, so that the range of the first decimal number in a Class B address is 128 to 191(binary 10000000 to 10111111). The second octet is also part of the Class B address, so that there are $2^{14} = 16,384$ Class B addresses. For Class C addresses, the first decimal number ranges from 192 to 223 (11000000 to 11011111). The total number of Class C addresses is $2^{21} = 2,097,152$.

SUBNETS AND SUBNET MASKS   The concept of subnet was introduced to address the following requirement. Consider an internet that includes one or more WANs and a number of sites, each of which has a number of LANs. We would like to allow arbitrary complexity of interconnected LAN structures within an organization while insulating the overall internet against explosive growth in network numbers and routing complexity. One approach to this problem is to assign a single network number to all of the LANs at a site. From the point of view of the rest of the internet, there is a single network at that site, which simplifies addressing and routing. To allow the routers within the site to function properly, each LAN is assigned a subnet number. The *host* portion of the internet address is partitioned into a subnet number and a host number to accommodate this new level of addressing.

Within the subnetted network, the local routers must route on the basis of an extended network number consisting of the *network* portion of the IP address and the subnet number. The address mask indicates the bit positions containing this extended network number. The use of the address mask allows the host to determine whether an outgoing datagram is destined for a host on the same LAN (send directly) or another LAN (send datagram to router). It is assumed that some other means (e.g., manual configuration) are used to create address masks and make them known to the local routers.

Table 14.2a shows the calculations involved in the use of a subnet mask. Note that the effect of the subnet mask is to erase the portion of the host field that refers to an actual host on a subnet. What remains is the network number and the subnet number.

Table 14.2   IPv4 Addresses and Subnet Masks

(a) Dotted decimal and binary representations of IP address and subnet masks

	Binary Representation	Dotted Decimal
IP address	11000000.11100100.00010001.00111001	192.228.17.57
Subnet mask	11111111.11111111.11111111.11100000	255.255.255.224
Bitwise AND of address and mask (resultant network/subnet number)	11000000.11100100.00010001.00100000	192.228.17.32
Subnet number	11000000.11100100.00010001.001	1
Host number	00000000.00000000.00000000.00011001	25

(b) Default subnet masks

	Binary Representation	Dotted Decimal
Class A default mask	11111111.00000000.00000000.00000000	255.0.0.0
Example Class A mask	11111111.11000000.00000000.00000000	255.192.0.0
Class B default mask	11111111.11111111.00000000.00000000	255.255.0.0
Example Class B mask	11111111.11111111.11111000.00000000	255.255.248.0
Class C default mask	11111111.11111111.11111111.00000000	255. 255. 255.0
Example Class C mask	11111111.11111111.11111111.11111100	255. 255. 255.252

EXAMPLE 14.2 Figure 14.7 shows an example of the use of subnetting. The figure shows a local complex consisting of three LANs and two routers. To the rest of the internet, this complex is a single network with a Class C address of the form 192.228.17.*x*, where the leftmost three octets are the network number and the rightmost octet contains a host number *x*. Both routers R1 and R2 are configured with a subnet mask with the value 255.255.255.224 (see Table 14.2a). For example, if a datagram with the destination address 192.228.17.57 arrives at R1 from either the rest of the internet or from LAN Y, R1 applies the subnet mask to determine that this address refers to subnet 1, which is LAN X, and so forwards the datagram to LAN X. Similarly, if a datagram with that destination address arrives at R2 from LAN Z, R2 applies the mask and then determines from its forwarding database that datagrams destined for subnet 1 should be forwarded to R1. Hosts must also employ a subnet mask to make routing decisions.

The default subnet mask for a given class of addresses is a null mask (Table 14.2b), which yields the same network and host number as the nonsubnetted address.

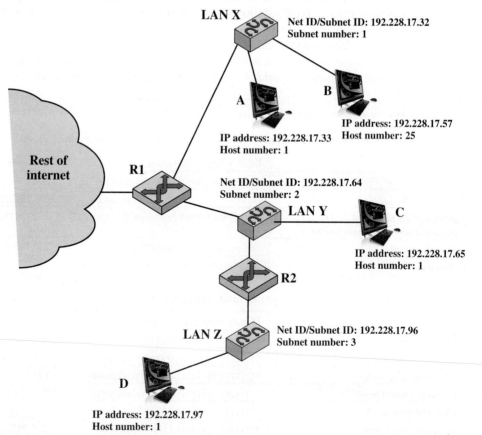

Figure 14.7 Example of Subnetworking

Internet Control Message Protocol (ICMP)

The IP standard specifies that a compliant implementation must also implement ICMP (RFC 792). ICMP provides a means for transferring messages from routers and other hosts to a host. In essence, ICMP provides feedback about problems in the communication environment. Examples of its use are when a datagram cannot reach its destination, when the router does not have the buffering capacity to forward a datagram, and when the router can direct the station to send traffic on a shorter route. In most cases, an ICMP message is sent in response to a datagram, either by a router along the datagram's path or by the intended destination host.

Although ICMP is, in effect, at the same level as IP in the TCP/IP architecture, it is a user of IP. An ICMP message is constructed and then passed down to IP, which encapsulates the message with an IP header and then transmits the resulting datagram in the usual fashion. Because ICMP messages are transmitted in IP datagrams, their delivery is not guaranteed and their use cannot be considered reliable.

Figure 14.8 shows the format of the various ICMP message types. An ICMP message starts with a 64-bit header consisting of the following:

- **Type (8 bits):** Specifies the type of ICMP message.
- **Code (8 bits):** Used to specify parameters of the message that can be encoded in one or a few bits.
- **Checksum (16 bits):** Checksum of the entire ICMP message. This is the same checksum algorithm used for IP.
- **Parameters (32 bits):** Used to specify more lengthy parameters.

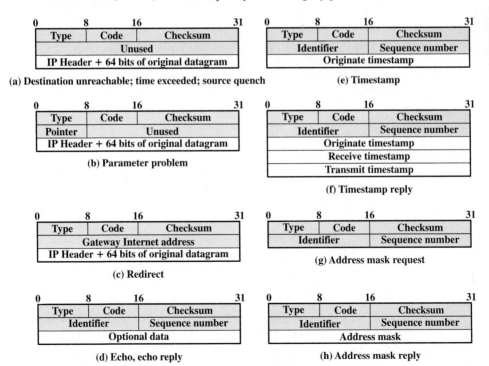

Figure 14.8   ICMP Message Formats

These fields are generally followed by additional information fields that further specify the content of the message.

In those cases in which the ICMP message refers to a prior datagram, the information field includes the entire IP header plus the first 64 bits of the data field of the original datagram. This enables the source host to match the incoming ICMP message with the prior datagram. The reason for including the first 64 bits of the data field is that this will enable the IP module in the host to determine which upper-level protocol or protocols were involved. In particular, the first 64 bits would include a portion of the TCP header or other transport-level header.

The **destination unreachable** message covers a number of contingencies. A router may return this message if it does not know how to reach the destination network. In some networks, an attached router may be able to determine if a particular host is unreachable and returns the message. The destination host itself may return this message if the user protocol or some higher-level service access point is unreachable. This could happen if the corresponding field in the IP header was set incorrectly. If the datagram specifies a source route that is unusable, a message is returned. Finally, if a router must fragment a datagram but the Don't Fragment flag is set, the datagram is discarded and a message is returned.

A router will return a **time exceeded** message if the lifetime of the datagram expires. A host will send this message if it cannot complete reassembly within a time limit.

A syntactic or semantic error in an IP header will cause a **parameter problem** message to be returned by a router or host. For example, an incorrect argument may be provided with an option. The Parameter field contains a pointer to the octet in the original header where the error was detected.

The **source quench** message provides a rudimentary form of flow control. Either a router or a destination host may send this message to a source host, requesting that it reduce the rate at which it is sending traffic to the internet destination. On receipt of a source quench message, the source host should cut back the rate at which it is sending traffic to the specified destination until it no longer receives source quench messages. The source quench message can be used by a router or host that must discard datagrams because of a full buffer. In that case, the router or host will issue a source quench message for every datagram that it discards. In addition, a system may anticipate congestion and issue source quench messages when its buffers approach capacity. In that case, the datagram referred to in the source quench message may well be delivered. Thus, receipt of a source quench message does not imply delivery or nondelivery of the corresponding datagram.

A router sends a **redirect** message to a host on a directly connected router to advise the host of a better route to a particular destination. The following is an example, using Figure 14.7. Router R1 receives a datagram from host C on network Y, to which R1 is attached. R1 checks its routing table and obtains the address for the next router, R2, on the route to the datagram's internet destination network, Z. Because R2 and the host identified by the internet source address of the datagram are on the same network, R1 sends a redirect message to C. The redirect message advises the host to send its traffic for network Z directly to router R2, because this is a shorter path to the destination. The router forwards the original datagram to its internet destination (via R2). The address of R2 is contained in the parameter field of the redirect message.

The **echo** and **echo reply** messages provide a mechanism for testing that communication is possible between entities. The recipient of an echo message is obligated to return the message in an echo reply message. An identifier and sequence number are associated with the echo message to be matched in the echo reply message. The identifier might be used like a service access point to identify a particular session, and the sequence number might be incremented on each echo request sent.

The **timestamp** and **timestamp reply** messages provide a mechanism for sampling the delay characteristics of the internet. The sender of a timestamp message may include an identifier and sequence number in the parameters field and include the time that the message is sent (originate timestamp). The receiver records the time it received the message and the time that it transmits the reply message in the timestamp reply message. If the timestamp message is sent using strict source routing, then the delay characteristics of a particular route can be measured.

The **address mask request** and **address mask reply** messages are useful in an environment that includes subnets. The address mask request and reply messages allow a host to learn the address mask for the LAN to which it connects. The host **broadcasts** an address mask request message on the LAN. The router on the LAN responds with an address mask reply message that contains the address mask.

Address Resolution Protocol (ARP)

Earlier in this chapter, we referred to the concepts of a global address (IP address) and an address that conforms to the addressing scheme of the network to which a host is attached (subnetwork address). For a local area network, the latter address is a MAC address, which provides a physical address for a host port attached to the LAN. Clearly, to deliver an IP datagram to a destination host, a mapping must be made from the IP address to the subnetwork address for that last hop. If a datagram traverses one or more routers between source and destination hosts, then the mapping must be done in the final router, which is attached to the same subnetwork as the destination host. If a datagram is sent from one host to another on the same subnetwork, then the source host must do the mapping. In the following discussion, we use the term *system* to refer to the entity that does the mapping.

For mapping from an IP address to a subnetwork address, a number of approaches are possible:

- Each system can maintain a local table of IP addresses and matching subnetwork addresses for possible correspondents. This approach does not accommodate easy and automatic additions of new hosts to the subnetwork.
- The subnetwork address can be a subset of the network portion of the IP address. However, the entire internet address is 32 bits long and for most subnetwork types (e.g., Ethernet) the host address field is longer than 32 bits.
- A centralized directory can be maintained on each subnetwork that contains the IP-subnet address mappings. This is a reasonable solution for many networks.
- An address resolution protocol can be used. This is a simpler approach than the use of a centralized directory and is well suited to LANs.

RFC 826 defines an Address Resolution Protocol, which allows dynamic distribution of the information needed to build tables to translate an IP address A into a 48-bit Ethernet address; the protocol can be used for any broadcast network. ARP exploits the broadcast property of a LAN; namely, that a transmission from any device on the network is received by all other devices on the network. ARP works as follows:

1. Each system on the LAN maintains a table of known IP-subnetwork address mappings.
2. When a subnetwork address is needed for an IP address, and the mapping is not found in the system's table, the system uses ARP directly on top of the LAN protocol (e.g., IEEE 802) to broadcast a request. The broadcast message contains the IP address for which a subnetwork address is needed.
3. Other hosts on the subnetwork listen for ARP messages and reply when a match occurs. The reply includes both the IP and subnetwork addresses of the replying host.
4. The original request includes the requesting host's IP address and subnetwork address. Any interested host can copy this information into its local table, avoiding the need for later ARP messages.
5. The ARP message can also be used simply to broadcast a host's IP address and subnetwork address, for the benefit of others on the subnetwork.

14.4 IPV6

IPv4 has been the foundation of the Internet and virtually all multivendor private internetworks. This protocol is reaching the end of its useful life and a new protocol, known as IPv6 (IP version 6), has been defined to ultimately replace IP.[5]

We first look at the motivation for developing a new version of IP and then examine some of its details.

IP Next Generation

The driving motivation for the adoption of a new version of IP was the limitation imposed by the 32-bit address field in IPv4. With a 32-bit address field, it is possible in principle to assign 2^{32} different addresses, which is over 4 billion possible addresses. One might think that this number of addresses was more than adequate to meet addressing needs on the Internet. However, in the late 1980s it was perceived that there would be a problem, and this problem began to manifest itself in the early 1990s. Reasons for the inadequacy of 32-bit addresses include the following:

- The two-level structure of the IP address (network number, host number) is convenient but wasteful of the address space. Once a network number is assigned to a network, all of the host-number addresses for that network

---

[5]The currently deployed version of IP is IP version 4; previous versions of IP (1 through 3) were successively defined and replaced to reach IPv4. Version 5 is the number assigned to the Stream Protocol, a connection-oriented internet-layer protocol. Hence the use of the label version 6.

number are assigned to that network. The address space for that network may be sparsely used, but as far as the effective IP address space is concerned, if a network number is used, then all addresses within the network are used.

- The IP addressing model generally requires that a unique network number be assigned to each IP network whether or not it is actually connected to the Internet.

- Networks are proliferating rapidly. Most organizations boast multiple LANs, not just a single LAN system. Wireless networks have rapidly assumed a major role. The Internet itself has grown explosively for years.

- Growth of TCP/IP usage into new areas will result in a rapid growth in the demand for unique IP addresses. Examples include using TCP/IP to interconnect electronic point-of-sale terminals and for cable television receivers.

- Typically, a single IP address is assigned to each host. A more flexible arrangement is to allow multiple IP addresses per host. This, of course, increases the demand for IP addresses.

So the need for an increased address space dictated that a new version of IP was needed. In addition, IP is a very old protocol, and new requirements in the areas of address configuration, routing flexibility, and traffic support had been defined.

In response to these needs, the Internet Engineering Task Force (IETF) issued a call for proposals for a next generation IP (IPng) in July 1992. A number of proposals were received, and by 1994 the final design for IPng emerged. A major milestone was reached with the publication of RFC 1752, "The Recommendation for the IP Next Generation Protocol," issued in January 1995. RFC 1752 outlines the requirements for IPng, specifies the PDU formats, and highlights the IPng approach in the areas of addressing, routing, and security. A number of other Internet documents defined details of the protocol, now officially called IPv6; these include an overall specification of IPv6 (RFC 2460), an RFC dealing with addressing structure of IPv6 (RFC 4291), and numerous others.

IPv6 includes the following enhancements over IPv4:

- **Expanded address space:** IPv6 uses 128-bit addresses instead of the 32-bit addresses of IPv4. This is an increase of address space by a factor of 2^{96}. It has been pointed out [HIND95] that this allows on the order of 6×10^{23} unique addresses per square meter of the surface of the Earth. Even if addresses are very inefficiently allocated, this address space seems inexhaustible.

- **Improved option mechanism:** IPv6 options are placed in separate optional headers that are located between the IPv6 header and the transport-layer header. Most of these optional headers are not examined or processed by any router on the packet's path. This simplifies and speeds up router processing of IPv6 packets compared to IPv4 datagrams.[6] It also makes it easier to add additional options.

---

[6]The protocol data unit for IPv6 is referred to as a packet rather than a datagram, which is the term used for IPv4 PDUs.

- **Address autoconfiguration:** This capability provides for dynamic assignment of IPv6 addresses.
- **Increased addressing flexibility:** IPv6 includes the concept of an anycast address, for which a packet is delivered to just one of a set of nodes. The scalability of multicast routing is improved by adding a scope field to multicast addresses.
- **Support for resource allocation:** IPv6 enables the labeling of packets belonging to a particular traffic flow for which the sender requests special handling. This aids in the support of specialized traffic such as real-time video.

All of these features are explored in the remainder of this section.

IPv6 Structure

An IPv6 protocol data unit (known as a packet) has the following general form:

← 40 octets →	←	0 or more	→	
IPv6 header	Extension header	• • •	Extension header	Transport-level PDU

The only header that is required is referred to simply as the IPv6 header. This is of fixed size with a length of 40 octets, compared to 20 octets for the mandatory portion of the IPv4 header (Figure 14.5a). The following extension headers have been defined:

- **Hop-by-Hop Options header:** Defines special options that require hop-by-hop processing
- **Routing header:** Provides extended routing, similar to IPv4 source routing
- **Fragment header:** Contains fragmentation and reassembly information
- **Authentication header:** Provides packet integrity and authentication
- **Encapsulating Security Payload header:** Provides privacy
- **Destination Options header:** Contains optional information to be examined by the destination node

The IPv6 standard recommends that when multiple extension headers are used, the IPv6 headers appear in the following order:

1. IPv6 header: Mandatory, must always appear first
2. Hop-by-Hop Options header
3. Destination Options header: For options to be processed by the first destination that appears in the IPv6 Destination Address field plus subsequent destinations listed in the Routing header
4. Routing header
5. Fragment header
6. Authentication header
7. Encapsulating Security Payload header
8. Destination Options header: For options to be processed only by the final destination of the packet

Figure 14.9 shows an example of an IPv6 packet that includes an instance of each header, except those related to security. Note that the IPv6 header and each extension header include a Next Header field. This field identifies the type of the immediately following header. If the next header is an extension header, then this field contains the type identifier of that header. Otherwise, this field contains the protocol identifier of the upper-layer protocol using IPv6 (typically a transport-level protocol), using the same values as the IPv4 Protocol field. In Figure 14.9, the upper-layer protocol is TCP; thus, the upper-layer data carried by the IPv6 packet consist of a TCP header followed by a block of application data.

We first look at the main IPv6 header and then examine each of the extensions in turn.

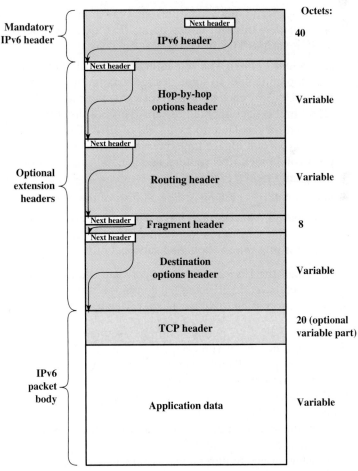

Figure 14.9 IPv6 Packet with Extension Headers (containing a TCP Segment)

IPv6 Header

The IPv6 header has a fixed length of 40 octets, consisting of the following fields (Figure 14.5b):

- **Version (4 bits):** Internet protocol version number; the value is 6.
- **DS/ECN (8 bits):** Available for use by originating nodes and/or forwarding routers for differentiated services and congestion functions, as described for the IPv4 DS/ECN field. This 8-bit field was originally referred to as the Traffic Class field, but the 6-bit DS and 2-bit ECN designation is now used.
- **Flow Label (20 bits):** May be used by a host to label those packets for which it is requesting special handling by routers within a network, discussed subsequently.
- **Payload Length (16 bits):** Length of the remainder of the IPv6 packet following the header, in octets. In other words, this is the total length of all of the extension headers plus the transport-level PDU.
- **Next Header (8 bits):** Identifies the type of header immediately following the IPv6 header; this will either be an IPv6 extension header or a higher-layer header, such as TCP or UDP.
- **Hop Limit (8 bits):** The remaining number of allowable hops for this packet. The hop limit is set to some desired maximum value by the source and decremented by 1 by each node that forwards the packet. The packet is discarded if Hop Limit is decremented to zero. This is a simplification over the processing required for the Time to Live field of IPv4. The consensus was that the extra effort in accounting for time intervals in IPv4 added no significant value to the protocol. In fact, IPv4 routers, as a general rule, treat the Time to Live field as a hop limit field.
- **Source Address (128 bits):** The address of the originator of the packet.
- **Destination Address (128 bits):** The address of the intended recipient of the packet. This may not in fact be the intended ultimate destination if a Routing header is present, as explained subsequently.

Although the IPv6 header is longer than the mandatory portion of the IPv4 header (40 octets versus 20 octets), it contains fewer fields (8 versus 12). Thus, routers have less processing to do per header, which should speed up routing.

FLOW LABEL   RFC 3697 defines a flow as a sequence of packets sent from a particular source to a particular (unicast, anycast, or multicast) destination for which the source desires special handling by the intervening routers. A flow is uniquely identified by the combination of a source address, destination address, and a nonzero 20-bit flow label. Thus, all packets that are to be part of the same flow are assigned the same flow label by the source.

From the source's point of view, a flow typically will be a sequence of packets that are generated from a single application instance at the source and that have the same transfer service requirements. A flow may comprise a single TCP connection or even multiple TCP connections; an example of the latter is a file transfer application, which could have one control connection and multiple data connections.

A single application may generate a single flow or multiple flows. An example of the latter is multimedia conferencing, which might have one flow for audio and one for graphic windows, each with different transfer requirements in terms of data rate, delay, and delay variation.

From the router's point of view, a flow is a sequence of packets that share attributes that affect how these packets are handled by the router. These include path, resource allocation, discard requirements, accounting, and security attributes. The router may treat packets from different flows differently in a number of ways, including allocating different buffer sizes, giving different precedence in terms of forwarding, and requesting different quality of service from networks.

There is no special significance to any particular flow label. Instead the special handling to be provided for a packet flow must be declared in some other way. For example, a source might negotiate or request special handling ahead of time from routers by means of a control protocol, or at transmission time by information in one of the extension headers in the packet, such as the Hop-by-Hop Options header. Examples of special handling that might be requested include some sort of nondefault quality of service and some form of real-time service.

In principle, all of a user's requirements for a particular flow could be defined in an extension header and included with each packet. If we wish to leave the concept of flow open to include a wide variety of requirements, this design approach could result in very large packet headers. The alternative, adopted for IPv6, is the flow label, in which the flow requirements are defined prior to flow commencement and a unique flow label is assigned to the flow. In this case, the router must save flow requirement information about each flow.

The following rules apply to the flow label:

1. Hosts or routers that do not support the Flow Label field must set the field to zero when originating a packet, pass the field unchanged when forwarding a packet, and ignore the field when receiving a packet.

2. All packets originating from a given source with the same nonzero flow label must have the same Destination Address, Source Address, Hop-by-Hop Options header contents (if this header is present), and Routing header contents (if this header is present). The intent is that a router can decide how to route and process the packet by simply looking up the flow label in a table and without examining the rest of the header.

3. The source assigns a flow label to a flow. New flow labels must be chosen (pseudo-) randomly and uniformly in the range 1 to $2^{20} - 1$, subject to the restriction that a source must not reuse a flow label for a new flow within the lifetime of the existing flow. The zero flow label is reserved to indicate that no flow label is being used.

This last point requires some elaboration. The router must maintain information about the characteristics of each active flow that may pass through it, presumably in some sort of table. To forward packets efficiently and rapidly, table lookup must be efficient. One alternative is to have a table with 2^{20} (about 1 million) entries, one for each possible flow label; this imposes an unnecessary memory burden on the router. Another alternative is to have one entry in the table per active flow, include the flow label with each entry, and require the router to search the entire table each time a packet is encountered. This imposes an unnecessary processing burden on the router. Instead, most router designs are likely to use some sort of hash table approach. With this approach a moderate-sized table is used, and each flow entry is mapped into the table using a hashing function on the flow label. The hashing function might simply be the low-order few bits (say 8 or 10) of the flow label or some simple calculation on the 20 bits of the flow label. In any case, the efficiency of the hash approach typically depends on the flow labels being uniformly distributed over their possible range. Hence requirement number 3 in the preceding list.

IPv6 Addresses

IPv6 addresses are 128 bits in length. Addresses are assigned to individual interfaces on nodes, not to the nodes themselves.[7] A single interface may have multiple unique unicast addresses. Any of the unicast addresses associated with a node's interface may be used to uniquely identify that node.

The combination of long addresses and multiple addresses per interface enables improved routing efficiency over IPv4. In IPv4, addresses generally do not have a structure that assists routing, and therefore a router may need to maintain huge table of routing paths. Longer internet addresses allow for aggregating addresses by hierarchies of network, access provider, geography, corporation, and so on. Such aggregation should make for smaller routing tables and faster table lookups. The allowance for multiple addresses per interface would allow a subscriber that uses multiple access providers across the same interface to have separate addresses aggregated under each provider's address space.

IPv6 allows three types of addresses:

- **Unicast** An identifier for a single interface. A packet sent to a unicast address is delivered to the interface identified by that address.
- **Anycast:** An identifier for a set of interfaces (typically belonging to different nodes). A packet sent to an anycast address is delivered to one of the interfaces identified by that address (the "nearest" one, according to the routing protocols' measure of distance).
- **Multicast** An identifier for a set of interfaces (typically belonging to different nodes). A packet sent to a multicast address is delivered to all interfaces identified by that address.

IPv6 addresses are represented by treating the 128-bit address as a sequence of 8 16-bit numbers, and representing this in the form of eight hexadecimal numbers divided by colons, for example:

2001:0DB8:0055:0000:CD23:0000:0000:0205

One to three zeroes that appear as the leading digits in any colon-delimited hexadecimal grouping may be dropped. For the preceding address, this yields:

2001:0DB8:55:0:CD23:0:0:0205

---

[7]In IPv6, a *node* is any device that implements IPv6; this includes hosts and routers.

Finally, a group of all zeroes, or consecutive groups of all zeroes, can be substituted by a double colon, but this may only be done once in an address. For our example address, we can write either:

2001:0DB8:55::CD23:0:0:0205 or 2001:0DB8:55:0:CD23::0205

The IPv6 address space is organized using format prefixes, similar to telephone country and area codes, that logically divide it in the form of a tree so that a route from one network to another can easily be found. The length of the prefix is variable and is specified in the address representation by the form

ipv6-address/prefix-length

where

ipv6-address is an IPv6 address and prefix-length is a decimal value specifying how many of the leftmost contiguous bits of the address comprise the prefix. Thus, if in our example address, the first 48 bits are to be interpreted as a prefix, then we could write

2001:0DB8:55:0:CD23::0205/48

Table 14.3 lists the major prefixes that have been assigned in the overall IPv6 address space. The address types in Table 14.3 can be described as follows:

- **Embedded IPv4 address:** Embeds an existing IPv4 address in an IPv6 format. This address type is used to represent the addresses of IPv4 nodes as IPv6 addresses.
- **Loopback:** Used by a node to send a packet to itself. This can be used to verify the operation for the IP software.
- **Multicast:** An identifier for a group of interfaces (typically on different nodes).
- **Link-local unicast:** For use on a single LAN or network link. Link-local addresses are designed to be used for addressing on a single link for purposes such as automatic address configuration neighbor discovery, or when no routers are present. Packets with link-local destination addresses are not routable and must not be forwarded off the local link.
- **Global unicast:** Encompasses unicast and anycast addresses.

Table 14.3   IPv6 Address Space Usage

Address Type	Binary Prefix	IPv6 Notation	Fraction of Address Space
Embedded IPv4 address	00...1111 1111 1111 1111 (96 bits)	::FFFF/96	2^{-96}
Loopback	00...1 (128 bits)	::1/128	2^{-128}
Link-local unicast	1111 1110 10	FE80::/10	1/1024
Multicast	1111 1111	FF00::/8	2/256
Global unicast	Everything else		

Hop-by-Hop Options Header

The Hop-by-Hop Options header carries optional information that, if present, must be examined by every router along the path. This header consists of (Figure 14.10a):

- **Next Header (8 bits):** Identifies the type of header immediately following this header.
- **Header Extension Length (8 bits):** Length of this header in 64-bit units, not including the first 64 bits.
- **Options:** A variable-length field consisting of one or more option definitions. Each definition is in the form of three subfields: Option Type (8 bits), which identifies the option; Length (8 bits), which specifies the length of the Option Data field in octets; and Option Data, which is a variable-length specification of the option.

It is actually the lowest-order five bits of the Option Type field that are used to specify a particular option. The high-order two bits indicate the action to be taken by a node that does not recognize this option type, as follows:

- 00—Skip over this option and continue processing the header.
- 01—Discard the packet.
- 10—Discard the packet and send an ICMP Parameter Problem message to the packet's Source Address, pointing to the unrecognized Option Type.
- 11—Discard the packet and, only if the packet's Destination Address is not a multicast address, send an ICMP Parameter Problem message to the packet's Source Address, pointing to the unrecognized Option Type.

The third highest-order bit specifies whether the Option Data field does not change (0) or may change (1) en route from source to destination. Data that may change must be excluded from authentication calculations, as discussed in Chapter 27.

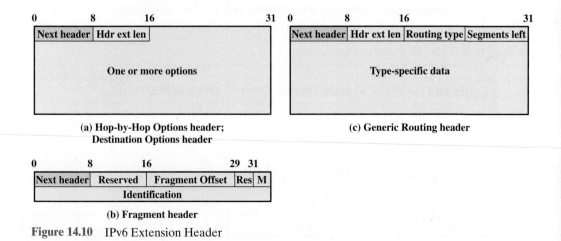

(a) Hop-by-Hop Options header;
Destination Options header

(c) Generic Routing header

(b) Fragment header

Figure 14.10   IPv6 Extension Header

These conventions for the Option Type field also apply to the Destination Options header.

Four hop-by-hop options have been specified so far:

- **Pad1:** Used to insert one byte of padding into the Options area of the header.

- **PadN:** Used to insert N bytes ($N \geq 2$) of padding into the Options area of the header. The two padding options ensure that the header is a multiple of 8 bytes in length.

- **Jumbo payload:** Used to send IPv6 packets with payloads longer than 65,535 octets. The Option Data field is 32 bits long and gives the length of the packet in octets, excluding the IPv6 header. For such packets, the Payload Length field in the IPv6 header must be set to zero, and there must be no Fragment header. With this option, IPv6 supports packet sizes up to more than 4 billion octets. This facilitates the transmission of large video packets and enables IPv6 to make the best use of available capacity over any transmission medium.

- **Router alert:** Informs the router that the contents of this packet is of interest to the router and to handle any control data accordingly. The absence of this option in an IPv6 datagram informs the router that the packet does not contain information needed by the router and hence can be safely routed without further packet parsing. Hosts originating IPv6 packets are required to include this option in certain circumstances. The purpose of this option is to provide efficient support for protocols such as RSVP (Chapter 22) that generate packets that need to be examined by intermediate routers for purposes of traffic control. Rather than requiring the intermediate routers to look in detail at the extension headers of a packet, this option alerts the router when such attention is required.

Fragmentation Header

In IPv6, fragmentation may only be performed by source nodes, not by routers along a packet's delivery path. To take full advantage of the internetworking environment, a node must perform a path discovery algorithm that enables it to learn the smallest maximum transmission unit (MTU) supported by any network on the path (RFC 1981). With this knowledge, the source node will fragment, as required, for each given destination address. Otherwise the source must limit all packets to 1280 octets, which is the minimum MTU that must be supported by each network.

The fragmentation header consists of the following (Figure 14.10b):

- **Next Header (8 bits):** Identifies the type of header immediately following this header.

- **Reserved (8 bits):** For future use.

- **Fragment Offset (13 bits):** Indicates where in the original packet the payload of this fragment belongs, measured in 64-bit units. This implies that fragments (other than the last fragment) must contain a data field that is a multiple of 64 bits long.

- **Res (2 bits):** Reserved for future use.

- **M Flag (1 bit):** 1 = more fragments; 0 = last fragment.
- **Identification (32 bits):** Intended to uniquely identify the original packet. The identifier must be unique for the packet's source address and destination address for the time during which the packet will remain in the internet. All fragments with the same identifier, source address, and destination address are reassembled to form the original packet.

The fragmentation algorithm is the same as that described in Section 14.2.

Routing Header

The Routing header contains a list of one or more intermediate nodes to be visited on the way to a packet's destination. All routing headers start with a 32-bit block consisting of four 8-bit fields, followed by routing data specific to a given routing type (Figure 14.10c). The four 8-bit fields are as follows:

- **Next Header:** Identifies the type of header immediately following this header.
- **Header Extension Length:** Length of this header in 64-bit units, not including the first 64 bits.
- **Routing Type:** Identifies a particular Routing header variant. If a router does not recognize the Routing Type value, it must discard the packet.
- **Segments Left:** Number of route segments remaining; that is, the number of explicitly listed intermediate nodes still to be visited before reaching the final destination.

Destination Options Header

The Destination Options header carries optional information that, if present, is examined only by the packet's destination node. The format of this header is the same as that of the Hop-by-Hop Options header (Figure 14.10a).

14.5 VIRTUAL PRIVATE NETWORKS AND IP SECURITY

In today's distributed computing environment, the **virtual private network (VPN)** offers an attractive solution to network managers. In essence, a VPN consists of a set of computers that interconnect by means of a relatively unsecure network and that make use of encryption and special protocols to provide security. At each corporate site, workstations, servers, and databases are linked by one or more LANs. The LANs are under the control of the network manager and can be configured and tuned for cost-effective performance. The Internet or some other public network can be used to interconnect sites, providing a cost savings over the use of a private network and offloading the wide area network management task to the public network provider. That same public network provides an access path for telecommuters and other mobile employees to log on to corporate systems from remote sites.

But the manager faces a fundamental requirement: security. Use of a public network exposes corporate traffic to eavesdropping and provides an entry point for unauthorized users. To counter this problem, the manager may choose from a variety of encryption and authentication packages and products. Proprietary solutions raise a number of problems. First, how secure is the solution? If proprietary encryption or authentication schemes are used, there may be little reassurance in the technical literature as to the level of security provided. Second is the question of compatibility. No manager wants to be limited in the choice of workstations, servers, routers, firewalls, and so on by a need for compatibility with the security facility. This is the motivation for the IP Security (IPsec) set of Internet standards.

IPsec

In 1994, the Internet Architecture Board (IAB) issued a report titled "Security in the Internet Architecture" (RFC 1636). The report stated the general consensus that the Internet needs more and better security and identified key areas for security mechanisms. Among these were the need to secure the network infrastructure from unauthorized monitoring and control of network traffic and the need to secure end-user-to-end-user traffic using authentication and encryption mechanisms.

To provide security, the IAB included authentication and encryption as necessary security features in the next-generation IP, which has been issued as IPv6. Fortunately, these security capabilities were designed to be usable both with the current IPv4 and the future IPv6. This means that vendors can begin offering these features now, and many vendors do now have some IPsec capability in their products. The IPsec specification now exists as a set of Internet standards.

Applications of IPsec

IPsec provides the capability to secure communications across a LAN, across private and public WANs, and across the Internet. Examples of its use include the following:

- **Secure branch office connectivity over the Internet:** A company can build a secure virtual private network over the Internet or over a public WAN. This enables a business to rely heavily on the Internet and reduce its need for private networks, saving costs and network management overhead.

- **Secure remote access over the Internet:** An end user whose system is equipped with IP security protocols can make a local call to an Internet service provider (ISP) and gain secure access to a company network. This reduces the cost of toll charges for traveling employees and telecommuters.

- **Establishing extranet and intranet connectivity with partners:** IPsec can be used to secure communication with other organizations, ensuring authentication and confidentiality and providing a key exchange mechanism.

- **Enhancing electronic commerce security:** Even though some Web and electronic commerce applications have built-in security protocols, the use of IPsec enhances that security. IPsec guarantees that all traffic designated by the network administrator is both encrypted and authenticated, adding an additional layer of security to whatever is provided at the application layer.

The principal feature of IPsec that enables it to support these varied applications is that it can encrypt and/or authenticate *all* traffic at the IP level. Thus, all distributed applications, including remote logon, client/server, e-mail, file transfer, Web access, and so on, can be secured.

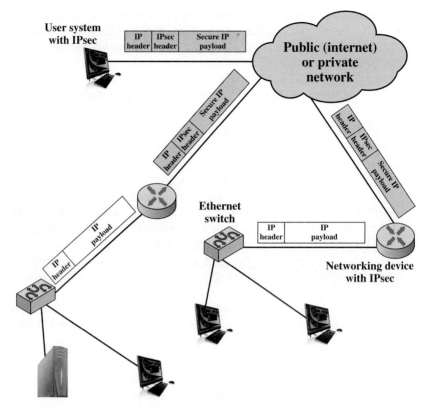

Figure 14.11   An IP Security Scenario

Figure 14.11 is a typical scenario of IPsec usage. An organization maintains LANs at dispersed locations. Nonsecure IP traffic is conducted on each LAN. For traffic offsite, through some sort of private or public WAN, IPsec protocols are used. These protocols operate in networking devices, such as a router or firewall, that connect each LAN to the outside world. The IPsec networking device will typically encrypt and compress all traffic going into the WAN, and decrypt and decompress traffic coming from the WAN; these operations are transparent to workstations and servers on the LAN. Secure transmission is also possible with individual users who dial into the WAN. Such user workstations must implement the IPsec protocols to provide security.

Benefits of IPsec

Some of the benefits of IPsec are as follows:

- When IPsec is implemented in a firewall or router, it provides strong security that can be applied to all traffic crossing the perimeter. Traffic within a company or workgroup does not incur the overhead of security-related processing.

- IPsec in a firewall is resistant to bypass if all traffic from the outside must use IP and the firewall is the only means of entrance from the Internet into the organization.

- IPsec is below the transport layer (TCP, UDP) and so is transparent to applications. There is no need to change software on a user or server system when IPsec is implemented in the firewall or router. Even if IPsec is implemented in end systems, upper-layer software, including applications, is not affected.

- IPsec can be transparent to end users. There is no need to train users on security mechanisms, issue keying material on a per-user basis, or revoke keying material when users leave the organization.

- IPsec can provide security for individual users if needed. This is useful for offsite workers and for setting up a secure virtual subnetwork within an organization for sensitive applications.

IPsec Functions

IPsec provides three main facilities: an authentication-only function referred to as Authentication Header (AH), a combined authentication/encryption function called Encapsulating Security Payload (ESP), and a key exchange function. For VPNs, both authentication and encryption are generally desired, because it is important both to (1) assure that unauthorized users do not penetrate the virtual private network and (2) assure that eavesdroppers on the Internet cannot read messages sent over the virtual private network. Because both features are generally desirable, most implementations are likely to use ESP rather than AH. The key exchange function allows for manual exchange of keys as well as an automated scheme.

IPsec is explored in Chapter 27.

14.6 RECOMMENDED READING AND ANIMATIONS

[PARZ06] provides clear coverage of all of the topics in this chapter. [SHAN02] and [KENT87] provide useful discussions of fragmentation. [BEIJ06] provides a good overview of IPv6. [METZ02] and [DOI04] describe the IPv6 anycast feature. Although its title suggests a focus on security, [FRAN10] has an excellent, detailed account of all aspects of IPv6.

BEIJ06   Beijnum, I. "IPv6 Internals." *The Internet Protocol Journal,* September 2006.

DOI04   Doi, S., et al. "IPv6 Anycast for Simple and Effective Communications." *IEEE Communications Magazine,* May 2004.

FRAN10   Frankel, S.; Graveman, R.; Pearce, J.; and Rooks, M. *Guidelines for the Secure Deployment of IPv6.* NIST Special Publication SP800-19, December 2010.

KENT87   Kent, C., and Mogul, J. "Fragmentation Considered Harmful." *ACM Computer Communication Review,* October 1987.

KESH98   Keshav, S., and Sharma, R. "Issues and Trends in Router Design." *IEEE Communications Magazine,* May 1998.

METZ02   Metz, C. "IP Anycast." *IEEE Internet Computing,* March 2002.

PARZ06   Parziale, L., et al. *TCP/IP Tutorial and Technical Overview.* IBM Redbook GG24-3376-07, 2006. http://www.redbooks.ibm.com/abstracts/gg243376.html.

SHAN02   Shannon, C.; Moore, D.; and Claffy, K. "Beyond Folklore: Observations on Fragmented Traffic." *IEEE/ACM Transactions on Networking,* December 2002.

SPOR03   Sportack, M. *IP Addressing Fundamentals.* Indianapolis, IN: Cisco Press, 2003.

Animations

A number of animations are available at the Premium Web site relating to the topics of this chapter. These include an IP simulator and animations relating to ARP, ICMP, and IP addressing. The reader is encouraged to view these animations to reinforce concepts from this chapter.

14.7 KEY TERMS, REVIEW QUESTIONS, AND PROBLEMS

Key Terms

broadcast	internetworking	segmentation
datagram lifetime	intranet	subnet
end system	IP security (IPsec)	subnet mask
fragmentation	IPv4	subnetwork
intermediate system (IS)	IPv6	Traffic class
Internet Control Message	multicast	unicast
Protocol (ICMP)	reassembly	virtual private network
Internet Protocol (IP)	router	(VPN)

Review Questions

14.1 List the requirements for an internetworking facility.

14.2 Give some reasons for using fragmentation and reassembly.

14.3 What are the pros and cons of limiting reassembly to the endpoint as compared to allowing en route reassembly?

14.4 Explain the function of the three flags in the IPv4 header.

14.5 How is the IPv4 header checksum calculated?

14.6 What is the difference between the Traffic class and Flow Label fields in the IPv6 header?

14.7 Briefly explain the three types of IPv6 addresses.

14.8 What is the purpose of each of the IPv6 header types?

Problems

14.1 Although not explicitly stated, the Internet Protocol (IP) specification, RFC 791, defines the minimum packet size a network technology must support to allow IP to run over it.

   a. Read Section 3.2 of RFC 791 to find out that value. What is it?

   b. Discuss the reasons for adopting that specific value.

14.2 In the discussion of IP, it was mentioned that the *identifier, don't fragment identifier,* and *time to live* parameters are present in the Send primitive but not in the Deliver primitive because they are only of concern to IP. For each of these parameters indicate whether it is of concern to the IP entity in the source, the IP entities in any intermediate routers, and the IP entity in the destination end systems. Justify your answer.

14.3   What is the address space and address range of a system with 10-byte addresses?

14.4   What will be the dotted decimal notation of the following IPv4 address?

10000011   01011010   00001111   11001011

14.5   IPv4 architecture is essentially classful architecture comprising five classes.

    a. Find the classes of the following addresses given in binary notation:

       1. 11000011   10101001   11110001   01010001
       2. 11111100   10100001   00001100   00110100
       3. 00011001   10011001   01100110   11000011

    b. Find the classes of the following addresses given in dotted decimal notation:

       1. 75.87.9.144
       2. 229.221.3.6
       3. 150.150.15.15

14.6   A 4480-octet datagram is to be transmitted and needs to be fragmented because it will pass through an Ethernet with a maximum payload of 1500 octets. Show the Total Length, More Flag, and Fragment Offset values in each of the resulting fragments.

14.7   Determine whether the following IPv4 addresses have any errors. If they are correct, then convert them to binary notation.

    a. 75. 264. 82. 7
    b. 32. 113. 49. 121
    c. 32. 03. 49. 120
    d. 231. 7. 8. 9. 42
    e. 134. 127. 4. 200

14.8   The IP checksum needs to be recalculated at routers because of changes to the IP header, such as the lifetime field. It is possible to recalculate the checksum from scratch. Suggest a procedure that involves less calculation. *Hint:* Suppose that the value in 16-bit word k is changed by $Z = $ new_value $-$ old_value; consider the effect of this change on the checksum.

14.9   An IP datagram is to be fragmented. Which options in the option field need to be copied into the header of each fragment, and which need only be retained in the first fragment? Justify the handling of each option.

14.10   In IPv4 addressing, the first three classes are divided into a fixed number of blocks. In Class A, the first byte denotes the number of blocks. In Class B, the first two bytes denote the number of blocks. In Class C, the first three bytes denote the number of blocks. Class D and Class E have a single block. Derive the number of blocks and the size of each block in every class.

14.11   The architecture suggested by Figure 14.1 is to be used. What functions could be added to the routers to alleviate some of the problems caused by the mismatched local and long-haul networks?

14.12   Should internetworking be concerned with a network's internal routing? Why or why not?

14.13   Provide the following parameter values for each of the network classes A, B, and C. Be sure to consider any special or reserved addresses in your calculations.

    a. Number of bits in network portion of address
    b. Number of bits in host portion of address
    c. Number of distinct networks allowed
    d. Number of distinct hosts per network allowed
    e. Integer range of first octet

14.14   Find the network identifier and host identifier of each of the following three IPv4 addresses: 130.30.13.10, 30.130.220.20, and 220.20.10.130.

14.15   An organization has been granted a block of 32 addresses. What is its subnet mask in dotted decimal notation and binary notations?

14.16   Is the subnet mask 255.255.240.0 valid for a Class C address?

14.17   In classless interdomain routing (CIDR) notation, the number of 1 bits in the mask is appended to the address preceded by a forward slash. If one of the addresses of a subnet is 255.230.64.47/26, what are the first and the last address of that subnet?

14.18   A block of addresses is granted to an organization. The last address of the block is 202.166.100.159/27. What is the first address of the block? How many addresses have been granted?

14.19   A service provider has been granted a block of addresses starting from 180.150.0.0/17. The provider needs to distribute these addresses in three groups as stated below:

   a.   The first group has 64 subnets; each needs 256 addresses.
   b.   The second group has 64 subnets; each needs 128 addresses.
   c.   The third group has 128 subnets; each needs 32 addresses.

   How many addresses are granted to the provider? How can the blocks of addresses be allotted to each group? How many unused addresses are there?

14.20   Find out about your network. Using the command "ipconfig," "ifconfig," or "winipcfg," we can learn not only our IP address but other network parameters as well. Can you determine your mask, gateway, and the number of addresses available on your network?

14.21   Using your IP address and your mask, what is your network address? This is determined by converting the IP address and the mask to binary and then proceeding with a bitwise logical AND operation. For example, given the address 172.16.45.0 and the mask 255.255.224.0, we would discover that the network address would be 172.16.32.0.

14.22   What are the abbreviated forms of the following IPv6 addresses?

   a.   56A7:0000:0000:00AA:0C03:0000:3003:FF22
   b.   0000:0000:0000:FFFF:0000:AAA7:0000:0000

14.23   What are the unabbreviated forms of the following IPv6 addresses?

   a.   F331:F3::3F
   b.   0:0:DD33:E::0

14.24   The IPv6 standard states that if a packet with a nonzero flow label arrives at a router and the router has no information for that flow label, the router should ignore the flow label and forward the packet.

   a.   What are the disadvantages of treating this event as an error, discarding the packet, and sending an ICMP message?
   b.   Are there situations in which routing the packet as if its flow label were zero will cause the wrong result? Explain.

14.25   The IPv6 flow mechanism assumes that the state associated with a given flow label is stored in routers, so they know how to handle packets that carry that flow label. A design requirement is to flush flow labels that are no longer being used (stale flow label) from routers.

   a.   Assume that a source always send a control message to all affected routers deleting a flow label when the source finishes with that flow. In that case, how could a stale flow label persist?
   b.   Suggest router and source mechanisms to overcome the problem of stale flow labels.

14.26   Table 14.3 gives the prefix for different address spaces of the IPv6 addressing scheme. Using the reference, determine the type of address for each of the following IPv6 addresses:

   a.   FF08::/8
   b.   ::AB34/96
   c.   FE91:22AA::/10
   d.   A123::234A/8

14.27   Link-local addresses are prefixed by FE80::/10 and site-local addresses are prefixed by FEC0::/10. What will be the global address of

   a.   A link-local address with node identifier 0::3A4/48.
   b.   A site-local address with node identifier 0::222/48.

CHAPTER 15

TRANSPORT PROTOCOLS

 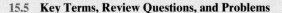

LEARNING OBJECTIVES

After studying this chapter, you should be able to:

◆ Explain the effect of the use of a reliable sequencing network on requirements for a reliable transport protocol.

◆ Present an overview of the principal functions needed in a transport protocol that operates over an unreliable network service.

◆ List and define the TCP services.

◆ Present an overview of TCP mechanisms.

◆ Understand the significance of the various TCP implementation policy options and how they relate to one another.

In a protocol architecture, the transport protocol sits above a network or internetwork layer, which provides network-related services, and just below application and other upper-layer protocols. The transport protocol provides services to transport service (TS) users, such as FTP, SMTP, and TELNET. The local transport entity communicates with some remote transport entity, using the services of some lower layer, such as the Internet Protocol. The general service provided by a transport protocol is the end-to-end transport of data in a way that shields the TS user from the details of the underlying communications systems.

We begin this chapter by examining the protocol mechanisms required to provide these services. We find that most of the complexity relates to reliable connection-oriented services. As might be expected, the less the network service provides, the more the transport protocol must do. The remainder of the chapter looks at two widely used transport protocols: Transmission Control Protocol (TCP) and User Datagram Protocol (UDP).

Refer to Figure 2.8 to see the position within the TCP/IP suite of the protocols discussed in this chapter.

15.1 CONNECTION-ORIENTED TRANSPORT PROTOCOL MECHANISMS

Two basic types of transport service are possible: connection oriented and connectionless or datagram service. A connection-oriented service provides for the establishment, maintenance, and termination of a logical connection between TS users. This has, so far, been the most common type of protocol service available and has a wide variety of applications. The connection-oriented service generally implies that the service is reliable. This section looks at the transport protocol mechanisms needed to support the connection-oriented service.

A full-feature connection-oriented transport protocol, such as TCP, is very complex. For clarity, we present the transport protocol mechanisms in an evolutionary fashion. We begin with a network service that makes life easy for the transport protocol by guaranteeing the delivery of all transport data units in order and defining the required mechanisms. Then we will look at the transport protocol mechanisms required to cope with an unreliable network service. All of this discussion applies in general to transport-layer protocols. In Section 15.2, we apply the concepts developed in this section to describe TCP.

Reliable Sequencing Network Service

Let us assume that the network service accepts messages of arbitrary length and, with virtually 100 percent reliability, delivers them in sequence to the destination. Examples of such networks include the following:

- An IEEE 802.3 LAN using the connection-oriented LLC service
- A highly reliable connection-oriented packet-switching network, such as a frame relay, with the reliable connection option

In such cases, the transport protocol is used as an end-to-end protocol between two systems attached to the same network, rather than across an internet.

The assumption of a reliable sequencing networking service allows the use of a quite simple transport protocol. Four issues need to be addressed:

- Addressing
- Multiplexing
- Flow control
- Connection establishment/termination

ADDRESSING   The issue concerned with addressing is simply this: A user of a given transport entity wishes either to establish a connection with or make a data transfer to a user of some other transport entity using the same transport protocol. The target user needs to be specified by all of the following:

- User identification
- Transport entity identification
- Host address
- Network number

The transport protocol must be able to derive the information listed above from the TS user address. Typically, the user address is specified as (Host, Port). The **Port** variable represents a particular TS user at the specified host. Generally, there will be a single transport entity at each host, so a transport entity identification is not needed. If more than one transport entity is present, there is usually only one of each type. In this latter case, the address should include a designation of the type of transport protocol (e.g., TCP, UDP). In the case of a single network, **Host** identifies an attached network device. In the case of an internet, *Host* is a global internet address. In TCP, the combination of port and host is referred to as a **socket**.

Because routing is not a concern of the transport layer, it simply passes the *Host* portion of the address down to the network service. *Port* is included in a transport header, to be used at the destination by the destination transport protocol entity.

One question remains to be addressed: How does the initiating TS user know the address of the destination TS user? Two static and two dynamic strategies suggest themselves:

1. The TS user knows the address it wishes to use ahead of time. This is basically a system configuration function. For example, a process may be running that is only of concern to a limited number of TS users, such as a process that collects statistics on performance. From time to time, a central network management routine connects to the process to obtain the statistics. These processes generally are not, and should not be, well known and accessible to all.

2. Some commonly used services are assigned "well-known addresses." Examples include the server side of FTP, SMTP, and some other standard protocols.

3. A name server is provided. The TS user requests a service by some generic or global name. The request is sent to the name server, which does a directory lookup and returns an address. The transport entity then proceeds with the connection. This service is useful for commonly used applications that change location from time to time. For example, a data entry process may be moved from one host to another on a local network to balance load.

4. In some cases, the target user is to be a process that is spawned at request time. The initiating user can send a process request to a well-known address. The user at that address is a privileged system process that will spawn the new process and return an address. For example, a programmer has developed a private application (e.g., a simulation program) that will execute on a remote server but be invoked from a local workstation. A request can be issued to a remote job-management process that spawns the simulation process.

MULTIPLEXING   With respect to the interface between the transport protocol and higher-level protocols, the transport protocol performs a multiplexing/demultiplexing function. That is, multiple users employ the same transport protocol and are distinguished by port numbers or service access points.

The transport entity may also perform a multiplexing function with respect to the network services that it uses. We define upward multiplexing as the multiplexing of multiple connections on a single lower-level connection, and downward multiplexing as the splitting of a single connection among multiple lower-level connections.

Consider, for example, a transport entity making use of a connection-oriented network service. Why should the transport entity employ upward multiplexing? One reason would be if the network provider determines what it charges in part on the number of connections, because each network-layer connection consumes some node buffer resources. Thus, if a network-layer connection provides sufficient throughput for multiple TS users, upward multiplexing is indicated.

On the other hand, downward multiplexing or splitting might be used to improve throughput. For example, the network layer connection may have a small sequence number space. A larger sequence space might be needed for high-speed, high-delay networks. Of course, throughput can only be increased so far. If there is a single host-node link over which all logical network connections are multiplexed, the throughput of a transport connection cannot exceed the data rate of that link.

FLOW CONTROL   Whereas flow control is a relatively simple mechanism at the link layer, it is a rather complex mechanism at the transport layer, for two main reasons:

- The transmission delay between transport entities is generally long compared to the actual transmission time. This means that there is a considerable delay in the communication of flow control information.

- Because the transport layer operates over a network or internet, the amount of the transmission delay may be highly variable. This makes it difficult to effectively use a timeout mechanism for retransmission of lost data.

In general, there are two reasons why one transport entity would want to restrain the rate of segment[1] transmission over a connection from another transport entity:

- The user of the receiving transport entity cannot keep up with the flow of data.
- The receiving transport entity itself cannot keep up with the flow of segments.

How do such problems manifest themselves? Presumably a transport entity has a certain amount of buffer space. Incoming segments are added to the buffer. Each buffered segment is processed (i.e., the transport header is examined) and the data are sent to the TS user. Either of the two problems just mentioned will cause the buffer to fill up. Thus, the transport entity needs to take steps to stop or slow the flow of segments to prevent buffer overflow. This requirement is difficult to fulfill because of the annoying time gap between sender and receiver. We return to this point subsequently. First, we present four ways of coping with the flow control requirement. The receiving transport entity can

1. Do nothing.
2. Refuse to accept further segments from the network service.
3. Use a fixed sliding-window protocol.
4. Use a credit scheme.

Alternative 1 means that the segments that overflow the buffer are discarded. The sending transport entity, failing to get an acknowledgment, will retransmit. This is a shame, because the advantage of a reliable network is that one never has to

---

[1]Recall from Chapter 2 that the blocks of data (protocol data units) exchanged by TCP entities are referred to as TCP segments.

retransmit. Furthermore, the effect of this maneuver is to exacerbate the problem. The sender has increased its output to include new segments plus retransmitted old segments.

The second alternative is a backpressure mechanism that relies on the network service to do the work. When a buffer of a transport entity is full, it refuses additional data from the network service. This triggers flow control procedures within the network that throttle the network service at the sending end. This service, in turn, refuses additional segments from its transport entity. It should be clear that this mechanism is clumsy and coarse grained. For example, if multiple transport connections are multiplexed on a single network connection (virtual circuit), flow control is exercised only on the aggregate of all transport connections.The third alternative is already familiar to you from our discussions of link-layer protocols in Chapter 7. The key ingredients, recall, are

- The use of sequence numbers on data units
- The use of a window of fixed size
- The use of acknowledgments to advance the window

With a reliable network service, the sliding-window technique would work quite well. For example, consider a protocol with a window size of 7. When the sender receives an acknowledgment to a particular segment, it is automatically authorized to send the succeeding seven segments (of course, some may already have been sent). When the receiver's buffer capacity gets down to seven segments, it can withhold acknowledgment of incoming segments to avoid overflow. The sending transport entity can send at most seven additional segments and then must stop. Because the underlying network service is reliable, the sender will not time out and retransmit. Thus, at some point, a sending transport entity may have a number of segments outstanding for which no acknowledgment has been received. Because we are dealing with a reliable network, the sending transport entity can assume that the segments will get through and that the lack of acknowledgment is a flow control tactic. This tactic would not work well in an unreliable network, because the sending transport entity would not know whether the lack of acknowledgment is due to flow control or a lost segment.

The fourth alternative, a credit scheme, provides the receiver with a greater degree of control over data flow. Although it is not strictly necessary with a reliable network service, a credit scheme should result in a smoother traffic flow. Further, it is a more effective scheme with an unreliable network service, as we shall see.

The credit scheme decouples acknowledgment from flow control. In fixed sliding-window protocols, such as X.25 and high-level data link control (HDLC), the two are synonymous. In a credit scheme, a segment may be acknowledged without granting new credit, and vice versa. For the credit scheme, each individual octet of data that is transmitted is considered to have a unique sequence number. In addition to data, each transmitted segment includes in its header three fields related to flow control: **sequence number (SN), acknowledgment number (AN)**, and **window (W)**. When a transport entity sends a segment, it includes the sequence number of the first octet in the segment data field. Implicitly, the remaining data octets are numbered sequentially following the first data octet. A transport entity acknowledges an incoming segment with a return segment that includes ($AN = i$, $W = j$), with the following interpretation:

- All octets through sequence number $SN = i - 1$ are acknowledged; the next expected octet has sequence number i.
- Permission is granted to send an additional window of $W = j$ octets of data; that is, the j octets corresponding to sequence numbers i through $i + j - 1$.

Figure 15.1 illustrates the mechanism (compare Figure 7.4). For simplicity, we show data flow in one direction only and assume that 200 octets of data are sent in each segment. Initially, through the connection establishment process, the sending and receiving sequence numbers are synchronized and A is granted an initial credit allocation of 1400 octets, beginning with octet number 1001. The first segment transmitted by A contains data octets numbered 1001 through 1200. After sending 600 octets in three segments, A has shrunk its window to a size of 800 octets (numbers 1601 through 2400). After B receives these three segments, 600 octets out of its original 1400 octets of credit are accounted for, and 800 octets of credit are outstanding. Now suppose that, at this point, B is capable of absorbing 1000 octets of incoming data on this connection. Accordingly, B acknowledges receipt of all octets through 1600 and issues a credit of 1000 octets. This means that A can send octets 1601 through 2600 (5 segments). However, by the time that B's message has arrived at A, A has already sent two segments, containing octets 1601 through 2000 (which was permissible under the initial allocation). Thus, A's remaining credit upon receipt of B's credit allocation is only 600

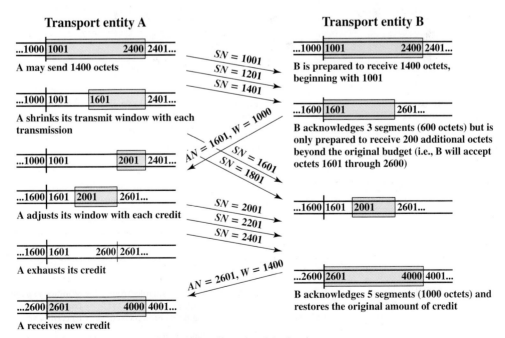

Figure 15.1 Example of TCP Credit Allocation Mechanism

octets (3 segments). As the exchange proceeds, A advances the trailing edge of its window each time that it transmits and advances the leading edge only when it is granted credit.

Figure 15.2 shows the view of this mechanism from the sending and receiving sides (compare Figure 7.3). Typically, both sides take both views because data may be exchanged in both directions. Note that the receiver is not required to immediately acknowledge incoming segments but may wait and issue a cumulative acknowledgment for a number of segments.

The receiver needs to adopt some policy concerning the amount of data it permits the sender to transmit. The conservative approach is to only allow new segments up to the limit of available buffer space. If this policy were in effect in Figure 15.1, the first credit message implies that B has 1000 available octets in its buffer, and the second message that B has 1400 available octets.

A conservative flow control scheme may limit the throughput of the transport connection in long-delay situations. The receiver could potentially increase throughput by optimistically granting credit for space it does not have. For example, if a receiver's buffer is full but it anticipates that it can release space for 1000 octets within a round-trip propagation time, it could immediately send a credit of 1000. If the receiver can keep up with the sender, this scheme may increase throughput and can do no harm. If the sender is faster than the receiver, however, some segments may be discarded, necessitating a retransmission. Because retransmissions are not

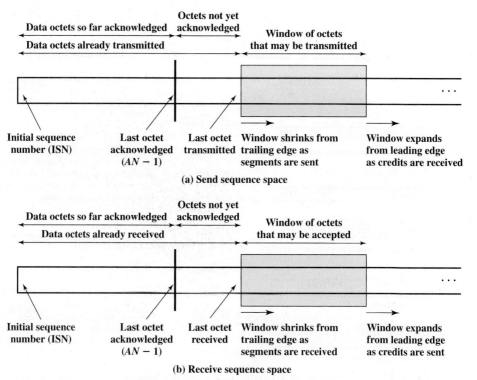

Figure 15.2 Sending and Receiving Flow Control Perspectives

otherwise necessary with a reliable network service (in the absence of internet congestion), an optimistic flow control scheme will complicate the protocol.

CONNECTION ESTABLISHMENT AND TERMINATION   Even with a reliable network service, there is a need for connection establishment and termination procedures to support connection-oriented service. Connection establishment serves three main purposes:

- It allows each end to assure that the other exists.
- It allows exchange or negotiation of optional parameters (e.g., maximum segment size, maximum window size, quality of service).
- It triggers allocation of transport entity resources (e.g., buffer space, entry in connection table).

Connection establishment is by mutual agreement and can be accomplished by a simple set of user commands and control segments, as shown in the state diagram of Figure 15.3. To begin, a TS user is in a CLOSED state (i.e., it has no open transport connection). The TS user can signal to the local TCP entity that it will passively wait for a request with a Passive Open command. A server program, such as time-sharing or a file transfer application, might do this. After the Passive Open command is issued, the transport entity creates a connection object of some sort

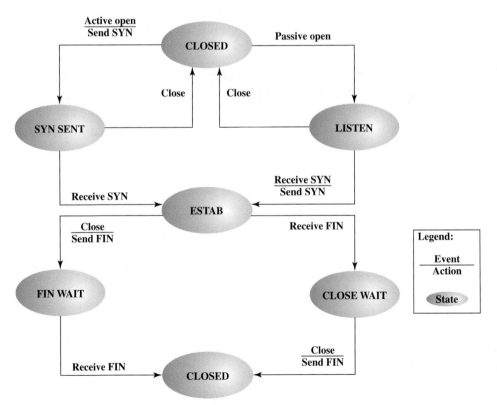

Figure 15.3   Simple Connection State Diagram

(i.e., a table entry) that is in the LISTEN state. The TS user may then change its mind by sending a Close command.

From the CLOSED state, a TS user may open a connection by issuing an Active Open command, which instructs the transport entity to attempt connection establishment with a designated remote TS user, which triggers the transport entity to send a SYN (for synchronize) segment. This segment is carried to the receiving transport entity and interpreted as a request for connection to a particular port. If the destination transport entity is in the LISTEN state for that port, then a connection is established by the following actions by the receiving transport entity:

- Signal the local TS user that a connection is open.
- Send a SYN as confirmation to the remote transport entity.
- Put the connection object in an ESTAB (established) state.

When the responding SYN is received by the initiating transport entity, it too can move the connection to an ESTAB state. The connection is prematurely aborted if either TS user issues a Close command.

Figure 15.4 shows the robustness of this protocol. Either side can initiate a connection. Further, if both sides initiate the connection at about the same time, it is established without confusion. This is because the SYN segment functions both as a connection request and a connection acknowledgment.

The reader may ask what happens if a SYN comes in while the requested TS user is idle (not listening). Three courses may be followed:

- The transport entity can reject the request by sending a RST (reset) segment back to the other transport entity.
- The request can be queued until the local TS user issues a matching Open.
- The transport entity can interrupt or otherwise signal the local TS user to notify it of a pending request.

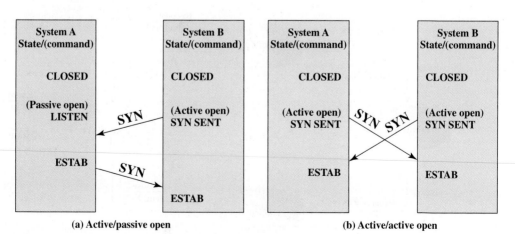

(a) Active/passive open   (b) Active/active open

Figure 15.4   Connection Establishment Scenarios

Note that if the third mechanism is used, a Passive Open command is not strictly necessary but may be replaced by an Accept command, which is a signal from the user to the transport entity that it accepts the request for connection.

Connection termination is handled similarly. Either side, or both sides, may initiate a close. The connection is closed by mutual agreement. This strategy allows for either abrupt or graceful termination. With abrupt termination, data in transit may be lost; a graceful termination prevents either side from closing the connection until all data have been delivered. To achieve the latter, a connection in the FIN WAIT state must continue to accept data segments until a FIN (finish) segment is received.

Figure 15.3 defines the procedure for graceful termination. First, consider the side that initiates the termination procedure:

1. In response to a TS user's Close primitive, a transport entity sends a FIN segment to the other side of the connection, requesting termination.

2. Having sent the FIN, the transport entity places the connection in the FIN WAIT state. In this state, the transport entity must continue to accept data from the other side and deliver that data to its user.

3. When a FIN is received in response, the transport entity informs its user and closes the connection.

From the point of view of the side that does not initiate a termination,

1. When a FIN segment is received, the transport entity informs its user of the termination request and places the connection in the CLOSE WAIT state. In this state, the transport entity must continue to accept data from its user and transmit it in data segments to the other side.

2. When the user issues a Close primitive, the transport entity sends a responding FIN segment to the other side and closes the connection.

This procedure ensures that both sides have received all outstanding data and that both sides agree to connection termination before actual termination.

Unreliable Network Service

A more difficult case for a transport protocol is that of an unreliable network service. Examples of such networks include the following:

- An internetwork using IP
- A frame relay network using only the LAPF core protocol
- An IEEE 802.3 LAN using the unacknowledged connectionless LLC service

The problem is not just that segments are occasionally lost, but that segments may arrive out of sequence due to variable transit delays. As we shall see, elaborate machinery is required to cope with these two interrelated network deficiencies. We shall also see that a discouraging pattern emerges. The combination of unreliability and nonsequencing creates problems with every mechanism we have discussed so far. Generally, the solution to each problem raises new problems. Although there are problems to be overcome for protocols at all levels, it seems that there are more difficulties with a reliable connection-oriented transport protocol than any other sort of protocol.

In the remainder of this section, unless otherwise noted, the mechanisms discussed are those used by TCP. Seven issues need to be addressed:

- Ordered delivery
- Retransmission strategy
- Duplicate detection
- Flow control
- Connection establishment
- Connection termination
- Failure recovery

ORDERED DELIVERY   With an unreliable network service, it is possible that segments, even if they are all delivered, may arrive out of order. The required solution to this problem is to number segments sequentially. We have seen that for data link control protocols, such as HDLC, each data unit (frame, packet) is numbered sequentially with each successive sequence number being one more than the previous sequence number. This scheme is used in some transport protocols, such as the ISO transport protocols. However, TCP uses a somewhat different scheme in which each data octet that is transmitted is implicitly numbered. Thus, the first segment may have a sequence number of 1. If that segment has 200 octets of data, then the second segment would have the sequence number 201, and so on. For simplicity in the discussions of this section, we will continue to assume that each successive segment's sequence number is 200 more than that of the previous segment; that is, each segment contains exactly 200 octets of data.

RETRANSMISSION STRATEGY   Two events necessitate the retransmission of a segment. First, a segment may be damaged in transit but nevertheless arrive at its destination. If a checksum is included with the segment, the receiving transport entity can detect the error and discard the segment. The second contingency is that a segment fails to arrive. In either case, the sending transport entity does not know that the segment transmission was unsuccessful. To cover this contingency, a positive acknowledgment scheme is used: The receiver must acknowledge each successfully received segment by returning a segment containing an acknowledgment number. For efficiency, we do not require one acknowledgment per segment. Rather, a cumulative acknowledgment can be used, as we have seen many times in this book. Thus, the receiver may receive segments numbered 1, 201, and 401, but only send $AN = 601$ back. The sender must interpret $AN = 601$ to mean that the segment with $SN = 401$ and all previous segments have been successfully received.

If a segment does not arrive successfully, no acknowledgment will be issued and a retransmission is in order. To cope with this situation, there must be a timer associated with each segment as it is sent. If the timer expires before the segment is acknowledged, the sender must retransmit.

So the addition of a timer solves that problem. Next problem: At what value should the timer be set? Two strategies suggest themselves. A fixed timer value could be used, based on an understanding of the network's typical behavior. This suffers from an inability to respond to changing network conditions. If the value is too small, there will be many unnecessary retransmissions, wasting network capacity. If the value is too large, the protocol will be sluggish in responding to a lost segment. The timer should be set at a value a bit longer than the round-trip time (send segment, receive ACK). Of course, this delay is variable even under constant network load. Worse, the statistics of the delay will vary with changing network conditions.

An adaptive scheme has its own problems. Suppose that the transport entity keeps track of the time taken to acknowledge data segments and sets its **retransmission timer** based on the average of the observed delays. This value cannot be trusted for three reasons:

- The peer transport entity may not acknowledge a segment immediately. Recall that we gave it the privilege of cumulative acknowledgments.
- If a segment has been retransmitted, the sender cannot know whether the received acknowledgment is a response to the initial transmission or the retransmission.
- Network conditions may change suddenly.

Each of these problems is a cause for some further tweaking of the transport algorithm, but the problem admits of no complete solution. There will always be some uncertainty concerning the best value for the retransmission timer. We return to this issue in Section 15.3.

Incidentally, the retransmission timer is only one of a number of timers needed for proper functioning of a transport protocol. These are listed in Table 15.1, together with a brief explanation.

DUPLICATE DETECTION   If a segment is lost and then retransmitted, no confusion will result. If, however, one or more segments in sequence are successfully delivered, but the corresponding ACK is lost, then the sending transport entity will time out and one or more segments will be retransmitted. If these retransmitted segments arrive successfully, they will be duplicates of previously received segments. Thus, the receiver must be able to recognize duplicates. The fact that each segment carries a sequence number helps, but, nevertheless, duplicate detection and handling is not simple. There are two cases:

- A duplicate is received prior to the close of the connection.
- A duplicate is received after the close of the connection.

The second case is discussed in the subsection on connection establishment. We deal with the first case here.

Table 15.1   Transport Protocol Timers

Retransmission timer	Retransmit an unacknowledged segment
MSL (maximum segment lifetime) timer	Minimum time between closing one connection and opening another with the same destination address
Persist timer	Maximum time between ACK/CREDIT segments
Retransmit-SYN timer	Time between attempts to open a connection
Keepalive timer	Abort connection when no segments are received

Notice that we say "a" duplicate rather than "the" duplicate. From the sender's point of view, the retransmitted segment is the duplicate. However, the retransmitted segment may arrive before the original segment, in which case the receiver views the original segment as the duplicate. In any case, two tactics are needed to cope with a duplicate received prior to the close of a connection:

- The receiver must assume that its acknowledgment was lost and therefore must acknowledge the duplicate. Consequently, the sender must not get confused if it receives multiple acknowledgments to the same segment.
- The sequence number space must be long enough so as not to "cycle" in less than the maximum possible segment lifetime (time it takes segment to transit network).

Figure 15.5 illustrates the reason for the latter requirement. In this example, the sequence space is of length 1600; that is, after $SN = 1600$, the sequence numbers cycle back and begin with $SN = 1$. For simplicity, we assume the receiving transport entity maintains a credit window size of 600. Suppose that A has transmitted data segments with $SN = 1, 201$, and 401. B has received the two segments with $SN = 201$ and $SN = 401$, but the segment with $SN = 1$ is delayed in transit. Thus, B does not send any acknowledgments. Eventually, A times out and retransmits segment $SN = 1$. When the duplicate segment $SN = 1$ arrives, B acknowledges 1, 201, and 401 with $AN = 601$. Meanwhile, A has timed out again and retransmits $SN = 201$, which B acknowledges with another $AN = 601$. Things now seem to have sorted themselves out and data transfer continues. When the sequence space is exhausted, A cycles back to $SN = 1$ and continues. Alas, the old segment $SN = 1$ makes a belated appearance and is accepted by B before the new segment $SN = 1$ arrives. When the new segment $SN = 1$ does arrive, it is treated as a duplicate and discarded.

It should be clear that the untimely emergence of the old segment would have caused no difficulty if the sequence numbers had not yet wrapped around. The larger the sequence number space (number of bits used to represent the sequence number), the longer the wraparound is avoided. How big must the sequence space be? This depends on, among other things, whether the network enforces a maximum packet lifetime, and the rate at which segments are being transmitted. Fortunately, each addition of a single bit to the sequence number field doubles the sequence space, so it is rather easy to select a safe size.

FLOW CONTROL   The credit allocation flow control mechanism described earlier is quite robust in the face of an unreliable network service and requires little enhancement. As was mentioned, a segment containing $(AN = i, W = j)$ acknowledges all octets through number $i - 1$ and grants credit for an additional j octets beginning with octet i. The credit allocation mechanism is quite flexible. For example, suppose that the last octet of data received by B was octet number $i - 1$ and that the last segment issued by B was $(AN = i, W = j)$. Then

- To increase credit to an amount k, where $(k > j)$, when no additional data have arrived, B issues $(AN = i, W = k)$.
- To acknowledge an incoming segment containing m octets of data $(m < j)$ without granting additional credit, B issues $(AN = i + m, W = j - m)$.

Transport
entity A

Transport
entity B

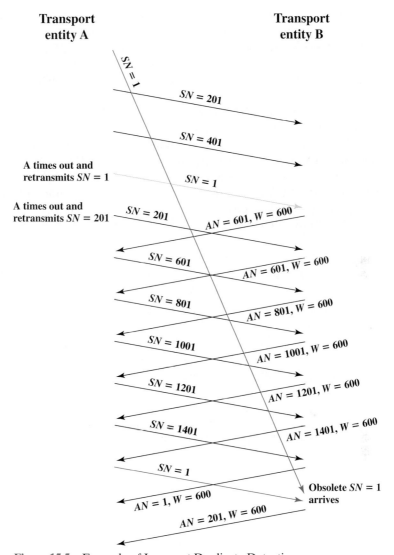

Figure 15.5 Example of Incorrect Duplicate Detection

If an ACK/CREDIT segment is lost, little harm is done. Future acknowledgments will resynchronize the protocol. Further, if no new acknowledgments are forthcoming, the sender times out and retransmits a data segment, which triggers a new acknowledgment. However, it is still possible for deadlock to occur. Consider a situation in which B sends ($AN = i$, $W = 0$), temporarily closing the window. Subsequently, B sends ($AN = i$, $W = j$), but this segment is lost. A is awaiting the opportunity to send data and B thinks that it has granted that opportunity. To overcome this problem, a **persist timer** can be used. This timer is reset with each outgoing segment (all segments contain the AN and W fields). If the timer ever expires, the protocol entity is required to send a segment, even if it duplicates a previous one. This breaks the deadlock and also assures the other end that the protocol entity is still alive.

CONNECTION ESTABLISHMENT As with other protocol mechanisms, connection establishment must take into account the unreliability of a network service. Recall that a connection establishment calls for the exchange of SYNs, a procedure sometimes referred to as a two-way handshake. Suppose that A issues a SYN to B. It expects to get a SYN back, confirming the connection. Two things can go wrong: A's SYN can be lost or B's answering SYN can be lost. Both cases can be handled by use of a **retransmit-SYN timer** (Table 15.1). After A issues a SYN, it will reissue the SYN when the timer expires.

This gives rise, potentially, to duplicate SYNs. If A's initial SYN was lost, there are no duplicates. If B's response was lost, then B may receive two SYNs from A. Further, if B's response was not lost, but simply delayed, A may get two responding SYNs. All of this means that A and B must simply ignore duplicate SYNs once a connection is established.

There are other problems to contend with. Just as a delayed SYN or lost response can give rise to a duplicate SYN, a delayed data segment or lost acknowledgment can give rise to duplicate data segments, as we have seen in Figure 15.5. Such a delayed or duplicated data segment can interfere with data transfer, as illustrated in Figure 15.6. Assume that with each new connection, each transport protocol

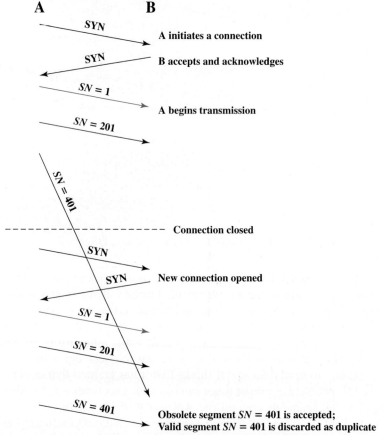

Figure 15.6 The Two-Way Handshake: Problem with Obsolete Data Segment

entity begins numbering its data segments with sequence number 1. In the figure, a duplicate copy of segment $SN = 401$ from an old connection arrives during the lifetime of a new connection and is delivered to B before delivery of the legitimate data segment $SN = 401$. One way of attacking this problem is to start each new connection with a different sequence number that is far removed from the last sequence number of the most recent connection. For this purpose, the connection request is of the form SYN $i + 1$, where i is the sequence number of the first data segment that will be sent on this connection.

Now consider that a duplicate SYN i may survive past the termination of the connection. Figure 15.7 depicts the problem that may arise. An old SYN i arrives at B after the connection is terminated. B assumes that this is a fresh request and responds with SYN j, meaning that B accepts the connection request and will begin transmitting with $SN = j + 1$. Meanwhile, A has decided to open a new connection with B and sends SYN k. B discards this as a duplicate. Now both sides have transmitted and subsequently received a SYN segment, and therefore think that a valid connection exists. However, when A initiates data transfer with a segment numbered $k + 1$, B rejects the segment as being out of sequence.

The way out of this problem is for each side to acknowledge explicitly the other's SYN and sequence number. The procedure is known as a **three-way handshake**. The revised connection state diagram, which is the one employed by TCP, is shown in the upper part of Figure 15.8. A new state (SYN RECEIVED) is added. In this state, the transport entity hesitates during connection opening to assure that the SYN segments sent by the two sides have both been acknowledged before the connection is declared established. In addition to the new state, there is a control segment (RST) to reset the other side when a duplicate SYN is detected.

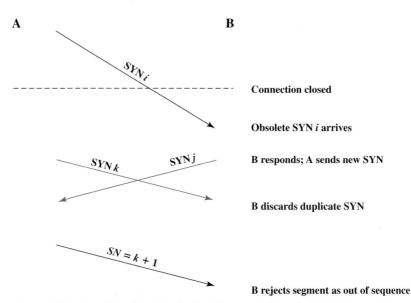

Figure 15.7 Two-Way Handshake: Problem with Obsolete SYN Segments

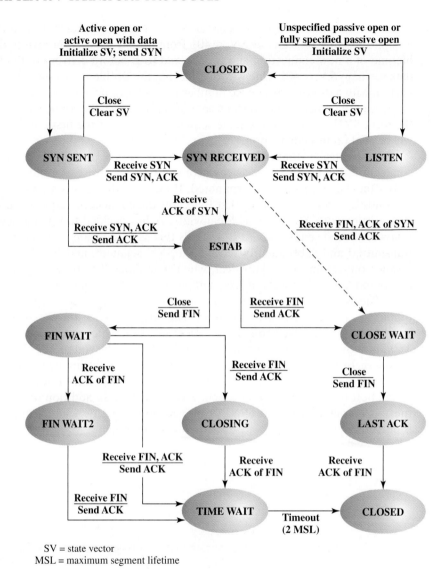

SV = state vector
MSL = maximum segment lifetime

Figure 15.8 TCP Entity State Diagram

Figure 15.9 illustrates typical three-way handshake operations. In Figure 15.9a, transport entity A initiates the connection, with a SYN including the sending sequence number, i. The value i is referred to as the initial sequence number (ISN) and is associated with the SYN; the first data octet to be transmitted will have sequence number $i + 1$. The responding SYN acknowledges the ISN with ($AN = i + 1$) and includes its ISN. A acknowledges B's SYN/ACK in its first data segment, which begins with sequence number $i + 1$. Figure 15.9b shows a situation in which an old SYN i arrives at B after the close of the relevant connection. B assumes that this is a fresh request and responds with SYN j, $AN = i + 1$. When A receives this message, it realizes that it has not requested a connection and therefore sends an RST, $AN = j$. Note that the

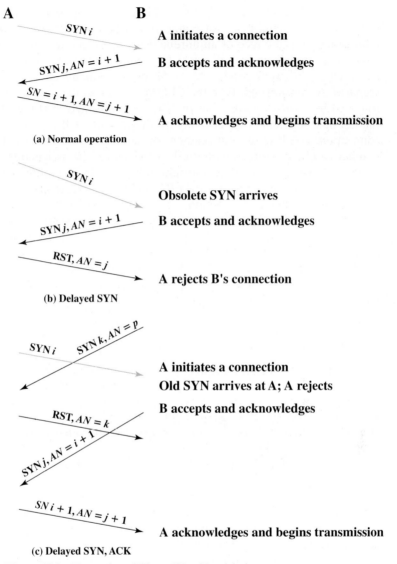

Figure 15.9 Examples of Three-Way Handshake

$AN = j$ portion of the RST message is essential so that an old duplicate RST does not abort a legitimate connection establishment. Figure 15.9c shows a case in which an old SYN/ACK arrives in the middle of a new connection establishment. Because of the use of sequence numbers in the acknowledgments, this event causes no mischief.

For simplicity, the upper part of Figure 15.8 does not include transitions in which RST is sent. The basic rule is as follows: Send an RST if the connection state is not yet OPEN and an invalid ACK (one that does not reference something that was sent) is received. The reader should try various combinations of events to see that this connection establishment procedure works in spite of any combination of old and lost segments.

Connection Termination   The state diagram of Figure 15.3 defines the use of a simple two-way handshake for connection establishment, which was found to be unsatisfactory in the face of an unreliable network service. Similarly, the two-way handshake defined in that diagram for connection termination is inadequate for an unreliable network service. Misordering of segments could cause the following scenario. A transport entity in the CLOSE WAIT state sends its last data segment, followed by a FIN segment, but the FIN segment arrives at the other side before the last data segment. The receiving transport entity will accept that FIN, close the connection, and lose the last segment of data. To avoid this problem, a sequence number can be associated with the FIN, which can be assigned the next sequence number after the last octet of transmitted data. With this refinement, the receiving transport entity, upon receiving a FIN, will wait if necessary for the late-arriving data before closing the connection.

A more serious problem is the potential loss of segments and the potential presence of obsolete segments. Figure 15.8 shows that the termination procedure adopts a similar solution to that used for connection establishment. Each side must explicitly acknowledge the FIN of the other, using an ACK with the sequence number of the FIN to be acknowledged. For a graceful close, a transport entity requires the following:

- It must send a FIN i and receive $AN = i + 1$.
- It must receive a FIN j and send $AN = j + 1$.
- It must wait an interval equal to twice the maximum expected segment lifetime.

Failure Recovery   When the system upon which a transport entity is running fails and subsequently restarts, the state information of all active connections is lost. The affected connections become *half open* because the side that did not fail does not yet realize the problem.

The still active side of a half-open connection can close the connection using a **keepalive timer**. This timer measures the time the transport machine will continue to await an acknowledgment (or other appropriate reply) of a transmitted segment after the segment has been retransmitted the maximum number of times. When the timer expires, the transport entity assumes that the other transport entity or the intervening network has failed, closes the connection, and signals an abnormal close to the TS user.

In the event that a transport entity fails and quickly restarts, half-open connections can be terminated more quickly by the use of the RST segment. The failed side returns an RST i to every segment i that it receives. When the RST i reaches the other side, it must be checked for validity based on the sequence number i, because the RST could be in response to an old segment. If the reset is valid, the transport entity performs an abnormal termination.

These measures clean up the situation at the transport level. The decision as to whether to reopen the connection is up to the TS users. The problem is one of synchronization. At the time of failure, there may have been one or more outstanding segments in either direction. The TS user on the side that did not fail knows how much data it has received, but the other user may not, if state information were lost. Thus, there is the danger that some user data will be lost or duplicated.

15.2 TCP

In this section, we look at TCP (RFC 793), first at the service it provides to the TS user and then at the internal protocol details.

TCP Services

TCP is designed to provide reliable communication between pairs of processes (TCP users) across a variety of reliable and unreliable networks and internets. TCP provides two useful facilities for labeling data: push and urgent.

- **Data stream push**: Ordinarily, TCP decides when sufficient data have accumulated to form a segment for transmission. The TCP user can require TCP to transmit all outstanding data up to and including that labeled with a push flag. On the receiving end, TCP will deliver these data to the user in the same manner. A user might request this if it has come to a logical break in the data.

- **Urgent data signaling**: This provides a means of informing the destination TCP user that significant or "urgent" data is in the upcoming data stream. It is up to the destination user to determine appropriate action.

As with IP, the services provided by TCP are defined in terms of primitives and parameters. The services provided by TCP are considerably richer than those provided by IP, and hence the set of primitives and parameters is more complex. Table 15.2 lists TCP service request primitives, which are issued by a TCP user to TCP, and Table 15.3 lists TCP service response primitives, which are issued by TCP to a local TCP user. Table 15.4 provides a brief definition of the parameters involved. The two passive open commands signal the TCP user's willingness to accept a connection request. The active open with data allows the user to begin transmitting data with the opening of the connection.

TCP Header Format

TCP uses only a single type of protocol data unit, called a TCP segment. The header is shown in Figure 15.10. Because one header must serve to perform all protocol mechanisms, it is rather large, with a minimum length of 20 octets. The fields are as follows:

- **Source Port (16 bits):** Source TCP user. Example values are Telnet = 23; TFTP = 69; HTTP = 80. A complete list is maintained at http://www.iana.org/assignments/port-numbers.

- **Destination Port (16 bits):** Destination TCP user.

- **Sequence Number (32 bits):** Sequence number of the first data octet in this segment except when the SYN flag is set. If SYN is set, this field contains the initial sequence number (ISN) and the first data octet in this segment has sequence number ISN + 1.

Table 15.2 TCP Service Request Primitives

Primitive	Parameters	Description
Unspecified Passive Open	source-port, [timeout], [timeout-action], [precedence], [security-range]	Listen for connection attempt at specified security and precedence from any remote destination.
Fully Specified Passive Open	source-port, destination-port, destination-address, [timeout], [timeout-action], [precedence], [security-range]	Listen for connection attempt at specified security and precedence from specified destination.
Active Open	source-port, destination-port, destination-address, [timeout], [timeout-action], [precedence], [security]	Request connection at a particular security and precedence to a specified destination.
Active Open with Data	source-port, destination-port, destination-address, [timeout], [timeout-action], [precedence], [security], data, data-length, PUSH-flag, URGENT-flag	Request connection at a particular security and precedence to a specified destination and transmit data with the request.
Send	local-connection-name, data, data-length, PUSH-flag, URGENT-flag, [timeout], [timeout-action]	Transfer data across named connection.
Allocate	local-connection-name, data-length	Issue incremental allocation for receive data to TCP.
Close	local-connection-name	Close connection gracefully.
Abort	local-connection-name	Close connection abruptly.
Status	local-connection-name	Query connection status.

Note: Square brackets indicate optional parameters.

- **Acknowledgment Number (32 bits):** Contains the sequence number of the next data octet that the TCP entity expects to receive.
- **Data Offset (4 bits):** Number of 32-bit words in the header.
- **Reserved (4 bits):** Reserved for future use.
- **Flags (8 bits):** For each flag, if set to 1, the meaning is

   CWR: congestion window reduced.

   ECE: ECN-Echo; the CWR and ECE bits, defined in RFC 3168, are used for the explicit congestion notification function; a discussion of this function is beyond our scope.

   URG: urgent pointer field significant.

   ACK: acknowledgment field significant.

   PSH: push function.

   RST: reset the connection.

   SYN: synchronize the sequence numbers.

   FIN: no more data from sender.

- **Window (16 bits):** Flow control credit allocation, in octets. Contains the number of data octets, beginning with the sequence number indicated in the acknowledgment field that the sender is willing to accept.

Table 15.3 TCP Service Response Primitives

Primitive	Parameters	Description
Open ID	local-connection-name, source-port, destination-port*, destination-address*,	Informs TCP user of connection name assigned to pending connection requested in an Open primitive
Open Failure	local-connection-name	Reports failure of an Active Open request
Open Success	local-connection-name	Reports completion of pending Open request
Deliver	local-connection-name, data, data-length, URGENT-flag	Reports arrival of data
Closing	local-connection-name	Reports that remote TCP user has issued a Close and that all data sent by remote user has been delivered
Terminate	local-connection-name, description	Reports that the connection has been terminated; a description of the reason for termination is provided
Status Response	local-connection-name, source-port, source-address, destination-port, destination-address, connection-state, receive-window, send-window, amount-awaiting-ACK, amount-awaiting-receipt, urgent-state, precedence, security, timeout	Reports current status of connection
Error	local-connection-name, description	Reports service-request or internal error

* = Not used for Unspecified Passive Open.

- **Checksum (16 bits):** The ones complement of the ones-complement sum of all the 16-bit words in the segment plus a pseudoheader, described subsequently.[2]
- **Urgent Pointer (16 bits):** This value, when added to the segment sequence number, contains the sequence number of the last octet in a sequence of urgent data. This allows the receiver to know how much urgent data is coming.
- **Options (Variable):** An example is the option that specifies the maximum segment size that will be accepted.

The **Sequence Number** and **Acknowledgment Number** are bound to octets rather than to entire segments. For example, if a segment contains sequence number 1001 and includes 600 octets of data, the sequence number refers to the first octet in the data field; the next segment in logical order will have sequence number 1601. Thus, TCP is logically stream oriented: It accepts a stream of octets from the user, groups them into segments as it sees fit, and numbers each octet in the stream.

The **Checksum** field applies to the entire segment plus a pseudoheader prefixed to the header at the time of calculation (at both transmission and reception).

---

[2]A discussion of this checksum is contained in Chapter 6.

Table 15.4 TCP Service Parameters

Source Port	Local TCP user
Timeout	Longest delay allowed for data delivery before automatic connection termination or error report; user specified
Timeout-action	Indicates whether the connection is terminated or an error is reported to the TCP user in the event of a timeout
Precedence	Precedence level for a connection. Takes on values zero (lowest) through seven (highest); same parameter as defined for IP
Security-range	Allowed ranges in compartment, handling restrictions, transmission control codes, and security levels
Destination Port	Remote TCP user
Destination Address	Internet address of remote host
Security	Security information for a connection, including security level, compartment, handling restrictions, and transmission control codes; same parameter as defined for IP
Data	Block of data sent by TCP user or delivered to a TCP user
Data Length	Length of block of data sent or delivered
PUSH flag	If set, indicates that the associated data are to be provided with the data stream push service
URGENT flag	If set, indicates that the associated data are to be provided with the urgent data signaling service
Local Connection Name	Identifier of a connection defined by a (local socket, remote socket) pair; provided by TCP
Description	Supplementary information in a Terminate or Error primitive
Source Address	Internet address of the local host
Connection State	State of referenced connection (CLOSED, ACTIVE OPEN, PASSIVE OPEN, ESTABLISHED, CLOSING)
Receive Window	Amount of data in octets the local TCP entity is willing to receive
Send Window	Amount of data in octets permitted to be sent to remote TCP entity
Amount Awaiting ACK	Amount of previously transmitted data awaiting acknowledgment
Amount Awaiting Receipt	Amount of data in octets buffered at local TCP entity pending receipt by local TCP user
Urgent State	Indicates to the receiving TCP user whether there are urgent data available or whether all urgent data, if any, have been delivered to the user

The pseudoheader includes the following fields from the IP header: source and destination internet address and protocol, plus a segment length field. By including the pseudoheader, TCP protects itself from misdelivery by IP. That is, if IP delivers a packet to the wrong host, even if the packet contains no bit errors, the receiving TCP entity will detect the delivery error.

By comparing the TCP header to the TCP user interface defined in Tables 15.2 and 15.3, the reader may feel that some items are missing from the TCP header—that is indeed the case. TCP is intended to work with IP. Hence, some TCP user

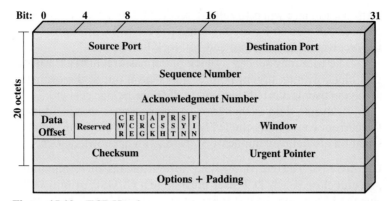

Figure 15.10   TCP Header

parameters are passed down by TCP to IP for inclusion in the IP header. The precedence parameter can be mapped into the Differentiated Services (DS) field, and the security parameter into the Optional Security field in the IP header.

It is worth observing that this TCP/IP linkage means that the required minimum overhead for every data unit is 40 octets.

TCP Mechanisms

We can group TCP mechanisms into the categories of connection establishment, data transfer, and connection termination.

CONNECTION ESTABLISHMENT   Connection establishment in TCP always uses a three-way handshake. When the SYN flag is set, the segment is essentially a request for connection and functions as explained in Section 15.1. To initiate a connection, an entity sends a SYN, $SN = X$, where X is the initial sequence number. The receiver responds with SYN, $SN = Y, AN = X + 1$ by setting both the SYN and ACK flags. Note that the acknowledgment indicates that the receiver is now expecting to receive a segment beginning with data octet $X + 1$, acknowledging the SYN, which occupies $SN = X$. Finally, the initiator responds with $AN = Y + 1$. If the two sides issue crossing SYNs, no problem results: Both sides respond with SYN/ACKs (Figure 15.4).

A connection is uniquely determined by the source and destination sockets (host, port). Thus, at any one time, there can only be a single TCP connection between a unique pair of ports. However, a given port can support multiple connections, each with a different partner port.

DATA TRANSFER   Although data are transferred in segments over a transport connection, data transfer is viewed logically as consisting of a stream of octets. Hence, every octet is numbered, modulo 2^{32}. Each segment contains the 32-bit sequence number of the first octet in the data field. Flow control is exercised using a credit allocation scheme in which the credit is a number of octets rather than a number of segments, as explained in Section 15.1.

Data are buffered by the transport entity on both transmission and reception. TCP normally exercises its own discretion as to when to construct a segment for transmission and when to release received data to the user. The PUSH flag is used to force the data so far accumulated to be sent by the transmitter and passed on by the receiver. This serves an end-of-block function.

The user may specify a block of data as urgent. TCP will designate the end of that block with an urgent pointer and send it out in the ordinary data stream. The receiving user is alerted that urgent data are being received.

If, during data exchange, a segment arrives that is apparently not meant for the current connection, the RST flag is set on an outgoing segment. Examples of this situation are delayed duplicate SYNs and an acknowledgment of data not yet sent.

CONNECTION TERMINATION   The normal means of terminating a connection is a graceful close. Each TCP user must issue a CLOSE primitive. The transport entity sets the FIN bit on the last segment that it sends out, which also contains the last of the data to be sent on this connection.

An abrupt termination occurs if the user issues an ABORT primitive. In this case, the entity abandons all attempts to send or receive data and discards data in its transmission and reception buffers. An RST segment is sent to the other side.

TCP Implementation Policy Options

The TCP standard provides a precise specification of the protocol to be used between TCP entities. However, certain aspects of the protocol admit several possible implementation options. Although two implementations that choose alternative options will be interoperable, there may be performance implications. The design areas for which options are specified are the following:

- Send policy
- Deliver policy
- Accept policy
- Retransmit policy
- Acknowledge policy

SEND POLICY   In the absence of both pushed data and a closed transmission window (see Figure 15.2a), a sending TCP entity is free to transmit data at its own convenience, within its current credit allocation. As data are issued by the user, they are buffered in the transmit buffer. TCP may construct a segment for each batch of data provided by its user or it may wait until a certain amount of data accumulates before constructing and sending a segment. The actual policy will depend on performance considerations. If transmissions are infrequent and large, there is low overhead in terms of segment generation and processing. On the other hand, if transmissions are frequent and small, the system is providing quick response.

DELIVER POLICY   In the absence of a Push, a receiving TCP entity is free to deliver data to the user at its own convenience. It may deliver data as each in-order segment is received, or it may buffer data from a number of segments in the receive buffer before delivery. The actual policy will depend on performance considerations. If deliveries are infrequent and large, the user is not receiving data as promptly as may be desirable. On the other hand, if deliveries are frequent and small, there may be unnecessary processing both in TCP and in the user software, as well as an unnecessary number of operating system interrupts.

ACCEPT POLICY   When all data segments arrive in order over a TCP connection, TCP places the data in a receive buffer for delivery to the user. It is possible, however, for segments to arrive out of order. In this case, the receiving TCP entity has two options:

- **In-order:** Accept only segments that arrive in order; any segment that arrives out of order is discarded.
- **In-window:** Accept all segments that are within the receive window (see Figure 15.2b).

The in-order policy makes for a simple implementation but places a burden on the networking facility, as the sending TCP must time out and retransmit segments that were successfully received but discarded because of misordering. Furthermore, if a single segment is lost in transit, then all subsequent segments must be retransmitted once the sending TCP times out on the lost segment.

The in-window policy may reduce transmissions but requires a more complex acceptance test and a more sophisticated data storage scheme to buffer and keep track of data accepted out of order.

RETRANSMIT POLICY   TCP maintains a queue of segments that have been sent but not yet acknowledged. The TCP specification states that TCP will retransmit a segment if it fails to receive an acknowledgment within a given time. A TCP implementation may employ one of three retransmission strategies:

- **First-only:** Maintain one retransmission timer for the entire queue. If an acknowledgment is received, remove the appropriate segment or segments from the queue and reset the timer. If the timer expires, retransmit the segment at the front of the queue and reset the timer.
- **Batch:** Maintain one retransmission timer for the entire queue. If an acknowledgment is received, remove the appropriate segment or segments from the queue and reset the timer. If the timer expires, retransmit all segments in the queue and reset the timer.
- **Individual:** Maintain one timer for each segment in the queue. If an acknowledgment is received, remove the appropriate segment or segments from the queue and destroy the corresponding timer or timers. If any timer expires, retransmit the corresponding segment individually and reset its timer.

The first-only policy is efficient in terms of traffic generated, because only lost segments (or segments whose ACK was lost) are retransmitted. Because the timer for the second segment in the queue is not set until the first segment is acknowledged, however, there can be considerable delays. The individual policy solves this problem at the expense of a more complex implementation. The batch policy also reduces the likelihood of long delays but may result in unnecessary retransmissions.

The actual effectiveness of the retransmit policy depends in part on the accept policy of the receiver. If the receiver is using an in-order accept policy, then it will discard segments received after a lost segment. This fits best with batch retransmission. If the receiver is using an in-window accept policy, then a first-only or individual retransmission policy is best. Of course, in a mixed network of computers, both accept policies may be in use.

ACKNOWLEDGE POLICY When a data segment arrives that is in sequence, the receiving TCP entity has two options concerning the timing of acknowledgment:

- **Immediate:** When data are accepted, immediately transmit an empty (no data) segment containing the appropriate acknowledgment number.
- **Cumulative:** When data are accepted, record the need for acknowledgment, but wait for an outbound segment with data on which to piggyback the acknowledgment. To avoid long delay, set a persist timer (Table 15.1); if the timer expires before an acknowledgment is sent, transmit an empty segment containing the appropriate acknowledgment number.

The immediate policy is simple and keeps the remote TCP entity fully informed, which limits unnecessary retransmissions. However, this policy results in extra segment transmissions, namely, empty segments used only to ACK. Furthermore, the policy can cause a further load on the network. Consider that a TCP entity receives a segment and immediately sends an ACK. Then the data in the segment are released to the application, which expands the receive window, triggering another empty TCP segment to provide additional credit to the sending TCP entity.

Because of the potential overhead of the immediate policy, the cumulative policy is typically used. Recognize, however, that the use of this policy requires more processing at the receiving end and complicates the task of estimating round-trip time (RTT) by the sending TCP entity.

15.3 UDP

In addition to TCP, there is one other transport-level protocol that is in common use as part of the TCP/IP suite: the User Datagram Protocol (UDP), specified in RFC 768. UDP provides a connectionless service for application-level procedures. Thus, UDP is basically an unreliable service; delivery and duplicate protection are not guaranteed. However, this does reduce the overhead of the protocol and may be adequate in many cases.

The strengths of the connection-oriented approach are clear. It allows connection-related features such as flow control, error control, and sequenced delivery. Connectionless service, however, is more appropriate in some contexts. At lower layers (internet, network), a connectionless service is more robust (e.g., see discussion in Section 9.5). In addition, it represents a "least common denominator" of service to be expected at higher layers. Further, even at transport and above there is justification for a connectionless service. There are instances in which the overhead of connection establishment and termination is unjustified or even counterproductive. Examples include the following:

- **Inward data collection:** Involves the periodic active or passive sampling of data sources, such as sensors, and automatic self-test reports from security

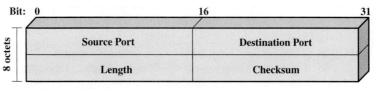

Figure 15.11 UDP Header

equipment or network components. In a real-time monitoring situation, the loss of an occasional data unit would not cause distress, because the next report should arrive shortly.

- **Outward data dissemination:** Includes broadcast messages to network users, the announcement of a new node or the change of address of a service, and the distribution of real-time clock values.

- **Request-response:** Applications in which a transaction service is provided by a common server to a number of distributed TS users, and for which a single request-response sequence is typical. Use of the service is regulated at the application level, and lower-level connections are often unnecessary and cumbersome.

- **Real-time applications:** Applications, such as voice and telemetry, that involve a degree of redundancy and/or a real-time transmission requirement. These must not have connection-oriented functions such as retransmission.

Thus, there is a place at the transport level for both a connection-oriented and a connectionless type of service.

UDP sits on top of IP. Because it is connectionless, UDP has very little to do. Essentially, it adds a port addressing capability to IP. This is best seen by examining the UDP header, shown in Figure 15.11. The header includes a source port and destination port. The Length field contains the length of the entire UDP segment, including header and data. The checksum is the same algorithm used for TCP and IP. For UDP, the checksum applies to the entire UDP segment plus a pseudoheader prefixed to the UDP header at the time of calculation and which is the same pseudoheader used for TCP. If an error is detected, the segment is discarded and no further action is taken.

The checksum field in UDP is optional. If it is not used, it is set to zero. However, it should be pointed out that the IP checksum applies only to the IP header and not to the data field, which in this case consists of the UDP header and the user data. Thus, if no checksum calculation is performed by UDP, then no check is made on the user data at either the transport or internet protocol layers.

15.4 RECOMMENDED READING AND ANIMATIONS

[IREN99] is a comprehensive survey of transport protocol services and protocol mechanisms, with a brief discussion of a number of different transport protocols.

IREN99   Iren, S.; Amer, P.; and Conrad, P. "The Transport Layer: Tutorial and Survey." *ACM Computing Surveys*, December 1999.

JACO88   Jacobson, V. "Congestion Avoidance and Control." *Proceedings, SIGCOMM '88, Computer Communication Review*, August 1988; reprinted in *Computer Communication Review*, January 1995; a slightly revised version is available at ftp. ee.lbl.gov/papers/congavoid.ps.Z

STEV94   Stevens, W. *TCP/IP Illustrated, Volume 1: The Protocols*. Reading, MA: Addison-Wesley, 1994.

Animations

Animations that illustrate the operation of TCP and IP are available at the Premium Web site. The reader is encouraged to view these animations to reinforce concepts from this chapter.

15.5 KEY TERMS, REVIEW QUESTIONS, AND PROBLEMS

Key Terms

checksum	retransmission	Transmission Control
credit	strategy	Protocol (TCP)
data stream push	sequence number	transport protocol
duplicate detection	socket	urgent data signaling
flow control	TCP implementation policy	User Datagram Protocol
multiplexing	options	(UDP)
port	three-way handshake	

Review Questions

15.1   What addressing elements are needed to specify a target transport service (TS) user?

15.2   Describe four strategies by which a sending TS user can learn the address of a receiving TS user.

15.3   Explain the use of multiplexing in the context of a transport protocol.

15.4   Briefly describe the credit scheme used by TCP for flow control.

15.5   What is the key difference between the TCP credit scheme and the sliding-window flow control scheme used by many other protocols, such as HDLC?

15.6   Explain the two-way and three-way handshake mechanisms.

15.7   What is the benefit of the three-way handshake mechanism?

15.8   Define the urgent and push features of TCP.

15.9   What is a TCP implementation policy option?

15.10   What does UDP provide that is not provided by IP?

Problems

15.1 It is common practice in most transport protocols (indeed, most protocols at all levels) for control and data to be multiplexed over the same logical channel on a per-user-connection basis. An alternative is to establish a single control transport connection between each pair of communicating transport entities. This connection would be used to carry control signals relating to all user-transport connections between the two entities. Discuss the implications of this strategy.

15.2 A file of size 40 KB is being sent over a TCP connection through 8 equal-sized segments. If the first byte is numbered 70,056, what are the sequence numbers of each segment? Also indicate the range of sequence numbers in each segment.

15.3 Two transport entities communicate across a reliable network. Let the normalized time to transmit a segment equal 1. Assume that the end-to-end propagation delay is 3, and that it takes a time 2 to deliver data from a received segment to the transport user. The sender is initially granted a credit of seven segments. The receiver uses a conservative flow control policy and updates its credit allocation at every opportunity. What is the maximum achievable throughput?

15.4 Someone posting to comp.protocols.tcp-ip complained about a throughput of 122 kbps on a 256-kbps link with a 128-ms round-trip delay between the United States and Japan, and a throughput of 33 kbps when the link was routed over a satellite.
   a. What is the utilization over the two links? Assume a 500-ms round-trip delay for the satellite link.
   b. What does the window size appear to be for the two cases?
   c. How big should the window size be for the satellite link?

15.5 Draw diagrams similar to Figure 15.4 for the following (assume a reliable sequenced network service):
   a. Connection termination: active/passive
   b. Connection termination: active/active
   c. Connection rejection
   d. Connection abortion: User issues an OPEN to a listening user, and then issues a CLOSE before any data are exchanged

15.6 With a reliable sequencing network service, are segment sequence numbers strictly necessary? What, if any, capability is lost without them?

15.7 Consider a connection-oriented network service that suffers a reset. How could this be dealt with by a transport protocol that assumes that the network service is reliable except for resets?

15.8 The discussion of retransmission strategy made reference to three problems associated with dynamic timer calculation. What modifications to the strategy would help to alleviate those problems?

15.9 Consider a transport protocol that uses a connection-oriented network service. Suppose that the transport protocol uses a credit allocation flow control scheme, and the network protocol uses a sliding-window scheme. What relationship, if any, should there be between the dynamic window of the transport protocol and the fixed window of the network protocol?

15.10 Packets of 512 bytes are being sent over a 64-kbps channel. How much time will it take to send 500 packets?

15.11 Is a deadlock possible using only a two-way handshake instead of a three-way handshake? Give an example or prove otherwise.

15.12 Listed are four strategies that can be used to provide a transport user with the address of the destination transport user. For each one, describe an analogy with the Postal Service user.
   a. Know the address ahead of time.
   b. Make use of a "well-known address."
   c. Use a name server.
   d. Addressee is spawned at request time.

15.13   In a network using a sliding-window scheme, if the receiver has a buffer of size 1000 bytes with 300 bytes of unprocessed data, what is the size of the receive window?

15.14   A network uses 128 byte-segments. If there is a congestion window of 8 segments and the receive window is 1500 bytes, what is the maximum size of data that a host can send?

15.15   A snapshot of a TCP header in hexadecimal format is:

541F7A20   00011310   0000002A   345D0023   00001122   43582ADE

   a. What is the length of the header?
   b. What is the address of the source port?
   c. What is the address of the destination port?
   d. What is the sequence number?
   e. What is the acknowledgement number?

15.16   Ordinarily, the Window field in the TCP header gives a credit allocation in octets. When the Window Scale option is in use, the value in the Window field is multiplied by a $2F$, where F is the value of the window scale option. The maximum value of F that TCP accepts is 14. Why is the option limited to 14?

15.17   The round-trip time between two hosts has been found out to be 64 ms. If the bit rate of the link between the hosts is 480 kbps, what will be the minimum TCP window size that will not cause overflow of buffers when data is continually being sent?

15.18   Two hosts are communicating using a 5-KB receive window. A packet takes 15 ms to go from one host to the other. The receiver takes 2 ms time to receive a packet and start sending the acknowledgement. What is the maximum data rate that can be achieved in this communication?

15.19   A host is receiving data from a remote peer by means of TCP segments with a payload of 1460 bytes. If TCP acknowledges every other segment, what is the minimum uplink bandwidth needed to achieve a data throughput of 1 Mbytes per second, assuming there is no overhead below the network layer? (*Note:* Assume no options are used by TCP and IP.)

15.20   A poor implementation of TCP's sliding-window scheme can lead to extremely poor performance. There is a phenomenon known as the Silly Window Syndrome (SWS), which can easily cause degradation in performance by several factors of 10. As an example of SWS, consider an application that is engaged in a lengthy file transfer, and that TCP is transferring this file in 200-octet segments. The receiver initially provides a credit of 1000. The sender uses up this window with 5 segments of 200 octets. Now suppose that the receiver returns an acknowledgment to each segment and provides an additional credit of 200 octets for every received segment. From the receiver's point of view, this opens the window back up to 1000 octets. However, from the sender's point of view, if the first acknowledgment arrives after five segments have been sent, a window of only 200 octets becomes available. Assume that at some point, the sender calculates a window of 200 octets but has only 50 octets to send until it reaches a "push" point. It therefore sends 50 octets in one segment, followed by 150 octets in the next segment, and then resumes transmission of 200-octet segments. What might now happen to cause a performance problem? State the SWS in more general terms.

15.21   The snapshot of a UDP header in hexadecimal format is

5A6A   00B0   0070   921E

   a. Check whether a correct snapshot has been taken on the basis of the length of the header.
   b. What is the source port number?
   c. What is the destination port number?
   d. What is the total length of the user datagram?
   e. What is the length of the data?

UNIT TWO
ADVANCED TOPICS IN DATA COMMUNICATIONS AND NETWORKING

ADVANCED DATA COMMUNICATIONS TOPICS

LEARNING OBJECTIVES

After studying this chapter, you should be able to:

◆ Present an overview of the basic methods of encoding analog data into a digital signal.

◆ Describe the two forms of angle modulation.

◆ Present an overview of FEC codes, including cyclic codes, BCH codes, and parity-check matrix codes.

◆ Understand the operation of an LDPC code.

◆ Discuss the key performance issues in ARQ protocols.

In this chapter, we examine three data communications topics referenced in Unit One, but which require a more advanced mathematical treatment. First, we complete the discussion of signal encoding techniques begun in Chapter 5, by discussing the use of analog signals to transmit analog data. Next, we elaborate on the discussion in Chapter 6 on forward error correction by looking at specific algorithms. Finally, the chapter examines some LAN performance issues.

16.1 ANALOG DATA, ANALOG SIGNALS

Modulation has been defined as the process of combining an input signal $m(t)$ and a carrier at frequency f_c to produce a signal $s(t)$ whose bandwidth is (usually) centered on f_c. For digital data, the motivation for modulation should be clear: When only analog transmission facilities are available, modulation is required to convert the digital data to analog form. The motivation when the data are already analog is less clear. After all, voice signals are transmitted over telephone lines at their original spectrum (referred to as baseband transmission). There are two principal reasons for analog modulation of analog signals:

• A higher frequency may be needed for effective transmission. For unguided transmission, it is virtually impossible to transmit baseband signals; the required antennas would be many kilometers in diameter.

• Modulation permits frequency-division multiplexing, an important technique explored in Chapter 8.

In this section we look at the principal techniques for modulation using analog data: amplitude modulation (AM), frequency modulation (FM), and phase modulation (PM). The three basic characteristics of a signal—amplitude, frequency, and phase—are used for modulation.

Amplitude Modulation

Amplitude modulation (AM) is the simplest form of modulation and is depicted in Figure 16.1. Mathematically, the process can be expressed as

$$\mathbf{AM} \quad s(t) = [1+n_a x(t)]\cos 2\pi f_c t \tag{16.1}$$

where $\cos 2\pi f_c t$ is the carrier and $x(t)$ is the input signal (carrying data), both normalized to unity amplitude. The parameter n_a, known as the **modulation index**, is the ratio of the amplitude of the input signal to the carrier. Corresponding to our previous notation, the input signal is $m(t) = n_a x(t)$. The "1" in Equation (16.1) is a dc component that prevents loss of information, as explained subsequently. This scheme is also known as double sideband transmitted carrier (DSBTC).

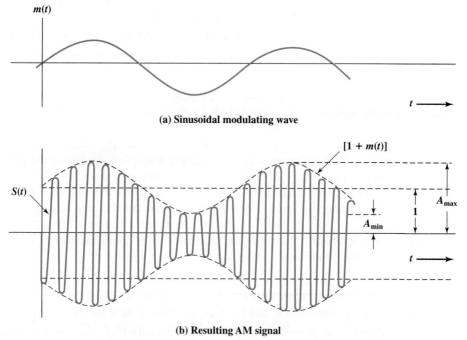

(a) Sinusoidal modulating wave

(b) Resulting AM signal

Figure 16.1 Amplitude Modulation

EXAMPLE 16.1 Derive an expression for $s(t)$ if $x(t)$ is the amplitude-modulating signal $\cos 2\pi f_m t$. We have

$$s(t) = [1 + n_a \cos 2\pi f_m t] \cos 2\pi f_c t$$

By trigonometric identity, this may be expanded to

$$s(t) = \cos 2\pi f_c t + \frac{n_a}{2} \cos 2\pi (f_c - f_m)t + \frac{n_a}{2} \cos 2\pi (f_c + f_m)t$$

The resulting signal has a component at the original carrier frequency plus a pair of components each spaced f_m Hz from the carrier.

From Equation (16.1) and Figure 16.1, it can be seen that AM involves the multiplication of the input signal by the carrier. The envelope of the resulting signal is $[1 + n_a x(t)]$ and, as long as $n_a < 1$, the envelope is an exact reproduction of the original signal. If $n_a > 1$, the envelope will cross the time axis and information is lost.

It is instructive to look at the spectrum of the AM signal. An example is shown in Figure 16.2. The spectrum consists of the original carrier plus the spectrum of the input signal translated to f_c. The portion of the spectrum for $|f| > |f_c|$ is the *upper sideband*, and the portion of the spectrum for $|f| < |f_c|$ is the *lower sideband*. Both the upper and lower sidebands are replicas of the original spectrum $M(f)$, with the lower sideband being frequency reversed.

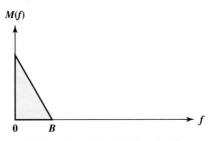

(a) Spectrum of modulating signal

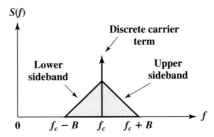

(b) Spectrum of AM signal with carrier at f_c

Figure 16.2   Spectrum of an AM Signal

EXAMPLE 16.2 Consider a voice signal with a bandwidth that extends from 300 to 3000 Hz being modulated on a 60-kHz carrier. The resulting signal contains an upper sideband of 60.3 to 63 kHz, a lower sideband of 57 to 59.7 kHz, and the 60-kHz carrier. If the carrier has an amplitude of 50 V and the audio signal has an amplitude of 20 V, then the modulation index is $n_a = 20/50 = 0.4$.

An important relationship is

$$P_t = P_c\left(1 + \frac{n_a^2}{2}\right)$$

where P_t is the total transmitted power in $s(t)$ and P_c is the transmitted power in the carrier. We would like n_a as large as possible so that most of the signal power is used to carry information. However, n_a must remain below 1.

EXAMPLE 16.3 Determine the power content of the carrier and each of the sidebands for an AM signal having a modulation index of 0.8 and a total power of 2500 W. Using the preceding equation, we have

$$2500 = P_c(1 + (0.8)^2/2) = 1.32\ P_c$$
$$P_c = 1893.9\ \text{W}$$

The remaining power is split evenly between the two sidebands, so that each sideband has a power content of $(2500 - 1893.9)/2 = 303$ W

It should be clear that $s(t)$ contains unnecessary components, because each of the sidebands contains the complete spectrum of $m(t)$. A popular variant of AM, known as single sideband (SSB), takes advantage of this fact by sending only one of the sidebands, eliminating the other sideband and the carrier. The principal advantages of this approach are as follows:

- Only half the bandwidth is required, that is, $B_T = B$, where B is the bandwidth of the original signal. For DSBTC, $B_T = 2B$.
- Less power is required because no power is used to transmit the carrier or the other sideband. Another variant is double sideband suppressed carrier (DSBSC), which filters out the carrier frequency and sends both sidebands. This saves some power but uses as much bandwidth as DSBTC.

The disadvantage of suppressing the carrier is that the carrier can be used for synchronization purposes. For example, suppose that the original analog signal is an ASK waveform encoding digital data. The receiver needs to know the starting point of each bit time to interpret the data correctly. A constant carrier provides a clocking mechanism by which to time the arrival of bits. A compromise approach is vestigial sideband (VSB), which uses one sideband and a reduced-power carrier.

Angle Modulation

Frequency modulation (FM) and phase modulation (PM) are special cases of **angle modulation**. The modulated signal is expressed as

$$\textbf{Angle Modulation} \qquad s(t) = A_c \cos[2\pi f_c t + \phi(t)] \qquad \textbf{(16.2)}$$

For phase modulation, the phase is proportional to the modulating signal:

$$\textbf{PM} \qquad \phi(t) = n_p m(t) \qquad \textbf{(16.3)}$$

where n_p is the phase modulation index.

For frequency modulation, the derivative of the phase is proportional to the modulating signal:

$$\textbf{FM} \qquad \phi'(t) = n_f m(t) \qquad \textbf{(16.4)}$$

where n_f is the frequency modulation index and $\phi'(t)$ is the derivative of $\phi(t)$.

For those who wish a more detailed mathematical explanation of the preceding, consider the following. The phase of $s(t)$ at any instant is just $2\pi f_c t + \phi(t)$. The instantaneous phase deviation from the carrier signal is $\phi(t)$. In PM, this instantaneous phase deviation is proportional to $m(t)$. Because frequency can be defined as the rate of change of phase of a signal, the instantaneous frequency of $s(t)$ is

$$2\pi f_i(t) = \frac{d}{dt}[2\pi f_c t + \phi(t)]$$

$$f_i(t) = f_c + \frac{1}{2\pi}\phi'(t)$$

and the instantaneous frequency deviation from the carrier frequency is $\phi'(t)$, which in FM is proportional to $m(t)$.

Figure 16.3 illustrates amplitude, phase, and frequency modulation by a sine wave. The shapes of the FM and PM signals are very similar. Indeed, it is impossible to tell them apart without knowledge of the modulation function.

Several observations about the FM process are in order. The peak deviation ΔF can be seen to be

$$\Delta F = \frac{1}{2\pi} n_f A_m \quad \text{Hz}$$

where A_m is the maximum value of $m(t)$. Thus an increase in the magnitude of $m(t)$ will increase ΔF, which, intuitively, should increase the transmitted bandwidth B_T. However, as should be apparent from Figure 16.3, this will not increase the average power level of the FM signal, which is $A_c^2/2$. This is distinctly different from AM, where the level of modulation affects the power in the AM signal but does not affect its bandwidth.

EXAMPLE 16.4 Derive an expression for $s(t)$ if $\phi(t)$ is the phase-modulating signal $n_p \cos 2\pi f_m t$. Assume that $A_c = 1$. This can be seen directly to be

$$s(t) = \cos\left[2\pi f_c t + n_p \cos 2\pi f_m t\right]$$

The instantaneous phase deviation from the carrier signal is $n_p \cos 2\pi f_m t$. The phase angle of the signal varies from its unmodulated value in a simple sinusoidal fashion, with the peak phase deviation equal to n_p.

The preceding expression can be expanded using Bessel's trigonometric identities:

$$s(t) = \sum_{n=-\infty}^{\infty} J_n(n_p) \cos\left(2\pi f_c t + 2\pi n f_m t + \frac{n\pi}{2}\right)$$

where, $J_n(n_p)$ is the nth-order Bessel function of the first kind. Using the property

$$J_{-n}(x) = (-1)^n J_n(x)$$

this can be rewritten as

$$s(t) = J_0(n_p) \cos 2\pi f_c t + \sum_{n=1}^{\infty} J_n(n_p)\left[\cos\left(2\pi(f_c + nf_m)t + \frac{n\pi}{2}\right)\right.$$

$$\left. + \cos\left(2\pi(f_c - nf_m)t + \frac{(n+2)\pi}{2}\right)\right]$$

The resulting signal has a component at the original carrier frequency plus a set of sidebands displaced from f_c by all possible multiples of f_m. For $n_p \ll 1$, the higher-order terms fall off rapidly.

EXAMPLE 16.5 Derive an expression for $s(t)$ if $\phi'(t)$ is the frequency modulating signal $-n_f \sin 2\pi f_m t$. The form of $\phi'(t)$ was chosen for convenience. We have

$$\phi(t) = -\int n_f \sin 2\pi f_m t \, dt = \frac{n_f}{2\pi f_m} \cos 2\pi f_m t$$

Thus

$$s(t) = \cos\left[2\pi f_c t + \frac{n_f}{2\pi f_m} \cos 2\pi f_m t\right]$$

$$= \cos\left[2\pi f_c t + \frac{\Delta F}{f_m} \cos 2\pi f_m t\right]$$

The instantaneous frequency deviation from the carrier signal is $-n_f \sin 2\pi f_m t$. The frequency of the signal varies from its unmodulated value in a simple sinusoidal fashion, with the peak frequency deviation equal to n_f radians/second.

The equation for the FM signal has the identical form as for the PM signal, with $\Delta F/f_m$ substituted for n_p. Thus the Bessel expansion is the same.

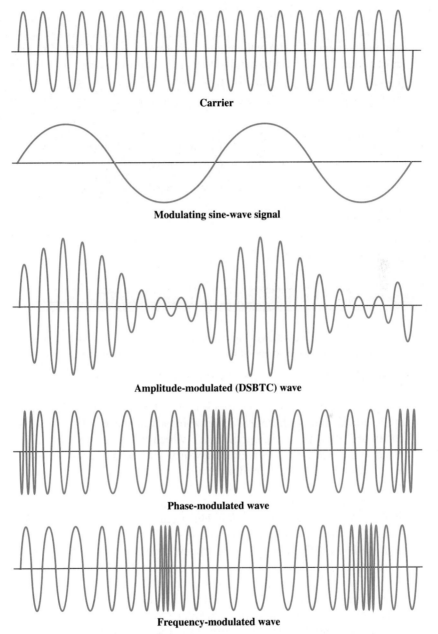

Carrier

Modulating sine-wave signal

Amplitude-modulated (DSBTC) wave

Phase-modulated wave

Frequency-modulated wave

Figure 16.3   Amplitude, Phase, and Frequency Modulation of a Sine-Wave Carrier by a Sine-Wave Signal

As with AM, both FM and PM result in a signal whose bandwidth is centered at f_c. However, we can now see that the magnitude of that bandwidth is very different. Amplitude modulation is a linear process and produces frequencies that are the sum and difference of the carrier signal and the components of the modulating signal. Hence, for AM,

$$B_T = 2B$$

However, angle modulation includes a term of the form $\cos(\phi(t))$, which is non-linear and will produce a wide range of frequencies. In essence, for a modulating sinusoid of frequency f_m, $s(t)$ will contain components at $f_c + f_m$, $f_c + 2f_m$, and so on. In the most general case, infinite bandwidth is required to transmit an FM or PM signal. As a practical matter, a very good rule of thumb, known as Carson's rule [COUC07], is

$$B_T = 2(\beta + 1)B$$

where

$$\beta = \begin{cases} n_p A_m & \text{for PM} \\ \dfrac{\Delta F}{B} = \dfrac{n_f A_m}{2\pi B} & \text{for FM} \end{cases}$$

We can rewrite the formula for FM as

$$B_T = 2\Delta F + 2B \tag{16.5}$$

Thus both FM and PM require greater bandwidth than AM.

16.2 FORWARD ERROR-CORRECTING CODES

Section 6.6 provided an overview of the principles of forward error correction. In this section, we introduce some of the most important forward error-correcting codes.

Cyclic Codes

Many of the error-correcting block codes that are in use are in a category called cyclic codes. For such codes, if the n-bit sequence $\mathbf{c} = (c_0, c_1, \ldots, c_{n-1})$ is a valid codeword, then $(c_{n-1}, c_0, c_1, \ldots, c_{n-2})$, which is formed by cyclically shifting $\mathbf{c}$ one place to the right, is also a valid codeword. This class of codes can be easily encoded and decoded using linear feedback shift registers (LFSRs). Examples of cyclic codes include the Bose–Chaudhuri–Hocquenghem (BCH) and Reed–Solomon codes.

The LFSR implementation of a cyclic error-correcting encoder is the same as that of the CRC (cyclic redundancy check) error-detecting code, illustrated in Figure 6.7. The key difference is that the CRC code takes an input of arbitrary length and produces a fixed-length CRC check code, while a cyclic error-correcting code takes a fixed-length input (k bits) and produces a fixed-length check code ($n - k$ bits).

Figure 16.4 shows the LFSR implementation of the decoder for a cyclic block code. Compare this to the encoder logic in Figure 6.7. Note that for the encoder, the k data bits are treated as input to produce an $(n - k)$ code of check bits in the shift register. For the decoder, the input is the received bit stream of n bits, consisting of k data bits followed by $(n - k)$ check bits. If there have been no errors, after the first k steps, the shift register contains the pattern of check bits that were transmitted. After the remaining $(n - k)$ steps, the shift register contains a syndrome code.

For decoding of a cyclic code, the following procedure is used:

1. Process received bits to compute the syndrome code in exactly the same fashion as the encoder processes the data bits to produce the check code.

2. If the syndrome bits are all zero, no error has been detected.

Received
(*n* bits)

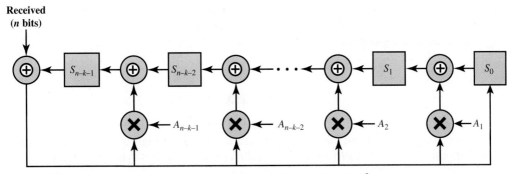

Figure 16.4 Block Syndrome Generator for Divisor $(1 + A_1X + A_2X^2 + \cdots + A_{n-k-1}X^{n-k-1} + X^{n-k})$

3. If the syndrome is nonzero, perform additional processing on the syndrome for error correction.

To understand the significance of the syndrome, let us examine the block code using polynomials. As in the case of the CRC, a particular cyclic code can be represented by a polynomial divisor, called the generator polynomial. For an (n, k) code, the generator polynomial has the form:

$$P(X) = 1 + \sum_{i=1}^{n-k-1} A_iX^i + X^{n-k}$$

where each coefficient A_i is either 0 or 1, corresponding to one bit position in the divisor. For example, for $P = 11001$, we have $P(X) = X^4 + X^3 + 1$. Similarly, the set of data bits is represented by the polynomial $D(X)$ and the check code by the polynomial $C(X)$. Recall from the CRC discussion that a check code is determined in the following way:

$$\frac{X^{n-k}D(X)}{P(X)} = Q(X) + \frac{C(X)}{P(X)}$$

That is, the data block $D(X)$ is shifted to the left by $(n - k)$ bits and divided by $P(X)$. This produces a quotient $Q(X)$ and a remainder $C(X)$ of length $(n - k)$ bits. The transmitted block is formed by concatenating $D(X)$ and $C(X)$:

$$T(X) = X^{n-k}D(X) + C(X) \tag{16.6}$$

If there is no error on reception, $T(X)$ will be exactly divisible by $P(X)$ with no remainder. This is easily demonstrated:

$$\frac{T(X)}{P(X)} = \frac{X^{n-k}D(X)}{P(X)} + \frac{C(X)}{P(X)}$$

$$= \left(Q(X) + \frac{C(X)}{P(X)}\right) + \frac{C(X)}{P(X)} = Q(X) \tag{16.7}$$

The last equality is valid because of the rules of modulo 2 arithmetic ($a + a = 0$, whether $a = 1$ or $a = 0$). Thus, if there are no errors, the division of $T(X)$ by $P(X)$ produces no remainder.

If one or more bit errors occur, then the received block $Z(X)$ will be of the form:

$$Z(X) = T(X) + E(X)$$

where $E(X)$ is an n-bit error polynomial with a value of 1 in each bit position that is in error in $Z(X)$. If we pass $Z(X)$ through the LFSR of Figure 16.4, we are performing the division $Z(X)/P(X)$, which produces the $(n - k)$ bit syndrome $S(X)$:

$$\frac{Z(X)}{P(X)} = B(X) + \frac{S(X)}{P(X)} \tag{16.8}$$

where $B(X)$ is the quotient and $S(X)$ is the remainder. Thus, $S(X)$ is a function of $Z(X)$. But how does this help us perform error correction? To see this, let us expand Equation (16.8).

$$\frac{Z(X)}{P(X)} = B(X) + \frac{S(X)}{P(X)}$$

$$\frac{T(X) + E(X)}{P(X)} = B(X) + \frac{S(X)}{P(X)}$$

$$Q(X) + \frac{E(X)}{P(X)} = B(X) + \frac{S(X)}{P(X)}$$

$$\frac{E(X)}{P(X)} = [Q(X) + B(X)] + \frac{S(X)}{P(X)} \tag{16.9}$$

What we see is that $E(X)/P(X)$ produces the same remainder as $Z(X)/P(X)$. Therefore, regardless of the initial pattern of bits (transmitted value of $T(X)$), the syndrome value $S(X)$ depends only on the error bits. If we can recover the error bits, $E(X)$, from $S(X)$, then we can correct the errors in $Z(X)$ by simple addition:

$$Z(X) + E(X) = T(X) + E(X) + E(X) = T(X)$$

Because $S(X)$ depends only on $E(X)$, we can easily determine the power of a cyclic block code. The syndrome pattern consists of $n - k$ bits and therefore takes on 2^{n-k} possible values. A value of all zeros indicates no errors. Therefore, a total of $2^{n-k} - 1$ different error patterns can be corrected. To be able to correct all possible single-bit errors with an (n, k) code, we must have $n \le (2^{n-k} - 1)$. To be able to correct all single- and double-bit errors, the relationship is $\left(n + \dfrac{n(n - 1)}{2}\right) \le (2^{n-k} - 1)$.

The way in which $E(X)$ is recovered from $S(X)$ may depend on the specific code involved. The most straightforward approach is to develop a table of all possible values of $E(X)$ with the corresponding values of $S(X)$. Then a simple table lookup is required.

EXAMPLE 16.6 Consider a $(7, 4)$ code with the generator polynomial $P(X) = X^3 + X^2 + 1$. We have $7 = 2^3 - 1$, so this code is capable of correcting all single-bit errors. Table 16.1a lists all of the valid codewords; note that d_{min} is 3, confirming that this is a single-error-correcting code. For example, for the data block 1010, we have $D(X) = X^3 + X$ and $X^{n-k}D(X) = X^6 + X^4$. Dividing as in Equation (16.7):

$$
\begin{array}{r}
X^3 + X^2 + 1 \quad\quad\quad\quad \leftarrow Q(X) \\
P(X) \to X^3 + X^2 + 1 \enclose{longdiv}{X^6 \quad\quad X^4 \quad\quad\quad\quad} \leftarrow 2^3 D(X) \\
\underline{X^3 + X^5 + \quad\quad X^3} \\
X^5 + X^4 + \quad X^3 \\
\underline{X^5 + X^4 + \quad\quad\quad X^2} \\
X^3 + X^2 \\
\underline{X^3 + X^2 + \quad 1} \\
1 \leftarrow C(X)
\end{array}
$$

Then, using Equation (16.6), we have $T(X) = X^6 + X^4 + 1$, which is the codeword 1010001.

For error correction, we need to construct the syndrome table shown in Table 16.1b. For example, for an error pattern of 1000000, $E(X) = X^6$. Using the last line of Equation (16.7), we calculate:

$$
\begin{array}{r}
X^3 + X^2 + X \quad\quad\quad \leftarrow Q(X) + B(X) \\
P(X) \to X^3 + X^2 + 1 \enclose{longdiv}{X^6 \quad\quad\quad\quad\quad\quad\quad\quad} \leftarrow E(X) \\
\underline{X^3 + X^5 + \quad\quad X^3} \\
X^5 + \quad\quad X^3 \\
\underline{X^5 + X^4 + \quad\quad X^2} \\
X^4 + \quad X^3 + X^2 \\
\underline{X^4 + \quad X^3 + \quad\quad X} \\
X^2 + X \leftarrow S(X)
\end{array}
$$

Therefore, $S = 110$. The remaining entries in Table 16.1b are calculated similarly. Now suppose the received block is 1101101, or $Z(X) = X^6 + X^5 + X^3 + X^2 + 1$. Using Equation (16.8):

$$
\begin{array}{r}
X^3 \quad\quad\quad\quad\quad\quad \leftarrow B(X) \\
P(X) \to X^3 + X^2 + 1 \enclose{longdiv}{X^6 + X^5 + \quad\quad X^3 + X^2 + 1} \leftarrow Z(X) \\
\underline{X^6 + X^5 + \quad\quad X^3} \\
X^2 + 1 \leftarrow S(X)
\end{array}
$$

Thus $S = 101$. Using Table 16.1b, this yields $E = 0001000$. Then,

$$T = 1101101 \oplus 0001000 = 1100101$$

Then, from Table 16.1a, the transmitted data block is 1100.

BCH Codes

BCH codes are among the most powerful cyclic block codes and are widely used in wireless applications. For any positive pair of integers m and t, there is a binary (n, k) BCH code with the following parameters:

$$\textbf{Block length:} \quad n = 2^m - 1$$

$$\textbf{Number of check bits:} \quad n - k \leq mt$$

$$\textbf{Minimum distance:} \quad d_{min} \geq 2t + 1$$

This code can correct all combinations of t or fewer errors. The generator polynomial for this code can be constructed from the factors of $(X^{2^m - 1} + 1)$. The BCH codes provide flexibility in the choice of parameters (block length, code rate). Table 16.2 lists the BCH parameters for code lengths up to $2^8 - 1$. Table 16.3 lists some of the BCH generator polynomials.

A number of techniques have been designed for BCH decoding that require less memory than a simple table lookup. One of the simplest was proposed by Berlekamp [BERL80]. The central idea is to compute an error-locator polynomial and solve for its roots. The complexity of the algorithm increases only as the square of the number of errors to be corrected.

Table 16.1   A Single-Error-Correcting (7, 4) Cyclic Code

(a) Table of valid codewords		(b) Table of syndromes for single-bit errors	
Data Block	**Codeword**	**Error Pattern E**	**Syndrome S**
0000	0000000	0000001	001
0001	0001101	0000010	010
0010	0010111	0000100	100
0011	0011010	0001000	101
0100	0100011	0010000	111
0101	0101110	0100000	011
0110	0110100	1000000	110
0111	0111001		
1000	1000110		
1001	1001011		
1010	1010001		
1011	1011100		
1100	1100101		
1101	1101000		
1110	1110010		
1111	1111111		

Table 16.2 BCH Code Parameters

n	k	t	n	k	t	n	k	t	n	k	t	n	k	t
7	4	1	63	30	6	127	64	10	255	207	6	255	99	23
15	11	1		24	7		57	11		199	7		91	25
	7	2		18	10		50	13		191	8		87	26
	5	3		16	11		43	14		187	9		79	27
31	26	1		10	13		36	15		179	10		71	29
	21	2		7	15		29	21		171	11		63	30
	16	3	127	120	1		22	23		163	12		55	31
	11	5		113	2		15	27		155	13		47	42
	6	7		106	3		8	31		147	14		45	43
63	57	1		99	4	255	247	1		139	15		37	45
	51	2		92	5		239	2		131	18		29	47
	45	3		85	6		231	3		123	19		21	55
	39	4		78	7		223	4		115	21		13	59
	36	5		71	9		215	5		107	22		9	63

Reed–Solomon Codes

Reed–Solomon (RS) codes are a widely used subclass of nonbinary BCH codes. With RS codes, data are processed in chunks of m bits, called symbols. An (n, k) RS code has the following parameters:

$$\textbf{Symbol length:}\quad m \text{ bits per symbol}$$
$$\textbf{Block length:}\quad n = 2^m - 1 \text{ symbols} = m(2^m - 1) \text{ bits}$$
$$\textbf{Data length:}\quad k \text{ symbols}$$
$$\textbf{Size of check code:}\quad n - k = 2t \text{ symbols} = m(2t) \text{ bits}$$
$$\textbf{Minimum distance:}\quad d_{\min} = 2t + 1 \text{ symbols}$$

Thus, the encoding algorithm expands a block of k symbols to n symbols by adding $n - k$ redundant check symbols. Typically, m is a power of 2; a popular value of m is 8.

Table 16.3 BCH Polynomial Generators

n	k	t	$P(X)$
7	4	1	$X^3 + X + 1$
15	11	1	$X^4 + X + 1$
15	7	2	$X^8 + X^7 + X^6 + X^4 + 1$
15	5	3	$X^{10} + X^8 + X^5 + X^4 + X^2 + X + 1$
31	26	1	$X^5 + X^2 + 1$
31	21	2	$X^{10} + X^9 + X^8 + X^6 + X^5 + X^3 + 1$

> **EXAMPLE 16.7** Let $t = 1$ and $m = 2$. Denoting the symbols as 0, 1, 2, 3 we can write their binary equivalents as $0 = 00$; $1 = 01$; $2 = 10$; $3 = 11$. The code has the following parameters.
>
> $$n = 2^2 - 1 = 3 \text{ symbols} = 6 \text{ bits}$$
> $$(n - k) = 2 \text{ symbols} = 4 \text{ bits}$$
>
> This code can correct any burst error that spans a symbol of 2 bits.

RS codes are well suited for burst error correction. They make highly efficient use of redundancy, and block lengths and symbol sizes can be easily adjusted to accommodate a wide range of message sizes. In addition, efficient coding techniques are available for RS codes.

Parity–Check Matrix Codes

An important type of FEC (forward error correction) is the low-density parity-check code (LDPC). LDPC codes are enjoying increasing use in high-speed wireless specifications, including the 802.11n and 802.11ac Wi-Fi standards and satellite digital television transmission. LDPC is also used for 10-Gbps Ethernet. LDPC codes exhibit performance in terms of bit error probability that is very close to the Shannon limit and can be efficiently implemented for high-speed use.

Before discussing LDPC, we introduce the more general class of parity-check codes, of which LDPC is a specific example. We discuss LDPC codes in the following section.

Consider a simple parity bit scheme used on blocks of n bits, consisting of $k = n - 1$ data bits and 1 parity-check bit, and that even parity is used. Let c_1 through c_n-1 be the data bits and c_n be the parity bit. Then the following condition holds:

$$c_1 \oplus c_2 \oplus \ldots \oplus c_n = 0 \qquad \textbf{(16.10)}$$

where addition is modulo 2 (equivalently, addition is the XOR function). Using the terminology from our discussion of block code principles in Chapter 6, there are 2^n possible codewords, of which 2^{n-1} are valid codewords. The valid codewords are those that satisfy Equation (16.10). If any of the valid codewords is received, the received block is accepted as free of errors, and the first $n-1$ bits are accepted as the valid data bits. This scheme can detect single-bit errors but cannot perform error correction.

We generalize the parity-check concept to consider codes whose words satisfy a set of $m = n - k$ simultaneous linear equations. A **parity-check code** that produces n-bit codewords is the set of solutions to the following equations:

$$h_{11}c_1 \oplus h_{12}c_2 \oplus \ldots + h_{1n}c_n = 0$$
$$h_{21}c_1 \oplus h_{22}c_2 \oplus \ldots \oplus h_{2n}c_n = 0$$
$$\vdots$$
$$h_{m1}c_1 \oplus h_{m2}c_2 \oplus \ldots \oplus h_{mn}c_n = 0 \qquad \textbf{(16.11)}$$

where the coefficients h_{ij} take on the binary values 0 or 1.

The $m \times n$ matrix $\mathbf{H} = [h_{ij}]$ is called the **parity-check matrix**. Each of the m rows of $\mathbf{H}$ corresponds to one of the individual equations in (16.11). Each of the n columns of $\mathbf{H}$ corresponds to one bit of the codeword. If we represent the codeword by the row vector $\mathbf{c} = [c_j]$, then the equation set (16.11) can be represented as:

$$\mathbf{H}\mathbf{c}^{\mathbf{T}} = \mathbf{c}\mathbf{H}^{\mathbf{T}} = \mathbf{0} \qquad (16.12)$$

An (n, k) parity-check code encodes k data bits into an n-bit codeword. Typically, and without loss of generality, the convention used is that that leftmost k bits of the codeword reproduce the original k data bits and the rightmost $(n - k)$ bits are the check bits (Figure 16.5). This form is known as a **systematic code**. Thus, in the parity-check matrix $\mathbf{H}$, the first k columns correspond to data bits and the remaining columns to check bits. To repeat what was said in Chapter 6, with an (n, k) block code, there are 2^k valid codewords out of a total of 2^n possible codewords. The ratio of redundant bits to data bits, $(n - k)/k$, is called the **redundancy** of the code, and the ratio of data bits to total bits, k/n, is called the **code rate**. The code rate is a measure of how much additional bandwidth is required to carry data at the same data rate as without the code.

The fundamental constraint on a parity-check code is that the code must have $(n - k)$ linearly independent equations. A code may have more equations, but only $(n - k)$ of them will be linearly independent. Without loss of generality, we can limit H to have the form:

$$\mathbf{H} = [\mathbf{A} \, \mathbf{I}_{n-k}]$$

where $\mathbf{I}_{n-k}$ is the $(n - k) \times (n - k)$ identity matrix, and $\mathbf{A}$ is a $k \times k$ matrix. The linear independence constraint is satisfied if and only if the determinant of $\mathbf{A}$ is nonzero.[1] With this constraint, the k data bits may be specified arbitrarily in the equation set (16.11). The set of equations can then be solved for the values of the check bits. Put another way, for each of the 2^k possible sets of data bits, it is possible to uniquely solve equation set (16.11) to determine the $(n - k)$ check bits.

Consider a $(7, 4)$ check code defined by the equations:

$$
\begin{array}{llllllll}
c_1 & \oplus c_2 & \oplus c_3 & & \oplus c_5 & & & = 0 \\
c_1 & & \oplus c_3 & \oplus c_4 & & \oplus c_6 & & = 0 \\
c_1 & \oplus c_2 & & \oplus c_4 & & & \oplus c_7 & = 0
\end{array}
\qquad (16.13)
$$

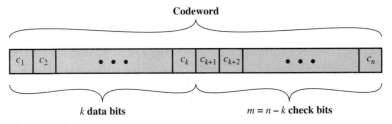

Figure 16.5 Structure of a Parity Check Codeword

---

[1]For the reader who needs a refresher on matrix multiplication and inversion, see Appendix L.

Using the parity-check matrix, we have:

$$
\underbrace{\begin{bmatrix} 1 & 1 & 1 & 0 & 1 & 0 & 0 \\ 1 & 0 & 1 & 1 & 0 & 1 & 0 \\ 1 & 1 & 0 & 1 & 0 & 0 & 1 \end{bmatrix}}_{\mathbf{H}} \begin{bmatrix} c_1 \\ c_2 \\ c_3 \\ c_4 \\ c_5 \\ c_6 \\ c_7 \end{bmatrix} = \begin{bmatrix} 0 \\ 0 \\ 0 \end{bmatrix} \tag{16.14}
$$

For a parity-check code, as with any FEC, there are three functions we need to perform:

- **Encoding:** For a given set of k data bits, generate the corresponding n-bit codeword.
- **Error detection:** For a given codeword, determine if there are one or more bits in error.
- **Error correction:** If an error is detected, perform error correction.

ENCODING   For our example, to form a codeword, we first choose values for data bits c_1, c_2, and c_3; for example, $c_1 = 1$, $c_2 = 1$, $c_3 = 0$, $c_4 = 0$. We then solve equation set (16.13) by rewriting them so that we show each check bit as a function of data bits:

$$
\begin{aligned}
c_5 &= c_1 \oplus c_2 \oplus c_3 \\
c_6 &= c_1 \oplus c_3 \oplus c_4 \\
c_7 &= c_1 \oplus c_2 \oplus c_4
\end{aligned} \tag{16.15}
$$

Thus the codeword is 1100010. With three information bits, there are a total of 16 valid codewords out of the $2^7 = 128$ possible codewords. We can solve for each of the 16 possible combinations of data bits to calculate these codewords. The results are shown in Table 16.4.

A more general approach to encoding is to create a $k \times n$ **generator matrix** for the code. Using equation set (16.13), we can write:

$$
\begin{bmatrix} c_1 & c_2 & c_3 & c_4 & c_5 & c_6 & c_7 \end{bmatrix} = \begin{bmatrix} c_1 & c_2 & c_3 & c_4 \end{bmatrix} \underbrace{\begin{bmatrix} 1 & 0 & 0 & 0 & 1 & 1 & 1 \\ 0 & 1 & 0 & 0 & 1 & 0 & 1 \\ 0 & 0 & 1 & 0 & 1 & 1 & 0 \\ 0 & 0 & 0 & 1 & 0 & 1 & 1 \end{bmatrix}}_{\mathbf{G}} \tag{16.16}
$$

By our convention, the first k bits of $\mathbf{c}$ are the data bits. Let us label the data bits of $\mathbf{c}$ as $\mathbf{u} = [u_i]$ where $u_i = c_i$, for $i = 1$ to k. Then, the codeword corresponding to a data block is determined by:

$$
\mathbf{c} = \mathbf{uG} \tag{16.17}
$$

Table 16.4   (7, 4) Parity-Check Code Defined by Equation (16.15)

Data Bits				Check Bits		
c_1	c_2	c_3	c_4	c_5	c_6	c_7
0	0	0	0	0	0	0
0	0	0	1	0	1	1
0	0	1	0	1	1	0
0	0	1	1	1	0	1
0	1	0	0	1	0	1
0	1	0	1	1	1	0
0	1	1	0	0	1	1
0	1	1	1	0	0	0
1	0	0	0	1	1	1
1	0	0	1	1	0	0
1	0	1	0	0	0	1
1	0	1	1	0	1	0
1	1	0	0	0	1	0
1	1	0	1	0	0	1
1	1	1	0	1	0	0
1	1	1	1	1	1	1

The first k columns of **G** are the identity matrix $\mathbf{I}_k$. **G** can be calculated from **H** as follows:

$$\mathbf{G} = [\mathbf{I}_k \mathbf{A}^\mathrm{T}]$$

ERROR DETECTION   Error detection is simply a matter of applying Equation (16.12). If $\mathbf{Hc}^\mathrm{T}$ yields a nonzero vector, then an error is detected. Using our example code, suppose that the codeword 1100010 is sent over a transmission channel and 1101010 is received. Applying the parity-check matrix to the received codeword, we have:

$$\underbrace{\begin{bmatrix} 1 & 1 & 1 & 0 & 1 & 0 & 0 \\ 1 & 0 & 1 & 1 & 0 & 1 & 0 \\ 1 & 1 & 0 & 1 & 0 & 0 & 1 \end{bmatrix}}_{\mathbf{H}} \begin{bmatrix} 1 \\ 1 \\ 0 \\ 1 \\ 0 \\ 1 \\ 0 \end{bmatrix} = \begin{bmatrix} 0 \\ 1 \\ 1 \end{bmatrix}$$

So the error is detected. Further, the resulting column vector is referred to as the **syndrome**. The syndrome indicates which of the individual parity-check equations do not equal 0. The result in our example indicates that the second and third parity-check equations in **H** are not satisfied. Thus at least one of the bits c_1, c_2, c_3, c_4, c_6, c_7 is in error.

ERROR CORRECTION   Referring back to our discussion of Chapter 6, one approach to error correction when an invalid codeword is received is to choose the valid codeword that is closest to the invalid codeword in terms of Hamming distance. This method works only in those instances in which there is a unique valid codeword at a minimum distance from the given invalid codeword. As was discussed in Chapter 6, define the minimum distance of a code as the minimum Hamming distance d_{min} between any two valid codewords. The code can detect all patterns of $(d_{min} - 1)$ or fewer bit errors and can correct all patterns of $\left\lfloor \dfrac{d_{min} - 1}{2} \right\rfloor$ or fewer bit errors.

A parity-check code $\mathbf{H}$ has a minimum distance d_{min} if some XOR sum of d_{min} columns of $\mathbf{H}$ is equal to zero, but no XOR sum of fewer than d_{min} columns of $\mathbf{H}$ is equal to zero. This property is of fundamental importance in the design of most parity-check codes. That is, the codes are designed so as to maximize d_{min}. An important exception to this approach is the low-density parity-check code, discussed in the next section.

For the example $\mathbf{H}$ that we have been using, no single column is the $\mathbf{0}$ vector, and no two columns sum to $\mathbf{0}$. But there are several instances where 3 columns sum to $\mathbf{0}$ (e.g., the 4th, 6th, and 7th columns). Thus, $d_{min} = 3$.

The brute-force approach to error correction would be to compare a received invalid codeword to all 2^k valid codewords and pick the one with minimum distance. This approach is only feasible for small k. For codes with thousands of data bits per codeword, a variety of approaches have been developed. A discussion of these is beyond our scope.

Low-Density Parity-Check Codes

A **regular LDPC code** is a parity-check code with parity-check matrix $\mathbf{H}$ with the following properties:

1. Each row of $\mathbf{H}$ contains w_r 1s.
2. Each column of $\mathbf{H}$ contains w_c 1s.
3. The number of 1s in common between any two columns is zero or one.
4. Both w_r and w_c are small compared to the number of columns (length of the codeword) and the number of rows.

Because of property 4, $\mathbf{H}$ has a small density of 1s. That is, the elements of $\mathbf{H}$ are almost all equal to 0. Hence the designation *low density*.

In practice, constraints 1 and 2 are often violated slightly in order to avoid having linearly dependent rows in H. For an **irregular LDPC code**, we can say that the average number of 1s per row and the average number of 1s per column are small compared to the number of columns and the number of rows.

CODE CONSTRUCTION   A number of approaches have been developed for the construction of LDPC codes, by defining the LDPC parity-check matrix. One of the earliest approaches was proposed by Robert Gallager [GALL62]. The code is constructed as a stack of w_c submatrices. The topmost submatrix has n columns and

n/w_r rows. The first row of this submatrix has 1s in the first w_r positions and 0s elsewhere. The second row has 1s in the second group of w_r positions and 0s elsewhere, and so on. The other submatrices are random column permutations of the first submatrix. Figure 16.6a is an example with $w_r = 4$.

An alternative approach, proposed by MacKay and Neal [MACK99], is illustrated with an example in Figure 16.6b. For this scheme, a transmitted block length n and a source block length k are selected. The initial value of w_c is set to an integer greater than or equal to 3, and the initial value of w_r is set to $w_c n/m$. Columns of **H** are created one at a time from left to right. The first column is initially generated randomly subject to the constraint that its weight equal the initial value of w_c. The nonzero entries for each subsequent column are chosen randomly subject to the constraint that each row weight does not exceed w_r. There may need to be some backtracking and relaxation of constraints to fill the entire matrix.

The two codes so for described are not systematic. That is, the data bits do not correspond to the first k columns of **H**. In general, with a nonsystematic code, it is more difficult to determine a technique for generating a codeword from a block of data bits. An LDPC construction technique that does result in a systematic code is called a **repeat-accumulate code** [DIVS98]. Construction begins with the rightmost column with a single one bit at the bottom of the column. The next column to the left has 1s in the lower 2 bit positions. For subsequent columns, the pair of 1s is shifted up one position, until the 1s reach the top of the column. The remaining k columns each have a single one bit per row. Figure 16.6c shows an example. The first parity bit can be computed as $c_4 = c_1$, the second as $c_5 = c_4 + c_1$, the third as $c_6 = c_5 + c_2$, and so on. Thus, after the first parity bit, each subsequent parity bit is a function of the preceding parity bit and one of the data bits.

ERROR CORRECTION As with any parity-check code, error detection of an LDPC code can be performed using the parity-check matrix. If $\mathbf{Hc}^T$ yields a nonzero vector, then an error is detected. Because there are relatively few 1s in the parity-check matrix, this computation is reasonably efficient.

Error detection is a more complex process. Depending on the nature of the construction of the LDPC code, a number of methods have been developed to provide reasonably efficient computation. Here we give a brief overview.

Many error-detection techniques make use of a representation of an LDPC code known as a **Tanner graph**. The graph contains two kinds of nodes: check nodes, which correspond to rows of **H**, and bit nodes, which correspond to columns of **H** and hence to the bits of the codeword. Construction is as follows: Check node j is connected to the variable node i if and only if element h_{ij} in H is 1. Figure 16.7 shows an example.

We now present a very simple error-correction technique using the LDPC example of Figure 16.7. This technique is not efficient and is not used in practice. However, it is simple and gives some idea of the basic mechanisms involved in a typical error-correction algorithm for LDPC codes.

Assume for our example that the source codeword is 1001010. This is a valid codeword because $\mathbf{Hc}^T = \mathbf{0}$. Assume that the second codeword bit is changed during

$$
\begin{bmatrix}
1 & 1 & 1 & 1 & 0 & 0 & 0 & 0 & 0 & 0 & 0 & 0 \\
0 & 0 & 0 & 0 & 1 & 1 & 1 & 1 & 0 & 0 & 0 & 0 \\
0 & 0 & 0 & 0 & 0 & 0 & 0 & 0 & 1 & 1 & 1 & 1 \\
\hline
1 & 0 & 1 & 0 & 0 & 1 & 0 & 0 & 0 & 1 & 0 & 0 \\
0 & 1 & 0 & 0 & 0 & 0 & 1 & 1 & 0 & 0 & 0 & 1 \\
0 & 0 & 0 & 1 & 1 & 0 & 0 & 0 & 1 & 0 & 1 & 0 \\
\hline
1 & 0 & 0 & 1 & 0 & 0 & 1 & 0 & 0 & 1 & 0 & 0 \\
0 & 1 & 0 & 0 & 0 & 1 & 0 & 1 & 0 & 0 & 1 & 0 \\
0 & 0 & 1 & 0 & 1 & 0 & 0 & 0 & 1 & 0 & 0 & 1
\end{bmatrix}
$$

(a) Gallager parity-check matrix with $w_c = 3$, $w_r = 4$

$$
\begin{bmatrix}
1 & 0 & 0 & 0 & 0 & 1 & 0 & 1 & 0 & 1 & 0 & 0 \\
1 & 0 & 0 & 1 & 1 & 0 & 0 & 0 & 0 & 0 & 1 & 0 \\
0 & 1 & 0 & 0 & 1 & 0 & 1 & 0 & 1 & 0 & 0 & 0 \\
0 & 0 & 1 & 0 & 0 & 1 & 0 & 0 & 0 & 0 & 1 & 1 \\
0 & 0 & 1 & 0 & 0 & 0 & 1 & 1 & 0 & 0 & 0 & 1 \\
0 & 1 & 0 & 0 & 1 & 0 & 0 & 0 & 1 & 0 & 1 & 0 \\
1 & 0 & 0 & 1 & 0 & 0 & 1 & 0 & 0 & 1 & 0 & 0 \\
0 & 1 & 0 & 0 & 0 & 1 & 0 & 1 & 0 & 1 & 0 & 0 \\
0 & 0 & 1 & 1 & 0 & 0 & 0 & 0 & 1 & 0 & 0 & 1
\end{bmatrix}
$$

(b) McKay-Neal parity-check matrix with $w_c = 3$, $w_r = 4$

$$
\begin{bmatrix}
1 & 0 & 0 & 1 & 0 & 0 & 0 & 0 & 0 & 0 & 0 & 0 \\
1 & 0 & 0 & 1 & 1 & 0 & 0 & 0 & 0 & 0 & 0 & 0 \\
0 & 1 & 0 & 0 & 1 & 1 & 0 & 0 & 0 & 0 & 0 & 0 \\
0 & 0 & 1 & 0 & 0 & 1 & 1 & 0 & 0 & 0 & 0 & 0 \\
0 & 0 & 1 & 0 & 0 & 0 & 1 & 1 & 0 & 0 & 0 & 0 \\
0 & 1 & 0 & 0 & 0 & 0 & 0 & 1 & 1 & 0 & 0 & 0 \\
1 & 0 & 0 & 0 & 0 & 0 & 0 & 0 & 1 & 1 & 0 & 0 \\
0 & 1 & 0 & 0 & 0 & 0 & 0 & 0 & 0 & 1 & 1 & 0 \\
0 & 0 & 1 & 0 & 0 & 0 & 0 & 0 & 0 & 0 & 1 & 1
\end{bmatrix}
$$

(c) Irregular repeat-accumulate parity-check matrix

Figure 16.6   Examples of LDPC Parity-Check Matrices

$$H = \begin{bmatrix} 0 & 1 & 0 & 1 & 1 & 0 & 0 & 1 \\ 1 & 1 & 1 & 0 & 0 & 1 & 0 & 0 \\ 0 & 0 & 1 & 0 & 0 & 1 & 1 & 1 \\ 1 & 0 & 0 & 1 & 1 & 0 & 1 & 0 \end{bmatrix}$$

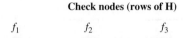

(a) Parity-check matrix

Check nodes (rows of H)

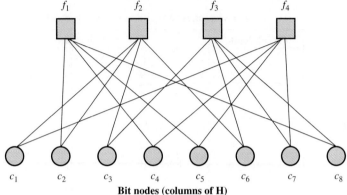

Bit nodes (columns of H)

(b) Tanner graph

Figure 16.7   Example LDPC Code

transmission so that the received codeword is 11010101. The error-detection algorithm detects that one or more bit errors have occurred:

$$\begin{bmatrix} 0 & 1 & 0 & 1 & 1 & 0 & 0 & 1 \\ 1 & 1 & 1 & 0 & 0 & 1 & 0 & 0 \\ 0 & 0 & 1 & 0 & 0 & 1 & 1 & 1 \\ 1 & 0 & 0 & 1 & 1 & 0 & 1 & 0 \end{bmatrix} \begin{bmatrix} 1 \\ 1 \\ 0 \\ 1 \\ 0 \\ 1 \\ 0 \\ 1 \end{bmatrix} = \begin{bmatrix} 1 \\ 1 \\ 0 \\ 0 \end{bmatrix}$$

Error correction proceeds with the following steps:

1. Using the Tanner graph of Figure 16.7b, each bit node sends its bit value to
   each linked check node (Table 16.5b). Thus, c_1, which has the codeword bit
   value 1 sends this value to nodes f_2 and f_4.

2. Each check node uses its corresponding constraint equation to calculate a
   bit value for each linked bit node and sends the value to the bit node. For
   example, the constraint equation for f_1, determined by the first row of **H**, is
   $c_2 \oplus c_4 \oplus c_5 \oplus c_8 = 0$. f_1 solves this equation 4 times, successively using each
   of its four inputs as the variable to be solved for. So, f_1 has received the values

Table 16.5 Example Error-Correction Technique for LDPC of Figure 16.7

(a) Constraint equations

Row of H	Check Node	Equation
1	f_1	$c_2 \oplus c_4 \oplus c_5 \oplus c_8 = 0$
2	f_2	$c_1 \oplus c_2 \oplus c_3 \oplus c_6 = 0$
3	f_3	$c_3 \oplus c_6 \oplus c_7 \oplus c_8 = 0$
4	f_4	$c_1 \oplus c_4 \oplus c_5 \oplus c_7 = 0$

(b) Messages sent and received by check nodes

Check Node		Messages
f_1	Received:	$c_2 \rightarrow 1\ c_4 \rightarrow 1\ c_5 \rightarrow 0\ c_8 \rightarrow 1$
	Sent:	$0 \rightarrow c_2\ 0 \rightarrow c_4\ 1 \rightarrow c_5\ 0 \rightarrow c_8$
f_2	Received:	$c_1 \rightarrow 1\ c_2 \rightarrow 1\ c_3 \rightarrow 0\ c_6 \rightarrow 1$
	Sent:	$0 \rightarrow c_1\ 0 \rightarrow c_2\ 1 \rightarrow c_3\ 0 \rightarrow c_6$
f_3	Received:	$c_3 \rightarrow 0\ c_6 \rightarrow 1\ c_7 \rightarrow 0\ c_8 \rightarrow 1$
	Sent:	$0 \rightarrow c_3\ 1 \rightarrow c_6\ 0 \rightarrow c_7\ 1 \rightarrow c_8$
f_4	Received:	$c_1 \rightarrow 1\ c_4 \rightarrow 1\ c_5 \rightarrow 0\ c_7 \rightarrow 0$
	Sent:	$1 \rightarrow c_1\ 1 \rightarrow c_4\ 0 \rightarrow c_5\ 0 \rightarrow c_7$

(c) Estimation of codeword bit values

Bit Node	Codeword Bit		Messages	Decision
c_1	1	$f_2 \rightarrow 0$	$f_4 \rightarrow 1$	1
c_2	1	$f_1 \rightarrow 0$	$f_2 \rightarrow 0$	0
c_3	0	$f_2 \rightarrow 1$	$f_3 \rightarrow 0$	0
c_4	1	$f_1 \rightarrow 0$	$f_4 \rightarrow 1$	1
c_5	0	$f_1 \rightarrow 1$	$f_4 \rightarrow 0$	0
c_6	1	$f_2 \rightarrow 0$	$f_3 \rightarrow 1$	1
c_7	0	$f_3 \rightarrow 0$	$f_4 \rightarrow 0$	0
c_8	1	$f_1 \rightarrow 0$	$f_3 \rightarrow 1$	1

$c_2 = 1$, $c_4 = 1$, $c_5 = 0$, $c_8 = 1$. First it solves $c_2 = c_4 \oplus c_5 \oplus c_8 = 0$ and sends the 0 to c_2. Then it solves $c_4 = c_2 \oplus c_5 \oplus c_8 = 0$ and sends the 0 to c_4, and so on for the remaining two variables.

3. Each of the incoming bit values to each bit node is an estimate of the corrected value for that node. The original bit value of the node is a third estimate. The bit node chooses the majority value as its final estimate of the value (Table 16.5c). Thus, for c_1, two of the three estimates are 1 and 1 is chosen as the final value for the first bit of the codeword.

These three steps are repeated until the codeword stops changing or until all the constraint equations are satisfied. In this case, the codeword stabilizes after just one iteration.

The same concept of message passing between bit nodes and check nodes can be used with a probabilistic basis. In essence, the probability of a codeword bit being 1 or 0 is calculated in each iteration and the loop stops when all of the probabilities pass a certain threshold.

There are a number of other approaches to error correction, many of which exploit the Tanner graph structure.

ENCODING   As was mentioned in our earlier discussions of the general case of parity-check codes, a straightforward method of encoding data bits to form a codeword is to calculate the generator matrix **G** from the parity-check matrix **H**. Typically, for LDPC codes, this is a difficult and resource-intensive operation. Accordingly, a variety of techniques have been developed for solving the parity-check constraint equations to show the parity bits as a function of the data bits. For the repeat-accumulate code, as we have seen, this is a simple process. For other forms of LDPC codes, the encoding process is considerably more complex and often involves the use of the Tanner graph.

One other point worth noting is that, in general, with the exception of the repeat-accumulate code, the LDCP code is not systematic. That is, the data bits are not necessarily grouped together at the beginning of the codeword. In essence, the code designer selects codeword bits to be the data bits and then the parity bits are calculated.

16.3 ARQ PERFORMANCE ISSUES

In this section, we examine some of the performance issues related to the use of sliding-window flow control.

Stop-and-Wait Flow Control

Let us determine the maximum potential efficiency of a half-duplex point-to-point line using the stop-and-wait scheme. Suppose that a long message is to be sent as a sequence of frames $F_1, F_2, ..., F_n$, in the following fashion:

- Station S_1 sends F_1.
- Station S_2 sends an acknowledgment.
- Station S_1 sends F_2.
- Station S_2 sends an acknowledgment.
- Station S_1 sends F_n.
- Station S_2 sends an acknowledgment.

The total time to send the data, T, can be expressed as $T = nT_F$, where T_F is the time to send one frame and receive an acknowledgment. We can express T_F as follows:

$$T_F = t_{prop} + t_{frame} + t_{proc} + t_{prop} + t_{ack} + t_{proc}$$

where

$$t_{prop} = \text{propagation time from } S_1 \text{ to } S_2$$

$$t_{frame} = \text{time to transmit a frame (time for the transmitter to send out all of the bits of the frame)}$$

$$t_{proc} = \text{processing time at each station to react to an incoming event}$$

$$t_{ack} = \text{time to transmit an acknowledgment}$$

Let us assume that the processing time is relatively negligible, and that the acknowledgment frame is very small compared to a data frame, both of which are reasonable assumptions. Then we can express the total time to send the data as

$$T = n(2t_{prop} + t_{frame})$$

Of that time, only $n \times t_{frame}$ is actually spent transmitting data and the rest is overhead. The utilization, or efficiency, of the line is

$$U = \frac{n \times t_{frame}}{n(2t_{prop} + t_{frame})} = \frac{t_{frame}}{2t_{prop} + t_{frame}} \qquad \textbf{(16.18)}$$

It is useful to define the parameter $a = t_{prop}/t_{frame}$ (see Figure 16.8). Then

$$U = \frac{1}{1 + 2a} \qquad \textbf{(16.19)}$$

This is the maximum possible utilization of the link. Because the frame contains overhead bits, actual utilization is lower. The parameter a is constant if both t_{prop} and t_{frame} are constants, which is typically the case: Fixed-length frames are often used for all except the last frame in a sequence, and the propagation delay is constant for point-to-point links.

To get some insight into Equation (16.19), let us derive a different expression for a. We have

$$a = \frac{\text{Propagation Time}}{\text{Transmission Time}} \qquad \textbf{(16.20)}$$

The propagation time is equal to the distance d of the link divided by the velocity of propagation V. For unguided transmission through air or space, V is the speed of light, approximately 3×10^8 m/s. For guided transmission, V is approximately 0.67 times the speed of light for optical fiber and copper media. The transmission time is equal to the length of the frame in bits, L, divided by the data rate R. Therefore,

$$a = \frac{d/V}{L/R} = \frac{Rd}{VL}$$

Thus, for fixed-length frames, a is proportional to the data rate times the length of the medium. A useful way of looking at a is that it represents the length of the medium in bits $[R \times (d/v)]$ compared to the frame length (L).

With this interpretation in mind, Figure 16.8 illustrates Equation (16.19). In this figure, transmission time is normalized to 1 and hence the propagation time,

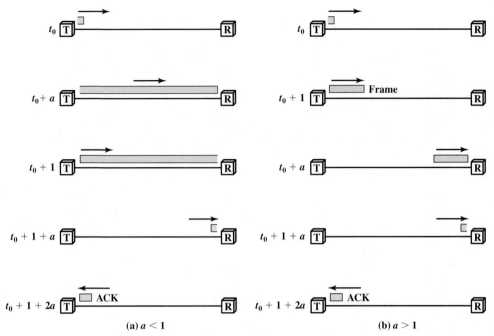

t_0 [T] □ [R] t_0 [T] □ [R]

$t_0 + a$ [T] [R] $t_0 + 1$ [T] Frame [R]

$t_0 + 1$ [T] [R] $t_0 + a$ [T] [R]

$t_0 + 1 + a$ [T] [R] $t_0 + 1 + a$ [T] [R]

$t_0 + 1 + 2a$ [T] □ ACK [R] $t_0 + 1 + 2a$ [T] □ ACK [R]

(a) $a < 1$ (b) $a > 1$

Figure 16.8 Stop-and-Wait Link Utilization (transmission time $= 1$; propagation time $= a$)

by Equation (16.20), is a. For the case of $a < 1$, the link's bit length is less than that of the frame. The station T begins transmitting a frame at time t_0. At t_0+a, the leading edge of the frame reaches the receiving station R, while T is still in the process of transmitting the frame. At t_0+1, T completes transmission. At t_0+1+a, R has received the entire frame and immediately transmits a small acknowledgment frame. This acknowledgment arrives back at T at t_0+1+2a. Total elapsed time: $1+2a$. Total transmission time: 1. Hence utilization is $1/(1+2a)$. The same result is achieved with $a > 1$, as illustrated in Figure 16.8.

> **EXAMPLE 16.8** First, consider a wide area network using asynchronous transfer mode (described in Part Three), with the two stations a thousand kilometers apart. The standard ATM frame size (called a cell) is 424 bits and one of the standardized data rates is 155.52 Mbps. Thus, transmission time equals $424/(155.52 \times 10^6) = 2.7 \times 10^{-6}$ s. If we assume an optical fiber link, then the propagation time is $(10^6 \text{ m})/(2 \times 10^8 \text{ m/s}) = 0.5 \times 10^{-2}$ s. Thus, $a = (0.5 \times 10^{-2})/(2.7 \times 10^{-6}) \approx 1850$, and efficiency is only $1/3701 = 0.00027$.
>
> At the other extreme, in terms of distance, is the local area network. Distances range from 0.1 to 10 km, with data rates of 10 Mbps to 1 Gbps; higher data rates tend to be associated with shorter distances. Using a value of $V = 2 \times 10^8$ m/s, a frame size of 1000 bits, and a data rate of 10 Mbps, the value of a is in the range of 0.005 to 0.5. This yields a utilization in the range of 0.5 to 0.99. For a 100-Mbps LAN, given the shorter distances, comparable utilizations are possible.

> We can see that LANs are typically quite efficient, whereas high-speed WANs are not. As a final example, let us consider digital data transmission via modem over a voice-grade line. A typical data rate is 56 kbps. Again, let us consider a 1000-bit frame. The link distance can be anywhere from a few tens of meters to thousands of kilometers. If we pick, say, as a short distance $d = 1000$ m, then $a = (56{,}000 \text{ bps} \times 1000 \text{ m})/(2 \times 10^8 \text{ m/s} \times 1000 \text{ bits}) = 2.8 \times 10^{-4}$, and utilization is effectively 1.0. Even in a long-distance case, such as $d = 5000$ km, we have $a = (56{,}000 \times 5 \times 10^6)/(2 \times 10^8 \times 1000 \text{ bits}) = 1.4$ and efficiency equals 0.26.

Error-Free Sliding-Window Flow Control

For sliding-window flow control, the throughput on the line depends on both the window size W and the value of a. For convenience, let us again normalize frame transmission time to a value of 1; thus, the propagation time is a. Figure 16.9 illustrates the efficiency of a full-duplex point-to-point line.[2] Station A begins to emit a sequence of frames at time $t = 0$. The leading edge of the first frame reaches station B at $t = a$. The first frame is entirely absorbed by $t = a + 1$. Assuming negligible processing time, B can immediately acknowledge the first frame (ACK). Let us also assume that the acknowledgment frame is so small that transmission time is negligible. Then the ACK reaches A at $t = 2a + 1$. To evaluate performance, we need to consider two cases:

- **Case 1:** $W \geq 2a + 1$. The acknowledgment for frame 1 reaches A before A has exhausted its window. Thus, A can transmit continuously with no pause and normalized throughput is 1.0.
- **Case 2:** $W < 2a + 1$. A exhausts its window at $t = W$ and cannot send additional frames until $t = 2a + 1$. Thus, normalized throughput is W time units out of a period of $(2a + 1)$ time units.

Therefore, we can express the utilization as

$$U = \begin{cases} 1 & W \geq 2a + 1 \\ \dfrac{W}{2a + 1} & W < 2a + 1 \end{cases} \qquad \textbf{(16.21)}$$

Typically, the sequence number is provided for in an n-bit field and the maximum window size is $W = 2^n - 1$ (not 2^n). Figure 16.10 shows the maximum utilization achievable for window sizes of 1, 7, and 127 as a function of a. A window size of 1 corresponds to stop and wait. A window size of 7 (3 bits) is adequate for many applications. A window size of 127 (7 bits) is adequate for larger values of a, such as may be found in high-speed WANs.

ARQ

We have seen that sliding-window flow control is more efficient than stop-and-wait flow control. We would expect that when error control functions are added that

---

[2]For simplicity, we assume that a is an integer, so that an integer number of frames exactly fills the line. The argument does not change for noninteger values of a.

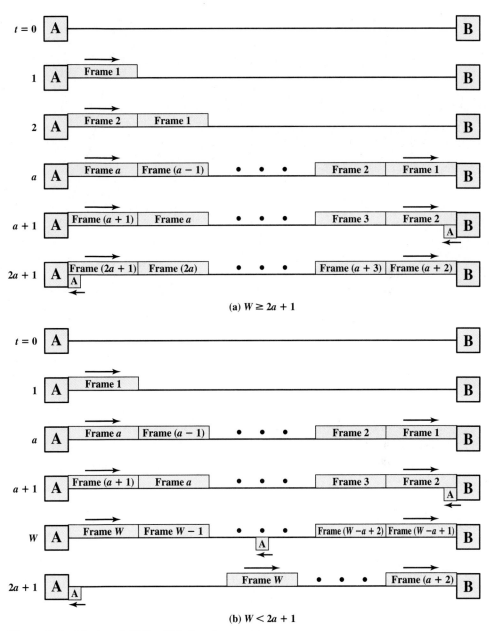

Figure 16.9   Timing of Sliding-Window Protocol

this would still be true: that is, that go-back-N and selective-reject **automatic repeat request** (ARQ) are more efficient than stop-and-wait ARQ. Let us develop some approximations to determine the degree of improvement to be expected.

First, consider stop-and-wait ARQ. With no errors, the maximum utilization is $1/(1+2a)$ as shown in Equation (16.19). We want to account for the possibility

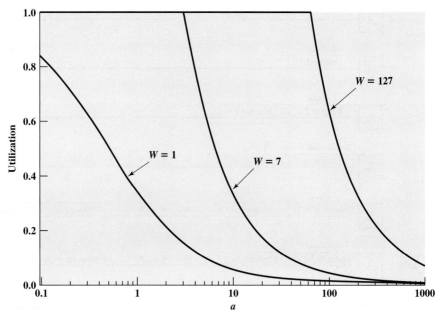

Figure 16.10 Sliding-Window Utilization as a Function of a

that some frames are repeated because of bit errors. To start, note that the utilization U can be defined as

$$U = \frac{T_f}{T_t} \qquad \text{(16.22)}$$

where

T_f = time for transmitter to emit a single frame

T_t = total time that line is engaged in the transmission of a single frame

For error-free operation using stop-and-wait ARQ:

$$U = \frac{T_f}{T_f + 2T_p}$$

where T_p is the propagation time. Dividing by T_f and remembering that $a = T_p/T_f$, we again have Equation (16.19). If errors occur, we must modify Equation (16.22) to

$$U = \frac{T_f}{N_r T_t}$$

where N_r is the expected number of transmissions of a frame. Thus, for stop-and-wait ARQ, we have

$$U = \frac{1}{N_r(1+2a)}$$

A simple expression for N_r can be derived by considering the probability P that a single frame is in error. If we assume that ACKs and NAKs are never in error, the probability that it will take exactly k attempts to transmit a frame successfully is $P^{k-1}(1-P)$. That is, we have $(k-1)$ unsuccessful attempts followed by one successful attempt; the probability of this occurring is just the product of the probability of the individual events occurring. Then,[3]

$$N_r = \text{E[transmissions]} = \sum_{i=1}^{\infty}(i \times \text{Pr}\,[i\text{transmissions}])$$

$$= \sum_{i=1}^{\infty}(iP^{i-1}(1-P)) = \frac{1}{1-P}$$

So we have

Stop-and-Wait:	$U = \dfrac{1-P}{1+2a}$

For the sliding-window protocol, Equation (16.21) applies for error-free operation. For selective-reject ARQ, we can use the same reasoning as applied to stop-and-wait ARQ. That is, the error-free equations must be divided by N_r. Again, $N_r = 1/(1-P)$. So

Selective-Reject:	$U = \begin{cases} 1-P & W \geq 2a+1 \\ \dfrac{W(1-P)}{2a+1} & W < 2a+1 \end{cases}$

The same reasoning applies for go-back-N ARQ, but we must be more careful in approximating N_r. Each error generates a requirement to retransmit K frames rather than just one frame. Thus

$$N_r = \text{E[number of transmitted frames to successfully transmit one frame]}$$

$$= \sum_{i=1}^{\infty}f(i)P^{i-1}(1-P)$$

where $f(i)$ is the total number of frames transmitted if the original frame must be transmitted i times. This can be expressed as

$$f(i) = 1 + (i-1)K$$
$$= (1-K) + Ki$$

Substituting yields[4]

$$N_r = (1-K)\sum_{i=1}^{\infty}P^{i-1}(1-P) + K\sum_{i=1}^{\infty}iP^{i-1}(1-P)$$

$$= 1 - K + \frac{K}{1-P}$$

$$= \frac{1-P+KP}{1-P}$$

---

[3]This derivation uses the equality $\displaystyle\sum_{i=1}^{\infty}(iX^{i-1}) = \frac{1}{(1-X)^2}$ for $(-1 < X < 1)$.

[4]This derivation uses the equality $\displaystyle\sum_{i=1}^{\infty}X^{i-1} = \frac{1}{1-X}$ for $(-1 < X < 1)$.

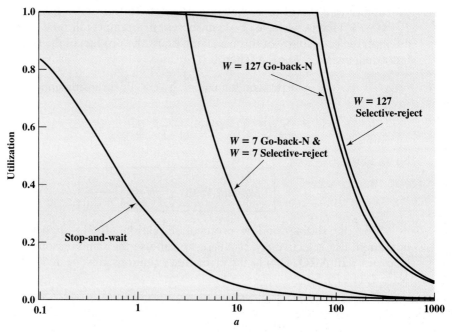

Figure 16.11 ARQ Utilization as a Function of a ($P = 10^{-3}$)

By studying Figure 16.9, the reader should conclude that K is approximately equal to $(2a + 1)$ for $W \geq (2a + 1)$, and $K = W$ for $W < (2a + 1)$. Thus

Go−back−N:	$U = \begin{cases} \dfrac{1 - P}{1 + 2aP} & W \geq 2a + 1 \\[2ex] \dfrac{W(1 - P)}{(2a + 1)(1 - P + WP)} & W < 2a + 1 \end{cases}$

Note that for $W = 1$, both selective-reject and go-back-N ARQ reduce to stop and wait. Figure 16.11[5] compares these three error control techniques for a value of $P = 10^{-3}$. This figure and the equations are only approximations. For example, we have ignored errors in acknowledgment frames and, in the case of go-back-N, errors in retransmitted frames other than the frame initially in error. However, the results do give an indication of the relative performance of the three techniques.

16.4 RECOMMENDED READING AND ANIMATIONS

[COUC13] provides solid coverage of analog signaling of analog data.

[LIN04] provides a thorough treatment of forward error-correcting codes, including LDPC codes. Two useful survey articles are [BERL87] and [BHAR83].

---

[5]For $W = 7$, the curves for go-back-N and selective-reject are so close that they appear to be identical in the figure.

A quite readable theoretical and mathematical treatment of error-correcting codes is [ASH90].

There is a large body of literature on the performance of ARQ link control protocols. Three classic papers, well worth reading, are [BENE64], [KONH80], and [BUX80]. A readable survey with simplified performance results is [LIN84]. Another good analysis is [ZORZ96]. A more thorough treatment can be found in [LIN04].

[KLEI92] and [KLEI93] are two key papers that look at the implications of gigabit data rates on performance.

ASH90   Ash, R. *Information Theory.* New York: Dover, 1990.

BENE64   Benice, R. "An Analysis of Retransmission Systems." *IEEE Transactions on Communication Technology*, December 1964.

BERL87   Berlekamp, E.; Peile, R.; and Pope, S. "The Application of Error Control to Communications." *IEEE Communications Magazine*, April 1987.

BHAR83   Bhargava, V. "Forward Error Correction Schemes for Digital Communications." *IEEE Communications Magazine*, January 1983.

BUX80   Bux, W.; Kummerle, K.; and Truong, H. "Balanced HDLC Procedures: A Performance Analysis." *IEEE Transactions on Communications*, November 1980.

COUC13   Couch, L. *Digital and Analog Communication Systems.* Upper Saddle River, NJ: Pearson, 2013.

KLEI92   Kleinrock, L. "The Latency/Bandwidth Tradeoff in Gigabit Networks." *IEEE Communications Magazine*, April 1992.

KLEI93   Kleinrock, L. "On the Modeling and Analysis of Computer Networks." *Proceedings of the IEEE*, August 1993.

KONH80   Konheim, A. "A Queuing Analysis of Two ARQ Protocols." *IEEE Transactions on Communications*, July 1980.

LIN84   Lin, S.; Costello, D.; and Miller, M. "Automatic-Repeat-Request Error-Control Schemes." *IEEE Communications Magazine*, December 1984.

LIN04   Lin, S, and Costello, D. *Error Control Coding.* Upper Saddle River, NJ: Prentice Hall, 2004.

ZORZ96   Zorzi, M., and Rao, R. "On the Use of Renewal Theory in the Analysis of ARQ Protocols." *IEEE Transactions on Communications*, September 1996.

Animations

Animations that illustrate Hamming code use are available at the Premium Web site. The reader is encouraged to view these animations to reinforce concepts from this chapter.

16.5 KEY TERMS, REVIEW QUESTIONS, AND PROBLEMS

Key Terms

amplitude modulation (AM)	forward error-correcting (FEC) codes	phase modulation (PM)
angle modulation	frequency modulation (FM)	Reed–Solomon code
automatic repeat request (ARQ)	generator matrix	regular LDPC code
BCH codes	go-back-N ARQ	redundancy
code rate	irregular LDPC code	repeat-accumulate code
cyclic codes	linear feedback shift register (LFSR)	selective-reject ARQ
double sideband suppressed carrier (DSBSC)	low-density parity-check (LDPC) codes	sideband
	modulation index	single sideband
		sliding-window flow control
double sideband transmitted carrier (DSBTC)	parity-check code	stop-and-wait ARQ
	parity-check matrix	stop-and-wait flow control
	parity-check matrix codes	syndrome
		systematic code
		Tanner graph

Review Questions

16.1 What are the differences among angle modulation, PM, and FM?

16.2 Is it possible to design an ECC that will correct some double-bit errors but not all double-bit errors? Why or why not?

16.3 In an (n, k) block ECC, what do n and k represent?

16.4 What function is performed by the matrices **H** and **G** in a parity-check matrix code?

16.5 What is the difference between a parity-check matrix code and an LDPC code?

16.6 Explain the significance of the parameter a in ARQ performance.

Problems

16.1 Consider the angle-modulated signal

$$s(t) = 10 \, \cos \left[(10^8)\pi t + 5 \, \sin \, 2\pi(10^3)t \right]$$

Find the maximum phase deviation and the maximum frequency deviation.

16.2 A signal has an amplitude of 30 V. It is being transmitted through a carrier that has amplitude of 40 V and power of 3000 W.

  a. What is the modulation index of this transmission?

  b. What is the total transmitted power?

16.3 A 30-Hz voice signal needs to be modulated. The maximum amplitude of this signal is 50 V.

  a. What will be the bandwidth if modulation is done using the amplitude modulation technique?

  b. Given a frequency modulation index of 0.9, what will be the bandwidth if modulation is done using the frequency modulation technique?

  c. Given a phase modulation index of 0.2, what will be the bandwidth if modulation is done using the phase modulation technique?

16.4 Can a C(29, 5) CRC code correct all single-bit errors? Is it capable of correcting all double-bits errors as well?

16.5　An RS code has 3 bits per symbol. If the length of data is 5 symbols, find the following parameters of the code:
  a. Block length
  b. Size of check code
  c. Maximum burst error that it can correct
  d. Minimum distance

16.6　A simple FEC code transmits every data bit 5 times. The receiver decides on the value of each data bit by choosing majority vote. If the uncoded bit error probability is 10^{-3}, what is the coded bit error probability?

16.7　A (6, 3) parity-check code is defined by the following equations:

$$c_1 \oplus c_3 \oplus c_4 = 0$$
$$c_1 \oplus c_2 \oplus c_3 \oplus c_5 = 0$$
$$c_1 \oplus c_2 \oplus c_6 = 0$$

  a. Determine the parity-check matrix **H**.
  b. Determine the generator matrix **G**.
  c. List all valid codewords.

16.8　A (6, 3) parity-check code is defined by the parity-check matrix

$$\mathbf{H} = \begin{bmatrix} 1 & 0 & 1 & 1 & 0 & 0 \\ 1 & 1 & 0 & 0 & 1 & 0 \\ 0 & 1 & 1 & 0 & 0 & 1 \end{bmatrix}$$

  a. Determine the generator matrix **G**.
  b. Find the codeword that begins 101.

16.9　Draw the Tanner graphs for each of the LDPC codes in Figure 16.6.

16.10　Hamming code is a category of error-correcting codes that can correct single-bit errors. A C(n, k) code has (n − k) redundant bits, say r. These are positioned in 1, 2, 4, 8,...; i.e., in a sequence of powers of 2 from the right of the code word. For clarity, let us name them r_1, r_2, r_4. The r_n values are calculated by checking the even parity of bits in positions in the following manner: start with the nth bit, check n bits, skip n bits, and so on. So, r_1 checks even parity of bit numbers 1, 3, 5, 7,...; r_2 checks even parity of 2, 3, 6, 7, 10, 11...; r_4 checks even parity of 4, 5, 6, 7, 12, 13, 14, 15...; and so on. How will you encode data of 1010110 using C(11, 7) code?

16.11　A 32-byte frame is being sent to a receiver 16 km away through a 400-kbps link. If the propagation speed is 2×10^8 m/s, what is the efficiency of the line?

16.12　Two hosts linked by a 200-km cable are communicating with each other using the sliding-window protocol. The data rate of the link is 1 Mbps. If the sender sends a 60-byte frame, what will be the utilization of the link in the following cases?
  a. The hosts use a window size of 3
  b. The hosts use a window size of 6
  Assume a propagation speed of 2×10^8 m/s.

16.13　The end-to-end propagation time of a 1-Mbps link has been found to be 1 ms. A host intends to send a 50-byte frame. The probability P that a single frame is in error is 0.01. What will the utilization of the line be when the following protocols are agreed upon by the hosts for communication?
  a. Stop-and-wait ARQ
  b. Selective-reject ARQ with a window size of 4
  c. Selective-reject ARQ with a window size of 8
  d. Go-back-N ARQ with a window size of 4
  e. Go-back-N ARQ with a window size of 8

CHAPTER **17**

WIRELESS TRANSMISSION TECHNIQUES

LEARNING OBJECTIVES

After studying this chapter, you should be able to:

♦ Explain the basic principles of MIMO antennas.

♦ Describe the issues involved in the use of MU-MIMO.

♦ Present an overview of OFDM, OFDMA, and SC-FDMA.

♦ Explain how multiple access is achieved using SC-FDMA.

♦ Present an overview of the principles of spread spectrum.

♦ Understand the operation of direct sequence spread spectrum.

♦ Understand the operation of code division multiple access.

This chapter examines some key transmission techniques and technologies that are relevant to wireless networks and that are key to the latest generations of Wi-Fi and cellular networks. The first section deals with multiple-input multiple-output (MIMO) antennas. Next, we examine orthogonal frequency-division multiplexing. The remainder of the chapter deals with several types of spread spectrum transmission.

17.1 MIMO ANTENNAS

Multiple-input-multiple-output (MIMO) antenna architecture has become a key technology in evolving high-speed wireless networks, including IEEE 802.11 Wi-Fi LANs and WiMAX. MIMO exploits the space dimension to improve wireless systems in terms of capacity, range, and reliability. Together, MIMO and OFDM technologies are the cornerstone of emerging broadband wireless networks.

MIMO Principles

In a MIMO scheme, the transmitter and receiver employ multiple antennas. The source data stream is divided into n substreams, one for each of the n transmitting antennas. The individual substreams are the input to the transmitting antennas (multiple input). At the receiving end, m antennas receive the transmissions from the n source antennas via a combination of line-of-sight transmission and multipath (Figure 17.1). The outputs from all of the m receiving antennas (multiple output) are combined. With a lot of complex math, the result is a much better receive signal than can be achieved with either a single antenna or multiple frequency channels.

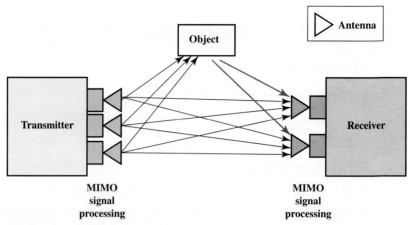

Figure 17.1 MIMO Scheme

Note that the terms *input* and *output* refer to the input to the transmission channel and the output from the transmission channel, respectively.

MIMO systems are characterized by the number of antennas at each end of the wireless channel. Thus a 8×4 MIMO system has 8 antennas at one end of the channel and 4 at the other end. In configurations with a base station, the first number typically refers to the number of antennas at the base station. There are two types of MIMO transmission schemes:

- **Spatial diversity:** The same data is coded and transmitted through multiple antennas, which effectively increases the power in the channel proportional to the number of transmitting antennas. This improves signal-to-noise (SNR) for cell edge performance. Further, diverse multipath fading offers multiple "views" of the transmitted data at the receiver, thus increasing robustness. In a multipath scenario where each receiving antenna would experience a different interference environment, there is a high probability that if one antenna is suffering a high level of fading, another antenna has sufficient signal level.

- **Spatial multiplexing:** A source data stream is divided among the transmitting antennas. The gain in channel capacity is proportional to the available number of antennas at the transmitter or receiver, whichever is less. Spatial multiplexing can be used when transmitting conditions are favorable and for relatively short distances compared to spatial diversity. The receiver must do considerable signal processing to sort out the incoming substreams, all of which are transmitting in the same frequency channel, and to recover the individual data streams.

For spatial multiplexing, there is a multilink channel that can be expressed as $\mathbf{y} = \mathbf{Hc} + \mathbf{n}$, where $\mathbf{y}$ is the vector of received signals, $\mathbf{c}$ is the vector of transmitted signals, $\mathbf{n}$ is an additive noise component, and $\mathbf{H} = [h_{ij}]$ is an $r \times t$ channel matrix, with r being the number of receiving antennas and t the number of transmitting

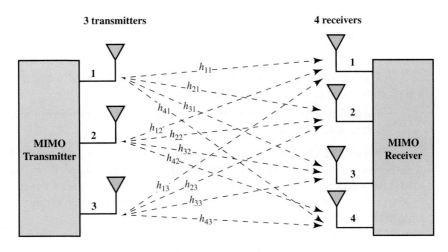

3 transmit antennas

$$H = \begin{bmatrix} h_{11} & h_{12} & h_{13} \\ h_{21} & h_{22} & h_{23} \\ h_{31} & h_{32} & h_{33} \\ h_{41} & h_{42} & h_{43} \end{bmatrix} \left.\right\} \text{ 4 receive antennas}$$

Figure 17.2 3×4 MIMO Scheme

antennas. The number of spatial data streams is $\min[r, t]$. For a channel with three transmitters and four receivers (Figure 17.2), the equation is:

$$\begin{bmatrix} y_1 \\ y_2 \\ y_3 \\ y_4 \end{bmatrix} = \begin{bmatrix} h_{11} & h_{12} & h_{13} \\ h_{21} & h_{22} & h_{23} \\ h_{31} & h_{32} & h_{33} \\ h_{41} & h_{42} & h_{43} \end{bmatrix} \begin{bmatrix} c_1 \\ c_2 \\ c_3 \end{bmatrix} + \begin{bmatrix} n_1 \\ n_2 \\ n_3 \end{bmatrix}$$

The h_{ij} are complex numbers $x + jz$ that represent both the amplitude attenuation (x) over the channel and the path dependent phase shift (z), and the n_i are additive noise components. The receiver measures the channel gains based on training fields containing known patterns in the packet preamble and can estimate the transmitted signal with the following equation:

$$\begin{bmatrix} \hat{c}_1 \\ \hat{c}_2 \\ \hat{c}_3 \end{bmatrix} = \mathbf{H}^{-1} \begin{bmatrix} y_1 \\ y_2 \\ y_3 \\ y_4 \end{bmatrix}$$

Multiple-User MIMO

Multiple-user MIMO (MU-MIMO) extends the basic MIMO concept to multiple endpoints, each with multiple antennas. The advantage of MU-MIMO compared to single-user MIMO is that the available capacity can be shared to meet time-varying demands. MU-MIMO techniques are used in both Wi-Fi and 4G cellular networks.

There are two applications of MU-MIMO:

- **Uplink—Multiple Access Channel, MAC:** Multiple end users transmit simultaneously to a single base station.
- **Downlink—Broadcast Channel, BC:** The base station transmits separate data streams to multiple independent users.

MIMO-MAC is used on the uplink channel to provide multiple access to subscriber stations. In general, MIMO-MAC systems outperform point-to-point MIMO, particularly if the number of receiver antennas is greater than the number of transmit antennas at each user. A variety of multiuser detection techniques are used to separate the signals transmitted by the users.

MIMO-BC is used on the downlink channel to enable the base station to transmit different data streams to multiple users over the same frequency band. MIMO-BC is more challenging to implement. The techniques employed involve processing of the data symbols at the transmitter to minimize interuser interference.

17.2 OFDM, OFDMA, AND SC-FDMA

This section looks at some FDM-based (frequency-division multiplexing) techniques that are of increasing importance in broadband wireless networks.

Orthogonal Frequency-Division Multiplexing

OFDM, also called *multicarrier modulation*, uses multiple carrier signals at different frequencies, sending some of the bits on each channel. This is similar to FDM. However, in the case of OFDM, all of the subcarriers are dedicated to a single data source.

Figure 17.3 illustrates OFDM. Suppose we have a data stream operating at R bps and an available bandwidth of Nf_b, centered at f_0. The entire bandwidth could be used to send the data stream, in which case each bit duration would be $1/R$. The alternative is to split the data stream into N substreams, using a serial-to-parallel converter. Each substream has a data rate of R/N bps and is transmitted on a separate subcarrier, with a spacing between adjacent subcarriers of f_b. Now the bit duration is N/R.

To gain a clearer understanding of OFDM, let us consider the scheme in terms of its base frequency, f_b. This is the lowest-frequency subcarrier. All of the other subcarriers are integer multiples of the base frequency, namely $2f_b$, $3f_b$, and so on, as shown in Figure 17.4a. The OFDM scheme uses advanced digital signal processing techniques to distribute the data over multiple carriers at precise frequencies. The relationship among the subcarriers is referred to as *orthogonality*. The result, as shown in Figure 17.4b, is that the peaks of the power spectral density of each subcarrier occur at a point at which the power of other subcarriers is zero. With OFDM, the subcarriers can be packed tightly together because there is minimal interference between adjacent subcarriers.

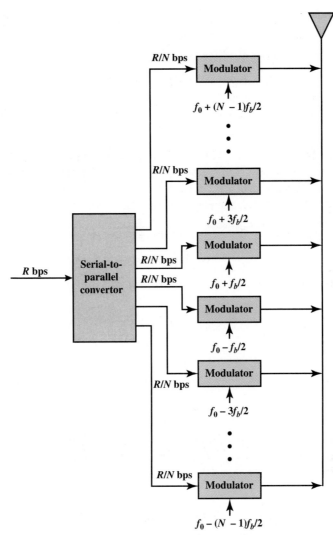

Figure 17.3 Orthogonal Frequency-Division Multiplexing

Note that Figure 17.3 depicts the set of OFDM subcarriers in a frequency band beginning with the base frequency. For transmission, the set of OFDM subcarriers is further modulated to a higher frequency band. For example, for the IEEE 802.11a LAN standard, the OFDM scheme consists of a set of 52 subcarriers with a base frequency of 0.3125 MHz. This set of subcarriers is then translated to the 5-GHz range for transmission.

OFDM has several advantages. First, frequency selective fading only affects some subcarriers and not the whole signal. If the data stream is protected by a forward error-correcting code, this type of fading is easily handled. More important, OFDM overcomes intersymbol interference (ISI) in a multipath environment. As discussed in Chapter 3, ISI has a greater impact at higher bit rates, because the

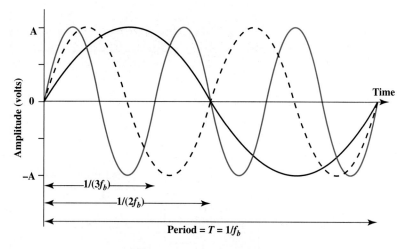

(a) Three subcarriers in time domain

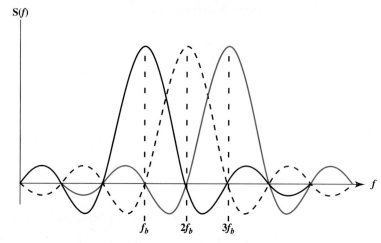

(b) Three subcarriers in frequency domain

Figure 17.4 Illustration of Orthogonality of OFDM

distance between bits, or symbols, is smaller. With OFDM, the data rate is reduced by a factor of N, which increases the symbol time by a factor of N. Thus, if the symbol period is T_s for the source stream, the period for the OFDM signals is NT_s. This dramatically reduces the effect of ISI. As a design criterion, N is chosen so that NT_s is significantly greater than the root-mean-square delay spread of the channel.

As a result of these considerations, with the use of OFDM, it may not be necessary to deploy equalizers, which are complex devices whose complexity increases with the number of symbols over which ISI is present.

A common modulation scheme used with OFDM is quadrature phase shift keying (QPSK). In this case, each transmitted symbol represents two bits. An example of an OFDM/QPSK scheme occupies 6 MHz made up of 512 individual carriers, with a carrier separation of a little under 12 kHz. To minimize ISI, data are transmitted in bursts, with each burst consisting of a cyclic prefix followed by data symbols. The cyclic prefix is used to absorb transients from previous bursts caused by multipath. For this system, 64 symbols constitute the cyclic prefix, followed by 512 QPSK symbols per burst. On each subcarrier, therefore, QPSK symbols are separated by a prefix, called a cyclic prefix (CP), of duration 64/512 symbol times. In general, by the time the prefix is over, the resulting waveform created by the combined multipath signals is not a function of any samples from the previous burst. Hence there is no ISI.

The signal processing for OFDM involves two functions known as **fast Fourier transform (FFT)** and **inverse fast Fourier transform (IFFT)**. The FFT is an algorithm that converts a set of uniformly spaced data points from the time domain to the frequency domain. FFT is in fact a family of algorithms that are able to perform a digital Fourier transform rapidly. They form a special case of the discrete Fourier transform (DFT), which refers to any algorithm that generates a quantized Fourier transform of a time-domain function.

The IFFT reverses the FFT operation. For OFDM, a source bit stream is mapped to a set of M subcarrier frequency bands. Then, to create the transmitted signal, an IFFT is performed on each subcarrier to create M time-domain signals. These in turn are vector-summed to create the final time-domain waveform used for transmission. The IFFT operation has the effect of ensuring that the subcarriers do not interfere with each other. On the receiving end, an FFT module is used to map the incoming signal back to the M subcarriers, from which the data streams are recovered.

Orthogonal Frequency–Division Multiple Access

Like OFDM, OFDMA employs multiple closely spaced subcarriers, but the subcarriers are divided into groups of subcarriers. Each group is named a subchannel. The subcarriers that form a subchannel need not be adjacent. In the downlink, a subchannel may be intended for different receivers. In the uplink, a transmitter may be assigned one or more subchannels. Figure 17.5 contrasts OFDM and OFDMA; in the OFDMA case the use of adjacent subcarriers to form a subchannel is illustrated.

Subchannelization defines subchannels that can be allocated to subscriber stations (SSs) depending on their channel conditions and data requirements. Using subchannelization, within the same time slot a 4G base station (BS) can allocate more transmit power to user devices (SSs) with lower SNR (signal-to-noise ratio), and less power to user devices with higher SNR. Subchannelization also enables the BS to allocate higher power to subchannels assigned to indoor SSs resulting in better in-building coverage. Subchannels are further grouped into bursts, which can be allocated to wireless users. Each burst allocation can be changed from frame to frame as well as within the modulation order. This allows the base station to dynamically adjust the bandwidth usage according to the current system requirements.

Subchannelization in the uplink can save user device transmit power because it can concentrate power only on certain subchannel(s) allocated to it. This power-saving feature is particularly useful for battery-powered user devices, the likely case in mobile 4G.

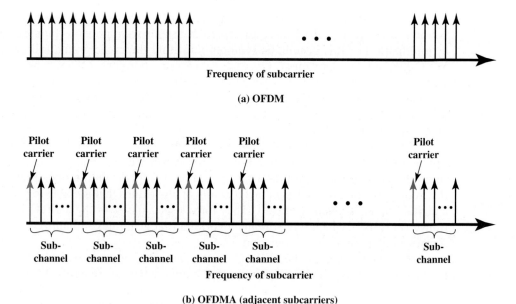

Figure 17.5   OFDM and OFDMA

Single-Carrier FDMA

Single-carrier FDMA is a relatively recently developed multiple access technique which has similar structure and performance to OFDMA. One prominent advantage of SC-FDMA over OFDMA is the lower peak-to-average power ratio (PAPR) of the transmit waveform, which benefits the mobile user in terms of battery life and power efficiency. OFDM signals have a higher PAPR because, in the time domain, a multicarrier signal is the sum of many narrowband signals. At some time instances, this sum is large and at other times is small, which means that the peak value of the signal is substantially larger than the average value.

Thus, SC-FDMA is superior to OFDMA. However, it is restricted to uplink use because the increased time-domain processing of SC-FDMA would entail considerable burden on the base station.

As shown in Figure 17.6, SC-FDMA performs a DFT prior to the IFFT operation, which spreads the data symbols over all the subcarriers carrying information and produces a virtual single-carrier structure. This is then passed through the OFDM processing modules to split the signal into subcarriers. Now, however, every data symbol is carried by every subcarrier. Figure 17.7 is an example of how the OFDM and SC-FDMA signals appear.

From Figure 17.7, we can make several observations. For OFDM, a source data stream is divided into N separate data streams and these streams are modulated and transmitted in parallel on N separate subcarriers each with bandwidth f_b. The source data stream has a data rate of R bps, and the data rate on each subcarrier is R/N bps. For SC-FDMA, it appears from Figure 17.7 that the source data stream is modulated on a single carrier (hence the SC prefix to the name) of bandwidth $N \times f_b$ and transmitted at a data rate of R bps. The data is transmitted at a higher rate, but

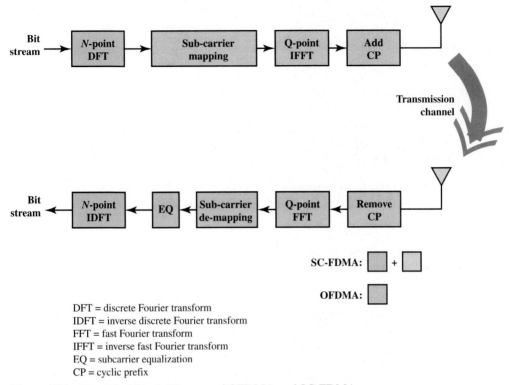

DFT = discrete Fourier transform
IDFT = inverse discrete Fourier transform
FFT = fast Fourier transform
IFFT = inverse fast Fourier transform
EQ = subcarrier equalization
CP = cyclic prefix

Figure 17.6   Simplified Block Diagram of OFDMA and SC-FDMA

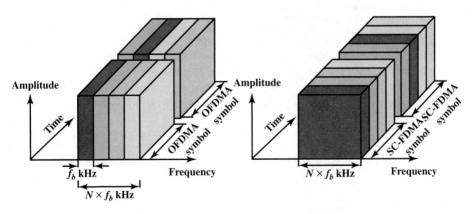

(a) **OFDM: Data symbols occupy f_b kHz for one OFDMA symbol period**   (b) **SC-FDMA: Data symbols occupy $N \times f_b$ kHz for $1/N$ SC-FDMA symbol period**

Figure 17.7   Example of OFDMA and SC-FDMA

over a wider bandwidth compared to the data rate on a single subcarrier of OFDM. However, because of the complex signal processing of SC-FDMA, the preceding description is not accurate. In effect, the source data stream is replicated N times, and each copy of the data stream is independently modulated and transmitted on a subcarrier, with a data rate on each subcarrier of R bps. Compared with OFDM, we are transmitting at a much higher data rate on each subcarrier, but because we are sending the same data stream on each subcarrier, it is still possible to reliably recover the original data stream at the receiver.

A final observation concerns the term *multiple access*. With OFDMA, it is possible to simultaneously transmit either from or to different users by allocating the subcarriers during any one time interval to multiple users. This is not possible with SC-FDMA: At any given point in time, all of the subcarriers are carrying the identical data stream and hence must be dedicated to one user. But over time, as illustrated in Figure 17.7, it is possible to provide multiple access. Thus, a better term for SC-FDMA might be SC-OFDM-TDMA, although that term is not used.

17.3 SPREAD SPECTRUM

Spread spectrum[1] is an important form of encoding for wireless communications. This technique does not fit neatly into the categories defined in Chapter 5, as it can be used to transmit either analog or digital data, using an analog signal.

The spread spectrum technique was developed initially for military and intelligence requirements. The essential idea is to spread the information signal over a wider bandwidth to make jamming and interception more difficult. The first type of spread spectrum developed is known as frequency hopping. A more recent type of spread spectrum is direct sequence. Both of these techniques are used in various wireless communications standards and products. For the subject matter of this book, direct sequence spread spectrum (DSSS) is by far the more important.

This section provides a brief overview. We then examine direct sequence spread spectrum. A final section looks at a multiple access technique based on spread spectrum.

Figure 17.8 highlights the key characteristics of any spread spectrum system. Input is fed into a channel encoder that produces an analog signal with a relatively narrow bandwidth around some center frequency. This signal is further modulated using a sequence of digits known as a spreading code or spreading sequence. Typically, but not always, the spreading code is generated by a pseudonoise, or

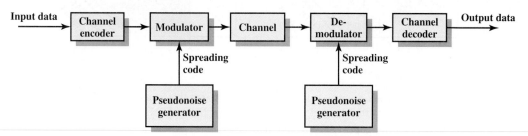

Figure 17.8   General Model of Spread Spectrum Digital Communication System

---

[1]Spread spectrum (using frequency hopping) was invented, believe it or not, by Hollywood screen siren Hedy Lamarr in 1940 at the age of 26. She and a partner who later joined her effort were granted a patent in 1942 (U.S. Patent 2,292,387; August 11, 1942). Lamarr considered this her contribution to the war effort and never profited from her invention.

pseudorandom number, generator. The effect of this modulation is to increase significantly the bandwidth (spread the spectrum) of the signal to be transmitted. On the receiving end, the same digit sequence is used to demodulate the spread spectrum signal. Finally, the signal is fed into a channel decoder to recover the data.

Several things can be gained from this apparent waste of spectrum:

- The signals gain immunity from various kinds of noise and multipath distortion. The earliest applications of spread spectrum were military, where it was used for its immunity to jamming.
- It can also be used for hiding and encrypting signals. Only a recipient who knows the spreading code can recover the encoded information.
- Several users can independently use the same higher bandwidth with very little interference. This property is used in cellular telephony applications, with a technique known as code division multiplexing (CDM) or code division multiple access (CDMA).

A comment about pseudorandom numbers is in order. These numbers are generated by an algorithm using some initial value called the seed. The algorithm is deterministic and therefore produces sequences of numbers that are not statistically random. However, if the algorithm is good, the resulting sequences will pass many reasonable tests of randomness. Such numbers are often referred to as pseudorandom numbers.[2] The important point is that unless you know the algorithm and the seed, it is impractical to predict the sequence. Hence, only a receiver that shares this information with a transmitter will be able to decode the signal successfully.

17.4 DIRECT SEQUENCE SPREAD SPECTRUM

With direct sequence spread spectrum (DSSS), each bit in the original signal is represented by multiple bits in the transmitted signal, using a spreading code. The spreading code spreads the signal across a wider frequency band in direct proportion to the number of bits used. Therefore, a 10-bit spreading code spreads the signal across a frequency band that is 10 times greater than a 1-bit spreading code.

One technique with direct sequence spread spectrum is to combine the digital information stream with the spreading code bit stream using an exclusive-OR (XOR). The XOR obeys the following rules:

$$0 \oplus 0 = 0 \qquad 0 \oplus 1 = 1 \qquad 1 \oplus 0 = 1 \qquad 1 \oplus 1 = 0$$

EXAMPLE 17.1 Figure 17.9 uses DSSS on a data input of 01001011. Note that an information bit of 1 inverts the spreading code bits in the combination, while an information bit of 0 causes the spreading code bits to be transmitted without inversion. The combination bit stream has the data rate of the original spreading code sequence, so it has a wider bandwidth than the information stream. In this example, the spreading code bit stream is clocked at four times the information rate.

2See [STAL05] for a more detailed discussion of pseudorandom numbers.

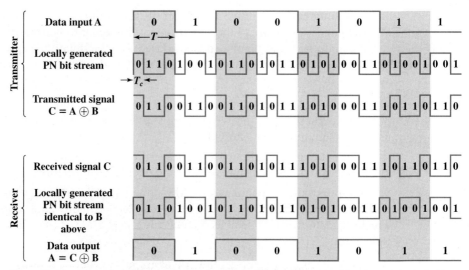

Figure 17.9 Example of Direct Sequence Spread Spectrum

DSSS Using BPSK

To see how this technique works out in practice, assume that a BPSK (binary phase shift keying) modulation scheme is to be used. Rather than represent binary data with 1 and 0, it is more convenient for our purposes to use +1 and −1 to represent the two binary digits. In that case, a BPSK signal can be represented as was shown in Equation (5.6):

$$s_d(t) = A\ d(t) \cos (2\pi f_c t) \tag{17.1}$$

where

A = amplitude of signal

f_c = carrier frequency

$d(t)$ = the discrete function that takes on the value of +1 for one bit time if the corresponding bit in the bit stream is 1 and the value of −1 for one bit time if the corresponding bit in the bit stream is 0

To produce the DSSS signal, we multiply the preceding by $c(t)$, which is the PN sequence taking on values of +1 and −1:

$$s(t) = A\ d(t)c(t) \cos (2\pi f_c t) \tag{17.2}$$

At the receiver, the incoming signal is multiplied again by $c(t)$. But $c(t) \times c(t) = 1$ and therefore the original signal is recovered:

$$s(t)c(t) = A\ d(t)c(t)c(t) \cos (2\pi f_c t) = s_d(t)$$

Equation (17.2) can be interpreted in two ways, leading to two different implementations. The first interpretation is to first multiply $d(t)$ and $c(t)$ together and then perform the BPSK modulation. That is the interpretation we have been discussing. Alternatively, we can first perform the BPSK modulation on

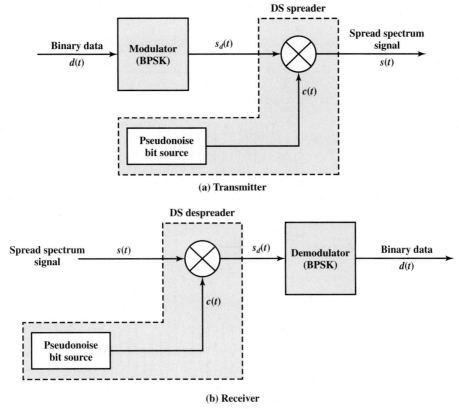

Figure 17.10   Direct Sequence Spread Spectrum System

the data stream $d(t)$ to generate the data signal $s_d(t)$. This signal can then be multiplied by $c(t)$.

An implementation using the second interpretation is shown in Figure 17.10.

EXAMPLE 17.2 Figure 17.11 uses the approach of Figure 17.10 on an input data of 1010, which is represented as $+1 -1 +1 -1$. The spreading code bit stream is clocked at three times the information rate.

DSSS Performance Considerations

The spectrum spreading achieved by the direct sequence technique is easily determined (Figure 17.12). In our example, the information signal has a bit width of T, which is equivalent to a data rate of $1/T$. In that case, the spectrum of the signal, depending on the encoding technique, is roughly $2/T$. Similarly, the spectrum of the PN signal is $2/T_c$. Figure 17.12c shows the resulting spectrum spreading. The amount of spreading that is achieved is a direct result of the data rate of the PN stream.

As with FHSS, we can get some insight into the performance of DSSS by looking at its effectiveness against jamming. Let us assume a simple

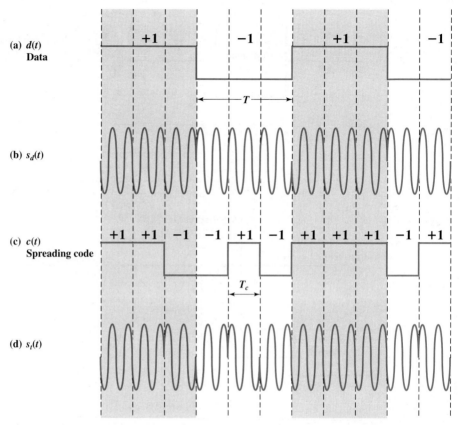

(a) $d(t)$
Data

(b) $s_d(t)$

(c) $c(t)$
Spreading code

(d) $s_t(t)$

Figure 17.11   Example of Direct Sequence Spread Spectrum Using BPSK

jamming signal at the center frequency of the DSSS system. The jamming signal has the form

$$s_j(t) = \sqrt{2S_j}\cos(2\pi f_c t)$$

and the received signal is

$$s_r(t) = s(t) + s_j(t) + n(t)$$

where

$\quad s(t) =$ transmitted signal

$\quad s_j(t) =$ jamming signal

$\quad n(t) =$ additive white noise

$\quad S_j =$ jammer signal power

The despreader at the receiver multiplies $s_r(t)$ by $c(t)$, so the signal component due to the jamming signal is

$$y_j(t) = \sqrt{2S_j}\,c(t)\cos(2\pi f_c t)$$

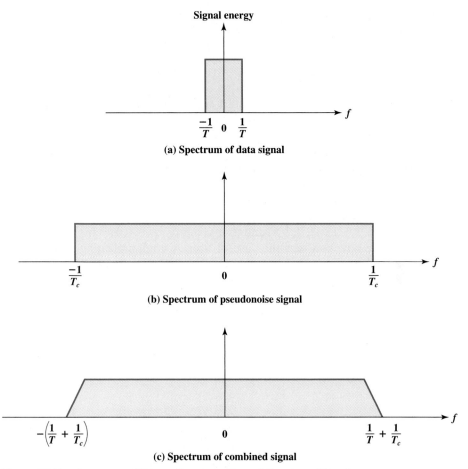

Figure 17.12 Spectrum of Direct Sequence Spread Spectrum Signal

This is simply a BPSK modulation of the carrier tone. Thus, the carrier power S_j is spread over a bandwidth of approximately $2/T_c$. However, the BPSK demodulator (Figure 17.9) following the DSSS despreader includes a bandpass filter matched to the BPSK data, with bandwidth of $2/T$. Thus, most of the jamming power is filtered. Although a number of factors come into play, as an approximation, we can say that the jamming power passed by the filter is

$$S_{iF} = S_j(2/T)/(2/T_c) = S_j(T_c/T)$$

The jamming power has been reduced by a factor of (T_c/T) through the use of spread spectrum. The inverse of this factor is the gain in signal-to-noise ratio:

$$G_P = \frac{T}{T_c} = \frac{R_c}{R} \approx \frac{W_s}{W_d} \qquad \textbf{(17.3)}$$

where R_c is the spreading bit rate, R is the data rate, W_d is the signal bandwidth, and W_s is the spread spectrum signal bandwidth.

17.5 CODE DIVISION MULTIPLE ACCESS

Basic Principles

CDMA is a multiplexing technique used with spread spectrum. The scheme works in the following manner. We start with a data signal with rate D, which we call the bit data rate. We break each bit into k **chips** according to a fixed pattern that is specific to each user, called the user's code, or **chipping code**. The new channel has a chip data rate, or **chipping rate**, of kD chips per second. As an illustration we consider a simple example with $k = 6$. It is simplest to characterize a chipping code as a sequence of 1s and −1s. Figure 17.13 shows the codes for three users, A, B, and C, each of which is communicating with the same base station receiver, R. Thus, the code for user A is $c_A = <1, -1, -1, 1, -1, 1>$. Similarly, user B has code $c_B = <1, 1, -1, -1, 1, 1>$, and user C has code $c_C = <1, 1, -1, 1, 1, -1>$.

We now consider the case of user A communicating with the base station. The base station is assumed to know A's code. For simplicity, we assume that communication is already synchronized so that the base station knows when to look for codes. If A wants to send a 1 bit, A transmits its code as a chip pattern <1, −1, −1, 1, −1, 1>. If a 0 bit is to be sent, A transmits the complement (1s and −1s reversed) of its code, <−1, 1, 1, −1, 1, −1>. At the base station the receiver decodes the chip patterns. In our simple version, if the receiver R receives a chip pattern $d = <d1, d2, d3, d4, d5, d6>$, and the receiver is seeking to communicate with a user u so that it

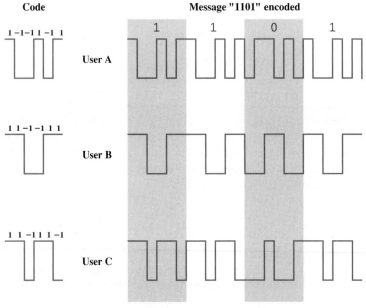

Figure 17.13 CDMA Example
Source: Based on example by Professor Richard Van Slyke of the Polytechnic University of Brooklyn.

has at hand u's code, <$c1, c2, c3, c4, c5, c6$>, the receiver performs electronically the following decoding function:

$$S_u(d) = d1 \times c1 + d2 \times c2 + d3 \times c3 + d4 \times c4 + d5 \times c5 + d6 \times c6$$

The subscript u on S simply indicates that u is the user that we are interested in. Let's suppose the user u is actually A and see what happens. If A sends a 1 bit, then d is <1, –1, –1, 1, –1, 1> and the preceding computation using S_A becomes

$$S_A(1, -1, -1, 1, -1, 1) = 1 \times 1 + (-1) \times (-1) + (-1) \times (-1)$$
$$+ 1 \times 1 + (-1) \times (-1) + 1 \times 1 = 6$$

If A sends a 0 bit that corresponds to d = <–1, 1, 1, –1, 1, –1>, we get

$$S_A(-1, 1, 1, -1, 1, -1) = -1 \times 1 + 1 \times (-1) + 1 \times (-1) + (-1) \times 1$$
$$+ 1 \times (-1) + (-1) \times 1 = -6$$

Please note that it is always the case that $-6 \leq S_A(d) \leq 6$ no matter what sequence of –1s and 1s that d is, and that the only d's resulting in the extreme values of 6 and –6 are A's code and its complement, respectively. So if S_A produces a +6, we say that we have received a 1 bit from A; if S_A produces a –6, we say that we have received a 0 bit from user A; otherwise, we assume that someone else is sending information or there is an error. So why go through all this? The reason becomes clear if we see what happens if user B is sending and we try to receive it with S_A, that is, we are decoding with the wrong code, A's. If B sends a 1 bit, then d = <1, 1, –1, –1, 1, 1>. Then

$$S_A(1, 1, -1, -1, 1, 1) = 1 \times 1 + 1 \times (-1) + (-1) \times (-1) + (-1) \times 1$$
$$+ 1 \times (-1) + 1 \times 1 = 0$$

Thus, the unwanted signal (from B) does not show up at all. You can easily verify that if B had sent a 0 bit, the decoder would produce a value of 0 for S_A again. This means that if the decoder is linear and if A and B transmit signals s_A and s_B, respectively, at the same time, then $S_A(s_A+s_B) = S_A(s_A)+S_A(s_B) = S_A(s_A)$ since the decoder ignores B when it is using A's code. The codes of A and B that have the property that $S_A(c_B) = S_B(c_A) = 0$ are called **orthogonal**.[3] Such codes are very nice to have but there are not all that many of them. More common is the case when $S_X(c_Y)$ is small in absolute value when $X \neq Y$. Then it is easy to distinguish between the two cases when $X = Y$ and when $X \neq Y$. In our example $S_A(c_C) = S_C(c_A) = 0$, but $S_B(c_C) = S_C(c_B) = 2$. In the latter case the C signal would make a small contribution to the decoded signal instead of 0. Using the decoder, S_u, the receiver can sort out transmission from u even when there may be other users broadcasting in the same cell.

Table 17.1 summarizes the example from the preceding discussion.

In practice, the CDMA receiver can filter out the contribution from unwanted users or they appear as low-level noise. However, if there are many users competing for the channel with the user the receiver is trying to listen to, or if the signal power of one or more competing signals is too high, perhaps because it is very near the receiver (the "near/far" problem), the system breaks down.

---

[3]See Appendix N for a discussion of orthogonality of chipping codes.

Table 9.1   CDMA Example

(a) User's codes

User A	1	−1	−1	1	−1	1
User B	1	1	−1	−1	1	1
User C	1	1	−1	1	1	−1

(b) Transmission from A

Transmit (data bit = 1)	1	−1	−1	1	−1	1	
Receiver codeword	1	−1	−1	1	−1	1	
Multiplication	1	1	1	1	1	1	= 6
Transmit (data bit = 0)	−1	1	1	−1	1	−1	
Receiver codeword	1	−1	−1	1	−1	1	
Multiplication	−1	−1	−1	−1	−1	−1	= −6

(c) Transmission from B, receiver attempts to recover A's transmission

Transmit (data bit = 1)	1	1	−1	−1	1	1	
Receiver codeword	1	−1	−1	1	−1	1	
Multiplication	1	−1	1	−1	−1	1	= 0

(d) Transmission from C, receiver attempts to recover B's transmission

Transmit (data bit = 1)	1	1	−1	1	1	−1	
Receiver codeword	1	1	−1	−1	1	1	
Multiplication	1	1	1	1	1	−1	= 2

(e) Transmission from B and C, receiver attempts to recover B's transmission

B (data bit = 1)	1	1	−1	−1	1	1	
C (data bit = 1)	1	1	−1	1	1	−1	
Combined signal	2	2	−2	0	2	0	
Receiver codeword	1	1	−1	−1	1	1	
Multiplication	2	2	2	0	2	0	= 8

CDMA for Direct Sequence Spread Spectrum

Let us now look at CDMA from the viewpoint of a DSSS system using BPSK. Figure 17.14 depicts a configuration in which there are n users, each transmitting using a different, orthogonal, PN sequence (compare Figure 17.10). For each user, the data stream to be transmitted, $d_i(t)$, is BPSK modulated to produce a signal with a bandwidth of W_s and then multiplied by the spreading code for that user, $c_i(t)$. All of the signals, plus noise, are received at the receiver's antenna. Suppose that the receiver is attempting to recover the data of user 1. The incoming signal is multiplied by the spreading code of user 1 and then demodulated. The effect of this

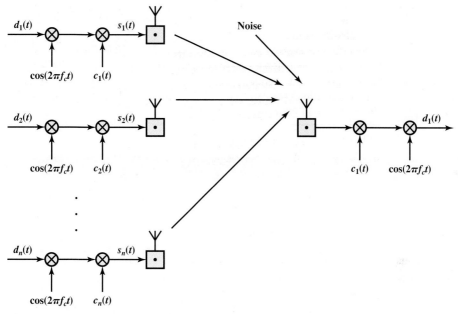

Figure 17.14   CDMA in a DSSS Environment for Receiving User 1

is to narrow the bandwidth of that portion of the incoming signal corresponding to user 1 to the original bandwidth of the unspread signal, which is proportional to the data rate. Incoming signals from other users are not despread by the spreading code from user 1 and hence retain their bandwidth of W_s. Thus the unwanted signal energy remains spread over a large bandwidth and the wanted signal is concentrated in a narrow bandwidth. The bandpass filter at the demodulator can therefore recover the desired signal.

17.6 RECOMMENDED READING

[GESB02] is a good overview of MIMO systems. [GESB03] covers both MIMO and MU-MIMO. Another useful overview of MU-MIMO is [KURV09].

[BERA08] and [MYUN06] provide a good treatment of OFDMA and SC-FDMA.

[PICK82] provides an excellent introduction to spread spectrum.

BERA08   Beradinelli, G., et al. "OFDMA vs SC-FDMA: Performance Comparison in Local Area IMT-A Scenarios." *IEEE Wireless Communications,* October 2008.

GESB02   Gesbert, D., and Akhtar, J. "Breaking the Barriers of Shannon's Capacity: An Overview of MIMO Wireless Systems." *Telektronikk,* January 2002.

GESB03   Gesbert, D., et al. "From theory to practice: An overview of MIMO space—Time coded wireless systems," *IEEE Journal on Selected Areas in Communications,* April 2003.

KURV09 Kurve, A. "Multi-User MIMO Systems: the Future in the Making." *IEEE Potentials,* November/December 2009.

MYUN06 Myung, H.; Lim, J.; and Goodman, D. "Single Carrier FDMA for Uplink Wireless Transmission." *IEEE Vehicular Technology,* September 2006.

PICK82 Pickholtz, R.; Schilling, D.; and Milstein, L. "Theory of Spread Spectrum Communications—A Tutorial." *IEEE Transactions on Communications,* May 1982. Reprinted in [TANT98].

17.7 KEY TERMS, REVIEW QUESTIONS, AND PROBLEMS

Key Terms

chip	inverse fast Fourier	orthogonal frequency
chipping code	transform (IFFT)	division multiple access
chipping rate	multiple-input multiple-	(OFDMA)
code division multiple	output (MIMO)	pseudonoise (PN)
access (CDMA)	multiple-user MIMO	single-carrier FDMA
direct sequence spread	(MU-MIMO)	(SC-FDMA)
spectrum (DSSS)	orthogonal	spread spectrum
fast Fourier transform (FFT)	orthogonal frequency	spreading code
frequency-hopping spread	division multiplexing	spreading sequence
spectrum (FHSS)	(OFDM)	

Review Questions

17.1 Briefly define MIMO and MU-MIMO.

17.2 Briefly define OFDM, OFDMA, and SC-FDMA

17.3 What is the relationship between the bandwidth of a signal before and after it has been encoded using spread spectrum?

17.4 List three benefits of spread spectrum.

17.5 What is direct sequence spread spectrum?

17.6 What is the relationship between the bit rate of a signal before and after it has been encoded using DSSS?

17.7 What is CDMA?

Problems

17.1 The DSSS physical layer often uses an 11-bit Barker Sequence to spread the data before it is transmitted. Each bit transmitted is modulated by the 11-bit sequence. This process spreads the energy across a wider bandwidth than would be required to transmit the raw data.

    a. In a wireless LAN, if the spreading code used is 111 0001 0010, how will data of 1001 be encoded?

    b. If the bandwidth of the original signal is 200 MHz, what will be the signal rate of the spread signal?

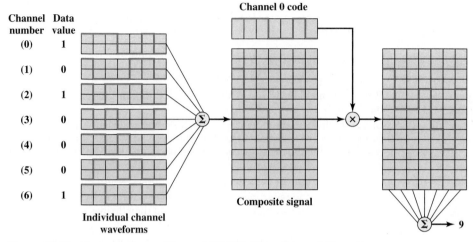

Figure 17.15 Example Seven-Channel CDMA Encoding and Decoding

17.2 Figure 17.15 depicts a simplified scheme for CDMA encoding and decoding. There are seven logical channels, all using DSSS with a spreading code of 7 bits. Assume that all sources are synchronized. If all seven sources transmit a data bit, in the form of a 7-bit sequence, the signals from all sources combine at the receiver so that two positive or two negative values reinforce and a positive and negative value cancel. To decode a given channel, the receiver multiplies the incoming composite signal by the spreading code for that channel, sums the result, and assigns binary 1 for a positive value and binary 0 for a negative value.

a. What are the spreading codes for the seven channels?
b. Determine the receiver output measurement for channel 1 and the bit value assigned.
c. Repeat part (b) for channel 2.

17.3 By far, the most widely used technique for pseudorandom number generation is the linear congruential method. The algorithm is parameterized with four numbers, as follows:

m	the modulus	$m > 0$
a	the multiplier	$0 \leq a < m$
c	the increment	$0 \leq c < m$
X_0	the starting value, or seed	$0 \leq X_0 < m$

The sequence of pseudorandom numbers $\{X_n\}$ is obtained via the following iterative equation:

$$X_{n+1} = (aX_n + c) \bmod m$$

If m, a, c, and X_0 are integers, then this technique will produce a sequence of integers with each integer in the range $0 \leq X_n < m$. An essential characteristic of a pseudorandom number generator is that the generated sequence should appear random. Although the sequence is not random, because it is generated deterministically, there is a variety of statistical tests that can be used to assess the degree to which a sequence exhibits randomness. Another desirable characteristic is that the function should be a full-period generating function. That is, the function should generate all the numbers between 0 and m before repeating.

With the linear congruential algorithm, a choice of parameters that provides a full period does not necessarily provide a good randomization. For example, consider the two generators:

$$X_{n+1} = (6X_n) \bmod 13$$
$$X_{n+1} = (7X_n) \bmod 13$$

Write out the two sequences to show that both are full period. Which one appears more random to you?

17.4   In a code division multiple access network, N stations are simultaneously communicating using one channel. A sending station places data on the common channel by multiplying the data with its code. A station can receive data from a sending station if it knows the latter's code.

  a. What multiplication technique do the stations use for encoding or decoding?
  b. Prove that the receiving station can get the data sent by the sender if it multiplies the entire data with the sender's code and then divides the result by N.

17.5   In any use of pseudorandom numbers, whether for encryption, simulation, or statistical design, it is dangerous to trust blindly the random number generator that happens to be available in your computer's system library. [PARK88] found that many contemporary textbooks and programming packages make use of flawed algorithms for pseudorandom number generation. This exercise will enable you to test your system.

The test is based on a theorem attributed to Ernesto Cesaro (see [KNUT98] for a proof), which states that the probability is equal to $\frac{6}{\pi^2}$ that the greatest commondivisor of two randomly chosen integers is 1. Use this theorem in a program to determine statistically the value of π. The main program should call three subprograms: the random number generator from the system library to generate the random integers, a subprogram to calculate the greatest common divisor of two integers using Euclid's algorithm, and a subprogram that calculates square roots. If these latter two programs are not available, you will have to write them as well. The main program should loop through a large number of random numbers to give an estimate of the aforementioned probability. From this, it is a simple matter to solve for your estimate of π.

If the result is close to 3.14, congratulations! If not, then the result is probably low, usually a value of around 2.7. Why would such an inferior result be obtained?

17.6   Walsh codes are the most common orthogonal codes used in CDMA applications. A set of Walsh codes of length n consists of the n rows of an $n \times n$ Walsh matrix. That is, there are n codes, each of length n. The matrix is defined recursively as follows:

$$\mathbf{W}_1 = (0) \quad \mathbf{W}_{2n} = \begin{pmatrix} \mathbf{W}_n & \mathbf{W}_n \\ \mathbf{W}_n & \overline{\mathbf{W}_n} \end{pmatrix}$$

where n is the dimension of the matrix and the overscore denotes the logical NOT of the bits in the matrix. The Walsh matrix has the property that every row is orthogonal to every other row and to the logical NOT of every other row. Show the Walsh matrices of dimensions 2, 4, and 8.

17.7   A certain network has 250 stations. What number of sequences in a Walsh table will suffice for this purpose?

17.8   Consider a CDMA system in which users A and B have the Walsh codes $(-1\ 1\ -1\ 1\ -1\ 1\ -1\ 1)$ and $(-1\ -1\ 1\ 1\ -1\ -1\ 1\ 1)$, respectively.

  a. Show the output at the receiver if A transmits a data bit 1 and B does not transmit.
  b. Show the output at the receiver if A transmits a data bit 0 and B does not transmit.
  c. Show the output at the receiver if A transmits a data bit 1 and B transmits a data bit 1. Assume the received power from both A and B is the same.
  d. Show the output at the receiver if A transmits a data bit 0 and B transmits a data bit 1. Assume the received power from both A and B is the same.

   e. Show the output at the receiver if A transmits a data bit 1 and B transmits a data bit 0. Assume the received power from both A and B is the same.

   f. Show the output at the receiver if A transmits a data bit 0 and B transmits a data bit 0. Assume the received power from both A and B is the same.

   g. Show the output at the receiver if A transmits a data bit 1 and B transmits a data bit 1. Assume the received power from B is twice the received power from A. This can be represented by showing the received signal component from A as consisting of elements of magnitude 1 (+1, −1) and the received signal component from B as consisting of elements of magnitude 2 (+2, −2).

   h. Show the output at the receiver if A transmits a data bit 0 and B transmits a data bit 1. Assume the received power from B is twice the received power from A.

CHAPTER 18

WIRELESS NETWORKS

LEARNING OBJECTIVES

After studying this chapter, you should be able to:

◆ Understand the issues involved and requirements for fixed broadband wireless access.

◆ Compare WiMAX with Wi-Fi and LTE-Advanced.

◆ Present an overview of the IEEE 802.16 network reference model and protocol architecture.

◆ Summarize the functionality of the IEEE 802.16 MAC layer.

◆ Explain the main differences among the three 802.16 physical layer specifications.

◆ Present an overview of the Bluetooth protocol architecture.

◆ Understand the key elements of the Bluetooth radio specification.

◆ Present an overview of the Bluetooth baseband specification.

◆ Understand the Bluetooth audio representation.

This chapter examines two important wireless network schemes. The chapter begins with an introduction to the concepts of fixed broadband wireless access, followed by a discussion of the WiMAX/IEEE 802.16 specifications that support this type of network. The remainder of the chapter deals with an important and widely used personal area network technology known as Bluetooth.

18.1 FIXED BROADBAND WIRELESS ACCESS

Traditionally, the provision of voice and data communications to the end user, over the local loop, or subscriber loop, has been provided by wired systems. As the demand for broadband Internet access has grown, providers of wired local loop service have responded with increasing reliance on optical fiber and coaxial cable.

However, increasing interest is being shown in competing wireless technologies for subscriber access. These approaches are generally referred to as **wireless local loop (WLL)**, or **fixed wireless access**. The most prominent **fixed broadband wireless access** (fixed BWA) system is referred to as WiMAX, based on the IEEE 802.16 standard. We examine WiMAX in the next section. In this section, we provide an overview of the concept of fixed BWA.

Figure 18.1 illustrates a simple fixed BWA configuration. A BWA provider services one or more cells. Each cell includes a base station (BS) antenna, mounted on top of a tall building or tower. In earlier systems, subscribers used a fixed antenna mounted on a building or pole that has an unobstructed line of sight to the BS antenna. The technology has evolved so that indoor wireless access points are possible. From the BS, there is a link, which may either be wired or wireless, to a switching center. The switching center is typically a telephone company local office, which provides connections to the local and long-distance telephone networks. An Internet service provider (ISP) may be collocated at the switch or connected to the switch by a high-speed link.

Figure 18.1 shows what amounts to a two-level hierarchy. More complex configurations have also been implemented, in which a BS may serve a number of subordinate BS antennas, each of which supports a number of subscribers.

The fixed WBA has a number of advantages over a wired approach to subscriber loop support:

- **Cost:** Wireless systems are less expensive than wired systems. Although the electronics of the wireless transmitter/receiver may be more expensive than those used for wired communications, with WBA the cost of installing kilometers of cable, either underground or on poles, is avoided, as well as the cost of maintaining the wired infrastructure.

- **Installation time:** WBA systems typically can be installed rapidly. The key stumbling blocks are obtaining permission to use a given frequency band and finding a suitable elevated site for the BS antennas. Once these hurdles are cleared, a WBA system can be installed in a small fraction of the time required for a new wired system.

- **Selective installation:** Radio units are installed only for those subscribers who want the service at a given time. With a wired system, typically cable is laid out in anticipation of serving every subscriber in a local area.

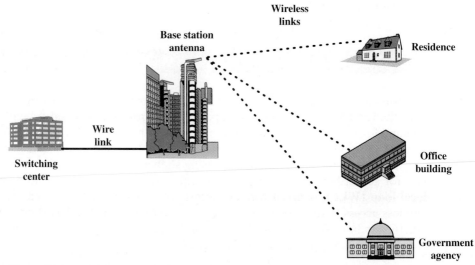

Figure 18.1   Fixed Broadband Wireless Configuration

WBA needs to be evaluated with respect to two alternatives:

- **Wired scheme using existing installed cable:** A large fraction of the earth's inhabitants do not have a telephone line. For high-speed applications, many subscribers with telephone lines do not have a line of sufficient quality or are too far from the central office to effectively use xDSL. Many of these same subscribers also do not have cable TV or their cable provider does not offer two-way data services. Finally, because WLL has become cost-competitive with wired schemes, new installations face a genuine choice between the wired and wireless approaches.
- **Mobile cellular technology:** 4G cellular systems provide broadband support. The primary advantages of a fixed WBA scheme are that the fixed WBA BS can cover a larger area, and that higher data rates can be achieved.

18.2 WIMAX/IEEE 802.16

With the growing interest in BWA services, a need was recognized within the industry to develop standards for this service. In response to this need the IEEE 802 committee set up the 802.16 working group in 1999 to develop broadband wireless standards. The charter for the group was to develop standards that:

- Use wireless links with microwave or millimeter wave radios
- Use licensed spectrum (typically)
- Are metropolitan in scale
- Provide public network service to fee-paying customers (typically)
- Use point-to-multipoint architecture with stationary rooftop or tower-mounted antennas
- Provide efficient transport of heterogeneous traffic supporting quality of service (QoS)
- Are capable of broadband transmissions (>2 Mbps)

In essence, IEEE 802.16 standardizes the air interface and related functions associated with BWA. In addition, an industry group, the WiMAX (Worldwide Interoperability for Microwave Access) Forum, was formed to promote the 802.16 standards and to develop interoperability specifications. Initially targeted at fixed BWA, IEEE 802.16 and the associated WiMAX specification now deal with both fixed and mobile BWA. In this section, we provide an overview of the 802.16 and WiMAX specifications, with an emphasis on the fixed BWA application. This section is based on the 2012 version of IEEE 802.16.

IEEE 802.16 Architecture

NETWORK REFERENCE MODEL   The WiMAX Forum has developed a logical representation of the architecture of a network that implements WiMAX, called the network reference model [WIMA12]. The model is useful in determining interface points between logical functional entities that can be used as a guide for developing interoperability standards. Figure 18.2 illustrates key elements of this model, which include the following:

- **Access Service Network (ASN):** The set of network functions needed to provide radio access to WiMAX subscribers.
- **Network Access Provider (NAP):** A business entity that provides WiMAX radio access infrastructure to one or more WiMAX Network Service Providers.
- **Connectivity Service Network (CSN):** A set of network functions that provide IP connectivity services to WiMAX subscribers. These functions include Internet access, authentication, and admission control based on user profiles.
- **Network Service Provider (NSP):** A business entity that provides IP connectivity and WiMAX services to WiMAX subscribers.
- **ASN Gateway:** Provides connectivity from an ASN to an NSP. The gateway performs such functions as routing and load balancing.

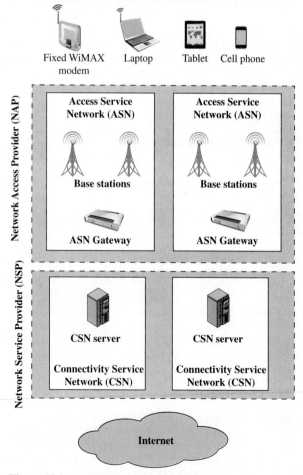

Figure 18.2 Elements of the WiMAX Network Reference Model

The network architecture logically divides into three parts: subscriber stations(SSs), the access service network, and the connectivity service networks. Subscribers may be fixed or mobile. Fixed subscribers are at a fixed geographic location and connect using a fixed WiMAX modem for broadband access. Fixed locations include residential, business, and government entities. An ASN consists of one or more BSs that are interconnected by a core network and connect to an ASN gateway. The gateway connects to one or more CSNs, which provide broadband access to the Internet. IEEE 802.16 standards are concerned with the air interface between the subscriber's transceiver station and the base transceiver station. The standards specify all the details of that interface, as discussed subsequently in this section. The system reference model also shows interfaces between the transceiver stations and the networks behind them. The details of these interfaces are beyond the scope of the 802.16 standards. The reason for showing these interfaces in the system reference model is that the subscriber and core network technologies (such as voice, ATM, etc.) have an impact on the technologies used in the air interface and the services provided by the transceiver stations over the air interface.

PROTOCOL ARCHITECTURE   Figure 18.3 illustrates the IEEE 802.16 protocol reference model. The **physical layer** includes the following:

- Encoding/decoding of signals
- Preamble generation/removal (for synchronization)
- Bit transmission/reception
- Frequency band and bandwidth allocation

The medium access control (MAC) layer is divided into three sublayers. The **security sublayer** includes authentication, secure key exchange, and encryption. Note that this sublayer is concerned with secure communication between the SS and the ASN base station. Secure communication between the SS and the CSN is handled at a higher layer.

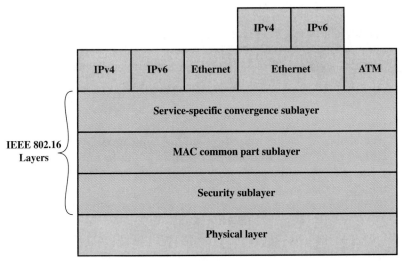

Figure 18.3   IEEE 802.16 Protocol Architecture

The **MAC common part sublayer** includes the basic functions of any MAC layer:

- On transmission, assemble data into a protocol data unit (PDU) with address and error detection fields.
- On reception, disassemble PDU, and perform address recognition and error detection.
- Govern access to the wireless transmission medium.

This sublayer, between the BS and the SS, is responsible for sharing access to the radio channel. Specifically, the MAC protocol defines how and when a BS or SS may initiate transmission on the channel. Because some of the layers above the MAC layer, such as ATM, require specified service levels (QoS), the MAC protocol must be able to allocate radio channel capacity so as to satisfy service demands. In the downstream direction (BS to SS), there is only one transmitter and the MAC protocol is relatively simple. In the upstream direction, multiple SSs are competing for access, resulting in a more complex MAC protocol.

The service-specific convergence sublayer provides functions specific to the service being provided. A convergence layer protocol may do the following:

- Encapsulate PDU framing of upper layers into the native 802.16 MAC PDUs.
- Map an upper layer's addresses into 802.16 addresses.
- Translate upper layer QoS parameters into native 802.16 MAC format.
- Adapt the time dependencies of the upper layer traffic into the equivalent MAC service.

IEEE 802.16 MAC Layer

Data transmitted over the 802.16 air interface from or to a given subscriber are structured as a sequence of MAC PDUs. The term **MAC PDU** as used in this context refers to the PDU that includes MAC protocol control information and higher-level data. This is not to be confused with a **TDMA burst**, which consists of a sequence of time slots, each dedicated to a given subscriber. A TDMA time slot may contain exactly one MAC PDU, a fraction of a MAC PDU, or multiple MAC PDUs. The sequence of time slots across multiple TDMA bursts that is dedicated to one subscriber forms a logical channel, and MAC PDUs are transmitted over that logical channel.

CONNECTIONS AND SERVICE FLOW The 802.16 MAC protocol is connection oriented. That is, a logical connection is set up between peer entities (MAC users) prior to the exchange of data between those entities. Each MAC PDU includes a connection ID, which is used by the MAC protocol to deliver incoming data to the correct MAC user. In addition, there is a one-to-one correspondence between a connection ID and service flow. The service flow defines the QoS parameters for the PDUs that are exchanged on the connection.

The concept of a service flow on a connection is central to the operation of the MAC protocol. Service flows provide a mechanism for upstream and downstream QoS management. In particular, they are integral to the bandwidth allocation process. The BS allocates both upstream and downstream bandwidth on the basis of the service flow for each active connection. Examples of service flow parameters are latency (maximum acceptable delay), jitter (maximum acceptable delay variation), and throughput (minimum acceptable bit rate).

PDU FORMAT   A good way to get a grasp of the MAC protocol is to examine the PDU format (Figure 18.4). The MAC PDU consists of three sections:

- **Header:** Contains protocol control information needed for the functioning of the MAC protocol.
- **Payload:** The payload may be either higher-level data (e.g., an ATM cell, an IP packet, a block of digital speech) or a MAC control message.
- **CRC:** The cyclic redundancy check field contains an error-detecting code. This optional CRC covers both the header and the payload and is applied after the payload is encrypted, if encryption is used.

Two types of headers are defined: the generic MAC header and the bandwidth request header. The **generic MAC header** is used in both the downlink (BS to SS) and uplink (SS to BS) directions. A MAC PDU with a generic header contains either MAC management messages or convergence sublayer data. The generic MAC header consists of the following fields:

- **Header type (1 bit):** This bit is set to zero indicating the header type is generic MAC PDU.

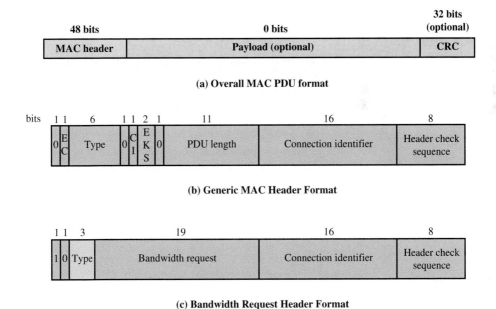

ATM = Asynchronous Transfer Mode
CI = CRC indicator
EC = encryption control
EKS = encryption key sequence

Figure 18.4   IEEE 802.16 MAC PDU Formats

- **Encryption control (1 bit):** Indicates whether the payload is encrypted.
- **Type (6 bits):** Indicates the subheaders and special payload types present in the message payload.
- **Reserved (1 bit):** Reserved bit, set to zero.
- **CRC indicator (1 bit):** Indicates whether there is a 32-bit CRC after the payload.
- **Encryption key sequence (2 bits):** An index into a vector of encryption key information, to be used if the payload is encrypted.
- **Reserved (1 bit):** Reserved bit, set to zero.
- **PDU length (11 bits):** Length in bytes of the entire MAC PDU.
- **Connection identifier (16 bits):** A unidirectional, MAC-layer address that identifies a connection to equivalent peers in the subscriber and base station MAC. A CID maps to an SFID, which defines the QoS parameters to the service flow associated with that connection.
- **Header check sequence (8 bits):** An 8-bit CRC used to detect errors in the header.

The Type field contains bits that indicate the presence or absence of each of the following subheaders at the beginning of the payload:

- **Fragmentation subheader:** Fragmentation is used to divide a higher-level block of data [called a service data unit (SDU)] into two or more fragments in order to reduce the size of MAC frames. This is done to allow efficient use of available bandwidth relative to the QoS requirements of a connection's service flow. If fragmentation is used, then all of the fragments are assigned the same fragment sequence number (FSN) in the fragmentation subheader. The MAC user at the destination is responsible for reassembling all of the fragments with the same FSN.
- **Packing subheader:** Packing is the process in which multiple MAC SDUs are packed into a single MAC PDU payload. This subheader contains the information needed for the receiving MAC entity to unpack the individual SDUs.
- **Fast feedback allocation subheader:** Only used in the downlink direction. It requests feedback from an SS with an advanced antenna system.
- **Grant management subheader:** Only used in the uplink direction. It conveys various information related to bandwidth management, such as polling request and additional-bandwidth request.

The **bandwidth request header** is used by the subscriber to request additional bandwidth. This header is for a MAC frame with no payload. As shown in Figure 18.4c, this header includes many of the fields in the generic MAC header. The 19-bit bandwidth request field indicates the number of bytes of capacity requested for uplink transmission. The type field allows the SS to request bandwidth for this connection only or aggregate bandwidth for all connections on this uplink.

SCHEDULING SERVICE AND QOS   An IEEE 802.16 network is designed to be able to transfer many different types of traffic simultaneously, including real-time flows such as voice, video, and bursty TCP flows. Although each such traffic flow is handled as a stream of PDUS traveling through a connection, the way in which each data flow is handled by the BS depends on the characteristics of the traffic flow and the requirements of the application. For example, real-time video traffic must be delivered within minimum variation in delay.

To accommodate the requirements of different types of traffic, IEEE 802.16 defines a number of different service classes. Each class is defined by certain general characteristics and a particular service flow is defined by assigning values to a set of QoS parameters. The most important of these parameters are the following:

- **Maximum sustained traffic rate:** The peak information rate, in bits per second of the service. The rate pertains to the service data units (SDUs) at the input to the system. The parameter is 6 bits in length and includes values in the range from 1200 bps to 1.921 Mbps.

- **Minimum reserved traffic rate:** The minimum rate, in bits per second, reserved for this service flow. The BS shall be able to satisfy bandwidth requests for a connection up to its minimum reserved traffic rate. If less bandwidth than its minimum reserved traffic rate is requested for a connection, the BS may reallocate the excess reserved bandwidth for other purposes. Values range from 1200 bps to 1.921 Mbps.

- **Maximum latency:** The maximum interval between the reception of a packet at the convergence sublayer of the BS or the SS and the forwarding of the SDU to its air interface. Values range from 1 ms to 10 s.

- **Tolerated jitter:** The maximum delay variation (jitter) for the connection. Values range from 1 ms to 10 s.

- **Traffic priority:** The priority of the associated service flow. Given two service flows identical in all QoS parameters besides priority, the higher-priority service flow should be given lower delay and higher buffering preference. For otherwise nonidentical service flows, the priority parameter should not take precedence over any conflicting service flow QoS parameter. Eight priority levels are used.

Table 18.1 lists the principal QoS parameters used for each of the five service classes defined in IEEE 802.16. The standard designates separate uplink and downlink services. Corresponding services use the same QoS parameter set. The principal difference is that for two of the service classes, polling is involved in the uplink transmission. Downlink transmission from the BS does not use polling, as there is a single transmitter, the BS.

The **unsolicited grant service (UGS)** is intended for real-time applications that generate fixed-rate data. A service flow with a data delivery service of UGS gets uplink resources assigned at uniform periodic intervals without requesting them each time (Figure 18.5a). UGS is commonly used for uncompressed audio and video information. On the downlink, the BS generates fixed-rate data as a uniform stream of PDUs. Examples of UGS applications include videoconferencing and distance learning.

The **real-time variable rate (RT-VR)** downlink service is intended for time-sensitive applications, that is, those requiring tightly constrained delay and delay variation. The principal difference between applications appropriate for RT-VR and those appropriate for UGS is that RT-VR applications transmit at a rate that varies with time. For example, the standard approach to video compression results in a sequence of image frames of varying sizes. Because real-time video requires

Table 18.1   IEEE 802.16 Service Classes and QoS Parameters

Scheduling Service (uplink)	Data Delivery Service (downlink)	Applications	QoS Parameters
Unsolicited grant service (UGS)	Unsolicited grant service (UGS)	VoIP	• Minimum reserved traffic rate • Maximum latency • Tolerated jitter
Real-time polling service (rtPS)	Real-time variable-rate service (RT-VR)	Streaming audio or video	• Minimum reserved traffic rate • Maximum sustained traffic rate • Maximum latency • Traffic priority
Non-real-time polling service (nrtPS)	Non-real-time variable-rate service (NRT-VR)	FTP	• Minimum reserved traffic rate • Maximum sustained traffic rate • Traffic priority
Best effort service (BE)	Best effort service (BE)	Data transfer, Web browsing, etc.	• Maximum sustained traffic rate • Traffic priority
Extended rtPS	Extended real-time variable-rate service (ERT-VR)	VoIP (voice with activity detection)	• Minimum reserved traffic rate • Maximum sustained traffic rate • Maximum latency • Tolerted jitter • Traffic priority

a uniform frame transmission rate, the actual data rate varies. On the downlink, RT-VR is implemented by transmitting the available data at uniform periodic intervals. On the uplink, the service is called **real-time polling service (rtPS)**. The BS issues a unicast poll (poll directed at a SS station) at periodic intervals, enabling the SS to transmit a block of data in each interval (Figure 18.5b). The RT-VR/rtPS service allows the network more flexibility than UGS. The network is able to statistically multiplex a number of connections over the same dedicated capacity and still provide the required service to each connection.

The **extended real-time variable rate (ERT-VR)** service is to support real-time applications with variable data rates, which require guaranteed data and delay, for example, VoIP with silence suppression. On the uplink, this service is called **extended rtPS**. As with UGS, the BS provides unicast grants of bandwidth in an unsolicited manner, thus saving the latency of a bandwidth request. However, in this case the allocations are variable in size, based on the amount of traffic so far carried. On the downlink side, the BS transmits PDUs over the service flow in varying sizes and at varying intervals, to keep up with the service flow QoS.

The **non-real-time variable-rate (NRT-VR)** service is intended for applications that have bursty traffic characteristics, do not have tight constraints on delay and delay variation, but for which it is possible to characterize the expected traffic flow and therefore set QoS parameters. An example is file transfer. On the downlink, the BS transmits data at variable intervals, to satisfy the minimum and maximum data rate requirements of the service flow. On the uplink, the service is

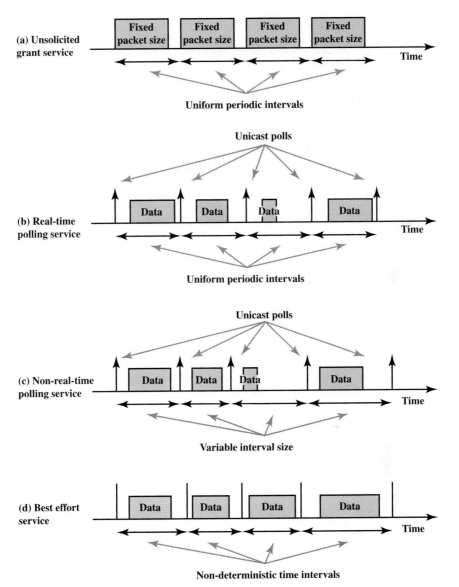

Figure 18.5   IEEE 802.16 Services

called **non-real-time polling service (nrtPS)**. The BS issues polls at varying intervals, depending on how much data has so far been transferred, so as to keep up with the required flow (Figure 18.5c).

At any given time, a certain amount of capacity between the BS and SSs is unused by the four classes of service so far discussed. This capacity is available for the **best effort (BE)** service. This service is suitable for applications that can tolerate variable delays and rates. Most applications running over TCP exhibit such tolerance. On the uplink, the SS sends requests for bandwidth in either random access slots (time slots in which SSs contend for access) or using dedicated transmission opportunities.

IEEE 802.16 Physical Layer

The IEEE 802.16 physical layer set of standards is still evolving, but is sufficiently stable to form the basis of widespread WiMAX implementation and deployment. The 2012 standard devotes almost 600 pages to the physical layer specification. Here we provide a brief overview.

The 802.16 specification defines three principal air interfaces, summarized in Table 18.2. All of these operate in licensed frequency bands. In addition, there are modifications to these specifications for operation in unlicensed bands below 11 GHz.

WIRELESSMAN-SC The **WirelessMAN-SC** interface is intended for use in the 10–66 GHz bands. In this region, due to the short wavelength, line-of-sight (LOS) is required and multipath is negligible. This environment is well suited for point-to-multipoint (PMP) access serving applications from small office/home office (SOHO) through medium- to large-office applications. Thus, this standard is suited for fixed wireless broadband access but does not support mobile stations.

Uplink transmission, from subscriber stations (SSs), is based on a combination of **time-division multiple access (TDMA)** and **demand-assignment multiple access (DAMA)**. As was defined in Chapter 8, TDMA employs a single, relatively large, uplink frequency band that is used to transmit a sequence of time slots. Repetitive time slots are assigned to an individual subscriber station to form a logical subchannel. When DAMA is employed, the time-slot assignment is changed as needed to respond optimally to demand changes among the multiple stations.

Downlink transmission from the base station is TDM, with the information for each SS multiplexed onto a single stream of data and received by all SSs within the same sector. To support SSs that operate in a half-duplex mode with frequency-division duplex (FDD), the standard makes provision for a TDMA portion of the

Table 18.2 IEEE 801.16 Physical Layer Modes

	WirelessMAN-SC	WirelessMAN-OFDM	WirelessMAN-OFDMA
Frequency band	10 to 66 GHz	≤ 11 GHz	≤ 11 GHz
LOS limitation	LOS	NLOS	NLOS
Duplexing technique	TDD, FDD	TDD, FDD	TDD, FDD
Uplink access	TDMA, DAMA	OFDM	OFDMA
Downlink access	TDM, TDMA	OFDM	OFDMA
Downlink modulation	QPSK, 16-QAM, 64-QAM	QPSK, 16-QAM, 64-QAM, BPSK	QPSK, 16-QAM, 64-QAM, BPSK
Uplink modulation	QPSK, 16-QAM, 64-QAM	QPSK, 16-QAM, 64-QAM, BPSK	QPSK, 16-QAM, 64-QAM, BPSK
Channel size	20 to 28 MHz	1.75 TO 20 MHZ	1.25 TO 20 MHZ
Subcarrier spacing	N/A	11.16 kHz	11.16 kHz
Data rate	32 to 134 Mbps	≤ 70 Mbps	≤ 70 Mbps
Downlink FEC	Reed-Solomon	Reed-Solomon	Convolutional
Uplink FEC	Reed-Solomon	Reed-Solomon	Convolutional

downlink. With TDMA, the downlink time slots are scheduled to coordinate the interchange with specific SSs.

WIRELESSMAN-OFDM   The **WirelessMAN-OFDM** interface operates below 11 GHz. In this region, due to the short wavelength, LOS is not necessary and multipath may be significant. The ability to support near-LOS and non-LOS (NLOS) scenarios requires additional physical-layer functionality, such as the support of advanced power management techniques, interference mitigation/coexistence, and MIMO antennas. Both uplink and downlink transmission use OFDM. Both WirelessMAN-OFDM and WirelessMAN-OFDMA are suitable for an environment that includes mobile SSs.

WirelessMAN-OFDM supports a range of channel bandwidths. Table 18.3 shows likely data rates achievable for various bandwidths.

WIRELESSMAN-OFDMA   **WirelessMAN-OFDMA** is an enhanced version of WirelessMAN-OFDM that provides added flexibility and efficiency by the use of OFDMA. Figure 18.6 is an example of how WirelessMAN-OFDMA operates using

Table 18.3   Data Rates Achieved at Various WirelessMAN-OFDM Bandwidths

Modulation	QPSK	QPSK	16-QAM	16-QAM	64-QAM	64-QAM
Code Rate	1/2	3/4	1/2	3/4	2/3	3/4
1.75 MHz	1.04	2.18	2.91	4.36	5.94	6.55
3.5 MHz	2.08	4.37	5.82	8.73	11.88	13.09
7.0 MHz	4.15	8.73	11.64	17.45	23.75	26.18
10.0 MHz	8.31	12.47	16.63	24.94	33.25	37.40
20.0 MHz	16.62	24.94	33.25	49.87	66.49	74.81

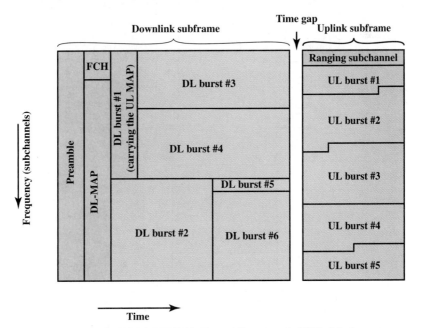

Figure 18.6   IEEE 802.16 OFDMA Frame Structure in TDD Mode

time-division duplex (TDD). Transmission is structure as a sequence of frames, each of which includes a downlink (DL) subframe followed by an uplink (UL) subframe. In each frame, a time gap is inserted between the DL and UL subframes and at the end of each frame to allow for transmission turnaround. Each DL subframe begins with a preamble used to synchronize all stations. This is followed by a DL-MAP pattern, which indicates how all of the subchannels are allocated in the DL subframe, and a frame control header (FCH). The FCH provides frame configuration information, such as the MAP message length, the modulation and coding scheme, and the usable subcarriers. The remainder of the DL subframe is divided into bursts, with each burst occupying a contiguous set of subchannels for a contiguous set of time intervals. One of these bursts is the UL-MAP pattern. The remaining bursts contain data, each burst intended for a specific SS. The UL subframe is similarly divided into bursts. One of these bursts is the ranging subchannel, which is allocated for SSs to perform closed-loop time, frequency, and power adjustment as well as bandwidth requests. The remaining bursts are allocated to SSs for transmission to the base station.

TDD, by its structure, readily supports half-duplex transmission, because UL and DL transmissions must alternate in time. This is not the case with FDD. Figure 18.7 shows how the structure of FDD WirelessMAN-OFDMA supports half-duplex operation. The FDD frame structure supports both full-duplex and

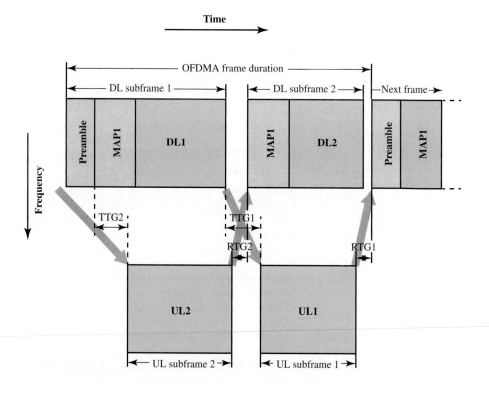

TTG = Transmitter-to-receiver gap
RTG = Receiver-to-transmitter gap

Figure 18.7   IEEE 802.16 OFDMA Frame Structure in FDD Mode

half-duplex SS types. The frame structure supports a coordinated transmission arrangement of two groups of half-duplex SSs (Group-1 and Group-2) that share the frame at distinct partitions of the frame. In each frame, one portion of the frequency band is devoted to DL transmission and one portion to UL transmission. The DL transmission consists of two subframes, the first for Group-1 and the second for Group-2. The UL transmission consists of a Group-2 subframe followed by a Group-1 subframe. Time gaps are inserted between subframes to enable both turnaround and half-duplex operation.

18.3 BLUETOOTH OVERVIEW

Bluetooth is an always-on, short-range radio hookup that resides on a microchip. The concept behind Bluetooth is to provide a universal short-range wireless capability. Using the 2.4-GHz band, available globally for unlicensed low-power uses, two Bluetooth devices within 10 m of each other can share up to 720 kbps of capacity. Bluetooth is intended to support an open-ended list of applications, including data (e.g., schedules and telephone numbers), audio, graphics, and even video. For example, audio devices can include headsets, cordless and standard phones, home stereos, and digital MP3 players. Examples of some of the capability Bluetooth can provide consumers are as follows:

- Make calls from a wireless headset connected remotely to a cell phone.
- Eliminate cables linking computers to printers, keyboards, and the mouse.
- Hook up MP3 players wirelessly to other machines to download music.
- Set up home networks so that a couch potato can remotely monitor air conditioning, the oven, and children's Internet surfing.
- Call home from a remote location to turn appliances on and off, set the alarm, and monitor activity.

Protocol Architecture

Bluetooth is defined as a layered protocol architecture (Figure 18.8) consisting of core protocols, cable replacement and telephony control protocols, and adopted protocols.
The **core protocols** form a five-layer stack consisting of the following elements:

- **Radio:** Specifies details of the air interface, including frequency, the use of frequency hopping, modulation scheme, and transmit power.
- **Baseband:** Concerned with connection establishment within a piconet, addressing, packet format, timing, and power control.
- **Link manager protocol (LMP)**: Responsible for link setup between Bluetooth devices and ongoing link management. This includes security aspects such as authentication and encryption, plus the control and negotiation of baseband packet sizes.
- **Logical Link Control and Adaptation Protocol (L2CAP)**: Adapts upper-layer protocols to the baseband layer. L2CAP provides both connectionless and connection-oriented services.

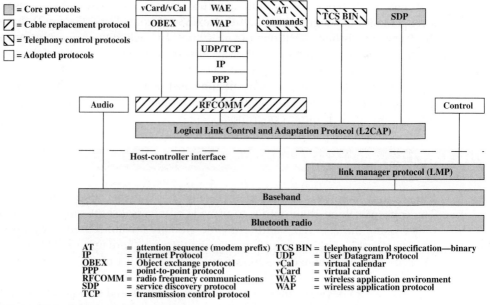

Figure 18.8 Bluetooth Protocol Stack

- **Service discovery protocol (SDP)**: Device information, services, and the characteristics of the services can be queried to enable the establishment of a connection between two or more Bluetooth devices.

RFCOMM is the **cable replacement protocol** included in the Bluetooth specification. RFCOMM presents a virtual serial port that is designed to make replacement of cable technologies as transparent as possible. Serial ports are one of the most common types of communications interfaces used with computing and communications devices. Hence, RFCOMM enables the replacement of serial port cables with the minimum of modification of existing devices. RFCOMM provides for binary data transport and emulates EIA-232 control signals over the Bluetooth baseband layer. EIA-232 (formerly known as RS-232) is a widely used serial port interface standard.

Bluetooth specifies a **telephony control protocol**. TCS BIN (telephony control specification—binary) is a bit-oriented protocol that defines the call control signaling for the establishment of speech and data calls between Bluetooth devices. In addition, it defines mobility management procedures for handling groups of Bluetooth TCS devices.

The **adopted protocols** are defined in specifications issued by other standards-making organizations and incorporated into the overall Bluetooth architecture. The Bluetooth strategy is to invent only necessary protocols and use existing standards whenever possible. The adopted protocols include the following:

- **PPP:** The point-to-point protocol is an Internet standard protocol for transporting IP datagrams over a point-to-point link.
- **TCP/UDP/IP:** These are the foundation protocols of the TCP/IP protocol suite (described in Chapter 4).

- **OBEX:** The object exchange protocol is a session-level protocol developed by the Infrared Data Association (IrDA) for the exchange of objects. OBEX provides functionality similar to that of HTTP, but in a simpler fashion. It also provides a model for representing objects and operations. Examples of content formats transferred by OBEX are vCard and vCalendar, which provide the format of an electronic business card and personal calendar entries and scheduling information, respectively.
- **WAE/WAP:** Bluetooth incorporates the wireless application environment and the wireless application protocol into its architecture.

Piconets and Scatternets

Bluetooth is designed to operate in an environment of many users. Up to eight devices can communicate in a small network called a **piconet**. Ten of these piconets can coexist in the same coverage range of the Bluetooth radio. To provide security, each link is encoded and protected against eavesdropping and interference. A piconet consists of a master and from one to seven active slave devices. The radio designated as the master makes the determination of the channel (frequency-hopping sequence) and phase (timing offset, i.e., when to transmit) that shall be used by all devices on this piconet. The radio designated as master makes this determination using its own device address as a parameter, while the slave devices must tune to the same channel and phase. A slave may only communicate with the master and may only communicate when granted permission by the master. A device in one piconet may also exist as part of another piconet and may function as either a slave or a master in each piconet (Figure 18.9). This form of overlapping is called a **scatternet**. Figure 18.10 contrasts the piconet/scatternet architecture with other forms of wireless networks.

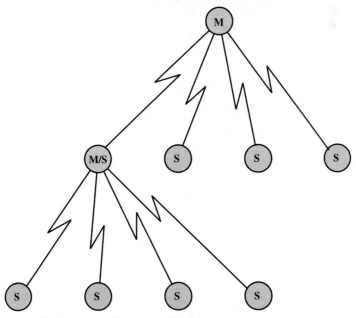

Figure 18.9   Master/Slave Relationships

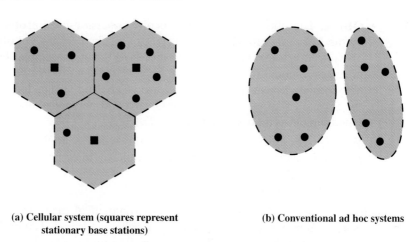

(a) Cellular system (squares represent
stationary base stations)

(b) Conventional ad hoc systems

(c) Scatternets

Figure 18.10 Wireless Network Configurations

The advantage of the piconet/scatternet scheme is that it allows many devices to share the same physical area and make efficient use of the bandwidth. A Bluetooth system uses a frequency-hopping scheme with a carrier spacing of 1 MHz. Typically, up to 80 different frequencies are used for a total bandwidth of 80 MHz. If frequency hopping were not used, then a single channel would correspond to a single 1-MHz band. With frequency hopping a logical channel is defined by the frequency-hopping sequence. At any given time, the bandwidth available is 1 MHz, with a maximum of eight devices sharing the bandwidth. Different logical channels (different hopping sequences) can simultaneously share the same 80-MHz bandwidth. Collisions will occur when devices in different piconets, on different logical channels, happen to use the same hop frequency at the same time. As the number of piconets in an area increases, the number of collisions increases, and performance degrades. In summary, the physical area and total bandwidth are shared by the scatternet. The logical channel and data transfer are shared by a piconet.

18.4 BLUETOOTH RADIO SPECIFICATION

The Bluetooth radio specification is a short document that gives the basic details of radio transmission for Bluetooth devices. Some of the key parameters are summarized in Table 18.4.

Bluetooth makes use of the 2.4-GHz band within the ISM (Industrial, Scientific, and Medical) band. In most countries, the bandwidth is sufficient to define 79 1-MHz physical channels. Power control is used to keep the devices from emitting any more RF power than necessary. The power control algorithm is implemented using the link management protocol between a master and the slaves in a piconet.

Modulation for Bluetooth is Gaussian FSK, with a binary one represented by a positive frequency deviation and a binary zero represented by a negative frequency deviation from the center frequency. The minimum deviation is 115 kHz.

18.5 BLUETOOTH BASEBAND SPECIFICATION

One of the most complex of the Bluetooth documents is the baseband specification. In this section we provide an overview of the key elements.

Frequency Hopping

Frequency hopping (FH) in Bluetooth serves two purposes:

1. It provides resistance to interference and multipath effects.
2. It provides a form of multiple access among co-located devices in different piconets.

The FH scheme works as follows. The total bandwidth is divided into 79 (in almost all countries) **physical channels**, each of bandwidth 1 MHz. FH occurs by jumping from one physical channel to another in a pseudorandom sequence. The same hopping sequence is shared by all of the devices on a single piconet; we will

Table 18.4   Bluetooth Radio and Baseband Parameters

Topology	Up to 7 simultaneous links in a logical star
Modulation	GFSK
Peak data rate	1 Mbps
RF bandwidth	220 kHz (−3 dB), 1 MHz (−20 dB)
RF band	2.4 GHz, ISM band
RF carriers	23/79
Carrier spacing	1 MHz
Transmit power	0.1 W
Piconet access	FH-TDD-TDMA
Frequency hop rate	1600 hops/s
Scatternet access	FH-CDMA

refer to this as an **FH channel**.[1] The hop rate is 1600 hops per second, so that each physical channel is occupied for a duration of 0.625 ms. Each 0.625-ms time period is referred to as a slot, and these are numbered sequentially.

Bluetooth radios communicate using a time division duplex (TDD) discipline. Because more than two devices share the piconet medium, the access technique is TDMA. Thus piconet access can be characterized as FH-TDD-TDMA. Figure 18.11 illustrates the technique. In the figure, k denotes the slot number, and $f(k)$ is the physical channel selected during slot period k.

Transmission of a packet starts at the beginning of a slot. Packet lengths requiring 1, 3, or 5 slots are allowed. For multislot packets, the radio remains at the same frequency until the entire packet has been sent. In the next slot after the multislot packet, the radio returns to the frequency required for its hopping sequence, so that during transmission, two or four hop frequencies have been skipped.

Using TDD prevents crosstalk between transmit and receive operations in the radio transceiver, which is essential if a one-chip implementation is desired. Note that because transmission and reception take place at different time slots, different frequencies are used.

The FH sequence is determined by the master in a piconet and is a function of the master's Bluetooth address. A rather complex mathematical operation involving permutations and exclusive-OR (XOR) operations is used to generate a pseudorandom hop sequence.

Because different piconets in the same area will have different masters, they will use different hop sequences. Thus, most of the time, transmissions on two devices on different piconets in the same area will be on different physical channels. Occasionally, two piconets will use the same physical channel during the same time slot, causing a collision and lost data. However, because this will happen infrequently, it is readily accommodated with forward error correction and error detection/ARQ techniques.

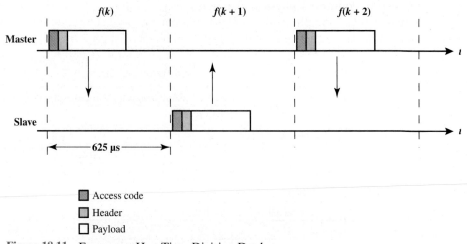

Figure 18.11   Frequency-Hop Time-Division Duplex

---

[1]The term *FH channel* is not used in the Bluetooth documents but is introduced here for clarity.

Thus, a form of code division multiple access (CDMA) is achieved between devices on different piconets in the same scatternet; this is referred to as FH-CDMA.

Physical Links

Two types of links can be established between a master and a slave:

- **Synchronous connection oriented (SCO)**: Allocates a fixed bandwidth between a point-to-point connection involving the master and a single slave. The master maintains the SCO link by using reserved slots at regular intervals. The basic unit of reservation is two consecutive slots (one in each transmission direction). The master can support up to three simultaneous SCO links, while a slave can support two or three SCO links. SCO packets are never retransmitted.

- **Asynchronous connectionless (ACL)**: A point-to-multipoint link between the master and all the slaves in the piconet. In slots not reserved for SCO links, the master can exchange packets with any slave on a per-slot basis, including a slave already engaged in an SCO link. Only a single ACL link can exist. For most ACL packets, packet retransmission is applied.

SCO links are used primarily to exchange time-bounded data requiring guaranteed data rate but without guaranteed delivery. One example, used in a number of Bluetooth profiles, is digitally encoded audio data with built-in tolerance to lost data. The guaranteed data rate is achieved through the reservation of a particular number of slots.

ACL links provide a packet-switched style of connection. No bandwidth reservation is possible and delivery may be guaranteed through error detection and retransmission. A slave is permitted to return an ACL packet in the slave-to-master slot if and only if it has been addressed in the preceding master-to-slave slot. For ACL links, 1-slot, 3-slot, and 5-slot packets have been defined. Data can be sent either unprotected (although ARQ can be used at a higher layer) or protected with a 2/3 forward error correction code. The maximum data rate that can be achieved is with a 5-slot unprotected packet with asymmetric capacity allocation, resulting in 721 kbps in the forward direction and 57.6 kbps in the reverse direction.

Packets

The packet format for Bluetooth packets is shown in Figure 18.12. It consists of three fields:

- **Access code:** Used for timing synchronization, offset compensation, paging, and inquiry
- **Header:** Used to identify packet type and to carry protocol control information
- **Payload:** If present, contains user voice or data and, in most cases, a payload header

The header format for all Bluetooth packets is shown in Figure 18.12b. It consists of six fields:

- **AM_ADDR:** The 3-bit AM_Addr contains the "active mode" address (temporary address assigned to this slave in this piconet) of one of the slaves.

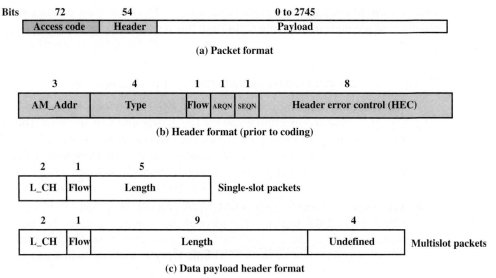

Figure 18.12 Bluetooth Baseband Formats

A transmission from the master to a slave contains that slave's address; a transmission from a slave contains its address. The 0 value is reserved for a broadcast from the master to all slaves in the piconet.

- **Type:** Identifies the type of packet. Four type codes are reserved for control packets common to both SCO and ACL links. The remaining packet types are used to convey user information. For SCO links, the HV1, HV2, HV3 packets each carry 64-kbps voice. The difference is the amount of error protection provided, which dictates how frequently a packet must be sent to maintain the 64-kbps data rate. The DV packet carries both voice and data. For ACL links, 6 different packets are defined. These, together with the DM1 packet, carry user data with different amounts of error protection and different data rates. There is another packet type common to both physical links; it consists of only the access code, with a fixed length of 68 bits (does not include trailer). This is referred to as the ID packet and is used in the inquiry and access procedures.

- **Flow:** Provides a 1-bit flow control mechanism for ACL traffic only. When a packet with Flow = 0 is received, the station receiving the packet must temporarily halt the transmission of ACL packets on this link. When a packet with Flow = 1 is received, transmission may resume.

- **ARQN:** Provides a 1-bit acknowledgment mechanism for ACL traffic protected by a CRC. If the reception was successful, an ACK (ARQN = 1) is returned; otherwise a NAK (ARQN = 0) is returned. When no return message regarding acknowledgment is received, a NAK is assumed implicitly. If a NAK is received, the relevant packet is retransmitted.

- **SEQN:** Provides a 1-bit sequential numbering scheme. Transmitted packets are alternately labeled with a 1 or 0. This is required to filter out retransmissions at the destination; if a retransmission occurs due to a failing ACK, the destination receives the same packet twice.

- **Header error control (HEC):** An 8-bit error detection code used to protect the packet header.

For some packet types, the baseband specification defines a format for the payload field. For voice payloads, no header is defined. For all of the ACL packets and for the data portion of the SCO DV packet, a header is defined. For data payloads, the payload format consists of three fields:

- **Payload header:** An 8-bit header is defined for single-slot packets, and a 16-bit header is defined for multislot packets.
- **Payload body:** Contains user information.
- **CRC:** A 16-bit CRC code is used on all data payloads except the AUX1 packet.

The payload header, when present, consists of three fields (Figure 18.12c):

- **L_CH:** Identifies the logical channel (described subsequently). The options are LMP message (11); an unfragmented L2CAP message or the start of a fragmented L2CAP message (10); the continuation of a fragmented L2CAP message (01); or other (00).
- **Flow:** Used to control flow at the L2CAP level. This is the same on/off mechanism provided by the Flow field in the packet header for ACL traffic.
- **Length:** The number of bytes of data in the payload, excluding the payload header and CRC.

Error Correction

At the baseband level, Bluetooth makes use of three error correction schemes:

- 1/3 rate FEC (forward error correction)
- 2/3 rate FEC
- ARQ (automatic repeat request)

These error correction schemes are designed to satisfy competing requirements. The error correction scheme must be adequate to cope with the inherently unreliable wireless link but must also be streamlined and efficient.

The **1/3 rate FEC** is used on the 18-bit packet header and also for the voice field in an HV1 packet. The scheme simply involves sending three copies of each bit. A majority logic is used: Each received triple of bits is mapped into whichever bit is in the majority.

The **2/3 rate FEC** is used in all DM packets, in the data field of the DV packet, in the FHS packet, and in the HV2 packet. The encoder is a form of Hamming code with parameters (15, 10). This code can correct all single errors and detect all double errors in each codeword.

The **ARQ scheme** is used with DM and DH packets, and the data field of DV packets. The scheme is similar to ARQ schemes used in data link control protocols (Chapter 7).

Bluetooth uses what is referred to as a *fast ARQ* scheme, which takes advantage of the fact that a master and slave communicate in alternate time slots. Figure 18.13 illustrates the technique. When a station receives a packet, it determines if an error has occurred using a 16-bit CRC. If so, the ARQN bit in the header is set to 0 (NAK); if no error is detected, then ARQN is set to 1 (ACK). When a station receives a NAK, it retransmits the same packet as it sent in the preceding slot, using the same 1-bit SEQN in the packet header. With this technique, a sender is notified in the next time slot if a transmission has failed and, if so, can retransmit. The use of 1-bit sequence numbers and immediate packet retransmission minimizes overhead and maximizes responsiveness.

Logical Channels

Bluetooth defines five types of logical data channels designated to carry different types of payload traffic.

- **Link control (LC):** Used to manage the flow of packets over the link interface. The LC channel is mapped onto the packet header. This channel carries low-level link control information like ARQ, flow control, and payload characterization. The LC channel is carried in every packet except in the ID packet, which has no packet header.

- **Link manager (LM):** Transports link management information between participating stations. This logical channel supports LMP traffic and can be carried over either an SCO or an ACL link.

- **User asynchronous (UA):** Carries asynchronous user data. This channel is normally carried over the ACL link but may be carried in a DV packet on the SCO link.

- **User isochronous (UI):** Carries isochronous user data.[2] This channel is normally carried over the ACL link but may be carried in a DV packet on the SCO link.

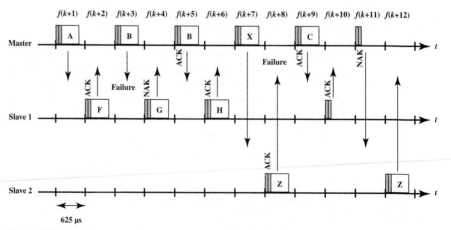

Figure 18.13 An Example of Retransmission Operation

---

[2]The term *isochronous* refers to blocks of data that recur with known periodic timing.

At the baseband level, the UI channel is treated the same way as a UA channel. Timing to provide isochronous properties is provided at a higher layer.

- **User synchronous (US):** Carries synchronous user data. This channel is carried over the SCO link.

Bluetooth Audio

The baseband specification indicates that either of two voice encoding schemes can be used: pulse code modulation (PCM) or continuously variable slope delta (CVSD) modulation. The choice is made by the link managers of the two communicating devices, which negotiate the most appropriate scheme for the application.

PCM was discussed in Chapter 5. CVSD is a form of delta modulation (DM), also discussed in Chapter 5. Recall that with delta modulation, an analog input is approximated by a staircase function that moves up or down by one quantization level (δ) at each sampling interval (T_s). Thus, the output of the delta modulation process can be represented as a single binary digit for each sample. In essence, a bit stream is produced by approximating the derivative of an analog signal rather than its amplitude: A 1 is generated if the staircase function is to go up during the next interval; a 0 is generated otherwise.

As was discussed, there are two forms of error in a DM scheme: quantizing noise, which occurs when the waveform is changing very slowly, and slope overload noise, when the waveform is changing rapidly (Figure 5.20). CVSD is designed to minimize both these types of error by using a variable quantization level, one that is small when the waveform is changing slowly and large when the waveform is changing rapidly (Figure 18.14). The slope is monitored by considering the K most recent

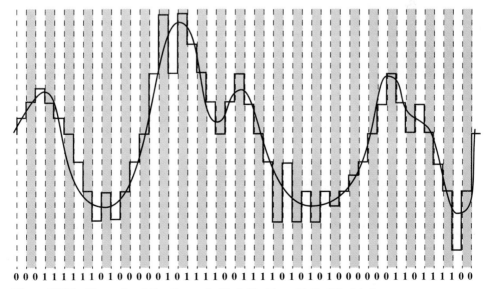

0 0 0 1 1 1 1 1 1 0 1 0 0 0 0 0 1 0 1 1 1 1 0 0 1 1 1 1 0 1 0 1 0 1 0 0 0 0 0 0 1 1 0 1 1 1 1 0 0

Figure 18.14 Example of Continuously Variable Slope Delta Modulation

output bits. The resulting scheme is more resistant to bit errors than PCM and more resistant to quantizing and slope overload errors than DM.

Figure 18.15 illustrates the CVSD encoding and decoding (compare Figure 5.21). As with DM, a binary output is converted into a staircase function that tracks the original waveform as closely as possible. For encoding, the following occurs: The input to the encoder is 64-kbps PCM. At each sampling time, the PCM input $x(k)$ is compared to the most recent value of the approximating staircase function, expressed as $\hat{x}(k - 1)$. The output of the comparator $b(k)$ is defined as

$$b(k) = \begin{cases} 1 & x(k) - \hat{x}(k - 1) \geq 0 \\ -1 & x(k) - \hat{x}(k - 1) < 0 \end{cases}$$

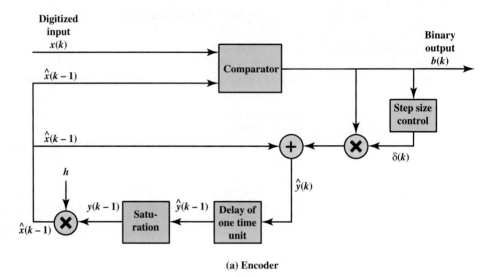

(a) Encoder

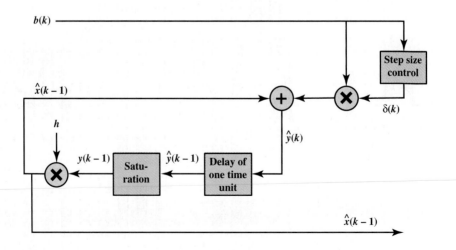

(b) Decoder

Figure 18.15   Continuously Variable Slope Delta Modulation

For transmission, these numbers are represented by the sign bit (negative numbers are mapped to binary 1; positive numbers are mapped to 0). The output $b(k)$ is used to produce the magnitude of the next step in the staircase, $\delta(k)$, as follows:

$$\delta(k) = \begin{cases} \min\left[\delta_{min} + \delta(k-1), \delta_{max}\right] & \text{if at least } J \text{ of the last } K \text{ output bits } b(\bullet) \text{ are the same} \\ \max\left[\beta \times \delta(k-1), \delta_{min}\right] & \text{otherwise} \end{cases}$$

Table 18.5 shows the default parameter values. The effect of the preceding definition is that if the waveform is changing rapidly (at least J of the last K steps have been in the same direction), then the magnitude of the step change, $\delta(k)$, increases in a linear fashion by a constant amount δ_{min}, up to some maximum magnitude δ_{max}. On the other hand, if the waveform is not changing rapidly, then the magnitude of the step change gradually decays by a *decay factor* β, down to a minimum value of δ_{min}. The sign of the step change is determined by the sign of the output $b(t)$.

The step change is then added to the most recent value of the staircase function to produce $\hat{y}(k)$.

$$\hat{y}(k) = \hat{x}(k-1) + b(k)\delta(k)$$

This value is then delayed one sample time, yielding $\hat{y}(k-1)$. Then a *saturation function* is applied, defined as

$$y(k-1) = \begin{cases} \min\left[\hat{y}(k-1), y_{max}\right] & \hat{y}(k-1) \geq 0 \\ \max\left[\hat{y}(k-1), y_{min}\right] & \hat{y}(k-1) < 0 \end{cases}$$

where y_{min} and y_{max} are the negative and positive saturation values for the encoder, limiting the total range of the staircase function.

Finally, $y(k-1)$ is multiplied by the decay factor h to yield the waveform estimate $\hat{x}(k-1)$. The decay factor determines how quickly the output of the CVSD decoder returns to zero in the absence of a strongly changing input.

Table 18.5   CVSD Parameter Values

Parameter	Value
h	$1 - \dfrac{1}{32} = 0.96875$
β	$1 - \dfrac{1}{1024} \approx 0.999$
J	4
K	4
δ_{min}	10
δ_{max}	1280
y_{min}	-2^{15} or $-2^{15}+1$
y_{max}	$2^{15}-1$

18.6 BLUETOOTH LOGICAL LINK CONTROL AND ADAPTATION PROTOCOL

Like Logical Link Control (LLC) in the IEEE 802 specification, L2CAP provides a link-layer protocol between entities across a shared-medium network. As with LLC, L2CAP provides a number of services and relies on a lower layer (in this case, the baseband layer) for flow and error control.

L2CAP makes use of ACL links; it does not provide support for SCO links. Using ACL links, L2CAP provides two alternative services to upper-layer protocols:

- **Connectionless service:** This is a reliable datagram style of service.
- **Connection-mode service:** This service is similar to that offered by HDLC. A logical connection is set up between two users exchanging data, and flow control and error control are provided.

Based on these services, L2CAP provides three types of logical channels:

- **Connectionless:** Supports the connectionless service. Each channel is unidirectional. This channel type is typically used for broadcast from the master to multiple slaves.
- **Connection oriented:** Supports the connection-oriented service. Each channel is bidirectional (full duplex). A quality of service (QoS) flow specification is assigned in each direction.
- **Signaling:** Provides for the exchange of signaling messages between L2CAP entities.

Associated with each logical channel is a channel identifier (CID). For connection-oriented channels, a unique CID is assigned at each end of the channel to identify this connection and associate it with an L2CAP user on each end. Connectionless channels are identified by a CID value of 2, and signaling channels are identified by a CID value of 1. Thus, between the master and any slave, there is only one connectionless channel and one signaling channel, but there may be multiple connection-oriented channels.

An important element of L2Cap is the provision of quality of service (QoS). The QoS parameter in L2CAP defines a traffic flow specification based on RFC 1363.[3] In essence, a **flow specification** is a set of parameters that indicate a performance level that the transmitter will attempt to achieve.

When included in a Configuration Request, this option describes the outgoing traffic flow from the device sending the request to the device receiving it. When included in a positive Configuration Response, this option describes the incoming traffic flow agreement as seen from the device sending the response. When included in a negative Configuration Response, this option describes the preferred incoming traffic flow from the perspective of the device sending the response.

---

[3]*A Proposed Flow Specification*, RFC 1363, September 1992.

The flow specification consists of the following parameters:

- Service type
- Token rate (bytes/second)
- Token bucket size (bytes)
- Peak bandwidth (bytes/second)
- Latency (microseconds)
- Delay variation (microseconds)

The **service type** parameter indicates the level of service for this flow. A value of 0 indicates that no traffic will be transmitted on this channel. A value of 1 indicates a best effort service; the device will transmit data as quickly as possible but with no guarantees about performance. A value of 2 indicates a guaranteed service; the sender will transmit data that conform to the remaining QoS parameters.

The **token rate** and **token bucket size** parameters define a token bucket scheme that is often used in QoS specifications. The advantage of this scheme is that it provides a concise description of the peak and average traffic load the recipient can expect and it also provides a convenient mechanism by which the sender can implement the traffic flow policy. The token bucket scheme is described in Chapter 20.

For L2CAP, a value of zero for the two parameters implies that the token scheme is not needed for this application and will not be used. A value of all 1s is the wild card value. For best effort service, the wild card indicates that the requestor wants as large a token or as large a token bucket size, respectively, as the responder will grant. For guaranteed service, the wild card indicates that the maximum data rate or bucket size, respectively, is available at the time of the request.

The **peak bandwidth**, expressed in bytes per second, limits how fast packets may be sent back-to-back from applications. Some intermediate systems can take advantage of this information, resulting in more efficient resource allocation. Consider that if the token bucket is full, it is possible for the flow to send a series of back-to-back packets equal to the size of the token bucket. If the token bucket size is large, this back-to-back run may be long enough to exceed the recipient's capacity. To limit this effect, the maximum transmission rate bounds how fast successive packets may be placed on the network.

The **latency** is the maximum acceptable delay between transmission of a bit by the sender and its initial transmission over the air, expressed in microseconds.

The **delay variation** is the difference, in microseconds, between the maximum and minimum possible delay that a packet will experience. This value is used by applications to determine the amount of buffer space needed at the receiving side in order to restore the original data transmission pattern. If a receiving application requires data to be delivered in the same pattern that the data were transmitted, it may be necessary for the receiving host briefly to buffer data as they are received so that the receiver can restore the old transmission pattern. An example of this is a case where an application wishes to send and transmit data such as voice samples, which are generated and played at regular intervals. The amount of buffer space that the receiving host is willing to provide determines the amount of variation in delay permitted for individual packets within a given flow.

18.7 RECOMMENDED READING

[PARE12] is an informative history of the evolution of IEEE 802.16 and WiMAX. [EKLU02] is a good technical overview of IEEE 802.16 developments up to 2002. [KOFF02] discusses OFDM in WiMAX. [HAAR00a], [HAAR00b], and [SAIR02] provide good overviews of Bluetooth.

EKLU02 Elkund, C., et al. "IEEE Standard 802.16: A Technical Overview of the WirelessMAN™ Air Interface for Broadband Wireless Access." *IEEE Communications Magazine*, June 2002.

HAAR00a Haartsen, J. "The Bluetooth Radio System." *IEEE Personal Communications*, February 2000.

HAAR00b Haartsen, J., and Mattisson, S. "Bluetooth—A New Low-Power Radio Interface Providing Short-Range Connectivity." *Proceedings of the IEEE*, October 2000.

KOFF02 Koffman, I., and Roman, V. "Broadband Wireless Access Solutions Based on OFDM Access in IEEE 802.16." *IEEE Communications Magazine*, April 2002.

PARE12 Pareit, D.; Moerman, I.; and Demester, P. "The History of WiMAX: A Complete Survey of the Evolution in Certification and Standardization for IEEE 802.16 and WiMAX." *IEEE Communications Surveys and Tutorials*, Fourth Quarter 2012.

SAIR02 Sairam, K.; Gunasekaran, N.; and Reddy, S. "Bluetooth in Wireless Communication." *IEEE Communications Magazine*, June 2002.

18.8 KEY TERMS, REVIEW QUESTIONS, AND PROBLEMS

Key Terms

adopted protocol	latency	scatternet
asynchronous connectionless (ACL)	Logical Link Control and Adaptation Protocol (L2CAP)	service discovery protocol (SDP)
best effort (BE)	link manager protocol (LMP)	synchronous connection oriented (SCO)
Bluetooth	MAC PDU	TDMA burst
cable replacement protocol	non-real-time polling service (nrtPS)	telephony control protocol
delay variation	non-real-time variable-rate (NRT-VR)	token bucket
extended real-time variable rate (ERT-VR)	piconet	unsolicited grant service (UGS)
extended rtPS	real-time polling service (rtPS)	WiMAX
fixed wireless access	real-time variable rate (RT-VR)	wireless local loop (WLL)
fixed broadband wireless access		WirelessMAN-OFDM
flow specification		WirelessMAN-OFDMA
frequency hopping		WirelessMAN-SC
IEEE 802.16		

Review Questions

18.1 Define fixed broadband wireless access.
18.2 List and briefly define IEEE 802.16 service classes.
18.3 List and briefly describe the three IEEE 802.16 physical layer options.
18.4 What is the relationship between master and slave in a piconet?
18.5 How is it possible to combine frequency hopping and time division duplex?
18.6 List and briefly define Bluetooth baseband logical channels.
18.7 What is a flow specification?

Problems

18.1 In Figure 18.6, the DL subframe contains both DL-MAP and UL-MAP. Why not make UL-MAP a preamble in the UL subframe?

18.2 **a.** Bluetooth uses FHSS with a hop rate of 1600 hops/s. What is the length of a time slot? What is the slot in bits with a 1-MHz bandwidth and 1 bit/Hz rate?
   b. In each time slot, 259 μs is needed for hopping and control mechanisms. Packets can be of 1, 3, or 5 slots. How long does a frame last in each type of packet?

18.3 A frame in the baseband layer has an access code of 72 bits, a header of 54 bits, and a payload. What will be the size of the payload for a 1-slot frame, 3-slot frame, and 5-slot frame? (Typical frame sizes are 1-slot frame $\rightarrow$ 366 bits, 3-slot frame $\rightarrow$ 1616 bits, and 5-slot frame $\rightarrow$ 2866 bits.)

18.4 The token bucket scheme places a limit on the length of time at which traffic can depart at the maximum data rate. Let the token bucket be defined by a bucket size B octets and a token arrival rate of R octets/second, and let the maximum output data rate be M octets/s.
   a. Derive a formula for S, which is the length of the maximum-rate burst. That is, for how long can a flow transmit at the maximum output rate when governed by a token bucket?
   b. What is the value of S for $b = 250$ KB, $r = 2$ MB/s, and $M = 25$ MB/s?

   Hint: The formula for S is not so simple as it might appear, because more tokens arrive while the burst is being output.

ROUTING

LEARNING OBJECTIVES

After studying this chapter, you should be able to:

♦ Understand the principal routing strategies used in switched data networks.

♦ Present an overview of the three generations of routing algorithms developed for Arpanet.

♦ Define the term *autonomous system.*

♦ Explain the key features of BGP.

♦ Explain the key features of OSPF.

♦ Compare and contrast Dijkstra's algorithm and the Bellman–Ford algorithm.

A key design issue in switched networks, including packet networks, the Internet, and private internets, is that of routing. In general terms, the routing function seeks to design routes through the network for individual pairs of communicating end nodes such that the network is used efficiently.

This chapter begins with a brief overview of issues involved in routing design. Next, we look at the routing function in packet-switching networks. Then we look at key routing algorithms for the Internet. Finally, the chapter examines least-cost algorithms that are a central part of routing in switched networks.

19.1 ROUTING IN PACKET-SWITCHING NETWORKS

One of the most complex and crucial design aspects of switched data networks is routing. This section surveys key characteristic that can be used to classify routing strategies.

Characteristics

The primary function of a packet-switching network is to accept packets from a source station and deliver them to a destination station. To accomplish this, a path or route through the network must be determined; generally, more than one route is possible. Thus, a routing function must be performed. The requirements for this function include the following:

• Correctness
• Simplicity

- Robustness
- Stability
- Fairness
- Optimality
- Efficiency

The first two items on the list, correctness and simplicity, are self-explanatory. Robustness has to do with the ability of the network to deliver packets via some route in the face of localized failures and overloads. Ideally, the network can react to such contingencies without the loss of packets or the breaking of virtual circuits. The designer who seeks robustness must cope with the competing requirement for stability. Techniques that react to changing conditions have an unfortunate tendency to either react too slowly to events or to experience unstable swings from one extreme to another. For example, the network may react to congestion in one area by shifting most of the load to a second area. Now the second area is overloaded and the first is underutilized, causing a second shift. During these shifts, packets may travel in loops through the network.

A trade-off also exists between fairness and optimality. Some performance criteria may give higher priority to the exchange of packets between nearby stations compared to an exchange between distant stations. This policy may maximize average throughput but will appear unfair to the station that primarily needs to communicate with distant stations.

Finally, any routing technique involves some processing overhead at each node and often a transmission overhead as well, both of which impair network efficiency. The penalty of such overhead needs to be less than the benefit accrued based on some reasonable metric, such as increased robustness or fairness.

With these requirements in mind, we are in a position to assess the various design elements that contribute to a routing strategy. Table 19.1 lists these elements. Some of these categories overlap or are dependent on one another. Nevertheless, an examination of this list serves to clarify and organize routing concepts.

PERFORMANCE CRITERIA The selection of a route is generally based on some performance criterion. The simplest criterion is to choose the minimum-hop route (one that passes through the least number of nodes) through the network.[1] This is an easily measured criterion and should minimize the consumption of network resources. A generalization of the minimum-hop criterion is least-cost routing. In this case, a cost is associated with each link, and, for any pair of attached stations, the route through the network that accumulates the least cost is sought.

---

[1]The term *hop* is used somewhat loosely in the literature. The more common definition, which we use, is that the number of hops along a path from a given source to a given destination is the number of links between network nodes (packet-switching nodes, ATM switches, routers, etc.) that a packet traverses along that path. Sometimes the number of hops is defined to include the link between the source station and the network and the link between the destination station and the network. This latter definition produces a value 2 greater than the definition we use.

Table 19.1 Elements of Routing Techniques for Packet-Switching Networks

Performance Criteria	Network Information Source
Number of hops	None
Cost	Local
Delay	Adjacent node
Throughput	Nodes along route
	All nodes
Decision Time	
Packet (datagram)	**Network Information Update Timing**
Session (virtual circuit)	Continuous
	Periodic
Decision Place	Major load change
Each node (distributed)	Topology change
Central node (centralized)	
Originating node (source)	

EXAMPLE 19.1 Figure 19.1 illustrates a network in which the two arrowed lines between a pair of nodes represent a link between these nodes, and the corresponding numbers represent the current link cost in each direction. The shortest path (fewest hops) from node 1 to node 6 is 1-3-6 (cost = 5 + 5 = 10), but the least-cost path is 1-4-5-6 (cost = 1 + 1 + 2 = 4).

Costs are assigned to links to support one or more design objectives. For example, the cost could be inversely related to the data rate (i.e., the higher the data rate on a link, the lower the assigned cost of the link) or the current queueing

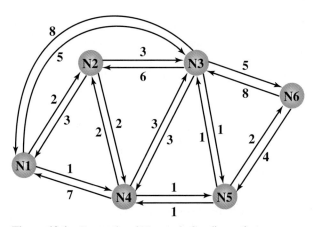

Figure 19.1 Example of Network Configuration

delay on the link. In the first case, the least-cost route should provide the highest throughput. In the second case, the least-cost route should minimize delay.

In either the minimum-hop or least-cost approach, the algorithm for determining the optimum route for any pair of stations is relatively straightforward, and the processing time would be about the same for either computation. Because the least-cost criterion is more flexible, this is more common than the minimum-hop criterion.

Several least-cost routing algorithms are in common use. These are described in Section 19.4.

DECISION TIME AND PLACE   Routing decisions are made on the basis of some performance criterion. Two key characteristics of the decision are the time and place that the decision is made.

Decision time is determined by whether the routing decision is made on a packet or virtual circuit basis. When the internal operation of the network is datagram, a routing decision is made individually for each packet. For internal virtual circuit operation, a routing decision is made at the time the virtual circuit is established. In the simplest case, all subsequent packets using that virtual circuit follow the same route. In more sophisticated network designs, the network may dynamically change the route assigned to a particular virtual circuit in response to changing conditions (e.g., overload or failure of a portion of the network).

The term *decision place* refers to which node or nodes in the network are responsible for the routing decision. Most common is distributed routing, in which each node has the responsibility of selecting an output link for routing packets as they arrive. For centralized routing, the decision is made by some designated node, such as a network control center. The danger of this latter approach is that the loss of the network control center may block operation of the network. The distributed approach is perhaps more complex but is also more robust. A third alternative, used in some networks, is source routing. In this case, the routing decision is actually made by the source station rather than by a network node and is then communicated to the network. This allows the user to dictate a route through the network that meets criteria local to that user.

The decision time and decision place are independent design variables. For example, in Figure 19.1, suppose that the decision place is each node and that the values depicted are the costs at a given instant in time: The costs may change. If a packet is to be delivered from node 1 to node 6, it might follow the route 1-4-5-6, with each leg of the route determined locally by the transmitting node. Now let the values change such that 1-4-5-6 is no longer the optimum route. In a datagram network, the next packet may follow a different route, again determined by each node along the way. In a virtual circuit network, each node will remember the routing decision that was made when the virtual circuit was established, and simply pass on the packets without making a new decision.

NETWORK INFORMATION SOURCE AND UPDATE TIMING   Most routing strategies require that decisions be based on knowledge of the topology of the network, traffic load, and link cost. Surprisingly, some strategies use no such information and yet manage to get packets through; flooding and some random strategies (discussed later) are in this category.

With distributed routing, in which the routing decision is made by each node, the individual node may make use of only local information, such as the cost of each outgoing link. Each node might also collect information from adjacent (directly connected) nodes, such as the amount of congestion experienced at that node. Finally, there are algorithms in common use that allow the node to gain information from all nodes on any potential route of interest. In the case of centralized routing, the central node typically makes use of information obtained from all nodes.

A related concept is that of information update timing, which is a function of both the information source and the routing strategy. Clearly, if no information is used (as in flooding), there is no information to update. If only local information is used, the update is essentially continuous. That is, an individual node always knows its local conditions. For all other information source categories (adjacent nodes, all nodes), update timing depends on the routing strategy. For a fixed strategy, the information is never updated. For an adaptive strategy, information is updated from time to time to enable the routing decision to adapt to changing conditions.

As you might expect, the more information available, and the more frequently it is updated, the more likely the network is to make good routing decisions. On the other hand, the transmission of that information consumes network resources.

Routing Strategies

A large number of routing strategies have evolved for dealing with the routing requirements of packet-switching networks. Many of these strategies are also applied to internetwork routing, which we cover in Part Five. In this section, we survey four key strategies: fixed, flooding, random, and adaptive.

FIXED ROUTING   For fixed routing, a single, permanent route is configured for each source–destination pair of nodes in the network. Either of the least-cost routing algorithms described in Section 19.3 could be used. The routes are fixed, or at least only change when there is a change in the topology of the network. Thus, the link costs used in designing routes cannot be based on any dynamic variable such as traffic. They could, however, be based on expected traffic or capacity.

> **EXAMPLE 19.2** Figure 19.2 suggests how fixed routing might be implemented for the network in Figure 19.1, with the associated link costs shown in Figure 19.1. A central routing matrix is created, to be stored perhaps at a network control center. The matrix shows, for each source–destination pair of nodes, the identity of the next node on the route.

Note that it is not necessary to store the complete route for each possible pair of nodes. Rather, it is sufficient to know, for each pair of nodes, the identity of the first node on the route. To see this, suppose that the least-cost route from X to Y begins with the X-A link. Call the remainder of the route R_1; this is the part from A to Y. Define R_2 as the least-cost route from A to Y. Now, if the cost of R_1 is greater than that of R_2, then the X-Y route can be improved by using R_2 instead. If the cost of R_1 is less than R_2, then R_2 is not the least-cost route from A to Y. Therefore, $R_1 = R_2$.

Central routing directory

From node

		1	2	3	4	5	6
	1	—	1	5	2	4	5
	2	2	—	5	2	4	5
To	3	4	3	—	5	3	5
node	4	4	4	5	—	4	5
	5	4	4	5	5	—	5
	6	4	4	5	5	6	—

Node 1 directory	
Destination	Next node
2	2
3	4
4	4
5	4
6	4

Node 2 directory	
Destination	Next node
1	1
3	3
4	4
5	4
6	4

Node 3 directory	
Destination	Next node
1	5
2	5
4	5
5	5
6	5

Node 4 directory	
Destination	Next node
1	2
2	2
3	5
5	5
6	5

Node 5 directory	
Destination	Next node
1	4
2	4
3	3
4	4
6	6

Node 6 directory	
Destination	Next node
1	5
2	5
3	5
4	5
5	5

Figure 19.2   Fixed Routing (using Figure 19.1)

Thus, at each point along a route, it is only necessary to know the identity of the next node, not the entire route. In our example, the route from node 1 to node 6 begins by going through node 4. Again consulting the matrix, the route from node 4 to node 6 goes through node 5. Finally, the route from node 5 to node 6 is a direct link to node 6. Thus, the complete route from node 1 to node 6 is 1-4-5-6.

From this overall matrix, routing tables can be developed and stored at each node. From the reasoning in the preceding paragraph, it follows that each node need only store a single column of the routing directory. The node's directory shows the next node to take for each destination.

With fixed routing, there is no difference between routing for datagrams and virtual circuits. All packets from a given source to a given destination follow the same route. The advantage of fixed routing is its simplicity, and it should work well in a reliable network with a stable load. Its disadvantage is its lack of flexibility. It does not react to network congestion or failures.

A refinement to fixed routing that would accommodate link and node outages would be to supply the nodes with an alternate next node for each destination. For example, the alternate next nodes in the node 1 directory might be 4, 3, 2, 3, 3.

FLOODING   Another simple routing technique is flooding. This technique requires no network information whatsoever and works as follows. A packet is sent by a source node to every one of its neighbors. At each node, an incoming packet is retransmitted on all outgoing links except for the link on which it arrived. For example, if node 1 in Figure 19.1 has a packet to send to node 6, it sends a copy of that packet (with a destination address of 6) to nodes 2, 3, and 4. Node 2 will send a copy to nodes 3 and 4. Node 4 will send a copy to nodes 2, 3, and 5. And so it goes. Eventually, a number of copies of the packet will arrive at node 6. The packet must have some unique identifier (e.g., source node and sequence number, or virtual circuit number and sequence number) so that node 6 knows to discard all but the first copy.

Unless something is done to stop the incessant retransmission of packets, the number of packets in circulation just from a single source packet grows without bound. One way to prevent this is for each node to remember the identity of those packets it has already retransmitted. When duplicate copies of the packet arrive, they are discarded. A simpler technique is to include a hop count field with each packet. The count can originally be set to some maximum value, such as the diameter (length of the longest minimum-hop path through the network)[2] of the network. Each time a node passes on a packet, it decrements the count by one. When the count reaches zero, the packet is discarded.

EXAMPLE 19.3 An example of the latter tactic is shown in Figure 19.3. The label on each packet in the figure indicates the current value of the hop count field in that packet. A packet is to be sent from node 1 to node 6 and is assigned a hop count of 3. On the first hop, three copies of the packet are created, and the hop count is decrement to 2. For the second hop of all these copies, a total of nine copies are created. One of these copies reaches node 6, which recognizes that it is the intended destination and does not retransmit. However, the other nodes generate a total of 22 new copies for their third and final hop. Each packet now has a hop count of 1. Note that if a node is not keeping track of packet identifier, it may generate multiple copies at this third stage. All packets received from the third hop are discarded, because the hop count is exhausted. In all, node 6 has received four additional copies of the packet.

The flooding technique has three remarkable properties:

- All possible routes between source and destination are tried. Thus, no matter what link or node outages have occurred, a packet will always get through if at least one path between source and destination exists.

- Because all routes are tried, at least one copy of the packet to arrive at the destination will have used a minimum-hop route.

- All nodes that are directly or indirectly connected to the source node are visited.

---

[2]For each pair of end systems attached to the network, there is a minimum-hop path. The length of the longest such minimum-hop path is the diameter of the network.

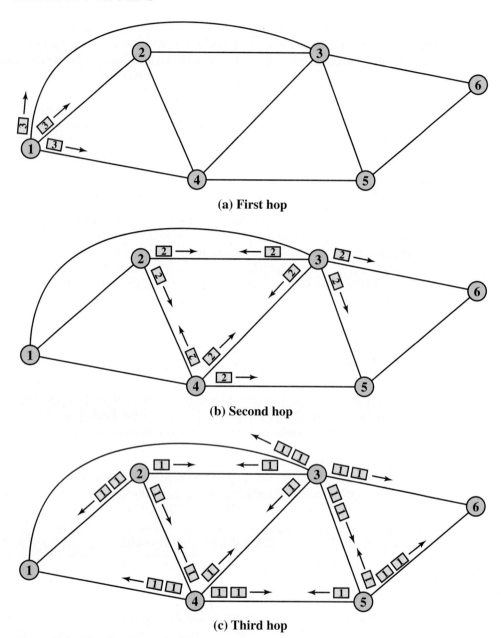

(a) First hop

(b) Second hop

(c) Third hop

Figure 19.3   Flooding Example (hop count = 3)

Because of the first property, the flooding technique is highly robust and could be used to send emergency messages. An example application is a military network that is subject to extensive damage. Because of the second property, flooding might be used initially to set up the route for a virtual circuit. The third property suggests that flooding can be useful for the dissemination of important information to all nodes; we will see that it is used in some schemes to disseminate routing information.

The principal disadvantage of flooding is the high traffic load that it generates, which is directly proportional to the connectivity of the network. Another disadvantage is that every node sees the routing data, which may create a security concern.

RANDOM ROUTING   Random routing has the simplicity and robustness of flooding with far less traffic load. With random routing, a node selects only one outgoing path for retransmission of an incoming packet. The outgoing link is chosen at random, excluding the link on which the packet arrived. If all links are equally likely to be chosen, then a node may simply utilize outgoing links in a round-robin fashion.

A refinement of this technique is to assign a probability to each outgoing link and to select the link based on that probability. The probability could be based on data rate, in which case we have:

$$P_i = \frac{R_i}{\sum_j R_j}$$

where

P_i = probability of selecting link i

R_i = data rate on link i

The sum is taken over all candidate outgoing links. This scheme should provide good traffic distribution. Note that the probabilities could also be based on fixed link costs.

Like flooding, random routing requires the use of no network information. Because the route taken is random, the actual route will typically be neither the least-cost route nor the minimum-hop route. Thus, the network must carry a higher-than-optimum traffic load, although not nearly as high as for flooding.

ADAPTIVE ROUTING   In virtually all packet-switching networks, some sort of adaptive routing technique is used. That is, the routing decisions that are made change as conditions on the network change. The principal conditions that influence routing decisions are given:

- **Failure:** When a node or link fails, it can no longer be used as part of a route.
- **Congestion:** When a particular portion of the network is heavily congested, it is desirable to route packets around rather than through the area of congestion.

For adaptive routing to be possible, information about the state of the network must be exchanged among the nodes. There are several drawbacks associated with the use of adaptive routing, compared to fixed routing:

- The routing decision is more complex; therefore, the processing burden on network nodes increases.
- In most cases, adaptive strategies depend on status information that is collected at one place but used at another. There is a trade-off here between the quality of the information and the amount of overhead. The more information that is exchanged, and the more frequently it is exchanged, the better will be the routing decisions that each node makes. On the other hand, this

information is itself a load on the constituent networks, causing a performance degradation.

- An adaptive strategy may react too quickly, causing congestion-producing oscillation, or too slowly, being irrelevant.

Despite these real dangers, adaptive routing strategies are by far the most prevalent, for two reasons:

- An adaptive routing strategy can improve performance, as seen by the network user.
- An adaptive routing strategy can aid in congestion control, which is discussed in Chapter 20. Because an adaptive routing strategy tends to balance loads, it can delay the onset of severe congestion.

These benefits may or may not be realized, depending on the soundness of the design and the nature of the load. By and large, adaptive routing is an extraordinarily complex task to perform properly. As demonstration of this, most major packet-switching networks, such as ARPANET and its successors, and many commercial networks, have endured at least one major overhaul of their routing strategy.

A convenient way to classify adaptive routing strategies is on the basis of information source: local, adjacent nodes, all nodes. An example of an adaptive routing strategy that relies only on local information is one in which a node routes each packet to the outgoing link with the shortest queue length, Q. This would have the effect of balancing the load on outgoing links. However, some outgoing links may not be headed in the correct general direction. We can improve matters by also taking into account preferred direction, much as with random routing. In this case, each link emanating from the node would have a bias B_i, for each destination i, such that lower values of B_i indicate more preferred directions. For each incoming packet headed for node i, the node would choose the outgoing link that minimizes $Q + B_i$. Thus a node would tend to send packets in the right direction, with a concession made to current traffic delays.

> **EXAMPLE 19.4** Figure 19.4 shows the status of node 4 of Figure 19.1 at a certain point in time. Node 4 has links to four other nodes. Packets have been arriving and a backlog has built up, with a queue of packets waiting for each of the outgoing links. A packet arrives from node 1 destined for node 6. To which outgoing link should the packet be routed? Based on current queue lengths and the values of bias (B_6) for each outgoing link, the minimum value of $Q + B_6$ is 4, on the link to node 3. Thus, node 4 routes the packet through node 3.

Adaptive schemes based only on local information are rarely used because they do not exploit easily available information. Strategies based on information from adjacent nodes or all nodes are commonly found. Both take advantage of information that each node has about delays and outages that it experiences.

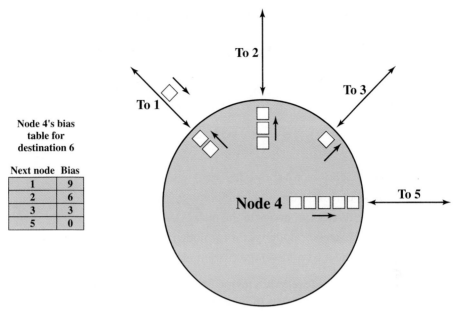

**Node 4's bias
table for
destination 6**

Next node	Bias
1	9
2	6
3	3
5	0

Figure 19.4 Example of Isolated Adaptive Routing

Such adaptive strategies can be either distributed or centralized. In the distributed case, each node exchanges delay information with other nodes. Based on incoming information, a node tries to estimate the delay situation throughout the network, and applies a least-cost routing algorithm. In the centralized case, each node reports its link delay status to a central node, which designs routes based on this incoming information and sends the routing information back to the nodes.

19.2 EXAMPLES: ROUTING IN ARPANET

In this section, we look at several examples of routing strategies. All of these were initially developed for ARPANET, which is a packet-switching network that was the foundation of the present-day Internet. It is instructive to examine these strategies for several reasons. First, these strategies and similar ones are also used in other packet-switching networks, including a number of networks on the Internet. Second, routing schemes based on the ARPANET work have also been used for internetwork routing in the Internet and in private internetworks. And finally, the ARPANET routing scheme evolved in a way that illuminates some of the key design issues related to routing algorithms.

First Generation—Distance Vector Routing

The original routing algorithm, designed in 1969, was a distributed adaptive algorithm using estimated delay as the performance criterion and a version of the Bellman–Ford algorithm (Section 19.4). The approach used is referred to as **distance-vector routing**. For this algorithm, each node maintains two vectors:

$$D_i = \begin{bmatrix} d_{i1} \\ \bullet \\ \bullet \\ \bullet \\ d_{iN} \end{bmatrix} \qquad S_i = \begin{bmatrix} s_{i1} \\ \bullet \\ \bullet \\ \bullet \\ s_{iN} \end{bmatrix}$$

Where

D_i = delay vector for node i

d_{ij} = current estimate of minimum delay from node i to node j ($d_{ii} = 0$)

N = number of nodes in the network

S_i = successor node vector for node i

s_{ij} = the next node in the current minimum-delay route from i to j

Periodically (every 128 ms), each node exchanges its delay vector with all of its neighbors. On the basis of all incoming delay vectors, a node k updates both of its vectors as follows:

$$d_{kj} = \min_{i \in A} [d_{ij} + l_{ki}]$$

$$s_{kj} = i \quad \text{using } i \text{ that minimizes the preceding expression}$$

where

A = set of neighbor nodes for k

l_{ki} = current estimate of delay from k to i

EXAMPLE 19.5 Figure 19.5 shows the data structures of the original ARPANET algorithm, using the network of Figure 19.6. This is the same network as that of Figure 19.1, with some of the link costs having different values (and assuming the same cost in both directions). Figure 19.5a shows the routing table for node 1 at an instant in time that reflects the link costs of Figure 19.6. For each destination, a delay is specified, and the next node on the route that produces that delay. At some point, the link costs change to those of Figure 19.1. Assume that node 1's neighbors (nodes 2, 3, and 4) learn of the change before node 1. Each of these nodes updates its delay vector and sends a copy to all of its neighbors, including node 1 (Figure 19.5b). Node 1 discards its current routing table and builds a new one, based solely on the incoming delay vector and its own estimate of link delay to each of its neighbors. The result is shown in Figure 19.5c.

The estimated link delay is simply the queue length for that link. Thus, in building a new routing table, the node will tend to favor outgoing links with shorter queues. This tends to balance the load on outgoing links. However, because queue lengths vary rapidly with time, the distributed perception of the shortest route could

Desti-nation	Delay	Next node			
1	0	—	3	7	5
2	2	2	0	4	2
3	5	3	3	0	2
4	1	4	2	2	0
5	6	3	3	1	1
6	8	3	5	3	3
	D_1	S_1	D_2	D_3	D_4

Desti-nation	Delay	Next node
1	0	—
2	2	2
3	3	4
4	1	4
5	2	4
6	4	4

$$I_{1,2} = 2$$
$$I_{1,3} = 5$$
$$I_{1,4} = 1$$

(a) Node 1's routing table before update

(b) Delay vectors sent to node 1 from neighbor nodes

(c) Node 1's routing table after update and link costs used in update

Figure 19.5   Original ARPANET Routing Algorithm

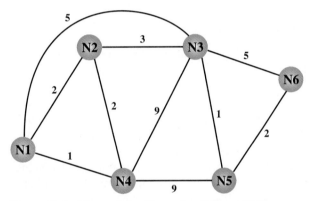

Figure 19.6   Network for Example of Figure 19.5a

change while a packet is en route. This could lead to a thrashing situation in which a packet continues to seek out areas of low congestion rather than aiming at the destination.

Second Generation—Link-State Routing

After some years of experience and several minor modifications, the original routing algorithm was replaced by quite a different one in 1979 [MCQU80]. The major shortcomings of the old algorithm were these:

- The algorithm did not consider line speed, merely queue length. Thus, higher-capacity links were not given the favored status they deserved.
- Queue length is, in any case, an artificial measure of delay, because some variable amount of processing time elapses between the arrival of a packet at a node and its placement in an outbound queue.
- The algorithm was not very accurate. In particular, it responded slowly to congestion and delay increases.

The new algorithm is also a distributed adaptive one, using delay as the performance criterion, but the differences are significant. Rather than using queue length as a surrogate for delay, the delay is measured directly. At a node, each incoming packet is timestamped with an arrival time. A departure time is recorded when the packet is transmitted. If a positive acknowledgment is returned, the delay for that packet is recorded as the departure time minus the arrival time plus transmission time and propagation delay. The node must therefore know link data rate and propagation time. If a negative acknowledgment comes back, the departure time is updated and the node tries again, until a measure of successful transmission delay is obtained.

Every 10 s, the node computes the average delay on each outgoing link. If there are any significant changes in delay, the information is sent to all other nodes using flooding. Each node maintains an estimate of delay on every network link. When new information arrives, it recomputes its routing table using Dijkstra's algorithm (Section 19.4).

The second-generation routing algorithm is referred to as a **link-state routing** algorithm.

Third Generation

Experience with this new strategy indicated that it was more responsive and stable than the old one. The overhead induced by flooding was moderate because each node does this at most once every 10 s. However, as the load on the network grew, a shortcoming in the new strategy began to appear, and the strategy was revised in 1987 [KHAN89].

The problem with the second strategy is the assumption that the measured packet delay on a link is a good predictor of the link delay encountered after all nodes reroute their traffic based on this reported delay. Thus, it is an effective routing mechanism only if there is some correlation between the reported values and those actually experienced after rerouting. This correlation tends to be rather high under light and moderate traffic loads. However, under heavy loads, there is little correlation. Therefore, immediately after all nodes have made routing updates, the routing tables are obsolete!

As an example, consider a network that consists of two regions with only two links, A and B, connecting the two regions (Figure 19.7). Each route between two nodes in different regions must pass through one of these links. Assume that a situation develops in which most of the traffic is on link A. This will cause the link delay on A to be significant, and at the next opportunity, this delay value will be reported to all other nodes. These updates will arrive at all nodes at about the same time, and all will update their routing tables immediately. It is likely that this new delay value for link A will be high enough to make link B the preferred choice for most, if not all, interregion routes. Because all nodes adjust their routes at the same time, most or all interregion traffic shifts at the same time to link B. Now the link delay value on B will become high, and there will be a subsequent shift to link A. This oscillation will continue until the traffic volume subsides.

There are a number of reasons why this oscillation is undesirable:

- A significant portion of available capacity is unused at just the time when it is needed most: under heavy traffic load.
- The overutilization of some links can lead to the spread of congestion within the network (this will be seen in the discussion of congestion in Chapter 20).

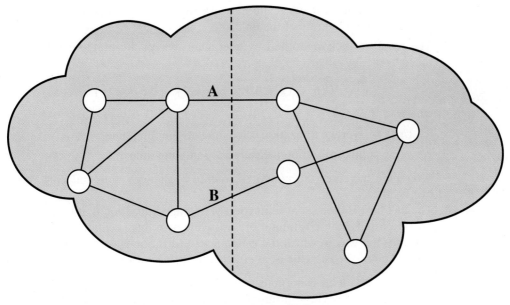

Figure 19.7   Packet-Switching Network Subject to Oscillations

- The large swings in measured delay values result in the need for more frequent routing update messages. This increases the load on the network at just the time when the network is already stressed.

The ARPANET designers concluded that the essence of the problem was that every node was trying to obtain the best route for all destinations, and that these efforts conflicted. It was concluded that under heavy loads, the goal of routing should be to give the average route a good path instead of attempting to give all routes the best path.

The designers decided that it was unnecessary to change the overall routing algorithm. Rather, it was sufficient to change the function that calculates link costs. This was done in such a way as to damp routing oscillations and reduce routing overhead. The calculation begins with measuring the average delay over the last 10 s. This value is then transformed with the following steps:

1. Using a simple single-server queueing model, the measured delay is transformed into an estimate of link utilization. From queueing theory, utilization can be expressed as a function of delay as follows:

$$\rho = \frac{2(T_s - T)}{T_s - 2T}$$

where
ρ = link utilization
T = measured delay
T_s = service time

2. The service time was set at the network-wide average packet size (600 bits) divided by the data rate of the link.

3. The result is then smoothed by averaging it with the previous estimate of utilization:

$$U(n + 1) = 0.5 \times \rho(n + 1) + 0.5 \times U(n)$$

where

$U(n)$ = average utilization calculated at sampling time n

$\rho(n)$ = link utilization measured at sampling time n

Averaging increases the period of routing oscillations, thus reducing routing overhead.

4. The link cost is then set as a function of average utilization that is designed to provide a reasonable estimate of cost while avoiding oscillation. Figure 19.8 indicates the way in which the estimate of utilization is converted into a cost value. The final cost value is, in effect, a transformed value of delay.

In Figure 19.8, delay is normalized to the value achieved on an idle line, which is just propagation delay plus transmission time. One curve on the figure indicates the way in which the actual delay rises as a function of utilization; the increase in delay is due to queueing delay at the node. For the revised algorithm, the cost value is kept at the minimum value until a given level of utilization is reached. This feature has the effect of reducing routing overhead at low traffic levels. Above a certain level of utilization, the cost level is allowed to rise to a maximum value that is equal to three times the minimum value. The effect of this maximum value is to dictate that traffic should not be routed around a heavily utilized line by more than two additional hops.

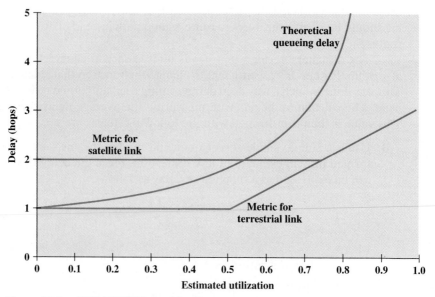

Figure 19.8   ARPANET Delay Metrics

Note that the minimum threshold is set higher for satellite links. This encourages the use of terrestrial links under conditions of light traffic, because the terrestrial links have much lower propagation delay. Note also that the actual delay curve is much steeper than the transformation curves at high utilization levels. It is this steep rise in link cost that causes all of the traffic on a link to be shed, which in turn causes routing oscillations.

In summary, the revised cost function is keyed to utilization rather than delay. The function acts similar to a delay-based metric under light loads and to a capacity-based metric under heavy loads.

19.3 INTERNET ROUTING PROTOCOLS

The routers in an internet are responsible for receiving and forwarding packets through the interconnected set of networks. Each router makes routing decision based on knowledge of the topology and traffic/delay conditions of the internet. In a simple internet, a fixed routing scheme is possible. In more complex internets, a degree of dynamic cooperation is needed among the routers. In particular, the router must avoid portions of the network that have failed and portions of the network that are congested. To make such dynamic routing decisions, routers exchange routing information using a special routing protocol for that purpose. Information is needed about the status of the internet, in terms of which networks can be reached by which routes, and the delay characteristics of various routes.

In considering the routing function, it is important to distinguish two concepts:

- **Routing information:** Information about the topology and delays of the internet
- **Routing algorithm:** The algorithm used to make a routing decision for a particular datagram, based on current routing information

Autonomous Systems

To proceed with our discussion of routing protocols, we need to introduce the concept of an **autonomous system (AS)**. An AS exhibits the following characteristics:

1. An AS is a set of routers and networks managed by a single organization.
2. An AS consists of a group of routers exchanging information via a common routing protocol.
3. Except in times of failure, an AS is connected (in a graph-theoretic sense); that is, there is a path between any pair of nodes.

A shared routing protocol, which we shall refer to as an **interior router protocol (IRP)**, passes routing information between routers within an AS. The protocol used within the AS does not need to be implemented outside of the system. This flexibility allows IRPs to be custom tailored to specific applications and requirements.

It may happen, however, that an internet will be constructed of more than one AS. For example, all of the LANs at a site, such as an office complex or campus, could be linked by routers to form an AS. This system might be linked through a

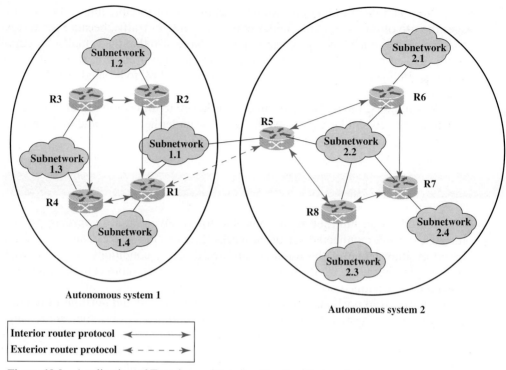

Figure 19.9 Application of Exterior and Interior Routing Protocols

wide area network to other ASs. The situation is illustrated in Figure 19.9. In this case, the routing algorithms and information in routing tables used by routers in different ASs may differ. Nevertheless, the routers in one AS need at least a minimal level of information concerning networks outside the system that can be reached. We refer to the protocol used to pass routing information between routers in different ASs as an **exterior router protocol (ERP)**.[3]

We can expect that an ERP will need to pass less information than an IRP for the following reason. If a datagram is to be transferred from a host in one AS to a host in another AS, a router in the first system need only determine the target AS and devise a route to get into that target system. Once the datagram enters the target AS, the routers within that system can cooperate to deliver the datagram; the ERP is not concerned with, and does not know about, the details of the route followed within the target AS.

In the remainder of this section, we look at what are perhaps the most important examples of these two types of routing protocols: **Border Gateway Protocol (BGP)** and **Open Shortest Path First (OSPF)** Protocol. But first, it is useful to look at a different way of characterizing routing protocols.

---

[3]In the literature, the terms *interior gateway protocol* (IGP) and *exterior gateway protocol* (EGP) are often used for what are referred to here as IRP and ERP. However, because the terms *IGP* and *EGP* also refer to specific protocols, we avoid their use when referring to general concepts.

Approaches to Routing

Internet routing protocols employ one of three approaches to gathering and using routing information: distance-vector routing, link-state routing, and path-vector routing.

Distance-vector routing requires that each node (router or host that implements the routing protocol) exchange information with its neighboring nodes. Two nodes are said to be neighbors if they are both directly connected to the same network. This approach is that used in the first-generation routing algorithm for ARPANET, as described in Section 19.2. For this purpose, each node maintains a vector of link costs for each directly attached network and distance and next-hop vectors for each destination. The relatively simple Routing Information Protocol (RIP) uses this approach.

Distance-vector routing requires the transmission of a considerable amount of information by each router. Each router must send a distance vector to all of its neighbors, and that vector contains the estimated path cost to all networks in the configuration. Furthermore, when there is a significant change in a link cost or when a link is unavailable, it may take a considerable amount of time for this information to propagate through the internet.

Link-state routing is designed to overcome the drawbacks of distance-vector routing. When a router is initialized, it determines the link cost on each of its network interfaces. The router then advertises this set of link costs to all other routers in the internet topology, not just neighboring routers. From then on, the router monitors its link costs. Whenever there is a significant change (e.g., a link cost increases or decreases substantially, a new link is created, or an existing link becomes unavailable), the router again advertises its set of link costs to all other routers in the configuration.

Because each router receives the link costs of all routers in the configuration, each router can construct the topology of the entire configuration and then calculate the shortest path to each destination network. Having done this, the router can construct its routing table, listing the first hop to each destination. Because the router has a representation of the entire network, it does not use a distributed version of a routing algorithm, as is done in distance-vector routing. Rather, the router can use any routing algorithm to determine the shortest paths. In practice, Dijkstra's algorithm is used. The OSPF protocol is an example of a routing protocol that uses link-state routing. The second-generation routing algorithm for ARPANET also uses this approach.

Both link-state and distance-vector approaches have been used for interior router protocols. Neither approach is effective for an exterior router protocol.

In a distance-vector routing protocol, each router advertises to its neighbors a vector listing each network it can reach, together with a distance metric associated with the path to that network. Each router builds up a routing database on the basis of these neighbor updates but does not know the identity of intermediate routers and networks on any particular path. There are two problems with this approach for an exterior router protocol:

1. This distance-vector protocol assumes that all routers share a common distance metric with which to judge router preferences. This may not be the case among different ASs. If different routers attach different meanings to a given metric, it may not be possible to create stable, loop-free routes.

2. A given AS may have different priorities from other ASs and may have restrictions that prohibit the use of certain other AS. A distance-vector algorithm gives no information about the ASs that will be visited along a route.

In a link-state routing protocol, each router advertises its link metrics to all other routers. Each router builds up a picture of the complete topology of the configuration and then performs a routing calculation. This approach also has problems if used in an exterior router protocol:

1. Different ASs may use different metrics and have different restrictions. Although the link-state protocol does allow a router to build up a picture of the entire topology, the metrics used may vary from one AS to another, making it impossible to perform a consistent routing algorithm.

2. The flooding of link-state information to all routers implementing an exterior router protocol across multiple ASs may be unmanageable.

An alternative, known as **path-vector routing**, is to dispense with routing metrics and simply provide information about which networks can be reached by a given router and the ASs that must be crossed to get there. The approach differs from a distance-vector algorithm in two respects: First, the path-vector approach does not include a distance or cost estimate. Second, each block of routing information lists all of the ASs visited in order to reach the destination network by this route.

Because a path vector lists the ASs that a datagram must traverse if it follows this route, the path information enables a router to perform policy routing. That is, a router may decide to avoid a particular path in order to avoid transiting a particular AS. For example, information that is confidential may be limited to certain kinds of ASs. Or a router may have information about the performance or quality of the portion of the internet that is included in an AS that leads the router to avoid that AS. Examples of performance or quality metrics include link speed, capacity, tendency to become congested, and overall quality of operation. Another criterion that could be used is minimizing the number of transit ASs.

Border Gateway Protocol

BGP was developed for use in conjunction with internets that employ the TCP/IP suite, although the concepts are applicable to any internet. BGP has become the preferred exterior router protocol for the Internet.

FUNCTIONS BGP was designed to allow routers, called gateways in the standard, in different autonomous systems (ASs) to cooperate in the exchange of routing information. The protocol operates in terms of messages, which are sent over TCP connections. The repertoire of messages is summarized in Table 19.2. The current version of BGP is known as BGP-4 (RFC 4271).

Three functional procedures are involved in BGP:

- Neighbor acquisition
- Neighbor reachability
- Network reachability

Table 19.2 BGP-4 Messages

Open	Used to open a neighbor relationship with another router.
Update	Used to (1) transmit information about a single route and/or (2) list multiple routes to be withdrawn.
Keepalive	Used to (1) acknowledge an Open message and (2) periodically confirm the neighbor relationship.
Notification	Send when an error condition is detected.

Two routers are considered to be neighbors if they are attached to the same network. If the two routers are in different autonomous systems, they may wish to exchange routing information. For this purpose, it is necessary first to perform **neighbor acquisition**. In essence, neighbor acquisition occurs when two neighboring routers in different autonomous systems agree to exchange routing information regularly. A formal acquisition procedure is needed because one of the routers may not wish to participate. For example, the router may be overburdened and does not want to be responsible for traffic coming in from outside the system. In the neighbor acquisition process, one router sends a request message to the other, which may either accept or refuse the offer. The protocol does not address the issue of how one router knows the address or even the existence of another router nor how it decides that it needs to exchange routing information with that particular router. These issues must be dealt with at configuration time or by active intervention of a network manager.

To perform neighbor acquisition, two routers send Open messages to each other after a TCP connection is established. If each router accepts the request, it returns a Keepalive message in response.

Once a neighbor relationship is established, the **neighbor reachability** procedure is used to maintain the relationship. Each partner needs to be assured that the other partner still exists and is still engaged in the neighbor relationship. For this purpose, the two routers periodically issue Keepalive messages to each other.

The final procedure specified by BGP is **network reachability**. Each router maintains a database of the networks that it can reach and the preferred route for reaching each network. When a change is made to this database, the router issues an Update message that is broadcast to all other routers implementing BGP. Because the Update message is broadcast, all BGP routers can build up and maintain their routing information.

BGP MESSAGES Figure 19.10 illustrates the formats of all of the BGP messages. Each message begins with a 19-octet header containing three fields, as indicated by the shaded portion of each message in the figure:

- **Marker:** Reserved for authentication. The sender may insert a value in this field that would be used as part of an authentication mechanism to enable the recipient to verify the identity of the sender.
- **Length:** Length of message in octets.
- **Type:** Type of message: Open, Update, Notification, Keepalive.

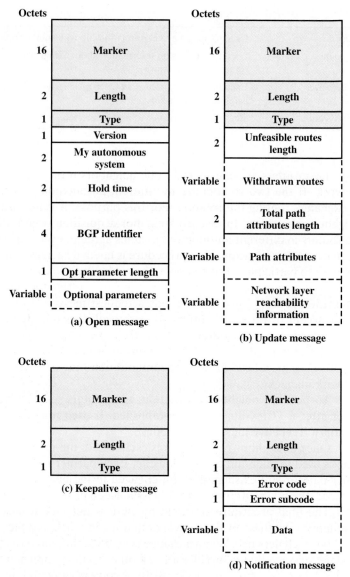

Figure 19.10   BGP Message Formats

To acquire a neighbor, a router first opens a TCP connection to the neighbor router of interest. It then sends an Open message. This message identifies the AS to which the sender belongs and provides the IP address of the router. It also includes a Hold Time parameter, which indicates the number of seconds that the sender proposes for the value of the Hold Timer. If the recipient is prepared to open a neighbor relationship, it calculates a value of Hold Timer that is the minimum of its Hold Time and the Hold Time in the Open message. This calculated value is the maximum number of seconds that may elapse between the receipt of successive Keepalive and/or Update messages by the sender.

The Keepalive message consists simply of the header. Each router issues these messages to each of its peers often enough to prevent the Hold Timer from expiring.

The Update message communicates two types of information:

- Information about a single route through the internet. This information is available to be added to the database of any recipient router.
- A list of routes previously advertised by this router that are being withdrawn.

An Update message may contain one or both types of information. Information about a single route through the network involves three fields: the Network Layer Reachability Information (NLRI) field, the Total Path Attributes Length field, and the Path Attributes field. The NLRI field consists of a list of identifiers of networks that can be reached by this route. Each network is identified by its IP address, which is actually a portion of a full IP address. Recall that an IP address is a 32-bit quantity of the form {network, host}. The left-hand or prefix portion of this quantity identifies a particular network.

The Path Attributes field contains a list of attributes that apply to this particular route. The following are the defined attributes:

- **Origin:** Indicates whether this information was generated by an interior router protocol (e.g., OSPF) or an exterior router protocol (in particular, BGP).
- **AS_Path:** A list of the ASs that are traversed for this route.
- **Next_Hop:** The IP address of the border router that should be used as the next hop to the destinations listed in the NLRI field.
- **Multi_Exit_Disc:** Used to communicate some information about routes internal to an AS. This is described later in this section.
- **Local_Pref:** Used by a router to inform other routers within the same AS of its degree of preference for a particular route. It has no significance to routers in other ASs.
- **Atomic_Aggregate, Aggregator:** These two fields implement the concept of route aggregation. In essence, an internet and its corresponding address space can be organized hierarchically (i.e., as a tree). In this case, network addresses are structured in two or more parts. All of the networks of a given subtree share a common partial internet address. Using this common partial address, the amount of information that must be communicated in NLRI can be significantly reduced.

The AS_Path attribute actually serves two purposes. Because it lists the ASs that a datagram must traverse if it follows this route, the AS_Path information enables a router to implement routing policies. That is, a router may decide to avoid a particular path to avoid transiting a particular AS. For example, information that is confidential may be limited to certain kinds of ASs. Or a router may have information about the performance or quality of the portion of the internet that is included in an AS that leads the router to avoid that AS. Examples of performance or quality metrics include link speed, capacity, tendency to become congested, and overall quality of operation. Another criterion that could be used is minimizing the number of transit ASs.

The reader may wonder about the purpose of the Next_Hop attribute. The requesting router will necessarily want to know which networks are reachable via the responding router, but why provide information about other routers? This is best explained with reference to Figure 19.9. In this example, router R1 in autonomous system 1 and router R5 in autonomous system 2 implement BGP and acquire a neighbor relationship. R1 issues Update messages to R5, indicating which networks it can reach and the distances (network hops) involved. R1 also provides the same information on behalf of R2. That is, R1 tells R5 what networks are reachable via R2. In this example, R2 does not implement BGP. Typically, most of the routers in an autonomous system will not implement BGP. Only a few routers will be assigned responsibility for communicating with routers in other autonomous systems. A final point: R1 is in possession of the necessary information about R2, because R1 and R2 share an interior router protocol.

The second type of update information is the withdrawal of one or more routes. In this case, the route is identified by the IP address of the destination network.

Finally, the Notification message is sent when an error condition is detected. The following errors may be reported:

- **Message header error:** Includes authentication and syntax errors.
- **Open message error:** Includes syntax errors and options not recognized in an Open message. This message can also be used to indicate that a proposed Hold Time in an Open message is unacceptable.
- **Update message error:** Includes syntax and validity errors in an Update message.
- **Hold timer expired:** If the sending router has not received successive Keepalive and/or Update and/or Notification messages within the Hold Time period, then this error is communicated and the connection is closed.
- **Finite state machine error:** Includes any procedural error.
- **Cease:** Used by a router to close a connection with another router in the absence of any other error.

BGP ROUTING INFORMATION EXCHANGE The essence of BGP is the exchange of routing information among participating routers in multiple ASs. This process can be quite complex. In what follows, we provide a simplified overview.

Let us consider router R1 in autonomous system 1 (AS1), in Figure 19.9. To begin, a router that implements BGP will also implement an internal routing protocol such as OSPF. Using OSPF, R1 can exchange routing information with other routers within AS1 and build up a picture of the topology of the networks and routers in AS1 and construct a routing table. Next, R1 can issue an Update message to R5 in AS2. The Update message could include the following:

- **AS_Path:** The identity of AS1
- **Next_Hop:** The IP address of R1
- **NLRI:** A list of all of the networks in AS1

This message informs R5 that all of the networks listed in NLRI are reachable via R1 and that the only autonomous system traversed is AS1.

Suppose now that R5 also has a neighbor relationship with another router in another autonomous system, say R9 in AS3. R5 will forward the information just received from R1 to R9 in a new Update message. This message includes the following:

- **AS_Path:** The list of identifiers {AS2, AS1}

- **Next_Hop:** The IP address of R5
- **NLRI:** A list of all of the networks in AS1

This message informs R9 that all of the networks listed in NLRI are reachable via R5 and that the autonomous systems traversed are AS2 and AS1. R9 must now decide if this is its preferred route to the networks listed. It may have knowledge of an alternate route to some or all of these networks that it prefers for reasons of performance or some other policy metric. If R9 decides that the route provided in R5's update message is preferable, then R9 incorporates that routing information into its routing database and forwards this new routing information to other neighbors. This new message will include an AS_Path field of {AS3, AS2, AS1}.

In this fashion, routing update information is propagated through the larger internet, consisting of a number of interconnected autonomous systems. The AS_Path field is used to assure that such messages do not circulate indefinitely: If an Update message is received by a router in an AS that is included in the AS_Path field, that router will not forward the update information to other routers.

Routers within the same AS, called internal neighbors, may exchange BGP information. In this case, the sending router does not add the identifier of the common AS to the AS_Path field. When a router has selected a preferred route to an external destination, it transmits this route to all of its internal neighbors. Each of these routers then decides if the new route is preferred, in which case the new route is added to its database and a new Update message goes out.

When there are multiple entry points into an AS that are available to a border router in another AS, the Multi_Exit_Disc attribute may be used to choose among them. This attribute contains a number that reflects some internal metric for reaching destinations within an AS. For example, suppose in Figure 19.9 that both R1 and R2 implement BGP and both have a neighbor relationship with R5. Each provides an Update message to R5 for network 1.3 that includes a routing metric used internal to AS1, such as a routing metric associated with the OSPF internal router protocol. R5 could then use these two metrics as the basis for choosing between the two routes.

Open Shortest Path First (OSPF) Protocol

The OSPF protocol (RFC 2328) is now widely used as the interior router protocol in TCP/IP networks. OSPF computes a route through the internet that incurs the least cost based on a user-configurable metric of cost. The user can configure the cost to express a function of delay, data rate, dollar cost, or other factors. OSPF is able to equalize loads over multiple equal-cost paths.

Each router maintains a database that reflects the known topology of the autonomous system of which it is a part. The topology is expressed as a directed graph. The graph consists of the following:

- Vertices, or nodes, of two types:
  1. Router
  2. Network, which is in turn of two types
     a. transit, if it can carry data that neither originate nor terminate on an end system attached to this network
     b. stub, if it is not a transit network

- Edges are of two types:
  1. Graph edges that connect two router vertices when the corresponding routers are connected to each other by a direct point-to-point link
  2. Graph edges that connect a router vertex to a network vertex when the router is directly connected to the network

Figure 19.11, based on one in RFC 2328, shows an example of an autonomous system, and Figure 19.12 is the resulting directed graph. The mapping is straightforward:

- Two routers joined by a point-to-point link are represented in the graph as being directly connected by a pair of edges, one in each direction (e.g., routers 6 and 10).
- When multiple routers are attached to a network (such as a LAN or packet-switching network), the directed graph shows all routers bidirectionally

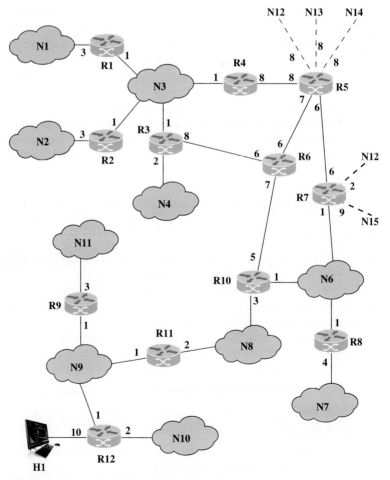

Figure 19.11 A Sample Autonomous System

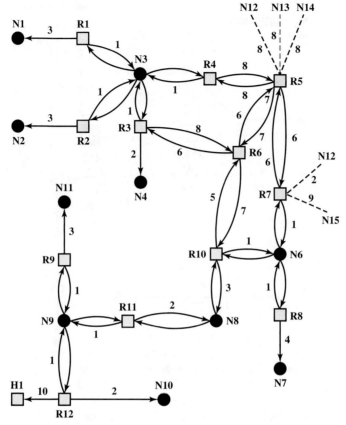

Figure 19.12 Directed Graph of Autonomous System of Figure 19.11

connected to the network vertex (e.g., routers 1, 2, 3, and 4 all connect to network 3).

- If a single router is attached to a network, the network will appear in the graph as a stub connection (e.g., network 7).

- An end system, called a host, can be directly connected to a router, in which case it is depicted in the corresponding graph (e.g., host 1).

- If a router is connected to other autonomous systems, then the path cost to each network in the other system must be obtained by some exterior router protocol. Each such network is represented on the graph by a stub and an edge to the router with the known path cost (e.g., networks 12 through 15).

A cost is associated with the output side of each router interface. This cost is configurable by the system administrator. Arcs on the graph are labeled with the cost of the corresponding router output interface. Arcs having no labeled cost have a cost of 0. Note that arcs leading from networks to routers always have a cost of 0.

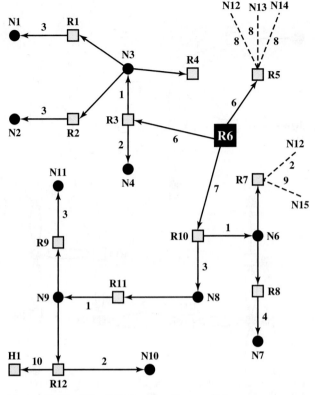

Figure 19.13 The SPF Tree for Router R6

A database corresponding to the directed graph is maintained by each router. It is pieced together from link-state messages from other routers in the internet. Using Dijkstra's algorithm (see Section 19.4), a router calculates the least-cost path to all destination networks. The result for router 6 of Figure 19.11 is shown as a tree in Figure 19.13, with R6 as the root of the tree. The tree gives the entire route to any destination network or host. However, only the next hop to the destination is used in the forwarding process. The resulting routing table for router 6 is shown in Table 19.3. The table includes entries for routers advertising external routes (routers 5 and 7). For external networks whose identity is known, entries are also provided.

19.4 LEAST-COST ALGORITHMS

Virtually all packet-switching networks and all internets base their routing decision on some form of least-cost criterion. If the criterion is to minimize the number of hops, each link has a value of 1. More typically, the link value is inversely proportional to the link capacity, proportional to the current load on the link, or some

Table 19.3   Routing Table for R6

Destination	Next Hop	Distance
N1	R3	10
N2	R3	10
N3	R3	7
N4	R3	8
N6	R10	8
N7	R10	12
N8	R10	10
N9	R10	11
N10	R10	13
N11	R10	14
H1	R10	21
R5	R5	6
R7	R10	8
N12	R10	10
N13	R5	14
N14	R5	14
N15	R10	17

combination. In any case, these link or hop costs are used as input to a least-cost routing algorithm, which can be simply stated as:

> Given a network of nodes connected by bidirectional links, where each link has a cost associated with it in each direction, define the cost of a path between two nodes as the sum of the costs of the links traversed. For each pair of nodes, find a path with the least cost.

Note that the cost of a link may differ in its two directions. This would be true, for example, if the cost of a link equaled the length of the queue of packets awaiting transmission from each of the two nodes on the link.

Most least-cost routing algorithms in use in packet-switching networks and internets are variations of one of two common algorithms, known as Dijkstra's algorithm and the Bellman–Ford algorithm. This section provides a summary of these two algorithms.

Dijkstra's Algorithm

Dijkstra's algorithm [DIJK59] can be stated as: Find the shortest paths from a given source node to all other nodes by developing the paths in order of increasing path length. The algorithm proceeds in stages. By the kth stage, the shortest paths to the k nodes closest to (least cost away from) the source node have been determined; these nodes are in set T. At stage $(k + 1)$, the node not in T that has the shortest path from the source node is added to T. As each node is added to T, its path from the source is defined. The algorithm can be formally described as follows. Define:

N = set of nodes in the network

s = source node

T = set of nodes so far incorporated by the algorithm

$w(i, j)$ = link cost from node i to node j; $w(i, i) = 0$; $w(i, j) = \infty$ if the two nodes are not directly connected; $w(i, j) \geq 0$ if the two nodes are directly connected

$L(n)$ = cost of the least-cost path from node s to node n that is currently known to the algorithm; at termination, this is the cost of the least-cost path in the graph from s to n

The algorithm has three steps; steps 2 and 3 are repeated until $T = N$. That is, steps 2 and 3 are repeated until final paths have been assigned to all nodes in the network:

1. **[Initialization]**

   $T = \{s\}$ i.e., the set of nodes so far incorporated consists of only the source node

   $L(n) = w(s, n)$ for $n \neq s$ i.e., the initial path costs to neighboring nodes are simply the link costs

2. **[Get Next Node]** Find the neighboring node not in T that has the least-cost path from node s and incorporate that node into T. Also incorporate the edge that is incident on that node and a node in T that contributes to the path. This can be expressed as:

   $$\text{Find } x \notin T \text{ such that } L(x) = \min_{j \notin T} L(j)$$

   Add x to T; add to T the edge that is incident on x and that contributes the least-cost component to $L(x)$, that is, the last hop in the path.

3. **[Update Least-Cost Paths]**

   $$L(n) = \min [L(n), L(x)+w(x, n)] \text{ for all } n \notin T$$

   If the latter term is the minimum, the path from s to n is now the path from s to x concatenated with the edge from x to n.

The algorithm terminates when all nodes have been added to T. At termination, the value $L(x)$ associated with each node x is the cost (length) of the least-cost path from s to x. In addition, T defines the least-cost path from s to each other node.

One iteration of steps 2 and 3 adds one new node to T and defines the least-cost path from s to that node. That path passes only through nodes that are in T. To see this, consider the following line of reasoning. After k iterations, there are k nodes in T, and the least-cost path from s to each of these nodes has been defined. Now consider all possible paths from s to nodes not in T. Among those paths, there is one of least cost that passes exclusively through nodes in T (see Problem 19.4), ending with a direct link from some node in T to a node not in T. This node is added to T and the associated path is defined as the least-cost path for that node.

EXAMPLE 19.6 Table 19.4a and Figure 19.14 show the result of applying this algorithm to the graph of Figure 19.1, using $s = 1$. The shaded edges define the spanning tree for the graph. The values in each circle are the current estimates of $L(x)$ for each node x. A node is shaded when it is added to T. Note that at each step the path to each node plus the total cost of that path is generated. After the final iteration, the least-cost path to each node and the cost of that path have been developed. The same procedure can be used with node 2 as source node, and so on.

Bellman–Ford Algorithm

The Bellman–Ford algorithm [FORD62] can be stated as: Find the shortest paths from a given source node subject to the constraint that the paths contain at most one link, then find the shortest paths with a constraint of paths of at most two links, and so on. This algorithm also proceeds in stages. The algorithm can be formally described as follows. Define:

s = source node

$w(i, j)$ = link cost from node i to node j; $w(i, i) = 0$; $w(i, j) = \infty$ if the two nodes are not directly connected; $w(i, j) \geq 0$ if the two nodes are directly connected

h = maximum number of links in a path at the current stage of the algorithm

$L_h(n)$ = cost of the least-cost path from node s to node n under the constraint of no more than h links

Table 19.4 Example of Least-Cost Routing Algorithms (using Figure 19.1)

(a) Dijkstra'a Algorithm ($s = 1$)

Iteration	T	L(2)	Path	L(3)	Path	L(4)	Path	L(5)	Path	L(6)	Path
1	{1}	2	1-2	5	1-3	1	1-4	∞	—	∞	—
2	{1, 4}	2	1-2	4	1-4-3	1	1-4	2	1-4-5	∞	—
3	{1, 2, 4}	2	1-2	4	1-4-3	1	1-4	2	1-4-5	∞	—
4	{1, 2, 4, 5}	2	1-2	3	1-4-5-3	1	1-4	2	1-4-5	4	1-4-5-6
5	{1, 2, 3, 4, 5}	2	1-2	3	1-4-5-3	1	1-4	2	1-4-5	4	1-4-5-6
6	{1, 2, 3, 4, 5, 6}	2	1-2	3	1-4-5-3	1	1-4	2	1-4-5	4	1-4-5-6

(b) Bellman–Ford Algorithm ($s = 1$)

h	$L_h(2)$	Path	$L_h(3)$	Path	$L_h(4)$	Path	$L_h(5)$	Path	$L_h(6)$	Path
0	∞	—	∞	—	∞	—	∞	—	∞	—
1	2	1-2	5	1-3	1	1-4	∞	—	∞	—
2	2	1-2	4	1-4-3	1	1-4	2	1-4-5	10	1-3-6
3	2	1-2	3	1-4-5-3	1	1-4	2	1-4-5	4	1-4-5-6
4	2	1-2	3	1-4-5-3	1	1-4	2	1-4-5	4	1-4-5-6

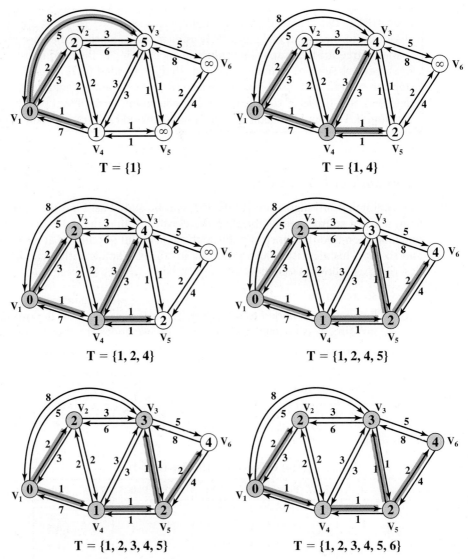

Figure 19.14 Dijkstra's Algorithm Applied to Graph of Figure 19.1

1. **[Initialization]**

$$L_0(n) = \infty, \text{ for all } n \neq s$$

$$L_h(s) = 0, \text{ for all } h$$

2. **[Update]**

For each successive $h \geq 0$:

For each $n \neq s$, compute

$$L_{h+1}(n) = \min_{j}[Lh(j) + w(j, n)]$$

Connect n with the predecessor node j that achieves the minimum, and eliminate any connection of n with a different predecessor node formed during an earlier iteration. The path from s to n terminates with the link from j to n.

For the iteration of step 2 with $h = K$, and for each destination node n, the algorithm compares potential paths from s to n of length $K + 1$ with the path that existed at the end of the previous iteration. If the previous, shorter, path has less cost, then that path is retained. Otherwise a new path with length $K + 1$ is defined from s to n; this path consists of a path of length K from s to some node j, plus a direct hop from node j to node n. In this case, the path from s to j that is used is the K-hop path for j defined in the previous iteration (see Problem 19.5).

EXAMPLE 19.7 Table 19.4b and Figure 19.15 show the result of applying this algorithm to Figure 19.1, using $s = 1$. At each step, the least-cost paths with a maximum number of links equal to h are found. After the final iteration, the least-cost path to each node and the cost of that path have been developed. The same procedure can be used with node 2 as source node, and so on. Note that the results agree with those obtained using Dijkstra's algorithm.

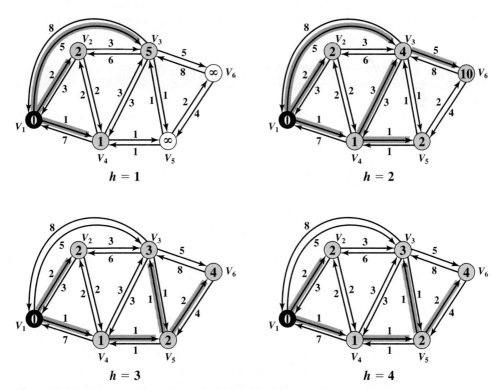

Figure 19.15 Bellman–Ford Algorithm Applied to the Graph of Figure 19.1

Comparison

One interesting comparison can be made between these two algorithms, having to do with what information needs to be gathered. Consider first the Bellman–Ford algorithm. In step 2, the calculation for node n involves knowledge of the link cost to all neighboring nodes to node n [i.e., $w(j, n)$] plus the total path cost to each of those neighboring nodes from a particular source node s [i.e., $L_h(j)$]. Each node can maintain a set of costs and associated paths for every other node in the network and exchange this information with its direct neighbors from time to time. Each node can therefore use the expression in step 2 of the Bellman–Ford algorithm, based only on information from its neighbors and knowledge of its link costs, to update its costs and paths. On the other hand, consider Dijkstra's algorithm. Step 3 appears to require that each node must have complete topological information about the network. That is, each node must know the link costs of all links in the network. Thus, for this algorithm, information must be exchanged with all other nodes.

In general, evaluation of the relative merits of the two algorithms should consider the processing time of the algorithms and the amount of information that must be collected from other nodes in the network or internet. The evaluation will depend on the implementation approach and the specific implementation.

A final point: Both algorithms are known to converge under static conditions of topology and link costs, and both will converge to the same solution. If the link costs change over time, the algorithm will attempt to catch up with these changes. However, if the link cost depends on traffic, which in turn depends on the routes chosen, then a feedback condition exists, and instabilities may result.

19.5 RECOMMENDED READING AND ANIMATIONS

[MAXE90] is a useful survey of routing algorithms. Another survey, with numerous examples, is [SCHW80].

A number of worthwhile books provide detailed coverage of various routing algorithms: [HUIT00], [BLAC00], and [PERL00].

[MOY98] provides a thorough treatment of OSPF.

[CORM09] contains a detailed analysis of the least-cost algorithms discussed in this chapter. [BERT92] also discusses these algorithms in detail.

BERT92 Bertsekas, D., and Gallager, R. *Data Networks*. Upper Saddle River, NJ: Prentice Hall, 1992.

BLAC00 Black, U. *IP Routing Protocols: RIP, OSPF, BGP, PNNI & Cisco Routing Protocols*. Upper Saddle River, NJ: Prentice Hall, 2000.

CORM09 Cormen, T., et al. *Introduction to Algorithms*. Cambridge, MA: MIT Press, 2009.

HUIT00 Huitema, C. *Routing in the Internet*. Upper Saddle River, NJ: Prentice Hall, 2000.

MAXE90 Maxemchuk, N., and Zarki, M. "Routing and Flow Control in High-Speed Wide-Area Networks." *Proceedings of the IEEE*, January 1990.

MOY98   Moy, J. *OSPF: Anatomy of an Internet Routing Protocol.* Reading, MA: Addison-Wesley, 1998.

PERL00   Perlman, R. *Interconnections: Bridges, Routers, Switches, and Internetworking Protocols.* Reading, MA: Addison-Wesley, 2000.

SCHW80   Schwartz, M., and Stern, T. "Routing Techniques Used in Computer Communication Networks." *IEEE Transactions on Communications*, April 1980.

Animations

Animations that illustrate the operation of BGP and OSPF are available at the Premium Web site. The reader is encouraged to view these animations to reinforce concepts from this chapter.

19.6 KEY TERMS, REVIEW QUESTIONS, AND PROBLEMS

Key Terms

adaptive routing	exterior router protocol	neighbor reachability
autonomous system (AS)	(ERP)	network reachability
Bellman–Ford algorithm	fixed routing	Open Shortest Path First
Border Gateway Protocol	flooding	(OSPF)
(BGP)	interior router protocol	random routing
Dijkstra's algorithm	least-cost algorithms	
distance-vector routing	link-state routing	

Review Questions

19.1   What are the key requirements for a routing function for a packet-switching network?

19.2   What is fixed routing?

19.3   What is flooding?

19.4   What are the advantages and disadvantages of adaptive routing?

19.5   What is a least-cost algorithm?

19.6   What is the essential difference between Dijkstra's algorithm and the Bellman–Ford algorithm?

19.7   What is an autonomous system?

19.8   What is the difference between an interior router protocol and an exterior router protocol?

19.9   Compare the three main approaches to routing.

19.10   List and briefly explain the three main functions of BGP.

Problems

19.1   Consider a packet-switching network of *N* nodes, connected by the following topologies:
  a. Star: one central node with no attached station; all other nodes attach to the central node.
  b. Loop: each node connects to two other nodes to form a closed loop.
  c. Fully connected: each node is directly connected to all other nodes.
  For each case, give the average number of hops between stations.

19.2   Consider a binary tree topology for a packet-switching network. The root node connects to two other nodes. All intermediate nodes connect to one node in the direction toward the root, and two in the direction away from the root. At the bottom are nodes with just one link back toward the root. If there are $2^N - 1$ nodes, derive an expression for the mean number of hops per packet for large *N*, assuming that trips between all node pairs are equally likely. *Hint:* You will find the following equalities useful:

$$\sum_{i=1}^{\infty} X^i = \frac{X}{1-X}; \sum_{i=1}^{\infty} iX^i = \frac{X}{(1-X)^2}$$

19.3   Dijkstra's algorithm, for finding the least-cost path from a specified node *s* to a specified node *t*, can be expressed in the following program:

```
for n := 1 to N do
    begin
        L[n] := ∞; final[n] := false; {all nodes are temporarily labeled with ∞}
        pred[n] := 1
    end;
L[s] := 0; final[s] := true; {node s is permanently labeled with 0}
recent := s;                {the most recent node to be permanently labeled is s}
path := true;
{initialization over }

while final[t] = false do
begin
    for n := 1 to N do {find new label}
        if (w[recent, n] < ∞) AND (NOT final[n]) then
        {for every immediate successor of recent that is not permanently labeled, do }
            begin {update temporary labels}
                newlabel := L[recent] + w[recent,n];
                if newlabel < L[n] then

                        begin L[n] := newlabel; pred[n] := recent end
                        {relabel n if there is a shorter path via node recent and make
                        recent the predecessor of n on the shortest path from s}

            end;
        temp := ∞;
        for x := 1 to N do {find node with smallest temporary label}
            if (NOT final[x]) AND (L[x] < temp) then
                    begin y := x; temp :=L[x] end;
        if temp < ∞ then {there is a path} then
                begin final[y] := true; recent := y end
                {y, the next closest node to s gets permanently labeled}
            else begin path := false; final[t] := true end
    end
```

In this program, each node is assigned a temporary label initially. As a final path to a node is determined, it is assigned a permanent label equal to the cost of the path from s. Write a similar program for the Bellman–Ford algorithm. *Hint:* The

Bellman–Ford algorithm is often called a label-correcting method, in contrast to Dijkstra's label-setting method.

19.4 In the discussion of Dijkstra's algorithm in Section 19.4, it is asserted that at each iteration, a new node is added to T and that the least-cost path for that new node passes only through nodes already in T. Demonstrate that this is true. *Hint:* Begin at the beginning. Show that the first node added to T must have a direct link to the source node. Then show that the second node to T must either have a direct link to the source node or a direct link to the first node added to T, and so on. Remember that all link costs are assumed nonnegative.

19.5 In the discussion of the Bellman–Ford algorithm, it is asserted that at the iteration for which $h = K$, if any path of length $K+1$ is defined, the first K hops of that path form a path defined in the previous iteration. Demonstrate that this is true.

19.6 The network given in Figure 19.6 has six nodes connected with links having the same costs in both directions. What will be the contents of the central routing directory and each node directory if the fixed routing strategy is used?

19.7 Using Dijkstra's algorithm, generate a least-cost route to all other nodes for nodes 2 through 6 of Figure 19.1. Display the results as in Table 19.4a.

19.8 Repeat Problem 19.7 using the Bellman–Ford algorithm.

19.9 Apply Dijkstra's routing algorithm to the networks in Figure 19.16. Provide a table similar to Table 19.4a and a figure similar to Figure 19.14.

19.10 Repeat Problem 19.9 using the Bellman–Ford algorithm.

19.11 If there are multiple least-cost paths between two nodes in a network, what factors do you consider while determining the route?

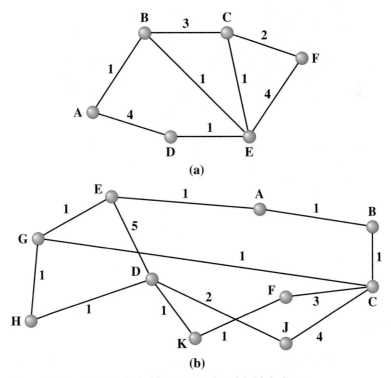

Figure 19.16 Packet-Switching Networks with Link Costs

19.12   Both Dijkstra's algorithm and the Bellman–Ford algorithm find the least-cost paths from one node to all other nodes. The Floyd–Warshall algorithm finds the least-cost paths between all pairs of nodes together. Define:

$N =$ set of nodes in the network

$w(i, j) =$ link cost from node i to node j; $w(i, i) = 0$; $w(i, j) = \infty$ if the two nodes are not directly connected

$L_n(i, j) =$ cost of the least-cost path from node i to node j with the constraint that only nodes $1, 2, ..., n$ can be used as intermediate nodes on paths

The algorithm has the following steps:

1. Initialize:

$$L_0(i, j) = w(i, j), \text{for all } i, j, \ i \neq j$$

2. For $n = 0, 1, \ldots, N - 1$

$$L_{n+1}(i, j) = \min[L_n(i, j), L_n(i, n + 1) + L_n(n + 1, j)] \quad \text{for all } i \neq j$$

Explain the algorithm in words. Use induction to demonstrate that the algorithm works.

19.13   In Figure 19.3, node 1 sends a packet to node 6 using flooding. Counting the transmission of one packet across one link as a load of one, what is the total load generated if:
    a. Each node discards duplicate incoming packets?
    b. A hop count field is used and is initially set to 5, and no duplicate is discarded?

19.14   The Floyd–Warshall algorithm has been stated in Problem 19.12. Write a pseudocode or a program in any language to implement it.

19.15   Explain with an example the difficulty of implementing distance-vector routing as an exterior routing protocol.

19.16   Another adaptive routing scheme is known as backward learning. As a packet is routed through the network, it carries not only the destination address but also the source address plus a running hop count that is incremented for each hop. Each node builds a routing table that gives the next node and hop count for each destination. How is the packet information used to build the table? What are the advantages and disadvantages of this technique?

19.17   Build a centralized routing directory for the networks of Figure 19.16.

19.18   Consider a system using flooding with a hop counter. Suppose that the hop counter is originally set to the "diameter" of the network. When the hop count reaches zero, the packet is discarded except at its destination. Does this always ensure that a packet will reach its destination if there exists at least one operable path? Why or why not?

19.19   BGP's AS_PATH attribute identifies the autonomous systems through which routing information has passed. How can the AS_PATH attribute be used to detect routing information loops?

19.20   Consider the autonomous system shown in Figure 19.11 and Figure 19.12. If the OSPF protocol is used, what will be the SPF tree and routing table for node R10?

CONGESTION CONTROL

 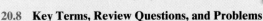
653

Congestion is a critical problem for all types of switched data networks. The phenomenon of congestion is a complex one, as is the subject of congestion control. In very general terms, congestion occurs when the number of packets[1] being transmitted through a network begins to approach the packet-handling capacity of the network. The objective of congestion control is to maintain the number of packets within the network below the level at which performance falls off dramatically.

To understand the issues involved in congestion control, we need to look at some results from queueing theory.[2] In essence, a data network or internet is a network of queues. At each node (data network switch, internet router), there is a queue of packets for each outgoing channel. If the rate at which packets arrive and queue up exceeds the rate at which packets can be transmitted, the queue size grows without bound and the delay experienced by a packet goes to infinity. Even if the packet arrival rate is less than the packet transmission rate, queue length will grow dramatically as the arrival rate approaches the transmission rate. As a rule of thumb, when the line for which packets are queueing becomes more than 80% utilized, the queue length grows at an alarming rate. This growth in queue length means that the delay experienced by a packet at each node increases. Further, since the size of any queue is finite, as queue length grows, eventually the queue must overflow.

This chapter focuses on congestion control in switched data networks, including packet-switching networks and the Internet. The chapter also

---

[1]In this chapter we use the term *packet* in a broad sense, to include packets in a packet-switching network, frames in a frame relay network, cells in an ATM network, or IP datagrams in an internet.

[2]Appendix H provides an overview of queueing analysis.

discusses TCP congestion control and a new protocol that provides congestion control with an unreliable service. The next three chapters look at additional congestion control mechanisms in our discussion of internetwork operation.

20.1 EFFECTS OF CONGESTION

Consider the queueing situation at a single packet switch or router, such as is illustrated in Figure 20.1. Any given node has a number of I/O ports[3] attached to it: one or more to other nodes, and zero or more to end systems. On each port, packets arrive and depart. We can consider that there are two buffers, or queues, at each

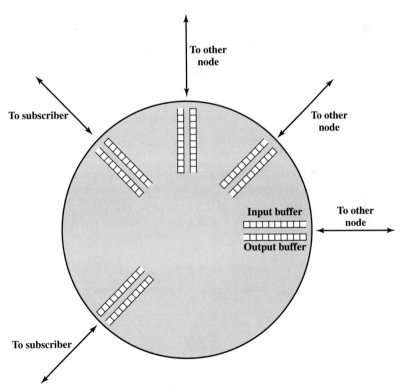

Figure 20.1   Input and Output Queues at Node

---

[3]In the case of a switch of a packet-switching, frame relay, or ATM network, each I/O port connects to a transmission link that connects to another node or end system. In the case of a router of an internet, each I/O port connects to either a direct link to another node or to a subnetwork.

port, one to accept arriving packets, and one to hold packets that are waiting to depart. In practice, there might be two fixed-size buffers associated with each port, or there might be a pool of memory available for all buffering activities. In the latter case, we can think of each port having two variable-size buffers associated with it, subject to the constraint that the sum of all buffer sizes is a constant.

In any case, as packets arrive, they are stored in the input buffer of the corresponding port. The node examines each incoming packet, makes a routing decision, and then moves the packet to the appropriate output buffer. Packets queued for output are transmitted as rapidly as possible; this is, in effect, statistical time division multiplexing. If packets arrive too fast for the node to process them (make routing decisions) or faster than packets can be cleared from the outgoing buffers, then eventually packets will arrive for which no memory is available.

When such a saturation point is reached, one of two general strategies can be adopted. The first such strategy is to discard any incoming packet for which there is no available buffer space. The alternative is for the node that is experiencing these problems to exercise some sort of flow control over its neighbors so that the traffic flow remains manageable. But, as Figure 20.2 illustrates, each of a node's neighbors is also managing a number of queues. If node 6 restrains the flow of packets from node 5, this causes the output buffer in node 5 for the port to node 6 to fill up. Thus, congestion at one point in the network can quickly propagate throughout a region or the entire network. While flow control is indeed a powerful tool, we need to use it in such a way as to manage the traffic on the entire network.

Ideal Performance

Figure 20.3 suggests the ideal goal for network utilization. The top graph plots the steady-state total throughput (number of packets delivered to destination end systems) through the network as a function of the offered load (number of packets

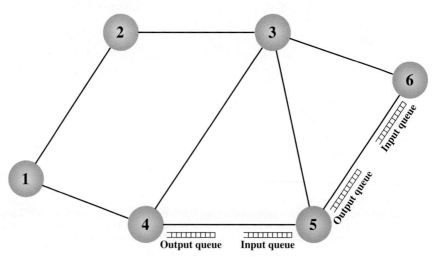

Figure 20.2 Interaction of Queues in a Data Network

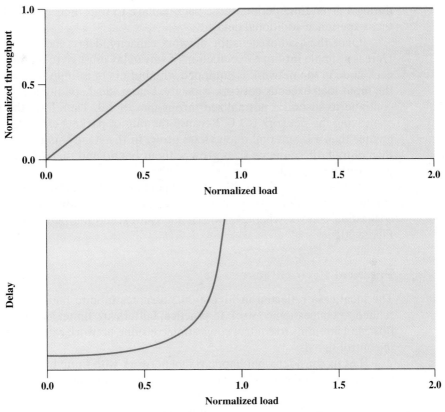

Figure 20.3 Ideal Network Utilization

transmitted by source end systems), both normalized to the maximum theoretical throughput of the network. For example, if a network consists of a single node with two full-duplex 1-Mbps links, then the theoretical capacity of the network is 2 Mbps, consisting of a 1-Mbps flow in each direction. In the ideal case, the throughput of the network increases to accommodate load up to an offered load equal to the full capacity of the network; then normalized throughput remains at 1.0 at higher input loads. Note, however, what happens to the end-to-end delay experienced by the average packet even with this assumption of ideal performance. At negligible load, there is some small constant amount of delay that consists of the propagation delay through the network from source to destination plus processing delay at each node. As the load on the network increases, queueing delays at each node are added to this fixed amount of delay. The reason for the increase in delay even when the total network capacity is not exceeded has to do with the variability in load at each node. With multiple sources supplying data to the network, even if each source produced packets at fixed intervals, there will be fluctuation in the input rate at each individual network node. When a burst of packets arrives at a node, it will take some time to clear the backlog. As it is clearing the backlog, it is sending out a sustained burst of packets, thus imposing packet bursts on downstream node. And once a queue builds up at a node, even if packets only arrive at a rate the node can handle during a given time period, those packets have to wait their turn in the queue, and thus experience additional delay.

Once the load exceeds the network capacity, delays increase without bound. Here is a simple intuitive explanation of why delay must go to infinity. Suppose that each node in the network is equipped with buffers of infinite size and suppose that the input load exceeds network capacity. Under ideal conditions, the network will continue to sustain a normalized throughput of 1.0. Therefore, the rate of packets leaving the network is 1.0. Because the rate of packets entering the network is greater than 1.0, internal queue sizes grow. In the steady state, with input greater than output, these queue sizes grow without bound and therefore queueing delays grow without bound.

It is important to grasp the meaning of Figure 20.3 before looking at real-world conditions. This figure represents the ideal, but unattainable, goal of all traffic and congestion control schemes. No scheme can exceed the performance depicted in Figure 20.3.

Practical Performance

The ideal case reflected in Figure 20.3 assumes infinite buffers and no overhead related to congestion control. In practice, buffers are finite, leading to buffer overflow, and attempts to control congestion consume network capacity in the exchange of control signals.

Let us consider what happens in a network with finite buffers if no attempt is made to control congestion or to restrain input from end systems. The details will, of course, differ depending on network configuration and on the statistics of the presented traffic. However, the graphs in Figure 20.4 depict the devastating outcome in general terms.

At light loads, throughput, and hence network utilization, increases as the offered load increases. As the load continues to increase, a point is reached (point A in the plot) beyond which the throughput of the network increases at a rate slower than the rate at which offered load is increased. This is due to network entry into a moderate congestion state. In this region, the network continues to cope with the load, although with increased delays. The departure of throughput from the ideal is accounted for by a number of factors. For one thing, the load is unlikely to be spread uniformly throughout the network. Therefore, while some nodes may experience moderate congestion, others may be experiencing severe congestion and may need to discard traffic. In addition, as the load increases, the network will attempt to balance the load by routing packets through areas of lower congestion. For the routing function to work, an increased number of routing messages must be exchanged between nodes to alert each other to areas of congestion; this overhead reduces the capacity available for data packets.

As the load on the network continues to increase, the queue lengths of the various nodes continue to grow. Eventually, a point is reached (point B in the plot) beyond which throughput actually drops with increased offered load. The reason for this is that the buffers at each node are of finite size. When the buffers at a node become full, the node must discard packets. Thus, the sources must retransmit the discarded packets in addition to new packets. This only exacerbates the situation:

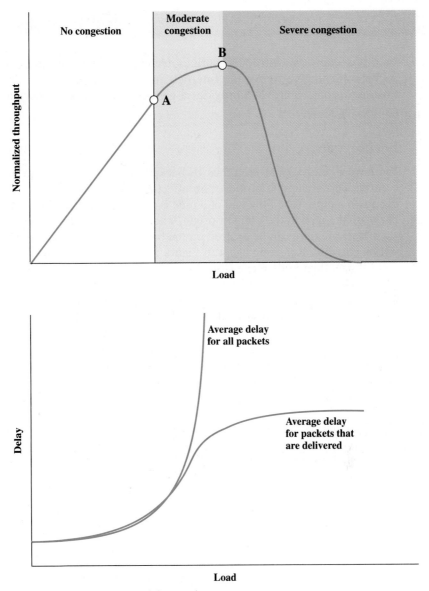

Figure 20.4 The Effects of Congestion

As more and more packets are retransmitted, the load on the system grows, and more buffers become saturated. While the system is trying desperately to clear the backlog, users are pumping old and new packets into the system. Even successfully delivered packets may be retransmitted because it takes too long, at a higher layer (e.g., transport layer), to acknowledge them: The sender assumes the packet did not get through and retransmits. Under these circumstances, the effective capacity of the system declines to zero.

20.2 CONGESTION CONTROL

In this section, we introduce various techniques for controlling congestion in packet-switching networks, the Internet, and private internets. To give context to this discussion, Figure 20.5 provides a general depiction of important congestion control techniques.

Backpressure

We have already made reference to backpressure as a technique for congestion control. This technique produces an effect similar to backpressure in fluids flowing down a pipe. When the end of a pipe is closed (or restricted), the fluid pressure backs up the pipe to the point of origin, where the flow is stopped (or slowed).

Backpressure can be exerted on the basis of links or logical connections (e.g., virtual circuits). Referring again to Figure 20.2, if node 6 becomes congested (buffers fill up), then node 6 can slow down or halt the flow of all packets from node 5 (or node 3, or both nodes 5 and 3). If this restriction persists, node 5 will need to slow down or halt traffic on its incoming links. This flow restriction propagates backward (against the flow of data traffic) to sources, which are restricted in the flow of new packets into the network.

Backpressure can be selectively applied to logical connections, so that the flow from one node to the next is only restricted or halted on some connections, generally the ones with the most traffic. In this case, the restriction propagates back along the connection to the source.

Choke Packet

A choke packet is a control packet generated at a congested node and transmitted back to a source node to restrict traffic flow. An example of a choke packet is the ICMP (Internet Control Message Protocol) Source Quench packet. Either a router or a destination end system may send this message to a source end system,

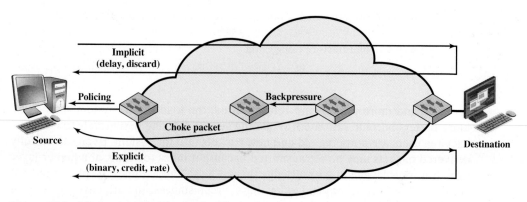

Figure 20.5 Mechanisms for Congestion Control

requesting that it reduce the rate at which it is sending traffic to the internet destination. On receipt of a source quench message, the source host should cut back the rate at which it is sending traffic to the specified destination until it no longer receives source quench messages. The source quench message can be used by a router or host that must discard IP datagrams because of a full buffer. In that case, the router or host will issue a source quench message for every datagram that it discards. In addition, a system may anticipate congestion and issue source quench messages when its buffers approach capacity. In that case, the datagram referred to in the source quench message may well be delivered. Thus, receipt of a source quench message does not imply delivery or nondelivery of the corresponding datagram.

The choke package is a relatively crude technique for controlling congestion. More sophisticated forms of explicit congestion signaling are discussed subsequently.

Implicit Congestion Signaling

When network congestion occurs, two things may happen: (1) The transmission delay for an individual packet from source to destination increases, so that it is noticeably longer than the fixed propagation delay, and (2) packets are discarded. If a source is able to detect increased delays and packet discards, then it has implicit evidence of network congestion. If all sources can detect congestion and, in response, reduce flow on the basis of congestion, then the network congestion will be relieved. Thus, congestion control on the basis of implicit signaling is the responsibility of end systems and does not require action on the part of network nodes.

Implicit signaling is an effective congestion control technique in connectionless, or datagram, configurations, such as datagram packet-switching networks and IP-based internets. In such cases, there are no logical connections through the internet on which flow can be regulated. However, between the two end systems, logical connections can be established at the TCP level. TCP includes mechanisms for acknowledging receipt of TCP segments and for regulating the flow of data between source and destination on a TCP connection. TCP congestion control techniques based on the ability to detect increased delay and segment loss are discussed in Section 20.5.

Implicit signaling can also be used in connection-oriented networks. For example, in frame relay networks, the LAPF control protocol, which is end to end, includes facilities similar to those of TCP for flow and error control. LAPF control is capable of detecting lost frames and adjusting the flow of data accordingly.

Explicit Congestion Signaling

It is desirable to use as much of the available capacity in a network as possible but still react to congestion in a controlled and fair manner. This is the purpose of explicit congestion avoidance techniques. In general terms, for explicit congestion avoidance, the network alerts end systems to growing congestion within the network and the end systems take steps to reduce the offered load to the network.

Typically, explicit congestion control techniques operate over connection-oriented networks and control the flow of packets over individual connections. Explicit congestion signaling approaches can work in one of two directions:

- **Backward:** Notifies the source that congestion avoidance procedures should be initiated where applicable for traffic in the opposite direction of the received notification. It indicates that the packets that the user transmits on this logical connection may encounter congested resources. Backward information is transmitted either by altering bits in a header of a data packet headed for the source to be controlled or by transmitting separate control packets to the source.

- **Forward:** Notifies the user that congestion avoidance procedures should be initiated where applicable for traffic in the same direction as the received notification. It indicates that this packet, on this logical connection, has encountered congested resources. Again, this information may be transmitted either as altered bits in data packets or in separate control packets. In some schemes, when a forward signal is received by an end system, it echoes the signal back along the logical connection to the source. In other schemes, the end system is expected to exercise flow control upon the source end system at a higher layer (e.g., TCP).

We can divide explicit congestion signaling approaches into three general categories:

- **Binary:** A bit is set in a data packet as it is forwarded by the congested node. When a source receives a binary indication of congestion on a logical connection, it may reduce its traffic flow.

- **Credit based:** These schemes are based on providing an explicit credit to a source over a logical connection. The credit indicates how many octets or how many packets the source may transmit. When the credit is exhausted, the source must await additional credit before sending additional data. Credit-based schemes are common for end-to-end flow control, in which a destination system uses credit to prevent the source from overflowing the destination buffers, but credit-based schemes have also been considered for congestion control.

- **Rate based:** These schemes are based on providing an explicit data rate limit to the source over a logical connection. The source may transmit data at a rate up to the set limit. To control congestion, any node along the path of the connection can reduce the data rate limit in a control message to the source.

20.3 TRAFFIC MANAGEMENT

There are a number of issues related to congestion control that might be included under the general category of traffic management. In its simplest form, congestion control is concerned with efficient use of a network at high load. The various mechanisms discussed in the previous section can be applied as the situation arises, without regard to the particular source or destination affected. When a node is saturated and must discard packets, it can apply some simple rule, such as discard the most recent arrival. However, other considerations can be used to refine the application of congestion control techniques and discard policy. We briefly introduce several of those areas here.

Fairness

As congestion develops, flows of packets between sources and destinations will experience increased delays and, with high congestion, packet losses. In the absence of other requirements, we would like to assure that the various flows suffer from congestion equally. Simply to discard on a last-in-first-discarded basis may not be fair. As an example of a technique that might promote fairness, a node can maintain a separate queue for each logical connection or for each source-destination pair. If all of the queue buffers are of equal length, then the queues with the highest traffic load will suffer discards more often, allowing lower-traffic connections a fair share of the capacity.

Quality of Service

We might wish to treat different traffic flows differently. For example, as [JAIN92] points out, some applications, such as voice and video, are delay sensitive but loss insensitive. Others, such as file transfer and electronic mail, are delay insensitive but loss sensitive. Still others, such as interactive graphics or interactive computing applications, are delay sensitive and loss sensitive. Also, different traffic flows have different priorities; for example, network management traffic, particularly during times of congestion or failure, is more important than application traffic.

It is particularly important during periods of congestion that traffic flows with different requirements be treated differently and provided a different quality of service (QoS). For example, a node might transmit higher-priority packets ahead of lower-priority packets in the same queue. Or a node might maintain different queues for different QoS levels and give preferential treatment to the higher levels.

Reservations

One way to avoid congestion and also to provide assured service to applications is to use a reservation scheme. Such a scheme is an integral part of ATM networks. When a logical connection is established, the network and the user enter into a traffic contract, which specifies a data rate and other characteristics of the traffic flow. The network agrees to give a defined QoS so long as the traffic flow is within contract parameters; excess traffic is either discarded or handled on a best-effort basis, subject to discard. If the current outstanding reservations are such that the network resources are inadequate to meet the new reservation, then the new reservation is denied. A similar type of scheme has now been developed for IP-based internets (RSVP, which is discussed in Chapter 22).

One aspect of a reservation scheme is traffic policing (Figure 20.5). A node in the network, typically the node to which the end system attaches, monitors the traffic flow and compares it to the traffic contract. Excess traffic is either discarded or marked to indicate that it is liable to discard or delay.

Traffic Shaping and Traffic Policing

Two important tools in managing network are traffic shaping and traffic policing. **Traffic shaping** is aimed at smoothing out traffic flow by reducing packet clumping that leads to fluctuations in buffer occupancy. In essence, if the input to a switch on a certain channel or logical connection or flow is bursty, traffic shaping produces an output packet stream that is less bursty and with a more regular flow of packets.

Traffic policing discriminates between incoming packets that conform to quality of service (QoS) agreement and those that don't. Packets that don't conform may be treated in one of the following ways:

1. Give the packet lower priority compared to packets in other output queues.
2. Label the packet as nonconforming by setting the appropriate bits in a header. Downstream switches may treat nonconforming packets less favorably if congestion occurs.
3. Discard the packet.

In essence, traffic shaping is concerned with traffic leaving the switch and traffic policing is concerned with traffic entering the switch. Two important techniques that can be used for traffic shaping or traffic policing are token bucket and leaky bucket.

TOKEN BUCKET   A widely used traffic management tool is token bucket. This is a way of characterizing and managing traffic that has three advantages:

1. Many traffic sources can be defined easily and accurately by a token bucket scheme.
2. The token bucket scheme provides a concise description of the load to be imposed by a flow, enabling the service to determine easily the resource requirement.
3. The token bucket scheme provides the input parameters to a policing function.

This scheme provides a concise description of the peak and average traffic load the recipient can expect and it also provides a convenient mechanism by which the sender can implement a traffic flow policy. Token bucket is used in the Bluetooth (Chapter 18) specification and in differentiated services (Chapter 22).

A token bucket traffic specification consists of two parameters: a token replenishment rate R and a bucket size B. The token rate R specifies the continually sustainable data rate; that is, over a relatively long period of time, the average data rate to be supported for this flow is R. The bucket size B specifies the amount by which the data rate can exceed R for short periods of time. The exact condition is as follows: during any time period T, the amount of data sent cannot exceed $RT + B$.

Figure 20.6 illustrates this scheme and explains the use of the term *bucket*. The bucket represents a counter that indicates the allowable number of bytes of data that can be sent at any time. The bucket fills with byte tokens at the rate of R

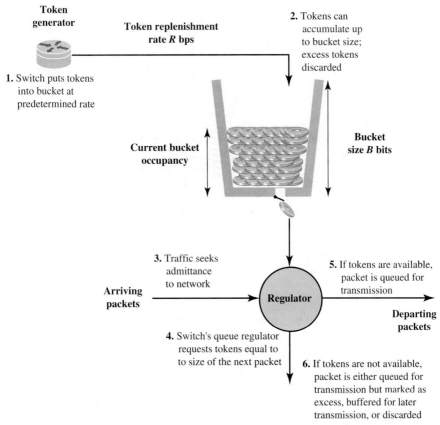

Figure 20.6 Token Bucket Scheme

(i.e., the counter is incremented R times per second), up to the bucket capacity (up to the maximum counter value). Data arrive from the user and are assembled into packets, which are queued for transmission. A packet may be transmitted if there are sufficient tokens to match the packet size. If so, the packet is transmitted and the bucket is drained of the corresponding number of tokens. If there are insufficient tokens available, then the packet exceeds the specification for this flow. The treatment for such packets is a design or implementation decision. Possible actions including:

- Queue the packet for transmission until sufficient tokens are available and then transmit.
- Queue the packet for transmission until sufficient tokens are available but label the packet as exceeding a threshold.
- Discard the packet.

The last option is generally not used with token bucket. Token bucket is typically used for traffic shaping but not traffic policing.

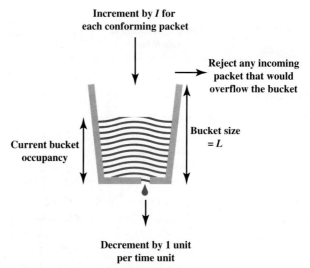

Figure 20.7 Leaky Bucket Algorithm

The result of this scheme is that if there is a backlog of packets and an empty bucket, then packets are emitted at a smooth flow of packets per second with no packet delay variation until the backlog is cleared. Thus, the token bucket smooths out bursts of cells. Over the long run, the rate of data allowed by the token bucket is R. However, if there is an idle or relatively slow period, the bucket capacity builds up, so that at most an additional B bytes above the stated rate can be accepted. Thus, B is a measure of the degree of burstiness of the data flow that is allowed.

LEAKY BUCKET   Another scheme, similar to token bucket, is leaky bucket. Leaky bucket is used in the asynchronous transfer mode (ATM) specification and in the ITU-T H.261 standard for digital video coding and transmission. The basic principle of leaky bucket is depicted in Figure 20.7. The algorithm maintains a running count of the cumulative amount of data sent in a counter X. The counter is decremented at a constant rate of one unit per time unit to a minimum value of zero; this is equivalent to a bucket that leaks at a rate of 1. The counter is incremented by I for each arriving packet, where I is the size of the packet, subject to the restriction that the maximum counter value is L. Any arriving cell that would cause the counter to exceed its maximum is defined as nonconforming; this is equivalent to a bucket with a capacity of L.

The token bucket and leaky bucket schemes operate in a similar fashion, but there are some differences. A token bucket fills at a constant rate up to the capacity of the bucket and empties at a rate dictated by the input data stream while the bucket is not empty. A leaky bucket empties at a constant rate while the bucket is not empty and fills at a rate dictated by the input stream up to the capacity of the bucket. Thus, for token bucket, as the rate of incoming packets rise, the output of the system speeds up. In effect, token bucket gives credit to a flow or connection that is underused, up to a point.

20.4 CONGESTION CONTROL IN PACKET-SWITCHING NETWORKS

A number of control mechanisms for congestion control in packet-switching networks have been suggested and tried. The following are examples:

1. Send a control packet from a congested node to some or all source nodes. This choke packet will have the effect of stopping or slowing the rate of transmission from sources and hence limit the total number of packets in the network. This approach requires additional traffic on the network during a period of congestion.

2. Rely on routing information. Routing algorithms, such as ARPANET's, provide link delay information to other nodes, which influences routing decisions. This information could also be used to influence the rate at which new packets are produced. Because these delays are being influenced by the routing decision, they may vary too rapidly to be used effectively for congestion control.

3. Make use of an end-to-end probe packet. Such a packet could be timestamped to measure the delay between two particular endpoints. This has the disadvantage of adding overhead to the network.

4. Allow packet-switching nodes to add congestion information to packets as they go by. There are two possible approaches here. A node could add such information to packets going in the direction opposite of the congestion. This information quickly reaches the source node, which can reduce the flow of packets into the network. Alternatively, a node could add such information to packets going in the same direction as the congestion. The destination either asks the source to adjust the load or returns the signal back to the source in the packets (or acknowledgments) going in the reverse direction.

20.5 TCP CONGESTION CONTROL

The credit-based flow control mechanism of TCP was designed to enable a destination to restrict the flow of segments from a source to avoid buffer overflow at the destination. This same flow control mechanism is now used in ingenious ways to provide congestion control over the Internet between the source and destination. Congestion, as we have seen a number of times in this book, has two main effects. First, as congestion begins to occur, the transit time across a network or internetwork increases. Second, as congestion becomes severe, network or internet nodes drop packets. The TCP flow control mechanism can be used to recognize the onset of congestion (by recognizing increased delay times and dropped segments) and to react by reducing the flow of data. If many of the TCP entities operating across a network exercise this sort of restraint, internet congestion is relieved.

Since the publication of RFC 793, a number of techniques have been implemented that are intended to improve TCP congestion control characteristics. Table 20.1 lists some of the most popular of these techniques. None of these

Table 20.1   Implementation of TCP Congestion Control Measures

Measure	RFC 1122	TCP Tahoe	TCP Reno	NewReno
RTT Variance Estimation	✓	✓	✓	✓
Exponential RTO Backoff	✓	✓	✓	✓
Karn's Algorithm	✓	✓	✓	✓
Slow Start	✓	✓	✓	✓
Dynamic Window Sizing on Congestion	✓	✓	✓	✓
Fast Retransmit		✓	✓	✓
Fast Recovery			✓	✓
Modified Fast Recovery				✓

techniques extends or violates the original TCP standard; rather the techniques represent implementation policies that are within the scope of the TCP specification. Many of these techniques are mandated for use with TCP in RFC 1122 (*Requirements for Internet Hosts*) while some of them are specified in RFC 5681. The labels Tahoe, Reno, and NewReno refer to implementation packages available on many operating systems that support TCP. The techniques fall roughly into two categories: retransmission timer management and window management. In this section, we look at some of the most important and most widely implemented of these techniques.

Retransmission Timer Management

As network or internet conditions change, a static retransmission timer is likely to be either too long or too short. Accordingly, virtually all TCP implementations attempt to estimate the current round-trip time by observing the pattern of delay for recent segments, and then set the timer to a value somewhat greater than the estimated round-trip time.

SIMPLE AVERAGE   A simple approach is to take the average of observed round-trip times over a number of segments. If the average accurately predicts future round-trip times, then the resulting retransmission timer will yield good performance. The simple averaging method can be expressed as:

$$\text{ARTT}(K + 1) = \frac{1}{K + 1}\sum_{i=1}^{K+1}\text{RTT}(i) \tag{20.1}$$

where $\text{RTT}(i)$ is the round-trip time observed for the ith transmitted segment, and $\text{ARTT}(K)$ is the average round-trip time for the first K segments.

This expression can be rewritten as

$$\text{ARTT}(K + 1) = \frac{K}{K + 1}\text{ARTT}(K) + \frac{1}{K + 1}\text{RTT}(K + 1) \tag{20.2}$$

With this formulation, it is not necessary to recalculate the entire summation each time.

EXPONENTIAL AVERAGE   Note that each term in the summation is given equal weight; that is, each term is multiplied by the same constant $1/(K + 1)$. Typically, we would like to give greater weight to more recent instances because they are more likely to reflect future behavior. A common technique for predicting the next value on the basis of a time series of past values, and the one specified in RFC 793, is exponential averaging:

$$\text{SRTT}(K + 1) = \alpha \times \text{SRTT}(K) + (1 - \alpha) \times \text{RTT}(K + 1) \quad \textbf{(20.3)}$$

where $\text{SRTT}(K)$ is called the smoothed round-trip time estimate, and we define $\text{SRTT}(0) = 0$. Compare this with Equation (20.2). By using a constant value of $\alpha(0 < \alpha < 1)$, independent of the number of past observations, we have a circumstance in which all past values are considered, but the more distant ones have less weight. To see this more clearly, consider the following expansion of Equation (20.3):

$$SRTT(K + 1) = (1 - \alpha)RTT(K + 1) + \alpha(1 - \alpha)RTT(K) +$$
$$\alpha^2(1 - \alpha)RRT(K - 1) + \dots + \alpha^K(1 - \alpha)RTT(1)$$

Because both α and $(1 - \alpha)$ are less than one, each successive term in the preceding equation is smaller. For example, for $\alpha = 0.8$, the expansion is

$$SRTT(K + 1) = (0.2)RTT(K + 1) + (0.16)RTT(K) +$$
$$(0.128)RTT(K - 1) + \dots$$

The older the observation, the less it is counted in the average.

The smaller the value of α, the greater the weight given to the more recent observations. For $\alpha = 0.5$, virtually all of the weight is given to the four or five most recent observations, whereas for $\alpha = 0.875$, the averaging is effectively spread out over the ten or so most recent observations. The advantage of using a small value of α is that the average will quickly reflect a rapid change in the observed quantity. The disadvantage is that if there is a brief surge in the value of the observed quantity and it then settles back to some relatively constant value, the use of a small value of α will result in jerky changes in the average.

Figure 20.8 compares simple averaging with exponential averaging (for two different values of α). In part (a) of the figure, the observed value begins at 1, grows gradually to a value of 10, and then stays there. In part (b) of the figure, the observed value begins at 20, declines gradually to 10, and then stays there. Note that exponential averaging tracks changes in RTT faster than does simple averaging and that the smaller value of α results in a more rapid reaction to the change in the observed value.

Equation (20.3) is used in RFC 793 to estimate the current round-trip time. As was mentioned, the retransmission timer should be set at a value somewhat greater than the estimated round-trip time. One possibility is to use a constant value:

$$\text{RTO}(K + 1) = \text{SRTT}(K + 1) + \Delta$$

where RTO is the retransmission timer (also called the retransmission time-out) and Δ is a constant. The disadvantage of this is that Δ is not proportional to SRTT. For large values of SRTT, Δ is relatively small and fluctuations in the actual RTT will result in unnecessary retransmissions. For small values of SRTT, Δ is relatively large

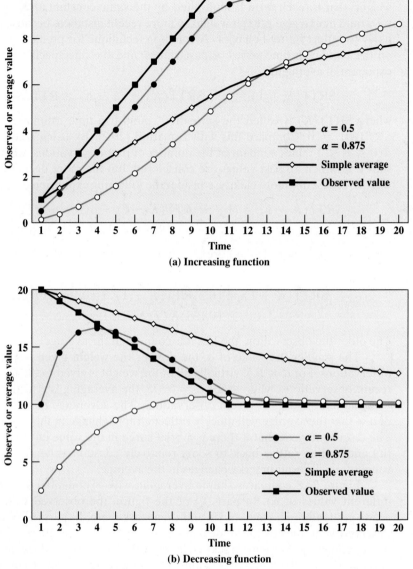

Figure 20.8 Use of Exponential Averaging

and causes unnecessary delays in retransmitting lost segments. Accordingly, RFC 793 specifies the use of a timer whose value is proportional to SRTT, within limits:

$$RTO(K + 1) = MIN(UBOUND, MAX(LBOUND, \beta \times SRTT(K + 1)))\quad (20.4)$$

where UBOUND and LBOUND are prechosen fixed upper and lower bounds on the timer value and β is a constant. RFC 793 does not recommend specific values but does list as "example values" the following: α between 0.8 and 0.9 and β between 1.3 and 2.0.

RTT VARIANCE ESTIMATION (JACOBSON'S ALGORITHM) The technique specified in the TCP standard, and described in Equations (20.3) and (20.4), enables a TCP entity to adapt to changes in round-trip time. However, it does not cope well with a situation in which the round-trip time exhibits a relatively high variance. [ZHAN86] points out three sources of high variance:

1. If the data rate on the TCP connection is relatively low, then the transmission delay will be relatively large compared to propagation time and the variance in delay due to variance in IP datagram size will be significant. Thus, the SRTT estimator is heavily influenced by characteristics that are a property of the data and not of the network.

2. Internet traffic load and conditions may change abruptly due to traffic from other sources, causing abrupt changes in RTT.

3. The peer TCP entity may not acknowledge each segment immediately because of its own processing delays and because it exercises its privilege to use cumulative acknowledgments.

The original TCP specification tries to account for this variability by multiplying the RTT estimator by a constant factor, as shown in Equation (20.4). In a stable environment, with low variance of RTT, this formulation results in an unnecessarily high value of RTO, and in an unstable environment a value of $\beta = 2$ may be inadequate to protect against unnecessary retransmissions.

A more effective approach is to estimate the variability in RTT values and to use that as input into the calculation of an RTO. A variability measure that is easy to estimate is the mean deviation, defined as

$$\text{MDEV}(X) = \text{E}[|X - \text{E}[X]|]$$

where $\text{E}[X]$ is the expected value of X.

As with the estimate of RTT, a simple average could be used to estimate MDEV:

$$\text{AERR}(K + 1) = \text{RTT}(K + 1) - \text{ARTT}(K)$$

$$\text{ADEV}(K + 1) = \frac{1}{K + 1} \sum_{i=1}^{K+1} |\text{AERR}(i)|$$

$$= \frac{1}{K + 1} \text{ADEV}(K) + \frac{1}{K + 1} |\text{AERR}(K + 1)|$$

where $\text{ARTT}(K)$ is the simple average defined in Equation (20.1) and $\text{AERR}(K)$ is the sample mean deviation measured at time K.

As with the definition of ARTT, each term in the summation of ADEV is given equal weight; that is, each term is multiplied by the same constant $1/(K + 1)$. Again, we would like to give greater weight to more recent instances because they are more likely to reflect future behavior. Jacobson, who proposed the use of a dynamic estimate of variability in estimating RTT [JACO88], suggests using the same exponential smoothing technique as is used for the calculation of SRTT. The complete algorithm proposed by Jacobson can be expressed as follows:

$$
\begin{aligned}
\text{SRTT}(K + 1) &= (1 - g) \times \text{SRTT}(K) + g \times \text{RTT}(K + 1) \\
\text{SERR}(K + 1) &= \text{RTT}(K + 1) - \text{SRTT}(K) \\
\text{SDEV}(K + 1) &= (1 - h) \times \text{SDEV}(K + h) \times |\text{SERR}(K + 1)| \\
\text{RTO}(K + 1) &= \text{SRTT}(K + 1) + f \times \text{SDEV}(K + 1) \qquad \textbf{(20.5)}
\end{aligned}
$$

As in the RFC 793 definition [Equation (20.3)], SRTT is an exponentially smoothed estimate of RTT, with $(1 - g)$ equivalent to α. Now, however, instead of multiplying the estimate SRTT by a constant [Equation (20.4)], a multiple of the estimated mean deviation is added to SRTT to form the retransmission timer. Based on his timing experiments, Jacobson proposed the following values for the constants in his original paper [JACO88]:

$$
\begin{aligned}
g &= 1/8 = 0.125 \\
h &= 1/4 = 0.25 \\
f &= 2
\end{aligned}
$$

After further research [JACO90a], Jacobson recommended using $f = 4$, and this is the value used in current implementations.

Figure 20.9 illustrates the use of Equation (20.5) on the same data set used in Figure 20.8. Once the arrival times stabilize, the variation estimate SDEV declines. The values of RTO for both $f = 2$ and $f = 4$ are quite conservative as long as RTT is changing but then begin to converge to RTT when it stabilizes.

Experience has shown that Jacobson's algorithm can significantly improve TCP performance. However, it does not stand by itself. Two other factors must be considered:

1. What RTO value should be used on a retransmitted segment? The exponential RTO backoff algorithm is used for this purpose.

2. Which round-trip samples should be used as input to Jacobson's algorithm? Karn's algorithm determines which samples to use.

EXPONENTIAL RTO BACKOFF   When a TCP sender times out on a segment, it must retransmit that segment. RFC 793 assumes that the same RTO value will be used for this retransmitted segment. However, because the time-out is probably due to network congestion, manifested as a dropped packet or a long delay in round-trip time, maintaining the same RTO value is ill advised.

Consider the following scenario. There are a number of active TCP connections from various sources sending traffic into an internet. A region of congestion develops such that segments on many of these connections are lost or delayed past the RTO time of the connections. Therefore, at roughly the same time, many segments will be retransmitted into the internet, maintaining or even increasing the congestion. All of the sources then wait a local (to each connection) RTO time and retransmit yet again. This pattern of behavior could cause a sustained condition of congestion.

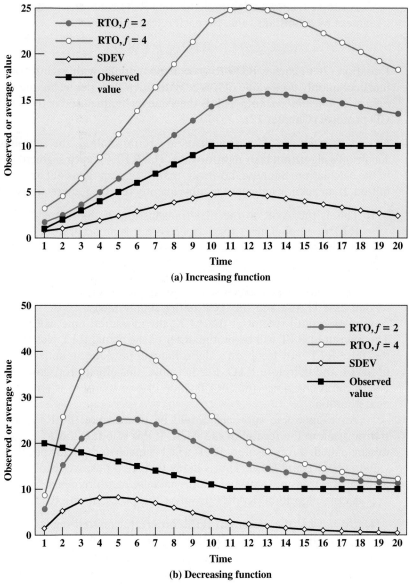

Figure 20.9 Jacobson's RTO Calculation

A more sensible policy dictates that a sending TCP entity increase its RTO each time a segment is retransmitted; this is referred to as a *backoff* process. In the scenario of the preceding paragraph, after the first retransmission of a segment on each affected connection, the sending TCP entities will all wait a longer time before performing a second retransmission. This may give the internet time to clear the current congestion. If a second retransmission is required, each sending TCP entity will wait an even longer time before timing out for a third retransmission, giving the internet an even longer period to recover.

A simple technique for implementing RTO backoff is to multiply the RTO for a segment by a constant value for each retransmission:

$$RTO = q \times RTO \qquad (20.6)$$

Equation (20.6) causes RTO to grow exponentially with each retransmission. The most commonly used value of q is 2. With this value, the technique is referred to as *binary exponential backoff*. This is the same technique used in the Ethernet CSMA/CD protocol (Chapter 12).

KARN'S ALGORITHM   If no segments are retransmitted, the sampling process for Jacobson's algorithm is straightforward. The RTT for each segment can be included in the calculation. Suppose, however, that a segment times out and must be retransmitted. If an acknowledgment is subsequently received, there are two possibilities:

1. This is the ACK to the first transmission of the segment. In this case, the RTT is simply longer than expected but is an accurate reflection of network conditions.
2. This is the ACK to the second transmission.

The sending TCP entity cannot distinguish between these two cases. If the second case is true and the TCP entity simply measures the RTT from the first transmission until receipt of the ACK, the measured time will be much too long. The measured RTT will be on the order of the actual RTT plus the RTO. Feeding this false RTT into Jacobson's algorithm will produce an unnecessarily high value of SRTT and therefore RTO. Furthermore, this effect propagates forward a number of iterations, since the SRTT value of one iteration is an input value in the next iteration.

An even worse approach would be to measure the RTT from the *second* transmission to the receipt of the ACK. If this is in fact the ACK to the first transmission, then the measured RTT will be much too small, producing a too low value of SRTT and RTO. This is likely to have a positive feedback effect, causing additional retransmissions and additional false measurements.

Karn's algorithm [KARN91] solves this problem with the following rules:

1. Do not use the measured RTT for a retransmitted segment to update SRTT and SDEV [Equation (20.5)].
2. Calculate the backoff RTO using Equation (20.6) when a retransmission occurs.
3. Use the backoff RTO value for succeeding segments until an acknowledgment arrives for a segment that has not been retransmitted.

When an acknowledgment is received to an unretransmitted segment, Jacobson's algorithm is again activated to compute future RTO values.

Window Management

In addition to techniques for improving the effectiveness of the retransmission timer, a number of approaches to managing the send window have been examined. The size of TCP's send window can have a critical effect on whether TCP can be used efficiently without causing congestion. We discuss two techniques found in virtually all modern implementations of TCP: slow start and **dynamic window sizing on congestion.**[4]

SLOW START The larger the send window used in TCP, the more segments that a sending TCP entity can send before it must wait for an acknowledgment. This can create a problem when a TCP connection is first established, because the TCP entity is free to dump the entire window of data onto the internet.

One strategy that could be followed is for the TCP sender to begin sending from some relatively large but not maximum window, hoping to approximate the window size that would ultimately be provided by the connection. This is risky because the sender might flood the internet with many segments before it realized from time-outs that the flow was excessive. Instead, some means is needed of gradually expanding the window until acknowledgments are received. This is the purpose of the slow-start mechanism.

With slow start, TCP transmission is constrained by the following relationship:

$$awnd = \text{MIN}[\,credit, cwnd\,] \tag{20.7}$$

where

$awnd$ = allowed window, in segments. This is the number of segments that TCP is currently allowed to send without receiving further acknowledgments.

$cwnd$ = congestion window, in segments. A window used by TCP during start-up and to reduce flow during periods of congestion.

$credit$ = the amount of unused credit granted in the most recent acknowledgment, in segments. When an acknowledgment is received, this value is calculated as $window/segment\_size$, where $window$ is a field in the incoming TCP segment (the amount of data the peer TCP entity is willing to accept).

When a new connection is opened, the TCP entity initializes $cwnd = 1$. That is, TCP is only allowed to send 1 segment and then must wait for an acknowledgment before transmitting a second segment. Each time an acknowledgment to new data is received, the value of $cwnd$ is increased by 1, up to some maximum value.

In effect, the slow-start mechanism probes the internet to make sure that the TCP entity is not sending too many segments into an already congested environment. As acknowledgments arrive, TCP is able to open up its window until the flow is controlled by the incoming ACKs rather than by $cwnd$.

The term *slow start* is a bit of a misnomer, because $cwnd$ actually grows exponentially. When the first ACK arrives, TCP opens $cwnd$ to 2 and can send two segments. When these two segments are acknowledged, TCP can slide the window 1 segment for each incoming ACK and can increase $cwnd$ by 1 for each incoming

---

[4]These algorithms were developed by Jacobson [JACO88] and are also described in RFC 2581. Van Jacobson describes things in units of TCP segments, whereas RFC 2581 relies primarily on units of TCP data octets, with some reference to calculations in units of segments. We follow the development in [JACO88].

ACK. Therefore, at this point TCP can send four segments. When these four are acknowledged, TCP will be able to send eight segments.

DYNAMIC WINDOW SIZING ON CONGESTION The slow-start algorithm has been found to work effectively for initializing a connection. It enables the TCP sender to determine quickly a reasonable window size for the connection. Might not the same technique be useful when there is a surge in congestion? In particular, suppose a TCP entity initiates a connection and goes through the slow-start procedure. At some point, either before or after *cwnd* reaches the size of the credit allocated by the other side, a segment is lost (time-out). This is a signal that congestion is occurring. It is not clear how serious the congestion is. Therefore, a prudent procedure would be to reset *cwnd* $= 1$ and begin the slow-start process all over.

This seems like a reasonable, conservative procedure, but in fact it is not conservative enough. Jacobson [JACO88] points out that "it is easy to drive a network into saturation but hard for the net to recover." In other words, once congestion occurs, it may take a long time for the congestion to clear.[5] Thus, the exponential growth of *cwnd* under slow start may be too aggressive and may worsen the congestion. Instead, Jacobson proposed the use of slow start to begin with, followed by a linear growth in *cwnd*. The rules are as follows. When a time-out occurs,

1. Set a slow-start threshold equal to half the current congestion window; that is, set *ssthresh* $=$ *cwnd*/2.

2. Set *cwnd* $= 1$ and perform the slow-start process until *cwnd* $=$ *ssthresh*. In this phase, *cwnd* is increased by 1 for every ACK received.

3. For *cwnd* $\geq$ *ssthresh*, increase *cwnd* by 1 for each round-trip time.

Figure 20.10 illustrates this behavior. Note that it takes 11 round-trip times to recover to the *cwnd* level that initially took 4 round-trip times to achieve.

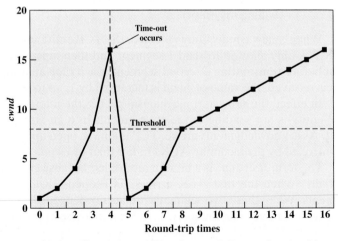

Figure 20.10 Illustration of Slow Start and Congestion Avoidance

---

[5]Kleinrock refers to this phenomenon as the long-tail effect during a rush-hour period. See Sections 2.7 and 2.10 of [KLEI76] for a detailed discussion.

FAST RETRANSMIT   The retransmission timer (RTO) that is used by a sending TCP entity to determine when to retransmit a segment will generally be noticeably longer than the actual round-trip time (RTT) that the ACK for that segment will take to reach the sender. Both the original RFC 793 algorithm and the Jacobson algorithm set the value of RTO at somewhat greater than the estimated round-trip time SRTT. Several factors make this margin desirable:

1. RTO is calculated on the basis of a prediction of the next RTT, estimated from past values of RTT. If delays in the network fluctuate, then the estimated RTT may be smaller than the actual RTT.

2. Similarly, if delays at the destination fluctuate, the estimated RTT becomes unreliable.

3. The destination system may not ACK each segment but cumulatively ACK multiple segments, while at the same time sending ACKs when it has any data to send. This behavior contributes to fluctuations in RTT.

A consequence of these factors is that if a segment is lost, TCP may be slow to retransmit. If the destination TCP is using an in-order accept policy (see Section 15.2), then many segments may be lost. Even in the more likely case that the destination TCP is using an in-window accept policy, a slow retransmission can cause problems. To see this, suppose that A transmits a sequence of segments, the first of which is lost. So long as its send window is not empty and RTO does not expire, A can continue to transmit without receiving an acknowledgment. B receives all of these segments except the first. But B must buffer all of these incoming segments until the missing one is retransmitted; it cannot clear its buffer by sending the data to an application until the missing segment arrives. If retransmission of the missing segment is delayed too long, B will have to begin discarding incoming segments.

Jacobson [JACO90b] proposed two procedures, called fast retransmit and fast recovery, that under some circumstances improve on the performance provided by RTO. Fast retransmit takes advantage of the following rule in TCP. If a TCP entity receives a segment out of order, it must immediately issue an ACK for the last in-order segment that was received. TCP will continue to repeat this ACK with each incoming segment until the missing segment arrives to "plug the hole" in its buffer. When the hole is plugged, TCP sends a cumulative ACK for all of the in-order segments received so far.

When a source TCP receives a duplicate ACK, it means that either (1) the segment following the ACKed segment was delayed so that it ultimately arrived out of order or (2) that segment was lost. In case (1), the segment does ultimately arrive and therefore TCP should not retransmit. But in case (2), the arrival of a duplicate ACK can function as an early warning system to tell the source TCP that a segment has been lost and must be retransmitted. To make sure that we have case (2) rather than case (1), Jacobson recommends that a TCP sender wait until it receives three duplicate ACKs to the same segment (i.e., a total of four ACKs to the same segment). Under these circumstances, it is highly likely that the following segment has been lost and should be retransmitted immediately, rather than waiting for a time-out.

FAST RECOVERY   When a TCP entity retransmits a segment using fast retransmit, it knows (or rather assumes) that a segment was lost, even though it has not yet timed out on that segment. Accordingly, the TCP entity should take congestion avoidance measures. One obvious strategy is the slow-start/congestion avoidance procedure used when a time-out occurs. That is, the entity could set *ssthresh* to *cwnd*/2, set*cwnd* $= 1$ and begin the exponential slow-start process until *cwnd* $=$ *ssthresh*, and then increase *cwnd* linearly. Jacobson [JACO90b] argues that this approach is unnecessarily conservative. As was just pointed out, the very fact that multiple ACKs have returned indicates that data segments are getting through fairly regularly to the other side. So Jacobson proposes a fast recovery technique: Retransmit the lost segment, cut *cwnd* in half, and then proceed with the linear increase of *cwnd*. This technique avoids the initial exponential slow-start process.

RFC 3782 (The NewReno Modification to TCP's Fast Recovery Mechanism) modifies the fast recovery algorithm to improve the response when two segments are lost within a single window. Using fast retransmit, a sender retransmits a segment before time-out because it infers that the segment was lost. If the sender subsequently receives an acknowledgment that does not cover all of the segments transmitted before fast retransmit was initiated, the sender may infer that two segments were lost from the current window and retransmit an additional segment. The details of both fast recovery and modified fast recovery are complex; the reader is referred to RFCs 5681 and 3782.

Explicit Congestion Notification

An example of explicit congestion signaling is the explicit congestion notification capability provided in IP and TCP and defined in RFC 3168. This mechanism was first proposed in [FLOY94]. The IP header includes the 2-bit Explicit Congestion Notification field, which enables routers to indicate to end nodes packets that are experiencing congestion, without the necessity of immediately dropping such packets. A value of 00 indicates a packet that is not using ECN. A value of 01 or 10 is set by the data sender to indicate that the end-points of the transport protocol are ECN-capable. A value of 11 is set by a router to indicate congestion has been encountered. The TCP header includes two one-bit flags: the ECN-Echo flag and the CWR (congestion window reduced) flag. A typical sequence of events involving all of these bits is as follows:

- The ECN field is set to 10 or 01 in packets transmitted by the sender to indicate that ECN is supported by the transport entities for these packets.
- An ECN-capable router detects impending congestion and detects that an ECN is set to 10 or 01 in the packet it is about to drop. Instead of dropping the packet, the router chooses to set the field to 11 in the IP header and forwards the packet.
- The receiver receives the packet with the 11 value set, and sets the ECN-Echo flag in its next TCP ACK sent to the sender.
- The sender receives the TCP ACK with ECN-Echo set, and reacts to the congestion as if a packet had been dropped.
- The sender sets the CWR flag in the TCP header of the next packet sent to the receiver to acknowledge its receipt of and reaction to the ECN-Echo flag. Typically, the reaction is to reduce the congestion window.

20.6 DATAGRAM CONGESTION CONTROL PROTOCOL

In this section, we introduce an important recent protocol, the **Datagram Congestion Control Protocol (DCCP)**. We start with a discussion of a key Internet concept known as TCP friendliness.

TCP Friendliness

An important challenge for maintaining the usefulness of the Internet is for it to be able to provide good service under heavy load. Even in the early days of the Internet, it was realized that severe congestion could occur if there were too many traffic flows operating independently and without regard to their effect on overall Internet performance, a situation referred to as **congestion collapse** [NAGL84], and illustrated in Figure 20.4. It was the phenomenon of congestion collapse that led to the development of the elaborate set of TCP congestion control procedures described in Section 20.5.

The TCP congestion control procedures do not support applications that do not use TCP. With the ever-increasing load from multimedia applications, much of the traffic on the Internet does not use TCP but rather uses UDP or some other connectionless protocol. These applications generally do not take into consideration overall Internet congestion effects and hence can contribute to congestion collapse. Thus, there has been an interest in developing a means of controlling data flows on the Internet from such applications in a way that is **TCP friendly**. The term *TCP friendly,* also known as TCP compatible, in rough terms refers to flows that will back off appropriately in the face of congestion. [BRAD98] defined the concept this way:

> We introduce the term "TCP-compatible" for a flow that behaves under congestion like a flow produced by a conformant TCP. A TCP-compatible flow is responsive to congestion notification, and in steady-state it uses no more bandwidth than a conformant TCP running under comparable conditions.

It is possible to quantify this requirement by deriving a **TCP-friendly equation** [FLOY99]:

$$T \le \frac{1.22 \times B}{R \times \sqrt{p}} \tag{20.8}$$

where

T = sending rate
B = maximum packet length
R = round-trip time experienced by the connection
p = packet drop rate

The equation makes intuitive sense. Larger packets are preferred compared to more numerous smaller packets because they require less cumulative processing.

An increase in either the round-trip time or the packet drop rate is an indication of increasing congestion and hence should lead to a reduction of the sending rate to help ease the congestion.

Thus the goal for applications that do not use TCP is to provide comparable congestion avoidance support so that the application conforms to Equation (20.8).

DCCP Operation

For multimedia applications, such as streaming audio or video, a reliable connection-oriented transport protocol, such as TCP, is not appropriate for two reasons: It imposes too much overhead and generally it is not desirable to delay the stream in order to retransmit dropped packets. On the other hand, it is difficult to see how an unreliable connectionless transport protocol, such as UDP, can detect and react to congestion so as to conform to the TCP-friendly equation. Accordingly, the Internet community has developed an unreliable connection-oriented protocol known as Datagram Congestion Control Protocol (DCCP), defined in RFC 4340. Because DCCP is connection-oriented, it can include mechanism for detecting congestion by determining round-trip time and packet drop rates. Because DCCP is unreliable, it does not include unwanted packet retransmission schemes.

DCCP runs on top of IP and serves as an alternative transport protocol for applications that would otherwise use UDP. DCCP consists of the following ten packet types:

- **DCCP-Request:** Sent by the client to initiate a connection (the first part of the three-way initiation handshake).
- **DCCP-Response:** Sent by the server in response to a DCCP-Request (the second part of the three-way initiation handshake).
- **DCCP-Data:** Used to transmit application data.
- **DCCP-Ack:** Used to transmit pure acknowledgments. That is, this packet is sent by one end of the connection to acknowledge an incoming data packet when there is no data packet available to send back.
- **DCCP-DataAck:** Used to transmit application data with piggybacked acknowledgment information.
- **DCCP-CloseReq:** Sent by the server to request that the client close the connection.
- **DCCP-Close:** Used by the client or the server to close the connection; elicits a DCCP-Reset in response.
- **DCCP-Reset:** Used to terminate the connection, either normally or abnormally.
- **DCCP-Sync, DCCP-SyncAck:** Used to resynchronize sequence numbers after large bursts of loss.

Figure 20.11 shows the normal exchange between two DCCP users. First, the two users must establish a logical full-duplex connection. This phase also includes a negotiation of options, such as which congestion control mechanism to use. Following this is a data transfer phase, in which each side can send data and each side must acknowledge incoming data. For this purpose each data and acknowledgment

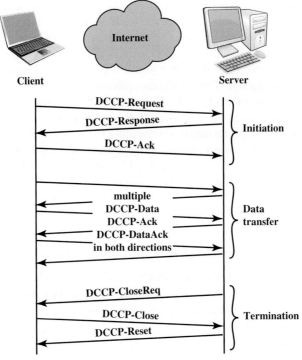

Figure 20.11   DCCP Packet Exchange

packet carries a sequence number that is incremented by one per packet. Finally, either side may terminate that connection. Note that both the initiation and termination phases involve three-way handshakes.

A single sequence number is maintained in each direction for all ten types of packets. The following exchange between DCCP entities A and B is an example:

A → B: DCCP-Data(seqno=1)

A → B: DCCP-Data(seqno=2)

B → A: DCCP-Ack(seqno=10, ackno = 2)

A → B: DCCP-DataAck(seqno=3, ackno = 10)

B → A: DCCP-DataACK(seqno=11, ackno =3)

The first two lines show that A sends two packets to B, numbered 1 and 2. Then B sends a pure acknowledgment with a sequence number of 10 and an acknowledgment of the last received packet. With A's next data packet, it increments its own sequence number and acknowledges the last packed from B by including an acknowledgment number. B's next packet is a data packet with a sequence number and an acknowledgment number. The use of a single sequence numbering scheme for all three types of packets enables the endpoints to detect all packet loss, including acknowledgment loss.

Since DCCP provides unreliable semantics, there are no retransmissions, and having a TCP-style cumulative acknowledgment field doesn't make sense. DCCP's

Acknowledgment Number field equals the greatest sequence number received, rather than the smallest sequence number not received. Separate options may be used to indicate any intermediate sequence numbers that weren't received.

If a network outage or large burst of dropped packets occurs, the two endpoints will receive sequence numbers and acknowledgment numbers very different from what was expected. This could complicate some of the congestion control mechanisms employed with DCCP. To bring the endpoints back into synchronization, an endpoint receiving an unexpected sequence or acknowledgment number sends a Sync packet asking its partner to validate that sequence number. The other endpoint processes the Sync and replies with a SyncAck packet. When the original endpoint receives a SyncAck with a valid ackno, it updates its expected sequence number windows based on that SyncAck's seqno.

DCCP Packet Format

Figure 20.12 shows the overall format of a DCCP packet. Every packet includes a generic header, which consists of the following fields:

- **Source and Destination Ports** (16 bits each): These fields identify the connection, similar to the corresponding fields in TCP and UDP.
- **Data Offset** (8 bits): The offset from the start of the packet's DCCP header to the start of its application data area, in 32-bit words.
- **CCVal** (4 bits): Reserved for use by the sender's congestion control mechanism. That is, it can be used by a congestion control mechanism to encode up to 4 bits of information in the generic header.

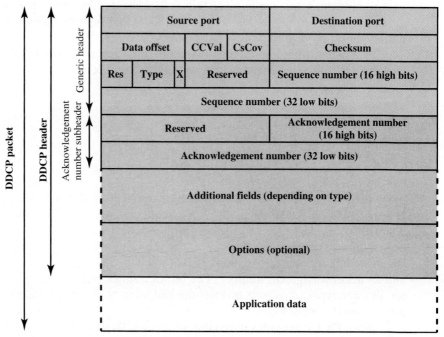

Figure 20.12   DCCP Packet Format ($X = 1$)

- **Checksum Coverage (CsCov)** (4 bits): Checksum Coverage determines the parts of the packet that are covered by the Checksum field. This always includes the DCCP header and options, but some or all of the application data may be excluded. This can improve performance on noisy links for applications that can tolerate corruption.
- **Checksum** (16 bits): The Internet checksum of the packet's DCCP header (including options), a network-layer pseudoheader, and, depending on Checksum Coverage, all, some, or none of the application data.
- **Reserved (Res)** (3 bits): Not used.
- **Type** (4 bits): Specifies the type of the packet.
- **Extended Sequence Numbers (X)** (1 bit): Set to one to indicate the use of an extended generic header with 48-bit Sequence and Acknowledgment Numbers. Figure 20.12 shows the format for $X = 1$.
- **Reserved** (8 bits): Not used if $X = 1$. This field is not present for $X = 0$, so that the 24-bit sequence number can be accommodated without an additional 32-bit word.
- **Sequence Number** (48 or 24 bits): Identifies the packet uniquely in the sequence of all packets the source sent on this connection. Sequence Number increases by one with every packet sent, including packets such as DCCP-Ack that carry no application data.

Connection initiation, synchronization, and teardown packets must use 48-bit sequence numbers. This ensures that the endpoints agree on sequence number and reduces the probability of success of some types of attacks. The 24-bit sequence number is simply the lower 24 bits of the sequence number and should suffice in most cases, providing greater efficiency in the transfer of data packets.

Following the generic header is the acknowledgment subheader, which contains the 24- or 48-bit acknowledgment number. All packets include this header except DCCP-Request and DCCP-Data. Allowing for DCCP-Data packets without including an acknowledgment number enables a data-intense user, such as a video stream, to transmit with the minimum of overhead.

The remainder of the packet includes additional fields required by various packet types, optional data for various functions, and optional application data.

DCCP Congestion Control

As with TCP, DCCP is a transport-layer protocol that defines the mechanisms and formats for connection establishment, data transfer, and connection termination but does not directly specify congestion control mechanisms. The DCCP packet format is sufficiently flexible to be able to support a variety of congestion control regimes. Accordingly, the Internet DCCP Working Group has defined two congestion control mechanisms, each assigned a congestion control identifier (CCID), and will define further mechanisms in the future. The two mechanisms so far defined are:

- **TCP-like congestion control (CCID 2):** This mechanism has behavior modeled directly on TCP, including congestion window, slow start, and time-outs. CCID 2 achieves maximum bandwidth over the long term, consistent with the use of end-to-end congestion control, but halves its congestion window in response to each congestion event. This leads to the abrupt rate changes typical of TCP. Applications should use CCID 2 if they prefer maximum bandwidth utilization to steadiness of rate. This is often the case for applications that are not streaming their data directly to the user.

- **TCP-friendly rate control (TFDC) (CCID 3):** This mechanism is based on the use of a variant of the TCP-friendly equation (Equation 20.8). TFRC is designed to be reasonably fair when competing for bandwidth with TCP-like flows, where a flow is "reasonably fair" if its sending rate is generally within a factor of two of the sending rate of a TCP flow under the same conditions. However, TFRC has a much lower variation of throughput over time compared with TCP, which makes CCID 3 more suitable than CCID 2 for applications such as streaming media, where a relatively smooth sending rate is important.

A CCID-compliant implementation must implement the appropriate congestion control algorithms and must include the appropriate fields and optional information in the DDCP packets. For example, TFRC requires that data senders attach to each data packet a coarse-grained "timestamp" that increments every quarter round-trip time. This timestamp allows the receiver to group losses and marks that occurred during the same round-trip time into a single congestion event.

20.7 RECOMMENDED READING AND ANIMATIONS

[YANG95] is a comprehensive survey of congestion control techniques. [JAIN90] and [JAIN92] provide excellent discussions of the requirements for congestion control, the various approaches that can be taken, and performance considerations. An excellent discussion of data network performance issues is provided by [KLEI93]. While somewhat dated, the definitive reference on flow control is [GERL80].

[MILL10] is a lengthy (570 pages) analysis of a wide variety of Internet congestion control mechanisms.

Perhaps the best coverage of the various TCP strategies for flow and congestion control is to be found in [FALL12]. An essential paper for understanding the issues involved is the classic [JACO88].

[KOLH06] is an excellent overview of DCCP.

FALL12 Fall, K., and Stevens, W. *TCP/IP Illustrated, Volume 1: The Protocols.* Reading, MA: Addison-Wesley, 2012.

GERL80 Gerla, M., and Kleinrock, L. "Flow Control: A Comparative Survey." *IEEE Transactions on Communications,* April 1980.

JACO88 Jacobson, V. "Congestion Avoidance and Control." *Proceedings, SIGCOMM '88, Computer Communication Review*, August 1988; reprinted in Computer Communication Review, January 1995; a slightly revised version is available at http://ee.lbl.gov/nrg-papers.html

JAIN90 Jain, R. "Congestion Control in Computer Networks: Issues and Trends." *IEEE Network Magazine,* May 1990.

JAIN92 Jain, R. "Myths About Congestion Management in High-Speed Networks." *Internetworking: Research and Experience*, Volume 3, 1992.

KLEI93 Kleinrock, L. "On the Modeling and Analysis of Computer Networks." *Proceedings of the IEEE*, August 1993.

KOHL06 Kohler, E.; Handley, M.; and Floyd, S. "Designing DCCP: Congestion Control Without Reliability." *ACM Computer Communication Review*, October 2006.

MILL10 Mill, K., et al. Study of Proposed Internet Congestion Control Mechanisms. NIST Special Publication 500-82, May 2010.

YANG95 Yang, C., and Reddy, A. "A Taxonomy for Congestion Control Algorithms in Packet Switching Networks." *IEEE Network*, July/August 1995.

Animations

Animations that illustrate the operation of TCP congestion control mechanisms are available at the Premium Web site. The reader is encouraged to view these animations to reinforce concepts from this chapter.

20.8 KEY TERMS, REVIEW QUESTIONS, AND PROBLEMS

Key Terms

backpressure	exponential average	retransmission timer
choke packet	exponential RTO backoff	RTT variance estimation
congestion	fairness	slow start
congestion collapse	fast recovery	TCP friendliness
congestion control	fast retransmit	token bucket
Datagram Congestion	implicit congestion signaling	traffic management
Control Protocol	Jacobson's algorithm	traffic policing
(DCCP)	leaky bucket	traffic shaping
dynamic window sizing	quality of service (QoS)	window management
explicit congestion signaling	reservations	

Review Questions

20.1 When a node experiences saturation with respect to incoming packets, what general strategies may be used?

20.2 Why is it that when the load exceeds the network capacity, delay tends to infinity?

20.3 Give a brief explanation of each of the congestion control techniques illustrated in Figure 20.5.

20.4 What is the difference between backward and forward explicit congestion signaling?

20.5 Briefly explain the three general approaches to explicit congestion signaling.

20.6 What are the differences between token bucket and leaky bucket?

20.7 How can TCP be used to deal with network or internet congestion?

20.8 Distinguish among TCP, UDP, and DCCP.

Problems

20.1 A proposed congestion control technique is known as isarithmic control. In this method, the total number of frames in transit is fixed by inserting a fixed number of permits into the network. These permits circulate at random through the frame relay network. Whenever a frame handler wants to relay a frame just given to it by an attached user, it must first capture and destroy a permit. When the frame is delivered to the destination user by the frame handler to which it attaches, that frame handler reissues the permit. List three potential problems with this technique.

20.2 When the sustained traffic through a packet-switching node exceeds the node's capacity, the node must discard packets. Buffers only defer the congestion problem; they do not solve it. Consider the packet-switching network in Figure 20.13. Five stations attach to one of the network's nodes. The node has a single link to the rest of the network with a normalized throughput capacity of $C = 1.0$. Senders 1 through 5 are sending at average sustained rates of r_i of 0.1, 0.2, 0.3, 0.4, and 0.5 respectively. Clearly the node is overloaded. To deal with the congestion, the node discards packets from sender i with a probability of p_i.

a. Show the relationship among p_i, r_i, and C so that the rate of undiscarded packets does not exceed C.

The node establishes a discard policy by assigning values to the pi such that the relationship derived in part (a) of this problem is satisfied. For each of the

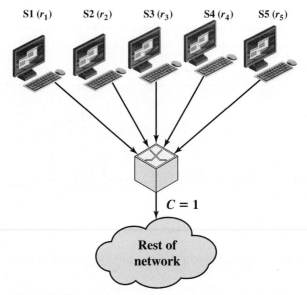

Figure 20.13 Stations Attached to a Packet-Switching Node

following policies, verify that the relationship is satisfied and describe in words the policy from the point of view of the senders.

b. $p_1 = 0.333; p_2 = 0.333; p_3 = 0.333; p_4 = 0.333; p_5 = 0.333$

c. $p_1 = 0.091; p_2 = 0.182; p_3 = 0.273; p_4 = 0.364; p_5 = 0.455$

d. $p_1 = 0.0; p_2 = 0.0; p_3 = 0.222; p_4 = 0.417; p_5 = 0.533$

e. $p_1 = 0.0; p_2 = 0.0; p_3 = 0.0; p_4 = 0.0; p_5 = 1.0$

20.3 A congestion control scheme used with ATM (Available Bit Rate) is to decrease the allowable data rate in response to congestion with the following equation.

$$\text{Ratenew} = \text{Rateold} - \text{Rateold} \times \text{RDF}$$

where RDF is the rate decrease factor.

a. Discuss how fast/slow does the sender respond to congestion for the various value of RDF.

b. If the equation was changed to Ratenew = Rateold − Rateold × α, do you think the response will be better or worse and why?

20.4 Consider the packet-switching network depicted in Figure 20.14. C is the capacity of a link in frames per second. Node A presents a constant load of 0.8 frames per second destined for A'. Node B presents a load λ destined for B'. Node S has a common pool of buffers that it uses for traffic both to A' and B'. When the buffer is full, frames are discarded, and are later retransmitted by the source user. S has a throughput capacity of 2. Plot the total throughput (i.e., the sum of A-A' and B-B' delivered traffic) as a function of λ. What fraction of the throughput is A-A' traffic for $\lambda > 1$?

20.5 For a frame relay network to be able to detect and then signal congestion, it is necessary for each frame handler to monitor its queueing behavior. If queue lengths begin to grow to a dangerous level, then either forward or backward explicit notification or a combination should be set to try to reduce the flow of frames through that frame handler. The frame handler has some choice as to which logical connections should be alerted to congestion. If congestion is becoming quite serious, all logical connections through a frame handler might be notified. In the early stages of congestion, the frame handler might just notify users for those connections that are generating the most traffic.

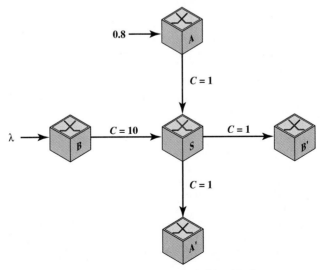

Figure 20.14 Network of Packet-Switching Nodes

The algorithm makes use of the following variables:

t = current time
t_i = time of ith arrival or departure event
q = number of frames in the system after the event
T_0 = time at the beginning of the previous cycle
T_1 = time at the beginning of the current cycle

The algorithm consists of three components:

1. Update: Beginning with $q_0 := 0$
   If the ith event is an arrival event, $q := q_{i-1} + 1$
   If the ith event is a departure event, $q := q_{i-1} - 1$

2.
$$A_{i-1} = \sum_{\substack{i \\ t_i \in [T_0, T_1)}} q_{i-1}(t_i - t_{i-1})$$

$$A_i = \sum_{\substack{i \\ t_i \in [T_1, t)}} q_{i-1}(t_i - t_{i-1})$$

3.
$$L = \frac{A_i + A_{i-1}}{t - T_0}$$

Figure 20.15   A Frame Relay Algorithm

In one of the frame relay specifications, an algorithm for monitoring queue lengths is suggested; this is shown in Figure 20.15. A cycle begins when the outgoing circuit goes from idle (queue empty) to busy (nonzero queue size, including the current frame). If a threshold value is exceeded, then the circuit is in a state of incipient congestion, and the congestion avoidance bits should be set on some or all logical connections that use that circuit. Describe the algorithm in words and explain its advantages.

20.6 The token bucket scheme places a limit on the length of time at which traffic can depart at the maximum data rate. Let the token bucket be defined by a bucket size B octets and a token arrival rate of R octets/second, and let the maximum output data rate be M octets/s.

  a. Derive a formula for S, which is the length of the maximum-rate burst. That is, for how long can a flow transmit at the maximum output rate when governed by a token bucket?

  b. What is the value of S for $b = 250$ KB, $r = 2$ MB/s, and $M = 25$ MB/s?

  Hint: the formula for S is not so simple as it might appear, because more tokens arrive while the burst is being output.

20.7 Consider a token bucket with a capacity of 1 Mb, a token replenishment rate of 2 Mbps, and an outgoing network link of capacity 10 Mbps. Suppose that an application produces 0.5-Mb burst every 250 ms for 3 seconds and that initially the bucket is full of tokens.

  a. Initially, what is the output rate that can be sustained?

  b. How long can the bucket sustain this rate?

  c. Show the output over the 3-second time interval.

20.8 A network has a committed bandwidth of 5 Mbps. The host sends a burst of data at the rate of 15 Mbps for 3 s, then remains silent for 4 s and then sends another burst of data at the rate of 6 Mbps for 3 s. If the leaky bucket technique is used,

    a. How much data will be in the bucket at each second?

    b. If the bucket size is 2.862 MB, what is the minimum bandwidth of the link required?

20.9 Analyze the advantages and disadvantages of performing congestion control at the transport layer, rather than at the network layer.

20.10 A TCP connection has 500-byte segments. The receiver window has a buffer of size 10,000 bytes. It has advertised the following window sizes with the acknowledgements: {6000, 7000, 7000, 8000, 6000, 6000, 5000, 8000}. Find the sizes of the congestion window and actual window with the dynamic window sizing technique.

20.11 One difficulty with the original TCP SRTT estimator is the choice of an initial value. In the absence of any special knowledge of network conditions, the typical approach is to pick an arbitrary value, such as 3 s, and hope that this will converge quickly to an accurate value. If this estimate is too small, TCP will perform unnecessary retransmissions. If it is too large, TCP will wait a long time before retransmitting if the first segment is lost. Also, the convergence may be slow, as this problem indicates.

    a. Choose $\alpha = 0.85$ and $SRTT(0) = 3$ s, and assume all measured RTT values $= 1$ s and no packet loss. What is $SRTT(19)$? *Hint:* Equation (20.3) can be rewritten to simplify the calculation, using the expression $(1 - \alpha^n)/(1 - \alpha)$.

    b. Now let $SRTT(0) = 1$ s and assume measured RTT values $= 3$ s and no packet loss. What is $SRTT(19)$?

20.12 Derive Equation (20.2) from Equation (20.1).

20.13 In Equation (20.5), rewrite the definition of $SRTT(K + 1)$ so that it is a function of $SERR(K+1)$. Interpret the result.

20.14 If the packet size is 512 bytes, average round-trip time is 30 ms, and packet drop rate is 5%, what is the TCP-compatible sending rate?

20.15 A snapshot of a DCCP header in hexadecimal format is:

441C7A24   00011310   00300000   0000A003   00000000   030000DE

    a. What is the length of the header?

    b. What is the address of the source port?

    c. What is the address of the destination port?

    d. What is the sequence number?

    e. What is the acknowledgement number?

Assume 48 bits for the sequence number as well as the acknowledgement number.

CHAPTER 21

INTERNETWORK OPERATION

LEARNING OBJECTIVES

After studying this chapter, you should be able to:

♦ List and explain the requirements for multicasting.

♦ Present an overview of IGMPv3.

♦ Summarize the key elements of a software-defined network.

♦ Understand the operation of OpenFlow.

♦ Present an overview of Mobile IP.

This chapter begins with a discussion of multicasting. Next we look at a new approach to managing Internet traffic known as software-defined network (SDN), and the related protocol OpenFlow. The chapter then introduces the topic of Mobile IP. Refer to Figure 21.8 to see the position within the TCP/IP suite of the protocols discussed in this chapter.

21.1 MULTICASTING

Typically, an IP address refers to an individual host on a particular network. IP also accommodates addresses that refer to a group of hosts on one or more networks. Such addresses are referred to as **multicast addresses**, and the act of sending a packet from a source to the members of a multicast group is referred to as **multicasting**.

Multicasting has a number of practical applications. For example,

• **Multimedia:** A number of users "tune in" to a video or audio transmission from a multimedia source station.

• **Teleconferencing:** A group of workstations form a multicast group such that a transmission from any member is received by all other group members.

• **Database:** All copies of a replicated file or database are updated at the same time.

• **Distributed computation:** Intermediate results are sent to all participants.

• **Real-time workgroup:** Files, graphics, and messages are exchanged among active group members in real time.

Multicasting done within the scope of a single LAN segment is straightforward. IEEE 802 and other LAN protocols include provision for MAC-level multicast addresses. A packet with a multicast address is transmitted on a LAN segment.

Those stations that are members of the corresponding multicast group recognize the multicast address and accept the packet. In this case, only a single copy of the packet is ever transmitted. This technique works because of the broadcast nature of a LAN: a transmission from any one station is received by all other stations on the LAN.

In an internet environment, multicasting is a far more difficult undertaking. To see this, consider the configuration of Figure 21.1; a number of LANs are interconnected by routers. Routers connect to each other either over high-speed links or across a wide area network (network N4). A cost is associated with each link or network in each direction, indicated by the value shown leaving the router for that link or network. Suppose that the multicast server on network N1 is transmitting packets to a multicast address that represents the workstations indicated on networks N3, N5, and N6. Suppose that the server does not know the location of the members of the multicast group. Then one way to assure that the packet is received by all members of the group is to **broadcast** a copy of each packet to each network in the configuration, over the least-cost route for each network. For example, one packet would be addressed to N3 and would traverse N1, link L3, and N3. Router B is responsible for translating the IP-level multicast address to a MAC-level multicast address before transmitting the MAC frame onto

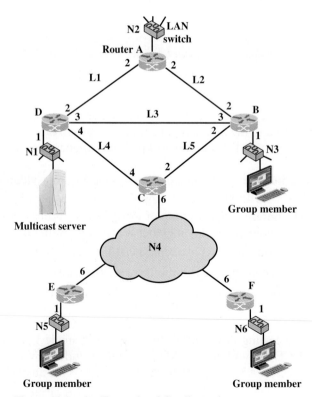

Figure 21.1 An Example of Configuration

Table 21.1   Traffic Generated by Various Multicasting Strategies

	Broadcast					Multiple Unicast				Multicast
	S→N2	S→N3	S→N5	S→N6	Total	S→N3	S→N5	S→N6	Total	
N1	1	1	1	1	4	1	1	1	3	1
N2										
N3	1	1	1					1	1	
N4			1	1	2		1	1	2	2
N5			1		1		1		1	1
N6			1	1			1	1	1	
L1	1				1					
L2										
L3		1			1	1			1	1
L4			1	1	2		1	1	2	1
L5										
Total	2	3	4	4	13	3	4	4	11	8

N3. Table 21.1 summarizes the number of packets generated on the various links and networks in order to transmit one packet to a multicast group by this method. In this table, the source is the multicast server on network N1 in Figure 21.1; the multicast address includes the group members on N3, N5, and N6. Each column in the table refers to the path taken from the source host to a destination router attached to a particular destination network. Each row of the table refers to a network or link in the configuration of Figure 21.1. Each entry in the table gives the number of packets that traverse a given network or link for a given path. A total of 13 copies of the packet are required for the broadcast technique.

Now suppose the source system knows the location of each member of the multicast group. That is, the source has a table that maps a multicast address into a list of networks that contain members of that multicast group. In that case, the source need only send packets to those networks that contain members of the group. We could refer to this as the **multiple unicast** strategy. Table 21.1 shows that in this case; 11 packets are required.

Both the broadcast and multiple unicast strategies are inefficient because they generate unnecessary copies of the source packet. In a true **multicast** strategy, the following method is used:

1. The least-cost path from the source to each network that includes members of the multicast group is determined. This results in a spanning tree[1] of the

---

[1]The concept of spanning tree was introduced in our discussion of bridges in Chapter 15. A spanning tree of a graph consists of all the nodes of the graph plus a subset of the links (edges) of the graph that provides connectivity (a path exists between any two nodes) with no closed loops (there is only one path between any two nodes).

configuration. Note that this is not a full spanning tree of the configuration. Rather, it is a spanning tree that includes only those networks containing group members.

2. The source transmits a single packet along the spanning tree.

3. The packet is replicated by routers only at branch points of the spanning tree.

Figure 21.2a shows the spanning tree for transmissions from the source to the multicast group, and Figure 21.2b shows this method in action. The source transmits a single packet over N1 to router D. D makes two copies of the packet, to transmit over links L3 and L4. B receives the packet from L3 and transmits it on N3, where it is read by members of the multicast group on the network. Meanwhile, C receives the packet sent on L4. It must now deliver that packet to both E and F. If network N4 were a broadcast network (e.g., an IEEE 802 LAN), then C would only need to transmit one instance of the packet for both routers to read. If N4 is a packet-switching WAN, then C must make two copies of the packet and address one to E and one to F. Each of these routers, in turn, retransmits the received packet on N5 and N6, respectively. As Table 21.1 shows, the multicast technique requires only eight copies of the packet.

Requirements for Multicasting

In ordinary unicast transmission over an internet, in which each datagram has a unique destination network, the task of each router is to forward the datagram along the shortest path from that router to the destination network. With multicast

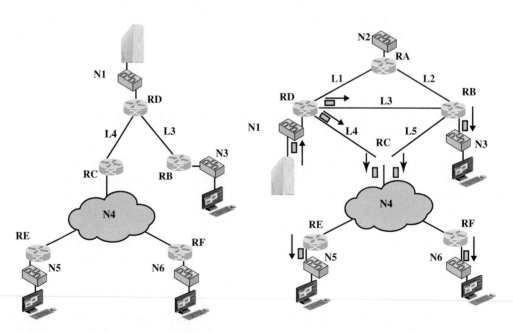

(a) Spanning tree from source to multicast group

(b) Packets generated for multicast transmission

Figure 21.2 Multicast Transmission Example

transmission, the router may be required to forward two or more copies of an incoming datagram. In our example, routers D and C both must forward two copies of a single incoming datagram.

Thus, we might expect that the overall functionality of multicast routing is more complex than unicast routing. The following is a list of required functions:

1. A convention is needed for identifying a multicast address. In IPv4, Class D addresses are reserved for this purpose. These are 32-bit addresses with 1110 as their high-order 4 bits, followed by a 28-bit group identifier. In IPv6, a 128-bit multicast address consists of an 8-bit prefix of all ones, a 4-bit flags field, a 4-bit scope field, and a 112-bit group identifier. The flags field, currently, only indicates whether this address is permanently assigned or not. The scope field indicates the scope of applicability of the address, ranging from a single network to global.

2. Each node (router or source node participating in the routing algorithm) must translate between an IP multicast address and a list of networks that contain members of this group. This information allows the node to construct a shortest-path spanning tree to all of the networks containing group members.

3. A router must translate between an IP multicast address and a network multicast address in order to deliver a multicast IP datagram on the destination network. For example, in IEEE 802 networks, a MAC-level address is 48 bits long; if the highest-order bit is 1, then it is a multicast address. Thus, for multicast delivery, a router attached to an IEEE 802 network must translate a 32-bit IPv4 or a 128-bit IPv6 multicast address into a 48-bit IEEE 802 MAC-level multicast address.

4. Although some multicast addresses may be assigned permanently, the more usual case is that multicast addresses are generated dynamically and that individual hosts may join and leave multicast groups dynamically. Thus, a mechanism is needed by which an individual host informs routers attached to the same network as itself of its inclusion in and exclusion from a multicast group. Internet Group Management Protocol (IGMP), described subsequently, provides this mechanism.

5. Routers must exchange two sorts of information. First, routers need to know which networks include members of a given multicast group. Second, routers need sufficient information to calculate the shortest path to each network containing group members. These requirements imply the need for a multicast routing protocol. A discussion of such protocols is beyond the scope of this book.

6. A routing algorithm is needed to calculate shortest paths to all group members.

7. Each router must determine multicast routing paths on the basis of both source and destination addresses.

The last point is a subtle consequence of the use of multicast addresses. To illustrate the point, consider again Figure 21.1. If the multicast server transmits a unicast packet addressed to a host on network N5, the packet is forwarded by router D to C, which then forwards the packet to E. Similarly, a packet addressed to a host on network N3 is forwarded by D to B. But now suppose that the server transmits a packet with a multicast address that includes hosts on N3, N5, and N6. As we have discussed, D makes two copies of the packet and sends one to B and one to C. What will C do when it receives a packet with such a multicast address? C knows that this packet is intended for networks N3, N5, and N6. A simple-minded approach would be for C to calculate the shortest path to each of these three networks. This produces the shortest-path spanning tree shown in Figure 21.3. As a result, C sends two copies of the packet out over N4, one intended for N5 and one intended for N6. But it also sends a copy of the packet to B for delivery on N3. Thus B will receive two copies of the packet, one from D and one from C. This is clearly not what was intended by the host on N1 when it launched the packet.

To avoid unnecessary duplication of packets, each router must route packets on the basis of both source and multicast destination. When C receives a packet intended for the multicast group from a source on N1, it must calculate the spanning tree with N1 as the root (shown in Figure 21.2a) and route on the basis of that spanning tree.

Internet Group Management Protocol (IGMP)

IGMP, defined in RFC 3376, is used by hosts and routers to exchange multicast group membership information over a LAN. IGMP takes advantage of the broadcast nature of a LAN to provide an efficient technique for the exchange of information among multiple hosts and routers. In general, IGMP supports two principal operations:

1. Hosts send messages to routers to subscribe to and unsubscribe from a multicast group defined by a given multicast address.
2. Routers periodically check which multicast groups are of interest to which hosts.

IGMP is currently at version 3. In IGMPv1, hosts could join a multicast group and routers used a timer to unsubscribe group members. IGMPv2 enabled a host to request to be unsubscribed from a group. The first two versions used essentially the following operational model:

- Receivers have to subscribe to multicast groups.
- Sources do not have to subscribe to multicast groups.
- Any host can send traffic to any multicast group.

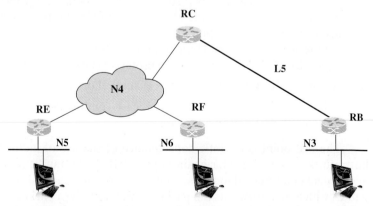

Figure 21.3   Spanning Tree from Router C to Multicast Group

This paradigm is very general, but it also has some weaknesses:

1. Spamming of multicast groups is easy. Even if there are application level filters to drop unwanted packets, still these packets consume valuable resources in the network and in the receiver that has to process them.
2. Establishment of the multicast distribution trees is problematic. This is mainly because the location of sources is not known.
3. Finding globally unique multicast addresses is difficult. It is always possible that another multicast group uses the same multicast address.

IGMPv3 addresses these weaknesses by

1. Allowing hosts to specify the list of hosts from which they want to receive traffic. Traffic from other hosts is blocked at routers.
2. Allowing hosts to block packets that come from sources that send unwanted traffic.

The remainder of this section discusses IGMPv3.

IGMP MESSAGE FORMAT   All IGMP messages are transmitted in IP datagrams. The current version defines two message types: Membership Query and Membership Report.

A **membership query** message is sent by a multicast router. There are three subtypes: a **general query**, used to learn which groups have members on an attached network; a **group-specific query**, used to learn if a particular group has any members on an attached network; and a **group-and-source specific query**, used to learn if any attached device desires reception of packets sent to a specified multicast address, from any of a specified list of sources. Figure 21.4a shows the message format, which consists of the following fields:

- **Type:** Defines this message type.
- **Max Response Code:** Indicates the maximum allowed time before sending a responding report in units of 0.1 s.
- **Checksum:** An error-detecting code, calculated as the 16-bit ones complement addition of all the 16-bit words in the message. For purposes of computation, the Checksum field is itself initialized to a value of zero. This is the same checksum algorithm used in IPv4.
- **Group Address:** Zero for a general query message; a valid IP multicast group address when sending a group-specific query or group-and-source-specific query.
- **S Flag:** When set to one, indicates to any receiving multicast routers that they are to suppress the normal timer updates they perform upon hearing a query.
- **QRV (querier's robustness variable):** If nonzero, the QRV field contains the RV value used by the querier (i.e., the sender of the query). Routers adopt the RV value from the most recently received query as their own RV value, unless that most recently received RV was zero, in which case the receivers use the default value or a statically configured value. The RV dictates how many times a host will retransmit a report to assure that it is not missed by any attached multicast routers.

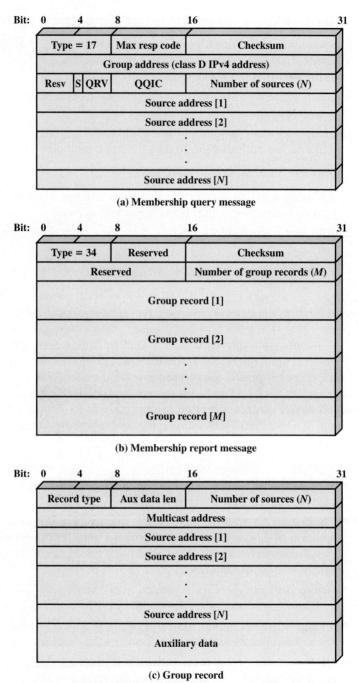

(a) Membership query message

(b) Membership report message

(c) Group record

Figure 21.4 IGMPv3 Message Formats

- **QQIC (querier's querier interval code):** Specifies the QI value used by the querier, which is a timer for sending multiple queries. Multicast routers that are not the current querier adopt the QI value from the most recently received query as their own QI value, unless that most recently received QI was zero, in which case the receiving routers use the default QI value.
- **Number of Sources:** Specifies how many source addresses are present in this query. This value is nonzero only for a group-and-source specific query.
- **Source Addresses:** If the number of sources is N, then there are N 32-bit unicast addresses appended to the message.

A **membership report** message consists of the following fields:

- **Type:** Defines this message type.
- **Checksum:** An error-detecting code, calculated as the 16-bit ones complement addition of all the 16-bit words in the message.
- **Number of Group Records:** Specifies how many group records are present in this report.
- **Group Records:** If the number of group records is M, then there are M 32-bit unicast group records appended to the message.

A group record includes the following fields:

- **Record Type:** Defines this record type, as described subsequently.
- **Aux Data Length:** Length of the auxiliary data field, in 32-bit words.
- **Number of Sources:** Specifies how many source addresses are present in this record.
- **Multicast Address:** The IP multicast address to which this record pertains.
- **Source Addresses:** If the number of sources is N, then there are N 32-bit unicast addresses appended to the message.
- **Auxiliary Data:** Additional information pertaining to this record. Currently, no auxiliary data values are defined.

IGMP Operation The objective of each host in using IGMP is to make itself known as a member of a group with a given multicast address to other hosts on the LAN and to all routers on the LAN. IGMPv3 introduces the ability for hosts to signal group membership with filtering capabilities with respect to sources. A host can either signal that it wants to receive traffic from all sources sending to a group except for some specific sources (called EXCLUDE mode) or that it wants to receive traffic only from some specific sources sending to the group (called INCLUDE mode). To join a group, a host sends an IGMP membership report message, in which the multicast address field is the multicast address of the group. This message is sent in an IP datagram with the same multicast destination address. In other words, the Multicast Address field of the IGMP message and the Destination Address field of the encapsulating IP header are the same. All hosts that are currently members of this multicast group will receive the message and learn of the new group member. Each router attached to the LAN must listen to all IP multicast addresses in order to hear all reports.

To maintain a valid current list of active group addresses, a multicast router periodically issues an IGMP general query message, sent in an IP datagram with an *all-hosts* multicast address. Each host that still wishes to remain a member of one or more multicast groups must read datagrams with the all-hosts address. When such a host receives the query, it must respond with a report message for each group to which it claims membership.

Note that the multicast router does not need to know the identity of every host in a group. Rather, it needs to know that there is at least one group member still active. Therefore, each host in a group that receives a query sets a timer with a random delay. Any host that hears another host claim membership in the group will cancel its own report. If no other report is heard and the timer expires, a host sends a report. With this scheme, only one member of each group should provide a report to the multicast router.

When a host leaves a group, it sends a leave group message to the all-routers static multicast address. This is accomplished by sending a membership report message with the INCLUDE option and a null list of source addresses; that is, no sources are to be included, effectively leaving the group. When a router receives such a message for a group that has group members on the reception interface, it needs to determine if there are any remaining group members. For this purpose, the router uses the group-specific query message.

GROUP MEMBERSHIP WITH IPv6 IGMP was defined for operation with IPv4 and makes use of 32-bit addresses. IPv6 internets need this same functionality. Rather than defining a separate version of IGMP for IPv6, its functions have been incorporated into the new version of the Internet Control Message Protocol (ICMPv6). ICMPv6 includes all of the functionality of ICMPv4 and IGMP. For multicast support, ICMPv6 includes both a group-membership query and a group-membership report message, which are used in the same fashion as in IGMP.

Protocol Independent Multicast (PIM)

IGMP provides a means of creating a group of multicast users, but is not itself a routing protocol. Over the years, a number of Internet multicast routing protocols have been proposed, but perhaps the most successful of these is the Protocol Independent Multicast (PIM)
Most multicast routing protocols have two characteristics:

1. The multicast protocol is an extension to an existing unicast routing protocol and requires that routers implement the unicast routing protocol. MOSPF as an extension to OSPF is an example.

2. In most cases, the multicast routing protocol is designed to be efficient when there is a relatively high concentration of multicast group members.

The use of a multicast extension to a unicast routing protocol is appropriate within a single autonomous system, where it is typical that a single unicast routing protocol is implemented. The assumption of a high concentration of multicast group members is often valid within a single autonomous system and for applications such as groupware. However, a different approach is needed to deal with a large internet of multiple autonomous systems and with applications such as multimedia, in which the size of a given multicast group may be relatively small and widely scattered.

To provide a more general solution to multicast routing, a new protocol has been developed, known as Protocol Independent Multicast (PIM). As the name suggests, PIM is a separate routing protocol, independent of any existing unicast routing protocol. PIM is designed to extract needed routing information from any unicast routing protocol and may work across multiple ASs with a number of different unicast routing protocols.

PIM STRATEGY   The design of PIM recognizes that a different approach may be needed to multicast routing depending on the concentration of multicast group members. When there are many multicast members and when many subnetworks within a configuration have members of a given multicast group, then the frequent exchange of group membership information is justified. In such an environment, it is desirable to build shared spanning trees, such as we saw in Figure 21.2b, so that packet duplication occurs as infrequently as possible. However, when there are a few widely scattered members to a given multicast group, different considerations apply. First, flooding of multicast group information to all routers is inefficient, because most routers will not be along the path of any members of a given multicast group. Second, there will be relatively little opportunity for using shared spanning trees, and therefore the focus should be on providing multiple shortest-path unicast routes.

To accommodate these differing requirements, PIM defines two modes of operation: dense-mode and sparse-mode operation. These are, in fact, two separate protocols. The dense-mode protocol is appropriate for intra-AS multicast routing and may be viewed as a potential alternative to a multicast version of OSPF known as MOSPF. The sparse-mode protocol is suited for inter-AS multicast routing. The remainder of this discussion concerns sparse-mode PIM (RFC 2362).

SPARSE-MODE PIM   The PIM specification defines a sparse group as one in which:

- The number of networks/domains with group members present is significantly smaller than the number of networks/domains in the internet.
- The internet spanned by the group is not sufficiently resource rich to ignore the overhead of current multicast routing schemes.

Before proceeding, let us define a group destination router to be a router with local group members (members attached to a subnetwork interfaced by that router). A router becomes a destination router for a given group when at least one local host joins that group using IGMP or a similar protocol. A group source router is a router that attaches to a network with at least one host that is transmitting packets on the multicast group address via that router. For some group, a given router will be both a source and a destination router. However, for broadcast types of applications, such as video distribution, there may be one or a small number of source routers with many destination routers.

The approach taken for sparse-mode PIM has the following elements:

1. For a multicast group, one router is designated as a *rendezvous point* (RP).
2. A group destination router sends a Join message toward the RP, requesting that its members be added to the group. The requesting router uses a unicast

shortest-path route to transmit the message toward the RP. The reverse of this path becomes part of the distribution tree from this RP to listeners in this group.

3. Any node that wishes to send to a multicast group sends packets toward the RP, using a shortest-path unicast route.

A transmission by this scheme, as defined so far, can be summarized as follows: A single packet follows the shortest unicast path from the sending node to the RP. From the RP, transmission occurs down the tree to the listeners, with each packet replicated at each split in the tree. This scheme minimizes the exchange of routing information, because routing information goes only from each router that supports group members to the RP. The scheme also provides reasonable efficiency. In particular, from the RP to the multicast receivers, a shared tree is used, minimizing the number of packets duplicated.

In a widely dispersed group, any RP will, of necessity, be remote from many of the group members, and paths for many group members will be much longer than the least-cost path. To help alleviate these drawbacks while maintaining the benefits of the PIM scheme, PIM allows a destination router to replace the group-shared tree with a shortest-path tree to any source. Once a destination router receives a multicast packet, it may elect to send a Join message back to the source router of that packet along a unicast shortest path. From then on, multicast packets between that source and all group members that are neighbors to that destination router follow the unicast shortest path.

Figure 21.5 illustrates the sequence of events. Once the destination begins to receive packets from the source by the shortest-path router, it sends a Prune

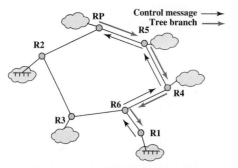

(a) R1 sends Join toward RP; RP adds path to distribution tree   (b) R2 sends Register to RP; RP returns Join; R2 builds path to RP

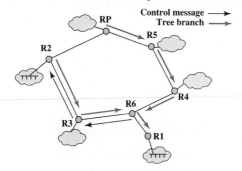

(c) R1 sends Join to R2; R2 prunes path to RP

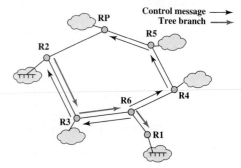

(d) R6 sends Prune to RP; RP prunes path to R1

Figure 21.5   Example of PIM Operation

message to the RP. This Prune message instructs the RP not to send any multi-cast packets from that source to this destination. The destination will continue to receive multicast packets from other sources via the RP-based tree, unless and until it prunes those sources. Any source router must continue to send multicast packets to the RP router for delivery to other multicast members.

The selection of an RP for a given multicast group is a dynamic process. The initiator of a multicast group selects a primary RP and a small ordered set of alternative RPs. In general, RP placement is not a critical issue because the RP-based tree will not be used for most receivers after shortest-path routers are followed.

21.2 SOFTWARE-DEFINED NETWORKS

A network organizing technique that has come to recent prominence is the software-defined network (SDN). In essence, an SDN separates the data and control functions of networking devices, such as routers, packet switches, and LAN switches, with a well-defined application programming interface (API) between the two. In contrast, in most large enterprise networks, routers and other network devices encompass both data and control functions, making it difficult to adjust the network infrastructure and operation to large-scale addition of end systems, virtual machines, and virtual networks.

Evolving Network Requirements

Before looking in more detail at SDNs, let us examine the evolving network requirements that lead to a demand for a flexible, responsive approach to controlling traffic flows within a network or internet.

One key driving factor is the increasingly widespread use of server virtualization. In essence, server virtualization masks server resources, including the number and identity of individual physical servers, processors, and operating systems, from server users. This makes it possible to partition a single machine into multiple independent servers, conserving hardware resources. It also makes it possible to quickly migrate a server from one machine to another for load balancing or for dynamic switchover in the case of machine failure. Server virtualization has become a central element in dealing with "big data" applications and in implementing cloud computing infrastructures. But it creates problems with traditional network architectures (e.g., see [LAYL10]). One problem is configuring virtual LANs. Network managers need to make sure the VLAN used by the virtual machine (VM) is assigned to the same switch port as the physical server running the VM. But with the VM being movable, it is necessary to reconfigure the VLAN every time that a virtual server is moved. In general terms, to match the flexibility of server virtualization, the network manager needs to be able to dynamically add, drop, and change network resources and profiles. This is difficult to do with conventional network switches, in which the control logic for each switch is collocated with the switching logic.

Another effect of server virtualization is that traffic flows differ substantially from the traditional client/server model. Typically, there is a considerable amount of traffic among virtual servers, for such purposes as maintaining consistent images of database and invoking security functions such as access control. These server-to-server flows change in location and intensity over time, demanding a flexible approach to managing network resources.

Another factor leading to the need for rapid response in allocating network resources is the increasing use by employees of mobile devices, such as smartphones, tablets, and notebooks to access enterprise resources. Network managers must be able to respond to rapidly changing resource, QoS, and security requirements.

Existing network infrastructures can respond to changing requirements for the management of traffic flows, providing differentiated QoS levels and security levels for individual flows, but the process can be very time consuming if the enterprise network is large and/or involves network devices from multiple vendors. The network manager must configure each vendor's equipment separately, and adjust performance and security parameters on a per-session, per-application basis. In a large enterprise, every time a new virtual machine is brought up, it can take hours or even days for network managers to do the necessary reconfiguration [ONF12].

This state of affairs has been compared to the mainframe era of computing [DELL12]. In the era of the mainframe, applications, the operating system, and the hardware were vertically integrated and provided by a single vendor. All of these ingredients were proprietary and closed, leading to slow innovation. Today, most computer platforms use the x86 instruction set and a variety of operating systems (Windows, Linux, Mac OS) run on top of the hardware. The OS provides APIs that enable outside providers to develop applications, leading to rapid innovation and deployment. In a similar fashion, commercial networking devices have proprietary features and specialized control planes and hardware, all vertically integrated on the switch. As will be seen, the SDN architecture and the OpenFlow standard provide an open architecture in which control functionality is separated from the network device, and placed in accessible control servers. This enables the underlying infrastructure to be abstracted for applications and network services, which can treat the network as a logical entity.

SDN Architecture

Figure 21.6 illustrates the logical structure of an SDN. A central controller performs all complex functionality, including routing, naming, policy declaration, and security checks. This constitutes the **SDN control plane**, and consists of one or more SDN servers.

The SDN controller defines the data flows that occur in the **SDN data plane**. Each flow through the network must first get permission from the controller, which verifies that the communication is permissible by the network policy. If the controller allows a flow, it computes a route for the flow to take, and adds an entry for that flow in each of the switches along the path. With all complex function subsumed by the controller, switches simply manage flow tables whose entries can only be populated by the controller. Communication between the controller and the switches uses a standardized protocol and API. Most commonly this interface is the OpenFlow specification, discussed in the next section.

The SDN architecture is remarkably flexible; it can operate with different types of switches and at different protocol layers. SDN controllers and switches can be implemented for Ethernet switches (layer 2), Internet routers (layer 3), transport

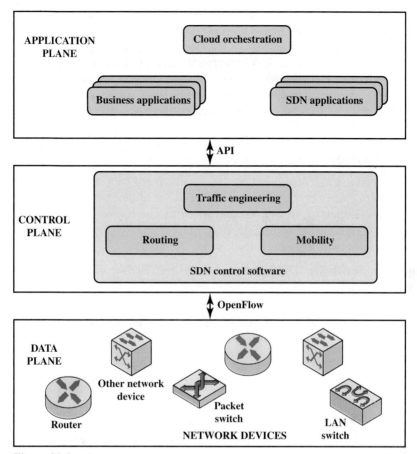

Figure 21.6 SDN Logical Structure

(layer 4) switching, or application-layer switching and routing. SDN relies on the common functions found on networking devices, which essentially involves forwarding packets based on some form of flow definition. In an SDN architecture, a switch performs the following functions:

1. The switch encapsulates and forwards a flow's first packet to an SDN controller, enabling the controller to decide whether the flow should be added to the switch's flow table.

2. The switch forwards incoming packets out the appropriate port based on the flow table. The flow table may include priority information dictated by the controller.

3. The switch can drop packets on a particular flow, temporarily or permanently, as dictated by the controller. Packet dropping can be used for security purposes, curbing denial-of-service attacks, or traffic management requirements.

In simple terms, the SDN controller manages the forwarding state of the switches in the SDN. This management is done through a vendor-neutral API that allows the controller to address a wide variety of operator requirements without changing any of the lower-level aspects of the network, including topology.

With the decoupling of the control and data planes, SDN enables applications to deal with a single abstracted network device, without concern for the details of how the device operates. Network applications see a single API to the controller. Thus it is possible to quickly create and deploy new applications to orchestrate network traffic flow to meet specific enterprise requirements for performance or security.

SDN Domains

In a large enterprise network, the deployment of a single controller to manage all network devices would prove unwieldy or undesirable. A more likely scenario is that the operator of a large enterprise or carrier network divides the whole network into a number of nonoverlapping SDN domains (Figure 21.7). Reasons for using SDN domains include the following:

- **Scalability:** The number of devices an SDN controller can feasibly manage is limited. Thus, a reasonably large network may need to deploy multiple SDN controllers.

- **Privacy:** A carrier may choose to implement different privacy policies in different SDN domains. For example, an SDN domain may be dedicated to a set of customers who implement their own highly customized privacy policies, requiring that some networking information in this domain (e.g., network topology) should not be disclosed to an external entity.

- **Incremental deployment:** A carrier's network may consist of portions of legacy and nonlegacy infrastructure. Dividing the network into multiple, individually manageable SDN domains allows for flexible incremental deployment.

The existence of multiple domains creates a requirement for individual controllers to communicate with each other via a standardized protocol, to exchange routing information. IETF is currently working on developing a protocol, called

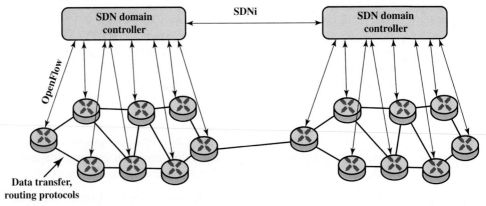

Figure 21.7 SDN Domain Structure

SDNi, for interfacing SDN domain controllers. SDNi functionality includes the following:

- Coordinate flow setup originated by applications, containing information such as path requirement, QoS, and service level agreements across multiple SDN domains.
- Exchange reachability information to facilitate inter-SDN routing. This will allow a single flow to traverse multiple SDNs and have each controller select the most appropriate path when multiple such paths are available.

The message types for SDNi tentatively include the following:

- Reachability update
- Flow setup/tear-down/update request (including application capability requirement such as QoS, data rate, latency, etc.)
- Capability update (including network-related capabilities, such as data rate and QoS, and system and software capabilities available inside the domain)

21.3 OPENFLOW

To turn the concept of SND into practical implementation, two requirements must be met. First, there must be a common logical architecture in all switches, routers, and other network devices to be managed by an SDN controller. This logical architecture may be implemented in different ways on different vendor equipment and in different types of network devices, so long as the SDN controller sees a uniform logical switch functionality. Second, a standard, secure protocol is needed between the SDN controller and the network device. Both of these requirements are addressed by OpenFlow, which is both a protocol between SDN controllers and network devices and a specification of the logical structure of the network switch functionality. OpenFlow is defined in the *OpenFlow Switch Specification*, published by the Open Networking Foundation (ONF). ONF is a consortium of software providers, content delivery networks, and networking equipment vendors whose purpose is to promote software-defined networking.

This section is based on the current OpenFlow specification, Version 1.3.0, June 25, 2012. The original specification, 1.0, was developed at Stanford University and was widely implemented. OpenFlow 1.2 was the first release from ONF after inheriting the project from Stanford. OpenFlow 1.3 significantly expands the functionality of the specification. Version 1.3 is likely to become the stable base upon which future commercial implementations for OpenFlow will be built. ONF intends for this version to be a stable target for chip and software vendors, so little if any change is planned for the foreseeable future [KERN12].

Logical Switch Architecture

Figure 21.8 illustrates the basic structure of the OpenFlow environment. An SDN controller communicates with OpenFlow-compatible switches using the OpenFlow protocol running over the Secure Sockets Layer (SSL). Each switch

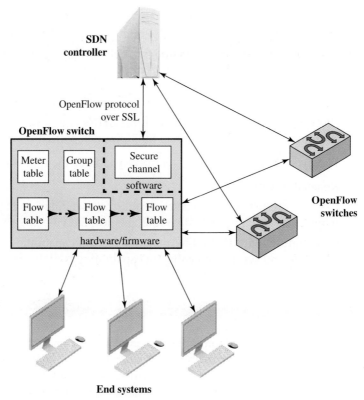

Figure 21.8   OpenFlow Switch

connects to other OpenFlow switches and, possibly, to end-user devices that are the sources and destinations of packet flows. Within each switch, a series of tables, typically implemented in hardware or firmware, are used to manage the flows of packets through the switch.

The OpenFlow specification defines three types of tables in the logical switch architecture. A **flow table** matches incoming packets to a particular flow and specifies what functions are to be performed on the packets. There may be multiple flow tables that operate in a pipeline fashion, as explained subsequently. A flow table may direct a flow to a **group table**, which may trigger a variety of actions that affect one or more flows. A **meter table** can trigger a variety of performance-related actions on a flow.

Before proceeding it is helpful to define what is meant by the term *flow*. Curiously, this term is not defined in the OpenFlow specification, nor is there an attempt to define it in virtually all of the literature on OpenFlow. In general terms, a **flow** is a sequence of packets traversing a network that share a set of header field values. For example, a flow could consist of all packets with the same source and destination IP addresses or all packets with the same virtual LAN (VLAN) identifier. We provide a more specific definition subsequently.

Flow Table Components

The basic building block of the logical switch architecture is the flow table. Each packet that enters a switch passes through one of more flow tables. Each flow table contains entries consisting of six components:

- **Match fields:** Used to select packets that match the values in the fields.
- **Priority:** Relative priority of table entries.
- **Counters:** Updated for matching packets. The OpenFlow specification defines a variety of timers. Examples include the number of received bytes and packets per port, per flow table, and per flow table entry; number of dropped packets; and duration of a flow.
- **Instructions:** Actions to be taken if a match occurs.
- **Time-outs:** Maximum amount of idle time before a flow is expired by the switch.
- **Cookie:** opaque data value chosen by the controller. May be used by the controller to filter flow statistics, flow modification and flow deletion; not used when processing packets.

A flow table may include a table-miss flow entry, which wildcards all match fields (every field is a match regardless of value) and has the lowest priority (priority 0).

MATCH FIELDS COMPONENT   The match fields component of a table entry consists of the following required fields:

- **Ingress port:** The identifier of the port on this switch on which the packet arrived. This may be a physical port or a switch-defined virtual port.
- **Ethernet source and destination addresses:** Each entry can be an exact address, a bitmasked value for which only some of the address bits are checked, or a wildcard value (match any value).
- **IPv4 or IPv6 protocol number:** A protocol number value, indicating the next header in the packet.
- **IPv4 or IPv6 source address, and destination address:** Each entry can be an exact address, a bitmasked value, a subnet mask value, or a wildcard value.
- **TCP source and destination ports:** Exact match or wildcard value.
- **UDP source and destination ports:** Exact match or wildcard value.

The preceding match fields must be supported by any OpenFlow-compliant switch. The following fields may be optionally supported.

- **Physical port:** Used to designate underlying physical port when packet is received on a logical port.
- **Metadata:** Additional information that can be passed from one table to another during the processing of a packet. Its use is discussed subsequently.
- **Ethernet type:** Ethernet Type field.
- **VLAN ID and VLAN user priority:** Fields in the IEEE 802.1Q virtual LAN header.
- **IPv4 or IPv6 DS and ECN:** Differentiated Services and Explicit Congestion Notification fields.

- **SCTP source and destination ports:** Exact match or wildcard value.
- **ICMP type and code fields:** Exact match or wildcard value.
- **ARP opcode:** Exact match in Ethernet Type field.
- **Source and target IPv4 addresses in ARP payload:** Can be an exact address, a bitmasked value, a subnet mask value, or a wildcard value.
- **IPv6 flow label:** Exact match or wildcard.
- **ICMPv6 type and code fields:** Exact match or wildcard value.
- **IPv6 neighbor discovery target address:** In an IPv6 Neighbor Discovery message.
- **IPv6 neighbor discovery source and target addresses:** Link-layer address options in an IPv6 Neighbor Discovery message.
- **MPLS label value, traffic class, and BoS:** Fields in the top label of an MPLS label stack.

Thus, OpenFlow can be used with network traffic involving a variety of protocols and network services. Note that at the MAC/link layer, only Ethernet is supported. Thus, OpenFlow as currently defined cannot control layer 2 traffic over wireless networks.

We can now offer a more precise definition of the term *flow*. From the point of view of an individual switch, a flow is a sequence of packets that matches a specific entry in a flow table. The definition is packet oriented, in the sense that it is function of the values of header fields of the packets that constitute the flow, and not a function of the path they follow through the network. A combination of flow entries on multiple switches defines a flow that is bound to a specific path.

INSTRUCTIONS COMPONENT   The instructions component of a table entry consists of a set of instructions that are executed if the packet matches the entry. Before describing the types of instructions, we need to define the terms *action* and *action set*. **Actions** describe packet forwarding, packet modification, and group table processing operations. The OpenFlow specification includes the following actions:

- **Output:** Forward packet to specified port.
- **Set-Queue:** Sets the queue id for a packet. When the packet is forwarded to a port using the output action, the queue id determines which queue attached to this port is used for scheduling and forwarding the packet. Forwarding behavior is dictated by the configuration of the queue and is used to provide basic Quality-of-Service (QoS) support.
- **Group:** Process packet through specified group.
- **Push-Tag/Pop-Tag:** Push or pop a tag field for a VLAN or MPLS packet.
- **Set-Field:** The various Set-Field actions are identified by their field type and modify the values of respective header fields in the packet.
- **Change-TTL:** The various Change-TTL actions modify the values of the IPv4 TTL, IPv6 Hop Limit, or MPLS TTL in the packet.

An **action set** is a list of actions associated with a packet that are accumulated while the packet is processed by each table and that are executed when the packet exits the processing pipeline.

Instructions are of four types:

- **Direct packet through pipeline:** The Goto-Table instruction directs the packet to a table farther along in the pipeline. The Meter instruction directs the packet to a specified meter.
- **Perform action on packet:** Actions may be performed on the packet when it is matched to a table entry.
- **Update action set:** Merge specified actions into the current action set for this packet on this flow, or clear all the actions in the action set.
- **Update metadata:** A metadata value can be associated with a packet. It is used to carry information from one table to the next.

Flow Table Pipeline

A switch includes one or more flow tables. If there is more than one flow table, they are organized as a pipeline (Figure 21.9), with the tables labeled with increasing numbers starting with 0. When a packet is presented to a table for matching, the input consists of the packet, the identity of the ingress port, the associated metadata value, and the associated action set. For Table , the metadata value is blank and the action set is null. Processing proceeds as follows:

1. Find the highest-priority matching flow entry. If there is no match on any entry and there is no table-miss entry, then the packet is dropped. If there is a match only on a table-miss entry, then that entry specifies one of three actions:
   a. Send packet to controller. This will enable the controller to define a new flow for this and similar packets, or decide to drop the packet.
   b. Direct packet to another flow table farther down the pipeline.
   c. Drop the packet.
2. If there is a match on one or more entries, other than the table-miss entry, then the match is defined to be with the highest-priority matching entry. The following actions may then be performed:
   a. Update any counters associated with this entry.
   b. Execute any instructions associated with this entry. This may include updating the action set, updating the metadata value, and performing actions.
   c. The packet is then forwarded to a flow table further down the pipeline, to the group table, to the meter table, or directed to an output port.

For the final table in the pipeline, forwarding to another flow table is not an option.

If and when a packet is finally directed to an output port, the accumulated action set is executed and then the packet is queued for output.

OpenFlow Protocol

The OpenFlow protocol describes message exchanges that take place between an OpenFlow controller and an OpenFlow switch. Typically, the protocol is implemented on top of SSL or TLS, providing a secure OpenFlow channel.

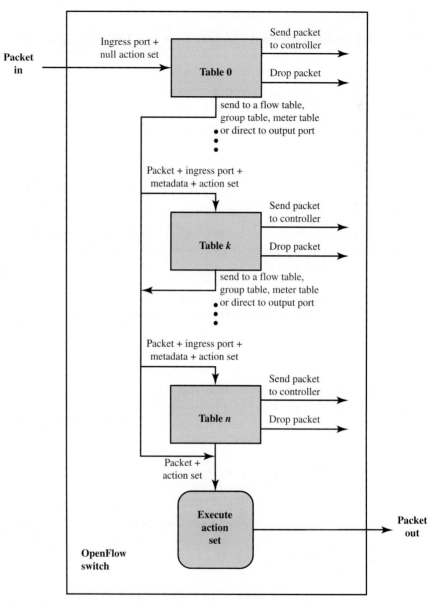

Figure 21.9 Packet Flow through OpenFlow-Compliant Switch

The OpenFlow protocol enables the controller to perform add, update, and delete actions to the flow entries in the flow tables. It supports 3 types of messages (Table 21.2):

- **Controller-to-Switch:** These messages are initiated by the controller and, in some cases, require a response from the switch. This class of messages enables the controller to manage the logical state of the switch, including its configuration and details of flow and group table entries. Also included in this class is

Table 21.2 OpenFlow Messages

Message	Description
Controller-to-Switch	
Features	Request the capabilities of a switch. Switch responds with a features reply that specifies its capabilities.
Configuration	Set and query configuration parameters. Switch responds with parameter settings
Modify-State	Add, delete, and modify flow/group entries and set switch port properties.
Read-State	Collect information from switch, such as current configuration, statistics, and capabilities.
Packet-out	Direct packet to a specified port on the switch.
Barrier	Barrier request/reply messages are used by the controller to ensure message dependencies have been met or to receive notifications for completed operations.
Role-Request	Set or query role of the OpenFlow channel. Useful when switch connects to multiple controllers.
Asynchronous-Configuration	Set filter on asynchronous messages or query that filter. Useful when switch connects to multiple controllers.
Asynchronous	
Packet-in	Transfer packet to controller.
Flow-Removed	Inform the controller about the removal of a flow entry from a flow table.
Port-Status	Inform the controller of a change on a port.
Error	Notify controller of error or problem condition.
Symmetric	
Hello	Exchanged between the switch and controller upon connection startup.
Echo	Echo request/reply messages can be sent from either the switch or the controller, and must return an echo reply.
Experimenter	For additional functionality.

the Packet-out message. This message is used when a switch sends a packet to the controller and the controller decides not to drop the packet but to direct it to a switch output port.

- **Asynchronous:** These types of messages are sent without solicitation from the controller. This class includes various status messages to the controller. Also included is the Packet-in message, which may be used by the switch to send a packet to the controller when there is no flow table match.

- **Symmetric:** These messages are sent without solicitation from either the controller or the switch. They are simple yet helpful. Hello messages are typically sent back and forth between the controller and switch when the connection is first established. Echo request and reply messages can be used by either the switch or controller to measure the latency or bandwidth of a controller-switch connection or just verify that the device is up and running. The Experimenter message is used to stage features to be built into future versions of OpenFlow.

The OpenFlow protocol enables the controller to manage the logical structure of a switch, without regard to the details of how the switch implements the OpenFlow logical architecture.

21.4 MOBILE IP

In response to the increasing popularity of palmtop and other mobile computers, Mobile IP was developed to enable computers to maintain Internet connectivity while moving from one Internet attachment point to another. Although Mobile IP can work with wired connections, in which a computer is unplugged from one physical attachment point and plugged into another, it is particularly suited to wireless connections.

The term *mobile* in this context implies that a user is connected to one or more applications across the Internet, that the user's point of attachment changes dynamically, and that all connections are automatically maintained despite the change. This is in contrast to a user, such as a business traveler, with a portable computer of some sort who arrives at a destination and uses the computer's notebook to dial into an Internet service provider (ISP). In this latter case, the user's Internet connection is terminated each time the user moves and a new connection is initiated when the user dials back in. Each time an Internet connection is established, software in the point of attachment (typically an ISP) is used to obtain a new, temporarily assigned IP address. This temporary IP address is used by the user's correspondent for each application-level connection (e.g., FTP, Web connection). A better term for this kind of use is *nomadic*.

We begin with a general overview of Mobile IP and then look at some of the details.

Operation of Mobile IP

Routers make use of the IP address in an IP datagram to perform routing. In particular, the **network portion** of an IP address (Figure 21.6) is used by routers to move a datagram from the source computer to the network to which the target computer is attached. Then the final router on the path, which is attached to the same network as the target computer, uses the **host portion** of the IP address to deliver the IP datagram to the destination. Further, this IP address is known to the next higher layer in the protocol architecture (Figure 14.1). In particular, most applications over the Internet are supported by TCP connections. When a TCP connection is set up, the TCP entity on each side of the connection knows the IP address of the correspondent host. When a TCP segment is handed down to the IP layer for delivery, TCP provides the IP address, and IP creates an IP datagram with that IP address in the IP header and sends the datagram out for routing and delivery. However, with a mobile host, the IP address may change while one or more TCP connections are active.

Figure 21.10 shows in general terms how Mobile IP deals with the problem of dynamic IP addresses. A mobile node is assigned to a particular network, known as its **home network**. Its IP address on that network, known as its **home address**, is static. When the mobile node moves its attachment point to another network, that

network is considered a **foreign network** for this host. Once the mobile node is reat-
tached, it makes its presence known by registering with a network node, typically
a router, on the foreign network known as a **foreign agent**. The foreign agent then
communicates with a similar agent on the user's home network, known as a **home
agent**, giving the home agent the **care-of address** of the mobile node; the care-of
address identifies the foreign agent's location. Typically, one or more routers on a
network will implement the roles of both home and foreign agents.

When IP datagrams are exchanged over a connection between the mobile
node and another host (a server in Figure 21.10), the following operations occur:

1. Server X transmits an IP datagram destined for mobile node A, with A's home
   address in the IP header. The IP datagram is routed to A's home network.

2. At the home network, the incoming IP datagram is intercepted by the home
   agent. The home agent encapsulates the entire datagram inside a new IP datagram that has the A's care-of address in the header, and retransmits the datagram. The use of an outer IP datagram with a different destination IP address
   is known as **tunneling**. This IP datagram is routed to the foreign agent.

3. The foreign agent strips off the outer IP header, encapsulates the original IP
   datagram in a network-level PDU (e.g., a LAN LLC frame), and delivers the
   original datagram to A across the foreign network.

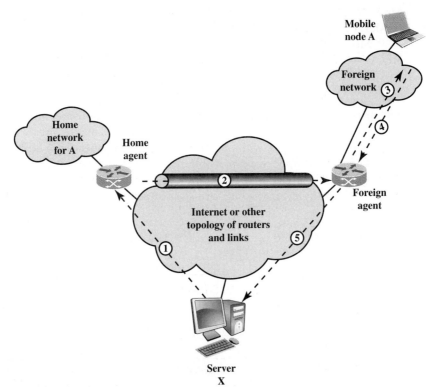

Figure 21.10   Mobile IP Scenario

4. When A sends IP traffic to X, it uses X's IP address. In our example, this is a fixed address; that is, X is not a mobile node. Each IP datagram is sent by A to a router on the foreign network for routing to X. Typically, this router is also the foreign agent.

5. The IP datagram from A to X travels directly across the Internet to X, using X's IP address.

To support the operations illustrated in Figure 21.10, Mobile IP includes three basic capabilities:

- **Discovery:** A mobile node uses a discovery procedure to identify prospective home agents and foreign agents.
- **Registration:** A mobile node uses an authenticated registration procedure to inform its home agent of its care-of address.
- **Tunneling:** Tunneling is used to forward IP datagrams from a home address to a care-of address.

Figure 21.11 indicates the underlying protocol support for the Mobile IP capability. The registration protocol communicates between an application on the mobile node and an application in the home agent and hence uses a transport-level protocol. Because registration is a simple request-response transaction, the overhead of the connection-oriented TCP is not required, and therefore UDP is used as the transport protocol. Discovery makes use of the existing Internet Control Message Protocol (ICMP) by adding the appropriate extensions to the ICMP header. Finally, tunneling is performed at the IP level.

Mobile IP is specified in a number of RFCs. The basic defining document is RFC 3344. Table 21.3 lists some useful terminology from RFC 3344.

Discovery

The discovery process in Mobile IP is very similar to the router advertisement process defined in ICMP. Accordingly, agent discovery makes use of ICMP router advertisement messages, with one or more extensions specific to Mobile IP.

The mobile node is responsible for an ongoing discovery process. It must determine if it is attached to its home network, in which case IP datagrams may be received without forwarding, or if it is attached to a foreign network. Because

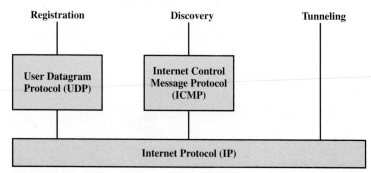

Figure 21.11 Protocol Support for Mobile IP

Table 21.3 Mobile IP Terminology (RFC 3334)

Mobile node	A host or router that changes its point of attachment from one network or subnetwork to another. A mobile node may change its location without changing its IP address; it may continue to communicate with other Internet nodes at any location using its (constant) IP address, assuming link-layer connectivity to a point of attachment is available.
Home address	An IP address that is assigned for an extended period of time to a mobile node. It remains unchanged regardless of where the node is attached to the Internet.
Home agent	A router on a mobile node's home network that tunnels datagrams for delivery to the mobile node when it is away from home, and maintains current location information for the mobile node.
Home network	A network, possibly virtual, having a network prefix matching that of a mobile node's home address. Note that standard IP routing mechanisms will deliver datagrams destined to a mobile node's Home Address to the mobile node's Home Network.
Foreign agent	A router on a mobile node's visited network that provides routing services to the mobile node while registered. The foreign agent detunnels and delivers datagrams to the mobile node that were tunneled by the mobile node's home agent. For datagrams sent by a mobile node, the foreign agent may serve as a default router for registered mobile nodes.
Foreign network	Any network other than the mobile node's Home Network.
Care-of address	The termination point of a tunnel toward a mobile node, for datagrams forwarded to the mobile node while it is away from home. The protocol can use two different types of care-of address: a "foreign agent care-of address" is an address of a foreign agent with which the mobile node is registered, and a "co-located care-of address" is an externally obtained local address which the mobile node has associated with one of its own network interfaces.
Correspondent node	A peer with which a mobile node is communicating. A correspondent node may be either mobile or stationary.
Link	A facility or medium over which nodes can communicate at the link layer. A link underlies the network layer.
Node	A host or a router.
Tunnel	The path followed by a datagram while it is encapsulated. The model is that, while it is encapsulated, a datagram is routed to a knowledgeable decapsulating agent, which decapsulates the datagram and then correctly delivers it to its ultimate destination.

handoff from one network to another occurs at the physical layer, a transition from the home network to a foreign network can occur at any time without notification to the network layer (i.e., the IP layer). Thus, discovery for a mobile node is a continuous process.

For the purpose of discovery, a router or other network node that can act as an agent periodically issues a router advertisement ICMP message (Figure 21.8d) with an advertisement extension. The router advertisement portion of the message includes the IP address of the router. The advertisement extension includes additional information about the router's role as an agent, as discussed subsequently. A mobile node listens for these **agent advertisement messages**. Because a foreign agent could be on the mobile node's home network (set up to serve visiting mobile nodes), the arrival of an agent advertisement does not necessarily tell the mobile node that it is on a foreign network. The mobile node must compare the network portion of the router's IP address with the network portion of its own home address. If these network portions do not match, then the mobile node is on a foreign network.

The **agent advertisement extension** follows the ICMP router advertisement fields. The extension includes the following 1-bit flags:

- **R:** Registration with this foreign agent is required (or another foreign agent on this network). Even those mobile nodes that have already acquired a care-of address from this foreign agent must re-register.
- **B:** Busy. The foreign agent will not accept registrations from additional mobile nodes.
- **H:** This agent offers services as a home agent on this network.
- **F:** This agent offers services as a foreign agent on this network.
- **M:** This agent can receive tunneled IP datagrams that use minimal encapsulation, explained subsequently.
- **G:** This agent can receive tunneled IP datagrams that use generic routing encapsulation (GRE), explained subsequently.
- **r:** Reserved.
- **T:** Foreign agent supports reverse tunneling.
- In addition, the extension includes zero or more **care-of addresses** supported by this agent on this network. There must be at least one such address if the F bit is set. There may be multiple addresses.

AGENT SOLICITATION   Foreign agents are expected to issue agent advertisement messages periodically. If a mobile node needs agent information immediately, it can issue an ICMP router solicitation message (Figure 21.8e). Any agent receiving this message will then issue an agent advertisement.

MOVE DETECTION   As was mentioned, a mobile node may move from one network to another due to some handoff mechanism, without the IP level being aware of it. The agent discovery process is intended to enable the agent to detect such a move. The agent may use one of two algorithms for this purpose:

- **Use of lifetime field:** When a mobile node receives an agent advertisement from a foreign agent that it is currently using or that it is now going to register with, it records the lifetime field as a timer. If the timer expires before the mobile node receives another agent advertisement from the agent, then the node assumes that it has lost contact with that agent. If, in the meantime, the mobile node has received an agent advertisement from another agent and that advertisement has not yet expired, the mobile node can register with this new agent. Otherwise, the mobile node should use agent solicitation to find an agent.
- **Use of network prefix:** The mobile node checks whether any newly received agent advertisement is on the same network as the node's current care-of address. If it is not, the mobile node assumes that it has moved and may register with the agent whose advertisement the mobile node has just received.

CO-LOCATED ADDRESSES The discussion so far has involved the use of a care-of address associated with a foreign agent; that is, the care-of address is an IP address for the foreign agent. This foreign agent will receive datagrams at this care-of address, intended for the mobile node, and then forward them across the foreign network to the mobile node. However, in some cases a mobile node may move to a network that has no foreign agents or on which all foreign agents are busy. As an alternative, the mobile node may act as its own foreign agent by using a co-located care-of address. A co-located care-of address is an IP address obtained by the mobile node that is associated with the mobile node's current interface to a network.

The means by which a mobile node acquires a co-located address is beyond the scope of Mobile IP. One means is to dynamically acquire a temporary IP address through an Internet service such as Dynamic Host Configuration Protocol (DHCP). Another alternative is that the co-located address may be owned by the mobile node as a long-term address for use only while visiting a given foreign network.

Registration

Once a mobile node has recognized that it is on a foreign network and has acquired a care-of address, it needs to alert a home agent on its home network and request that the home agent forward its IP traffic. The registration process involves four steps:

1. The mobile node requests the forwarding service by sending a registration request to the foreign agent that the mobile node wants to use.
2. The foreign agent relays this request to the mobile node's home agent.
3. The home agent either accepts or denies the request and sends a registration reply to the foreign agent.
4. The foreign agent relays this reply to the mobile node.

If the mobile node is using a co-located care-of address, then it registers directly with its home agent, rather than going through a foreign agent.

The registration operation uses two types of messages carried in UDP segments. The **registration request message** includes the following 1-bit flags:

- **S:** Simultaneous bindings. The mobile node is requesting that the home agent retain its prior mobility bindings. When simultaneous bindings are in effect, the home agent will forward multiple copies of the IP datagram, one to each care-of address currently registered for this mobile node. Multiple simultaneous bindings can be useful in wireless handoff situations to improve reliability.
- **B:** Broadcast datagrams. Indicates that the mobile node would like to receive copies of broadcast datagrams that it would have received if it were attached to its home network.
- **D:** Decapsulation by mobile node. The mobile node is using a co-located care-of address and will decapsulate its own tunneled IP datagrams.
- **M:** Indicates that the home agent should use minimal encapsulation, explained subsequently.
- **G:** Indicates that the home agent should use GRE, explained subsequently.
- **T:** Reverse tunneling requested.

In addition, the message includes the following fields:

- **Home Address:** The home IP address of the mobile node. The home agent can expect to receive IP datagrams with this as a destination address, and must forward those to the care-of address.
- **Home Agent:** The IP address of the mobile node's home agent. This informs the foreign agent of the address to which this request should be relayed.
- **Care-of Address:** The IP address at this end of the tunnel. The home agent should forward IP datagrams that it receives with mobile node's home address to this destination address.
- **Identification:** A 64-bit number generated by the mobile node, used for matching registration requests to registration replies and for security purposes, explained subsequently.
- **Extensions:** The only extension so far defined is the authentication extension, explained subsequently.

The **registration reply message** includes a code that indicates whether the request is accepted and, if not, the reason for denial.

SECURING THE REGISTRATION PROCEDURE   A key concern with the registration procedure is security. Mobile IP is designed to resist two types of attacks:

1. A node may pretend to be a foreign agent and send a registration request to a home agent so as to divert traffic intended for a mobile node to itself.
2. A malicious agent may replay old registration messages, effectively cutting the mobile node from the network.

The technique that is used to protect against such attacks involves the use of message authentication and the proper use of the identification field of the registration request and reply messages.

For purposes of message authentication, each registration request and reply contains an **authentication extension**, which includes the following fields:

- **Security Parameter Index (SPI):** An index that identifies a security context between a pair of nodes. This security context is configured so that the two nodes share a secret key and parameters relevant to this association (e.g., authentication algorithm).
- **Authenticator:** A code used to authenticate the message. The sender inserts this code into the message using a shared secret key. The receiver uses the code to ensure that the message has not been altered or delayed. The authenticator protects the entire registration request or reply message, any extensions prior to this extension, and the type and length fields of this extension.

The default authentication algorithm is HMAC-MD5, defined in RFC 2104, which produces a 128-bit message digest. HMAC-MD4 is an example of what is known as a keyed hash code. Appendix Q describes such codes. The digest is computed over a shared secret key, and the protected fields from the registration message.

Three types of authentication extensions are defined:

- **Mobile-home:** This extension must be present and provides for authentication of the registration messages between the mobile node and the home agent.
- **Mobile-foreign:** The extension may be present when a security association exists between the mobile node and the foreign agent. The foreign agent will strip this extension off before relaying a request message to the home agent and add this extension to a reply message coming from a home agent.
- **Foreign-home:** The extension may be present when a security association exists between the foreign agent and the home agent.

Note that the authenticator protects the identification field in the request and reply messages. As a result, the identification value can be used to thwart replay types of attacks. As was mentioned, the identification value enables the mobile node to match a reply to a request. Further, if the mobile node and the home agent maintain synchronization, so that the home agent can distinguish a reasonable identification value from a suspicious one, then the home agent can reject suspicious messages. One way to do this is to use a timestamp value. As long as the mobile node and home agent have reasonably synchronized values of time, the timestamp will serve the purpose. Alternatively, the mobile node could generate values using a pseudorandom number generator. If the home agent knows the algorithm, then it knows what identification value to expect next.

Tunneling

Once a mobile node is registered with a home agent, the home agent must be able to intercept IP datagrams sent to the mobile node's home address so that these datagrams can be forwarded via tunneling. The standard does not mandate a specific technique for this purpose but references the Address Resolution Protocol (ARP) as a possible mechanism. The home agent needs to inform other nodes on the same network (the home network) that IP datagrams with a destination address of the mobile node in question should be delivered (at the link level) to this agent. In effect, the home agent steals the identity of the mobile node in order to capture packets destined for that node that are transmitted across the home network.

For example, suppose that R3 in Figure 21.12 is acting as the home agent for a mobile node that is attached to a foreign network elsewhere on the Internet. That is, there is a host H whose home network is LAN Z that is now attached to some foreign network. If host D has traffic for H, it will generate an IP datagram with H's home address in the IP destination address field. The IP module in D recognizes that this destination address is on LAN Z and so passes the datagram down to the link layer with instructions to deliver it to a particular MAC-level address on Z. Prior to this time, R3 has informed the IP layer at D that datagrams destined for that particular address should be sent to R3. Thus, D inserts the MAC address of R3 in the destination MAC address field of the outgoing MAC frame. Similarly, if an IP datagram with the mobile node's home address arrives at router R2, it recognizes that the destination address is on LAN Z and will attempt to deliver the datagram to a MAC-level address on Z. Again, R2 has previously been informed that the MAC-level address it needs corresponds to R3.

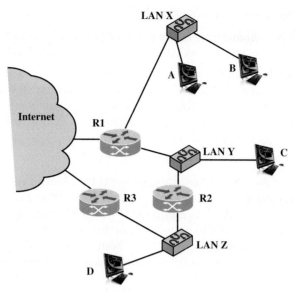

Figure 21.12   A Simple Internetworking Example

For traffic that is routed across the Internet and arrives at R3 from the Internet, R3 must simply recognize that for this destination address, the datagram is to be captured and forwarded.

To forward an IP datagram to a care-of address, the home agent puts the entire IP datagram into an outer IP datagram. This is a form of encapsulation, just as placing an IP header in front of a TCP segment encapsulates the TCP segment in an IP datagram. Three options for encapsulation are allowed for Mobile IP:

- **IP-within-IP encapsulation:** This is the simplest approach, defined in RFC 2003.
- **Minimal encapsulation:** This approach involves fewer fields, defined in RFC 2004.
- **Generic routing encapsulation (GRE):** This is a generic encapsulation procedure that was developed prior to the development of Mobile IP, defined in RFC 1701.

We review the first two of these methods.

IP-WITHIN-IP ENCAPSULATION   With this approach, the entire IP datagram becomes the payload in a new IP datagram (Figure 21.13a). The inner, original IP header is unchanged except to decrement Time to Live (TTL) by 1. The outer header is a full IP header. Two fields (indicated as unshaded in the figure) are copied from the inner header: The version number is 4, which is the protocol identifier for IPv4, and the type of service requested for the outer IP datagram is the same as that requested for the inner IP datagram.

In the inner IP header, the source address refers to the host that is sending the original datagram, and the destination address is the home address of the intended recipient. In the outer IP header, the source and destination addresses refer to the entry and exit points of the tunnel. Thus, the source address typically is the IP address of the home agent, and the destination address is the care-of address for the intended destination.

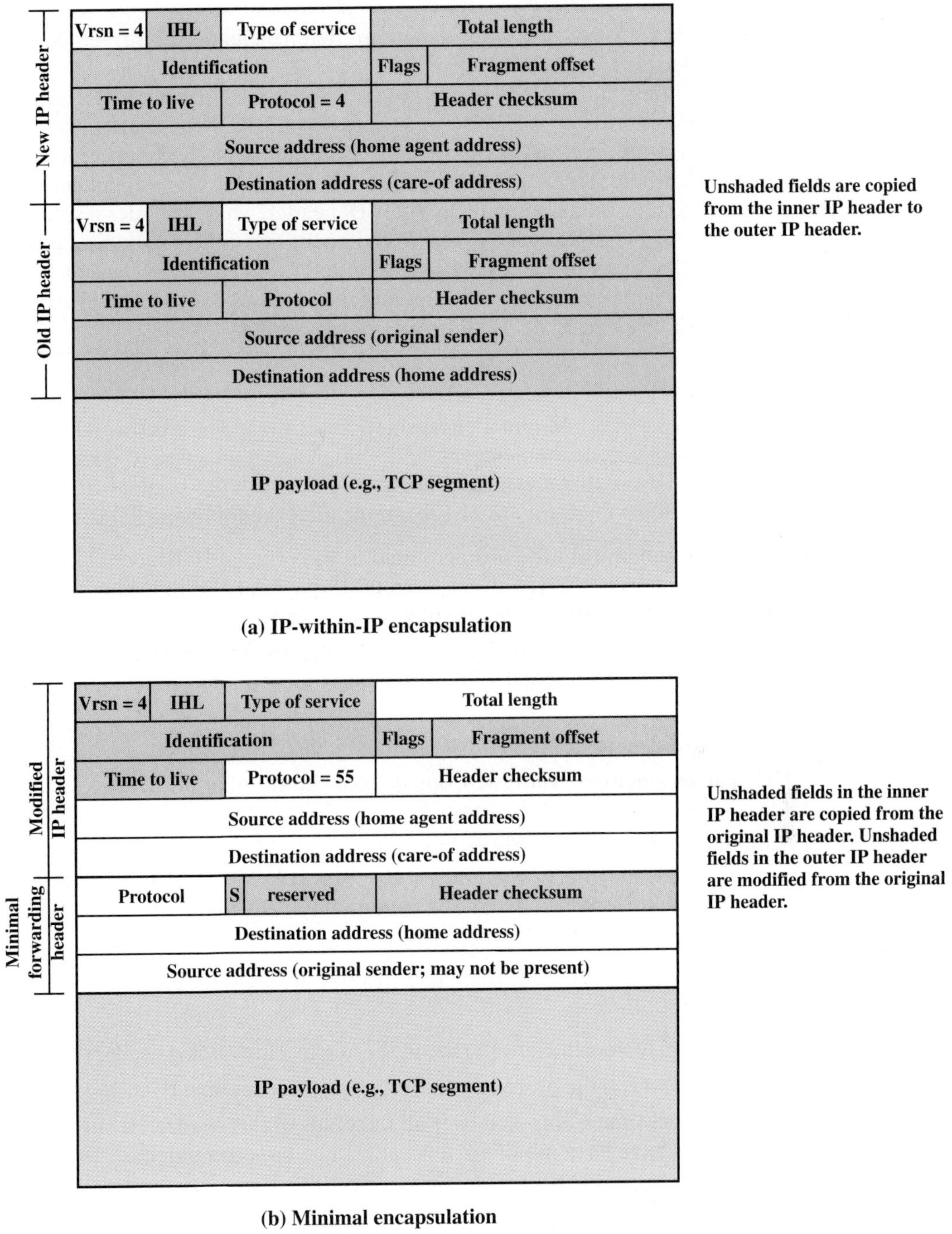

Vrsn = 4	IHL	Type of service	Total length	
Identification			Flags	Fragment offset
Time to live		Protocol = 4	Header checksum	
Source address (home agent address)				
Destination address (care-of address)				
Vrsn = 4	IHL	Type of service	Total length	
Identification			Flags	Fragment offset
Time to live		Protocol	Header checksum	
Source address (original sender)				
Destination address (home address)				
IP payload (e.g., TCP segment)				

New IP header / *Old IP header*

Unshaded fields are copied from the inner IP header to the outer IP header.

(a) IP-within-IP encapsulation

Vrsn = 4	IHL	Type of service	Total length	
Identification			Flags	Fragment offset
Time to live		Protocol = 55	Header checksum	
Source address (home agent address)				
Destination address (care-of address)				
Protocol		S	reserved	Header checksum
Destination address (home address)				
Source address (original sender; may not be present)				
IP payload (e.g., TCP segment)				

Modified IP header / *Minimal forwarding header*

Unshaded fields in the inner IP header are copied from the original IP header. Unshaded fields in the outer IP header are modified from the original IP header.

(b) Minimal encapsulation

Figure 21.13 Mobile IP Encapsulation

EXAMPLE 21.1 Consider an IP datagram that originates at server X in Figure 21.10 and that is intended for mobile node A. The original IP datagram has a source address equal to the IP address of X and a destination address equal to the IP home address of A. The network portion of A's home address refers to A's home network, and so the datagram is routed through the Internet to A's home network, where it is intercepted by the home agent. The home agent encapsulates the incoming datagram with an outer IP header, which includes a source address equal to the IP address of the home agent and a destination address equal to the IP address of the foreign agent on the foreign network to which A is currently attached. When this new datagram reaches the foreign agent, it strips off the outer IP header and delivers the original datagram to A.

MINIMAL ENCAPSULATION Minimal encapsulation results in less overhead and can be used if the mobile node, home agent, and foreign agent all agree to do so. With minimal encapsulation, the new header is inserted between the original IP header and the original IP payload (Figure 21.13b). It includes the following fields:

- **Protocol:** Copied from the protocol field in the original IP header. This field identifies the protocol type of the original IP payload and thus identifies the type of header that begins the original IP payload.
- **S:** If 0, the original source address is not present, and the length of this header is 8 octets. If 1, the original source address is present, and the length of this header is 12 octets.
- **Header Checksum:** Computed over all the fields of this header.
- **Original Destination Address:** Copied from the destination address field in the original IP header.
- **Original Source Address:** Copied from the source address field in the original IP header. This field is present only if the S bit is 1. The field is not present if the encapsulator is the source of the datagram (i.e., the datagram originates at the home agent).

The following fields in the original IP header are modified to form the new outer IP header:

- **Total Length:** Incremented by the size of the minimal forwarding header (8 or 12).
- **Protocol:** 55; this is the protocol number assigned to minimal IP encapsulation.
- **Header Checksum:** Computed over all the fields of this header; because some of the fields have been modified, this value must be recomputed.
- **Source Address:** The IP address of the encapsulator, typically the home agent.
- **Destination Address:** The IP address of the exit point of the tunnel. This is the care-of address and may either be the IP address of the foreign agent or the IP address of the mobile node (in the case of a co-located care-of address).

The processing for minimal encapsulation is as follows. The encapsulator (home agent) prepares the encapsulated datagram with the format of Figure 21.13b.

This datagram is now suitable for tunneling and is delivered across the Internet to the care-of address. At the care-of address, the fields in the minimal forwarding header are restored to the original IP header and the forwarding header is removed from the datagram. The total length field in the IP header is decremented by the size of the minimal forwarding header (8 or 12) and the header checksum field is recomputed.

21.5 DYNAMIC HOST CONFIGURATION PROTOCOL

The Dynamic Host Configuration Protocol (DHCP) is an Internet protocol, defined in RFC 2131, that enables dynamic allocation of IP addresses to hosts.

DHCP was developed to deal with the shortage of IP addresses, a shortage that will remain an issue until the wholesale conversion to the longer IPv6 addresses. DHCP enables a local network, such as in a business enterprise, to assign IP addresses from a pool of available IP addresses to hosts currently in use. When a host is not in use, its IP address is returned to the pool managed by a DHCP server.

Even when there is not a shortage of IP addresses, DHCP is useful in environments with mobile systems, such as laptops and tablets, that travel among different networks or that are only used sporadically. DHCP also can assign permanent IP addresses to some systems, such as servers, so that the address remains the same when the system is rebooted.

DHCP operates on a client/server model, with any host acting as a client that needs an IP address upon booting up, and a DHCP server that provides the request IP address along with related configuration parameters (Figure 21.14). The configuration parameters may include the network address of a default router for communication outside the local network and the address of a local DNS server.

The following DHCP messages are used for protocol operation:

- **DHCPDISCOVER:** Client broadcast to locate available servers.
- **DHCPOFFER:** Server to client in response to DHCPDISCOVER with offer of configuration parameters.
- **DHCPREQUEST:** Client message to servers either (a) requesting offered parameters from one server and implicitly declining offers from all others, (b) confirming correctness of previously allocated address after, for example, system reboot, or (c) extending the lease on a particular network address.
- **DHCPACK:** Server to client with configuration parameters, including committed network address.
- **DHCPNACK:** Server to client indicating client's notion of network address is incorrect (e.g., client has moved to new subnet) or client's lease has expired.
- **DHCPDECLINE:** Client to server indicating network address is already in use. DHCP server should then notify sysadmin.
- **DHCPRELEASE:** Client to server relinquishing network address and canceling remaining lease.
- **DHCPINFORM:** Client to server, asking only for local configuration parameters; client already has externally configured network address.

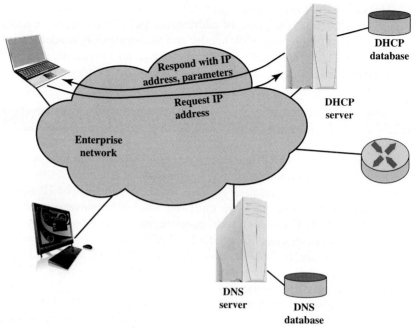

Figure 21.14 DHCP Role

Figure 21.15 illustrates a typical message exchange. The following steps are involved:

1. The client broadcasts a DHCPDISCOVER message on its local physical network. The message may include options that suggest values for the network address and lease duration. Relay agents may pass the message on to DHCP servers not on the same physical network.

2. Each server may respond with a DHCPOFFER message that includes an available network address.

3. The client receives one or more DHCPOFFER messages from one or more servers. The client may choose to wait for multiple responses. The client chooses one server from which to request configuration parameters, based on the configuration parameters offered in the DHCPOFFER messages. The client broadcasts a DHCPREQUEST message that includes the server identifier option to indicate which server it has selected, and that may include other options specifying desired configuration values. This DHCPREQUEST message is broadcast and relayed through DHCP relay agents. The client times out and retransmits the DHCPDISCOVER message if the client receives no DHCPOFFER messages.

4. The servers receive the DHCPREQUEST broadcast from the client. Those servers not selected by the DHCPREQUEST message use the message as notification that the client has declined that server's offer. The server selected in the DHCPREQUEST message commits the binding for the client to

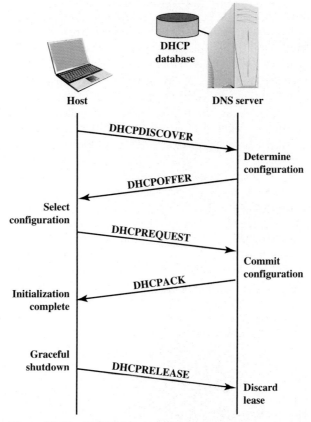

Figure 21.15 DHCP Message Exchange

persistent storage and responds with a DHCPACK message containing the configuration parameters for the requesting client.

5. The client receives the DHCPACK message with configuration parameters. At this point, the client is configured.

6. The client may choose to relinquish its lease on a network address by sending a DHCPRELEASE message to the server.

21.6 RECOMMENDED READING AND ANIMATIONS

[LI05] provides an overview of Mobile IP. A more detailed discussion is found in [VENK05].

[LI02] and [RAMA00] are two excellent surveys of multicast routing protocols. [DEER96] is a detailed account of sparse-mode PIM.

[GOTH11] provides an overview of SDN and OpenFlow. [VAUG11] and [LIMO12] are useful overviews of OpenFlow. [JARS11] examines the performance of OpenFlow-based SDN architectures.

DEER96 Deering, S., et al. " The PIM Architecture for Wide-Area Multicast Routing." *IEEE/ACM Transactions on Networking*, April 1996.

GOTH11 Goth, G. "Software-Defined Networking Could Shake Up More than Packets." *IEEE Internet Computing*, July/August 2011.

JARS11 Jarschel, M., et al. "Modeling and Performance Evaluation of an OpenFlow Architecture." *Proceedings, International Teletraffic Congress*, 2011

LIMO12 Limoncelli, T. "OpenFlow: A Radical New Idea in Networking." *Communications of the ACM*, August 2012.

LI02 Li, V., and Zhang, Z. "Internet Multicast Routing and Transport Control Protocols." *Proceedings of the IEEE*, March 2002.

LI05 Li, J., and Chen, H. "Mobility Support for IP-Based Networks." *IEEE Communications Magazine*, October 2005.

RAMA00 Ramalho, M. "Intra- and Inter-Domain Multicast Routing Protocols: A Survey and Taxonomy." *IEEE Communications Surveys and Tutorials*, First Quarter 2000.

VAUG11 Vaughan-Nichols, S. "OpenFlow: The Next Generation of the Network?" *Computer*, August 2011.

VENK05 Venkataraman, N. "Inside Mobile IP." *Dr. Dobb's Journal*, September 2005.

Animations

Animations that illustrate multicasting and the operation of DHCP are available at the Premium Web site. The reader is encouraged to view these animations to reinforce concepts from this chapter.

21.7 KEY TERMS, REVIEW QUESTIONS, AND PROBLEMS

Key Terms

action	meter table	SDN control plane
action set	Mobile IP	SDN data plane
application programming interface (API)	multicast address	SDN domain
	multicasting	SDNi
flow	OpenFlow	server virtualization
flow table	Protocol Independent Multicast (PIM)	software-defined networks (SDN)
group table	Sparse-Mode PIM	unicast address
Internet Group Management Protocol	SDN application plane	

Review Questions

21.1 List some practical applications of multicasting.

21.2 Summarize the differences among unicast, multicast, and broadcast addresses.

21.3 List and briefly explain the functions that are required for multicasting.

21.4 What operations are performed by IGMP?

21.5 What network requirements led to the development of SDN?

21.6 What is an SDN domain?

21.7 What is Openflow?

21.8 List and briefly define the capabilities provided by Mobile IP.

21.9 What is the relationship between Mobile IP discovery and ICMP?

21.10 What are the two different types of destination addresses that can be assigned to a mobile node while it is attached to a foreign network?

21.11 Under what circumstances would a mobile node choose to use each of the types of address referred to in the preceding question?

Problems

21.1 Most operating systems include a tool named "traceroute" (or "tracert") that can be used to determine the path packets follow to reach a specified host from the system the tool is being run on. A number of sites provide web access to the "traceroute" tool, for example:

http://www.supporttechnique.net/traceroute.ihtml
http://www.t1shopper.com/tools/traceroute

Use the "traceroute" tool to determine the path packets follow to reach the host williamstallings.com.

21.2 Given the following undirected graph, draw minimum spanning trees for each node as the root node:

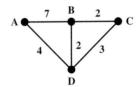

21.3 In the discussion of Figure 21.1, three alternatives for transmitting a packet to a multicast address were discussed: broadcast, multiple unicast, and true multicast. In the multiple unicast strategy, multiple copies of the packets start from the source to the destinations. On the other hand, in multicasting, a single packet is transmitted from the source and is replicated by routers in the branch points if required. Can you identify the advantages associated with this mechanism? Are there any disadvantages in multicasting?

21.4 In a manner similar to Figure 21.3, show the spanning tree from router B to the multicast group.

21.5 IGMP specifies that query messages are sent in IP datagrams that have the Time to Live field set to 1. Why?

21.6 At the network layer, an IGMP message has a Class D IP address that is changed to an Ethernet multicast address in the MAC layer. To do this, 23 LSBs of the IP address are added to the starting Ethernet multicast address, which ranges from 01:00:5E:00:00:00 to 01:00:5E:7F:FF:FF. Change the IP address 237:47:1:9 to a MAC address.

21.7 IGMP membership queries include a "Max Resp Code" field that specifies the maximum time allowed before sending a responding report. The actual time allowed, called the Max Resp Time, is represented in units of 0.1 s and is derived from the Max Resp Code as follows:

If MaxRespCode $<$ 128, MaxRespTime $=$ Max Resp Code

If MaxRespCode $\geq$ 128, MaxRespTime is a floating-point value as follows:

0	1	2	3	4	5	6	7
1	exp			mant			

$$\text{MaxRespTime} = (\text{mant}|0 \times 10) \ll (\text{exp} + 3) \text{ in C notation}$$

$$\text{MaxRespTime} = (\text{mant OR } 16) \times 2^{(\text{exp}+3)}$$

Explain the motivation for the smaller values and the larger values.

21.8 Multicast applications call an API function on their sockets in order to ask the IP layer to enable or disable reception of packets sent from some specific IP address(es) to a specific multicast address.

For each of these sockets, the system records the desired multicast reception state. In addition to these per-socket multicast reception states, the system must maintain a multicast reception state for each of its interfaces, which is derived from the per-socket reception states.

Suppose four multicast applications run on the same host, and participate in the same multicast group, M1. The first application uses an EXCLUDE{A1, A2, A3} filter. The second one uses an EXCLUDE{A1, A3, A4} filter. The third one uses an INCLUDE{A3, A4} filter. And the fourth one uses an INCLUDE{A3} filter. What's the resulting multicast state (multicast-address, filter-mode, source-list) for the network interface?

21.9 Multicast applications commonly use UDP or RTP (Real-Time Transport Protocol) as their transport protocol. Multicast applications do not use TCP as its transport protocol. What's the problem with TCP?

21.10 With multicasting, packets are delivered to multiple destinations. Thus, in case of errors (such as routing failures), one IP packet might trigger multiple ICMP error packets, leading to a packet storm. How is this potential problem avoided? *Hint:* consult RFC 1122.

21.11 Most multicast routing protocols, such as MOSPF, minimize the path cost to each group member, but they do not necessarily optimize the use of the Internet as a whole. This problem demonstrates this fact.
   a. Sum the hop costs incurred by each packet involved in a multicast transmission of a source packet using the spanning tree of Figure 21.2a.
   b. Design an alternative spanning tree that minimizes the total cost. Show the tree and the total cost.

21.12 "In sparse-mode PIM, for the route between a given source and a given destination, the RP-based tree may be replaced with a path that is the shortest unicast path from source to destination." This is not quite accurate. What is wrong with the statement?

21.13 The Protocol Independent Multicast (PIM) defines two independent multicast protocols: PIM dense-mode and PIM sparse-mode. List their differences with respect to the areas of application and the strategies applied.

21.14 This problem refers to Figure 21.12. Suppose that LAN Z is the home network for host E and that D sends a block of data to E via IP.

   a. Show the PDU structure, including the fields of the IP header and the lower-level headers (MAC, LLC) with the contents of address fields indicated for the case in which E is on its home network.

   b. Repeat part (a) for the case in which E is on a foreign network reachable via the Internet through R3. Show formats for the MAC frame leaving D and the IP datagram leaving R3. Assume that IP-to-IP encapsulation is used.

   c. Repeat part (b) for the IP datagram leaving R3, but now assume that minimal encapsulation is used.

21.15 Again referring to Figure 21.12, assume that A is a mobile node and that LAN X is a foreign network for A. Assume that an IP datagram arrives at R1 from the Internet to be delivered to A. Show the format of the IP datagram arriving at R1 and the MAC frame leaving R1 (include the IP header or headers) for the following cases:

   a. IP-to-IP encapsulation is used and R1 is the care-of address.

   b. Minimal encapsulation is used and R1 is the care-of address.

   c. IP-to-IP encapsulation is used and A is the care-of address.

   d. Minimal encapsulation is used and A is the care-of address.

21.16 In a typical Mobile IP implementation in a home agent, the agent maintains a mobility binding table to map a mobile node's home address to its care-of address for packet forwarding. What entries are essential for each row of the table?

21.17 Consider a TCP segment of 5000 bytes that has a 20-byte IP header. What will its size be if it is encapsulated using IP-within-IP encapsulation and mobile encapsulation?

   Hint: consult RFC 2003 and RFC 2004.

INTERNETWORK QUALITY OF SERVICE

LEARNING OBJECTIVES

After studying this chapter, you should be able to:

◆ Summarize the key concepts of the Integrated Services Architecture.

◆ Compare and contrast elastic and inelastic traffic.

◆ Present an overview of RSVP.

◆ Explain the concept of differentiated services.

◆ Understand the use of service level agreements.

◆ Describe IP performance metrics.

The traffic that the Internet and other internetworks must carry continues to grow and change. The demand generated by traditional data-based applications, such as electronic mail, Usenet news, file transfer, and remote logon, is sufficient to challenge these systems. But the driving factors are the heavy use of the World Wide Web, which demands real-time response, and the increasing use of audio, image, and video over internetwork architectures.

These internetwork schemes are essentially datagram packet-switching technology with routers functioning as the switches. This technology was not designed to handle voice and video and is straining to meet the demands placed on it.

To cope with these demands, it is not enough to increase Internet capacity. Sensible and effective methods for managing the traffic and controlling congestion are needed. Historically, IP-based internets have been able to provide a simple best-effort delivery service to all applications using an internet. But the needs of users have changed. A company may have spent millions of dollars installing an IP-based internet designed to transport data among LANs but now finds that new real-time, multimedia, and multicasting applications are not well supported by such a configuration.

Thus, there is a strong need to be able to support a variety of traffic with a variety of quality-of-service (QoS) requirements, within the TCP/IP architecture. This chapter begins with a look at an overall QoS architecture, which describes internetwork functions and services designed to meet this need.

Next, we look at the Integrated Services Architecture (ISA), which provides a framework for current and future internet services. We then look at a key protocol related to ISA called RSVP. Then, we examine differentiated services. Finally, we introduce the topics of service level agreements and IP performance metrics.

22.1 QOS ARCHITECTURAL FRAMEWORK

Before looking at the Internet standards that deal with provision of quality of service (QoS) in the Internet and private internetworks, it is useful to consider an overall architectural framework that relates the various elements that go into QoS provision. Such a framework has been developed by the Telecommunication Standardization Sector of the International Telecommunication Union (ITU-T) as part of its Y series of Recommendations.[1] The Recommendation, Y.1291 (*An Architectural Framework for Support of Quality of Service in Packet Networks*), gives a "big picture" overview of the mechanisms and services that comprise a QoS facility.

The Y.1291 framework comprises a set of generic network mechanisms for controlling the network service response to a service request, which can be specific to a network element, or for signaling between network elements, or for controlling and administering traffic across a network. Figure 22.1 shows the relationship

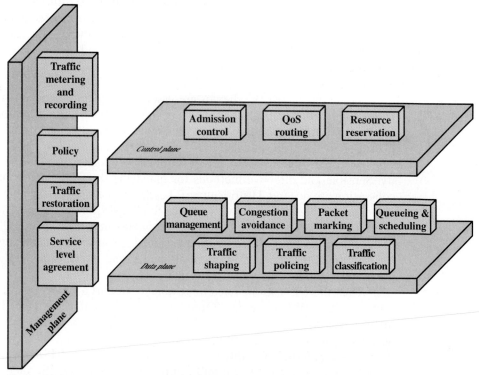

Figure 22.1   Architectural Framework for QoS Support

---

[1]The Y series, entitled *Global Information Infrastructure, Internet Protocol Aspects and Next-generation Networks*, contains a number of very useful documents dealing with QoS, congestion control, and traffic management.

among these elements, which are organized into three planes: data, control, and management.

Data Plane

The data plane includes those mechanisms that operate directly on flows of data. We briefly comment on each.

Queue management algorithms manage the length of packet queues by dropping packets when necessary or appropriate. Active management of queues is concerned primarily with congestion avoidance. In the early days of the Internet, the queue management discipline was to drop any incoming packets when the queue was full, referred to as the **tail drop** technique. There are a number of drawbacks to tail drop, including [BRAD98]:

1. There is no reaction to congestion until it is necessary to drop packets, whereas a more aggressive congestion avoidance technique would likely improve overall network performance.

2. Queues tend to be close to full, which causes an increase in packet delay through a network and which can result in a large batch of drop packets for bursty traffic, necessitating many packet retransmissions.

3. Tail drop may allow a single connection or a few flows to monopolize queue space, preventing other connections from getting room in the queue.

One noteworthy example of queue management is random early detection (RED). RED drops incoming packets probabilistically based on an estimated average queue size. The probability for dropping increases as the estimated average queue size grows. RED is described in Appendix P.

Queueing and scheduling algorithms, also referred to as queueing discipline algorithms, determine which packet to send next and are used primarily to manage the allocation of transmission capacity among flows. Queueing discipline is discussed in Section 22.2

Congestion avoidance deals with means for keeping the load of the network under its capacity such that it can operate at an acceptable performance level, not experiencing congestion collapse. Congestion avoidance is discussed in detail in Chapter 20.

Packet marking encompasses two distinct functions. First, packets may be marked by edge nodes of a network to indicate some form of QoS that the packet should receive. An example is the Differentiated Services (DS) field in the IPv4 and IPv6 packets (Figure 14.5) and the Traffic Class field in MPLS labels, discussed in Chapter 23. Such markings may be used by intermediate nodes to provide differential treatment to incoming packets. Packet marking can also be used to mark packets as nonconformant, which may be dropped later if congestion is experienced.

Traffic classification can be done on a packet or flow basis. All traffic assigned to a particular flow or other aggregate can then be treated similarly. The flow label in the IPv6 header (Figure 14.5b) can be used for traffic classification.

Traffic policing, discussed in Chapter 20, deals with the determination of whether the traffic being presented is on a hop-by-hop basis compliant with prenegotiated policies or contracts. Nonconformant packets may be dropped, delayed, or labeled as nonconformant. ITU-T Recommendation Y.1221 (*Traffic Control and Congestion Control in IP-based Networks*) recommends the use of token bucket to characterize traffic for purposes of traffic policing.

Traffic shaping, also discussed in Chapter 20, deals with controlling the rate and volume of traffic entering and transiting the network on a per-flow basis. The entity responsible for traffic shaping buffers nonconformant packets until it brings the respective aggregate in compliance with the traffic. The resulted traffic thus is not as bursty as the original and is more predictable. Y.1221 recommends the use of leaky bucket and/or token bucket for traffic shaping.

Control Plane

The control plane is concerned with creating and managing the pathways through which user data flows. It includes admission control, QoS routing, and resource reservation.

Admission control determines what user traffic may enter the network. This may be in part determined by the QoS requirements of a data flow compared to the current resource commitment within the network. RSVP, described in Section 22.3, implements this form of admission control. But beyond balancing QoS requests with available capacity to determine whether to accept a request, there are other considerations in admission control. Network managers and service providers must be able to monitor, control, and enforce use of network resources and services based on policies derived from criteria such as the identity of users and applications, traffic/bandwidth requirements, security considerations, and time-of-day/week. RFC 2753 (*A Framework for Policy-based Admission Control*) discusses such policy-related issues.

QoS routing is a routing technique that determines a network path that is likely to accommodate the requested QoS of a flow. This contrasts with the philosophy of the routing protocols described in Chapter 19, which generally are looking for a least-cost path through the network. RFC 2386 (*A Framework for QoS-based Routing in the Internet*) provides an overview of the issues involved in QoS routing, which is an area of ongoing study.

Resource reservation is a mechanism that reserves network resources on demand for delivering desired network performance to a requesting flow. The resource reservation mechanism that has been implemented for the Internet is RSVP, described in Section 22.3.

Management Plane

The management plane contains mechanisms that affect both control plane and data plane mechanisms. The control plane deals with the operation, administration, and management aspects of the network. It includes service level agreement (SLA), traffic restoration, traffic metering and recording, and policy.

A **service level agreement (SLA)** typically represents the agreement between a customer and a provider of a service that specifies the level of availability, serviceability, performance, operation, or other attributes of the service. SLAs are discussed in Section 22.5.

Traffic metering and recording concerns monitoring the dynamic properties of a traffic stream using performance metrics such as data rate and packet loss rate. It involves observing traffic characteristics at a given network point and collecting and storing the traffic information for analysis and further action. Depending on the conformance level, a meter can invoke necessary treatment (e.g., dropping or shaping) for the packet stream. Section 22.6 discusses the types of metrics that are used in this function.

Traffic restoration refers to the network response to failures. This encompasses a number of protocol layers and techniques.

Policy is a category that refers to a set of rules for administering, managing, and controlling access to network resources. They can be specific to the needs of the service provider or reflect the agreement between the customer and service provider, which may include reliability and availability requirements over a period of time and other QoS requirements.

22.2 INTEGRATED SERVICES ARCHITECTURE

To meet the requirement for QoS-based service, the IETF is developing a suite of standards under the general umbrella of the Integrated Services Architecture (ISA). ISA, intended to provide QoS transport over IP-based internets, is defined in overall terms in RFC 1633, while a number of other documents fill in the details. Already, a number of vendors have implemented portions of the ISA in routers and end-system software.

This section provides an overview of ISA.

Internet Traffic

Traffic on a network or internet can be divided into two broad categories: elastic and inelastic. A consideration of their differing requirements clarifies the need for an enhanced internet architecture.

ELASTIC TRAFFIC   Elastic traffic is that which can adjust, over wide ranges, to changes in delay and throughput across an internet and still meet the needs of its applications. This is the traditional type of traffic supported on TCP/IP-based internets and is the type of traffic for which internets were designed. Applications that generate such traffic typically use TCP or UDP as a transport protocol. In the case of UDP, the application will use as much capacity as is available up to the rate that the application generates data. In the case of TCP, the application will use as much capacity as is available up to the maximum rate that the end-to-end receiver can accept data. Also with TCP, traffic on individual connections adjusts to congestion by reducing the rate at which data are presented to the network; this is described in Chapter 20.

Applications that can be classified as elastic include the common applications that operate over TCP or UDP, including file transfer (FTP), electronic mail (SMTP), remote login (TELNET), network management (SNMP), and Web access (HTTP). However, there are differences among the requirements of these applications. For example,

- E-mail is generally insensitive to changes in delay.

- When file transfer is done interactively, as it frequently is, the user expects the delay to be proportional to the file size and so is sensitive to changes in throughput.

- With network management, delay is generally not a serious concern. However, if failures in an internet are the cause of congestion, then the need for SNMP messages to get through with minimum delay increases with increased congestion.

- Interactive applications, such as remote logon and Web access, are sensitive to delay.

It is important to realize that it is not per-packet delay that is the quantity of interest. As noted in [CLAR95], observation of real delays across the Internet suggests that wide variations in delay do not occur. Because of the congestion control mechanisms in TCP, when congestion develops, delays only increase modestly before the arrival rate from the various TCP connections slow down. Instead, the QoS perceived by the user relates to the total elapsed time to transfer an element of the current application. For an interactive TELNET-based application, the element may be a single keystroke or single line. For a Web access, the element is a Web page, which could be as little as a few kilobytes or could be substantially larger for an image-rich page. For a scientific application, the element could be many megabytes of data.

For very small elements, the total elapsed time is dominated by the delay time across the internet. However, for larger elements, the total elapsed time is dictated by the sliding-window performance of TCP and is therefore dominated by the throughput achieved over the TCP connection. Thus, for large transfers, the transfer time is proportional to the size of the file and the degree to which the source slows due to congestion.

It should be clear that even if we confine our attention to elastic traffic, a QoS-based internet service could be of benefit. Without such a service, routers are dealing evenhandedly with arriving IP packets, with no concern for the type of application and whether a particular packet is part of a large transfer element or a small one. Under such circumstances, and if congestion develops, it is unlikely that resources will be allocated in such a way as to meet the needs of all applications fairly. When inelastic traffic is added to the mix, the results are even more unsatisfactory.

INELASTIC TRAFFIC   Inelastic traffic does not easily adapt, if at all, to changes in delay and throughput across an internet. The prime example is real-time traffic. The requirements for inelastic traffic may include the following:

- **Throughput:** A minimum throughput value may be required. Unlike most elastic traffic, which can continue to deliver data with perhaps degraded service, many inelastic applications absolutely require a given minimum throughput.

- **Delay:** An example of a delay-sensitive application is stock trading; someone who consistently receives later service will consistently act later, and with greater disadvantage.

- **Jitter:** The magnitude of delay variation, called jitter, is a critical factor in real-time applications. Because of the variable delay imposed by the Internet, the interarrival times between packets are not maintained at a fixed interval at the destination. To compensate for this, the incoming packets are buffered, delayed sufficiently to compensate for the jitter, and then released at a constant rate to the software that is expecting a steady real-time stream. The larger the allowable delay variation, the longer the real delay in delivering the data and the greater the size of the delay buffer required at receivers. Real-time interactive applications, such as teleconferencing, may require a reasonable upper bound on jitter.

- **Packet loss:** Real-time applications vary in the amount of packet loss, if any, that they can sustain.

These requirements are difficult to meet in an environment with variable queueing delays and congestion losses. Accordingly, inelastic traffic introduces two new requirements into the internet architecture. First, some means is needed to give preferential treatment to applications with more demanding requirements. Applications need to be able to state their requirements, either ahead of time in some sort of service request function or on the fly, by means of fields in the IP packet header. The former approach provides more flexibility in stating requirements, and it enables the network to anticipate demands and deny new requests if the required resources are unavailable. This approach implies the use of some sort of resource reservation protocol.

An additional requirement in supporting inelastic traffic in an internet architecture is that elastic traffic must still be supported. Inelastic applications typically do not back off and reduce demand in the face of congestion, in contrast to TCP-based applications. Therefore, in times of congestion, inelastic traffic will continue to supply a high load, and elastic traffic will be crowded off the internet. A reservation protocol can help control this situation by denying service requests that would leave too few resources available to handle current elastic traffic.

ISA Approach

The purpose of ISA is to enable the provision of QoS support over IP-based internets. The central design issue for ISA is how to share the available capacity in times of congestion.

For an IP-based internet that provides only a best-effort service, the tools for controlling congestion and providing service are limited. In essence, routers have two mechanisms to work with:

- **Routing algorithm:** Most routing protocols in use in internets allow routes to be selected to minimize delay. Routers exchange information to get a picture of the delays throughout the internet. Minimum-delay routing helps to balance loads, thus decreasing local congestion, and helps to reduce delays seen by individual TCP connections.
- **Packet discard:** When a router's buffer overflows, it discards packets. Typically, the most recent packet is discarded. The effect of lost packets on a TCP connection is that the sending TCP entity backs off and reduces its load, thus helping to alleviate internet congestion.

These tools have worked reasonably well. However, as the discussion in the preceding subsection shows, such techniques are inadequate for the variety of traffic now coming to internets.

ISA is an overall architecture within which a number of enhancements to the traditional best-effort mechanisms are being developed. In ISA, each IP packet can be associated with a flow. RFC 1633 defines a flow as a distinguishable stream of related IP packets that results from a single user activity and requires the same QoS. For example, a flow might consist of one transport connection or one video stream distinguishable by the ISA. A flow differs from a TCP connection in two respects: A flow is unidirectional, and there can be more than one recipient of a flow (multicast). Typically, an IP packet is identified as a member of a flow on the basis of source and destination IP addresses and port numbers, and protocol type. The flow identifier in the IPv6 header is not necessarily equivalent to an ISA flow, but in future the IPv6 flow identifier could be used in ISA.

ISA makes use of the following functions to manage congestion and provide QoS transport:

- **Admission control:** For QoS transport (other than default best-effort transport), ISA requires that a reservation be made for a new flow. If the routers collectively determine that there are insufficient resources to guarantee the requested QoS, then the flow is not admitted. The protocol RSVP is used to make reservations.

- **Routing algorithm:** The routing decision may be based on a variety of QoS parameters, not just minimum delay. For example, the routing protocol OSPF, discussed in Section 19.3, can select routes based on QoS.

- **Queueing discipline:** A vital element of the ISA is an effective queueing policy that takes into account the differing requirements of different flows.

- **Discard policy:** A discard policy determines which packets to drop when a buffer is full and new packets arrive. A discard policy can be an important element in managing congestion and meeting QoS guarantees.

ISA Components

Figure 22.2 is a general depiction of the implementation architecture for ISA within a router. Below the thick horizontal line are the forwarding functions of the router; these are executed for each packet and therefore must be highly optimized. The remaining functions, above the line, are background functions that create data structures used by the forwarding functions.

The principal background functions are as follows:

- **Reservation protocol:** This protocol is to reserve resources for a new flow at a given level of QoS. It is used among routers and between routers and end systems. The reservation protocol is responsible for maintaining flow-specific state information at the end systems and at the routers along the path of the flow. RSVP is used for this purpose. The reservation protocol updates the traffic control database used by the packet scheduler to determine the service provided for packets of each flow.

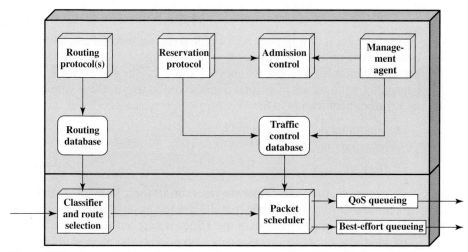

Figure 22.2 Integrated Services Architecture Implemented in Router

- **Admission control:** When a new flow is requested, the reservation protocol invokes the admission control function. This function determines if sufficient resources are available for this flow at the requested QoS. This determination is based on the current level of commitment to other reservations and/or on the current load on the network.

- **Management agent:** A network management agent is able to modify the traffic control database and to direct the admission control module in order to set admission control policies.

- **Routing protocol:** The routing protocol is responsible for maintaining a routing database that gives the next hop to be taken for each destination address and each flow.

These background functions support the main task of the router, which is the forwarding of packets. The two principal functional areas that accomplish forwarding are the following:

- **Classifier and route selection:** For the purposes of forwarding and traffic control, incoming packets must be mapped into classes. A class may correspond to a single flow or to a set of flows with the same QoS requirements. For example, the packets of all video flows or the packets of all flows attributable to a particular organization may be treated identically for purposes of resource allocation and queueing discipline. The selection of class is based on fields in the IP header. Based on the packet's class and its destination IP address, this function determines the next-hop address for this packet.

- **Packet scheduler:** This function manages one or more queues for each output port. It determines the order in which queued packets are transmitted and the selection of packets for discard, if necessary. Decisions are made based on a packet's class, the contents of the traffic control database, and current and past activity on this outgoing port. Part of the packet scheduler's task is that of policing, which is the function of determining whether the packet traffic in a given flow exceeds the requested capacity and, if so, deciding how to treat the excess packets.

ISA Services

ISA service for a flow of packets is defined on two levels. First, a number of general categories of service are provided, each of which provides a certain general type of service guarantees. Second, within each category, the service for a particular flow is specified by the values of certain parameters; together, these values are referred to as a traffic specification (TSpec). Currently, three categories of service are defined:

- Guaranteed
- Controlled load
- Best effort

An application can request a reservation for a flow for a guaranteed or controlled load QoS, with a TSpec that defines the exact amount of service required. If the reservation is accepted, then the TSpec is part of the contract between the data flow and the service. The service agrees to provide the requested QoS as long as the flow's data traffic continues to be described accurately by the TSpec. Packets that are not part of a reserved flow are by default given a best-effort delivery service.

GUARANTEED SERVICE   The key elements of the guaranteed service are as follows:

- The service provides assured capacity, or data rate.
- There is a specified upper bound on the queueing delay through the network. This must be added to the propagation delay, or latency, to arrive at the bound on total delay through the network.
- There are no queueing losses. That is, no packets are lost due to buffer overflow; packets may be lost due to failures in the network or changes in routing paths.

With this service, an application provides a characterization of its expected traffic profile, and the service determines the end-to-end delay that it can guarantee.

One category of applications for this service is those that need an upper bound on delay so that a delay buffer can be used for real-time playback of incoming data, and that do not tolerate packet losses because of the degradation in the quality of the output. Another example is applications with hard real-time deadlines.

The guaranteed service is the most demanding service provided by ISA. Because the delay bound is firm, the delay has to be set at a large value to cover rare cases of long queueing delays.

CONTROLLED LOAD   The key elements of the controlled load service are as follows:

- The service tightly approximates the behavior visible to applications receiving best-effort service under unloaded conditions.
- There is no specified upper bound on the queueing delay through the network. However, the service ensures that a very high percentage of the packets do not experience delays that greatly exceed the minimum transit delay (i.e., the delay due to propagation time plus router processing time with no queueing delays).
- A very high percentage of transmitted packets will be successfully delivered (i.e., almost no queueing loss).

As was mentioned, the risk in an internet that provides QoS for real-time applications is that best-effort traffic is crowded out. This is because best-effort types of applications employ TCP, which will back off in the face of congestion and delays. The controlled load service guarantees that the network will set aside sufficient resources so that an application that receives this service will see a network that responds as if these real-time applications were not present and competing for resources.

The controlled service is useful for applications that have been referred to as adaptive real-time applications [CLAR92]. Such applications do not require an *a priori* upper bound on the delay through the network. Rather, the receiver measures the jitter experienced by incoming packets and sets the playback point to the minimum delay that still produces a sufficiently low loss rate (e.g., video can be adaptive by dropping a frame or delaying the output stream slightly; voice can be adaptive by adjusting silent periods).

Queueing Discipline

An important component of an ISA implementation is the queueing discipline used at the routers. Routers traditionally have used a first-in-first-out (FIFO) queueing discipline at each output port. A single queue is maintained at each output port. When a new packet arrives and is routed to an output port, it is placed at the end of the queue. As long as the queue is not empty, the router transmits packets from the queue, taking the oldest remaining packet next.

There are several drawbacks to the FIFO queueing discipline:

* No special treatment is given to packets from flows that are of higher priority or are more delay sensitive. If a number of packets from different flows are ready to be forwarded, they are handled strictly in FIFO order.

* If a number of smaller packets are queued behind a long packet, then FIFO queueing results in a larger average delay per packet than if the shorter packets were transmitted before the longer packet. In general, flows of larger packets get better service.

* A greedy TCP connection can crowd out more altruistic connections. If congestion occurs and one TCP connection fails to back off, other connections along the same path segment must back off more than they would otherwise have to do.

To overcome the drawbacks of FIFO queueing, some sort of fair queueing scheme is used, in which a router maintains multiple queues at each output port (Figure 22.3). With simple fair queueing, each incoming packet is placed in the queue for its flow. The queues are serviced in round-robin fashion, taking one packet from each nonempty queue in turn. Empty queues are skipped over. This scheme is fair in that each busy flow gets to send exactly one packet per cycle. Further, this is a form of load balancing among the various flows. There is no advantage in being greedy. A greedy flow finds that its queues become long, increasing its delays, whereas other flows are unaffected by this behavior.

A number of vendors have implemented a refinement of fair queueing known as weighted fair queueing (WFQ). In essence, WFQ takes into account the amount

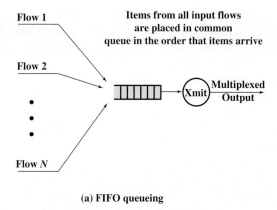

(a) FIFO queueing

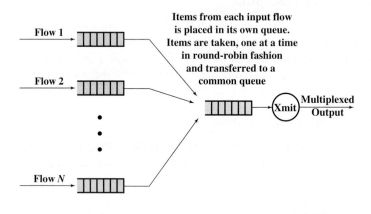

(b) Fair queueing

Figure 22.3 FIFO and Fair Queueing

of traffic through each queue and gives busier queues more capacity without completely shutting out less busy queues. In addition WFQ can take into account the amount of service requested by each traffic flow and adjust the queueing discipline accordingly. Details on the algorithms mentioned in this section can be found in Appendix P.

22.3 RESOURCE RESERVATION PROTOCOL

RFC 2205 defines Resource ReSerVation Protocol (RSVP), which provides supporting functionality for ISA. This subsection provides an overview.

A key task, perhaps the key task, of an internet is to deliver data from a source to one or more destinations with the desired QoS (throughput, delay, delay variance, etc.). This task becomes increasingly difficult on any internet with increasing number of users, data rate of applications, and use of multicasting. One tool for coping with a high demand is dynamic routing. A dynamic routing scheme, supported by protocols such as OSPF and BGP (Chapter 19), can respond quickly to failures in the internet by routing around points of failure. More important, a dynamic routing scheme can, to some extent, cope with congestion, first by load balancing to smooth out the load across the internet, and second by routing around areas of developing congestion using least-cost routing. In the case of multicasting, dynamic routing schemes have been supplemented with multicast routing capabilities that take advantage of shared paths from a source to multicast destinations to minimize the number of packet duplications.

Another tool available to routers is the ability to process packets on the basis of a QoS label. We have seen that routers can (1) use a queue discipline that gives preference to packets on the basis of QoS; (2) select among alternate routes on the basis of QoS characteristics of each path; and (3) when possible, invoke QoS treatment in the subnetwork of the next hop.

All of these techniques are means of coping with the traffic presented to the internet but are not preventive in any way. Based only on the use of dynamic routing and QoS, a router is unable to anticipate congestion and prevent applications from causing an overload. Instead, the router can simply supply a best-effort delivery service, in which some packets may be lost and others delivered with less than the requested QoS.

As the demands on internets grow, it appears that prevention as well as reaction to congestion is needed. As this section shows, a means to implement a prevention strategy is resource reservation.

Preventive measures can be useful in both unicast and multicast transmission. For **unicast**, two applications agree on a specific QoS for a session and expect the internet to support that QoS. If the internet is heavily loaded, it may not provide the desired QoS and instead deliver packets at a reduced QoS. In that case, the applications may have preferred to wait before initiating the session or at least to have been alerted to the potential for reduced QoS. A way of dealing with this situation is to have the unicast applications reserve resources in order to meet a given QoS. Routers along an intended path could then preallocate resources (queue space, outgoing capacity) to assure the desired QoS. If a router could not meet the resource reservation because of prior outstanding reservations, then the applications could be informed. The applications may then decide to try again at a reduced QoS reservation or may decide to try later.

Multicast transmission also presents a compelling case for implementing resource reservation. A multicast transmission can generate a tremendous amount of internet traffic if either the application is high volume (e.g., video) or the group of multicast destinations is large and scattered, or both. What makes the case for multicast resource reservation is that much of the potential load generated by a multicast source may easily be prevented. This is so for two reasons:

1. Some members of an existing multicast group may not require delivery from a particular source over some given period of time. For example, there may be two "channels" (two multicast sources) broadcasting to a particular multicast group at the same time. A multicast destination may wish to "tune in" to only one channel at a time.

2. Some members of a group may only be able to handle a portion of the source transmission. For example, a video source may transmit a video stream that consists of two components: a basic component that provides a reduced picture quality, and an enhanced component. Some receivers may not have the processing power to handle the enhanced component, or may be connected to the internet through a subnetwork or link that does not have the capacity for the full signal.

Thus, the use of resource reservation can enable routers to decide ahead of time if they can meet the requirement to deliver a multicast transmission to all designated multicast receivers and to reserve the appropriate resources if possible.

Internet resource reservation differs from the type of resource reservation that may be implemented in a connection-oriented network, such as ATM or frame relay. An internet resource reservation scheme must interact with a dynamic routing strategy that allows the route followed by packets of a given transmission to change. When the route changes, the resource reservations must be changed. To deal with this dynamic situation, the concept of *soft state* is used. A soft state is simply a set of state information at a router that expires unless regularly refreshed from the entity that requested the state. If a route for a given transmission changes, then some soft states will expire and new resource reservations will invoke the appropriate soft states on the new routers along the route. Thus, the end systems requesting resources must periodically renew their requests during the course of an application transmission.

We now turn to the protocol that has been developed for performing resource reservation in an internet environment: RSVP, defined in RFC 2205.

RSVP Goals and Characteristics

Based on these preceding considerations, RFC 2205 lists the following characteristics of RSVP:

- **Unicast and multicast:** RSVP makes reservations for both unicast and multicast transmissions, adapting dynamically to changing group membership as well as to changing routes, and reserving resources based on the individual requirements of multicast members.

- **Simplex:** RSVP makes reservations for unidirectional data flow. Data exchanges between two end systems require separate reservations in the two directions.

- **Receiver-initiated reservation:** The receiver of a data flow initiates and maintains the resource reservation for that flow.

- **Maintaining soft state in the internet:** RSVP maintains a soft state at intermediate routers and leaves the responsibility for maintaining these reservation states to end users.

- **Providing different reservation styles:** These allow RSVP users to specify how reservations for the same multicast group should be aggregated at the intermediate switches. This feature enables a more efficient use of internet resources.

- **Transparent operation through non-RSVP routers:** Because reservations and RSVP are independent of routing protocol, there is no fundamental conflict in a mixed environment in which some routers do not employ RSVP. These routers will simply use a best-effort delivery technique.

It is worth elaborating on two of these design characteristics: receiver-initiated reservations, and soft state.

RECEIVER-INITIATED RESERVATION   In previous attempts at resource reservation, including the approach taken in frame relay and ATM networks, the source of a data flow requests a given set of resources. In a strictly unicast environment, this approach is reasonable. A transmitting application is able to transmit data at a certain rate and has a given QoS designed into the transmission scheme. However, this approach is inadequate for multicasting. As was mentioned, different members of the same multicast group may have different resource requirements. If the source transmission flow can be divided into component subflows, then some multicast members may only require a single subflow. If there are multiple sources transmitting to a multicast group, then a particular multicast receiver may want to select only one or a subset of all sources to receive. Finally, the QoS requirements of different receivers may differ depending on the output equipment, processing power, and link speed of the receiver.

It therefore makes sense for receivers rather than senders to make resource reservations. A sender needs to provide the routers with the traffic characteristics of the transmission (data rate, variability), but it is the receivers that must specify the desired QoS. Routers can then aggregate multicast resource reservations to take advantage of shared path segments along the distribution tree.

SOFT STATE   RSVP makes use of the concept of a soft state. This concept was first introduced by David Clark in [CLAR88]. Clark makes several points in his paper[2]:

1. When a gateway treats each datagram in isolation, it is difficult to perform any sort of intelligent resource allocation and performance management at the level of the gateway, or router.

2. Most datagrams are part of some sequence of packets from source to destination, rather than isolated units at the application level. We can refer to each such sequence as a **flow**.

3. The flow, rather than the datagram, is a better building block for the next generation of Internet architecture, which must provide better performance management and over more flexible quality of service.

4. To make use of flows, each router would have to maintain state information for each flow passing through the router, so as to remember the nature of the flows passing through.

5. The flow state information is not critical in maintaining the described type of service associated with the flow. Instead, that type of service can be enforced by the end points, which can periodically send messages to routers to ensure that the proper type of service is being associated with the flow.

6. Therefore, the state information associated with the flow could be lost in a crash without permanent disruption of the service features being used. Thus, Clark refers to such a flow state as a **soft state**.

---

[2]*Gateway* is the term used for *router* in most of the earlier RFCs and TCP/IP literature; it is still occasionally used today (e.g., Border Gateway Protocol).

In essence, a connection-oriented scheme takes a hard-state approach, in which the nature of the connection along a fixed route is defined by the state information in the intermediate switching nodes. RSVP takes a soft-state, or connectionless, approach, in which the reservation state is cached information in the routers that is installed and periodically refreshed by end systems. If a state is not refreshed within a required time limit, the router discards the state. If a new route becomes preferred for a given flow, the end systems provide the reservation to the new routers on the route.

Data Flows

Three concepts relating to data flows form the basis of RSVP operation: session, flow specification, and filter specification.

A session is a data flow identified by its destination. The reason for using the term *session* rather than simply *destination* is that it reflects the soft-state nature of RSVP operation. Once a reservation is made at a router by a particular destination, the router considers this as a session and allocates resources for the life of that session. In particular, a session is defined by:

> **Session:**   Destination IP address
> IP protocol identifier
> Destination port

The destination IP address may be unicast or multicast. The protocol identifier indicates the user of IP (e.g., TCP or UDP), and the destination port is the TCP or UDP port for the user of this transport-layer protocol. If the address is multicast, the destination port may not be necessary, because there is typically a different multicast address for different applications.

A reservation request issued by a destination end system is called a *flow descriptor* and consists of a *flowspec* and a *filter spec*. The flowspec specifies a desired QoS and is used to set parameters in a node's packet scheduler. That is, the router will transmit packets with a given set of preferences based on the current flowspecs. The filter spec defines the set of packets for which a reservation is requested. Thus, the filter spec together with the session define the set of packets, or flow, that are to receive the desired QoS. Any other packets addressed to the same destination are handled as best-effort traffic.

The content of the flowspec is beyond the scope of RSVP, which is merely a carrier of the request. In general, a flowspec contains the following elements:

> **Flowspec:**   Service class
> RSpec
> TSpec

The service class is an identifier of a type of service being requested; it includes information used by the router to merge requests. The other two parameters are sets of numeric values. The RSpec (R for reserve) parameter defines the desired QoS, and the TSpec (T for traffic) parameter describes the data flow. The contents of Rspec and TSpec are opaque to RSVP.

In principle, the filter spec may designate an arbitrary subset of the packets of one session (i.e., the packets arriving with the destination specified by this session). For example, a filter spec could specify only specific sources, or specific source protocols, or in general only packets that have a match on certain fields in any of the protocol headers in the packet. The current RSVP version uses a restricted filter spec consisting of the following elements:

> **Filter spec:**   Source address
>   UDP/TCP source port

Figure 22.4 indicates the relationship among session, flowspec, and filter spec. Each incoming packet is part of at most one session and is treated according to the logical flow indicated in the figure for that session. If a packet belongs to no session, it is given a best-effort delivery service.

RSVP Operation

Much of the complexity of RSVP has to do with dealing with multicast transmission. Unicast transmission is treated as a special case. In what follows, we examine the general operation of RSVP for multicast resource reservation. The internet configuration shown in Figure 22.5a is used in the discussion. This configuration consists of four routers connected as shown. The link between two routers, indicated by a line, could be a point-to-point link or a subnetwork. Three hosts, G1, G2, and G3, are members of a multicast group and can receive datagrams with the corresponding destination multicast address. Two hosts, S1 and S2, transmit data to this multicast address. The thick black lines indicate the routing tree for source S1 and this

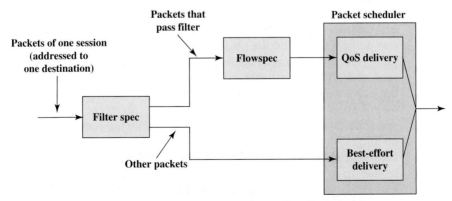

Figure 22.4   Treatment of Packets of One Session at One Router

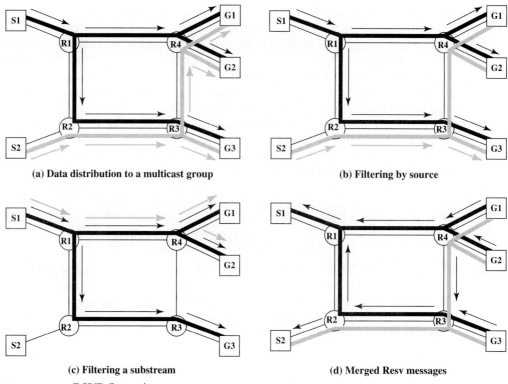

(a) Data distribution to a multicast group (b) Filtering by source

(c) Filtering a substream (d) Merged Resv messages

Figure 22.5   RSVP Operation

multicast group, and the thick shaded lines indicate the routing tree for source S2 and this multicast group. The arrowed lines indicate packet transmission from S1 (black) and S2 (gray).

We can see that all four routers need to be aware of the resource reservations of each multicast destination. Thus, resource requests from the destinations must propagate backward through the routing trees toward each potential host.

FILTERING   Figure 22.5b shows the case that G3 has set up a resource reservation with a filter spec that includes both S1 and S2, whereas G1 and G2 have requested transmissions from S1 only. R3 continues to deliver packets from S2 for this multicast address to G3 but does not forward such packets to R4 for delivery to G1 and G2. The reservation activity that produces this result is as follows. Both G1 and G2 send an RSVP request with a filter spec that excludes S2. Because G1 and G2 are the only members of the multicast group reachable from R4, R4 no longer needs to forward packets for this session. Therefore, it can merge the two filter spec requests and send these in an RSVP message to R3. Having received this message, R3 will no longer forward packets for this session to R4. However, it still needs to forward such packets to G3. Accordingly, R3 stores this reservation but does not propagate it back up to R2.

Data packets that are addressed to a particular session but do not match any of the filter specs are treated as best-effort traffic.

A more fine-grained example of filtering is illustrated in Figure 22.5c. Here we only consider transmissions from S1, for clarity. Suppose that two types of packets are transmitted to the same multicast address representing two substreams (e.g., two parts of a video signal). These are illustrated by black and gray arrowed lines. G1 and G2 have sent reservations with no restriction on the source, whereas G3 has used a filter spec that eliminates one of the two substreams. This request propagates from R3 to R2 to R1. R1 then blocks transmission of part of the stream to G3. This saves resources on the links from R1 to R2, R2 to R3, and R3 to G3, as well as resources in R2, R3, and G3.

RESERVATION STYLES   The manner in which resource requirements from multiple receivers in the same multicast group are aggregated is determined by the reservation style. These styles are, in turn, characterized by two different options in the reservation request:

- **Reservation attribute:** A receiver may specify a resource reservation that is to be shared among a number of senders (shared) or may specify a resource reservation that is to be allocated to each sender (distinct). In the former case, the receiver is characterizing the entire data flow that it is to receive on this multicast address from the combined transmission of all sources in the filter spec. In the latter case, the receiver is saying that it is simultaneously capable of receiving a given data flow from each sender characterized in its filter spec.

- **Sender selection:** A receiver may either provide a list of sources (explicit) or implicitly select all sources by providing no filter spec (wild card).

Based on these two options, three reservation styles are defined in RSVP, as shown in Table 22.1. The **wildcard-filter (WF) style** specifies a single resource reservation to be shared by all senders to this address. If all of the receivers use this style, then we can think of this style as a shared pipe whose capacity (or quality) is the largest of the resource requests from all receivers downstream from any point on the distribution tree. The size is independent of the number of senders using it. This type of reservation is propagated upstream to all senders. Symbolically, this style is represented in the form $WF(*\{Q\})$, where the asterisk represents wildcard sender selection and Q is the flowspec.

To see the effects of the WF style, we use the router configuration of Figure 22.6 taken from the RSVP specification. This is a router along the distribution tree that forwards packets on port y for receiver R1 and on port z for receivers R2 and R3. Transmissions for this group arrive on port w from S1 and on port x from S2

Table 22.1   Reservation Attributes and Styles

Sender Selection	Reservation Attribute	
	Distinct	**Shared**
Explicit	Fixed-filter (FF) style	Shared-explicit (SE) style
Wildcard	—	Wildcard-filter (WF) style

and S3. Transmissions from all sources are forwarded to all destinations through this router.

Figure 22.6b shows the way in which the router handles WF requests. For simplicity, the flowspec is a one-dimensional quantity in multiples of some unit resource B. The *Receive* column shows the requests that arrive from the receivers. The *Reserve* column shows the resulting reservation state for each outgoing port. The *Send* column indicates the requests that are sent upstream to the previous-hop nodes. Note that the router must reserve a pipe of capacity 4B for port y and of capacity 3B for port z. In the latter case, the router has merged the requests from R2 and R3 to support the maximum requirement for that port. However, in passing requests upstream the router must merge all outgoing requests and send a request for 4B upstream on both ports w and x.

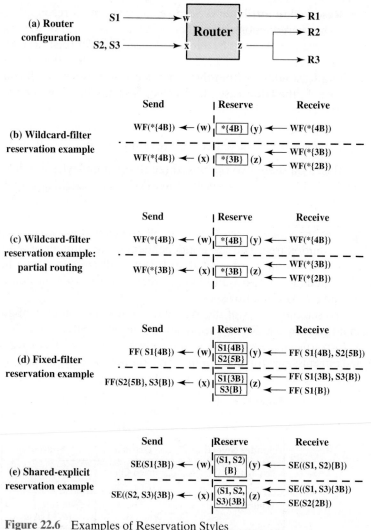

Figure 22.6 Examples of Reservation Styles

Now suppose that the distribution tree is such that this router forwards packets from S1 on both ports y and z but forwards packets from S2 and S3 only on port z, because the internet topology provides a shorter path from S2 and S3 to R1. Figure 22.6c indicates the way in which resource requests are merged in this case. The only change is that the request sent upstream on port x is for 3B. This is because packets arriving from this port are only to be forwarded on port z, which has a maximum flowspec request of 3B.

A good example of the use of the WF style is for an audio teleconference with multiple sites. Typically, only one person at a time speaks, so a shared capacity can be used by all senders.

The **fixed-filter (FF) style** specifies a distinct reservation for each sender and provides an explicit list of senders. Symbolically, this style is represented in the form $FF(S1\{Q1\}, S2\{Q2\}, \ldots)$, where Si is a requested sender and Qi is the resource request for that sender. The total reservation on a link for a given session is the sum of the Qi for all requested senders.

Figure 22.6d illustrates the operation of the FF style. In the *Reserve* column, each box represents one reserved pipe on the outgoing link. All of the incoming requests for S1 are merged to send a request for 4B out on port w. The flow descriptors for senders S2 and S3 are packed (not merged) into the request sent of port x; for this request, the maximum requested flowspec amount for each source is used.

A good example of the use of the FF style is for video distribution. To receive video signals simultaneously from different sources requires a separate pipe for each of the streams. The merging and packing operations at the routers assure that adequate resources are available. For example, in Figure 22.5a, R3 must reserve resources for two distinct video streams going to G3, but it needs only a single pipe on the stream going to R4 even though that stream is feeding two destinations (G1 and G2). Thus, with FF style, it may be possible to share resources among multiple receivers but it is never possible to share resources among multiple senders.

The **shared-explicit (SE) style** specifies a single resource reservation to be shared among an explicit list of senders. Symbolically, this style is represented in the form $SE(S1,S2, \ldots \{Q\})$. Figure 22.6e illustrates the operation of this style. When SE-style reservations are merged, the resulting filter spec is the union of the original filter specs, and the resulting flowspec is the largest flowspec.

As with the WF style, the SE style is appropriate for multicast applications in which there are multiple data sources but they are unlikely to transmit simultaneously.

RSVP Protocol Mechanisms

RSVP uses two basic message types: Resv and Path. Resv messages originate at multicast group receivers and propagate upstream through the distribution tree, being merged and packed when appropriate at each node along the way. These messages create soft states within the routers of the distribution tree that define the resources reserved for this session (this multicast address). Ultimately, the merged Resv messages reach the sending hosts, enabling the hosts to set up appropriate traffic control parameters for the first hop. Figure 22.5d indicates the flow of Resv messages. Note that messages are merged so that only a single message flows upstream along any branch of the combined distribution trees. However, these messages must be repeated periodically to maintain the soft states.

The Path message is used to provide upstream routing information. In all of the multicast routing protocols currently in use, only a downstream route, in the form of a distribution tree, is maintained. However, the Resv messages must propagate upstream through all intermediate routers and to all sending hosts. In the absence of reverse routing information from the routing protocol, RSVP provides this with the Path message. Each host that wishes to participate as a sender in a multicast group issues a Path message that is transmitted throughout the distribution tree to all multicast destinations. Along the way, each router and each destination host creates a path state that indicates the reverse hop to be used for this source. Figure 22.5a indicates the paths taken by these messages, which is the same as the paths taken by data packets.

Figure 22.7 illustrates the operation of the protocol, with events numbered from the perspective of each host. The following events occur:

a. A receiver joins a multicast group by sending an IGMP (Internet Group Message Protocol) join message to a neighboring router.

b. A potential sender issues a Path message to the multicast group address.

c. A receiver receives a Path message identifying a sender.

d. Now that the receiver has reverse path information, it may begin sending Resv messages, specifying the desired flow descriptors.

e. The Resv message propagates through the internet and is delivered to the sender.

f. The sender starts sending data packets.

g. The receiver starts receiving data packets.

Events a and b may happen in either order.

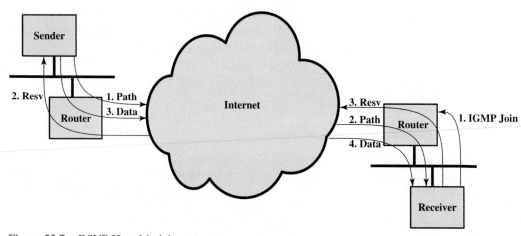

Figure 22.7   RSVP Host Model

22.4 DIFFERENTIATED SERVICES

ISA and RSVP are intended to support QoS capability in the Internet and in private internets. Although ISA in general and RSVP in particular are useful tools in this regard, these features are relatively complex to deploy. Further, they may not scale well to handle large volumes of traffic because of the amount of control signaling required to coordinate integrated QoS offerings and because of the maintenance of state information required at routers.

As the burden on the Internet grows, and as the variety of applications grow, there is an immediate need to provide differing levels of QoS to different traffic flows. The differentiated services (DS) architecture (RFC 2475) is designed to provide a simple, easy-to-implement, low-overhead tool to support a range of network services that are differentiated on the basis of performance.

Several key characteristics of DS contribute to its efficiency and ease of deployment:

- IP packets are labeled for differing QoS treatment using the existing IPv4 or IPv6 DS field (Figure 14.5). Thus, no change is required to IP.
- A Service Level Specification (SLS) is established between the service provider (Internet domain) and the customer prior to the use of DS. This avoids the need to incorporate DS mechanisms in applications. Thus, existing applications need not be modified to use DS. The SLS is a set of parameters and their values which together define the service offered to a traffic stream by a DS domain.
- A Traffic Conditioning Specification (TCS) is a part of the SLS that specifies traffic classifier rules and any corresponding traffic profiles and metering, marking, discarding, and/or shaping rules which are to apply to the traffic stream.
- DS provides a built-in aggregation mechanism. All traffic with the same DS octet is treated the same by the network service. For example, multiple voice connections are not handled individually but in the aggregate. This provides for good scaling to larger networks and traffic loads.
- DS is implemented in individual routers by queueing and forwarding packets based on the DS octet. Routers deal with each packet individually and do not have to save state information on packet flows.

Today, DS is the most widely accepted QoS mechanism in enterprise networks.

Although DS is intended to provide a simple service based on relatively simple mechanisms, the set of RFCs related to DS is relatively complex. Table 22.2 summarizes some of the key terms from these specifications.

Services

The DS type of service is provided within a DS domain, which is defined as a contiguous portion of the Internet over which a consistent set of DS policies are administered. Typically, a DS domain would be under the control of one

Table 22.2   Terminology for Differentiated Services

Behavior Aggregate	A set of packets with the same DS codepoint crossing a link in a particular direction.
Classifier	Selects packets based on the DS field (BA classifier) or on multiple fields within the packet header (MF classifier).
DS Boundary Node	A DS node that connects one DS domain to a node in another domain
DS Codepoint	A specified value of the 6-bit DSCP portion of the 8-bit DS field in the IP header.
DS Domain	A contiguous (connected) set of nodes, capable of implementing differentiated services, that operate with a common set of service provisioning policies and per-hop behavior definitions.
DS Interior Node	A DS node that is not a DS boundary node.
DS Node	A node that supports differentiated services. Typically, a DS node is a router. A host system that provides differentiated services for applications in the host is also a DS node.
Dropping	The process of discarding packets based on specified rules; also called **policing**.
Marking	The process of setting the DS codepoint in a packet. Packets may be marked on initiation and may be re-marked by an en route DS node.
Metering	The process of measuring the temporal properties (e.g., rate) of a packet stream selected by a classifier. The instantaneous state of that process may affect marking, shaping, and dropping functions.
Per-Hop Behavior (PHB)	The externally observable forwarding behavior applied at a node to a behavior aggregate.
Service Level Agreement (SLA)	A service contract between a customer and a service provider that specifies the forwarding service a customer should receive.
Shaping	The process of delaying packets within a packet stream to cause it to conform to some defined traffic profile.
Traffic Conditioning	Control functions performed to enforce rules specified in a TCA, including metering, marking, shaping, and dropping.
Traffic Conditioning Agreement (TCA)	An agreement specifying classifying rules and traffic conditioning rules that are to apply to packets selected by the classifier.

administrative entity. The services provided across a DS domain are defined in an SLA, which is a service contract between a customer and the service provider that specifies the forwarding service that the customer should receive for various classes of packets. A customer may be a user organization or another DS domain. Once the SLA is established, the customer submits packets with the DS octet marked to indicate the packet class. The service provider must assure that the customer gets at least the agreed QoS for each packet class. To provide that QoS, the service provider must configure the appropriate forwarding policies at each router (based on DS octet value) and must measure the performance being provided for each class on an ongoing basis.

   If a customer submits packets intended for destinations within the DS domain, then the DS domain is expected to provide the agreed service. If the destination is beyond the customer's DS domain, then the DS domain will attempt to forward the packets through other domains, requesting the most appropriate service to match the requested service.

A draft DS framework document lists the following detailed performance parameters that might be included in an SLA:

- Detailed service performance parameters such as expected throughput, drop probability, latency
- Constraints on the ingress and egress points at which the service is provided, indicating the scope of the service
- Traffic profiles that must be adhered to for the requested service to be provided, such as token bucket parameters
- Disposition of traffic submitted in excess of the specified profile

The framework document also gives some examples of services that might be provided:

1. Traffic offered at service level A will be delivered with low latency.
2. Traffic offered at service level B will be delivered with low loss.
3. Ninety percent of in-profile traffic delivered at service level C will experience no more than 50 ms latency.
4. Ninety-five percent of in-profile traffic delivered at service level D will be delivered.
5. Traffic offered at service level E will be allotted twice the bandwidth of traffic delivered at service level F.
6. Traffic with drop precedence X has a higher probability of delivery than traffic with drop precedence Y.

The first two examples are qualitative and are valid only in comparison to other traffic, such as default traffic that gets a best-effort service. The next two examples are quantitative and provide a specific guarantee that can be verified by measurement on the actual service without comparison to any other services offered at the same time. The final two examples are a mixture of quantitative and qualitative.

DS Field

Packets are labeled for service handling by means of the 6-bit DS field in the IPv4 header or the IPv6 header. The value of the DS field, referred to as the **DS codepoint**, is the label used to classify packets for differentiated services. Figure 22.8a shows the DS field.

With a 6-bit codepoint, there are in principle 64 different classes of traffic that could be defined. These 64 codepoints are allocated across three pools of codepoints, as follows:

- Codepoints of the form xxxxx0, where x is either 0 or 1, are reserved for assignment as standards.
- Codepoints of the form xxxx11 are reserved for experimental or local use.
- Codepoints of the form xxxx01 are also reserved for experimental or local use but may be allocated for future standards action as needed.

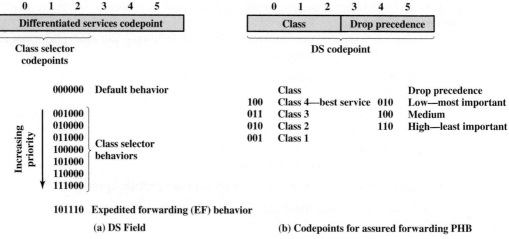

Figure 22.8 DS Field

Within the first pool, several assignments are made in RFC 2474. The code-point 000000 is the default packet class. The default class is the best-effort forwarding behavior in existing routers. Such packets are forwarded in the order that they are received as soon as link capacity becomes available. If other higher-priority packets in other DS classes are available for transmission, these are given preference over best-effort default packets.

Codepoints of the form xxx000 are reserved to provide backward compatibility with the IPv4 precedence service. To explain this requirement, we need to digress to an explanation of the IPv4 precedence service. The IPv4 type of service (TOS) field includes two subfields: a 3-bit precedence subfield and a 4-bit TOS subfield. These subfields serve complementary functions. The TOS subfield provides guidance to the IP entity (in the source or router) on selecting the next hop for this datagram, and the precedence subfield provides guidance about the relative allocation of router resources for this datagram.

The precedence field is set to indicate the degree of urgency or priority to be associated with a datagram. If a router supports the precedence subfield, there are three approaches to responding:

- **Route selection:** A particular route may be selected if the router has a smaller queue for that route or if the next hop on that route supports network precedence or priority (e.g., a token ring network supports priority).
- **Network service:** If the network on the next hop supports precedence, then that service is invoked.
- **Queueing discipline:** A router may use precedence to affect how queues are handled. For example, a router may give preferential treatment in queues to datagrams with higher precedence.

RFC 1812, Requirements for IP Version 4 Routers, provides recommendations for queueing discipline that fall into two categories:

- **Queue service**
  - a. Routers SHOULD implement precedence-ordered queue service. Precedence-ordered queue service means that when a packet is selected for output on a (logical) link, the packet of highest precedence that has been queued for that link is sent.
  - b. Any router MAY implement other policy-based throughput management procedures that result in other than strict precedence ordering, but it MUST be configurable to suppress them (i.e., use strict ordering).
- **Congestion control**. When a router receives a packet beyond its storage capacity, it must discard it or some other packet or packets.
  - a. A router MAY discard the packet it has just received; this is the simplest but not the best policy.
  - b. Ideally, the router should select a packet from one of the sessions most heavily abusing the link, given that the applicable QoS policy permits this. A recommended policy in datagram environments using FIFO queues is to discard a packet randomly selected from the queue. An equivalent algorithm in routers using fair queues is to discard from the longest queue. A router MAY use these algorithms to determine which packet to discard.
  - c. If precedence-ordered queue service is implemented and enabled, the router MUST NOT discard a packet whose IP precedence is higher than that of a packet that is not discarded.
  - d. A router MAY protect packets whose IP headers request the maximize reliability TOS, except where doing so would be in violation of the previous rule.
  - e. A router MAY protect fragmented IP packets, on the theory that dropping a fragment of a datagram may increase congestion by causing all fragments of the datagram to be retransmitted by the source.
  - f. To help prevent routing perturbations or disruption of management functions, the router MAY protect packets used for routing control, link control, or network management from being discarded. Dedicated routers (i.e., routers that are not also general purpose hosts, terminal servers, etc.) can achieve an approximation of this rule by protecting packets whose source or destination is the router itself.

The DS codepoints of the form xxx000 should provide a service that at minimum is equivalent to that of the IPv4 precedence functionality.

DS Configuration and Operation

Figure 22.9 illustrates the type of configuration envisioned in the DS documents. A DS domain consists of a set of contiguous routers; that is, it is possible to get from any router in the domain to any other router in the domain by a path that does not include routers outside the domain. Within a domain, the interpretation of DS codepoints is uniform, so that a uniform, consistent service is provided.

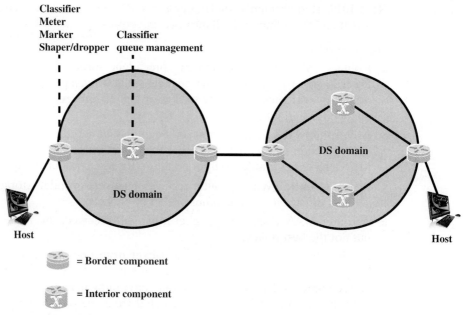

Figure 22.9 DS Domains

Routers in a DS domain are either boundary nodes or interior nodes. Typically, the interior nodes implement simple mechanisms for handling packets based on their DS codepoint values. This includes queueing discipline to give preferential treatment depending on codepoint value, and packet-dropping rules to dictate which packets should be dropped first in the event of buffer saturation. The DS specifications refer to the forwarding treatment provided at a router as per-hop behavior (PHB). This PHB must be available at all routers, and typically PHB is the only part of DS implemented in interior routers.

The boundary nodes include PHB mechanisms but more sophisticated traffic conditioning mechanisms are also required to provide the desired service. Thus, interior routers have minimal functionality and minimal overhead in providing the DS service, while most of the complexity is in the boundary nodes. The boundary node function can also be provided by a host system attached to the domain, on behalf of the applications at that host system.

The traffic conditioning function consists of five elements:

- **Classifier:** Separates submitted packets into different classes. This is the foundation of providing differentiated services. A classifier may separate traffic only on the basis of the DS codepoint (behavior aggregate classifier) or based on multiple fields within the packet header or even the packet payload (multifield classifier).

- **Meter:** Measures submitted traffic for conformance to a profile. The meter determines whether a given packet stream class is within or exceeds the service level guaranteed for that class.

- **Marker:** Re-marks packets with a different codepoint as needed. This may be done for packets that exceed the profile; for example, if a given throughput is guaranteed for a particular service class, any packets in that class that exceed the throughput in some defined time interval may be re-marked for best-effort handling. Also, re-marking may be required at the boundary between two DS domains. For example, if a given traffic class is to receive the highest supported priority, and this is a value of 3 in one domain and 7 in the next domain, then packets with a priority 3 value traversing the first domain are remarked as priority 7 when entering the second domain.

- **Shaper:** Delays packets as necessary so that the packet stream in a given class does not exceed the traffic rate specified in the profile for that class.

- **Dropper:** Drops packets when the rate of packets of a given class exceeds that specified in the profile for that class.

Figure 22.10 illustrates the relationship between the elements of traffic conditioning. After a flow is classified, its resource consumption must be measured. The metering function measures the volume of packets over a particular time interval to determine a flow's compliance with the traffic agreement. If the host is bursty, a simple data rate or packet rate may not be sufficient to capture the desired traffic characteristics. A token bucket scheme, (Figure 20.7) is an example of a way to define a traffic profile to take into account both packet rate and burstiness.

If a traffic flow exceeds some profile, several approaches can be taken. Individual packets in excess of the profile may be re-marked for lower-quality handling and allowed to pass into the DS domain. A traffic shaper may absorb a burst of packets in a buffer and pace the packets over a longer period. A dropper may drop packets if the buffer used for pacing becomes saturated.

Per–Hop Behavior

As part of the DS standardization effort, specific types of PHB need to be defined, which can be associated with specific differentiated services. Currently, two standards-track PHBs have been issued: expedited forwarding PHB (RFCs 3246 and 3247) and assured forwarding PHB (RFC 2597).

EXPEDITED FORWARDING PHB   RFC 3246 defines the expedited forwarding (EF) PHB as a building block for low-loss, low-delay, and low-jitter end-to-end services

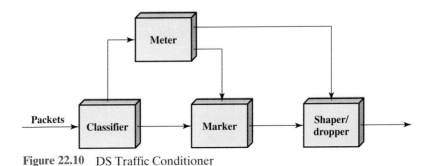

Figure 22.10   DS Traffic Conditioner

through DS domains. In essence, such a service should appear to the endpoints as providing close to the performance of a point-to-point connection or leased line.

In an internet or packet-switching network, a low-loss, low-delay, and low-jitter service is difficult to achieve. By its nature, an internet involves queues at each node, or router, where packets are buffered waiting to use a shared output link. It is the queueing behavior at each node that results in loss, delays, and jitter. Thus, unless the internet is grossly oversized to eliminate all queueing effects, care must be taken in handling traffic for EF PHB to assure that queueing effects do not result in loss, delay, or jitter above a given threshold. RFC 3246 declares that the intent of the EF PHB is to provide a PHB in which suitably marked packets usually encounter short or empty queues. The relative absence of queues minimizes delay and jitter. Furthermore, if queues remain short relative to the buffer space available, packet loss is also kept to a minimum.

The EF PHB is designed to configuring nodes so that the traffic aggregate[3] has a well-defined minimum departure rate. (*Well-defined* means "independent of the dynamic state of the node." In particular, independent of the intensity of other traffic at the node.) The general concept outlined in RFC 3246 is this: The border nodes control the traffic aggregate to limit its characteristics (rate, burstiness) to some predefined level. Interior nodes must treat the incoming traffic in such a way that queueing effects do not appear. In general terms, the requirement on interior nodes is that the aggregate's maximum arrival rate must be less than the aggregate's minimum departure rate.

RFC 3246 does not mandate a specific queueing policy at the interior nodes to achieve the EF PHB. The RFC notes that a simple priority scheme could achieve the desired effect, with the EF traffic given absolute priority over other traffic. So long as the EF traffic itself did not overwhelm an interior node, this scheme would result in acceptable queueing delays for the EF PHB. However, the risk of a simple priority scheme is that packet flows for other PHB traffic would be disrupted. Thus, some more sophisticated queueing policy might be warranted.

ASSURED FORWARDING PHB   The assured forwarding (AF) PHB is designed to provide a service superior to best effort but one that does not require the reservation of resources within an internet and does not require the use of detailed discrimination among flows from different users. The concept behind the AF PHB was first introduced in [CLAR98] and is referred to as explicit allocation. The AF PHB is more complex than explicit allocation, but it is useful to first highlight the key elements of the explicit allocation scheme:

1. Users are offered the choice of a number of classes of service for their traffic. Each class describes a different traffic profile in terms of an aggregate data rate and burstiness.

2. Traffic from a user within a given class is monitored at a boundary node. Each packet in a traffic flow is marked *out* or *in* based on whether it does or does not exceed the traffic profile.

---

[3]The term *traffic aggregate* refers to the flow of packets associated with a particular service for a particular user.

3. Inside the network, there is no separation of traffic from different users or even traffic from different classes. Instead, all traffic is treated as a single pool of packets, with the only distinction being whether each packet has been marked *in* or *out*.

4. When congestion occurs, the interior nodes implement a dropping scheme in which *out* packets are dropped before *in* packets.

5. Different users will see different levels of service because they will have different quantities of *in* packets in the service queues.

The advantage of this approach is its simplicity. Very little work is required by the internal nodes. Marking of the traffic at the boundary nodes based on traffic profiles provides different levels of service to different classes.

The AF PHB defined in RFC 2597 expands on the preceding approach in the following ways:

1. Four AF classes are defined, allowing the definition of four distinct traffic profiles. A user may select one or more of these classes to satisfy requirements.

2. Within each class, packets are marked by the customer or by the service provider with one of three drop precedence values. In case of congestion, the drop precedence of a packet determines the relative importance of the packet within the AF class. A congested DS node tries to protect packets with a lower drop precedence value from being lost by preferably discarding packets with a higher drop precedence value.

This approach is still simpler to implement than any sort of resource reservation scheme but provides considerable flexibility. Within an interior DS node, traffic from the four classes can be treated separately, with different amounts of resources (buffer space, data rate) assigned to the four classes. Within each class, packets are handled based on drop precedence. Thus, as RFC 2597 points out, the level of forwarding assurance of an IP packet depends on the following:

• How much forwarding resources has been allocated to the AF class to which the packet belongs

• The current load of the AF class, and, in case of congestion, within the class

• The drop precedence of the packet

RFC 2597 does not mandate any mechanisms at the interior nodes to manage the AF traffic. It does reference the RED algorithm as a possible way of managing congestion.

Figure 22.8b shows the recommended codepoints for AF PHB in the DS field.

22.5 SERVICE LEVEL AGREEMENTS

A service level agreement (SLA) is a contract between a network provider and a customer that defines specific aspects of the service that is to be provided. The definition is formal and typically defines quantitative thresholds that must be met. An SLA typically includes the following information:

- **A description of the nature of service to be provided:** A basic service would be IP-based network connectivity of enterprise locations plus access to the Internet. The service may include additional functions such as Web hosting, maintenance of domain name servers, and operation and maintenance tasks.
- **The expected performance level of the service:** The SLA defines a number of metrics, such as delay, reliability, and availability, with numerical thresholds.
- **The process for monitoring and reporting the service level:** This describes how performance levels are measured and reported.

The types of service parameters included in an SLA for an IP network are similar to those provided for frame relay and ATM networks. A key difference is that, because of the unreliable datagram nature of an IP network, it is more difficult to realize tightly defined constraints on performance, compared to the connection-oriented frame relay and ATM networks.

Figure 22.11 shows a typical configuration that lends itself to an SLA. In this case, a network service provider maintains an IP-based network. A customer has a number of private networks (e.g., LANs) at various sites. Customer networks are connected to the provider via access routers at the access points. The SLA dictates service and performance levels for traffic between access routers across the provider network. In addition, the provider network links to the Internet and thus provides

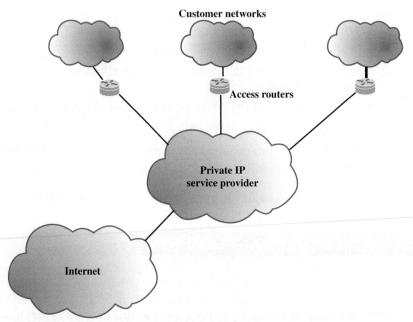

Figure 22.11 Typical Framework for Service Level Agreement

Internet access for the enterprise. For example, for the Internet Dedicated Service provided by MCI, the SLA includes the following items:

- **Availability:** 100% availability.
- **Latency (delay):** Average round-trip transmissions of $\leq$ 45 ms between access routers in the contiguous U.S. Average round-trip transmissions of $\leq$ 90 ms between an access router in the New York metropolitan area and an access router in the London metropolitan area. Latency is calculated by averaging sample measurements taken during a calendar month between routers.
- **Network packet delivery (reliability):** Successful packet delivery rate of $\geq$99.5%.
- **Denial of service (DoS):** Responds to DoS attacks reported by customer within 15 minutes of customer opening a complete trouble ticket. MCI defines a DoS attack as more than 95% bandwidth utilization.
- **Network jitter:** Jitter is defined as the variation or difference in the end-to-end delay between received packets of an IP or packet stream. Jitter performance will not exceed 1 ms between access routers.

An SLA can be defined for the overall network service. In addition, SLAs can be defined for specific end-to-end services available across the carrier's network, such as a virtual private network, or differentiated services.

22.6 IP PERFORMANCE METRICS

The IP Performance Metrics Working Group (IPPM) is chartered by IETF to develop standard metrics that relate to the quality, performance, and reliability of Internet data delivery. Two trends dictate the need for such a standardized measurement scheme:

1. The Internet has grown and continues to grow at a dramatic rate. Its topology is increasingly complex. As its capacity has grown, the load on the Internet has grown at an even faster rate. Similarly, private internets, such as corporate intranets and extranets, have exhibited similar growth in complexity, capacity, and load. The sheer scale of these networks makes it difficult to determine quality, performance, and reliability characteristics.
2. The Internet serves a large and growing number of commercial and personal users across an expanding spectrum of applications. Similarly, private networks are growing in terms of user base and range of applications. Some of these applications are sensitive to particular QoS parameters, leading users to require accurate and understandable performance metrics.

A standardized and effective set of metrics enables users and service providers to have an accurate common understanding of the performance of the Internet and private internets. Measurement data is useful for a variety of purposes, including

- Supporting capacity planning and troubleshooting of large complex internets
- Encouraging competition by providing uniform comparison metrics across service providers

- Supporting Internet research in such areas as protocol design, congestion control, and quality of service
- Verification of service level agreements

Table 22.3 lists the metrics that have been defined in RFCs at the time of this writing. Table 22.3a lists those metrics which result in a value estimated based on a sampling technique. The metrics are defined in three stages:

- **Singleton metric:** The most elementary, or atomic, quantity that can be measured for a given performance metric. For example, for a delay metric, a singleton metric is the delay experienced by a single packet.
- **Sample metric:** A collection of singleton measurements taken during a given time period. For example, for a delay metric, a sample metric is the set of delay values for all of the measurements taken during a one-hour period.
- **Statistical metric:** A value derived from a given sample metric by computing some statistic of the values defined by the singleton metric on the sample. For example, the mean of all the one-way delay values on a sample might be defined as a statistical metric.

The measurement technique can be either active or passive. **Active techniques** require injecting packets into the network for the sole purpose of measurement. There are several drawbacks to this approach. The load on the network is increased. This in turn can affect the desired result. For example, on a heavily loaded network, the injection of measurement packets can increase network delay, so that the measured delay is greater than it would be without the measurement traffic. In addition, an active measurement policy can be abused for denial-of-service attacks disguised as legitimate measurement activity. **Passive techniques** observe and extract metrics from existing traffic. This approach can expose the contents of Internet traffic to unintended recipients, creating security and privacy concerns. So far, the metrics defined by the IPPM working group are all active.

For the sample metrics, the simplest technique is to take measurements at fixed time intervals, known as periodic sampling. There are several problems with this approach. First, if the traffic on the network exhibits periodic behavior, with a period that is an integer multiple of the sampling period (or vice versa), correlation effects may result in inaccurate values.

Also, the act of measurement can perturb what is being measured (e.g., injecting measurement traffic into a network alters the congestion level of the network), and repeated periodic perturbations can drive a network into a state of synchronization (e.g., [FLOY94]), greatly magnifying what might individually be minor effects. Accordingly, RFC 2330 (*Framework for IP Performance Metrics*) recommends Poisson sampling. This method uses a Poisson distribution to generate random time intervals with the desired mean value.

Most of the statistical metrics listed in Table 22.3a are self-explanatory. The percentile metric is defined as follows: The xth percentile is a value y such that $x\%$ of measurements $\geq y$. The inverse percentile of x for a set of measurements is the percentage of all values $\leq x$.

Table 22.3 IP Performance Metrics

(a) Sampled metrics

Metric Name	Singleton Definition	Statistical Definitions
One-Way Delay	Delay = dT, where Src transmits first bit of packet at T and Dst received last bit of packet at $T + dT$	Percentile, median, minimum, inverse percentile
Round-Trip Delay	Delay = dT, where Src transmits first bit of packet at T and Src received last bit of packet immediately returned by Dst at $T + dT$	Percentile, median, minimum, inverse percentile
One-Way Loss	Packet loss = 0 (signifying successful transmission and reception of packet); = 1 (signifying packet loss)	Average
One-Way Loss Pattern	Loss distance: Pattern showing the distance between successive packet losses in terms of the sequence of packets Loss period: Pattern showing the number of bursty losses (losses involving consecutive packets)	Number or rate of loss distances below a defined threshold, number of loss periods, pattern of period lengths, pattern of inter-loss period lengths.
Packet Delay Variation	Packet delay variation (pdv) for a pair of packets with a stream of packets = difference between the one-way-delay of the selected packets	Percentile, inverse percentile, jitter, peak-to-peak pdv

Src = IP address of a host

Dst = IP address of a host

(b) Other metrics

Metric Name	General Definition	Metrics
Connectivity	Ability to deliver a packet over a transport connection.	One-way instantaneous connectivity, Two-way instantaneous connectivity, one-way interval connectivity, two-way interval connectivity, two-sway temporal connectivity
Bulk Transfer Capacity	Long-term average data rate (bps) over a single congestion-aware transport connection.	BTC = (data sent)/(elapsed time)

Figure 22.12 illustrates the packet delay variation metric. This metric is used to measure jitter, or variability, in the delay of packets traversing the network. The singleton metric is defined by selecting two packet measurements and measuring the difference in the two delays. The statistical measures make use of the absolute values of the delays.

Table 22.3b lists two metrics that are not defined statistically. Connectivity deals with the issue of whether a transport-level connection is maintained by the

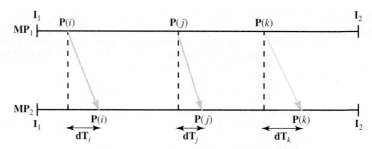

I_1, I_2 = times that mark that beginning and ending of the interval
          in which the packet stream from which the singleton
          measurement is taken occurs.
MP_1, MP_2 = source and destination measurement points
$P(i)$ = ith measured packet in a stream of packets
dT_i = one-way delay for $P(i)$

Figure 22.12   Model for Defining Packet Delay Variation

network. The current specification (RFC 2678) does not detail specific sample and statistical metrics but provides a framework within which such metrics could be defined. Connectivity is determined by the ability to deliver a packet across a connection within a specified time limit. The other metric, bulk transfer capacity, is similarly specified (RFC 3148) without sample and statistical metrics but begins to address the issue of measuring the transfer capacity of a network service with the implementation of various congestion control mechanisms.

22.7 RECOMMENDED READING AND WEB SITES

[XIAO99] provides an overview and overall framework for Internet QoS as well as integrated and differentiated services. [MEDD10] is a more recent survey. [CLAR92] and [CLAR95] provide valuable surveys of the issues involved in internet service allocation for real-time and elastic applications, respectively. [SHEN95] is a masterful analysis of the rationale for a QoS-based internet architecture. [ZHAN95] is a broad survey of queueing disciplines that can be used in an ISA, including an analysis of FQ and WFQ.

   [ZHAN93] is a good overview of the philosophy and functionality of RSVP, written by its developers. [WHIT97] is a broad survey of both ISA and RSVP.

   [CARP02] and [WEIS98] are instructive surveys of differentiated services, while [KUMA98] looks at differentiated services and supporting router mechanisms that go beyond the current RFCs.

   Two papers that compare IS and DS in terms of services and performance are [BERN00] and [HARJ00].

   [VERM04] is an excellent survey of service level agreements for IP networks. [BOUI02] covers the more general case of data networks. [MART02] examines limitations of IP network SLAs compared to data networks such as frame relay.

   [CHEN02] is a useful survey of Internet performance measurement issues. [PAXS96] provides an overview of the framework of the IPPM effort.

BERN00 Bernet, Y. "The Complementary Roles of RSVP and Differentiated Services in the Full-Service QoS Network." *IEEE Communications Magazine*, February 2000.

BOUI02 Bouillet, E.; Mitra, D.; and Ramakrishnan, K. "The Structure and Management of Service Level Agreements in Networks." *IEEE Journal on Selected Areas in Communications*, May 2002.

CARP02 Carpenter, B., and Nichols, K. "Differentiated Services in the Internet." *Proceedings of the IEEE*, September 2002.

CHEN02 Chen, T. "Internet Performance Monitoring." *Proceedings of the IEEE*, September 2002.

CLAR92 Clark, D.; Shenker, S.; and Zhang, L. "Supporting Real-Time Applications in an Integrated Services Packet Network: Architecture and Mechanism." *Proceedings, SIGCOMM '92*, August 1992.

CLAR95 Clark, D. *Adding Service Discrimination to the Internet.* MIT Laboratory for Computer Science Technical Report, September 1995, http://groups.csail.mit.edu/ana/Publications/index.html

HARJ00 Harju, J., and Kivimaki, P. "Cooperation and Comparison of DiffServ and IntServ: Performance Measurements." *Proceedings, 23rd Annual IEEE Conference on Local Computer Networks*, November 2000.

KUMA98 Kumar, V.; Lakshman, T.; and Stiliadis, D. "Beyond Best Effort: Router Architectures for the Differentiated Services of Tomorrow's Internet." *IEEE Communications Magazine*, May 1998.

MART02 Martin, J., and Nilsson, A. "On Service Level Agreements for IP Networks." *Proceedings, IEEE INFOCOMM'02*, 2002.

MEDD10 Meddeb, A. "Internet QoS: Pieces of the Puzzle." *IEEE Communications Magazine*, January 2010.

PAXS96 Paxson, V. "Toward a Framework for Defining Internet Performance Metrics." *Proceedings, INET '96*, 1996, http://www-nrg.ee.lbl.gov

SHEN95 Shenker, S. "Fundamental Design Issues for the Future Internet." *IEEE Journal on Selected Areas in Communications*, September 1995.

VERM04 Verma, D. "Service Level Agreements on IP Networks." *Proceedings of the IEEE*, September 2004.

WEIS98 Weiss, W. "QoS with Differentiated Services." *Bell Labs Technical Journal*, October–December 1998.

WHIT97 White, P., and Crowcroft, J. "The Integrated Services in the Internet: State of the Art." *Proceedings of the IEEE*, December 1997.

XIAO99 Xiao, X., and Ni, L. "Internet QoS: A Big Picture." *IEEE Network*, March/April 1999.

ZHAN93 Zhang, L.; Deering, S.; Estrin, D.; Shenker, S.; and Zappala, D. "RSVP: A New Resource ReSerVation Protocol." *IEEE Network*, September 1993.

ZHAN95 Zhang, H. "Service Disciplines for Guaranteed Performance Service in Packet-Switching Networks." *Proceedings of the IEEE*, October 1995.

22.8 KEY TERMS, REVIEW QUESTIONS, AND PROBLEMS

Key Terms

classifier	Integrated Services	quality of service (QoS)
differentiated services	Architecture (ISA)	queueing discipline
(DS)	jitter	Resource ReSerVation
dropper	marker	Protocol (RSVP)
elastic traffic flow	meter	service level agreement (SLA)
inelastic traffic	per-hop behavior (PHB)	shaper soft state

Review Questions

22.1 What is the Integrated Services Architecture?

22.2 What is the difference between elastic and inelastic traffic?

22.3 What are the major functions that are part of an ISA?

22.4 List and briefly describe the three categories of service offered by ISA.

22.5 What is the difference between FIFO queueing and WFQ queueing?

22.6 What is the purpose of a DS codepoint?

22.7 List and briefly explain the five main functions of DS traffic conditioning.

22.8 What is meant by per-hop behavior?

Problems

22.1 When multiple equal-cost routes to a destination exist, OSPF may distribute traffic equally among the routes. This is called *load balancing*. What effect does such load balancing have on a transport layer protocol, such as TCP?

22.2 It is clear that if a router gives preferential treatment to one flow or one class of flows, then that flow or class of flows will receive improved service. It is not as clear that the overall service provided by the internet is improved. This question is intended to illustrate an overall improvement. Consider a network with a single link modeled by an exponential server of rate $T_s = 1$, and consider two classes of flows with Poisson arrival rates of $\lambda 1 = \lambda 2 = 0.25$ that have utility functions $U_1 = 4 - 2\,T_{q1}$ and $U_2 = 4 - T_{q2}$, where T_{qi} represents the average queueing delay to class i. Thus, class 1 traffic is more sensitive to delay than class 2. Define the total utility of the network as $V = U_1 + U_2$.

  a. Assume that the two classes are treated alike and that FIFO queueing is used. What is V?

  b. Now assume a strict priority service so that packets from class 1 are always transmitted before packets in class 2. What is V? Comment.

22.3 How is the Internet traffic required by an email application different from that required by a teleconferencing session?

22.4 In RSVP, because the UDP/TCP port numbers are used for packet classification, each router must be able to examine these fields. This requirement raises problems in the following areas:

  a. IPv6 header processing
  b. IP-level security

  Indicate the nature of the problem in each area, and suggest a solution.

22.5   A differentiated services (DS) domain consists of a set of routers that operate with a common set of service provisioning policies. How can you categorize these routers on the basis of the functions that they perform?

22.6   One way to quantify the EF PHB performance requirement is with the following set of equations relating to packets leaving a node through some interface I to an external communications link:

$$d_j \le f_j > 0 + E_a \quad j > 0$$
$$f_0 = d_0 = 0$$
$$f_j = MAX[a_j, MIN(d_{j-1}, f_{j-1})] + (L_j/R)$$

where

d_j = departure time of the jth EF packet to depart from I; measured at the time the last bit leaves the node

f_j = target departure time for the jth EF packet to depart from I; the ideal time at or before which the last bit of that packet leaves the node

E_a = Error term for the treatment of individual EF packets; it represents the worst case deviation between actual departure time of an EF packet and the ideal departure time of the same packet

a_j = arrival time at this node of the last bit of the jth EF packet destined to depart from I

L_j = length in bits of the jth EF packet destined to depart from I

R = EF configured rate at I in bps; this is not the actual data rate on the line but rather the desired data rate for this EF PHB

This definition assumes that EF packets should ideally be served at a rate R or faster. It must take into account these cases: (1) An EF packet arrives when all previous EF packets have already departed; (2) an EF packet arrives at a device that still contains waiting EF packets. With these facts in mind, explain the equations. *Hint:* For the second case, there are two subcases.

22.7   Now consider an alternative set of equations for EF PHB:

$$D_j \le F_j + E_p \quad j > 0$$
$$F_0 = D_0 = 0$$
$$F_j = MAX[A_j, MIN(D_{j-1}, F_{j-1})] + (L_j/R)$$

where

D_j = departure time of the jth EF packet to arrive at this node and destined to depart from I; measured at the time the last bit leaves the node

F_j = target departure time for the jth EF packet to arrive at this node and destined to depart from I; the ideal time at or before which the last bit of that packet leaves the node

E_p = Error term for the treatment of individual EF packets; it represents the worst case deviation between actual departure time of an EF packet and the ideal departure time of the same packet

A_j = arrival time at this node of the last bit of the jth EF packet to arrive at this node and destined to depart from I

L_j = length in bits of the jth EF packet to arrive at this node and destined to depart from I

R = EF configured rate at I in bps; this is not the actual data rate on the line but rather the desired data rate for this EF PHB

Explain the difference between this definition and that of Problem 9.9.

22.8 What are the three stages in which IP performance metrics can be defined? If you are required to define metrics for jitters, what will be your metric for each of the stages that you have defined?

22.9 RFC 2330 (*Framework for IP Performance Metrics*) defines percentile in the following way. Given a collection of measurements, define the function $F(x)$, which for any x gives the percentage of the total measurements that were $\leq x$. If x is less than the minimum value observed, then $F(x) = 0\%$. If it is greater or equal to the maximum value observed, then $F(x) = 100\%$. The yth percentile refer to the smallest value of x for which $F(x) \geq y$. Consider that we have the following measurements: $-2, 7, 7, 4, 18, -5$. Determine the following percentiles: 0, 25, 50, 100.

22.10 For the one-way and two-way delay metrics, if a packet fails to arrive within a reasonable period of time, the delay is taken to be undefined (informally, infinite). The threshold of reasonable is a parameter of the methodology. Suppose we take a sample of one-way delays and get the following results: 100 ms, 110 ms, undefined, 90 ms, 500 ms. What is the 50th percentile?

22.11 RFC 2330 defines the median of a set of measurements to be equal to the 50th percentile if the number of measurements is odd. For an even number of measurements, sort the measurements in ascending order; the median is then the mean of the two central values. What is the median value for the measurements in the preceding two problems?

22.12 RFC 2679 defines the inverse percentile of x for a set of measurements to be the percentage of all values $\leq x$. What is the inverse percentile of 103 ms for the measurements in Problem 22.14?

CHAPTER 23

MULTIPROTOCOL LABEL SWITCHING

LEARNING OBJECTIVES

After studying this chapter, you should be able to:

- Discuss the role of MPLS in an Internet traffic management strategy.
- Explain at a top level how MPLS operates.
- Understand the use of labels in MPLS.
- Present an overview of how the function of label distribution works.
- Present an overview of MPLS traffic engineering.
- Understand the difference between layer 2 and layer 3 VPNs.

In Chapter 19, we examined a number of IP-based mechanisms designed to improve the performance of IP-based networks and to provide different levels of quality of service (QoS) to different service users. Although the routing protocols discussed in Chapter 19 have as their fundamental purpose dynamically finding a route through an internet between any source and any destination, they also provide support for performance goals in two ways:

1. Because these protocols are distributed and dynamic, they can react to congestion by altering routes to avoid pockets of heavy traffic. This tends to smooth out and balance the load on the Internet, improving overall performance.
2. Routes can be based on various metrics, such as hop count and delay. Thus a routing algorithm develops information that can be used in determining how to handle packets with different service needs.

More directly, some of the mechanisms discussed in Chapter 22 (IS, DS) provide enhancements to an IP-based internet that explicitly provide support for QoS. However, none of the mechanisms or protocols discussed in Chapter 22 directly addresses the performance issue: How to improve the overall throughput and delay characteristics of an internet. MPLS is intended to provide connection-oriented QoS with features similar to those found in differentiated services, and support traffic management to improve network throughput and retain the flexibility of an IP-based networking approach.

Multiprotocol Label Switching (MPLS) is a set of Internet Engineering Task Force (IETF) specifications for including routing and traffic engineering information in packets. Thus, MPLS comprises a number of interrelated protocols, which can be referred to as the MPLS protocol suite. It can be used in IP networks but also in other types of packet-switching networks. MPLS is used to ensure that all packets in a particular flow take the same route over a backbone. Deployed by many telecommunication companies and service providers, MPLS delivers the quality of service required to support real-time voice and video as well as service level agreements (SLAs) that guarantee bandwidth.

We begin this chapter with an overview of the current status of MPLS as a networking technology.

Although the basic principles of MPLS are straightforward, the set of protocols and procedures that have been built up around MPLS is formidable. As of this writing, the IETF MPLS working group has issued 70 RFCs and has 29 active Internet Drafts. In addition, there are five other IETF working groups developing RFCs on topics related to MPLS. The goal of this chapter is to present the fundamental concepts and an overview of the breadth of MPLS.

23.1 THE ROLE OF MPLS

In essence, MPLS is an efficient technique for forwarding and routing packets. MPLS was designed with IP networks in mind, but the technology can be used without IP to construct a network with any link-level protocol, including ATM and frame relay. In an ordinary packet-switching network, packet switches must examine various fields within the packet header to determine destination, route, quality of service, and any traffic management functions (such as discard or delay) that may be supported. Similarly, in an IP-based network, routers examine a number of fields in the IP header to determine these functions. In an MPLS network, a fixed-length label encapsulates an IP packet or a data link frame. The MPLS label contains all the information needed by an MPLS-enabled router to perform routing, delivery, QoS, and traffic management functions. Unlike IP, MPLS is connection oriented.

The IETF MPLS working group is the lead organization in developing MPLS-related specifications and standards. A number of other working groups deal with MPLS-related issues. Briefly, the objectives of these groups are as follows:

- **MPLS:** Responsible for standardizing a base technology for using label switching and for the implementation of label switched paths over various packet-based link-level technologies, such as Packet-over-SONET, Frame Relay, ATM, and LAN technologies (e.g., all forms of Ethernet, Token Ring, etc.). This includes procedures and protocols for the distribution of labels between routers and encapsulation.

- **Common control and measurement plane (CCAMP):** Responsible for defining a common control plane and a separate common measurement plane for physical path and core tunneling technologies of Internet and telecom service providers (ISPs and SPs), for example, O-O and O-E-O optical switches, TDM switches, Ethernet switches, ATM and frame relay switches, IP encapsulation tunneling technologies, and MPLS.

- **Layer 2 Virtual Private Networks (L2VPN):** Responsible for defining and specifying a limited number of solutions for supporting provider-provisioned Layer- 2 Virtual Private Networks (L2VPNs). The objective is to support link layer interfaces, such as ATM and Ethernet, for providing VPNs for an MPLS-enabled IP packet- switched network.

- **Layer 3 Virtual Private Networks (L3VPN):** Responsible for defining and specifying a limited number of solutions for supporting provider-provisioned Layer- 3 (routed) Virtual Private Networks (L3VPNs). Standardization includes supporting VPNs for end systems that have an IP interface over an MPLS-enabled IP packet-switched network.

- **Pseudowire Emulation Edge to Edge (pwe3):** Responsible for specifying protocols for pseudowire emulation over an MPLS network. A pseudowire emulates a point-to-point or point-to-multipoint link, and provides a single service that is perceived by its user as an unshared link or circuit of the chosen service.

- **Path Computation Element (PCE):** Focuses on the architecture and techniques for constraint-based path computation.

The magnitude of this effort suggests the importance, indeed the coming dominance, of MPLS. A 2009 survey found that 84% of companies are now using MPLS for their wide area networks [REED09]. MPLS is deployed in almost every major IP network. [MARS09] lists the following reasons for the dramatic growth in MPLS acceptance.

1. MPLS embraced IP. In the early 1990s, the telecom industry was pinning their hopes on ATM as the network backbone technology of the future, and made substantial investment. But as Internet usage exploded, carriers needed to refocus their efforts. At the same time, IETF was looking for ways to make circuit-oriented ATM technology run over IP. The result was the MPLS effort, which was quickly adopted by ATM proponents.

2. MPLS has built-in flexibility in several ways. MPLS separates out a control component, which enables various applications to directly manipulate label bindings, and a forwarding component, which uses a simple label-swapping paradigm. Also, MPLS allows labels to be stacked, enabling multiple control planes to act on a packet.

3. MPLS is protocol neutral. MPLS is designed to work in a multiple protocol environment. This enables MPLS to work with ATM, frame relay, SONET, or Ethernet at the core.

4. MPLS is pragmatic. The architecture created only two new protocols: Label Distribution Protocol and Link Management Protocol. Everything else incorporates or adapts existing protocols.

5. MPLS is adaptable. MPLS has evolved over time to support new applications and services, including layer 2 and layer 3 virtual private networks, Ethernet services, and traffic engineering.

6. MPLS supports metrics. MPLS allows carriers to collect a wide variety of statistics that can be used for network traffic trend analysis and planning. With

MPLS, it is possible to measure traffic volume, latency, and delay between two routers. Carriers also can measure traffic between hubs, metropolitan areas, and regions.

7. MPLS scales. For example, Verizon uses MPLS for several global networks including its public and private IP networks. Verizon's Public IP network spans 410 points of presence on six continents and spans more than 150 countries.

It is clear that MPLS will permeate virtually all areas of networking. Hence the need for students to gain a basic understanding of its technology and protocols.

23.2 BACKGROUND

The roots of MPLS go back to a number of efforts in the mid-1990s to provide a comprehensive set of QoS and traffic engineering capabilities in IP-based networks. The first such effort to reach the marketplace was IP switching, developed by Ipsilon. To compete with this offering, numerous other companies announced their own products, notably Cisco Systems (tag switching), IBM (aggregate route-based IP switching), and Cascade (IP navigator). The goal of all these products was to improve the throughput and delay performance of IP, and all took the same basic approach: Use a standard routing protocol such as OSPF to define paths between endpoints and assign packets to these paths as they enter the network.

In response to these proprietary initiatives, the IETF set up the MPLS working group in 1997 to develop a common, standardized approach. The working group issued its first set of Proposed Standards in 2001. The key specification is RFC 3031. MPLS reduces the amount of per-packet processing required at each router in an IP-based network, enhancing router performance even more. More significantly, MPLS provides significant new capabilities in four areas that have ensured its popularity: QoS support, traffic engineering, virtual private networks, and multiprotocol support. Before turning to the details of MPLS, we briefly examine each of these.

Connection-Oriented QoS Support

Network managers and users require increasingly sophisticated QoS support for a number of reasons. [SIKE00] lists the following key requirements:

- Guarantee a fixed amount of capacity for specific applications, such as audio/video conference.
- Control latency and jitter and ensure capacity for voice.
- Provide very specific, guaranteed, and quantifiable service level agreements, or traffic contracts.
- Configure varying degrees of QoS for multiple network customers.

A connectionless network, such as in IP-based internet, cannot provide truly firm QoS commitments. A differentiated service (DS) framework works in only a general way and upon aggregates of traffic from a number of sources. An integrated services (IS) framework, using RSVP, has some of the flavor of a connection-oriented approach but is nevertheless limited in terms of its flexibility and scalability. For services such as voice and video that require a network with high predictability, the DS and IS approaches, by themselves, may prove inadequate on a heavily loaded network. By contrast, a connection-oriented network, as we have seen with ATM, has powerful traffic management and QoS capabilities. MPLS imposes a connection-oriented framework on an IP-based internet and thus provides the foundation for sophisticated and reliable QoS traffic contracts.

Traffic Engineering

MPLS makes it easy to commit network resources in such a way as to balance the load in the face of a given demand and to commit to differential levels of support to meet various user traffic requirements. The ability to define routes dynamically, plan resource commitments on the basis of known demand, and optimize network utilization is referred to as **traffic engineering**. Prior to the advent of MPLS, the one networking technology that provided strong traffic engineering capabilities was ATM.

With the basic IP mechanism, there is a primitive form of automated traffic engineering. Specifically, routing protocols such as OSPF enable routers to dynamically change the route to a given destination on a packet-by-packet basis to try to balance load. But such dynamic routing reacts in a very simple manner to congestion and does not provide a way to support QoS. All traffic between two endpoints follows the same route, which may be changed when congestion occurs. MPLS, on the other hand, is aware of not just individual packets but flows of packets in which each flow has certain QoS requirements and a predictable traffic demand. With MPLS, it is possible to set up routes on the basis of these individual flows, with two different flows between the same endpoints perhaps following different routers. Further, when congestion threatens, MPLS paths can be rerouted intelligently. That is, instead of simply changing the route on a packet-by-packet basis, with MPLS, the routes are changed on a flow-by-flow basis, taking advantage of the known traffic demands of each flow. Effective use of traffic engineering can substantially increase usable network capacity.

Virtual Private Network (VPN) Support

MPLS provides an efficient mechanism for supporting VPNs. With a VPN, the traffic of a given enterprise or group passes through an internet in a way that effectively segregates that traffic from other packets on the internet, proving performance guarantees and security.

Multiprotocol Support

MPLS can be used on a number of networking technologies. Our focus in this chapter is on IP-based internets, and this is likely to be the principal area of use. MPLS is an enhancement to the way a connectionless IP-based internet is operated, requiring an upgrade to IP routers to support the MPLS features. MPLS-enabled routers can coexist with ordinary IP routers, facilitating the evolution to MPLS schemes. MPLS is also designed to work in ATM and frame relay networks. Again, MPLS-enabled ATM switches and MPLS-enabled frame relay switches can be configured to coexist with ordinary switches. Furthermore, MPLS can be used in a pure

Table 23.1   MPLS Terminology

Forwarding equivalence class (FEC) A group of IP packets that are forwarded in the same manner (e.g., over the same path, with the same forwarding treatment).	**Label stack** An ordered set of labels.
	Merge point A node at which label merging is done.
Frame merge Label merging, when it is applied to operation over frame-based media, so that the potential problem of cell interleave is not an issue.	**MPLS domain** A contiguous set of nodes that operate MPLS routing and forwarding and that are also in one Routing or Administrative Domain.
Label merging The replacement of multiple incoming labels for a particular FEC with a single outgoing label.	**MPLS edge node** An MPLS node that connects an MPLS domain with a node that is outside of the domain, either because it does not run MPLS, and/or because it is in a different domain. Note that if an LSR has a neighboring host that is not running MPLS, then that LSR is an MPLS edge node.
Label swap The basic forwarding operation consisting of looking up an incoming label to determine the outgoing label, encapsulation, port, and other data handling information.	**MPLS egress node** An MPLS edge node in its role in handling traffic as it leaves an MPLS domain.
Label swapping A forwarding paradigm allowing streamlined forwarding of data by using labels to identify classes of data packets that are treated indistinguishably when forwarding.	**MPLS ingress node** An MPLS edge node in its role in handling traffic as it enters an MPLS domain.
	MPLS label A short, fixed-length physically contiguous identifier that is used to identify a FEC, usually of local significance. A label is carried in a packet header.
Label switched hop The hop between two MPLS nodes, on which forwarding is done using labels.	
Label switched path The path through one or more LSRs at one level of the hierarchy followed by a packets in a particular FEC.	**MPLS node** A node that is running MPLS. An MPLS node will be aware of MPLS control protocols, will operate one or more L3 routing protocols, and will be capable of forwarding packets based on labels. An MPLS node may optionally be also capable of forwarding native L3 packets.
Label switching router (LSR) An MPLS node that is capable of forwarding native L3 packets.	

IP-based internet, a pure ATM network, a pure frame relay network, or an internet that includes two or even all three technologies. This universal nature of MPLS should appeal to users who currently have mixed network technologies and seek ways to optimize resources and expand QoS support.

For the remainder of this discussion, we focus on the use of MPLS in IP-based internets, with brief comments about formatting issues for ATM and frame relay networks. Table 23.1 defines key MPLS terms used in our discussion.

23.3   MPLS OPERATION

An MPLS network or internet[1] consists of a set of nodes, called **label switching routers (LSRs)**, capable of switching and routing packets on the basis of a label appended to each packet. Labels define a flow of packets between two endpoints or, in the case of multicast, between a source endpoint and a multicast group of destination endpoints. For each distinct flow, called a **forwarding equivalence class (FEC)**,

---

[1]For simplicity, we will use the term *network* for the remainder of this section. In the case of an IP-based internet, we are referring to the Internet or a private internet, where the IP routers function as MPLS nodes.

a specific path through the network of LSRs is defined, called a **label switched path (LSP)**. In essence, an FEC represents a group of packets that share the same transport requirements. All packets in an FEC receive the same treatment en route to the destination. These packets follow the same path and receive the same QoS treatment at each hop. In contrast to forwarding in ordinary IP networks, the assignment of a particular packet to a particular FEC is done just once, when the packet enters the network of MPLS routers.

Thus, MPLS is a connection-oriented technology. Associated with each FEC is a traffic characterization that defines the QoS requirements for that flow. The LSRs need not examine or process the IP header but rather simply forward each packet based on its label value. Each LSR builds a table, called a **label information base (LIB)**, to specify how a packet must be treated and forwarded. Thus, the forwarding process is simpler than with an IP router.

Label assignment decisions (i.e., the assignment of a packet to a give FEC and hence a given LSP) may be based on the following criteria:

- **Destination unicast routing:** In the absence of other criteria, packets flowing from one source to one destination may be assigned to the same FEC.
- **Traffic engineering:** Packet flows may be split up or aggregated to accommodate traffic engineering requirements.
- **Multicast:** Multicast routes through the network may be defined.
- **Virtual private network (VPN):** Traffic among end systems for a particular customer may be segregated from other traffic on a public MPLS network by means of a dedicated set of LSPs.
- **QoS:** Traffic may be assigned different FECs for different QoS requirements.

Figure 23.1 depicts the operation of MPLS within a domain of MPLS-enabled routers. The following are key elements of the operation:

1. Prior to the routing and delivery of packets in a given FEC, a path through the network, known as a **label switched path (LSP)**, must be defined and the QoS parameters along that path must be established. The QoS parameters determine (1) how much resources to commit to the path, and (2) what queuing and discarding policy to establish at each LSR for packets in this FEC. To accomplish these tasks, two protocols are used to exchange the necessary information among routers:

   a. An interior routing protocol, such as OSPF, is used to exchange reachability and routing information.

   b. Labels must be assigned to the packets for a particular FEC. Because the use of globally unique labels would impose a management burden and limit the number of usable labels, labels have local significance only, as discussed subsequently. A network operator can specify explicit routes manually and assign the appropriate label values. Alternatively, a protocol is used to determine the route and establish label values between adjacent LSRs. Either of two protocols can be used for this purpose: the Label Distribution Protocol (LDP) or an enhanced version of RSVP. LDP is now considered the standard technique.

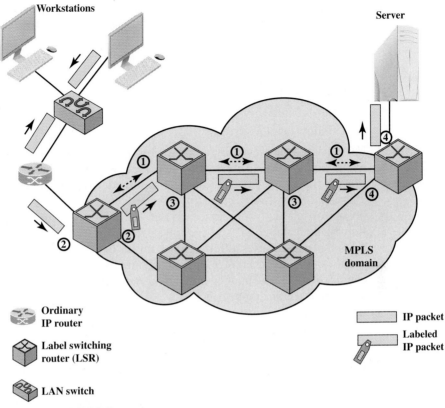

Workstations

Server

Ordinary
IP router

Label switching
router (LSR)

LAN switch

IP packet

Labeled
IP packet

MPLS
domain

Figure 23.1 MPLS Operation

2. A packet enters an MPLS domain through an ingress edge LSR, where it is processed to determine which network-layer services it requires, defining its QoS. The LSR assigns this packet to a particular FEC, and therefore a particular LSP; appends the appropriate label to the packet; and forwards the packet. If no LSP yet exists for this FEC, the edge LSR must cooperate with the other LSRs in defining a new LSP.

3. Within the MPLS domain, as each LSR receives a labeled packet, it

   a. removes the incoming label and attaches the appropriate outgoing label to the packet

   b. forwards the packet to the next LSR along the LSP

4. The egress edge LSR strips the label, reads the IP packet header, and forwards the packet to its final destination.

   Several key features of MLSP operation can be noted at this point:

1. An MPLS domain consists of a contiguous, or connected, set of MPLS-enabled routers. Traffic can enter or exit the domain from an endpoint on a directly connected network, as shown in the upper-right corner of Figure 23.1. Traffic may also arrive from an ordinary router that connects to a portion of the internet not using MPLS, as shown in the upper-left corner of Figure 23.1.

2. The FEC for a packet can be determined by one or more of a number of parameters, as specified by the network manager. Some of the possible parameters are the following:
   - Source and/or destination IP addresses or IP network addresses
   - Source and/or destination port numbers
   - IP protocol ID
   - Differentiated services codepoint
   - IPv6 flow label

3. Forwarding is achieved by doing a simple lookup in a predefined table that maps label values to next hop addresses. There is no need to examine or process the IP header or to make a routing decision based on destination IP address. This not only makes it possible to separate types of traffic, such as best-effort traffic from mission-critical traffic, it also renders an MPLS solution highly scalable. MPLS decouples packet forwarding from IP header information because it uses different mechanisms to assign labels. Labels have local significance only; therefore, it is nearly impossible to run out of labels. This characteristic is essential to implementing advanced IP services such as QoS, VPNs, and traffic engineering.

4. A particular per-hop behavior (PHB) can be defined at an LSR for a given FEC. The PHB defines the queuing priority of the packets for this FEC and the discard policy.

5. Packets sent between the same endpoints may belong to different FECs. Thus, they will be labeled differently, will experience different PHB at each LSR, and may follow different paths through the network.

Figure 23.2 shows the label-handling and forwarding operation in more detail. Each LSR maintains a forwarding table for each LSP passing through the LSR. When a labeled packet arrives, the LSR indexes the forwarding table to determine the next hop. For scalability, as was mentioned, labels have local significance only. Thus, the LSR removes the incoming label from the packet and attaches the matching outgoing label before forwarding the packet. The ingress edge LSR determines the FEC for each incoming unlabeled packet and, on the basis of the FEC, assigns the packet to a particular LSP, attaches the corresponding label, and forwards the packet. In this example, the first packet arrives at the edge LSR, which reads the IP header for the destination address prefix, 128.89. The LSR then looks up the destination address in the switching table, inserts a label with a 20-bit label value of 19, and forwards the labeled packet out interface 1. This interface is attached via a link to a core LSR, which receives the packet on its interface 2. The LSR in the core reads the label and looks up its match in its switching table, replaces label 19 with label 24, and forwards it out interface 0. The egress LSR reads and looks up label 24 in its table, which says to strip the label and forward the packet out interface 0.

Let us now look at an example that illustrates the various stages of operation of MPLS, using Figure 23.3. We examine the path of a packet as it travels from a source workstation to a destination server. Across the MPLS network, the packet enters at ingress node LSR 1. Assume that this is the first occurrence of a packet

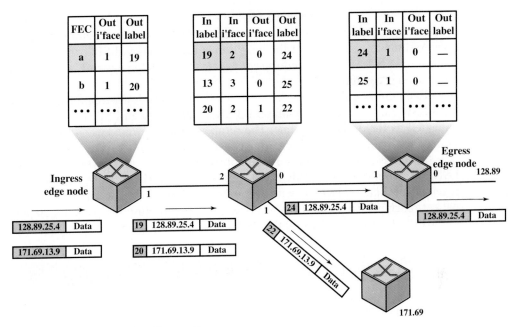

Figure 23.2 MPLS Packet Forwarding

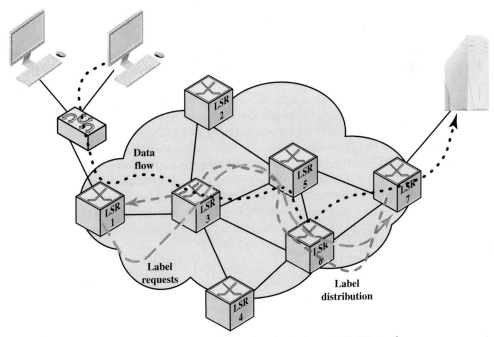

Figure 23.3 LSP Creation and Packet Forwarding through an MPLS Domain

on a new flow of packets, so that LSR 1 does not have a label for the packet. LSR 1 consults the IP header to find the destination address and then determine the next hop. Assume in this case that the next hop is LSR 3. Then, LSR 1 initiates a label request toward LSR 3. This request propagates through the network as indicated by the dashed green line.

Each intermediate router receives a label from its downstream router starting from LSR 7 and going upstream until LSR 1, setting up an LSP. The LSP setup is indicated by the dashed gray line. The setup can be performed using LDP and may or may not involve traffic engineering considerations.

LSR 1 is now able to insert the appropriate label and forward the packet to LSR 3. Each subsequent LSR (LSR 5, LSR 6, LSR 7) examines the label in the received packet, replaces it with the outgoing label, and forwards it. When the packet reaches LSR 7, the LSR removes the label because the packet is departing the MPLS domain and delivers the packet to the destination.

23.4 LABELS

Label Stacking

One of the most powerful features of MPLS is label stacking. A labeled packet may carry a number of labels, organized as a last-in-first-out stack. Processing is always based on the top label. At any LSR, a label may be added to the stack (push operation) or removed from the stack (pop operation). Label stacking allows the aggregation of LSPs into a single LSP for a portion of the route through a network, creating a tunnel. The term *tunnel* refers to the fact that traffic routing is determined by labels, and is exercised below normal IP routing and filtering mechanisms. At the beginning of the tunnel, an LSR assigns the same label to packets from a number of LSPs by pushing the label onto each packet's stack. At the end of the tunnel, another LSR pops the top element from the label stack, revealing the inner label. This is similar to ATM, which has one level of stacking (virtual channels inside virtual paths) but MPLS supports unlimited stacking.

Label stacking provides considerable flexibility. An enterprise could establish MPLS-enabled networks at various sites and a number of LSPs at each site. The enterprise could then use label stacking to aggregate multiple flows of its own traffic before handing it to an access provider. The access provider could aggregate traffic from multiple enterprises before handing it to a larger service provider. Service providers could aggregate many LSPs into a relatively small number of tunnels between points of presence. Fewer tunnels mean smaller tables, making it easier for a provider to scale the network core.

Label Format

An MPLS label is a 32-bit field consisting of the following elements (Figure 23.4), defined in RFC 3032:

- **Label value:** Locally significant 20-bit label. Values 0 through 15 are reserved.
- **Traffic class (TC):** 3 bits used to carry traffic class information.

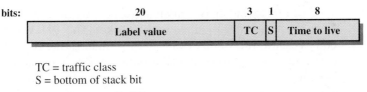

TC = traffic class
S = bottom of stack bit

Figure 23.4   MPLS Label Format

- **S:** Set to one for the oldest entry in the stack, and zero for all other entries. Thus, this bit marks the bottom of the stack.
- **Time to live (TTL):** 8 bits used to encode a hop count, or time to live, value.

TRAFFIC CLASS   RFCs 3270 and 5129 discuss the use of the TC field to convey information to support differentiated services and explicit congestion notification (ECN), respectively. With respect to DS, one approach is to assign a unique label value to each DS per-hop-behavior scheduling class, in which case, the TC field is not necessarily needed. The other approach is to map the drop precedence or some other DS information into the TC field. With respect to ECN, the three possible ECN values (not ECN capable, ECN capable, congestion marked) are mapped into the TC field. RFC 5129 discusses strategies in which both DS and ECN might be supported in the TC field. At present, no unique definition of the TC bits has been standardized.

TIME TO LIVE PROCESSING   A key field in the IP packet header is the TTL field (IPv4, Figure 14.5), or hop limit (IPv6, Figure 14.5). In an ordinary IP-based inter- net, this field is decremented at each router and the packet is dropped if the count falls to zero. This is done to avoid looping or having the packet remain too long in the Internet due to faulty routing. Because an LSR does not examine the IP header, the TTL field is included in the label so that the TTL function is still supported. The rules for processing the TTL field in the label are as follows:

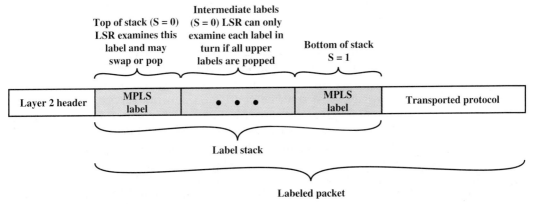

Figure 23.5   Encapsulation for Labeled Packet

1. When an IP packet arrives at an ingress edge LSR of an MPLS domain, a single label stack entry is added to the packet. The TTL value of this label stack entry is set to the value of the IP TTL value. If the IP TTL field needs to be decremented, as part of the IP processing, it is assumed that this has already been done.

2. When an MPLS packet arrives at an internal LSR of an MPLS domain, the TTL value in the top label stack entry is decremented. Then

   a. If this value is zero, the MPLS packet is not forwarded. Depending on the label value in the label stack entry, the packet may be simply discarded, or it may be passed to the appropriate "ordinary" network layer for error processing (e.g., for the generation of an ICMP error message).

   b. If this value is positive, it is placed in the TTL field of the top label stack entry for the outgoing MPLS packet, and the packet is forwarded. The outgoing TTL value is a function solely of the incoming TTL value and is independent of whether any labels are pushed or popped before forwarding. There is no significance to the value of the TTL field in any label stack entry that is not at the top of the stack.

3. When an MPLS packet arrives at an egress edge LSR of an MPLS domain, the TTL value in the single label stack entry is decremented and the label is popped, resulting in an empty label stack. Then

   a. If this value is zero, the IP packet is not forwarded. Depending on the label value in the label stack entry, the packet may be simply discarded, or it may be passed to the appropriate "ordinary" network layer for error processing.

   b. If this value is positive, it is placed in the TTL field of the IP header, and the IP packet is forwarded using ordinary IP routing. Note that the IP header checksum must be modified prior to forwarding.

Label Placement

The label stack entries appear after the data link layer headers, but before any network layer headers. The top of the label stack appears earliest in the packet (closest to the data link header), and the bottom appears latest (closest to the network layer header), as shown in Figure 23.5. The network layer packet immediately follows the label stack entry that has the S bit set. In data link frames, such as for PPP (point-to-point protocol), the label stack appears between the IP header and the data link header (Figure 23.6a). For an IEEE 802 frame, the label stack appears between the IP header and the LLC (logical link control) header (Figure 23.6b).

If MPLS is used over a connection-oriented network service, a slightly different approach may be taken, as shown in Figures 23.6c and d. For ATM cells, the label value in the topmost label is placed in the VPI/VCI field in the ATM cell header. The entire top label remains at the top of the label stack, which is inserted between the cell header and the IP header. Placing the label value in the ATM cell header facilitates switching by an ATM switch, which would, as usual, only need to look at the cell header. Similarly, the topmost label value can be placed in the DLCI (data link connection identifier) field of a frame relay header. Note that in

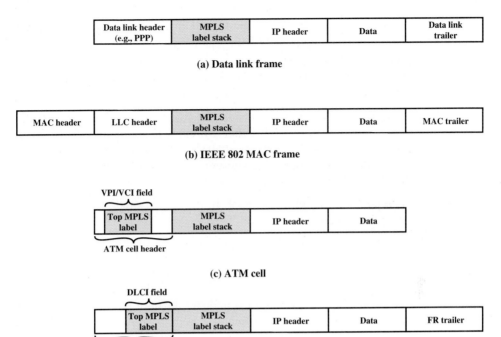

(a) Data link frame

(b) IEEE 802 MAC frame

(c) ATM cell

(d) Frame relay frame

Figure 23.6 Position of MPLS Label Stack

both these cases, the time to live field is not visible to the switch and so is not decremented. The reader should consult the MPLS specifications for the details of the way this situation is handled.

23.5 FECS, LSPS, AND LABELS

To understand MPLS, it is necessary to understand the operational relationship among FECs, LSPs, and labels. The specifications covering all of the ramifications of this relationship are lengthy. In the remainder of this section, we provide a summary.

The essence of MPLS functionality is that traffic is grouped into FECs. The traffic in an FEC transits an MPLS domain along an LSP. Individual packets in an FEC are uniquely identified as being part of a given FEC by means of a locally significant label. At each LSR, each labeled packet is forwarded on the basis of its label value, with the LSR replacing the incoming label value with an outgoing label value.

The overall scheme described in the previous paragraph imposes a number of requirements:

1. Each traffic flow must be assigned to a particular FEC.
2. A routing protocol is needed to determine the topology and current conditions in the domain so that a particular LSP can be assigned to an FEC. The

routing protocol must be able to gather and use information to support the QoS requirements of the FEC.

3. Individual LSRs must become aware of the LSP for a given FEC, must assign an incoming label to the LSP, and must communicate that label to any other LSR that may send it packets for this FEC.

The first requirement is outside the scope of the MPLS specifications. The assignment needs to be done either by manual configuration, or by means of some signaling protocol, or by an analysis of incoming packets at ingress LSRs. Before looking at the other two requirements, let us consider topology of LSPs. We can classify these in the following manner:

- **Unique ingress and egress LSR:** In this case a single path through the MPLS domain is needed.

- **Unique egress LSR, multiple ingress LSRs:** If traffic assigned to a single FEC can arise from different sources that enter the network at different ingress LSRs, then this situation occurs. An example is an enterprise intranet at a single location but with access to an MPLS domain through multiple MPLS ingress LSRs. This situation would call for multiple paths through the MPLS domain, probably sharing a final few hops.

- **Multiple egress LSRs for unicast traffic:** RFC 3031 states that, most commonly, a packet is assigned to an FEC based (completely or partially) on its network layer destination address. If not, then it is possible that the FEC would require paths to multiple distinct egress LSRs. However, more likely, there would be a cluster of destination networks all of which are reached via the same MPLS egress LSR.

- **Multicast:** RFC 5332 defines techniques for handling multicast packets.

Route Selection

Route selection refers to the selection of an LSP for a particular FEC. The MPLS architecture supports two options: hop-by-hop routing and explicit routing.

With **hop-by-hop routing**, each LSR independently chooses the next hop for each FEC. RFC 3031 implies that this option makes use of an ordinary routing protocol, such as OSPF. This option provides some of the advantages of MPLS, including rapid switching by labels, the ability to use label stacking, and differential treatment of packets from different FECs following the same route. However, because of the limited use of performance metrics in typical routing protocols, hop-by-hop routing does not readily support traffic engineering or policy routing (defining routes based on some policy related to QoS, security, or some other consideration).

With **explicit routing**, a single LSR, usually the ingress or egress LSR, specifies some or all of the LSRs in the LSP for a given FEC. For strict explicit routing, an LSR specifies all of the LSRs on an LSP. For loose explicit routing, only some of the LSRs are specified. Explicit routing provides all of the benefits of MPLS, including the ability to do traffic engineering and policy routing.

Explicit routes can be selected by configuration, that is, set up ahead of time, or dynamically. Dynamic explicit routing would provide the best scope for traffic engineering. For dynamic explicit routing, the LSR setting up the LSP would need information about the topology of the MPLS domain as well as QoS-related information about that domain. An MPLS traffic engineering specification (RFC 2702) suggests that the QoS-related information falls into two categories:

- A set of attributes associated with an FEC or a collection of similar FECs that collectively specify their behavioral characteristics
- A set of attributes associated with resources (nodes, links) that constrain the placement of LSPs through them

A routing algorithm that takes into account the traffic requirements of various flows and that takes into account the resources available along various hops and through various nodes is referred to as a **constraint-based routing algorithm**. In essence, a network that uses a constraint-based routing algorithm is aware of current utilization, existing capacity, and committed services at all times. Traditional routing algorithms, such as OSPF and BGP, do not employ a sufficient array of cost metrics in their algorithms to qualify as constraint based. Furthermore, for any given route calculation, only a single-cost metric (e.g., number of hops, delay) can be used. For MPLS, it is necessary either to augment an existing routing protocol or to deploy a new one. For example, an enhanced version of OSPF has been defined (RFC 2676) that provides at least some of the support required for MPLS. Examples of metrics that would be useful to constraint-based routing are as follows:

- Maximum link data rate
- Current capacity reservation
- Packet loss ratio
- Link propagation delay

23.6 LABEL DISTRIBUTION

Requirements for Label Distribution

Route selection consists of defining an LSP for an FEC. A separate function is the actual setting up of the LSP. For this purpose, each LSR on the LSP must do the following:

1. Assign a label to the LSP to be used to recognize incoming packets that belong to the corresponding FEC.
2. Inform all potential upstream nodes (nodes that will send packets for this FEC to this LSR) of the label assigned by this LSR to this FEC, so that these nodes can properly label packets to be sent to this LSR.
3. Learn the next hop for this LSP and learn the label that the downstream node (LSR that is the next hop) has assigned to this FEC. This will enable this LSR to map an incoming label to an outgoing label.

The first item in the preceding list is a local function. Items 2 and 3 must either be done by manual configuration or require the use of some sort of label distribution protocol. Thus, the essence of a label distribution protocol is that it enables one LSR to inform others of the label/FEC bindings it has made. In addition, a label distribution protocol enables two LSRs to learn each other's MPLS capabilities. The MPLS architecture does not assume a single label distribution protocol but allows for multiple such protocols. Specifically, RFC 3031 refers to a new label distribution protocol and to enhancements to existing protocols, such as RSVP and BGP, to serve the purpose.

The relationship between label distribution and route selection is complex. It is best to look at in the context of the two types of route selection.

With hop-by-hop route selection, no specific attention is paid to traffic engineering or policy routing concerns, as we have seen. In such a case, an ordinary routing protocol such as OSPF is used to determine the next hop by each LSR. A relatively straightforward label distribution protocol can operate using the routing protocol to design routes.

With explicit route selection, a more sophisticated routing algorithm must be implemented, one that does not employ a single metric to design a route. In this case, a label distribution protocol could make use of a separate route selection protocol, such as an enhanced OSPF, or incorporate a routing algorithm into a more complex label distribution protocol.

Label Distribution Protocol

Protocols that communicate which label goes with which FEC are called label distribution protocols. A number of label distribution protocols exist, most commonly Label Distribution Protocol (LDP; RFC 5036), Resource Reservation Protocol-Traffic Engineering (RSVP-TE; RFC 3209), and multiprotocol BGP as extended for Layer 3 VPNs (L3VPNs; RFC 4364). LDP has emerged as the preferred solution and we provide a brief introduction here.

LDP has a simple objective: It is a protocol defined for distributing labels. It is the set of procedures and messages by which label switching routers (LSRs) establish label switched paths (LSPs) through a network by mapping network-layer routing information directly to data-link layer switched paths. These LSPs may have an endpoint at a directly attached neighbor (comparable to IP hop-by-hop forwarding), or may have an endpoint at a network egress node, enabling switching via all intermediary nodes. LDP associates a forwarding equivalence class (FEC) with each LSP it creates. The FEC associated with an LSP specifies which packets are mapped to that LSP. LSPs are extended through a network as each LSR splices incoming labels for a FEC to the outgoing label assigned to the next hop for the given FEC.

Two LSRs that use LDP to exchange FEC label binding information are known as LDP peers. In order to exchange information, two LDP peers first establish a session over a TCP connection. LDP includes a mechanism by which an LSR can discover potential LDP peers. The discovery mechanism makes it unnecessary for operators to explicitly configure each LSR with its LDP peers. When an LSR discovers another LSR it follows the LDP session setup procedure to establish an LDP session. By means of this procedure the LSRs establish a session TCP connection and use it to negotiate parameters for the session, such as the label distribution method to be used. After the LSRs agree on the parameters, the session is operational and the LSRs use the TCP connection for label distribution.

LDP supports two different methods for label distribution. An LSR using Downstream Unsolicited distribution advertises FEC-label bindings to its peers when it is ready to forward packets in the FEC by means of MPLS. An LSR using Downstream on Demand distribution provides FEC-label bindings to a peer in response to specific requests from the peer for a label for the FEC.

LDP depends on a routing protocol, such as OSPF, to initially establish reachability between two LSRs. The routing protocol can also be used to define the route for the LSP. Alternatively, traffic engineering considerations can determine the exact route of the LSP, as discussed in Section 23.7. Once a route is identified for an LSP, LDP is used to establish the LSP and assign labels. Figure 23.7 suggests the operation of LDP. Each LSP is unidirectional, and label assignment propagate back from the end point of the LSP to the originating point.

LDP Messages

LDP operates by the exchange of messages over a TCP connection between LDP peers. There are four categories of messages, reflecting the four major functions of LDP:

- **Discovery:** Each LSR announces and maintains its presence in a network. LSRs indicate their presence in a network by sending Hello messages periodically. Hello messages are transmitted as UDP packets to the LDP port at the group multicast address for all routers on the subnet.

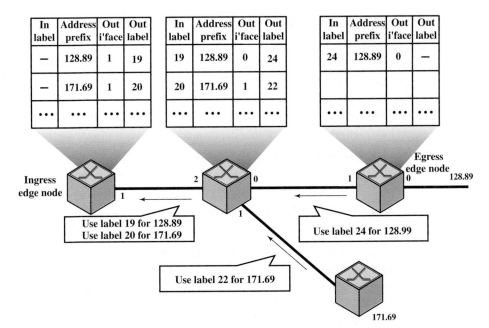

Figure 23.7   Assigning Labels Using LDP Downstream Allocation

- **Session establishment and maintenance:** If two LSRs have discovered each other by means of the LDP Hellos, they can then establish, maintain, and terminate sessions as LDP peers. When a router establishes a session with another router learned through the Hello message, it uses the LDP initialization procedure over TCP transport. When the initialization procedure is completed successfully, the two routers are LDP peers and can exchange advertisement messages.

- **Advertisement:** Advertising label mappings or label bindings is the main purpose of LDP. Advertisement messages are used to create, change, and delete label mappings for FECs. Requesting a label or advertising a label mapping to a peer is a decision made by the local router. In general, the router requests a label mapping from a neighboring router when it needs one and advertises a label mapping to a neighboring router when it wants the neighbor to use a label.

- **Notification messages:** Used to provide advisory information and to signal error information. LDP sends notification messages to report errors and other events of interest. There are two kinds of LDP notification messages:

  —Error notifications, which signal fatal errors. If a router receives an error notification from a peer for an LDP session, it terminates the LDP session by closing the TCP transport connection for the session and discarding all label mappings learned through the session.

  —Advisory notifications, which pass information to a router about the LDP session or the status of some previous message received from the peer.

LDP Message Format

Figure 23.8 illustrates the format of LDP messages. Each LDP protocol data unit (PDU) consists of an LDP header followed by one or more LDP messages. The header contains three fields:

- **Version:** Version number for this protocol. The current version is 1.
- **PDU length:** Length of this PDU in octets.
- **LDP identifier:** Identifies the LSR uniquely.

Each message consists of the following fields:

- **U bit:** Indicates how to handle a message of an unknown type (forward or discard). This facilitates backward compatibility.
- **Message type:** Identifies the specific type of message (e.g., Hello).
- **Message length:** Length of this message in octets.
- **Message ID:** Identifies this specific message with a sequence number. This is used to facilitate identifying subsequent notification messages that may apply to this message.

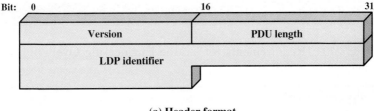

(a) Header format

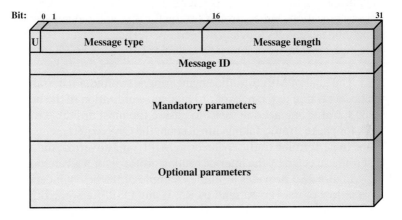

(b) Message format

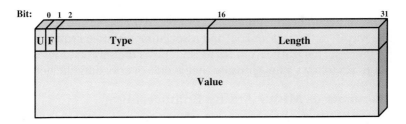

(c) Type-length-value (TLV) parameter encoding

Figure 23.8   LDP PDU Formats

- **Mandatory parameters:** Variable length set of required message parameters. Some messages have no required parameters.
- **Optional parameters:** Variable length set of optional message parameters. Many messages have no optional parameters.

Each parameter has a type-length-value (TLV) format. An LDP TLV is encoded as a 2-octet field that uses 14 bits to specify a Type and 2 bits to specify behavior when an LSR doesn't recognize the Type, followed by a 2-octet Length field, followed by a variable length Value field.

23.7 TRAFFIC ENGINEERING

RFC 2702 (Requirements for Traffic Engineering Over MPLS) describes traffic engineering as follows:

> **TRAFFIC ENGINEERING.** Traffic Engineering (TE) is concerned with performance optimization of operational networks. In general, it encompasses the application of technology and scientific principles to the measurement, modeling, characterization, and control of Internet traffic, and the application of such knowledge and techniques to achieve specific performance objectives. The aspects of traffic engineering that are of interest concerning MPLS are measurement and control[2].

The goal of MPLS traffic engineering is twofold. First, traffic engineering seeks to allocate traffic to the network to maximize utilization of the network capacity. And second, traffic engineering seeks to ensure the most desirable route through the network for packet traffic, taking into account the QoS requirements of the various packet flows. In performing traffic engineering, MPLS may override the shortest path or least-cost route selected by the interior routing protocol for a given source-destination flow.

Figure 23.9 provides a simple example of traffic engineering. Both R1 and R8 have a flow of packets to send to R5. Using OSPF or some other routing protocol, the shortest path is calculated as R2-R3-R4. However, if we assume that R8 has a steady-state traffic flow of 20 Mbps and R1 has a flow of 40 Mbps, then the aggregate flow over this route will be 60 Mbps, which will exceed the capacity of the R3-R4 link. As an alternative, a traffic engineering approach is to determine a route from source to destination ahead of time and reserve the required resources along the way by setting up an LSP and associating resource requirements with that LSP. In this case, the traffic from R8 to R5 follows the shortest route, but the traffic from R1 to R5 follows a longer route that avoids overloading the network.

Elements of MPLS Traffic Engineering

MPLS TE works by learning about the topology and resources available in a network. It then maps the traffic flows to a particular path based on the resources that the traffic flow requires and the available resources. MPLS TE builds unidirectional LSPs from a source to the destination, which are then used for forwarding traffic. The point where the LSP begins is called LSP headend or LSP source, and the node where the LSP ends is called LSP tailend or LSP tunnel destination.

LSP tunnels allow the implementation of a variety of policies related to network performance optimization. For example, LSP tunnels can be automatically or manually routed away from network failures, congestion, and bottlenecks. Furthermore, multiple parallel LSP tunnels can be established between two nodes, and traffic between the two nodes can be mapped onto the LSP tunnels according to local policy. The following components work together to implement MPLS TE:

- **Information distribution:** A link state protocol, such as Open Shortest-Path First, is necessary to discover the topology of the network. OSPF is enhanced

---

[2]RFC 2702, IETF Trust.

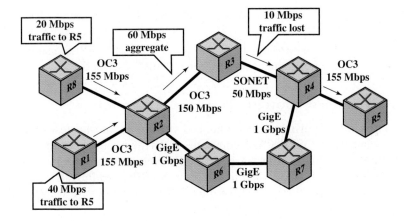

(a) A shortest-path solution

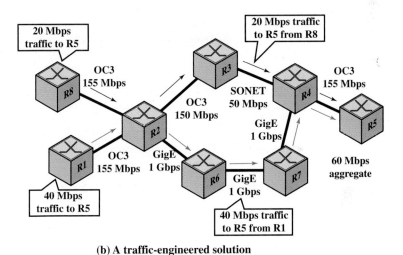

(b) A traffic-engineered solution

Figure 23.9 Traffic Engineering Example

to carry additional information related to TE, such as bandwidth available and other related parameters. OSPF uses Type 10 (opaque) Link State Advertisements (LSAs) for this purpose.

- **Path calculation:** Once the topology of the network and the alternative routes are known, a constraint-based routing scheme is used for finding the shortest path through a particular network that meets the resource requirements of the traffic flow. The constrained shortest-path first algorithm (discussed subsequently), which operates on the LSP headend is used for this functionality.

- **Path setup:** A signaling protocol to reserve the resources for a traffic flow and to establish the LSP for a traffic flow. IETF has defined two alternative protocols for this purpose. RSVP has been enhanced with TE extensions for carrying labels and building the LSP. The other approach is an enhancement to LDP known as Constraint-based Routing Label Distribution Protocol (CR-LDP).

- **Traffic forwarding:** This is accomplished with MPLS, using the LSP set up by the traffic engineering components just described.

Constrained Shortest–Path First Algorithm

The CSPF algorithm is an enhanced version of the shortest-path first (SPF) algorithm used in OSPF. CSPF computes paths taking into account multiple constraints. When computing paths for LSPs, CSPF considers the topology of the network, the attributes of the individual links between LSRs, and the attributes of existing LSPs. CSPF attempts to satisfy the requirements for a new LSP while minimizing congestion by balancing the network load.

Figure 23.10 suggests the context in which CSPF is used. In setting up a new LSP, CSPF operates on the basis of three inputs:

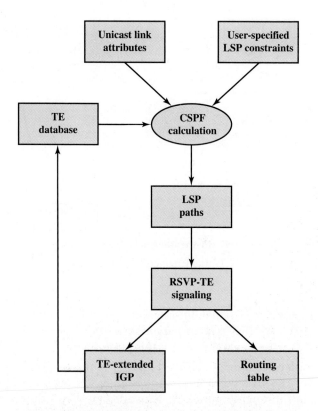

RSVP-TE = Resource Reservation Protocol-Traffic Engineering
CSPF = constrained shortest-path first
IGP = interior gateway protocol (interior routing protocol; e.g., OSPF)
LSP = label switching path
TE = traffic engineering

Figure 23.10   CSPF Flowchart

- **Unicast link attributes:** These include the capacity of the link and the administrative groups that are allowed to use this link. For example, some links may be reserved for the exclusive use of one or several groups or, alternatively, some groups may be specifically excluded from using this link. The term *color* is used to refer to a unique administrative group.
- **User-specified LSP constraints:** When an application requests an LSP to a given unicast destination, the application specifies the required attributes of the path, including data rate, hop limitations, link color requirements, priority, and explicit route requirements.
- **Traffic engineering database:** The TE database maintains current topology information, current reservable capacity of links, and link colors.

Based on these three inputs, the CSPF algorithm selects a route for the requested LSP. This information is used by RSVP-TE to set up the path and to provide information to the routing algorithm, which in turn updates the TE database.

In general terms, the CSPF path selection procedure involves the following steps:

1. If multiple LSPs are to be determined, calculate LSPs one at a time, beginning with the highest priority LSP. Among LSPs of equal priority, CSPF starts with those that have the highest capacity requirement.
2. Prune the TE database of all the links that do not have sufficient reservable capacity. If the LSP configuration includes the include statement, prune all links that do not share any included colors. If the LSP configuration includes the exclude statement, prune all links that contain excluded colors and do not contain a color.
3. Find the shortest path toward the LSP's egress router, taking into account explicit-path constraints. For example, if the path must pass through Router A, two separate SPFs are computed, one from the ingress router to Router A, the other from Router A to the egress router.
4. If several equal-cost paths remain, select the one with the fewest number of hops.
5. If several equal-cost paths remain, apply the CSPF load-balancing rule configured on the LSP.

RSVP-TE

Early in the MPLS standardization process, it became clear that a protocol was needed that would enable providers to set up LSPs that took into account QoS and traffic engineering parameters. Development of this type of signaling protocol proceeded on two different tracks:

- Extensions to RSVP for setting up MPLS tunnels, known as RSVP-TE [RFC 3209]
- Extensions to LDP for setting constraint-based LSPs [RFC 3212]

The motivation for the choice of protocol in both cases was straightforward. Extending RSVP-TE to do in an MPLS environment what it already was doing (handling QoS information and reserving resources) in an IP environment is comprehensible; you only have to add the label distribution capability. Extending a native

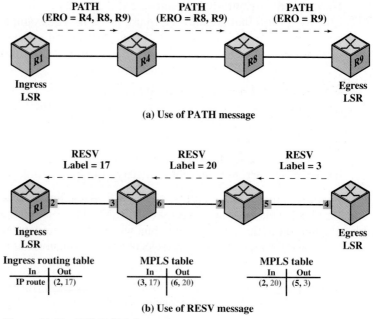

Figure 23.11   RSVP-TE Operation

MPLS protocol like LDP, which was designed to do label distribution, to handle some extra TLVs with QoS information is also not revolutionary. Ultimately, the MPLS working group announced, in RFC 3468, that RSVP-TE is the preferred solution.

In general terms, RSVP-TE operates by associating an MPLS label with an RSVP flow. RSVP is used to reserve resources and to define an explicit route for an LSP tunnel. Figure 23.11 illustrates the basic operation of RSVP-TE. An ingress node uses the RSVP PATH message to request an LSP to be defined along an explicit route. The PATH message includes a label request object and an explicit route object (ERO). The ERO defines the explicit route to be followed by the LSP.

The destination node of a label switched path responds to a LABEL_ REQUEST by including a LABEL object in its response RSVP Resv message. The LABEL object is inserted in the filter spec list immediately following the filter spec to which it pertains. The Resv message is sent back upstream toward the sender, following the path state created by the Path message, in reverse order.

23.8 VIRTUAL PRIVATE NETWORKS

A virtual private network is a private network that is configured within a public network (a carrier's network or the Internet) in order to take advantage of the economies of scale and management facilities of large networks. VPNs are widely used by enterprises to create wide area networks that span large geographic areas, to provide site-to-site connections to branch offices, and to allow mobile users to dial up their company LANs. From the point of view of the provider, the pubic network facility is shared by many customers, with the traffic of each customer segregated from other traffic. Traffic designated as VPN traffic can only go from a VPN source to a destination in the same VPN. It is often the case that encryption and authentication facilities are provided for the VPN.

The subject of VPNs, even when limited to MPLS-enabled VPNs, is extraordinarily complex. In this section, we provide a brief overview of two of the most common approaches to VPN implementation using MPLS: the layer 2 VPN (L2VPN) and the layer 3 VPN (L3VPN).

Table 23.2, based on RFC 4026 (*Provider Provisioned Virtual Private Network Terminology*), defines key VPN terms used in our discussion.

Layer 2 Virtual Private Network

With a layer 2 VPN, there is mutual transparency between the customer network and the provider network. In effect, the customer requests a mesh of unicast LSPs among customer switches that attach to the provider network. Each LSP is viewed as a layer 2 circuit by the customer. In an L2VPN, the provider's equipment forwards customer data based on information in the Layer 2 headers, such as an Ethernet MAC address, an ATM virtual channel identifier, or a frame relay data link connection identifier.

Figure 23.12 depicts key elements in an L2VPN. Customers connect to the provider by means of a layer 2 device, such as an Ethernet switch, or a frame relay or ATM node; the customer device that connects to the MPLS network is generally referred to as a customer edge (CE) device. The MPLS edge router is referred to as a provider edge (PE) device. The link between the CE and the PE operates at the link layer (e.g., Ethernet), and is referred to as an attachment circuit. The MPLS network then sets up an LSP that acts as a tunnel between two edge routers (i.e., two PEs) that attach to two networks of the same enterprise. This tunnel can carry multiple virtual channels (VCs) using label stacking.

Table 23.2 VPN Terminology

Attachment circuit (AC) In a Layer 2 VPN the CE is attached to PE via an AC. The AC may be a physical or logical link.	packets from one PE to another. Separation of one customer's traffic from another customer's traffic is done based on tunnel multiplexers.
Customer edge (CE) A device or set of devices on the customer premises that attaches to a provider provisioned VPN.	**Tunnel multiplexer** An entity that is sent with the packets traversing the tunnel to make it possible to decide which instance of a service a packet belongs to and from which sender it was received. In an MPLS network, the tunnel multiplexor is formatted as an MPLS label.
Layer 2 VPN (L2VPN) An L2VPN interconnects sets of hosts and routers based on Layer 2 addresses.	
Layer 3 VPN (L3VPN) An L3VPN interconnects sets of hosts and routers based on Layer 3 addresses.	**Virtual channel (VC)** A VC is transported within a tunnel and identified by its tunnel multiplexer. In an MPLS-enabled IP network, a VC label is an MPLS label used to identify traffic within a tunnel that belongs to a particular VPN; i.e., the VC label is the tunnel multiplexer in networks that use MPLS labels.
Packet switched network (PSN) A network through which the tunnels supporting the VPN services are set up.	
Provider edge (PE) A device or set of devices at the edge of the provider network with the functionality that is needed to interface with the customer.	**Virtual private network (VPN)** A generic term that covers the use of public or private networks to create groups of users that are separated from other network users and that may communicate among them as if they were on a private network.
Tunnel Connectivity through a PSN that is used to send traffic across the network from one PE to another. The tunnel provides a means to transport	

When a link-layer frame arrives at the PE from the CE, the PE creates an MPLS packet. The PE pushes a label that corresponds to the VC assigned to this frame. Then the PE pushes a second label onto the label stack for this packet that corresponds to the tunnel between the source and destination PE for this VC. The packet is then routed across the LSP associated with this tunnel, using the top label for label switched routing. At the destination edge, the destination PE pops the tunnel label and examines the VC label. This tells the PE how to construct a link-layer frame to deliver the payload across to the destination CE.

If the payload of the MPLS packet is, for example, an ATM AAL5 PDU, the VC label will generally correspond to a particular ATM VC at PE2. That is, PE2 needs to be able to infer from the VC label the outgoing interface and the VPI/VCI (virtual path identifier/virtual circuit identifier) value for the AAL5 PDU. If the payload is a frame relay PDU, then PE2 needs to be able to infer from the VC label the outgoing interface and the DLCI (data link connection identifier) value. If the payload is an Ethernet frame, then PE2 needs to be able to infer from the VC label the outgoing interface, and perhaps the VLAN identifier. This process is unidirectional, and will be repeated independently for bidirectional operation.

The virtual circuits in the tunnel can all belong to a single enterprise, or it is possible for a single tunnel to manage virtual circuits from multiple enterprises. In any case, from the point of view of the customer, a virtual circuit is a dedicated link-layer point-to-point channel. If multiple VCs connect a PE to a CE this is logically the multiplexing of multiple link-layer channels between the customer and the provider.

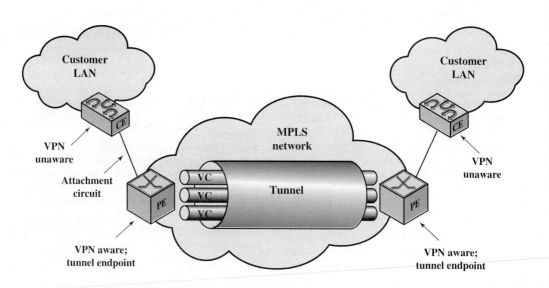

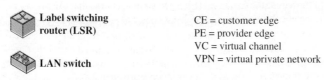

Figure 23.12   Layer 2 VPN Concepts

Layer 3 Virtual Private Network

Whereas L2VPNs are constructed based on link level addresses (e.g., MAC addresses), L3VPNs are based on VPN routes between CEs based on IP addresses. As with an L2VPN, an MPLS-based L3VPN typically uses a stack of two labels. The inner label identifies a specific VPN instance; the outer label identifies a tunnel or route through the MPLS provider network. The tunnel label is associated with an LSP and is used for label swapping and forwarding. At the egress PE, the tunnel label is stripped off and the VPN label is used to direct the packet to the proper CE and to the proper logical flow at that CE.

For an L3VPN, the CE implements IP and is thus a router, such as is illustrated in Figure 23.1. The CE routers advertise their networks to the provider. The provider network can then use an enhanced version of BGP to establish VPNs between CEs. Inside the provider network, MPLS tools, such as CR-LDP, are used to establish routes between edge PEs supporting a VPN. Thus, the provider's routers participate in the customer's L3 routing function.

23.9 RECOMMENDED READING

[VISW98] includes a concise overview of the MPLS architecture and describes the various proprietary efforts that preceded MPLS. [LAWR01] looks at the design of MPLS switches. ITU-T Recommendation Y.1370 is an excellent introduction to the operation of MPLS [ITUT05].

ITUT05 ITU-T. *MPLS Layer Network Architecture*. ITU-T Recommendation Y.1370, 2005.

LAWR01 Lawrence, J. "Designing Multiprotocol Label Switching Networks." *IEEE Communications Magazine*, July 2001.

VISW98 Viswanathan, A., et al. "Evolution of Multiprotocol Label Switching." *IEEE Communications Magazine*, May 1998.

23.10 KEY TERMS, REVIEW QUESTIONS, AND PROBLEMS

Key Terms

constrained shortest-path first algorithm	label stacking	Multiprotocol Label Switching (MPLS)
constraint-based routing algorithm	label switched path (LSP)	pseudowire
forwarding equivalence class (FEC)	label switching router (LSR)	Resource Reservation Protocol-Traffic Engineering (RSVP-TE)
label distribution	Layer 2 Virtual Private Network (L2VPN)	traffic engineering
Label Distribution Protocol (LDP)	Layer 3 Virtual Private Network (L3VPN)	
	LSP tunnel	

Review Questions

23.1 What is traffic engineering?

23.2 What is an MPLS forwarding equivalence class?

23.3 What is an MPLS label switched path?

23.4 Explain label stacking.

23.5 What is meant by a constraint-based routing algorithm?

Problems

23.1 The MPLS specification allows an LSR to use a technique known as *penultimate hop popping*. With this technique, the next-to-last LSR in an LSP is allowed to remove the label from a packet and send it without the label to the last LSR in that LSP.

    a. Explain why this action is possible; that is, why it results in correct behavior.

    b. What is the advantage of penultimate hop popping?

23.2 In the TCP/IP protocol suite, it is standard practice for the header corresponding to a given protocol layer to contain information that identifies the protocol used in the next higher layer. This information is needed so that the recipient of the PDU, when stripping off a given header, knows how to interpret the remaining bits so as to identify and process the header portion. For example, the IPv4 and IPv6 headers have a Protocol and Next Header field, respectively (Figure 14.5); TCP and UDP both have a Port field (Figures 15.10 and 15.14), which can be used to identify the protocol on top of TCP or UDP. However, each MPLS node processes a packet whose top element is the MPLS label field, which contains no explicit information about the protocol that is encapsulated. Typically, that protocol is IPv4, but it could be some other network-layer protocol.

    a. Along an LSP, which MPLS nodes would need to identify the packet's network layer protocol?

    b. What conditions must we impose on the MPLS label in order for proper processing to occur?

    c. Are such restrictions needed on all of the labels in an MPLS label stack or, if not, which ones?

23.3 Suppose an MPLS packet has arrived at an internal label switching router of an MPLS domain. On receiving the packet, the TTL value in the top label stack entry is decremented. It is found that the value is equal to zero. What could be done with this packet? What would have been done if the value was positive?

23.4 What are the metrics that determine routes in a constraint-based routing algorithm like the CSPF algorithm?

23.5 Consider that we have two applications using MPLS with traffic engineering. One application is delay sensitive (DS), such as a real-time voice or video application. The other application is throughput sensitive (TS), such as a file transfer application or a high-volume remote sensor feed. Now consider the following settings defined by the user for the ingress node of a requested LSP:

	PDR	PBS	CDR	CBS	EBS	Frequency
1	S	S	=PDR	=PBS	0	Frequent
2	S	S	S	S	0	Unspecified

Where the S values are user specified and may differ for each entry.

    a. Which row is more appropriate for DS and which for TS?

    b. Consider the following two policies: (1) drop packet if PDR is exceeded. (2) drop packet if PDR or PBS is exceeded; mark packet as potentially to be dropped, if needed, if CDR or CBS is exceeded. Which policy is more appropriate for DS and which for TS?

ELECTRONIC MAIL, DNS, AND HTTP

LEARNING OBJECTIVES

After reading this chapter, you should be able to:

◆ Discuss the applications for electronic mail.

◆ Explain that basic functionality of SMTP.

◆ Explain the need for MIME as an enhancement to ordinary e-mail.

◆ Describe the key elements of MIME.

◆ Explain Internet domains and domain names.

◆ Discuss the operation of the Domain Name System.

◆ Explain the role of HTTP in the operation of the Web.

◆ Describe the functions of proxies, gateways, and tunnels in HTTP.

◆ Explain Web caching.

The chapter begins with electronic mail, with the SMTP and MIME standards as examples; SMTP provides a basic e-mail service, while MIME adds multimedia capability to SMTP. The chapter then examines DNS, which is an essential name/address directory lookup service for the Internet. Finally, we look at HTTP, which is the support protocol on which the World Wide Web (WWW) operates.

24.1 ELECTRONIC MAIL—SMTP AND MIME

Electronic mail is a facility that allows users at workstations and terminals to compose and exchange messages. The messages need never exist on paper unless the user (sender or recipient) desires a paper copy of the message. Some e-mail systems only serve users on a single computer; others provide service across a network of computers.

In this section, we look at the standard Internet mail architecture and then examine the key protocols to support e-mail applications.

Internet Mail Architecture

To understand the operation of an electronic mail system and its supporting protocols, it is useful to have a basic grasp of the Internet mail architecture, which is currently defined in RFC 5598 (*Internet Mail Architecture*). At its most fundamental level, the Internet mail architecture consists of a user world, in the form of Message User Agents (MUA), and the transfer world, in the form of the **Message Handling Service (MHS)**, which is composed of Message Transfer Agents (MTA). The MHS accepts a message from one user and delivers it to one or more other users, creating a virtual MUA-to-MUA exchange environment. This architecture involves three types of interoperability. One is directly between users: Messages must be formatted by the MUA on behalf of the message author so that the message can be displayed to the message recipient by the destination MUA. There are also interoperability requirements between the MUA and the MHS—first when a message is posted from an MUA to the MHS and later when it is delivered from the MHS to the destination MUA. Interoperability is required among the MTA components along the transfer path through the MHS.

Figure 24.1 illustrates the key components of the Internet mail architecture, which include the following.

- **Message User Agent (MUA):** Works on behalf of user actors and user applications. It is their representative within the e-mail service. Typically, this function is housed in the user's computer and is referred to as a client e-mail program or a local network e-mail server. The author MUA formats a message and performs initial submission into the MHS via an MSA. The recipient MUA processes receive mail for storage and/or display to the recipient user.

- **Mail Submission Agent (MSA):** Accepts the message submitted by an MUA and enforces the policies of the hosting domain and the requirements of Internet standards. This function may be located together with the MUA or as a separate functional model. In the latter case, the Simple Mail Transfer Protocol (SMTP) is used between the MUA and the MSA.

- **Message Transfer Agent (MTA):** Relays mail for one application-level hop. It is like a packet switch or IP router in that its job is to make routing assessments and to move the message closer to the recipients. Relaying is performed by a sequence of MTAs until the message reaches a destination MDA. An MTA also adds trace information to the message header. SMTP is used between MTAs and between an MTA and an MSA or MDA.

- **Mail Delivery Agent (MDA):** Responsible for transferring the message from the MHS to the MS.

- **Message Store (MS):** An MUA can employ a long-term MS. An MS can be located on a remote server or on the same machine as the MUA. Typically, an MUA retrieves messages from a remote server using POP (Post Office Protocol) or IMAP (Internet Message Access Protocol).

Two other concepts need to be defined. An **administrative management domain (ADMD)** is an Internet e-mail provider. Examples include a department

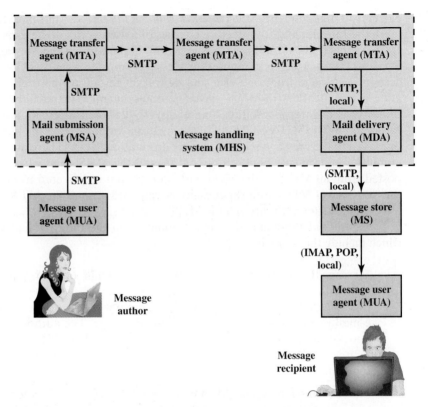

Figure 24.1 Function Modules and Standardized Protocols Used Between Them in the Internet Mail Architecture

that operates a local mail relay (MTA), an IT department that operates an enterprise mail relay, and an ISP that operates a public shared e-mail service. Each ADMD can have different operating policies and trust-based decision making. One obvious example is the distinction between mail that is exchanged within an organization and mail that is exchanged between independent organizations. The rules for handling the two types of traffic tend to be quite different.

The **Domain Name System (DNS)** is a directory lookup service that provides a mapping between the name of a host on the Internet and its numerical address. DNS is discussed in Chapter 7.

The user agent functions are visible to the e-mail user. These include facilities for preparing and submitting messages for routing to the destination(s), as well as utility functions to assist the user in filing, retrieving, replying, and forwarding. The MHS accepts messages from the user agent for transmission across a network or internetwork. The MHS is concerned with the protocol operation needed to transmit and deliver messages.

The user does not directly interact with the MHS. If the user designates a local recipient for a message, the MUA stores the message in the local recipient's mailbox. If a remote recipient is designated, the MUA passes the message to the MHS for transmission to a remote MTA and ultimately to a remote mailbox.

To implement the Internet mail architecture, a set of standards is needed. Four standards are noteworthy:

- **Post Office Protocol (POP3):** POP3 allows an e-mail client (user agent) to download an e-mail from an e-mail server (MTA). POP3 user agents connect via TCP/IP to the server (typically port 110). The user agent enters a username and password (either stored internally for convenience or entered each time by the user for stronger security). After authorization, the UA can issue POP3 commands to retrieve and delete mail.

- **Internet Mail Access Protocol (IMAP):** As with POP3, IMAP also enables an e-mail client to access mail on an e-mail server. IMAP also uses TCP/IP, with server TCP port 143. IMAP is more complex than POP3. IMAP provides stronger authentication than POP3 and provides other functions not supported by POP3.

- **Simple Mail Transfer Protocol (SMTP):** This protocol is used for transfer of mail from a user agent to an MTA and from one MTA to another.

- **Multipurpose Internet Mail Extensions (MIME):** MIME supplements SMTP and allows the encapsulation of multimedia (nontext) messages inside of a standard SMTP message.

In the remainder of this section, we elaborate on these standards.

Simple Mail Transfer Protocol (SMTP)

SMTP is the standard protocol for transferring mail between hosts in the TCP/IP suite; it is defined in RFC 821.

Although messages transferred by SMTP usually follow the format defined in RFC 822, described later, SMTP is not concerned with the format or content of messages themselves, with two exceptions. This concept is often expressed by saying that SMTP uses information written on the *envelope* of the mail (message header), but does not look at the contents (message body) of the envelope. The two exceptions are as follows:

1. SMTP standardizes the message character set as 7-bit ASCII.
2. SMTP adds log information to the start of the delivered message that indicates the path the message took.

BASIC ELECTRONIC MAIL OPERATION   Figure 24.2 illustrates the overall flow of mail in a typical system. Although much of this activity is outside the scope of SMTP, the figure illustrates the context within which SMTP typically operates.

To begin, mail is created by a user agent program in response to user input. Each created message consists of a header that includes the recipient's e-mail address and other information, and a body containing the message to be sent. These messages are then queued in some fashion and provided as input to an SMTP sender program, which is typically an always-present server program on the host.

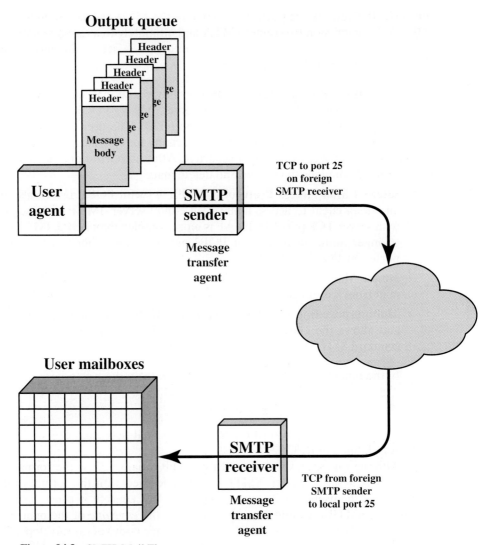

Figure 24.2   SMTP Mail Flow

Although the structure of the outgoing mail queue will differ depending on the host's operating system, each queued message conceptually has two parts:

1. The message text, consisting of
   - The RFC 822 header: This constitutes the message envelope and includes an indication of the intended recipient or recipients.
   - The body of the message, composed by the user.

2. A list of mail destinations.

The list of mail destinations for the message is derived by the user agent from the RFC 822 message header. In some cases, the destination or destinations are literally specified in the message header. In other cases, the user agent may need to expand mailing list names, remove duplicates, and replace mnemonic names with actual mailbox names. If any blind carbon copies (BCCs) are indicated, the user agent needs to prepare messages that conform to this requirement. The basic idea is that the multiple formats and styles preferred by humans in the user interface are replaced by a standardized list suitable for the SMTP send program.

The **SMTP sender** takes messages from the outgoing mail queue and transmits them to the proper destination host via SMTP transactions over one or more TCP connections to port 25 on the target hosts. A host may have multiple SMTP senders active simultaneously if it has a large volume of outgoing mail, and should also have the capability of creating SMTP receivers on demand so that mail from one host cannot delay mail from another.

Whenever the SMTP sender completes delivery of a particular message to one or more users on a specific host, it deletes the corresponding destinations from that message's destination list. When all destinations for a particular message are processed, the message is deleted from the queue. In processing a queue, the SMTP sender can perform a variety of optimizations. If a particular message is sent to multiple users on a single host, the message text needs to be sent only once. If multiple messages are ready to send to the same host, the SMTP sender can open a TCP connection, transfer the multiple messages, and then close the connection rather than opening and closing a connection for each message.

The SMTP sender must deal with a variety of errors. The destination host may be unreachable, out of operation, or the TCP connection may fail while mail is being transferred. The sender can requeue the mail for later delivery but give up after some period rather than keep the message in the queue indefinitely. A common error is a faulty destination address, which can occur due to user input error or because the intended destination user has a new address on a different host. The SMTP sender must either redirect the message if possible or return an error notification to the message's originator.

SMTP is used to transfer a message from the SMTP sender to the SMTP receiver over a TCP connection. SMTP attempts to provide reliable operation but does not guarantee to recover from lost messages. SMTP does not return an end-to-end acknowledgment to a message's originator to indicate that a message is successfully delivered to the message's recipient. Also, SMTP does not guarantee to return error indications. However, the SMTP-based mail system is generally considered reliable.

The **SMTP receiver** accepts each arriving message and either places it in the appropriate user mailbox or copies it to the local outgoing mail queue if forwarding is required. The SMTP receiver must be able to verify local mail destinations and deal with errors, including transmission errors and lack of storage capacity.

The SMTP sender is responsible for a message up to the point where the SMTP receiver indicates that the transfer is complete; however, this simply means that the message has arrived at the SMTP receiver, not that the message has been delivered to and retrieved by the intended final recipient. The SMTP receiver's error-handling responsibilities are generally limited to giving up on TCP connections that fail or are inactive for very long periods. Thus, the sender has most of the error recovery responsibility. Errors during completion indication may cause duplicate, but not lost, messages.

In most cases, messages go directly from the mail originator's machine to the destination machine over a single TCP connection. However, mail will occasionally go through intermediate machines via an SMTP forwarding capability, in which case the message must traverse a series of TCP connections between source and destination. One way for this to happen is for the sender to specify a route to the destination in the form of a sequence of servers. A more common event is forwarding required because a user has moved.

It is important to note that SMTP is limited to the conversation that takes place between the SMTP sender and the SMTP receiver. SMTP's main function is the transfer of messages, although there are some ancillary functions dealing with mail destination verification and handling. The rest of the mail-handling apparatus depicted in Figure 24.2 is beyond the scope of SMTP and may differ from one system to another.

RFC 822   RFC 822 defines a format for text messages that are sent using electronic mail. The SMTP standard adopts RFC 822 as the format for use in constructing messages for transmission via SMTP. In the RFC 822 context, messages are viewed as having an envelope and contents. The envelope contains whatever information is needed to accomplish transmission and delivery. The contents comprise the object to be delivered to the recipient. The RFC 822 standard applies only to the contents. However, the content standard includes a set of header fields that may be used by the mail system to create the envelope, and the standard is intended to facilitate the acquisition of such information by programs.

An RFC 822 message consists of a sequence of lines of text and uses a general "memo" framework. That is, a message consists of some number of header lines, which follow a rigid format, followed by a body portion consisting of arbitrary text.

A header line usually consists of a keyword, followed by a colon, followed by the keyword's arguments; the format allows a long line to be broken up into several lines. The most frequently used keywords are From, To, Subject, and Date. Here is an example message:

```
Date: Mon, 10 Mar 2008 10:37:17 (EDT)
From: "William Stallings" <ws@host.com>
Subject: The Syntax in RFC 822
To: Smith@Other-host.com
Cc: Jones@Yet-Another-Host.com

Hello. This section begins the actual message body, which is delimited from the message heading by a blank line.
```

Another field that is commonly found in RFC 822 headers is Message-ID. This field contains a unique identifier associated with this message.

Multipurpose Internet Mail Extensions (MIME)

MIME is an extension to the RFC 822 framework that is intended to address some of the problems and limitations of the use of SMTP and RFC 822 for electronic mail. [PARZ06] lists the following limitations of the SMTP/822 scheme:

1. SMTP cannot transmit executable files or other binary objects. A number of schemes are in use for converting binary files into a text form that can be used by SMTP mail systems, including the popular UNIX UUencode/UUdecode scheme. However, none of these is a standard or even a de facto standard.

2. SMTP cannot transmit text data that includes national language characters because these are represented by 8-bit codes with values of 128 decimal or higher, and SMTP is limited to 7-bit ASCII.

3. SMTP servers may reject mail messages over a certain size.

4. SMTP gateways that translate between the character codes ASCII and EBCDIC do not use a consistent set of mappings, resulting in translation problems.

5. SMTP gateways to X.400 electronic mail networks cannot handle nontextual data included in X.400 messages.

6. Some SMTP implementations do not adhere completely to the SMTP standards defined in RFC 821. Common problems include
   - Deletion, addition, or reordering of carriage return and line feed
   - Truncating or wrapping lines longer than 76 characters
   - Removal of trailing white space (tab and space characters)
   - Padding of lines in a message to the same length
   - Conversion of tab characters into multiple space characters

MIME is intended to resolve these problems in a manner that is compatible with existing RFC 822 implementations. The specification is provided in RFCs 2045 through 2049.

OVERVIEW The MIME specification includes the following elements:

1. Five new message header fields are defined, which may be included in an RFC 822 header. These fields provide information about the body of the message.

2. A number of content formats are defined, thus standardizing representations that support multimedia electronic mail.

3. Transfer encodings are defined that enable the conversion of any content format into a form that is protected from alteration by the mail system.

In this subsection, we introduce the five message header fields. The next two subsections deal with content formats and transfer encodings.

The five header fields defined in MIME are as follows:

- **MIME-Version:** Must have the parameter value 1.0. This field indicates that the message conforms to the RFCs.

- **Content-Type:** Describes the data contained in the body with sufficient detail that the receiving user agent can pick an appropriate agent or mechanism to present the data to the user or otherwise deal with the data in an appropriate manner.

- **Content-Transfer-Encoding:** Indicates the type of transformation that has been used to represent the body of the message in a way that is acceptable for mail transport.
- **Content-ID:** Used to uniquely identify MIME entities in multiple contexts.
- **Content-Description:** A plaintext description of the object with the body; this is useful when the object is not displayable (e.g., audio data).

Any or all of these fields may appear in a normal RFC 822 header. A compliant implementation must support the MIME-Version, Content-Type, and Content-Transfer-Encoding fields; the Content-ID and Content-Description fields are optional and may be ignored by the recipient implementation.

MIME CONTENT TYPES The bulk of the MIME specification is concerned with the definition of a variety of content types. This reflects the need to provide standardized ways of dealing with a wide variety of information representations in a multimedia environment.

Table 24.1 lists the MIME content types. There are seven different major types of content and a total of 14 subtypes. In general, a content type declares the general type of data, and the subtype specifies a particular format for that type of data.

Table 24.1 MIME Content Types

Type	Subtype	Description
Text	Plain	Unformatted text; may be ASCII or ISO 8859.
Multipart	Mixed	The different parts are independent but are to be transmitted together. They should be presented to the receiver in the order that they appear in the mail message.
	Parallel	Differs from Mixed only in that no order is defined for delivering the parts to the receiver.
	Alternative	The different parts are alternative versions of the same information. They are ordered in increasing faithfulness to the original and the recipient's mail system should display the "best" version to the user.
	Digest	Similar to Mixed, but the default type/subtype of each part is message/rfc822
Message	rfc822	The body is itself an encapsulated message that conforms to RFC 822.
	Partial	Used to allow fragmentation of large mail items, in a way that is transparent to the recipient.
	External-body	Contains a pointer to an object that exists elsewhere.
Image	jpeg	The image is in JPEG format, JFIF encoding.
	gif	The image is in GIF format.
Video	mpeg	MPEG format.
Audio	Basic	Single-channel 8-bit ISDN mu-law encoding at a sample rate of 8 kHz.
Application	PostScript	Adobe Postscript.
	octet-stream	General binary data consisting of 8-bit bytes.

Table 24.2 MIME Transfer Encodings

7 bit	The data are all represented by short lines of ASCII characters.
8 bit	The lines are short, but there may be non-ASCII characters (octets with the high-order bit set).
binary	Not only may non-ASCII characters be present but the lines are not necessarily short enough for SMTP transport.
quoted-printable	Encodes the data in such a way that if the data being encoded are mostly ASCII text, the encoded form of the data remains largely recognizable by humans.
base64	Encodes data by mapping 6-bit blocks of input to 8-bit blocks of output, all of which are printable ASCII characters.
x-token	A named nonstandard encoding.

MIME TRANSFER ENCODINGS The other major component of the MIME specification, in addition to content-type specification, is a definition of transfer encodings for message bodies. The objective is to provide reliable delivery across the largest range of environments.

The MIME standard defines two methods of encoding data. The Content-Transfer-Encoding field can actually take on six values, as listed in Table 24.2. However, three of these values (7bit, 8bit, and binary) indicate that no encoding has been done but provide some information about the nature of the data. For SMTP transfer, it is safe to use the 7-bit form. The 8-bit and binary forms may be usable in other mail transport contexts. Another Content-Transfer-Encoding value is x-token, which indicates that some other encoding scheme is used, for which a name is to be supplied. This could be a vendor-specific or application-specific scheme. The two actual encoding schemes defined are quoted-printable and base64. Two schemes are defined to provide a choice between a transfer technique that is essentially human readable, and one that is safe for all types of data in a way that is reasonably compact.

The **quoted-printable** transfer encoding is useful when the data consist largely of octets that correspond to printable ASCII characters. In essence, it represents nonsafe characters by the hexadecimal representation of their code and introduces reversible (soft) line breaks to limit message lines to 76 characters. The encoding rules are as follows:

1. **General 8-bit representation:** This rule is to be used when none of the other rules apply. Any character is represented by an equal sign followed by a two-digit hexadecimal representation of the octet's value. For example, the ASCII form feed, which has an 8-bit value of decimal 12, is represented by "=0C".

2. **Literal representation:** Any character in the range decimal 33 ("!") through decimal 126 ("~"), except decimal 61 ("="), is represented as that ASCII character.

3. **White space:** Octets with the values 9 and 32 may be represented as ASCII tab and space characters, respectively, except at the end of a line. Any white

space (tab or blank) at the end of a line must be represented by rule 1. On decoding, any trailing white space on a line is deleted. This eliminates any white space added by intermediate transport agents.

4. **Line breaks:** Any line break, regardless of its initial representation, is represented by the RFC 822 line break, which is a carriage-return/line-feed combination.

5. **Soft line breaks:** If an encoded line would be longer than 76 characters (excluding <CRLF>), a soft line break must be inserted at or before character position 75. A soft line break consists of the hexadecimal sequence 3D0D0A, which is the ASCII code for an equal sign followed by carriage return, line feed.

The **base64 transfer encoding**, also known as radix-64 encoding, is a common one for encoding arbitrary binary data in such a way as to be invulnerable to the processing by mail transport programs. This technique maps arbitrary binary input into printable character output. The form of encoding has the following relevant characteristics:

1. The range of the function is a character set that is universally representable at all sites, not a specific binary encoding of that character set. Thus, the characters themselves can be encoded into whatever form is needed by a specific system. For example, the character "E" is represented in an ASCII-based system as hexadecimal 45 and in an EBCDIC-based system as hexadecimal C5.

2. The character set consists of 65 printable characters, one of which is used for padding. With $2^6 = 64$ available characters, each character can be used to represent 6 bits of input.

3. No control characters are included in the set. Thus, a message encoded in radix 64 can traverse mail-handling systems that scan the data stream for control characters.

4. The hyphen character ("-") is not used. This character has significance in the RFC 822 format and should therefore be avoided.

Table 24.3 shows the mapping of 6-bit input values to characters. The character set consists of the alphanumeric characters as well as "+" and "/". The "=" character is used as the padding character.

Figure 24.3 illustrates the simple mapping scheme. Binary input is processed in blocks of 3 octets, or 24 bits. Each set of 6 bits in the 24-bit block is mapped into a character. In the figure, the characters are shown encoded as 8-bit quantities. In this typical case, each 24-bit input is expanded to 32 bits of output.

For example, consider the 24-bit raw text sequence 00100011 01011100 10010001, which can be expressed in hexadecimal as 235C91. We arrange this input in blocks of 6 bits:

001000 110101 110010 010001

Table 24.3 Radix-64 Encoding

6-Bit Value	Character Encoding	6-Bit Value	Character Encoding	6-Bit Value	Character Encoding	6-Bit Value	Character Encoding
0	A	16	Q	32	G	48	w
1	B	17	R	33	H	49	x
2	C	18	S	34	I	50	y
3	D	19	T	35	J	51	z
4	E	20	U	36	K	52	0
5	F	21	V	37	L	53	1
6	G	22	W	38	M	54	2
7	H	23	X	39	N	55	3
8	I	24	Y	40	O	56	4
9	J	25	Z	41	P	57	5
10	K	26	a	42	Q	58	6
11	L	27	b	43	R	59	7
12	M	28	c	44	S	60	8
13	N	29	d	45	T	61	9
14	O	30	e	46	U	62	+
15	P	31	f	47	V	63	/
						(pad)	=

The extracted 6-bit decimal values are 8, 53, 50, and 17. Looking these up in Table 24.3 yields the radix-64 encoding as the following characters: I1yR. If these characters are stored in 8-bit ASCII format with parity bit set to zero, we have

01001001 00110001 01111001 01010010

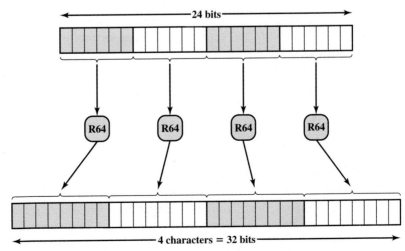

Figure 24.3 Printable Encoding of Binary Data into Radix-64 Format

In hexadecimal, this is 49317952. To summarize,

Input Data	
Binary representation	00100011 01011100 10010001
Hexadecimal representation	235C91
Radix-64 Encoding of Input Data	
Character representation	I1yR
ASCII code (8 bit, zero parity)	01001001 00110001 01111001 01010010
Hexadecimal representation	49317952

POP and IMAP

The Post Office Protocol and the Internet Message Access Protocol support retrieval of mail between a client system (message user agent) and a server that holds the mail for the client (message store).

POST OFFICE PROTOCOL   Version 3 of POP, identified as POP3, is an Internet standard defined in RFC 1939. POP3 supports the basic functions of download and delete for e-mail retrieval. To perform a function from the client (MUA) to the server (MS), the MUA establishes a TCP connection to the MS, using port 110. Then, the interaction passes through three distinct states:

- **Authentication state:** During this state, the client must authenticate itself to the user. This is often done with a simple user ID/password combination, although more sophisticated options are available.
- **Transaction state:** Once the server successfully authenticates the client, the client can access the mailbox to retrieve and delete messages.
- **Update state:** During this state, the server enacts all of the changes requested by the client's commands and then closes the connection.

INTERNET MESSAGE ACCESS PROTOCOL   IMAP version 4 is defined by RFC 3501. Similar to POP, IMAP4 servers store messages for multiple users to be retrieved upon client requests, but the IMAP4 model provides more functionality to users than does the POP model, including the following features:

- Clients can have multiple remote mailboxes from which messages can be retrieved.
- Clients can also specify criteria for downloading messages, such as not transferring large messages over slow links.
- IMAP always keeps messages on the server and replicates copies to the clients.
- IMAP4 allows clients to make changes both when connected and when disconnected. When disconnected (referred to as a disconnected client), changes made on the client take effect on the server by periodic re-synchronization of the client and server.

24.2 INTERNET DIRECTORY SERVICE: DNS

The Domain Name System (DNS) is a directory lookup service that provides a mapping between the name of a host on the Internet and its numerical address. DNS is essential to the functioning of the Internet. It is defined in RFCs 1034 and 1035.

Four elements comprise the DNS:

- **Domain name space:** DNS uses a tree-structured name space to identify resources on the Internet.
- **DNS database:** Conceptually, each node and leaf in the name space tree structure names a set of information (e.g., IP address, type of resource) that is contained in a resource record (RR). The collection of all RRs is organized into a distributed database.
- **Name servers:** These are server programs that hold information about a portion of the domain name tree structure and the associated RRs.
- **Resolvers:** These are programs that extract information from name servers in response to client requests. A typical client request is for an IP address corresponding to a given domain name.

In the next two sections, we examine domain names and the DNS database, respectively. We then describe the operation of DNS, which includes a discussion of name servers and resolvers.

Domain Names

The IP address provides a way of uniquely identifying devices attached to the Internet. This address is interpreted as having two components: a network number, which identifies a network on the Internet, and a host address, which identifies a unique host on that network. The practical use of IP addresses presents two problems:

1. Routers devise a path through the Internet on the basis of the network number. If each router needed to keep a master table that listed every network and the preferred path to that network, the management of the tables would be cumbersome and time consuming. It would be better to group the networks in such a way as to simplify the routing function.
2. The 32-bit IPv4 address is usually written as four decimal numbers, corresponding to the four octets of the address. This number scheme is effective for computer processing but is not convenient for users, who can more easily remember names than numerical addresses.

These problems are addressed by the concept of **domain**. In general terms, a domain refers to a group of hosts that are under the administrative control of a single entity, such as a company or government agency. Domains are organized hierarchically, so that a given domain may consist of a number of subordinate domains. Names are assigned to domains and reflect this hierarchical organization.

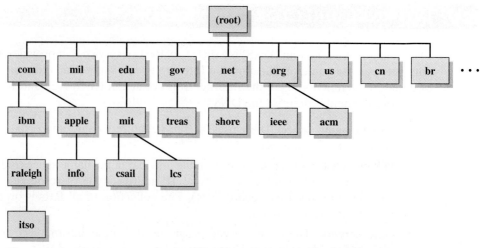

Figure 24.4 Portion of Internet Domain Tree

Figure 24.4 shows a portion of the domain naming tree. At the very top level are a small number of domains that encompass the entire Internet. Additionally, at the top level are various country codes, such as us (United States), cn (People's Republic of China), and br (Brazil). Table 24.4 lists non-country top-level domains.

Table 24.4 Top-Level Internet Domains

Domain	Contents
com	Commercial organizations
edu	Educational institutions
gov	U.S. federal, state, and local government agencies
mil	U.S. military
net	Network support centers, Internet service providers, and other network-related organizations
org	Nonprofit organizations
us	U.S. state and local government agencies, schools, libraries, and museums
country code	ISO standard 2-letter identifier for country-specific domains (e.g., au, ca, uk)
biz	Dedicated exclusively for private businesses
info	Unrestricted use
name	Individuals, for e-mail addresses and personalized domain names.
museum	Restricted to museums, museum organizations, and individual members of the museum profession
coop	Member-owned cooperative organizations, such as credit unions
aero	Aviation community
pro	Medical, legal, and accounting professions
arpa	Address and routing parameter area; used for technical infrastructure purposes, such as reverse domain name resolution
int	International organizations

Each subordinate level is named by prefixing a subordinate name to the name at the next highest level. For example,

- edu is the domain of college-level U.S. educational institutions.
- mit.edu is the domain for MIT (Massachusetts Institute of Technology)
- csail.mit.edu is the domain for the MIT Computer Science and Artificial Intelligence Laboratory.

As you move down the naming tree, you eventually get to leaf nodes that identify specific hosts on the Internet. These hosts are assigned Internet addresses. Domain names are assigned hierarchically in such a way that every domain name is unique. At a top level, the creation of new top-level names and the assignment of names and addresses are administered by the Internet Corporation for Assigned Names and Numbers (ICANN). The actual assignment of addresses is delegated down the hierarchy. Thus, the mil domain is assigned a large group of addresses. The U.S. Department of Defense (DoD) then allocates portions of this address space to various DoD organizations for eventual assignment to hosts.

For example, the main host at MIT, with a domain name of mit.edu, has the IP address 18.7.22.69. The subordinate domain csail.mit.edu has the IP address 128.30.2.121.[1]

The DNS Database

DNS is based on a hierarchical database containing **resource records (RRs)** that include the name, IP address, and other information about hosts. The key features of the database are as follows:

- **Variable-depth hierarchy for names:** DNS allows essentially unlimited levels and uses the period (.) as the level delimiter in printed names, as described earlier.
- **Distributed database:** The database resides in DNS servers scattered throughout the Internet and private intranets.
- **Distribution controlled by the database:** The DNS database is divided into thousands of separately managed zones, which are managed by separate administrators. The database software controls distribution and update of records.

Using this database, DNS servers provide a name-to-address directory service for network applications that need to locate specific servers. For example, every time an e-mail message is sent or a Web page is accessed, there must be a DNS name lookup to determine the IP address of the e-mail server or Web server.

---

[1]You should be able to demonstrate the name/address function by connecting your Web browser to your local ISP's Web server. The ISP should provide a ping or nslookup tool that allows you to enter a domain name and retrieve an IP address. Such a tool is typically available on user operating systems as well.

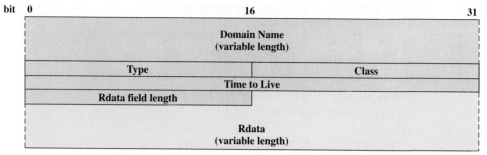

Figure 24.5   DNS Resource Record Format

Figure 24.5 shows the structure of an RR. It consists of the following elements:

- **Domain Name:** Although the syntax of domain names in messages, described subsequently, is precisely defined, the form of the domain name in an RR is described in general terms. In essence, the domain name in an RR must correspond to the human-readable form, which consists of a series of labels of alphanumeric characters or hyphens, with each pair of labels separated by a period.

- **Type:** Identifies the type of resource in this RR. The various types are listed in Table 24.5.[2]

- **Class:** Identifies the protocol family. The only commonly used value is IN, for the Internet.

Table 24.5   Resource Record Types

Type	Description
A	A host address. This RR type maps the name of a system to its IPv4 address. Some systems (e.g., routers) have multiple addresses, and there is a separate RR for each.
AAAA	Similar to A type, but for IPv6 addresses.
CNAME	Canonical name. Specifies an alias name for a host and maps this to the canonical (true) name.
HINFO	Host information. Designates the processor and operating system used by the host.
MINFO	Mailbox or mail list information. Maps a mailbox or mail list name to a host name.
MX	Mail exchange. Identifies the system(s) via which mail to the queried domain name should be relayed.
NS	Authoritative name server for this domain.
PTR	Domain name pointer. Points to another part of the domain name space.
SOA	Start of a zone of authority (which part of naming hierarchy is implemented). Includes parameters related to this zone.
SRV	For a given service, provides name of server or servers in domain that provide that service.
TXT	Arbitrary text. Provides a way to add text comments to the database.
WKS	Well-known services. May list the application services available at this host.

---

[2]*Note*: The SRV RR type is defined in RFC 2782.

- **Time to Live:** Typically, when an RR is retrieved from a name server, the retriever will cache the RR so that it need not query the name server (NS) repeatedly. This field specifies the time interval that the RR may be cached before the source of the information should again be consulted. A zero value is interpreted to mean that the RR can only be used for the transaction in progress and should not be cached.
- **Rdata Field Length:** Length of the Rdata field in octets.
- **Rdata:** A variable length string of octets that describes the resource. The format of this information varies according to the type of the RR. For example, for the A type, the Rdata is a 32-bit IPv4 address, and for the CNAME type, the Rdata is a domain name.

DNS Operation

DNS operation typically includes the following steps (Figure 24.6):

1. A user program requests an IP address for a domain name.
2. A resolver module in the local host or local ISP queries a local name server in the same domain as the resolver.
3. The local name server checks to see if the name is in its local database or cache, and, if so, returns the IP address to the requestor. Otherwise, the name server queries other available name servers, if necessary going to the root server, as explained subsequently.
4. When a response is received at the local name server, it stores the name/address mapping in its local cache and may maintain this entry for the amount of time specified in the time to live field of the retrieved RR.
5. The user program is given the IP address or an error message.

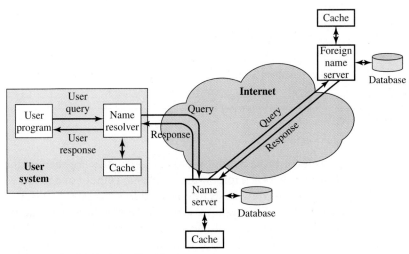

Figure 24.6 DNS Name Resolution

```
telnet locis.loc.gov
Trying 140.147.254.3...
Connected to locis.loc.gov.
Escape character is '^]'.
          L O C I S:  LIBRARY OF CONGRESS INFORMATION SYSTEM

          To make a choice: type a number, then press ENTER

   1   Copyright Information     -- files available and up-to-date

   2   Braille and Audio         -- files frozen mid-August 1999

   3   Federal Legislation       -- files frozen December 1998

 *    *    *    *    *    *    *    *    *    *    *    *    *    *    *

              The LC Catalog Files are available at:
                  http://lcweb.loc.gov/catalog/

 *    *    *    *    *    *    *    *    *    *    *    *    *    *    *

   8   Searching Hours and Basic Search Commands
   9   Library of Congress General Information
  10   Library of Congress Fast Facts

  12   Comments and Logoff
       Choice:
   9
              LIBRARY OF CONGRESS GENERAL INFORMATION

LC is a research library serving Congress, the federal government, the
library community world-wide, the US creative community, and any researchers
beyond high school level or age.  On-site researchers request materials by
filling out request slips in LC's reading rooms; requesters must present a
photo i.d.  Staff are available for assistance in all public reading rooms.

------------------------------------------------------------------------------
The following phone numbers offer information about hours and other services:

General Research Info:    202-707-6500    Reading Room Hours:   202-707-6400
Exhibits/Tours/Gift Shop: 202-707-8000    Location/Parking:     202-707-4700
Copyright Information:    202-707-3000    Cataloging Products:  202-707-6100
Copyright Forms:          202-707-9100         "      "  fax:   202-707-1334

------------------------------------------------------------------------------
For information on interlibrary loan, see:  http://lcweb.loc.gov/rr/loan/

12  Return to LOCIS MENU screen

Choice:
```

Figure 24.7   A Telnet Session

The results of these behind-the-scenes activities are seen by the user in a way illustrated in Figure 24.7. Here, a user issues a Telnet connection request to locis. loc.gov. This is resolved by DNS to the IP address of 140.147.254.3.

The distributed DNS database that supports the DNS functionality must be updated frequently because of the rapid and continued growth of the Internet. Further, the DNS must cope with dynamic assignment of IP addresses, such as is done for home DSL users by their ISP. Accordingly, dynamic updating functions for DNS have been defined. In essence, DNS name servers automatically send out updates to other relevant name servers as conditions warrant.

THE SERVER HIERARCHY The DNS database is distributed hierarchically, residing in DNS name servers scattered throughout the Internet. Name servers can be operated by any organization that owns a domain or subdomain; that is, any organization that has responsibility for a subtree of the hierarchical domain name space. Each name server is configured with a subset of the domain name space, known as a **zone**, which is a collection of one or more (or all) subdomains within a domain, along with the associated RRs. This set of data is called authoritative, because this name server is responsible for maintaining an accurate set or RRs for this portion of the domain name hierarchy. The hierarchical structure can extend to any depth. Thus, a portion of the name space assigned to an authoritative name server can be delegated to a subordinate name server in a way that corresponds to the structure of the domain name tree. For example, a name server corresponds to the domain ibm.com. A portion of that domain is defined by the name watson.ibm.com, which corresponds to the node watson.ibm.com and all of the branches and leaf nodes underneath the node watson.ibm.com.

At the top of the server hierarchy are 13 **root name servers** that share responsibility for the top-level zones (Table 24.6). This replication is to prevent the root server from becoming a bottleneck, and for reliability. Even so, each individual root server is quite busy. For example, the Internet Software Consortium reports that its server (F) answers almost 300 million DNS requests daily (www.isc.org/services/public/F-root-server.html). Note that some of the root servers exist as multiple servers that are geographically distributed. When there are multiple root servers with the same name, each has an identical copy of the database for that server and the same IP address. When a query is made to that root server, the IP routing protocol and algorithm directs the query to the most convenient server, which is generally the nearest server physically.

Consider a query by a program on a user host for watson.ibm.com. This query is sent to the local server and the following steps occur:

1. If the local server already has the IP address for watson.ibm.com in its local cache, it returns the IP address.

2. If the name is not in the local name server's cache, it sends the query to a root server. The root server in turn forwards the request to a server with an NS record for ibm.com. If this server has the information for watson.ibm.com, it returns the IP address.

3. If there is a delegated name server just for watson.ibm.com, then the ibm.com name server forwards the request to the watson.ibm.com name server, which returns the IP address.

Typically, single queries are carried over UDP. Queries for a group of names are carried over TCP.

NAME RESOLUTION As Figure 24.6 indicates, each query begins at a name resolver located in the user host system (e.g., gethostbyname in UNIX). Each resolver is configured to know the name and address of a local DNS name server. If the resolver does

Table 24.6   Internet Root Servers

Server	Operator	Cities	IP Addr
A	VeriSign Global Registry Services	6 sites in the United States, Germany, Hong Kong	IPv4: 198.41.0.4 IPv6: 2001:503:BA3E::2:30
B	Information Sciences Institute	Marina Del Rey, CA, USA	IPv4: 192.228.79.201 IPv6: 2001:478:65::53
C	Cogent Communications	6 sites in the United States, Germany, Spain	192.33.4.12
D	University of Maryland	College Park, MD, USA	128.8.10.90
E	NASA Ames Research Center	Mountain View, CA, USA	192.203.230.10
F	Internet Software Consortium	49 sites in the United States and other countries	IPv4: 192.5.5.241 IPv6: 2001:500::1035
G	U.S. DOD Network Information Center	6 sites in United States, Japan, Germany, Italy	192.112.36.4
H	U.S. Army Research Lab	Aberdeen, MD, USA San Diego, CA, USA	IPv4: 128.63.2.53 IPv6: 2001:500:1::803f:235
I	Netnod	38 sites in the United States and other countries	IPv4: 192.36.148.17 IPv6: 2001:7fe::53
J	VeriSign Global Registry Services	70 sites in the United States and other countries	IPv4: 192.58.128.30 IPv6: 2001:503:C27::2:30
K	Reseaux IP Europeens—Network Coordination Centre	18 sites in the United States and other countries	IPv4: 193.0.14.129 IPv6: 2001:7fd::1
L	Internet Corporation for Assigned Names and Numbers	55 sites in the United States and other countries	IPv4: 199.7.83.42 IPv6: 2001:500:3::42
M	WIDE Project	6 sites in the United States, Japan, Korea, France	IPv4: 202.12.27.33 IPv6: 2001:dc3::35

not have the requested name in its cache, it sends a DNS query to the local DNS server, which either returns an address immediately or does so after querying one or more other servers. Again, resolvers use UDP for single queries and TCP for group queries.

There are two methods by which queries are forwarded and results returned. Suppose a resolver issues a request to local name server (A). If A has the name/address in its local cache or local database, it can return the IP address to the resolver. If not, then A can do either of the following:

1. Query another name server for the desired result and then send the result back to A. This is known as a **recursive technique**.

2. Return to A the address of the next server (C) to whom the request should be sent. A then sends out a new DNS request to C. This is known as the **iterative technique**.

In exchanges between name servers, either the iterative or recursive technique may be used. For requests sent by a name resolver, the recursive technique is used.

DNS MESSAGES   DNS messages use a single format, shown in Figure 24.8. There are five possible sections to a DNS message: header, question, answer, authority, and additional records.

The **header section** is always present and consists of the following fields:

- **Identifier:** Assigned by the program that generates any kind of query. The same identifier is used in any response, enabling the sender to match queries and responses.
- **Query Response:** Indicates whether this message is a query or response.
- **Opcode:** Indicates whether this is a standard query, an inverse query (address to name), or a server status request. This value is set by the originator and copied into the response.
- **Authoritative Answer:** Valid in a response and indicates whether the responding name server is an authority for the domain name in question.
- **Truncated:** Indicates whether the response message was truncated due to length greater than permitted on the transmission channel. If so, the requestor will use a TCP connection to resend the query.
- **Recursion Desired:** If set, directs the server to pursue the query recursively.
- **Recursion Available:** Set or cleared in a response to denote whether recursive query support is available in the name server.
- **Response Code:** Possible values are: no error, format error (server unable to interpret query), server failure, name error (domain name does not exist), not implemented (this kind of query not supported), and refused (for policy reasons).
- **QDcount:** Number of entries in question section (zero or more).
- **ANcount:** Number of RRs in answer section (zero or more).
- **NScount:** Number of RRs in authority section (zero or more).
- **ARcount:** Number of RRs in additional records section (zero or more).

The **question section** contains the queries for the name server. If present, it typically contains only one entry. Each entry contains the following:

- **Domain Name:** A domain name represented as a sequence of labels, where each label consists of a length octet followed by that number of octets. The domain name terminates with the zero-length octet for the null label of the root.
- **Query Type:** Indicates type of query. The values for this field include all values valid for the Type field in the RR format (Figure 24.5), together with some more general codes that match more than one type of RR.
- **Query Class:** Specifies the class of query, typically the Internet.

The **answer section** contains RRs that answer the question; the **authority section** contains RRs that point toward an authoritative name server; the **additional records section** contains RRs that relate to the query but are not strictly answers for the question.

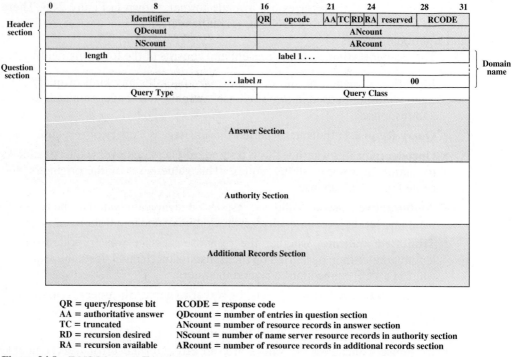

Figure 24.8 DNS Message Format

24.3 WEB ACCESS AND HTTP

The Hypertext Transfer Protocol is the foundation protocol of the World Wide Web and can be used in any client/server application involving hypertext. The name is somewhat misleading in that HTTP is not a protocol for transferring hypertext; rather it is a protocol for transmitting information with the efficiency necessary for making hypertext jumps. The data transferred by the protocol can be plaintext, hypertext, audio, images, or any Internet-accessible information.

We begin with an overview of HTTP concepts and operation and then look at some of the details, basing our discussion on the most recent version to be put on the Internet standards track, HTTP 1.1 (RFC 2616). A number of important terms defined in the HTTP specification are summarized in Table 24.7; these will be introduced as the discussion proceeds.

HTTP Overview

HTTP is a transaction-oriented client/server protocol. The most typical use of HTTP is between a Web browser and a Web server. To provide reliability, HTTP makes use of TCP. Nevertheless, HTTP is a **stateless protocol**: Each transaction is treated independently. Accordingly, a typical implementation will create a new TCP connection between client and server for each transaction and then terminate the connection as soon as the transaction completes, although the specification

Table 24.7 Key Terms Related to HTTP

Cache A program's local store of response messages and the subsystem that controls its message storage, retrieval, and deletion. A cache stores cacheable responses in order to reduce the response time and network bandwidth consumption on future, equivalent requests. Any client/server may include a cache, though a cache cannot be used by a server while it is acting as a tunnel.	**Origin Server** The server on which a given resource resides or is to be created. **Proxy** An intermediary program that acts as both a server and a client for the purpose of making requests on behalf of other clients. Requests are serviced internally or by passing them, with possible translation, on to other servers. A proxy must interpret and, if necessary, rewrite a request message before forwarding it. Proxies are often used as client-side portals through network firewalls and as helper applications for handling requests via protocols not implemented by the user agent.
Client An application program that establishes connections for the purpose of sending requests.	
Connection A transport-layer virtual circuit established between two application programs for the purposes of communication.	
Entity A particular representation or rendition of a data resource, or reply from a service resource, that may be enclosed within a request or response message. An entity consists of entity headers and an entity body.	**Resource** A network data object or service which can be identified by a URI. **Server** An application program that accepts connections in order to service requests by sending back responses.
Gateway A server that acts as an intermediary for some other server. Unlike a proxy, a gateway receives requests as if it were the original server for the requested resource; the requesting client may not be aware that it is communicating with a gateway. Gateways are often used as server-side portals through network firewalls and as protocol translators for access to resources stored on non-HTTP systems.	**Tunnel** An intermediary program that is acting as a blind relay between two connections. Once active, a tunnel is not considered a party to the HTTP communication, though the tunnel may have been initiated by an HTTP request. A tunnel ceases to exist when both ends of the relayed connections are closed. Tunnels are used when a portal is necessary and the intermediary cannot, or should not, interpret the relayed communication.
Message The basic unit of HTTP communication, consisting of a structured sequence of octets transmitted via the connection.	**User Agent** The client that initiates a request. These are often browsers, editors, spiders, or other end-user tools.

does not dictate this one-to-one relationship between transaction and connection lifetimes.

The stateless nature of HTTP is well suited to its typical application. A normal session of a user with a Web browser involves retrieving a sequence of Web pages and documents. The sequence is, ideally, performed rapidly, and the locations of the various pages and documents may be a number of widely distributed servers.

Another important feature of HTTP is that it is flexible in the formats that it can handle. When a client issues a request to a server, it may include a prioritized list of formats that it can handle, and the server replies with the appropriate format. For example, a Lynx browser cannot handle images, so a Web server need not transmit any images on Web pages. This arrangement prevents the transmission of unnecessary information and provides the basis for extending the set of formats with new standardized and proprietary specifications.

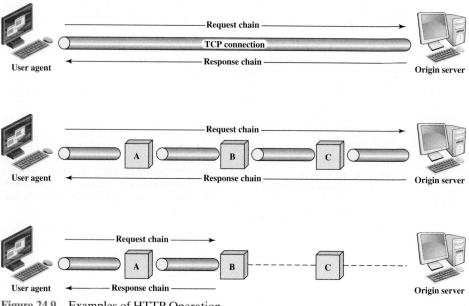

Figure 24.9 Examples of HTTP Operation

Figure 24.9 illustrates three examples of HTTP operation. The simplest case is one in which a user agent establishes a direct connection with an origin server. The **user agent** is the client that initiates the request, such as a Web browser being run on behalf of an end user. The **origin server** is the server on which a resource of interest resides; an example is a Web server at which a desired Web home page resides. For this case, the client opens a TCP connection that is end-to-end between the client and the server. The client then issues an HTTP request. The request consists of a specific command, referred to as a method, an address [referred to as a uniform resource locator (URL)],[3] and a MIME-like message containing request parameters, information about the client, and perhaps some additional content information.

When the server receives the request, it attempts to perform the requested action and then returns an HTTP response. The response includes status information, a success/error code, and a MIME-like message containing information about the server, information about the response itself, and possible body content. The TCP connection is then closed.

The middle part of Figure 24.9 shows a case in which there is not an end-to-end TCP connection between the user agent and the origin server. Instead, there are one or more intermediate systems with TCP connections between logically adjacent systems. Each intermediate system acts as a relay, so that a request initiated by the client is relayed through the intermediate systems to the server, and the response from the server is relayed back to the client.

Three forms of intermediate system are defined in the HTTP specification: proxy, gateway, and tunnel, all of which are illustrated in Figure 24.10.

---

[3]Appendix R contains a discussion of URLs.

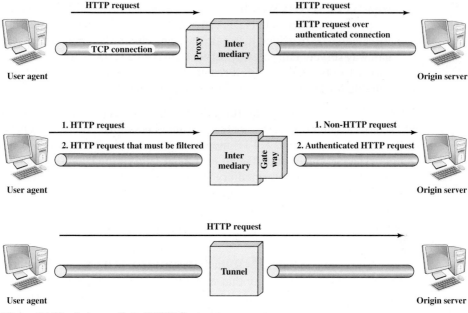

Figure 24.10   Intermediate HTTP Systems

PROXY   A proxy acts on behalf of other clients and presents requests from other clients to a server. The proxy acts as a server in interacting with a client and as a client in interacting with a server. There are two scenarios that call for the use of a proxy:

- **Security intermediary:** The client and server may be separated by a security intermediary such as a firewall, with the proxy on the client side of the firewall. Typically, the client is part of a network secured by a firewall and the server is external to the secured network. In this case, the server must authenticate itself to the firewall to set up a connection with the proxy. The proxy accepts responses after they have passed through the firewall.
- **Different versions of HTTP:** If the client and server are running different versions of HTTP, then the proxy can implement both versions and perform the required mapping.

In summary, a proxy is a forwarding agent, receiving a request for a URL object, modifying the request, and forwarding the request toward the server identified in the URL.

GATEWAY   A gateway is a server that appears to the client as if it were an origin server. It acts on behalf of other servers that may not be able to communicate directly with a client. There are two scenarios in which gateways can be used.

- **Security intermediary:** The client and server may be separated by a security intermediary such as a firewall, with the gateway on the server side of the firewall. Typically, the server is connected to a network protected by a firewall, with the client external to the network. In this case the client must authenticate itself to the gateway, which can then pass the request on to the server.

- **Non-HTTP server:** Web browsers have built-in capability to contact servers for protocols other than HTTP, such as FTP and Gopher servers. This capability can also be provided by a gateway. The client makes an HTTP request to a gateway server. The gateway server then contacts the relevant FTP or Gopher server to obtain the desired result. This result is then converted into a form suitable for HTTP and transmitted back to the client.

TUNNEL   Unlike the proxy and the gateway, the tunnel performs no operations on HTTP requests and responses. Instead, a tunnel is simply a relay point between two TCP connections, and the HTTP messages are passed unchanged as if there were a single HTTP connection between user agent and origin server. Tunnels are used when there must be an intermediary system between client and server but it is not necessary for that system to understand the contents of messages. An example is a firewall in which a client or server external to a protected network can establish an authenticated connection and then maintain that connection for purposes of HTTP transactions.

CACHE   Returning to Figure 24.9, the lowest portion of the figure shows an example of a cache. A cache is a facility that may store previous requests and responses for handling new requests. If a new request arrives that is the same as a stored request, then the cache can supply the stored response rather than accessing the resource indicated in the URL. The cache can operate on a client or server or on an intermediate system other than a tunnel. In the figure, intermediary B has cached a request/response transaction, so that a corresponding new request from the client need not travel the entire chain to the origin server, but is handled by B.

Not all transactions can be cached, and a client or server can dictate that a certain transaction may be cached only for a given time limit.

Messages

The best way to describe the functionality of HTTP is to describe the individual elements of the HTTP message. HTTP consists of two types of messages: requests from clients to servers and responses from servers to clients. Figure 24.11 provides an example. More formally, using enhanced BNF (Backus-Naur Form) notation[4] (Table 24.8), we have:

HTTP-Message = Simple-Request | Simple-Response | Full-Request | Full-Response
Full-Request = Request-Line
   *(General-Header | Request-Header | Entity-Header)
   CRLF
   [Entity-Body]
Full-Response = Status-Line
   *(General-Header | Response-Header | Entity-Header)
   CRLF
   [Entity-Body]
Simple-Request = "GET" SP Request-URL CRLF
Simple-Response = [Entity-Body]

---

[4]A description of BNF is contained in Appendix S.

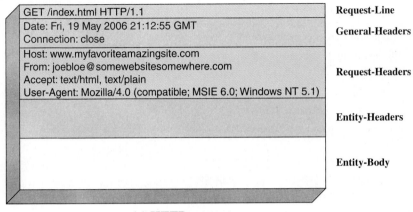

(a) HTTP request

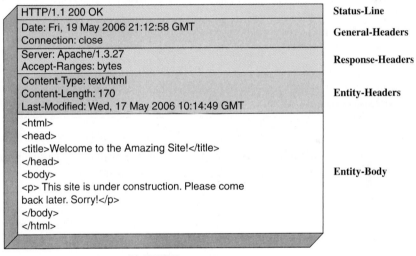

(b) HTTP response

Figure 24.11 Examples of HTTP Message Format

The Simple-Request and Simple-Response messages were defined in HTTP/0.9. The request is a simple GET command with the requested URL; the response is simply a block containing the information identified in the URL. In HTTP/1.1, the use of these simple forms is discouraged because it prevents the client from using content negotiation and the server from identifying the media type of the returned entity.

All of the HTTP headers consist of a sequence of fields following the same generic format as RFC 822 (described in Section 24.1). Each field begins on a new line and consists of the field name followed by a colon and the field value.

A full request uses the following fields:

- **Request-Line:** Indicates the requested action, the resource on which the action is to be performed, and the version of HTTP used in this message.

Table 24.8 Augmented BNF Notation Used in URL and HTTP Specifications

- Words in lowercase represent variables or names of rules.
- A rule has the form

  name = definition

- DIGIT is any decimal digit; CRLF is carriage return, line feed; SP is one or more spaces.
- Quotation marks enclose literal text.
- Angle brackets, "<" ">", may be used within a definition to enclose a rule name when their presence will facilitate clarity.
- Elements separated by bar (" | ") are alternatives.
- Ordinary parentheses are used simply for grouping.
- The character "*" preceding an element indicates repetition. The full form is:

  <I>*<J>element

  indicating at least I and at most J occurrences of element. *element allows any number, including 0; 1*element requires at least one element; and 1*2element allows 1 or 2 elements; <N>element means exactly N elements.
- Square brackets, "[" "]," enclose optional elements.
- The construct "#" is used to define, with the following form:

  <I>#<J>element

  indicating at least I and at most J elements, each separated by a comma and optional linear white space.
- A semicolon at the right of a rule starts a comment that continues to the end of the line.

- **General-Headers:** Contains fields that are applicable to the request message but that do not apply to the entity being transferred.
- **Request-Headers:** Contains information about the request and the client. For example, a request may be conditional, specifying under what conditions the requested action is to be determined. A field in this header may also indicate which formats and encodings the client is able to handle.
- **Entity-Header:** Contains information about the resource identified by the request and information about the entity body, if any.
- **Entity-Body:** The body of the message.

A response message has the same structure as a request message, but substitutes the following headers for the request line and the request headers:

- **Status-Line:** Indicates the version of HTTP used in this message and provides status information about this response. For example, "OK" means that the request was successfully completed.
- **Response-Headers:** Provide additional data that expand on the status information in the status line.

Although the basic transaction mechanism is simple, there is a large number of fields and parameters defined in HTTP. In the remainder of this section, we look at the general header fields. Following sections describe request headers, response headers, and entities.

GENERAL HEADER FIELDS General header fields can be used in both request and response messages. These fields are applicable in both types of messages and contain information that does not directly apply to the entity being transferred. The fields are as follows:

- **Cache-Control:** Specifies directives that must be obeyed by any caching mechanisms along the request/response chain. The purpose is to prevent a cache from adversely interfering with this particular request or response.

- **Connection:** Contains a list of keywords and header field names that only apply to this TCP connection between the sender and the nearest nontunnel recipient.

- **Date:** Date and time at which the message originated.

- **Forwarded:** Used by gateways and proxies to indicate intermediate steps along a request or response chain. Each gateway or proxy that handles a message may attach a Forwarded field that gives its URL.

- **Keep-Alive:** May be present if the keep-alive keyword is present in an incoming Connection field, to provide information to the requester of the persistent connection. This field may indicate a maximum time that the sender will keep the connection open waiting for the next request or the maximum number of additional requests that will be allowed on the current persistent connection.

- **MIME-Version:** Indicates that the message complies with the indicated version of MIME.

- **Pragma:** Contains implementation-specific directives that may apply to any recipient along the request/response chain.

- **Upgrade:** Used in a request to specify what additional protocols the client supports and would like to use; used in a response to indicate which protocol will be used.

Request Messages

A full request message consists of a status line followed by one or more general, request, and entity headers, followed by an optional entity body.

REQUEST METHODS A full request message always begins with a Request-Line, which has the following format:

> Request-Line = Method SP Request-URL SP HTTP-Version CRLF

The Method parameter indicates the actual request command, called a method in HTTP. Request-URL is the URL of the requested resource, and HTTP-Version is the version number of HTTP used by the sender.

The following request methods are defined in HTTP/1.1:

- **OPTIONS:** A request for information about the options available for the request/response chain identified by this URL.

- **GET:** A request to retrieve the information identified in the URL and return it in a entity body. A GET is conditional if the If-Modified-Since header field is included and is partial if a Range header field is included.

- **HEAD:** This request is identical to a GET, except that the server's response must not include an entity body; all of the header fields in the response are the same as if the entity body were present. This enables a client to get information about a resource without transferring the entity body.
- **POST:** A request to accept the attached entity as a new subordinate to the identified URL. The posted entity is subordinate to that URL in the same way that a file is subordinate to a directory containing it, a news article is subordinate to a newsgroup to which it is posted, or a record is subordinate to a database.
- **PUT:** A request to accept the attached entity and store it under the supplied URL. This may be a new resource with a new URL or a replacement of the contents of an existing resource with an existing URL.
- **PATCH:** Similar to a PUT, except that the entity contains a list of differences from the content of the original resource identified in the URL.
- **COPY:** Requests that a copy of the resource identified by the URL in the Request-Line be copied to the location(s) given in the URL-Header field in the Entity-Header of this message.
- **MOVE:** Requests that the resource identified by the URL in the Request-Line be moved to the location(s) given in the URL-Header field in the Entity-Header of this message. Equivalent to a COPY followed by a DELETE.
- **DELETE:** Requests that the origin server delete the resource identified by the URL in the Request-Line.
- **LINK:** Establishes one or more link relationships from the resource identified in the Request-Line. The links are defined in the Link field in the Entity-Header.
- **UNLINK:** Removes one or more link relationships from the resource identified in the Request-Line. The links are defined in the Link field in the Entity-Header.
- **TRACE:** Requests that the server return whatever is received as the entity body of the response. This can be used for testing and diagnostic purposes.
- **WRAPPED:** Allows a client to send one or more encapsulated requests. The requests may be encrypted or otherwise processed. The server must unwrap the requests and process accordingly.
- **Extension-method:** Allows additional methods to be defined without changing the protocol, but these methods cannot be assumed to be recognizable by the recipient.

REQUEST HEADER FIELDS   Request header fields function as request modifiers, providing additional information and parameters related to the request. The following fields are defined in HTTP/1.1:

- **Accept:** A list of media types and ranges that are acceptable as a response to this request.
- **Accept-Charset:** A list of character sets acceptable for the response.
- **Accept-Encoding:** List of acceptable content encodings for the entity body. Content encodings are primarily used to allow a document to be compressed

or encrypted. Typically, the resource is stored in this encoding and only decoded before actual use.

- **Accept-Language:** Restricts the set of natural languages that are preferred for the response.
- **Authorization:** Contains a field value, referred to as *credentials*, used by the client to authenticate itself to the server.
- **From:** The Internet e-mail address for the human user who controls the requesting user agent.
- **Host:** Specifies the Internet host of the resource being requested.
- **If-Modified-Since:** Used with the GET method. This header includes a date/ time parameter; the resource is to be transferred only if it has been modified since the date/time specified. This feature allows for efficient cache update. A caching mechanism can periodically issue GET messages to an origin server and will receive only a small response message unless an update is needed.
- **Proxy-Authorization:** Allows the client to identify itself to a proxy that requires authentication.
- **Range:** In a GET message, a client can request only a portion of the identified resource by specifying a range of bytes in the entity body.
- **Referrer:** The URL of the resource from which the Request-URL was obtained. This enables a server to generate lists of back-links.
- **Unless:** Similar in function to the If-Modified-Since field, with two differences: (1) It is not restricted to the GET method, and (2) comparison is based on any Entity-Header field value rather than a date/time value.
- **User-Agent:** Contains information about the user agent originating this request. This is used for statistical purposes, the tracing of protocol violations, and automated recognition of user agents for the sake of tailoring responses to avoid particular user agent limitations.

Response Messages

A full response message consists of a status line followed by one or more general, response, and entity headers, followed by an optional entity body.

STATUS CODES A full response message always begins with a Status-Line, which has the following format:

Status-Line = HTTP-Version SP Status-Code SP Reason-Phrase CRLF

The HTTP-Version value is the version number of HTTP used by the sender. The Status-Code is a three-digit integer that indicates the response to a received request, and the Reason-Phrase provides a short textual explanation of the status code.

HTTP/1.1 includes a rather large number of status codes, organized into the following categories:

- **Informational:** The request has been received and processing continues. No entity body accompanies this response.

- **Successful:** The request was successfully received, understood, and accepted. The information returned in the response message depends on the request method, as follows:
  - GET: The contents of the entity body correspond to the requested resource.
  - HEAD: No entity body is returned.
  - POST: The entity describes or contains the result of the action.
  - TRACE: The entity contains the request message.
  - Other methods: The entity describes the result of the action.
- **Redirection:** Further action is required to complete the request.
- **Client Error:** The request contains a syntax error or the request cannot be fulfilled.
- **Server Error:** The server failed to fulfill an apparently valid request.

RESPONSE HEADER FIELDS   Response header fields provide additional information related to the response that cannot be placed in the Status-Line. The following fields are defined in HTTP/1.1:

- **Location:** Defines the exact location of the resource identified by the Request-URL.
- **Proxy-Authenticate:** Included with a response that has a status code of Proxy Authentication Required. This field contains a "challenge" that indicates the authentication scheme and parameters required.
- **Public:** Lists the nonstandard methods supported by this server.
- **Retry-After:** Included with a response that has a status code of Service Unavailable and indicates how long the service is expected to be unavailable.
- **Server:** Identifies the software product used by the origin server to handle the request.
- **WWW-Authenticate:** Included with a response that has a status code of Unauthorized. This field contains a "challenge" that indicates the authentication scheme and parameters required.

Entities

An entity consists of an entity header and an entity body in a request or response message. An entity may represent a data resource, or it may constitute other information supplied with a request or response.

ENTITY HEADER FIELDS   Entity header fields provide optional information about the entity body or, if no body is present, about the resource identified by the request. The following fields are defined in HTTP/1.1:

- **Allow:** Lists methods supported by the resource identified in the Request-URL. This field must be included with a response that has a status code of Method Not Allowed and may be included in other responses.
- **Content-Encoding:** Indicates what content encodings have been applied to the resource. The only encoding currently defined is zip compression.
- **Content-Language:** Identifies the natural language(s) of the intended audience of the enclosed entity.

- **Content-Length:** The size of the entity body in octets.
- **Content-MD5:** For future study. MD5 refers to the MD5 hash code function, described in Appendix Q.
- **Content-Range:** For future study. The intent is that this will indicate a portion of the identified resource that is included in this response.
- **Content-Type:** Indicates the media type of the entity body.
- **Content-Version:** A version tag associated with an evolving entity.
- **Derived-From:** Indicates the version tag of the resource from which this entity was derived before modifications were made by the sender. This field and the Content-Version field can be used to manage multiple updates by a group of users.
- **Expires:** Date/time after which the entity should be considered stale.
- **Last-Modified:** Date/time that the sender believes the resource was last modified.
- **Link:** Defines links to other resources.
- **Title:** A textual title for the entity.
- **Transfer-Encoding:** Indicates what type of transformation has been applied to the message body to transfer it safely between the sender and the recipient. The only encoding defined in the standard is *chunked*. The chunked option defines a procedure for breaking an entity body into labeled chunks that are transmitted separately.
- **URL-Header:** Informs the recipient of other URLs by which the resource can be identified.
- **Extension-Header:** Allows additional fields to be defined without changing the protocol, but these fields cannot be assumed to be recognizable by the recipient.

ENTITY BODY   An entity body consists of an arbitrary sequence of octets. HTTP is designed to be able to transfer any type of content, including text, binary data, audio, images, and video. When an entity body is present in a message, the interpretation of the octets in the body is determined by the entity header fields Content-Encoding, Content-Type, and Transfer-Encoding. These define a three-layer, ordered encoding model:

entity-body: = Transfer-Encoding(Content-Encoding(Content-Type(data)))

The data are the content of a resource identified by a URL. The Content-Type field determines the way in which the data are interpreted. A Content-Encoding may be applied to the data and stored at the URL instead of the data. Finally, on transfer, a Transfer-Encoding may be applied to form the entity body of the message.

24.4 RECOMMENDED READING AND ANIMATIONS

[KHAR98] provides an overview of SMTP.

[MOGU02] discusses the design strengths and weaknesses of HTTP. [GOUR02] provides comprehensive coverage of HTTP. Another good treatment is [KRIS01]. [MOCK88] is an overview of DNS.

GOUR02 Gourley, D., et al. *HTTP: The Definitive Guide.* Sebastopol, CA: O'Reilly, 2002.

KHAR98 Khare, R. "The Spec's in the Mail." *IEEE Internet Computing*, September/October 1998.

KRIS01 Krishnamurthy, B., and Rexford, J. *Web Protocols and Practice: HTTP/1.1, Networking Protocols, Caching, and Traffic Measurement.* Upper Saddle River, NJ: Prentice Hall, 2001.

MOCK88 Mockapetris, P., and Dunlap, K. "Development of the Domain Name System." *ACM Computer Communications Review*, August 1988.

MOGU02 Mogul, J. "Clarifying the Fundamentals of HTTP." *Proceedings of the Eleventh International Conference on World Wide Web*, 2002.

Animations

Animations that illustrate SMTP, DNS, and HTTP are available at the Premium Web site. The reader is encouraged to view these animations to reinforce concepts from this chapter.

24.5 KEY TERMS, REVIEW QUESTIONS, AND PROBLEMS

Key Terms

Backus-Naur Form (BNF)	HTTP tunnel	recursive technique
base64 transfer encoding	Hypertext Transfer Protocol (HTTP)	resolver
domain		resource record (RR)
domain name	iterative technique	root name server
Domain Name System (DNS)	Multipurpose Internet Mail Extensions (MIME)	Simple Mail Transfer Protocol (SMTP)
electronic mail		
HTTP gateway	name server	Uniform Resource Locator (URL)
HTTP message	origin server	
HTTP proxy	radix-64 encoding	Zone

Review Questions

24.1 What is the difference between RFC 821 and RFC 822?

24.2 What are the SMTP and MIME standards?

24.3 What is the difference between a MIME content type and a MIME transfer encoding?

24.4 Briefly explain radix-64 encoding.

24.5 What is DNS?

24.6 What is the difference between a name server and a resolver in DNS?
24.7 What is a DNS resource record?
24.8 Give a brief description of DNS operation.
24.9 What is the difference between a domain and a zone?
24.10 Explain the difference between the recursive technique and the iterative technique in DNS.
24.11 What is meant by saying that HTTP is a stateless protocol?
24.12 Explain the differences among HTTP proxy, gateway, and tunnel.
24.13 What is the function of the cache in HTTP?

Problems

Note: For some of the problems in this chapter, you will need to consult the relevant RFCs.

24.1 Suppose that two persons in two different cities are sending and receiving e-mails. In the first situation, they are at home and are using their personal computers, which are directly connected to the Internet. In the second situation, they are using computers at their workplaces. Suppose that a workplace has a LAN and uses one mail server connected to the Internet. Users need to send and receive their emails using this mail server. Use diagrams to show how the various components of e-mail architecture are involved in each of the message transfers.

24.2 Give an example of how you can directly use SMTP to send an e-mail to a single recipient.

24.3 Two of the MIME headers of a message have the following contents: Content-Type: Multipart/Mixed, Content-Transfer-Encoding: 7 bits. What do you understand from this?

24.4 Suppose a single email message from email ID magenta@colors.net is to be sent to three recipients with the email IDs violet@colors.net, indigo@colors.net, and lilac@colors.net. What will be the SMTP conversation if lilac@colors.net is an invalid ID?

24.5 We've seen that the character sequence "<CR><LF>.<CR><LF>" indicates the end of mail data to an SMTP-server. What happens if the mail data itself contains that character sequence?

24.6 Users are free to define and use additional header fields other than the ones defined in RFC 822. Such header fields must begin with the string "X-". Why?

24.7 If you need to download only the text portion of a multimedia email, will you choose POP3 or IMAP4? Justify your choice.

24.8 Although TCP is a full-duplex protocol, SMTP uses TCP in a half-duplex fashion. The client sends a command and then stops and waits for the reply. How can this half-duplex operation fool the TCP slow-start mechanism when the network is running near capacity?

24.9 Identify the need for dynamic DNS in the current online climate.

24.10 A DNS resolver typically issues a query using UDP but may also use TCP. Is there a problem using TCP for this purpose? If so, what do you suggest is the solution? *Hint:* Consider the TCP and UDP headers.

24.11 Can you classify domain names according to their sequence of labels?

24.12 A DNS resolver has prior knowledge that the size of the response message is 1 KB. Does it use a UDP or TCP connection?

24.13 We query an authoritative name server for the example.com zone in order to get the IP address of www.example.com, the Web site of a large company. We get eight A records in response to our query. We repeat this query several times, and note that we continue getting the same eight A records, but in a different order each time. Suggest a reason why.

24.14   The dig tool provides easy interactive access to the DNS. The dig tool is available for UNIX and Windows operating systems. It can also be used from the Web. Here are two sites that, at the time of this writing, provided free access to dig:

http://www.gont.com.ar/tools/dig
http://www.webmaster-toolkit.com/dig.shtml

Use the dig tool to get the list of root servers.

24.15   A problem of the resolver with caching is that it may give outdated mapping information if the mapping is used for too long. What techniques may be used to counter this?

24.16   Choose a root server, and use the dig tool to send it a query for the IP address of www.example.com, with the RD (Recursion Desired) bit set. Does it support recursive lookups? Why or why not?

24.17   Type dig www.example.com A in order to get the IP address of www.example.com. What's the TTL of the A record returned in the response? Wait a while, and repeat the query. Why has the TTL changed?

24.18   With the widespread use of x-DSL and cable-modem technologies, many home users now host Web sites on their own desktop computers. As their IP addresses are dynamically assigned by their Internet service providers (ISPs), users must update their DNS records every time their IP addresses change (it's usually done by some computer software on the user machine that automatically contacts the name server to update the corresponding data whenever the assigned IP address changes). This service is usually called Dynamic DNS. However, in order for these updates to work as expected, there's one field of each resource record that must be set to a quite different value from the typical ones. Which one, and why?

24.19   Secondary name servers periodically query the primary to check whether the zone data has been updated. Regardless of how many resource records the zone data contains, the secondary name servers need to query the primary only one resource record to detect any changes on the zone data. Which resource record will they query? How will they use the requested information to detect changes?

24.20   A user on the host 170.210.17.145 is using a Web browser to visit www.example.com. In order to resolve the "www.example.com" domain to an IP address, a query is sent to an authoritative name server for the "example.com" domain. In response, the name server returns a list of four IP addresses in the following order {192.168.0.1, 128.0.0.1, 200.47.57.1, 170.210.10.130}. Even though it is the last IP address in the list returned by the name server, the Web browser creates a connection to 170.210.17.130. Why?

24.21   Before the deployment of DNS, a simple text file (HOSTS.TXT) centrally maintained at the SRI Network Information Center was used to enable mapping between host names and addresses. Each host connected to the Internet had to have an updated local copy of it to be able to use host names instead of having to cope directly with their IP addresses. Discuss the main advantages of the DNS over the old centralized HOSTS.TXT system.

24.22   A client using an HTTP connection intends to download five different small images from five different locations. How many times is a TCP connection made if they use HTTP 1.0? What improvement would they notice if HTTP 1.1 is used instead?

CHAPTER 25

INTERNET MULTIMEDIA SUPPORT

LEARNING OBJECTIVES

After studying this chapter, you should be able to:

♦ Understand the transmission requirements for real-time traffic.

♦ Present an overview of VoIP networks.

♦ Summarize the key elements of RTP.

♦ Explain the complementary roles of RTP and RTCP.

With the increasing availability of broadband access to the Internet has come an increased interest in Web-based and Internet-based multimedia applications. The term *multimedia* refers to the use of multiple forms of information, including text, still images, audio, and video. The reader may find it useful to review Section 2.6 before proceeding.

An in-depth discussion of multimedia applications is well beyond the scope of this book. In this chapter, we focus on a few key topics. First, we examine some of the key characteristics of real-time traffic. Next we look at SIP (Session Initiation Protocol) and its use to support voice over IP. Finally, we examine the Real-Time Transport Protocol.

25.1 REAL-TIME TRAFFIC

The widespread deployment of high-speed LANs and WANs and the increase in the line capacity on the Internet and other internets have opened up the possibility of using IP-based networks for the transport of real-time traffic. However, it is important to recognize that the requirements of real-time traffic differ from those of high-speed but non-real-time traffic.

With traditional Internet applications, such as file transfer, electronic mail, and client/server applications including the Web, the performance metrics of interest are generally throughput and delay. There is also a concern with reliability, and mechanisms are used to make sure that no data are lost, corrupted, or misordered during transit. By contrast, real-time applications are more concerned with timing issues. In most cases, there is a requirement that data be delivered at a constant rate equal to the sending rate. In other cases, a deadline is associated with each block of data, such that the data are not usable after the deadline has expired.

Real-Time Traffic Characteristics

Figure 25.1 illustrates a typical real-time environment. Here, a server is generating audio to be transmitted at 64 kbps. The digitized audio is transmitted in packets containing 160 octets of data, so that one packet is issued every 20 ms. These packets are passed through an internet and delivered to a multimedia PC, which plays the audio in real time as it arrives. However, because of the variable delay imposed by the Internet, the interarrival times between packets are not maintained at a fixed 20 ms at the destination. To compensate for this, the incoming packets are buffered, delayed slightly, and then released at a constant rate to the software that generates the audio.

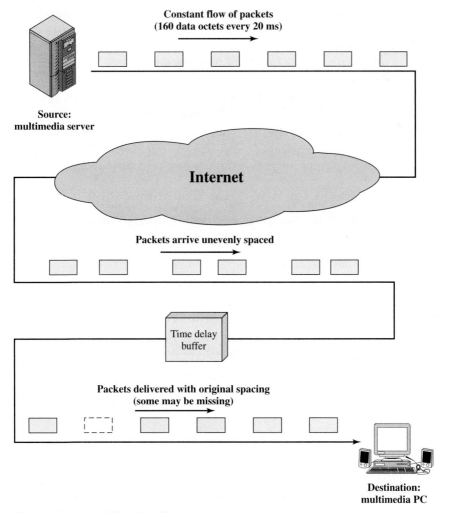

Figure 25.1 Real-Time Traffic

The compensation provided by the delay buffer is limited. To understand this, we need to define the concept of *delay jitter*, which is the maximum variation in delay experienced by packets in a single session. For example, if the minimum end-to-end delay seen by any packet is 1 ms and the maximum is 6 ms, then the delay jitter is 5 ms. As long as the time delay buffer delays incoming packets by at least 5 ms, then the output of the buffer will include all incoming packets. However, if the buffer delayed packets only by 4 ms, then any incoming packets that had experienced a relative delay of more than 4 ms (an absolute delay of more than 5 ms) would have to be discarded so as not to be played back out of order.

The description of real-time traffic so far implies a series of equal-size packets generated at a constant rate. This is not always the profile of the traffic. Figure 25.2 illustrates some of the common possibilities:

- **Continuous data source:** Fixed-size packets are generated at fixed intervals. This characterizes applications that constantly generate data, have few redundancies, and that are too important to compress in a lossy way. Examples are air traffic control radar and real-time simulations.

- **On/off source:** The source alternates between periods when fixed-size packets are generated at fixed intervals and periods of inactivity. A voice source, such as in telephony or audio conferencing, fits this profile.

- **Variable packet size:** The source generates variable-length packets at uniform intervals. An example is digitized video in which different frames may experience different compression ratios for the same output quality level.

Requirements for Real–Time Communication

[ARAS94] lists the following as desirable properties for real-time communication:

- Low jitter
- Low latency
- Ability to easily integrate non-real-time and real-time services
- Adaptable to dynamically changing network and traffic conditions
- Good performance for large networks and large numbers of connections
- Modest buffer requirements within the network
- High effective capacity utilization
- Low overhead in header bits per packet
- Low processing overhead per packet within the network and at the end system

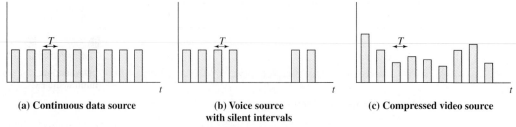

(a) Continuous data source   (b) Voice source with silent intervals   (c) Compressed video source

Figure 25.2 Real-Time Packet Transmission (based on [ARAS94])

These requirements are difficult to meet in a wide area IP-based network or internet. Neither TCP (Transport Control Protocol) nor UDP (User Datagram Protocol) by itself is appropriate. We will see that RTP provides a reasonable foundation for addressing these issues.

Hard versus Soft Real-Time Applications

A distinction needs to be made between hard and soft real-time communication applications. Soft real-time applications can tolerate the loss of some portion of the communicated data, while hard real-time applications have zero loss tolerance. In general, soft real-time applications impose fewer requirements on the network, and it is therefore permissible to focus on maximizing network utilization, even at the cost of some lost or misordered packets. In hard real-time applications, a deterministic upper bound on jitter and high reliability takes precedence over network utilization considerations.

25.2 VOICE OVER IP

We have referred a number of times in this text to the trend toward the convergence of data, voice, and video transmission using IP-based networks. This convergence enables the delivering of advanced services at lower cost for residential users, business customers of varying sizes, and service providers. One of the key technologies underlying this convergence is VoIP (voice over IP), which has become increasingly prevalent in organizations of all sizes.

In essence, VoIP is the transmission of speech across IP-based network. VoIP works by encoding voice information into a digital format, which can be carried across IP networks in discrete packets. VoIP has two main advantages over traditional telephony.

1. A VoIP system is usually cheaper to operate than an equivalent telephone system with a PBX and conventional telephone network service. There are several reasons for this. Whereas traditional telephone networks allocate dedicated circuits for voice communications using circuit switching, VoIP uses packet switching, allowing the sharing of transmission capacity. Further, packetized voice transmission fits well in the framework of the TCP/IP protocol suite, enabling the use of application- and transport-level protocols to support communications.

2. VoIP readily integrates with other services, such as combining Web access with telephone features through a single PC or terminal.

VoIP Signaling

Before voice can be transferred using VoIP, a call must be placed. In a traditional phone network, the caller enters the digits of the called number. The telephone number is processed by the provider's signaling system to ring the called number. With VoIP, the calling user (program or individual) supplies the phone number of a URI (Universal Resource Indicator, a form of URL), which then triggers a set of protocol interactions resulting in the placement of the call.

The heart of the call placement process for VoIP is the Session Initiation Protocol (SIP). SIP supports not only VoIP but also many multimedia applications. Section 25.3 discusses SIP.

VoIP Processing

Once a called party responds, a logical connection is established between the two parties (or more for a conference call), and voice data may be exchanged in both directions. Figure 25.3 illustrates the basic flow of voice data in one direction in a VoIP system. On the sending side, the analog voice signal is first converted into a digital bit stream and then segmented into packets. The packetization is performed, typically, by RTP. This protocol includes mechanisms for labeling the packets so that they can be reassembled in the proper order at the receiving end, plus a buffering function to smooth out reception and deliver the voice data in a continuous flow. The RTP packets are then transmitted across the Internet or a private internet using the User Datagram Protocol and IP protocols.

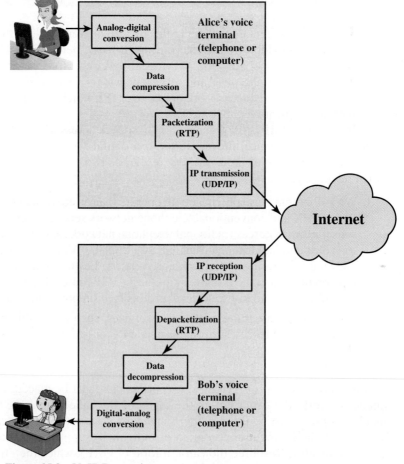

Figure 25.3 VoIP Processing

At the receiving end, the process is reversed. The packet payloads are reassembled by RTP and put into the proper order. The data are then decompressed and the digitized voice is processed by a digital-to-analog converter to produce analog signals for the receiver's telephone or headset speaker.

VoIP Context

Ultimately, VoIP using IP-based networks may replace the public circuit-switched networks in use today. But for the foreseeable future, VoIP must coexist with the existing telephony infrastructure. Figure 25.4 suggests some of the key elements involved in the coexistence of the older and newer technologies.

The deployment of the VoIP infrastructure has been accompanied by a variety of end-user products including the following:

- **Traditional telephone handset:** These corded or cordless units function much like a traditional telephone but are VoIP capable. They typically have many additional features, making use of a screen, and providing capabilities found in smart mobile phones.

- **Conferencing units:** These provide the same basic service of conventional conference calling phone systems. These units also allow users to coordinate other data communications services, such as text, graphics, video, and whiteboarding.

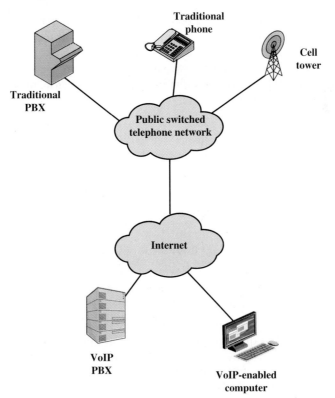

Figure 25.4   VoIP Context

- **Mobile units:** Smart phones and other cell phones with VoIP capability can tie directly into a VoIP network without going through any kind of gateway system.
- **Softphone:** The term *softphone* refers to software operating on a PC that implements VoIP. Typically, the PC is configured with a headset or a telephone that makes use of a USB connection to the PC.

There is a wide variety of infrastructure equipment developed to support VoIP. Here we mention two noteworthy types:

- **IP PBX:** The IP PBX is designed to support digital and analog phones and connect to IP-based networks using VoIP, as well as provide if needed a connection to the public switched telephone network using traditional technology.
- **Media gateway:** The media gateway connects different physical networks in order to provide end-to-end connectivity. An important type of media gateway connects a VoIP network to a circuit-switched telephone network, providing the necessary conversion and signaling.

The VoIP environment continues to evolve with a large number of products being developed for service providers, businesses, and residential/personal users.

25.3 SESSION INITIATION PROTOCOL

The Session Initiation Protocol (SIP), defined in RFC 3261, is an application-level control protocol for setting up, modifying, and terminating real-time sessions between participants over an IP data network. The key driving force behind SIP is to enable Internet telephony, also referred to as voice over IP (VoIP). SIP can support any type of single media or multimedia session, including teleconferencing.

SIP supports five facets of establishing and terminating multimedia communications:

- **User location:** Users can move to other locations and access their telephony or other application features from remote locations.
- **User availability:** Determination of the willingness of the called party to engage in communications.
- **User capabilities:** Determination of the media and media parameters to be used.
- **Session setup:** Set up point-to-point and multiparty calls, with agreed session parameters.
- **Session management:** Including transfer and termination of sessions, modifying session parameters, and invoking services.

SIP employs design elements developed for earlier protocols. SIP is based on an HTTP-like request/response transaction model. Each transaction consists of a client request that invokes a particular method, or function, on the server and at least one response. SIP uses most of the header fields, encoding rules, and status codes of HTTP. This provides a readable text-based format for displaying information. SIP also uses concepts similar to the recursive and iterative searches of DNS

(Domain Name System). SIP incorporates the use of a Session Description Protocol (SDP), which defines session content using a set of types similar to those used in MIME (Multipurpose Internet Mail Extension).

SIP Components and Protocols

An SIP network can be viewed of consisting of components defined on two dimensions: client/server and individual network elements. RFC 3261 defines **client** and **server** as follows:

- **Client:** A client is any network element that sends SIP requests and receives SIP responses. Clients may or may not interact directly with a human user. User agent clients and proxies are clients.
- **Server:** A server is a network element that receives requests in order to service them and sends back responses to those requests. Examples of servers are proxies, user agent servers, redirect servers, and registrars.

The individual elements of a standard SIP network are as follows:

- **User Agent:** Resides in every SIP end station. It acts in two roles:
  - **User agent client (UAC):** Issues SIP requests
  - **User agent server (UAS):** Receives SIP requests and generates a response that accepts, rejects, or redirects the request
- **Redirect Server:** Used during session initiation to determine the address of the called device. The redirect server returns this information to the calling device, directing the UAC to contact an alternate URI. This is analogous to iterative searches in DNS.
- **Proxy Server:** An intermediary entity that acts as both a server and a client for the purpose of making requests on behalf of other clients. A proxy server primarily plays the role of routing, which means its job is to ensure that a request is sent to another entity closer to the targeted user. Proxies are also useful for enforcing policy (e.g., making sure a user is allowed to make a call). A proxy interprets, and, if necessary, rewrites specific parts of a request message before forwarding it. This is analogous to recursive searches in DNS.
- **Registrar:** A server that accepts REGISTER requests and places the information it receives (the SIP address and associated IP address of the registering device) in those requests into the location service for the domain it handles.
- **Location Service:** A location service is used by a SIP redirect or proxy server to obtain information about a callee's possible location(s). For this purpose, the location service maintains a database of SIP-address/IP-address mappings.
- **Presence Server:** Accepts, stores, and distributes presence information. The presence server has two distinct sets of clients:
  - Presentities (producers of information) provide presence information to the server to be stored and distributed.
  - Watchers (consumers of information) receive presence information from the server.

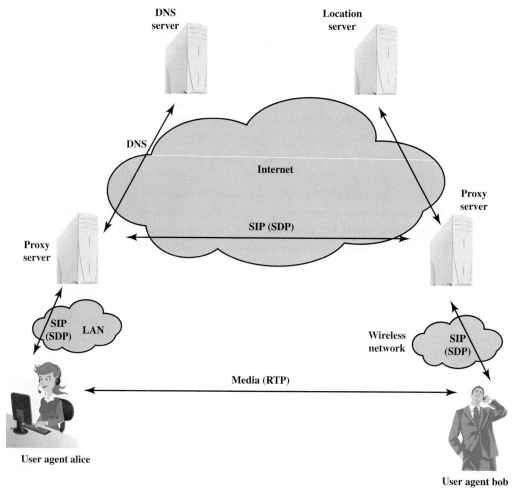

Figure 25.5   SIP Components and Protocols

The various servers are defined in RFC 3261 as logical devices. They may be implemented as separate servers configured on the Internet or they may be combined into a single application that resides in a physical server.

Figure 25.5 shows how some of the SIP components relate to one another and the protocols that are employed. A user agent acting as a client (in this case UAC alice) uses SIP to set up a session with a user agent that will act as a server (in this case UAS bob). The session initiation dialogue uses SIP and involves one or more proxy servers to forward requests and responses between the two user agents. The user agents also make use of the Session Description Protocol, which is used to describe the media session.

The proxy servers may also act as redirect servers as needed. If redirection is done, a proxy server will need to consult the location service database, which may be collocated with a proxy server or not. The communication between the proxy server and the location service is beyond the scope of the SIP standard. DNS is also an important part of SIP operation. Typically, a UAC will make a request using the domain name of the UAS, rather than an IP address. A proxy server will need to consult a DNS server to find a proxy server for the target domain.

SIP typically runs on top of UDP for performance reasons, and provides its own reliability mechanisms, but may also use TCP. If a secure, encrypted transport mechanism is desired, SIP messages may alternatively be carried over the Transport Layer Security (TLS) protocol, described in Chapter 27.

Associated with SIP is the Session Description Protocol, defined in RFC 4566. SIP is used to invite one or more participants to a session, while the SDP-encoded body of the SIP message contains information about what media encodings (e.g., voice, video) the parties can and will use. Once this information is exchanged and acknowledged, all participants are aware of the participants' IP addresses, available transmission capacity, and media type. Then data transmission begins, using an appropriate transport protocol. Typically, the Real-Time Transport Protocol (RTP), described subsequently, is used. Throughout the session, participants can make changes to session parameters, such as new media types or new parties to the session, using SIP messages.

SIP Uniform Resource Identifier

A resource within a SIP network is identified by a Uniform Resource Identifier (URI). Examples of communications resources include the following:

- A user of an online service
- An appearance on a multiline phone
- A mailbox on a messaging system
- A telephone number at a gateway service
- A group (such as "sales" or "helpdesk") in an organization

SIP URIs have a format based on e-mail address formats, namely user@ domain. There are two common schemes. An ordinary SIP URI is of the form

sip: bob@biloxi.com

The URI may also include a password, port number, and related parameters. If secure transmission is required, "sip:" is replaced by "sips:". In the latter case, SIP messages are transported over TLS.

Session Description Protocol

The Session Description Protocol (SDP) describes the content of sessions, including telephony, Internet radio, and multimedia applications. SDP includes information about the following [SCHU99]:

- **Media streams:** A session can include multiple streams of differing content. SDP currently defines audio, video, data, control, and application as stream types, similar to the MIME types used for Internet mail (Table 24.1).
- **Addresses:** Indicates the destination addresses, which may be a multicast address, for a media stream.

- **Ports:** For each stream, the UDP port numbers for sending and receiving are specified.
- **Payload types:** For each media stream type in use (e.g., telephony), the payload type indicates the media formats that can be used during the session.
- **Start and stop times:** These apply to broadcast sessions, like a television or radio program. The start, stop, and repeat times of the session are indicated.
- **Originator:** For broadcast sessions, the originator is specified, with contact information. This may be useful if a receiver encounters technical difficulties.

25.4 REAL-TIME TRANSPORT PROTOCOL (RTP)

The most widely used transport-level protocol is TCP. Although TCP has proven its value in supporting a wide range of distributed applications, it is not suited for use with real-time distributed applications. By a real-time distributed application, we mean one in which a source is generating a stream of data at a constant rate, and one or more destinations must deliver that data to an application at the same constant rate. Examples of such applications include audio and video conferencing, live video distribution (not for storage but for immediate play), shared workspaces, remote medical diagnosis, telephony, command and control systems, distributed interactive simulations, games, and real-time monitoring. A number of features of TCP disqualify it for use as the transport protocol for such applications:

1. TCP is a point-to-point protocol that sets up a connection between two endpoints. Therefore, it is not suitable for multicast distribution.
2. TCP includes mechanisms for retransmission of lost segments, which then arrive out of order. Such segments are not usable in most real-time applications.
3. TCP contains no convenient mechanism for associating timing information with segments, which is another real-time requirement.

The other widely used transport protocol, UDP, does not exhibit the first two characteristics listed but, like TCP, does not provide timing information. By itself, UDP does not provide any general-purpose tools useful for real-time applications.

Although each real-time application could include its own mechanisms for supporting real-time transport, there are a number of common features that warrant the definition of a common protocol. A protocol designed for this purpose is the Real-Time Transport Protocol (RTP), defined in RFC 3550. RTP is best suited to soft real-time communication. It lacks the necessary mechanisms to support hard real-time traffic.

This section provides an overview of RTP. We begin with a discussion of real-time transport requirements. Next, we examine the philosophical approach of RTP. The remainder of the section is devoted to the two protocols that make up RTP: The first is simply called RTP and is a data transfer protocol; the other is a control protocol known as RTCP (RTP Control Protocol).

RTP Protocol Architecture

In RTP, there is close coupling between the RTP functionality and the application-layer functionality. Indeed, RTP is best viewed as a framework that applications can use directly to implement a single protocol. Without the application-specific information, RTP is not a full protocol. On the other hand, RTP imposes a structure and defines common functions so that individual real-time applications are relieved of part of their burden.

RTP follows the principles of protocol architecture design outlined in a paper by Clark and Tennenhouse [CLAR90]. The two key concepts presented in that paper are application-level framing and integrated layer processing.

APPLICATION-LEVEL FRAMING In a traditional transport protocol, such as TCP, the responsibility for recovering from lost portions of data is performed transparently at the transport layer. [CLAR90] lists two scenarios in which it might be more appropriate for recovery from lost data to be performed by the application:

1. The application, within limits, may accept less than perfect delivery and continue unchecked. This is the case for real-time audio and video. For such applications, it may be necessary to inform the source in more general terms about the quality of the delivery rather than to ask for retransmission. If too much data are being lost, the source might perhaps move to a lower-quality transmission that places lower demands on the network, increasing the probability of delivery.

2. It may be preferable to have the application rather than the transport protocol provide data for retransmission. This is useful in the following contexts:

    a. The sending application may recompute lost data values rather than storing them.

    b. The sending application can provide revised values rather than simply retransmitting lost values, or send new data that "fix" the consequences of the original loss.

To enable the application to have control over the retransmission function, Clark and Tennenhouse propose that lower layers, such as presentation and transport, deal with data in units that the application specifies. The application should break the flow of data into application-level data units (ADUs), and the lower layers must preserve these ADU boundaries as they process the data. The application-level frame is the unit of error recovery. Thus, if a portion of an ADU is lost in transmission, the application will typically be unable to make use of the remaining portions. In such a case, the application layer will discard all arriving portions and arrange for retransmission of the entire ADU, if necessary.

INTEGRATED LAYER PROCESSING In a typical layered protocol architecture, such as TCP/IP or OSI, each layer of the architecture contains a subset of the functions to be performed for communications, and each layer must logically be structured as a separate module in end systems. Thus, on transmission, a block of data flows down through and is sequentially processed by each layer of the architecture. This structure restricts the implementer from invoking certain functions in parallel or out of the layered order to achieve greater efficiency. Integrated layer processing,

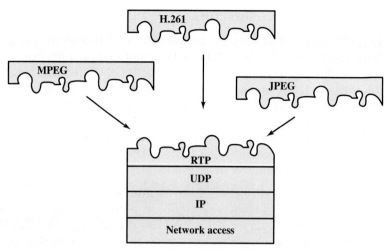

Figure 25.6 RTP Protocol Architecture [THOM96]

as proposed in [CLAR90], captures the idea that adjacent layers may be tightly coupled and that the implementer should be free to implement the functions in those layers in a tightly coupled manner.

The idea that a strict protocol layering may lead to inefficiencies has been propounded by a number of researchers. For example, [CROW92] examined the inefficiencies of running a remote procedure call (RPC) on top of TCP and suggested a tighter coupling of the two layers. The researchers argued that the integrated layer processing approach is preferable for efficient data transfer.

Figure 25.6 illustrates the manner in which RTP realizes the principle of integrated layer processing. RTP is designed to run on top of a connectionless transport protocol such as UDP. UDP provides the basic port addressing functionality of the transport layer. RTP contains further transport-level functions, such as sequencing. However, RTP by itself is not complete. It is completed by modifications and/or additions to the RTP headers to include application-layer functionality. The figure indicates that several different standards for encoding video data can be used in conjunction with RTP for video transmission.

RTP Data Transfer Protocol

We first look at the basic concepts of the RTP data transfer protocol and then examine the protocol header format. Throughout this section, the term *RTP* will refer to the RTP data transfer protocol.

RTP CONCEPTS RTP supports the transfer of real-time data among a number of participants in a session. A session is simply a logical association among two or more RTP entities that is maintained for the duration of the data transfer. A session is defined by the following:

- **RTP port number:** The destination port address is used by all participants for RTP transfers. If UDP is the lower layer, this port number appears in the Destination Port field (see Figure 2.6) of the UDP header.

- **RTCP port number:** The destination port address is used by all participants for RTCP transfers.
- **Participant IP addresses:** This can either be a multicast IP address, so that the multicast group defines the participants, or a set of unicast IP addresses.

The process of setting up a session is beyond the scope of RTP and RTCP.

Although RTP can be used for unicast real-time transmission, its strength lies in its ability to support multicast transmission. For this purpose, each RTP data unit includes a source identifier that identifies which member of the group generated the data. It also includes a timestamp so that the proper timing can be re-created on the receiving end using a delay buffer. RTP also identifies the payload format of the data being transmitted.

RTP allows the use of two kinds of RTP relays: translators and mixers. First we need to define the concept of relay. A relay operating at a given protocol layer is an intermediate system that acts as both a destination and a source in a data transfer. For example, suppose that system A wishes to send data to system B but cannot do so directly. Possible reasons are that B may be behind a firewall or B may not be able to use the format transmitted by A. In such a case, A may be able to send the data to an intermediate relay R. R accepts the data unit, makes any necessary changes or performs any necessary processing, and then transmits the data to B.

A **mixer** is an RTP relay that receives streams of RTP packets from one or more sources, combines these streams, and forwards a new RTP packet stream to one or more destinations. The mixer may change the data format or simply perform the mixing function. Because the timing among the multiple inputs is not typically synchronized, the mixer provides the timing information in the combined packet stream and identifies itself as the source of synchronization.

An example of the use of a mixer is to combine a number of on/off sources such as audio. Suppose that a number of systems are members of an audio session and each generates its own RTP stream. Most of the time only one source is active, although occasionally more than one source will be "speaking" at the same time. A new system may wish to join the session, but its link to the network may not be of sufficient capacity to carry all of the RTP streams. Instead, a mixer could receive all of the RTP streams, combine them into a single stream, and retransmit that stream to the new session member. If more than one incoming stream is active at one time, the mixer would simply sum their PCM values. The RTP header generated by the mixer includes the identifier(s) of the source(s) that contributed to the data in each packet.

The **translator** is a simple device that produces one or more outgoing RTP packets for each incoming RTP packet. The translator may change the format of the data in the packet or use a different lower-level protocol suite to transfer from one domain to another. Examples of translator use include the following:

- A potential recipient may not be able to handle a high-speed video signal used by the other participants. The translator converts the video to a lower-quality format requiring a lower data rate.

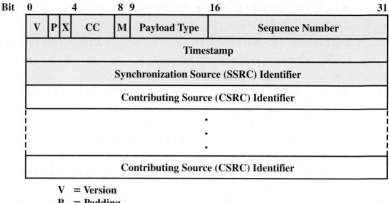

V = Version
P = Padding
X = Extension
CC= CSRC count
M = Marker

Figure 25.7   RTP Header

- An application-level firewall may prevent the forwarding of RTP packets. Two translators are used, one on each side of the firewall, with the outside one tunneling all multicast packets received through a secure connection to the translator inside the firewall. The inside translator then sends out RTP packets to a multicast group protected by the firewall.

- A translator can replicate an incoming multicast RTP packet and send it to a number of unicast destinations.

RTP FIXED HEADER   Each RTP packet includes a fixed header and may also include additional application-specific header fields. Figure 25.7 shows the fixed header. The first 12 octets (shaded portion) are always present and consist of the following fields:

- **Version (2 bits):** Current version is 2.
- **Padding (1 bit):** Indicates whether padding octets appear at the end of the payload. If so, the last octet of the payload contains a count of the number of padding octets. Padding is used if the application requires that the payload be an integer multiple of some length, such as 32 bits.
- **Extension (1 bit):** If set, the fixed header is followed by exactly one extension header, which is used for experimental extensions to RTP.
- **CSRC Count (4 bits):** The number of CSRC (contributing source) identifiers that follow the fixed header.
- **Marker (1 bit):** The interpretation of the marker bit depends on the payload type; it is typically used to indicate a boundary in the data stream. For video, it is set to mark the end of a frame. For audio, it is set to mark the beginning of a talk spurt.
- **Payload Type (7 bits):** Identifies the format of the RTP payload, which follows the RTP header.

- **Sequence Number (16 bits):** Each source starts with a random sequence number, which is incremented by one for each RTP data packet sent. This allows for loss detection and packet sequencing within a series of packets with the same timestamp. A number of consecutive packets may have the same timestamp if they are logically generated at the same time; an example is several packets belonging to the same video frame.
- **Timestamp (32 bits):** Corresponds to the generation instant of the first octet of data in the payload. The time units of this field depend on the payload type. The values must be generated from a local clock at the source.
- **Synchronization Source Identifier:** A randomly generated value that uniquely identifies the source within a session.

Following the fixed header, there may be one or more of the following field:

- **Contributing Source Identifier:** Identifies a contributing source for the payload. These identifiers are supplied by a mixer.

The Payload Type field identifies the media type of the payload and the format of the data, including the use of compression or encryption. In a steady state, a source should only use one payload type during a session but may change the payload type in response to changing conditions, as discovered by RTCP. Table 25.1 summarizes the payload types defined in RFC 3551.

RTP Control Protocol (RTCP)

The RTP data transfer protocol is used only for the transmission of user data, typically in multicast fashion among all participants in a session. A separate control protocol (RTCP) also operates in a multicast fashion to provide feedback to RTP data sources as well as all session participants. RTCP uses the same underlying

Table 25.1 Payload Types for Standard Audio and Video Encodings (RFC 3551)

0	PCMU audio		15	G728 audio
1	1016 audio		16–23	unassigned audio
2	G721 audio		24	unassigned video
3	GSM audio		25	CelB video
4	unassigned audio		26	JPEG video
5	DV14 audio (8 kHz)		27	unassigned
6	DV14 audio (16 kHz)		28	nv video
7	LPC audio		29–30	unassigned video
8	PCMA audio		31	H261 video
9	G722 audio		32	MPV video
10	L16 audio (stereo)		33	MP2T video
11	L16 audio (mono)		34–71	unassigned
12	QCELP wireless		72–76	reserved
13	Comfort noise		77–95	unassigned
14	MPA audio		96–127	dynamic

transport service as RTP (usually UDP) and a separate port number. Each participant periodically issues an RTCP packet to all other session members. RFC 3550 outlines four functions performed by RTCP:

- **Quality of Service (QoS) and congestion control:** RTCP provides feedback on the quality of data distribution. Because RTCP packets are multicast, all session members can assess how well other members are performing and receiving. Sender reports enable receivers to estimate data rates and the quality of the transmission. Receiver reports indicate any problems encountered by receivers, including missing packets and excessive jitter. For example, an audio–video application might decide to reduce the rate of transmission over low-speed links if the traffic quality over the links is not high enough to support the current rate. The feedback from receivers is also important in diagnosing distribution faults. By monitoring reports from all session recipients, a network manager can tell whether a problem is specific to a single user or more widespread.

- **Identification:** RTCP packets carry a persistent textual description of the RTCP source. This provides more information about the source of data packets than the random SSRC identifier and enables a user to associate multiple streams from different sessions. For example, separate sessions for audio and video may be in progress.

- **Session size estimation and scaling:** To perform the first two functions, all participants send periodic RTCP packets. The rate of transmission of such packets must be scaled down as the number of participants increases. In a session with few participants, RTCP packets are sent at the maximum rate of one every five seconds. RFC 3550 includes a relatively complex algorithm by which each participant limits its RTCP rate on the basis of the total session population. The objective is to limit RTCP traffic to less than 5% of total session traffic.

- **Session control:** RTCP optionally provides minimal session control information. An example is a participant identification to be displayed in the user interface.

An RTCP transmission consists of a number of separate RTCP packets bundled in a single UDP datagram (or other lower-level data unit). The following packet types are defined in RFC 3550:

- Sender Report (SR)
- Receiver Report (RR)
- Source Description (SDES)
- Goodbye (BYE)
- Application Specific

Figure 25.8 depicts the formats of these packet types. Each type begins with a 32-bit word containing the following fields:

- **Version (2 bits):** Current version is 2.
- **Padding (1 bit):** If set, indicates that this packet contains padding octets at the end of the control information. If so, the last octet of the padding contains a count of the number of padding octets.

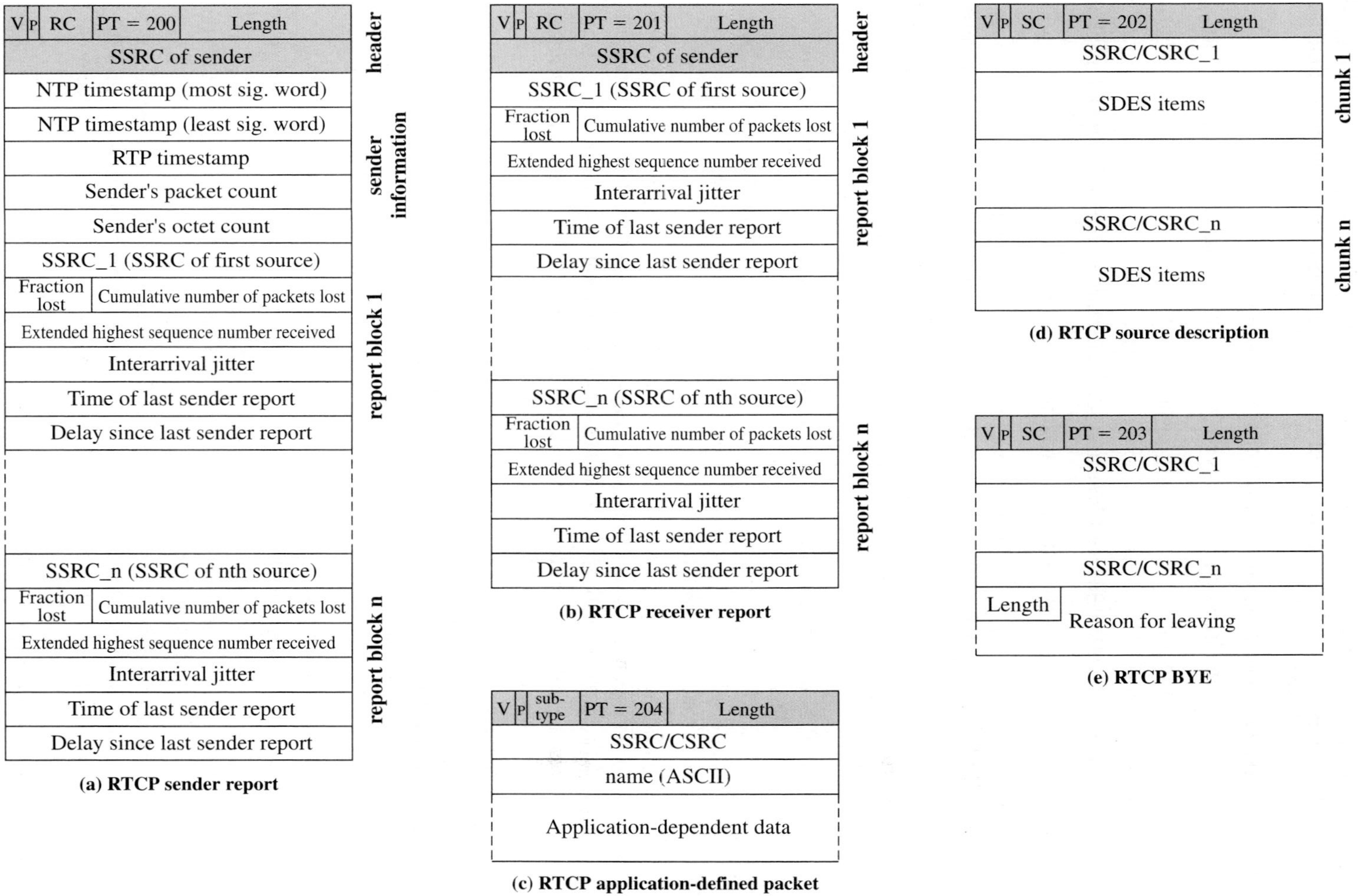

(d) RTCP source description

(e) RTCP BYE

(b) RTCP receiver report

(c) RTCP application-defined packet

(a) RTCP sender report

Figure 25.8 RTCP Formats

859

- **Count (5 bits):** The number of reception report blocks contained in an SR or RR packet (RC), or the number of source items contained in an SDES or BYE packet.
- **Packet Type (8 bits):** Identifies RTCP packet type.
- **Length (16 bits):** Length of this packet is 32-bit words, minus one.

In addition, the Sender Report and Receiver Report packets contain the following field:

- **Synchronization Source Identifier:** Identifies the source of this RTCP packet.

We now turn to a description of each packet type.

SENDER REPORT (SR) RTCP receivers provide reception quality feedback using a Sender Report or a Receiver Report, depending on whether the receiver is also a sender during this session. Figure 25.8a shows the format of a Sender Report. The Sender Report consists of a header, already described; a sender information block; and zero or more reception report blocks. The sender information block includes the following fields:

- **NTP Timestamp (64 bits):** The absolute wall clock time when this report was sent; this is an unsigned fixed-point number with the integer part in the first 32 bits and the fractional part in the last 32 bits. This may be used by the sender in combination with timestamps returned in receiver reports to measure round-trip time to those receivers.
- **RTP Timestamp (32 bits):** This is the relative time used to create timestamps in RTP data packets. This lets recipients place this report in the appropriate time sequence with RTP data packets from this source.
- **Sender's Packet Count (32 bits):** Total number of RTP data packets transmitted by this sender so far in this session.
- **Sender's Octet Count (32 bits):** Total number of RTP payload octets transmitted by this sender so far in this session.

Following the sender information block are zero or more reception report blocks. One reception block is included for each source from which this participant has received data during this session. Each block includes the following fields:

- **SSRC_n (32 bits):** Identifies the source referred to by this report block.
- **Fraction lost (8 bits):** The fraction of RTP data packets from SSRC_n lost since the previous SR or RR packet was sent.
- **Cumulative Number of Packets Lost (24 bits):** Total number of RTP data packets from SSRC_n lost during this session.
- **Extended Highest Sequence Number Received (32 bits):** The least significant 16 bits record the highest RTP data sequence number received from SSRC_n. The most significant 16 bits record the number of times the sequence number has wrapped back to zero.
- **Interarrival Jitter (32 bits):** An estimate of the jitter experienced on RTP data packets from SSRC_n, explained later.

- **Last SR Timestamp (32 bits):** The middle 32 bits of the NTP timestamp in the last SR packet received from SSRC_n. This captures the least significant half of the integer and the most significant half of the fractional part of the time-stamp and should be adequate.
- **Delay Since Last SR (32 bits):** The delay, expressed in units of 2^{-16} s, between receipt of the last SR packet from SSRC_n and the transmission of this report block. These last two fields can be used by a source to estimate round-trip time to a particular receiver.

Recall that delay jitter was defined as the maximum variation in delay experienced by packets in a single session. There is no simple way to measure this quantity at the receiver, but it is possible to estimate the average jitter in the following way. At a particular receiver, define the following parameters for a given source:

$S(I)$ = Timestamp from RTP data packet I.

$R(I)$ = Time of arrival for RTP data packet I, expressed in RTP time stamp units. The receiver must use the same clock frequency (increment interval) as the source but need not synchronize time values with the source.

$D(I)$ = The difference between the interarrival time at the receiver and the spacing between adjacent RTP data packets leaving the source.

$J(I)$ = Estimated average interarrival jitter up to the receipt of RTP data packet I.

The value of $D(I)$ is calculated as

$$D(I) = (R(I) - R(I - 1)) - (S(I) - S(I - 1))$$

Thus, $D(I)$ measures how much the spacing between arriving packets differs from the spacing between transmitted packets. In the absence of jitter, the spacings will be the same and $D(I)$ will have a value of 0. The interarrival jitter is calculated continuously as each data packet I is received, according to the formula

$$J(I) = \frac{15}{16} J(I - 1) + \frac{1}{16} |D(I)|$$

In this equation, $J(I)$ is calculated as an exponential average[1] of observed values of $D(I)$. Only a small weight is given to the most recent observation, so that temporary fluctuations do not invalidate the estimate.

The values in the Sender Report enable senders, receivers, and network managers to monitor conditions on the network as they relate to a particular session. For example, packet loss values give an indication of persistent congestion, while the jitter measures transient congestion. The jitter measure may provide a warning of increasing congestion before it leads to packet loss.

---

[1] For comparison, see Equation (22.3).

Table 25.2   SDES Types (RFC 3550)

Value	Name	Description
0	END	End of SDES list
1	CNAME	Canonical name: unique among all participants within one RTP session
2	NAME	Real user name of the source
3	EMAIL	E-mail address
4	PHONE	Telephone number
5	LOC	Geographic location
6	TOOL	Name of application generating the stream
7	NOTE	Transient message describing the current state of the source
8	PRIV	Private experimental or application-specific extensions

RECEIVER REPORT *(RR)*   The format for the Receiver Report (Figure 25.8b) is the same as that for a Sender Report, except that the Packet Type field has a different value and there is no sender information block.

SOURCE DESCRIPTION *(SDES)*   The Source Description packet (Figure 25.8d) is used by a source to provide more information about itself. The packet consists of a 32-bit header followed by zero or more chunks, each of which contains information describing this source. Each chunk begins with an identifier for this source or for a contributing source. This is followed by a list of descriptive items. Table 25.2 lists the types of descriptive items defined in RFC 3550.

GOODBYE *(BYE)*   The BYE packet indicates that one or more sources are no longer active. This confirms to receivers that a prolonged silence is due to departure rather than network failure. If a BYE packet is received by a mixer, it is forwarded with the list of sources unchanged. The format of the BYE packet consists of a 32-bit header followed by one or more source identifiers. Optionally, the packet may include a textual description of the reason for leaving.

APPLICATION-DEFINED PACKET   This packet is intended for experimental use for functions and features that are application specific. Ultimately, an experimental packet type that proves generally useful may be assigned a packet type number and become part of the standardized RTCP.

25.5 RECOMMENDED READING

[SPAR07] and [SCHU98] are good overviews of SIP. [GOOD02] and [SCHU99] discuss SIP in the context of VoIP. [DIAN02] looks at SIP in the context of the support of multimedia services over the Internet. [SHER04] provides a readable overview of VoIP.

DIAN02 Dianda, J.; Gurbani, V.; and Jones, M. "Session Initiation Protocol Services Architecture." *Bell Labs Technical Journal*, Volume 7, Number 1, 2002.

GOOD02 Goode, B. "Voice Over Internet Protocol (VoIP)." *Proceedings of the IEEE*, September 2002.

SCHU98 Schulzrinne, H., and Rosenberg, J. "The Session Initiation Protocol: Providing Advanced Telephony Access Across the Internet." *Bell Labs Technical Journal*, October–December 1998.

SCHU99 Schulzrinne, H., and Rosenberg, J. "The IETF Internet Telephony Architecture and Protocols." *IEEE Network*, May/June 1999.

SHER04 Sherburne, P., and Fitzgerald, C. "You Don't Know Jack About VoIP." *ACM Queue*, September 2004.

SPAR07 Sparks, R., and Systems, E. "SIP—Basics and Beyond." *ACM Queue*, March 2007.

25.6 KEY TERMS, REVIEW QUESTIONS, AND PROBLEMS

Key Terms

Real-Time Transport Protocol (RTP)	Session Description Protocol (SDP)	SIP proxy server
RTP Control Protocol (RTCP)	Session Initiation Protocol (SIP)	SIP redirect server
	SIP location service	SIP registrar
		voice over IP (VoIP)

Review Questions

25.1 What are the five key services provided by SIP?
25.2 List and briefly define the major components in an SIP network.
25.3 What is the Session Description Protocol?
25.4 What are some desirable properties for real-time communications?
25.5 What is the difference between hard and soft real-time applications?
25.6 What is the purpose of RTP?
25.7 What is the difference between RTP and RTCP?

Problems

25.1 A single video source transmits 30 frames per second, each containing 2 Mbits of data. The data experiences a delay jitter of 1 s. What size of delay buffer is required at the destination to eliminate the jitter?

25.2 Argue the effectiveness, or lack thereof, of using RTP as a means of alleviating network congestion for multicast traffic.

25.3 While sending an audio file, the difference in milliseconds between the interarrival time at the receiving end and the spacing at the source of adjacent RTP data packets for 30 observations is {4, 6, 7, 5, 8, 6, 5, 3, 3, 4, 4, 6, 7, 12, 9, 6, 5, 4, 3, 4, 5, 6, 5, 8, 14, 6, 5, 3, 3, 4}. What is the exponential average interarrival jitter?

25.4 Illustrate how the last two fields in an RTCP SR or RR receiver report block can be used to calculate round-trip propagation time.

APPENDIX

FOURIER ANALYSIS

In this appendix, we provide an overview of key concepts in Fourier analysis.

A.1 FOURIER SERIES REPRESENTATION OF PERIODIC SIGNALS

With the aid of a good table of integrals, it is a remarkably simple task to determine the frequency domain nature of many signals. We begin with periodic signals. Any periodic signal can be represented as a sum of sinusoids, known as a Fourier series:[1]

$$x(t) = \frac{A_0}{2} + \sum_{n=1}^{\infty} [A_n \cos{(2\pi n f_0 t)} + B_n \sin{(2\pi n f_0 t)}]$$

where f_0 is the reciprocal of the period of the signal ($f_0 = 1/T$). The frequency f_0 is referred to as the **fundamental frequency** or **fundamental harmonic**; integer multiples of f_0 are referred to as **harmonics**. Thus a periodic signal with period T consists of the fundamental frequency $f_0 = 1/T$ plus integer multiples of that frequency. If $A_0 \neq 0$, then $x(t)$ has a **dc component**.

The values of the coefficients are calculated as follows:

$$A_0 = \frac{2}{T} \int_0^T x(t)\, dt$$

[1]Mathematicians typically write Fourier series and transform expressions using the variable w_0, which has a dimension of radians per second and where $w_0 = 2\pi f_0$. For physics and engineering, the f_0 formulation is preferred; it makes for simpler expressions, and it is intuitively more satisfying to have frequency expressed in Hz rather than radians per second.

864

$$A_n = \frac{2}{T} \int_0^T x(t) \cos(2\pi n f_0 t) \, dt$$

$$B_n = \frac{2}{T} \int_0^T x(t) \sin(2\pi n f_0 t) \, dt$$

This form of representation, known as the sine-cosine representation, is the easiest form to compute but suffers from the fact that there are two components at each frequency. A more meaningful representation, the amplitude-phase representation, takes the form

$$x(t) = \frac{C_0}{2} + \sum_{n=1}^{\infty} C_n \cos(2\pi n f_0 t + \theta_n)$$

This relates to the earlier representation as follows:

$$C_0 = A_0$$

$$C_n = \sqrt{A_n^2 + B_n^2}$$

$$\theta_n = \tan^{-1}\left(2\frac{-B_n}{A_n}\right)$$

Examples of the Fourier series for periodic signals are shown in Figure A.1.

A.2 FOURIER TRANSFORM REPRESENTATION OF APERIODIC SIGNALS

For a periodic signal, we have seen that its spectrum consists of discrete frequency components, at the fundamental frequency and its harmonics. For an aperiodic signal, the spectrum consists of a continuum of frequencies. This spectrum can be defined by the Fourier transform. For a signal $x(t)$ with a spectrum $X(f)$, the following relationships hold:

$$x(t) = \int_{-\infty}^{\infty} X(f) e^{j2\pi ft} df$$

$$X(f) = \int_{-\infty}^{\infty} X(t) e^{-j2\pi ft} dt$$

where $j = \sqrt{-1}$. The presence of an imaginary number in the equations is a matter of convenience. The imaginary component has a physical interpretation having to do with the phase of a waveform, and a discussion of this topic is beyond the scope of this book

Figure A.2 presents some examples of Fourier transform pairs.

Power Spectral Density and Bandwidth

The absolute bandwidth of any time-limited signal is infinite. In practical terms, however, most of the power in a signal is concentrated in some finite band, and

Signal Fourier Series

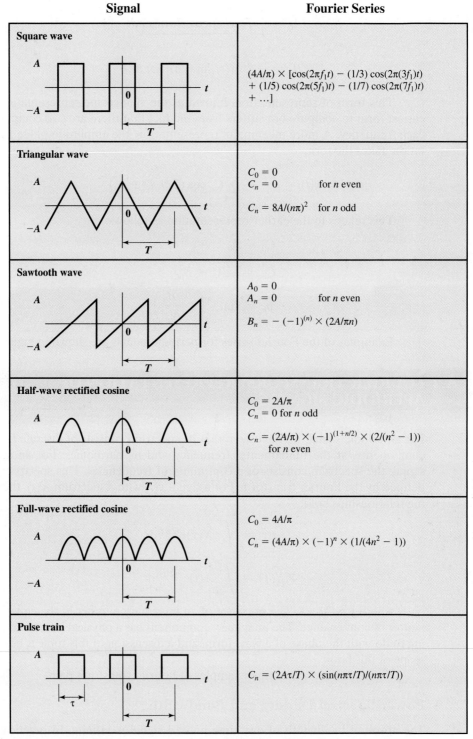

Square wave

$(4A/\pi) \times [\cos(2\pi f_1 t) - (1/3) \cos(2\pi(3f_1)t)$
$+ (1/5) \cos(2\pi(5f_1)t) - (1/7) \cos(2\pi(7f_1)t)$
$+ \ldots]$

Triangular wave

$C_0 = 0$
$C_n = 0 \qquad$ for n even

$C_n = 8A/(n\pi)^2 \quad$ for n odd

Sawtooth wave

$A_0 = 0$
$A_n = 0 \qquad$ for n even

$B_n = -(-1)^{(n)} \times (2A/\pi n)$

Half-wave rectified cosine

$C_0 = 2A/\pi$
$C_n = 0$ for n odd

$C_n = (2A/\pi) \times (-1)^{(1+n/2)} \times (2/(n^2 - 1))$
$\qquad$ for n even

Full-wave rectified cosine

$C_0 = 4A/\pi$

$C_n = (4A/\pi) \times (-1)^n \times (1/(4n^2 - 1))$

Pulse train

$C_n = (2A\tau/T) \times (\sin(n\pi\tau/T)/(n\pi\tau/T))$

Figure A.1 Some Common Periodic Signals and Their Fourier series

Signal $x(t)$ **Fourier Transform $X(f)$**

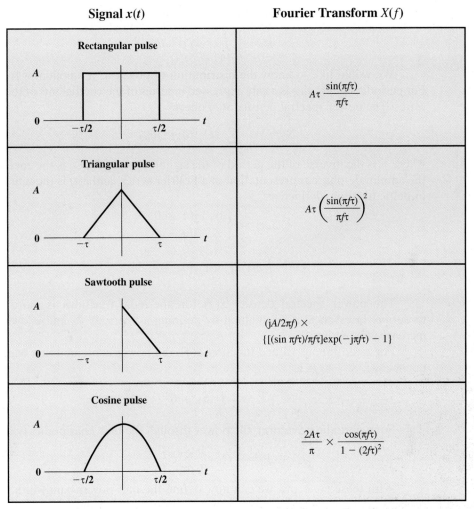

Figure A.2   Some Common Aperiodic Signals and Their Fourier Transforms

the effective bandwidth consists of that portion of the spectrum that contains most of the power. To make this concept precise, we need to define the power spectral density (PSD). In essence, the PSD describes the power content of a signal as a function of frequency, so that it shows how much power is present over various frequency bands.

First, we observe the power in the time domain. A function $x(t)$ usually specifies a signal in terms of either voltage or current. In either case, the instantaneous power in the signal is proportional to $|x(t)|^2$. We define the average power of a time-limited signal as

$$P = \frac{1}{t_1 - t_2} \int_{t_1}^{t_2} |x(t)|^2 \, dt$$

For a periodic signal the average power in one period is

$$P = \frac{1}{T} \int_0^T |x(t)|^2 \, dt$$

We would like to know the distribution of power as a function of frequency. For periodic signals, this is easily expressed in terms of the coefficients of the Fourier series. The power spectral density $S(f)$ obeys

$$S(f) = \sum_{n=-\infty}^{\infty} |C_n|^2 \delta(f - nf_0)$$

where f_0 is the inverse of the period of the signal ($f_0 = 1/T$), C_n is the coefficient in the amplitude-phase representation of a Fourier series, and $\delta(t)$ is the unit impulse, or delta, function, defined as:

$$\delta(t) = \begin{cases} 0 & \text{if } t \neq 0 \\ \infty & \text{if } t = 0 \end{cases}$$

$$\int_{-\infty}^{\infty} \delta(t) dt = 1$$

The power spectral density $S(f)$ for aperiodic functions is more difficult to define. In essence, it is obtained by defining a "period" T_0 and allowing T_0 to increase without limit.

For a continuous valued function $S(f)$, the power contained in a band of frequencies, $f_1 < f < f_2$, is

$$P = 2 \int_{f_1}^{f_2} S(f) \, df$$

For a periodic waveform, the power through the first j harmonics is

$$P = \frac{1}{4} C_0^2 + \frac{1}{2} \sum_{n=1}^{j} C_n^2$$

With these concepts, we can now define the half-power bandwidth, which is perhaps the most common bandwidth definition. The half-power bandwidth is the interval between frequencies at which $S(f)$ has dropped to half of its maximum value of power, or 3 dB below the peak value.

A.3 RECOMMENDED READING

A very accessible treatment of Fourier series and Fourier transforms is [JAME11]. For a thorough understanding of Fourier series and transforms, the book to read is [KAMM07]. [BHAT05] is a useful short introduction to Fourier series.

BHAT05   Bhatia, R. *Fourier Series.* Washington, DC: Mathematical Association of America, 2005.

JAME11   James, J. *A Student's Guide to Fourier Transforms.* Cambridge, England: Cambridge University Press, 2011.

KAMM07   Kammler, D. *A First Course in Fourier Analysis.* Cambridge, England: Cambridge University Press, 2007.

PROJECTS AND OTHER STUDENT EXERCISES FOR TEACHING DATA AND COMPUTER COMMUNICATIONS

Many instructors believe that research or implementation projects are crucial to the clear understanding of the concepts of data and computer communications. Without projects, it may be difficult for students to grasp some of the basic concepts and interactions among components. Projects reinforce the concepts introduced in the book, give the student a greater appreciation of how protocols and transmission schemes work, and can motivate students and give them confidence that they have mastered the material.

In this text, I have tried to present the concepts as clearly as possible and have provided nearly 400 homework problems to reinforce those concepts. Many instructors will wish to supplement this material with projects. This appendix provides some guidance in that regard and describes the support material available in the **Instructor's Resource Center (IRC)** for this book, accessible from Pearson for instructors. The support material covers nine types of projects and other student exercises:

- Animations and animation assignments
- Practical exercises
- Sockets programming projects
- Wireshark projects
- Simulation projects
- Performance modeling projects
- Research projects

- Reading/report assignments
- Writing assignments
- Discussion topics

B.1 ANIMATIONS AND ANIMATION ASSIGNMENTS

Animations provide a powerful tool for understanding the complex mechanisms discussed in this book, including forward error correction, signal encoding, and protocols. Over 150 Web-based animations are used to illustrate many of the data communications and protocol concepts in this book. The animations are available at the Premium Web site. For those chapters for which animations are available, the icon next to this paragraph appears at the beginning of the chapter.

Twelve of the animations have been designed to allow for two types of assignments. First, the student can be given a specific set of steps to invoke and watch the animation, and then be asked to analyze and comment on the results. Second, the student can be given a specific end point and required to devise a sequence of steps that achieve the desired result. The IRC includes a set of assignments for each of these animations, plus suggested solutions so that instructors can assess the student's work. These animations were developed at the University of Stirling in Scotland by Iain Robin and Ken Turner, with contributions from Paul Johnson and Kenneth Whyte. Larry Tan of the University of Stirling developed the animation assignments.

B.2 PRACTICAL EXERCISES

The IRC includes Web pages that provide a set of practical exercises for an introduction to the use of IP over a LAN. The exercises naturally follow one another and build on the experience of the previous exercises. They do not, however, need to be attempted one after another. The four exercises may more easily be done on four separate occasions. The practical exercises are designed to help the student understand the operation of an Ethernet LAN and an IP network. The exercises involve using simple network commands available on most computers. About an hour is needed to perform all four exercises. The exercises cover the following topics: your own network connection, computers on your LAN, computers on remote networks, and the Internet.

B.3 SOCKETS PROJECTS

The Berkeley Sockets Interface is the de facto standard application programming interface (API) for developing networking applications, spanning a wide range of operating systems. The Sockets API provides generic access to interprocess communications services. Thus, the sockets capability is ideally suited for students to learn the principles of protocols and distributed applications by hands-on program development.

The IRC includes a set of programming projects together with sample solution programs.

B.4 WIRESHARK PROJECTS

Wireshark, formerly known as Ethereal, is used by network professionals around the world for troubleshooting, analysis, software and protocol development, and education. It has all of the standard features you would expect in a protocol analyzer and several features not seen in any other product. Its open-source license allows talented experts in the networking community to add enhancements. It runs on all popular computing platforms, including UNIX, Linux, Windows, and Mac OS X.

Wireshark is ideal for allowing students to study the behavior of protocols not only because of its many features and multiplatform capability but also because students may subsequently use Wireshark in their professional life.

The IRC includes a Student User's Manual and a set of project assignments for Wireshark created specifically for use with the book. In addition, there is a very useful video tutorial that introduces the student to the use of Wireshark.

Michael Harris of Indiana University initially developed the Ethereal exercises and user's guide. Dave Bremer of Otago Polytechnic in New Zealand updated the material for the most recent Wireshark release; he also developed the online video tutorial.

B.5 SIMULATION AND MODELING PROJECTS

An excellent way to obtain a grasp of the operation of communication protocols and network configurations, and to study and appreciate some of the design trade-offs and performance implications, is by simulating key elements. A tool that is useful for this purpose is *cnet*.

Compared to actual hardware/software implementation, simulation provides two advantages for both research and educational use:

- With simulation, it is easy to modify various elements of a network configuration or various features of a protocol, to vary the performance characteristics of various components and then to analyze the effects of such modifications.

- Simulation provides for detailed performance statistics collection, which can be used to understand performance trade-offs.

The *cnet* network simulator [MCDO91] enables experimentation with various data link layer, network layer, routing and transport layer protocols, and with various network configurations. It has been specifically designed for undergraduate computer networking courses and used worldwide by thousands of students since 1991.

The *cnet* simulator was developed by Professor Chris McDonald at the University of Western Australia. Professor McDonald has developed a Student User's Manual and a set of project assignments specifically for use with *Data and Computer Communications* and available to professors on request.

The *cnet* simulator runs under a variety of UNIX and Linux platforms. The software can be downloaded from the *cnet* Web site. It is available at no cost for noncommercial use.

B.6 PERFORMANCE MODELING

An alternative to simulation for assessing the performance of a communications system or networking protocol is analytic modeling. As used here, a nalytic modeling refers to tools for doing queuing analysis, as well as tools for doing simple statistical tests on network traffic data and tools for generating time series for analysis.

A powerful and easy-to-use set of tools has been developed by Professor Kenneth Christensen at the University of South Florida. His *tools page* contains downloadable tools primarily related to performance evaluation of computer networks and to TCP/IP sockets programming. Each tool is written in ANSI C. The format for each tool is the same, with the program header describing tool purpose, general notes, sample input, sample output, build instructions, execution instructions, and author/contact information. The code is documented with extensive inline comments and header blocks for all functions. The goal for each tool is that it can serve as a teaching tool for the concept implemented by the tool (and as a model for good programming practices). Thus, the emphasis is on simplicity and clarity. It is assumed that the student will have access to a C compiler and have at least moderate experience in C programming.

Professor Christensen has developed a Student User's Manual and a set of project assignments specifically for use with *Data and Computer Communications* and available to professors on request. The software can be downloaded from the *tools* Web site. It is available at no cost for noncommercial use.

In addition, OPNET, a professional modeling tool for networking configurations, can be used. An academic version is available and a student lab manual prepared for this book is available from Pearson.

B.7 RESEARCH PROJECTS

An effective way of reinforcing basic concepts from the course and for teaching students research skills is to assign a research project. Such a project could involve a literature search as well as a Web search of vendor products, research lab activities, and standardization efforts. Projects could be assigned to teams or, for smaller projects, to individuals. In any case, it is best to require some sort of project proposal early in the term, giving the instructor time to evaluate the proposal for appropriate topic and appropriate level of effort. Student handouts for research projects should include the following:

- A format for the proposal
- A format for the final report
- A schedule with intermediate and final deadlines
- A list of possible project topics

The students can select one of the listed topics or devise their own comparable project. The IRC includes a suggested format for the proposal and final report plus a list of possible research topics.

B.8 READING/REPORT ASSIGNMENTS

Another excellent way to reinforce concepts from the course and to give students research experience is to assign papers from the literature to be read and analyzed. The IRC includes a suggested list of papers, one or two per chapter, to be assigned. A PDF copy of each of the papers is available at box.com/dcc10e. The IRC also includes a suggested assignment wording.

B.9 WRITING ASSIGNMENTS

Writing assignments can have a powerful multiplier effect in the learning process in a technical discipline such as cryptography and network security. Adherents of the Writing Across the Curriculum (WAC) movement (http://wac.colostate.edu/) report substantial benefits of writing assignments in facilitating learning. Writing assignments lead to more detailed and complete thinking about a particular topic. In addition, writing assignments help to overcome the tendency of students to pursue a subject with a minimum of personal engagement, just learning facts and problem-solving techniques without obtaining a deep understanding of the subject matter.

The IRC contains a number of suggested writing assignments, organized by chapter. Instructors may ultimately find that this is an important part of their approach to teaching the material. I would greatly appreciate any feedback on this area and any suggestions for additional writing assignments.

B.10 DISCUSSION TOPICS

One way to provide a collaborative experience is discussion topics, a number of which are included in the IRC. Each topic relates to material in the book. The instructor can set it up so that students can discuss a topic in a class setting, an online chat room, or a message board. Again, I would greatly appreciate any feedback on this area and any suggestions for additional discussion topics.

REFERENCES

ABBREVIATIONS

ACM	Association for Computing Machinery
IBM	International Business Machines Corporation
IEEE	Institute of Electrical and Electronics Engineers
NIST	National Institute of Standards and Technology

ADAM91   Adamek, J. *Foundations of Coding.* New York: Wiley, 1991.

ALSA13   Alsabbagh, E.; Yu, H.; and Gallagher, K. "802.11ac Design Consideration for Mobile Devices." *Microwave Journal*, February 2013.

ANDE95   Anderson, J.; Rappaport, T.; and Yoshida, S. "Propagation Measurements and Models for Wireless Communications Channels." *IEEE Communications Magazine*, January 1995.

ARAS94   Aras, C.; Kurose, J.; Reeves, D.; and Schulzrinne, H. "Real-Time Communication in Packet-Switched Networks." *Proceedings of the IEEE*, January 1994.

ASH90   Ash, R. *Information Theory.* New York: Dover, 1990.

BAI12   Bai, D., et al. "LTE-Advanced Modem Design: Challenges and Perspectives." *IEEE Communications Magazine*, February 2012.

BAKE12   Baker, M. "From LTE-Advanced to the Future." *IEEE Communications Magazine*, February 2012.

BALL89   Ballart, R., and Ching, Y. "SONET: Now It's the Standard Optical Network." *IEEE Communications Magazine*, March 1989.

BARA02   Baran, P. "The Beginnings of Packet Switching: Some Underlying Concepts." *IEEE Communications Magazine*, July 2002.

BEIJ06   Beijnum, I. "IPv6 Internals." *The Internet Protocol Journal*, September 2006.

BELL90   Bellcore (Bell Communications Research). *Telecommunications Transmission Engineering, Volume 2: Facilities.* 1990

BELL00   Bellamy, J. *Digital Telephony.* New York: Wiley, 2000.

BENE64   Benice, R. "An Analysis of Retransmission Systems." *IEEE Transactions on Communication Technology*, December 1964.

BENN48   Bennet, W. "Noise in PCM Systems." *Bell Labs Record*, December 1948.

BERA08   Beradinelli, G., et al. "OFDMA vs SC-FDMA: Performance Comparison in Local Area IMT-A Scenarios." *IEEE Wireless Communications*, October 2008.

BERN00   Bernet, Y. "The Complementary Roles of RSVP and Differentiated Services in the Full-Service QoS Network." *IEEE Communications Magazine*, February 2000.

BERL80   Berlekamp, E. "The Technology of Error-Correcting Codes." *Proceedings of the IEEE*, May 1980.

BERL87   Berlekamp, E.; Peile, R.; and Pope, S. "The Application of Error Control to Communications." *IEEE Communications Magazine*, April 1987.

BERT92   Bertsekas, D., and Gallager, R. *Data Networks.* Englewood Cliffs, NJ: Prentice Hall, 1992.

BERT94   Bertoni, H.; Honcharenko, W.; Maciel, L.; and Xia, H. "UHF Propagation Prediction for Wireless Personal Communications." *Proceedings of the IEEE*, September 1994.

BHAR83   Bhargava, V. "Forward Error Correction Schemes for Digital Communications." *IEEE Communications Magazine*, January 1983.

BHAT05   Bhatia, R. *Fourier Series.* Washington, DC: Mathematical Association of America, 2005.

BLAC00   Black, U. *IP Routing Protocols: RIP, OSPF, BGP, PNNI & Cisco Routing Protocols.* Upper Saddle River, NJ: Prentice Hall, 2000.

BOEH90   Boehm, R. "Progress in Standardization of SONET." *IEEE LCS*, May 1990.

BORE97   Borella, M., et al. "Optical Components for WDM Lightwave Networks." *Proceedings of the IEEE*, August 1997.

BOUI02   Bouillet, E.; Mitra, D.; and Ramakrishnan, K. "The Structure and Management of Service Level Agreements in Networks." *IEEE Journal on Selected Areas in Communications*, May 2002.

BRAD98   Braden, B., et al. *Recommendations on Queue Management and Congestion Avoidance in the Internet.* RFC 2309, April 1998.

BUX80   Bux, W.; Kummerle, K.; and Truong, H. "Balanced HDLC Procedures: A Performance Analysis." *IEEE Transactions on Communications*, November 1980.

CARN99   Carne, E. *Telecommunications Primer: Data, Voice, and Video Communications.* Upper Saddle River, NJ: Prentice Hall, 1999.

CARP02   Carpenter, B., and Nichols, K. "Differentiated Services in the Internet." *Proceedings of the IEEE*, September 2002.

CERF74   Cerf, V., and Kahn, R. "A Protocol for Packet Network Interconnection." *IEEE Transactions on Communications,* May 1974.

CHAN06   Chan, P., et al. "The Evolution Path of 4G Networks: FDD or TDD?" *IEEE Communications Magazine*, December 2006.

CHEN02   Chen, T. "Internet Performance Monitoring." *Proceedings of the IEEE*, September 2002.

CICI01   Ciciora, W. "The Cable Modem Traffic Jam." *IEEE Spectrum*, June 2001.

CISC07   Cisco Systems, Inc. "802.11n: The Next Generation of Wireless Performance." Cisco White Paper, 2007. cisco.com

CISC12a   Cisco Systems, Inc. *Cisco Visual Networking Index: Forecast and Methodology, 2011–2016.* Cisco White Paper, May 30, 2012.

CISC12b   Cisco Systems, Inc. *802.11ac: The Fifth Generation of Wi-Fi.* Cisco White Paper, August 2012.

CLAR88   Clark, D. "The Design Philosophy of the DARPA Internet Protocols." *ACM SIGCOMM Computer Communications Review*, August 1988.

CLAR90   Clark, D., and Tennenhouse, D. "Architectural Considerations for a New Generation of Protocols." *Proceedings, SIGCOMM '90, Computer Communication Review*, September 1990.

CLAR92   Clark, D.; Shenker, S.; and Zhang, L. "Supporting Real-Time Applications in an Integrated Services Packet Network: Architecture and Mechanism." *Proceedings, SIGCOMM '92*, August 1992.

CLAR95   Clark, D. *Adding Service Discrimination to the Internet.* MIT Laboratory for Computer Science Technical Report, September 1995. http://groups.csail.mit.edu/ana/Publications/index.html

CLAR98   Clark, D., and Fang, W. "Explicit Allocation of Best-Effort Packet Delivery Service." *IEEE/ACM Transactions on Networking*, August 1998.

COME99   Comer, D., and Stevens, D. *Internetworking with TCP/IP, Volume II: Design Implementation, and Internals.* Upper Saddle River, NJ: Prentice Hall, 1999.

COME01   Comer, D., and Stevens, D. *Internetworking with TCP/IP, Volume III: Client-Server Programming and Applications.* Upper Saddle River, NJ: Prentice Hall, 2001.

COME14   Comer, D. *Internetworking with TCP/IP, Volume I: Principles, Protocols, and Architecture.* Upper Saddle River, NJ: Prentice Hall, 2013.

CORD10   Cordeiro, C.; Akhmetov, D.; and Park, M. "IEEE 802.11ad: Introduction and Performance Evaluation of the First Multi-Gbps WiFi Technology." *Proceedings of the 2010 ACM International Workshop on mmWave Communications: From Circuits to Networks*, 2010.

CORM09   Cormen, T., et al. *Introduction to Algorithms.* Cambridge, MA: MIT Press, 2009.

CROW92   Crowcroft, J.; Wakeman, I.; Wang, Z.; and Sirovica, D. "Is Layering Harmful?" *IEEE Network Magazine*, January 1992.

COUC13   Couch, L. *Digital and Analog Communication Systems.* Upper Saddle River, NJ: Pearson, 2013.

DIAN02   Dianda, J.; Gurbani, V.; and Jones, M. "Session Initiation Protocol Services Architecture." *Bell Labs Technical Journal*, Volume 7, Number 1, 2002.

DEBE07   Debeasi, P. "802.11n: Beyond the Hype." *Burton Group White Paper*, July 2007. www.burtongroup.com

DELL12   Dell, Inc. *Software Defined Networking: A Dell Point of View.* Dell White Paper, October 2012.

DEER96   Deering, S., et al. "The PIM Architecture for Wide-Area Multicast Routing." *IEEE/ACM Transactions on Networking*, April 1996.

DIJK59   Dijkstra, E. "A Note on Two Problems in Connection with Graphs." *Numerical Mathematics*, October 1959.

DINA98   Dinan, E., and Jabbari, B. "Spreading Codes for Direct Sequence CDMA and Wideband CDMA Cellular Networks." *IEEE Communications Magazine*, September 1998.

DIVS98   Divsalar, D.; Jin, H.; and McEliece, J. "Coding Theorems for 'Turbo-Like' Codes." Proceedings, 36th Allerton Conference on Communication, Control, and Computing, September 1998.

DOI04   Doi, S., et al. "IPv6 Anycast for Simple and Effective Communications." *IEEE Communications Magazine*, May 2004.

DONA01   Donahoo, M., and Clavert, K. *The Pocket Guide to TCP/IP Sockets.* San Francisco, CA: Morgan Kaufmann, 2001.

EKLU02   Elkund, C., et al. "IEEE Standard 802.16: A Technical Overview of the WirelessMAN™ Air Interface for Broadband Wireless Access." *IEEE Communications Magazine*, June 2002.

FALL12   Fall, K., and Stevens, W. *TCP/IP Illustrated, Volume 1: The Protocols*. Reading, MA: Addison-Wesley, 2012.

FELL01   Fellows, D., and Jones, D. "DOCSIS Cable Modem Technology." *IEEE Communications Magazine*, March 2001.

FIOR95   Fiorini, D.; Chiani, M.; Tralli, V.; and Salati, C. "Can We Trust HDLC?" *ACM Computer Communications Review*, October 1995.

FLOY94   Floyd, S. "TCP and Explicit Congestion Notification." *ACM Computer Communication Review*, October 1994.

FLOY99   Floyd, S., and Fall, K. "Promoting the Use of End-to-End Congestion Control in the Internet." *IEEE/ACM Transactions on Networking*, August 1999.

FORD62   Ford, L., and Fulkerson, D. *Flows in Networks*. Princeton, NJ: Princeton University Press, 1962.

FRAN10   Frankel, S.; Graveman, R.; Pearce, J.; and Rooks, M. *Guidelines for the Secure Deployment of IPv6*. NIST Special Publication SP800-19, December 2010.

FRAZ99   Frazier, H., and Johnson, H. "Gigabit Ethernet: From 100 to 1,000 Mbps." *IEEE Internet Computing*, January/February 1999.

FREE98a   Freeman, R. "Bits, Symbols, Baud, and Bandwidth." *IEEE Communications Magazine*, April 1998.

FREE98b   Freeman, R. *Telecommunication Transmission Handbook*. New York: Wiley, 1998.

FREE02   Freeman, R. *Fiber-Optic Systems for Telecommunications*. New York: Wiley, 2002.

FREE04   Freeman, R. *Telecommunication System Engineering*. New York: Wiley, 2004.

FREE05   Freeman, R. *Fundamentals of Telecommunications*. New York: Wiley, 2005.

FREE07   Freeman, R. *Radio System Design for Telecommunications*. New York: Wiley, 2007.

FREN13   Frenzel, L. "An Introduction to LTE-Advanced: The Real 4G." *Electronic Design*, February 2013.

FURH94   Furht, B. "Multimedia Systems: An Overview." *IEEE Multimedia*, Spring 1994.

GALL62   Gallager, R. "Low-Density Parity-Check Codes." *IRE Transactions on Information Theory*, January 1962.

GEIE01   Geier, J. "Enabling Fast Wireless Networks with OFDM." *Communications System Design*, February 2001. http://www.csdmag.com

GERL80   Gerla, M., and Kleinrock, L. "Flow Control: A Comparative Survey." *IEEE Transactions on Communications*, April 1980.

GESB02   Gesbert, D., and Akhtar, J. "Breaking the Barriers of Shannon's Capacity: An Overview of MIMO Wireless Systems." *Telektronikk*, January 2002.

GESB03   Gesbert, D., et al. "From theory to practice: An overview of MIMO space—Time coded wireless systems." *IEEE Journal on Selected Areas in Communications*, April 2003.

GHOS10   Ghosh, A., et al. "LTE-Advanced: Next-Generation Wireless Broadband Technology." *IEEE Wireless Communications*, June 2010.

GONZ00   Gonzalez, R. "Disciplining Multimedia." *IEEE Multimedia*, July–September 2000.

GOOD02   Goode, B. "Voice Over Internet Protocol (VoIP)." *Proceedings of the IEEE*, September 2002.

GOTH11   Goth, G. "Software-Defined Networking Could Shake Up More than Packets." *IEEE Internet Computing*, July/August, 2011.

GOUR02   Gourley, D., et al. *HTTP: The Definitive Guide.* Sebastopol, CA: O'Reilly, 2002.

GREE80   Green, P. "An Introduction to Network Architecture and Protocols." *IEEE Transactions on Communications*, April 1980.

HAAR00a   Haartsen, J. "The Bluetooth Radio System." *IEEE Personal Communications*, February 2000.

HAAR00b   Haartsen, J., and Mattisson, S. "Bluetooth—A New Low-Power Radio Interface Providing Short-Range Connectivity." *Proceedings of the IEEE*, October 2000.

HALL01   Hall, B. *Beej's Guide to Network Programming Using Internet Sockets.* 2001. http://beej.us/guide/bgnet

HALP10   Halperin, D., et al. "802.11 with Multiple Antennas for Dummies." *Computer Communication Review*, January 2010.

HARJ00   Harju, J., and Kivimaki, P. "Cooperation and Comparison of DiffServ and IntServ: Performance Measurements." *Proceedings, 23rd Annual IEEE Conference on Local Computer Networks*, November 2000.

HATA80   Hata, M. "Empirical Formula for Propagation Loss in Land Mobile Radio Services." *IEEE Transactions on Vehicular Technology*, March 1980.

HAWL97   Hawley, G. "Systems Considerations for the Use of xDSL Technology for Data Access." *IEEE Communications Magazine*, March 1997.

HAYK09   Haykin, S. *Communication Systems.* New York: Wiley, 2009.

HEGG84   Heggestad, H. "An Overview of Packet Switching Communications." *IEEE Communications Magazine*, April 1984.

HELL01   Heller, R., et al. "Using a Theoretical Multimedia Taxonomy Framework." *ACM Journal of Educational Resources in Computing*, Spring 2001.

HIND83   Hinden, R.; Haverty, J.; and Sheltzer, A. "The DARPA Internet: Interconnecting Heterogeneous Computer Networks with Gateways." *Computer*, September 1983.

HOFF00   Hoffman, P. "Overview of Internet Mail Standards." *The Internet Protocol Journal*, June 2000.

HUIT00   Huitema, C. *Routing in the Internet.* Upper Saddle River, NJ: Prentice Hall, 2000.

HUMP97   Humphrey, M., and Freeman, J. "How xDSL Supports Broadband Services to the Home." *IEEE Network*, January/March 1997.

IBM95   IBM International Technical Support Organization. *Asynchronous Transfer Mode (ATM) Technical Overview.* IBM Redbook SG24-4625-00, 1995. http://www.redbooks.ibm.com

IEEE12   IEEE 802.3 Ethernet Working Group. *IEEE 802.3 Industry Connections Ethernet Bandwidth Assessment.* July 2012. http://www.ieee802.org/3/ad_hoc/bwa/

IREN99   Iren, S.; Amer, P.; and Conrad, P. "The Transport Layer: Tutorial and Survey." *ACM Computing Surveys*, December 1999.

ITUT05   ITU-T. *MPLS Layer Network Architecture.* ITU-T Recommendation Y.1370, 2005.

IWAM10   Iwamura, M., et al. "Carrier Aggregation Framework in 3GPP LTE-Advanced." *IEEE Communications Magazine*, August 2010.

JACO88   Jacobson, V. "Congestion Avoidance and Control." *Proceedings, SIGCOMM '88, Computer Communication Review*, August 1988; reprinted in *Computer Communication Review*, January 1995; a slightly revised version is available at http://ee.lbl.gov/nrg-papers.html

JACO90a   Jacobson, V. "Berkeley TCP Evolution from 4.3 Tahoe to 4.3-Reno." *Proceedings of the Eighteenth Internet Engineering Task Force*, September 1990.

JACO90b   Jacobson, V. "Modified TCP Congestion Avoidance Algorithm." *end2end-interest mailing list*, April 20, 1990, ftp://ftp.ee.lbl.gov/email/vanj.90apr30.txt

JAIN90   Jain, R. "Congestion Control in Computer Networks: Issues and Trends." *IEEE Network Magazine*, May 1990.

JAIN92   Jain, R. "Myths About Congestion Management in High-Speed Networks." *Internetworking: Research and Experience*, Volume 3, 1992.

JAME11   James, J. *A Student's Guide to Fourier Transforms.* Cambridge, England: Cambridge University Press, 2011.

JARS11   Jarschel, M., et al. "Modeling and Performance Evaluation of an OpenFlow Architecture." *Proceedings, International Teletraffic Congress*, 2011.

KAMM07   Kammler, D. *A First Course in Fourier Analysis.* Cambridge, England: Cambridge University Press, 2007.

KANE98   Kanel, J.; Givler, J.; Leiba, B.; and Segmuller, W. "Internet Messaging Frameworks." *IBM Systems Journal*, Number 1, 1998.

KARN91   Karn, P., and Partridge, C. "Improving Round-Trip Estimates in Reliable Transport Protocols." *ACM Transactions on Computer Systems*, November 1991.

KENT87   Kent, C., and Mogul, J. "Fragmentation Considered Harmful." *ACM Computer Communication Review*, October 1987.

KERN12   Kern, S. "OpenFlow Protocol 1.3.0 Approved." *Enterprise Networking Planet*, May 17, 2012.

KHAN89   Khanna, A., and Zinky, J. "The Revised ARPANET Routing Metric." *Proceedings, SIGCOMM '89 Symposium*, 1989.

KHAR98   Khare, R. "The Spec's in the Mail." *IEEE Internet Computing*, September/October 1998.

KLEI76   Kleinrock, L. *Queueing Systems, Volume II: Computer Applications.* New York: Wiley, 1976.

KLEI92   Kleinrock, L. "The Latency/Bandwidth Tradeoff in Gigabit Networks." *IEEE Communications Magazine*, April 1992.

KLEI93   Kleinrock, L. "On the Modeling and Analysis of Computer Networks." *Proceedings of the IEEE*, August 1993.

KNUT98   Knuth, D. *The Art of Computer Programming, Volume 2: Seminumerical Algorithms.* Reading, MA: Addison-Wesley, 1998.

KOFF02   Koffman, I., and Roman, V. "Broadband Wireless Access Solutions Based on OFDM Access in IEEE 802.16." *IEEE Communications Magazine*, April 2002.

KOHL06   Kohler, E.; Handley, M.; and Floyd, S. "Designing DCCP: Congestion Control Without Reliability." *ACM Computer Communication Review*, October 2006.

KONH80   Konheim, A. "A Queuing Analysis of Two ARQ Protocols." *IEEE Transactions on Communications*, July 1980.

KRIS01   Krishnamurthy, B., and Rexford, J. *Web Protocols and Practice: HTTP/1.1, Networking Protocols, Caching, and Traffic Measurement.* Upper Saddle River, NJ: Prentice Hall, 2001.

KUMA98   Kumar, V.; Lakshman, T.; and Stiliadis, D. "Beyond Best Effort: Router Architectures for the Differentiated Services of Tomorrow's Internet." *IEEE Communications Magazine*, May 1998.

KURV09   Kurve, A. "Multi-User MIMO Systems: The Future in the Making." *IEEE Potentials*, November/December 2009.

LAWR01   Lawrence, J. "Designing Multiprotocol Label Switching Networks." *IEEE Communications Magazine*, July 2001.

LAYL04   Layland, R. "Understanding Wi-Fi Performance." *Business Communications Review*, March 2004.

LAYL10   Layland, R. "The Dark Side of Server Virtualization." *Network World*, July 7, 2010.

LEIN85   Leiner, B.; Cole, R.; Postel, J.; and Mills, D. "The DARPA Internet Protocol Suite." *IEEE Communications Magazine*, March 1985.

LIMO12   Limoncelli, T. "OpenFlow: A Radical New Idea in Networking." Communications of the ACM, August 2012.

LIN84   Lin, S.; Costello, D.; and Miller, M. "Automatic-Repeat-Request Error-Control Schemes." *IEEE Communications Magazine*, December 1984.

LI02   Li, V., and Zhang, Z. "Internet Multicast Routing and Transport Control Protocols." *Proceedings of the IEEE*, March 2002.

LI05   Li, J., and Chen, H. "Mobility Support for IP-Based Networks." *IEEE Communications Magazine*, October 2005.

LIN04   Lin, S., and Costello, D. *Error Control Coding.* Upper Saddle River, NJ: Prentice Hall, 2004.

MACK99   Mackay, D., and Neal, R. "Good Error-Correcting Codes Based on Very Sparse Matrices." *IEEE Transactions on Information Theory*, May 1999.

MARS09   Marsan, C. "7 Reasons MPLS Has Been Wildly Successful." *Network World*, March 27, 2009.

MART02   Martin, J., and Nilsson, A. "On Service Level Agreements for IP Networks." *Proceedings, IEEE INFOCOMM'02*, 2002.

MAXE90   Maxemchuk, N., and Zarki, M. "Routing and Flow Control in High-Speed Wide-Area Networks." *Proceedings of the IEEE*, January 1990.

MAXW96   Maxwell, K. "Asymmetric Digital Subscriber Line: Interim Technology for the Next Forty Years." *IEEE Communications Magazine*, October 1996.

MCDO91   McDonald, C. "A Network Specification Language and Execution Environment for Undergraduate Teaching." *Proceedings of the ACM Computer Science Educational Technical Symposium*, March 1991.

MCFA03   McFarland, B., and Wong, M. "The Family Dynamics of 802.11." *ACM Queue*, May 2003.

MCQU80   McQuillan, J.; Richer, I.; and Rosen, E. "The New Routing Algorithm for the ARPANET." *IEEE Transactions on Communications,* May 1980.

MEDD10   Meddeb, A. "Internet QoS: Pieces of the Puzzle." *IEEE Communications Magazine*, January 2010.

METC76   Metcalfe, R., and Boggs, D. "Ethernet: Distributed Packet Switching for Local Computer Networks." *Communications of the ACM*, July 1976.

METZ02   Metz, C. "IP Anycast." *IEEE Internet Computing*, March 2002.

MILL10   Mill, K., et al. *Study of Proposed Internet Congestion Control Mechanisms.* NIST Special Publication 500-82, May 2010.

MOCK88   Mockapetris, P., and Dunlap, K. "Development of the Domain Name System." *ACM Computer Communications Review*, August 1988.

MOGU02   Mogul, J. "Clarifying the Fundamentals of HTTP." *Proceedings of the Eleventh International Conference on World Wide Web*, 2002.

MOY98   Moy, J. *OSPF: Anatomy of an Internet Routing Protocol.* Reading, MA: Addison-Wesley, 1998.

MUKH00   Mukherjee, B. "WDM Optical Communication Networks: Progress and Challenges." *IEEE Journal on Selected Areas in Communications*, October 2000.

MYUN06   Myung, H.; Lim, J.; and Goodman, D. "Single Carrier FDMA for Uplink Wireless Transmission." *IEEE Vehicular Technology*, September 2006.

NOWE07   Nowell, M.; Vusirikala, V.; and Hays, R. "Overview of Requirements and Applications for 40 Gigabit and 100 Gigabit Ethernet." *Ethernet Alliance White Paper*, August 2007.

NAGL84   Nagle, J. *Congestion Control in IP/TCP Internetworks.* RFC 896, 6 January 1984.

OJAN98   Ojanpera, T., and Prasad, G. "An Overview of Air Interface Multiple Access for IMT-2000/UMTS." *IEEE Communications Magazine*, September 1998.

OKUM68   Okumura, T., et al. "Field Strength and Its Variability in VHF and UHF Land Mobile Radio Service." *Review of the Electrical Communications Laboratory*, 1968.

OLIV09   Oliviero, A., and Woodward, B. *Cabling: The Complete Guide to Copper and Fiber-Optic Networking.* Indianapolis: Sybex, 2009.

ONF12   Open Networking Foundation. *Software-Defined Networking: The New Norm for Networks.* ONF White Paper, April 12, 2012.

PARE12   Pareit, D.; Moerman, I.; and Demester, P. "The History of WiMAX: A Complete Survey of the Evolution in Certification and Standardization for IEEE 802.16 and WiMAX." *IEEE Communications Surveys and Tutorials*, Fourth Quarter 2012.

PARK88   Park, S., and Miller, K. "Random Number Generators: Good Ones Are Hard to Find." *Communications of the ACM*, October 1988.

PARK11   Parkvall, S.; Furuskar, A.; and Dahlman, E. "Evolution of LTE Toward IMT-Advanced." *IEEE Communications Magazine*, February 2011.

PARZ06   Parziale, L., et al. *TCP/IP Tutorial and Technical Overview.* IBM Redbook GG24-3376-07, 2006. http://www.redbooks.ibm.com/abstracts/gg243376.html

PAXS96   Paxson, V. "Toward a Framework for Defining Internet Performance Metrics." *Proceedings, INET '96*, 1996. http://www-nrg.ee.lbl.gov

PERA10   Perahia, E., et al. "IEEE 802.11ad: Defining the Next Generation Multi-Gbps Wi-Fi." *Proceedings, 7th IEEE Consumer Communications and Networking Conference*, 2010.

PERL00   Perlman, R. *Interconnections: Bridges, Routers, Switches, and Internetworking Protocols.* Reading, MA: Addison-Wesley, 2000.

PETE61   Peterson, W., and Brown, D. "Cyclic Codes for Error Detection." *Proceedings of the IEEE*, January 1961.

PETR00   Petrick, A. "IEEE 802.11b—Wireless Ethernet." *Communications System Design*, June 2000. http://www.commsdesign.com

PICK82   Pickholtz, R.; Schilling, D.; and Milstein, L. "Theory of Spread Spectrum Communications—A Tutorial." *IEEE Transactions on Communications*, May 1982.

PROA05   Proakis, J. *Fundamentals of Communication Systems.* Upper Saddle River, NJ: Prentice Hall, 2005.

RAJA97   Rajaravivarma, V. "Virtual Local Area Network Technology and Applications." *Proceedings, 29th Southeastern Symposium on System Theory*, 1997.

RAMA88   Ramabadran, T., and Gaitonde, S. "A Tutorial on CRC Computations." *IEEE Micro*, August 1988.

RAMA00   Ramalho, M. "Intra- and Inter-Domain Multicast Routing Protocols: A Survey and Taxonomy." *IEEE Communications Surveys and Tutorials*, First Quarter 2000.

RAMA06   Ramaswami, R. "Optical Network Technologies: What Worked and What Didn't." *IEEE Communications Magazine*, September 2006.

RAPP02   Rappaport, T. *Wireless Communications.* Upper Saddle River, NJ: Prentice Hall, 2002.

REED09   Reed, B. "What's Next for MPLS?" *Network World*, December 21, 2009.

REEV95   Reeve, W. *Subscriber Loop Signaling and Transmission Handbook.* Piscataway, NJ: IEEE Press, 1995.

ROBE78   Roberts, L. "The Evolution of Packet Switching." *Proceedings of the IEEE*, November 1978.

SAIR02   Sairam, K.; Gunasekaran, N.; and Reddy, S. "Bluetooth in Wireless Communication." *IEEE Communications Magazine*, June 2002.

SCHU98   Schulzrinne, H., and Rosenberg, J. "The Session Initiation Protocol: Providing Advanced Telephony Access Across the Internet." *Bell Labs Technical Journal*, October–December 1998.

SCHU99   Schulzrinne, H., and Rosenberg, J. "The IETF Internet Telephony Architecture and Protocols." *IEEE Network*, May/June 1999.

SCHW80   Schwartz, M., and Stern, T. "Routing Techniques Used in Computer Communication Networks." *IEEE Transactions on Communications*, April 1980.

SHAN48   Shannon, C. "A Mathematical Theory of Communication." *Bell System Technical Journal*, July 1948 and October 1948.

SHAN02 Shannon, C.; Moore, D.; and Claffy, K. "Beyond Folklore: Observations on Fragmented Traffic." *IEEE/ACM Transactions on Networking*, December 2002.

SHEN95 Shenker, S. "Fundamental Design Issues for the Future Internet." *IEEE Journal on Selected Areas in Communications*, September 1995.

SHER04 Sherburne, P., and Fitzgerald, C. "You Don't Know Jack About VoIP." *ACM Queue*, September 2004.

SHOE02 Shoemake, M. "IEEE 802.11g Jells as Applications Mount." *Communications System Design*, April 2002. http://www.commsdesign.com.

SIKE00 Siket, J., and Proch, D. "MPLS—Bring IP Networks and Connection-Oriented Networks Together." *Business Communications Review*, April 2000.

SKLA93 Sklar, B. "Defining, Designing, and Evaluating Digital Communication Systems." *IEEE Communications Magazine*, November 1993.

SKLA01 Sklar, B. *Digital Communications: Fundamentals and Applications*. Englewood Cliffs, NJ: Prentice Hall, 2001.

SKOR08 Skordoulis, D., et al. "IEEE 802.11n MAC Frame Aggregation Mechanisms for Next-Generation High-Throughput WLANs." *IEEE Wireless Communications*, February 2008.

SPAR07 Sparks, R., and Systems, E. "SIP—Basics and Beyond." *ACM Queue*, March 2007.

STAL99 Stallings, W. *ISDN and Broadband ISDN, with Frame Relay and ATM*. Upper Saddle River, NJ: Prentice Hall, 1999.

STAL00 Stallings, W. *Local and Metropolitan Area Networks, Sixth Edition*. Upper Saddle River, NJ: Prentice Hall, 2000.

STAL05 Stallings, W. *Wireless Communications and Networks, Second Edition*. Upper Saddle River, NJ: Prentice Hall, 2005.

STEV96 Stevens, W. *TCP/IP Illustrated, Volume 3: TCP for Transactions, HTTP, NNTP, and the UNIX(R) Domain Protocol*. Reading, MA: Addison-Wesley, 1996.

TANT98 Tantaratana, S., and Ahmed, K., eds. *Wireless Applications of Spread Spectrum Systems: Selected Readings*. Piscataway, NJ: IEEE Press, 1998.

TEKT01 Tektronix. *SONET Telecommunications Standard Primer*. Tektronix White Paper, 2001. http://www.tek.com/document/primer/sonet-telecommunications-standard-primer

THOM96 Thomas, S. *IPng and the TCP/IP Protocols: Implementing the Next Generation Internet*. New York: Wiley, 1996.

TOYO10 Toyoda, H.; Ono, G.; and Nishimura, S. "100 GbE PHY and MAC Layer Implementation." *IEEE Communications Magazine*, March 2010.

VAUG11 Vaughan-Nichols, S. "OpenFlow: The Next Generation of the Network?" *Computer*, August 2011.

VENK05 Venkataraman, N. "Inside Mobile IP." *Dr. Dobb's Journal*, September 2005.

VERM04 Verma, D. "Service Level Agreements on IP Networks." *Proceedings of the IEEE*, September 2004.

VIN98 Vin, H. "Supporting Next-Generation Distributed Applications." *IEEE Multimedia*, July–September 1998.

VISW98 Viswanathan, A., et al. "Evolution of Multiprotocol Label Switching." *IEEE Communications Magazine*, May 1998.

VOGE95   Vogel, A., et al. "Distributed Multimedia and QoS: A Survey." *IEEE Multimedia*, Summer 1995.

WEIS98   Weiss, W. "QoS with Differentiated Services." *Bell Labs Technical Journal*, October–December 1998.

WHIT97   White, P., and Crowcroft, J. "The Integrated Services in the Internet: State of the Art." *Proceedings of the IEEE*, December 1997.

WIDM83   Widmer, A., and Franaszek, P. "A DC-Balanced, Partitioned, 8B/10B Transmission Code." *IBM Journal of Research and Development*, September 1983.

WILL97   Willner, A. "Mining the Optical Bandwidth for a Terabit per Second." *IEEE Spectrum*, April 1997.

WIMA12   WiMAX Forum. *WiMAX Forum Network Architecture: Architecture Tenets, Reference Model and Reference Points.* WMF-T32-001-R021v01, December 3, 2012.

WRIG95   Wright, G., and Stevens, W. *TCP/IP Illustrated, Volume 2: The Implementation.* Reading, MA: Addison-Wesley, 1995.

XI11   Xi, H. "Bandwidth Needs in Core and Aggregation Nodes in the Optical Transport Network." IEEE 802.3 Industry Connections Ethernet Bandwidth Assessment Meeting, November 8, 2011. http://www.ieee802.org/3/ad_hoc/bwa/public/nov11/index_1108.html

XIAO99   Xiao, X., and Ni, L. "Internet QoS: A Big Picture." *IEEE Network*, March/April 1999.

XIAO04   Xiao, Y. "IEEE 802.11e: QoS Provisioning at the MAC Layer." *IEEE Communications Magazine*, June 2004.

XION00   Xiong, F. *Digital Modulation Techniques.* Boston: Artech House, 2000.

YANG95   Yang, C., and Reddy, A. "A Taxonomy for Congestion Control Algorithms in Packet Switching Networks." *IEEE Network*, July/August 1995.

ZENG00   Zeng, M.; Annamalai, A.; and Bhargava, V. "Harmonization of Global Third-generation Mobile Systems." *IEEE Communications Magazine*, December 2000.

ZHAN86   Zhang, L. "Why TCP Timers Don't Work Well." *Proceedings, SIGCOMM '86 Symposium*, August 1986.

ZHAN93   Zhang, L.; Deering, S.; Estrin, D.; Shenker, S.; and Zappala, D. "RSVP: A New Resource ReSerVation Protocol." *IEEE Network*, September 1993.

ZHAN95   Zhang, H. "Service Disciplines for Guaranteed Performance Service in Packet-Switching Networks." *Proceedings of the IEEE*, October 1995.

ZORZ96   Zorzi, M., and Rao, R. "On the Use of Renewal Theory in the Analysis of ARQ Protocols." *IEEE Transactions on Communications*, September 1996.

INDEX

885

ACRONYMS

AAL	ATM Adaptation Layer	ITU	International Telecommunication Union
ADSL	Asymmetric Digital Subscriber Line	ITU-T	ITU Telecommunication Standardization
AES	Advanced Encryption Standard		Sector
AM	Amplitude Modulation	LAN	Local Area Network
AMI	Alternate Mark Inversion	LAPB	Link Access Procedure—Balanced
ANS	American National Standard	LAPD	Link Access Procedure on the D
ANSI	American National Standard		Channel
	Institute	LAPF	Link Access Procedure for Frame Mode
ARP	Address Resolution Protocol		Bearer Services
ARQ	Automatic Repeat Request	LLC	Logical Link Control
ASCII	American Standard Code for	MAC	Medium Access Control
	Information Interchange	MAN	Metropolitan Area Network
ASK	Amplitude-Shift Keying	MIME	Multi-Purpose Internet Mail Extension
ATM	Asynchronous Transfer Mode	MPLS	Multiprotocol Label Switching
BER	Bit Error Rate	NRZI	Nonreturn to Zero, Inverted
BGP	Border Gateway Protocol	NRZL	Nonreturn to Zero, Level
CBR	Constant Bit Rate	NT	Network Termination
CCITT	International Consultative Committee	OSI	Open Systems Interconnection
	on Telegraphy and Telephony	OSPF	Open Shortest Path First
CIR	Committed Information Rate	PBX	Private Branch Exchange
CMI	Coded Mark Inversion	PCM	Pulse-Code Modulation
CRC	Cyclic Redundancy Check	PDU	Protocol Data Unit
CSMA/CD	Carrier Sense Multiple Access with	PM	Phase Modulation
	Collision Detection	PSK	Phase-Shift Keying
DCE	Data Circuit-Terminating Equipment	PTT	Postal, Telegraph, and Telephone
DEA	Data Encryption Algorithm	QAM	Quadrature Amplitude Modulation
DES	Data Encryption Standard	QoS	Quality of Service
DS	Differentiated Services	QPSK	Quadrature Phase Shift Keying
DTE	Data Terminal Equipment	RBOC	Regional Bell Operating Company
FCC	Federal Communications Commission	RF	Radio Frequency
FCS	Frame Check Sequence	RSA	Rivest, Shamir, Adleman Algorithm
FDM	Frequency-Division Multiplexing	RSVP	Resource ReSerVation Protocol
FSK	Frequency-Shift Keying	SAP	Service Access Point
FTP	File Transfer Protocol	SDH	Synchronous Digital Hierarchy
FM	Frequency Modulation	SDU	Service Data Unit
GFR	Guaranteed Frame Rate	SLA	Service Level Agreement
GPS	Global Positioning System	SMTP	Simple Mail Transfer Protocol
HDLC	High-Level Data Link Control	SNMP	Simple Network Management Protocol
HTML	Hypertext Markup Language	SONET	Synchronous Optical Network
HTTP	Hypertext Transfer Protocol	SS7	Signaling System Number 7
IAB	Internet Architecture Board	STP	Shielded Twisted Pair
ICMP	Internet Control Message Protocol	TCP	Transmission Control Protocol
ICT	Information and Communications	TDM	Time-Division Multiplexing
	Technology	TE	Terminal Equipment
IDN	Integrated Digital Network	UBR	Unspecified Bit Rate
IEEE	Institute of Electrical and Electronics	UDP	User Datagram Protocol
	Engineers	UNI	User-Network Interface
IETF	Internet Engineering Task Force	UTP	Unshielded Twisted Pair
IGMP	Internet Group Management Protocol	VAN	Value-Added Network
IP	Internet Protocol	VBR	Variable Bit Rate
IPng	Internet Protocol—Next Generation	VCC	Virtual Channel Connection
IRA	International Reference Alphabet	VLAN	Virtual LAN
ISA	Integrated Services Architecture	VPC	Virtual Path Connection
ISDN	Integrated Services Digital Network	WDM	Wavelength Division Multiplexing
ISO	International Organization for	Wi-Fi	Wireless Fidelity
	Standardization	WWW	World Wide Web

THE WILLIAM STALLINGS BOOKS ON COMPUTER AND DATA COMMUNICATIONS TECHNOLOGY

BUSINESS DATA COMMUNICATIONS, SEVENTH EDITION
(with Tom Case)

A comprehensive presentation of data communications and telecommunications from a business perspective. Covers voice, data, image, and video communications and applications technology and includes a number of case studies. Topics covered include data communications, TCP/IP, cloud computing, Internet protocols and applications, LANs and WANs, network security, and network management.

OPERATING SYSTEMS, SEVENTH EDITION

A state-of-the art survey of operating system principles. Covers fundamental technology as well as contemporary design issues, such as threads, micro-kernels, SMPs, real-time systems, multiprocessor scheduling, embedded OSs, distributed systems, clusters, security, and object-oriented design. **Third, fourth, and sixth editions received the Text and Academic Authors Association (TAA) award for the best Computer Science and Engineering Textbook of the year.**

CRYPTOGRAPHY AND NETWORK SECURITY, SIXTH EDITION

A tutorial and survey on network security technology. Each of the basic building blocks of network security, including conventional and public-key cryptography, authentication, and digital signatures, are covered. Provides a thorough mathematical background for such algorithms as AES and RSA. The book covers important network security tools and applications, including S/MIME, IP Security, Kerberos, SSL/TLS, network access control, and Wi-Fi security. In addition, methods for countering hackers and viruses are explored. **Second edition received the TAA award for the best Computer Science and Engineering Textbook of 1999.**

COMPUTER ORGANIZATION AND ARCHITECTURE, NINTH EDITION

A unified view of this broad field. Covers fundamentals such as CPU, control unit, microprogramming, instruction set, I/O, and memory. Also covers advanced topics such as multicore, superscalar, and parallel organization. **Five-time winner of the TAA award for the best Computer Science and Engineering Textbook of the year.**

COMPUTER SECURITY, SECOND EDITION
(with Lawrie Brown)

A comprehensive treatment of computer security technology, including algorithms, protocols, and applications. Covers cryptography, authentication, access control, database security, intrusion detection and prevention, malicious software, denial of service, firewalls, software security, physical security, human factors, auditing, legal and ethical aspects, and trusted systems. **Received the 2008 TAA award for the best Computer Science and Engineering Textbook of the year.**

NETWORK SECURITY ESSENTIALS, FIFTH EDITION

A tutorial and survey on network security technology. The book covers important network security tools and applications, including S/MIME, IP Security, Kerberos, SSL/TLS, network access control, and Wi-Fi security. In addition, methods for countering hackers and viruses are explored.

WIRELESS COMMUNICATIONS AND NETWORKS, SECOND EDITION

A comprehensive, state-of-the art survey. Covers fundamental wireless communications topics, including antennas and propagation, signal encoding techniques, spread spectrum, and error-correction techniques. Examines satellite, cellular, wireless local loop networks and wireless LANs, including Bluetooth and 802.11. Covers Mobile IP and WAP.

COMPUTER NETWORKS WITH INTERNET PROTOCOLS AND TECHNOLOGY

An up-to-date survey of developments in the area of Internet-based protocols and algorithms. Using a top–down approach, this book covers applications, transport layer, Internet QoS, Internet routing, data link layer and computer networks, security, and network management.

HIGH-SPEED NETWORKS AND INTERNETS, SECOND EDITION

A state-of-the art survey of high-speed networks. Topics covered include TCP congestion control, ATM traffic management, Internet traffic management, differentiated and integrated services, Internet routing protocols and multicast routing protocols, resource reservation and RSVP, and lossless and lossy compression. Examines important topic of self-similar data traffic.